'WE WUNT
BE DRUV'

'WE WUNT BE DRUV'

THE ROYAL SUSSEX REGIMENT ON THE WESTERN FRONT 1914 – 1918

BY HUGH MILLER

Reveille
PRESS

Reveille Press is an imprint of
Tommies Guides Military Booksellers & Publishers

Gemini House
136-140 Old Shoreham Road
Brighton
BN3 7BD

www.tommiesguides.co.uk

First published in Great Britain by
Reveille Press 2012

For more information please visit
www.reveillepress.com

978-1-908336-30-9

Cover design by Reveille Press

Printed and bound by CPI Group (UK) Ltd, Croydon,
CR0 4YY

This book is dedicated to the memory of all those men who served with The Royal Sussex Regiment on the Western Front and especially to the following:

Lieutenant-Colonel William Colsey Millward, D.S.O., Croix-de-Guerre, who served throughout with the 11th Battalion, joining as a Private and becoming Commanding Officer from 1st March, 1917. A severe wound on Good Friday, 28th March, 1918, necessitated the amputation of his left leg but he survived. He died in 1956 and is buried in St.Nicolas Churchyard, Pevensey, Sussex.

Charlie Roffe of Pevensey Bay, Sussex, a Regular Soldier who served with the 2nd Battalion before and throughout the war, gained the rank of Sergeant and survived.

Private George Herbert Wratten of Isfield, Sussex, who survived after serving throughout with the 5th (Cinque Ports) Battalion on the Western Front and, later, in Italy.

The brothers, all of Pevensey, Sussex:

Private Arthur John (Jack) Miller who joined the 11th Battalion, received 'Blighty' wounds at 'The Boar's Head', Richebourg-L'Avoué, and later returned to be killed-in-action near Morlancourt, Somme, serving with the 7th Battalion. He has no known grave but is commemorated on the Vis-en-Artois Memorial, Haucourt, Pas-de-Calais, France.

Private Frederick George Miller who, although wounded in 1917, survived the war, having served, at various times, with all three 'Lowther's Lambs' Battalions and also, for a period, with the 8th Battalion The Royal Sussex Regiment.

Private Stephen Miller who joined the 11th Battalion but was discharged and died at home from tuberculosis.

Private Wilfred Lawrence Miller who served with the 11th Battalion and was killed-in-action at Mailly-Maillet Wood, Somme; he is buried at Englebelmer Communal Cemetery Extension, Somme, France.

Contents

List of Sketch Maps
Drawn by the author

List of Illustrations

Acknowledgments

The research and other preparation for a work such as this cannot be completed without the ready help, co-operation, encouragement and support of a significant number of individuals and organisations. Thus, I place on record my sincere appreciation and thanks to those who have assisted me over a number of years past.

The main written and photographic records of The Royal Sussex Regiment are held at the West Sussex Record Office at Chichester. It was there that I spent many hours trawling and dredging through masses of papers created so long ago and where I received, on every visit and in response to every written enquiry, the ready and enthusiastic help of Richard Childs, County Archivist, and his staff.

For the Commonwealth War Graves Commission I have every praise and gratitude. The Commission has responsibility for maintaining the many war graves, cemeteries and memorials throughout the world. On the Western Front, as elsewhere, the cemeteries are kept, without exception, in immaculate condition. Whenever I visit a cemetery and find one of the teams of French or Belgian gardeners working there on behalf of the Commission, it is my privilege to seek them out and to express my individual heartfelt thanks for the work they do and for the beautiful and peaceful settings they create and maintain around the last resting places and memorials of the war dead.

At its Maidenhead offices, the Commission has a vast store of records relating to service personnel who were killed or lost their lives in other ways during the war. From those records I have obtained invaluable information concerning men of The Royal Sussex Regiment, the cemeteries in which they lie and the memorials on which their names are inscribed abroad and at home. I have been grateful, particularly, for the assistance of Mr.D.Butler and Mr.B.J.Murphy of the Commission's Records Section.

Other organisations who deserve thanks for their help in my research are the British Library Newspaper Library, the Imperial War Museum and the Reference Services Section of the House of Commons Library.

For permission to use extracts from that excellent book "Undertones of War" by the author and poet, Edmund Blunden, I am most grateful to Harper-Collins Publishers Ltd.

My acknowledgements would not be complete without sincere thanks to my friend Geoff Bridger for first encouraging and leading me towards publication of this book. Also, I thank Terry Cave who kindly read my manuscript and provided me with valuable editorial comments, suggestions and advice.

The service provided over some years by Ray Westlake, together with his experienced and freely given ideas concerning publishing possibilities have been much appreciated; a goodly number of 'Ray Westlake Military Books' line my shelves.

Almost last, but certainly not least, I express my sincere thanks to those who have sustained me during frequent visits to the Western Front. Before their retirement, Monsieur and Madame Duthoit of the Hôtel-Restaurant de la Paix in Albert always provided a warm welcome to their family establishment and an excellent menu of local delicacies in their restaurant. Since then, the Hôtel and restaurant have continued to function to the same warmth of welcome in the care of their niece and her husband, Isabelle and Frederic Daudigny-Duthoit. After long days of battlefield research, often in the still-glutinous Somme mud, their haven of replenishment and rest has been invaluable. Similarly, the Hôtel Ariane, its proprietors and staff have always provided a most welcoming and comfortable 'home' and splendid restaurant within a short walk of

Ypres centre when the focus of research has been the Ypres Salient.

Finally, I shall be grateful always to my wife, Diana, for spending with me many hours on the battlefields of the Western Front; searching, reading, recording, investigating, checking and re-checking. All this she has done in fine weather and foul, not only with the best of good grace but also frequently with a determination and persistence that has brought unbounded rewards.

Preface

My father, mercifully too young to serve during the events of 1914 – 1918, was a soldier in the Second World War. At that time, some twenty-five years after the Great War ended with the 1918 Armistice, my mother took me occasionally to visit a great- aunt and uncle who also lived in our Sussex village. There, I now realise, the seed of my eventual fascination with the earlier war was sown as, bored with adult conversation, I spent hours sitting on the floor examining my uncle's 'The War Illustrated' volumes of that earlier conflict. I remember that my schoolboy questions were answered by my great-uncle in no great depth. I did not realise that my enthusiasm evoked no matching response from 'Uncle Fred', probably because he felt his own awful experiences and memories formed no suitable story for one so young.

As time passed and I grew to be a teenage Grammar School boy introduced to the team challenges of sport, I became adept at the game of cricket. At thirteen years of age, soon after the Second World War, I was playing for my village team and, at seventeen, I had progressed sufficiently to have trials for Sussex County Cricket Club. One man above all others was instrumental in arranging those trials and in giving me the greatest sporting encouragement; he was an upright and imposing figure though, for all the years that I knew him, he used a walking stick and his artificial leg creaked at the knee. He was known to everyone fondly and simply as 'Colonel Millward' and he was President of my local village club. I formed a great respect for 'The Colonel' but it was only much later that I came to know of this man's greatness and that, in the Great War, he had risen from Private to Lieutenant-Colonel Commanding the 11th Battalion, The Royal Sussex Regiment. It was after the Colonel's death that the earlier-sown seed of my interest in the Great War germinated and began its slow but steady growth. Alas, it was too late to gain from my great-uncle and from the Colonel the information I craved; by then, both had passed on to re-join their comrades.

Another gap of twenty-five years occured before my own son, Richard, was studying the 1914-1918 war in preparation for his grammar school examinations. He and I planned a trip by car to the battlefields so that he might secure a better insight for his studies. Our preparations prompted some research into the involvement of our ancestors. I knew that four of my great-uncles, all brothers, had taken part. One, Stephen, was discharged from the service to die at home from tuberculosis; two, Wilfred and Jack, were killed in action and the fourth, 'Uncle Fred', survived into old age. At Stephen's grave in our village churchyard, the reverse of the headstone is inscribed to the memory of the two brothers killed in action. The details for Wilfred end with the inscription 'Buried at Beaussart, France.'

In response to my enquiry, the Commonwealth War Graves Commission provided information that Jack, who has no known grave, is commemorated on the the Vis-en-Artois Memorial at Haucourt, Pas-de-Calais and that Wilfred's grave is at Englebelmer, Somme. Why Englebelmer, we wondered ? Why not Beaussart ? For us, one of the fascinating mysteries related to the Great War was born. Time has shown that such mysteries are legion; they continue to surface; they continue to invoke amateur detective work, sometimes with success and elation, sometimes with failure and the understanding that such a momentous era of so many years ago must inevitably retain some secrets for ever.

Father and son visited the battlefields and were much moved and impressed. At Vis-en-Artois, a dismal and sombre place, we felt close to Jack though we knew from our churchyard headstone that he had been killed some thirty miles away 'near Morlancourt'. His name appeared on the Vis-en-Artois memorial together with those of many of his Royal Sussex Regiment comrades killed 'during the great Advance to Victory', that is on, or after, 8th August,1918.

At Englebelmer, in one of those corners of "a foreign field that is forever England", we found

Wilfred's grave. We found, too, in the cemetery record book and on a specially erected stone within the cemetery, the solution to our mystery. Wilfred, together with others, had been buried initially at Beaussart but, later in the conflict, that cemetery had been so heavily damaged by shellfire that, after the war, all the bodies there, except two that could not be found, were moved for re-burial at Englebelmer.

That short week-end proved to be the first of many trips made by me to the Western Front. It was, more than anything else, the moving experiences of that first visit that brought my flower of fascination for the Great War to full bloom; it is proving to be an everlasting flower; may its bloom, my memories and my gratitude never fade.

From that time onwards, I have continued to undertake research for my own interest. In so doing, I have obtained and read many books on the First World War, particularly the Western Front. Many and varied are the topics covered by a miriad of authors: causes, strategies, armaments, successes, failures, incompetences; armies, corps, brigades, regiments, battalions. There are many regiments whose exploits have been faithfully written, bound and published but I have been able to find only two substantial books of record on The Royal Sussex Regiment. Both are chronological records; one is entitled *'The History of the Seventh (Service) Battalion The Royal Sussex Regiment 1914 – 1918'* compiled by a Committee of Officers of that Battalion and published in 1934. The other is *'The Sussex Yeomanry and 16th (Sussex Yeomanry) Battalion Royal Sussex Regiment 1914 – 1919'* by Lieutenant Colonel H.I.Powell-Edwards D.S.O. Another book , that splendid work by the author and poet Edmund Blunden, published in 1928 and entitled *'Undertones of War '*, tells of the author's experiences as an officer in the 11th Battalion. In many instances, however, place names, dates and times are omitted from Edmund Blunden's narrative thus initiating a number of those post-war-time mysteries.

So it was that my thoughts turned towards making my own contribution by producing a book about those battalions of The Royal Sussex Regiment that served on the Westen Front. Research material has been gathered from far and wide. Wherever possible, accounts of personal stories and happenings have been included because it was the individuals, brought together in great numbers, who bore the brunt and who, collectively, formed the great armies of the British Expeditionary Force on the Western Front. I believe that, for The Royal Sussex Regiment at least, this is the first time that one book has brought together the chronological history of a Regiment's Battalions and a full list of all those who lost their lives, including where known, details of each man's full name; place of birth; place of enlistment; rank; service number; decorations; date and form of death; cemetery of burial or place of memorial inscription; age; names and address of next-of-kin and other pieces of related information. Any man killed while serving in an 'Acting Rank' is regarded in this book as holding that higher rank. For example, a sustantive corporal who, at the time of his death, was an 'Acting Sergeant' will be recorded in this book as a sergeant. To my mind it is only fair and proper that the rank recorded should be the full rank in which a man was undertaking his duties at the time of death.

The First World War ranks supreme in the historical annals of this land and its former Empire. Only 1066 and the Battle of Hastings is etched so deeply in the memories of succeeding generations. It is my humble wish that this book may, in some small way, nourish those memories so that the Great War of 1914-1918, its sacrifices, failures and achievements may remain in the collective remembrances of the English speaking peoples.

Hugh Miller,
Pevensey,
East Sussex.

2012.

Introduction

In the year 1701, King William III, formerly the Prince of Orange, decreed that a number of new regiments should be raised in order to strengthen the British army. One of the eminent persons commissioned by the King to raise the new regiments was the Third Earl of Donegal. His home was in Belfast and it was from there that many of his recruits were drawn. So prominent were the Ulstermen that the new regiment was called 'The Belfast Regiment' or 'The Earl of Donegal's Regiment'. Unofficially, they became known as 'The Orange Lilies'.

The Regiment was first posted overseas in 1704 to the West Indies but was soon sent from there, in haste, to defend Gibraltar against a large Franco-Spanish force. So successful was the regiment that it was awarded its first Battle Honour 'Gibraltar 1704-1705'. The tide was turned in 1707, however, when the Regiment was almost annihilated by a Franco-Spanish force nearly double its number at Almansa.

Fifty years later, in 1757, during the seven-years war with France, the Regiment was sent to Canada and there, 3,000 strong, defended Fort William Henry against 10,000 French until, short of ammunition and food, and with the garrison including many women and children, it was forced to surrender. The following year, with many survivors from Fort William Henry included, the Regiment captured the 'impregnable' French stronghold of Louisburg.

On 13th September,1759, the Regiment was proud to take part in General Wolfe's famous capture of Quebec. During fierce hand-to-hand fighting in this engagement, the French 'Royal Roussillon Regiment' whose soldiers had worn in their headgear the white plume of Navarre, was throughly defeated. It was there that the victors picked up many of the plumes from the battleground and stuck them in their own hats. As a result, the plume was later incorporated into the regimental badge and remained there throughout the many years the Regiment continued in existence.

In 1782, the Regiment was told that, under a new government recruiting drive, it was to be re-named 'The 35th (Dorsetshire) Regiment'. There was no great enthusiasm for this among the officers and men; the Regiment had not the slightest connection with the county of Dorset. Five years later, the Regiment received a new Commanding Officer, Charles Lennox, who was a member of an old and distinguished Sussex family. At the beginning of the 19th century several regiments, including the 35th (Dorsetshire) Regiment, were ordered to increase recruitment by raising two battalions. Of these, the 2/35th comprised mainly volunteers from the county of Sussex, recruited by Charles Lennox, by then promoted to Major-General. This forceful man obtained Royal Assent to replace '(Dorsetshire)' with '(Sussex)'. Under its new title, the 35th (Sussex) Regiment was present at the 1815 Battle of Waterloo.

So high was the esteem and reputation of the Regiment by 1832 that King William IV granted that, henceforth, it should be called 'The Royal Sussex Regiment of Foot'. As a result of this high honour, the orange colours were replaced by the traditional blue of 'Royal Regiments'.

During the Indian Mutiny, which began in 1857, the Regiment had contact with the 107th Bengal Infantry which was a regiment of the East India Company. This contact was renewed twentyfour years later when the two regiments were united, the 35th Foot becoming the 1st Battalion and the 107th Bengal's forming the 2nd Battalion. The 1st Battalion subsequently took part in the South African Boer War of 1899-1902.

At the outbreak of the First World War on 4th August,1914, The Royal Sussex Regiment comprised only two battalions, the 1st and 2nd, both regular battalions. The 1st Battalion was then serving in India and, to the chagrin of many of its men, there it was destined to remain throughout the whole war.

During the 1914-1918 war the Regiment fielded no less than 26 battalions which, between them, served on every front of that war, gaining 69 Battle Honours. The 1914 – 1918 memorial panels in the Regimental Chapel at Chichester Cathedral are inscribed with 6,800 names.

The training of troops during the Great War was intense. Rivalry and competition was deliberately fostered at all levels from regiments down to platoons in order to promote the essential qualities of comradeship and morale. Inter-regimental pride was universal. Naturally, the long-established, regular units considered themselves superior initially but, with the progress of the war, the inevitable replacement of men as battles took their toll, and with the creation of Lord Kitchener's 'New Army', a parity gradually became established. Even so, rivalry continued, particularly amongst the 'county' regiments. In this rivalry, Sussex had a lead because of its 'Royal' designation. A story of the time, changed over the years, perhaps, told of a senior staff officer being seconded temporarily to a Sussex battalion. He had the full battalion drawn up on the huge parade ground where, after suitably introducing himself, he determined to put the men through some of their paces himself. Placing himself at the head of the troops, he gave the order: "In column of route, Sussex Regiment, by the left, quick march." Not one man moved. Outraged, the officer summoned to stand before him the battalion's commanding officer and demanded to know the reason why the battalion had not followed his direct order. In equally forceful tones, so that every man could hear, the Commanding Officer, Lieutenant-Colonel Impey replied, "Sir, with respect, the ROYAL Sussex Regiment will follow you anywhere."

Traditionally, after its very early days, The Royal Sussex Regiment was made up, predominently, of Sussex men and that tradition continued when the 'New Armies' began to be enlisted in September,1914. Of course, many men came from the large seaside towns of the county but by far the greatest number came from the hinterland; the picturesque villages of the rolling South Downs, the country parishes of the Weald and the isolated farms and hamlets of the lowland grazing areas. Most were Sussex born and bred; most had been instilled at school with a proud and patriotic love of family, county and country; most had never ventured outside their county boundaries.

There were exceptions, of course, but the majority had received only a basic education in the "3 R's". That marvellously slow, broad Sussex dialect pervaded the units. Every man was loyal to, and firmly supportive of, his close comrades. As individuals, and as a body, the men exhibited the Sussex trait of a certain stubbornness. They were happy and relaxed when properly instructed and encouraged, but when unduly coerced or put upon they could dig in their collective heels. It was due to their determination not to be pushed around by the enemy during the early battles around Ypres, that they earned from the Germans the title 'The Iron Regiment'.

This determination and stubbornness is beautifully described in a well known saying in their beloved Sussex dialect: "We dunt mind bein' led but we wunt be druv !". Interpreted for the benefit of anyone not well versed in the Sussex language, this means, "We do not mind being led but we will NOT be driven !"

It should be remembered that the main text of the book includes, at the appropriate dates of death, the rank, surname and initials of each man together with a reference number in brackets. This number may be used to refer to a particular man's details in the Alphabetical Lists to be found at the end of the book. Conversely, reference to a name in the Alphabetical List will provide the Battalion and date of death which, in turn, will enable the reader to find, within the main text, the Battalion's situation at that time.

It should be remembered, also, that not every man was killed outright in action. Thus, some names listed within the text will relate to deaths from wounds which, in many cases, occured after the dates of action; sometimes after a number of days; sometimes after many months. The names include, also, those who died during the war from natural causes such as tuberculosis, influenza or pneumonia.

After the war the Imperial (now Commonwealth) War Graves Commission sent questionnaires to all known next-of-kin seeking information that would enable existing records to be confirmed or corrected and, where possible, augmented for every man who lost his life. The records which stand today owe much to the willingness of relatives to complete and return those questionnaires. Many questionnaires were never returned, with the result that only the most basic details are available; some were completed only in the most formal manner e.g. "Son of A.Smith of London" and some were completed after a wife had re-married e.g. "Husband of Mrs.A.Jones, formerly Smith".

Thus, the Battalion Alphabetical Lists at the end of the book contain all the information available for each man, sometimes with interesting extra information but sometimes with only the barest details.

The spellings of some place names, particularly in Belgium, have changed during the intervening years; generally, the spellings used by the Battalions are used also throughout this book.

PART ONE

The 2nd Battalion
('Old Contemptibles')

CHAPTER 1
1914
AUGUST-DECEMBER

Upon the declaration of war with Germany on Tuesday 4th August,1914, The Royal Sussex Regiment consisted of two regular infantry battalions. The Regiment had originated in 1701 as the '35th Regiment of Foot' and, after a number of reorganisations and changes of name, had been formed into two battalions in 1881. During the years leading up to 1914, most of the British 'County' and other infantry regiments were made up of two regular battalions, the 1st and 2nd., and The Royal Sussex Regiment conformed with this arrangement.

The 1st Battalion had taken part in the South African 'Boer War' of 1899 – 1902. In 1914, however, this battalion was serving in India where, much to the frustration of many of its soldiers, it remained throughout the whole of the First World War.

The 2nd Battalion, on the other hand, was based in England during the early months of 1914. There, at various locations, was continued that form of peacetime training which bore no resemblance to what the battalion would be required to face and experience before the year's end. Bell-tented camps, set out in immaculately straight lines on grassy, dry, rolling tracts of the English countyside provided pleasant living quarters during that summer of 1914. Purpose-built rifle ranges and assault courses taxed the skill and fitness of the men, as did the long and frequent route marches, but there was no enemy, no true battleground terrain and no in-coming shells or bullets.

Despite the lack of battlefield reality, the Battalion was well taught in the rigours of parades, drills, fatigues, 'bull' and accompanying army discipline. These sometimes unpopular aspects of army life, together with the relatively exciting and pleasurable experiences of marksmanship, would stand the men in good stead before long.

During the weeks prior to the outbreak of war, the 2nd battalion was stationed in Surrey at Inkerman Barracks, Woking. The complex political situation in Europe pointed more and more closely to the likelihood of hostilities into which Britain would be drawn from the outset. Rumours abounded and it was due, in part, to such circulating stories that the 2nd Battalion, together with many other battalions around the country, began active preparation. At Woking, all the men were medically examined to confirm their 'fighting fitness', especially those specialist officers and N.C.O's who were likely to be transferred to train other army units. The horses, too, were made ready and the transport wagons were prepared and positioned for loading.

Britain had only a 'gentlemen's agreement' to assist France but had a full treaty with Belgium to come to her aid if attacked. Germany, the most likely protagonist, had been prepared since 1905 with its comprehensive 'Schlieffen Plan' for attacking France. In England, the plan of campaign, which included arrangements for dispatch of the British Expeditionary Force (B.E.F.) to the continent, was known as 'The War Book'. Consisting of several millions of words, 'The War Book' set out in detail who should do what, and when, and it served Britain well. Its plan for mobilising Britain's available army and transporting it to France and Belgium in a relatively short space of time was wholly successful.

Germany struck first. True to the plan drawn up by its former Chief of the General Staff, General Count Alfred von Schlieffen, the common Franco-German border in the north-east of France was ignored in order to avoid the line of 'impregnable' forts constructed there by the French following the Franco-Prussian War. Instead, France was to be invaded across its northern border. This meant that Germany would need to obtain Belgium's agreement to cross its territory or would have to molest Belgium's neutrality. Belgium stood up defiantly to the German's demands, refused right of passage and paid the price of invasion. The German army crossed into Belgium on 4th August. Britain's demand that Germany withdraw her troops immediately from Belgium was ignored and, as a result, Britain formally declared war on Germany.

On that fateful day, Tuesday 4th August, 1914, one of the many orders sent out by telegram from the War Office under the requirements of 'The War Book' was addressed to the Commanding Officer, 2nd Battalion The Royal Sussex Regiment, Battalion Headquarters, Inkerman Barracks, Woking, Surrey. The telegram contained one stark and momentous word: "MOBILISE".

The Battalion swung into every aspect of preparation. All peacetime battalions consisted of between half and two-thirds of their fighting strength of men. The remainder were reservists who, having served their time as professional soldiers, had reverted to civilian life with a requirement to serve so many years in the reserve.

During each of these years, the reservists were required to attend annual camp in order to refresh their competence. The receipt of the reservists into annual camp was not a task particularly enjoyed by their full-time serving comrades but the experience now began to prove its worth. On 6th August, two batches of reservists, in total more that 450 men, arrived at Woking station and were absorbed into the Battalion. Additional horses direct from the purchaser arrived that morning. These animals were two days behind 'The War Book' schedule but the delay was overcome without difficulty.

Two other problems were dealt with; several reservists were transferred from the battalion as 'unfit' and no less than 163 pairs of boots were found too small for their wearers and had to be exchanged.

By the 10th August all wagons were loaded and ready to move. Two days later the Battalion marched out of Inkerman Barracks and, in two trains, one at 11.30am and the other at 12.40pm, left Woking station for Southampton. The Battalion was not alone. Within one week of the declaration of war the whole of the 1st Division of the British Expeditionary Force began to leave for France. The Division was made up as follows:

1st (Guards)Brigade :
    1st Coldstream Guards; 1st Scots Guards;
    1st Black Watch; 2nd Royal Munster
    Fusiliers;
2nd Brigade:
    2nd Royal Sussex; 1st Loyal North Lancs;
    1st Northants; 2nd Kings Royal Rifle Corps.
3rd Brigade:
    1st Queen's; 1st South Wales Borderers; 1st
    Glosters; 2nd Welsh.

Less than nine hours after leaving Woking station, the first party of the 2nd Battalion The Royal Sussex Regiment sailed from Southampton aboard the "S.S. Olympia". Three hours later, at 11.30pm, the remainder of the battalion set sail on the "S.S. Agapenor". This second ship ran into, and holed, a collier soon after leaving Southamption but continued undamaged on her voyage to Le Havre where she docked at noon on 13th, only thirty minutes after the "Olympia". After disembarkation, the Battalion marched to Bleville Camp where the night was spent some five miles from the port.

There was no respite because the Division was urgently required at the front. On the evening of the 14th, the 2nd Battalion was back at Le Havre ready to leave by train.

The Commander in Chief of the B.E.F., General Sir John French, had given considerable thought and planning to the movement of large numbers of men and materials over long distances by train. His solution was that each train should be made up of the same rolling stock. Thus, wherever possible on the continent, every troop train comprised a carriage for officers, 40 box-cars for men or horses, and flat trucks for guns or wagons. In this way a single train could move a whole battalion and its transport. It was on this basis that the 2nd Battalion left Le Havre.

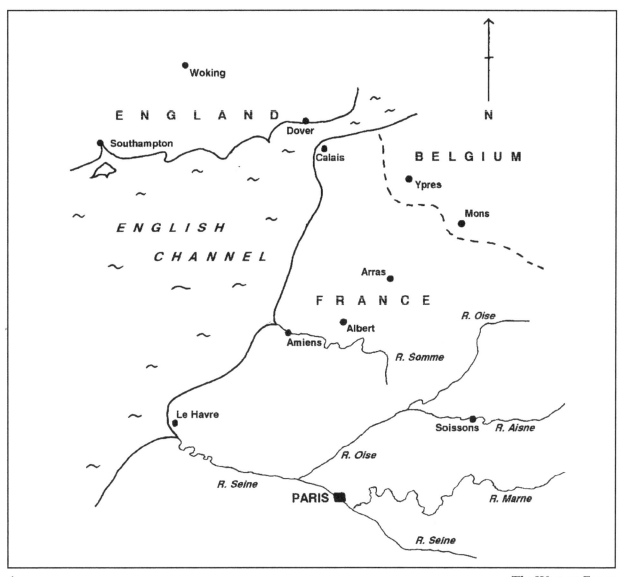

1.   *The Western Front*

Every box-car was marked "Quarante Hommes. Huit Chevaux", in English "40 men or 8 horses". It was a tight squeeze to accommodate 40 men and all their equipment in one box-car and most uncomfortable over long periods of time. It was no wonder the men considered that they were travelling in cattle trucks. As their train slowly pulled out of Le Havre to the cheering of large French crowds waving Union Jacks and Tricolours, the soldiers, unable to respond in the French language, replied in good humour with "moo-o-o's" and "baa-a-a's".

The train journey was slow because of the great demands being made upon the French railway system at that time. After a lengthy stop at Arras, the train eventually arrived at Etreux where the men were billeted for the night more than 21 hours after leaving Le Havre.

Early the next day, the 16th August, the Battalion marched some five miles to Esqueheries where it met up with the remainder of the 2nd Brigade. The next five days were spent there in scattered but reasonably comfortable billets. During this period, training and route marches were undertaken and the men were inoculated against typhoid fever.

On the 21st August the Battalion had the honour of moving out at the head of the whole of the 2nd Brigade for the march of about 14 miles to Avesnes. On the following day the march was continued another 16 miles. Then, after only two hours rest, orders were received to move immediately and, within 20 minutes, the Battalion was moving again by way of Maubeuge to Villers-Sire-Nicole where the men arrived just before midnight after an exhausting march. Even then, there was no respite for "D" Company which had to provide two piquets on roads north of the village.

Matters were certainly beginning to boil. Feelings of expectation and excitement began to grip the men; they felt that the time for real action was fast approaching. Extra rounds of ammunition had been issued and a sudden order to move again was received at 3.15am on the 23rd August. Within two hours the Battalion had marched across the border into Belgium to billet at Rouveroy. During the late evening the Battalion advanced along the road leading to Mons and took up position just short of the village of Givry. From there, heavy German artillery fire on Mons could be heard and seen

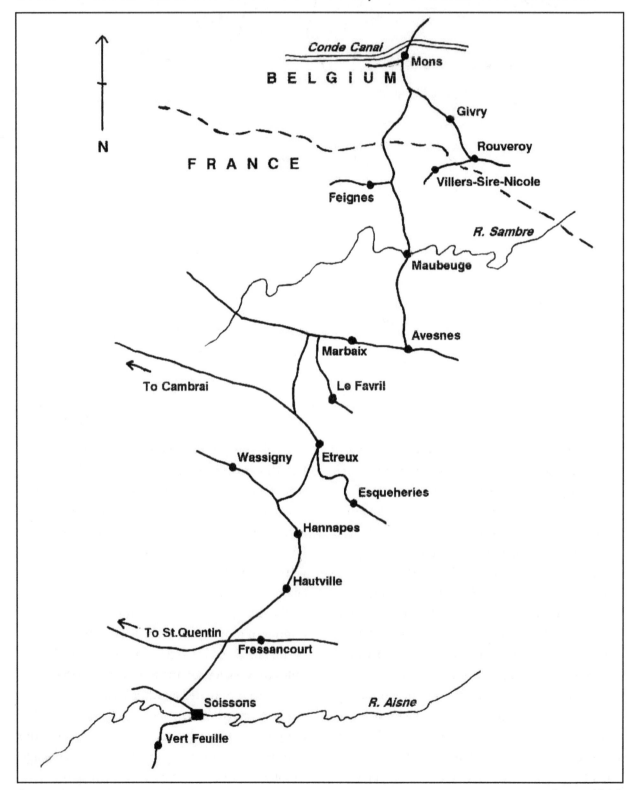

2.

August 1914

clearly and, close-by, guns of the Royal Artillery were brought into action.

Soon after dawn on the 24th August the rival artillery duels began again and the Battalion was ordered to march south-west, first to Bonnet and, later, to Feignes. The great British retreat from Mons had begun. Of this retreat the battalion was part and, at this stage, was leading the way. On the 25th the Battalion marched south all day and experienced, for the first time, some of the confusion that a retreat can engender. French troops nearby wrongly identified a number of British aircraft and began to fire excitedly upon the planes with small arms. During the excitement thus created, Sgt. A.J.Hitchman became the Battalion's first casualty of the war when he sustained a thigh wound. After dark, French troops inadvertently opened fire on Battalion wagons drawn up in the street at Marbaix. This firing created something of a stampede amongst the horses and one nearby animal bolted, throwing its French gendarme rider to his death beneath the wheels of a watercart.

For the next two days the relentless southward march was maintained. The sound of artillery fire was almost continuous and the men knew full well that the B.E.F. was being forced back with the Germans close on their heels.

At this time, the procurement of adequate food and water was a real problem because it was prudent to keep the wagons and horses safely away from the front. Accordingly, the transport dropped supplies at the roadside and then withdrew. The result was that troops at the head of the retreating columns reached the dumps first and did well, while those at the rear were able to obtain little, or nothing, in the way of food or drink. In addition, the relentless marching was hard for the men, all of whom were carrying heavy loads. To provide some relief, they were allowed to leave behind their greatcoats in the charge of ten men chosen for the purpose. Later, it was learned that most of the ten men had been over-run and captured by the Germans; the greatcoats were never seen again !

The Battalion had marched south in two days by way of Wassigny, Hannapes and Hautville. After a further march of 21 hours on 28th August, the men enjoyed the luxury of one day's rest at Fressancourt. On the 30th and 31st the retreat continued and, by the end of the month, the Battalion had marched through Premontre and Soissons to Verte Feuille. By this time the men were tired, weary and, above all, frustrated; "When", they asked, "shall we turn and fight ?"

The southwards march continued for 17 miles on the first day of September. That evening the troops were ordered to sleep in their accoutrements but, by 11.30pm., they were moving again. Soon, they crossed the River Marne, after which the bridges and some river barges were blown up by the Sappers. Through the following day, the march lasted for over 17 hours with the men receiving no rations to sustain them. By late afternoon, the Battalion billeted at Vareddes. At the time, it was not realised that the long retreat was over. The Battalion had marched more than 60 miles in 65 hours.

Although movement on the 3rd was south-easterly, it was an advance in so far as it was a move towards the enemy. That night was spent in billets at Romeny. Early next morning, positions were taken up on the high ground around Aulnoy and, during the day, heavy exchanges of artillery fire brought shrapnel shells crashing all around. Fortunately there were no Battalion casualties on this, the first day of the Battle of the Marne. For the next five days the Battalion formed part of the reserve forces and moved, during that time, by way of Bernay, Rozoy-Vaudoy, Jouy-sur-Morin and Flagny to La Croisette.

On Thursday 10th September the Battalion formed the Brigade's advance guard. Just before reaching Priez, there was a ripple of excitement and anticipation as the enemy actually came into sight on high ground beyond the village. The Battalion advanced through the village in heavy rain and, as it moved out on the far side, the Germans opened such intensive rifle fire that the Battalion was forced to retire. By mid-afternoon, with assistance from the remainder of the Brigade and from French troops rushed from Paris, the Germans were driven back. At 6pm the Battalion moved into billets at Paissy with some sense of shock at their experience and the realisation that, for the first time, so many casualties had been sustained. In addition to those known to be dead, 83 men had been wounded and a number were missing.

SEPTEMBER:
10th:
Captain: (833) Capt. A.E.Jemmett-Brown.
Regimental Sergeant Major: (313) W.Cleare.
Sergeant: (876) W.H.Kettle.
Corporal: (294) T.E.Chessell.
Lance Corporals: (278) E.Cato, (417) G.W.Davey, (1145) C.H.Pankhurst.
Privates: (504) F.Enticknapp, (577) S.A.Funnell, (665) J.Hancock, (697) F.E.Heasman, (816) H.Isaacs, (1204) G.N.Piper, (1246) W.L.Read, (1641) C.E.Wheeler.
Drummers: (1278) S.Richardson, (1655) G.B.Whittington.
Over the following three days a number of men died of wounds received on the 10th September. During this period, movement was through Coincy, Bourg and Paars to Moulins.

SEPTEMBER:
11th:
Lance Corporal: (24) F.J.Ansell.
Privates: (496) W.E.Ellis, (810) P.Inkpen, (990) J.Martin.

High-ground positions beyond Moulins were taken up on 13th September and a heavy artillery duel resulted in the death by shrapnel of Pte. Swaine and the wounding of seven others. The enemy made a further withdrawal.

SEPTEMBER:
13th:
Privates: (554) F.Fowle, (1476) T.Swaine.

The Battle of the Aisne began on 14th September with a vengeance that would result in many Battalion casualties. The Battalion was sent to occupy high ground above Vendresse where it captured 250 German prisoners who were taken by surprise in their bivouacs and surrendered under a white flag. While these prisoners were being marshalled, other Germans opened fire causing the deaths of many soldiers, including their own men. There is no record of the response to this act of treachery. Then the Battalion, ordered to hold its position at all costs, dug itself into trenches.

Thus, for the Battalion, the brief period of open warfare had ended; the long months of

trench warfare were about to begin. In spite of heavy losses, the remainder hung on until evening when the fighting died down. The wounded totalled 79 and there were 114 missing including many dead and wounded. Men in front of the British trenches could not be brought in because of close-quarter fire from the Germans.

SEPTEMBER:
14th:
Lieutenant Colonel: (1048) E.H.Montresor.
Major: (351) M.E.Cookson.
Captain: (1390) L.Slater.
Lieutenants: (413) E.C.Darren, (416) E.C.Daun, (784) W.S.Hughes, (1180) Hon.H.L.Pelham.
Sergeants: (246) T.Butfoy, (309) A.Clarke, (800) G.W.Hutson, (884) J.J.King, (1189) W.Peters.
Corporals: (57) G.H.Baker, (721) H.W.Hider.
Lance Corporals: (291) H.Chatfield, (1222) F.G.Price, (1299) A.A.Rowberry.
Privates: (59) J.Baker, (64) W.J.Baker, (69) H.Baldwin, (71) J.F.Ballard, (127) G.Blackman, (286) S.Chappell, (324) S.G.Colbran, (428) T.Deacon, (432) A.C.Dedman, (437) A.Denyer, (488) H.H.Edwards, (560) J.W.Fraser, (573) E.Funnell, (605) H.E.Glyde, (638) A.Greenfield, (691) W.Haylor, (698) W.J.Heaste, (733) D.S.Hilton, (741) J.Hodge, (853) E.Keates, (859) J.W.Kember, (874) S.Kenward, (882) H.A.King, (914) A.J.Lassetter, (932) V.A.Letchford, (959) J.Luxford, (1182) E.A.Pelling, (1219) F.H.Powell, (1225) A.Pullen, (1310) G.Sageman, (1325) E.Saunders, (1360) D.Shirley, (1451) T.Still, (1452) C.E.Stoffell, (1479) C.W.Sygrove, (1516) G.Tomlin, (1528) W.Townsend, (1530) H.G.Tree, (1536) A.Trussler, (1549) E.Tween, (1579) E.Walter, (1663) F.H.G.Willey, (1704) A.T.Yeatman.

On the 15th September the enemy dug themselves into trenches 600 yards from the Battalion line. The Germans attacked during the afternoon but were easily repulsed; they then retired to a distance of about 1,500 yards. During the night the Germans attacked again, but having been spotted by scouts, one of whom was killed, were beaten back once more. Throughout the 16th there was a general artillery bombardment. The weather was very wet.

SEPTEMBER:
15th:
Private: (1575) J.Walker.
16th:
Private: (1361) W.H.Shoosmith.

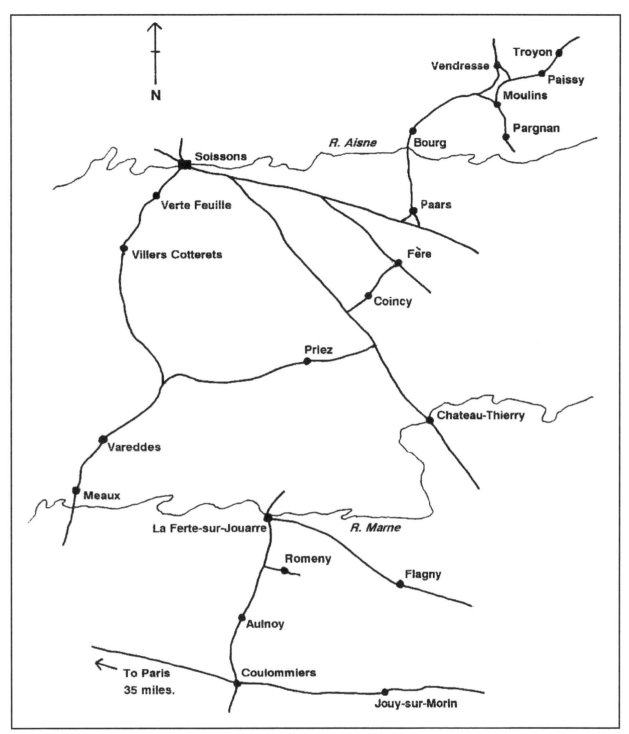

3.   *September 1914*

Throughout the 17th, 18th and 19th, September artillery bombardments continued. On the last of these days the Battalion was relieved from the front line and sent to take up an outpost position at Paissy where they sheltered in available caves. At dawn on the 20th, the enemy bombardment was continued and, in the early afternoon, the Battalion drove back Germans who had forced French troops and the West Yorks to retire on the right. Twelve men were wounded and two others could not be located by stretcher bearers. The bodies of these two men, Cpl. Peacock and Private Boniface, were later found and buried by the Royal Artillery. On the 21st, a shell dropped into a yard where men were billeted, wounding four and killing Pte. Kenward. At 6am on 22nd, the Battalion was relieved and joined the rest of the Brigade at Pargnan. The next day saw the Battalion in reserve at Moulins before it returned, in the evening, to billet again at Pargnan.

SEPTEMBER:
18th:
Sergeants: (65) W.Balcombe, (170) G.Breeds.
Corporals: (719) S.Hickmott, (1398) A.H.Smith.
Privates: (182) A.Broadbridge, (870) E.H.Kenward.
19th:
Company Quartermaster Sergeant: (122) E.T.Bish.
Private: (216) G.Bryant.
20th:
Corporal: (1175) F.J.Peacock.
Private: (139) A.Boniface.
21st:
Private: (869) C.Kenward.
22nd:
Private: (1670) A.T.Willins.
23rd:
Lance Corporal: (843) C.J.Jones.

A welcome rest was taken for the next two days, the 24th and 25th September, but, on the second evening, the Battalion moved up to trenches at Troyon. A shell explosion on the morning of the 26th buried, or partially buried, three men, of whom one was killed. A similar explosion buried Sgt. Butcher in the afternoon but he was dug out unharmed after one and a half hours.

A Battalion machine gun was knocked out by a shell on the 27th killing three gunners; the bombardment continued most of the day. Two other men, injured by stray bullets, died of wounds the following day. Enemy shelling continued during the last three days of the month. In particular, on the 29th, shrapnel shelling of the road where the transport was situated killed several men and eight horses.

SEPTEMBER:
26th:
Private: (1169) A.G.Payne.
27th:
Lance Corporal: (705) G.M.Henderson.
Privates: (205) H.Brown, (400) R.Croft, (423) G.Day, (531) W.J.Fissi, (1322) W.Sansome, (1703) F.C.Yeates
28th:
Privates: (454) W.H.Dowson, (645) A.Griffith.
29th:
Privates: (814) L.Irish, (1036) H.D.Mitchell, (1181) H.Pellett, (1554) T.Uwins, (1627) W.Wells.
30th:
Privates: (1664) C.A.Williams, (1702) C.D.G.Wyatt.

The hamlet of Troyon and its immediate area was to remain the Battalion's location for the first half of October. At that place they were some 15 miles east of Soissons and two or three miles north of the River Aisne with alternate steep hillsides and deep valleys running south-west to north-east from the river. Heavy artillery fire from both sides continued each day. On the 3rd, a machine gunner, Lance Corporal Wicks, was trying his utmost to quieten a particularly troublesome enemy sniper when he lost the deadly game, being shot himself by that very sniper and dying from his wounds soon after. During the early morning of the 4th October, German shells found the Battalion positions and six men were killed. The following two days were uneventful and quiet.

OCTOBER:
3rd:
Private: (1659) J.Wicks.
4th:
Privates: (574) E.E.Funnell, (650) W.Gumbrill, (1212) H.W.Poole, (1423) S.Spencer, (1497) H.Theobald, (1629) A.West.

The Battalion had spent some considerable effort in constructing, at a safe distance, a number of dummy trenches containing several 'men of straw' dressed in old rags and clothing. The 'men of straw' were positioned so as to be just on view; one 'man' was even reading a copy of the 'Daily Mail'! At 6am on the 7th the trap was sprung when, to the delight of witnesses, heavy and prolonged German machine gun fire was opened on the dummies. Later, much to everyone's amusement, the newspaper reader was found to have been shot 40 times!

On two occasions later the same day, the general seriousness of the situation was restored when the Germans began to send over a new type of high-trajectory heavy shell which caused casualties. These shells were later nicknamed 'coalboxes' on account of the distinctive pall of dense black smoke emitted upon explosion. More casualties were sustained in similar fashion on the 8th October.

OCTOBER:
7th:
Captain: (12) R.J.P.D.Aldridge.
Lance Corporal: (1072) J.Mustchin.

Privates: (33) J.Askew, (447) A.Doe, (961) W.E.Maccabee, (1482) W.Tarling.

8th:

Company Quartermaster Sergeant: (445) T.Diplock.

Privates: (771) F.C.House, (1543) C.Turner, (1585) T.Ward.

From the 9th to the 15th October, bombardments continued apace and a number of casualties were caused thereby. The 15th, however, was to be the Battalion's last day of fighting on the River Aisne. Preparations to move were made and, during that evening, French troops arrived to take over the positions. At midnight, the Battalion began to move southwards, much assisted by a heavy mist which enabled the withdrawal to be completed without interference from the enemy. On the 16th, the Battalion billeted and rested at Vauxcere before marching farther south, late that evening, to the railway station at Fismes.

OCTOBER:

12th:

Private: (162) J.Bradford.

13th:

Private: (772) H.A.Howard.

14th:

Private: (289) A.E.Chatfield.

OCTOBER:

16th:

Private: (1087) A.E.V.Newnham.

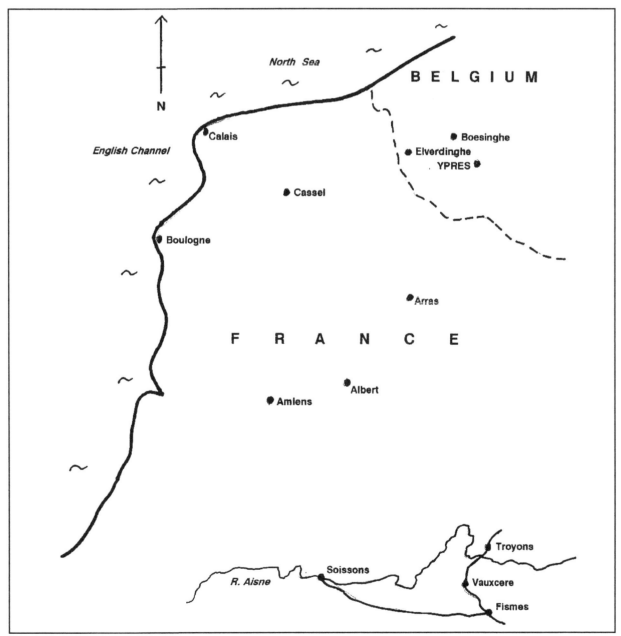

4.   *October 1914*

At 3am on 17th October the Battalion left Fismes by train on what was to be a protracted and weary journey northwards back into Belgium. The journey, by way of Amiens, Boulogne and Calais, was much delayed by a breakdown on the line ahead and they finally detrained, after 48 uncomfortable hours, at Cassel where they dropped thankfully into billets. Unknown to them, they were approaching the First Battle of Ypres which started on the 18th October.

Throughout the 20th October the whole Brigade was on the march, re-entering Belgium and reaching Elverdinghe. The following day saw the march continue to Boesinghe. There, the Battalion was placed in reserve until it marched, on the 25th, into the town of Ypres. Billets were taken in the town which was still relatively undamaged at that stage. The next day was spent in bivouacs just outside the town before the Battalion marched eastwards on the 27th to entrench in Château Wood, immediately to the north of the Menin Road, about two miles from the centre of Ypres.

OCTOBER:
23rd:
Private: (1561) O.O.Vincent.

From Château Wood, the Battalion moved forward almost one mile on the 28th October to entrench themselves once more, this time in Polygon Wood. There, enemy shelling accounted for several casualties amongst men and horses, including those bringing small arms ammunition carts across open ground to the wood. Early morning on the 29th brought an enemy attack all along the line, forcing the Battalion to fall back to its trenches in Château Wood.

OCTOBER:
29th:
Privates: (1273) F.Richardson, (1665) C.E.Williams.

Beginning at 10am on the 30th October, the Battalion found itself fighting hard over a two-day period. Heavy German shells fell among the men's dugouts and, at that time, orders were received for an immediate move to stem a crisis and restore the line at Zandvoorde. Early in this move, the Commanding Officer, Lt.Col. Crispin, tried to take a short cut across country. Almost

immediately, the enemy opened a concentrated shrapnel fire which caused the Colonel's horse to bolt carrying the C.O. on under heavy fire until he was shot and killed instantaneously.

Following this sad and serious loss of its Commanding Officer, the Battalion was led on by Major Green along the main road so far as Hooge where a left turn was taken. Soon, the Battalion was ordered to attack and make good the line along the nearby road but so concentrated was the German artillery, rifle and machine gun fire, some in enfilade from the left, that no progress could be made. However, the position was held until mid-day on the 31st October. At that time, news was received that the British line had been broken near Gheluvelt and, as a result, it was necessary for the 2nd Battalion to move back to a safer position. Even then it was reported that the enemy were advancing. The Germans came on in large numbers but were met and forced right back by the Battalion until, by early evening, the Sussex men were able to move forward with fixed bayonets to re-occupy their earlier trenches with the welcome news that a counter-attack by the 2nd Worcesters had restored the situation at Gheluvelt.

All was not secure, however, because another serious situation developed quickly when scouts found that the Germans, with a number of machine guns, had occupied a nearby trench and part of Château Wood. A hazardous plan was formulated by which 'D' Company would attack the trench while the remainder of the Battalion would advance across open country to the enemy positions in the wood. The Germans allowed the cross-country advance to proceed to a point where the attackers were too-far committed. Heavy rifle and machine gun fire was then opened on the unprotected men of the Battalion. Some fared better than others but the general result was a withdrawal under such covering fire as colleagues farther back could bring to bear. Heavy casualties were sustained during these two days fighting.

OCTOBER:
30th:
Lieutenant Colonel: (396) H.T.Crispin.
Lieutenant: (952) E.A.Lousada.
Second Lieutenants: (975) F.C.J.Marillier, (1352) C.F.Shaw.

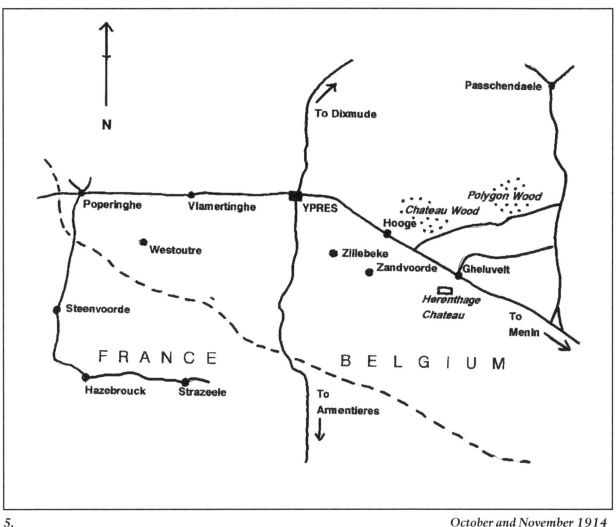

5. *October and November 1914*

Sergeants: (433) M.Delaney, (875) A.H.Kerswill, (1020) C.L.Miller.

Corporal: (1449) H.L.Stevens.

Lance Corporals: (403) D.Crowley, (624) E.Gorringe, (700) R.J.Heather, (795) F.Hurst, (1550) J.J.Twyman.

Privates: (30) H.T.Ash, (54) F.Baker, (201) F.Brown, (210) T.Brown, (225) G.Burchell, (235) W.F.Burt, (238) T.J.Burton, (242) F.Bushby, (365) S.Coppard, (399) L.R.Croft, (541) A.Foord, (635) H.Green, (752) F.C.Holland, (786) C.C.Humphrey, (909) E.Lambourne, (978) A.Marsh, (982) C.Martin, (1003) G.McCready, (1055) W.Moore, (1066) A.J.Mullins, (1070) E.Murphy, (1150) R.Parker, (1207) J.Plater, (1287) R.F.Rodell, (1340) S.Seale, (1344) W.G.Selby, (1518) W.Tompsett, (1584) J.B.Ward, (1694) J.Worsell, (1709) F.J.Young.

31st:

Privates: (152) T.C.Bourne, (338) J.Collins, (393) F.A.Creed, (439) H.Denyer, (657) A.H.Hall, (702) J.Hemmings, (858) F.Kember, (953) A.C.Love, (1128) F.Ovenden, (1147) E.Pannifer, (1164) W.Pattenden, (1244) E.Read, (1492) H.Tennent.

At one minute after midnight on the 1st day of November, three Companies, which had formed up in a line just south of Château Wood, advanced in silence with bayonets fixed. The plan was to clear the Germans from the wood but the whereabouts of friend and foe was not entirely certain. As the men neared the trench for which they were aiming, enemy small arms fire was opened against them. The charge immediately commenced but when the men reached the trench they found it occupied by the Northamptons! The necessary withdrawal to the previous position was covered successfully by Battalion machine guns. There, the line was held and improved until a further withdrawal into a reserve position was made on the 2nd. At 8pm that evening, the enemy, giving vent to wild yells, made a determined attack. The Battalion held fire until the Germans were close and then caused serious damage, quickly aborting the attack. The next morning, four German corpses were found inside and about 100 more outside the Battalion's protective wire.

NOVEMBER:
1st:
Sergeants: (1296) A.Routhan, (1667) F.Williams.
Privates: (482) J.J.G.Eckert, (980) E.Marshall, (993) E.Maryan.
2nd:
Privates: (219) F.W.Bugler, (330) S.F.Coleman, (335) T.E.Collings.

Apart from the usual outbreaks of shelling, the four day period commencing on the 3rd November was relatively quiet. On Saturday 7th another attempt, this time successful, was made to dislodge the Germans from Château Wood by pushing them out through the south-east corner. This episode cost over 20 casualties, killed, wounded and missing. More casualties were sustained on the 8th, some almost certainly from 'friendly fire' when our own shells dropped very close to the Battalion trenches before being redirected.

NOVEMBER:
3rd:
Lieutenant: (461) B.P.Duke.
Privates: (5) G.Adams, (514) C.E.Farley.
4th:
Private: (1564) H.A.Vivash.
5th:
Corporal: (1117) A.J.Oliver.
Private: (1221) T.R.Pratt.
6th:
Corporal: (314) H.G.Clevett.
Privates: (1321) E.G.Sangster, (1648) G.A.White.
7th:
Corporal: (852) W.J.Jupp.
Privates: (126) E.C.Blackman, (534) A.J.Fleet, (1693) H.E.Worsell.
8th:
Sergeant: (824) F.James.
Corporal: (972) C.Manville.
Privates: (507) W.G.Etherington, (863) E.Kennard, (902) W.Knight, (998) H.Matthews, (1279) E.Riddle, (1581) P.Wanstall.

On the 9th November, a move was made through Zillebeke to dig-in near Hooge where the 10th was spent in reflection and welcome rest. A return was made on the 11th to Château Wood where, next day, the situation became critical

for a while until the trench line, which was badly broken, had been repaired. Shelling continued on the 13th and 14th. Then, on the 15th, the Battalion was at last relieved from the First Battle of Ypres and moved back to bivouac about one mile from the town itself.

NOVEMBER:
10th:
Private: (970) H.F.Manser.
11th:
Private: (989) J.Martin.
12th:
Lieutenant: (1638) R.C.Westall.
Private: (497) B.C.Elmes.
13th:
Privates: (353) R.Coomber, (1073) F.Muzzall, (1226) H.L.Pullen, (1567) E.C.Waite.
14th:
Privates: (643) E.H.Grender, (1201) A.E.Pilbeam.
15th:
Privates: (522) G.Felton, (1541) J.Tugnut.

The move continued on the 16th November around Ypres to Vlamertinghe and then to Westoutre. On the 17th, Strazeele was reached by marching and there, billeted in a warm, strongly fragrant malt house for two days, the men received a bountiful supply of comforts in the way of good food, beer, confectionery, cigarettes and tobacco. Hazebrouck was reached in a blizzard on the 19th and there the Battalion remained for the rest of the month, being kept occupied by training and the occasional route march. More reinforcements arrived during this period; they were sorely needed to replace the many who had been lost as casualties. Indeed, in keeping with all other battalions of the B.E.F. at that time, the 2nd Battalion could no more be regarded as a fully professional soldier force. Too many regulars had been lost and their places would be taken mainly by territorials sent out from England.

NOVEMBER:
17th:
Private: (776) E.E.Howell.
20th:
Private: (973) H.Manville.
22nd:
Privates: (1574) C.J.Walker, (1684) S.Wood.
26th:
Private: (55) F.J.Baker.
30th:
Private: (1330) W.Saunders.

The Battalion had fought hard and well at the First Battle of Ypres. Because of its absolute refusal to be budged from its positions there, despite overwhelming odds, it was proud to have been given the name 'The Iron Regiment' by none other than its German adversaries.

Route marches, musketry, machine gun, Company and general training occupied the first three weeks of December. During that period a few isolated bombs were dropped by enemy aircraft without causing damage and there was a highlight on Thursday 3rd when King George V inspected troops at Hazebrouck and the Battalion lined the streets.

DECEMBER:
18th:
Lieutenant: (1234) D.G.Ramsay.
DECEMBER:
20th:
Private: (546) H. J. Ford.

At 7am on the 21st December, the Battalion boarded motor buses at Hazebrouck with all their tools and 40 boxes of ammunition. Travelling south-eastwards, and marching the last few miles, they arrived at the village of Le Touret. On the 22nd, relief of the Seaforth Highlanders began at 7.30am but, owing to the appalling mud and very bad state of the communication trench, the relief was not completed until 3.20pm. That night, some of the Germans entered trenches on the left. Barriers were constructed quickly and both sides bombed each other with vigour. To the right, a fire trench was flooded and 2nd Battalion men there had to stand in water waist deep until relieved on the evening of the 23rd.

DECEMBER:
22nd:
Lieutenant: (1559) C.F.Verrall.
Private: (1158) T.S.Patchen.
23rd:
Lance Corporal: (1191) A.Petty.
Privates: (599) W.Gilbey, (606) F.Goddard, (723) R.E.Hilder, (779) C.G.Hudson, (910) A.Langford, (1146) J.Pankhurst.

On Christmas Eve the Battalion was relieved and marched back to Le Hamel. Christmas Day was spent peacefully, although in readiness to move at one hour's notice. Christmas cards from the King and Queen were issued. In addition, every man received one of the special presents sent by Princess Mary; these were gold-coloured metal tins measuring 5" x 3" x 1" and containing either cigarettes or chocolate, a pencil in the shape of a bullet, and a small card inscribed "With Best Wishes for a Happy Christmas and a Victorious New Year from the Princess Mary and Friends at Home". The Battalion diary makes no mention of the food and drink provided nor of the famous 'Christmas Truce' during which British and German troops met and fraternised in 'No-Man's-Land' along some sections of the front on that Christmas Day of 1914.

There was no luxury of a long Christmastide break because, at 6am on Boxing Day, the Battalion moved off to take over trenches between the La Bassée Canal and the village of Givenchy. Again, the change-over was lengthy and difficult owing to the poor state of the ground. Conditions were so bad that, during the period 24th to 31st December, no fewer than 160 men were admitted to hospital with "rheumatism, ague and trench feet". Much time was spent attempting to improve the condition and effectiveness of the trenches. On the 28th, Sergeant Milton was shot by a sniper and, on the 29th, the Battalion's complement of machine guns was increased from two to four, still a woefully inadequate number. Casualties were sustained on the final day of the year during a British counter attack made to recover an observation and machine gun post from the Germans.

DECEMBER:
28th:
Sergeant: (1030) E.Milton.
30th:
Private: (525) E.Finch.
31st:
Privates: (206) H.H.Brown, (1358) W.J.Sheppard, (1365) J.Short.

By this time, the heavy toll in casualties sustained during the last three months of 1914 meant that few of the original 'Old Contemptibles' remained with this, or any other, British regular army Battalion. Great were the losses in experienced men and, sadly, the current methods of waging trench warfare were to deplete numbers even more dramatically and critically during the year to come. Already, at home, the huge waves of recruits to Lord Kitchener's 'New Armies' were being gathered and trained but it would be many months, yet, before they were ready to play their part. In the meantime, the gaps were being filled manfully by men from the territorial forces; theirs would be the heavy task of making good the losses.

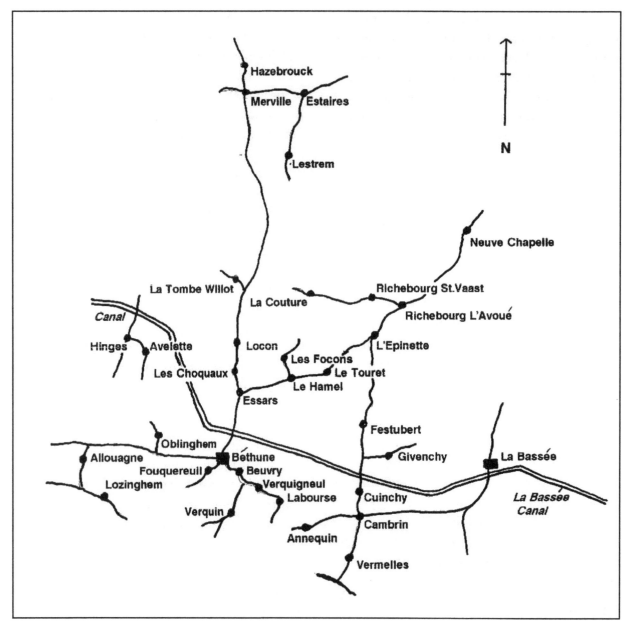

6.   *December 1914 – August 1915*

CHAPTER 2
1915
JANUARY – JUNE

During the counter attack made by the Battalion on New Year's Eve 21 casualties were sustained including wounded and missing. At daylight there began an allied bombardment of the enemy posts still held in the La Bassée Canal embankment.

JANUARY:
1st:
Second Lieutenant: (1371) A.L.Silvester.
Lance Corporals: (50) A.Baker, (878) G.W.Kinch, (966) W.Manley.
Privates: (190) C.F.Brooker, (464) T.Dunk, (732) H.G.Hillyer, (879) A.H.King, (1285) H.Robins.

With general ground conditions so bad and trenches deep with mud and water, a system of relief every 24 hours was introduced. Heavy allied bombardments continued, particularly against enemy positions in the canal bank. At one point, on the 4th January, observers witnessed portions of the nearby railway lines and seven Germans hurtling through the air. Battalion positions were close to a brick kiln with several large nearby brick stacks. By joining a number of these brick stacks, a redoubt, or keep, was built to advantage. On the 12th, the Germans shelled the brick stacks and got close enough to throw a few bombs. At mid-day Cuinchy was bombarded and a German shell fell into the Battalion Headquarters' kitchen while the officers were lunching in the next room; nobody was injured. The next day, these officers were busy assimilating a welcome draft of 130 men as replacements for those lost. Much time continued to be spent on trench improvements in this, the worst winter's weather for many years; mid-month was reached in this way on the 15th.

JANUARY:
2nd:
Private: (575) F.Funnell.
6th:
Privates: (458) R.Dudfield, (718) J.A.M.Heyes.

12th:
Privates: (68) A.B.Baldwin, (934) C.W.Levett, (1315) P.Samson.
13th:
Privates: (455) A.Dray, (1523) G.W.Topp.
15th:
Lance Corporal: (1033) W.H.Minns.

Medical advice resulted in the system of relief being changed to 48 hours starting on the 16th January. Although this meant longer periods in the line, there was greater advantage by having longer periods for rest and recuperation at Givenchy and Annequin. These villages were close to the fighting, however, so that rest there was only relative and could be disturbed at any time.

JANUARY:
17th:
Private: (1580) W.K.Walton.
20th:
Private: (143) G.H.Boniface.
22nd:
Private: (607) F.J.Goddard.

A greater sense of rest and relaxation was welcomed on the 21st January when the Battalion marched farther back from the fighting and into the town of Béthune. Cleaning of billets, men and equipment was the first requirement. Baths, which had not been possible for a considerable time, were enjoyed by everyone. All underclothing, much of it verminous with lice, was handed in prior to bathing and the luxury of new clothing was received afterwards. Sunday the 24th was a day of complete freedom and rest following the church parade in the town theatre attended by 100 men at 10.30am.

Rest and relative peace were rudely shattered on the 25th January by the sound of a heavy and persistent cannonade at 9.30am. Very quickly came the order to move to Beuvry. The Germans had exploded six mines and rushed trenches held by the Guards, pushing the British back almost to the villages of Cuinchy and Givenchy. By 5.30pm the Battalion had reached Cambrin from Beuvry. Moving on to Cuinchy, the Battalion attacked at 7.30pm in an effort to regain lost ground. Some ground was re-taken although the Germans were clearly expecting a counter-attack and opened a heavy fire aided by the near-full moon. By the end of the second day, the 26th, things had quietened down and the allies had consolidated their position by a long period of trench digging.

JANUARY:
25th:
Second Lieutenant: (627) R.W.R.Gramshaw.
Lance Corporals: (566) G.Frisch, (933) H.J.Leverett.
Privates: (215) F.M.Bryan, (317) W.Clifton, (336) C.F.Collins, (368) J.J.Cork, (372) R.A.Cosson, (381) L.J.Cox, (414) J.C.Dartnell, (489) J.Edwards, (512) S.Fairbank, (513) A.Farley, (626) A.R.Gower, (963) J.M.C.Mackay, (1021) G.Miller, (1054) P.H.Moore, (1205) H.Piper, (1331) H.H.Sawyers, (1383) W.G.Skeggs, (1454) A.L.Stone, (1613) A.E.Wedge, (1651) W.J.White.
26th:
Corporals: (135) E.W.Blunden, (239) F.Busby, (579) E.S.Gadsden.
Lance Corporals: (1188) A.R.Pestel, (1688) H.J.Woodley.
Privates: (23) E.S.Anscombe, (337) G.W.Collins, (905) J.Lallyett, (1045) H.Monk, (1433) F.V.Stead, (1501) P.Thompson.

Shell, sniping and machine gun fire continued from the enemy on the 27th January. The following day, when a German motor machine gun battery was detected, allied heavy siege guns were brought to bear, during which Battalion troops took extra shelter in a culvert. The Germans quickly moved their mobile battery. The Keep came under determined enemy attack on the morning of the 29th, first by use of bombs and minenwerfers, then by massed infantry carrying with them scaling ladders and hatchets. Although the Germans got to within 20 or 30 yards of the Keep they were repelled by concentrated rifle fire and by an effective bombing party. Despite this, the enemy regrouped behind the brick stacks for a

further attack but were so accurately shelled by allied artillery that the attempt was apparently cancelled. Spasmodic bombing and shelling continued on the 30th January before the Battalion was relieved and moved back, once more, to Béthune. On this occasion, the whole Battalion was billeted together in the tobacco factory. Sunday the 31st was spent resting and trying to remove some of the all-pervading mud.

JANUARY:
27th:
Second Lieutenant: (801) H.V.Hutt.
Corporal: (742) W.T.Hodge.
Lance Corporal: (633) C.Green.
Privates: (36) B.R.Attree, (154) W.E.Bourne, (1195) W.J.Philpott, (1350) W.Sharp.
28th:
Private: (367) W.F.Coppard.
29th:
Second Lieutenant: (85) S.A.N.S.Barthropp.
Sergeants: (1277) J.Richardson, (1485) A.Taylor.
Corporal: (1252) E.Reed.
Lance Corporal: (1511) H.Tippett.
Privates: (274) W.T.Carter, (535) H.Flesher, (667) A.E.Hanks, (971) W.Manvell, (1014) F.Meredith, (1140) G.Page, (1341) S.J.Sealey, (1621) R.J.Weller.
30th:
Privates: (191) H.Brooker, (377) E.Coulstock, (585) L.V.Gasson, (817) C.Isden.
31st:
Lance Corporal: (249) J.A.Butt.
Private: (304) G.Clark.

In written messages, the Brigadier General Commanding the 2nd Infantry Brigade, and General Sir John French, Commander in Chief of the British Expeditionary Force, congratulated the 2nd Battalion, The Royal Sussex Regiment "... in the magnificent defence of the Keep and the beating off of the German attack this morning (29th) ...". It was fortunate that, during what remained of the deep winter of 1914 – 15, the Battalion remained out of the immediate front line areas. Indeed, February,1915, was to prove one of the least active months allowed to the Battalion throughout the whole of its four years and four months on the Western Front. All forms of instruction and training continued, however, and a number of reinforcement drafts were received. On the 27th, the Battalion paraded for inspection by the 1st Army Corps Commander, Lt.Gen.Sir C.Monro, K.C.B.

A steady trickle of losses, including those dying from wounds and from natural causes, continued to be sustained. On the last day of the month the Battalion marched to Les Choquaux and went into Corps Reserve.

FEBRUARY:
1st:
Private: (1589) H.P.Warton.
3rd:
Lance Corporal: (203) G.W.Brown.
4th:
Lance Corporal: (1291) E.T.Rooks.
Privates: (463) E.F.Duncan, (1043) J.C.B.Mohr.
7th:
Private: (708) H.Henshaw.
8th:
Privates: (373) C.J.Cotten, (1133) W.T.Padbury, (1571) A.Walder.
9th:
Lance Corporal: (211) W.G.C.Brown.
10th:
Private: (781) F.P.Hughes.
12th:
Lance Corporal: (690) A.J.Hayes.
Privates: (1110) G.Nutley, (1406) O.Smith, (1471) J.Sumner.
13th:
Private: (578) R.Furness.
16th:
Corporals: (750) L.Holden, (1259) R.J.Relph.
Privates: (45) A.Bailey, (256) E.Cain, (426) J.Deacon, (462) G.W.Dumbrell, (701) F.Hedger, (984) G.Martin, (1297) M.Routhan, (1389) A.E.Slater.
22nd:
Private: (378) P.Covey.

For the period 1st – 9th March, the Battalion was billeted and undergoing further training at Les Choquaux. On the 10th, a march was made to La Cassan where the day was spent in Army Reserve well within hearing of an extensive allied bombardment all along the line from Cuinchy to Armentières. At midnight, a return march was made to billets in La Couture and Le Touret. The 11th and 12th were spent in tactical movement between Locon, La Couture, Le Touret and Les Choquaux before moving into the front line at Festubert on the 14th March. The German opponents at this point were Saxons and one

of them, who spoke excellent English, shouted across to remonstrate against British sniping at night. Certainly, sniping was a continuous danger because there were no trenches, only breastworks, in this area. The absence of communication trenches meant that all reliefs could be accomplished only under cover of darkness.

The 15th, 16th and 17th March proved relatively inactive save for concealed efforts to improve the defences. Sleep was difficult, however, because the Germans persisted in shelling a nearby farm where a cluster of British dummy guns had been placed. On the 18th March the Battalion was relieved by the 5th (Cinque Ports) Battalion, The Royal Sussex Regiment, and marched back to Essars for a few days rest, training and inter-company football matches.

MARCH:
1st:
Private: (341) C.G.Colwell.
2nd:
Private: (1600) A.E.Watts (alias Thomas).
6th:
Private: (1261) P.Remnant.
16th:
Private: (431) I.G.Dean.
17th:
Private: (600) J.Gill.

At 5pm on the 23rd March, the Battalion paraded and marched to Richebourg L'Avoué to take over the front line of breastworks. The 24th March was a quiet day but, on the 25th, the Germans shelled the rear areas with lyddite. It was relatively quiet again for the next two days. On the 27th, two Companies went to Richeboug St.Vaast and two, plus Headquarters, returned to Le Touret.

All Companies provided working parties on Sunday 28th March, the day before a strange occurrence. A mysterious individual dressed as a priest was found at Richebourg St.Vaast on the Monday. This man was apprehended and handed over to the neighbouring 3rd Brigade as a suspected spy but he was released after examination of his papers. The Battalion's own 2nd Brigade was not satisfied with this and caused further checks to be made on the man whereupon the French confirmed that he was, in fact, a local man of the cloth. All this somewhat disappointed the men because the Colonel had offered a prize of £5 for the first true spy captured by the Battalion.

All Battalion Companies were relieved from Richebourg St.Vaast and from Le Touret on the 30th March and went back to billets at La Tombe Willot. There they were to remain for the next week with time for training, football and athletics.

MARCH:
25th:
Private: (1130) C.H.Overton.
27th:
Private: (25) H.E.Applegate.

The Battalion remained 'at rest' until the 7th April when a move was made to take over the line with half the Battalion at Neuve Chapelle and half at Richebourg St.Vaast. No-Man's-Land in this area was between 300 and 400 yards wide. The Germans appeared to have no offensive intentions but concentrated, instead, on improving their defensive positions. The Battalion, too, had much work to do for the improvement of their own conditions. The parapets were dangerously low and had to be raised. Also, there was still much hardship from mud and water in these low-lying Artois fields where the natural water table was only some two feet below the ground. Efforts to divert and clear water by the use of spades and mud scoops, known in Sussex as ' scuppets' or 'jutts', had only a marginal effect. Through all this there were spasmodic shelling episodes from both sides. Reinforcements continued to arrive including men from Kitchener's 'New Army' and some re-enlisted soldiers.

Sunday 11th April brought a respite with a move back to billets in Les Choquaux. A march to more billets in Pont Hinges was made on the 15th for an eight day period of further rest and training.

A return to the former front line area near Richebourg St.Vaast was made on the 24th April. The enemy shelled the area a good deal on the following day and then, at night, sent out a working party to improve their wire entanglements. A burst of rapid fire was sent in the workers' direction; this must have had some

effect because, during the day on the 26th, the Germans were seen to throw three of their dead forward over their parapet into No-Man's-Land.

APRIL:
11th:
Private: (364) A.Coppard.
25th:
Privates: (297) H.Childs, (352) E.Coomber, (889) H.Kingett.
26th:
Private: (832) J.Jefery.

There was a good deal of enemy shelling during the next two days before, on the evening of the 28th April, a relief began and the Battalion reached billets at Pont Avelette by 3am. In that place, the month ended with some rest and continued training.

APRIL:
27th:
Privates: (1381) J.E.Sjoquist, (1425) C.Spooner.
28th:
Private: (1196) R.Phoenix.
30th:
Privates: (44) F.Bacon, (830) O.Jarvis.

Now began one of the heaviest months for casualties sustained by the 2nd Battalion throughout the war. After the severe winter, the spring and early summer encouraged the allies, in particular, to turn their attentions to offensive actions. After all, the Germans were in possession of large tracts of Belgium and Northern France and could well afford to stand on the defensive until Russia was defeated; something had to be done to dislodge the Germans and force them back.

From Pont Avelette a march was made to Alluagne on the 2nd May for training until the 6th when movement was effected to Les Facons. There, on the 7th, orders for an assault on the enemy lines opposite Richebourg L'Avoué were received. On the following evening the breastworks near Richebourg L'Avoué were taken over by the Battalion and, during the night, bombs and wooden bridges for crossing the stream, called the 'Riviere des Laies', in No-Man's-Land were brought forward in readiness.

On Sunday the 9th May,1915, took place the bloody, one-day Battle of Aubers Ridge. The day began at 3.30am with an issue of tea and rum. The Battalion's front of attack was to be about 400 yards wide across fields immediately opposite, and to the south-east of, the village of Richebourg L'Avoué which straggled along both sides of the main road known as the 'Rue du Bois'. At 5.00am the British preliminary bombardment commenced. This bombardment intensified at 5.30am and, at that hour, men of the Battalion went 'over the top' followed, at a distance of 50 yards, by the second wave. The men were slowed by the weight of their equipment; some were carrying sandbags and barbed wire for use if enemy positions were taken. Soon, men from the nearby Royal Sussex Regiment's 5th Battalion arrived and many of them went straight over the top to become intermingled with 2nd Battalion men.

The plan was that, directly the German front line was entered, special parties should bomb the enemy communication trench in the rear. On the right, 'A' and 'C' Companies advanced to within 40 yards of the enemy's wire. At this time several officers were wounded, one being Lt.R.T.Shaw who was later killed while efforts were being made to bring him in to safety. The right of the line was being subjected to enfilade fire from enemy machine guns. Second Lieutenant Roberts of 'D' Company was killed whereupon Company Sergeant Major Butcher assumed command and ordered the men to dig themselves in as best they could.

The left of the line also suffered heavily from German enfilade fire at a point where an early retirement by the Munster Fusiliers left the Battalion flank exposed. At 6.30am, just one hour after the initial assault, orders were issued for a general retirement behind the breastworks from which the attack had started. In the afternoon another senseless assault was ordered to be carried out by the 1st Guards Brigade; this, too, ended in predictable failure. At 7.30pm the remnants of the shocked and shattered 2nd Battalion marched off back to billets at Les Choquaux. The roll calls were answered only by the pathetic few. The strength of a British battalion at that time normally would have been about 1,000 men of whom some 850 would have been fully armed and fighting infantrymen.

Set against that, then, the numbers of killed, wounded and missing recorded for that day in the Battalion War Diary: 14 officers and 548 other ranks. Included among those killed in action were brothers Aubrey and Jack Brooks of Newick, Sussex. Such was the tragedy of that day's fighting that the B.E.F. generally was in no fit state to take further action; this may be judged from the fact that most of the bodies could not be recovered from No-Man's-Land. Over 93% of the 2nd Battalion men killed that day have no known graves; their names are recorded on the Memorial at Le Touret.

The fact was that the the artillery bombardment had been inadequate both in weight and accuracy. Although the German breastworks and trenches had been blown in at some points, no serious damage sufficient adequately to aid the attack had been achieved. There is little doubt that a serious shortage of shells was a contributing factor but this situation had been known to British senior officers beforehand. Also, the experience and expertise of the British gunners at that relatively early stage of the war was lacking. The result was that the brave infantrymen were required to make an assault over open, flat ground against an enemy well prepared and with many machine guns strategically sighted, especially in enfilade positions.

From the first whistle sending men 'over the top', tragedy struck. Many brave infantrymen were mown down on, or just beyond, their breastworks. The ground within 50 yards of the start line was quickly littered with the dead and wounded. Whole waves of men simply crumpled and fell. Within a few minutes it must have been plain that failure was inevitable and that heavy casualties could be the only outcome. Yet it was a terrible period of 60 minutes before the reality sunk home to those officers with sufficient authority to recall the Battalion.

The fact that Haig, in overall command, ordered further attacks later in the day when nothing out there had changed and when he must have known the outcome of the morning would be repeated, was nothing short of murderous. Literally to throw away so many men of Britain's experienced regular army was a disaster of major

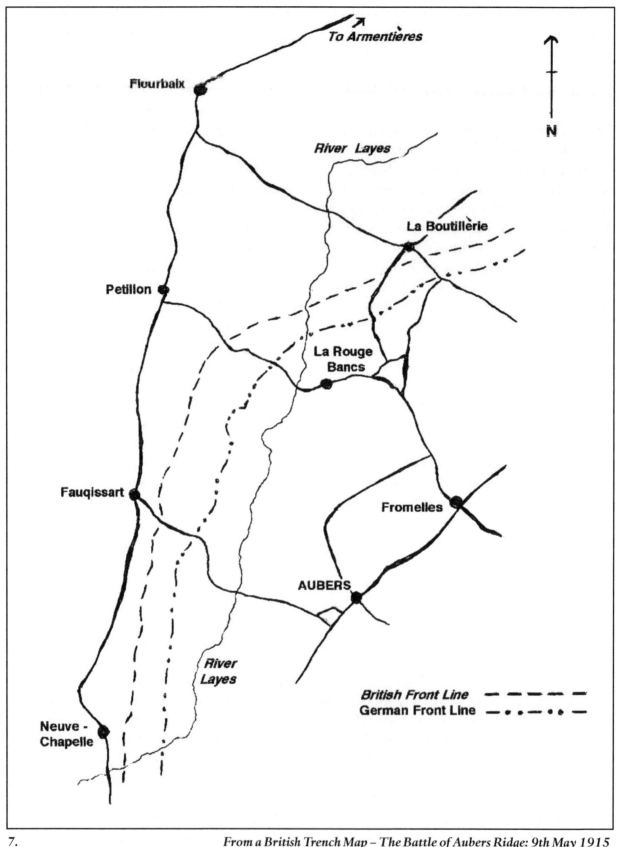

7.   *From a British Trench Map – The Battle of Aubers Ridge: 9th May 1915*

and far-reaching proportions. Yet, incredibly, no big heads rolled. Haig sheltered behind the ammunition shortage and his claim that the effort was necessary in order to assist the French who were attacking to the south. Eventually, the

British official history was to state blandly that the Battle of Aubers Ridge had been "a serious disappointment".

Total British losses for 9th May, recorded at the time, were 145 officers and 9,400 other ranks. Later examination of Divisional and other records suggest over 400 officers and more than 10,400 other ranks: a serious disappointment, indeed !

Thus ended one of several such ill-concieved frontal infantry assaults of 1915 ordered to send mere men across open ground against enemy machine guns and strengthened enemy defensive positions. Sadly, the salutary lesson went unheeded by the allied High Command with further unnecessary slaughter of brave and valuable men in much the same manner later in the year.

MAY:
9th:
Captain: (526) R.F.Finke.
Lieutenants: (848) T.R.Juckes, (1354) R.T.Shaw.
Second Lieutenants: (41) O.Austin, (295) G.R.G.Child.
Sergeants: (222) C.Bulman, (310) C.P.P.Clay, (611) A.W.Godden, (917) A.Lavender, (1257) O.J.Reeves, (1357) H.W.Sheppard, (1573) C.Wales, (1662) B.Wilkins.
Corporals: (35) A.Attreall, (270) C.Carter, (319) E.Coatsworth, (631) G.M.Greaves, (773) W.Howard, (938) F.G.Lewry, (1137) C.Page, (1172) J.J.Payne, (1417) W.J.R.Somers, (1546) G.Turner, (1558) L.Venus, (1685) W.Wood.
Lance Corporals: (108) E.H.Bennett, (146) C.F.Booth, (192) A.Brooks, (366) W.J.Coppard, (409) J.E.Damerell, (636) J.Green, (1100) G.H.Nicks, (1194) F.T.B.Philp, (1333) F.G.Scott, (1346) A.J.Sellings, (1377) T.H.Singleton, (1387) J.Skipper, (1415) J.L.H.Smyth, (1616) M.J.H.Welch, (1707) B.C.Young.
Privates: (10) P.Ainsworth, (19) W.W.Amos, (26) W.Arben, (29) D.Arthur, (42) G.Awcock, (43) S.Axell, (49) J.Bailey, (52) C.H.Baker, (63) W.Baker, (88) R.Bassett, (91) N.H.Batt, (94) E.Beal, (105) F.J.Bell, (129) M.H.Blackman, (134) F.Bloore, (144) W.Boniface, (153) W.Bourne, (161) S.E.Brackpool, (171) C.Brett, (193) J.Brooks, (213) E.Browning, (221) T.R.Bull, (222) C.Bulman, (229) R.Burge, (247) A.Butler, (254) R.G.Caesar, (259) F.V.Campbell, (263) G.Caplen, (264) J.Caplin, (267) P.G.Carpenter, (268) W.Carr, (272) C.H.Carter, (273) L.Carter, (276) W.Carver, (280) E.A.Chaffer, (283) E.Chandler, (290) F.Chatfield, (293) A.Cheesman, (298) P.G.Childs, (325) T.G.Colbran, (327) W.A.Cole, (342) W.E.Comber, (354) W.E.Coomber, (355) F.G.Coombes, (360) W.H.Cooper, (361)

W.Coote, (370) J.Cornwell, (374) G.Cottington, (382) R.W.Cox, (389) E.Crassweller, (404) C.T.Curd, (410) F.R.Dancy, (443) H.Dine, (444) E.Diplock, (449) R.H.Doo, (452) W.Downer, (456) J.Driscoll, (476) E.Easton, (481) J.F.W.Eckert, (486) F.S.Edwards, (498) W.F.Elmes, (501) E.A.Elphick, (506) P.Etherington, (508) J.A.F.Eustes, (515) A.G.Farmer, (527) G.W.Fish, (533) A.E.Fleet, (545) F.J.Ford, (551) E.C.Foster, (561) C.H.Freegard, (571) G.Fuller, (572) T.Fuller, (581) A.H.W.Garbutt, (586) G.H.Gaston, (591) J.Gearing, (598) A.V.Gilbey, (603) H.S.Glazier, (610) A.T.Godden, (618) C.E.Goldsmith, (625) W.C.Gourd, (628) A.J.Grant, (630) E.T.Gravett, (640) A.Greening, (653) C.Gurr, (656) F.T.Halfacre, (658) F.Hall, (660) J.Hall, (664) T.W.Hammond, (669) R.J.Hansford, (674) E.Harding, (675) J.Hargreaves, (678) J.Harper, (682) C.Harrison, (683) R.H.Harrison, (685) J.W.Hart, (693) C.G.Hayward, (706) T.Hennessy, (710) A.Henty, (727) W.C.Hill, (730) R.Hills, (734) G.Hilton, (736) L.Hiscock, (737) L.W.Hoad, (740) F.Hobbs, (744) G.Hodges, (748) W.H.Hokings, (754) C.J.Hollebone, (758) R.E.Holman, (762) T.Honeysett, (763) W.Honeysett, (790) C.R.Hunt, (797) E.C.Hutchings, (799) T.H.Hutchinson, (807) B.H.Ide, (808) W.G.Ingleton, (826) W.James, (827) A.Jardon, (834) T.J.Jenner, (846) W.W.Jones, (850) G.H.Jupp, (860) C.A.Kemp, (865) G.E.Kennaugh, (873) R.T.Kenward, (887) W.King, (890) W.H.Kinnard, (897) L.J.Knight, (898) P.F.Knight, (899) R.Knight, (916) J.Latter, (921) A.F.Lee, (928) A.W.Lennard, (941) H.F.Linfield, (945) A.Lloyd, (977) H.Marment, (979) E.Marsh, (983) E.G.Martin, (994) G.H.Maskell, (996) F.Mathias, (1016) D.Miles, (1019) A.E.Miller, (1029) T.H.Mills, (1039) S.E.Mitchell, (1040) A.V.Mockett, (1041) A.H.G.Mockett, (1052) J.Moore, (1057) H.J.Morfee, (1060) W.Morris, (1064) L.Mott, (1071) W.Murray, (1074) A.Muzzell, (1076) W.G.Neal, (1080) E.Netley, (1085) P.C.Newman, (1086) T.Newman, (1092) B.T.Newton, (1096) S.G.Nicholls, (1104) E.J.Norris, (1109) F.Noyce, (1111) G.R.Nuttman, (1129) W.Ovenden, (1134) E.J.Paddon, (1142) W.J.Page, (1144) W.H.Pallett, (1152) J.A.Parlett, (1160) G.Pate, (1161) J.Patten, (1166) H.S.Paxman, (1167) C.Pay, (1173) A.Peachy, (1179) E.B.Peerless, (1183) W.H.Pelling, (1187) W.J.Pescott, (1192) C.W.Phillips, (1198) H.Pierce, (1218) C.Powell, (1233) W.J.Ralph, (1248) J.Reader, (1250) A.Redford, (1251) C.Reed, (1258) T.Regan, (1275) H.C.Richardson, (1280) J.A.J.Ridley, (1290) E.J.Rooke, (1294) G.Rossiter, (1303) E.Ruff, (1305) W.Rushmore, (1314) J.Salvage, (1320) M.D.Sands, (1339) W.H.Seacey,

(1347) H.Selmes, (1356) C.Shelton, (1384)
A.E.Skinner, (1388) G.P.Skuse, (1393) A.M.Smale,
(1395) J.V.Smethurst, (1397) A.E.Smith, (1401)
G.Smith, (1404) H.Smith, (1409) T.J.Smith, (1412)
W.C.Smith, (1440) J.Stemp, (1457) J.Stoneham,
(1459) S.Stonestreet, (1460) A.Strange, (1468)
A.H.Styles, (1473) J.W.P.Sutton, (1490) E.A.Tedbury,
(1504) W.H.Thorpe, (1506) A.Ticehurst, (1514)
H.W.Todman, (1517) A.E.Tompsett, (1519)
T.W.Tomsett, (1551) E.J.Umpleby, (1557) J.Veness,
(1560) W.Vine, (1565) A.Wain, (1569) E.Wakeham,
(1576) W.E.Walker, (1587) J.H.C.Wareham,
(1590) J.E.Waterman, (1593) M.C.Waters, (1596)
A.E.Watson, (1603) W.Watts, (1605) B.A.Waymark,
(1607) A.E.Weaver, (1609) A.W.Webb, (1611)
G.Webb, (1615) J.Weekley, (1633) E.D.West, (1634)
F.West, (1640) D.Wheatley, (1646) D.G.White,
(1660) G.R.Wilcox, (1675) G.A.Winborn.

For several days men continued to die from wounds received on the dreadful 9th May. Monday the 10th was a day of complete rest but on the following day a march was made to Oblinghem where a badly needed draft of 120 men joined the Battalion. During the morning of the 12th, the Battalion was inspected and addressed by the Brigadier who, no doubt, did his best to raise spirits and morale. The afternoon was taken up by a march to billets in Béthune where, over two days, bathing parades at the town swimming baths were enjoyed. A move to fresh billets in Labourse was made on the 15th. There, over a restful four-day period, further bathing was possible and a concert was enjoyed in the courtyard of Château Labourse.

MAY:
10th:
Privates: (167) G.T.Brazil, (326) E.Cole, (483) S.A.Ede, (648) A.J.Groombridge, (766) W.Hopper, (950) T.Longlands, (1015) W.Message.
11th:
Corporal: (632) A.Green.
Privates: (1676) J.G.Winckle, (1690) A.Woolley.

MAY:
12th:
Sergeant: (768) A.G.Hounsom.
Privates: (28) W.G.Arnold, (260) E.Campkin.
13th:
Private: (1588) S.Warner.
16th:
Private: (212) H.Browne.

17th:
Second Lieutenant: (804) H.W.Hyde.
Private: (499) C.Elms.
18th:
Private: (115) C.A.Bignell.

The Battalion marched back to the front on the 20th May, this time to a position south of the Béthune – La Bassée Road. That day and the three following days were quiet enough for work to be undertaken improving the front line fire steps. Relief to billets in Cambrin took place on the 24th. The following three days were spent at rest there but, even so, casualties were sustained when the village was shelled on one occasion.

A return was made on the 28th May to the trenches where, although the enemy threw bombs the following morning and partially buried Company Sergeant Major Butcher, there was little hostile activity on either side and the situation remained the same until the end of the month.

MAY:
23rd:
Private: (609) W.H.Goddard.
25th:
Privates: (204) H.Brown, (1534) A.C.Tringham.
26th:
Privates: (32) W.Ashdown, (208) N.B.Brown, (255) A.J.Cager.
29th:
Private: (544) C.Ford.
31st:
Private: (713) S.T.Heselden.

Throughout the whole of the summer month of June the Battalion undertook front line duties mainly to the south of the Béthune – La Bassée Road. Short tours in the front line were interspersed by similarly short breaks at rest or in reserve a few miles back in such resorts as Béthune, Annequin, Fourquereuil, Lozinghem, and Cambrin. At these places time was spent at swimming, sports and training, concentrating particularly in assimilating incoming drafts of men into the requirements of the Battalion and trench life.

Unusually for a summer month, warfare activity was low on both sides and it was almost a case of 'All Quiet on the Western Front' in this area. Not entirely so, however; for example, on the 3rd June, everyone was brought to their senses at 4.30am by the blowing of a German mine. Fortunately, the enemy had made a miscalculation and caused damage only by blowing in their own parapet. Then, on the night of the 17th, a rumour of an expected attack by the enemy in celebration of the Battle of Waterloo caused the Battalion to sleep with its boots on but nothing came of the circulating story.

Spasmodic shelling and bombing took a relatively light toll of casualties during June..

JUNE:
2nd:
Private: (1272) F.Richardson.
3rd:
Lance Corporal: (836) A.H.Jex.
Private: (904) S.Laker.
4th:
Lance Corporal: (1031) E.Milton.
16th:
Private: (649) E.Grossman.

At Cambrin, another month of relative inactivilty commenced. It is well documented that, from the viewpoint of individual units, duty in the war on the Western Front tended to be made up of relatively short periods of actual fighting interspersed by long spells of inactivity and boredom. For the 2nd Battalion, June, July, August and most of September, 1915, proved to be just such a time of inactivity. That is not to say that periods of shelling, bombing, trench raids and night-time forays into No-Man's-Land were not experienced. Men also lost their lives during these weeks but the casualties were sustained in a trickle rather than en-masse as had been the case on the 9th May.

Time spent in the front line trenches was always harrowing to a lesser or greater extent. There was the place of exposure to the greatest danger where the mind could seldom rest from alertness in means of self-preservation should

the unexpected happen at any moment: a sudden enemy raid; the sickly sweet smell of gas; the air-splitting sound of artillery shells or the tumbling approach of trench mortar missiles. Nerves remained taught throughout the long hours, or days, in the trenches. Short periods of relaxation were provided by the arrival and distribution of rations such as sweet tea tainted by the taste of petrol from the cans in which the infusion was carried. On some fortunate occasions food arrived in relatively hot condition: perhaps stew of dubious and frequently repetative origin accompanied by dry bread or biscuits.

Except after spells of action when casualties had been sustained, the rations were seldom sufficient to quell the appetites of all the young active men on duty. On the other hand, soldiers remarked that 'bully beef' was so often provided that the men could no longer face eating it and it was not uncommon for the tin to be opened, the top slice taken off and the tin, still containing the remainder, either discarded or used to line the trench sides. This at a time when severe meat shortages were being experienced at home.

The hours of trench duty were spent longing for news of relief. When, eventually, the good news came and men of some other Unit began to arrive to take over, the outgoing troops, often exhausted from lack of sleep, summoned new strength and cheerfulness to tramp out along a communication trench and then above ground on tracks or pave roads back to their allotted place of rest. Frequently, however, they got little, or no, rest. It seemed that there was always work to be done cleaning equipment and billets or undertaking various tasks of a pioneering nature. Also, they were seldom allowed to remain in one place for long. They were always being marched from one place to another, often for no apparent reason, and significant were the frustrations, grumbles and lowering of morale thereby caused.

CHAPTER 3
1915
JULY – DECEMBER

Some indication of the soldiers' inactivity and the need to relieve boredom may be appreciated from the Battalion War Diary's record that, on the 4th July, the first number of the 'Dugout Despatch' was published.

JULY:
4th:
Private: (282) R.Champ.

The routine of moving in and out of the front line area continued with respite being taken in the town of Béthune, where billets were in the Avenue de Bruay, the Avenue des Lens, and in the nearby suburbs or villages of Verquigneul and Verquin.

JULY:
21st:
Major: (542) Forbes.

Four officers of the 'New Army' arrived on 20th July for attachment and instruction. These were Colonel MacDougal, his adjutant and two machine gun officers. The following day, Colonel MacDougal's second in command, Major Forbes arrived.

A start was made by the Battalion's Captain Cameron who took Colonel MacDougal and Major Forbes on a tour of the trenches. Over to the left, they were passing along the lines when a stray enemy howitzer shell dropped right among the party. Most unfortunately, Colonel MacDougal was killed outright, Major Forbes was fatally wounded and Captain Cameron was also wounded but survived.

Based in billets at Verquin, the Battalion continued training into August, especially with the replacement drafts still being received. A newly-introduced 'West Bomb Thrower' went on trial in a nearby wood without any record of its success or failure.

Something of a gala day was held on Thursday the 5th August in the form of an inter-Battalion Horse Show, again in an attempt to keep the men entertained and to raise their spirits. The Battalion was successful by gaining first prizes for N.C.O's Horse Riding, Heavy Draft Horse Pairs, Cooker Turn-out and Small Arms Ammunition Cart Turn-out. Unfortunately, less success came to Captain F.G.Stammers who, having been thrown from his horse, was admitted to hospital with concussion !

AUGUST:
5th:
Private: (614) H.Godwin.

During the night of the 8th August there occured a short but vicious period of bomb throwing by the enemy. In retaliation, British heavy guns shelled known German billets the following morning before the Battalion went into reserve at Labourse. From there, fatigue parties were sent out to the trenches from time to time to assist the Royal Engineers. This was the position on the 13th August, the first anniversary of the Battalion's arrival in France.

AUGUST:
9th:
Privates: (457) J.P.Duane, (1386) W.Skinner.
13th:
Private: (1622) A.W.Wells.

The pattern of interchange between trench duty, rest and training continued until the end of the month. A tragedy occured on the 21st August, however, when Private James Tiller was accidentally killed while undergoing bomb throwing practice.

AUGUST:
21st:
Private: (1509) J.Tiller.

27

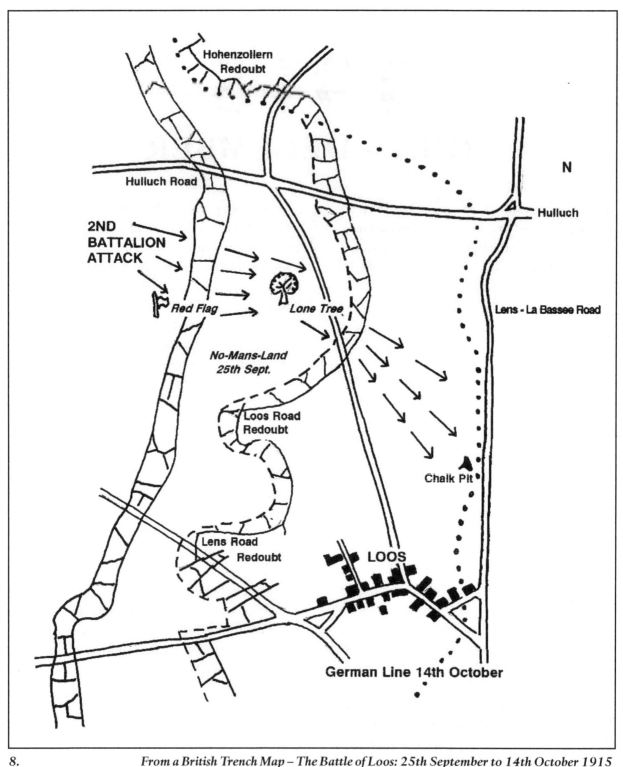

8.   *From a British Trench Map – The Battle of Loos: 25th September to 14th October 1915*

26th:
Privates: (100) H.C.Beeching, (296) C.W.Childs.
29th:
Lance Corporal: (1619) R.F.Wellen.
Privates: (637) W.Green, (829) H.Jarvis, (942)
     W.R.Lintott, (1538) C.G.Tubb.

The month of September, which began so quietly in billets at Vermelles, was to develop into further tragedy for the Battalion at the ill-fated Battle of Loos. From Vermelles, the men marched away west beyond Béthune to billet at Ecquedecques on the 8th and there they stayed until the 20th when they began their return in preparation for the coming battle. That night they billeted at Marles-les-Mines, moving again the next day. They were forced to spend the following night, which was very wet, in most uncomfortable bivouacs near Verquin. On the 24th the Battalion moved into trenches at Vermelles.

SEPTEMBER:
4th:
Lance Corporal: (346) C.E.J.Cook.
7th:
Private: (301) E.F.Churcher.
19th:
Private: (113) G.Bigland.

At 1.50am on fateful Saturday 25th September, the 2nd Battalion took up position in trenches opposite Hulluch. Orders were to occupy the front line trenches directly they had been vacated by the Brigade's first assaulting battalions, the 1st Loyal North Lancs and 2nd Kings Royal Rifle Corps, and then to push on in support directly the assaulting battalions had gained a foothold in the German front line. The assault began at 6.30am in a grey drizzle and, due to the wind veering and blowing smoke and gas back towards the British line at this point, it was not possible to observe how the initial assault had progressed. On the initiative of Company Commanders, the Battalion immediately advanced to support the attack thus becoming part of the assaulting line at an early stage.

This advance was pushed right up to the enemy wire which was found to be uncut, and every officer and man who reached, or got near to, the wire was either killed or wounded. The Royal Sussex Machine Gun Section attempted to reach the German line but was annihilated about 50 yards in front of 'Lone Tree', a well known isolated cherry tree which bloomed in 1915 on the Loos battlefield (see Sketch Map 8).

One line of men dwindled in number under the fierce enemy rifle and shell fire until only two or three were left and they, sensibly, flung themselves to the ground. Looking back, these men could see their next line advancing. This line, too, was shot to pieces and its three survivors also stopped and hugged the ground. Then a third line was seen advancing but so concentrated was the German fire that every man in that line was killed or wounded.

Units to the left and right had succeeded in dislodging the Germans from their front line trench but the line in front of the 2nd Battalion was clearly being held in strength by the enemy.

Owing to the fact that almost all of the Battalion officers and N.C.O's had been killed or wounded, Major Willett was sent forward to obtain information on progress. However, the enemy machine gun and rifle fire was so intense that the major was unable to get beyond 'Lone Tree'.

At 11.45am 'Green's Force', a separate and special unit formed for this assault under the command of Lt.Col. Green, attempted to attack but also got no farther than 'Lone Tree'. Another attempt by the Force during the afternoon was more successful, however, and succeeded in pushing the enemy back. At about 3.15pm, the available four officers of the 2nd Battalion gathered together all their remaining men, only about 70 in total, to form a line close to 'Lone Tree'. Soon afterwards, the Germans opposite the Battalion surrendered, whereupon the Royal Sussex men occupied the enemy's former front line. From there, this small group still representing the 2nd Battalion pushed on to entrench themselves along the Lens – La Bassée Road with their right flank resting on the Chalk Pit. There they held on until they were relieved at 3.00am on the 26th September and moved back to the old British line.

As on the 9th May,1915, the Battalion had suffered grievous losses. It seemed that nothing had been learned by the army high command about allaying the excessive casualty level which they should have known would be the repeated result of attacking well prepared enemy defences across mainly level, open ground with insufficient artillery. Forced into such a hopeless situation, the 2nd Battalion had acquitted itself well in the circumstances despite enormous self-sacrifice. Two-thirds of the Battalion men killed that day have no known graves; most are commemorated on the Loos Memorial. The dead included brothers, Privates E.F. and G.W.Short of Southwick, Sussex.

Also, on that day, the Battalion's L 8088 Sergeant Harry Wells, born at Herne Bay, Kent, on 19th September,1888, won the Victoria Cross. His citation reads:

"Sergeant Harry Wells V.C., 2nd Bn. R.Sx. Regt.

For the most conspicuous bravery near Le Routier on 25/9/15. When his platoon officer had been killed, he took command and led his men forward to within 15 yards of the German wire. Nearly half the platoon were killed or wounded, and the remainder were much shaken, but with the utmost coolness and bravery Sergeant Wells rallied them and led them forward. Finally, when very few were left, he stood up and urged them forward once more, but while doing so he himself was killed. He gave a magnificent display of courage and determination. London Gazette 18/11/15."

The body of Sergeant Wells was later retrieved from the battlefield and he was buried at Dud Corner Cemetery where he is surrounded by the names of so many colleagues inscribed on the Loos Memorial which forms part of that cemetery.

SEPTEMBER:
25th:
Captain: (1583) G.E.Ward.
Lieutenants: (937) R.R.Lewin, (1635) G.W.West.
Second Lieutenants: (93) R.F.Baxter, (176) J.L.Bright, (184) H.F.Bromley, (460) J.H.Dugnolle, (479) J.D.Eaton-Richards, (672) A.J.V.Harden, (815) W.Ireland, (1566) G.L.Wainwright.
Company Sergeant Major: (569) F.S.Fry.
Sergeants: (312) A.T.Cleare, (344) W.Constable, (949) L.J.Lock, (1170) A.H.Payne, (1625) H.Wells, V.C.
Corporals: (56) F.J.Baker, (714) G.Hesmer, (861) T.Kemp.
Lance Corporals: (22) C.Anning, (84) W.T.Bartholomew, (130) H.A.Blackmore, (257) A.Camp, (299) T.Childs, (434) A.Dellar, (448) A.B.Donovan, (769) A.Hounsome, (849) C.E.Judge, (871) J.Kenward, (930) W.J.Leonard, (936) E.Levick, (955) A.C.Lovelock, (1068) A.E.Munson, (1081) G.Neve, (1353) G.J.Shaw, (1399) C.Smith, (1512) A.J.Titheridge, (1656) G.Wickenden, (1672) W.Willmott.
Privates: (20) E.R.T.Andrews, (80) W.Barnes, (81) H.B.Barrand, (114) A.T.Bignell, (136) C.Boarer, (138) C.H.Bolt, (140) C.W.Boniface, (141) F.A.Boniface, (149) H.Bourn, (155) B.Bowley, (165) J.Bradshaw, (189) W.H.Brook, (200) C.Brown, (207) J.Brown, (236) W.J.Burt, (250) W.Butt, (258) W.C.E.Campany, (300) E.Chowne, (315) J.Clevett, (331) T.H.Coleman, (332) W.V.Coleman, (333) W.J.T.Coles, (334) W.T.Coles, (349) S.Cooke, (350) W.E.Cooke, (356) G.Cooper, (358) R.G.K.Cooper, (380) J.Cox, (387) E.A.Cranham, (392) F.L.Creasey, (397) A.E.Crittenden, (402) C.W.Croucher, (412)

W.E.Dapp, (421) A.E.Davison, (430) F.Dean, (459) J.R.Duffield, (467) A.Dyer, (472) T.Earl, (494) C.W.Ellis, (510) J.Evans, (518) J.Farnes, (530) W.E.Fisher, (532) C.R.Fitsell, (536) H.Fletcher, (589) F.J.Gates, (594) H.Gibbs, (596) T.Gibbs, (601) C.Glanfield, (620) A.L.Goodacre, (622) T.E.Goodwin, (668) F.W.Hanks, (676) D.Harlen, (677) G.Harman, (696) J.Hearn, (717) R.H.Hewitt, (720) A.W.Hide, (728) W.N.Hillman, (739) F.T.Hobbs, (746) A.J.Hogg, (751) F.Holdstock, (756) R.B.Holloway, (761) F.V.Honeysett, (765) I.T.Hopkins, (782) L.E.Hughes, (818) E.Izzard, (820) G.J.Jackson, (828) W.Jarman, (838) F.S.Johnson, (847) W.T.Jones, (881) G.H.King, (903) H.Knowles, (906) E.Lambert, (915) C.Lassiter, (922) J.Lee, (927) E.C.Lelliott, (935) J.J.Levett, (954) A.Lovell, (958) J.E.Luck, (965) J.Manktelow, (969) A.E.Mansbridge, (1001) J.McCall, (1017) H.Miles, (1024) W.H.Miller, (1027) E.G.Mills, (1028) F.A.Mills, (1034) J.Misselbrook, (1049) J.R.Moody, (1075) E.G.H.R.Myers, (1077) W.E.Neale, (1084) M.E.Newman, (1094) B.J.Nicholls, (1103) H.L.Norman, (1114) W.G.Oasgood, (1118) J.Oliver, (1125) R.Orton, (1138) E.Page, (1155) W.E.C.Parrott, (1163) J.Pattenden, (1203) E.S.Piper, (1220) C.Pratt, (1241) L.G.Rawlinson,(1264) A.Rice, (1265) A.Rice, (1266) E.J.Rice, (1283) W.R.Roberts, (1289) A.F.Rooke, (1298) T.Routhan, (1301) P.F.Rowe, (1306) P.J.W.Russell, (1316) C.J.Sanders, (1319) G.H.Sands, (1323) R.Sargent, (1327) G.T.Saunders, (1329) J.W.Saunders, (1337) A.Scutt, (1362) E.F.Short, (1364) G.W.Short, (1366) R.Short, (1367) E.J.Shorter, (1378) G.Sivyer, (1418) E.Spain, (1428) H.G.Standen, (1432) H.Stapley, (1438) F.Steer, (1442) E.J.Sternell, (1462) A.Stratford, (1465) A.Streeter, (1491) R.A.Tee, (1494) J.Terry, (1498) B.E.Thomas, (1521) W.Toole, (1526) F.Town, (1531) H.Treherne, (1544) C.H.Turner, (1547) H.J.Turner, (1568) A.Wakeham, (1572) C.Walder, (1604) H.J.Way, (1606) C.Wearing, (1636) L.West, (1639) W.J.Weston, (1668) H.E.Williams.

It is, perhaps, indicative of the intensity of the conflict and the lack of opportunity to bring in casualties afterwards, that only six men died from wounds during the week following the first day of the Battle of Loos. So serious were the losses amongst the British army, and so desperate was the need for manpower, that the relatively few men of the Battalion who remained fit for duty were required, with only a few hours snatched rest, to remain in the line until the end of the month.

SEPTEMBER:
27th:
Privates: (770) E.M.House, (1000) J.Maynard, (1335)
    H.Scrase, (1400) F.Smith, (1477) C.Swannell.
28th:
Private: (1577) E.Waller.
29th:
Private: (169) G.H.Breed.

Shortly before midnight on the 1st October
the Battalion was relieved by the 114th French
Infantry Regiment and marched out, thankfully,
to billets at Noeux-les-Mines. There, the
disturbing news was received that, earlier in the
day, Brigade Major R.J.A.Terry, D.S.O., M.V.O.,
had been hit by a shell while in Loos and had died
from his wounds.

Before moving to Mazingarbe on the 6th
October the sadly depleted Battalion was
strengthened by the arrival of a draft of 10
officers and 392 men. These men had little time
to settle in before, on the very next day, the
Battalion was back, once more, in the trenches
near Loos. On the afternoon of the 8th the
Germans attacked but were beaten off.

OCTOBER:
1st:
Lieutenant-Colonel: (1495) R.J.A.Terry.
3rd:
Sergeant: (1692) W.Woolvin.
Private: (16) F.J.Allen.
8th:
Lance Corporal: (716) T.E.Hewett.
Private: (1430) W.Stanford.
9th:
Private: (1441) W.Stenning.
10th:
Privates: (749) C.F.Holden, (1444) E.W.Stevens.
12th:
Privates: (450) J.W.Dorsett, (813) G.Irish.

The weather at this time was good and the
opportunity was taken to improve conditions
with nightly digging parties. A few casualties
were sustained almost every day until, on the
13th October, another major attack was launched
on the German positions. Once more, the
Battalion was opposite the German-held village
of Hulluch and, this time, was to provide one
Company as a strong patrol while the remainder
was held ready to give support to the attacking
troops by following up to occupy the German

trench and houses immediately to the west of
Hulluch. The initial attack, carried out by the
Cameron Highlanders, was launched at 2.00pm.
Twenty minutes later a message was received that
the attack, again over open ground, had failed.
The 2nd Royal Sussex were sent forward to assist
but no general progress was possible.

OCTOBER:
13th:
Captain: (230) W.Burgess.
Sergeant: (1308) S.Rutherford.
Privates: (4) F.Adams, (7) W.Adams, (39) H.Austen,
    (104) A.E.Beeston, (117) J.Billington, (160) W.Boyne,
    (188) W.Brook, (343) P.Conlon, (475) J.J.East, (485)
    C.Edwards, (487) G.Edwards, (490) R.B.Edwards,
    (558) H.Franklin, (659) J.Hall, (729) E.A.Hills, (792)
    J.W.Hunt, (823) S.D.Jackson, (831) E.A.Jay, (923)
    J.H.Lee, (960) P.E.G.Luxford, (1121) L.E.Orford,
    (1165) J.Pavey, (1260) T.W.A.Relf, (1271)
    D.Richardson, (1411) W.Smith, (1446) F.T.Stevens,
    (1489) W.R.Taylor, (1507) R.Ticehurst, (1520)
    C.F.Toogood, (1617) W.Welfare.

No further offensive was undertaken until
5.30am on the 14th October when the Battalion
was ordered to support an attack by the
Northamptonshire Regiment. Incredibly, with
everyone in position in the British front line
trench, the attack was called off because it was
now daylight ! It was not until late that evening
that the Battalion was relieved and was able to
entrain for Lillers. The remainder of the month
was spent 'at rest' but with plenty of training and
route marching. More replacement officers and
men joined the Battalion.

OCTOBER:
14th:
Private: (502) C.E.Elworthy.
15th:
Second Lieutenant: (1529) H.C.Toye.
Private: (1313) A.Saltmarsh.
16th:
Privates: (612) G.W.Godden, (1373) W.C.Simmonds.
17th:
Private: (615) J.H.Godwin.

The first two weeks of November, the month
approaching winter, were spent happily enough
at Lillers where there were plenty of drill parades,
sessions of musketry and physical training. By
way of entertainment, several concerts were held

in the town theatre. Time passed all too quickly, however, and, on the 13th, there was a move by train back to Noeux-les-Mines from where a march was made to billets in Mazingarbe.

On the 15th November it was time to return to the well known area of trenches opposite the village of Hulluch where the old German lines were occupied for four days. A move up to the firing line was made on the 19th but, with the onset of winter, the situation continued relatively quiet with neither side considering any serious offensive activity.

The Battalion strength continued to be replenished during the month with seven officers and 106 other ranks joining.

NOVEMBER:
9th:
Private: (440) P.F.Denyer.
21st:
Private: (1602) T.S.Watts.
23rd:
Private: (1422) C.Spencer.
30th:
Private: (1035) W.W.Missing.

With the weather gradually deteriorating, no major offensives were launched from either side, but skirmishes, spasmodic shelling and sniping continued resulting in a number of casualties. The Battalion remained in, or near, the front line of the Loos sector until the 6th December when it moved back to billets in the village of Philosophe. Much time was spent there in removing mud from clothing in an effort to smarten up appearances.

Monday the 8th December was time for a return to the trenches until relief came late at night on the 14th. During these days, long and arduous periods of work were undertaken in an attempt to keep the trenches free from mud and water. This work entailed the removal of all duck boards and the digging of deeper sump pits.

Very tired men struggled thankfully into buses which took them for five days much-needed rest. On the 20th December, came a move into reserve at Philosophe and a return to trenches on the 22nd.

This year the Battalion was forced to spend the whole of the Christmas period in the trenches in cold, dark and wet conditions. There was no Christmas truce or fraternisation with the enemy as there had been in 1914; all contact of such a nature this year was stictly forbidden. Not until the 30th December was the Battalion freed from the trenches and, only then, to fall back in reserve at Philosophe.

DECEMBER:
3rd:
Private: (1302) W.H.Rowland.
13th:
Privates: (60) J.Baker, (738) W.Hoare.
14th:
Private: (809) J.Ingram.
28th:
Private: (398) A.Crockett.
31st:
Private: (842) J.Jolly.

CHAPTER 4
1916
JANUARY – JUNE

In the depth of winter there remained little activity in the area of Loos. On New Year's Day the Battalion moved back to Divisional Reserve at Noeux-les-Mines. With the 25th December having been spent in the trenches where little joy was to be had, a special effort, though still necessarily limited, was made on the 3rd January with a free day and late Christmas festivities but the War Diary gives no details of what was provided in the way of food, drink and other 'comforts'.

At midnight on the 4th January the Battalion was ordered to move up to join its Royal Sussex Regiment sister battalion, the 5th (Cinque Ports), as Brigade support. Once again, the old German front line in the vicinity of Hulluch was occupied. A further move, closer to Loos, was made on the 6th and there everyone remained until relieved on the 14th. During this period the German artillery became unusually active but, fortunately, there were few casualties.

JANUARY:
12th:
Private: (580) W.H.E.Gallard.

A march to Philosophe on the 14th January was followed by a motor bus journey to Noeux-les-Mines from where the train was taken to Lillers the following day. The remainder of January was taken up with training, especially for the 'specialist' men such as trench pioneers, bombers, wirers, trench mortar teams and machine gunners. Even this training was restricted for the last four days of the month

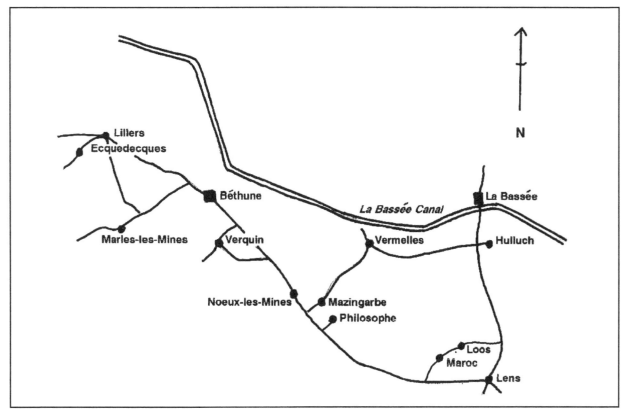

September 1915 to June 1916

by orders placing the Battalion on readiness to move at three, sometimes two, hour's notice. Nonetheless, recreation was enjoyed in the form of concerts and a Brigade football tournament.

The first two weeks of the deep-winter month of February saw the Battalion remaining at Lillers undergoing training, recreation and receiving new drafts of men. During this time the opportunity was taken by the Medical Officer, Lieutenant F.Joscelyne, to inoculate the whole Battalion against Para-Typhoid. With the winter's enforcement of relative inactivity, 14 lucky men were allowed to go on leave to England.

On Wednesday 2nd February, The Royal Sussex Regiment football team participated in the Brigade final which resulted in a draw after extra time. In the replay, on Sunday 6th February, the Regiment ran out winners by 1 – 0 and the victors received medals presented by Brigadier General Thuillier.

FEBRUARY:
12th:
Private: (1552) W.E.Unicombe.

Noeux-les-Mines was the destination when the Battalion entrained from Lillers on the 15th February. From there a march was made by way of Braquemont and Les Brebis to trenches near Maroc. From Noeux-les-Mines another 16 men went off on leave to England.

The wind changed to blow from the direction of the enemy lines on the 18th February and a gas alert was issued. Then a move to the firing line was completed, at which point the Battalion had, on its left, the 3rd Brigade and, to its right, the French. The following day brought minenwerfer trench mortar bombs from the Germans. During a patrol out to the enemy wire after dark, Private John Henry was mortally wounded but he was brought in by colleagues.

FEBRUARY:
20th:
Private: (707) J.Henry.

The relief came on the 21st February, a bitterly cold day with snow falls. For the next three days and nights the temperature remained below freezing and there was more snow. Night work was carried out by fatigue parties in these awful conditions but a lucky group of 15 men escaped

with leave passes to England. The hard weather prompted the commencement of lectures by stretcher bearers in the use of massage with whale oil to ward off frostbite.

A new draft of 57 N.C.O's and other ranks joined before the end of the month which saw the Battalion back in trenches near Loos.

FEBRUARY:
26th:
Private: (686) C.E.W.Hartt.

The first two days of March saw a re-awakening of activity on the part of the enemy. The use of minenwerfers and heavy calibre shells caused considerable disruption, especially to work being carried out in the trenches in an attempt to keep them free from water. A particularly hostile bombardment was received on the afternoon of the 2nd with three heavy shells dropping into the Battalion's front line trench.

MARCH:
1st:
Private: (228) F.Burford.
2nd:
Sergeant: (1334) F.Scrase.
Lance Corporal: (103) A.V.Beesley.
Privates: (384) G.Craighead, (891) C.F.Kirby, (1689) J.E.Woolfitt.

The 3rd March was a quiet day with the exception of some shelling in the evening.

Several days were then spent in various trenches working on improvements. On the 8th the enemy shelled with six inch high explosives killing Private Stephen Crompton from Birkenhead. Further shelling on the 9th killed Sergeant Sidney Simpson; another three wounded men died on subsequent days.

MARCH:
3rd:
Private: (964) W.Malkowski.
7th:
Privates: (83) E.E.Bartholomew, (1618) A.W.Wellard.
8th:
Private: (401) S.Crompton.
9th:
Sergeant: (1375) S.Simpson.
10th:
Sergeant: (1089) H.Newnham.

Lance Corporal: (1276) I.G.Richardson.
15th:
Private: (711) T.Henty.

Trenches opposite the Double Crassier, two coal mining slag heaps, were taken over on the 18th March. In this position on the 20th at about 7.00pm the Germans sent up a green rocket. The rocket signal was followed immediately by the blowing of an enemy mine at the end of the southernmost Crassier. Although part of the Battalion's front line trench was blown in, no casualties were suffered.

After three days in support at Maroc, a return was made to the Double Crassier trenches on the 24th March. Approaching midnight on the 25th, four or five Germans crept up to attack a Battalion sap-head at the Southern Crassier. The enemy crawled along both sides of the sap trench and reached a point about 15 yards distant without being heard before throwing bombs. Two men were severely wounded and one of these was taken prisoner by the Germans. Battalion bombers quickly retaliated killing one German. Another German was shot and was seen to roll down between the Crassiers.

The 8th Royal Berks arrived as relief on the 27th March and the Battalion moved back to Petit Sains in Divisional Reserve. There, until the end of the month, training was carried out and welcome baths were taken at the mine works. Unfortunately, on the 31st, bathing had to be curtailed when the Germans shelled the area with a long- range heavy gun.

At this time, also, a Battalion N.C.O. was instrumental in bringing about the arrest of two civilians seen in the vicinity and suspected of being spies.

MARCH:
21st:
Private: (320) R.L.Cobbold.
24th:
Private: (82) J.Barry.
25th:
Lance Corporal: (1595) A.Watson.

Saturday 1st April gave an opportunity for inter-company football matches to be played and the men remained 'at rest' until the 5th when they relieved the Loyal North Lancs in the front line. At about midnight the enemy exploded a small mine and followed up with trench mortar and much rifle fire but, within a half hour, all was quiet.

Sporadic shelling by both sides was carried out over the next two days. On the 7th a small camouflet mine, designed to destroy enemy underground workings, was sprung by the British but this brought retaliatory machine gun and rifle fire which severely wounded Second Lieutenant C.N.Broad who died two days later in hospital at Noeux-les-Mines.

APRIL:
4th:
Private: (1652) G.C.Whiting.
6th:
Privates: (995) W.Masters, (1671) J.Willis,
8th:
Privates: (726) R.Hill, (1700) R.Wright.
9th:
Second Lieutenant: (181) C.N.Broad.

During the two or three days leading up to the 13th April, a scheme was planned for making a small raid on a part of the enemy line where a machine gun emplacement was suspected. Volunteers were called for and there was great competition for selection to the party of 15 N.C.O's and men to be led by Second Lieutenant Osmaston. Every man was instructed carefully in the part he had to play. In essence, the raid was to be carried out in silence using only bayonets and bludgeons. The line of advance had been reconnoitred and marked the previous evening when it had been confirmed that a known gap in the German wire still existed. The only anxiety was caused by the knowledge that the moon would not set until 3.00am thus giving only about one hour of darkness before dawn.

APRIL:
12th:
Private: (451) F.Downer.

At 2.25am on the 13th April, with a cloud bank obscuring the moon, the party set out. A few hundred yards to the left there was considerable bombing activity by way of diverting enemy attention from the raid area. Those left behind watched and listened as best they could but only faint sounds of movement and digging were heard from the direction of the enemy trenches. After what seemed a very long time, the raiding party, with the exception of Second Lieutenant Osmaston and three men, returned; they had been away for 50 minutes. Five minutes later the others, who had been covering the retreat of their comrades, also returned. Not one man had been killed or wounded.

Second Lieutenant Osmaston, who was later awarded the Military Cross for this action, described how they crept up silently to within a short distance of the enemy wire where they had to wait because some German wirers were at work a little to the left. After a while, the party moved forward again, cut the enemy wire and dropped into the trench. The suspected machine gun post was then reached and inspected but was found to be incomplete and without a gun. Meanwhile, two Germans who approached along the trench were surprised and killed. There was then no more to be achieved so the party withdrew. For gallant support in this venture Lance Corporal Adams received the D.C.M. while Lance Corporal Kent and Private Moore were commended by the Divisional Commander.

The following day a German shell of heavy calibre struck one of the nearby twin mine shaft structures known as 'Tower Bridge' with the result that the tall shaft collapsed in spectacular fashion. That evening the Battalion was relieved and moved back to Les Brebis. There, for the next six days, training was continued, particularly in the use of smoke bombs and gas helmets. The men also availed themselves of the luxurious opportunity to take baths. One officer and 69 men arrived to join the Battalion.

From the 20th April until the end of the month the Battalion was in and around Maroc and the Double Crassier. From time to time, particularly on the 23rd, the enemy sent over shrapnel shells. On the 25th the British 18 pounder guns destroyed a large portion of German barbed wire entanglements which were three rows deep to the right of the Double Crassier. Then, the next day, troops were withdrawn to greater safety while British heavy howitzers fired 40 rounds onto what was suspected of being a German mine sap near the Southern Crassier.

APRIL:
23rd:
Private: (1696) E.E.J.Wren.
24th:
Private: (111) R.J.Berry.
27th:
Private: (548) G.Foreman.

A gas alert was sounded on the 29th April and a pungent smell of chlorine was evident in and around Maroc. Gas helmets were worn for about 15 minutes by which time the air had cleared.

APRIL:
29th:
Private: (474) T.Eason.

On the afternoon of the 1st May the Germans caused problems by firing trench mortars and shrapnel shells killing Sergeant W.Couchman, D.C.M. and Private F.A.White and wounding several others. During the previous night some Germans entered a front line trench and tried to take away a Lewis machine gun but failed. Three of the enemy were killed, one of whom, for some strange, unknown reason, was found to have his hands tied together and a rope round his neck.

MAY:
1st:
Sergeant: (375) W.Couchman, D.C.M.
Private: (1647) F.A.White.

The Battalion was relieved on the evening of the 2nd May and moved back to billets at Les Brebis, remaining there under training until the 8th when a return was made to the line at cellars in Loos, where it was exceptionally quiet.

MAY::
2nd:
Private: (576) J.Funnell.
3rd:
Private: (1673) G.Wilson.
4th:
Privates:: (900) T.H.Knight, (1037) R.A.Mitchell.

For the next three days things remained relatively quiet but on the 11th May the enemy became more active with machine guns, snipers and gas shells, the latter causing little discomfort. The following day, more shelling caused considerable damage to the Battalion's front line, reserve and communication trenches. One man was shot through the head by a sniper. That night, large working parties were organised to repair the trench damage.

MAY:
12th:
Privates: (662) J.Hallam, (1223) R.Price, (1513) A.Tobutt.

The enemy guns were quieter for much of the 14th May, perhaps because of a British bombardment the previous evening, but late in the day shelling was resumed. Captain MacDonald fired an S.O.S. emergency rocket which brought down a British barrage on the enemy. Within 15 minutes all was quiet once more and the Battalion was moved back to Loos in support.

MAY:
14th:
Corporal: (1274) G.W.Richardson.
Private: (985) G.Martin.

Working and wiring parties on the nights of the 15th and 16th May sustained casualties. On the 17th there occured a 10 minutes fierce bombing fight which caused more deaths before a move back to Les Brebis billets was made.

MAY:
15th:
Private: (37) L.Attridge.
16th:
Private: (77) H.W.Barnard.
MAY:
17th:
Privates: (484) A.P.Eden, (747) T.W.Hogwood, (825) T.James, (892) C.Knapp, (1487) F.E.Taylor.
18th:
Sergeant: (284) A.J.Chapman.

During this period at Les Brebis all the men had the opportunity to take baths. On the 21st May a German bombardment of the village lasted five hours from 3pm. Although several shells penetrated the building used as the officers mess, little damage was done. This bombardment apparently was in conjunction with an enemy attack farther south, at Vimy, and was designed to prevent the movement of British reinforcements to that area.

At this point must be recorded a 'blot on the landscape' of the 2nd Battalion. It was on the 22nd May that the only soldier to be sentenced to death by court martial while serving with this proud Battalion was shot at dawn. He was L 10414 Private William Henry Burrell, aged 21 years and a native of Pulborough, Sussex. Although he had joined soon after the war began in 1914, he went missing after only two months from the trenches near the brick stacks at Cuinchy. He was absent for some time but was eventually captured. He was court martialled and condemned to death but, on 5th May,1915, his sentence was commuted to imprisonment. On 4th April, 1916, that sentence was suspended, he was released from custody and returned to the Battalion. However, he soon deserted again and was recaptured. This time the death sentence, his second, was carried out by firing squad at Mazingarbe, Pas-de-Calais and it is there that he is buried.

MAY:
22nd:
Private: (233) W.H.Burrell.

For the remainder of May there was no unusual activity. On the 25th a move was made to Maroc. At this time, three officers and more than 100 other ranks, including eight drummers, joined the Battalion. The month ended on a sad note when, on the 30th, a German shell fell on a Battalion stables killing six horses and wounding another.

MAY:
23rd:
Lance Corporal: (692) G.Haynes.
29th:
Private: (75) F.Barker.

By the 1st June, the Battalion had moved into the firing line at South Maroc where they occupied houses and cellars.

JUNE:
1st:
Privates: (202) G.A.Brown, (1044) O.A.Monery, (1480) L.Taplin.

On the 4th June the Battalion returned to the support line and, there, the men heard news of the following Birthday Honour Awards:

C.M.G.:   Lieutenant-Colonel R.F.Villiers, D.S.O.
Military Cross: Captain and Quartermaster T.A.Jones

	Captain E.A.Baker
	Captain M.Wallington
	Captain E.H.Preston.
D.C.M.:	Regimental Sergeant Major W.F.Rainsford
	Quartermaster Sergeant W.Hearn
	Company Sergeant Major W.Soughton.
Military Medal:	Sergeant Young
	Corporal Larby
	Lance Corporal Horscroft
	Private Hughes
	Private Offler.

The weather then became very wet for a number of days and literally dampened down most of the activity from both sides. On the 10th June, the Battalion took up billets in Les Brebis as Divisional Reserve. The opportunity was taken generally to clean up equipment, uniforms and to take welcome baths. The Battalion was represented on the 13th by two officers and 45 men at the memorial service held at Braquemont to Lord Kitchener, Secretary of State for War, who had died aboard a torpedoed British warship.

Until the 18th June, training was carried out intermingled with periods of relaxation. A very successful concert was held on the evening of the 15th in the new Divisional Recreation Hut. The North Maroc firing line was the venue on the 18th. Heavy German shelling filled in parts of the trench system on the 19th and, on the following day, two German camouflets were sprung causing slight damage to a British mine gallery. Sporadic shelling caused a number of casualties over the next few days.

JUNE:
20th:
Lance Corporal: (1242) A.H.Raworth.
21st:
Private: (1687) F.Woodhams.
22nd:
Private: (862) B.Kennard.

During the 26th June, working parties were employed on improving the concertina barbed wire entanglements and, following very heavy rain in the afternoon, the trenches had to be cleaned up so far as possible. Unfortunately, 2nd Lt. W.F.Scandrett, who was attached to the Brigade Trench Mortar Battery, was himself killed by a German trench mortar bomb on the 27th. The following two days were taken up with preparations for the major attack planned for the last day of the month.

JUNE:
26th:
Sergeant: (125) A.H.Blackman.
Privates: (116) W.T.Billings, (1202) H.Pinyoun.
27th:
Second Lieutenant: (1332) W.F.Scandrett.

The operations planned to be carried out by the Battalion in conjunction with the 2nd King's Royal Rifle Corps (K.R.R.C.) on the night of the 30th June were timed to begin at 9.10pm. All troops were in position by 8.30pm and, at 9.00pm, the enemy, who seemed to have been forewarned, began a bombardment of the British front and support line trenches. A number of casualties were caused at this time because the trenches were crowded with men ready to go 'over the top'.

The assault was to be against the German position known as the 'Triangle' and against the northern arm of the Double Crassier. In the initial assault the K.R.R.C. attacked two supposed enemy tunnels but the defensive wire there, which should have been cut by British artillery, remained impassable and the men were forced to advance along the front of the entanglements. Not only did they capture an enemy post at the Crassier but also they took a mine crater blown by the British.

Meanwhile, the Royal Sussex men had attacked along the top of the Crassier and some, including 2nd Lt. Goddard and Sgt.Baker (both of whom were killed), got into a German sap-head. Repeated efforts were then made to advance along the sap which had been almost levelled by shellfire. Some 50 yards along, the enemy had constructed a barricade into which they had fitted a loophole at low level. Through this loophole a machine gun was able to fire directly down the trench. It appeared that the barricade also had a stout roof because continuous attempts to bomb the enemy machine gunners proved unsuccessful and they kept firing.

The Germans brought up a second machine gun which began firing at a range of only 30 yards. Under cover of this machine gun fire the Germans tried to bomb our men out of the sap-head but they were thwarted by Sergeant Weal and his men who were stationed there and who inflicted a number of enemy casualties.

At 11.10am Captain McDonald sent a message to say that he could hold his position but could make no more progress because the K.R.R.C. had been unable to capture the enemy trench in the Triangle. In response, the Commanding Officer, Lieutenant Colonel Villiers, relayed the Brigadier's order that the Royal Sussex men were to withdraw to their original position. This withdrawal was carried out in good order, the enemy making no attempt to follow.

In comparison with casualties sustained by other units in this day's attack, the 2nd Battalion Royal Sussex Regiment came off relatively lightly. At the same time, a short distance north, opposite the village of Richebourg L'Avoué , a German salient known as 'The Boar's Head' had been attacked by the 'New Army' 11th, 12th and 13th Battalions of The Royal Sussex Regiment. Those Battalions, too, were repulsed with heavy losses of men.

Most of the casualties suffered by the 2nd Battalion appear to have been caused by rifle and machine gun fire from the Triangle and the Crassier, except in the sap-head where a number of men had been hit by bomb splinters. In keeping with the considerable length of front line to north and south in this area, no gains of ground had been made. If the total British casualty list is assessed, this attack would appear to have been another failure, wasteful of manpower but, if the action is considered to have been a 'holding attack' designed to keep German troops occupied and away from the great Somme offensive to be launched some 30 miles to the south at 7.30am the next day, the 1st July, the effort may be regarded as having at least some merit.

JUNE:
30th:
Second Lieutenant: (608) S.G.Goddard.
Sergeant: (53) F.Baker.
Corporal: (1051) H.Moore.
Lance Corporals: (1162) C.T.H.Pattenden, (1439) F.A.Stemp, (1542) W.G.Tupper.
Privates: (40) B.Austin, (217) G.H.Buckwell, (265) J.Caplin, (394) R.F.Cripps, (438) G.Denyer, (469) W.S.Dyer, (509) H.J.Evans, (529) A.E.Fisher, (629) S.J.Grant, (646) A.Griffiths, (767) S.R.Hore, (839) T.R.Johnston, (913) F.J.V.La Roche, (1101) F.Norman, (1342) J.Searle, (1628) L.Were, (1706) B.W.Young.

CHAPTER 5
1916
JULY – DECEMBER

Saturday 1st July, 1916, dawned with the promise of a beautifully hot and bright summer's day, yet it would go down as the blackest day in the history of the British army. On that day, some 30 miles south from the Battalion's position, began the Battle of the Somme. On that single day Britain and her Empire would take over 57,000 casualties on the Somme including 19,240 dead.

For the Battalion, July,1916, was to be the end of seven long, grinding months in the vicinity of Loos. On the 2nd July, the Battalion left Maroc and marched away through Les Brebis, Mazingarbe and Noeux-les-Mines to Houchin where the night was spent under canvas. Next day the march continued by way of Hallicourt and Bruay to Division where, after two days of training and parades, movement continued on foot for six miles to Lillers. Already they were on their way south to the dreaded Somme.

At Lillers, on the 6th July, the Battalion and the whole of its transport entrained for a journey of six hours to Candas, north of Amiens. A six miles march was then made to Flesselles where most of the troops were billeted in barns. Two more days marching at eight miles each day brought the troops to Frechencourt on the 8th and to Brésle on the 9th. They were then some five miles west of the town of Albert, to the east of which the battle still raged.

JULY:
1st:
Sergeant: (1467) F.J.Sturt.
4th:
Private: (1229) J.Puttock.
7th:
Second Lieutenant: (872) R.Kenward.
8th:
Lieutenant: (347) C.E.Cook.

On the 10th July, the Battalion, in fighting order, entered the immediate area of the Somme battlefields, marching through the town of Albert to bivouac about two miles beyond, in Bécourt Wood. This wood, described then as 'a big rubbish tip', was to be 'home' for several days during which heavy rain fell and German shells were received from time to time. In particular, casualties were sustained from gas shelling during the night of 14th / 15th.

JULY:
13th:
Privates: (87) W.H.Barton, (521) G.Fellows, (1061) H.J.Mortimer, (1159) A.W.Patching.
15th:
Sergeant: (17) H.J.Allen.
Lance Corporal: (220) J.Bull.
Privates: (106) R.R.Bellham, (670) E.Hanson, (1177) A.E.Pearson, (1288) H.Rogers, (1649) H.M.White, (1695) T.Wragg.
16th:
Private: (1710) G.Young.

The 17th July was very misty and, after wet conditions the previous day, the Battalion struggled along in the infamous Somme mud to positions near the village of Fricourt. On the 18th, following a day-long British bombardment, a move forward and north was effected to trenches near the village of Contalmaison. On successive days Contalmaison was shelled by the enemy. On the 19th a draft of 83 other ranks, including men from the 10th and 12th Battalions, The Royal Sussex Regiment, were welcomed and absorbed. On the 21st, news was received of the well justified award of the D.C.M. to Sergeant Weal and Corporal Sloan for their sterling work on the 30th June,1916. Sadly, Corporal Sloan was to die of wounds only three days later on 24th July,1916.

JULY:
19th:
Private: (1372) F.Simmonds.
20th:
Private: (1336) H.Scruby.

At last, on the 22nd July, the Somme firing line was reached to the right of the village of Pozières, with the Australian 1st Division on the left. There, an attack was ordered for 12.30am on the 23rd after an intense five minutes bombardment. Unfortunately, the Germans, assisted by Very

Lights, were in a good position to see the leading Companies moving to their positions of deployment. As a result, such heavy shelling and fire from machine guns hidden in the long grass was brought down by the Germans from both flanks that confusion reigned and the attack never got properly under way. The Battalion was forced to withdraw and, the following day, returned to bivouac in Bécourt Wood. Over 20 men died as a result of this aborted effort.

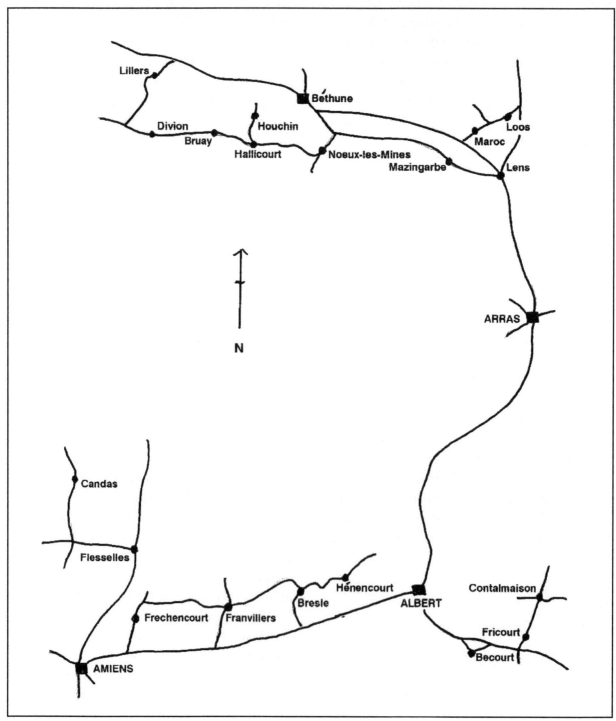

10. *July 1916*

JULY:
23rd:
Second Lieutenant: (1396) A.C.Smith.
Lance Sergeant: (1503) W.Thornton.
Corporal: (1666) E.Williams.
Lance Corporals: (735) G.Hilton, (1338) F.Scutt.
Privates: (27) C.Archer, (142) F.G.Boniface, (187)
    E.B.Brook, (209) S.E.Brown, (241) R.S.Bush, (302)
    E.E.Clark, (755) J.T.Holloway, (854) A.Keep, (920)
    C.Ledword, (940) T.J.Lind, (1115) E.Ockenden,
    (1141) O.Page, (1197) A.E.Pierce, (1227) G.Pumfrey,
    (1348) H.K.Sendall, (1349) C.O.Shambrook, (1382)
    A.L.Skeet, (1677) A.W.Windmill.
24th:
Corporal: (1392) R.H.S.Sloan, D.C.M.
Private: (1488) J.H.Taylor.

Franvillers was the Battalion's destination
on the 26th. There they billeted, received a new
draft of 31 men, cleaned up, took baths at nearby
Mérville, paraded and received the following
show prizes at the Brigade Sports afternoon:
Water Carts – 1st; Cookers – 1st, 2nd and 3rd;
Pack Horse – 3rd; Limbered Wagons – 3rd. On
the 30th, a five miles march was made to bivouacs
at Hénencourt where, the following day, the
Battalion was inspected by the General Officer
Commanding 2nd Brigade.

For the first 12 days of August the Battalion
undertook some very intensive training
interspersed with occasions of relaxation and
enjoyment. Another draft of 46 men joined
on the 2nd. An evening concert, bathing and
boxing tournaments were organised. Physical
training, drill, musketry and, particularly night
time operations and wood fighting exercises,
were carried out. A number of men lost their lives
during this period, possibly during realistic night
time wood skirmishes, although the Battalion
War Diary mentions no such accidents.

AUGUST:
1st:
Sergeant: (520) W.E.Fellingham.
4th:
Sergeant: (785) E.Hulkes.
5th:
Private: (1427) F.Stace.
6th:
Privates: (1156) C.H.Partridge, (1644) A.White.
7th:
Privates: (183) E.G.Bromley, (251) F.Byford, (385)

L.Cramp, (466) J.W.Dunton, (492) E.C.Eldridge,
(666) R.G.Hands, (957) J.E.Lucas, (1168) A.Payne,
(1414) W.J.Smith.

On the evening of the 13th August the
Battalion marched through Albert and returned,
once more, to Bécourt Wood. Next day a march
was made eastward by way of Mametz Wood,
the scene of such bitter fighting during the
previous month, and on to take over, from the
Suffolk Regiment, the front line at High Wood.
Casualties were sustained from enemy shelling
during the night of 14th / 15th and, late on the
evening of the 15th, a patrol reported that the
German trench running south-west from High
Wood was not wired and that an attack should be
feasible.

An assault using men from the 2nd Royal
Sussex and 1st Northamptons was made without
artillery support. This attack proved to be
unsuccessful, mainly because direction was lost
in the darkness. There were some 30 casualties
including 2nd Lieutenant Collins who was killed.
Next evening another attempt was made under
intense bombardment. This time the trench was
occupied with few casualties and 12 Germans
were taken prisoner.

AUGUST:
15th:
Second Lieutenant: (339) N.L.Collins.
Privates: (199) C.E.Brown, (570) S.E.Fryer.
16th:
Captain: (34) L.de B.Atkinson.
Sergeant: (559) W.Frape.
Corporal: (1239) C.G.Rapley.
Privates: (157) R.A.Boxall, (218) H.A.Budd, (420)
    A.G.Davis, (724) A.Hill, (855) G.F.Kellaway-Smith,
    (1237) W.J.Ransom, (1269) H.Richards, (1402)
    G.Smith, (1453) W.R.Stokes, (1678) W.W.Winsor.

Towards morning on the 17th August, the
Germans made a determined counter-attack
using a flame-thrower and hand-grenades.
Considerable confusion ensued and a good
number of men were killed and wounded. Second
Lieutenant Wright, the sole remaining officer,
together with a few men, held on to the trench
even though they were bombarded all day,
taking further casualties, until relieved by the
1st Northamptons. The exhausted Royal Sussex
men, together with their 1st Northampton

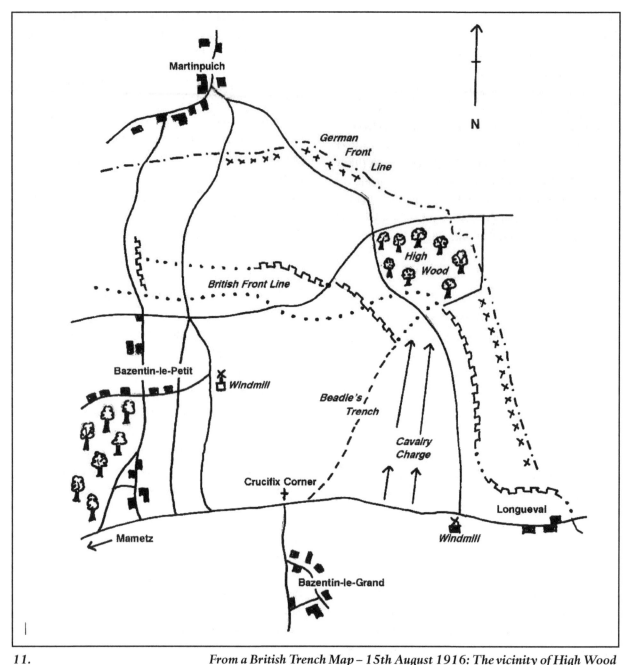

11.   *From a British Trench Map – 15th August 1916: The vicinity of High Wood*

colleagues, then trudged back to Brigade Reserve in Mametz Wood.

AUGUST:

17th:

Sergeants: (1256) G.C.Reeves, (1326) G.Saunders.

Corporal: (1539) F.Tucknott.

Lance Corporals: (307) J.G.Clark, (411) A.G.Dann, (415) G.E.Datlen, (896) G.S.Knight, (1127) S.D.Osborne.

Privates: (89) J.Bassford, (101) H.F.Beer, (123) J.Bishop, (151) H.Bourne, (305) J.Clark, (311) F.Clayton, (376) T.A.Couldry, (418) H.Davies, (425) G.Deacon, (524) W.J.Figg, (563) F.J.French, (568) E.Fry, (753) W.Holland, (1095) E.Nicholls, (1199) H.Pierce, (1328) H.Saunders, (1431) W.R.Staplehurst, (1469) J.J.Suggitt, (1475) E.Swain, (1478) G.Swift, (1537) F.Trussler, (1699) I.Wright.

18th:

Private: (1113) S.Oakman.

'A' and 'D' Companies went, on the 19th August, to support the Northamptons who had occupied the slightly higher ground west of High Wood. Early in the morning of the 20th, the Battalion received welcome news of its withdrawal to billets in Albert but, to everyone's dismay, the arrangements were cancelled. Instead, a move back to the firing line in support of the Northamptons took place. At 2.30pm the Battalion launched an attack which quickly came under enfilade machine gun fire from left and right. One post was established but no further progress could be made.

Heavy casualties were sustained this day before the Battalion was relieved and returned to a point south of Mametz Wood. Even there, the troops came under a gas shell bombardment but took no further casualties. Then a cheery march was made back to those previously-mentioned and even more welcome billets in Albert.

At the time of this relief from the front line positions, the Battalion strength had been severely reduced, by the previous seven days of attacks, to only four officers and approximately 150 other ranks. In recognition of the hardships endured, a message was received from the General Officer Commanding 2nd Infantry Brigade expressing his "...intense admiration of the gallant manner in which all ranks have responded to the severe calls made upon them..." and stating that he was "...proud to have troops under his command who have so splendidly maintained the famous traditions of the Units to which they belong."

AUGUST:

19th:
Lance Corporal: (1661) S.G.Wilcox.
Privates: (232) F.G.Burrell, (634) E.E.Green, (780) M.Huggett, (997) C.Matthews, (1102) G.Norman, (1470) A.Sullivan.

20th:
Second Lieutenant: (1714) N.L.Young.
Sergeants: (1058) F.Morley, (1132) J.L.Packet.
Corporals: (185) C.A.Brook, (1626) J.G.Wells.
Lance Corporals: (386) S.E.Crane, (987) H.R.Martin, (1447) G.E.Stevens, (1496) J.Tester,M.M.
Privates: (110) J.Bennett, (133) E.Bliss, (197) B.Brown, (243) A.J.Buss, (292) W.G.Cheal, (383) W.Cox, (567) F.Frost, (924) A.Leggatt, (1178) W.F.Pearson, (1193) P.E.Phillips, (1262) M.V.Renard, (1408) S.Smith, (1434) F.G.Steadman, (1486) E.J.Taylor, (1553) J.T.Urry, (1623) A.Wells, (1642) J.F.Wheeler, (1643) W.F.H.Wheeler, (1712) J.Young.

In addition to those killed during the previous seven days of attacks in the vicinity of High Wood, 14 officers and 320 men were wounded and 87 other ranks were missing.

On 21st August an enemy aircraft dropped bombs on the town of Albert but caused little damage. For that and the following six days the Battalion remained in Albert enjoying baths, generally cleaning equipment, undergoing training, physical exercises, drills and inspections. During those days, 185 other ranks, including 97 men from the Royal East Kent Reserve Yeomanry, joined the Battalion. Several more men succumbed to their wounds received in the recent fighting.

AUGUST:

23rd:
Private: (1545) E.Turner.
24th:
Lance Corporals: (173) W.A.Bridger, (348) T.H.Cook.
Privates: (137) E.Bold, (986) G.C.Martin, (1135) A.E.Padgham, (1436) E.Steel.
26th:
Private: (1683) M.Wood.

The Companies moved off independently from Albert to Mametz Wood on the evening of the 27th August. There, all was quiet owing to the inclement weather. On the final day of the month the Battalion moved forward again, this time to take over the firing line immediately to the right of High Wood.

AUGUST:

27th:
Private: (992) W.T.Martin.
29th:
Lance Corporal: (796) H.G.Hussey.

September began with heavy German shelling of the front line held by the Battalion. Remarkably, this bombardment, which continued for most of the morning on the 1st, and was renewed during the evening, killed only one man, Private A.P.W.Bourne, although the trench was filled in at several points and a number of men were buried. In retaliation, Battalion snipers accounted for some of the enemy when they attempted to leave shell holes to return to their own trenches.

SEPTEMBER:

1st:
Private: (150) A.P.W.Bourne.

On the 2nd September, a British bombardment of three hours took place during the afternoon. The Germans replied with very accurate heavy shells on Battalion lines which, again, filled in the trenches in places. One of those particularly severe family tragedies occured this day when the twins, Privates Frank and Thomas Bindoff of 76, Coventry Street, Brighton, were killed, probably together. Too late for these men came the relief which allowed the Battalion to return to Reserve in Bécourt Wood.

SEPTEMBER:

2nd:

Privates: (118) F.E.Bindoff, (119) H.T.Bindoff, (196) A.E.Brown, (371) C.Cosham, (880) A.King.

The burying of telephone cables in Mametz Wood occupied a working party of 250 men on the 4th September. On that day, too, a draft of 328 other ranks joined the Battalion. Nine more men joined the following day, during which a move to bivouac in Lozenge Wood was made. At 3pm on the 7th a move of great portent occured when the front line trenches to the right of High Wood were taken over.

SEPTEMBER:

6th:

Sergeant: (1599) L.L.Watson.

Corporal: (597) R.W.Gibson.

Privates: (1154) W.G.Parmenter, (1355) G.Shelley.

7th:

Privates: (493) J.Eldridge, (821) G.W.Jackson.

On the 8th September, the enemy, perhaps with knowledge of the British attack planned for the following day, shelled the Battalion's front trenches heavily, filling them in here and there and causing casualties. During the evening, ammunition and bombs were carried up in considerable quantities to the front line.

SEPTEMBER:

8th:

Sergeant: (1524) W.T.Torrance.

Privates: (867) J.H.Kent, (1363) G.A.V.Short, (1630) C.N.West.

Orders were received that, on the 9th September, the main German trench in High Wood and to its east would be attacked and captured. That day, at 4.45pm, with the 1st Northamptons on its left and the Kings Royal Rifle Corps on its right, the Battalion advanced to the attack, the objective being part of the trench known as Wood Lane. Despite

heavy artillery and machine gun fire from the Germans, 'C' and 'D' Companies, closely followed by 'A' and 'B' Companies, advanced steadily and in splendid order. 'D' Company secured its objective with few losses but 'C' Company was less fortunate and suffered heavy casualties from a machine gun in High Wood. 'A' Company pushed through and advanced some distance in front of the captured line, accounting for a number of the enemy as they ran back. On the right, the Rifle Corps took its objectives but, on the left, the Northamptons were driven back by intense fire, leaving the 2nd Battalion's flank exposed. As a consequence it was necessary to dig a defensive flank; this proved successful and, by dark, consolidation of the position was well under way. Several German prisoners had been taken and the Battalion Scout Sergeant secured a Maxim Gun.

Good work had been accomplished but the Battalion's casualties, which included 154 wounded and 63 missing, were the heaviest sustained for almost a year.

SEPTEMBER:

9th:

Captain: (687) R.d'A.Harvey.

Second Lieutenants: (306) J.T.Clark, (329) H.E.E.Coleman, (540) A.M.Foley, (547) C.F.Forder, (788) W.G.Humphreys, (1247) C.L.R.Reade.

Sergeants: (277) A.G.Catchpole, (671) T.Hanwell, (1046) W.C.Monk, (1705) A.Young, (1711) G.T.Young.

Corporals: (379) E.F.Cowling, (408) E.S.Dale, (794) W.Hurmson, (895) G.E.Knight, (1005) A.W.McGregor, (1624) F.Wells.

Lance Corporals: (72) F.G.Banfield, (120) S.J.Birch, (163) E.A.Bradley, (582) P.J.Gardiner, (655) W.Haig, (775) H.Howe, (835) M.J.Jennings, (837) C.A.Johnson, (918) A.Lavender, (1093) W.J.Newton, (1124) A.C.Orrin, (1217) H.Potter, (1324) C.H.Saunders, (1450) E.E.Stevenson, (1500) E.Thompson, (1669) T.P.Williams.

Privates: (1) E.E.Abbott, (38) H.W.Aucock, (74) R.Barcock, (102) T.W.Beer, (107) F.P.Beniston, (131) F.W.Blake, (166) E.S.Brandom, (177) P.Bristow, (198) B.F.Brown, (261) J.R.Cannon, (275) H.W.Cartner, (323) J.H.Colbear, (363) A.K.Coplestone, (369) W.G.Cork, (422) W.Dawes, (424) E.A.Deacon, (429) A.Deadman, (446) F.A.Dixon, (477) C.H.Eastwood, (491) W.J.Edwards, (528) W.F.Fish, (538) W.G.Foard, (556) P.J.Francis,

(557) W.Francis, (619) C.J.Goldsmith, (621)
C.H.Goodwin, (651) W.W.Gunfield, (652) A.Gurr,
(695) A.J.Head, (789) C.W.Humphries, (793)
F.Hurlock, (811) B.W.Inskip, (841) A.Johnstone,
(856) M.Kelly, (943) C.S.Little, (988) H.G.Martin,
(1007) E.Mead, (1013) G.Melton, (1023) P.Miller,
(1047) A.Montague, (1053) J.Moore, (1063) A.Moss,
(1067) W.E.Muncey, (1079) C.W.Nelson, (1082)
E.A.Newby, (1108) H.J.Noviss, (1120) J.Orbell,
(1148) T.B.Parfect, (1186) W.H.Perry, (1200)
L.C.Pike, (1213) G.Pope, (1216) A.E.Potter, (1281)
J.Ridley, (1282) L.A.Robere, (1286) E.Robinson,
(1345) H.L.Sellen, (1376) W.Simpson, (1403)
G.F.Smith, (1407) P.W.Smith, (1413) W.H.Smith,
(1421) H.J.Speed, (1424) A.Spooner, (1437)
W.R.Steele, (1578) F.A.Wallis.(1686) R.C.Wooden.

The captured ground was maintained on the
10th September and the situation remained
relatively quiet. The Battalion, with the exception
of 'D' Company which had to remain until the
following day, was relieved and withdrew to
Bécourt Wood.

SEPTEMBER:
10th:
Corporal: (1525) J.Tottman.
Privates: (911) W.E.Large, (1505) R.E.Tibbitt.

At 5am on the 12th September the Battalion
marched about eight miles via Albert to bivouac
in a wood just outside the village of Baizieux.
The next day some tents became available and
the men were able to camp more comfortably
in a field opposite the wood. A rest period of
one week in safety well behind the lines was
then thoroughly enjoyed by all ranks. Physical
exercises, musketry and other training were
undertaken in a relaxed atmosphere. A Church
Parade was attended on Sunday 17th followed
by Inter-Company football matches. Then, later
that day, news was received that the villages of
Courcelette, Martinpuich and Flers had been
captured from the Germans. This was welcome
news, indeed, especially as the advent of the
tank at Flers had made a great impact. Rumours
about the new steel monsters caused great
excitement.

SEPTEMBER:
11th:
Lance Sergeant: (1268) E.K.Richards.
Private: (1304) C.J.Rummery.

12th:
Privates: (553) W.P.Foster, (1006) J.McGuiness, (1026)
E.A.Mills, (1032) J.Milton, (1379) F.C.Sizeland.
13th:
Lance Corporal: (511) F.E.Ewer.
14th:
Sergeant: (234) A.Burt.
15th:
Private: (98) H.Beaton.
18th:
Sergeant: (673) W.C.Hardiman.

A circular from Divisional Headquarters
on the 19th September brought to an end the
period of rest and returned the Battalion by way
of Hénencourt and Albert to Bécourt Wood. In
fact, six days were spent in bivouacs there while
the weather turned exceedingly wet and everyone
became uncomfortable. To make matters worse,
the wood was heavily shelled late on the 22nd
with seven horses being killed and four wounded.
Of five men wounded, Regimental Quartermaster
Sergeant Hearn was the only survivor, the others
dying over the next few days.

SEPTEMBER:
22nd:
Lance Corporal: (468) J.Dyer.
23rd:
Private: (564) E.Friend.
24th:
Private: (321) W.R.Cobby.
25th:
Private: (227) G.W.Burdett.

Later on the 25th September the Battalion
moved up to support trenches in front of High
Wood. On their right, considerable enemy
shelling was in progress but their front was
relatively quiet. The next day, the good news
was received that the formidable Thiepval
fortress, some three miles to the north-west
had been captured at last. Then, with only six
hours' notice, the Battalion launched an attack at
11pm. The effort was unsuccessful and was soon
discontinued.

SEPTEMBER:
26th:
Corporals: (128) J.Blackman, (1263) B.Reynolds.
Private: (1011) W.F.Megnin.

Next day, the 27th September, with somewhat
longer to prepare, the Battalion renewed its

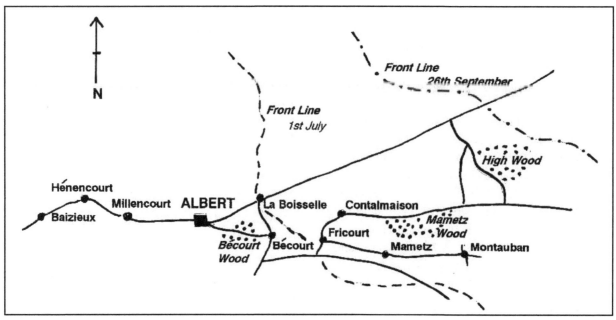

12.   *August and September 1916*

attack. In spite of much hostile artillery, the Companies advanced steadily and secured their objectives. By nightfall the captured position was consolidated. Patrols then reported that the next German line to the front had been evacuated. Immediately, an officer, 12 bombers and a Lewis Gun party moved forward to occupy the position and form a barricade. At one time it appeared that the enemy were massing for a counter attack but our artillery was turned on to the area concerned and no attempt was made by the Germans that night to regain their lost ground. In addition to those men of the Battalion killed in this action, six officers and 99 other ranks were recorded as wounded and 36 men as missing.

SEPTEMBER:

27th:

Sergeant: (61) J.W.Baker.

Lance Corporals: (709) G.R.Henson, (888) W.R.King, (1025) C.W.Millington.

Privates: (3) F.Adams, (18) W.A.Allwright, (21) H.B.Annenberg, (164) W.A.Bradley, (179) A.H.Britton, (595) H.Gibbs, (661) L.Hall, (715) P.G.Hewett, (774) F.W.Howe, (956) G.Lower, (962) D.S.MacGregor, (1062) H.G.Morton, (1088) G.V.Newnham, (1091) A.Newstead, (1131) H.V.Owen, (1309) J.Sadler, (1426) J.J.Spooner, (1458) C.H.Stoner, (1535) H.C.Trow, (1570) F.Wakeling.

Late at night on the 28th September, the Battalion was relieved and made its weary way back to bivouac in the familiar Bécourt Wood.

After a somewhat fitful rest, a welcome march was made next day away from the wood, through the town of Albert and on to much-appreciated billets at Millencourt. There, the month ended with valiant attempts to clean up and with the issue of new clothing.

SEPTEMBER:

28th:

Corporal: (1231) A.C.Quinton.

Lance Corporals: (593) F.C.Gibbs, (1270) A.H.Richardson.

Privates: (145) H.Bonnett, (240) J.Bush, (252) P.Byford, (362) S.Cope, (406) E.Dack, (470) W.Eagle, (1209) E.J.Poll, (1224) R.W.Proctor, (1461) J.Strange, (1654) W.Whittacker.

29th:

Privates: (266) F.H.Cardey, (617) A.Goldsmith.

30th:

Privates: (503) C.G.Ennals, (1474) S.Sutton.

At Millencourt on the 1st October the Battalion was not aware that this was to be the beginning of a period of seven weeks away from the fighting areas. For the most part, the relative luxury of billets would be enjoyed and, although much time was to be spent on training, drilling, route marching and exercising, removal to safety at a fair distance from the Somme front lines provided a general relaxation of benefit to everyone.

The Battalion transport left Millencourt at 5am on the 2nd October and took two days to reach the Battalion's next destination. On the morning of the 3rd, the remaining officers and men marched so far as the Albert – Amiens Road. From there, motor buses took them in the direction of Amiens and to billets at Toeuflies. Once everyone was settled, the cleaning of equipment and clothing was renewed. The men, too, enjoyed the rare luxury of baths.

By Sunday the 8th October everyone was sufficiently presentable to attend Church Parade which was held in the orchard opposite Battalion Headquarters. This parade was repeated on the 15th, during which service the names were read out of every friend and colleague who had fallen on the Somme front.

Leave began to be authorised at this stage. Initially, 26 lucky men were given leave passes each week but, later in the month, this was reduced to 15. At the same time, drafts of replacement soldiers continued to arrive, totalling 15 officers and over 80 other ranks during October.

Recreational events were organised in a further effort to boost morale. The Divisional Band played in the orchard and football matches were arranged, the Battalion team drawing with No.141 Field Artillery and beating the 1st Northamptons 2 – 0.

Large scale manoeuvres were carried out in night fighting and wood fighting. There was also training, both theoretical and actual, in musketry, bombing, bayonet fighting, consolidation, re-organisation and various methods of communication.

During October the Battalion was proud to receive honours and awards for past achievements; three officers were awarded the Military Cross and 22 men the Military Medal. By month end, however, preparations were under way for a gradual return towards the front.

OCTOBER:
1st:
Private: (1691) F.Woolnough.
4th:
Lance Corporal: (391) A.W.Creasey.
Private: (939) F.A.Lilley.
8th:
Lance Corporal: (587) G.N.Gastrell.

On the morning of the 1st November the Battalion awoke in the tented camp outside the village of Brésle where it had arrived the previous day by bus. Three days of lectures and manoeuvres followed before the Battalion, with cookers, water-carts, mess-carts and Lewis Guns, moved up to billets in the remnants of the town of Albert.

Much time was spent in cleaning the billets. Then, on the 9th November, the Germans dropped shells near the station and there was considerable air activity as a reminder, if such was needed, that the war was still in progress.

NOVEMBER:
9th:
Private: (901) T.J.Knight.
14th:
Private: (1249) W.A.Rebbeck.

The long period of absence from the fighting zone ended on the 18th November when a long march brought the Battalion into Reserve at canvas huts close to the well known area of High Wood. Another forward move was made on the 21st to relieve the 5th Australian Brigade in front line trenches to the right of Eaucourt L'Abbaye. Because of the wet weather, trenches were in a very bad state. The infamous, heavy, cloying Somme mud made appalling conditions for everyone. In addition, casualties, the first in direct action since the 28th September, were sustained from heavy enemy shelling on the 22nd, two days after the official end of the Battle of the Somme.

NOVEMBER:
22nd:
Lance Corporal: (613) H.Godfrey.
Privates: (340) S.Collins, (357) H.Cooper, (500) E.J.Elms.

On the 23rd November, British artillery carried out a concentrated bombardment on the Butte de Warlencourt, an ancient mound which, in later times, would be regarded as being on the final line of the Somme battle. The enemy retaliated with 4.2" and 5.9" shells on that and the succeeding day.

NOVEMBER:
23rd:
Private: (178) R.Britt.
24th:
Private: (684) J.Harryman.

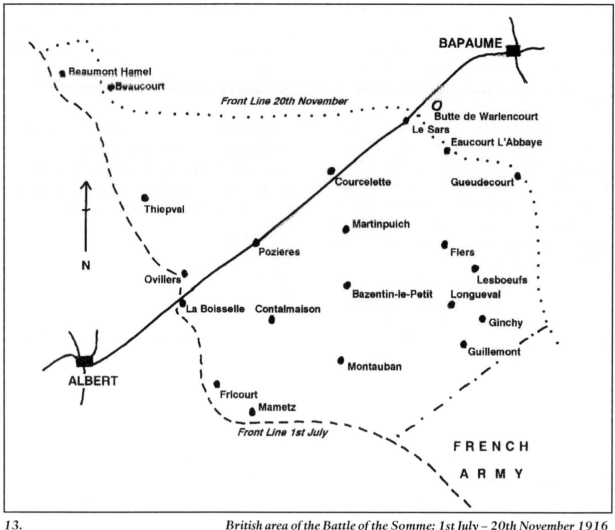

13.   *British area of the Battle of the Somme: 1st July – 20th November 1916*

Further continuous and steady rain began on the 25th November and, soon, the front line became so muddy that it was virtually impassable. Whole sections of the trenches began to crumble and fall. Despite much hard work the line became more than knee deep in mud and many men became stuck. Relief by the 2nd Royal Munster Fusiliers commenced during the evening of the 27th but such were the appalling conditions that the Battalion was unable to move out until the following morning. That day a long, exhausting trek was made back to Mametz Wood. On arrival there, the only shred of comfort had to be found in a pathetic camp of tents. Everyone was in a very filthy state and much time was spent in an attempt to get dry and clean. These efforts were fulfilled eventually with opportunities for the men to take baths and obtain new clothing.

NOVEMBER:
27th:
Lance Corporals: (214) J.J.Browning, (866) F.H.Kent.

Privates: (802) R.H.Hutt, (968) D.W.Manners, (1004) E.McDougald.
28th:
Privates: (764) T.G.Hook, (1238) A.W.Ranson.
30th:
Privates: (639) W.H.Greenfield, (1153) G.T.Parmenter.

Training and wood gathering for fires were the orders of the first four days of December. Then, on the 5th, at intervals of ten minutes, the Battalion Companies moved out on their way to a hutted camp at High Wood. The following day saw another forward move to the old German trench known as 'Flers Line' in the direction of that village.

On the 8th and 9th December the British artillery was very active. The enemy replied causing four casualties and damaging a Lewis Gun. The trenches remained in a very muddy condition and it was necessary to provide working parties for repairs and the laying of duckboards.

DECEMBER:
8th:
Private: (562) W.E.Freeman.
9th:
Lance Corporal: (1284) W.T.Roberts.
Private: (908) H.J.Lambert.

By the 11th December, a further 30 yards of the collapsed Flers Line had been reclaimed and dugouts reconstructed. In the late afternoon the Battalion was relieved by the 2nd Kings Royal Rifle Corps and moved back to a camp of huts at Bazentin-le-Petit. Snow which fell on the following morning turned to rain later and the men were forced, for their own betterment, to work on camp drainage systems.

On the 15th December the whole Battalion, with the exception of 160 men and N.C.O.'s drawn equally from each Company, who remained in camp, moved up again to the front line. At night, fatigue parties were provided and, on the 16th, four of these men were killed and three wounded by enemy shelling. In some places the distance between the opposing front lines was only 40 yards so that the sporadic fighting was limited to the use of bombs and rifle grenades.

DECEMBER:
16th:
Privates: (62) W.Baker, (262) C.F.Capelin, (288) W.Chase, (1059) G.Morley.

In the early morning of the 18th December, when the Commanding Officer and Second Lieutenant King were visiting posts in the line, a burst of enemy machine gun fire killed Second Lieutenant King instantly and narrowly missed the C.O.

DECEMBER:
18th:
Second Lieutenant: (885) P.D.A.King.
Private: (244) F.G.A.Bussey.

A move back to the camp at Bazentin-le-Petit was made on the 19th December. Much time was spent in cleaning the camp. Working parties also cleared and mended roads while very clear visibility following early frost encouraged shelling on both sides.

On the 23rd December, a return was made to the line where Christmas was spent in miserable conditions with relief coming again on the 27th. Then, on the 30th, a move farther back, to Fricourt, was effected and there a hard winter's month ended quietly.

DECEMBER:
27th:
Corporal: (1610) A.B.Webb.
29th:
Private: (1419) F.Sparkes.

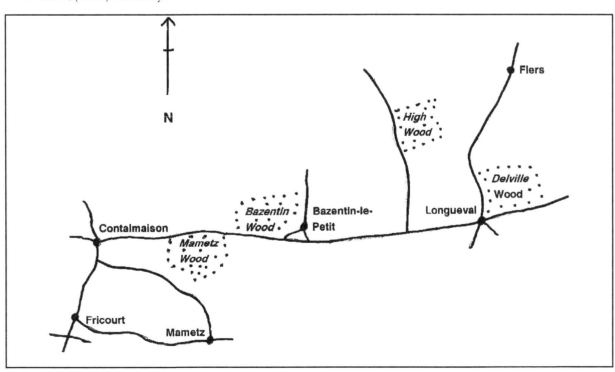

14.   *December 1916*

CHAPTER 6
1917
JANUARY – JUNE

The first nine days of the new year were spent in camp at Fricourt. During that time large working parties were employed in mending roads which had been broken up by the rain, mud and frost. On the 8th January a late Christmas dinner was enjoyed by all ranks and a regimental concert was held in the new Y.M.C.A. hut which formed part of the camp.

The Battalion left Fricourt camp on the 10th January and proceeded through Albert to Millencourt. Although at a safe distance from the limited winter fighting, accommodation at Millencourt was under canvas, not the most comfortable of overhead coverings for winter weather. Two days were spent cleaning up, and the Companies were issued with new clothing and boots. The Battalion looked really smart once more when church parade was attended on Sunday 14th. On the 24th January, a move was made to Brésle where billets vacated by the Australians were taken over. One Military Medal and four Distinguished Conduct Medals were awarded to the Battalion this month.

JANUARY:
25th:
Private: (946) H.Lloyd.

After beginning the month of February at Brésle, the Battalion marched out on the 3rd at 10.30am with its destination as Méricourt-sur-Somme, some 10 miles to the south-east. The march, accompanied by Battalion transport, was by way of Ribémont-sur-Ancre, where that river was crossed. Next came another Méricourt, this time Méricourt-l'Abbé, then Sailly-le-Sec, Sailly Laurette, where a crossing was made for the first time to south of the River Somme, and on to Cérisy and Morcourt.

All went well until a long, gradual slope in the road was reached at 11.30am soon after passing through Méricourt-L'Abbé. At that point considerable congestion with transport of other battalions was encountered owing to the severe frost which had made the road incline very slippery. To avert further delay it was necessary to set the men to work helping the Battalion's own transport to negotiate the hill. It was not until 2.30pm that the march could continue. Thereafter, good progress was made and billets at Méricourt-sur-Somme were reached, thankfully, at 6.0pm. Immediately, dinner, which had been cooked on route, was served to the hungry men.

The following day the march continued for some three miles to Chuignolles within the former French Army area of the conflict. On the way, as a sign of welcome for Britain's allies, the Battalion marched past the Officer Commanding the 12th French Army Corps. Billets were available at Chuignolles where, for the remainder of the day and throughout the 6th February, preparations were made for taking over the line.

On the 7th February marching continued towards Dompièrre with gas helmets worn in the 'alert' position. At 6.00pm French guides were met and progress was made until the entance to the main communication trench was reached. By 10.30pm the front line had been taken over from the 108th Regiment, 24th Division, 12th French Army Corps.

For the next five days of February the Battalion remained in the line improving and strengthening the positions. Although use of gas by the Germans was expected, and precautions such as the setting up of 'Strombus' Horns, gongs and the use of wetted blankets hung over dugout entrances were taken, gas does not appear to have been a problem. On the other hand, enemy shelling continued intermittently, especially by

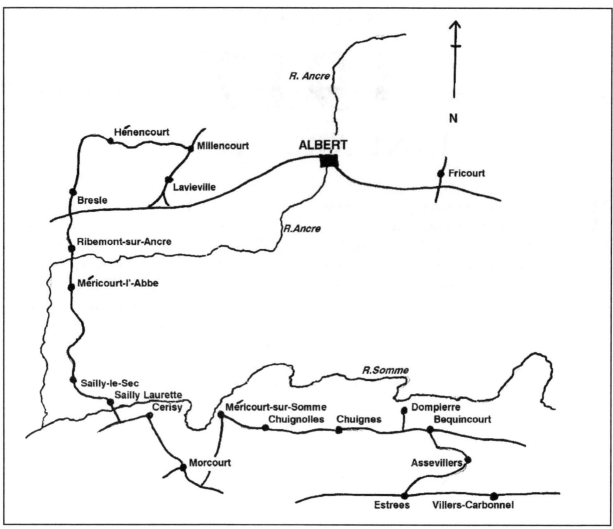

15.   *January to April 1917*

5.9's on the 10th when one man, the first in the new area, was killed.

FEBRUARY:
10th:
Private: (435) F.E.Dellow.

It seemed that, when relief came eventually on the 12th February, the Germans had some indication of the change over because a very heavy and sweeping shrapnel fire on the British communication trenches was commenced. The Commanding Officer and his staff had just started the trench passage at that time and they were obliged to run the gauntlet of fire, fortunately without casualties. In due course the Battalion billeted in dugouts at Assevillers about three miles to the rear.

FEBRUARY:
12th:
Lance Corporal: (868) L.Kent.

A move farther back, to Chuignolles, was made on the 14th February, and there the Battalion was destined to remain for eight days. During that time, training was undertaken in a variety of aspects but movement became increasingly difficult owing to a steady thaw which brought very muddy conditions. However, the men enjoyed baths, a complete change of clothes and passage through the anti-frostbite foot bath devised by, and copied from, the French.

FEBRUARY:
22nd:
Private: (226) A.J.Burdett.

A move into reserve at the twin villages of Dompièrre and Béquincourt was effected on the 23rd February. The thaw was completed and the all-pervading mud created much hardship by the time the Battalion went into the front line to relieve the 1st Loyal North Lancs on the 26th.

Many men became stuck in the mud and had to be released by the active assistance of colleagues.

Despite the use of trench mortars and sniping by the Germans on the 27th February, no casualties were sustained. It was the turn of the British artillery to launch a bombardment on the 28th as part of a sham attack to assist activities farther north. In case of retaliation, the Battalion's front line was evacuated. Although this move was successful, one man, Private George Jupp of Chichester, was killed by a sniper.

FEBRUARY:
28th:
Privates: (851) G.J.Jupp, (1645) A.A.White.

The month of March began with much improved ground conditions. Mud clearing continued in the front line to some extent but, in general, most places were drier. Thursday the 1st was a clear day and there was much aircraft activity from both sides.

MARCH:
1st:
Private: (109) G.F.Bennett.

On the 2nd March, the Battalion moved back to 'support' where daily working parties were found, particularly for road repairs. Two inches of snow fell on the 5th, after which the weather turned fine and clear. A return was made to the front line on the 7th and, on the 8th and 9th, snow fell again and the front remained quiet, hardly a shell being fired. Rumour spread that the Germans were preparing to retire but the reason and intent were unclear. It was at this time, too, that a discovery was made that the Germans were using a new mixture in their gas shells. By use of a vacuum bulb a sample of gas was obtained from an unexploded shell and the sample was sent off to Brigade Headquarters for analysis.

MARCH:
10th:
Private: (73) A.Barbrook.

Casualties occured on the 11th March before a night-time relief to a support position was made. During the following evening, a move back to Chuignes brought the Battalion to welcome hutted accommodation and rest. Several days were spent there cleaning and training.

MARCH:
11th:
Sergeant: (1508) J.F.Tickner.
Private: (1228) S.C.Purser.
14th:
Private: (644) C.W.Griffin.

On the 17th March, more definite news of the German withdrawal was received and preliminary preparations for a follow-up move were made. What was taking place, not only in front of the Battalion but also for many miles all along the line, was the large German strategic withdrawal to their new, heavily fortified line known by them as the Siegfried Stellung. As a result of the Battle of the Somme the Germans found themselves pushed back to positions not of their choosing and certainly not to their liking. Accordingly, during the winter of 1916-17, they had finished preparing their 'impregnable' line some 20 or 25 miles to the east. Known to the allies as the Hindenburg Line, this was a position which had enabled the Germans to shorten their front line considerably and also to re-establish it along the most favourable terrain for defence. Here was strength in depth: a strongly constructed line with many deep dugouts, troop accommodation chambers, advantageous fields of fire and extensive barbed wire entanglements; a formidible position and obstacle indeed.

Naturally, the allies were required to follow-up on this enemy withdrawal. It was soon found, however, that the Germans had operated a 'scorched earth' policy as they withdrew. All villages were burned or otherwise completely destroyed. Important points such as crossroads and railway installations were blown up. Many trees were cut down across the roads, and almost all water sources were poisoned or contaminated. In addition, a variety of ingenious booby-traps were laid and these caused many injuries and fatalities to allied troops until the dangers were fully realised and made known to all units.

The 2nd Battalion, The Royal Sussex Regiment, however, was not to take part in the follow-up operation. Instead, the 2nd Brigade, of which the Battalion formed an integral part, remained behind to continue, in the areas of

Chuignes and Assevillers, road repairs and the collection of useful salvage.

During this month of March, 1917, Lance Corporal Madgwick was awarded a bar to his Military Medal for bombing a German machine gun.

With much of the British Expeditionary Force having moved away eastwards following up the Germans to the Hindenburg Line, the Battalion remained behind spending its time repairing roads during the first week of April. Particular attention was given to the main highway from Amiens to St.Quentin at a stretch between Estrées and Villers-Carbonel. With the Hindenburg Line running through the area around St.Quentin, this road had become a vitally extended supply route for the B.E.F.

The Battalion marched back to billets in Chuignes on the 8th April and, on the 16th, moved farther to the rear and a hutted camp in a wood just outside the village of Morcourt. From then until the end of the month training was carried out and a Brigade sports event was held at which the Battalion won races over one and three miles.

APRIL:
8th:
Private: (453) W.H.Downes.
APRIL:
24th:
Second Lieutenant: (14) G.R.Alexander.
Private: (78) A.Barnes.

Training, incorporating several relatively small new drafts of men who had arrived during April, continued around the base at Morcourt Camp for the first half of May. The weather was warm and, in contrast to the recent hard winter, the men enjoyed the relative relaxation. Many had now become hardened to the loss of friends and colleagues and they had learned to concentrate their minds only on the present and the immediate future.

On the 19th May the whole 1st Division moved westward from the Morcourt – Chuignes area to be concentrated on land between Warfusée and Villers-Bretonneux. The Battalion marched on the main Péronne – Amiens road to billets actually in the village of Villers-Bretonneux. At a point along this route the Major

General took the salute from the Battalion as it marched past.

MAY:
5th:
Private: (99) G.Beck.
6th:
Private: (1099) E.Nicholson.

News came that the Division was to leave the 4th Army and there were many speculations and rumours concerning the likely whereabouts of the Battalion following its transfer. On the 20th May, the Army Commander visited the Battalion's Commanding Officers at Brigade Headquarters to bid formal farewell. On that day, too, the following letter was sent by Sir Henry Rawlinson, Commander of the 4th Army, to all Units:

"1st Division.
Fourth Army No. G.S. 697.
It is now 10 months since the 1st Division joined the Fourth Army, and I cannot allow them to leave without expressing my gratitude for all the excellent services they have rendered during that time.

The conspicuous part played by the Division in the heavy fighting around CONTALMAISON, POZIÈRES, HIGH WOOD and EAUCOURT L'ABBAYE was beyond praise and reflects the highest credit on all concerned. Though they lost over 10,000 officers and men, and have suffered much over an exceptionally cold and trying winter, yet they are today, if possible, in a higher state of fighting efficiency than they were last July. The result is in the highest degree satisfactory.

There is no Division in the British Army which holds a finer record than the 1st Division, and I can never forget the conspicuous gallantry they displayed at the Battle of LOOS when in the VI Corps. It is a matter of deep regret to me that they are now leaving the Fourth Army.

In thanking all ranks for what they have done, and in wishing them the best of good fortune in the future I shall hope that at no distant date I may again have the good fortune to find them under my Command.
    H.Rawlinson, General.
    Commanding Fourth Army.
    H.Q. Fourth Army,
    20th May,1917."

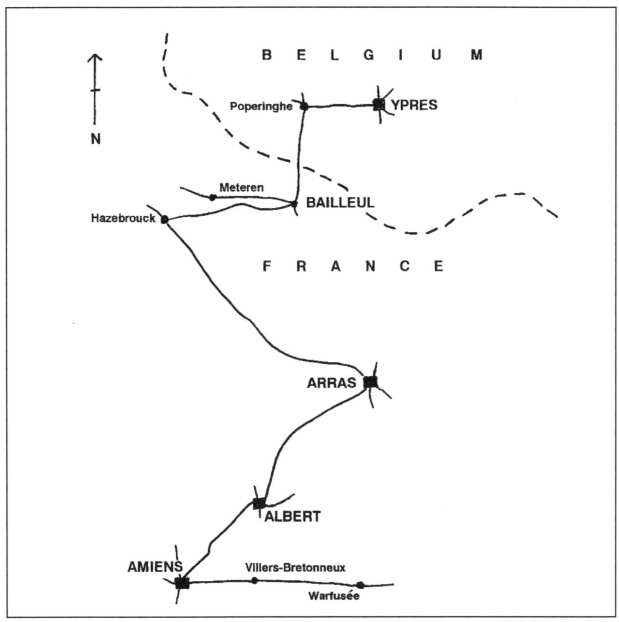

16.   *May 1917*

Naturally, because it formed part of the 1st Division, the Battalion, and The Royal Sussex Regiment as a whole, rightly and worthily basked in the praise expressed in the Army Commander's letter of congratulation and farewell. So it was with a continuing sense of euphoria that the Battalion, with the rest of the Division, entrained at Villers-Bretonneux on the 26th May for the long journey back to the northern part of the Western Front; 'A' Company entrained at 5.55pm and the remainder of the Battalion at 9.00pm.

The destination of Bailleul was eventually reached at 8.00am the following morning and a march was made to billets in, and tents just outside, the village of Meteren. There the

Battalion was duly inspected in full marching order on the last day of the month by Brigadier-General A.B.Hubback, C.M.G., General Officer Commanding 2nd Brigade.

The Battalion was at Meteren for the first part of June. On the morning of the 7th, however, when a large scale attack was delivered by the British Expeditionary Force against the Messines ridge, the Battalion was held in tactical reserve and expectations of involvement were high. Such was the success of the attack, however, that the Battalion was not needed.

On the 11th June, the Battalion moved back to the area around Hazebrouck and, having been on the move for more than 16 hours that day, arrived at scattered billets in the vicinity of St.Marie Cappel. For the next week small drafts of new men were absorbed and training continued. Then, on the 20th, the Battalion moved again, this time in stages, by way of Wormhoudt and Coudekerque Branche to Leffrinckoucke. At Leffrinckoucke the Battalion entrained. Eventually, Coxyde Bains, on the North Sea coast, was reached and billets there were occupied.

JUNE:
11th:
Private: (441) A.Deves.

On the evening of the 24th June, the Battalion marched to Oost Dunkerque Bains and there took over the Coastal Defences. This was an entirely new experience because the Coastal Defences consisted of a series of posts along the sea shore which were manned only at night. Thus, the task could be accomplished by just one Company while the others remained in billets. The relatively undemanding nature of these duties allowed the men ample chance for relaxation and sea bathing.

During this month of June the Military Cross was awarded to Second Lieutenant. (Temporary Captain) H.Roberts and the Distinguished Conduct Medal to Acting Sergeant C.S.Kenward.

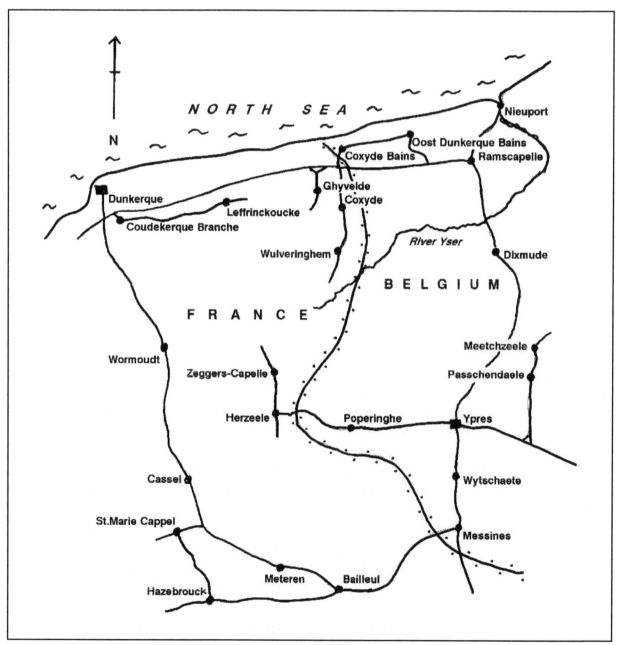

17. *June to September 1917*

CHAPTER 7
1917
JULY – DECEMBER

From Oost Dunkerque Bains, the Battalion moved up to a support position west of the River Yser where working parties were found nightly. On the 5th July, the Germans began an artillery bombardment and caused a good deal of damage to the Battalion defences. Each day, the enemy artillery became more active, and a number of casualties were sustained.

JULY:
5th:
Privates: (812) A.Inverarity, (1098) L.W.Nichols, (1106) D.Norton.
6th:
Private: (1253) W.Reed.
8th:
Privates: (1562) S.Virgoe, (1597) F.G.Watson.
9th:
Private: (1143) C.Pain.

The Battalion disposition on the 10th July was east of the River Yser when, at 5.30am, the enemy began a heavy bombardment of the whole 1st Divisional area on both sides of the river. The intensity of fire increased during the day and an attack seemed imminent, especially as, by mid-afternoon, all three bridges near the river mouth were down. Men of the 2nd Battalion, The Royal Sussex Regiment were in support and immediately took up defensive positions to the west of the river. During lulls in the enemy bombardment German planes flew low and unmolested over the area using their machine guns against any British movement.

The enemy attack was launched at 7.30pm and German troops were seen on the sand dunes just east of the river. The 1st Northamptonshires and the 2nd Kings Royal Rifles had been cut off on the east side of the Yser and messages were received from them only by carrier pigeon. A few of their officers and men managed to swim the river back to safety but the remainder of both battalions were either killed or taken prisoner.

The enemy advanced in small groups and in three lines behind a creeping barrage. A number of flammenwerfer (flame-throwers) were employed to fire British dugouts. Other dugouts were blown in with their occupants either killed, wounded or imprisoned. Officers who succeeded in getting back estimated that casualties were between 70% and 80%.

The Battalion 'stood to' all night and, by dawn on the 11th July, the situation had quietened, the enemy apparently being satisfied to have captured all the British defences to the east of the River Yser along a length of almost a mile from its mouth. The situation remained quiet with no opportunity to counter-attack across the river.

JULY:
10th:
Privates: (31) W.J.Ash, (90) A.Bates, (159) W.H.Boxall, (602) F.G.Glaysher, (641) F.Gregory, (722) J.Higgins, (1022) M.Miller, (1455) D'A.V.S.Stone, (1493) J.Terry, (1533) F.Trimmer, (1598) H.Watson, (1653) F.Whittaker.
11th:
Private: (583) T.H.Gardner.

The Battalion remained in the front line until relieved on the 16th July, on which day the move out was hampered by enemy gas shelling. By the 28th, billets at Ghyvelde were reached and month-end was spent in further training following a move on to a camp at Le Clipon. In addition to those killed during July, 60 men had been wounded and three were missing.

JULY:
13th:
Privates: (743) D.Hodges, (1540) A.Tuckwell.
14th:
Private: (427) R.St.J.P.Deacon.

16th:
Private: (803) G.H.Hyde.
18th:
Private: (11) R.Albery.
22nd:
Private: (516) C.H.Farmer.
25th:
Lance Corporal: (465) S.E.Dunn.

Throughout the whole of the summer month of August the Battalion remained at Le Clipon camp. The main task was that of special training for a projected combined military and naval offensive involving certain monitor vessels of the fleet and the entire 1st Division. The task entailed the disembarkation from monitor vessels and pontoons and the scaling of a sea wall. So secretive were these preparations that Le Clipon camp was closed and all communication with the outside world was prohibited.

Commanding Officers returned from a special visit to the Thames Estuary where they had inspected in detail the monitors and pontoons envisaged for the assault. On the 21st August more representatives of units also made the journey to the Thames Estuary for the same purpose.

As all ranks were confined to camp, varying interests were organised by way of sports and recreation. These included sea bathing, football and boxing. Also, a cinema and a concert marquee were erected. A competition over an obstacle course was held, for which the prize, won by the Battalion's No.8 platoon, was a 75mm shell fashioned as a clock.

A Divisional parade was held on the 23rd August when, on the sands at Le Clipon camp, the whole 1st Division marched past the Army Commander, General Sir Henry Rawlinson. Royal Sussex Regiment marched past, not to its own musical march but to the official march of the 1st Division. Two days after the parade, the following letter was received from the Army Commander:

" 1st Division.
I want to let the 1st Division know how pleased I was with their appearance on parade this morning. The turn out of all ranks was particularly good, the handling of the arms was very smart and the march past struck me as quite

excellent, especially in three battalions which marched with a swing and a precision I have seldom seen equalled.

It is very evident that there is a high standard of discipline maintained in all units and I congratulate the Division as a whole on their fine spirit and soldier-like appearance on parade. Whatever duty they may be called upon to perform I know that they will do it right well and that none could do it better.

H.Rawlinson,
General Commanding Fourth Army."

After all the hard training that had been put in towards the combined assault, it was learned on the 24th August that the projected operations had been postponed indefinitely.

Notwithstanding the report that the proposed special operations had been shelved, the Battalion continued training within Clipon Camp throughout the whole of September. The knowledge that they remained enclosed within the camp and that their training efforts probably would come to nought had a frustrating effect upon the men and, before month end, there set in a certain amount of boredom.

AUGUST:
3rd:
Private: (1435) H.A.L.Steed.
13th:
Private: (174) W.P.Bridger.

Long afterwards, it became known that the special operation for which the Battalion had been selected and put under such secretive training was to have been a daring seaborne invasion attack on the harbour mole at Zeebrugge.

Continuing on through the first three weeks of October, the Battalion remained at Le Clipon camp in relative security. The Germans 'rested on their laurels' and were content to hold the gains they had made as a result of their attack on the 10th August.

So far as the Battalion was concerned, training continued but, by the 10th October, it was almost certain that the previously planned joint operations with the Naval Division would not take place. Accordingly, on that date and much to the men's relief, secrecy was relaxed and the camp was re-opened.

OCTOBER:
5th:
Private: (132) W.B.Blake.
10th:
Private: (1369) H.Sillis.
23rd:
Private: (1380) G.G.Sizer.

On the 24th October, after 12 weeks at Le Clipon camp, the Battalion marched off to billets in the area of Zeggers-Capel. On the following day, the march continued to Hertzeele and, on the 25th, to School Camp some one and a half miles west of Poperinghe. It was to the Battalion's credit that, during the whole of this long, three-days march from Le Clipon, not one man fell out.

For the last few days of October, training was carried out at the appropriately named School Camp in preparation for taking over a portion of the line in the area of Ypres.

November was to bring, for the Battalion, a return to active fighting and the taking of casualties once more. This time, the position was to be in that dreadful salient where Field Marshall Douglas Haig was persisting with his forlorn effort to break through the German lines at the 3rd Battle of Ypres, otherwise known as Passchendaele.

Billets in Poperinghe were occupied on the 5th November and, the following day, the Battalion travelled by train to Reigersburg. The only accommodation there was of tents and bivouacs in a camp which was a wasteland of mud.

A move on the 9th November was made up to the canal bank where, to the surprise of everyone, conditions were quite good in the available dugouts, many of which contained the luxury of electric lighting. The 11th brought a march up to the support line and, two days later, the Battalion relieved the 1st Loyal North Lancs in the front line. The 'line', such as it was, consisted only of a series of mud and water-filled shell holes joined, here and there, by duckboard tracks, the only means of movement in that seascape of liquid mud.

The conditions which the Battalion then had to endure were recognised, later, as being the worst of the whole war. Throughout that

period, until welcome relief came, eventually, on the night of the 15th / 16th November, artillery activity on both sides was very great. Many casualties were sustained from this cause and from low flying aircraft which machine-gunned along the duckboard tracks. After relief, the Battalion retired to a hutted camp at Irish Farm.

During this tour of duty in the front line, the Battalion had lost, in addition to those killed, two officers and 111 men wounded and four men who were posted as missing.

NOVEMBER:
12th:
Private: (1592) H.A.Waters.
13th:
Second Lieutenant: (981) C.E.Marten-Smith.
Lance Corporals: (592) J.George, (777) T.H.Howes.
Privates: (237) G.J.Burton, (912) A.G.Lark.
14th:
Second Lieutenant: (1185) A.B.Perks-Morris.
Privates: (15) F.G.Allen, (76) E.T.Barnard, (95) W.Beard, (147) W.G.Booty, (345) A.Cook, (886) S.W.King, (1300) B.Rowe, (1499) A.C.Thompson, (1502) T.Thompson.
15th:
Corporal: (1464) L.J.Stredwick.
Privates: (223) F.G.Bundy, (495) W.Ellis, (604) A.Glenister, (1214) C.J.Popplewell, (1351) G.Shatock, (1556) H.G.Venables, (1631) C.E.West.
16th:
Private: (699) H.Heath.

Even the position at Irish Farm was not entirely safe because it was shelled from a considerable distance almost daily by enemy high velocity guns. These caused some havoc, particularly on the 19th November when they inflicted 18 casualties.

NOVEMBER:
17th:
Privates: (407) C.Dadswell, (929) A.E.Leonard.
19th:
Lance Corporal: (845) H.S.J.Jones.
Privates: (478) W.Eastwood, (1697) A.Wright.
20th:
Private: (926) F.J.Leighton.

On the evening of the 21st November the Battalion marched to an area just north of what remained of the village of Passchendaele. Unfortunately, the guides lost their way, which, in the prevailing conditions, was not too surprising, and the change-over was long delayed. For two dreary days the line was held. Although no positive operations were undertaken, artillery activity on both sides remained considerable. Some patrols were carried out and, during one of these, a German machine-gun of a new pattern was found and brought back. On another patrol, Second Lieutenant Knifton went missing and it was found, later, that he had been killed. His brother, also a Second Lieutenant, was to be killed serving with the Battalion in July,1918.

NOVEMBER:
21st:
Privates: (195) J.Broom, (1295) H.Rothwell, (1601) H.Watts, (1657) T.H.Wickenden.

22nd:
Privates: (47) F.J.Bailey, (1232) W.C.L.Radford, (1317) F.Sanders, (1456) P.Stone, (1632) E.A.West.
23rd:
Second Lieutenant: (893) C.W.McK.Knifton.
Privates: (328) G.T.Coleman, (543) A.W.Ford, (688) J.Hatcher, (822) J.E.Jackson, (919) L.E.Lawrence, (1176) D.Pearman alias R.J.F.Comporo, (1215) V.C.H.Portsmouth, (1445) F.Stevens.

On the night of the 23rd / 24th November relief came in the form of a march back to Irish Farm. From there, at noon on the 24th, the Battalion entrained, travelled to Poperinghe and there marched to occupy Tunnellers Camp. Training and refitting were carried out until the end of the month with a move being made to

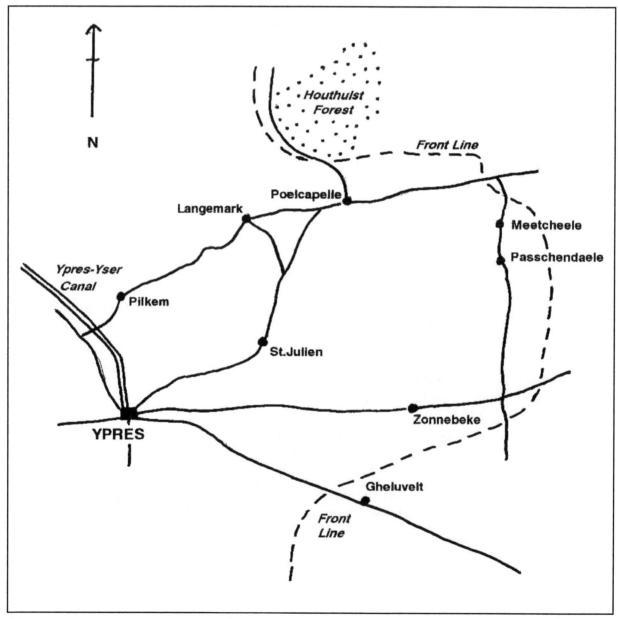

18. *November 1917 – The Third Battle of Ypres, Passchendaele: The final position*

scattered but good billets at Herzeele on the 27th.

With the Third Battle of Ypres, or Passchendaele, officially ended and with winter drawing on, offensive activities were mostly curtailed. For the first week of December training was undertaken at, and around, Herzeele. Then, on the 7th, a move was made to billets at Crombeke and a further move to a French camp at Eykhoek on the 9th.

DECEMBER:
6th:
Private: (281) H.H.Chalton.

The 13th December brought a Battalion move, without its transport, to a support area north of Elverdinghe where accommodation was found in dugouts and concrete shelters built under, and against, the remains of houses. It was necessary to find large working parties every day until Christmas Eve when the front line at the south-west edge of Houthulst Forest was taken over from the Loyal North Lancs. Christmas Day was spent there in the front line, without any seasonal comforts, although the situation remained quiet for the most part. Relief came from the 8th Royal Berks on the 28th and a move back to Eykhoek was carried out with an overnight stop north of Elverdinghe.

During this last month of 1917 the decorations awarded to the Battalion amounted to one Military Cross, one Distinguished Conduct Medal and 10 Military Medals.

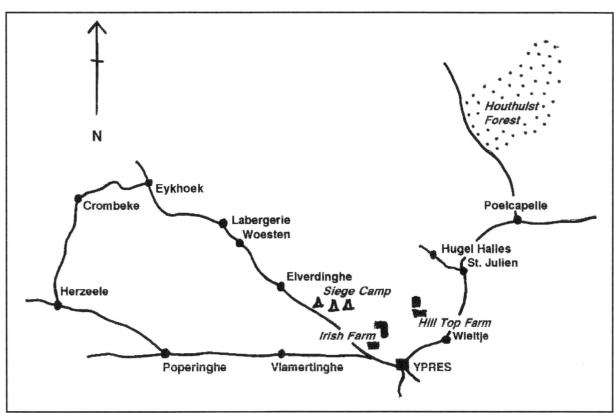

19.   *December 1917 to March 1918*

CHAPTER 8
1918
JANUARY – JUNE

With 25th December, 1917, having been spent in considerable discomfort in the front line, the Christmas dinner was served to the Battalion at Eykhoek on 1st January, 1918, in celebration, also, of the New Year. This, of course, was to be the final year of the war although, as yet, there was no such general realisation, or even hope.

The 6th day of the new year brought a move forward to the support areas. From then on, large working parties were found every night and a number of casualties were suffered.

JANUARY:
10th January:
Lance Corporal: (1466) A.Stoud.
Privates: (186) C.Brook, (844) F.Jones.
12th January:
Private: (1680) H.T.Winton.

On the evening of the 17th January a return was made to the south-west corner of Houthulst Forest and the front line. Recent rains had again made for atrocious ground conditions but, as a result, the enemy did not show himself and the artillery was quiet. Thus, there had been no front line casualties throughout this tour of duty when it came to an end, on the evening of 21st January, with relief effected by the 8th Battalion Royal Berkshire Regiment. A train journey brought the Battalion for an overnight stop at Vlamertinghe and a return, next day, to familiar billets in the Eykhoek area.

JANUARY:
24th January:
Private: (175) F.J.Bridges.

The end of January saw a further move to billets at Labergerie and news that awards for January had included one Military Cross and four Distinguished Conduct Medals. In addition,

two officers, Second Lieutenants J.T.Pratt and C.Clements, and 152 other ranks still serving with the Battalion received the 1914 Star.

For the first week of February, army training was carried out each morning and recreational training during the afternoons. A move by train was taken on the 8th to enable support areas to be manned at Hugel Halles, north-west of St.Julien. From there, the inevitable progression to the front line took place on the 10th but the following four days of duty were very quiet.

A brief spell back in reserve began on the 14th February but the front line was manned, once more, on the 16th for a further four days. This time, the enemy used a number of gas shells at night but no fatalities were sustained during February, although 10 men were wounded.

Another rail journey took the Battalion, this time, on its way back to Siege Camp, south-east of Elverdinghe on the 20th February and there everyone remained taking part in training and recreation until the end of the month. Belgian awards were made this month; the Decoration Militaire to Private A.V.Coppard and the Croix de Guerre to Corporal E.Tucker, M.M.

Another month of shuttling movement between support, front line and rest areas began with a train journey to Wieltje on the 4th March. From there, reserve trenches almost a mile to the north-east were occupied. Again, the provision of large working parties for the forward Army Defence Line had to be found.

MARCH:
2nd:
Lance Sergeant: (436) G.Denney.
Lance Corporal: (419) W.H.Davies.
4th:
Private: (1008) J.Mearing.

The front line itself was manned from the 16th to the 18th, from the 20th to the 24th and from the 26th to the 28th March. A number of patrols were carried out during these tours of front line duty and, on one of these patrols, Second Lieutenant A.J.A.Hutchins went missing, later to be confirmed as killed.

The system of short periods in forward positions where ground conditions were bad, had been re-introduced to ease the load on officers and men but the frequent moves, to and fro, themselves imposed undue strains and fatigues.

MARCH:
17th:
Private: (1674) R.Wilson.
19th:
Private: (405) W.Cutting.
22nd:
Second Lieutenant: (798) A.J.A.Hutchins.
Private: (1429) D.L.Standing.
23rd:
Private: (1563) S.Vinter.

The Battalion's final departure from the front line in this area of the Ypres Salient came on the 28th March with a move back to Hill Top Farm, one mile north-west of Wieltje. However, the enemy shelled the farm area so heavily on the 30th that a prudent move was made to a safer position in dugouts along the canal bank.

MARCH:
29th:
Privates: (194) S.Brooks, (271) C.Carter, (1385) H.Skinner.
30th:
Privates: (1443) E.Stevens, (1708) F.G.Young.
31st:
Private: (1448) H.Stevens.

So, a five months period in the areas north and north-east of Ypres was almost at an end. This situation, although not known to the men at the time, was being brought about as a result of the German's Spring Offensive launched from the Hindenburg Line farther south on the 21st March. An effective breakthrough of the British line had been forced by the enemy with the result that the allied divisions were being driven back westward in what was little short of a rout. The 2nd Battalion, The Royal Sussex Regiment was needed southward.

The Canal Bank dugouts north of Ypres were 'home' until the 4th of April when orders were received that the Battalion must be ready to leave by train at short notice. In fact, it was on the following day that the men entrained at Boesinghe, leaving the transport to follow on by road. Originally, the train's destination was Mérville but, even during the journey, this was changed and they came to Choques where they detrained during the early afternoon of the 5th. From the rail head they marched to billets in Marles-les-Mines where they were joined by the transport on its arrival the following day after a two day drive by way of Godewaersvelde and Mérville. Thus, the whole Battalion was now back in the area from which it had last moved in July,1916.

On Sunday the 7th April, after morning Church Parade and dinner, the Battalion marched to Hesdigneul where they boarded buses and were driven to Beuvry. They marched on to Cambrin where they were to remain until the 13th.

The enemy opened a very heavy bombardment using gas shells on the 7th April and this bombardment continued for 10 hours. Gas shelling was resumed by the enemy at intervals on the 8th and, on the 9th, became intense once more. News came that the Germans had achieved some attacking success and were on the high ground above Givenchy. The situation then became confused with the result that the Battalion 'stood to' in battle positions along the Noyelles – Grenay Line the whole day. Casualties were sustained by the Battalion, chiefly from gas shells.

APRIL:
9th:
Lieutenant: (70) A.H.Ball.
Privates: (2) P.Abbott, (92) A.W.Battley, (783) W.Hughes, (1010) G.R.Meek, (1105) J.H.North.
10th:
Privates: (308) W.Clark, (745) W.H.J.Hodges.

While back at Cambrin from the 10th to the 13th April, many men began to lose their voices and it was evident that this was due to the delayed action of exposure to gas during the previous three days. On the night of the 13th / 14th the stretch of front line between the

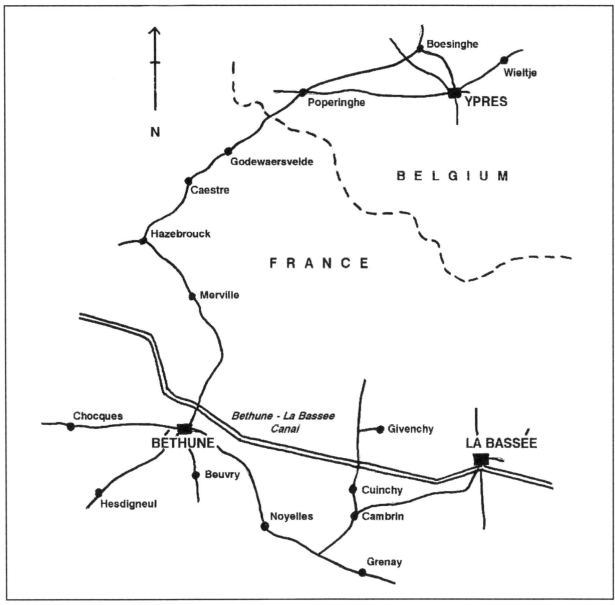

20. *April 1918*

Cambrin – La Bassée Road and the Béthune – La Bassée Canal was taken over. Thus began, for the Battalion, an inordinate length of 20 days in the front line. The situation on the left, that is on the far side of the canal, continued to remain uneasy with the expectancy of another German assault. South of the canal, around the Battalion's position, it remained fairly quiet, however, until the early morning of the 18th when a violent bombardment of the position was sustained. The enemy attacked north of the canal but no assault developed to the south where the Battalion was holding the line up to the important canal lock and crossing at Port Fixe.

By the evening of the 18th April the situation had quietened and work began on repairs to

the trenches where they had been damaged considerably by the enemy shelling. Many trench sections had been blow flat but the number of casualties were relatively light considering the weight and intensity of the bombardment received.

APRIL:
18th:
Captain: (1311) F.C.Sainton.
Privates: (158) S.C.Boxall, (395) A.Crisp, (712)
    A.W.Herbert, (1012) F.W.Mellersh, (1136)
    F.Padgham, (1318) H.M.W.Sandford.
20th:
Private: (1637) W.R.West.

Throughout the remaining days of April many of the men who had been affected by gas became worse and 79 had to be designated "Wounded Gas" and evacuated to hospital. These men were replaced by others sent to join the Battalion. Enemy activity subsided to a considerable extent although he showed trench mortar activity from time to time.

APRIL:
27th:
Private: (523) W.Fenn.
28th:
Private: (1002) G.E.McComas.

It is a fact that the Battalion was relatively little occupied in active duties during the coming three summer months. This may be regarded as strange following Germany's great spring effort to break through to Amiens and the channel ports. Most of that activity and the consequent retreat of the allied armies, particularly the British, occurred farther south, however, and did not concern, or draw in, The Royal Sussex Regiment's 2nd Battalion. In any case, that German offensive was largely spent by mid-April and, for want of good

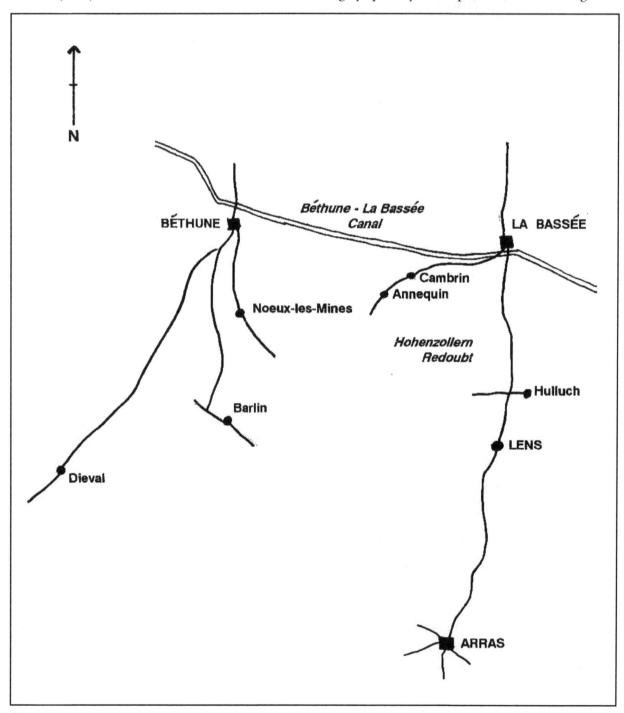

21.   *May to August 1918*

communications and supplies, had been brought to a standstill by the British still some miles short of the enemy's railhead objective of Amiens.

Indeed, by now, the German High Command had been forced to acknowledge failure farther south and had turned their attentions and efforts, once again, to the northern areas of the Western Front. It was these enemy efforts that the Battalion was helping to withstand during this summer period.

It was on the 3rd May that the Battalion was relieved from the front line near Cambrin and moved back to rest in camp along the Route d'Arras at Noeux-les-Mines. On the morning of the 8th, a German offensive was felt to be imminent and the Battalion 'stood to' ready to move off at a moment's notice. Nothing came of this expectation, however, and it was not until the 12th that the front line was taken over and manned until the 20th in the area of the German's extensive stronghold at the Hohenzollern Redoubt. Those days proved to be relatively quiet, the main problem coming from leaky gas cylinders left in the Battalion's own trenches. A number of patrols were sent out but they experienced great difficulties in No-Man's-Land from the condition of the ground which remained dotted with numerous old mine craters and spent equipment.

MAY:
13th:
Private: (1211) J.E.Pollington.
15th:
Company Quarter Master Sergeant: (1293) T.Rose.
19th:
Private: (1056) A.Moorey.
28th:
Lance Corporal: (13) F.R.Alexander.

Following a few days in support at Annequin, a return to the front line was effected on the 25th May. Three days later the Commanding Officer, Lieutenant Colonel D.G.Johnson, D.S.O., M.C., was wounded by a machine gun bullet and had to be evacuated. That same day the Battalion was relieved and returned to end the month of May in former billets at Noeux-les-Mines.

The front line at Cuinchy was taken over on the 5th June. This tour of duty, although of a quiet nature, was marked by a particularly unfortunate incident when a chance enemy rifle grenade hit a box of bombs in one of the Battalion's positions and knocked out a Lewis Gun team. A few casualties were also sustained during active patrols.

JUNE:
6th:
Lance Corporal: (1658) P.A.Wickens.
Private: (180) S.G.Britton.
8th:
Second Lieutenant: (1370) H.W.Silver.
Private: (1612) S.Webb.
12th:
Lieutenant: (442) J.M.Dickinson.
Lance Corporal: (1405) J.H.Smith.
Privates: (66) E.E.Baldey, (806) A.C.Hyland.

On the 13th June the Battalion went back to support at Cambrin and, on the 21st, retired farther to Noeux-les-Mines where they remained until the end of the month.

13th:
Private: (616) F.Golding.
20th:
Lance Corporal: (663) H.Hammond.
Private: (1240) A.E.Rasey.

Image 1: First Battle of Ypres: An enemy shell exploding near British positions.

Image 2: First Battle of Ypres: 'Old Contemptibles' attacking over sandbagged breastworks.

Image 3: A contemporary silk postcard.

Image 4: Bombing Germans out of a deep dugout at Martinpuich, Somme, September 1916.

Image 5: An Officer in a British Headquarters dugout. Note the revolver placed with immediate reach on the table.

Image 6: German dead on the British wire following an attack at Givenchy.

Image 7: Germans surrendering from a blockhouse on Pilkem Ridge, 1917.

Image 8: 1915. Route marches normally allowed ten minutes rest in each hour. Here, other ranks relax while Officers gather for instructions.

CHAPTER 9
1918
JULY – THE ARMISTICE

An important parade was organised and held on the 1st July when the 2nd Brigade formed up in hollow square and was inspected by His Royal Highness the Duke of Connaught who then presented ribbons. Later, a letter was received from the Duke expressing his satisfaction at the smart appearance and soldierly bearing of the Brigade. The remainder of July was spent in shuttling between the front line, Annequin and Noeux-les-Mines.

JULY:
2nd:
Private: (819) W.H.Izzard.
10th:
Lance Corporal: (390) H.J.Craythorn.

The most conspicuously active event of July occured on the night of the 20th / 21st. 'B' Company was chosen to undertake a raid on the enemy positions and, with a few days' notice, special training was given in preparation not only of the attack but also in the necessary close co-operation with artillery, trench mortar and machine gun support. Despite this, not all went according to plan.

On the night of the raid the preparatory bombardment commenced too early and not simultaneously. This relatively minor problem was redeemed with a very accurate high explosive shelling of the enemy front line. The infantry went over the top and, following up close behind the barrage, easily rushed the first objective. Seven dugouts were found in the German front line and enemy soldiers were seen at most of the entrances. These Germans retreated into their underground recesses where they were left for the time being, care being taken, so far as possible, that they did not reappear to inflict damage.

The second wave of infantry then leapfrogged the first and quickly captured the German second line. Two machine guns, one in a shell crater, were captured before the signal to withdraw was given. Again, dugouts were found and, at one point, rifle fire came from two of them. Attempts were made at all these dugouts, without success, to induce the enemy to come up and surrender. Consequently, all the dugouts were then bombed or destroyed with mobile charges before 'B' Company returned to their lines.

The raid was regarded as a success although there had been 17 casualties, including two officers and two men killed. One of the officers was Second Lieutenant J.W.McK.Knifton whose brother had been killed serving with the Battalion during November,1917. The other officer, Captain H.C.Barnes, M.C., was killed by the explosion of a small bomb dump during the raid.

JULY:
21st:
Lieutenant: (79) H.C.Barnes.
Second Lieutenant: (894) J.McK.Knifton.
Privates: (505) A.J.Etherington, (1107) H.V.Nott.

During the day after the raid, relief came with a move back to Noeux-les-Mines. There, on the 28th July, spirits were restored to some extent when the Battalion did well in the Brigade eliminating contest for the Divisional Horse Show. No less than four first prizes were secured, these being for (1) Battalion Transport Turn Out; (2) Limbered General Service Wagon and pair of Light Draught Horses in Marching Order; (3) Heavy Draught Horse, Stripped; and (4) Lewis Gun Limber and pair of Light Draught Mules in Marching Order.

July came to an end with a return to the front line on the 31st, this time in the Cambrin sector.

The Battalion remained in the front line for the first four days of August during which time things were very quiet and marked only by the undertaking of patrols. After a four day return to Cambrin village, when day and night working parties were provided, a longer tour in the front line was forthcoming from the 8th to the 17th.

This tour was marked by considerable patrol activity on the Battalion's part and, in particular, by an attempted German raid on the 10th August. At 7.30am that morning two Germans were seen moving along a trench and, at 8.15am, No.6977 Private Golds spotted seven of the enemy about 20 yards on the far side of a crater opposite the Battalion's 'Argyle Sap' leading out from No.3 Brick Stack. Private Golds, thinking a raid was probable, seized his Lewis Gun, ran down the brick stack, giving the alarm as he went, and brought his gun into action.

Lieutenant Lane, who was in command of the platoon, ordered his men into their battle positions. He then took the nearest six men and advanced to the attack but, coming into contact with a superior force, probably 40 men, at close quarters and separated only by an old parapet, he withdrew after an exchange of bombs during which he used up his whole supply. This spirited action by Lieutenant Lane and his men undoubtedly thwarted the German plan to enter the Battalion line.

This action prompted the 2nd Infantry Brigade Commander to send the following letter of congratulation:

"2nd. Bde. No.G.3/3/21.
2nd Royal Sussex Regt.

With reference to the attempted hostile raid on the morning of the 10th instant, I wish to congratulate Lieut. Lane and the men of his platoon on their success in teaching the 369th Regt. of the 10th Ersatz Division the risks that have to be run in any attempt to raid the 2nd Royal Sussex Regiment.

It is most satisfactory to note that the enemy's movements were immediately spotted, and this speaks well for the vigilance and alertness of the sentries.

I am especially pleased to see that as soon as the enemy had been met with fire from the troops in the forward post, the first idea in the mind of the Platoon Commander was to take offensive action, and to seek for an identification at considerable risk and under circumstances by no means favourable. The result was that although it was not possible to secure a wounded prisoner, a dead German was found and identification established.

Please convey to Lieutenant Lane and to all the men of his platoon engaged in this creditable little affair, my thanks, and my appreciation of their good work.

Signed: G.C.Kelly, Brigadier-General, Commanding 2nd Infantry Brigade. 11th August,1918."

Other patrols also gained good results including one at night on the 10th August led by Second Lieutenant Kirkby which penetrated deeply into enemy held territory, passing even beyond the German's second line and returning with useful information.

AUGUST:
13th:
Corporal: (1119) W.Oliver.
Lance Corporal: (1236) W.M.Ranger.
19th:
Corporal: (1208) A.Pledge.
Private: (1548) S.A.Turton.
24th:
Private: (1149) A.Park.

Within the first two hours of September the Battalion arrived by train at Arras and was billeted in the Rue d'Amiens. The day was spent cleaning and resting before marching off south-eastwards at 11.30pm to an assembly position in the open just west of the village of Wancourt.

The Division was in reserve to the Canadian Corps which launched an attack at 5.00am on the 2nd September. During this operation, the Canadians were very successful, capturing many German prisoners and much enemy equipment. Indeed, the attack went so well that the 1st Division was not required. However, the Battalion moved forward to a second assembly position in the valley just south of Vis-en-Artois.

Late on the 3rd September a move was made to the area around Etaing and a section of the line which had been captured only that morning. A relatively quiet time ensued partly due to the fact that the River Sensée separated the opposing sides.

SEPTEMBER:
6th:
Lance Corporal: (1420) R.T.Sparshott.
Private: (480) C.R.Eccleston.

The Battalion was relieved on the 7th September and, after a relatively short march, boarded buses which took them to Habarcq, west of Arras. From Habarcq, the whole Battalion, including the transport, entrained on the 10th and, after a very slow journey which took them south beyond the River Somme, detrained the following day at Guillaucourt and marched to accommodation in huts and bivouacs near Proyart.

SEPTEMBER:
9th:
Lance Corporal: (1206) A.E.Pitchford.

The task of the 1st Division at this time was to follow-up on the retiring German army and consequently there was little time to settle in any one place. Thus, the Battalion travelled by bus on the 13th September and took over an old camp just south of Mons-en-Chaussée. The next day saw a move to billets in Estrées and, on the 15th, a march to Reserve at a camp south of Poeuilly.

During the evening of the 16th September, the Battalion took over the front line in the vicinity of Vadancourt some six miles north-west of St.Quentin. There, over the next two days, preparations were made for an attack which was to be launched at 5.00am on the 18th in conjunction with the Australians, on the left, and the 2nd Kings Royal Rifle Corps on the right. This attack was to be part of a large operation carried out by the 3rd and 4th Armies as part of Field Marshall Haig's aim of keeping up continuous pressure on the failing Germans and to force their army ever-farther eastward.

By 4.30am on the 18th the Battalion was in the jumping off position in artillery formation to a depth of 400 yards along a frontage of 1,100 yards. The jumping off position was a line running north-west to south-east through a point about 700 yards south-west of the road junction in Vadancourt. The assaulting troops were supported by a Section of the Machine Gun Corps and by a Trench Mortar Battery.

At 5.20am the creeping barrage came down 200 yards in front of the jumping off line. Ten minutes later, at zero hour, the leading troops went over the top, keeping close behind, and advancing with, the creeping barrage. On the left, little opposition was met until the first objective, the 'Green Line', an enemy trench system some 1,000 yards east of the Vadancourt road junction, was reached. To the right, however, the expected enemy resistance was met in Vadancourt with the result that the troops attempting to advance there were unable to keep up with the barrage as it crept forwards over the marshy ground between the village and the 'Green Line' trenches. This problem was overcome by the planned move of a platoon passing north of the marsh and then working its way to the right and southwards down the trench. This platoon was involved in a stiff fight but overcame all resistance so that the 'Green Line' was fully occupied some 30 minutes ahead of the planned advance to the second objective, the 'Red Line'.

At zero plus 190 minutes, that is at 8.40am, the advance began towards the second objective, the high ground and slopes overlooking Pontruet from the north-west. From this advance, many of the enemy tried to escape but so swift was the Battalion's onslaught that large numbers of them were captured about Pontruet and the nearby quarry. The 'Red Line' was captured to time and quickly consolidated for defence. The slopes around were swept by enemy machine gun fire from Pontruet but retaliatory fire by Lewis and Vickers machine guns kept them subdued.

Further exploitation of the Battalion's success was attempted at 1.00pm when two platoons of 'C' Company started to work small patrols down into the valley ahead and up the opposite slope. Just as one of these small patrols was about to enter the next German trench the enemy launched a counter-attack but this was repulsed.

The Australians, to the left, continued their advance beneath a barrage at 11.00pm on the 18th September and, at short notice, the 2nd Battalion, The Royal Sussex Regiment was ordered to conform by attacking at midnight to secure a footing in a sunken road ahead. This attack was only partially successful with one platoon gaining access into the northern end of the sunken road. Farther south along the sunken road, very heavy German machine gun fire from Pontruet precluded any more advance so a line was established with a flank thrown back to connect with the 2nd Kings Royal Rifle Corps.

Although relatively heavy casualties had been taken by the Battalion, this had been a successful, though very hard day's fighting. Battalion troops had captured completely their first objectives, a rare achievement indeed during this war when the aims set by senior staff were normally over-ambitious to the point of absurdity. In addition, several mortars, nine field guns, about 300 prisoners and numerous machine guns and rifles had been captured.

Letters of congratulation were received from the Army, Corps and Brigade Commanders, while the Divisional Commander not only sent the following congratulatory letter but also made a personal visit to congratulate and thank the Battalion.

"1st Division No. G 586.
21.9.18.
I am most glad to convey to you the attached congratulations and thanks of the Army Commander and Corps Commander on your splendid work in the recent fighting.

You have now been engaged with the enemy since September 2nd with but a short interval spent in travelling, and during all this time you have been called upon to undergo very considerable exposure and hard work. It ended with two days of very severe fighting, on the 18th and 19th, when you advanced your line on an average depth of 3,000 yards, took several strong positions and captured several hundred prisoners in the face of very determined opposition, during which a large number of the enemy were killed. It is a record that you may well be proud of – You have once again shown that fine fighting spirit, determination and Espirit de Corps which makes you what you are, and every Unit has well maintained the fine traditions that are theirs.

I realise to the full all that you have gone through, and I thank you all very deeply for the great gallantry, sense of duty, and determination that you have shown.

The Staffs of all Units have had an exceptionally trying time and the smoothness of all arrangements is proof of their excellent work.

Much hard fighting is ahead of us in the near future, and at no period of the war were greater efforts required of us than now, when the enemy is suffering from defeat, morally and physically, and every blow now will render his final and complete defeat nearer and surer.

I am full of confidence that you will more than maintain the reputation of the 1st Division in the fighting that is before you, and that you will again acquit yourselves with distinction as you have done so often before.

I feel great pride in commanding you, and great gratitude for the grand work you have done under continued severe conditions.

E.P.Stickland,
Major General,
Commanding 1st Division."

SEPTEMBER:
18th:
Second Lieutenants: (471) H.W.Earl, (623) R.G.Gordon, (944) H.E.Little, (1555) J.M.Vaughan, (1650) J.S.White.
Sergeants: (112) G.E.Bevan, D.C.M., (172) F.Bridger.
Corporal: (689) J.Haydon.
Lance Corporals: (322) A.W.Coe, (549) G.W.Foreman, (679) W.G.Harrington, (1069) W.A.Munson.
Privates: (124) A.J.Blackman, (168) A.G.Breck, (253) J.H.Byles, (359) T.G.Cooper, (552) W.Foster, (565) F.Friend, (642) S.P.Gregory, (681) F.Harris, (791) F.H.Hunt, (883) H.King, (931) S.J.Lepper, (974) W.Marchant, (1018) J.Miles, (1116) W.Offin, (1171) C.C.Payne, (1184) J.B.Penfold, (1230) A.C.Quaife, (1254) D.S.Rees, (1582) A.V.Ward, (1586) W.Ward, (1591) A.G.Waters.
19th:
Privates: (96) W.Beard, (287) T.G.Chapple.

The Battalion was relieved on the 19th and moved back eventually to a position south of Poeuilly and into Divisional Reserve. Everyone was much looking forward to a period of relaxation.

After only one day's rest, however, the Battalion was warned to prepare for a further attack, this time against the enemy position to the north of Gricourt. This was to be part of an offensive being made by the 1st Division to secure the villages of Gricourt and Fresnoy together with the high ground north of Gricourt which provided the Germans with good fields of observation.

SEPTEMBER:
20th:
Private: (1515) P.Tolley.
22nd:
Private: (318) C.A.Coates.

During the evening of the 23rd September the Battalion made an approach march to the quarries east of Vermand. At 11.00pm an enemy barrage was falling on crossroads in the direct line of route so a move was made across country around Maissemy to the desired forming up position.

Zero hour was 5.00am on the 24th September and, at that time, the Battalion moved forward once more behind a creeping barrage. Although considerable opposition was met in the trenches and sunken roads, all was overcome and many prisoners were captured. However, the 46th Division, to the left, had failed to take the village of Pontruet, as a result of which the Northampton Regiment was exposed and was forced to withdraw. In turn, that withdrawal completely exposed the left flank of the Battalion's 'C' Company on the hillside. This Company was subjected to very heavy artillery and machine gun fire and, inevitably, took many casualties, with the remnants being forced to withdraw down the slopes.

At about 11.20am a large force of about 400 enemy soldiers was seen advancing to make a counter-attack against the Battalion's 'A' Company. Captain Roberts, commanding 'A' Company, ordered his men to open fire. As a result of this concentrated rifle fire the enemy began to waiver when at a distance of about 50 yards. At that instant, upon an order from Captain Roberts, the men fixed bayonets, rose from their positions in shell holes and charged the enemy. The Germans were utterly routed and over 40 of their men were taken prisoner. The artillery, in response to 'A' Company S.O.S. signals, shelled the retreating enemy causing many more casualties amongst them. This action, which had been a fine example in the use of infantry weapons, with dash and fighting spirit, was mentioned in a communique by Sir Douglas Haig. The total number of all ranks in 'A'

Company at the time had been only 80 and they had been out-numbered by 5 to 1.

Following this splendid overall effort the Divisional Commander paid a special visit to congratulate the Battalion. Also, letters and telegrams were received from other higher commanders and past officers of the regiment. In particular, the following short letter was received:

"1st Division No. G.A.5/1.
The Field Marshal Commanding in Chief has today personally directed me to convey to all ranks of the 1st Division his congratulations on their splendid successes in the recent fighting, with which he is much pleased.
E.P.Strickland, Major-General, Commanding 1st Division."

Captured during the 24th September had been two field guns, much other equipment and some 400 prisoners. In addition to those killed, the Battalion sustained seven officers wounded and two missing, plus 117 other ranks wounded and 39 missing.

SEPTEMBER:
24th:
Captain: (1472) G.Sunderland.
Lieutenant: (1698) B.C.Wright.
Company Sergeant Major: (1112) G.F.Oakley.
Second Lieutenants: (8) F.E.Adkin, M.M., (584) A.Garton, (1359) Sir J.B.Shifner, Bart.
Sergeants: (248) H.J.Butler, (925) E.Leggatt, (999) T.Matthias, M.M., (1151) J.L.Parks.
Lance Sergeants: (1527) F.E.Townsend, (1713) J.T.Young.
Corporals: (731) W.R.Hillsdon, (1532) F.Tribe, (1682) J.Wood.
Lance Corporals: (67) F.Baldock, (86) R.Barton, (1065) W.Muggeridge.
Privates: (148) J.Botten, (245) P.Butcher, (316) W.Clifford, (473) P.Earthey, (537) E.C.Flower, (588) E.A.Gater, (647) S.Grinstead, (757) W.R.Hollox, (760) S.Honeyball, (805) W.Hyghgate, (857) R.C.Kelsey, (877) H.J.Key, (907) E.Lambert, (947) W.G.Lloyd, (967) M.P.Mann, M.M., (976) J.Mark, (1009) E.A.Meek, (1038) R.J.Mitchell, (1083) H.J.Newman, (1097) W.E.Nicholls, (1122) P.Orme, (1126) A.Osborne, (1139) E.Page, (1157) L.Parvin, (1243) A.Raynsford, (1255) E.Reeves, (1312) W.F.Salisbury, (1394) W.Smart, (1416) A.E.Sole, (1484) A.F.R.Taylor, (1510) E.Tiltman, (1522) C.Toon.

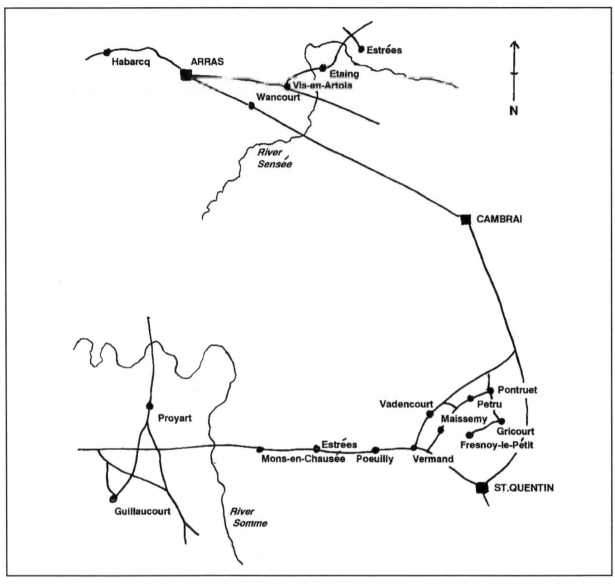

22.   *September 1918*

The Battalion remained holding its position until relieved on the night of the 28th / 29th September. A weary march then brought the men back to Brigade Reserve at Vermand. There they rested beyond the end of the month and re-organised from four into only three Companies owing to the casualties suffered on the 24th September.

SEPTEMBER:
26th:
Second Lieutenant: (555) W.M.Fowler.
Lance Corporal: (9) J.B.Aikman.
Private: (694) H.R.T.Haywood.
28th:
Lance Corporal: (703) S.H.Hemsley, M.M.
Privates: (864) F.J.Kennard, (1681) H.J.Wood.
30th:
Company Sergeant Major: (519) W.Farrell.

Some confusion or, at least, uncertainty seems to have occured on the 4th October when the Battalion marched north-east for about four miles to Pontruet. Later they were ordered to march back to Vermand which they did, remaining there for their dinners. After eating, they marched again, this time south-west, some three miles to Caulaincourt where they were accommodated in shelters.

OCTOBER:
3rd:
Private: (48) H.C.Bailey.
4th:
Private: (1307) G.B.Rustell.
5th:
Private: (1614) C.R.Weekes.
8th:
Private: (1210) G.E.Pomfrett.

Training was undertaken and rest was enjoyed at Caulaincourt for five days until, on the 9th October, an 11 miles march was made north-westwards so far as Bellenglise. There, an unfortunate railway accident of some sort, with unrecorded details, occured on the 13th resulting in the death of Private T.A.Martin.

OCTOBER:

13th:

Privates: (46) F.J.Bailey, (279) W.G.Cattermole, (303) E.J.Clark, (654) J.W.Guymer, M.M., (991) T.A.Martin.

Training around Bellenglise continued until, on the 16th October, reconnoitering officers went forward by lorry while the remainder of the Battalion followed on foot to bivouac in a field just north-west of Bohain.

OCTOBER:

16th:

Private: (1463) A.R.Stratford.

At 1.00am on the 17th October, the Battalion marched forward to Becquigny and there took up artillery formation in Brigade Reserve immediately south of the railway. The plan was that the 2nd Brigade would leap-frog through the 16th Brigade after that Brigade's first bound eastwards from Vaux Andigny had been completed to a line through the north-west edge of La Vallée Mulâtre. At that point the barrage was to stop for 30 minutes to give the 2nd Brigade time to pass through and continue the advance to a line running just east of the La Vallée Mulâtre – Ribeauville Road. Then, after a three hours halt, a further advance was to be attempted to the high ground overlooking the Sambre Canal.

At zero hour, 5.20am on the 17th October, the advance began with the Battalion following closely along the southern edge of the Bois de Busigny. The railway was reached west of Vaux Andigny. There was a thick fog at the time which, together with the wearing of gas masks because the enemy was gas shelling Vaux Andigny, made for slow progress. After passing the eastern outskirts of Vaux Andigny, however, the advance continued with the Battalion's right flank on the railway.

As the leading troops approached Molain, the fog began to lift. With improved vision, enemy

machine guns, which had not been dealt with, opened fire from Molain and the high ground south of the railway. The machine gun in Molain was put out of action by 'B' Company thus allowing the advance to continue towards La Vallée Mulâtre.

Another hold up developed due to a nest of enemy machine guns sited in houses at the north-west of La Vallée Mulâtre. Two Vickers machine guns were brought up to engage them and they were captured by an encircling movement carried out by 'D' Company.

At 2.00pm further progress was halted by the strength of the enemy's position around Demi Lieu. At 4.00pm, with this hold-up continuing, the Brigade Major arrived and ordered the advance to continue at 5.15pm behind a barrage. When the renewed attack began, considerable enemy machine gun fire from Demi Lieu was met but this was overcome and the Battalion captured 10 machine guns and one field gun.

Advances continued but a report was received that the Northamptonshires had been prevented from making further progress and had withdrawn through the outskirts of La Vallée Mulâtre. The implication of this was that the 2nd Battalion, The Royal Sussex Regiment was about 1,000 yards forward of any troops on either side, and the front Companies were being fired on by enemy machine guns in the rear of their flanks. This difficulty was overcome by the front Companies establishing a line along the railway with 'D' Company thrown back along a line to connect with the Northamptonshires at La Vallée Mulâtre.

OCTOBER:

17th:

Lance Corporal: (285) J.Chapman.

Privates: (550) H.G.Fossey, (680) A.J.Harris, (1235) G.Ranger, M.M., (1343) C.Secker.

On the morning of the 18th October, the 1st and 3rd Brigades passed through the Battalion to take, respectively, Wassigny and the high ground about Ribeauville. Before these moves by other Brigades could be accomplished, a number of enemy machine guns had to be located and successfully engaged by Lewis gun teams of the Battalion. Later, several of these enemy machine guns were found knocked out with men of their teams lying dead beside, and around, the guns.

OCTOBER:
18th:
Privates: (231) H.R.Burr, (725) P.J.Hill.

The following telegram was received at Battalion Headquarters in connection with the action of the 17th and 18th October:

" From General Braithwaite, Commanding XI Corps.
Well done 1st Division your work yesterday and today is in accordance with your best traditions. It enhances even your reputation. I congratulate you heartily."

The 'rolling' operation in which the Brigade was engaged continued on the afternoon of the 19th October when the Battalion relieved the 120th American Regiment in the area of Mazinghein and remained in support. Relief during the night of the 20th / 21st served only to allow preparations for a Brigade attack to capture La Haie Tonnolle Farm and the high ground to its east, overlooking Catillon.

OCTOBER:
20th:
Private: (224) L.Burberry.

21st:
Private: (1481) A.Tapner, M.M.

The next forward move had its zero hour set for 1.20am on the 23rd October and support by tanks had been promised by the Tank Commander. That night the moon was bright but a thick ground mist restricted visibility to about 50 yards. Directions were taken by compass bearings and the findings were communicated to every section so that they could follow their directions by the stars.

Two minutes before zero a friendly machine gun barrage opened followed, precisely at zero, by the artillery. The enemy retaliated with high explosive and phosgene shells. The German infantry, however, offered no resistance and ran back so fast as they could before the creeping barrage could catch them. So rapid was the German retreat that they left behind their rifles, eight machine guns, equipment and rations. Of those troops too slow to get away, 20 were taken prisoner. A line was formed along the objective and consolidated before dawn. Not one single tank had appeared to provide the help promised in this operation.

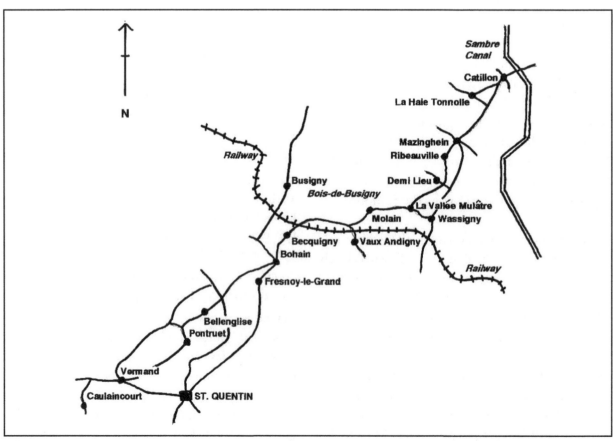

23.   *October to November 1918*

OCTOBER:

23rd:

Privates: (156) S.Box, (388) O.Cranmer, (704) T.C.Hemsley, (778) R.W.Howlett, M.M., (1078) A.H.Nelson, (1174) A.Peacock, (1483) H.Tasker, (1679) S.J.Winter.

On the night of the 24th October the Battalion was finally relieved from its part in the recent extended operations. This long and complicated series of actions had been completed successfully by the depleted Battalion, then numbering only 17 officers and 353 other ranks, with surprisingly few casualties. Two officers, Lieutenant C.L.Mitchell, M.C., and Second Lieutenant Homewood had been wounded and 53 other ranks were killed, wounded or missing.

OCTOBER:

24th:

Sergeant: (517) I.H.Farmer, M.M.

25th:

Private: (1190) W.Pettet.

A new draft of 93 men, bringing the month's total to 202, arrived on the 27th October in time to join the Battalion when it took over the front line of 1,200 yards that evening. A group of enemy soldiers attempted to rush one of the Battalion posts on the 28th but they were driven off by Lewis gun fire.

The Northamptonshire Regiment, to the right, assisted by 'D' Company of the 2nd Battalion, The Royal Sussex Regiment, reached and occupied the line of the Sambre Canal on the 29th October. Despite an attempted penetration by the enemy on the 30th, the canal line was held, with 'D' Company killing 12 Germans and capturing one prisoner and one machine gun.

OCTOBER:

29th:

Private: (97) H.J.Beasley.

The Battalion was relieved on the night of the 30th / 31st October and moved back to Molain, where it received notification of awards for October; these amounted to one Bar to the D.S.O., five Bars to Military Medals and no less than 45 Military Medals, the latter, in particular, indicating what sterling work had been carried out by other ranks. The Battalion marched out from Molain to La Vallée Mulâtre on the 1st

November and remained there while plans were finalised for the attempted forcing of the Canal de la Sambre. This relatively new canal, which was deep and wide with very steep and high banks, would prove a formidable obstacle. Even before the canal itself was reached it would be necessary to ascend a steep bank, some 100 yards short of the canal proper, which led up to a lock.

Soon after dawn, the attack was launched only to be met by withering fire from the enemy as the troops breasted the top of the bank at the approach to the canal. Severe casualties were sustained by the Brigade and, for a time, there was considerable confusion. Order was restored by Lieutenant Colonel D.G.Johnson who rallied the men and led them onwards. Again, the assault was broken up by heavy fire from the Germans but, once more, Lieutenant Colonel Johnson urged the bridging parties on to the lock which they reached enabling a crossing of the canal to be accomplished.

In fact Lieutenant Colonel Johnson's Regiment was the South Wales Borderers but, for this particular operation, he was attached to the 2nd Battalion, The Royal Sussex Regiment. For his part in the canal assault he was awarded the Victoria Cross for which the citation reads as follows:

"Lt.Col.Dudley Graham Johnson, V.C., D.S.O., M.C.

Lt.Col.Dudley Graham Johnson, D.S.O., M.C., South Wales Borderers, attached 2nd Bn. Royal Sussex, for most conspicuous bravery and leadership during the forcing of the Sambre Canal on November 4th 1918.

The 2nd Infantry Brigade, of which 2nd Bn.R.Sx. formed part, was ordered to cross the lock south of Catillon. The position was strong, and before the bridge could be thrown, a steep bank leading up to a lock and a waterway about 100 yards short of the canal had to be crossed.

Upon their arrival at the waterway, the Battalion's assaulting platoons, together with bridging parties of the Royal Engineers, were thrown into confusion by a heavy barrage and machine gun fire and heavy casualties were caused.

At this moment Lieutenant Colonel Johnson arrived. With great presence of mind and determination he quickly assessed the situation. Realising the serious predicament, he at once collected men to man the bridges and to assist the Royal Engineers; the Lieutenant Colonel personally led the assault.

In spite of his efforts, heavy fire again broke up the assaulting and bridging parties.

Without any hesitation he again organised the platoons and bridging parties and led them at the lock, this time succeeding in effecting a crossing after which all went well. During all this time Lieutenant Colonel Johnson was under heavy fire, which, though it nearly decimated the assault columns, left him untouched.

His conduct was a fine example of great valour, coolness and intrepidity, which, added to the splendid leadership and offensive spirit that he had inspired in his Bn. were entirely responsible for the successful crossing.

London Gazette 6/1/19."

So, fittingly, upon this splendid note of success, came to an end the fighting experiences of the 2nd Battalion in the Great War. Sadly, a number of men were killed in the operation on the 4th November, or died from their wounds the following day, literally only hours from the war's end and their personal survival. Such are the tragedies and misfortunes of war.

NOVEMBER:
3rd:
Private: (1267) C.Richards.
4th:
Second Lieutenant: (948) E.S.Loader.
Lance Sergeant: (1368) W.Shufflebottom.
Corporal: (590) A.H.Gausden.
Privates: (121) A.Bird, (539) E.Folds, (759) J.T.Holmes, (787) E.Humfreys, (951) G.Longley, (1410) W.Smith, M.M., (1594) G.V.Watling, (1608) J.Weaver, (1620) E.Weller, (1701) N.Wrist.
5th:
Corporal: (58) G.W.Baker.
Lance Corporal: (840) W.Johnston.
Privates: (51) A.Baker, (1090) T.C.Newsome, (1245) G.E.Read, (1292) H.Roper.

What was to be the final relief from the front line came on the 6th November when the Battalion marched by way of Bohain to billets in Fresnoy-le-Grand. It was while they were at Fresnoy-le-Grand that, first rumours, then confirmation came of the armistice which was to take place with all firing halted at 11.00am on the 11th November.

Interestingly, the Battalion War Diary makes no mention at all of the actual ending of the war. Perhaps the diarist was numbed by all that had taken place over the past 51 months and could not bring himself to believe that the end had come; or perhaps he was too overcome by feelings of euphoria to record the events. It is a fact that many men were too shattered, mentally, to take in the implications of their survival. Whatever the reason, the Battalion War Diary contains no individual entry for that momentous day, the 11th November, 1918.

NOVEMBER:
12th:
Private: (1374) P.W.Simpson.

2nd Battalion Epilogue

The 2nd Battalion, The Royal Sussex Regiment had served on the Western Front so long as any other British or Empire regiment. The Battalion first arrived in France on 13th August,1914, only nine days after the declaration of war. The Battalion had remained on the Western Front without interruption from then until the armistice, a total of 51 months or 1,552 days.

The alphabetical reference list at the end of this book forms the Battalion's 'Roll of Honour' with details of more than 1,700 men who lost their lives while the Battalion was serving on the Western Front. Thus, the average death rate was in excess of one each day. Looked at another way, and appreciating that a battalion's initial strength was about 1,000 men, of whom some 850 were fully armed and trained infantrymen, the Battalion lost in death, while on The Western Front, more than twice its original fighting strength.

This Battalion of Britain's regular army was justly proud of its achievements during the Great War. Those achievements, many and varied, were crowned by the award of the Victoria Cross, the country's highest honour for bravery, to Sergeant Harry Wells, V.C., and to Lieutenant Colonel Dudley Graham Johnson, V.C., D.S.O., M.C., both serving with the 2nd Battalion, the Lieutenant Colonel being attached at the time from the South Wales Borderers.

PART TWO

The 4th Battalion
('Territorials')

CHAPTER 10

1918

JUNE – THE ARMISTICE

The 4th Battalion The Royal Sussex Regiment was a Territorial unit raised, with others, during 1908. The service numbers of many of its men were prefixed by the Territorial Force initials 'TF'.

At the outbreak of war the Battalion was attached to the Home Counties Division but it had been transferred to the 160th Brigade, 53rd Division, at Cambridge on 24th April, 1915. Following a spell at Bedford, the Battalion embarked in July, 1915, for the Mediterranean. On 9th August, 1915, the Battalion had landed at Suvla Bay in the Dardanelles and, by December that year, had moved to Egypt. The period of service in the Middle East did not end until June, 1918, by which time over 300 officers and men of the Battalion had lost their lives.

On 17th June, 1918, the Battalion left Alexandria aboard His Majesty's Transport "Malwa" which made a four-day passage to arrive in Italy at the port of Taranto on 22nd. From the dockside a long and slow train journey began northwards through Italy and by way of Genoa to the French Mediterranean port of Marseilles. From there, with no respite, the train journey continued north-westwards across France until Étaples was reached on 29th June and the Battalion sank thankfully into Rest Camp for one night. Such was the urgent need for reinforcements on the Western Front following the German's 'Spring Offensive' that the Battalion went on again, the very next day, to de-train at Proven, join the 101st Brigade, 34th Division, and move on to Herzeele on what was the last day of the month. It is evident that a number of 4th Battalion personnel lost their lives on the Western Front before the full Battalion arrived, no doubt when, for various reasons, they had been attached to other Units.

Reference details of those men are recorded here:

JUNE,1916:
Private: (1784) A.A.Hedgecock.
JULY,1916:
Privates: (1776) E.S.Grant, (1822) P.J.Phillips.
OCTOBER,1916:
Private: (1793) G.H.Johnson.
MARCH,1917:
Sergeant: (1863) W.T.Walsham.
APRIL,1917:
Second Lieutenant: (1727) E.L.Bostock.
MAY,1917:
Second Lieutenant: (1843) W.Smith.
JUNE,1917:
Lieutenant: (1827) V.Richardson.
AUGUST,1917:
Second Lieutenant: (1773) A.H.Golby.
SEPTEMBER,1917:
Second Lieutenant: (1741) J.E.Charman.
OCTOBER,1917:
Lieutenant: (1860) A.H.Tucker.
MARCH,1918:
Second Lieutenant: (1845) C.T.Squires.
APRIL,1918:
Second Lieutenant: (1868) C.A.Wilmshurst.
JUNE,1918:
Private: (1749) J.G.Deadman.

At the commencement of this period on the Western Front the Battalion's strength was 29 officers and 941 other ranks. On the 2nd July a march was made from billets near Herzeele to a hutted camp at Proven. Over the next 10 days close order drill and gas training were undertaken. Then, on the 13th July, the men marched to School Camp at St.Jan-ter-Biezen and rested for two days.

JULY:
1st:
Private: (1788) W.H.Holder.

On the 16th July it was back to Proven from where a long train journey was taken to arrive on the 18th at Chantilly and onward march to bivouac near Vineuil. The following day the Battalion was taken by buses to Vauciennes and a night in billets.

JULY:
17th:
Private: (1831) G.S.Rossiter.

The whole Brigade set out, on the 20th July, to march together to Pusieux where they did not arrive until 5.00am the following morning. After two days in billets at Pusieux, the Battalion marched to a point west of Parcy Tigny where it came into Brigade Reserve bivouaced in a wood. During the day on the 23rd, three Companies were sent forward to support the Loyal North Lancs in an attack but were not needed so returned. The enemy heavily shelled the wood this day with disasterous results. Second Lieutenant E.W.Austin, who was on attachment from the 1st Battalion Cheshire Regiment, and a number of men were killed, while Second Lieutenant H.Burrows and 47 other men were wounded.

JULY:
23rd:
Second Lieutenant:: (1716) E.W.Austin.
Corporal: (1865) A.Watson.
Privates: (1736) A.Butler, (1742) C.Chipper, (1746) E.Cooper, (1752) C.A.W.Donno, (1764) A.J.G.Francis, (1798) W.Kenyon, (1800) H.I.Kilduff, (1802) E.F.Kirby, (1803) H.T.Knapp, (1804) A.G.Lee, (1817) E.Owen, (1818) W.P.Parsons, (1821) H.E.Phillips, (1839) D.J.Smith.

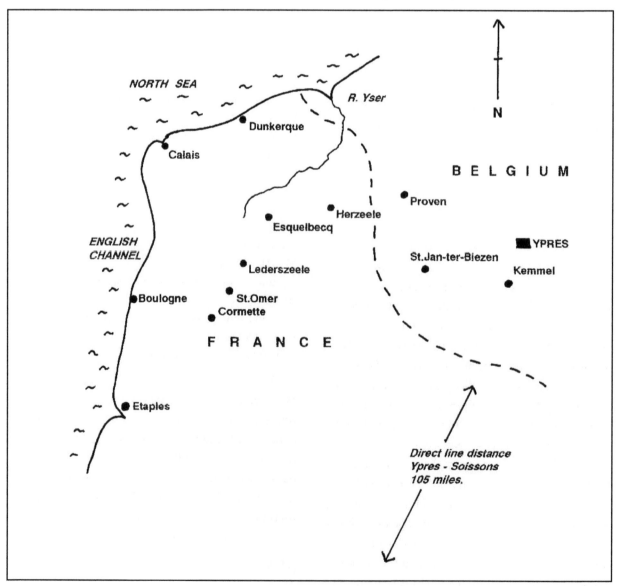

July and August 1918 (Northern Area)

24.

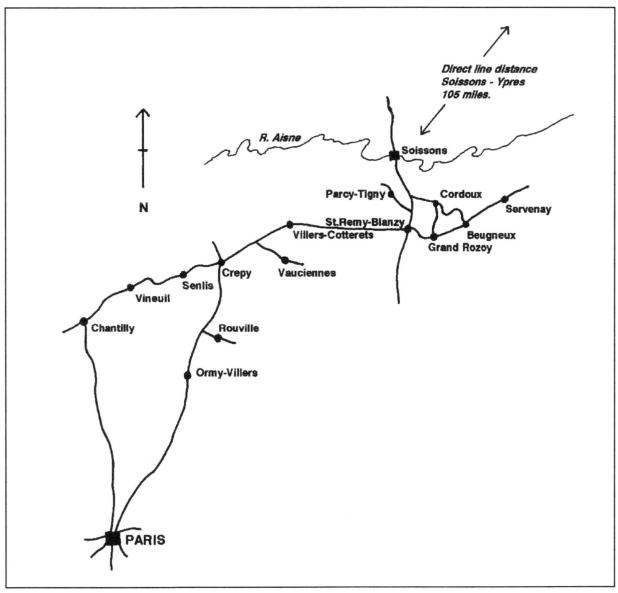

25.   *July and August 1918 (Southern Area)*

The Battalion remained in Reserve until the 27th July when relief by French troops was effected and a march made to bivouac in the Bois de Boeuf, west of St.Remy Blanzy.

JULY:
24th:
Private: (1725) H.Bond.
27th:
Private: (1728) F.G.Brake.

On the 28th July, orders for an attack early the following morning were received. The plan required the Battalion to move to an assembly point along the railway line south-west of Bois du Mortceau. This move started at 9.10pm but the French guide became completely lost and the destination was not reached until 2.45am on the 29th. At 3.00am an enemy shell killed Captain A.M.H.Weekes, M.C. and mortally wounded Captain S.K.Reid, M.C. Command of the Battalion was then taken over by Captain Middleton, M.C. Precisely as planned, the advance began at 4.10am. Keeping in touch with Units to the left and right, the wood was cleared with little opposition and the advance continued to within 300 yards of the Grand Rozoy – Beugneux Road. Casualties to this point had been very light.

At 6.00am the advance was continued across the road and into the Bois de Beugneux but enemy machine gun fire from within the wood was so concentrated that a withdrawal back to the road was made. Lack of communication prevented artillery support so, after some reorganisation, the wood was charged with the bayonet and carried; several Germans were killed and machine guns captured.

The north-east corner of the wood was reached at 7.00am but enfilade machine gun fire was taken from both flanks. A further small advance was made but, in addition to machine gun fire, field artillery salvoes were taken from point blank range causing a withdrawal to the wood. British troops on the flanks had been forced back making it necessary for the Battalion to draw back to a previous line of defence north of the Bois du Mortceau. This line was consolidated and held for the remainder of the day.

In addition to those killed, four officers and 125 other ranks had been wounded and another 29 men were missing.

JULY:
29th:
Captains: (1825) S.K.Reid, M.C., (1866) A.N.H.Weekes, M.M.

Second Lieutenants: (1722) S.Blagg, (1723) F.J.Bleeze.

Regimental Sergeant Major: (1838) J.Simmons, D.C.M.

Sergeant: (1814) H.T.Neighbour.

Corporal: (1873) C.M.Woollven.

Lance Corporals: (1738) J.Campbell, (1795) A.G.Jolly, (1837) A.C.Shier, (1855) W.Tabour, (1859) A.W.Tree.

Privates: (1726) F.E.Boniface, (1731) J.Brow, (1733) G.H.Bryant, (1735) A.J.Burch, (1739) P.W.Chalcraft, (1745) G.Coomber, (1747) T.E.Cooper, (1748) F.Cross, (1753) H.E.Dowers, (1757) G.Ellis, (1759) H.H.Everest, (1760) E.A.Evitt, (1763) F.A.E.Flecknell, (1765) H.J.Francis, (1767) J.W.Gabbitas, (1775) E.G.M.Graham, (1786) J.Hislop, (1787) E.L.Holder, (1790) R.H.Holton, (1796) F.K.Jones, (1799) O.J.A.Kerwood, (1805) P.J.Leftwich, (1808) P.F.Manwaring, (1812) M.Mepham, (1819) G.Perry, (1826) E.G.Richardson, (1828) W.Rist, (1832) W.Rowland, (1836) A.P.Shaw, (1841) F.H.Smith, (1842) W.Smith, (1844) O.N.Spencer, (1847) P.Standing, (1848) G.M.Steele, (1850) G.S.Stoner, (1852) W.J.Styles, (1854) G.Swain, (1858) W.S.Tizzard, (1861) J.Verrall, (1862) F.Vidler, (1869) F.H.Windebank, (1870) H.F.Winkle.

On the following day, the 30th July, outposts were pushed forward to the Grand Rozoy – Beugneux Road. German artillery was active but there was no infantry engagement. The last day of the month was quiet.

By the beginning of August, and as a result of deaths and injuries, the strength of the Battalion had dropped to 23 officers and 636 men, this being more than 300 men less than on arrival at the Western Front. The early part of the month was to involve intense activity and action before a retirement for rest was granted.

The very first day of August saw preparation for an attack as part of the overall strategy of the allies to maintain heavy and continuous pressure on an enemy now considered to be 'on the run' at last. At 4.45am four lines of Companies assembled on the Grand Rozoy – Beugneux Road and advanced through the Bois de Beugneux. The enemy retired in disorder. Some Germans were killed with the bayonet, others taken prisoner and several of their machine guns siezed. After a period of consolidation, orders were received for a further 600 yards advance. This advance began at 7.00am and was successful, six more machine guns being captured. From this time, the enemy seemed to have retired from the immediate front and French troops passed through the Battalion in pursuit. There was a general euphoria that the British army was in the ascendancy.

AUGUST:
1st:
Sergeant: (1758) F.Elms.

Lance Corporal: (1806) A.T.Lillywhite.

Privates: (1732) E.C.Brown, (1740) S.H.V.Chaplin, (1751) L.Dixon, (1761) H.A.Feast, (1762) J.W.Fisher, (1772) H.J.Godden, (1797) A.E.Kemp, (1816) G.A.B.Nutley, (1833) E.C.Rudderham, (1840) E.H.Smith.

2nd:
Privates: (1743) C.F.Chitty, (1810) G.E.Martin

3rd:
Privates: (1729) A.V.Brand, (1770) H.G.Giddings, (1853) G.F.Summersell.

Two days later, on the 4th August, the Battalion, having consolidated its position and resided in bivouacs, travelled by bus from the Beugneux area to Rouville. Billets in Rouville were left on the 6th August for a train journey arriving in Esquelbecq the following day. From Esquelbecq the men marched on the 12th by way of Lederszeele to a camp at Cormette. From there, the Battalion had the honour to march past H.M. King George V at St.Omer on the 13th; on that day, too, a cadre of the disbanded 13th Battalion Royal Sussex Regiment was absorbed into the 4th Battalion.

AUGUST:
6th:
Private: (1754) L.Dowling.
7th:
Second Lieutenant: (1871) H.F.Wixcey.
Privates: (1750) C.D.D.Denyer, (1829) R.H.Roberts, (1856) P.F.Targett.
11th:
Private: (1785) A.F.Hills.
17th:
Private: (1846) H.Stace.
23rd:
Private: (1791) E.Humphrey.
27th:
Corporal: (1809) H.Markwick.

Ten days later, after a period of rest and training, the Battalion entrained at St.Omer for Proven where huts were occupied in relative luxury. A welcome draft of 119 other ranks arrived to join the Battalion and soon found themselves, by month's end, in Divisional, then Brigade, Reserve. It was reported at this time that the enemy had retired from Kemmel Hill.

September saw the Battalion back nearer to full strength with 40 officers and 919 other ranks when they advanced through the Loyal North Lancs at 5.00pm on the 1st. Soon, a halt to the advance was called owing to fire from a large number of enemy machine guns in Petit Bois and the fact that Units on either flank had made insufficient progress. That night, several minor patrol encounters took place. The line was held but its position was dangerously exposed and, during daylight on the 2nd September, casualties were taken from continued machine gun fire from the flanks.

SEPTEMBER:
2nd.:
Second Lieutenant: (1737) – Byrne.
Privates: (1717) B.Bailie, (1720) S.A.Bird, (1721) F.Blackman, (1768) C.W.Gennery, (1792) S.A.Jay, (1794) S.Johnson, (1834) A.D.Sales, (1864) G.S.Warn, (1875) F.C.Yeates.

After a day in Reserve on the 3rd September, the Battalion once more held the line without too much activity. The line was pushed forward after dusk on the 8th but work was made difficult by the darkness and heavy rain.

SEPTEMBER:
3rd.:
Privates: (1807) W.Macklin, (1857) A.Tickner.
4th.:
Corporal: (1756) A.E.Durrant.
Privates: (1801) D.A.King, (1867) E.A.Wilkes.
5th.:
Private: (1874) S.G.Wye.
6th.:
Lieutenant: (1823) F.A.Pierssene.
Private: (1724) J.Bolton.
8th.:
Private: (1755) C.F.B.Dowman.

A move back to Reserve in the Kemmel Defences was made on the 10th September. Then, after another two day spell in the line, the Battalion went out to Divisional Reserve in the Scherpenberg – La Clytte area on the 15th. The weather was very pleasant at this period and the men enjoyed a good rest until relieving the 4th Battalion Cheshire Regiment in the line on the 22nd.

SEPTEMBER:
12th:
Private: (1730) A.Brandi.
14th:
Private: (1783) N.W.Hazell.

The nearby Spanbroekmolen Crater was the object of attention from the 23rd to 25th September.

On the first of those days Lieutenant P.W.Lovering made a personal reconnaissance and found no German lookout at the crater. The Lieutenant entered the crater alone, shooting one German and finding it to be garrisoned by about 15 men. Patrols pushed out on the afternoon of the 25th and, by stealth and determination, drove out the enemy and occupied the crater. Heavy small-arms fire had been experienced and, at one point, it had been necessary for the men to run the gauntlet of dashing singly across a road. The new positions were consolidated and held for the next two days.

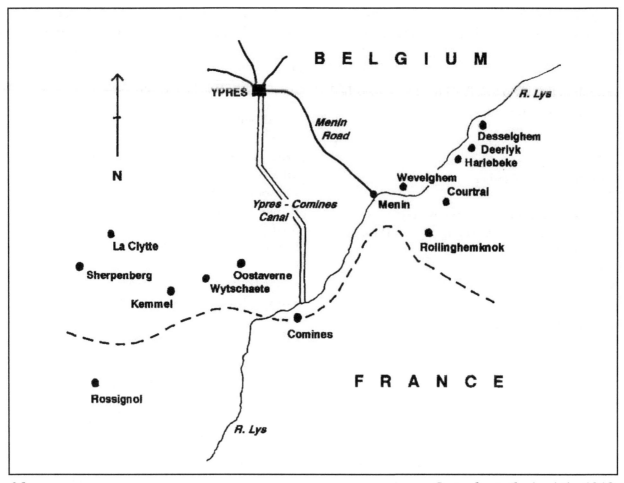

26.   *September to the Armistice 1918*

SEPTEMBER:
25th:
Sergeant: (1782) J.Harwood.
Privates: (1719) B.Bentley, (1811) G.W.Mc Intyre,
    (1824) C.Proctor.
27th:
Corporal: (1718) J.Bennett.

By the 28th September it was time for another
forward push and, at 7.30pm, a move towards
an allotted portion of the Wytschaete Ridge
began. The ground was so pitted with shell
holes and strewn with old wire and equipment
that little progress could be made in the pitch
darkness of the night. The advance continued
early next morning when, with little opposition
being experienced, the move carried forward to
Oostaverne where the Battalion was ordered to
halt while the 7th Battalion Cheshire Regiment
passed through to carry on the move.

SEPTEMBER:
29th:
Corporal: (1820) A.H.Pettifer.
Privates: (1780) D.H.Hamer, (1789) F.Holman.

In addition to those killed during the month
of September, 5 officers and 68 other ranks had
been wounded and 86 had been lost through
sickness.

Although the Battalion alternated with spells
in the front line and spells back in Reserve
throughout October, its fighting activities
gradually faded out during the month and were
not to be resumed. Movement by marching
started away from a bivouac area east of the
Ypres – Comines Canal on the 1st October
and eventually brought the Battalion to a line
advanced to about 300 yards from the River
Lys. The canal was crossed by footbridge
at dusk on the 16th October. Little activity,
save for occasional light enemy shelling, was
experienced before the Battalion entered
Reserve on the 20th, occupying billets in
Rollinghemknok. On the 26th October a march
was made to Desselghem where the line was
taken over from the 9th Royal Irish Fusiliers
and the 12th Royal Irish Rifles.

OCTOBER:
8th:
Private: (1849) G.M.Stevens.
9th:
Privates: (1715) W.J.Ashby, (1872) T.Woolford.
10th:
Private: (1779) F.A.Hall.
11th:
Private: (1774) F.Goldthorpe.
15th:
Private: (1766) F.Fuller.
16th:
Corporal: (1744) J.Compton.
17th:
Private: (1835) W.J.Saunders.

The Battalion's final departure from the front line occurred on the 28th October with a return to billets in Desselghem from where a march to billets at Harlebeke on the 29th and to Deerlyck on 31st brought the month to an end.

OCTOBER:
28th:
Corporal: (1771) W.P.Giles.

From Deerlyck on 1st November the Battalion marched to billets in Harlebeke and from there to Wevelghem on the 3rd. It was at Wevelghem, with a strength of 38 officers and 730 other ranks, that the Armistice news came to the 4th Battalion.

4th Battalion Epilogue

The 4th Battalion was the only Royal Sussex Regiment battalion to be sent to the Western Front following service in other theatres of the Great War. Those officers and men who made the journey from Egypt to France had to readjust, mentally and physically, to the differences between the arid terrain of the Middle East and the man-made wet and muddy desolations of the Western Front.

Counting from the day that it arrived by train at Étaples, the 4th Battalion The Royal Sussex Regiment was on active duty on the Western Front for a little over four months or, to be precise, only 137 days. During that relatively short period of time, the need, a vital one, had been for the Battalion to supplement the allied forces which had already stemmed the German 'Spring Offensive' aimed at capturing the great rail head at Amiens and sweeping on to the crucial channel ports. For that purpose the Battalion had been brought all the way from the Middle East; the Battalion did not fail. Soon, the tide would be turned, the great allied 'advance to victory' would begin and, in that, the 4th Battalion would play its vital part.

From the last week of July,1918, until mid-October the Battalion took part in a number of sharp actions aimed at pushing back the enemy at a steady pace. Several bouts of fighting, often at close quarters, were bloody and, in all during the period from 28th June to the Armistice on 11th November,1918, 159 officers and men of the Battalion lost their lives.

The Armistice itself, the great end to the war and, for those left, the realisation of survival, went unrecorded, almost as if unnoticed, in the Battalion's War Diary. Even though subsequent historical records have been modest in their acclaim of this 'unsung' Unit, the 4th Battalion can stand justly proud of its contribution and its sacrifices.

PART THREE

The 5th (Cinque Ports) Battalion (Territorials and Pioneers)

PART THREE

CHAPTER 11
1915
FEBRUARY – JUNE

Six months after the war began on the 4th August, 1914, the 1/5th Battalion The Royal Sussex Regiment was stationed at one of the most prestigious places of English history, namely the Tower of London. It was from there that the move to France and action began. While Britain's regular army battalions had been bearing the brunt of the fighting, at first and briefly, across the border in Belgium, and then in France, the 5th Battalion had been waiting, training and speculating.

As a Territorial Battalion, the 5th had its origins prior to the outbreak of war. Its men, who had been enlisted predominently at the Sussex seaside town of Hastings, one of England's historic and important Cinque Ports, were proud to have the designation "(Cinque Ports)" incorporated formally into the Battalion's title. The enthusiastic volunteers had been drawn, to a very large extent, from Sussex, particularly the eastern part of that county, and from the nearer parts of Kent. They had always known that they were to be in readiness to be called to support and reinforce the Units of the regular army if, and after, those 'regulars' had become engaged in any conflict.

The men, most of whom held full-time employment, spent much of their leisure time training and rehearsing as Territorial troops. The necessary training was undertaken at various drill halls and other suitable buildings scattered and established at places to which the men could gather during the evenings and at week-ends. Those living in relatively isolated country communities, sometimes had to travel many miles either by bicycle or on foot to and from their training bases.

At the outbreak of war, men of the Battlion were called to muster at Hastings where their main base was at the Drill Hall in Middle Street. Billets were found in boarding houses, Hôtels and private homes throughout the town and the adjoining St.Leonards-on-Sea.

By February,1915, however, the Battalion had moved to the Tower of London, and there, during the morning of the 16th, the men were inspected by General Monck. That afternoon, orders were received that the Battalion was to join the British Expeditionary Force (B.E.F.) in France. Final preparations ran smoothly, particularly on the 18th February when, within the space of eight hours, the Battalion entrained at Waterloo Station, travelled to the dockside at Southampton, embarked on the "S.S.Pancras" at 6.00pm and almost immediately set sail.

Virtually without exception, the men, many of whom had rarely travelled outside their own home areas, felt this to be a thrilling experience as the steamer moved down the Solent, butted out into the English Channel and, in darkness, set course for France. At 4.00am the following morning, the "S.S.Pancras" dropped anchor outside the entrance to the port of Le Havre. There, as the ship 'stood-to' until mid-day, dawn broke to reveal the first sight of the foreign land that was to be the Battalion's 'home' for the foreseeable future. At noon the ship moved in to tie up at the dock and, three hours later, the Battalion had disembarked and was marching off to the nearby No.1 Rest Camp.

From Le Havre at 7.00am next day, 19th February, the Battalion, with all its equipment and transport, began a slow and tortuous train journey north-eastwards which ended 26 hours later at Choques some three miles west of the town of Béthune. From Choques a march was made west and south-west for some three miles to billets in the village of Allouagne. There, on the 21st, the Battalion was officially attached to the 1st Division's 2nd Infantry Brigade where it joined the 1st Northamptons, 1st Loyal North Lancs, 2nd Kings Royal Rifle Corps and the 2nd Battalion The Royal Sussex Regiment, all under the command of General Westmacott.

Following an inspection on the 27th February by the General Officer Commanding the 1st Army Corps, a march was made, next day, by way of Choques, Vendin-les-Béthune and Hinges to billets on either side of the Canal d'Aire at Hingette.

On the 2nd March the Battalion moved to Avelette on the east side of the canal. From there a northward march on the 10th brought

the whole Brigade to Le Cornet Malo where it remained in Army Reserve while the major allied attack took place some five miles to the east at Neuve Chapelle. Although a move back to Hingette was made on the 13th, everyone was held in a state of such high alert that, when orders came to advance, the Battalion with all its transport was on the move within 11 minutes. The village of Gorre was reached and, from there, working parties were provided for the next three nights.

One of the tragedies which happened in training from time to time took place on the 17th March. Three men of the Battalion's transport were shot while exercising. Privates Foster and

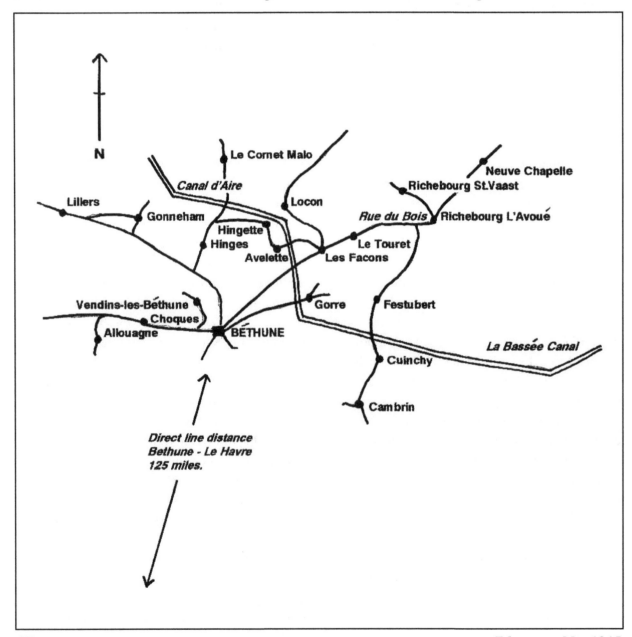

Stone received severe chest wounds while Private Bishop was wounded in the armpit; fortunately, none of these wounds proved fatal. That day, also, however, Private Frank Mushett of Rye was shot in the head by a German while with a working party in the tenches; he was transported back to military hospital in Boulogne where he died on 17th April,1915.

On the 18th March, men of 'C' and 'D' Companies took over front line trenches near Festubert with the remainder of the Battalion in Reserve in that village. Private Percy Vince, the first man of the Battalion to die in action, was shot in the head and killed on the 19th. The following day, shellfire wounded three men of whom one, Private Archibald Dunster, died on the 21st March.

MARCH:
19th:
Private: (2160) P.W.Vince.
20th:
Private: (1930) B.Catt.
21st:
Privates: (1939) M.Copland, (1956) A.Dunster.

From the 23rd to the 26th March the Battalion remained in support at Le Touret and Richebourg St.Vaast. Then, on the 27th, the trenches and breastworks were taken over at Richebourg L'Avoué . The next day a shell burst in a dugout killing Privates Swain and Garner while Privates Taylor and Hayward were killed in an advanced trench by rifle fire.

MARCH::
28th:
Privates: (1975) W.W.Garner, (2003) A.Hayward, (2140) J.Swain, (2145) F.Taylor.

On the 31st March, Corporal Carnaghan and Private Tester were also killed by rifle fire in the advanced trench which was too shallow to give full protection. Such an unsatisfactory situation was caused by the ground conditions in this part of the front. The natural water table was so near the surface that only very shallow trenches could be dug before water started to percolate. It was therefore necessary to build above-ground breastworks of earth-filled sandbags immediately in front of these shallow trenches in order to give improved concealment and safety. The last day of

the month saw relief from the line and a return to rest in Hingette. There was some sense of shock at the first loss of comrades in action.

MARCH:
30th:
Corporal: (1929) S.Carnaghan.
Private: (2150) C.C.Tester.
31st:
Privates: (1974) P.A.Gander, (1994) E.Harman.

The first week of April was spent 'at rest' although there always seemed plenty of work to be done. On the 7th of the month, a move was made to positions at Neuve Chapelle where the German lines were about 400 to 500 yards distant except at one point where they closed to 250 yards. Captain T.N.Hornblower was wounded at this point the following day while bravely trying to assist a severely wounded man under fire.

APRIL:
8th:
Private: (2122) T.Simmons.
9th:
Private: (2175) R.Winchester.

On the 11th April a gradual move back began to various rest billets in villages along the Rue du Bois. Rest and training continued until month's end. On the 29th, the front line trenches were bombarded in the early morning by German 'minenwerfers' and, in the evening by heavy shelling. Although the 'minenwerfers' were silenced on the 30th by Battalion rifle grenades and trench mortars, enemy shelling was heavy again during the afternoon.

APRIL:
11th:
Private: (1978) W.C.Gilbert.
13th:
Private: (2052) E.Manser.
17th:
Private: (2069) F.Mushett.
29th:
Private: (2024) C.Jarrett.

Side by side with colleagues of the 2nd Battalion The Royal Sussex Regiment, the 5th (Cinque Ports) Battalion was to suffer heavily this month during the ill-conceived, badly planned and disasterous Battle of Aubers Ridge on the 9th May. Even so early as the 1st May it seemed that the enemy had knowledge of the coming allied offensive because a violent bombardment, particularly on allied second line and communication trenches where preparations were likely to be in progress, was launched. During this bombardment a shell dropped into his dugout killing Company Sergeant Major Bull instantly. Then, the following day, immediately before relief by the Scots Guards, Second Lieutenant Price was standing outside his dugout when he was killed by a rifle bullet. His body was taken back with the relief about eight miles to Gonneham where it was buried beneath a crucifix in the south-west corner of the village churchyard where it remains, undisturbed, to this day.

MAY:

1st:

Company Sergeant Major: (1925) H.Bull.
Private: (1959) S.J.Elphick.

2nd:

Second Lieutenant: (2099) W.E.Price.

During the evening of the 8th May the Battalion moved up and into trenches beside the road known as Rue du Bois at Richebourg L'Avoué . At 4.00am the following morning, the fateful day of the 9th, a heavy allied bombardment opened on the enemy barbed wire, parapets and buildings in the rear. Events were to prove that this bombardment failed the waiting infantry in its weight, concentration and accuracy.

In the first line of attack were the 2nd Royal Sussex on the left and the 1st Northamptons on the right. Behind them in the second line were, to the left, the 5th Royal Sussex and, to the right, the 2nd Kings Royal Rifle Corps. Farther back, in the third line, were the 1st Loyal North Lancs and the 9th Kings Liverpools. The first line went over the top to attack a stretch of German trenches and nearby buildings. The aim of the second line, which included the 5th Battalion, was to follow immediately behind the assaulting wave, to clear hostile trenches left in rear of the attacking troops, to secure and send back prisoners and then to dig in to make a strong point.

Following, as planned, behind the 2nd Royal Sussex, the 5th (Cinque Ports) troops had

to cross about 250 yards of open No-Man's-Land. The enemy had already opened heavy rifle, machine gun and shell fire and many men were killed during this initial advance. The first attacking wave was already held up by intensive fire particularly from the left flank. It was quickly realised that to continue across such flat, open ground against well prepared defensive positions was suicidal, and it was to their credit that Battalion platoon commanders sensibly called a halt. Unfortunately it was too late to stop 'C' Company from attempting to advance farther and very heavy casualties were sustained to no avail. (See Sketch Map 7).

At 7.00am orders to retire were received and Sergeant Roberts bravely went out three times to the firing line with messages. Those men who were able came back from the open ground to some form of protection, many of them wounded. Incredibly, orders were received that the Battalion should collect its available men and be ready to continue the attack in the afternoon. At this point it was realised that some nine officers and 230 other ranks were already killed, wounded or missing.

Senior commanders, including French and Rawlinson, either had not appreciated, or chose to ignore, the seriousness and hopelessness of the situation. The result was that the futile attack was re-launched at 4.30pm. This time, although a few men from the Black Watch, the 2nd and 5th Royal Sussex got into the enemy's front line trench, very few got back and the attack inevitably failed as it had done earlier in the day. Not until 6.00pm did the Battalion receive orders to march back to Le Touret. Ironically, it was to be at that spot after the war that the attractive and colonnaded Le Touret Memorial would be erected to bear the inscribed names of so many Royal Sussex men who perished during the one-day Battle of Aubers Ridge. So many men have no known graves because it was impossible to bring in bodies over such open bullet-swept terrain.

This 9th May,1915, had brought what was to be the highest number of casualties for a single day suffered by the Battalion throughout the whole of its time on the Western Front. Amongst the killings, two poignant family tragedies were wrought when two sets of brothers, Albert and William Hawkins, and Arthur and George Pilbeam, all of whom were Privates who had enlisted at Wadhurst, Sussex, were killed in this action; not one of the four has a known grave and all four names appear on the Le Touret Memorial. Such events, and the loss of so many lives in total, bring into unfavourable focus the official history which later described the day mildly as 'a serious disappointment'. The men who fought through the disaster called Aubers Ridge would, no doubt, have found more colourful and accurate language with which to describe the events and the Senior Commanders responsible for the debacle.

MAY:
9th:
Captains: (1985) F.N.Grant, (2135) T.A.Stewart-Jones.
Second Lieutenants: (1951) R.E.McK.Dennison, (1962) R.Fazan, (2097) R.H.Powell.
Sergeants: (1892) R.Balcombe, (1916) A.E.Bovis, (2065) A.G.Moore, (2070) W.J.Neve, (2109) F.Robinson.
Corporal: (2105) T.Riches.
Lance Corporals: (1946) C.B.Croft, (2040) G.G.R.Laughton, (2087) G.E.Peel, (2113) F.Saunders.
Privates: (1878) A.J.Akehurst, (1882) G.Allen, (1884) C.J.Andrew, (1885) A.E.Anscombe, (1887) H.W.Avard, (1890) G.Baker, (1893) S.J.Baldwin, (1897) A.C.Barrow, (1901) A.Beale, (1902) E.Beney, (1909) C.E.Bissenden, (1912) A.J.Blagrove, (1917) F.O.Brazier, (1919) H.H.Breach, (1921) A.Britt, (1922) R.H.Brooks, (1928) M.L.Carley, (1931) A.H.Chandler, (1934) S.Clouting, (1940) G.Cornwall, (1942) G.L.Cox, (1950) A.Dence, (1952) F.H.Develin, (1957) R.F.Edwards, (1958) H.J.Ellis, (1964) G.Fillery, (1973) C.E.Gander, (1979) J.O.Gladman, (1980) H.E.Goldsmith, (1989) R.Griffin, (1990) W.T.Griffiths, (1997) S.H.Harmer, (2000) A.Hawkins, (2001) W.Hawkins, (2002) L.Haydon, (2004) W.H.A.Hazelden, (2017) G.Huggett, (2026) G.E.Johnson, (2028) W.L.Judge, (2029) H.L.Kendall, (2031) G.A.Kenward, (2035) H.W.Lancaster, (2037) A.T.Langridge, (2048) C.Mankelow, (2050) H.V.Mann, (2056) H.D.Marriott, (2061) E.Message, (2064) A.Moore, (2074) S.A.Oliver, (2089) A.J.Pilbeam, (2090) G.H.Pilbeam, (2094) E.B.Poole, (2095) H.J.Pope, (2108) E.Riglesford, (2110) E.W.Russell, (2117)

A.C.Shanks, (2118) J.H.Shepherd, (2121) R.T.Simmonds, (2132) W.Stedman, (2134) A.Stevens, (2136) T.Stone, (2156) G.Turner, (2159) W.Vidler, (2164) G.Waller, (2165) H.Wallis, (2166) T.G.Wells, (2177) C.E.Woods, (2179) H.W.Wright, (2181) W.J.Wright.
Bugler: (1970) H.G.Funnell.

At Le Touret, amongst motley crowds of men from many other Units back from the shambles of the battle, the Battalion was ordered onwards and rearwards through Avelette to rest billets at Gonneham. Next day, a further march brought the weary men to billets at the Chocolate Factory in Rue de Lille, Béthune. There they stayed in Corps, then Brigade, Reserve until several days later when they moved to a position just south of Cuinchy.

MAY:
10th:
Sergeant: (1896) J.H.Barrett.
Corporal: (1981) P.Goodsell.
11th:
Privates: (1894) A.L.Barker, (2025) F.H.Jarrett, (2093) A.Poole.
12th:
Private: (1955) P.J.Dudeney.
17th:
Lance Sergeant: (2143) E.A.Sweetman.
Privates: (1961) T.F.Farrier, (1977) W.Gibbs.
Drummer: (2151) J.Thorpe.
MAY:
18th:
Private: (2163) R.D.Walder.
19th:
Captain: (2012) A.A.Holmes.
24th:
Privates: (2005) J.T.W.Hicks, (2075) A.V.Osborne.

It was from Cuinchy by the end of May that, as a result of their experiences, Captains Dawes and Lloyd were sent to hospital suffering from 'nervous breakdowns', and what remained of the Battalion was warned again for the firing line. At 31st May the Battalion's total strength was a mere 566 of which only 6 officers and 360 men were fit for front line active duty.

The 1st Northamptons were relieved from the line between Cuinchy and the Béthune – La Bassée canal on the 1st June. There, the Battalion's line was quiet but two German mines were blown to the right while a heavy enemy bombardment fell on the left.

Following relief on the 4th June, the men marched back to billets in Labeuvrière where they arrived, thankfully, at 11.00pm. At a parade on the 8th, the General Officer Commanding 1st Corps spoke well of the Battalion's efforts. 'Rest', including route marches, outpost work, wood fighting, field fighting and ceremonial parades for disciplinary training continued until the 16th when a move was made to bivouac in Le Quesnoy

Wood. After three more days, various billets at Verquin, Allouagne and Verquigneul were used until the end of June.

JUNE:
8th:
Lance Corporal: (1880) H.E.Alce.
16th:
Private: (1898) F.Bartlett.

CHAPTER 12
1915
JULY – DECEMBER

Having been in billets at Verquigneul for the first week of July, the whole Battalion moved into the front line on the 7th to take over the Cambrin sector. Sporadic activity but no attacks took place during this tour of duty. Relief and a move to billets at Verquin were effected on the 13th.

JULY:
8th:
Privates: (1996) A.Harmer, (2112) A.Sales, (2119) E.B.Shoesmith, (2139) F.G.Stubberfield.
12th:
Private: (1932) F.J.A.Chapman.
16th:
Drummer: (2092) W.E.Plester.

On the 19th July the Vermelles sector of front line was taken over and, although day and night working parties were active, no casualties were sustained there before a move out to Labourse billets on the 25th. For three nights from the 27th July digging took place to provide a trench 400 yards long to connect two existing systems. The last day of the month brought a move out of the line in order to commence work completing and extending a new camp called 'Garden City'.

JULY:
27th:
—: (2128) J.Smith.
28th:
Privates: (2007) P.E.Hoad, (2041) W.J.Lavender.

Throughout the first week of August work continued on 'Garden City' camp. Roads were made and drains laid. Also, buildings for the Orderly Room and Officers' Quarters were erected; even a swimming pool was dug.

AUGUST:
5th:
Private: (2125) C.Smith.

Sailly-la-Bourse was the march destination on the 6th August. There, the Control Post orders and arrangements were found to be chaotic and it was necessary to re-organise them as a matter of urgency in order to relieve the roadway congestion for traffic heading for Vermelles and Mazingarbe.

On the 8th August the Battalion returned to the front line trenches and, on the 12th, took part in an intensive machine-gun barrage on enemy positions at Haisnes, some 3,100 yards distant, and on trenches near Cuinchy, a distance of 1,800 yards. During the afternoon, following removal of the machine-gun team, the spot was heavily and accurately shelled by the Germans who had evidently taken cross-bearings earlier in the day. A new type of 4.2 inch German shrapnel shell with double explosion was used but Battalion personnel were by this time at a safe distance and no casualties were sustained. Later that day the Battalion marched slowly and wearily to billets in Annequin.

On the 17th August, while working parties were digging a new support trench in the second line defences at Cambrin, orders were received warning the Battalion to make ready to entrain. The following day a march was made to Fouquereuil where, on the 19th August, a full parade was held at which the Battalion was inspected by the General Officer Commanding 1st Division and the General Officer Commanding the 2nd Infantry Brigade. The Battalion was congratulated on its performance over the past six months. Now, however, there was to be a major change: the 5th (Cinque Ports) Battalion The Royal Sussex Regiment would henceforth be transferred to become a Pioneer Battalion.

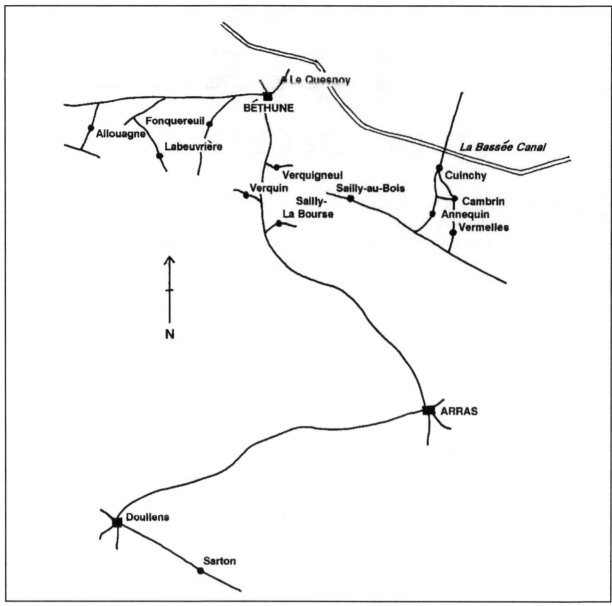

28.   *June to August 1915*

True it is that, over a good many weeks past, much of the work assigned to the Battalion had been of a pioneering nature. Trench digging, road repairing and camp construction had formed the major part of duties. Whether that had been a deliberate move to accustom the Battalion to pioneering tasks or whether the competent performance of such duties had resulted in the Battalion being chosen to be pioneers is a matter for conjecture.. The result, however, was that the Battalion would no longer be first and foremost an infantry unit. Its primary task now would be one of hard labour in support of engineers and the fighting units although its men would still be expected to take up front line fighting positions at times of crisis.

On Friday 20th August the Battalion entrained at Fouquereuil in the afternoon and, after a journey of six hours, came to the town of Doullens north-west from the area of the Somme battlefields. An immediate march was made through the night to Sarton which was reached at 1.00am on the 21st. At this point it was made known that attachment to the 48th (South Midland) Division as its Pioneer Battalion was to take immediate effect.

Over the next five days, marches were made to Louvencourt, from where working parties were provided to Bois de Marnimont near Authie, and then on to Sailly-au-Bois where Headquarters was established. Parties of men were then set to work daily on a second trench line from the Mill at Colincamps to a point north of the Château de la Haie and also on the Sailly-au-Bois village defences. It was at Sailly-au-Bois that the Battalion was to make its base for several months to come.

At the beginning of September the Battalion was given charge of all pioneering tasks in the Sailly-au-Bois area, about 12 miles of trench work altogether. As a result of good work done, the Battalion was given a two day rest starting on the 19th September. Sailly-au-Bois was lightly shelled by the enemy on the 21st and Private Blackman was killed.

SEPTEMBER:
21st:
Private: (1910) H.W.Blackman.

For a period of four days at the end of September, the Battalion was moved into the front line to gain knowledge of the positions in case of enemy attack. During this period a general clearing and tidying up of trench stores and equipment was undertaken.

October brought work for the Battalion on several nearby 'forts' with associated barbed wire defences, trenches and underground

accommodation for up to 50 men. On the 8th October a combined canteen and institute for use by all units was opened and welcomed at Sailly-au-Bois. This venture immediately gained the support of the men and did much to raise morale.

OCTOBER:
9th:
Private: (2086) H.J.Payne.
10th:
Private: (2057) R.Marshall.
16th:
Private: (2137) A.J.Strange.

On the 17th October Sailly-au-Bois was heavily shelled from the direction of Serre by the Germans using 4.2 and 5.9 inch high explosive and incendiary shells. One house was set alight and a number of casualties sustained, none of which was fatal.

Work on the 'forts' and related defences continued until month's end by which time almost all was completed.

OCTOBER:
24th:
Corporal: (2127) H.Smith.

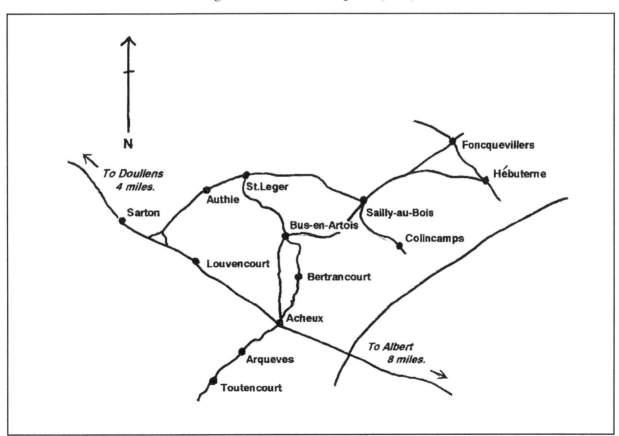

29.   *August 1915 to June 1916*

During the month of November the weather became most inhospitable. Because working conditions became so bad following heavy rain, relief from the heavy work was organised every eight hours. Wintery weather on the 15th made it necessary for the men to be employed clearing snow from the trenches and from the roads around Sailly-au-Bois. A draft of 40 other ranks was received on the 22nd and the new men soon received their 'baptism of fire' when incendiary shells were fired into, and around, the village on the 26th.

The winter weather continued through December, and Sailly-au-Bois was subjected to enemy shelling on several days, fortunately without casualties. Trench boards had to be laid over open ground because everywhere was so muddy and all movement difficult. A drainage gulley had to be dug from one trench which was holding about four feet of water and was collapsing seriously from the sides.

On the 20th December news of the Battalion's next major task was received. This was to erect 10 corrugated iron shelters and about 100 steel casemates in a trench west of Hébuterne and Fonquevillers. Work commenced but proved very difficult and demanding because the ground was so heavy, the available space cramped and the area frequently under enemy fire.

There was little comfort on Christmas Day especially when Sailly-au-Bois was subjected to heavy German fire over a one hour period during which about 200 shells rained down. No Battalion casualties were sustained but, close by, the Royal Garrison Artillery had three men and five horses killed on this day of 'Peace and Goodwill to Men'.

CHAPTER 13
1916
JANUARY – JUNE

On the very first day of this New Year the Battalion's stores area was heavily bombarded for a short period during the afternoon. Approximately, some 60 shells fell causing some damage and injuring two men one of whom, Private Palmer, died of his wounds.

JANUARY:
2nd:
Private: (2080) S.E.Palmer.
5th:
Private: (2049) C.Manktelow.

Battalion Headquarters and two Companies moved to Authie and St.Léger-les-Authie on the 6th January, the remainder staying at Sailly-au-Bois. Heartening news was received on the 15th that Captain Fazan had been awarded the Military Cross and that Quartermaster Sergeant Roberts and Private Weston had received the D.C.M.

By the end of January four Lewis Guns had been received together with reinforcements of 50 men. The erection of 18 casemates had been completed and work had commenced on site digging and collecting materials for others.

During February, road works were taken over in the vicinity of Toutencourt and Arqueves. Then, moves to start similar work behind the forward areas in and around Bértrancourt and Souastre were made. On the 10th, Lieutenant Bingen was killed instantly by the explosion of a 5.9" shell in the trench where he was superintending work.

FEBRUARY:
10th:
Lieutenant: (1906) C.A.M.Bingen.
12th:
Private: (2027) A.Joy.

During the latter half of February a move was made to the areas of Souastre and Bértrancourt so that work could be carried on behind the Divisional front lines. For a time on the 29th, it became necessary for the men to garrision the Southern Keep at Foncquevillers ('Funky Villas' to the troops) because of an expected attack. However, work continued and there was no pressure from the enemy. By this time, the Battalion's strength was reduced to 31 officers and 747 other ranks; a new draft of 250 men was urgently needed so that all necessary work could continue on schedule.

A number of moves were made, sometimes by single or twin Companies, during March. 'D' Company went from Bértrancourt to Bus-en-Artois and then back to Sailly-au-Bois. 'C' Company moved to Bayencourt from Souastre and 'A' Company relieved 'B' Company in the Keep at Hébuterne. On the 21st March the Battalion was even given a portion of the front line to hold with the help of two Lewis Guns. Two days later a heavy German bombardment killed Private Raven and wounded seven other men.

MARCH:
23rd:
Private: (2101) W.G.Raven.

Again, as April came, the Battalion was seldom in one place for long, although they remained in the same area. General pioneering and front line trench work was undertaken. On the 10th April Second Lieutenant Adams and 45 men were sent off for a spell to dig emplacements at the Army Trench Mortar School at Valheureux. Some men were sent out to fell and cut timber; others manned the Hébuterne Keep. A welcome draft of 22 men arrived from Base on the 22nd.

APRIL:
13th:
Private: (2010) J.Hodges.
14th:
Private: (2079) J.Palmer.

A gradual local withdrawal into training with the Royal Engineers was effected during May. Under expert guidance, useful knowledge was gained in the construction of pontoons, rafts and trestle bridges. Two more drafts totalling 118 men brought Battalion strength back to a respectable level of 32 officers and 908 other ranks by the end of this month.

The month of June, 1916, saw a major build-up in the strength of the Battalion as may have been expected as the launch of the great Somme Offensive approached. Although now not a 'pure' infantry Battalion, the 5th Royal Sussex would have much hard work of maintenance and repair to do once the battle started. The Battalion was augmented by 147 new men drafted in, and 35 more rejoined from other places.

Even so, the Battalion's available strength was no more than required. Throughout the month, continuous heavy work, particularly in conjunction with Corps Signallers who were laying and burying communication cables in readiness for the big offensive, continued day and night. Often, the men worked non-stop for up to 14 hours soaked to the skin by the heavy rain, exhausted by the muddy conditions and frequently under enemy fire.

The heavy and continuous pre-Somme bombardment set up by the allies was responded to by the Germans using 'Percy', a 5.11inch naval gun, which shelled the Battalion's bivouac area near Sailly-au-Bois on the 27th killing Company Sergeant Major Hart, Private Fletcher and injuring others.

JUNE:
27th:
Company Sergeant Major: (1998) W.J.Hart.
Private: (1965) T.S.Fletcher.
28th:
Private: (1915) A.G.Botting.
29th:
Privates: (1920) T.Brett, (2018) P.S.Huggett, (2157) A.C.Twitchett.

On the 30th June orders were received to prepare to move forward next day into Corps Reserve for the ensuing major operations.

CHAPTER 14
1916
JULY – DECEMBER

On fateful Saturday 1st July, 1916, the first day of the Battle of the Somme, the Battalion marched from Sailly-au-Bois to bivouac in a wood to the south-west of the village of Mailly-Maillet, there to form part of Corps Reserve and be ready to fight as infantry if necessary. Already, this summer's day was hot and dusty as the march proceeded with the clear sounds of thunderous artillery and small arms fire coming from the battleground only some two miles distant from Mailly-Maillet.

Mercifully, being held in Reserve, the 5th Battalion, the only Royal Sussex Battalion, save the 7th Battalion, to be on the Somme at that time, was spared the horror of that first day of slaughter. The Battalion's 'parent' 48th (South Midland) Division faired badly, however, on this 'The Blackest Day in the History of the British Army'. The Divisional attack between Beaumont Hamel and the River Ancre failed miserably against strongly fortified German defences and the Division suffered 1,060 men killed.

On Sunday 2nd July the Battalion was ordered forward to support an attack on German trenches between Beaumont Hamel and the River Ancre. Fortunately, this attack was cancelled at the last moment, even as Battalion men waited in the front line trenches.

No doubt it was because the expected Somme breakthrough had not materialised that the Battalion moved back to Sailly-au-Bois on the 3rd July. At this point, the intended use of the Battalion as a temporary infantry Unit was abandoned and, on the 4th, a return to pioneering duties was effected. This involved sending 600 men to Mailly-Maillet from where they moved out to commence digging a long and traversed trench line right down towards the River Ancre from where the 5th Battalion Monmouthshire

Regiment pioneers would start digging from the opposite direction. In all probability this was to be the communication trench which was to become well known as 'Jacob's Ladder' and would be used significantly later by the 11th, 12th and 13th Battalions The Royal Sussex Regiment. 'Jacob's Ladder' stretched from the direction of Englebelmer and Mesnil down to the village of Hamel on the River Ancre and was so steep in places that flights of steps had to be cut.

This work was completed by mid-July, much of the time under heavy fire during which casualties were sustained and the officers and men showed great coolness and gallantry in continuing their tasks.

JULY:
6th:
Privates: (2042) W.Leeves, (2115) G.Scott, (2178) A.E.Wright.
7th:
Privates: (1937) D.Coleman, (2158) R.W.Vidler.
12th:
Privates: (2131) W.Starnes, (2170) F.A.Wettle.
13th:
Private: (1971) W.Funnell.
14th:
Private: (2107) H.J.Riddle.

The Battalion moved, on the 15th July, to billets in Bouzincourt where, below many of the houses, were cellars giving good protection from the occasional enemy shelling. From there during the late afternoon a detachment was sent to 'Crucifix Corner', just across the River Ancre and east of the village of Aveluy, in order to deepen a new communication trench towards the enemy front line. The remainder of the Battalion moved in the evening through the town of Albert and out on the approach to the battlefield. There, they positioned themselves at the roadside ready

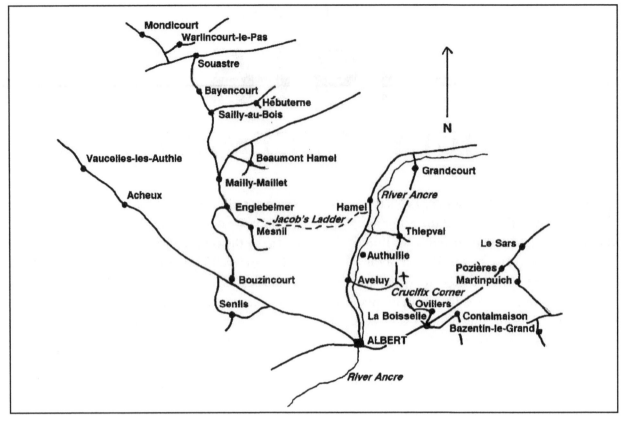

30.   *July to December 1916*

to assist in any consolidating work that might become necessary. After a wait and inaction which lasted a whole day and night, a move back to billets in Albert was ordered.

For the remainder of July much trench work was undertaken in the areas around Albert, which were behind the battlefield eastward advances made by allied Units. Trenches were deepened and barbed wire was set out around the destroyed villages of La Boisselle, Ovillers and Aveluy. Enemy shelling was still experienced and casualties were sustained. Second Lieutenant Symons was killed in his dugout close to 'Crucifix Corner' on the 18th and, four days later, Second Lieutenant L. Blunden was killed while with a working party.

JULY:
18th:
Second Lieutenant: (2144) J.A.Symons.
19th:
Private: (1986) E.Grantham.
22nd:
Second Lieutenant: (1914) L.Blunden.
23rd:
Private: (2084) E.Parks.
24th:
Private: (2044) H.W.Lester.

26th:
Private: (2126) E.G.Smith.

Work was interrupted by a gas shell attack on the 26th July and then, on the 29th, after an early morning march to Bouzincourt, relief and rest came by way of a journey by buses back some 35 miles to Domqueur.

JULY:
28th:
Private: (2016) F.W.Howell.
31st:
Private: (1900) S.F.Bateup.

Of the 10 days rest allotted, two days were taken up receiving Royal Engineers' instruction on bridging techniques. A return journey, again by buses, brought the Battalion to the familiar areas of Aveluy and Bouzincourt on the 8th August. By this time, the fighting had moved on from Ovillers and it was in, and around, the rubble of that former village that work was carried out over a number of days and nights to improve trenches, construct dugouts and improve barbed wire defences. By mid-August maintenance of Tramways in and around Albert were taken over together with management of the Tram Depot and the care of mules.

AUGUST:
9th:
Second Lieutenant: (1881) G.H.Alington.
Private: (1968) E.Fuller.

On the 15th August began a period of 10 hectic days during which much work was carried out under shell fire, sometimes so heavy that tasks had to be curtailed and the men withdrawn. Inevitably casualties increased in proportion to the severity of the situation. Despite this, a number of dugouts were constructed between the villages of Ovillers and Pozières, also in front of the German fortress at Thiepval. On the 21st, Battalion Lewis Guns were sent out and, in covering the 6th Glosters, very effective fire was brought to bear which broke up an enemy counter attack. Men of the Battalion assisted in carrying up many bombs and themselves taking part in bombing forays. The Lewis Guns of 'B' and 'C' Companies were eventually relieved on the 22nd and those of 'A' and 'D' Companies on the 24th; they had all done good work.

AUGUST:
15th:
Private: (2014) A.Horsecroft.
16th:
Privates: (1903) F.Benham, (1954) J.E.Drury, (2030) W.E.Kent, (2047) C.Mackellow, (2060) H.R.Martin, (2111) J.T.Russell, (2149) A.E.Tester, (2153) R.C.Trimmer.
17th:
Private: (2077) W.H.Page.
18th:
Privates: (2021) A.Hyland, (2100) A.F.Ransome.
19th:
Privates: (1963) T.W.Field, (2072) L.O'Beirne.
21st:
Sergeant: (1883) B.G.Anderson.
Private: (2076) R.F.Page.
24th:
Private: (2168) J.E.West.

By the end of August the Battalion had marched a long distance back to Vauchelles-les-Authie for a well-earned rest.

AUGUST:
31st:
Private: (1941) H.C.Cowley.

The 'rest' with which the month of September began was interrupted by daily training in Companies and groups of men detailed for specific purposes. During the night of the 15th, buses took the Battalion to Senlis where they arrived the following morning and marched on down into the Ancre Valley, crossed the river and arrived on the eastern side of the village of Aveluy. From there they moved out across the 1st July front line where they worked on a tramway which ran across the torn battlefield from Ovillers to Pozières a distance of about three-quarters of a mile.

SEPTEMBER:
4th:
Privates: (2114) O.Saunders, (2155) G.E.Turk.
5th:
Private: (2120) F.H.W.Shoesmith.
16th:
Lance Corporal: (1879) W.C.Akehurst.
Privates: (1877) H.J.Adams, (2039) P.Larkin.

On the 22nd September work was taken over from the Battalion's sister pioneers, the 8th Royal Sussex on a light railway which also ran from Ovillers to Pozières. In addition, work was carried out on a tramway from its sidings at Aveluy, and work was commenced on a trestle bridge on, or close to, the River Ancre.

SEPTEMBER:
23rd:
Private: (1984) R.J.Grabham.

The Thiepval fortress, including its formidable Schwarben Redoubt, which had denied capture since the first British attempt on 1st July, was finally taken on 26th September. The very next day, the Battalion was helping to construct a road from Pozières to Grandcourt by way of the newly-taken Thiepval area. A march out of the battlefields took place on the 29th September for an over-night stay in huts at Acheux before moving on, next day, to Bayencourt.

SEPTEMBER:
29th:
Private: (1982) T.J.Goodsell.

Souastre was the destination on the 1st October. From there, over the next two to three weeks, much trench work was carried out in the Hébuterne area.

OCTOBER:
8th:
Private: (1924) E.O.Bull.

9th:
Private: (2180) J.L.Wright.
19th:
Private: (2023) A.J.Jarrett.

The Battalion marched to huts at Warlincourt-les-Pas on the 20th October, and stayed there for five days before being taken by buses on a circuitous journey via Doullens and Amiens arriving, eventually, at Albert. From there, fifty men were put to work on a light railway at Contalmaison under direction of the 7th Field Company Royal Engineers. The Battalion moved to Bazentin-le-Grand Wood on the 28th October only to find that their bivouac camp had been cut through by a newly-laid light railway. Wood cutting and the laying of wooden 'corduroy' roads in the vicinity of Bazentin, Martinpuich and Le Sars were the main duties continued until the end of the month.

By the beginning of November the allies had pushed the Germans back eastwards a distance of four miles or so and the Battalion had followed-up behind the front line advance roughly in the direction of Bapaume. From the Battalion's base in Bazentin-le-Petit Wood there was much pioneering work of a varied nature to be done to consolidate the positions behind the front line and to improve the lines of communication so that men, supplies and materials could be more easily moved over the devastated battlefield areas. The weather had broken during this month and operations took place in awful conditions of rain, cold and heavy clinging mud. Every move across country was exhausting and slow. German observation of the area was still good with the result that artillery fire was frequently brought to bear on the allies. The Battalion received its share of shelling and casualties were fairly high.

Work consisted of constructing roads of brick rubble through the destroyed village of Martinpuich and the laying of a tramway track. Construction began nearby of a hutted camp consisting of 28 huts, roadways, trenchboarding, canteen, soup kitchen, cooker shelters, stores, tool sheds, stable, horse standings, ablution and latrine facilities. The work continued by day and night until the end of the month. The Battle of the

Somme had officially ended on 20th November but sporadic fighting, skirmishing and artillery duels continued.

NOVEMBER:
8th:
Privates: (2022) A.E.Ives, (2146) L.W.Taylor.
11th:
Private: (2053) W.H.March.
14th:
Lieutenant: (2173) A.B.Wilkinson.
Second Lieutenant: (1891) W.G.Baker.
Lance Sergeant: (1948) J.L.Dash.
Corporal: (2059) E.W.Martin.
Lance Corporal: (2106) F.Rickard.
Privates: (1918) J.H.Brazil, (1967) A.Ford, (1976) H.Garton, (2043) A.E.G.Leggatt, (2063) G.H.Miller, (2091) H.M.Piper, (2116) R.J.Seddon, (2123) G.Slarks, (2154) E.R.Tucker, (2171) W.Whillock.
16th:
Private: (2073) A.Oliver.

At the beginning of December the Battalion was still camped in Bazentin-le-Petit Wood. Gangs were sent out from there to do road works in the devastated battlefield triangle area between the destroyed villages of Contalmaison, Bazentin-le-Petit and Martinpuich, with dugouts also being constructed near the latter village.
DECEMBER:
3rd:
Second Lieutenant: (2009) J.C.A.Hobart.
5th:
Private: (2081) C.Panter.

By the end of the month of December much work had been completed in the construction of three new camps for use by the troops during the winter that was almost upon the army. Two Company Headqaurters, 23 Amiens Huts, 12 Nissen Huts, stores, cooker shelters, orderlies' quarters, bath house, stables, tailors' shop, armourers' shop, pioneers' shop and bootmakers' shop had been erected. Trench-board tracks had been laid and ablution and latrine blocks built. As the dreadful year of 1916 came to a close, the health of the men was generally much improved as a result of foot care and a rest from constant night work. The Battalion's War Diary makes no mention of Christmas or attempts at related festivities.

CHAPTER 15
1917
JANUARY – NOVEMBER

On New Year's Day the men were very happy to learn that their camp in Bazentin-le-Grand Wood was to be known officially as 'Cinque Ports Camp'. By mid-month work allotted to the Battalion on construction of various other camps had been completed. There was some regret on the 15th January when the very clean and sanitary 'Cinque Ports Camp' was handed over to the 15th Division.

The Battalion was formally inspected by the General Officer Commanding 48th Division on the 27th January. He complimented everyone for the splendid and arduous work carried out over the past three months and praised the way that 'Cinque Ports Camp' had been planned, constructed and left in such an exemplary condition. On the 28th January the Battalion arrived at Cérisy-sur-Somme to relieve the 152nd French Division which had been in position in front of the town of Péronne.

On the 1st February, 'C' Company moved up to dugouts north of Hérbecourt and, on the following day, 'A' and 'B' Companies marched to Froissy. The weather was very hard at this time, temperatures falling to 30 degrees Fahrenheit (16 degrees Centigrade) below freezing. Work consisted of maintaining considerable lengths of communication trenches and signal lines, laying trench board tracks, constructing dugouts and trench mortar emplacements. A thaw at the end of February after six weeks of heavy frost made conditions and work very difficult and heavy.

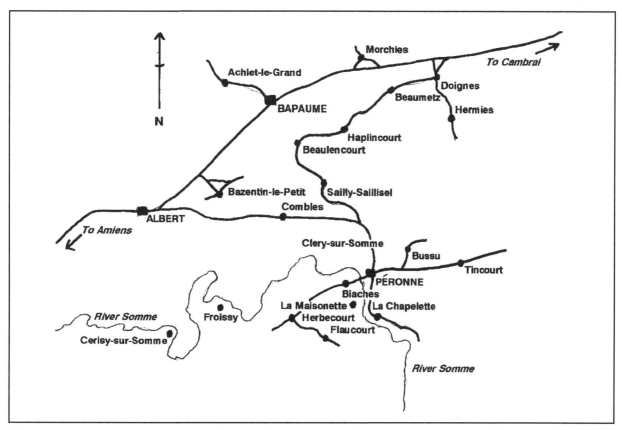

31.

FEBRUARY:
7th:
Private: (1953) C.Dray.
26th:
Private: (2172) W.J.White.

March, with its improving weather conditions, was spent almost exclusively on road works in the areas around Hérbecourt, Flaucourt, Biaches, Péronne, Tincourt and Bussu. However, for a few days, 'B' Company worked on a 24 inch gauge tramway from Flaucourt. It was noted that the enemy had evacuated areas to the front; this was as a result of the general German withdrawal eastwards some 25 miles to the newly-constructed and fortified Hindenburg Line.

MARCH:
1st:
Privates: (1969) E.D.Funnell, (1999) A.B.Haselgrove.
10th:
Private: (1899) C.E.Bates.

As a result of a short move during early April, the Battalion settled in and around Tincourt. Work continued on many roads in the forward areas. In addition, the filling in of numerous craters, the digging of strong points and communication trenches, and the erection of barbed wire entanglements were tasks for the month.

APRIL:
25th:
Lance Corporal: (1944) V.T.Crawford.
Private: (2058) A.Martin.

Selected men from the Battalion had been working continuously for three months as Scouts for the 48th Division; on the 7th May they were withdrawn to Flammicourt for rest and training. For the remainder of the Battalion, work ceased on the 11th May after 15 consecutive all-night sessions. Over the next few days moves were made to the area around Péronne. On the 15th, a march was made to Combles by way of Clery and the following day to Haplincourt by way of Sailly-Saillisel.

By the end of May two officers and 87 other ranks re-joined from secondment to Corps Light Railway Companies. Battalion strength was then 39 officers and 1040 other ranks. There were no fatal casualties this month.

June, 1917, was to prove the last month to be spent by the Battalion in the area of the Somme battlefields. General pioneering and labouring duties continued around Haplincourt, Morchies and Beaumetz. On the 28th June the Battalion was warned to make ready to move back north into Belgium.

JUNE:
12th:
Private: (1991) J.T.Groombridge.

On the 3rd July the Battalion was relieved and its duties taken over by the 20th Kings Royal Rifle Corps, Pioneer battalion to the 3rd Division. At an inspection the following day, the General Officer Commanding 48th Division expressed his satisfaction of all the work done.

By train on the 5th July the Battalion travelled north to Hoputre then marched to spend two days in bivouac at Costhuer. There, the enemy provided a 'welcome' back to Belgium with a heavy bombardment which killed five men.

JULY:
7th:
Lance Corporal: (2011) W.G.Hollebon.
Privates: (1923) F.J.Brown, (2038) F.H.Langridge, (2067) H.J.Morris, (2088) W.G.Phillips.

Billets at Poperinghe provided relative luxury for a one night stay before movement, on the 9th July, to Camp 'Z' at St.Jan-ter-Biezen two miles westward. Clearly, the Battalion had been brought north to assist with preparations for the planned and forthcoming Third Battle of Ypres, otherwise known as Passchendaele. Officers soon went forward to make a reconnaissance of advanced work areas, and construction of a light railway and causeway began immediately.

'B' and 'C' Companies were badly gassed while working along the canal bank during the 25th July and had to move back to Peselhoek but there were no fatalities. On the 30th, a general move rearwards was made to bivouac near Vlamertinghe but, even there, some gassing was experienced during the night. In fact about 100 men with gas symptoms were admitted to hospital during the month.

JULY:
29th:
Privates: (2015) A.E.Horton, (2034) J.W.Laker.

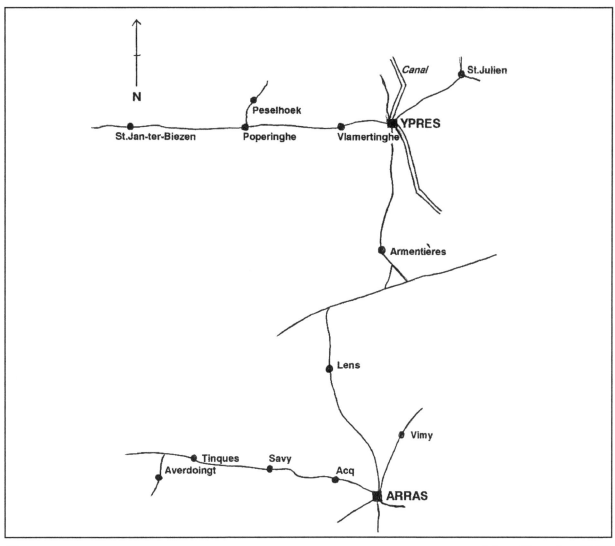

32.   *July to November 1917*

The Third Battle of Ypres opened on 31st July and the Battalion moved out at 2.45am for what was to be a long and hard day's work keeping roads open for the movement of traffic, mainly guns. Efforts were successful and made possible the vital forward passage of 60 pounder guns, howitzers, field guns, wagons and pack transport.

For a pioneer battalion not normally required for front line fighting, casualties became relatively heavy during August. Road maintenance of all kinds continued to be essential for the first half of the month. In addition, the laying began of one of the 'corduroy' tracks which were to become the only means of any purposeful movement over the quagmire of the battlefield.

AUGUST:
2nd:
Privates: (1908) H.G.Bishop, (1933) F.W.T.Churcher.
7th:
Privates: (1888) W.H.Axell, (1911) J.S.G.Blackman.

Pressure was such on the 16th August that five platoons from the Battalion, under Captain C.R.Langham, were sent forward to assist the attacking troops by consolidating any gains as a result of a renewed offensive on enemy positions east of the Steenbeek, one of the drainage streams crossing the battlefield. Heavy enemy fire prevented any positive allied advance. The Battalion sustained casualties including Captain Langham and Second Lieutenant Green killed. Following the loss of these officers, Sergeant Cannon led the men to some small success by consolidating a slight rise known as Jew Hill.

AUGUST:
16th:
Captain: (2036) C.R.Langham.
Second Lieutenant: (1987) H.W.Green.
Lance Corporal: (2008) M.Hoare.
Privates: (1945) H.Creed, (1988) P.Griffen, (2045) I.Ling, (2138) J.Stratford.

17th:
Privates: (1895) O.Barnes, (2142) A.E.Sweetman.

Heavy and continuous work was carried on until the end of the month of August by which time the Battalion had been relieved and had moved back to bivouac east of Vlamertinghe. A trickle of casualties had continued and more men were affected by gas during the month. Reinforcements were badly needed, as overall strength had diminished, the equivalent of two platoons having practically disappeared.

AUGUST:
18th:
Private: (1995) W.Harman.
22nd:
Private: (2169) R.L.West.
23rd:
Private: (2006) A.Hill.
24th:
Corporal: (2019) H.J.Humphrey.
25th:
Lance Corporal: (2152) H.Tiltman.
Privates: (2104) P.Richards, (2167) W.H.Wenham.
26th:
Private: (2032) A.F.Kinnard.
28th:
Quartermaster Sergeant: (1876) R.H.Abraham.
29th:
Private: (2062) C.Miller.
31st:
Sergeant: (2020) F.Hunt.

Work continued on forward roads and shelters through September. Casualties were sustained from enemy shelling and air-raid bombing of the Battalion's base camp. A move to the west bank of the canal north of Ypres was made on the 26th. From there, work was done on roads around St.Julien. Only a few reinforcements were received during the month and overall strength continued to fall.

SEPTEMBER:
10th:
Privates: (1927) L.Cane, (1943) A.St.S.Cramp.
12th:
Sergeant: (1966) S.Foord.
15th:
Privates: (2055) H.Markie, (2082) T.A.Park, (2141) J.H.Sweatman, (2148) J.S.Teague, (2162) W.M.Wadey, (2176) J.Wood.
16th:
Private: (2130) J.W.Spice.

22nd:
Lance Corporal: (2147) S.Taylor.
Privates: (1889) C.Baker, (1907) A.Bishop, (2013) R.H.Horne, (2054) A.E.Marchant, (2066) A.Mordaunt.
23rd:
Private: (2133) H.S.Stephens.
SEPTEMBER:
24th:
Private: (2174) F.M.Wilmshurst.
26th:
Private: (2078) I.Paling.
27th:
Private: (1936) E.Cockerill.
30th:
Privates: (1938) T.Connolly, (2046) P.A.Lynch, (2124) A.Smith.

Throughout the first half of October work continued as before, mainly on roads. A move to 'Siege Camp' was made on the 10th and there, two days later, a single high explosive shell fell killing four and wounding 18 other ranks. These men were to be the last of the Battalion killed-in-action on the Western Front. The carnage on that occasion, including 47 horses killed and 12 wounded, was pitiful.

OCTOBER:
3rd:
Private: (2083) W.R.Parker.
4th:
Privates: (1905) A.J.Berry, (1992) A.V.Gurr, (2129) G.Spencer.
5th:
Private: (1935) H.Clover.
7th:
Private: (1947) J.Crouch.
12th:
Lance Corporal: (1904) W.Bennett.
Privates: (1960) C.W.Evenden, (1972) A.E.Furner, (2051) W.Manners, (2085) D.Parsons, (2103) T.W.Reed, (2161) B.Vine.

On Sunday 14th October the Battalion entrained at Peselhoek and travelled to Maroeil from where they marched to Acq just to the west of Arras. A camp north of Neuville St.Vaast was occupied on the 17th except by 'C' Company which took over dugouts west of Thélus. Work was done on trench-board tracking and concrete gun emplacements until month's end.

The 7th November saw the Battalion withdrawn to Headquarters and dugouts north

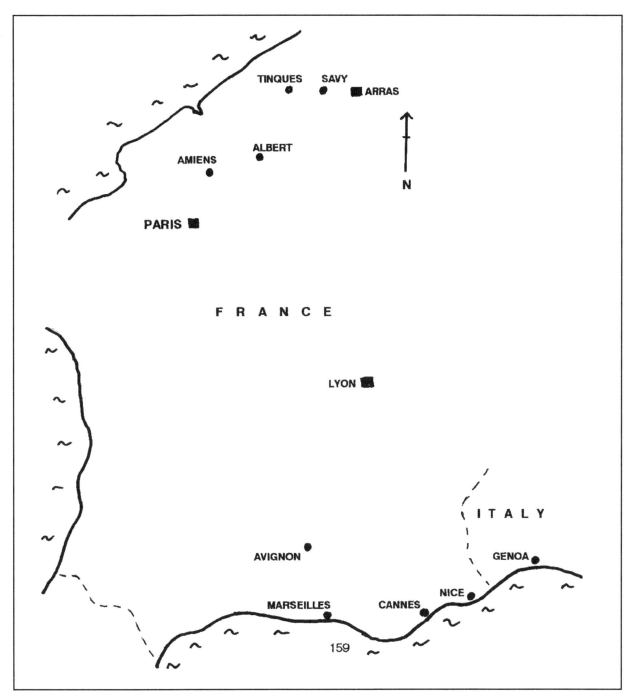

33.   *23rd to 29th November 1917*

of Vimy. Ten days later a march was made to
Averdoingt. Then, on the 23rd November, 1917,
Battalion Headquarters, together with 'A' and
'C' Companies entrained at Savy while 'B' and
'D' Companies entrained at Tinques. Amid
much rumour, speculation and excitement, the
whole Battalion was on the move headed for an
unknown destination.

NOVEMBER:
14th:
Lieutenant: (1949) A.R.Deane.

5th Battalion Epilogue

The Battalion then undertook an extraordinarily
long journey by train. Their route was, at first,
southward by way of Albert and Amiens to Paris.
There was great excitement for the men at seeing
the French capital but they had no time to enjoy
its attractions before they continued, south-east
this time, across central France to its second
city, Lyon, before turning south to Avignon and,
eventually, to Marseilles where they caught their
first glimpse of the Mediterranean.

Eastward, along the beautiful Côte d'Azure, the journey continued by way of Cannes and Nice before crossing the border into the country of their destination: Italy. It was, by then, 29th November; the journey from Vimy had taken no less than six days and nights.

The Battalion formed part of the British Expeditionary Force which, it had been decreed, was to be transferred to help stem the setbacks experienced by our allies in Italy. Splendid work continued to be done in the mountainous regions of Italy but the 5th Battalion, The Royal Sussex Regiment, had seen the last of The Western Front.

Although, for the most part, the Battalion had served behind the front lines as pioneers, the officers and men remembered with sadness that over 300 of their colleagues had been left behind in the war cemeteries of Belgium and France.

PART FOUR

The 7th (Service) Battalion ('New Army')

CHAPTER 16
1914
AUGUST – DECEMBER

Secretary of State for War, Lord Kitchener, quickly realised that, if ultimate success was to be achieved, Britain's relatively small regular army must be augmented by a massive recruitment of men into a 'New Army' which would be some months in training before it could be of use to the British Expeditionary Force. So early as 7th August, 1914, only three days after war was declared, Kitchener launched his famous nation-wide appeal for 'the first 100,000' volunteers.

The very next day, two specially picked officers and 15 N.C.O.'s left the regular army's 2nd Battalion The Royal Sussex Regiment stationed at Woking and travelled to Chichester to organise and set up The Royal Sussex Regiment's first 'New Army' battalion.

On 21st August the embryo Battalion transferred to Colchester where it was officially designated the '7th (Service) Battalion the Royal Sussex Regiment' and became part of the 36th Infantry Brigade belonging to the 12th (Eastern) Division. The 36th Infantry Brigade was made up as follows:

7th Royal Sussex
8th Royal Fusiliers
9th Royal Fusiliers
11th Middlesex

With the help of an appeal poster signed by senior officers, and as a result of several recruiting tours through Sussex using private motor cars lent by their enthusiastic owners, recruitment to the 7th Battalion began to gather pace. In particular, ex-regular officers and N.C.O.'s of the Royal Sussex Regiment were promised their previous rank if they re-joined. Many ex-personnel did re-join, bringing with them that much-needed leavening of invaluable experience into the fledgling Battalion.

Soon, there was a great inflow of recruits of whom the vast majority were Sussex men. Organisation and training continued apace until, on the 2nd October, the Battalion left Colchester by train for a well know Territorial Camp area at Shorncliffe near Folkestone in Kent. For a time, there remained a serious shortage of all types of equipment; in particular the number of useable rifles did not exceed 200 for any of the battalions, each of about 1,100 men, in the whole Brigade.

During November there was almost continual rain and a considerable amount of resulting sickness. Happily, arrangements were made, shortly before Christmas, for the whole Battalion to be billeted in Folkestone.

Recruiting Poster

7th SERVICE BATTALION
THE ROYAL SUSSEX REGIMENT

THIS BATTALION OF
LORD KITCHENER'S
SECOND EXPEDITIONARY FORCE OF
100,000

is forming at COLCHESTER, and is short of men.

Major W.L.OSBORN, Royal Sussex Regiment, who

is in Command,

APPEALS TO ALL SUSSEX MEN,

including EX-N.C.O's and SOLDIERS

TO COME FORWARD NOW, WITHOUT ANY DELAY,

To join the Battalion and

FILL THE RANKS WITH SUSSEX MEN

Who will sustain the honour of the Regiment Abroad.

The four Double Company Commanders are Captains

E.C.BEETON, J.L.SLEEMAN,
R.M.BIRKETT, G.H.IMPEY,

ROYAL SUSSEX REGIMENT.

Report at nearest Recruiting Office, and

INSIST ON SERVING IN THE 7th BATTALION
FOR THE PERIOD OF THE WAR.
GOD SAVE THE KING !

CHAPTER 17
1915
JANUARY – DECEMBER

Intensive and almost continuous training from the beginning of the year, together with the provision of more and better equipment, had brought the Battalion to much greater efficiency by the beginning of March. At that time, Sir John French, Commanding the British Expeditionary Force, had ruled that, before any 'New Army' unit moved to the Western Front, it must be proficient at working, moving, billeting and supplying itself. Thus, it was decided that the Battalion, in company with the remainder of the 36th Infantry Brigade, should gain such experience by marching from Folkestone all the way to Aldershot. The march, by way of Ashford, Maidstone, Edenbridge, Dorking and Guildford, took six days. The march proved successful and, during the 25 miles stretch from Dorking to Guildford, the whole 12th (Eastern) Division had the honour of marching past Lord Kitchener himself.

Training continued with drills; parades; night and daytime manoeuvres; field exercises; simulated trench warfare, bombing, machine gunning and poison gas attacks. By May all of this preparation had brought the Battalion's 1,100 men to fighting readiness and an anxious desire to get abroad to start the task before them.

A final 'home' honour was received when His Majesty King George V, Her Majesty Queen Mary and Her Royal Highness Princess Mary attended a Divisional Church Parade. Finally, the following message was received from His majesty:

"You are about to join your comrades at the front in bringing to a successful conclusion this relentless war of over nine months' duration. Your prompt and patriotic answer to the Nation's call to arms will never be forgotten. The keen exertions of all ranks during the period of training have brought you to a state of efficiency not unworthy of my Regular Army. I am confident that in the field you will nobly uphold the tradtions of the fine regiments whose names you bear. Ever since your enrollment I have closely watched the growth and steady progress of all units. I shall continue to follow with interest the fortunes of your Division.

In bidding you farewell, I pray that God may bless you in all your undertakings."

The first Units of the Division began to move out from Aldershot on 29th May. The following day, the 7th Battalion's Transport and Machine Gun Sections went from Farnborough to Southampton and then on the 'S.S.City of Dunkirk' to Le Havre. The main Battalion took another route on 31st May, first by two trains to Folkestone, from where they left the pier aboard the 'S.S.Victoria' at 11.00pm.

The 'S.S.Victoria' ploughed across the dark, moonless but smooth English Channel in good time and, at 1.00 am on 1st June, docked at Boulogne. There the troops disembarked and marched to Ostrahove Camp at the north-east outskirts of the town. A two miles march brought them to Pont de Brique next day where they were reunited with the Transport and Machine Gun Sections which had travelled up the coast from Le Havre. From Pont de Brique a slow train journey of almost four hours carried the Battalion to Arques. Then came a one mile march to Blendeques two miles south-east of St.Omer where they occupied their first billets in France.

On the 5th June, the whole of the 36th Brigade marched almost 13 miles to Les Cinque Rues just west of Hazebrouck. The hot and oppressive weather made marching with full equipment exhausting and 37 men dropped out along the way. Even worse was to come next day when, in

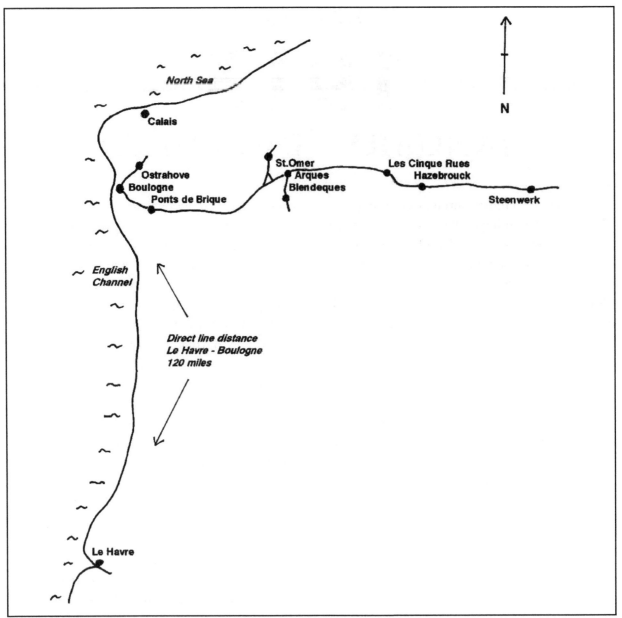

34.   *1st to 6th June 1915*

similar conditions, a 15 miles march was made eastward to Steenwerk. This time no less than 156 men fell out with exhaustion but they all rejoined by evening. The experiences of these two days brought commanders to realise that the previously recognised route-marching pace of three and a half miles per hour was unrealistic, especially over stone 'pave' roads, and that two and a half miles was the proper expectation.

Three days' training at Steenwerk was followed, on the 10th June, by an onward march to the sizeable town of Armentières. This time, the Battalion progressed through heavy rain for half the distance. At Armentières, immediate attachment to established regular army units was effected so that front line trench experience

could be obtained quickly. Those regular units included the Devonshire Regiment, the Royal Irish Fusiliers and the Duke of Cornwall's Light Infantry.

On the 13th June, the first casualties were sustained when a sergeant and two privates were injured by shrapnel splinters. Later, the Battalion's first fatal casualty was Private George King, killed while working in the Irish Fusiliers' trenches. Here, it should be remembered throughout that it was the policy of the 7th Battalion to record at noon casualties sustained during the previous 24 hours. Thus, the date of death recorded for some men may be inaccurate by one day.

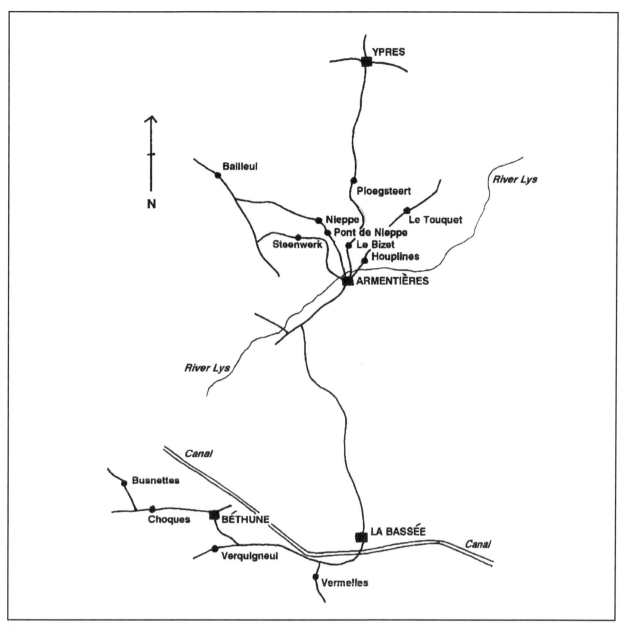

35. *June to September 1915*

JUNE:
13th:
Private: (2760) G.King.

It was fortunate that more men were not killed on 14th June when five shells fell on 'C' Company's billet in the school at Rue de Quesnoy but everyone was out in the trenches. A lucky escape had also occured three days earlier. On that occasion Captain Sleeman, Second in Command, and Captain Thompson, Medical Officer, had been standing talking with other officers when a shell dropped right amongst the group killing one and seriously injuring two; Captains Sleeman and Thompson escaped unharmed.

During the next fortnight training and practice continued. Also, there was an opportunity for the men to take baths at Bailleul and to enjoy the luxury of a change of underclothes.

On the 21st June, a march was made to Pont de Nieppe and, the next day, the Battalion made its first appearance in the front line as a complete unit, taking up position near the River Lys and along the Armentières – Comines railway. At this point there were small houses on both sides of the line, some occupied by Battalion men and some by the enemy. In such a situation it was difficult to avoid enemy rifle fire, one officer and one private being killed by snipers before the end of the month.

JUNE:
28th:
Captain: (2351) J.G.Bussell.
30th:
Private: (2675) H.Holland.

The early days of July were spent by numerous working parties, large and small, at various spots improving the front and support trenches. This work was undertaken in the areas of Le Touquet and Le Bizet north of Armentières. At last, after days of very hard work, the Battalion moved back a short distance on the 10th July to billets in Pont de Nieppe. Training continued there until a move to Houplines on the 15th. Trench work was recommenced and carried on each day, more or less, until the end of July. During the last few days of the month heavy artillery bombardments were carried out by both sides and several casualties were sustained. In particular, a number of enemy 4.5 inch shells fell in the vicinity during the evening of the 31st July killing three men. This month, the Battalion strength was recorded as 1,045 all ranks.

JULY:
3rd:
Private: (2855) G.T.Merritt.
8th:
Private: (3156) A.J.Thompson.
22nd:
Private: (2904) W.Newton.
23rd:
Corporal: (2784) H.T.Lea.
25th:
Sergeant: (2185) C.Adams.
Private: (2734) W.J.Johnson.
26th:
Privates: (2382) J.E.Cherriman, (3157) F.B.Tiffin.
31st:
Privates: (2292) J.Botting, (2453) D.Crouch, (3080) H.Simmons.

August began with the Battalion in Reserve. There continued to be much rifle fire and a number of men were killed. A mine was blown by the Royal Engineers at a point where the Germans had come close to a Battalion trench but its success could not be gauged accurately. Then, on the 6th August, a generally quiet day, the enemy were heard singing patriotic songs to celebrate their capture of Warsaw. To dampen the celebrations, bombing parties approached under cover and threw two bombs into the enemy trench.

Mid-August brought a period of heavy rain and thunder storms. The communication trenches soon began to deteriorate and, along some trenches, the duckboards were afloat. Although this weather made conditions most unpleasant, it had the advantage of reducing belligerent activity on both sides. Normal activity resumed on the 19th August, however, when the Germans used incendiary shells against the Battalion for the first time. Several such shells fell in Armentières and a number of houses were set alight.

Fatigues and working parties continued. While Lieutenant Cox was returning from one of these working parties at 1.00 am on the 23rd August he was unluckily shot through the head and killed by a chance bullet. Lieutenant Cox had been a splendid footballer and his brother also served with the Battalion.

An unusual occurrence was witnessed on the 26th August when Saxon soldiers in the enemy trenches tried to fraternize. One brave German even stood openly on his trench parapet and shouted apologies about recent shelling by the Prussians. The Germans referred to the 1914 Christmas truce and suggested a meeting in No-Man's-Land but strict Battalion orders prevented any such thing. Two days later a party of men bathing in the River Lys was spotted by the enemy and fired upon. Captain Osborne was wounded in the thigh and was absent from the Battalion for the next five months as a result.

During August, artillery ammunition ran very low and restricted activity. Lack of shells generally had been a great British weakness at this time. Also, the British had been very slow to appreciate the importance of the machine gun, most infantry battalions of about 1,000 men being supplied with only two, a pitifully inadequate number. This month, however, the 7th Battalion's machine guns were increased to four, still woefully insufficient. At month's end the Battalion's area around Houplines was quiet.

AUGUST:
4th:
Corporal: (3243) L.P.Worth.
Private: (2468) E.Davis.

5th:
Lance Corporal: (2247) H.Barron.
6th:
Privates: (2219) E.A.Avis, (2519) P.Ellis, (2618) A.H.Grover, (3083) H.Sims.
10th:
Private: (3245) E.V.Wright.
23rd:
Lieutenant: (2441) N.J.Cox.
28th:
Private: (2270) S.Berryman.

For the first week of September the Battalion was in Reserve. An appreciable amount of rain fell during this period and it was necessary to find working parties to carry out repairs to front line and communication trenches. Activity on both sides was dampened down by the weather.

General Sir Herbert Plumer K.C.B., inspected the Battalion on the 7th September and expressed himself satisfied with all that he had seen. Later that day, the Battalion relieved the 8th Fusiliers in the front line trenches. Enemy machine guns and searchlights were active during the night and a man was killed at 5.00 am while at a listening post.

SEPTEMBER:
8th:
Lance Corporal: (2680) P.L.Holloway.

All remaining civilians were evacuated from Houplines on the 9th September. That day, too, civilians were seen apparently working as carrying parties behind the German lines. There was some persistent enemy shelling of Battalion Headquarters on the 11th September and two men were killed. Morale was raised considerably at this time by the welcome opening of a Regimental Coffee Shop and Canteen.

SEPTEMBER:
11th:
Privates: (2213) W.C.Attwood, (2672) J.H.Hogan.

Sounds of enemy mining nearby were heard on the 12th September. Arrangements were made for a counter-charge which was blown at 9.00 pm. One British miner was reported gassed inside the shaft. Immediately, Lieutenant E.G.Sutton, attached to the 36th Brigade Mining Section from the 8th Battalion, The Royal Sussex Regiment, without gas protection and

without knowing how far inside the tunnel the man was, went into the shaft and brought out the casualty. For this action, Lieutenant Sutton received the first Military Cross to be awarded to the 12th Division. The Battalion was relieved the following day and went back to billets in Reserve. Fatigues, training and route marching were undertaken daily until the front line was occupied, once more, on the 19th September.

Farther south, the Battle of Loos began on the 25th September. Early that morning a smoke curtain was put up along the Battalion's front by the burning of damp straw placed in bundles at appropriate intervals. This, together with smoke candles, phosphorus bombs and a fortuitously foggy morning, proved effective visually. However, the apparent attempt to divert German attention from the Loos area not only brought casualties but also, with hindsight, proved unsuccessful in its main purpose.

SEPTEMBER:
25th:
Privates: (2436) S.Court, (2510) T.Earl, (2685) P.Hopkins, (2902) W.J.Newman, (2922) H.Osborne, (2946) H.Pearson.

Along the Battalion's front, all was absolutely quiet on the 26th September as if both sides were catching their breath, although they knew nothing, at that stage, of the slaughter amongst regular, territorial and 'New Army' units on the battlefields at Loos. After this one day of relative relaxation, enemy heavy howitzers shelled Battalion billets on the 27th, killing three mules and five men, including the Machine Gun Section sergeant. Of the 18 men wounded, two died the following day. It was only slowly that news of the Loos debacle, farther south, reached the battalion.

SEPTEMBER:
27th:
Sergeant: (2252) A.J.Basson.
Privates: (2229) C.Baker, (2434) F.Cotterill, (2641) E.A.C.Harris, (2909) A.Niederaller.
28th:
Privates: (2374) R.G.Chapman, (3203) G.F.Watts.

The Battalion was relieved on the 28th September, marching off early in the morning to Steenwerk from where they travelled by train to

Choques and then marched to billets in Busnettes. This movement proved to be of little respite because a march to Verquigneul took place on the 29th. The front line east of Vermelles and opposite Hulluch was occupied at month's end.

SEPTEMBER:
30th:
Private: (2324) J.Brown.

For the whole of the first week of October the Battalion was occupied consolidating the front line and communication trenches. Intermittent enemy shelling continued throughout and this made particularly difficult conditions for the men who were detailed to water-carrying parties and had to fetch their precious commodity from water carts a mile away. Relief in the form of a move back to billets in Verquin did not come until the 8th October.

OCTOBER:
1st:
Private: (2829) R.S.Marsh.
2nd:
Lance Corporal: (2495) S.T.Dollery.
Private: (2961) S.Phillips.
4th:
Privates: (2727) D.Jenner, (2867) J.R.Mills.
5th:
Private: (2897) J.Naisbitt.
6th:
Private: (2511) H.Eason.
7th:
Private: (2968) E.J.Pockney.
8th:
Private: (2752) G.Kensett.
9th:
Private: (2956) E.Perry.

After remaining in billets for three days, the Battalion marched to Noyelles on the 12th October. There they remained while a heavy British bombardment of the enemy at Hulluch and at the Hohenzollern Redoubt strongpoint took place. The bombardment was followed by an unsuccessful attack by the 46th Division supported by the 35th and 37th Infantry Brigades. Because the attack had failed in its main objectives, the Battalion moved, on the 13th, to billets in Philosophe.

Next day the trenches were taken over opposite Hulluch and just south of the Hulluch – Vermelles Road. Work was carried out on trench traverses and wiring. This tour in the front line lasted eight days and nights with occasional heavy shelling from the enemy. Not until the 21st October did the Battalion move out to Noyelles from where they were taken in motor buses to Fouquereuil. On this day, supplies of a new innovation, which was to save many lives during the remainder of the war, were issued to the men. These were none other than the 'Battle Bowlers' or 'tin hats'.

Whether, or not, the 'tin hats' were being worn at live bomb-throwing practice is not recorded but Lieutenant Cox and another man were accidentally injured at Fouquereuil on the 24th October during such a bombing exercise. A further, bizarre, accident occured before the end of October when Private 'Barney' Cain, a boxer of considerable repute, was wounded when he lit a Mills bomb detonator in mistake for a cigarette!

The last week of October brought heavy rain and moves by the Battalion, first to Annequin and then to Noyelles.

OCTOBER:
15th:
Privates: (2184) A.Adams, (2467) T.B.Davidson.
16th:
Private: (3199) A.Watson.
17th:
Private: (2850) G.Meeten.
18th:
Private: (2738) B.H.Joy.
19th:
Lance Corporal: (2669) W.L.Hoadley.
Privates: (2874) F.G.Mitchell, (3101) W.Smith.
20th:
Private: (3113) J.E.Squires.
21st:
Private: (2883) A.L.Morgan.
23rd:
Corporal: (2488) A.N.De.St.Croix.
24th:
Corporal: (3096) A.W.Smith.
Lance Corporal: (2291) A.Borrow.

In wet and muddy conditions, the Battalion entered Reserve on the 1st November in trenches opposite the Hohenzollern Redoubt. Next day, when a Royal Engineers' dump near Battalion Headquarters was struck by German shellfire, one man was killed; another, who was seriously

---

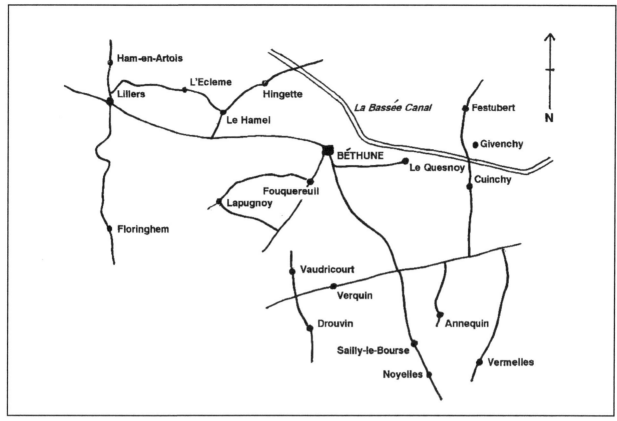

36. *October 1915 to June 1916*

injured, died from his wounds the following day.

NOVEMBER:
2nd:
Private: (2528) C.J.Evans.
3rd:
Private: (2391) L.Clark.

Heavy and frequent German shelling was experienced during the 4th, 5th and 6th November. The weather continued wet and trenches were deep in mud. For the first time, the Battalion occupied part of the Hohenzollern Redoubt. Many bodies were still lying out in the surrounding area since the 25th September Battle of Loos. When conditions permitted, some of the corpses were given rudimentary burials by being rolled into shallow scrape holes. The last fatalities in action this month were as a result of heavy shelling on the 9th.

NOVEMBER:
4th:
Private: (2424) A.J.Cooper.
5th:
Privates: (2465) J.Dann, (2735) E.Johnson.
6th:
Private: (2579) E.George.

9th:
Privates: (2952) H.L.J.Penfold, (3104) A.Soal.

The Battalion had been in the line continuously from the 28th October to the 12th November. Frequent heavy rain had brought the trenches to an appalling condition and, for the men, there was no overhead shelter from the downpours. Despite the daily use of whale oil and anti-frostbite grease, there were many cases of 'trench feet'. In one trench bay a sign was erected stating 'This bay reserved for the greasing and rubbing of feet'. Not unexpectedly, a comedian put up an unofficial notice round the next corner: 'This bay reserved for the wailing and gnashing of teeth!'

Battalion telephone communications worked well during this period and was most fortunate because the use of 'runners' carrying messages was severely curtailed by the muddy conditions. On one occasion it took the Commanding Officer 45 minutes to reach a neighbouring Headquarters a half mile distant.

It came as a great relief when the Battalion left the trenches on the 12th November and went back to billets in Sailly-La-Bourse. By this time, night time frosts had set in and a

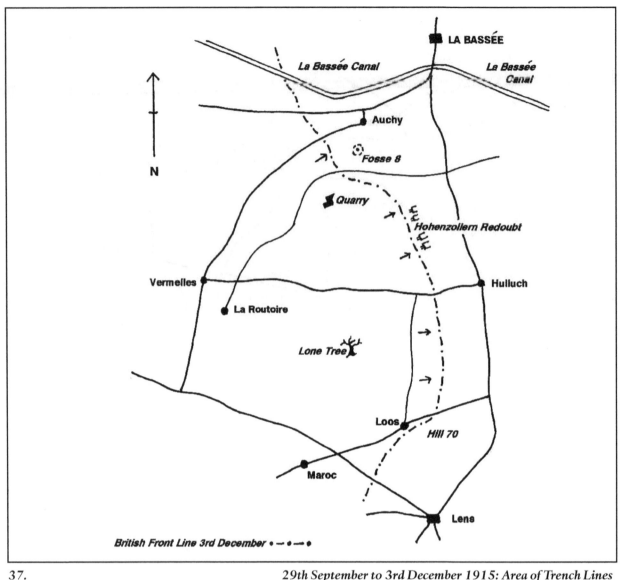

37.   *29th September to 3rd December 1915: Area of Trench Lines*

further move to warmer billets in Béthune was welcomed on the 16th. Some 50 men, who were unable to march because of 'trench feet', were transported by motor bus. It was mainly due to 'trench feet' and other related problems that about 200 men had to be evacuated from the trenches and the Battalion's strength was reduced to 33 officers and 799 men by the end of November.

It was to the trench areas near Festubert and Givenchy, north of the La Bassée Canal, that the Battalion moved on the 3rd December. This area was to be 'home' for the next two, hard-winter months. However, as additional protection from cold weather, the men were issued with mittens, vests, waterproof capes, and jerkins made from a variety of dogs' skins. As a direct result of this foresight, general health and morale were much improved.

The front line approximately one mile east of the village of Festubert was taken over on the 11th December. So flat and wet was the terrain that there were no trenches as such because the water table was so near the surface. The line consisted of intermittent sections of sandbagged, above-ground parapets or breastworks surrounded by water and mud. Not unreasonably, the descriptive name 'island' was given to each of these parapet sections and they were numbered 1 – 16 over a distance of about 500 yards. These 'islands', manned by between six and 24 men, according to parapet length, were themselves interspersed by tiny raised posts known as 'Grouse Butts'. Neither the 'islands' nor the 'Grouse Butts' could be supported in daylight. Night-time relief was organised to take place every 48 hours.

Relief back to Festubert came at mid-December but not before Captain L.F.Cass, Commanding 'A' Company, had been shot dead by a German sniper on the 13th.

Five days later, a man on permanent fatigue duties in Givenchy was unluckily killed by shellfire.

DECEMBER:
13th:
Captain: (2365) L.F.Cass.
18th:
Private: (3018) W.A.Roberts.

Gas cylinders were carried into the line on the 20th December. So great was this tasks in terms of human effort that a fatigue party of no less than 18 officers and 720 men was required. Fortunately, the work was completed without casualties.

Christmas Eve saw considerable activity which commenced at 7.15 am when the Germans blew a mine close to the Battalion's trenches burying men and causing considerable damage. The enemy occupied the mine crater during the afternoon and there was British retaliation by machine gun, bombs and rifle grenade fire which eventually forced the Germans to retire from the crater.

DECEMBER:
24th:
Corporal: (2214) G.W.Auberton.
Private: (2342) A.H.Burgess.

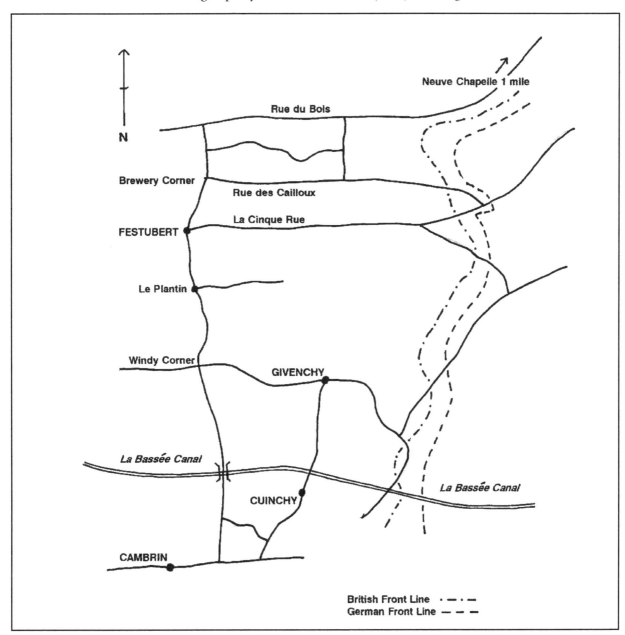

38. *3rd December 1915 to 10th February 1916: Area of Trench Lines*

Relief by the 8th Royal Fusiliers on Christmas Morning allowed the battalion to retire to Givenchy but there was no opportunity for anything in the way of festive celebration. In turn, the Battalion relieved the 8th Royal Fusiliers in the front line on the 27th December. The next day saw a tragic accident when the safety pin was inadvertently removed from a grenade before it was inserted into the rifle. The resulting explosion wounded several men and killed Company Quartermaster Sergeant Faircloth, one of the N.C.O.'s originally sent from the 2nd Battalion, The Royal Sussex Regiment to help set up the 7th Battalion.

DECEMBER:
28th:
Company Quartermaster Sergeant: (2534) H.L.Faircloth.
Privates: (2733) G.Johnson, (2799) J.R.Little.

The enemy blew another mine on the 29th December. Four men were buried by fallout but they were dug out unharmed. Thus the year 1915 drew to a close with the Battalion withdrawn to Hingette for a thankful period of rest.

CHAPTER 18

1916

JANUARY – JUNE

The first half of January in the ominous year of 1916 was spent in and out of the line in front of Festubert every five or six days. When the battalion departed on the 13th January for a relatively lengthy rest, the very last platoon to leave the front was caught by shellfire which wounded four men, two of whom died later. On the way out, the Battalion was fed at Le Hamel and then continued the march to Béthune where billets were taken up at the tobacco factory.

JANUARY:
13th:
Private: (2944) M.Patten.
14th:
Private: (2335) G.Budgen.

A six miles train journey on the 16th January took the Battalion, together with the rest of the 36th Infantry Brigade, to Lillers. The onward journey four miles north-westward was made by road to the village of Ham-en-Artois. From then until the end of January, a relatively restful time, sprinkled with parades, training and route marches, was enjoyed in safety. The most notable day was the 20th when the Brigade paraded and was inspected by General Joffre with General Sir Douglas Haig present.

JANUARY:
20th:
Private: (3085) J.Sinclair.

February saw the withdrawal of the Battalion's four relatively old type machine guns and their replacement with Lewis Guns. Thus it was seventeen months into the war before this, and most other battalions, began to be supplied with the guns they needed; even then the weapons supplied were too few. The Battalion's own Trench Mortar Battery was also formed this month.

It was not until the 11th February that a move back towards the front commenced with a march to Sailly-la-Bourse. The next day the old, well known trench lines opposite the Hohenzollern Redoubt were occupied. From time to time the Germans were active with artillery and trench mortars. Not until the 21st February was a move made back to Fouquereuil. From there the men marched through heavy snow to take welcome baths in Béthune. This was leap year and so it was on the 29th February that the Battalion, having billeted one night in Annequin, returned to trenches in front of the Hohenzollern Redoubt.

FEBRUARY:
14th:
Private: (2477) J.Dean.
15th:
Private: (2620) W.J.Grover.

March came in like a lamb on the Battalion's sector but the relative quiet was not to last. Things hotted up on the 2nd and reached a crescendo during the night of the 3rd / 4th March. The Germans opened a barrage on Battalion positions. Heavy trench mortars, field guns and howitzers were used and a great deal of close quarter bomb fighting ensued. After some time the enemy withdrew leaving the Battalion with the advantage but both sides had suffered significant casualties. In addition to those killed, the Battalion had two missing and 181 wounded. Relief was completed on the 5th March.

MARCH:
2nd:
Privates: (2350) J.Buss, (2440) G.Cox, (3200) C.J.Watson.
3rd:
Lieutenant: (2258) C.W.Beale.
Sergeant: (2308) R.Brewster.
Lance Corporal: (2835) J.Martin.

Privates: (2223) E.Bacon, (2295) C.J.Bowley, (2996) E.A.Ransome, (3034) A.J.Sadler.

4th:

Lieutenant: (3210) R.G.Wells.

Second Lieutenant: (2878) E.A.Montesole.

Sergeants: (2585) F.S.M.Gillham, (2744) J.Keegan, D.C.M.

Lance Corporals: (2671) J.B.Hodkinson, (3022) E.T.Rogers, (3068) W.J.Sheppard.

Privates: (2272) S.Biggs, (2319) S.Brooks, (2574) J.A.Gearing, (2595) G.Godden, (2616) S.Grender, (2634) T.Harbour, (2654) W.Hearsay, (2833) H.S.Martin, (3021) W.Rodgers, (3089) F.Skinner, (3202) A.G.Watts.

5th:

Lance Corporal: (2407) P.Coleman.

Private: (2683) S.M.Hooper.

In continuing bad weather the Battalion moved out of the line to Annequin on the 5th March and made a route march return to Fouquereuil the next day. Baths were allocated on the 8th and then, in the afternoon, the Battalion was inspected and complimented on its defence of the line in front of the Hohenzollern Redoubt by Lieutenant General Sir Hubert Gough, General Officer Commanding 1st Corps.

A return to trenches was completed on the 11th March. On the 13th the enemy used trench mortars to some effect but retaliation by British howitzers brought the German fire to a halt. On that day a new draft of four officers and 100 men joined, bringing the Battalion strength to 20 officers and 737 other ranks. Over the past months, the Battalion numbers had been whittled away by a trickle of casualties sustained, not during any particular set-piece battle but by routine skirmishes, patrols and tours of duty in the front line or when within reach of enemy fire farther back.

MARCH:

13th:

Privates: (2862) A.Miller, (2976) W.Pratt.

14th:

Private: (2361) C.P.Carn.

Over the next several days, sporadic mortar and rifle grenade fire was troublesome. On the 19th a small British mine was blown and men of the Battalion attacked the resulting crater. Casualties were sustained and, while helping in a wounded man, Captain Woodhams was killed and Lieutenant Richardson was wounded.

MARCH:

15th:

Private: (2392) W.Clark.

17th:

Lance Corporal: (3124) W.G.Stenner.

Private: (2898) M.E.Napper.

18th:

Privates: (2679) T.Hollman, (3145) G.E.Taylor, (3236) A.Wood.

19th:

Captain: (3240) G.Woodhams.

Privates: (2501) J.Driscoll, (2677) G.Hollingsworth.

There was a heavy fall of snow on the 24th March, after which activity on both sides subsided noticeably. On that, and the previous, day there was some shell and mortar fire which caused a number of casualties. However, the German's heavy trench mortar, which had been causing particular damage, apparently moved off after its location was found and bombarded by our guns.

MARCH:

23rd:

Privates: (2317) H.W.Britt, (2462) C.Dadswell, (2523) F.J.Elsey.

24th:

Privates: (2305) F.Bray, (2667) F.Hilton, (2761) F.Kingshott, (2914) G.North.

Before the end of March the prolonged exposure to snow and slush brought a number of 'trench feet' cases despite the regular use of gumboots and grease. The last few days of the month were spent in billets at the orphanage in Béthune.

A Church Parade was held in Béthune's Municipal Theatre on Sunday 2nd April. Afterwards, the Battalion, together with the 11th Middlesex, marched past General Sir Charles Monro, Commanding 1st Army. Next day it was back to the reserve trenches of the Hohenzollern sector. A draft of 23 men was welcomed to those trenches on the 5th April, even though the Medical Officer rejected two as unfit.

APRIL:

2nd:

Lieutenant: (2555) P.G.Foster.

4th:

Second Lieutenant: (2550) T.Fitzsimons.

After returning to front line trenches on the 3rd April, a small British mine was blown as a defensive measure. During the German retaliation, four men were wounded. Of these, Sergeant Skerrett, another of the Battalion's original N.C.O's, died a week later. Another calamity befell the Battalion on the 8th April when, as a result of an enemy mine explosion, 17 miners were buried in dugouts and their own mine shaft. All were dug out alive with the exception of one man who broke under the stress of his ordeal and shot himself. Later that day Lieutenant Sutton, who had been the first man in the Battalion to receive a bravery award, was shot while climbing over a filled in portion of a crater in an attempt to ascertain the situation. This day, also, 39 men were wounded and one was gassed.

APRIL:
8th:
Lieutenant: (3136) E.G.Sutton.
Lance Corporal: (3120) G.Stear.
Privates: (2554) A.Foster, (2602) H.Gooderson, (2651) A.Haylor, (2890) C.Muir, (3181) A.Voice, (3231) V.C.Winkworth.

Two men were killed by enemy trench mortar fire on the 9th April and, two days later, falling debris from a German mine explosion killed Second Lieutenant Field.

APRIL:
9th:
Lance Sergeant: (2714) D.F.Isted.
Private: (2497) J.F.Down.
11th:
Second Lieutenant: (2540) J.M.Field.

The blowing of so many mines by both sides during this period produced a moonscape, the largest combined chasm being some 50 to 70 feet deep, 60 to 100 yards wide and 200 yards long. On the 16th April British miners broke into a German mine shaft and removed a potentially dangerous charge weighing 2,000 lbs. The Royal West Kents came up to relieve on the 17th allowing the Battalion to return to billets in Annequin.

APRIL:
12th:
Private: (2848) F.Measor.
14th:
Sergeant: (3088) A.Skerrett.

15th:
Privates: (2206) A.Arrowsmith, (3075) C.Silsby.
17th:
Lance Corporal: (2212) W.H.Atkinson.

Following a return to billets at the Tobacco Factory, Béthune's Municipal Theatre became the venue for a Good Friday Parade Service on the 12th April. On Easter Monday, trenches in the Quarries Sector were occupied and found to be deep in water after the heavy rain of the past week. These conditions were borne until relief on the 26th April and a move back to Annequin. Next day, early, Strombus Horns sounded to warn of an enemy gas attack. Everyone donned their primitive gas helmets made from chemical-soaked flannel which, with eye pieces which quickly misted, made life very unpleasant. These conditions were tolerated only in the knowledge that, in all probability, one's life was being preserved thereby. On this occasion helmets had to be worn for one hour while a very thick cloud of gas passed through the Battalion's position on the slow-moving air. Although primitive, the helmets worked exceedingly well and, although every piece of metal was coated with a blue-green pigment, not one of the 700 men was harmed. Although quickly moved away from the course of the main gas cloud, a few unprotected horses in the vicinity seemed to be slightly affected and lethargic. Later that day the battalion marched 12 miles to Lapugnoy where the last few days of the month were spent at relative ease.

The whole of the month of May was to be spent away from the tensions of the front line. Time was spent at parades, lectures, route marching and training. So early as the 2nd may, cases of measles began to be diagnosed amongst the men. Straight way a programme of protection was instituted whereby, almost every day through the month, batches of 40, or more, men were inoculated. Greater danger was experienced on the 17th May when a bomb exploded prematurely on the training ground and three men were injured.

MAY:
3rd:
Private: (2484) A.O.Dennis.

The Battalion moved to Estrée Blanche on 22nd May and on to Floringhem on the 27th. Men who had been inoculated recently were unable to march and were conveyed by buses the next day. Billets at Lapugnoy were the destination on the 29th and, while there, the Battalion's machine gun complement was increased to 16.

The inoculations programme continued into June until all the men had been protected. Intensive training was also carried out in every aspect. A move was made on the 8th June to Bully Grenay. Sick and recently inoculated men were excused the march and travelled, instead, by buses to Maroc. The villages of Drovin and Vaudricourt were the shared destinations on the 13th. Two days later came news of a significant move which began on the 16th with a march to Fouquereuil. From there, they left at noon by train and at 7.45 pm arrived at Longneau near the railhead city of Amiens in the Département de la Somme. Immediately after detraining the Battalion marched through the city and north-

westward some 15 miles to Vignaucourt where they fell thankfully into billets at 4.00 am.

Gradually more intensive training was undertaken as the summer days of June ticked past. It was during this period that Captains Clarke and Hinds hit upon a splendid idea for cheering and raising the morale of the men, many of whom had been dispirited by the almost impossible task of obtaining cigarettes. With a joint capital of just 200 francs, the two officers set up a 'Regimental Canteen'. So popular and successful was this exercise that it soon developed into a 'Department Store' and its increasing profits were used to purchase newspapers, other special items, treats and even Christmas Dinners.

During the last week of June the rumble of continuous artillery fire away to the east could be heard from time to time. The build-up to the Battle of the Somme had begun. Surely, everyone thought, it could not be long now before the Battalion was called upon to play its part.

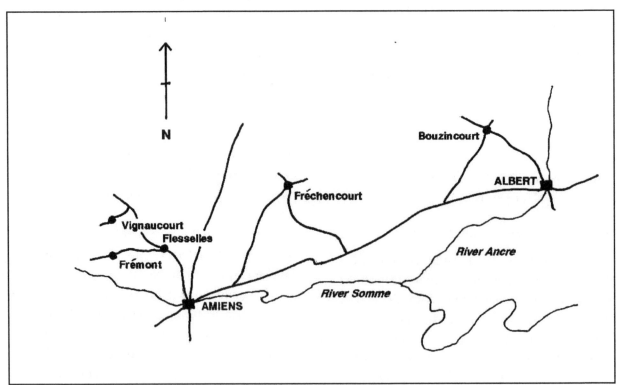

39.   *June 1916*

CHAPTER 19
1916
JULY – DECEMBER

At 7.30 am on the momentous day of the 1st July, 1916, British troops all along the front of 15 miles between Gommecourt and Maricourt went 'over the top' to commence the battle of the Somme. This was to prove the worst day in the history of the British army, with some 57,000 casualties, 19,200 of them fatal and 40% of them in the first hour. Pre-planning and orders had had the effect of sending the unprotected chests of thousands of men walking across open, featureless terrain against German shells, machine guns and rifles.

Many army units were decimated but, at that fateful hour of 7.30 am, the 7th Battalion The Royal Sussex Regiment was in the rear areas some seven miles behind the front line and marching forward towards Baizieux Wood. Later that day, with the noise of battle in their ears, they moved forward again to take over the intermediate line between Bouzincourt village and the town of Albert.

It was not until 11.15 am on the 6th July that the Battalion moved into the Somme front line trenches. Their orders, received that morning, were to launch an attack the following day on the German stronghold village of Ovillers. Here was a place where other units had sustained horrendous casualties to no avail during the preceding days. Here, the twin villages of Ovillers and La Boisselle were separated by 'Mash Valley', a shallow defile some 400 yards wide where there was no shelter or cover, except in the many shell holes caused by the seven days' pre-battle bombardment.

JULY:
6th:
Private: (2708) T.E.Huteson.

A narrow, partly sunken, road ran parallel to 'Mash Valley' along the lower part of its northern

slope and into Ovillers village. The Battalion's assembly trenches ran at right-angles to this road and continued up the slope but not to its crest. This wise precaution was to prevent enemy fire being brought to bear on the assembly trenches from the German stronghold of the Leipzig Salient to the north. Thus, so far as the Leipzig Salient was concerned, the Battalion's assembly trenches were in unseen or 'dead ground'. The assembly positions were facing Ovillers village and the final objective of enemy trenches just beyond what remained of the church which, with part of one gable still intact, acted as an orientation marker.

Zero hour was to be 8.30 am but the Germans were aware of the impending attack and, well before that time, laid down a heavy barrage on and around the assembly trenches causing many casualties even before the advance began. Precisely on time, men of the Battalion went 'over the top' and, together with the remainder of the 36th Brigade, advanced in steady formation.

The Battalion met a heavy bombardment and also machine gun fire but they pressed on to reach the third line of enemy trenches. Among the first officers to go over were Lieutenant Colonel Osborn, Lieutenant Stocks, and Captain Thomson the Medical Officer. In 'No-Man's-Land', the first of this group to be hit was Lieutenant Stocks whose femur was broken. The M.O. quickly dressed and bound the wound, using his own cane as a splint. Having been very busy treating the wounded all morning, Captain Thomson arrived back, around mid-day, to where Lieutenant Stocks was lying in a dangerously exposed position. Under heavy rifle and machine gun fire, the M.O. managed to get his injured colleague onto a groundsheet and began dragging the Lieutenant towards safety. Suddenly, and

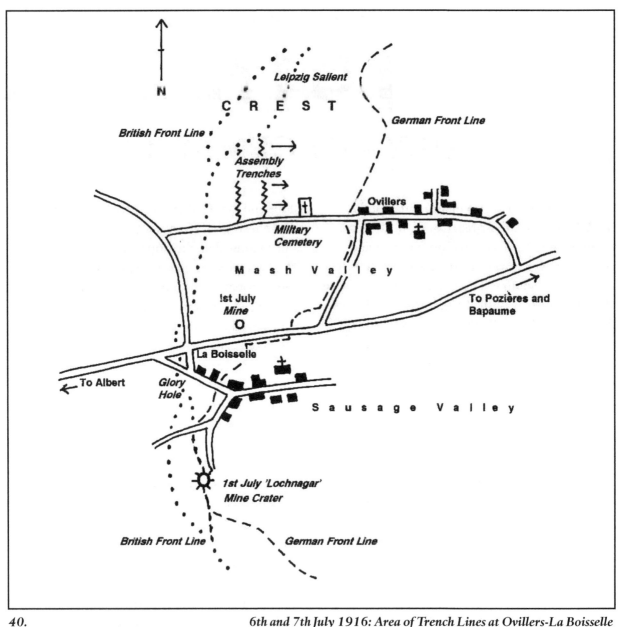

40.   *6th and 7th July 1916: Area of Trench Lines at Ovillers-La Boisselle*

without a sound, Captain Thomson fell forward to the ground. He had been shot through the heart and died instantly. His exemplary bravery was later recommended for high honour but he remained one of the many unsung heroes of that day.

There followed a good deal of confused action in, and around, Ovillers. Skirmishes, close quarter fighting, bomb throwing and the taking of German prisoners went on throughout the morning.

Captain H.Sadler reported that, having impressed upon his men the importance of speed in crossing 'No-Man's-Land', he ran across 'like a scalded cat' and reached the enemy trench line alone because his men were carrying heavy equipment and could not match his pace. He realised that he had arrived before the enemy soldiers had left their dugouts. He sat down to wait briefly and, as the Germans came up into the trench, he 'accounted' for them all.

It was Captain Sadler who reported another act of heroism and self-sacrifice: about 15 minutes before zero hour Captain May of 'A' Company was wounded by a bullet which passed through his steel helmet. Undoubtedly it was this wound which killed him but he remained in the trench urging on his men until they went 'over the top', then he fell.

By afternoon, the Commanding Officer, Lieutenant Colonel Osborn, decided to abandon the third objective and consolidate the first two lines of captured German trenches. Thus, the night passed without undue incident although it rained throughout. This had been a momentous and hard-fought day in the annals of the 7th Battalion which had performed with great credit. The Battalion suffered this day its highest number of deaths for any single day of the war. Twenty five officers and 650 other ranks went into the attack but only five officers and 220 other ranks remained unscathed by the end of the day.

JULY:
7th:
Captains: (2845) R.T.May, (3155) A.M.Thomson.

Lieutenant: (2603) H.B.Gordon.

Second Lieutenants: (2463) C.I.Dadswell, (2599) J.C.R.Godwin, (3196) F.R.Waring.

Sergeants: (2527) A.J.Evans, M.M., (2755) J.C.Kent, (2815) W.Madge, (3176) W.Unsted.

Corporals: (2380) W.Cheeseman, (2446) F.J.Crawley, (3183) E.Wady.

Lance Corporals: (2226) A.F.Bailey, (2304) H.Brain, (2795) W.J.Light, (2796) E.Lillywhite, (2900) J.E.New, (2935) M.W.Palmer, (2971) E.G.Pope, (2984) G.C.Pullen, (3013) H.T.B.Richardson, (3108) R.Southon, (3132) H.J.Sturt, (3149) J.E.Tee, (3168) C.T.Trill, (3218) J.Whiteman, (3219) A.Whitenstall.

Privates: (2190) J.Ahern, (2193) W.N.Aldridge, (2221) A.O.Ayling, (2222) J.A.Back, (2231) G.Baker, (2243) G.Barnes, (2265) P.Bell, (2275) C.Binstead, (2277) J.Bird, M.M., (2280) H.Bissmire, (2281) C.Blackhurst, (2284) F.G.Boakes, (2296) P.J.Bowra, (2297) J.Boxall, (2298) A.Boyde, (2318) J.Brooks, (2330) J.G.Bryant, (2336) F.H.Bumstead, (2339) R.C.Bunning, (2341) A.W.P.Burden, (2348) J.Burt, (2356) D.Callaghan, (2368) W.N.Catt, (2370) G.Chaffey, (2376) G.R.Chapple, (2397) G.Clifton, (2412) J.W.Collings, (2415) T.J.Comper, (2423) W.G.Coombes, (2449) H.A.Crittenden, (2450) E.F.Croft, (2452) M.J.Crooke, (2461) W.H.Daborn, (2487) G.C.Denyer, (2491) J.G.Dickinson, (2504) A.W.Duke, (2521) G.W.Elms, (2529) O.Evans, (2546) F.W.Fitch, (2561) A.Frost, (2590) A.C.Gocher, (2592) P.W.Goddard, (2598) R.Godfree, (2613) H.Greenfield, (2643) H.O.Harrison, (2652) F.Hazeldine, (2674) F.W.Holden, (2676) L.H.Hollingdale, (2691) J.Howard, (2696) J.T.Hubbold, (2717) F.W.Jackson, (2722) T.Jarman, (2731) R.F.Jerome, (2757) H.Kewell, (2777) W.Latham, (2794) J.Lewis, (2810) P.Luxford, (2817) T.G.Main, (2828) H.Marks, (2847) L.McCaul, (2858) A.E.Midmore, (2861) F.W.Millard, (2894) J.G.Murray, (2920) L.Oram, (2926) G.R.Pack,

(2955) L.l.Pepper, (2964) E.Pirie, (2965) H.Playford, (2983) W.J.Prior, (2990) A.L.Quelch, (2993) A.E.Ralph, (2999) W.Raven, (3012) C.Richardson, (3020) A.Robinson, (3027) G.Rowe, (3077) F.Simmonds, (3084) D.Sinclair, (3095) A.H.T.Smith, (3114) H.W.Stampe, (3118) F.C.Starling, (3119) C.Steadman, (3123) C.A.Steedman, (3131) T.Stubbs, (3140) S.Sylvester, (3143) F.Taylor, (3159) J.C.Timmins, (3161) G.A.Tingley, (3173) H.J.Twine, (3188) G.E.Walker, (3189) P.C.Wall, (3190) C.W.Waller, (3194) J.Walls, (3212) W.West, (3215) A.G.Weston, (3242) A.S.Wooler.

There was only occasional shelling during the night which was spent uncomfortably in the rain. Bombing posts were set up on the flanks and consolidation work took place so far as possible in the circumstances. This position was held throughout the following day, the 8th July, and during that evening the Battalion was relieved. The men moved out and back to Crucifix Corner near Aveluy where they were provided with tea before continuing their march to welcome billets in Albert.

JULY:
8th:
Private: (3244) W.Wrapson.

A march of about five miles on the 9th July took the Battalion back to bivouac near the village of Senlis. Baths were enjoyed there and the men recovered as best they could from their recent ordeal and the loss of so many colleagues. Over the next three weeks the Battalion recuperated although continual disturbance moved them variously between the villages of Forceville, Bus-les-Artois, Sailly-au-Bois, Mailly-Maillet, Hédauville and Martinsart.

As a result of the severe losses suffered by the 36th Brigade, the remnants of the 7th Royal Sussex and the 9th Royal Fusiliers were amalgamated to form a composite battalion. During these days, also, men wounded in the recent attack continued to die from their wounds. In particular, Lance Corporal George Edwin Chevis, whose brother was to be killed with the Battalion on the last day of the month, was badly wounded as he sought shelter in a shell hole. Shrapnel fragments had passed through his thigh and, later, he was wounded again in the same leg. Lance Corporal Chevis died from his wounds and Captain Wilson said that no words could describe this man's bravery through the inevitable pain he suffered.

JULY:
9th:
Private: (3023) J.V.Rogers.
10th:
Lance Corporal: (2851) H.Meeton,
Privates: (2506) W.A.Dykes, (2805) W.J.Longhurst.
11th:
Lance Corporal: (2493) A.E.Dixon.
Privates: (3049) H.T.Sayers, (3138) A.D.Swayne.
12th:
Lance Corporal: (2384) G.E.Chevis.
13th:
Private: (2907) S.Nicholson.
14th:
Private: (2402) A.G.Coe.
18th:
Privates: (2482) G.H.De Gruchy, (2729) G.A.Jenner.

19th:
Lance Corporal: (2553) G.F.Foord.
26th:
Private: (2200) B.Ansell.

A sad but proud day was marked on the 24th July when Lieutenant Colonel Osborn, who had commanded the Battalion since its inception and brought it to its current high level of operation and experience, left to take up his promotional move to command the 16th Brigade, 6th Division, at Poperinghe. Lieutenant Colonel Osborn drove away from the assembled Battalion to the generous cheers of the men and the sound of 'Sussex by the Sea' played by the band.

By the late afternoon of the 28th July, the Battalion was once more in position supporting the front line, this time between La Boisselle and Ovillers. The immediate task was to provide large carrying parties to move bombs up to the 11th

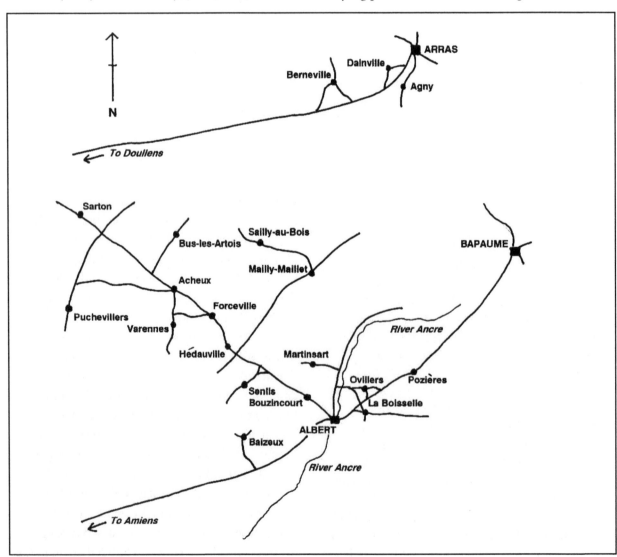

41.

July to September 1916

Middlesex situated west of Pozières village. On the 30th July, the Battalion made a diversionary demonstration while the 11th Middlesex attacked a strong German position on the left flank. Unfortunately, the main attack lost direction and failed completely. On the next evening, this attack was resumed in exactly the same manner. Not surprisingly, the Germans were ready and thwarted this renewed effort with concentrated rifle and machine gun fire. Four men, including J.H.Chevis, whose brother had been killed with the Battalion earlier in the month, lost their lives in this short-sighted venture.

JULY;
29th:
Private: (2464) J.Daniels.
30th:
Private: (3054) L.R.Scott.
31st:
Corporal: (2385) J.H.Chevis.
Privates: (2189) A.Adsett, (2399) G.E.Cobb, (2959) A.Phillips.

The first day of August found the Battalion occupying trenches to the west of Pozières where they were heavily shelled for two days and nights. During this period there were a number of casualties and several men, including Sergeant Tyrell, were killed by one particular shell burst. Second Lieutenant C.F.Rolfe, having been hit by a sniper's bullet, was bandaged by stretcher bearers who then had to abandon him in No-Man's-Land because it was too dangerous to try to bring him in. After 14 hours, Second Lieutenant Rolfe was picked up by Germans who treated him well in the circumstances and he survived the war as a prisoner.

AUGUST:
1st:
Sergeant: (3175) G.W.Tyrrell.
Corporal: (2797) W.Linden.
Lance Corporal: (2532) E.W.Everett.
Privates: (2719) C.E.Jacobs, (2818) J.D.Malcher, (2838) H.Maskell, (2917) W.E.Oakley, (3066) E.H.Shawyer, (3126) H.Stevens.
2nd:
Private: (2188) S.Adkin.

On the 4th August an attack was launched on Ration Trench which included an enemy strong point. Heavy machine gun fire prevented capture

of the strong point but Ration Trench was taken and consolidated. At one stage, Lance Corporal Peters, who was a man of relatively small build, jumped into the enemy trench almost on top of a heavily built German who promptly surrendered and was taken back with several others under the watchful eye and fixed bayonet of the proud Lance Corporal. Three other Germans were brought back, this time by Regimental Sergeant Major Joy who had forced their surrender using only an empty Verey Light pistol.

AUGUST:
4th:
Second Lieutenants: (2419) H.F.Cooke, (2787) G.D.Le Doux Veitch, (3239) T.V.Wood.
Sergeant: (2701) E.Hulkes.
Lance Sergeant: (3167) G.G.Tozer.
Lance Corporals: (2586) W.Gladwish, (3005) W.G.Reed.
Privates: (2266) D.Bellamy, (2445) T.H.Cramphorn, (2457) A.Cundell, (2478) W.W.Dean, (2496) A.Dorset, (2589) J.Goble, (2609) C.Grant, (2782) F.Lawson, (2820) G.W.Manktelow, (2860) A.J.Miles, (2887) E.F.Morris, (2891) W.C.R.Muirhead, (2906) F.V.Nichols, M.M., (2928) H.G.Padfield, (2978) G.M.Preater, (3057) T.W.Scutt.

On the following day, the 5th August, at dawn, the Germans made a counter attack using a flame thrower. Quickly bringing his Lewis Gun to bear, Sergeant F.Tooms killed both operators and the attack crumbled. After this incident it was reported that a large number of Germans were lying out in No-Man's-Land near Ration Trench. Men from the Battalion who had a knowledge of the German language were sent out and they managed to induce no less than 180 of the enemy to surrender. During the evening following this unusual but successful occurrence the Battalion was relieved and moved back, well pleased with its efforts, to the Tara-Usna Line east of Albert.

AUGUST:
5th:
Lance Corporal: (3069) L.S.Sherman.
Privates: (2753) G.A.J.Kent, (2970) H.G.Poole, (3135) A.S.Summons.
6th:
Private: (3117) G.Staplehurst.

The Battalion had well-earned the rest that it was to enjoy for the next fortnight. An honour

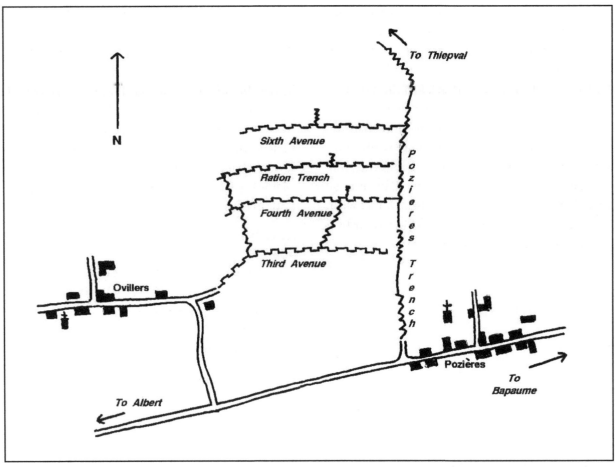

42. *30th July to 5th August 1916: Area of Trench Lines*

was bestowed on the 10th August when, near Senlis, the Battalion formed up and was inspected by H.M.King George V accompanied by the Prince of Wales. After the formalities, the men of the Battalion gave the Royal visitors three rousing cheers.

AUGUST:
8th:
Second Lieutenant: (2567) H.W.Gale.
Privates: (3102) F.J.Smithers, (3234) R.E.Winter.
10th:
Sergeant: (2371) W.E.Chalk.
Private: (2606) J.Gould.

A series of daily marches away from the Somme battlefields began on the 11th August, first to Varenne and then onwards, north-west, by way of Puchevillers, Sarton and Bérneville to Agny just south-west of the strategic and important rail junction town of Arras. There, on the 20th August, began six very quiet days in the trenches before the Battalion was relieved and moved out to billets in Dainville where it remained until the end of the month.

AUGUST:
11th:
Private: (2425) G.Cooper.
13th:
Private: (2460) J.Cusack.
22nd:
Private: (2475) W.W.Deadman.
24th:
Private: (2632) H.Hand.

Throughout the month of September the Battalion remained in the area of Agny which, on the whole, remained almost unrealistically quiet. A raid was attempted by the Battalion on the 24th but, as it was found impossible to penetrate the German wire, all available bombs were thrown towards the enemy trench and the raiding party withdrew. This relatively half-hearted effort seemed to epitomise the easy conditions near Arras at this time.

SEPTEMBER:
1st:
Second Lieutenant: (2552) J.A.Flowers.
4th:
Private: (2768) A.H.Knowles.

9th:
Private: (2960) R.C.Phillips.
12th:
Private: (3186) P.Walder.
26th:
Private: (2250) G.A.Bartup.

Having been relieved on the 28th September, the Battalion travelled by lorries from Wanquetin the following day to Bouquemaison and, on the 29th, moved on by buses to arrive at Pommièrs Redoubt camp near Mametz Wood by month end. The 'rest' near Arras was over; the Battalion was back for its third spell of duty on the Somme battlefields.

October 1st brought the Battalion into the Somme front line once more. Since they were last there the battle had been moved slowly but inexorably eastward and the front line was now between the villages of Flers and Gueudecourt. Front, support and reserve trenches were shelled by the Germans throughout the first ten days of the month. Attempts to move forward were hazardous and almost impossible because of the terrible ground conditions. Hardly a square foot of land had not been churned up by shellfire, and the heavy rains that had now set in turned everywhere into a moonscape of heavy mud. The narrow, over-used roads became almost impassable to men, horses, limbers and lorries. Only pack mules were able to carry supplies in an endless struggle against the elements. Thankfully, on the 10th, the Battalion was relieved and moved back to a camp in Bernafay Wood.

OCTOBER:
1st:
Private: (2985) W.R.Pullen.
2nd:
Private: (2182) C.Abear.
3rd:
Sergeant: (3030) F.J.Russell.
Corporal: (2702) J.A.Hulme.
Private: (2307) E.Breed.
5th:
Second Lieutenant: (2600) F.Golds.
Corporals: (2379) R.Cheeseman, D.C.M., (2673) C.Holden, (2912) J.C.Norman.
Lance Corporals: (2932) E.W.Paice, (3158) E.G.Till.
Privates: (2197) W.Allen, (2199) A.W.Andress, (2310) J.Bridger, (2352) P.B.Buswell, (2772) R.Kohler, (2791) H.Lewcock, (2812) R.S.Mace,

(2814) J.Mackey, (2819) R.H.R.Man, (2840) F.G.A.Matthews, (2859) A.E.Miles, (3053) G.L.Scopes, (3076) F.Silsby, (3187) F.C.Walker.
6th:
Sergeant: (2981) R.Prevett, D.C.M.
Private: (3028) C.F.Roxbee.
7th:
Corporal: (2653) A.H.Head.
Lance Corporals: (2278) S.G.E.Bishop, (2989) G.H.Quaife, (3128) R.W.Stone.
Privates: (2483) H.Dell, (2732) C.Jinks, (2816) F.Maher.
8th:
Privates: (2422) W.Coombes, (2692) W.A.Howard, (3019) E.Robin, (3052) E.W.Scarce, (3122) A.G.Stedman
9th:
Private: (3152) R.G.Thacker.
10th:
Private: (2245) H.W.Barnes.

For six consecutive days beginning on the 11th October large working parties were provided to dig assembly trenches. So awful were the ground conditions that these duties quickly proved exhausting for every man. A draft of 108 men arrived on the 18th and were soon in action during the early hours of the following morning. It appeared that the enemy had seen men moving up to their assembly trenches, however, because they opened up such a heavy barrage that the attack was cancelled.

A move out to camp at Mametz Wood was made on the 19th October and a further move the following day to another camp, this time at Fricourt. The last few days of the month were spent in moving by marching and by buses back to the area around Arras. The Somme offensive was slowly being forced to an end by the atrocious weather and ground conditions; the Battalion was not altogether sorry to be moving north.

OCTOBER:
13th:
Private: (2924) W.J.Osborne.
15th:
Private: (2769) C.W.Knowles.
16th:
Private: (3160) J.H.Tindell.
18th:
Private: (2195) A.Allcorn.
19th:
Private: (2623) R.Hack.

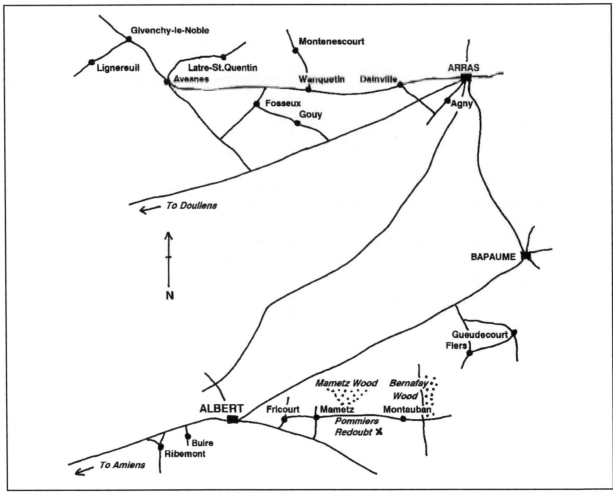

43.   *October 1916 to March 1917*

20th:
Private: (2636) V.B.Harding.
21st:
Private: (2750) R.Kennard.

The month of November was quiet as had been the case when the Battalion left the Arras sector in September. Of course, the area was well known from that previous experience and, throughout the month, a general routine of regular movement in and out of the line was operated. With activity continuing at such a low level, casualties were very few indeed. On the 23rd, all men of the Battalion were provided, and tested under gas, with the new box respirator. This innovation was a great improvement on the old makeshift mask of chemical-soaked flannel. Not only would many more casualties be avoided but also working conditions when compelled to wear the respirators would be far more tolerable.

NOVEMBER:
2nd:
Private: (2661) W.Hendry, M.M.

10th:
Private: (2340) G.Burchell.
14th:
Private: (2642) J.Harris.

The first half of December continued in similar vein until, on the 14th, a move farther back for a proper, more lengthy and very well deserved period of 'rest' some 20 miles west of Arras began. This was the first occasion for six months that the Battalion had been out of the front line areas. It was there that Christmas was spent using the largest available accommodation, which happened to be a huge barn where 'D' Company was billeted. Two Church Parades, each of two Companies, were held on Christmas Eve. Then, on Christmas Day, 'B' and 'D' Companies enjoyed their dinner followed by a concert. 'A' and 'C' Companies had to wait until Boxing Day for their dinner and concert but enjoyed both nonetheless.

Image 9: An Officer encourages his men "over the top" for a night-time attack.

Image 10: Contemporary souvenir postcard featuring a photograph of a Royal Sussex Regiment Private.

Image 11: Moving along a communication trench towards the front line on the Somme, July 1916.

Image 12: Searching a German prisoner flushed from a deep dugout at Martinpuich, Somme, September 1916.

Image 13: An Officer leading an attack through Trônes Wood, July 1916.

Image 14: A stretcher case is carried with difficulty to an Aid Post.

Image 15: The Third Battle of Ypres, (Passchendaele). Reinforcements moving up to the front line at St Julien on the first day of the battle 31st July 1917.

Image 16: The Third Battle of Ypres: Attempting to remove a field gun and limber from the quagmire.

CHAPTER 20
1917
JANUARY – JUNE

The Battalion's period of 'rest' continued on through the deep winter month of January. Although parades and training programmes were undertaken, much time was allocated for sports and recreation. Football matches were played, the band entertained and the officers held a concert for the benefit of the N.C.O's.

JANUARY:
8th:
Private: (2320) W.Brooks.

A very cold 15 miles march was made to Wanquetin, on the route back towards Arras, on the 16th January. This march proved to be very trying because the conditions on the roads were so slippery. Many men in full marching order found it difficult to keep their feet. There was much slipping and sliding and many falls. The situation was amusing at first and there was much banter and laughter. Before long, however, the whole Battalion was irritated by this wintery experience and everyone was glad to fall into billets at the end of the march.

JANUARY:
21st:
Private: (2724) C.Jarvis.

On the 23rd January, a further move, this time to billets in the city of Arras was made and this heralded a period of intensive digging activity. Work was undertaken within the many large natural caves which existed below Arras. These caves were extended into cellars of properties in the Grand Place, the Petit Place and into the extensive system of sewers. This was a tremendous undertaking by many units of the British army in preparation for the Battle of Arras offensive planned for the spring of 1917. The huge and extensive cave and gallery system was fitted with tramways, electric light, water, sanitation and living quarters. In all, there was

accommodation for 40,000 men, and galleries were driven far out into No-Man's-Land so that, with a quick breakthrough to the surface, many men could be disgorged at zero hour to attack the unsuspecting enemy.

Much trench digging work was carried out on the surface, too, and, with frequent snow and sometimes a foot of frozen soil, the labour was intensive, back-breaking, exhausting and never-to-be-forgotten by those who took part.

Digging and general working parties continued to be found during the first half of February. A number of casualties were sustained from German shelling of Arras and, to everyone's considerable distress, the Battalion's Medical Officer, Captain A.A.Rees, died in hospital at 41st Casualty Clearing Station, Wanquetin. A couple of spells in reserve trenches relieved, to some extent, the hard labour of trench digging. A steady trickle of men lost their lives during the month.

FEBRUARY:
1st:
Private: (2666) J.Hill.
3rd:
Private: (3090) J.Slade.
4th:
Captain: (3006) A.A.Rees.
9th:
Privates: (2557) E.W.J.Framp, (2706) H.B.Humphreys.
10th:
Privates: (2788) P.Lee, (3059) H.G.Sears.
17th:
Private: (2831) F.Marshall.
19th:
Private: (2205) F.Arnott.
23rd:
Private: (2901) P.Newington.
26th:
Private: (2268) F.Bennett.
28th:
Private: (2915) A.Norton.

It had been in continuing bitterly cold conditions that this period of heavy labour had been undertaken. It was morale-lifting for the men, therefore, when, at about this time, the successful Regimental Canteen, which had been started towards the end of June, 1916, was augmented by the service of a 'Wet Canteen'. From this addition, beer was made available not only to Battalion men but also to other units within reach. This undertaking was operated in a most efficient manner; it made a considerable profit which, together with the items supplied, was of great benefit to the Battalion.

Sir Douglas Haig inspected the Battalion on the 6th March at Givenchy-le-Noble. Then, under the British plan for the forthcoming offensive operations east of Arras, virtually the whole of March was taken up by training and practice exercises over ground prepared as a model of the enemy lines to be attacked. Working parties were provided to dig these model trenches which, it has to be said, were of small scale and of little practical help in assimilating what, in due course, would be the real conditions of battle.

Two serious and unfortunate accidents happened during practice on the 9th and 10th March. On the first of these days Second Lieutenants R.J.Ledger and H.C.Bowler were severely wounded by the explosion of a bomb. On the second day, during practice over assault trenches, six men were wounded by the explosion of a rifle grenade. Sadly, Second Lieutenant Ledger died on the 11th from his injuries.

MARCH:
11th:
Second Lieutenant: (2786) R.J.Ledger.
15th:
Private: (2886) A.G.W.Morris.

For the last few days of March, Companies were ordered up for digging duties at Arras. During these duties in the early hours of the 31st, a chance German shell killed eight men in 'A' Company.

MARCH:
31st:
Lance Corporal: (2627) W.J.Hall.
Privates: (2253) J.T.Batchelor, (2395) W.G.D.Clarkson, (2448) J.H.Cripps, (2808) H.E.Luck, (2877) N.Mockford, (3092) G.F.Smissen, (3162) E.Tinsley.

By the beginning of April, preparations for the Arras offensive were almost complete. The Battalion was to take part and moved, on the 3rd, to safe concealment in the subterranean cellars and caves beneath Arras. At 6.00 am the following day the British barrage, which was to continue unabated for the next five days and nights, commenced. The Battalion moved out into trenches on the 4th and undertook preliminary patrols and trench raids over the following few days. Removal of wire and obstacles from the front of the Battalion trenches was completed on Easter Sunday, the 8th. Trench ladders and bridges were put in place.

36th Brigade Operational Order No. 177 confirmed the February voluntary withdrawal of enemy forces to their newly constructed and fortified 'Hindenburg Line' and that the British 5th Army and VII Corps, to the right, had followed up to face the Germans in their new 'impregnable' positions. In fact, the northern end of the 'Hindenburg Line' joined the old trench lines near the Arras battle zone.

At zero hour, 5.30 am on Easter Sunday 9th April, the Battalion went 'over the top' along a frontage of 250 yards. The action went particularly well. Quickly, the good effect of the preliminary bombardment was appreciated when it was seen that little of the German barbed wire defences and front line trench remained. Little difficulty was experienced in gaining the first objective at which time two machine guns were captured and about 100 prisoners taken.

After such a promising start, a serious flaw in the operational plan resulted in the loss of many men. Senior officer planners had decreed that, after capturing the German front line trench, the men were to reorganise and consolidate while the British barrage paused in front of their position. Sadly, the holding barrage line was short of the enemy positions with the result that, virtually unmolested, German riflemen and machine gunners took heavy toll.

Despite the setback, the Battalion was well established by 7.30 am. In the afternoon, as planned, the 35th Brigade and, later, the 37th Division passed through to continue the attack. During the evening, two Battalion Companies were sent forward to support but, owing to the difficulties of darkness and a driving snow storm, they had to withdraw until dawn. Thus ended the successful first day of the battle.

APRIL:

9th:

Sergeants: (2217) H.J.Austin, (2257) A.W.Beale, (2873) F.Mitchell, (3129) E.Stoner.

Lance Corporal: (2725) F.Jeffery.

Privates: (2215) A.E.Aukett, (2263) A.W.Beeching, (2276) A.Bird, (2326) L.M.Brown, (2367) J.Cate, (2372) A.E.Chambers, (2437) A.J.Covell, (2516) R.W.R.Eells, (2547) T.Fitt, (2601) G.T.Goldsmith, (2610) W.C.G.Grant, (2611) F.Gratwicke, (2657) E.Heasmer, (2681) E.Hook, (2763) A.H.Kirby, (2802) W.Lloyd, (2825) J.H.Marchant, (2865) F.Mills, (2910) L.Nightingale, (2913) W.E.Norris, (2916) C.Nurden, (2969) A.Pocock, (3004) T.J.Reed, (3015) J.F.Ridley, (3038) J.A.Salvage, (3063) H.A.Selden, (3082) A.E.Simons, (3112) D.Squires, (3121)

W.H.Stebbings, (3169) A.J.Trotman, (3191) F.Waller, (3222) E.B.Wightwick, (3238) L.D.Wood, (3241) E.G.Wooff.

'B', 'C' and 'D' Companies advanced in support of the 5th Royal Berkshires when they resumed the attack at 6.00 am on the 10th April. The Royal Berkshires were quickly successful and the 7th Royal Sussex were not required to take part in the fighting. Instead, they passed the remainder of the day sitting in the snow and bitterly cold wind of the 'Brown Line' trench.

Following this action, the Battalion Commander, Lieutenant Colonel Sansom, received from Brigadier C.Owen, Commanding the 36th Brigade, the following letter:

'Dear Sansom,
Please convey my very best congratulations to all ranks who took part in the attack today.

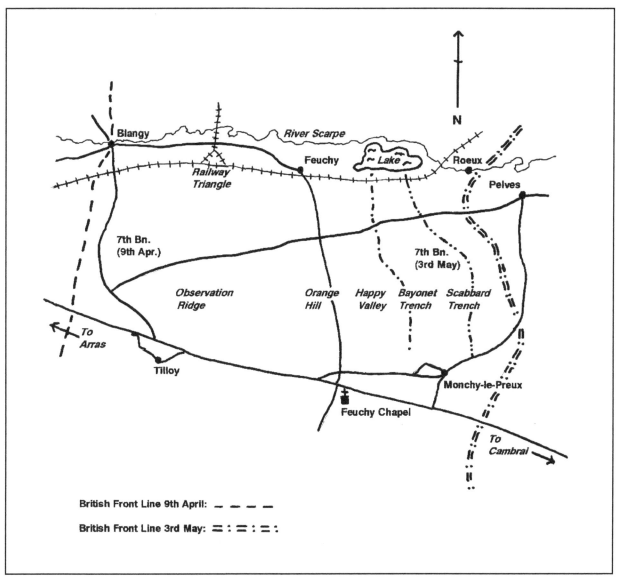

44.   *9th April and 3rd May 1917: Area of Trench Lines East of Arras*

They did magnificent work. They went forward and carried out their job as if they were on the practice trenches at Lignereuil. Whilst one cannot but regret the number of casualties experienced, yet considering the successful results achieved they have on the whole proved remarkably small. I hope you will bring to my notice all officers and other ranks who distinguished themselves.
Yours sincerely,
Signed: C.Owen.'

APRIL:
10th:
Lance Corporal: (2240) L.M.Barker,
Privates: (2286) G.F.Bonas, (2414) B.Comber, (2427) C.Coote, (2533) C.Eyles, (2571) G.Gates, (2608) H.Graham, (2614) W.J.Greenway, (2834) J.Martin, (2933) G.M.Pain, (3105) G.Soffe.

The Battalion marched up to relieve the 5th Royal Berkshires in trenches around Feuchy Chapel on the 11th April with 'A' Company holding an outpost line on nearby Orange Hill. That night was spent in digging and improving the trenches. The following day was relatively quiet, and relief in the form of the 1st Newfoundland Regiment enabled the 7th Royal Sussex to march back to the safety of the caves beneath Arras.

APRIL:
11th:
Privates: (2220) G.H.Avis, (3207) T.Webber.
12th:
Major: (3237) A.Wood.
Privates: (2630) W.M.Hampton, (2813) A.Mackey, (3000) L.J.Rawling.

From the Arras caves a march was made to Lattre St.Quentin on the 14th and to Mondicourt on the 15th April. There, a week's rest was enjoyed before a march to Wanquetin and a journey by buses back to the strategic Railway Triangle east of Arras. For the remainder of April, work was undertaken filling in shell holes and trenches, and the last day of the month saw the Battalion established in trenches on Orange Hill.

APRIL:
13th:
Lance Corporal: (2514) G.T.Edmunds.
Private: (2954) J.Penrith.

15th:
Private: (2947) T.Peart.
16th:
Private: (3064) H.C.Sewell,
20th:
Private: (3228) W.H.Wills.
25th:
Private: (2531) G.Evenden.
26th:
Private: (2345) B.L.Burgins.
27th:
Privates: (2289) M.J.Boniface, (2444) A.Cracknell.

A further attack in the continuing, but by now less successful, Battle Of Arras was to be made by the Battalion on the 3rd May. Companies moved forward to occupy Bayonet Trench which was so damaged as to be barely waist high. This trench ran south from a lake close to the River Scarpe and, while there, the men were subjected to a heavy and accurate enemy shrapnel bombardment which caused many casualties.

It was then discovered that the next trench line, Scabbard Trench, had been re-occupied by the Germans. After an intense 10 minutes British bombardment the Battalion attacked and successfully recaptured Scabbard Trench taking 45 prisoners and three enemy machine guns. While in Scabbard Trench the Battalion brought rifle and machine gun fire to bear on an enemy aircraft which was shot down, dropped near Pelves and was destroyed there by our artillery fire.

Later in the day the enemy ahead were seen to be withdrawing, so the Battalion made another successful move forward. However, word came from Headquarters that units to the right and left had not been able to keep abreast with the result that the 7th Royal Sussex were 'in the air'. Disappointingly, this situation meant that the Battalion was forced to withdraw to Scabbard and Bayonet Trenches which were consolidated and held until relief arrived on the 7th May.

MAY:
3rd:
Corporals: (2242) E.Barnes, (2560) E.W.French.
Lance Corporals: (2198) H.H.Ames,(2389) E.V.Chunn, (2503) O.S.Duffield, (2551) F.G.Flecknoe, (2868) W.W.Milstead, (2936) P.A.Palmer, (3014) W.H.Richardson, (3046) C.R.Savage.

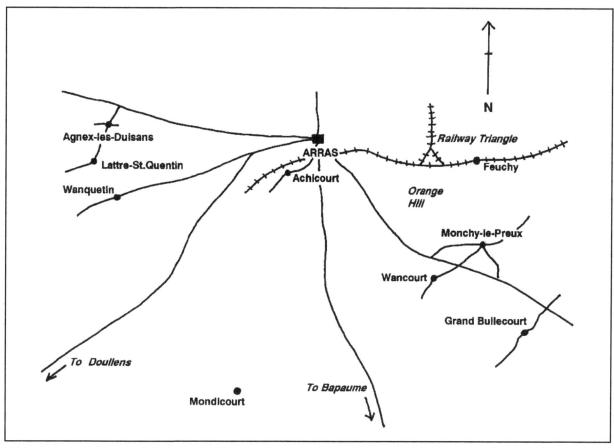

45.   *April to October 1917*

Privates: (2187) B.H.Ades, (2191) J.S.Aitkin, (2216) J.F.Aukett, (2235) G.W.Balcombe, (2239) E.J.Barber, (2241) E.R.Barnes, (2302) A.H.Brackstone, (2311) P.W.Bridger, (2323) F.Brown, (2413) V.J.Coltman, (2474) S.H.Deadman, (2476) A.C.G.Dean, (2538) J.T.Feist, (2564) A.Funnell, (2577) W.H.Gell, (2580) W.George, (2596) G.H.Godden, (2638) P.H.Hare, (2647) T.F.Hawkins, (2703) E.O.B.Humberstone, (2709) G.Hyde, (2739) L.Jukes, (2762) A.Kingsland, (2807) F.G.Lucas, (2895) W.E.Murrell, (2905) C.H.Nicholls, (2911) J.Noble, (2977) W.G.Pratt, (2986) G.Pumphrey, (2998) A.Ratcliffe, (3072) J.D.Shorten, (3091) F.M.Small, (3233) J.Winter, (3246) G.H.Wright.

4th:

Privates: (2312) R.Brigdgstock, (3195) T.W.Ware.

5th:

Privates: (2479) T.H.J.Deane, (2659) W.J.Hedger, (2881) S.Moore, (3214) W.Westgate.

6th:

Corporal: (2809) A.E.Luxford.

7th:

Private: (2953) C.Pennell.

The relief was only partial because, apart from one night in Arras billets, the Battalion continued to occupy trenches and provide working parties.

On the 14th May the British opened a so-called 'Chinese Bombardment', that is a feint to make the enemy believe that an attack was imminent. The unwelcome result was retaliation by German guns at an intensity of 100 shells per minute which inflicted casualties. The Battle of Arras officially ended on the 17th May. Although of relatively short duration, the severity of infantry actions made this the bitterest and bloodiest battle of the war. The ratio of British casualties per day was higher between the 9th April and the 17th May than any other battle during the 1914 – 1918 conflict.

MAY:

8th:

Private: (3036) F.C.Sales.

9th:

Private: (2490) W.G.Dewley.

10th:

Private: (2690) F.Houghton.

14th:

Privates: (2536) T.E.Faulkner, (2581) C.A.Gibbs, (2593) C.T.R.Godden, (3099) H.Smith.

17th:

Private: (2443) A.E.Crabb.

With the severity of the Arras campaign now greatly diminished, there began what was to become known as the Defence of Monchy, that is the village of Monchy-le-Preux. For the time being, however, the Battalion was leaving all this behind. First, on the 16th May, a long day's march was made westward to a camp just west of Agnex-les-Duisans where parades and cleaning duties were carried out over the next week. Then came a move to Grand Bullicourt where the most beautiful countryside and the perfect calm was appreciated to the full for a period of three weeks. During this time everyone was able to relax and enjoy, amongst other events, the Battalion Sports Day and the Brigade Gymkhana.

Of course, these good things had to come to an end and this they did with a move back towards Arras on the 17th June, arriving in the city the following day. From Arras, trenches around Monchy-le-Preux were occupied in what was known as a condition of 'active defence'. It was in this relatively quiet state of affairs that the hot summer month of June closed.

JUNE:
26th:
Private: (2455) J.F.Croucher.

CHAPTER 21
1917
JULY – DECEMBER

The defences around Monchy-le-Preux were the Battalion's 'home' at the beginning of July. On the 4th, an attack was ordered against a range of shell holes occupied by the enemy. The assault began at 2.30 am but the attackers were heavily bombed and were forced to retire with several of their number dead and missing. Amongst the missing, who were never seen again, were Lieutenant A.E.Willard, and an 'Old Contemptible', Private Benjamin Engleton, who went out to France originally with the 2nd Battalion. On that day, too, Private J.E.Barnes, a Battalion man 'not of good character', was shot at dawn at Arras for his second desertion, already being under a suspended Court Martial sentence of 15 years penal servitude.

JULY:
3rd:
Corporal: (2588) G.W.Goble.
Privates: (2792) A.J.Lewis, (3094) A.Smith.
4th:
Lieutenant: (3226) A.E.Willard.
Sergeant: (3147) G.W.E.Taylor.
Privates: (2246) J.E.Barnes, (2454) W.C.Crouch, (2517) B.Engleton, (3206) F.P.Webber.

A particular tragedy befell the Battalion on the 5th July. During a fierce bombardment, during which a number of casualties were sustained, the Commanding Officer, Lieutenant Colonel A.J.Sansom, and the Adjutant, Captain G.Nagle, came up from their Headquarters dugout in Shrapnel Trench to witness the enemy sequence of signal flares. Hardly had they emerged when a shell dropped between them in the trench killing both men. Lieutenant Colonel Sansom was not a professional regular soldier; he had left his school in Bexhill-on-Sea, initially to join the 5th Battalion. Although he was of mature years he was a vigorous and brave man. Ironically, a letter arrived from General Headquarters on the day of his death recalling him for duty in England. It was with sad hearts that the Battalion moved out after relief on the 7th.

JULY:
5th:
Lieutenant Colonel: (3045) A.J.Sansom.
Captain and Adjutant: (2896) G.Nagle.
Privates: (2211) A.E.Aslett, (3032) W.A.Russell, (3079) H.Simmons.
7th:
Second Lieutenant: (3086) C.M.Sing.

For the next two weeks the Battalion was variously resting at billets in Achicourt or providing working parties in the Wancourt – Feuchy trench line system. Then, suddenly, on the 25th July at 3.00 am, approximately 400 Germans made a surprise attack on the Battalion's trenches. Using a heavy barrage, trench mortars, bombs, gas and flame throwers, the enemy drove the British from both Long and Spoon trenches, neither of which was of great strategic importance but 22 men were lost to the Battalion.

JULY:
25th:
Sergeants: (2185) C.Adams, (2203) A.C.Arnell.
Lance Corporals: (2432) C.S.J.Cornford, (2486) C.G.Denyer, (2612) H.J.Gray, (3180) H.Voak.
Privates: (2249) H.Bartholomew, (2254) S.G.Bateman, (2279) G.Bishopp, (2287) F.J.Bone, (2400) B.J.Cobby, (2421) P.G.Coomber, (2469) T.S.Davis, (2607) C.H.Gower, (2745) G.W.Kehlbacher, (2852) W.J.Mein, (2864) E.R.Mills, (2951) E.A.Pelling, (3009) H.Relf, (3130) W.Strudwick, (3221) E.H.Wickham, (3225) E.Wilkins.

Three days later, on the 28th July, and quite by co-incidence, the enemy fired coloured flares almost identical to the Battalion's S.O.S. signal.

British guns responded to what they thought was a call for their help. The Germans replied causing a number of casualties. The final three days of the month were relatively quiet, although there was some enemy trench mortar and artillery fire.

On the 31st July began, farther north, in the Ypres salient, the Third Battle of Ypres, otherwise known as Passchendaele. Fortunately for the Battalion, they were not called upon to play any part in that action which was fought in the most atrocious quagmire conditions, later acknowledged as the worst of the whole war.

JULY:
27th:
Private: (2375) E.Chappell.
28th:
Lance Corporal: (3172) R.Twibill.
29th:
Privates: (2591) J.Goddard, (2882) W.O.Moore, (3039) G.F.Sambrook.
30th:
Private: (3151) H.Tester.
31st:
Corporal: (3208) T.Webster.

The months of August, September and most of October continued to be spent in the areas around Arras. Some time was enjoyed in billets at Achicourt, some in providing working parties and some in the Monchy Defence trenches. On the whole, there was little fighting activity but a few men were killed, mainly by spasmodic shelling.

AUGUST:
3rd:
Private: (2943) E.H.Partington.
10th:
Lance Corporal: (3106) F.H.Souch.
17th:
Privates: (2420) L.Cooksey, (2748) J.Kempton.
18th:
Private: (2470) B.Dawes.
30th:
Private: (3204) W.Weatherley.
SEPTEMBER:
5th:
Private: (2684) A.G.Hopkins.
24th:
Private: (2260) G.J.P.Beck.
25th:
Private: (2232) L. J. H.Baker.

OCTOBER:
1st:
Lance Sergeant: (2938) F.L.Pannell.
Lance Corporal: (2334) T.W.Budd.
Private: (2929) A.Page.

At last, after 18 weeks in and near the Monchy-le-Preux trenches, the Battalion moved out by train from Arras on the 24th October for a well-deserved rest. In easy stages over the next five days the Battalion eventually arrived and settled at Vieil Hesdin some 30 miles west of Arras and close to the 15th Century battlefield of Agincourt. For the remainder of October and the first half of November intensive training was carried out, particularly in connection with the relatively new military science of operating with tanks. Real live tanks were a scarce resourse, however, and, in the early stages, it was necessary for the huge iron monsters to be represented by wheelbarrows and two-wheeled stretchers !

Following this relatively long period of intensive training in the infantry role of support in tank warfare, the Battalion was moved by way of Péronne, Moslains and Équancourt to a position just north of Gonnelieu by the 18th November. Here, they prepared to help boost the war's first major tank offensive in the Battle of Cambrai. Here, also, during the night of the 19th / 20th November, they heard the distant rumbling of heavy engines as 380 tanks trundled noisily up into position.

At 6.20 am on the 20th November an unusually short barrage from over 1,000 British guns roared forth while low-flying aircraft assisted in drowning from the Germans the noise from the tank engines as they moved to the attack. The iron monsters drove forward with small groups of infantry following closely behind each tank for maximum protection. The enemy were taken by surprise; in many cases they were panic stricken at the sight of the tanks and, everywhere, resistance was feeble.

Such was the menace of the tanks, that men of the Battalion and other units found it possible to advance casually across No-Man's-Land, even stopping to light cigarettes as they followed the slow-moving iron-clads. The Battalion's front was approximately 800 yards wide; all went to plan and proved to be the most successful

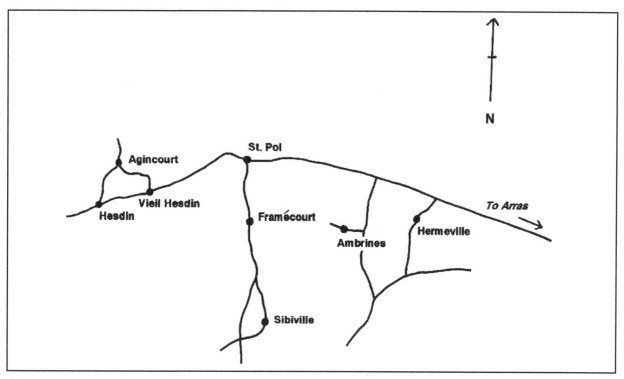

46.   *October to November 1917*

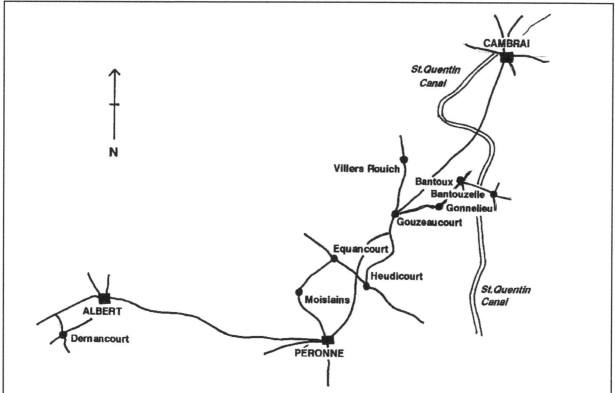

47.   *November to December 1917*

attack ever made by the Battalion. Indeed, every objective allotted by the 12th Division's High Command was attained.

The Battalion had, of course, taken its share of casualties. In the early stages an enemy machine gun in a pillbox of the Hindenburg Line swept No-Man's-Land and, later, another caused more

casualties. The tanks performed wonderfully in the ideal conditions. They flattened barbed wire, gunning German trenches and machine gun posts with impunity.

The whole first day of the battle was a success and should have been even more so if the Senior Commanders had played their cards.

One incident illustrates the point admirably. By careful observation, the Battalion's Captain Le Hardy could see that the villages of Banteux and Bantouzelle appeared to have been evacuated by the enemy. The patrol he sent forward walked unmolested through both villages confirming the situation which Captain Le Hardy immediately reported to Brigade. Through poor communications and the lack of incisiveness of higher commanders this great opportunity to move forward unopposed to a vital canal crossing was lost. There were other such opportunities, also lost. The British Reserves, too, were held so far behind the attack that their vital introduction was not possible quickly enough. The resulting delay allowed the Germans to re-group and re-inforce. The Battle of Cambrai degenerated into yet another wasted chance of real success and the war continued.

NOVEMBER:
19th:
Private: (2962) E.Pickering.
20th:
Second Lieutenants: (2403) D.T.Cohen, (2771) J.L.Knox.
Corporal: (2980) G.W.Preston, M.M.
Lance Corporals: (2321) E.W.Broomfield, (2357) T.H.Cane, (2662) J.Henson.
Privates: (2300) G.T.Braban, (2332) E.G.C.Buckman, (2428) T.K.Copping, (2431) W.Corke, (2665) H.H.Hill, (2678) H.L.Hollis, (2689) C.A.Hosier, (2742) W.F.Kaye, (2822) W.Mansbridge, (2857) W.Middleton, (2884) A.T.Morgan, (2949) J.R.Peen, (3024) J.Rogers, (3093) A.Smith.

After four days respite, the Battalion was ordered to attack Pelican and Bitch Trenches. The attack began at 7.00 am and all objectives were gained. However, the ground conditions and withering German machine gun fire made great difficulties for the carrying parties. Thus, a lack of bombs and the fact that very muddy conditions made Lewis Guns and many rifles unuseable, meant that the men were driven out by the enemy. Incredibly, despite strong protests to Brigade, the depleted and exhausted men were ordered again to attack Pelican Trench at 10.50 pm the same day. This second attack resulted in heavy hand-to-hand fighting and the weary British were forced back to their starting line. All of the slaughter this day would have been averted if only the higher commanders had taken the marvellous opportunity to follow up the German withdrawal on the 20th November when Captain Le Hardy had perceived and reported the villages of Banteux and Bantouzelle, which areas included Pelican and Bitch Trenches, empty. Such were the wasted opportunities and unnecessary losses of life imposed by lack-lustre leadership in some higher echelons of the British army.

NOVEMBER:
21st:
Sergeant: (2923) W.J.Osborne, M.M.
23rd:
Private: (3211) H.E.West.
24th:
Lance Corporal: (2537) J.H.Fearnley.
25th:
Captain: (2237) C.W.Ballard.
Company Quartermaster Sergeant: (3016) W.Robbins.
Sergeants: (2535) F.C.Fairhall, (2931) A.E.Paice.
Lance Sergeant: (2565) D.Funnell.
Lance Corporals: (2626) R.Hall, (2664) H.Hill, (2811) H.P.S.Lyddall, (2842) H.Maughan, M.M.
Privates: (2194) E.A.Alexander, (2261) A.S.Beckettt, (2337) G.W.Bumstead, (2515) A.W.Edwards, (2518) S.J.Elliott, (2524) A.Emblen, (2649) F.B.Haydock, (2655) J.Heasman, (2686) W.C.Hopkins, (2694) W.Howell, (2711) G.Hyland, (2754) H.Kent, (2764) G.S.Kirk, (2803) C.S.Long, (2846) S.C.Maynard, (3110) F.R.Springett, (3201) E.Watson.

After these events, all was relatively quiet until the 30th November when, during a surprise German counter attack which commenced at 7.00 am, considerable confusion arose and the Battalion was fired upon by German and British guns. Undoubtedly, some lost their lives to 'friendly fire' on this occasion. By noon, the Battalion had stemmed the attack by taking up a defensive position in the reserve trenches.

NOVEMBER:
26th:
Lance Corporal: (2839) G.Maslin.
Privates: (3042) J.Sands, (3229) F.W.Wilson.
29th:
Private: (2366) A.Cassidy.
30th:
Corporal: (3074) C.S.Sickelmore.

Privates: (2306) S.Brazier, (2542) L.Finch, (2726) E.R.P.Jeffery, (2774) P.A.Lake, (2800) G.E.Littlechild, (3026) E.G.Routledge, (3209) R.G.Weeden.

On the 1st December the enemy made a determined bombing attack along the Hindenburg Line but, with difficulty, was prevented from crossing the Cambrai Road. This was a close run thing because all the Battalion's S.O.S. rockets had been fired and only a small reserve of ammunition and bombs remained. This proved to be the Battalion's last throw in what had been its most critically difficult period of the war.

DECEMBER:
1st:
Privates: (2668) H.A.Hiscock, (2713) A.Ireson.

The Battle of Cambrai officially ended on the 3rd December. Almost all the gains made in the successful early stages of the battle were lost through poor planning and missed opportunities. Recriminations rumbled on for many months but, surprisingly, no Senior Officer heads rolled. In the House of Commons there was a violent attack upon the role of Sir Douglas Haig who, as Commander in Chief, was ultimately responsible. In a blatant attempt to shield the Government, Secretary of State for War, Mr.J.I.Macpherson, refused to accept that the blame should be placed on the higher command; this implied that the fault was that of the fighting troops.

Indeed, the Senior Officers of Higher Command succeeded in white-washing themselves although with a considerable loss of esteem then, and over the following years of close historical examination of the facts. Even worse was to come when General Byng, the Battalion's own Army Commander, declared: "I attribute the reason of the local success on the part of the enemy to one cause and one alone, namely – the lack of training on the part of junior officers, N.C.O's and men." Such a blatantly disgraceful declaration quite rightly enraged not only every man in the Battalion but also many in other units and outside the army. Such was the quality of this particular Senior Officer who, far from supporting his troops, turned in this cowardly way upon them in an effort towards his own self-preservation.

The Battalion was now moving slowly but purposefully away from the Cambrai area. First, movement was southward, eventually to Péronne, then west for a brief stay at the village of Dernancourt just south of Albert, on the Somme battlefield. This move by road transport in beautifully fine weather was much enjoyed by

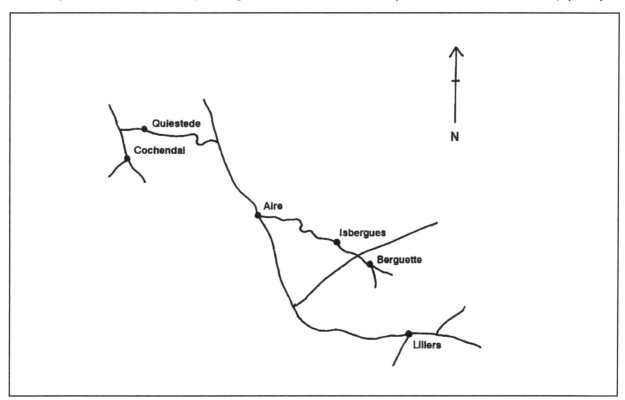

48.   *December 1917 to January 1918*

the men. On the 7th December the direction of movement, this time in snowy conditions, was north, once more, until they arrived at the twin villages of Quiestede and Cochendal north-west of Lillers in northern France. Two days before Christmas another move, relatively short this time, was made to Berguette. Prior to this transfer many items for the anticipated Christmas celebrations had been purchased from the successful canteen funds. Incredibly, an order was received to dump all unnecessary items before the move. It was much to the men's ingenuity, however, that turkeys, geese, beer, fruit and even pigs somehow found their way onto Lewis Gun and other limbers before the journey. As a result of these concealed efforts and receipt of a large consignment of Christmas puddings from funds raised by national newspapers at home, all the men enjoyed an excellent Christmas dinner in the village school at Isbergues.

DECEMBER:
2nd:
Lance Corporal: (2358) A.Cannon.
4th:
Lance Corporal: (2500) S.Drake.
8th:
Private: (2405) W.Colburn.
14th:
Private: (3164) A.E.Tooke.
22nd:
Lance Corporal: (2594) E.Godden.
25th:
Private: (2988) W.Putman.
27th:
Private: (2381) A.Cheesemore.
29th:
Lieutenant: (2841) J.L.Matthews.

CHAPTER 22
1918
JANUARY – JUNE

The old year having ended with a Smoking Concert organised and provided by the Battalion sergeants, 1918 began with a period of training, re-training and practice at bombing, machine gunning, sniping and general musketry. At one point, Second Lieutenant Atkinson was even sent on a one-day course in the care and use of pigeons ! Then, on the 13th January, the Battalion arrived back at the village of La Boulillerie between Fromelles and Fleurbaix, a sector last occupied two years previously. The ground was still the same; flat, open, inclined to be wet, and devoid of trenches. With the natural water table so near to the surface it was not possible to dig to any reasonable depth. Instead, the front and support lines were entirely of sandbagged breastworks and parapets, now in a most derelict and perished condition.

Work was put in hand to improve the situation and much was done before the 21st January when the Battalion was relieved and moved to Doulieu. By month end the Fleurbaix defences and the sector near Bois Grenier were being manned.

It was at this time that the army's losses of men and the reluctance of the Government, led by Lloyd-George, to send more soldiers to the Western Front, forced Sir Douglas Haig to implement reductions to conserve manpower and reorganise his Divisions. Infantry Brigades were reduced from four to three battalions. This meant that some battalions were moved, amalgamated or even disbanded. The 36th Brigade lost the 8th Royal Fusiliers and the 11th Middlesex but gained the 5th Royal Berkshires. Fortunately, the 7th Royal Sussex were otherwise unaffected.

At 5.30 am on the 4th February the Germans raided a post held by 'A' Company. The first fatalities of 1918 were sustained in this skirmish and one man died of wounds two days later.

FEBRUARY:
4th:
Corporals: (2559) W.C.Freeland, (2758) W.Kewell.
Privates: (2327) S.J.Brown, (2827) E.Mardle.
6th:
Private: (2459) P.Curtis.

There then passed a quiet period of 10 days before the Battaion marched to rest at Sailly-sur-la-Lys. Large working parties were provided almost daily until a return to the front line was made on the 22nd February. Even then it was 'all quiet' on the Battalion's front.

The recent pattern of inactivity and the provision of working parties continued into March, 1918, the month of menace. Throughout the British army concern was afoot about a threatening German build-up along the front, particularly along the Hindenburg Line. It was from there that the threat would become reality on the 21st March and the Battalion was moved back to help stem the inevitable enemy attack. As the German assault was launched, the Battalion travelled over a three-day period by way of Caudescure, Steenbecque, Pérnes, St.Pol, Frevent, Doullens and Warloy to Aveluy Wood on the old Somme battlefield. Aveluy Wood was to have great significance for the Battalion while it played its part in bringing to a halt the great German Spring Offensive which aimed to reach the major railhead at Amiens and break through to the channel ports.

MARCH:
5th:
Private: (3111) A.E.Squires.
7th:
Private: (2401) A.H.Cody.
8th:
Private: (2605) J.Gough.
18th:
Private: (2773) J.H.Lake.

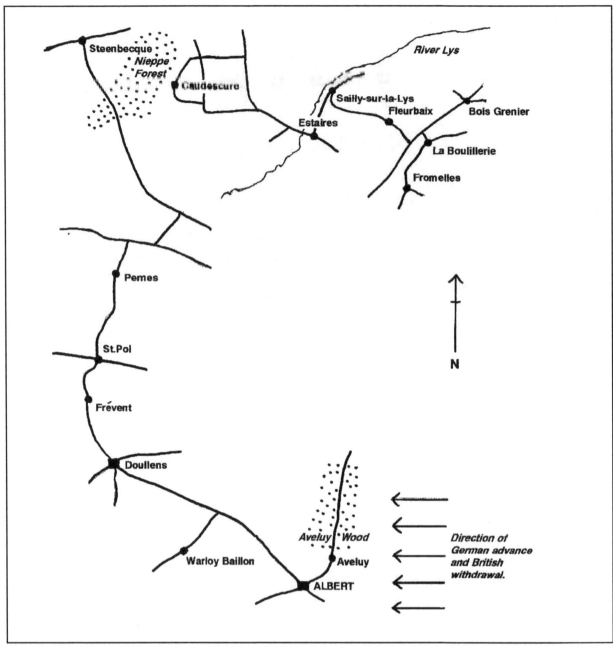

49.

Just in time, the Battalion took up its position in Aveluy Wood immediately on the west side of the River Ancre on the 26th March. During that night it was an awsome sight to look eastward and witness the whole of the old Somme battlefield in front of them lit up by the fires of many stores and dumps set ablaze by the British armies as they fell back under the weight and speed of the German onslaught. The Battalion knew clearly what was coming their way and felt fortunate, indeed, that within the last three weeks they had been issued with an additional 20 machine guns.

MARCH:
26th:
Lance Corporal: (2369) H.S.Cave.
Private: (2201) J.W.Ansell.

The retreating forces, now immediately in front of the Battalion, were falling back with the enemy in hot pursuit. At 9.30 am on the 27th March the Germans arrived and attacked on the Battalion's right. Two Companies quickly set up a defensive flank along the southern edge of Aveluy Wood while the other two Companies continued to face east. Late in the afternoon the enemy attacked in force and entered the south-east corner of the wood.

Although a good number of Germans were killed, they succeeded in surrounding Battalion Headquarters which was established at Quarry Post within the wood.

The Commanding Officer was there directing and supporting the defence by distributing ammunition as a tremendous fight took place. Every man there used rifles against repeated German rushes until, eventually, the enemy retired. For this action Lieutenant Colonel Impey was awarded the D.S.O.

MARCH:
27th:
Second Lieutenants: (2543) H.F.Finnemore, (2821) H.D.Manley.
Sergeants: (2775) H.Lambert, (2869) E.G.Minall.
Lance Corporals: (2192) J.A.Alderton, (2210) G.Ashman, (2426) J.Cooper.
Privates: (2285) J.Boater, (2331) W.Bryder, (2360) G.Canton, (2406) B.Coleman, (2411) W.S.Collier, (2539) W.Fickling, (2548) H.Fitzell, (2705) G.F.Humphreys, (2721) G.James, (2723) W.Jarrett, (2743) J.Keating, (2747) A.A.Kelly, (2995) L.V.Randall, (3031) F.W.Russell, (3033) G.W.Rutland, (3055) W.F.Scrivens.

During the following day, the 28th March, the Battalion continued to be hard pressed but retained its vital hold on Aveluy Wood. Second Lieutenant V.E.Rogers later reported that, at one point, he and his men heard a voice in good English ordering them to raise their hands. They quickly complied, realising that enemy soldiers were covering them at close range with a machine gun. Taken prisoner, the group trudged through the wood escorted by Germans with revolvers. Second Lieutenant Rogers was walking in front with the German officer who asked the whereabouts of British positions. At this, Second Lieutenant Rogers, who knew the wood very well, gradually led the group towards the nearby railway line where he knew the 6th Royal West Kents were positioned. Too late at about 100 yards distance, the German officer realised the trap. He tried to save himself by pointing his revolver at his prisoner as a hostage but was promptly shot and killed by a Royal West Kent sniper. The grateful British officer and his eight men quickly rejoined their comrades.

MARCH:
28th:
Lance Corporal: (2728) E.Jenner.
Privates: (2225) E.V.Baggett, (2344) J.Burgess, (2485) W.Denton, (2704) J.T.Humphrey, (2972) D.R.Porteous, (3070) D.W.Shoesmith, (3142) A.H.Taylor, (3185) P.Wakeham.

It was on this day, the 28th March, that the German advance was halted along the western edge of the town of Albert. One German officer, who could not understand why, later told how he entered the town to find the cause of the hold up. There he saw many German soldiers who clearly had no wish to go onward. In the town they had discovered huge stocks of food and particularly wine; commodities they themselves had been denied for so long. Another German officer also claimed that the reason they failed to reach Amiens was the looting of Albert by German troops. Many men were found lying about in rooms and cellars drunk and unfit to fight. However, this was not the whole story. Ironically for the Germans, a major reason was the success of their own offensive; so quick and so far reaching was their advance of some 30 or 35 miles, over a devastated previous battlefield with no roads, railways or other means of supply and communication, that the momentum dwindled and, with grit and determination displayed by the British, was brought to a standstill.

The Battalion was still holding Aveluy Wood doggedly when it was relieved on the 29th March and moved back to Warloy. So ended March, 1918, and with it the main and final German threat to break through to the English Channel.

MARCH:
29th:
Privates: (2779) E.A.Lawes, (3071) H.Short.
30th:
Privates: (2230) C.Baker, (2899) E.R.New.

The front line just north of Albert was taken over on the 2nd April. The following day was quiet but, on the next afternoon, increased enemy shelling foretold the likelihood of an impending attack. At 7.00 am on the 5th April, the German barrage increased with the use of many gas shells. When the attack finally came it penetrated the front line held by the 5th Royal Berkshires. An ill-conceived counter attack was then ordered to be carried out by 'A' and 'B' Companies of the 7th Royal Sussex.

These two Companies were sent in under cover of darkness wearing full fighting order. Their clanking equipment forewarned the enemy who were ready and waiting. There was no British artillery support. As the men crossed a sunken road enemy Very Lights illuminated the scene and numerous casualties were taken immediately from rifle and machine gun fire. Further advance was impossible and the remnants of the two Companies somehow got back to their starting points.

The Battalion held its position through the rest of the night and the following day before being relieved and retiring to Senlis.

APRIL:
5th:
Corporal: (2780) J.P.Lawes.
Lance Corporals: (2328) A.J.Browne, (2386) W.H.Child, (2992) J.Quinn, (3040) J.E.Sammonds.
Privates: (2196) R.G.Allen, (2202) A.F.Appleby, (2238) C.Banger, (2255) W.J.Bateman, (2288) G.Boniface, (2314) H.J.Bright, (2417) F.Cook, (2430) C.Corder, (2480) A.R.Dearling, (2505) F.Dumsday, (2520) R.Ellis, (2569) H.Gallard, (2622) G.Gutsell, (2639) T.W.Harper, (2656) W.G.Heasman, (2693) S.C.Howden, (2698) G.Huggett, (2736) A.J.J.Jones, (2766) T.Knight, (2798) W.D.Linfield, (2823) C.W.March, (2824) F.Marchant, (2830) T.Marsh, (2875) H.J.Mitchell, (2876) J.F.Mitchell, (2979) S.Preece, (3048) G.H.Sawyer, (3107) J.Southon, (3115) J.Stanley, (3179) J.Vincent, (3182) A.Wade.
6th:
Lance Sergeant: (2688) R.Horney.
Lance Corporal: (3001) J.Ray.
Privates: (2541) F.Filtness, (2570) T.Gander, (2843) G.E.Maxwell.

The Germans gas shelled Senlis during the next two days so it was little hardship to return to the front line at Bouzincourt on the 9th April. While they were there an alarming but, in retrospect, amusing incident occured. One night, no guides arrived to lead the transport to the Battalion's position. Eager to deliver the men's rations, the transport stopped at the roadside while trying to decide the right direction. At that moment a salvo of enemy shells exploded overhead. The noise stampeded the horses, all of which were quickly checked with the exception

of two. These animals, Jerry and Jumbo, were pulling the field kitchen and they charged out of control towards the German lines. The field kitchen was soon completely wrecked but the driver, Private Laker, held firm and did a wonderful job by pulling up the horses in front of the enemy wire. Extricating the animals from the shattered kitchen, Private Laker returned to laughter, cheers and hoots of derision.

APRIL:
8th:
Private: (2770) H.Knowles.
9th:
Privates: (2790) J.Levett, (2826) P.H.Marchant, (2919) A.G.W.Onslow, (2921) H.C.Osborn.

On the 12th April the Battalion moved out to Warloy Baillon, enjoyed baths at Contay and then established itself at Mirvaux. From Mirvaux a quick sojourn was taken at Piérregot before a succession of moves, to Harponville on the 19th, to Acheux on the 22nd and finally back to the line for the last few days of the month.

APRIL:
13th:
Private: (2313) W.F.Bridle.
16th:
Corporal: (2404) G.Colburn.
19th:
Private: (2248) A.R.Barrs.
21st:
Private: (2273) C.S.Billing.
22nd:
Private: (2269) A.Berry.
25th:
Privates: (2349) D.Bushell, (2562) J.A.Frost.
26th:
Private: (2987) C.Purchase.
28th:
Privates: (2660) R.Hemsley, (3166) C.A.Townsend.
30th:
Private: (3047) A.D.H.Sawyer.

The month of May proved to be relatively quiet. The German spring offensive advance had been halted and the new line was being held by the British while they reorganised and brought themselves slowly into readiness for their own counter attack offensive later in the summer. The Battalion held the line east of Mailly-Maillet during the month, interspersed with periods

50.   *April to August 1918*

of rest at Acheux. Time was spent in cleaning, training and providing various working parties. There was spasmodic German shelling and also some bombing by their aircraft which caused a number of casualties.

Another of those incidents, serious at the time but amusing with hindsight, occured at this period. Because enemy bombing was causing problems around the transport lines at Mailly-Maillet, the drivers were being taught how to use the three Lewis Guns provided for anti-aircraft purposes. One of the drivers was being shown how to aim his gun without touching the trigger. In his excitement and nervousness, however, he inadvertently fired a short burst. At that

moment there happened to be a British balloon high overhead, and the observers in its basket, thinking they were being machine gunned by an unseen enemy aircraft, jumped for their lives and floated to earth on their parachutes.

The Battalion marched from Mailly-Maillet to Beauquesne, in the direction of Doullens, on the 25th May and there remained until the end of the month.

MAY:
1st:
Private: (3073) A.Shorter.
3rd:
Second Lieutenant: (2283) C.E.Blencowe.
Private: (2974) A.H.Powell.

10th:
Private: (2720) E.A.James.
15th:
Lance Corporal: (2621) H.V.Gunton.
16th:
Privates: (2633) H.Harbour, (3065) W.H.S.Seymour.
19th:
Privates: (2218) T.Avey, (2338) J.Bunker.
20th:
Privates: (2234) R.D.Baker, (2507) W.J.Eade, (2942) W.J.F.Parkinson, (3127) F.E.Stone.
21st:
Private: (2388) S.C.Chpperfield.
24th:
Corporal: (2625) H.F.Hall.
Private: (3230) J.Wingfield.
27th:
Privates: (2259) T.H.Beall, M.M., (2966) F.Plummer.

The British army continued to hold the line, reinforce, train and bide its time throughout the month of June, and the 7th Battalion was no exception. The strength and morale of personnel were improved with range finding, courses, sports days and opportunities to bathe. New drafts of men were received and incorporated into Battalion life. On the 17th June a move began back to the front line by way of Toutencourt, Harponville and Warloy Baillon. The front trenches were taken over from the 9th Royal Fusiliers on the 21st.

On the 23rd June, while supervising a working party, Lieutenant S.C.Boys was killed by enemy machine gun fire. British guns and trench mortars were active on the 27th and 28th, following the policy of keeping pressure on the enemy. A move back to a valley north of Warloy Baillon on the 29th put the Battalion into Divisional Reserve, giving them a time to rest and clean up generally.

JUNE:
23rd:
Lieutenant: (2299) S.C.Boys.
29th:
Private: (2316) F.Bristow.

Within five hours of arrival at Warloy Baillon, the Battalion was ordered to 'stand to' ready to assist in any emergency while the 37th Brigade made an attack on enemy positions. The attack proved successful so, as a result, the Battalion 'stood down'.

JUNE:
30th:
Lance Corporals: (2549) L.V.Fitzpatrick, (2576) F.Gear.
Private: (2228) A.W.Baker.

CHAPTER 23
1918
JULY – THE ARMISTICE

The position east of Senlis, taken by the 37th Brigade on the 30th June, was conter-attacked and reclaimed by the Germans on the 2nd July. In response to this, the Battalion, having been placed under the orders of the General Officer Commanding 37th Brigade, were ordered by him at 1.35 am on the 3rd July to attack and reclaim the position from the enemy. Heavy German artillery fire was experienced on the move forward to starting positions and 'D' Company was severely affected by the explosion amongst them of an eight inch shell. Fortunately, the hasty and ill-conceived attack was cancelled just 15 minutes before zero hour. Undoubtedly, the cancellation saved the Battalion from a massacre because the Germans were clearly ready and waiting for them. Thankfully, by 5.00 am, the Battalion, although still east of Senlis, was farther back for a while but, that night, they returned to the familiar front line at Aveluy Wood.

JULY;
3rd:
Lance Corporal: (3198) G.Washer.
Privates: (2233) M.Baker, (2650) H.Hayes, (2870) J.Minnis, (2940) L.Papworth.

For the next few days the front line was fairly quiet but, during the early hours of the 9th July, the Germans dropped about 100 gas shells on the right hand trenches. The fact that large numbers of casualties were not sustained bears evidence to the effectiveness of the new gas masks and the quick actions of the troops. Relief came the following day and the Battalion marched out to Toutencourt Wood. From there, on the 14th July, the transport set off by road and, later by rail, to the Battalion's new destination, the village of Oresmaux some eight miles south of Amiens. The remaining officers and men travelled by buses and the whole Battalion met up again at Oresmaux on

the 15th where they came into support of the IX and XXXI French Corps.

JULY:
4th:
Private: (2186) C.E.Adams.
9th:
Corporal: (3087) C.L.Sisley.
11th:
Privates: (2687) J.F.Horn, (2948) C.W.Peckham.
14th:
Private: (3037) H.Salvage.
18th:
Private: (2566) C.Furner.

At Oresmaux, which was quite a large village, training continued much as before but with particular emphasis on gas precautions. A large training and demonstration ground was available and this was fully utilised throughout the stay of 15 days. During that time, a filly was born to one of the mares. The young horse became a firm favourite; she was named 'Somme' and she was destined to accompany the Battalion to victory. In due time there was a happy ending to this story because 'Somme' returned to England with the Battalion and there, being put up for sale at Chichester market, she was purchased for £40 by Captain H.Sadler who had served the Battalion so well, especially and appropriately at Ovillers on the Somme.

The month of August saw the British and French re-strengthened, re-prepared, re-trained and ready to launch their own offensive which, unkown to them at the time, was to become known as 'The Battle of Amiens' and, later, the 'Great Advance to Victory'. The great attack was launched on the 8th August with massive artillery, tank and Royal Air Force support and co-operation.

By the time the attack was made, the Battalion had left Oresmaux for Lahoussoye on the

Amiens – Albert Road from where it moved into position to play its part south-west of the village of Morlancourt. Casualties were incurred on the day before the actual attack when German heavy shells fell as the Battalion moved up to its assembly positions which were on very open, relatively high, rolling countryside reminiscent of Sussex Downland. The men wounded at this time were attended to by the 8th Royal Sussex who were billeted nearby in their capacity as pioneers to the 18th Division.

AUGUST:
7th:
Lieutenant: (2494) P.S.Dixon.
Second Lieutenant: (2893) A.Murray.

The plan was that the Battalion, now attached to the 18th Division, and part of the British army's III Corps, was to capture ground between the Rivers Ancre and Somme as a defensive northern flank to the main attack which was to be undertaken south of the River Somme by the Australians and Canadians.

Zero hour was fixed for 4.20 am, an hour before sunrise on the 8th August. The Battalion was to attack on a front of 500 yards. As the time approached, the sound of tank engines could be heard but the noise was soon blotted out, as planned, by low flying aircraft. The Battalion would have no tank support as that was to be concentrated south of the River Somme. The ground was unfamiliar and, by zero hour, a thick mist had formed reducing visibility in the pre-dawn darkness to only about 10 yards.

In these conditions the advance was slow. At the far side of No-Man's-Land it was found that the enemy was manning short lengths of trench but it was difficult to find and identify them. A considerable number of men fell as casualties in the confusion of firing and bombing. The fog lifted about 10.00 am and many men who went missing in the fog rejoined their units later in the day. The attack was halted somewhat short, and to the right of, the Battalion's objectives and the remainder of the day was relatively quiet.

AUGUST:
8th:
Second Lieutenants: (2934) H.J.Palmer, (3025) W.S.Rousell.

Sergeants: (2209) A.H.Ashenden, (3062) A.E.Selby, M.M.
Corporals: (2958) T.W.Philcox, (3235) E.H.Wise.
Privates: (2301) F.W.Brace, (2343) A.Burgess, (2387) R.W.Children, (2429) H.Corbett, (2435) F.W.Court, (2447) W.T.Creighton, (2451) H.G.Croft, (2492) J.J.Dinmore, (2498) L.J.Downham, (2631) T.Hamson, (2741) A.Kay, (2767) W.H.Knight, (2908) T.A.Nickless, (2927) R.Packham, (2939) F.Papworth, (2975) J.W.Pratt, (2994) J.Rand, (3171) F.T.Turner, (3184) H.Wakeford.

After a relatively quiet time on the 8th August and the following morning, there was some German shelling which caused casualties during the afternoon of the 9th. Later that day the Battalion moved back to rest shelters near Méricourt-l'Abbé. Everyone was clearly in need of a night's sleep but at midnight, only two hours after arrival, they were sent forward again, this time in Reserve along the old front lines west of Morlancourt.

AUGUST:
9th:
Second Lieutenant: (2346) C.P.Burley.
Company Sergeant Major: (3178) E.N.Venn.
Lance Sergeants: (2471) L.Dawson, (3050) H.Sayers.
Lance Corporal: (2256) H.J.C.Battensby.
Privates: (2363) P.G.Carstairs, (2410) R.J.Coles, (2563) C.Fuller, (2730) G.W.A.J.Jenner, (2756) A.L.Kerswill, (2759) C.J.King, (3008) W.H.Reickie, (3058) J.S.Seamark, (3217) A.T.White, (3223) G.Wild.

The Battalion moved east of Morlancourt to the front line on the 10th August where they experienced two quiet days on the 11th and 12th. On the 13th a local operation was launched at 4.55 am. The men of 'C' and 'D' Companies were to attack over open ground while 'A' Company advanced along a trench which led towards the enemy positions.. Second Lieutenant W.T.Trowell, the only officer remaining with 'C' Company, was lying out with his men in front of their trench ready to attack. As the arranged bombardment commenced, the men of 'C' Company rose to their feet and began to advance. Immediately, the whole Company was overwhelmed tragically by 'friendly fire' and suffered heavy losses. It had been impossible for the British artillery to register their guns prior to this attack and the results were catostrophic.

Although 'A' Company drove back the enemy along his trench for about 300 yards, capturing two machine guns and 12 prisoners, the attack generally met fierce German resistence and could not continue once the allied bombardment had passed ahead.

All units were compelled to make their way back as best they could to their original lines. The Battalion was relieved shortly before midnight and moved back west of Morlancourt heartbroken and angry that so many colleagues had been killed by 'friendly fire'. Even then there was to be a 'sting in the tail' when, on the march back, just after midnight, Lieutenant Clements was killed by a single stray German bullet.

AUGUST:
11th:
Privates: (2844) H.May, (3109) J.H.Spencerly.
12th:
Private: (3232) H.H.Winter.
13th:
Lance Corporals: (2309) W.T.Bridgland, (2697) G.E.Hudson.
Privates: (2227) A.G.Bailey, (2353) T.H.Butcher, (2373) E.Chapman, (2442) S.Cox, (2481) H.Debenham,(2749) J.C.Kennaby, (2783) T.A.Lawson, (2863) A.J.Miller.
14th:
Lieutenant: (2396) R.F.Clements.
Privates: (2472) F.G.Day, (2889) A.Mountstephens.

On the 16th August the Battalion moved back to rest at Méricourt-l'Abbé. In the previous nine days of action since the Brirish attack was launched, the Battalion had to its credit the capture of one 77mm gun, 11 machine guns and 120 prisoners. On the debit side, casualties had amounted to 14 officers and 235 other ranks.

On the first full day of this spell at Méricourt-l'Abbé, a few heavy shells fell nearby. There then followed three quiet days before the inevitable return to the front line. It was from midnight onwards on the night of the 21st / 22nd August that heavy enemy gas shelling was received. The Battalion attacked once more that morning, at about 4.45 am, with the support of three heavy tanks and a contact aircraft. After initial enemy shelling there was surprisingly little resistance. At one point 'C' Company formed up in echelon on either side of a tank and completed the advance to take all objectives including the ridge to the east of the Albert – Bray-sur-Somme road. This day had seen the nearest the Battalion had been so far to 'open warfare'. The successful advance of three miles with little sign of opposition had been exhilerating.

AUGUST:
17th:
Lance Corporal: (2746) S.Keigwin.
18th:
Private: (2329) E.M.Browne.
21st:
Second Lieutenant: (2776) F.C.Lanaway.
Private: (2715) A.E.Ives.
22nd:
Sergeant: (2274) E.V.Billings.
Lance Sergeant: (3165) F.J.Tooms.
Privates: (2359) G.H.Cannons, (2645) G.Harwood, (3041) A.G.Sanders, (3174) W.W.Twinn.

With the Germans at last 'on the run' or, at worst, fighting a rearguard retreat, the British army was anxious to maintain its pressure. Thus, at 1.00 am on the 24th August, the Battalion was again moving forward. Inevitably, casualties were sustained during the advance which was continued into the next day when the Battalion moved round south of Albert to a position close to the village of Fricourt.

AUGUST:
24th:
Lance Corporal: (2804) J.Longbottom.
Privates: (2315) A.G.Brind, (2325) J.F.Brown, (2525) W.Emery, (2648) W.Howorth, (2737) H.C.Jones, (2789) T.G.Lee, (3007) F.J.Reeve, (3100) W.W.Smith, (3205) B.F.Webb.
25th:
Private: (3061) W.Secker.

Once more the attack continued, this time at 4.30 am on the 26th August. The aim was to press forward through the line east of Mametz reached earlier by the 35th Brigade, the new front line being more that a mile beyond Mametz Wood. Unlike the previous few days, very strong German opposition, particularly with clever and concealed use of machine guns, was encountered and it was almost impossible to make headway once daylight came. It was at this time that Lieutenant Lavender was killed and Second Lieutenant Honeyman was shot in the stomach.

The Medical Officer, Captain O'Malley, was soon attending several wounded men while they lay in the open under heavy machine gun fire; he was awarded the D.S.O. for this gallantry. However, the enemy began a further withdrawal during the afternoon. British units followed up and with direction that day changing from north-east to almost due east, the Battalion was positioned, by nightfall, on a ridge some 500 yards west of the Maricourt – Montauban Road.

AUGUST:
26th:
Lieutenant: (2778) H.R.Lavender.
Sergeant: (2456) H.J.Cruttenden.
Lance Corporals: (2251) W.R.Barwick, (2390) E.A.Clark, (2573) S.G.Geall, (3017) R.A.Roberts, (3051) W.R.Sayers.
Privates: (2393) W.F.Clark, (2438) H.Cowdrey, (2617) V.Griffiths, (2837) F.C.Maskell, (2888) O.C.Morris, (2930) S.W.Page-Mitchell, (3125) M.Stephenson, (3150) J.O.Tegerdine, (3220) F.A.Whittemore, M.M. and Bar.

The remaining days of August were spent in rest and reorganisation. In the evenings there were some happy 'sing-songs' following the acquisition by one of the cooks of a concertina which proved very popular. For the last three weeks the Battalion had been almost continually on the move forward having covered, with the Division, approximately eight and a half miles.

AUGUST:
27th:
Privates: (2271) P.J.Bianchi, (3078) C.Simmons.
28th:
Lance Corporals: (2856) S.G.Merritt, (3035) S.V.Sadler.
Privates: (2615) H.Gregory, (2700) C.Hughes.
29th:
Corporal: (3043) W.Sands.
Lance Corporal: (2670) F.G.Hodges.

September began with further moves forward. The Battalion settled, on the 4th, in a position south-east of St.Piérre Vaast Wood, north of Péronne. It was agonising to see that the wood

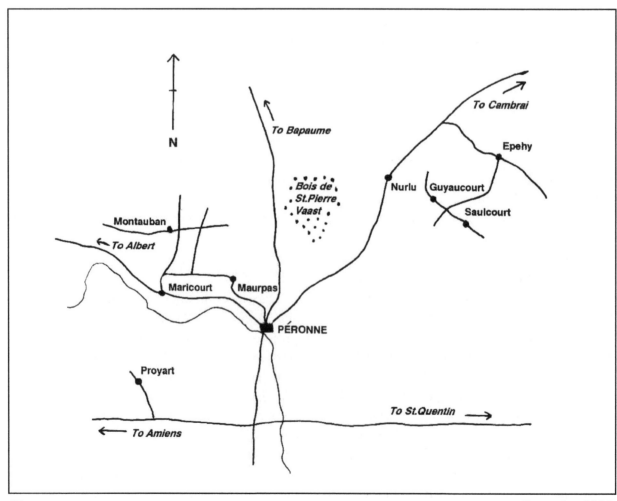

51.   *September 1918*

itself was littered with dead horses, mostly gun teams, many of whom were still in their traces.

SEPTEMBER: 2nd:
Corporal: (2473) G.Day.
Private: (2244) G.J.Barnes.
4th:
Private: (2880) A.Moore.

Again at short notice, orders came for an attack on Vesta and Ajax Trenches which were south of the village of Nurlu. The first attack at zero hour, 5.00 am, was to cross the Canal du Nord which was being continually gas shelled. The crossing was accomplished by use of a number of foot bridges, all of which were in reach of long- range German small arms fire. Next came an advance up a long grassy slope, which was situated west of Signal Copse and was devoid of cover. On reaching a line opposite Signal Copse, no further advance was possible because of sweeping fire from enemy machine guns.

The attack was ordered to recommence at 7.00 pm by which time there was torrential rain which made it difficult to keep direction and in touch with other units in the darkness. Once again, the attack was held up by machine guns, and the Battalion remained in the valley in front of Nurlu. The village was taken, next day, by the 5th Royal Berkshires. During the two attacks on the 5th September, two officers and seven other ranks were killed. In addition, three officers and 60 other ranks were wounded, three of whom died over the next two days.

SEPTEMBER:
5th:
Captain: (2604) E.C.Gorringe.
Second Lieutenant: (2207) T.P.Ashby.
Sergeants: (2347) C.G.Burrough, (2885) W.L.Morley.
Privates: (2333) H.Buckwalter, (2378) F.G.Chatfield, (2416) B.G.Convoy, (2619) R.Grover, (2950) E.G.Pegram.
6th:
Private: (2918) J.G.G.Olley.
7th:
Privates: (2364) A.W.Carver, (2973) F.Potter.

Since the British offensive was launched on the 8th August, the Battalion had done its share of the splendid work. They had delivered 17 attacks, advanced 17 miles, captured 194 machine guns, 17 other guns, 102 trench mortars and 1,027 prisoners. They now enjoyed a well-earned period, from the 7th to the 16th September, cleaning, bathing, training and reorganising. During these 10 days the British advance had maintained its momentum so that, by the time the Battalion was brought into action again, on the 17th, they had moved north-eastwards and were assembled in front of the village of Epéhy.

The next attack, planned for 6.50 am on the 18th September, was a complicated manoeuvre and depended on the early taking of Epéhy by the 35th Brigade. All was made worse by very heavy rain which, together with the darkness, made hard going for the infantry and tanks. At dawn a heavy mist, and a smoke barrage put down by our own artillery, added greatly to the problems. As a result, and almost inevitably, platoons lost direction and this was realised only when the men came up to a very thick barrier of barbed wire which was not expected and was not shown on the maps. At this point concentrated enemy machine gun fire was received from Epéhy which had not been taken as planned and many casualties were the cumulative result.

All the Company officers, with the exception of Captain Andrews and second Lieutenant Coxhead, together with over 200 other ranks had become casualties. The loss of one officer, Lieutenant J.A.Wright, Commanding 'A' Company, was a result of enemy treachery for which they paid dearly. Approaching an enemy post, Lieutenant Wright saw several Germans with their hands raised in surrender. He was moving towards them without firing when, suddenly, at very close range, other Germans in the post opened fire killing Lieutenant Wright instantly and killing and wounding several of his men. Understandably, the remaining Royal Sussex men 'dealt' with the situation and no Germans in the post survived.

Not until 7.45 pm was Epéhy cleared of the enemy and the devastating fire from that village halted. Further progress by the tattered Battalion was not possible in the circumstances so they held on where they were situated. At that time, the Battalion's four Companies consisted of only three officers and 197 other ranks.

SEPTEMBER:
18th:
Lieutenant: (3247) J.A.Wright.
Second Lieutenants: (2526) E.C.Ericson, (2695) W.Howett, (2699) S.G.Huggett, (2853) J.Mennie.
Sergeant: (2635) G.Hardham.
Corporal: (2903) F.Newton.
Lance Corporals: (2458) H.Curd, (3227) J.Williams.
Privates: (2183) H.Abrams, (2290) A.Boorman, (2355) R.Caddow, (2394) C.A.Clarkson, (2398) G.Cluff, (2408) A.E.Coles, (2409) E.W.Coles, (2522) W.Elphick, (2530) S.C.Evans, (2544) F.C.Fish, (2572) W.Gaunt, (2575) S.Gearing, (2583) S.J.Gibson, (2584) W.C.Gibson-Lee, (2628) W.Hallam, (2644) A.Harvey, (2658) G.J.Heath, (2707) W.S.Hutchinson, (2740) G.W.Jupp, (2751) H.Kennedy, (2793) E.V.Lewington, (2801) G.B.Lloyd, (2806) A.J.Lucas, (2849) H.J.Meekings, (2871) S.Misselbrook, (2872) F.Mitchell, (2957) H.W.Peters, (2963) W.Pink, (2967) J.R.Plummer, (2982) A.G.Prevost, (3002) J.W.Rayment, (3011) F.A.Rich, (3056) F.Scutt, (3067) F.Sheppard, (3081) S.J.Simmons, (3097) B.F.Smith, (3134) H.Summers, (3139) F.Swift, (3153) E.Thake, (3163) L.Titman, (3177) E.Utting, (3213) J.W.G.Westgate.

So depleted was the Battalion at this time that it was re-organised into a two-Company Unit. Even so, there was to be no respite because a relatively minor attack was carried out on the 21st September and this was followed by two days of heavy enemy shelling. Somewhat surprisingly, the Germans counter-attacked on the 24th supported by a heavy barrage but they were driven off with many casualties.

By the morning of the 19th September the enemy had withdrawn about one mile. Men of the Battalion remained in position and were heavily shelled.

SEPTEMBER:
19th:
Privates: (3116) E.Staplehurst, (3137) E.A.Swain.
20th:
Lance Corporal: (3098) H.Smith.
21st:
Second Lieutenant: (2466) B.Daunt.
Privates: (2499) A.W.Doyle, (2854) H.Mercer, (3010) P.E.Relf, (3103) F.Snell.
22nd:
Private: (2354) G.B.Byles.
23rd:
Lance Sergeant: (2710) H.P.Hygate.
Privates: (2418) H.J.L.Cook, (3003) R.Reed.

24th Second Lieutenant: (2781) T.E.Lawrence.
Privates: (2383) A.Cherryman, (2512) F.B.East, (2545) E.Fisher, (2556) W.H.Foster, (2582) A.W.Gibby, (2991) A.W.Quested, (3197) F.Warrington, (3216) D.Wharton.

Although relieved on the 25th September, there was to be no immediate move back to rest. As the tide of the British offensive swept onward, units stayed where they were for some respite. There, enemy shell fire continued to be a problem and a cause of casualties until the last day of the month when the Battalion was ordered back to Guyencourt ready to travel by bus the following day. In truth, the Battalion had fought itself to a standstill since the 8th August British offensive and, in essence, virtually ceased to exist. Since that time, casualties had totalled no less than 40 officers and 800 other ranks.

SEPTEMBER:
26th:
Lance Sergeant: (2785) A.J.Le Chevalier.
Private: (3148) J.E.Teague.
27th:
Lance Corporal: (2502) E.Dudman.
29th:
Privates: (2712) A.Hylands, (3044) W.Sands, (3060) G.Secker.

Men of the Battalion boarded buses at Saulcourt on the 1st October and were driven to Péronne and then on to Proyart, south of the River Somme. At the time they did not know that they were about to leave the Somme battlefield areas for the last time. The whole Battalion boarded a train on the 2nd and chugged off at 11.00 pm moving slowly but steadily northwards.

OCTOBER:
2nd:
Privates: (2489) G.N.Dewar, (2937) S.A.Palmer.

The train journey of 13 hours brought them, by mid-day on the 3rd October, to Acq north-west of Arras and just behind the infamous Vimy Ridge. A short bus journey on the 4th took the Battalion to a cross-roads near the village of Thélus at a time when patrols indicated that the enemy seemed ready to withdraw and all local British units were attempting to advance. A definite German withdrawal was confirmed on

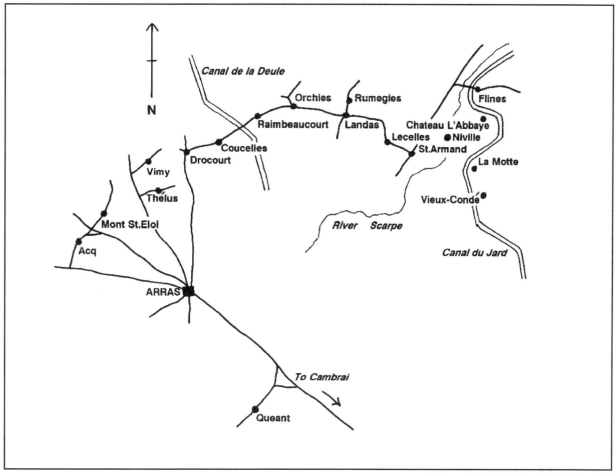

52. *October to the Armistice 1918*

the 8th. The Battalion was placed in Reserve for two days and then, on the 12th moved forward to take up position in the Drocourt – Queant Line, moving on again, next day, to approach the Canal de la Deule from which heavy enemy fire was being received.

OCTOBER:
4th:
Private: (3154) W.Thirst, M.M.
7th:
Sergeant: (2997) F.J.Ransome, D.C.M., M.M., Croix de Guerre.
13th:
Private: (2637) W.A.Hardy.

For three days, the crossing of the canal was found impossible but the time was spent by the Royal Engineers in constructing an ingenious floating bridge made of trench boards lashed to large slabs of cork. During the early hours of the 17th October the canal was bridged, by use of the Royal Engineers' brainchild, and crossed, surprisingly without opposition. A general advance was continued throughout the whole

of that day until the village of Raimbeaucourt was reached. Many civilians were found in Raimbeaucourt and they were overjoyed at this first glimpse of British soldiers.

OCTOBER:
16th:
Privates: (2208) T.C.Ashdown, (2718) R.J.Jackson, (3141) A.E.Taylor.
17th:
Private: (2267) A.A.Bennett.
18th:
Private: (3144) G.Taylor.

Still the advance continued, now in a steadily north-east direction. On the 20th October the village of Orchies was reached. A long day on the 22nd brought the Battalion to Rumegies and then to Lecelles where it was found that road and canal bridges had been blown. A British barrage on the 24th brought a determined response from the enemy which prevented planned movement.

What was to prove the Battalion's last action of the war was ordered to take place on the 26th October against the village of Château l'Abbaye which was to be cleared of the enemy. Much of the surrounding land, together with many roads in the vicinity, had been flooded and only two 'dry' tracks remained leading towards the objective. At 2.30 am the platoons set off supported by only a very light field gun barrage directed at Château l'Abbaye. They were fearful that strong opposition might be stationed in the village, particularly in the houses which remained. To everyone's relief, however, not a single shot was received; the enemy had withdrawn and the objective was taken without opposition.

Billets in Vieux Condé on the eastern side of the Canal du Jard were reached on the 28th October. The following day, Private F.F.Hammocks died of wounds received earlier. Although, later, one man died of natural causes, and three died of wounds at home, Private Hammocks was the last Battalion man to die on active service.

OCTOBER:
23rd:
Private: (2508) J.Ealdon.
24th:
Corporal: (2282) A.W.Blake.
Lance Corporal: (2941) C.A.M.Park.
25th:
Second Lieutenant: (2293) R.H.Bourne.
Private: (3029) A.Russell.
26th:
Second Lieutenant: (2303) J.Bradley.
29th:
Private: (2629) F.F.Hammocks.

The first few days of November were spent in general cleaning, bathing, training and inspections at Fines. A move back to the village of Landas was made on the 10th and this, for the 7th Battalion, was the place where the war would cease.

On the morning of the 11th November a signal was received that the war would end officially at 11.00 am. So physically and mentally exhausted were the men that the news was greeted with only the feeblest of cheers. Much more impressive, however, was the Thanksgiving Service held that day actually at 11.00 am. The whole of the 36th Brigade paraded at almost full strength for the Thanksgiving.

Throughout the Service, an elderly Frenchman, an old warrior of the Franco-Prussian War of 1870, stood stiffly to attention in the centre of the village square holding aloft a large Tricolour. When the parade was dismissed, the Frenchman led off followed immediately by the officers marching in close ranks with all the men of the Brigade behind. The symbolism of the old man's proud action brought tears to the eyes of many battle-hardened and battle-weary Englishmen, officers and men alike. At the 36th Field Ambulance Mess 'medical comforts' were provided to all present, and the old Frenchman joined the numerous enthusiastic toasts to the Victorious Allies.

NOVEMBER:
1st:
Lance Corporal: (2832) A.Martin.
Privates: (2362) W.J.Carson, (2439) S.F.Cowtan, (2640) E.A.Harris.

7th Battalion Epilogue

The 7th Battalion had served continuously on the Western Front for just three weeks short of two and a half years. During that time, more than the Battalion's original strength of around 1,000 officers and men had lost their lives. The Battalion had set out as part of 'Kitchener's New Army', inexperienced and untried. As part of the British Expeditionary Force, the officers and men acquitted themselves magnificently. Through periods of inactivity, boredom, exhaustion and the most exhilarating and fearful fighting they did their duty well.

On the 25th November, 1918, the Battalion moved from Landas to Hornaing between the towns of Douai and Valenciennes. This area was to be its home until March, 1919. Arrangements for demobilisation began almost at once with miners and students being given first priority. Those less lucky spent their time salvaging and clearing the surrounding areas of war debris.

On the 4th Februaary, 1919, the King's Colour for the Battalion was consecrated by the Senior Chaplain of the Division and, afterwards, presented by His Royal Highness the Prince of Wales. The Prince then addressed the battalions of the 36th Infantry Brigade in these words:

"It gives me very great pleasure to be here today and to have the honour to present the King's Colour to the battalions before me.

You were raised in August, 1914, and came out to France in the 12th Division in May, 1915.

Since that date, in addition to much hard fighting in minor engagements and long periods of strenuous work in the trenches, you have taken a conspicuous part in the following battles:-

Loos, Hohenzollern Craters, Somme 1916, Arras, Cambrai, Somme 1918, Epéhy, and the German retreat to the Scheldt, which culminated in the final victory of our arms. I know full well that these Colours will always be honoured and cherished by you and that you will worthily uphold in the future, as you have always done in the past, the glorious traditions of the regiments to which you belong.

These Colours are emblems of the heroic deeds performed by your battalions. I now entrust them to you, confident that you will guard them as worthy successors of those gallant soldiers who have so gloriously fallen in the service of their King and Country."

On the 2nd March, 1919, the first of several drafts of officers and men left to join the 4th Battalion The Royal Sussex Regiment as part of the Army of Occupation on the River Rhine in Germany, and the remainder were formed into one composite Company.

This composite Company, the remnants of the Battalion, set out from the port of Dunkirk to return to England on the 7th June, 1919. A warm welcome was received at the home barracks in Chichester and it was there, almost three years after its inception, that the 7th Battalion was disbanded and ceased to exist. Yet another glorious part of the history of The Royal Sussex Regiment had ended.

PART FIVE

The 8th (Service) Battalion ('New Army' Pioneers)

CHAPTER 24
1914 and 1915

The 8th Battalion The Royal Sussex Regiment was formed as a 'New Army' Unit under the recruitment drive launched soon after the outbreak of war by Secretary of State Lord Kitchener. The Battalion was placed within the 18th (Eastern) Division and began as part of that Division's 54th Infantry Brigade. Although the Battalion commenced as a purely infantry unit it was destined to be converted to a Pioneer Battalion within the 18th (Eastern) Division in February, 1915.

Every infantry Division was comprised of three Brigades, each made up of four infantry Battalions. It was in this manner that the Royal Sussex Regiment's 8th Battalion found itself forming part of the 18th (Eastern) Division under the command of Major-General Sir Ivor Maxse. The full Division was constituted as follows:

18th (EASTERN) DIVISION
53rd. Infantry Brigade:
8th Norfolk, 8th Suffolk, 10th Essex, 6th Royal Berkshire
54th Infantry Brigade:
11th Royal Fusiliers, 8th Royal Sussex, 6th Northamptonshire, 12th Middlesex
55th Infantry Brigade:
7th Queens, 7th Buffs, 8th East Surrey, 7th Royal West Kent

Thus, the 8th Battalion The Royal Sussex Regiment was destined to play a less active fighting part in the various theatres of Western Front warfare. Its main role was to be one of support and, in large measure, hard physical work. Expertise was gained through various pioneering tasks undertaken on the training grounds of England, often with guidance from, and under the supervision and instruction of, Royal Engineer units.

Although the Battalion's main duties were to be of a pioneering nature, every officer and man had to be capable of serving in an active fighting capacity should conditions demand.

Emergency situations at the front could mean that every available combatant would be required to take up weapons and fight. To this end, every soldier of the Battalion was provided with rifle, ammunition, gas mask, 'iron rations' and other basic equipment carried by infantrymen. The working tools of their pioneering 'trade' were provided and made available for use as required. The Battalion's own transport was capable of carrying every sort of implement and material that might be required for pioneering duties.

Thus trained and prepared, the Battalion was ready for active service by mid-1915. The 'War Diary', however, the document written up on a regular basis by the adjutant or other competent officer in every battalion while on active service, was to contain, in the case of the 8th Battalion, a record of massed detail mainly concerning map references, geographical positions and a minutiae of technical information on all aspects of the pioneering work carried out. The result was a voluminous document, sadly providing relatively little information concerning the non-pioneering experiences of the Battalion.

It was on 24th July, 1915, however, that the Battalion left Codford on Salisbury Plain in three trains, the first departing at 5.05am., and travelled to Southampton where they arrived at the docks after a journey lasting 12 hours. Boarding and loading all equipment onto a transport ship, the 'Empress Queen', the Battalion made an uneventful overnight crossing of the English Channel to arrive during the early morning at Le Havre. Disembarkation began at 7.00am on the 25th and a move was made to a rest camp. On the following day a first journey by French railways was made and the related inexplicable delays were experienced. The direct-line distance of approximately 100 miles took more than 10 hours to accomplish before the travel-weary Battalion detrained at Amiens and began to tramp north-eastward towards the Somme battlefields.

A march of five hours on the 8th August brought the Battalion to Béthencourt. On the following day the march was continued, this time for four hours, partly through a heavy thunder storm which resulted in everyone arriving very wet at Bouzincourt, a village some three miles north-west of the town of Albert. Work began that same day preparing and improving trenches between Albert and Aveluy along the banks of the River Ancre. The inconvenience of life near the front line was brought home straight away when it became necessary to transport all usable water by cart from Albert.

Base was moved a couple of miles south of Albert to Méaulte on the 20th August from where training and wood cutting took place. The Battalion was to remain based at Méaulte for some months while the infantry Brigades of the Division took over responsibility for the front lines established some two or three miles distant between Fricourt and Mametz.

The Battalion continued with a great variety of pioneering duties. This work was certainly carried on frequently in, or close to, the front lines where new trenches had to be dug, altered, strengthened or repaired; where communications had to be set out and maintained; where dugouts had to be hewn and overhead protection erected.

The first Battalion casualty was sustained on 24th August when Private James Chandler was mortally wounded and died the next day. During September, trench and communication work was continued and two more men were fatally wounded. Other men were also wounded by rifle grenades and bullets while at work.

AUGUST:
25th:
Private: (3290) J.Chandler.
SEPTEMBER:
13th:
Private: (3404) G.H.Parsons.
22nd:
Lance Corporal: (3344) E.Hatchett.

Throughout October, November and December, general work on defences including trenches, dugouts, intermediate lines, shelters and billets continued as the men became accustomed to their life and duties north of the River Somme. The hard work was rewarded, occasionally, with the opportunity for the men to take baths in Albert.

Four more men were killed during those last months of 1915.

OCTOBER:
13th:
Private: (3419) D.Richards.
NOVEMBER:
24th:
Sergeant: (3347) C.F.Henley.
DECEMBER:
14th:
Private: (3403) A.J.Parsons.
23rd:
Private: (3317) W.Edgar.

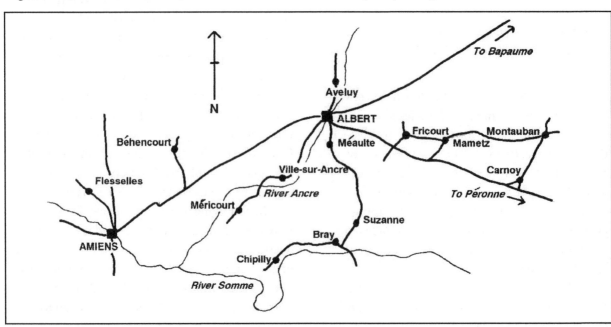

53.   *July 1915 to 21st July 1916*

CHAPTER 25
1916

Work of a general nature continued around the town of Albert and Bécourt village during the first months of 1916 so far as the weather permitted. Heavy snow at the end of February made working and living conditions utterly miserable.

By now, though, preparations for the planned major offensive in the area were beginning to get under way. The idea was for a massive attack jointly with the French to help relieve pressures on the French at Verdun; the French were to attack south of the River Somme and the British along a line running roughly north-west from the river. During March, the Commander of the British Fourth Army, General Sir Henry Rawlinson, who was to be responsible for the Battle of the Somme, arrived to set up his headquarters in the château at Querrieu some 12 miles behind the front line.

The 8th Battalion began its own preparatory work during March as directed by the Divisional Commander, Major-General Sir Ivor Maxse. The work was undertaken in the sector of front line between Mametz and Montauban. Maxse was probably the greatest tactical British commander on the Western Front. He gave much thought and full consideration to the likely events and their consequences. There is no doubt that he was an outstanding and inspirational trainer of soldiers. Everything that could be achieved by way of planning and preparation was done to give his troops the best possible advantage and, above all, the best chance for their own protection.

Thus, while Rawlinson and his Senior Staff Officers were making plans for the great attack, Maxse was making his own. Officially, it was decided that everything should be staked on a fierce five day-and-night bombardment of the German lines that would blow away the enemy's barbed wire defences and smash trenches and dugouts thus reducing enemy manpower to an insignificant minimum of survivors. That

achieved, the British army would rise from its trenches, go 'over the top' carrying between 60 and 80 lbs. of equipment per man and simply walk across No-Man's-Land to capture the enemy positions.

Maxse was to see things differently; his men would not take part in the 'easy walk' towards the enemy which was compelled upon almost every other battalion for the 'First Day of the Battle of the Somme'. From March, 1916, Maxse began to make his own arrangements for attacking when the time came. His 8th Battalion pioneers began to dig 'Russian Saps' from the Divisional front line and out beneath No-Man's-Land. These 'Russian Saps' were shallow underground tunnels through which men could pass to the attack unseen by the enemy. The far end of each tunnel was left as a dead-end for the time being so that a breakthrough could be made easily and swiftly at zero hour. By the time the battle was launched on 1st July, 1916, the 8th Battalion had completed, on the 18th (Eastern) Division front, eight 'Russian Saps' to within 20 yards of the German front line.

JANUARY:
14th:
Private: (3364) S.A.Knight.
26th:
Private: (3324) W.D.Ford.
29th:
Corporal: (3387) H.T.Miller.
FEBRUARY:
7th:
Private: (3260) W.H.Banks.
MARCH:
22nd:
Second Lieutenant: (3249) F.Addison.
APRIL:
10th:
Private: (3472) C.W.Whimhurst.
MAY:
17th:
Private: (3433) C.R.Smith.

Only a limited number of men could work at any one time on the 'Russian Saps', digging the tunnels and carefully disposing of the spoil out of sight of the Germans and German aircraft. Other units from the Battalion carried on with general works in the vicinity of Bray, Suzanne, Chipilly, Carnoy and at Bernafay Farm.

On the 25th June, with the day-and-night British bombardment of German positions well under way, the 18th (Eastern) Division was given its instructions for taking part in the forthcoming general offensive; the 8th Royal Sussex officers and troops came under orders to be prepared to forsake pioneering duties and to fight as infantrymen.

JUNE:
18th:
Lance Corporal: (3289) A.G.Challen.
30th:
Privates: (3296) F.J.Comber, (3434) J.Smith.

Bad weather caused the major assault, the 'Big Push', to be postponed until Saturday 1st July, 1916. At 7.30am on that day British and French forces went 'over the top'.

Because of pressures and hardships elsewhere, the French force, on the right of the British, had been greatly reduced from the original numbers envisaged. In the event, the French achieved some success whereas the British, bearing the lions' share of the attack, failed along almost all of its 15 miles of attacking lines. Only at the far right of the British line, where the 18th (Eastern) Division and the 30th Divison were operating, did anything like success result.

At 7.28am on Saturday 1st July, 1916, the great British barrage which, because of bad weather in the later stages, had been extended to seven days and nights, lifted. Two minutes later, all along the 15 miles of front, the signal whistles blew and thousands of soldiers clambered out of their trenches and went 'over the top'. On the 18th (Eastern) Division front, to the west of Montauban, most men had already left their trenches; they had been sent forward early and under cover of darkness to lie out in No-Man's-Land, concealed so close as possible to the German line. It was accepted that casualties at a level of six per cent might be sustained from short-fall British shells as a result of this early

move but that this would be preferable to obeying blindly the official order for a 'steady walk' across No-Man's-Land. Many other 18th (Eastern) Division men broke through from the 'Russian Sap' heads and poured out only 20 yards, or so, from the enemy trenches. By this forethought, preparation and readiness, 18th (Eastern) Division men were in the German trenches before the enemy could come up from their dugouts in readiness to fight. Within five minutes the first German prisoners were being sent back. Pommiers Redoubt, a German stronghold just south of the Mametz – Montauban road, was overwhelmed and captured by 9.30am. Only along this part of the line, and as a result of these sensibly thought-out tactics, were all objectives for the day taken; the whole of the Montauban Ridge had been captured by the Division.

The tactics, carried out as instructed, along all of the remaining sections of the British line, brought total disaster and the description of the 1st July, 1916, as the worst day in the history of the British Army. To this extent the battle plans were fundamentally flawed; they sent thousands of heavily laden men at a slow walking pace to their deaths, mainly from machine gun and rifle fire. On that sunny and hot summer's day the British sustained 57,000 casualties, 19,200 of them fatal and approximately 40 per cent of them during the first hour.

Senior Officer planners knew, before the battle commenced, that the long bombardment upon which they had staked so much, including the lives of so many young men, had not been the success anticipated. Late reports from patrolling soldiers and officers had told that, in many places, the barrage had failed to 'blow away' the German barbed wire defences. A shortage of big guns meant that there were insufficient heavy shells with the power to reach down to the known German deep dugouts. Yet still the flawed plan was doggedly maintained. Much has been written elsewhere concerning who was responsible and who should have taken the blame. This, perhaps, is not the place to pursue those arguments and recriminations.

It has been said with much truth that the British chance of success on the first day of the Somme battle was squandered by three minutes.

That was the time it might have taken lightly equipped and running infantry attackers to cross No-Man's-Land and reach the German trenches. It was the time considerably in excess of three minutes that gave the enemy opportunity to rush up from their deep, protective dugouts and, with their machine guns and rifles, begin to mow down in their thousands the slowly advancing British. If, as should have been foreseen, the British infantry had been lightly laden and had attacked at speed, running across the open spaces between the opposing front lines, they could have won the race and been able to confront the unprepared Germans as they appeared from below ground. That was not to be, however, and there were reports of German soldiers, in their excitement and eagerness, standing up to fire from their parapets upon the waves of slowly approaching British.

To their great credit and the initiative, common sense and foresight of their Commander, the 18th (Eastern) Division, which had never been in battle before, won the race to the German front line trenches, took all their objectives, maintained their position by the end of the day and sustained relatively few casualties. From their starting off positions along a front of 2,500 yards they had cleared No-Man's-Land together with the German trenches at this point, and considerable numbers of the enemy could be seen retreating beyond the new British-held front. The 8th Battalion pioneers had taken part, quickly following behind their attacking comrades and working hard and successfully all day to consolidate captured strongpoints.

With several hours of daylight remaining, a chance of further success was at hand. None other than the Corps Commander, Lieutenant-General Congreve, delighted with what had been achieved, went forward and saw for himself the open ground ahead together with the silent woods of Mametz, Bernafay and Trônes with no Germans in sight. Excitedly he hurried back and, from his headquarters, contacted Rawlinson, seeking permission to re-commence the advance. Controversially, to say the least, Rawlinson refused permission and the chance was lost. This almost numbed response was to lose many more lives later when those same dark woods had to be

wrested, yard by yard, from the enemy which, by then, had returned to them and reorganised. Thus, for the Division, the first vital day ended on a mixed note of euphoria at the success achieved but of disappointment at a golden opportunity denied.

JULY:
1st:
Corporal: (3301) P.J.Court.
Lance Corporals: (3316) A.H.Dyer, (3402) H.Parkes.
Privates: (3262) B.Bayton, (3271) F.E.Boxall, (3300) F.S.Cottingham, (3328) W.P.Freeman, (3331) C.A.Gasson, (3369) H.Lelliott, (3405) W.Parsons, (3466) J.Watson, (3468) W.H.Wenham.

No further attack was made on the 2nd July but repair and strengthening work on captured positions continued round the clock. Former German trenches near Montauban were wired on the 3rd for British defence and the occupation of Caterpillar Wood by the 53rd Brigade entailed more work of consolidation by the 8th Battalion pioneers. By this time, with hardly a break since the start of the battle, everyone was almost completely exhausted. It was, therefore, necessary to provide some form of rest by platoons in turn. These short periods of relative relaxation enabled the men to continue with their vital manual duties for a full week until, on the 8th July, the 8th Battalion thankfully moved back to Grovetown Camp, a collection of huts that it had erected during March just north of Bray-sur-Somme.

JULY:
2nd:
Private: (3435) W.Smith.
7th:
Private: (3368) R.Lee.
16th:
Private: (3421) H.Ridgway.

The few days rest at Grovetown Camp, a safe distance from the fighting, was welcomed by all men and officers. Opportunity was taken to effect a general cleaning of clothes, kit and equipment. Several times the men were given the pleasure of swimming in the tranquil waters of the River Somme at Bray. By such pleasures, spirits were much refreshed and stimulated.

All too soon, on the 13th July, came the order that the 18th (Eastern) Division was to be given the difficult task of capturing Trônes Wood. In particular, the 8th Battalion would be required to assist by consolidating a line through the eastern edge of Bernafay Wood, thence south to a sunken road and, from there, north-east to join up with the French. This work commenced at 11.00pm and continued through a heavy German barrage laid down in the vicinity, particularly on Bernafay Wood. The 8th Battalion War Diary recorded three officers and 24 men killed, 85 wounded and eight missing. Several of these wounded men were destined to die over the following week. However, the supporting work enabled the Division to go on, next day, and clear Trônes Wood despite the chaotic conditions created by dense thickets of undergrowth within the wood and many trees felled by the British preparatory bombardment. Work completed, the 8th Battalion moved out to a safer position in Copse Valley. From there, at least one return working visit was made to the area around Trônes Wood. Further support was given as the Division's Infantry Brigades moved forward to make attacks in, and around, Longueval.

JULY:
13th:
Captains: (3381) H.W.Meade, (3476) J.D.Whyte.
Lieutenant: (3478) E.R.Willis.
Lance Corporal: (3283) C.Caiger.
Privates: (3427) W.G.Scutt, (3467) G.Webb
14th:
Corporals: (3359) H.J.N.Kenward, (3415) A.Putland.
Lance Corporals: (3394) L.Newnham(3439) S.Stacey, (3442) H.Stevens, (3465) T.W.Ward.
Privates: (2350) E.Adsett, (3254) G.J.Andrews, (3297) H.Coombs, (3304) A.Croucher, (3314) A.R.Durrant, (3323) C.E.Ford, (3329) L.Gabell, (3333) G.Gibson, (3335) F.Goodsell, (3343) J.Hart, (3352) P.Hurn, (3354) H.Jeal, (3361) F.Knaggs, (3383) E.J.Merryweather, (3399) W.F.Palmer, (3416) R.Rees, (3423) C.Rothwell, (3428) J.W.Seaman, (3441) C.Stevens.
15th:
Privates: (3253) A.E.Allwright, (3392) H.Newman.
16th:
Privates: (3457) F.Tulett, (3463) G.J.Vincent.
17th:
Private: (3366) H.J.Langridge.
21st:
Lance Corporal: (3456) C.V.Trayhurn.

Somewhat surprisingly, and certainly abruptly, the 8th Battalion was moved out of the Somme area altogether on the 21st July. During that afternoon they entrained at Méricourt and, at 8.00pm., arrived at Longpré north-west of Amiens where they detached themselves from the train and marched five miles to Hallencourt. The following day, after a march of a similar distance, they crossed the River Somme to Pont Remy and entrained once more. Heading north through the evening, the train brought the Battalion to the town of St.Omer by 2.00am on the 24th July. The remainder of the night was spent on the march until they reached Renescure at 7.00am.

After a rest of four days, the Battalion was marching again; on the 28th July four miles to Staple and, on the 29th, a further 18 miles to Berthen where they enjoyed another relatively restful spell. In warm conditions on the 5th August the men were marching again, this time to Erquinghem-sur-Lys immediately to the west of Armentières. There they spent nearly three weeks training and constructing gun pits with guidance from engineers.

On the 22nd August yet another move was ordered, this time to Estaires from where, three days later, the Battlion moved to Mérville and thence by train, eventually arriving at Averdoingt on the 25th. Four days of further training followed before a march to Rebreuviette and then to Doullens by the last day of the month. There, they could sense again the nearness of the Somme.

AUGUST:
3th:
Private: (3265) G.W.Bishop.
6th:
Lance Corporal: (3396) J.E.Nye.
31st:
Second Lieutenant: (3358) H.D.Kemp.

Buses took the Battalion south-east from Doullens to Acheux on the 1st September. The remainder of that day was spent in marching onward to Forceville and, the following day, to Aveluy Wood where they were well and truly back on the Somme battlefields. One wonders at the aim of such continuous wanderings as the Battalion had experienced over a period in excess of six weeks. The last thing achieved, if indeed

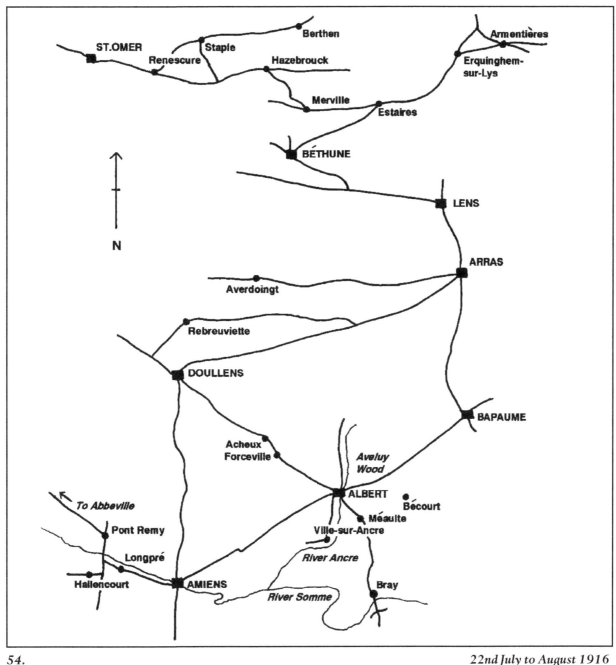

54.   *22nd July to August 1916*

that had been the aim in removing the Unit from the Somme in July, was rest and recuperation. On the contrary, the continuous movement from one place to the next produced amongst all ranks ever-growing exhaustion and irritation.

In Aveluy Wood, bivouacs and a camp were constructed during the first week of September. Work was also carried out on the road leading to Ovillers and along the railway line at Aveluy and Authuille. On the 12th September two men, on the 13th one man and on the 15th one man were all injured by the premature explosion of allied shells, the last of those men, Private C.E.Ketcher, dying from his wounds. Two more men were

killed on the 20th, this time by hostile enemy shelling of the Aveluy Wood camp which was situated close to the River Ancre along the valley running north from Albert.

SEPTEMBER:
8th:
Private: (3461) F.W.Veness.
11th:
Company Sergeant Major: (3277) D.Burchell.
19th:
Private: (3360) C.E.Ketcher.
20th:
Privates: (3389) C.D.Moon, (3452) W.G.Taylor.

General pioneering duties were handed over, on the 22nd September, to the 5th (Cinque Ports) Battalion The Royal Sussex Regiment in order that the 8th Battalion could be free to support the 18th (Eastern) Division in its important attack on the German stronghold village of Thiepval which contained, in its immediate vicinity, no less than 144 enemy deep dugouts. By the 26th September the Division had triumphantly captured Thiepval which had held out against all previous allied attempts since the 1st July. One brilliant part of the advance planning for this attack was for the Division's 8th Battalion pioneers to clear the two miles of road from Authuille to Thiepval and then to line it with a brushwood screen to thwart enemy observation. The effect was a dramatic reduction in German shelling of this road so that it could be used throughout for the essential transportation of men, supporting equipment and supplies. It was during this period that the men obtained, at Crucifix Corner near Aveluy, their first exciting view of a tank, four of which had been detailed to assist the attack on Thiepval.

Immediately following this successful infantry attack, the 8th Battalion men were at work in and around Thiepval repairing and improving roads and communications. Heavy fighting was continuing at the nearby Schwaben Redoubt but

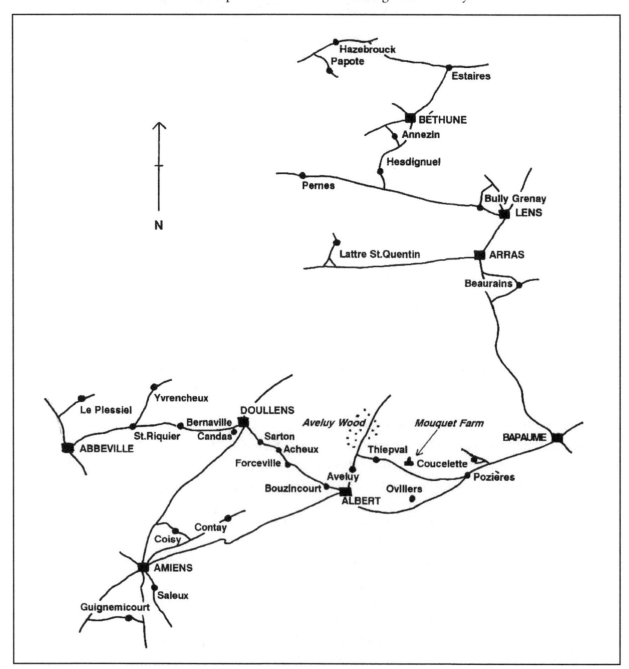

55.   *September 1916 to 21st June 1917*

the pioneering work continued until relief by the 13th Gloucestershire pioneers came on the 5th October.

SEPTEMBER:
27th:
Private: (3464) W.A.Walker.
30th:
Private: (3280) C.V.Buss.
OCTOBER:
1st:
Lance Corporal: (3306) J.Daughtry, M.M.
Private: (3264) W.Bish.
4th:
Private: (3469) H.H.Were.

By the 7th October the Battalion had moved back to Acheux from where they entrained for Candas, south-west of the town of Doullens, then marched on to Bérnaville.

After only five days' rest the Battalion was back east of Albert on the 12th October working on dugouts and communication trenches that had been in use on 1st July. The following week, a move forward was made so that work could be carried out at the former German stronghold at Mouquet Farm on the road running from Thiepval to Pozières. Later, pioneering work was undertaken farther east at Courcelette.

OCTOBER:
23rd:
Private: (3438) G.Spencer.

28th:
Private: (3420) W.Richards.

Several men were killed, one from the effects of gas, during November and others died of wounds. Much work was undertaken, mainly on the important Thiepval to Pozières Road until the 21st December when the Battalion made a welcome move by train out of the battle zone from Albert to St.Riquier, north-west of Amiens. By road, they continued to Le Plessiel on the 22nd and there, training and resting, they spent Christmas and saw in the New Year.

NOVEMBER:
1st
Private: (3418) W.Rice.
4th:
Private: (3346) J.Heap.
19th:
Private: (3390) J.Muir.
20th:
Sergeant: (3378) L.Martin.
22nd:
Private: (3450) E.J.Stunt.
25th:
Private: (3477) T.Williams.
29th:
Private: (3313) R.E.Dunster.
DECEMBER:
18th:
Lance Corporal: (3391) R.Murray.

CHAPTER 26
1917

So, for the 8th Battalion The Royal Sussex Regiment, the new year and deep winter began at Le Plessiel some 40 miles west of the battle lines. Even this far back pioneering hands were not allowed to lie idle, and work repairing roads and billets was found. On the 11th January the Battalion moved to Yvrencheux and, the following day, to Bérnaville. After one day's rest it was south-east to Sarton, then back to familiar Aveluy by the 16th.

By 22nd January the weather was freezing cold with occasional snow falls. The men kept warm with their labouring work setting ballast for a communication tramline running from Ovillers to Mouquet Farm. That work was finished by the end of the month and attention was turned to clearing and extending old trench lines.

JANUARY:
29th:
Private: (3430) E.Simcox.

Throughout February, work continued on an extension of the tramline. A welcome rota was established whereby men could take turns to enjoy baths in Albert. Twelve men were wounded and one killed at duty during the month.

FEBRUARY:
5th:
Private: (3473) F.W.Whitehead.
20th:
Private: (3263) W.J.Berry.
25th:
Private: (3356) J.W.Keeley.

The usual routine of work continued during March. Several men were wounded, one accidentally when a bullet exploded from a live cartridge in an incinerator fire. On the 10th a serious blow befell the Battalion at 5.00pm. When Lieutenant Colonel A.A.Chase, D.S.O., was in the front line a German shell fell very close by and the Lieutenant Colonel was severely wounded. He was brought back but died at No. 45 Casualty Clearing Station on the 11th. At 5.30pm that day he was buried with full Military Honours at Aveluy.

MARCH:
11th:
Lieutenant Colonel: (3292) A.A.Chase, D.S.O.

The Division route-marched out to Contay on the first day of spring. Next day, the 22nd March, the move continued to Guignemicourt south of Amiens. Then, on the 25th, they moved the short distance to Saleux and entrained. After a protracted rail journey of almost 36 hours the tired Division arrrived at Papote just south of Hazebrouck.

The first two weeks of April were spent resting and training. Then orders were received to be prepared to move at short notice. On the 14th, move they did, first to Annezin, close to the town of Béthune, then on to Bully-Grenay, west of Lens. Roadwork repairs were the orders for the next 12 days at the end of which period the 8th Battalion marched to Hesdigneul and then on to Pérnes. On the 28th, a very hot and dusty day, the Battalion marched 21 miles to Lattre St.Quentin. So oppressive were the conditions that relief was allowed by all packs being carried by lorry. The very next day the march was continued, this time to Beaurains just south of Arras. At Beaurains the Battalion bivouaced in a field which was very pleasant in the warming spring weather.

APRIL:
12th:
Private: (3307) E.Davey.
22nd:
Private: (3279) H.G.Burtenshaw.
24th:
Private: (3481) H.Woods.

By this time, the Germans had completed their move back east to their newly fortified Hindenburg Line. The Battalion's pioneering task was thus to improve the road from Héninel eastward in the direction of the Hindenburg Line to which the allies had moved up behind the enemy. On the 3rd May the 18th (Eastern) Division attacked the Hindenburg Line and, although they took early objectives, they were forced back by a determined German counter-attack. Such was the emergency that the 8th Battalion was put into the line to help stop the spread of this serious rebuff.

From this point onwards the Battalion casualties increased markedly bearing in mind that this was a pioneering, not an infantry, Unit. After the emergency of the 5th May had passed, work started on the digging of a new communication trench between Cherisy and Héninel. The work continued despite frequent heavy shelling of the area by the enemy. A move to a new base south of Mercatel was made on the 10th May. Trench digging continued and, on the 13th, four men were wounded and three killed while they were off duty and sleeping actually in the Hindenburg Line trench.

MAY:
5th:
Second Lieutenant: (3326) A.D.Foster.
Corporal: (3355) P.J.Keeble.
Privates: (3310) G.C.Doidge, (3398) A.V.Paish.
13th:
Privates: (3268) A.H.Bourne, (3293) J.Cobby, (3322) J.Field, (3432) A.Smart, (3482) S.A.Worcester.

At camp, the Battalion then enjoyed a period of relative rest. There was work to do, however, mainly improving their own conditions by the erection of a baths building with horse trough baths !

At the end of May the Battalion moved forward to a camp at Hénin from where they began more trench improvement work. Heavy machine gun and shell fire during the night of the 1st June killed three, with another dying later from wounds. On the 17th, the Battalion marched from Hénin and, by train, moved off north once again.

JUNE:
1st:
Captain: (3443) H.E.Stewart.
Corporal: (3348) A.J.Hill.
Privates: (3312) W.Dunn, (3480) R.D.Wood.

11th:
Private: (3425) C.W.Scott.
16th:
Private: (3363) C.G.Knight.

The Battalion detrained at Hopoutre and marched to 'Dominion Camp' on the Ouderdom – Vlamertinghe Road south-east of Ypres. For the remainder of this summer month the men were employed dismantling Nissen huts and working on nearby dugouts and a railway line.

JUNE:
29th:
Sergeant: (3270) T.F.Bowling.
30th:
Private: (3401) F.L.F.Parker.

Much preparatory work in the Ypres areas was being carried out in readiness for the big offensive to be launched by the British from the infamous Ypres Salient. In particular, great store dumps had sprung up all around containing every kind of equipment, supplies and ammunition. Battalion tasks included erecting huts, digging ditches and trenches. On the 29th July the Battallion moved to an Advanced Reinforcement Camp.

For the most part, pioneering work was required at varying distances behind the lines, although almost always within reach of enemy shelling which, with a tendancy to be spasmodic and unannounced, could be all the more unnerving. The main aim was the keeping open of the vital lines of communication, especially roadways which were heavily used by marching, often weary, men and by motorised and horse transport moving to and fro in a continuous stream conveying to the fighting units the unending material requirements of war. Without the provision of such vital commodities as ammunition, artillery pieces and rations, and without the evacuation of wounded men by ambulances, disasters involving much loss of life could evolve quickly.

Roads and railways, road and rail junctions, bridges, camps, duckboard tracks and many important places besides, were always under threat of enemy bombardment. Disruption by shelling was an important part of the strategy of both sides. Shells produced craters in these lines of communication with monotonous regularity, often causing casualties, general mayhem and serious obstruction. Pioneers had to be on hand to clear these obstructions, fill in the craters and repair other damage in order to get the thoroughfares open for use again quickly.

Ahead of the Battalion, on the 31st July, was launched the major 3rd Battle of Ypres otherwise known as Passchendaele. At first, the Battalion repaired tracks used by advancing tanks. Soon, a barrage of enemy bullets failed to inconvenience the tanks but created an anxious time for the relatively unprotected pioneers. At 9.30am the German counter-barrage started in earnest; so heavy did it become by 10.30am that further work was impossible and the men were forced to take whatever cover they could find. The barrage, which included gas shells, killed several Battalion men and eventually forced an abandonment of its work schedule and retirement to a less dangerous location.

JULY;
5th:
Privates: (3371) C.H.Longland, (3384) A.H.Middleton, (3406) R.W.Pavey, (3453) R.Thompson, (3462) W.E.Venn.
12th:
Privates: (3365) F.J.Laker, (3372) N.Lord.
14th:
Lance Corporal: (3451) H.Stunt.

16th:
Lance Corporal: (3261) W.Bannister.
20th:
Lance Corporal: (3474) A,Whittington.
21st:
Private: (3375) J.McIntyre.
23rd:
Lieutenant: (3377) J.Marsland, M.C.
31st:
Privates: (3295) H.Collins, (3309) G.W.Dobson, (3318) C.Edwards, (3336) R.Goodsell, (3410) E.T.Penfold, (3454) J.Titheridge, (3470) A.T.West.

On the 2nd August it had been possible for a working party, under Lieutenant Dutton,to go out and spend some time burying the dead. Much of the remainder of the month was taken up with heavy pioneering work, often under fire, while the main battle began to bog down in the quagmire at the approaches to Passchendaele. The vital duckboard tracks, which were the only means of movement for any distance across the morass, required continuous repair because they were frequently obliterated by shellfire. Tracks along Observatory Ridge were also maintained.

Respite was gained by a move back to Connaught Camp at Wippenhoek in mid-August. There, some work was undertaken at night on trenches, and baths were erected for welcome use by the men. Time was available for Church

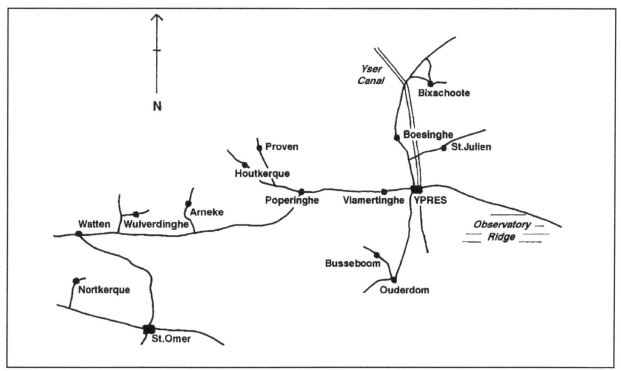

56.   *2nd June 1917 to 8th February 1918*

Parades on two consecutive Sundays and a lucky group of 400 officers and men were even taken in lorries to the seaside for the day on the 27th.

AUGUST·
6th:
Private: (3437) C.G.Sparshott.
8th:
Second Liuetenant: (3284) E.R.Calvert.

The first day of September brought a march from Wulverdinghe to Arneke and thence by train into Ypres. After a short march from the station the Battalion arrived at the Yser Canal bank north of the town. Two days were spent there repairing bridges crossing the canal but an attempted move to work at St.Julien on the 5th was thwarted by heavy German shelling. Instead, the men filled sandbags with bricks and rubble while under some cover.

From the 9th September all work was hampered by the fast-deteriorating ground and consequent lack of materials because movement was all but impossible. Pioneering needs were now directed towards attempts to improve conditions underfoot. The drainage of excess water by means of ditching and gulleying was attempted with limited success. With difficulty, roads were made passable by horse transport but use of motorised vehicles was impossible at this stage. The work that could be undertaken was frequently hampered by shelling and by the attentions of enemy aircraft, both of which caused casualties.

The exhausted Battalion was allowed to rest on the 26th September and, the following day, moved back to Poperinghe. After a rest for two more days, a further move away from the battle zone was made to Nortkerque some 30 miles west from Ypres. So ended the month of September.

SEPTEMBER:
5th:
Lance Corporal: (3305) W.Daragon.
Privates: (3351) A.G.Humphrey, (3393) R.J.Newman, (3446) F.J.Strevens, (3445) J.Stratford.
6th:
Corporal: (3449) T.Stroud.
Lance Corporals: (3299) P.Cornwall, (3340) H.Halford.
8th:
Sergeant: (3308) H.R.Diplock, M.M.

Lance Corporal: (3339) A.Greenshields.
Privates: (3266) P.A.Bleach, (3353) W.J.James, (3429) F.W.Shipton, (3431) J.M.Slater.
10th   11th:
Second Lieutenant: (3315) G.Dutton.
13th:
Privates: (3275) C.E.Brown, (3287) C.S.Castle.
22nd:
Lance Sergeant: (3269) F.Bowles.
Corporal: (3311) F.Dudman.
Lance Corporal: (3424) D.Russell.
23rd:
Private: (3303) F.Cowstick.
24th:
Private: (3386) H.H.Miller.
25th:
Privates: (3332) H.W.Gault, (3341) G.C.Hammer.

It was found that there were insufficient billets at Nortkerque and so the Battalion returned eastwards on the 8th October to Poperinghe which was somewhat less healthy because it was well within reach of enemy guns. Maintenance and repair work continued throughout October as conditions allowed. Mud clearance and the filling of shell holes took up much time, as did drainage and the construction of shelters. Some days only a half hour of work was possible because of enemy shelling. More duckboard tracks were laid towards the end of the month.

OCTOBER:
14th:
Lance Corporal: (3272) J.Boxall.
16th:
Private: (3334) C.H.Godley.
19th:
Lieutenant: (3357) J.R.Keen.
20th:
Private: (3327) H.Fowler.
23rd:
Lance Corporal: (3256) H.Bailey.
29th:
Privates: (3367) A.Lee, (3440) F.P.Standing.

Work during November reflected Field Marshal Sir Douglas Haig's unwise decision to persist with the Passchendaele battle despite the atrocious ground conditions and the ever-worsening weather as winter approached. With the exception of work on a cookhouse and maintenance of a tramway, all tasks were a consequence of the ground conditions: drainage, laying duckboards and the repair of collapsed trenches.

NOVEMBER:
14th:
Privates: (3374) J.C.Lyle, (3444) C.T.Stranes.
26th:
Corporal: (3281) W.Cade.
27th:
Private: (3458) A.Turner.

With fighting activity curtailed as winter hardened around the Ypres Salient, direct fighting support work was proportionately reduced. Instead, duties related more to domestic needs such as generally improving the camp and draining flooded Nissen huts. Local rail and road repairs also continued but, on Christmas Day, the whole Battalion rested.

DECEMBER:
12th:
Private: (3267) H.G.Bond.

CHAPTER 27
1918
JANUARY – THE ARMISTICE

During the cold winds, frost and snow of January, work was started on construction of a new 250 yards trench line near Bixschoote. All the dugouts, shelters and barbed wire systems forming part of this line were carried out satisfactorily with little disturbance. There were no casualties within the Battalion this month.

By the 4th February the new Bixschoote trench line had been completed and, although the Battalion did not know it at the time, this was the last pioneering task it would have to undertake in, and around, the Ypres Salient. On the 9th February the 8th Battalion marched from Boesinghe to Proven station. From there, a long southward train journey was made to Noyons about 15 miles north-east of the town of Compiegne. In fact, the whole of the 18th (Eastern) Division, the 20th and 66th Divisions, were on the move from the Ypres area to bolster the Fifth Army which had taken over an extension of the British line to the south.

From Noyons station a march of five miles took the Battalion to Grandru. After two days' rest, all men who had not been inoculated for more than 18 months were re-inoculated. At that time, also, a draft of 39 men was welcomed from the 12th Battalion The Royal Sussex Regiment, one of the battalions to be disbanded under the British army's early 1918 reorganisation which reduced all Brigades from four to three battalions.

On the 15th February the 8th Battalion moved by road transport to Chauny where a late, desperate effort was being made to improve the allied defences along the southern-most part of its line. By this time it was known that a major German attack was imminent. Where the attack would fall was not known but Haig had kept his major forces farther north as protection for the channel ports. Consequently, this southern area was relatively weakly manned and its defences inadequate.

Behind the allied front line was an area known as the 'Battle Zone' and it was this zone that needed the urgent pioneering attentions of the Battalion. With Battalion Headquarters at Bichencourt, an early task for the men was construction and strengthening of a strongpoint named 'Rond de l'Epinois' which was situated in the Basse Foret de Courcy, a forested area about 10 square miles in extent south-east of the River Oise. That strongpoint completed, so far as time would allow, the Battalion returned to Chauny. Then, on 27th February, movement was by way of Villequier and Faillouel to the west bank of the St.Quentin Canal immediately to the east of the village of Mennessis.

British intelligence sources were now convinced that the German onslaught would come within a matter of days. There, along the St.Quentin Canal, it was a question, not literally but metaphorically, of 'all hands to the pumps'. Every Unit was warned of the forthcoming German attack and the 8th Battalion was ordered to be prepared to forsake its pioneering role and take up arms as an infantry unit. The Battalion 'stood to' in battle order with extra ammunition issued, tools ready and transport loaded. Yet, after a while, the order was received to stand down and resume normal duties. There had been no casualties during February.

Construction work, particularly in the provision of defensive shelters, was carried out during the first half of March. Then, once again, this time on the 20th March, the Division, including the 8th Battalion pioneers, was ordered to man battle positions. This was the real thing; the German 'Spring Offensive' was launched in the misty dawn on the 21st March along a front of approximately 70 miles between Arras in the

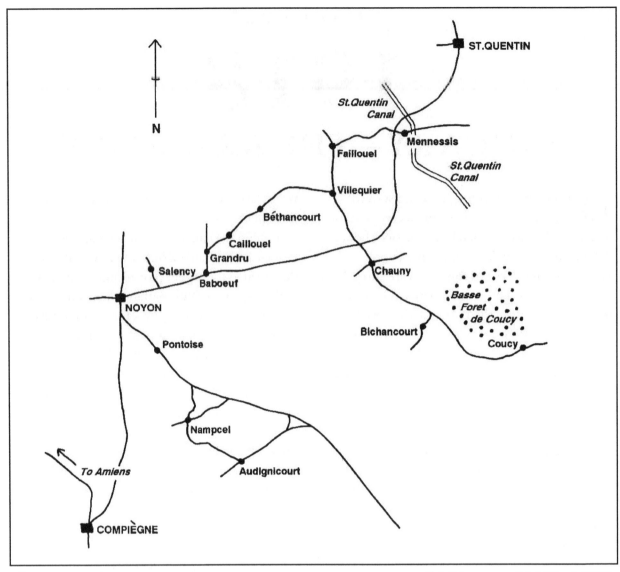

57.

north and Fére in the south. In the event, the
18th (Eastern) Division together with the 36th
(Ulster) Division, the 14th (Light) Division and
just one Brigade of the 58th (London) Division,
found itself to be in the weakest and most
vulnerable British position. Those Units formed
part of the Fifth Army which was thinly and
weakly spread along the southern-most stretch of
the line just north of Fére.

By the end of the first day, most British troops
in the southern area had been pushed right out
of the so called 'Battle Zone' and significant gaps
were left between the units that did remain. The
8th Battalion took its own share of casualties.

MARCH:
21st:
Second Lieutenant: (3422) G.L.Roberson.
Sergeant: (3459) J.F.Turner, M.M.

Privates: (3259) H.J.Baker, (3330) E.G.Gane, (3362)
A.E.Knight, (3385) G.W.Miles, (3471) L.D.Wheeler,
(3475) G.Whittington.

The German offensive and the British retreat
were gaining momentum. Next day, the 22nd
March, the 8th Battalion fell back across the
St.Quentin Canal to Villequier Aumont.

MARCH:
22nd:
Private: (3379) W.Martin.

For the most part, the British withdrawal was
reasonably well organised, with one unit standing
firm or retiring slowly, fighting a rearguard
action, while other units retired through its
position and rearwards. In turn, another unit
stood firm while others retired. The 8th Battalion
found itself caught up in this form of retreat
on the 23rd when it fought a rearguard action

before making its own retirement under cover of darkness to Béthancourt.

MARCH:
23rd:
Sergeant: (3376) E.J.Manvell, M.M.
Privates: (3302) F.T.Cousins, (3436) J.Sparrow.

On the 24th March, the 8th Battalion's 'A' Company left Béthancourt at 10.00am and, at dusk, did well to repulse a German attack just north of Caillouel. However, the general situation remained one of withdrawal and the Company made its way back through a wood at midnight to Grandru, continuing, next day, to Baboeuf and then to Salency. 'B' Company also continued to retreat on the 25th to Baboeuf and then across the canal to Pontoise. Baboeuf was also the destination for 'C' Company that day.

MARCH:
24th:
Private: (3414) E.J.Punnett.
25th:
Private: (3273) W.Breach.

On the 26th March the 8th Battalion came together once more and, at 6.00pm., set off marching to Averdoingt, arriving at 9.30pm. The next night was spent in caves which provided a comforting feeling of protection. A further march, this time through Nampcel, was made

on the 30th to a fleet of lorries which were boarded. Surprisingly, the Battalion found itself moving out of the immediate battle area, east to Compiegne and then north-west through Bretieul to Boves some six miles short of Amiens. They were glad to go: in addition to those killed since the German offensive began nine days previously, 89 men had been wounded and eight were missing. This month proved to be the heaviest, in terms of casualties, sustained by the 8th Battalion during the war.

MARCH:
30th:
Privates: (3276) E.Bryant, (3373) J.H.Lower.

Not surprisingly, men continued to die during April from wounds received during their enforced fighting the previous month. The time was spent at a number of locations around the south of Amiens and ten days' work was undertaken on the Gentelles – Cachy road before the Battalion moved to Dreuil-les-Molliens and Oissy.

The 18th (Eastern) Division had been brought to the area east of Amiens to protect that city from the threatened German advance which, if successful, would pave an open way to the vital channel ports. The Division's three Infantry Brigades, together with the 8th

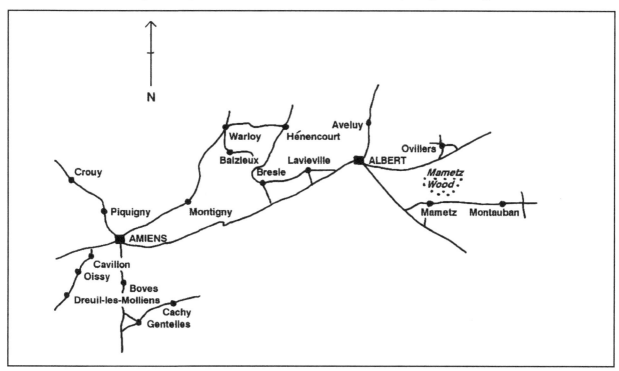

Division and the 5th Australian Division, were positioned east of the city along the 'Amiens Defence Line' which ran through Villers-Bretonneux. The enemy attack there came on the 4th April. Heavy fighting took place all day but the Germans were held back on Villers-Bretonneux's eastern fringes.

The Germans attacked with determination and gained more ground on the 24th April but the following day the British counter-attacked with the Australians and the 18th (Eastern) Division in the forefront. By a surprise attack at 10.00pm the allies struck without preliminary artillery bombardment and successfully regained most of the ground lost the previous day.

APRIL:
1st:
Private: (3342) G.A.R.Harbour.
4th:
Lieutenant: (3285) I.McK.Campbell.
6th:
Privates: (3291) H.Chant, (3448) W.Stringer.
7th:
Private: (3380) E.L.Maskrey.
12th:
Private: (3413) W.Poile.
30th:
Private: (3286) A.W.Care.

A very happy day was spent by the Battalion on the 1st May. Company sports competitions were held through the day, the Division band played during the afternoon and everyone enjoyed an evening concert. However, it was soon time for more work and movement. On the 5th it was time to clamber aboard old, requisitioned London buses near Cavillon and trundle along on solid tyres to Montigny east of Amiens. From Montigny the Battalion marched on eastward to Baizieux. Lavieville, west of Albert, was the destination on the 7th and, there, trench work was performed under the inconvenience of occasional gas shelling. Casualties were sustained as trench work continued through the month. On the last day of the month a short move was made to Hénencourt.

MAY:
9th:
Corporal: (3460) F.Tyler.
Lance Corporal: (3298) A.Cornwall.

Privates: (3252) F.C.Allen, (3278) C.E.Burridge, (3321) P.L.Farrant.
10th:
Privates: (3397) W.Osborn, (3407) A.W.Peake.
12th:
Second Lieutenant: (3409) C.H.Peerless.
Privates: (3255) T.Armstrong, (3417) F.W.Rice.
14th:
Sergeant: (3447) E.Stringer, M.M.
Private: (3248) J.T.Abley.
15th:
Private: (3400) B.Parker.

During the month of June casualties dropped considerably while trench work continued around Hénencourt and Warloy. For a time, the pioneers turned their skills to tunneling at a redoubt in the vicinity. All of this took place while the Germans were being held and while the allies drew breath in readiness for their forthcoming major counter-attack.

JUNE:
1st:
Private: (3320) H.Elsey.
6th:
Private: (3426) S.Scott.
24th:
Privates: (3274) A.J.Brown, (3382) R.J.Mellish.

As the month of July began, three Companies were at Hénencourt and the fourth Company nearby at Warloy. While the Battalion was widening and deepening trenches near the Lavieville – Millancourt Road on the 2nd July they were fired upon by the enemy using gas shells. Nine other ranks were so badly affected by the gas that they had to be taken from duty but there is no record of any deaths for this month. The Battalion boarded buses along the Warloy – Contay Road on the 12th and travelled back to Picquigny, west of Amiens. They marched to Crouy where the weather was so bad on the following Sunday that the Church Parade was cancelled. On the last day of the month buses moved everyone to Heilly just south of the Amiens – Albert Road.

Much time was spent during the first week of August in demolition and salvaging. Time was even found to assist with the cutting of crops but commencement of this relatively pleasant and, to some Sussex men, familiar, task was delayed because of the late arrival of sickles ! These tasks continued for some days after the Allies had launched their 'Advance to Victory' attack on the 8th August. On the second day of the battle the 18th (Eastern) Division captured the village of Morlancourt and the advance gradually gained momentum.

AUGUST:
7th:
Sergeant: (3282) G.Caesar, M.M., M.S.M.
13th:
Private: (3251) A.J.Allen.
16th:
Second Lieutenant: (3288) W.H.Cater.
17th:
Private: (3325) P.J.Forster.

The Division re-captured the town of Albert on the 22nd August after hard fighting. The 8th Battalion pioneers then began to follow-up behind the fighting Brigades of their Division.

First, craters were filled in along the Amiens – Albert Road. This work was followed by improvement to tracks across the River Ancre, then a move onward to repair the Albert – Bapaume Road. By month end the 8th Battalion had followed-up to Mametz Wood, then to Trônes Wood before moving on towards Montauban repairing roads and burying dead horses.

The 8th Battalion pioneers followed the advancing allies ever-eastward during September repairing roads around Sailly-Saillisel and St.Pierre Vaast Wood north of Péronne. Later, similar work was carried out on the Villers-Faucon – Ronssoy Road.

There was an unfortunate occurrence for the Battalion's record on the 18th when, at a court martial, 11071 Private W.Stephen was tried and found guilty of the following act: 'When on Active Service wilfully maiming himself with intent thereby to render himself unfit for

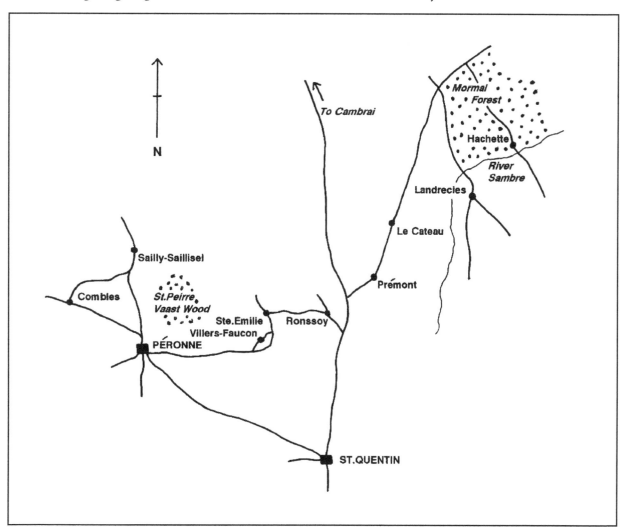

59.   *5th September to the Armistice 1918*

service.' Private Stephen was sentenced to two years intensive hard labour. This incident shows that, even during the 'Advance to Victory' with the Germans in steady retreat and Battalion casualties at their lowest for several months, there could still be such intensive psychological pressures on the men that some cracked under the strain.

SEPTEMBER:
24th:
Private: (3319) S.A.Edwards.

Relief in the form of a few days' rest at Combles was welcomed before the end of September.

Early October brought several quick and successive moves by bus and march in order to keep pace with the continuing general advance. By way of St.Emilie and Prémont the Battalion arrived, on the 22nd, at Le Cateâu, the place where the great British stand had been made during the retreat from Mons in August, 1914. Once again, at this place, the allies were within easy reach of enemy shelling and a number of casualties were taken while the men struggled to maintain the vital roadways along which essential supplies passed to the front line fighting troops.

OCTOBER:
10th:
Private: (3337) S.G.Gore.
23rd:
Lance Corporals: (3411) J.P.Perkins, M.M., (3455) J.Town.
Privates: (3257) F.Baines, (3294) F.C.Coles, (3338) R.J.Gover, (3345) J.E.T.Hayward, (3350) A.J.Hodges, (3395) P.H.Norman, (3408) H.T.Pearson, (3412) P.E.Pettitt, (3479) N.J.Wilson.
26th:
Major: (3349) E.A.Hill.
31st:
Private: (3258) F.Baker.

Work continued around Le Cateâu for the first week of November. On the 8th a final move was made, this time some eight miles north-east to the hamlet of Hachette sandwiched between the great forest of Mormal to the north and the Canal de la Sambre et Oise to the south. There, on the 11th November, the momentous and last message that everyone awaited was received: "HOSTILITIES will cease at 1100 hours."

8th Battalion Epilogue

There is little doubt that the British Army Pioneer Battalions on the Western Front received few expressions of great praise for their efforts. The fact that, for the most part, they were non-combatant has tended to reduce the perceived value of their contribution in the minds of many people, historians and authors. Yet both the existence and the work of these 'behind-the-scenes' battalions were vital in supporting the fighting infantry; in providing accommodation, protection and, above all, in keeping open the essential supply routes along roads, railways and canals. Often, they were required to work close up behind the front lines in the very areas where the enemy were shelling in deliberate attempts to prevent just such work, movement and reinforcements. Their labour-intensive work throughout many hours, day and night, often in the most dreadful weather and ground conditions, was exhausting and morale-sapping. On occasions of heavy pressure on the fighting colleagues of their Divisions they were required to fight in the front positions; testimony to this is shown in the sudden increase of deaths within the 8th Battalion at various times during the war.

The 8th Battalion The Royal Sussex Regiment had been formed as part of Lord Kitchener's 'New Army' and it had been trained and sent to war on the Western Front as a pioneer battalion. For three years and three months the Battalion undertook its duties with no significant periods of respite. To its honour, the Battalion formed part of the 18th (Eastern) Division, justifiably regarded as the most successful Divison to fight on the Somme battlefields and one of the most successful in the whole war. To its detriment, the 18th (Eastern) Division bore severe fighting hardships purely as a result of its own battle successes. The splendid reputation gained led to the Division being used repeatedly in the forefront of subsequent attacks. The Division was led by Major General Sir Ivor Maxse who was undoubtedly one of the most able commanders on the Western Front, his superiors included. He was a man who was prepared to ignore military convention and even disregard the orders of those in higher command if he felt that to do so meant that common sense prevailed against the oft-stupidity that he knew would put his men in senseless and unnecessary danger. Despite his genuine regard for his troops and his efforts to protect them to the best of his ability, the Division suffered 46,503 casualties during the war.

There are three memorials specifically to the 18th (Eastern) Division on the Western Front. Appropriately, one memorial, is at Thiepval, the village taken by the Division at the end of September, 1916. The obelisk stands virtually on the site of the Thiepval Château which was totally destroyed during the fighting. A second memorial to the Divison, also on the Somme, stands beside the road at the southern end of Trônes Wood. The 18th (Eastern) Division brilliantly captured this wood on the 14th July, 1916, and, quite by co-incidence, was to capture it from the Germans again in August, 1918. The third memorial is in the Ypres Salient and stands at 'Clapham Junction' on the infamous Menin Road. The 8th Battalion The Royal Sussex Regiment justifiably basks in these glories and its memories are maintained in these memorials.

PART SIX

The 9th Service Battalion ('New Army')

PART SIX

CHAPTER 28
1914 and 1915

The 'Service' Battalions raised during August and September, 1914, following the call to arms made by Secretary of State for War, Lord Kitchener, had formed the necessary 18 Divisions of the three so-called 'New Armies'. The 9th (Service) Battalion The Royal Sussex Regiment was formed at Chichester in September, 1914, and, continuing its early training, had been established by the end of that year in billets at Portslade just west of Brighton on the Sussex coast. The Battalion was allocated to the 24th Division and, in particular, to its 73rd Infantry Brigade. The whole Division was made up initially as follows:

24th DIVISION
71st Infantry Brigade:
9th Norfolk, 9th Suffolk, 8th Bedfordshire, 11th Essex
72nd Infantry Brigade:
8th Queens, 9th East Surrey, 8th Royal West Kent, 1st North Staffordshire
73rd Infantry Brigade:
9th Royal Sussex, 7th Northamptonshire, 13th Middlesex, 2nd Leinster

Training continued into 1915 on the nearby South Downs and became more intensive after the Battalion left its Portslade billets and moved a short distance to the army training camp at Shoreham. In June, a move north was made to Woking in Surrey where final aspects of the Battalion's 'home' training programme were completed. Towards the end of August news came of the move to France and, on the 31st, the Battalion travelled to Southampton where it embarked on the 'S.S. La Marguerite', arriving at Le Havre on the 1st September.

After a day at the reception camp, a train journey of some 20 hours brought them to Maresquel on the 3rd September. There they detrained in very wet and miserable conditions to billets in barns and outhouses at Embrey

and Rimboval. Over succeeding days it was possible slowly to dry clothes and equipment as the weather improved. All forms of training and instruction were continued, including trench digging, musketry, bomb throwing, route marching and night time work and movement by compass. On one occasion a lecture was given on the effects of gas, following which all ranks had to pass through a gass filled trench. Apparently, the 'smoke helmet' gas masks provided full protection during this exercise.

With other battalions participating, training progressed to Brigade manoeuvres on the 11th September, a very hot and sunny day. The temperature was so high that, on return to billets, the men were allowed to parade in 'shirt sleeve order' and without their heavy packs. Practice at boarding and leaving requisitioned London buses was undertaken with particular note being taken of the best methods of getting the fully armed and equipped men onto, and off, the buses. By the end of the day the average time taken to load and unload a bus was reduced to a commendable 35 seconds!

The Battalion's first death on active service was sustained on the 19th September when Second Lieutenant A.D.Stewart was killed accidentally by the explosion of a bomb (grenade) at a training school at Quilen.

SEPTEMBER:
19th:
Second Lieutenant: (4153) A.D.Stewart.

On the 21st September the Battalion set out on a seven hours march towards the front, arriving in Laires in the early hours of the following morning. Next evening another tiring march, again of seven hours, and over rough 'pavé' roads, brought them to billets at Busnes. On the 24th the Battalion marched to Beuvry and, the following day, moved up to the battle trenches at Vermelles.

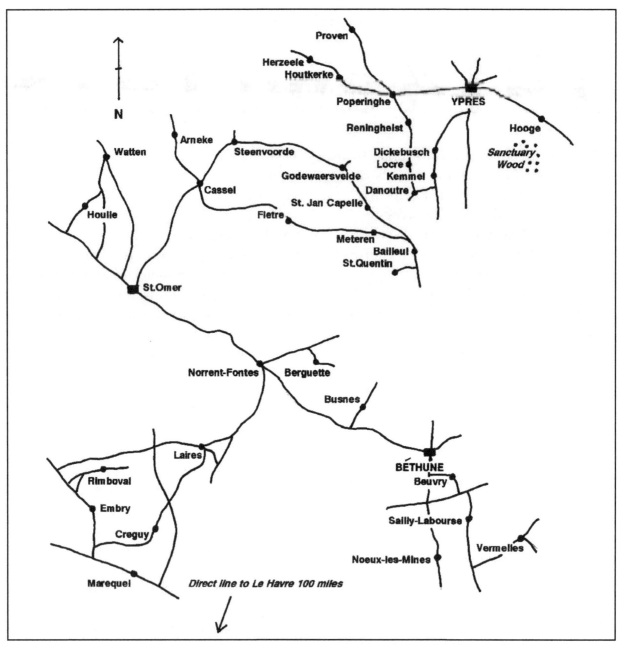

60. *September 1915 to 24th July 1916*

For their part in this, the disastrous Battle of Loos, the 24th and 21st Divisions, both totally untried Units, were mishandled by Field Marshal Sir John French who not only kept the British Reserves, at 16 miles distant, too far in the rear but also failed to release them in time. As a result, both Divisions were forced to endure three exhausting successive night marches and arrived too late to fight when support was sorely needed on the 25th September. Much criticism was levelled at the Commander in Chief for attempting to use these inexperienced Units when other, more experienced Regulars and Territorials were standing not far away in 'quiet' sectors.

Thus, on the morning of the 25th September, the Battalion moved by way of Sailly-Labourse and Vermelles to the trenches soon after midday. By that time all other attacking Units, which had launched the main assault in the early hours, had been repulsed. Such was the general confusion that the Battalion was held in readiness throughout the remainder of the day. The Brigade Major then ordered the Battalion to advance on 'Fosse 8', a large and conspicuous mining slag heap. The move began at 11.30pm to the east and over the Fosse which was to be 'held at all costs'. Despite several German attacks, including heavy artillery and machine gun fire, and the fact that the men were without food and water, the Battalion held on until withdrawn to Sailly-Labourse during the night of the 27th / 28th. Throughout, heavy and continuous enemy artillery fire had been directed against the Fosse area. Many casualties had been sustained but the Battalion had done well in very difficult circumstances. In torrential rain on the 29th the Battalion marched to Noeux-les-Mines and entrained for Berquette from where a march was made to billets in the village of Norrent Fontes. There, as the Battalion rested and absorbed the enormity of its first fierce action, an officer and 23 men who had lost contact during the fighting, rejoined their comrades.

SEPTEMBER:

25th:
Lieuteneant: (4031) F.R.Pring.
Second Lieutenant: (3492) D.W.Armitage.
Lance Sergeant: (4261) H.T.Wickersham.
Corporal: (4155) W.E.Still.
Lance Corporals: (3821) R.J.Hobbs, (3964) W.G.Moss, (4217) P.D.Wadey.
Privates: (3502) D.Avis, (3508) H.Baker, (3511) C.Baldock, (3512) L.J.Baldock, (3543) A.Bishop, (3546) W.Blades, (3576) E.Brooker, (3599) W.Burton, (3605) A.E.Callow, (3617) W.T.Chandler, (3618) L.Channing, (3629) A.Clements, (3632) J.Coldman, (3642) H.Cook, (3667) T.David, (3670) C.W.L.Dawson, (3702) H.Edwards, (3715) W.Findlay, (3728) W.Franks, (3767) W.J.Griffiths, (3771) A.G.Gumbrell, (3787) H.M.Harman, (3808) E.Henley, (3817) F.Hillman, (3859) C.H.Jepson, (3862) J.F.Jervis, (3869) A.V.Jones, (3889) H.Knight, (3894) H.Laker, (3899) H.Lee, (3904) H.Leppard, (3939) G.Maskell, (3940) A.Mason, (3954) C.Milham, (3968) R.Mustchin, (4003) F.J.Pearce, (4006) J.Peat, (4015) F.J.Pettit, (4038) T.G.Putnam, (4042) D.Quigley, (4054) G.E.Remnant, (4063) H.Riddle, (4068) R.F.Robinson, (4107) F.A.Simmonds, (4122) G.W.Smith, (4127) J.Smith, (4141) L.Squelch, (4149) A.Stevens, (4166) J.Strickett, (4183) F.Thatcher, (4209) G.A.Upton, (4218) A.Waite, (4234) C.H.Webb, (4253) W.White, (4263) R.Wilkin, (4265) G.A.Willey, (4280) W.T.Woolven.

26th:
Sergeant: (3801) R.S.Hazell.
Privates: (3584) C.Browning, (3713) W.J.Fieldwick, (4171) H.Strudwick.

27th:
Captains: (3628) J.G.Clarke, (3829) B.H.Holloway.

Lieutenant: (3805) H.R.Heldman.
Second Lieutenant: (4010) H.E.Pennington.
Privates: (3826) R.Holland, (4130) J.Smith, (4159) A.P.Stofer.

28th:
Sergeants: (3944) G.O.Matthews, (4041) S.Quaife.
Lance Sergeant: (3521) O.S.Barnes.
Corporals: (3764) A.O.Griffiths, (3843) J.Hoy.
Lance Corporal: (3538) E.S.Bigg.
Privates: (3490) W.J.Andrews, (3509) W.J.Baker, (3533) H.W.Bell, (3547) H.C.Blattman, (3551) E.Blunt, (3555) J.C.Boniface, (3564) W.C.Bowley, (3610) A.B.Carpenter, (3766) H.Griffiths, (3770) W.J.Grover, (3778) F.Hall, (3795) E.T.Havell, (3806) A.Helme, (3824) A.Holding, (3930) R.S.H.Marsh, (3967) W.G.Murrell, (4022) E.Pitman, (4055) J.Reynolds, (4079) A.Sadler, (4139) R.Spriggs, (4143) F.W.Staker, (4185) O.Thompson, (4186) W.E.Thompson, (4198) J.Trill, (4202) F.E.Turkington, (4216) G.H.Vogel, (4219) F.C.Wakley, (4243) E.West.

29th:
Lance Corporal: (4001) F.A.Payne.
Private: (4074) L.Ross.

Berquette railway station was reached by march on the 2nd October. From there, the Battalion travelled by train to Godewaersvelde in Belgium and then marched to billets at Herzeele. After three days' rest the Battalion marched by way of Houtkerke to new billets at Proven and, from there, on the same day, six officers and 400 other ranks set off by bus for 48 hours in the trenches near Ypres. At Proven, instruction, training and inspections continued and a new draft of two officers and 50 other ranks arrived.

OCTOBER:

1st:
Privates: (3672) W.Dawtrey, (4114) W.Skinner.
2nd:
Private: (3721) H.E.Ford.
7th:
Privates: (3531) W.E.Beeching, (3841) A.Howes, (4084) A.Sandalls.
9th:
Lieutenant: (3879) L.W.Kennelly.

Camp 'C' at Rosenhill near Reninghelst was the march destination on the 11th October and, on the 14th, trenches were taken over from the Duke of Cornwall's Light Infantry. The Germans were relatively quiet at this period and the opportunity was taken to improve the trench lines with sandbags, some 200 of which were filled every day. Five men were wounded, none seriously, during this period before relief and return to Camp 'C' occured on the 19th. Over the next two days the whole Battalion enjoyed the luxury of baths and changes of underclothing at Reninghelst. Several wet days were experienced towards the end of the month and, when trenches were taken over from the 1st Leinsters on the 27th, the conditions were very bad with trench sides collapsing in many places. A small ditch nearby was dangerously full and attempts were made to reduce the flooding by the use of 5,000 sandbags. Men became exhausted working day and night to repair damage and improve conditions. Collapsed support trenches meant that cover for the men was seriously reduced with the result that two were killed on the 29th, one by a sniper and the other unluckily by a stray bullet.

OCTOBER:
21st:
Private: (4000) J.C.Paterson.
29th:
Privates: (3820) F.E.Hinton, (4223) J.Walters.

November began with almost continuous rain and, soon, trench sides were falling in again and the men were struggling to create some sort of effective drainage. By the evening of the 2nd, the Battalion had marched by way of Dickebusch to a rest camp near Reninghelst. The weather improved for the so-called 'rest' which was interrupted by parades and inspections. News was received that Lance Sergeant W.C.Dennet had been awarded the Distinguished Conduct Medal (D.C.M.). On the 6th a return to the trenches was made. Artillery duels took place on several days before the next relief and move back to rest at Reninghelst. At mid-month, by

which time the Battalion had moved into billets at Dickebusch, long range German guns were hitting the area causing wounds from shrapnel shells. Also, eight high explosive shells dropped within 30 yards of the billets but fortunately did no harm.

NOVEMBER:
9th:
Private: (3953) F.Miles.

A welcome march began on the 24th November as the Battalion retired to 'Divisional Rest'. After three days marching by way of Steenvoorde, Arneke and Cassel they were billeted in Houlle and the nearby maltery. The remainder of the month was taken up with the inevitable parades and inspections which did much to interrupt the rest so desperately needed by the men. On the 28th the first party to be allowed to go on leave departed in high spirits.

NOVEMBER:
16th:
Private: (3901) J.W.Leek.
19th:
Lance Corporal: (4251) H.White.
25th:
Private: (4105) W.G.Shoesmith.
26th:
Private: (3920) W.B.Mahy.

The whole of December was spent at Houlle, some 35 miles west of the fighting zones. Intensive training by way of lectures, manoeuvres and attendances at specialist schools was organised for all ranks. Physical fitness through route marching was maintained. Thus, Christmas and the New Year were spent cheerfully and safely in that quiet area of north-west France.

DECEMBER:
11th:
Private: (4116) W.Slater.

CHAPTER 29
1916

With its band playing and leading the way, the Battalion marched out from its rest period at Houlle on the 7th January heading for St.Omer from where a journey by train was taken to Quintin. After detraining, the Battalion marched to a camp beyond Poperinghe, a point close enough to the enemy for gas helmets to be worn compulsorily day and night.

On the 12th January two Taub enemy aircraft flew over the camp and dropped two bombs. Aiming was poor, however, and the bombs dropped on open ground some 200 yards from the camp. The Battalion entered the trenches near Zouave Wood on the 18th where significant enemy shell and sniper fire was experienced. Relief came on the 22nd but, on two consecutive days, the Battalion had to find fatigue parties of 400 and 500 men for trench repair work. Ground conditions were so bad that the men visited the Asylum in Ypres for the purpose of drawing and returning Wellington boots as they moved in and out of the sodden trench system. January ended with the Battalion out of the line at rest camp.

JANUARY:
16th:
Private: (4017) L.Phillips.
20th:
Private: (4215) A.Virgo.
28th:
Second Lieutenant: (3528) R.A.Bazeley.
Privates: (3579) A.Brown, (3800) A.H.Hayward.

There were two welcome occurrences on the 2nd February. The Battalion had use of baths at Poperinghe and, later that day, a gift of many tins of sausages and peppermints was received from the 'Sussex Soldiers Cigarettes and Comforts Fund'. That splendid fund, through its Honorary Secretary, Miss Adams of St.Leonards-on-Sea, at various times distributed to the Units of The Royal Sussex Regiment, more than 60,000 Woodbine cigarettes. Well armed with supplies of comforts, the men enjoyed, next day, an excellent Regimental Concert. These combined treats did much to improve morale and put the men in great good humour.

A draft of 46 men joined the Battalion on the 7th February. These were mainly men who had been recovering and recuperating since being wounded at Loos at the end of September, 1915. Shelters in cellars within Ypres were taken over on the 9th and parties of men had to be found for work in and around the town. On the evening of the 11th the Battalion marched to the trenches at Hooge where all was relatively quiet. Two days later, however, the Germans put down a tremendous bombardment for over eight hours on the British front line areas. A great deal of damage was suffered and there were 30 casualties including several fatalities. Second Lieutenant C.H.Tisdall was killed at this time while attempting to dig out a man who had been buried alive by the shelling.

FEBRUARY:
11th:
Lance Corporal: (3695) W.J.Dunkley.
12th:
Private: (3583) R.R.Brown.
13th:
Second Lieutenant: (4190) C.H.Tisdall.
Sergeant: (3984) F.J.Orchin.
Privates: (3524) A.G.H.Bartlett, (3626) G.H.Clark, (3740) J.L.George, (3958) H.Mitchell, (4240) F.G.Weller.

Heavy enemy shelling continued at Hooge during the 14th February and then, at 5.45pm, the Germans exploded two mines. Several mines were blown near Hooge Château during the war and the two on this occasion produced both disaster and heroism within the 9th Battalion. A number of men, including Lieutenant Eric Archibald McNair, were flung into the air by one of the mine explosions. All were severely shaken but Lieutenant McNair, quickly regaining his composure, immediately organised machine gunners to defend the craters' rims and drive back the inevitable enemy infantry attack. McNair then made the perilous crossing of No-Man's-Land to fetch reinforcements which, under heavy fire, he led back across the open and torn landscape to the overlapping mine craters. Through his presence of mind and bravery Lieutenant McNair had saved a desperate situation; for these actions he was later awarded the Victoria Cross, one of only three to be awarded to The Royal Sussex Regiment on the Western Front. Sadly, Lieutenant McNair was severely wounded and died while serving in Italy during 1918.

The disaster caused to the 9th Battalion by the enemy mines at Hooge on the 14th February involved the men of one platoon of 'D' Company and their officer, Second Lieutenant C.D.Hill, all of whom were completely buried alive without chance of rescue. Second Lieutenant Hill's body was subsequently recovered and re-buried at Menin Road South Military Cemetery. The shaken Battalion was relieved on the 15th and returned to cellars in Ypres. During this period of four days in the trenches at Hooge, casualties had totalled seven officers and 134 other ranks, some of whom died on following days from their wounds.

FEBRUARY:
14th:
Lieutenant: (3680) G.Le B. De Wolf.
Second Lieutenant: (3815) C.D.L.Hill.
Sergeants: (3570) R.Bryce, (3754) L.Gordon, (4051) H.Reeves.
Corporals: (4036) W.Pullen, (4077) E.W.Rubidge.
Lance Corporals: (3734) H.J.Funnell, (3737) J.C.Gardner.
Privates: (3571) E.J.Bridger, (3606) F.Calway, (3651) G.E..Cowdrey, (3661) J.E.Dadswell, (3691) A.A.Dray, (3709) J.E.Farrant, (3712) J.Fergus, (3773) R.E.Haddington, (3783) A.Hammond, (3788) G.S.Harris, (3804) S.G.Heather, (3900) J.W.Lee, (3922) T.Mallows, (3927) J.Marchant, (3937) R.Martin, (3972) J.J.Newbery, (3994) J.E.Parker, (4016) J.Phillips, (4027) C.Poulter, (4066) J.H.W.Robbins, (4177) T.H.Tann, (4235) B.Webber, (4260) J.D.Whittome, (4282) A.E.Wren.
15th:
Lieutenant: (3957) F.S.Mitchell.
Private: (3813) A.E.Herrington.

After one day's complete rest 200 men had to be detailed for working parties. Finding so

many men was difficult because, in addition to the recent heavy casualties, a significant number reported sick and were sent to hospital. The Hooge trenches were occupied again from the 19th February until the 24th when relief came followed by a train journey to comfortable but cold billets in Poperinghe. At the end of the month, while still 'at rest', the Battalion was congratulated by the General Officer Commanding on its fine performance during its recent tour of front line duties.

FEBRUARY:
18th:
Private: (4191) D.Todman.
20th:
Privates: (3516) R.F.Banks, (3981) C.V.Oliver, (4255) H.P.Whitehouse.
21st:
Lance Corporal: (3625) W.J.Churcher.
Private: (4050) A.J.Reeves.
23rd:
Lieutenant: (3905) R.J.M.Lias.
Private: (3769) H.Grover.
24th:
Lance Corporal: (3883) F.King.

The third day of March brought a move from Poperinghe back to the area around the château at Hooge. The weather was bitterly cold and there were heavy falls of snow. The men were kept warm by means of frequent working party duties. The Battalion moved back to 'Camp F' on the 15th and, on the 17th, was allocated the exclusive use of hot baths for the whole day. A move by road on the 19th was made to Meteren where, over a period of four days, training and route marching took place to 'harden' the men who had done very little 'foot slogging' of late. An unusually quiet period was experienced in the trenches from the 24th to the end of March.

MARCH:
6th:
Private: (3595) E.Burrell.
8th:
Private: (3600) W.H.A.Butcher.
9th:
Private: (4032) C.J.Pringle.
11th:
Private: (4168) W.S.Stringer.
13th:
Private: (4163) W.Stoner.

14th:
Private: (3545) E.A.Blackwell.
24th:
Privates: (3830) J.Holman, (4254) J.Whitehead.
27th:
Private: (4046) J.Raffle.
28th:
Private: (4211) G.W.P.Verion.

April proved to be a surprisingly quiet month with relatively few casualties. For some obscure reason all leave was cancelled at mid-month and Captain McNair, promoted from Lieutenant since his exploits of the 14th February, was unable to depart for England to be presented with his Victoria Cross. Towards the end of April the gas alarms were sounded on two occasions and the Battalion had to 'stand-to' in case of attack. The first was a false alarm but, on the 30th, about 20 minutes of thick gas was experienced. There had been plenty of warning to allow gas helmets to be put on and no serious effects were felt. Morale had been raised this month by a concert held in the Y.M.C.A hut on the 4th and a football match on the 28th with the result: Officers 3 The Rest 2.

APRIL:
8th:
Private: (3908) F.Lintott.
18th:
Lance Corporal: (3748) F.Golding.
Private: (3961) C.Moore.
22nd:
Private: (3650) C.Cottam.
24th:
Private: (3540) G.J.Birchmore.
29th:
Private: (3701) H.Eastwood.

Many days comparatively free from war-like activity occured in May and the weather improved considerably. Moves in and out of the trenches were carried out but, again, casualties were light.

MAY:
5th:
Company Sergeant Major: (3822) F.J.Hodge.
Privates: (3671) E.T.Dawson, (4106) J.H.Silverton.
10th:
Sergeant: (4018) A.Pike.
Privates: (3786) A.Harding, (3895) J.H.Lancaster.

15th:
Lance Corporal: (3674) W.G.Day.
17th:
Sergeant: (4126) H.S.Smith.
Privates: (3535) F.Berriman, (3729) H.J.Freeland, (4011) A.J.Pepper.
MAY:
27th:
Private: (4069) R.Robinson.

The unusually quiet period continued until the 17th June when the Germans decided to liven up the situation. Just after midnight, the first of three waves of gas crossed the Battalion's position over a period of approximately 40 minutes. The men wore their gas masks uncomfortably for one hour during which heavy shell and machine gun fire came their way; in all there were 15 fatalities. Later that day the Battalion was relieved by the 7th Australian Brigade and moved out by motor lorries to St.Jan Capelle. Over the next two days, two more men died from the effects of gas inhalation. A move to huts at Locre was made on the 20th but June ended with the Battalion experiencing shelling, minenwerfers and trench mortars back in the front line.

JUNE:
1st:
Privates: (3794) L.H.Harwood, (4118) C.Smith.
3rd:
Private: (3665) F.J.E.Dann.
5th:
Private: (3580) B.Brown.
6th:
Private: (3969) T.Nally.
9th:
Privates: (4062) R.Ricketts, (4123) H.Smith.
13th:
Private: (4082) B.Sageman.
17th:
Lance Sergeants: (4090) E.E.Sayer, (4229) A.Warriner.
Privates: (3572) G.Bridger, (3664) A.G.Dann, (3699) J.Eames, (3722) J.Ford, (3724) W.Foster, (3874) A.Joseph, (3915) S.Luscombe, (3921) A.L.Malcolm, (4002) G.A.Payne, (4029) A.Pratt, (4131) W.C.Smith, (4162) F.Stoner, (4208) G.Upton.
18th:
Privates: (3500) P.Atherall, (3542) J.J.Birtle, (3550) E.W.Blunden, (4007) W.E.Peck, (3604) T.G.Callcut, (3640) R.G.Constable, (4151) H.J.Stevens.
23rd:
Privates: (3755) E.Gorringe, (4065) E.S.Ridley.

28th:
Privates: (3537) R.C.Betts, (3563) F.H.Bowler, (4045) H.S.Radford, (4083) G.Salvage, (4230) A.G.Waters.
29th:
Private: (3875) J.Joyes.
30th:
Privates: (3577) J.H.Brookfield, (3839) A.D.T.Hough.

The 6th July brought a Battalion move out of the trenches to bivouacs and huts near Kemmel and, on the 8th, a further move to more comfortable barns and huts at Dranoutre. From there, a nine day tour in the trenches began on the 11th. All was quiet and, although preparations for the discharge of gas were made, unfavourable winds sprang up and the discharge was cancelled. Relief by the Duke of Cornwall's Light Infantry on the 20th allowed the Battalion to move by lorries and buses to Fletre. Then the Battalion marched to Godewaersvelde on the 25th and, by train, left the area of the Ypres Salient behind them as they travelled south to Saleux, some six miles south-west of Amiens, arriving during the early evening and marching to good billets at Montagne.

JULY:
2nd:
Private: (4110) W.J.Skeites.
13th:
Sergeant: (4009) E.J.R.Pelling.
15th:
Corporal: (4140) H.J.Spurgin.
16th:
Private: (3519) J.Barlow.
17th:
Private: (3991) S.Padwick.
19th:
Privates: (3962) F.G.Morley, (4021) C.G.Pitman.
30th:
Private: (3716) H.A.Fisher.

Having marched away from Montagne the previous day, the Battalion underwent a day's bayonet fighting practice at Corbie on the 1st August, exactly one month after the disastrous start of the Battle of the Somme; the Battalion was about to join that battle. By way of Sailly-le-Sec, moves were made in stages until the 10th when the defences at Montauban were occupied, extending to an area of craters near Carnoy the next day. Two or three days were then spent in the forward areas salvaging re-useable items of equipment and materials; this, however, was a lull before the storm.

AUGUST:
6th:
Private: (3733) T.B.Fuller.
8th:
Private: (3988) E.C.Owen.
13th:
Corporal: (4284) T.Wynne.
17th:
Private: (3673) J.Day.

A significant British attack was launched on the 18th August against the village of Guillemont. The plan was for the 9th Battalion to follow up with its own attack at 5.00am on the 19th with the aim of advancing half way through the fortified village. In the event, the 7th Northamptonshires lost so heavily in hand-to-hand fighting on the 18th that the 9th Royal Sussex were called in as reinforcements. They, too, took considerable casualties including Captain McNair who was wounded attempting to find a route across No-Man's-Land. Another officer, Second Lieutenant K.C.Bright, was killed while leading his men across as reinforcements.

AUGUST:
18th:
Second Lieutenants: (3573) K.C.Bright, (4030) C.M.Prince.
Sergeants: (3647) J.W.Cornford, (3846) W.C.Hughes, (3861) G.Jerrold, (3959) W.J.Mittell.
Lance Sergeant: (3556) M.J.Boniface.
Corporals: (3997) R.W.Parris, (4173) E.Stunell.
Lance Corporals: (3831) T.Holmes, (3833) G.T.Hope, (3945) E.W.May, (4044) F.A.Radford, (4246) A.J.White.
Privates: (3487) G.Allfrey, (3532) M.H.R.Beeton, (3552) W.C.H.Bond, (3553) H.W.Bones, (3568) J.Bradshaw, (3582) H.Brown, (3641) C.A.Cook, (3657) G.W.Cuddington, (3659) G.E.Curtis, (3791) P.J.Harrod, (3855) J.James, (3872) W.J.Jones, (3881) S.G.Kent, (3911) G.Longhurst, (3936) J.Martin, (3941) W.Mason, (4012) J.W.Perkins, (4014) A.C.Pettitt, (4047) G.H.Randall, (4076) A.J.Rouse, (4085) E.W.Sanders, (4129) J.Smith, (4136) H.A.Sopp.

The following day Units from elsewhere and groups of men from the Battalion acted as

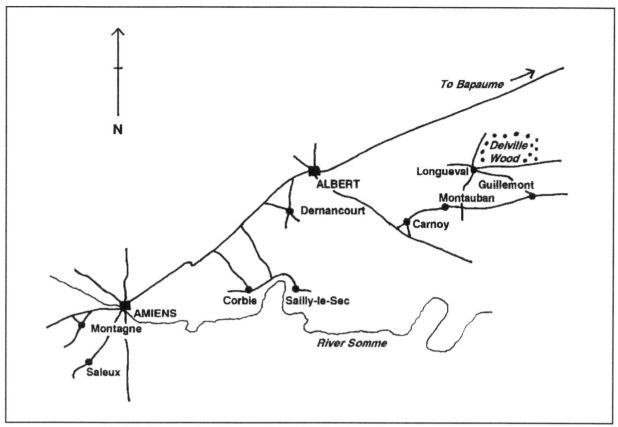

61.   *25th July to 5th September 1916*

reinforcements to the 7th Northamptonshires, holding their position and hurriedly constructing a strong point on the right flank. That night the Battalion was relieved by the 8th Royal West Kent and moved back to an area near Carnoy. During the two day's heavy fighting for Guillemont the Battalion sustained seven officer and 183 other rank casualties.

AUGUST:
19th:
Captain: (4072) E.S.Rogerson.
Lance Corporals: (3522) V.Barratt, (3975) L.Newman.
Private: (4034) H.C.Pryor.
20th:
Privates: (3925) A.Manville, (3929) H.J.Marden, (4158) W.J.Stockford, (4174) F.S.Sturmey, (4178) W.G.Tapper.
21st
Privates: (4064) P.E.Riddles, (4145) F.C.Stanley.
22nd:
Private: (3638) C.F.Comber.
23rd:
Privates: (3756) R.Grant, (4204) G.Turner.
25th:
Lance Corporal: (4268) H.L.Willson.
29th:
Private: (3598) H.Burton.

Seven days of recuperation followed. At the end of that period the Battalion moved into trenches on the left of Delville Wood where they were attacked by the Germans after a heavy bombardment on the 31st August. Although the enemy broke through to the left of the Battalion, the 9th Royal Sussex held on after repulsing a determined bombing party. The Battalion had another 30 men killed and 80 wounded during, and as a result of, this successful holding operation.

AUGUST:
31st:
Sergeants: (3601) G.Butler, (3819) G.Hingston, (3876) M.G.C.Jupp, D.C.M., (4165) T.Street.
Corporal: (4271) J.Winchester.
Privates: (3530) S.Bedford, (3559) J.W.Boucher, (3660) T.Dacey, (3703) F.Eldridge, (3736) G.Gardner, (3739) H.Gearing, (3768) J.Grist, (3782) R.A.Hames, (3799) H.Hayler, (3807) C.Hemsley, (3828) A.Holloway, (3836) F.J.Hopkins, (3870) A.Jones, (3943) E.J.Maton, (3950) J.Meredith, (3982) W.G.Oliver, (3987) J.H.Overy, (4081) J.W.Sage, (4144) J.P.Standen, (4146) F.G.Stedman, (4156) J.Stillwell, (4247) F.White, (4250) G.White, (4270) C.Winch.

On the 1st September the Battalion held on

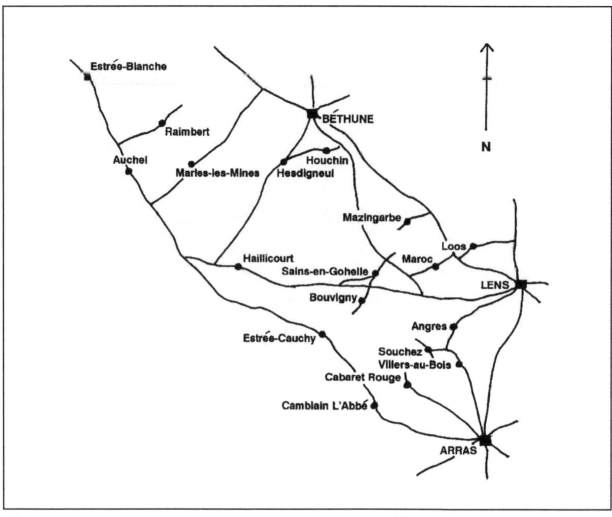

62.   *6th September 1916 to 12th May 1917*

through several more German attacks. Almost the worst problem was the complete lack of food and water. A valiant attempt to bring up rations was led by Regimental Sergeant Major Williams who was wounded in so doing. In the afternoon the Germans were driven back by a battalion over to the left and this considerably eased the situation. The 9th Battalion was relieved on the 3rd. A move was made back to Dernancourt on the 5th and then the Battalion went by train to Brucamps and billets. Over the next fortnight much training and reorganisation was accomplished. The Battalion travelled onwards to Marles-les-Mines on the 20th, marched to Haillicourt on the 22nd and onwards to Camblain- l'Abbé next day. On the 24th, Villers-au-Bois was the final march destination for the month. Drafts totalling seven officers and 199 men arrived during the latter half of September; these were sorely needed to help replace those recently lost to the Battalion.

SEPTEMBER:
1st:
Private (4104) T.Sherwood.
4th:
Privates: (3612) E.A.Carr, (4142) A.Stagles.
6th:
Lance Corporal: (4222) W.G.Walter.
9th:
Lance Corporal: (3877) A.G.Kelly.
15th:
Private: (3823) A.W.Holcombe.
28th:
Private: (4004) R.W.Pearce.

The only fatal casualties during October occured when, during the first week, three men died from wounds while the Battalion held the line in front of Souchez, north-west of Arras. A move back to billets in Camblain-l'Abbé and nearby Villers-au-Bois was effected on the 10th. After a nine days spell in support at Cabaret Rouge, the Battalion marched to Estrée Cauchie and then northwards to Mazingarbe before moving into the trenches near Loos before the end of the month.

OCTOBER:
1st:
Private: (4274) W.Winyard.
3rd:
Lance Corporal: (4070) R.Robson.
Private: (3685) C.Dival.
9th:
Private: (3653) W.J.Cozens.

November proved to be a month of little fighting activity and just a few casualties. A trickle of men continued to arrive as replacement drafts. Time was spent in and out of the Loos front line trenches, with support and reserve spells at Maroc and Les Brebis respectively.

NOVEMBER:
6th:
Second Lieutenant: (3797) J.A.Hawkridge.
12th:
Private: (4182) S.Terry.
17th:
Private: (4252) J.White.
21st:
Private: (4199) W.Trodd.

26th:
Corporal: (3758) G.F.Gray.
29th:
Private: (4125) H.S.Smith.

December continued quietly in the Battalion's area. Again, casualties were few while duties were undertaken in the trenches, on working parties and fatigues. The year ended with the Battalion in the trenches at Loos after Christmas dinners had been enjoyed by two Companies on Christmas Day and the remainder on the 28th.

DECEMBER:
6th:
Private: (4221) S.Wallis.
7th:
Private: (4109) N.Simmons.
10th:
Private: (3608) C.Card.
13th:
Sergeant: (4080) H.Sage.
30th:
Private: (3951) C.F.Merton.

CHAPTER 30
1917

An enemy gas shell bombardment welcomed in the New Year, fortunately without serious casualties. With the exception of a German raid on the 24th January there was little other hostile activity from either side in this period of deep winter. The enemy raid was repulsed before it could reach the Battalion's trenches and one wounded German was brought in to captivity.

It was in connection with this relatively minor skirmish that one of those poignant wartime stories was recorded. Brothers Tom and Alfred Alexander Macdonald were serving together at the time as members of the same team of Lewis gunners. A burst of enemy fire was heard and Tom was wounded but only slightly. With a colleague, Tom was helping to move a more seriously wounded man to a medical aid post when he heard the familiar shout for 'Stretcher Bearers'. Tom had a strange feeling that his brother may also have been hit and, while at the aid post, he asked a stretcher bearer to go back with him. The two men returned along the trench in the dark and soon they found 'Alex', as Tom's brother was known. After just one glance the stretcher bearer set off saying that he must get help. Alex was lying face-down and motionless and Tom saw immediately a bad wound in the back of his brother's head. Tom waited in a state of much anxiety until his brother was carefully moved by the stretcher bearers and Tom himself went back to an Advanced Dressing Station. The injection Tom was given for his hand wound made him very sleepy for a time. Sadly, by then, Alex was dead. Next day Tom made what he described as the longest walk of his life to bury his brother at the village of Philosophe. Tom was supported by his officer, Lieutenant Dudley, and by the Padre as his brother was buried at what was then a new cemetery. In 1918 Tom had the chance to visit that cemetery again. He then found many graves there and was pleased to see that Alex's best pals had placed a wooden cross at the grave with his name, rank, number, battalion and the words, 'One of the Best'.

JANUARY:
3rd:
Private: (4206) W.E.Twine.
13th:
Private: (3796) E.W.Hawkins.
15th:
Private: (4088) L.C.Saunders.
17th:
Private: (4244) A.J.Weston.
24th:
Privates: (3745) F.W.Godden, (3918) A.A.Macdonald, (4091) W.Scott.

For the fifth consecutive month things remained relatively 'all quiet' during February on the Battalion's sector of the Western Front. On the 12th, a move out to 'rest' at Hesdigneul was made, Field Marshal Sir Douglas Haig taking the salute along the line of march. After a period of reorganisation and the replenishment of kit, an inspection was undertaken by General Nivelle, at that time Commander-in-Chief of the French Army, whose over-ambitious plans, marred by lack of foresight and judgement, were to launch so many French soldiers to their useless deaths later at the ill-conceived attack farther south, along the Chemin-des-Dames.

FEBRUARY:
2nd:
Private: (3562) H.V.Bowden.
4th:
Private: (3690) F.Downard.
5th:
Private: (3548) C.Bleach.
12th:
Private: (4020) H.Pilcher.
15th:
Private: (3621) J.Cheesman.
23rd:
Private: (3913) T.G.Lown.

Casualty levels increased during March as, after a period of rest, recuperation and preparation, the Battalion returned to the line, this time in the area around the Lorette Spur, Sains-en-Gohelle and Souchez, north-west of Arras. At Souchez, an enemy raid was thwarted by Lewis Gun and rifle fire on the 10th but the accompanying German bombardment caused several casualties. Further periods of extended shell fire without infantry involvement occured on the 26th, 27th and 28th.

MARCH:
11th:
Lance Corporal: (4112) H.H.Skinner.
Privates: (3578) J.Brooman, (3812) C.Hepden, (3938) A.C.Maskell, (4161) F.R.Stone.
27th:
Lance Sergeant: (3689) E.A.Doggett.
Privates: (3515) J.E.Banks, (3529) H.R.Beck, (3891) S.Knight, (4089) R.J.Sawyer, (4160) C.H.Stone.
28th:
Privates: (3596) A.H.Burt, (4239) C.C.Weller.
29th:
Private: (4179) G.Tapsell.
30th:
Private: (3999) F.G.Partridge.
31st:
Private: (3914) L.G.Luck.

The Battalion was back in full action on the 12th and 13th April when a British attack was launched on the German positions in the Bois-en-Hache. The attack, which included the Brigade's 2nd Leinster Battalion, was undertaken in conjunction with the Canadian Corps, the objective being the enemy 1st and 2nd lines. All Units moved into position without difficulty or casualties on the 12th. Tea and rum were served to the men. The difficult night time task of forming up in correct alignment for the assault was hampered, five minutes before zero hour, by a driving blizzard.

As the whistles sounded all along the line and men went 'over the top', casualties were immediately taken from enemy machine gun fire. At the cost of 60 Battalion casualties, the enemy's first line was taken. Half a dozen Germans who stayed to fight were bayoneted while the remainder ran off or were captured. The attack was continued, through a blinding snow storm over ground churned into a sea of mud by shelling and bad weather, until the objectives were taken. The bad ground conditions made

communications difficult but the positions were held on the 13th. During the afternoon of that day it was noticed that the Germans appeared to be shelling their own line and the village of Angres.

Consequently, patrols were sent out and these established that, apart from a machine gun and two snipers, the enemy had withdrawn. Accordingly, an outpost line was established on the River Souchez and held through the night until relief by the Royal Fusiliers at 7.00am. During this two-day action, and in addition to those killed, four officers and 63 men had been wounded.

APRIL:
7th:
Private: (4205) W.E.Turner.
12th:
Lieutenants: (3622) W.D.Chepmell, (4102) W.B.Shaw.
Second Lieutenants: (3613) A.Carter, (4033) G.M.W.Prowse, (4213) B.H.Vidler.
Sergeants: (3890) J.Knight, (4187) W.G.Thompson.
Corporal: (4207) A.E.Tyrrell.
Privates: (3506) A.J.Baker, (3738) A.Garrod, (3765) F.C.Griffiths, (3998) B.W.Parsons.
13th:
Company Sergeant Major: (3520) F.Barnard, D.C.M.
Sergeants: (4193) S.A.Toplis, (4277) T.H.Woodhams.
Corporals: (3541) W.J.Bird, (3636) J.C.Collins, (3893) S.Lake.
Lance Corporals: (3589) A.J.Buckland, (3679) F.T.Denyer, (3882) A.W.King, (4094) C.Searle.
Privates: (3485) A.Agate, (3495) J.E.Arundel, (3507) E.Baker, (3510) E.J.W.Balcombe, (3534) C.L.Bennett, (3558) R.Bottoms, (3567) W.H.Bradley, (3585) R.Brunton, (3624) A.J.Christian, (3637) L.Colvin, (3648) A.H.Cornock, (3741) W.Gilbert, (3753) W.H.Goodwin, (3856) M.Jamieson, (3907) J.H.Lines, (3912) R.T.Loop, (3917) W.Lytharby, (3924) H.G.Mant, (3980) A.W.Nottage, (3986) H.J.Overy, (4019) H.J.Pike, (4037) F.C.Purdy, (4100) E.Sharp, (4101) F.Sharp, (4245) F.Weston, (4267) W.J.Willie.

The Battalion moved back on the 14th April, reaching Hesdigneul on the 17th, Auchel on the 18th and Estrée Blanche on the 19th. There, at last, rest and reorganisation were possible and were enjoyed for a whole week. On the 26th, however, a march was made to Raimbert and, on the following day, to Houchin in Brigade Support.

APRIL:
14th:
Private: (4148) G.Stephens.
15th:
Sergeant: (3909) P.O.Lock.
Private: (3603) S.C.Cadman.
24th:
Private: (3607) F.Cannon.
26th:
Private: (3776) J.W.Haigh.

The month of April ended happily with recreational football matches on consecutive days: 9th Battalion 4, Brigade Headquarters 1; 9th Battalion 2, 2nd Leinsters 0.

May began, as it was to continue throughout, with rest, training, fieldwork, working parties and the integration of men newly drafted to the Battalion.

MAY:
5th:
Sergeant: (3708) L.Evans.
28th:
Private: (3993) H.Page.

June, 1917, saw the undertaking of one of the most successful British attacks of the war, at the Battle of Messines Ridge in which the

9th Battalion was to take part. At 11.30pm on the 6th the Battalion marched to its assembly trenches at Château Segard near Dickebusch. As the men arrived they were shelled with gas, one man being killed and three incapacitated as a result of inhalation. The Battalion's role was not in the first attack at 3.10am which followed the blowing of 19 British mines along the crest of the Messines Ridge. It was at 11.30am on the 7th that the Battalion moved steadily forward in artillery formation to what had been the British front line and, at 2.00pm, continued ahead over open ground captured earlier by the 41st Division. By the appointed time of 3.30pm Battalion troops were deployed beneath the British barrage. The advance under protection of the barrage was accomplished in 20 minutes and the objectives were taken with little opposition.

JUNE:
6th:
Privates: (3677) J.Dennis, (3742) W.G.Glaysher, (3814) F.G.Hewson.
7th:
Privates: (3575) L.F.W.Bromley, (3707) A.J.Etheridge.

From the 8th to the 11th June the Battalion held the line it had attained, consolidating and

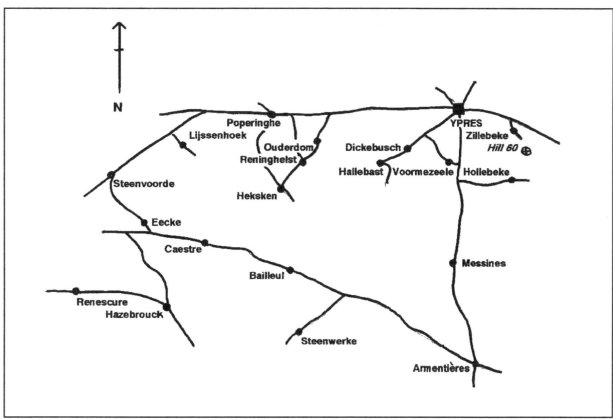

13th May to 21st September 1917

strengthening its position despite increased enemy shelling. The battle as a whole had been a great success although the Battalion suffered 134 wounded and three missing in addition to those killed. Unfortunately the senior officer planners had not made preparations for onward movement and the great chance was lost. Instead, a general halt of six weeks followed while arrangements were made for the launch of the next major stage, the 3rd Battle of Ypres. By that time the Germans had recovered and were, once more, well prepared.

JUNE:
8th:
Privates: (3497) F.Ashenden, (3903) H.Legg.
10th:
Sergeant: (3635) S.C.Coleman.
11th:
Sergeant: (3560) C.W.Bourne.
Corporals: (3935) J.Martin, (3750) E.H.Goldsmith.
Privates: (3503) P.F.Aylard, (3592) P.G.Burden, (3602) S.Button, (3655) W.Cross, (3717) H.H.Fisher, (3759) W.C.Gray, (3789) R.Harris, (3802) F.Hearne, (3844) A.W.Hughes, (3853) J.Jackson, (3857) B.Jarvis, (3897) W.Langridge, (3923) B.Mansfield, (3978) P.Noakes, (3989) G.Packham, (4059) R.G.Richardson, (4119) E.Smith, (4188) G.N.Thorpe, (4201) B.Tuesley, (4212) G.Verrall, (4241) W.A.S.Wenban, (4248) F.S.White.

After the Battle of Messines Ridge the Battalion moved back to Ouderdom but soon returned in support to the Hill 60 area at the northern end of the Ridge. On the 23rd June Ouderdom was a familiar spot once more. From there, on the 27th, the Battalion travelled by train to billets in the rest area at Nielles-les-Blequin where, as the month ended, the welcome and proud news of awards to the Battalion was received: Military Cross: Captain C.V.Newton and Second Lieutenant R.W.Rumsby; Distinguished Conduct Medal: Private A.J.Dell; Military Medal: Sergeants C.Fuller and W.G.Tickner, Corporal H.G.Sivyer, Private E.Isard; Medaille Militaire: Sergeant Chillman.

JUNE:
15th:
Privates: (3816) E.A.Hill, (4049) J.Read.
19th:
Private: (3946) J.McArthur.

20th:
Privates: (3488) G.E.Almond, (3749) A.E.Goldring.
21st:
Lance Corporal: (3837) J.Horsley.
Privates: (3536) E.Berwick, (4172) J.E.Stubbs.
22nd:
Privates: (3704) C.G.P.Ellis, (3916) A.Lynn, (4099) J.F.Seymour.
23rd:
Corporal: (3711) W.Fennelow.
Lance Corporal: (4152) A.L.Stevenson.
Privates: (3730) N.H.Freeman, (3840) E.Howard, (3858) H.R.Jarvis, (3867) F.A.Johnson, (3906) P.W.Lincoln, (3932) J.Marshall, (3995) P.W.F.Parker, (4060) W.G.Richardson, (4087) T.W.Sargent, (4103) J.Sheriff, (4147) J.W.Steed, (4189) A.Thurlow, (4195) T.Townsend.
24th:
Sergeant: (3658) F.A.Cuddon.
Corporal: (4262) W.Wiles.
28th:
Private: (4040) J.Puttock.

While recuperating and training at Nielles-les-Blequin during the first half of July, the largest draft ever received by the Battalion arrived in the form of 150 men, all young and with previous experience in France. Some were returning after wounds or recuperation and they were all welcomed warmly to the Battalion. In considerable summer heat on the 17th a 16 miles march was made to Renescure, continuing to Caestre, Eecke, Lijssenthoek and Reninghelst on successive days. Gradually, the Battalion moved closer to the area of the coming battle so disastrously delayed since the successful assault along the Messines Ridge six weeks earlier. The next expected attack, the 3rd Battle of Ypres, otherwise known as Passchendaele, was to be dogged by heavy rains which began even before the battle itself was launched.

On the 30th July, the day before the battle commenced, the Battalion suffered from gas shelling. The mustard gas used caused huge blisters on exposed flesh and 'A' Company, in particular, was badly affected. The Battalion was not to be in the first wave of assaulting troops but moved up to its assault positions on the 31st, even as that first day of the battle was raging. Great difficulty was experienced getting through congested Voormezeele, especially with two cookers and two water carts, but the effort was worth while with the later benefit of hot food and drink. At that spot, also, they had to pass close by, and suffer the deafening noise of, a firing 11" gun.

JULY:
14th:
Private: (3809) H.Hennessey.
18th:
Private: (3865) C.C.Jewers.
24th:
Private: (3779) W.F.Hall.
25th:
Private: (3868) H.Johnson.
26th:
Second Lieutenant: (3639) G.Compton.
27th:
Lance Sergeant: (3566) O.Brackpool.
28th:
Privates: (3845) J.Hughes, (4095) C.C.Searle.
29th:
Private: (3693) W.Driver.
30th:
Private: (4242) F.P.Wenham.

Having been moved up in close support for the beginning of the battle, the Battalion took over the front line on the 3rd August. Bad weather continued and all duties were carried out only with the greatest difficulty as the ground degenerated into a vast morass. Movement over all but the shortest distance was an enormous effort with men sinking knee, even thigh-deep, into the porridge-like liquid mud at the bottom of every shallow trench. Welcome relief came on the 8th with a move to a position 800 yards north-west of Dickebusch Church where three days were spent resting and reorganising.

AUGUST:
2nd:
Private: (3662) G.T.Dale.
3rd:
Sergeant: (3863) F.W.Jestico.
Lance Corporals: (3649) G.Cornwall, (4275) E.C.Wood.
Privates: (3586) H.Bryant, (3587) J.Bryant, (3687) S.C.Dix, (3960) E.J.Mitten, (4169) W.H.Stringer.
4th:
Privates: (3588) E.Buck, (3611) J.S.Carpenter, (3850) A.Hutchings, (4026) J.W.Pope, (4132) W.J.Smith.
6th:
Privates: (3780) W.H.Hall, (3864) A.W.Jewell.
7th:
Private: (3525) A.T.Bassett.

8th:
Privates: (3591) S.Burchett, (4266) D.Williams.
10th:
Lance Corporal: (3554) H.Boniface.

The inevitable return to the line was made on the 8th August. The weather had improved to the extent that some work on the posts, trenches and dugouts was possible. In particular, a scheme for the naming and marking of dugouts proved very successful enabling guides, runners and others to find their way much more quickly. Three German bombing attacks were driven off and, on the whole, casualties were light. From a minor offensive viewpoint a raiding party reached an enemy post, found it to be occupied only by a single sentry and promptly took him prisoner. The Battalion moved out to rest on the night of the 15th / 16th but were back in the line by the 23rd.

AUGUST:
12th:
Privates: (3634) J.Coleman, (3896) R.Langley, (4228) E.F.Warren.
13th:
Private: (4028) F.J.Powell.
15th:
Privates: (3798) A.H.Hayler, (4025) C.O.T.Pope.
16th:
Private: (3619) F.Charlton.
17th:
Private: (3928) W.Marchant.

During the second half of August enemy aircraft were considerably more active. As a protective measure, sandbag walls were built between the tents of the 'rest areas' to minimise the effect of any bomb blasts. On the 31st a flight of German 'Gotha' planes flew over; this was the first occasion on which those large machines had been seen.

The following letter of praise was received from Brigadier General W.Duncan, Commanding 73rd Infantry Brigade: 'I would like the officers and men to be told how very much the Brigade appreciates the work done by your Battalion in the trenches during the preparations for the recent operations. A great deal of hard work had to be done in a very short time, stores had to be carried up and dumps made. During this period the Battalion was exposed to heavy shell fire day and night but, in spite of all, arrangements were complete and up to time. Difficulties were overcome with cheerfulness and everything was carried out with that thoroughness and soldierly spirit which is a special feature of the Battalion.'

AUGUST:
26th:
Corporal: (4035) C.H.Pull.
Privates: (3483) J.W.Adlington, (4124) H.G.Smith.
28th:
Private: (3910) W.J.Long.

The first half of September was spent either in the line or resting at familiar Dickebusch. Front line activity was generally less than previously during the battle although enemy shelling, including gas, occured at times. By mid-month the Battalion had moved to Hallebast, then to Heksken where time for a football match, with the score 9th Battalion 1, Siege Battery 1, was found.

SEPTEMBER:
3rd:
Privates: (3574) C.Bristow, (3990) W.Padgham, (4285) J.Young.
6th:
Private: (3985) G.H.Osborne.

A journey by buses and a march of eight miles brought the Battalion to Steenwerke on the 15th September. The next week was spent at training during the mornings and sport in the afternoons. From Bailleul, a train journey on the 21st September took the Battalion some 40 miles south to Bapaume, a town previously held by the Germans to the east of the old Somme Battlefields. During early 1917, however, the Germans had withdrawn voluntarily eastward to their new and heavily fortified Hindenburg Line, leaving the allies to follow-up and occupy Bapaume. From Bapaume, the Battalion marched five miles south-east to camp at the village of Barastre. On the 23rd, Battalion Sports were held followed by an excellent evening concert. Next day, in considerable heat, an exhausting march through hilly country, much of it laid waste by the 'scorched earth' policy of the German withdrawal, was made to Haut Allaines, to the north of the town of Péronne. On arrival the men

were able to relax by bathing in the cool waters of the Canal du Nord.

Buses conveyed the Battalion ten miles eastward to Hervilly on the 25th September and, on the following day, a march three miles north-east brought the troops to Hargicourt where they relieved the Nothumberland Fusiliers in the trenches close up to the enemy's Hindenburg Line. Unlike those in the Ypres Salient, the trenches here were in good order but, nonetheless, amidst sporadic shelling and sniper fire, work was put in hand to strengthen the defences in order to withstand the coming winter.

SEPTEMBER:
25th:
Lance Corporal: (4135) J.G.Soper.
Private: (3871) F.Jones.
29th:
Private: (4167) J.W.Strike.

October was a very quiet month with only one man being killed in action. Near Hargicourt, the line was held around Malakoff Farm for a few days at a time, interspersed with periods in support, or at rest, near Hervilly. It was significant, however, that this stretch of the British line was inadequately fortified against attack and too thinly held in terms of men. Along the Battalion's front of 1,500 yards, for example, the line was held by only 100 soldiers, or only one man for every 15 yards of trench. Working parties toiled every day erecting barbed wire defences and keeping trenches and dugouts in good condition. Time was granted for a well supported football match on the 18th with the score Officers 1, Other Ranks 2.

OCTOBER:
12th:
Captain: (3746) F.T.Godman.
24th:
Private: (3627) H.G.Clarke.

The Battalion's line was extended, in November, to an overall length of one mile. Trench improvement and wiring work continued. Another football match was played, this time 'away' at Roisel with the result Sherwood Foresters 2, 9th Battalion 1. Duties continued to alternate between Hervilly, 'at rest', and Malakoff Farm in the line. On the 20th the Battalion staged

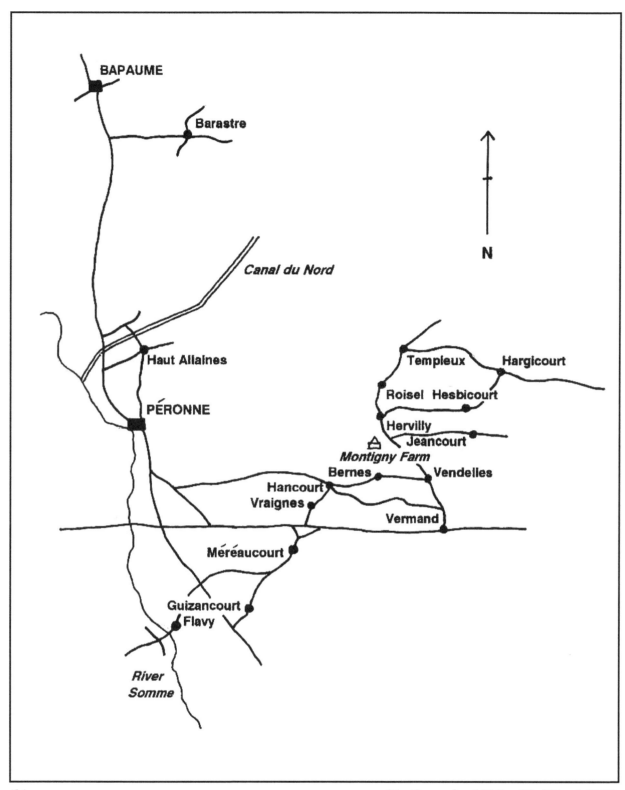

64.   *21st September 1917 to 23rd March 1918*

diversionary demonstrations, first by use of
dummy figures and, later, with smoke bombs.
Both efforts drew a certain amount of harmless
German retaliatory gun fire.

NOVEMBER:
20th:
Private: (4098) G.Sephton.

21st:
Privates: (3792) C.W.Harvey, (4071) J.A.Rogers.
29th:
Private: (3725) D.Fowler.

The same areas were inhabited and similar
tours of duty and rest continued through
December. A raid on enemy posts found them

unoccupied on the 12th; one man was killed during that enterprise. A new venue of Vendelles as Brigade Reserve was visited on the 18th after a heavy snow fall. Christmas was celebrated with a good dinner for the men at mid-day. Warrant Officers and Sergeants dined in the evening while the officers attended a Divisional Dinner. Unfortunately no seasonal concert could be held for lack of a suitable venue. The whole Battalion spent Boxing Day carrying wire for use at the Jeancourt Switch line. Then followed four days rest before the New Year was welcomed while in the line at Hargicourt.

DECEMBER:
11th:
Private: (3656) C.J.Crowhurst.

Image 17: TF 240778 Private George Herbert Wratten 5th (Cinque Ports) Battalion.

Image 18: A British machine gun team operating from the ruins of a German blockhouse.

Image 19: A soldier offering his waterbottle to a wounded comrade at a destroyed enemy blockhouse at Hooge, September 1917.

Image 20: From the lip of a mine crater troops are repelling an enemy counter-attack.

Image 21: Spring 1917. Makeshift bunk beds in the labyrinth of caves below Arras. Note the stacked rifles ready for immediate collection.

Image 22: The grave of the 2nd Battalion's Sergeant Harry Wells V.C. at Dud Corner Cemetery.

Image 23: Changing fortunes of 1918. British dead overwhelmed by the "German Spring Offensive".

Image 24: Changing fortunes of 1918. British troops go "over the top" between Epéhy and Bellicourt during the "Advance to Victory", September 1918.

CHAPTER 31
1918

Extreme cold and falls of snow that remained on the ground kept activity low for most of January, even after a thaw set in on the 20th. Working parties were found for the Jeancourt – Hesbecourt trench line. After the thaw a suitable ground was found for inter-battalion league and cup football: 'A' Company 9th Battalion 5, 'B' Company 2nd Leinsters 2; 'B' Company 9th Battalion 0, 73rd Infantry Brigade Headquarters 3; 'C' Company 9th Battalion 2, 'C' Company 2nd Leinsters 4; 'D' Company 9th Battalion 2, 'D' Company 7th Northamptonshire 4. After completion of these matches, a move into Brigade Support at Vendelles was made on the 29th. The relative quiet of this winter period allowed 10 officers and 101 men to be granted home leave to England.

JANUARY:
27th:
Private: (4133) A.Smitherman.
28th:
Private: (3762) W.G.Griffin.

The following awards to Battalion personnel were notified during January: Military Cross: Major R.P.Dodd and Captain H.C.Coleman; Distinguished Conduct Medal: Company Sergeant Major J.Bartlett; Belgian Croix de Guerre: Sergeant F.Wood.

The first half of February was spent at Vendelles camp. Large working parties of up to 250 men were found to protect and improve the camp with brick walls, paths and ovens. The Battalion lost football matches to the Household Cavalry 3 – 1, the 13th Middlesex 5 – 0, and the Brigade Headquarters 2 – 1. Better success was attained at Rugby Football and Hockey. The camp had a good Y.M.C.A. hut where several successful concerts and boxing tournaments were held. A draft containing one officer and 94 other ranks was received from the 12th Battalion Royal Sussex Regiment which had been disbanded under the army re-organisation which reduced all Infantry Brigades from four to three battalions.

FEBRUARY:
5th:
Private: (4184) G.Theobald.
15th:
Private: (3501) J.Attwood.

On the 17th February a successful silent raid was made by two officers and 18 other ranks following close examination of recent aerial photographs. The party departed at 10.30pm and passed through a known area of weak enemy wire to the parapet of the German trench. Two German soldiers patrolling the far side of the empty enemy trench were allowed to pass. The two officers plus two N.C.O's then crossed the trench to lie down spread out beyond. All four were holding on to a length of string as they awaited the return of the enemy patrolmen. When the two enemy soldiers came back and were in the midst of our men, a tug on the string was the signal for our chaps to spring up and charge forward. A brief struggle ensued before the two Germans were overpowered and taken back as prisoners for interrogation. Not one shot had been fired and not one man had been harmed. Later, a German raid, perhaps in retaliation, was spotted and broken up with Lewis Gun and rifle fire. By the end of February the British positions were so well protected as the meagre allocation of materials and men permitted. Each of the 24th Division's three Brigades were in the line, each having one battalion in the 'Outpost Zone', one in the 'Battle Zone' and one in Reserve. The last days of the month brought increasing levels of enemy bombardments.

FEBRUARY:
21st:
Lieutenant: (3594) R.Burnier.
Private: (3810) E.E.Henniker.
22nd:
Private: (3983) A.T.Oram.

It was known full well that a German major attack would be launched soon from some part of the long Hindenburg Line. Thus, early March was a time for consolidation and last efforts in preparatory training around Hancourt. Battle positions were taken up at 5am on the 21st March at Hesbecourt and a heavy gas shell bombardment signalled that the great 'German Spring Offensive', with the object of breaking through to Amiens and the channel ports, had begun.

MARCH:
8th;
Private: (4196) T.J.P.Tratt.

By 7.30am on that fateful day of the 21st March, the 9th Battalion, together with the 7th Northamptonshire and the 13th Middlesex, had occupied the line of British redoubts between Hesbecourt and Vermand. As it happened, the 9th Battalion was little involved with the fighting that day except for one Company holding a position east of Hesbecourt which suffered a number of casualties from enemy shelling.

MARCH:
21st:
Second Lieutenants: (3544) A.W.Bishop, (4052) E.C.Regan.
Sergeant: (4257) F.W.Whitner.
Corporal: (4176) B.C.Symons.
Lance Corporal: (4249) G.C.D.White.
Privates: (3630) A.O.Clift, (3643) J.Cook, (3652) W.H.Cozens, (3714) W.L.Finch, (3718) F.G.Fleckney, (3719) W.L.Fleet, (3720) W.W.Follett, (3732) J.A.Fuller, (3803) A.Heather, (3818) T.Hinch, (3842) W.Howlett, (3884) J.King, (3977) F.E.Nicholls, (4023) J.F.Playford, (4043) C.Radford, (4048) H.Randall, (4061) R.Riches, (4086) W.A.Santer, (4097) S.J.Seeley.

The Battalion became heavily involved with the fighting on the 22nd March. Their 'Trinket Redoubt' was attacked under cover of a thick mist at 6.00am but managed to hold out until 11am. Nearby 'Trinity Redoubt' was almost cut off but the men that remained managed to withdraw down a shallow trench to 'Triple Redoubt', the next closest strongpoint. As the day drew on, the Battalion was compelled to withdraw through Hesbecourt to Hervilly while the enemy got onto the higher ground in the region of Hervilly Wood. During the afternoon the Battalion was withdrawn along the Roisel – Montigny Road where a rearguard action by 30 men, on high ground south-west of Hervilly, for some time held up large numbers of Germans. One man later reported that, while they still waited for their first sight of the enemy, a long line of Germans in extended order came over the hill. At a steady pace, the first line was followed by a second line and then by others until several waves were moving down the slopes towards the waiting British. The 9th Battalion men were impatient to open fire but they were ordered to wait. Fire was ordered and opened on the enemy with good effect when they were about 300 yards distant. Orders had been received that the Brigade would withdraw to concentrate at Mereaucourt. By evening, the move had been carried out in good order to bivouacs west of that village.

MARCH:
22nd:
Corporals: (3847) S.A.Humfress, (3851) J.Hyder, (4150) F.Stevens.
Lance Corporals: (3526) H.S.Batehup, (3849) E.Hurrell, (3979) E.H.Norris.
Privates: (3597) C.E.Burtenshaw, (3681) H.J.Dexter, (3698) F.E.Dye, (3735) F.Gardner, (3772) C.F.Gurney, (3811) E.W.Henson, (3832) P.E.Homewood, (3902) J.Leeves, (3934) H.L.Martin, (3992) C.H.Page, (4005) W.R.Pearcy, (4111) E.A.Skinner, (4203) A.S.Turner, (4224) E.Ward, (4225) F.J.Ward.

As the 9th Battalion had received severe casualties over previous days, men of the 73rd Light Trench Mortar Battery were attached to the Battalion as infantrymen on the 23rd March. By 6.00am that day the Battalion had taken up position in a thick mist at Guisancourt. The enemy was not engaged, however, and three hours later a further withdrawal was ordered and carried out to Flavy. After standing in a defensive position before the bridge at Flavy for one hour, the Battalion crossed over the River Somme and marched four miles to Marchelpot before retracing its steps for a mile to end the day at Licourt.

MARCH:
23rd:
Sergeant: (3505) W.B.Bailey.
Privates: (4170) W.J.Strong, (4231) A.M.Watkins.

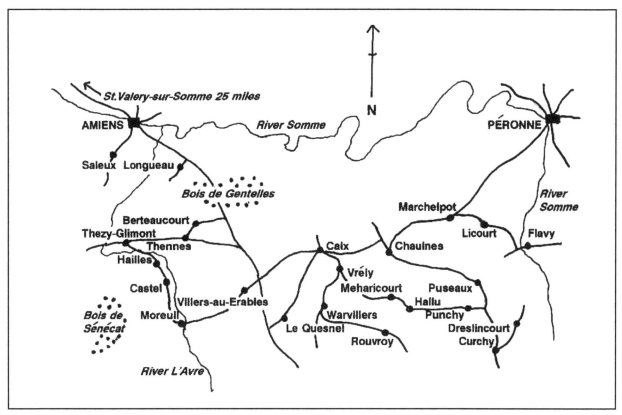

65. *23rd March to 16th April 1918*

The westward withdrawal re-commenced at 6.00am on the 24th March with a five miles treck to Chaulnes by 7.30am. At 1.30pm a move, this time south-east, was carried out to set up a defensive position in front of Puseaux but no contact with the enemy was made that day. The Battalion was ordered forward some three miles eastward on the 25th and there encountered heavy enemy machine gun fire east and north-east of Curchy. Dreslincourt was already in German occupation. The French, who should have joined to effect an allied counter-attack, failed to take any part. This left the 9th Battalion's right flank completely 'in the air' and a withdrawal became imperative. This withdrawal was to a point west of Puseaux where reorganisation took place with difficulty because so many officers had been lost through woundings. Thankfully, during the night, 300 men arrived from the Corps Reinforcement Camp and were absorbed into the Brigade's three battalions.

MARCH:
24th:
Lance Corporal: (3676) A.J.Dell, D.C.M.
Privates: (4113) J.Skinner, (4283) J.G.Wrighton.
25th:
Second Lieutenant: (3747) A.W.Golden.

Lance Corporals: (3793) E.M.Harvey, (4093) R.D.J.Seal, (4194) E.F.Towler.
Privates: (3616) A.H.Chambers, (3666) A.David, (3996) W.Parker, (4128) J.Smith.

The Germans were pressing so hard that the Battalion was ordered, at 15 minutes past midnight, to withdraw to a line between Chaulnes and Hallu. Later that day, the 26th March, the Battalion dropped back, yet again, this time to a position overlooking Meharicourt. Next morning the Germans attacked and managed to enter trenches on the right and bombed their way along them towards 'A' Company. The Company had no bombs and so kept the enemy back with repeated bayonet charges along the trench. Finally it was possible to make a trench block from which the enemy was held back by Lewis Gun fire. A fresh supply of bombs arrived at 5.00pm and from then on the enemy was thwarted with little difficulty. During this action the Battalion's Commanding Officer, Lieutenant Colonel M.V.B.Hill, D.S.O., was wounded and the Second-in-Command, Major J.J.Banham, killed. When evening came, the Battalion, which had been heavily engaged the whole day, was withdrawn to a wood between Warvillers and Caix.

MARCH:
26th:
Private: (3517) H.Barber.
27th:
Major: (3514) J.J.Banham.
Second Lieutenant: (3777) E.L.Hall.
Lance Corporals: (3705) F.Ellis, (3873) S.A.E.Joseph.
Privates: (3644) F.Coote, (3775) W.T.Hadlow, (3825) A.Holland, (4067) G.Robins.

Three more withdrawals were accomplished on the 28th March. First, at noon, a move was made to a line between Caix and Le Quesnel. Then, by late afternoon, it was noticed that the battalions on both flanks were moving back. It was soon established that a general order to withdraw had failed to reach the 9th Battalion. Consequently, an immediate retirement was made to Villers-aux-Erables where the whole Brigade concentrated. The day's final withdrawal began during the evening and ended about midnight in bivouacs within the Bois-de-Senecat, a mile west of Castel where the small River L'Avre had been crossed.

MARCH:
28th:
Corporal: (3631) R.M.Clybouw.
Privates: (3620) E.Cheeseman, (4137) H.Spencer, (4226) H.S.Ward.

The 29th March dawned as Good Friday and, that afternoon, the Battalion marched back westward to high ground overlooking Castel and Moreuil, both on the River L'Avre. However, there was no activity there and the Battalion was withdrawn from the outpost to march three miles north-west to the luxury of billets in Thezy-Glimont. The following day passed without incident and, on the 31st, Easter Sunday, having covered the bridge at Hailles for five hours, a return was made to Thezy-Glimont.

MARCH:
29th:
Private: (4078) J.A.Russell.
31st:
Privates: (3675) E.H.M.Deakin, (4138) C.A.Spicknell.

In addition to those who had lost their lives since the German Spring Offensive began on the 21st March, it was recorded at the end of March that there had been, amongst the officers,

13 wounded; 2 wounded and missing; 1 missing believed Prisoner of War. For other ranks the record showed 167 wounded; 13 wounded and missing; 105 missing; 67 missing believed Prisoners of War.

By this time, having spent 11 consecutive days and nights almost continually on the move, pausing only for the occasional rearguard or covering action, every man was exhausted from lack of sleep and the pressure of the enemy onslaught. It came as a great relief, therefore, that the beginning of April was relatively quiet but, on the night of the 3rd / 4th, the Battalion moved forward once more, this time to the Bois-de-Gentelles. There was now beginning to dawn the realisation that the almost continuous and frantic withdrawals of the last two weeks had come to an end. Indeed, the enemy pressure had been so effectively held that men of the Corps Reinforcement Battalion left the Brigade on the 4th to rejoin their own Units.

The enemy had been halted, at last; the German efforts to break through to Amiens had been arrested. So certain of this considerable achievement were the British Commanders that, after dusk on the 5th April, the 73rd Infantry Brigade was withdrawn from its positions without being relieved or replaced. The Battalion marched to Longneau from where, on the 6th, the officers and men were taken by buses to Saleux. Here, finally, ended 17 days of desperate fighting withdrawal. Sadly, over many more days men continued to die from their wounds.

APRIL:
1st:
Private: (3834) G.V.Hope.
3rd:
Corporal: (3663) L.A.W.Dancer.
Lance Corporal: (4075) A.Rous.
Privates: (3484) W.Adsett, (3513) R.Baldwin, (3886) J.Kipling, (4108) B.A.Simmons.
5th:
Private: (4278) W.H.Woodhouse.
6th:
Privates: (4192) H.Tomlinson, M.M., (4197) T.Trevett.

Having left Saleux by train the previous day, the Battalion arrived at St.Valery-sur-Somme at 3.00am on the 7th April. Tea taken in a

Church Army hut was welcome before moving into billets. An afternoon march was made to Friville where a draft of one officer and 365 men joined the Battalion. The next week was spent at intensive training before a march to Woincourt on the 16th. Next day everyone and everything was moved on an eight hour train journey to Pérnes from where the men marched to La Comte. Twelve days of training and parades followed. One platoon formed a parade 'Honour Guard' when Monsieur Clemenceau, the French Prime Minister, visited the area.

APRIL:
9th:
Private: (4175) A.Swan.
10th:
Private: (3933) H.Martin.
12th:
Private: (4232) R.Watson.
25th:
Lieutenant: (4115) B.W.Skipworth.

The 29th April proved to be a day of fiasco with much hilarity and annoyance. After a 9.00am parade everyone spent the morning loading and boarding lorries and buses for a journey to Les Brebis. With the men finally seated and quite looking forward to their trip, a cyclist messenger rode up at speed with an order cancelling the move. All of this was re-enacted the following day, the last of the month. On eventual arrival at Les Brebis the Battalion was billeted there and at nearby Maroc.

May began quietly in, and out of, the trenches but stress was ever-present for some men and a case of self-inflicted wound was reported on the 12th. Wiring, trench improvements and active patrols were carried out. On the 29th, during one of the patrols, Second Lieutenant F.H.Bray was killed accidentally in a manner not recorded. During the very last hour of the month more than 400 enemy gas projectiles fell in the Battalion's area. A great concentration of gas was experienced with 21 other ranks being affected, eight of them fatally.

MAY:
3rd:
Private: (3645) A.R.Coppard.
6th:
Lance Corporal: (3926) J.Marchant.

10th:
Privates: (3694) V.A.Dunkerley, (4096) I.A.Secretan.
17th:
Private: (4073) P.E.Rolling.
18th:
Private: (3887) E.Knight.
28th:
Second Lieutenant: (3569) F.H.Bray.
Private: (4273) F.Winter.
30th:
Private: (3970) H.E.Neal.
31st:
Lance Corporal: (4121) G.E.Smith.
Privates: (3491) P.Anson, (3523) G.Barrett, (3688) A.R.Dodman, (3784) F.Hammond, (3860) G.W.Jermy, (3880) H.G.P.Kennett, (4181) A.G.Taylor.

The following awards were made to the Battalion for gallantry and devotion to duty during the recent retreat south of the Somme: Bar to Distinguished Service Order: Lieutenant Colonel M.V.B.Hill, D.S.O., M.C.; Bar to Military Cross: Captain D.W.G.May, M.C.; Military Cross: Captain A.V.Rewell, Lieutenant H.H.L'Estrange, Second Lieutenants D.Fraser, S.Horscroft, J.Mann and P.V.Pullinger; Distinguished Conduct Medal: Company Sergeant Major G.F.Head; Military Medal: Sergeant V.G.Maskell, Corporals R.Ashford, C.J.Bliss, W.H.Hadley, F.Pestell, Lance Corporals A.Parkes, C.Taplin, S.Wilkinson; Privates H.Bagge, J.Bourne, J.Dunk, W.Issard, O.Leighton, E.Paley, S.Stokes and R.H.Weeks.

Two main occurences, both of very different nature, marked the month of June. On the 3rd, a raid by two officers and 30 men was devised by Brigade with the aim of taking a known German machine gun post and capturing prisoners for the purpose of enemy regiment identification. Elaborate operational orders were issued for execution by the raiding party and supporting artillery. The raid was a success in that two Germans of the 1st Bavarian Division were captured but at the cost of two Battalion men wounded and two missing. The second occurence was an outbreak of the 1918 influenza pandemic when five officers and 250 men had to be sent to hospital. Honours awarded during June were: Military Cross: Captain C.Harris (attached from Royal Army Medical Corps), Second Lieutenant

R.Hudson (for the 3rd June raid); Distinguished Conduct Medal: Regimental Sergeant Major H.A.Coles; Military Medal (all for the 3rd June raid). Sergeant W.C.Norman, Lance Corporal R.E.Stuart and Private A.S.Lightfoot.

JUNE:
1st:
Lance Corporal: (3752) F.G.Goodwin.
Privates: (3498) S.P.Ashford, (3696) J.Dunn, (3697) W.J.Duxbury, (3794) L.H.Harwood.
2nd:
Privates: (4120) F.Smith, (4164) E.T.Stopps, (4214) S.J.Vine.
3rd:
Privates: (3557) S.E.Boothby, (3731) W.Frost.
4th:
Private: (3683) W.M.Dickinson.
5th:
Sergeant: (3827) W.Hollebon.
Privates: (3838) J.Hoskins, (4258) H.W.B.Whitsey.
7th:
Private: (3527) E.Baxendale.
10th:
Private: (3539) R.H.Billington.

13th:
Private: (4082) B.Sageman.
17th:
Lance Corporal: (4279) H.Wooler.
Privates: (3835) J.E.Hope, (3878) H.Kennedy, (3917) M.McDermott.
18th:
Private: (3955) W.Miller.
22nd:
Private: (3790) A.E.Harrison.
23rd:
Private: (3581) F.Brown.
26th:
Private: (3682) J.W.Dickerson.

July was a very quiet month which was still spent in the areas around Les Brebis and Loos. A draft of 20 men was received to replace, in part, those suffering from influenza. The Corps Commander inspected the Battalion on two occasions and expressed himself to be well satisfied. Baths and changes of underclothing were provided for all the men. In the Sergeants' Mess was held on the 16th a very successful and enjoyable Smoking Concert to which all officers were invited.

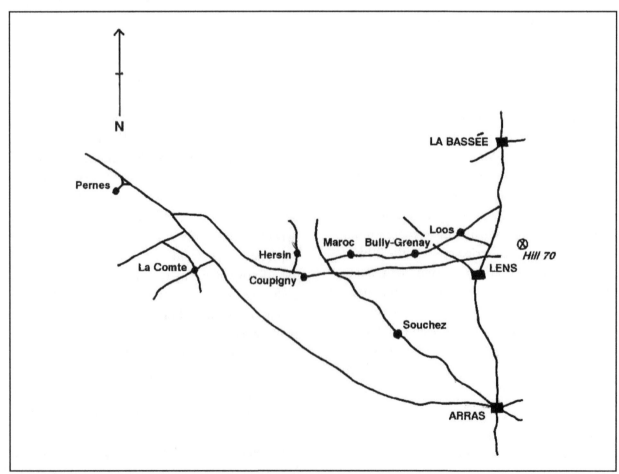

66. *17th April to September 1918*

JULY:
1st:
Private: (3609) R.Careless.
5th:
Private: (3781) W.A.Halley.
12th:
Private: (3971) H.Neil.
18th:
Private: (3760) W.Green.
29th:
Private: (3623) F.Childs.

August began with the Battalion in Brigade Reserve at Les Brebis. Training continued and included visits to the range where, unfortunately, Captain R.G.Duffield was wounded by a blow-back from a defective rifle and had to be evacuated to a Casualty Clearing Station. The Battalion moved out to rest at Bully-Grenay on the 27th but, the very next day, had to return to the line in front of Loos. It was on the 12th of this month that Captain E.A.McNair, V.C., having gained his gallantry award and been wounded later while with the 9th Battalion, died, having been transferred to serve in Italy.

AUGUST:
12th
Captain: (3949) E.A.McNair, **V.C.**
23rd:
Private: (3633) F.J.Cole.
27th:
Private: (3898) A.Lawrence.
30th:
Private: (4272) A.J.Wink.
31st:
Private: (4024) J.R.Pont.

From its position in the line on the western outskirts of Lens, the Battalion obtained information on the 1st September, from German prisoners captured by the 7th Northamptonshires, that the enemy had evacuated the town of Lens leaving their pioneers to blow up dugouts. Accordingly, patrols were pushed forward to set up posts on the La Bassée Road. On the 4th, one of three patrols sent out came across a section of men from the Scottish Rifles who had been cut off and missing for two days. That day, too, Battalion Headquarters was visited by Mr.Harry Lauder, the famous Music Hall artist, whose son had been killed and buried

at Ovillers on the Somme. The following night a shower of enemy mustard gas shells was received but there were no casualties.

On the 13th the Battalion was relieved and remained out of the line training and route marching until the 22nd when trenches in the Lens sector were taken over from the 7th Northamptonshires. For several days German aircraft were in evidence. One plane flew low over the trenches and was engaged, unsuccessfully, by anti-aircraft and small arms fire. On the 26th, a successful raid killed a German officer, captured a machine gun and blew up a dugout. A 'tit-for-tat' retaliation by an enemy raiding party, on the 28th, captured one Battalion man, wounded two others and made off with a Lewis Gun. The Battalion moved to Souchez on the 30th and were conveyed from there by buses to huts at Coupigny. Only three fatal casualties had been sustained during September.

SEPTEMBER:
8th:
Private: (4238) G.F.Welland.
13th:
Privates: (3561) C.H.Bowden, (3852) A.Isaacson.
18th:
Private: (4269) E.G.Wiltshire.

A seven hour train journey from Hersin took the Battalion to Mondicourt by late evening on the 1st October. Training was instituted there until the 6th when the Battalion left Mondicourt by train for Hermies and then marched on to a bivouac staging area just east of Moeuvres. An eastward march to a position south-west of Cantaing was made on the following day. On the 8th, the 73rd Infantry Brigade concentrated east of the Canal de St.Quentin. The 'Advance to Victory' continued on the 9th with the 72nd Infantry Brigade attacking, with heavy artillery support, and capturing Awoingt and the railway to its east. The 9th Battalion followed-up in close support before relieving the 72nd Brigade. At noon orders were received that the 9th Royal Sussex would lead the next attack to be made by the 73rd Infantry Brigade, interestingly and unusually supported by the Corps Cyclist Battalion, one group of the 6th Dragoon Guards, two Machine Gun Companies and the 56th and 181st Brigades Royal Field Arrtillery.

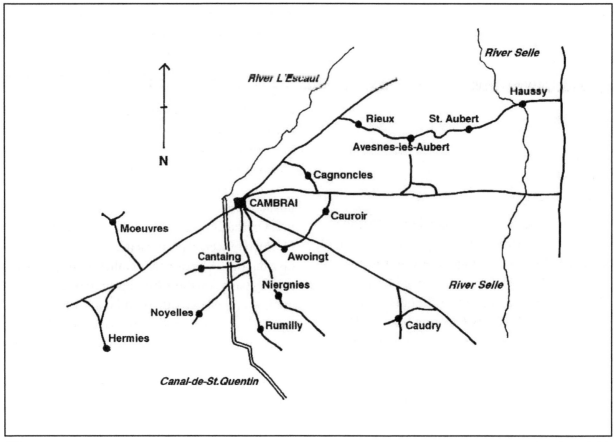

67.   *October 1918*

Accordingly, the 9th Battalion moved forward from its position just east of Niergnies at 9.45am and led the way across the Cambrai – Caudry Road at 11.00am. By evening the Battalion had passed through to the cemetery east of Cauroir. The Battalion had enjoyed a very successful day and had taken few casualties, only two of which were fatal.

OCTOBER:
9th:
Privates: (3565) T.Bracegirdle, (3761) L.W.Greengrass.

With no respite given or received, the attack was resumed early on the 10th October with the Battalion on the right flank. At 6.40am reports were received that leading Units were encountering no enemy opposition so the advance continued. By 9.00am cyclists and cavalry patrols entered Rieux and Avesnes-les-Aubert. Pressing forward, cavalry scouts found that the high ground to the north was strongly held by the Germans. The 9th Battalion then came under heavy artillery and machine gun fire from that high ground as it approached the two villages.

Two Companies were then sent forward to support an attack by the 13th Middlesex and a third Company occupied the railway station at Avesnes-les-Aubert. By evening advanced troops of the Battalion had reached the outskirts of St.Aubert. The remainder of the Battalion soon caught up and remained in position overnight.

Early morning orders on the 11th October were that the present position was to be maintained; respite at last ! Later that day the whole Brigade was withdrawn to billets in Avesnes-les-Aubert. During that night the enemy withdrew to the line of the River Selle, closely followed by British Units which soon succeeded in constructing crossings over the river.

Next day, with the arrival of Headquarters and Quartermaster's Stores, the whole Battalion was together once more. Thankfully, everyone rested for several days before route marching up to Cauroir on the 17th. The men were kept occupied and alert with training. Relaxation was augmented by football matches and several evening concerts over the next week. On the 23rd, as part of a fairly universal salvaging programme, the men were sent out on an unusual pastime, namely a 'Nail Hunt' around the billets. Some idea of the tremendous amount of wartime discarded impedimenta may be gained from the fact that this single 'hunt' produced over 80 lbs. of nails for re-use !

OCTOBER:

10th:

Privates: (3486) J.Agate, (3726) H.W.Fox, (3848) P.Hunt, (3956) E.Milward.

11th:

Privates: (3743) W.N.Glew, (3919) A.Maffret, (3966) P.J.Moylan, (3973) L.Newell.

12th:

Private: (3710) J.E.Faulkner.

15th:

Private: (3614) P.C.Carter.

17th:

Private: (3744) A.R.Goddard.

18th:

Private: (3700) R.J.Eastman.

22nd:

Private: (4057) E.B.Richardson.

25th:

Private: (3499) G.J.Atfield.

The Battalion paraded at 7.40am on the 26th October and marched by way of Avesnes-les-Aubert and St.Aubert to Haussy, where it arrived at 12.15pm and was allowed to rest for the remainder of the day. The 29th was designated Brigade Sports Day and, on the 30th, attack training manoeuvres were carried out using dummy tanks. At the end of the month Private W.A.Hyde was awarded the Military Medal.

At 2.00pm on the 1st November the Battalion left Haussy on a two and a half hours march through Maison Blanche, Maison Bleue and St.Martin to Bermarain. On the 3rd, a further march was made to Sepmeries where a halt was ordered until 6.00pm before moving on to Maresches.

NOVEMBER:

3rd:

Privates: (3654) J.A.Cronshaw, (3668) C.H.Davis.

One of the most costly days in terms of 9th Battalion casualties started with an attack through the 13th Middlesex Battalion at 5.30am on the 4th November. The aim was to gain the crossings over the River Rhonelle and take the high ground north of Wargnies-le-Petit and Wargnies-le-Grand. Also, if possible, crossings over the River Rhonelle were to be made good ready for the following troops and transport.

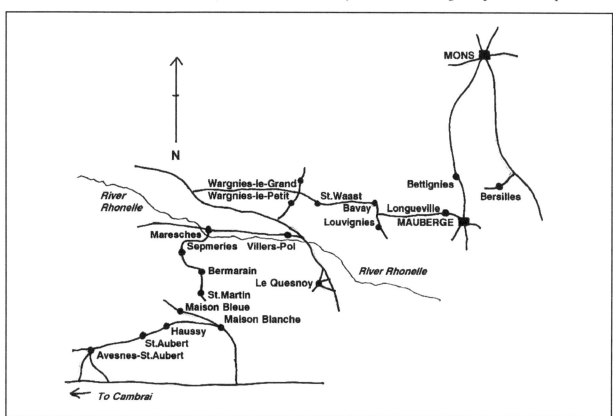

The advance to assembly positions was made behind a creeping barrage despite significant enemy shelling in the vicinity. Even before zero hour, casualties were sustained from shell and machine gun fire. Enemy artillery proved less of a problem during the advance but their machine guns were particularly troublesome. 'A' and 'B' Companies were held up until 11.00am by machine guns on both sides of the river. Eventually, however, the Germans were forced to retire and the Battalion's two Companies consolidated on the high ground as planned. The 13th Middlesex and the 7th Northamptonshire pushed respectively through Wargnies-le-Grand and Wargnies-le-Petit during the afternoon. The 9th Battalion's 'D' Company pushed patrols forward at 5.30pm but found no sign of the enemy. In addition to those killed, the Battalion lost 95 other ranks wounded and five missing that day. Those who died, and those who succumbed to wounds over the next few days, did not know that they had paid the supreme sacrifice so close to the end of hostilities.

NOVEMBER:
4th:
Lieutenant: (4237) H.G.Welham.
Sergeants: (3549) C.J.Bliss, M.M., (3678) C.G.Denton, (3774) W.H.Hadley, M.M., (4256) A.E.Whitlock, M.M.
Corporals: (3723) J.O.Forryan, (3948) J.McGregor, (4092) F.J.Scrivener.
Lance Corporals: (3686) E.Divall, (3757) J.Gravett, (3854) S.G.Jacob, (4154) C.A.Still, (4281) F.H.Worsfold.
Privates: (3489) G.E.Ambrose, (3493) S.E.A.Arnold, (3496) H.Ashburner, (3504) E.S.Bailey, (3518) F.E.Barker, (3590) H.Bullett, (3646) F.Coppard, (3669) C.Dawson, (3684) H.Dimes, (3706) W.Emery, (3727) W.Fox, (3763) S.J.Griffen, (3885) J.Kingham, (3888) H.J.Knight, (3892) W.Knowles, (3963) W.J.Mortimer, (4008) A.J.Peer, (4013) W.A.Pettingill, (4039) F.Puttock, (4056) J.E.Reynolds, (4134) F.L.F.SoMérville, (4157) P.W.Stocker, (4180) A.Taylor, (4200) W.Trusler, (4220) A.Walker, (4233) S.J.Watson, (4236) C.W.Welch, (4259) G.Whittaker, (4264) A.Wilkinson, (4276) S.Wood.

The 73rd Infantry Brigade came into Divisional Support in billets at Wargnies-le-Petit on the 5th November. They remained in support, experiencing occasional shelling when they marched in the wake of the 72nd Brigade to Bavay. The transport column was held up at St.Waast for a time because the enemy had blown bridges but it continued, later, across country. The 9th Battalion's destination on the 9th November was the Mons – Mauberge Road which it reached at noon without opposition. Orders were received that the Battalion was to advance no farther except that 'B' Company was to occupy Bersilles which was done.

Next day, the 10th, November, the 73rd Infantry Brigade was relieved by the 60th Brigade. The relief was completed by 1.30pm and the 9th Battalion marched by Companies to Les Vents and relatively comfortable billets for the night. 'B' Company was separated from the rest, following relief, and sent off to march to Bersilles.

On the eleventh day of the eleventh month, at 9.30am, the whole Battalion came together at Louvignies after 'B' Company had marched from Bersilles and the remainder from Les Vents. The last action of the war had been fought and it was at Louvignies that the great conflict ended for the 9th Battalion.

The area of Louvignies is situated immediately to the south-east of Bavay and is on the main road which leads south-west to Le Cateâu and north-east to Mons, the line of the war's first great retreat by the British army following the Battle of Mons at the end of August, 1914. Thus, the 9th Battalion ended its war a mere 10 miles from the spot, at Mons, where the conflict began for the British four years and three months previously.

The end came swiftly. With only one hour's notice, orders were received on the 11th November that hostilities were to cease at 11.00am.

NOVEMBER:
5th:
Privates: (3942) G.H.Mathew, (3952) R.Midgley, (4117) J.Smethurst.
6th:
Privates: (3615) A.Castel, (3751) J.C.Gooderham, (3931) D.S.Marshall, (3974) W.Newell.
8th:
Private: (3692) B.Driver.
10th:
Corporal: (3976) E.G.Newton.
Lance Corporal: (4210) H.Usher.
13th:
Private: (3785) J.Hampson.

It was one of the tragedies of war that the euphoria of victory and the Armistice was tinged with sadness for the pals of Private John Hampson. Wounded during the last skirmish, Private Hampson lived to see the jubillant end to the conflict, only to die from his wounds two days later, on the 13th November.

9th Battalion Epilogue

From the 1st September, 1915, to the Armistice the 9th Battalion served on the Western Front. This period of three years, two months and ten days was the longest served in Belgium and France by any of The Royal Sussex 'New Army' Battalions. Before the British final 1918 advance, the Battalion had not appeared in the front areas east of Arras but had divided its time mainly between the Ypres Salient and the Somme before pushing forward, with its parent 24th Division during the 'Advance to Victory', almost to Mons, the starting point of the conflict in the west.

Within three weeks of its arrival in France the Battalion was put, without any previous fighting experience of any sort, into the Battle of Loos. It was only on the day the battle was launched that the Battalion first entered front line trenches. This was at Vermelles where, in the process, it suffered 64 fatalities, its highest number in any one day throughout the war. Strangely, it was to be within one week of the Armistice before the second highest fatality figure of 43 was to be suffered in a single day.

The Country's highest honour, 'For Valour', was awarded to an officer of the 9th Battalion, Lieutenant Eric Archibald McNair V.C., who won the award for his gallantry at Hooge in the Ypres Salient. Sadly he was later transferred to the Italian front where he was wounded and subsequently died.

Altogether the Battalion had just over 800 fatalities, either killed-in-action, died of wounds or of natural causes. Throughout, service had been with the 73rd Infantry Brigade as part of the 24th Division. The Battalion had achieved much to be proud of and could hold its head high amongst the many Units of the British Army.

PART SEVEN

The 11th, 12th and 13th (Service) Battalions ('New Army' – 'Lowther's Lambs')

CHAPTER 32

1914 and 1915

Immediately following the declaration of war on the 4th August, 1914, Lord Kitchener, who was Secretary of State for War, realised that many more men would need to be recruited to augment Britain's Regular Army in order to give the allies a realistic chance of victory in the longer term. Thus, Kitchener was personally responsible for launching a recruiting drive, a national appeal for the 'First 100,000 Men'. Formal authority for the formation of the New Divisions, known as 'Kitchener's Army' or the 'New Army', was given by Army Order 324 dated 21st August, 1914. That Army Order declared that '. . . The new battalions will be raised as additional battalions of the regiments of Infantry of the Line and will be given numbers following consecutively on the existing battalions of their regiments. They will be further distinguished by the word 'Service' after the number . . .'

Before long, Kitchener's immense task of recruitment, organisation, provision of accommodation and equipment came to be assisted considerably by a number of prominent men up and down the country who took it upon themselves to raise and organise their own battalions. One such man was Colonel Lowther whose home was at Herstmonceux Castle in East Sussex.

Born in 1872, Colonel Claude William Henry Lowther M.P., was Member of Parliament for the Eskdale Division of Cumberland. He had served with distinction in the Boer War as Second in Command of the Cumberland and Westmorland Yeomanry and, during that campaign, had been recommended unsuccessfully for the Victoria Cross for his bravery in saving the life of a comrade at the Battle of Faber's Spruit.

Colonel Lowther set out to raise, from the young men of Sussex, an infantry battalion, expected to be of about 1,000 men, for Kitchener's 'New Army'. He formed and headed a Committee which set up recruiting offices at

Herstmonceux Castle and at a number of towns throughout the county of Sussex. The Territorial Army Drill Hall at 'The Downs', Bexhill-on-Sea, some ten miles from Herstmonceux, was taken over as a reception centre.

All over the country, men with a patriotic fervour instilled into them at school, flocked to join up; flocked to fight for their country; flocked for a chance of excitement. Many of the men previously had hardly been outside the immediate areas of their own villages or towns, let alone out of the country, and they saw this as an opportunity to spread their wings, exhibit their manhood, gain a chance of perceived glory and shake off the shackles of everyday life. Soon it was being mooted that the war would be 'all over by Christmas' and so, in order to be part of it, there was no time to be lost.

To Lord Kitchener's call-to-arms there was a massive nation-wide surge of response; his appeal for the first 100,000 men soon developed into 1,000,000 volunteers. In turn, Lowther's single battalion became three battalions and his reception base soon overflowed. The men of Sussex who had been told that, if they joined, they could serve together and be led by Colonel Lowther, quickly had to be found accommodation. First, the school immediately adjoining the Bexhill-on-Sea reception base was used. When the school overflowed, the men were provided with billets in the town's Hôtels and boarding houses until a tented, later hutted, camp could be set up for them all on land given for the purpose at Cooden Mount a couple of miles to the west.

Gradually a programme of training and equipping was introduced. At first the men were issued with obsolete blue serge uniforms and no rifles were available. The pace of progress quickened, however, and a marked degree of smartness and competence was instilled. The Colonel, as Officer Commanding, gave them the name 'South Down Battalions', the 1st Battalion being raised officially on the 7th September, the 2nd Battalion on the 3rd November and the 3rd Battalion on the 20th November, 1914, all at Bexhill-on-Sea. To give the men even more pride and a sense of 'togetherness', every man's service number was prefixed by the letters 'SD' and the three battalions became known collectively and affectionately as 'Lowther's Lambs'. While at Cooden Mount, a lamb of the 'Southdown' breed of sheep, was provided by Mr.J.Passmore of Applesham Farm, Lancing, Sussex, and became the official mascot of the three battalions. The lamb, named 'Peter', remained as mascot but did not go overseas; he was buried honourably in the grounds of Herstmonceux Castle upon his eventual death in 1928.

Training and preparation continued until, on the 1st July, 1915, the 1st, 2nd and 3rd South Down Battalions were taken over officially by the War Office and became the 11th, 12th and 13th Battlions The Royal Sussex Regiment. Sadly for the men, and very disappointingly for their Commanding Officer, the War Office decreed that Colonel Claude Lowther, at the age of 43, was too old to continue his leadership of the Battalions he had raised with such enthusiasm. He followed closely throughout the war the fortunes and misfortunes of 'his men', and his great pride in them and their achievements remained steadfast until his death in 1929.

By the time they became Royal Sussex Regiment Battalions in July, 1915, khaki uniforms, together with regimental 'Roussillon Plume' badges, had arrived to be worn proudly by all officers and men. That month, too, 'Lowther's Lambs' left Cooden Mount Camp for Detling Camp at Maidstone, Kent. Two months later, following a brief stay at Malplaquet Barracks, Aldershot, Hampshire, the three Battalions moved to Witley Camp on the London – Portsmouth Road near Godalming in Surrey. There, 'Lowther's Lambs' were constituted formally as part of the New Army's 39th Division as follows:

39th Division
116th Infantry Brigade:
    11th Royal Sussex, 12th Royal Sussex, 13th Royal Sussex, 14th Hampshire.
117th Infantry Brigade:
    16th Sherwood Foresters, 17th Sherwood Foresters, 17th Kings Royal Rifle Corps, 16th Rifle Brigade.
118th Infantry Brigade:
    13th, East Surreys, 20th Middlesex, 21st Middlesex, 14th Argyll and Sutherland Highlanders
Pioneers:
    13th Gloucestershire.

The 11th, 12th and 13th Battalions were destined to remain together throughout the whole of their existence on the Western Front. In this text, also, they will be considered together. To avoid lengthy repetition, the three Battalions collectively will be referred to as 'Lowther's Lambs'.

CHAPTER 33

1916

JANUARY – JUNE

At Witley Camp training continued throughout the winter and into the spring of that fateful year 1916. For some, there was growing impatience for action; for others, feelings of trepidation, even foreboding, grew as news of steadily increasing casualties was received from the Western Front. At last, word came that Lowther's Lambs were to move to France and, at 3.30am on 4th March, 1916, the three Battalions marched out of Witley Camp and occupied three trains which left Milford at one hour intervals for Southampton. There, at the dockside, everything was prepared for embarkation. Each Battalion comprised 30 officers, 1,000 men, 60 horses, 16 Lewis guns, 4 carts and 14 wagons or lorries. Consequently it required two ships, the 'Australind' and the 'Viper' to convey them on an exciting but uneventful channel crossing to Le Havre where disembarkation took place at 7.00am on the 5th March. After a few hours in No.5 Docks Rest Camp, they entrained at Le Havre and set off north-east across France. With officers in the few coaches and men and horses cramped into the many goods wagons, they arrived eventually at Steenbecque. The train journey had taken 22 hours and, after a relatively short march, everyone fell exhausted into billets which were houses, farm houses, barns, schools and sheds in the village of Morbeque.

After three days rest, during which everyone gradually got used to the sights, sounds and smells of a new and somewhat strange country, Lowther's Lambs marched to Estaires on the 11th March. An onward move the following day brought the Battalions to the trenches for the first time and there, at Fleurbaix, they were attached to experienced occupying Units for instruction. While entering the trenches for the first time,

Private David Dunk, from the Battalions' 'home' town of Bexhill-on-Sea, was shot through the head by a sniper; he was the first of more than 2,000 of Lowther's Lambs' lives to be lost while they were on the Western Front.

MARCH:

12th:
Private: (4493) D.T.Dunk.

On the 13th March Festubert received a dozen 5.9" enemy shells, one of which fell on an 11th Battalion billet resulting in four fatalities and nine wounded of whom one man died later in the day.

MARCH:

13th:
Sergeant: (4626) W.J.Hitchman.
Privates: (4628) F.Hobbs, (4718) C.C.Martin, (4773) A.T.Newman, (4866) W.S.Seall.
14th:
Private: (4414) F.J.Catt.
18th:
Privates: (4439) C.Collins, (5447) A.W.Roper, (5616) F.C.Bennett.
19th:
Privates: (5070) W.E.Bourner, (4800) C.H.Peckham.
21st:
Lance Corporal: (5515) H.Tier.

On the 23rd March Lowther's Lambs were relieved from the trenches and marched back to billets in the vicinity of Estaires. During the intervening days the Battalions had variously manned trenches, undertaken patrols, provided working parties and 'rested' in billets. By the end of March, their first month of action, Lowther's Lambs had moved to billets a little farther west, near Mérville.

MARCH:

27th:
Captain: (4578) G.M.J.A.Grisewood.

29th:
Lance Corporal: (6032) J.W.Oliver.
30th:
Privates: (5013) J.F.Aldridge, (5835) G.Gray.
31st:
Private: (6084) S.S.Pollard.

During exceptionally fine and warm weather over the first half of April the Battalions undertook training including night operations and firing on the ranges. From Mérville (11th Bn.), Cordescure (12th Bn.) and Estaires (13th Bn.), they all came together in the trenches at Givenchy, some 10 miles south. These trenches, at an area known as the 'Duck's Bill', were in poor condition with weak barbed wire defences, the whole requiring a significant amount of improvement work. A direct hit on the parapet by an enemy shell on the 16th killed four and wounded six 13th Battalion men of whom one died. While a wiring party from the same Battalion was out next day, three men were wounded and fell upon the wire. One of those men extricated himself and crawled back to tell Second Lieutenant Roberts who immediately went out and managed to bring back the remaining two wounded soldiers.

APRIL:
10th:
Private: (5175) R.A.I.Evershed.
16th:
Lance Corporal: (5664) F.H.Buckland.
Privates: (5739) S.A.Dabbs, (5906) F.Hyder, (6266) A.Voice, (6319) W.A.Winchester.
17th:
Private: (6187) J.Stevenson.

Although the moon was bright on the 20th April, an 11th Battalion patrol went out and returned delighted with a number of German rifle grenades and a forage cap ! On the following day, Good Friday, an officer and two men were killed by a rifle grenade fired by the enemy. Under the growing pressure, Lance Corporal Crane of 11th Battalion induced a self-inflicted wound on the 25th at Givenchy. On the 26th, William Colsey Millward, who had joined the 1st South Down Battalion as a Private in August, 1914, re-joined the 11th Battalion, this time as a Captain. Traces of gas, the first experienced by Lowther's Lambs, was detected

on the 27th and all men were warned. A trickle of casualties continued from enemy shell and machine gun fire.

APRIL:
20th:
Private: (5556) W.Widgery.
21st:
Second Lieutenant: (4336) F.W.Battley.
Lance Corporal: (4851) B.Rouse.
Privates: (4477) H.Diplock, (5389) S.T.Muggridge.
22nd:
Sergeant: (4847) R.H.Roberts.
Lance Sergeant: (5033) W.G.Baker.
Private: (5142) G.S.Culver.
24th:
Private: (5932) B.Jones.
27th:
Private: (5441) E.Reeves.
28th:
Privates: (4300) A.Ashdown, (4434) T.Clifton, (5425) H.F.Poiney.
29th:
Sergeant: (5089) G.Brown.
Corporal: (5046) F.T.Beale.
30th:
Lance Corporal: (4964) C.A.Ward.
Private: (5119) J.Collins.

At the beginning of May all three Battalions were behind the lines 'at rest' at Hingette (11th Bn.), Les Choquaux (12th Bn.) and Hinges (13th Bn.). It was normal practice for the Battalions to rotate with each other in their various periods of rest, reserve and front line duties so that they were not often all in the line at the same time. The 11th Battalion went into the trenches at Festubert on the 14th May where sporadic machine gun, shrapnel and 'Whizz Bang' fire was experienced. A draft of 99 men was received from the Cyclist Corps on the 19th. On the 29th, an enemy mine was blown and about 600 shells fell in the area.

The mine explosion, some 20 yards in front of 13th Battalion trench, buried several men of whom one was killed. Bombers were sent forward immediately to occupy the near lip of the crater but no enemy soldiers were seen. That night, after a heavy bombardment, a German raiding party entered part of the 13th Battalion line, capturing and dragging away an N.C.O. The following night a small search party found and retrieved the body of a German soldier and that of Lance Sergeant Daws, the N.C.O. who had been hauled from his trench.

MAY:
1st:
Lance Corporal: (5277) J.F.G.Hollobone.
9th:
Lance Corporal: (5517) H.Titchener.
10th:
Privates: (5160) W.Dixon, (5237) W.Habberjam, (5312) W.Johnston.
11th:
Lance Sergeant: (5857) G.Harriott.
Lance Corporals: (4759) T.B.Morling, (5848) E.Hamilton.
Privates: (5654) A.E.Brooks, (4646) J.Huggett, (6302) H.White.
12th:
Private: (4695) A.T.Langmaid.
14th:
Private: (4710) J.Lowndes
16th:
Privates: (5230) H.C.Griffiths, (5346) H.Lewis.
Lance Coporal: (4684) W.King.
17th:
Privates: (5497) J.Steere, (5563) H.Winton.
20th:
Second Lieutenant: (5772) G.E.Elliott.
Lance Corporal: (5719) H.Collins.
21st:
Privates: (4783) P.J.Oliver, (5462) I.Settatree, (6174) A.Spring.
22nd:
Privates: (4644) A.Huckstep, (4951) G.G.Veness.
24th:
Lance Corporal: (4725) C.May.
Private: (4411) W.T.Carter.
25th:
Private: (5485) W.Smith.
28th:
Private: (5274) F.Holcombe.
29th:
Second Lieutenant: (5731) J.Cornwell.
Private: (6095) E.Punch.
30th:
Lance Sergeant: (5743) G.W.Daws.
Private: (6326) W.Wood.

On the 1st June Lieutenant H.S.Lewis received the Military Cross for his gallantry at Givenchy on 27th April, 1916; this was the first honour awarded to Lowther's Lambs although, the following day, Lance Corporals G.Compton and

W.Booth received Military Medals for the parts they played, also on the 27th April.

For three consecutive days commencing on the 2nd June, the 11th Battalion suffered casualties from shelling, 'Whizz Bangs', Minenwerfers and rifle grenades. On the last of those days another German mine was blown but was not followed by any attack. Just before midnight on the 6th, Second Lieutenant McRoberts, an Engineer Officer, and 36 men left 13th Battalion trenches and advanced to the German wire. They took with them, somewhat experimentally, a device known as a 'Bangalore Torpedo', the aim of which was not entirely explained. The device was placed at a gap in the enemy wire and a sapper returned to report that all was ready. After a slight pause the 'torpedo' was fired electrically from the Battalion's front line and our artillery opened fire. Second Lieutenant McRoberts and his men rushed forward through the gap but the enemy retaliated strongly by throwing many bombs. After bombing along the German parapet and inflicting casualties, the Battalion's party withdrew with Second Lieutenant McRoberts and 14 men slightly wounded. The success, or otherwise, of the 'Bangalore Torpedo' seems not to have been recorded.

JUNE:
2nd:
Second Lieutenant: (4841) R.H.Richards.
Privates: (4530) E.F.Foulkes, (4564) A.Gratwicke.
3rd:
Lance Corporals: (5785) F.J.Firrell, (4858) A.Sambucci, (4938) E.W.H.Tompsett.
Privates: (4457) S.Creasey, (4483) E.Dorling, (5000) E.Wood.
4th:
Sergeant: (4835) R.Relf.
Corporal: (4906) T.N.Stevenson.
Lance Corporal: (4840) G.E.Richards.
Privates: (4315) A.Baker, (5658) A.E.Brown, (4441) J.A.Collison, (4720) R.N.Martin.
5th:
Second Lieutenant: (5071) A.C.Boud.
Corporal: (5443) A.E.Richford.
7th:
Sergeant: (6160) H.W.Smith.
9th:
Private: (5414) W.Pattenden.

10th:
Private: (4929) E.C.P.Thomas.
11th:
Private: (5091) R.Buckwell.
12th;
Private: (4894) S.H.Standen.
13th:
Private: (4713) J.MacFarlane.
14th:
Private: (4936) A.W.Tilbury.

Trenches close to the Ferme-du-Bois, an isolated farmstead opposite a small German salient, produced by a significant bend in the line, known as the 'Boar's Head', were occupied on the 16th June (13th Bn.), 21st June (11th Bn.) and 28th June (13th Bn.). There, opposite the village of Richebourg L'Avoué which straggled along the Rue-du-Bois, Lowther's Lambs were to take part together in their first large attack and they were about to receive their first major 'blooding'. More, or less, unknown to them the great Battle of the Somme was to be launched by the British and French farther south on the 1st July. On the previous day Lowther's Lambs were to launch a 'holding attack' aimed at no specifically important objective but principally to keep the Germans occupied and prevent them from sending reinforcements to the Somme.

JUNE:
18th:
Captain: (5816) F.S.Gillespie.
20th:
Privates: (4619) H.Hill, (5422) G.H.Pitcher.
21st:
Lance Corporal: (5856) A.G.Harman.
Privates: (5611) J.E.B.Beacher, (6212) H.W.Tapp.
22nd:
Private: (6313) P.L.Willmer.
23rd:
Private: (4942) A.Turner.
25th:
Lance Corporal: (4771) H.C.Newell.
Private: (4528) W.A.Foord.
26th:
Private: (5003) S.A.Wood.
29th:
Private: (4629) H.H.Hobbs.

The 12th and 13th Battalions, who were to be in the forefront of the attack, assembled at 1.30am on Friday 30th June. The preliminary bombardment commenced at 2.50am and, at 3.05am, the first wave scaled the parapet and moved forward in line. No-Man's-Land was crossed with light casualties except on the left where heavy enemy machine gun fire held up the advance. At an early stage a smoke cloud, designed to mask the attack, drifted across the front making it impossible for the men to see more than a few yards. As a direct result of this planning blunder direction was lost completely and the advance degenerated into small groups of men struggling to move forward towards their objectives. Although there was general confusion, some groups engaged the enemy with bombs and bayonets but relatively few succeeded in reaching the enemy trenches. The Germans were by now thoroughly prepared and for two and a half hours brought to bear on the assailants a tremendous fire using every means available. With the likelihood that many attackers would be cut off or completely annihilated, the order to withdraw was given and remnants of the Brigade struggled back to their starting lines.

The 11th Battalion, which had been detailed to act in support by providing carrying parties for small arms ammunition, bombs and water, followed their sister Battalions to the enemy front line but also were forced to withdraw. Great numbers of dead and wounded men lay out in the No-Man's-Land areas of flat, unprotected grassland. Little could be done to help them, at least until nightfall.

There had been many instances of bravery that day, none more so than of a man born in Hailsham, Sussex, who lived, and worked as a cinema commissionaire, in Eastbourne. That man's citation read: 'Nelson Victor Carter, Company Sergeant Major, 4th Company 12th Bn. R. Sx. Regt. Date of act of bravery: 30/6/16, for most conspicuous bravery. During an attack he was in command of the fourth wave of the assault. Under intense shell and machine gun fire he penetrated, with a few men, into the enemy's second line and inflicted heavy casualties with bombs. When forced to retire to the enemy's first line, he captured a machine gun and shot the gunner with his revolver. Finally, after carrying several wounded men into safety, he was himself mortally wounded, and died in a few minutes.

His conduct throughout the day was magnificent. London Gazette 9/9/16.'

Nelson Victor Carter, V.C., had enlisted in the Royal Field Artillery in 1903 at the age of 16 under the false name of Nelson Smith. The alias was used probably so that his true age could not be checked. Later, after his eighteenth birthday, he re-enlisted under his real name. He was invalided out of the army in 1906 following a serious hernia operation. On the 14th October, 1914, he re-enlisted, this time with Colonel Lowther's 2nd South Down Battalion, later to become the 12th Royal Sussex. His previous service and experience were acknowledged immediately and he was made a corporal on the day he joined. This man, one of only three Royal Sussex men to be awarded the Victoria Cross during the First World War, is buried at the Royal Irish Rifles Graveyard, Laventie.

The 30th June, 1916, proved to be the costliest day for Lowther's Lambs throughout the whole war. The number of fatalities recorded at the time were 11th Battalion 31, 12th Battalion 145, 13th Battalion 167, with another 25 dying from wounds over the following week. No less than six sets of brothers were killed and one set died from wounds received that day. This was a foretelling of the terrible loss of life within individual families and close-knit communities that was to be suffered by Units, especially of the north of England 'Pals' Battalions, where men and groups of men who worked together, were encouraged to join and serve together. After the Battle of the Somme this practice was stopped when it was realised that these groups of men would, in many instances, not only join and serve together but also die together. Whole streets of northern towns were bereft of their young manhood as a result of this early-war practice.

The 12th Battalion, whose obligatory 'War Diary' was generally far less detailed than the other two Battalions, was on this occasion, strangely, the only one to record its casualties in addition to those killed. Those figures, which give some indication of the position likely in the 13th Battalion and, because of its less active role, somewhat lower level in the 11th Battalion, were 7 Officers and 236 Other Ranks wounded; 5 Officers and 120 Other Ranks missing.

JUNE:
30th:
Captains: (5130) A.N.Cotton, (5747) M.C.Diggens, (5902) C.M.Humble-Crofts, (6307) R.D'A.Whittaker.
Lieutenants: (5788) H.L.Fitzherbert, (5490) C.Sparks.
Second Lieutenants: (5022) F.T.Arkcoll, (4461) A.C.Cushen, (5755) E.W.Dudley, (5185) G.J.Fenchelle, (4577) F.Grisewood, (5241) F.J.Hanby, (5386) L.L.Moody, (6016) D.N.Morgan, (6031) H.P.G.Oliver, (6090) L.A.Prior, (5451) J.B.Salberg.
Company Sergeant Majors: (5102) N.V.Carter, **V.C.**, (5395) G.A.Nicholas.
Sergeants: (5606) W.Bassett, (5057) I.C.M.Bishop, (5672) W.S.Burns, (5100) W.T.Carlin, (5104) F.Casey, (5738) A.E.Cutler, (5758) W.C.Duly, (5781) E.L.Farnden, (5191) F.Fisher, (5793) C.H.Fogden, (5800) J.French, (4569) H.P.Green, (5250) A.T.Harris, (6321) H.Wingfield.
Lance Sergeants: (5060) C.Blackman, (5066) T.P.Blurton, (5073) S.Brackell, (5852) W.J.Harding, (4726) G.E.May, (4890) T.W.Spurge, (5502) J.G.Sumner.
Corporals: (5628) J.Bishop, (5084) C.M.Bromwich, (5771) A.Elliott, (5864) H.I.Hayes, (5299) G.H.Jackson, (5371) E.G.Mason, (6051) P.Parsons, (5453) W.J.Saunders, (6285) W.Watts.
Lance Corporals: (5574) R.Agate, (4311) C.H.Aynsworth, (5043) W.H.Bayless, (5630) W.J.Blackford, (4363) A.Botting, (5651) F.Bristow, (5108) F.W.Chandler, (5700) S.E.M.Charman, (5728) W.R.Cooper, (5131) S.A.Cousins, (5135) F.W.Creasy, (4484) G.Dorling, (5172) H.Etherton, (5780) R.V.Farminer, (5206) R.D.Frape, (4540) J.Fuller, (5802) C.H.Funnell, (4541) E.G.Funnell, (5811) C.Gell, (5827) J.E.Goldsmith, (5850) H.Hand, (5298) A.Isted, (5941) C.Kelly, (5947) J.Kent, (5339) G.T.Lawrence, (4764) F.W.Murrell, (6040) E.Page, (6047) J.H.Parkhouse, (6056) S.A.Peacham, (6062) F.Perkins, (6075) L.Pierce, (5431) A.V.Randell, (4855) R.Russell, (6172) A.Sparks, (6197) A.J.Street, (4927) E.W.Tester, (6225) D.Thick, (6241) C.L.Toye, (6251) E.R.Turner, (6259) R.C.Veness, (6299) A.V.Whibley.
Privates: (5571) E.A.Adams, (5012) J.S.Akehurst, (5015) P.Alford, (4296) H.W.Amos, (5017) C.C.Andrews, (5585) W.V.Awcock, (5587) N.Ayling, (5028) W.Aylward, (5596) J.Banks, (5603) T.Barrow, (5042) K.Barton, (5605) R.Bashford, (5045) F.Beagley, (5612) G.Beale, (5047) L.Beaton, (5048) W.F.Bedding, (5613) C.Beesley, (5615) P.J.Belcher, (5049) A.E.Bennett, (5619) W.A.Bennett, (5623) H.T.Billinghurst, (5061) F.Blaker, (5633) L.Blaker, (5063) E.Blight, (5065) E.B.Blurton, (5067) W.Bonas,

(5637) A.J.Bond, (5639) J.Botting, (5640) R.Botting, (5075) F.Bradford, (5076) G.Bradford, (5078) W.J.Bradley, (5080) A.E.Brett, (5650) E. Bristow, (5651) F. Bristow, (5086) S.Brooks, (4377) A. W. Brown, (5087) C.J.Brown, (4379) D.O.Brown, (5661) F.W.Browning, (5662) A.Brunning, (4388) J.H.Budgen, (5666) C.H.Burchell, (5670) H.T.Burgess, (5095) A.Butler, (5098) H.Callingham, (5103) W.Carver, (5106) F.Catton, (5107) F.J.Cawte, (5694) W.S.Chalcraft, (5703) W.E.Cheeseman, (5113) W.H.Clarke, (5710) G.Cloake, (5711) E.A.Clout, (5712) G.R.Coates, (5713) W.Coates, (5118) E.G.Collins, (5122) F.M.Coombs, (5125) E.J.Coppard, (5126) A.H.Corke, (5127) R.Corke, (5132) A.W.Cowley, (5136) A.C.Crittenden, (5137) G.Croft, (5143) S.Culver, (4462) S.H.Dadswell, (5742) F.W.Dann, (5150) L.Davis, (5159) B.Diggens, (5162) H.J.Doyle, (4489) H.Duke, (5757) V.G.Duke, (5759) G.Dummer, (5760) A.E.Dunk, (5774) F.Ellis, (5782) W.Faulkener, (5790) F.A.Fleet, (5194) H.Fletcher, (4526) W.T.Foat, (5198) A.Foord, (5199) W.C.Foord, (5795) A.S.Ford, M.M., (4529) A.J.Foster, (5203) A.J.Fowler, (5208) R.Fry, (5211) P.Fuller, (5212) E.G.Funnell, (5803) J.E.Funnell, (5805) J.G.Gadd, (5808) H.E.K.Garbett, (5809) S.A.Garrett, (5215) P.B.J.Gaut, (5216) J.Gearing, (5813) E.Gent, (5819) E.F.H.Gillman, (5219) F.Goddard, (5840) A.Greenaway, (5841) F.H.Greenfield, (5227) A.H.Gregory, (5228) A.C.Grenyer, (5229) H.Griffiths, (5844) E.S.Gumbrell, (5849) R.Hamper, (5240) A.Hampshire, (4596) F.T.Harbour, (5245) W.T.Hards, (5855) R.Hargreaves, (5247) T.Harlott, (5858) E.C.Harris, (5860) E.Hartley, (5254) E.W.Hawes, (5865) W.R.Haylar, (5867) L.Heasman, (5870) T.Henley, (5872) G.H.Henshaw, (5874) E.Hewitt, (5268) T. Hicks, (5269) W. B. Hide, (5882) H. Hobday, (5272) C. Hodges, (5276) G. Holland, (5280) E. J. Honeybun, (5892) C.Honeysett, (5893) J.G.Honeysett, (5898) G.L.Horton, (5286) C.A.Howlett, (5288) W.E.Hubbard, (5295) F.Hutley, (5296) A.J.Hutson, (5909) A.Ide, (5910) C.Ireland, (5911) P.J.Isard, (5301) H.James, (5302) A.W.Jarman, (5922) B.Jempson, (5923) C.S.Jempson, (5926) J.C.Jenner, (5307) W.Jenner, (5930) G.Johnson, (5324)

F.Kirk, (4692) H.Langford, (5331) P.F.Langton, (5969) H.H.Legge, (5350) W.E.Linfield, (5977) W.H.Long, (5357) W.E.Lucas, (5983) A.W.Lydford, (5361) J.Mace, (5364) R.C.Manwaring, (5990) C.Mardell, (5991) A.V.Marsh, (5996) H.Maskell, (5372) A.A.Matthews, (5375) E.L.Mepham, (4733) H.Mercer, (5376) W.G.Mercer, (6007) G.H.Merricks, (5378) A.G.Mewett, (4737) F.A.Middleton, (6009) L.Miles, (6011) S.Miller, (4746) A.T.Mitchell, (5388) A.D.Morley, (6018) J.A.Morriss, (6020) J.Mustchin, (5391) C.A.Nevell, (4781) E.W.Nunne, (6037) H.Osborne, (6041) A.F.Paige, (5405) C.H.Palmer, (6044) A.Pannell, (6045) C.J.Pannell, (5406) W.Pannell, (5411) D.Parsons, (6053) R.G.Patching, (6055) H.H.Pavey, (5416) W.W.Pelling, (5417) H.Peregoe, (6064) P.P.Perrin, (6069) A.G.Phillips, (6072) S.Phippen, (6078) H.Playford, (6081) H.P.Pocock, (6093) F.Pullen, (5428) W.N.Pumphrey, (5433) F.W.Ray, (6100) T.J.Raynsford, (5438) N.J.Reed, (5442) F.Richards, (5444) F.G.Richford, (6121) B.Rogers, (6124) L.T.Rolfe, (5450) F.Russell, (5455) G.S.Saville, (6130) W.Saxby, (6136) H.C.Scott, M.M., (5460) J.Searle, (5463) F.W.Sexton, (6138) R.J.E.Shearing, (6139) W.T.Shepherd, (6142) A.E.Simmonds, (5468) H.A.Simmons, (6145) G.A.Sinnock, (5472) G.E.Slater, (5474) C.R.Smart, (6152) A.Smith, (6162) T.Smith, (6165) W.S.Smith, (6169) H.S.South, (6171) W.T.Sparkes, (6176) W.A.Squires, (5492) W.A.Stace, (5494) H.J.Staplehurst, (6184) E.G.Stevens, (6188) J.Stevenson, (5493) F.J.Stangemore, (6203) A.H.Stubberfield, (6205) H. Sumner, (6213) F.J.Tasker, (6219) W. Taylor, (6226) E.L.Thomas, (6227) R.W.Thomas, (6229) T.H.Tice, (5516) A.Tingley, (6238) R.Toon, (4939) R.Topping, (5522) W.G.Tugwell, (4940) R.T.Tully,(5523) J.Tuppen, (6249) A.C.Turner, (5525) F.Turner, (6265) E.Vine, (5534) A.E.Virgo, (5537) S.Walker, (5538) W.R.Walker, (5540) G.E.Walls, (6280) H.E.T.Walters, (5544) C.Watts, (6289) R.L.Webb, (4988) A.White,(5553) W.J.Wickens, (5558) H.Williams, (5561) G.H.R.Wilson, (6317) S.Wilson, (6318) H.Winchester, (6320) W.F.Winchester, (6324) G.Wood, (6325) H.J.Wood, (6327) A.Woodford, (5566) E.Wooler.

CHAPTER 34
1916
JULY – DECEMBER

As a result of the bloody nose received at the 'Boar's Head' on the last day of June, Lowther's Lambs retired to rest and re-organise over the first week of July at Richebourg and Le Touret (11th Bn.), Les Brebis and Béthune (12th Bn.) and Vieille Chapelle and Béthune (13th Bn.). All men who had been engaged on the 30th June were inspected on the 3rd July by the Corps and Divisional Commanders. By the 12th July all three Battalions were back in the normal trench routines with sporadic firing being carried out by both sides. During a heavy bombardment on the 12th, Sergeant Joseph White was buried by a heavy Minenwerfer explosion and, although a digging party tried long and hard to save him, all hope had to be abandoned.

JULY:
1st:
Privates: (4487) A.Driver, (5824) R.E.Godin, (5297) W.Irons, (5978) M.Longhurst, (5356) R.H.Lucas, (5382) R.R.Mills, (6058) J.F.Pellett, (5439) W.Reed, (4924) E.C.Taylor, (6244) C.Trill.
2nd:
Corporal: (5031) G.E.Baines.
Lance Corporals: (5709) C.Clayton, (6079) A.Plummer.
Privates: (5429) C.Rabson, (5466) G.Shore, (5486) W.F.Smith, (5524) C.N.Turner.
3rd:
Privates: (5913) R.Jackson, (5914) R.H.Jackson, (5925) A.E.Jenner, (5419) E.B.Phipps, (5440) A.B.Reeves. (4888) F.G.Softley.
4th:
Privates: (4586) A.Gurr, (5385) C.A.J.A.Moncur, (5491) A.Sprange.
6th:
Sergeant: (5413) H.Pattenden.
7th:
Captain: (5789) W.W.Fitzherbert.
Company Sergeant Major: (5917) E.James.
Sergeant: (6151) L.Slaughter.

Lance Corporal: (6067) H.Pettitt.
8th:
Drummer: (4589) E.A.Haffenden.
Private: (4815) C.A.Piper.
9th:
Privates: (4594) P.Hall, (5935) P.D.Joy.
10th:
Sergeant: (4291) S.W.Akehurst.
Privates: (4507) W.Elphick, (5265) H.A.Henty.
11th:
Sergeant: (5458) E.J.Scott.
Privates: (4476) L.Dennis, (4499) G.Edwards, (4656) J.H.Isted.
12th:
Sergeant: (6304) J.White.
Lance Corporal: (5723) S.H.Coombs.
Privates: (4330) G.A.E.Barnes, (5238) A.J.Hake, (6104) E.T.Reed, (5533) A.J.Vine.
13th:
Sergeant: (4970) G.E.Watling.
Lance Corporal: (4497) T.J.Earl.
Private: (5483) J.Smith.
14th:
Corporal: (5912) R.Ivermee.
Private: (6036) F.Osborne.
15th:
Lance Corporal: (5178) H.E.Fairs.
Private: (6014) W.Moon.
16th:
Private: (6291) W.Wellcome.
17th:
Sergeant: (5420) W.A.Phypers.
Private: (5035) T.Baldwin.
18th:
Private: (4831) W.T.Ralph.
19th:
Private: (5584) F.Austin.
21st:
Private: (4609) A.Hayler.
22nd:
Second Lieutenant: (5686) N.C.Carter.
Privates: (5158) F.Dewey, (6068) J.Philby.

It is interesting to note that a considerable growth of summer grass had occured in the former meadows of No-Man's-Land. Determined efforts at grass cutting were made by both sides at night in order to deprive opponents of the chance of concealment. On the night of the 23rd / 24th July, men of the 11th Battalion undertook a raid aimed at securing an enemy prisoner or other form of German Unit identification. In the event, the available gap in the enemy wire was small thus reducing the speed of movement and attack to such a degree that the Germans had time to draw in reinforcements from their flanks and mount a determined defence with fusilades of rifle grenades. The attackers pressed on to the German parapet and bombed along the trench for some distance. Shouting and groans from the enemy indicated that damage had been inflicted upon them. German resistence increased, however, and it was decided to call a halt to the raid. Its leader, Second Lieutenant Gammons received two wounds, two men were wounded and two killed while returning to their lines.

JULY:
23rd:
Privates: (4368) A.G.Brackpool, (5224) A.J.Grainger.
24th:
Lance Corporal: (4747) B.Mitchell.
Privates: (4533) R.Francis, (4657) S.J.Isted.
25th:
Private: (4565) P.Gratwicke.
27th:
Private: (4875) H.Sloman.
28th:
Private: (4703) J.J.Lee.
29th:
Corporal: (5891) P.Homer.

Another raid, this time by the 13th Battalion took place with tragic results on the night of the 30th / 31st July. It should have been realised that the particularly dark night and misty conditions, reducing visibility to no more than a yard or so, would cause difficulties but the plan was put into operation. Orders were soon issued for the party to stand fast but the message took time to reach everyone involved. A party of men was detected in front of the Battalion's wire and a voice was heard to shout, 'come on boys, let's give it them', followed by receipt of a shower of

bombs. Retaliatory bombs and Lewis Gun fire were used. The firing ceased abruptly when it was realised that a patrol under Second Lieutenant MacNaughton had gone out but not returned. Eventually, several of the patrol did return and, from the reports, it was realised that the patrol had lost all direction in the poor visibility and had wandered about until they reached what they thought was the German trench. It was then that the confrontational fire was opened, as it transpired, between friendly forces. Second Lieutenant MacNaughton and three men lost their lives because of this disasterously bad planning and inevitable confusion.

JULY:
31st:
Second Lieutenant: (5985) A.E.H.MacNaughten.
Sergeant: (5617) H.Bennett.
Private: (6260) H.Venni.

Much of the first half of August was spent out of the line training, route marching and attending to domestic necessities within billets. Large contingents from each Battalion attended a commemorative Church Parade in the main square at Béthune to mark the second anniversary of the outbreak of the war and the last appearance in France of the First Army's General Sir Charles Monro. With the weather still quite hot, Lowther's Lambs rested and underwent feet inspections on the 12th. This was a precursor to the move south from the region of Artois where they had been for the past five months. Two days of marching brought them to the training areas around the village of Monchy Breton, known as 'Monkey Britain' by the troops, some 12 miles south-west of Béthune and 15 miles north-west of Arras. There, they underwent ten days and nights of intensive training. As yet, they did not know officially that they were on their way to participate in the continuing Battle of the Somme.

AUGUST:
6th:
Sergeant: (4600) F.R.Harmer.
Private: (5801) C.Frost.
9th:
Lance Sergeant: (4466) H.Davey.
13th:
Lance Corporal: (4928) A.J.Thomas.

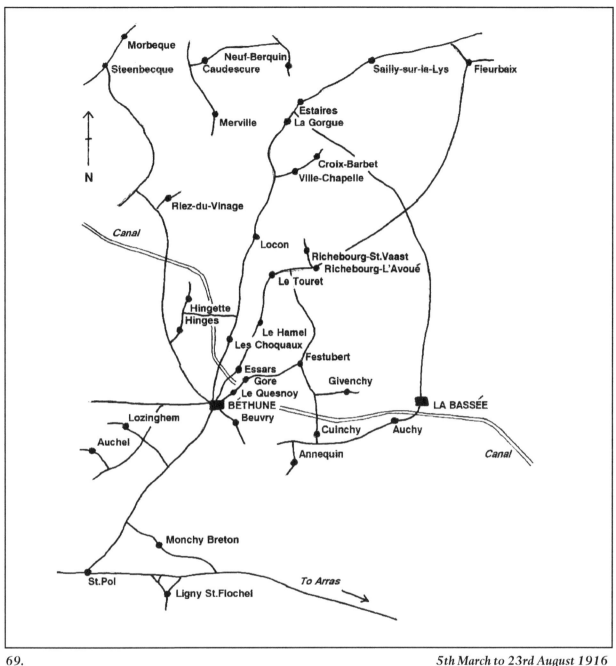

69. *5th March to 23rd August 1916*

AUGUST:
16th:
Private: (6073) A.Pierce.
17th:
Private: (4749) R.Mitchell.
20th:
Private: (5088) F.Brown.

The move farther south began on the 23rd August, each Battalion taking a slightly different route of march after a relatively short rail journey from Ligny-St.Flochel to Bouquemaison. After de-training they marched by way of Le Souich (11th Bn.), Sibiville and Sus-St.Leger (12th Bn.), Moncheaux and Ivergny (13th Bn.).

Serving as an officer with the 11th Battalion throughout most of its time in Belgium and France was the celebrated poet and author, Edmund Blunden. Some ten years after the war he published 'Undertones of War', a splendid book outlining his experiences on the Western Front. His officer colleagues included Major William Colsey Millward, a great sportsman who had played football for Dulwich Hamlet and cricket at county level for Worcestershire and Sussex. It is worth quoting here Edmund Blunden's charming recollections of one of the nights they spent on the way to the Somme battlefields. 'Leaving the railway, we were

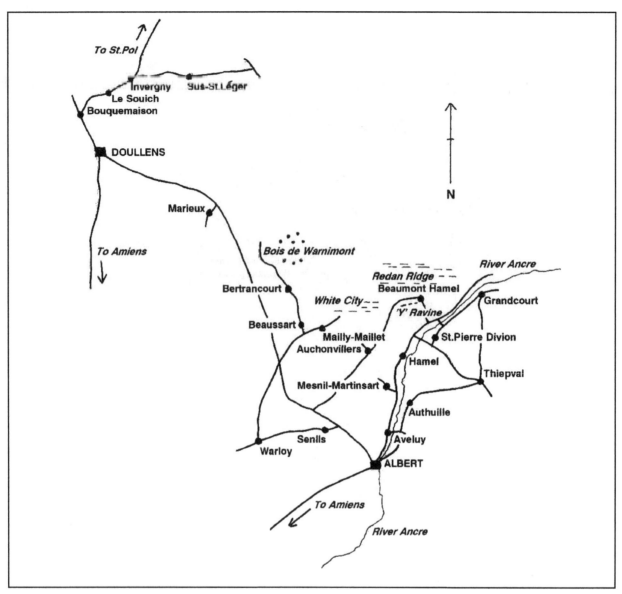

70.   *23rd August to 17th November 1916*

billeted one night in the village of Le Souich. The occasion was marked at Battalion Headquarters by a roast goose, which the old farmer whose house we had invaded had shot at shortest range with the air of a mighty hunter ... and I joyfully recollect how Millward, that famed cricketer, gave a few of us an hour's catching practice in the orchard with apples instead of cricket balls ...'

By their different routes, Lowther's Lambs came together again at the Bois de Warnimont to which they marched in great heat and dust and where they trained for two days while officers, including Edmund Blunden, reconnoitred the nearby area of front lines. Next day, the 27th August, they arrived to bivouac just two miles west of the front, the 12th Battalion near Englebelmer and the other two Battalions in

Mailly-Maillet Wood. The following three days were very wet as the men prepared to take part in a planned attack which was postponed twice on account of the bad weather. As they waited, the Germans shelled the vicinity of Mailly-Maillet Wood with shrapnel, the shells, filled with many marble-sized lead or iron balls, bursting in the air for maximum tortuous effect against men and horses. Edmund Blunden graphically described just such a shelling as this: ' ... the savage rush of shrapnel shells uncoiling their dingy green masses of smoke downwards while their white-hot darts scoured the acre below.' The casualties on the 30th were sustained in this manner.

AUGUST:

25th:

Corporal: (5180) G.Farley.

29th:
Private: (4298) F.L.Andrews.
30th:
Privates: (5147) P.Daughtrey, (4496) W.Dyer, (5329) G.Lambert, (4742) W.L.Miller, (4860) H.G.Saunders.

Over the first two days and nights of September Lowther's Lambs made final preparations for the major attack in which they were to take part on the 3rd at 5.10am. The main assault was to be undertaken by the 11th Battalion with the 12th and 13th in support. On the evening of the 2nd the Battalions moved off to make their way across country and down to the village of Hamel on the west side of the River Ancre, a northern tributary of the River Somme. The long and steep communication trench they used on the approach was called 'Jacob's Ladder'. Edmund Blunden again: 'If ever there was a vile, unnerving and desperate place in the battle zone, it was the Mesnil end of 'Jacob's Ladder', among the heavy battery positions, and under perfect enemy observation. 'Jacob's Ladder' was a long trench, good in parts, stretching from Mesnil with many angles down to Hamel on the River Ancre, requiring flights of stairs at one or two steep places.'

Lieutenant Blunden's part had been to plan the siting, and organise the stocking, of stores dumps in forward positions for use by the Battlions supporting the attack. Following the opening barrage, men of the 11th Battalion went 'Over the Top' to attack uphill and over a ridge in fairly open country between the villages of Beaumont Hamel and Beaucourt-sur-l'Ancre. The first wave of the assault succeeded in entering the enemy front line but the Germans opened a fearsome bombardment across 'No-Man's-Land' causing heavy casualties amongst the second and third waves. A few men, led on by Captain Northcote, even managed to get into the German's second line but they could do little but hang on desperately against great odds. The bombardment effectively prevented the attacking waves from being supplied and re-inforced throughout the day. Captain Mitchell, with surviving men from the second and third waves, consolidated a line of shell holes between the enemy wire and front line but, in such an exposed position, took many more casualties from shrapnel and bombs as the long daylight hours ticked slowly away.

By early evening and into the early hours of darkness, the inevitable withdrawal got under way. The most forward men were led back by Captain Northcote who was killed in the process and, in fact, only one soldier from that group returned. Others got back as best they could but, in addition to the 11th Battalion men killed that day, 160 were recorded as wounded and 123 missing.

In attempting to provide support, part of the 13th Battalion unfortunately waivered in direction and lost all contact with the 11th Battalion. Patrols were pushed out to left and right but the enemy fire across 'No-Man's-Land' prevented any communication with other Units. Men of 'A' Company of the 13th Battalion were getting into their support trench when shouts of 'Retire. Retire' were heard and a confused mob of men, mainly from the 117th Infantry Brigade, came rushing back from their part in the attack. Captain Fabian rallied his men by shouting, 'Come on 'A' Company 13th' and leading them out in support of the 11th Battalion. Within 70 yards of the German line this gallant officer had two fingers blown from his right hand but pressed on until he was killed by a shot through the head. His men took what cover they could get in shell holes until they could withdraw.

In turn Lieutenant Cheape took over control of 'A' Company and did well, even attending to wounded men at the end of the action. It was while undertaking his last humane task of helping to carry away a wounded man on a stretcher, that he himself was targetted and deliberately killed with a shot from an enemy sniper. All three battalions re-assembled at day's end and made their weary way back up the long slope of 'Jacob's Ladder'. On the way they passed the military cemetery already started at Hamel, a burial place that Edmund Blunden described poignantly as 'open all hours.'

SEPTEMBER:
1st:
Lieutenants: (4638) O.Hood, (5310) A.H.Johns.
Private: (4511) E.Evenden.
2nd:
Captain: (5527) L.W.Tuttiet.

Second Lieutenant: (5505) T.C.Tate.
3rd:
Captains: (5779) A.S.Fabian, (4779) E.S.Northcote, (4803) C.P.Penruddocke.
Lieutenants: (5702) J.De C. Cheape, (4580) L.A.Groves, (6228) S.E.B.Thomas.
Second Lieutenants: (5602) F.W.Barrow, (4522) B.E.Fish, (4538) A.A.French, (5315) W.L.Kennedy, (4754) H.P.Mole, (6034) F.J.Ormsby.
Company Sergeant Majors: (5117) W.T.Coleman, (4902) E.Stevens.
Sergeants: (4321) D.Barham, (4386) R.Budd, D.C.M., (4620) R.Hill, (4627) F.A.Hoad, (6054) W.M.Patching, (4883) R.E.Smither, (4891) E.Squires.
Lance Sergeants: (4303) E.W.Atkins, (5594) C.E.Ball, (5859) W.P.G.Harrold.
Corporals: (5025) A.E.Austin, (4360) M.F.Booth, (4403) H.J.Burton, (4451) F.Cosstick, (4745) G.Minns, (4846) R.C.Roberts,.
Lance Corporals: (4309) W.Avis, (4413) A.G.Catt, (4456) E.S.Creasey, (5740) D.J.Dadswell, (4491) P.Dummer, (5853) A.Hards, (4637) R.Honeysett, (4679) J.W.Justice, (4688) E.Lambert, (4690) F.Lander, (5982) A.J.Lydford, (4719) E.P.Martin, (4769) H.Neville, (5424) E.W.Plummer, (4853) G.E.Rowland, (4914) H.G.Sutton, (4923) C.H.Taylor, (4948) E.P.Upperton, (4971) G.W.F.Watson, (4980) C.F.West,
Privates: (4289) W.A.Agnew, (4290) H.R.Aitken, (5582) V.C.Ascott, (4314) H.W.Bailey, (4317) C.J.Ballard, (4326) T.Barnard, (5609) A.J.Bates, (4337) H.E.Beal, (4342) A.Benton, (4344) P.M.Best, (4346) C.H.Bignell, (4354) P.R.Blackford, (5064) L.Blunden, (4371) G.Braiden, (4373) F.Bray, (4374) A.S.Bromley, (4385) E.T.Brunige, (4392) W.Burchett, (4394) J.C.D.Burgess, (4399) E.W.Burr, (5689) F.Caselden, (4416) T.A.Ceeney, (4423) E.R.Cheal, (4429) J.Clark, (4433) W.Clifford, (4436) E.E.Coleman, (4454) W.Coward, (4470) J.C.Dawes, (5155) H.Dean, (5156) A.E.De Boo, (5157) E.W.Deeprose, (4474) S.V.Delphine, (4478) F.Divall, (4485) A.Dorrington, (4490) W.H.Duke, (4494) J.Dunning, (4502) E.W.Elliott, (4504) R.Ellis, (4513) O.Farmer, (4514) W.R.Farnes, (5186) C.Fieldwick, (4537) E.T.Freeland, (4547) A.J.George, (4550) C.O.Gilbert, (5225) J.H.Grant, (4573) G.Griffiths, (5231) W.Grinstead, (4583) C.Gunn, (4591) J.Haggar, (4595) A.G.Hambrook, (4599) A.Harman, (4610) E.Heasman, (4611) T.Heasman, (4612) P.Heather, (4615) J.R.Henty, (4634) A.E.Holman, (5278) C.Holter, (4639) A.H.Hook, (4640) F.V.Hook, (4641) A.A.Hoskins, (4645) G.Hudson, (4655) M.Irwin, (4662) H.B.James,

(4665) C.J.Jarvis, (4667) H.Jocelyn, (5931) W.Johnson, (4672) W.J.Jones, (4673) A.Jordan, (4682) S.Kensett, (5338) M.T.Lawrence, (5341) J.Leaney, (4711) W.Lucas, (4721) T.Martin, (4741) T.Miller, (6019) G.Moseley, (4776) H.C.Nicholls, (5396) M.E.Norris, (4786) S.Padgham, (4810) C.E.Phillips, (4818) F.H.Plummer, (4843) M.Roach, (4844) C.D.Roberts, (4861) P.A.T.Saunders, (6132) J.Sayers, (4869) J.Sharpe, (4880) H.Smith, (4895) J.Stanford, (6179) V.J.Stapleton, (4905) W.T.Stevens, (5500) W.G.Stone, (5499) W.H.Stone, (6202) S.V.Strong, (5510) A.Tester, (5512) J.Thomas, (4949) F.E.Upton, (6274) F.J.Waller, (4965) E.Ward, (5545) T.Webb, (4982) P.West, (4983) T.H.West, (5552) A.H.Whiting, (4995) C.H.Williams.
Drummer: (5817) C.W.Gillett.

Lowther's Lambs had been hit hard and, once again, family tragedies were caused when sets of brothers, all Sussex men, who had enlisted together, this time Edgar and Thomas Heasman of Shipley, Albert and Frederick Hook of Hastings, and Ernest and Thomas Martin from Willingdon, died during the same action. Inevitably, a number of wounded men died over susequent days, increasing the death toll.

So hard had the 11th Battalion suffered on the 3rd September that it was re-formed, temporarily, into only two Companies. After two days rest in billets at Englebelmer, new drafts of replacement men began to arrive from other Units; 481 for the 11th, 260 for the 12th and 219 for the 13th Battalion, necessitating further training in order to absorb the new men.

SEPTEMBER:
4th:
Privates: (4624) A.F.Hilton, (5504) F.Tadd, (4977) A.E.Weller,.
5th:
Privates: (5128) E.T.Cornford, (4676) H.T.Judge, (5962) W.Latter.
6th:
Privates: (4567) C.Gray, (4618) E.B.Hide, (5270) F.G.Hills, (5907) D.Hyland, (5393) A.F.J.Newman, (4833) F.S.E.Reed.
8th:
Private: (5701) W,C.Chatfield.

For the remainder of September Lowther's Lambs took their normal turns in the front line and back in Brigade Reserve at Beaussart (11th Bn.), Englebelmer (12th Bn.) and Mailly-

Maillet (13th Bn.). Times in the line were taken up improving barbed wire defences and repairing rain-affected trenches to the right of Auchonvillers and on the Redan Ridge to the left of Beaumont Hamel. Days were punctuated by enemy heavy trench mortar fire and a few lachrymatory gas shells. On the 23rd a single enemy trench mortar killed nine 13th Battalion men in the front trench on the Redan Ridge; eight of those men, including two sets of brothers, Arthur and Walter Smith from Eastbourne, and Henry and Frederick Walsgrove of Hastings, had only just arrived with a new draft.

SEPTEMBER:
9th:
Private: (5010) A.G.Addy.
11th:
Corporal: (5449) F.F.Rumbelow.
Privates: (5026) A.Ayling, (5368) A.W.Martin, (5408) A.W.Parker.
12th:
Sergeant: (6333) W.G.Yeatman.
13th:
Lieutenant: (4955) C.A.Vorley.
Sergeant: (4975) R.S.Welchman.
Privates: (4822) W.A.Povey, (6308) R.Whitwell.
16th:
Privates: (4446) C.J.Cooke, (5007) R.Wright.
18th:
Private: (4508) A.Emery.
20th:
Sergeants: (4450) C.N.Cosstick, (4452) F.Couchman.
Privates: (5578) W.F.Allen, (4449) J.A.Cornish, (5179) A.F.Farley, (5201) A.Foster, (4561) H.Goodrich, (6216) J.B.Tatlow.
21st:
Privates: (5548) J.T.West, (5564) L.Woodford.
22nd:
Private: (4531) C.Fowler.
23rd:
Lance Corporal: (4390) A.Bunn.
Privates: (5597) E.F.Barber, (4362) C.T.Bosworth, (5871) R.Henrys, (5970) H.Leverton, (6066) C.H.Pettit, (6153) A.Smith, (6163) W.Smith, (6209) S.Swatton, (6277) F.Walsgrove, (6278) H.Walsgrove.

On the 26th September Lowther's Lambs participated in the support given to an attack towards Thiepval on the high ground beyond the River Ancre. Divisional artillery bombarded the enemy trenches continuously during the afternoon. Dummy figures were hoisted onto the parapets but a proposed smoke demonstration was cancelled because the wind was unfavourable. These efforts to deceive the enemy seem to have been to little avail as only slight retaliatory fire was drawn.

SEPTEMBER:
25th:
Lance Sergeant: (4306) F.N.Austin.
26th
Privates: (5352) A.Lingham, (6223) F.Terry.
27th:
Privates: (4542) F.W.Funnell, (5487) W.H.Smith.
28th:
Privates: (5929) A.V.Jinkerson, (5006) D.C.A.Wortley.
29th:
Private: (6085) H.J.Pope.
30th:
Private: (5110) W.H.Chapman.

The first half of October was spent in the same areas of Auchonvillers, Englebelmer and Mailly-Maillet when out of the line, and in the vicinity of Redan Ridge, 'White City', 'Y' Ravine and Hamel when on trench duty. Significant bouts of trench mortar and shelling activity were inflicted by both sides. A new area of activity was approached on the 15th when the River Ancre was crossed and Lowther's Lambs made their way ominously towards the German fortress area of Thiepval which had been taken, on the 26th September, by the 18th Division for the British who had first made the attempt so long ago as the 1st July.

OCTOBER:
1st:
Privates: (5572) S.H.Adams, (4464) J.Daniels, (4558) W.Godden.
4th:
Private: (4717) F.E.Marker.
5th:
Private: (5687) J.Carver.
6th:
Reverend: (5565) D.C.Woodhouse.
8th:
Lance Corporal: (5314) P.S.C.Jones.
Privates: (4345) H.J.Benyon, (5167) E.G.Ellis, (5946) E.Kent, (5334) G.J.Large, (5409) H.C.Parker, (5426) E.G.Pope, (4958) P.E.Walker.
10th:
Privates: (5244) A.Hards, (5275) A.Holland, (5279) A.W.Homewood, (5337) W.J.Larkin.

12th:
Lance Corporal: (4381) E.J.Brown.
Privates: (5223) F.E.Gore, (4516) T.R.Fayers, (5290) W.T.Hughes, (5410) B.E.Parnell, (5473) H.Sloman, (5509) W.W.Teale.
14th:
Privates: (5399) J.G.Oldham, (6131) A.B.Sayers.
15th:
Private: (6309) C.H.Wilkins.
18th:
Lance Corporals: (4512) W.G.Faires, (4651) A.F.Hunt.
15th:
Private: (5221) E.C.Goodburn.
16th:
Privates: (5164) C.A.Easton, (5367) J.Marshall, (5543) E.Watson.

The 12th Battalion took heavy casualties when they were in the line on the 17th October from a particularly heavy and prolonged enemy bombardment with 5.9" and 8" shells which lasted from 3.00pm until 8.30pm. Caught during a relief by the 14th Hampshires, the 12th Battalion casualties amounted to 5 officers and 156 other ranks, including brothers Alfred and Clement Andrews.

OCTOBER:
17th:
Second Lieutenant: (5134) L.F.Coxon.
Sergeant: (5058) F.J.Bissenden.
Lance Corporals: (5394) C.Newman, (5432) T.Rawlings.
Privates: (5016) A.F.Andrews, (5018) C.C.Andrews, (5024) F.Ashton, (5059) H.R.Blackford, (5138) H.R.Cross, (5140) I.R.Croxon, (5152) S.Dawes, (5154) A.Deadman, (5170) G.Empringham, (5197) W.C.Follett, (5234) W.Grunnell, (5246) W.Harland, (5284) H.Howard, (5300) H.James, (5313) F.C.Jones, (5319) W.Killick, (5342) E.A.Le Blancq, (5345) E.H.Levy, (5370) W.Martin, (5374) J.H.Mawer, (5387) B.Moon, (5403) B.Packham, (5454) W.W.Savage, (5456) F.W.Sawyer, (5482) J.V.Smith, (5519) C.R.Toynbee.
18th:
Second Lieutenant: (5488) K.O.H.Smith-Howard.
Privates: (5069) J.T.Botterill, (5253) S.G.Haulkham, (5448) R.S.Ruff.
19th:
Lance Corporal: (5715) B.B.Colbourne.
Privates: (5933) W.C.Jones, (6242) G.H.Toyne, (5521) J.F.Tritton.
20th:
Private: (5495) C.J.Steel.

To the north of Thiepval was the massive German underground labyrinth fortress of the Schwaben Redoubt. After the capture of that Redoubt attention had to be turned to the right where an enemy-held line known as 'Stuff Trench' ran uphill across a ridge of open ground.

The 21st October was the day for the important attack on 'Stuff Trench'. Preparatory work, together with the disposition of men was good. At 12.06pm Lowther's Lambs went 'Over the Top' following closely behind a creeping barrage. The assault was over quite quickly with Lowther's Lambs taking possession of 'Stuff Trench'. However, heavy casualties were sustained by both sides and many German prisoners were taken. The British casualties amounted to three officers and 209 men. In addition the 13th Battalion had 30 men missing. Consolidation of the trench was effected and no enemy couter-attack was forthcoming.

Several succeeding days were spent bringing back wounded men and in burying the dead, many of whom now lie in the isolated Grandcourt Road Cemetery not far from the old line of 'Stuff Trench'.

OCTOBER:
21st:
Captain: (4658) F.H.H.Ivens.
Lieutenant: (4482) G.W.Doogan.
Second Lieutenant: (4857) F.H.Salter.
Company Sergeant Major; (4699) G.E.Lawrence.
Sergeants: (5692) R.Catt, (4575) H.Grimley, (4588) W.R.Habgood, (4625) A.Hiscock, (4867) A.G.Seamer.
Corporals: (4302) E.C.Astley, (5317) C.H.Kewell, (4798) S.Pearce.
Lance Corporals: (5676) E.E.Calver, (5124) R.Copeland, (4501) F.W.Eke, (4562) F.S.Gosling, (6094) W.H.Pullen, (4834) H.Relf, (4878) E.E.Smith, (4946) C.T.Tyler.
Privates: (4292) U.Alcock, (4295) F.G.Alvis, (4299) H.Arnold, (5588) F.S.W.Bagot, (4347) G.E.Bilbie, (5055) H.E.Bishop, (5068) A.P.Booles, (4361) W.Boswell, (4365) H.Bower, (4366) G.Bowers, (4370) W.G.Bradbury, (5649) T.G.Bridgewater, (4382) T.H.Brown, (4391) L.A.Burch, (4395) W.H.Burgess, (5097) A.J.Butters, (4415) J.Cawley, (5697) P.W.Chambers, (5705) G.W.Clark, (4438) L.Coley, (4444) A.Cook, (4445) J.Cook, (5736) S.T.Cullen, (4460) A.W.Currey, (4472) A.E.Day, (5153) A.W.Day, (4473) T.Dean, (4481) S.F.Dodds,

(5756) G.W.Duke, (5765) A.J.East, (5776) J.Ellis, (4518) G.I.Fenn, (5190) E.F.Fisher, (4524) L.Fisher, (4527) F.M.Folkard, (5794) E.Foord, (5797) C.A.Francis, (4535) A.E.Fredman, (5207) W.J.French, (5806) W.E.Gadd, (4544) A.Gallup, (5810) T.W.Geal, (5822) W.Goble, (4568) E.J.Green, D.C.M., (4570) T.J.Green, (5843) W.Grout, (4601) H.E.Harmer, (5252) C.Hartwell, (5878) C.W.Hills, (5879) F.C.Hills, (4630) G.H.Hobday, (4635) O.E.Holmwood, (5900) T.Hull, (5905) F.H.Hyde, (4664) J.Jarrett, (4670) E.A.Jones, (4680) W.R.Keates, (5332) H.Lapwood, (5344) S.Leeke, (5363) A.Manley, (4715) E.Mansell, (5993) J.W.Martin, (4722) D.Matthews, (4723) A.Mattin, (4730) J.H.Meekings, (6005) T.Mepham, (4734) B.W.Merricks, (4751) W.T.Mitchell, (4770) P.Neville, (6026) A.Norris, (4788) A.H.Paget, (6042) W.T.Pain, (6049) A.Parsons, (4804) R.C.Perham, (6061) H.S.Perigoe, (6071) H.G.Philpott, (4813) F.Pilbeam, (4820) A.W.Potter, (4826) H.J.Prior, (4838) A.Rice, (6106) C.H.J.Rice, (4839) E.L.Richards, (6108) A.E.Richardson, (4848) A.Robey, (4849) L.Rogers, (4850) F.Ross, (4854) J.H.Rush, (4864) J.Scarterfield, (6137) L.Scutt, (5459) F.Searle, (5461) A.B.Selsby, (4870) F.E.Shirley, M.M., (6143) E.G.Simpson, (5470) A.J.Sippets, (6150) E.J.Skipp, (6159) H.H.Smith, (4885) R.G.Snelling, (4892) H.Stace, (6181) L.Stenning, (4911) A.Street, (4913) C.Sullivan, (6204) A.W.Sumner, (6207) A.N.Sutton, (6210) W.S.Tailby, (4922) A.F.E.Taylor, (4933) W.Thorpe, (6239) B.R.Topliss, (6267) E.A.Voites, (6269) S.Waight, (6270) F.G.Waldock, (4967) S.T.Warner, (6297) J.H.West, (6303) H.White, (4989) W.G.A.White, (5002) S.Wood, (6330) B.G.Wright.

22nd:

Privates: (5032) S.Baker, (4652) S.J.Hunt, (5965) G.H.Laws, (5397) T.Oakley, (4879) G.R.Smith, (4998) R.W.Wisker.

23rd:

Lance Sergeant: (6002) E.Mead.

Privates: (4352) J.Bishop, M.M., (5638) J.W.Booker, (5691) F.A.Catherwood, (4426) D.Churchill, (5169) E.G.Elsey, (4752) W.J.Moates.

25th:

Private: (4736) T.F.Messer.

26th:

Lance Corporal: (5727) W.Cooper.

Privates: (5716) E.H.Coleman, (5746) J.Denyer, (5768) F.R.Edwards, (5950) J.Killick, (6273) A.Waller, (6292) H.W.Weller.

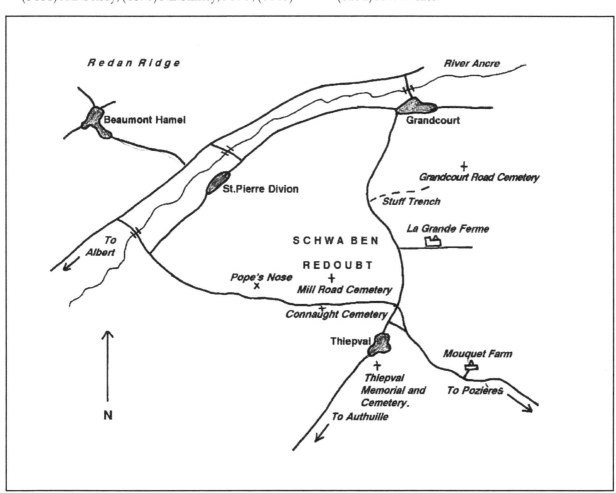

71.   *Thiepval, Schwaben Redoubt and Stuff Trench 21st October 1916*

27th:

Privates: (4397) S.F.Burnard, (5704) A.T.Clanford, (5187) H.C.Fifield, (6170) B.H.Spalding, (6189) S.W.Stewart.

30th:

Sergeants: (4961) W.J.Waller, (4994) H.S.Wilkinson, M.M.

Privates: (5112) H.Clarke, (4523) H.H.A.Fisher.

31st:

Corporal: (5121) E.Coombe.

Privates: (5021) S.J.Arbon, (5074) J.Brackenbury, (4486) G.J.Dowen, (5889) G.W.Holland, (4780) A.Nunn, (4852) W.C.Rowe.

In deteriorating weather and ground conditions, the Battle of the Somme was being wound down during the first half of November. Lowther's Lambs spent their time between rest periods at Senlis and front line occupation, including burials, salvaging and minor attacks. The 11th Battalion was entertained at Senlis by a concert put on by the '18th Division Follies' on the 3rd. Two days later a medical scare led to one platoon being isolated for fear of diphtheria. On the 13th, other Units of the Division, with support from the 12th and 13th Battalions, captured the village of St.Pierre Divion, on the bank of the River Ancre, completely surprising the enemy through a dripping autumn fog. Sadly, the loss in action of another set of brothers, George and William Newnham from Brighton, dampened the 13th Battalion's satisfaction.

NOVEMBER:

1st:

Second Lieutenant: (4807) K.G.Perry.

Private: (4909) J.Stoner.

3rd:

Privates: (5591) W.W.Bailey, (5034) E.Baldwin, (5825) C.F.Godson, (4579) F.R.Groom, (4689) R.C.A.Lambert, (6021) G.F.Newnham, (6023) W.J.Newnham, (6140) J.Shoesmith.

4th:

Privates: (4488) A.R.Duffield, (6063) J.H.Perkins, (5445) J.Ripley, M.M.

5th:

Privates: (5210) H.Fulcher, (5220) J.W.Goddard.

6th:

Privates: (5652) T.E.Brooker, (5717) S.Coleman.

11th:

Private: (4931) G.F.Thomas.

12th:

Lance Corporal: (4375) R.Brookes.

Private: (5023) D.Arnold.

13th:

Corporal: (4557) C.V.Godden.

Lance Corporal: (5507) A.Taylor.

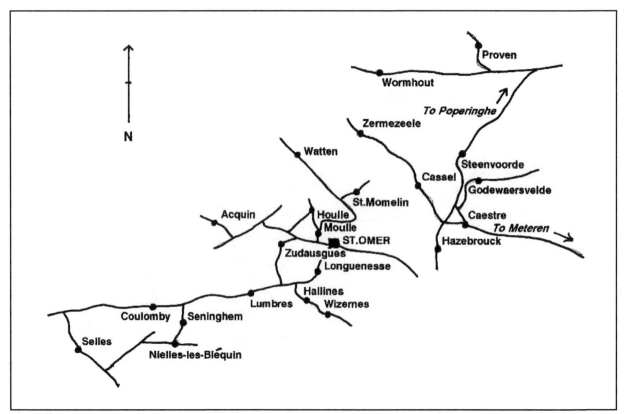

72.   *17th November 1916 to 26th January 1918 (West)*

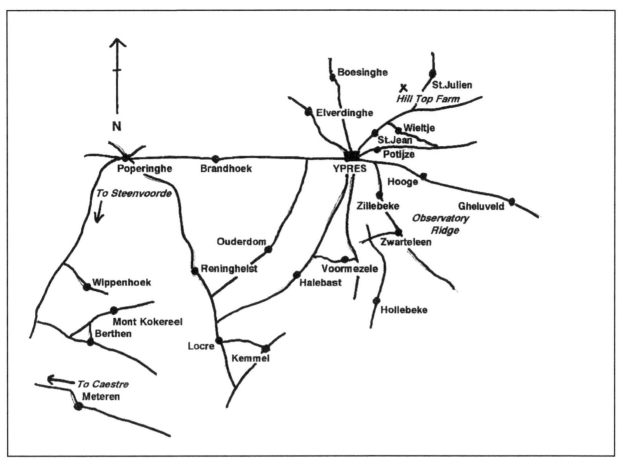

72.   *17th November 1916 to 26th January 1918 (East)*

Privates: (4587) G.D.Gurr, (5239) J.Hale, (5326) A.D.Knight, (5508) P.J.Taylor, (5539) F.Waller, (5542) J.R.Ward.

The successful capture of St.Pierre Divion was the last action undertaken by the Divison on the Somme for the time being. The three Battalions moved back west to Warloy on the 14th November and onwards, next day, to enter the town of Doullens with a swinging step and an enthusiastic rendering of 'Sussex by the Sea'.

NOVEMBER:
14th:
Lance Sergeant: (5099) W.R.F.Canning.

In bitterly cold weather, Lowther's Lambs entrained in cattle trucks at Doullens on the 17th November and arrived, frozen, the following morning at Poperinghe where they knew they were back in Belgium and due, sooner or later, for another dose of the infamous Ypres Salient. Taken with them under close guard on that train journey was Private R.T.Tite of the 13th Battalion who had been tried by Court Martial at Aveluy on the 2nd November and found guilty of 'cowardice and failing in his soldierly duties'

by leaving the trenches without permission while they were under heavy fire on 9th October. A previous conviction of four years penal servitude for disobeying an order weighed against him and he was sentenced to death. He was 'shot at dawn' at Poperinghe on the 25th November, the second Royal Sussex man to be so punished.

NOVEMBER:
18th
Private: (5531) E.Venis.
20th:
Sergeant: (5379) R.S.Millard.
22nd:
Private: (4740) S. Miller.
25th:
Private: (6233) R.T.Tite.
26th:
Private: (5549) F.Westgate.
28th:
Company Sergeant Major: (5328) A.J.Laker.
DECEMBER:
2nd:
Private: (4706) F.P.Livings.

Rest, recreation and training continued in camp at Poperinghe until the 5th December when, for the first time, the Lowther's Lamb Battalions were split up by movement of the 11th Battalion by train from Poperinghe to St.Omer from where they marched to billets at Moulle. About two miles from their billets, the men were set to work digging rifle ranges. That strenuous work, which took eight consecutive days, was interspersed with time for football and other recreational games. The work having been completed, the 11th Battalion marched from Moulle to St.Momelin on the 15th and entrained back to Poperinghe. From then until Christmas, time was spent in the line near Hill Top Farm and 'at rest' just north of Ypres in canal-side dugouts.

While the 11th Battalion had been away, training continued for the 12th and 13th Battalions. They, too, were allowed some ease, notably with a splendid concert in the camp recreation hut on the 5th December. Both of these two Battalions were also established in canal-side dugouts while undertaking trench duties which were relatively quiet as winter took hold and wet weather made trench conditions very trying and uncomfortable. It was particularly sad that, on Christmas Eve, three men lost their lives, two from the 13th Battalion being killed by shell fire just before their trench relief was due.

The three Battalions were accommodated in Camps 'E' (11th Bn.), 'D' (12th Bn.) and 'G' (13th Bn.) for Christmas Day and great efforts were made, in the circumstances, to provide enjoyable dinners. Training re-commenced after Christmas, and New Year's Eve found them all back in the line, the 12th at Machine Gun Farm, near Elverdinge, the 11th and 13th at Boesinghe.

DECEMBER:
11th:
Sergeant: (5202) C.Foster.
13th:
Sergeant: (4862) F.J.Saxby.
Private: (5749) C.Doble.
14th:
Private: (5038) B.T.Barnett.
16th:
Private: (5182) C.Fearn.
20th:
Private: (5282) W.Horton.
21st:
Corporal: (5842) L.A.Grisbrook.
24th:
Privates: (5883) A.A.T.Hobden, (5551) W.White, (6335) E.G.Young.
26th:
Private: (5214) G.Gale.
31st:
Private: (6043) M.Palmer.

CHAPTER 35
1917
JANUARY – JUNE

Routine trench duties continued well into January, the weather turning colder with heavy falls of snow on the 12th and 15th. Soon after the second snow fall, a thaw set in resulting in collapses along the entire length of trenches. By the 16th, all three Battalions had moved into Ypres itself where they shared accommodation in the Ramparts, a convent near the station and a school on the Menin Road. From those various billets, moves out to the line north of Ypres were made for their periods of trench duty. On the 25th, an early morning violent enemy Minenwerfer and 'Whiz-Bang' barrage near Potijze was followed by a 30-man raid in strength. The raiders were beaten off leaving their commanding officer and two men dead on the parapet which enabled identification to be made. Four men of the 11th Battalion were killed.

JANUARY:
3rd:
Private: (4447) W.T.Cooper.
8th:
Private: (5823) T.H.Godden.
14th:
Private: (5665) J.Bulbeck.
25th:
Privates: (4677) C.W.Jupp, (4687) W.C.C.Laker, (4727) W.May, (4729) B.Meadwell.

The remainder of this winter month of January produced more snow, more trench misery and little comfort in the billets of Ypres. The men were kept busy with parades, inspections and provision of trench working parties. Major W.C.Millward returned from a course to take over duties as Second in Command of the 11th Battalion. Having re-gained the services of this senior officer, Lowther's Lambs lost another on the 31st when Major W.T.Heagerty of the 13th Battalion was wounded in the back by a shell which dropped close to Battalion Headquarters. He was evacuated speedily but died later that day at No.2 Canadian Hospital.

JANUARY:
26th:
Private: (4384) W.R.Bruley.
27th:
Private: (4801) A.W.Pelling.
29th:
Private: (5318) H.Kiff.
30th:
Privates: (5589) C.Bailey, (5886) H.W.Holden, (4694) C.Langley, (6052) E.S.Partridge.
31st:
Major: (5866) W.T.Heagerty.
Private: (5881) F.Hoath.

The first days of February were relatively quiet except that, on the 3rd, the 12th Battalion lost two officers and 13 men as a result of the blowing of an enemy mine and the desperate and immediate need to capture its crater, a feat that was accomplished successfully. On the 4th all three Battalions moved by train from Ypres to Brandhoek for a period of rest, training, lectures, baths and medical inspections. By the 25th, the 13th Battalion and, by month end, the other two battalions had taken up a new sector of line, this time at Observatory Ridge some two miles east of Ypres and south of the Menin Road.

FEBRUARY:
2nd:
Private: (5072) C.E.Bracher.
3rd:
Second Lieutenants: (5526) R.R.Turner, (5547) C.J.Wentworth.
Sergeants: (5081) W.C.Brett, (5434) G.Reading.
Privates: (5037) J.E.Barnes, (5294) R.Hutchinson, (5303) G.F.Jarrold, (5305) G.W.Jeffery, (5311)

W.Johnson, (5320) F.King, (5327) J.E.Knight, (5347) L.P.Lewis, (5383) G.H.Mingay.

13th:
Privates: (4525) A.B.Fleet, (4631) F.E.Hodgins, (4691) E.W.Lane, (5407) A.E.Parker, (4984) W.H.West.

17th:
Private: (6122) C.Rogers.

26th:
Private: (5217) E.B.Giles.

28th:
Corporal: (5027) R.T.Ayling.
Privates: (4343) L.Berresford, (5083) E.J.Bringloe, (4407) A.E.Bye, (4576) A.Grimsey.

Lowther's Lambs were delighted on the 1st March when the popular William Colsey Millward, who had enlisted as a Private in September, 1914, took over as Officer Commanding the 11th Battalion, being promoted to Lieutenant Colonel on the 23rd March. A feature of the new Commanding Officer's tenure, which did much to raise and keep high the morale of his men, was his early introduction of cricket, football, sports and entertainments of all kinds at every reasonable opportunity. His philosophy undoubtedly was 'all fight and no play makes 'Tommy' a poor soldier'. The Battalion's splendid achievements under his leadership certainly proved that philosophy to be correct in the circumstances.

The three Battalions alternated between the Observatory Ridge trenches and the cellars of Kruisstraat in Ypres. On clear days there was much aerial activity and it was evident, at that stage, that the enemy in the air had the upper hand. On one occasion, two British planes were seen to be brought down. From one of those planes, the observer was seen to fall, or jump, before the plane crashed into the moat at Ypres. On another day an enemy plane was seen to be brought down in flames.

Artillery shelling from both sides continued along the whole front during March. In the late evening of the 21st several enemy 4.2" high explosive shells fell into Sanctuary Wood, one scoring a direct hit on the 13th Battalion's 'A' and 'D' Company cookhouse. Fortunately there was only one man inside at the time but he was killed instantly. There was another unusual occurrence on the 24th, this time at Poperinghe where Major du Moulin was attending a demonstration

of signalling with aircraft. The Major took the opportunity to go up in a plane which, from a height of 100 feet suddenly crashed to the ground. The officer was pinned beneath the machine but help arrived quickly and he was extricated suffering from a head wound and concussion. He was taken to the No.10 Casualty Clearing Station and, happily, survived his injuries.

MARCH:
1st:
Lance Corporal: (5575) J.Akehurst.
Private: (6268) E.Waby.
2nd:
Regimental Sergeant Major: (4465) J.W.Daniels.
Lance Corporal: (5177) P.G.Fairman.
Privates: (5019) P.D.B.Apps, (4760) W.B.G.Muddle, (5476) A.E.Smith.
3rd:
Private: (5077) E.J.Bradley.
7th:
Private: (5590) C.F.Bailey.
9th:
Private: (4598) A.Hare.
14th:
Colour Sergeant: (5358) W.Luck.
Lance Corporal: (5777) J.Enticknap.
Private: (5555) R.Wicker.
15th:
Privates: (6004) A.B.Meek, (4735) G.E.Merritt, (4898) W.Stebbings.
17th:
Private: (4915) W.R.Sutton.
20th:
Private: (6013) A.J.Mitchell.
21st:
Lance Corporal: (5573) E.S.Ade.
Private: (5830) A.Goodman.
22nd:
Private: (5903) A.Hunt.
24th:
Private: (4972) B.Waymark.
26th:
Private: (4617) C.A.Hide.
27th:
Private: (4674) S.C.Joyce.

Trench duties at Observatory Ridge continued into April with periods of rest taken at Brandhoek, at Kruisstraat, Ypres, and in canal bank dugouts. Snow fell heavily during the first week of the month and, on one occasion, a sharp-eyed 13th Battalion sentry spotted two men in white overalls leaving the enemy trench. A Battalion sniper was sent out into No-Man's-Land from where he fired, hitting one of the enemy and frightening off the other. On the 4th, German rifle grenades fell along the 13th Battalion front. Second Lieutenant H.C.Keogh decided to direct retaliatory fire by viewing from the fire step but he had been in position only a few minutes when he was shot through the head and killed by an enemy sniper. All three Battalions were back at Poperinghe by the end of the month and, on the 1st May, they all travelled by train to St.Omer.

APRIL:
1st:
Private: (5829) C.E.Goodfellow
2nd:
Private: (6113) F.Roberts.
3rd:
Private: (5769) W.Edwards.
4th:
Second Lieutenant: (5948) H.C.Keogh.
Lance Corporal: (6098) C.Ratcliff.
13th:
Captain: (5133) C.R.Cox.
Privates: (5029) C.E.Bagley, (5369) L.J.Martin, (6008) H.Merrydew.
18th:
Second Lieutenant: (6099) L.K.Rayner.
Private: (5189) B.J.Finbow.
19th:
Private: (5054) A.H.Bingham.
22nd:
Lance Corporal: (4789) T.Paige.
Private: (4649) H.Hulme.
23rd:
Private: (5355) B.H.W.Long.
26th:
Private: (5195) H.Fletcher.
30th:
Private: (6097) J.W.R.Ransley.

Within a few miles of St.Omer, around the villages of Hallines, Wizernes and Zudausques, Lowther's Lambs spent virtually the whole of May training with the emphasis, optimistically, on preparation for 'open warfare'. This was the period when the British were getting ready for Field Marshal Haig's over-enthusiastic attempt to break out from the confines of the Ypres Salient.

Only on the very last day of the month did the three Battalions return to the line north of Ypres.

MAY:
29th:
Lance Corporal: (5971) R.C.Lightfoot.
Private: (5109) W.Chapman.

Canal bank dugouts and Hill Top Farm were familiar places during early June. To the rear, Ypres was bombarded frequently with gas and incendiary shells. The Battle of Messines Ridge, one of the most successful British offensives of the war, began early on the 7th and, although Lowther's Lambs took no part other than with efforts at deception, the explosion of many mines away to the south were clearly heard. Next day, a Field General Court Martial found Second Lieutenant W.R.Botting guilty of an unrecorded misdemeanour and sentenced him to be 'severely censured'; he was destined to be killed-in-action on the 25th September that same year. Two of his officer colleagues were wounded while leading night-time working parties on the 11th and 13th June. First, Second Lieutenant R.M.Herron was hit and evacuated to No.2 Canadian Casualty Clearing Station at Poperinghe but died there the following day. Second, a shell exploded in front of Captain A.C.Taylor as he was leading his men back from their night's work. He, too, was evacuated to No.2 C.C.C.S. where his lower leg had to be amputated but he survived. These formed a portion of the steady trickle of casualties sustained by all three Battalions during June.

JUNE:
2nd:
Private: (5336) E.Larkin.
3rd:
Privates: (4427) G.A.F.Chuter, (4702) C.Lee, (6217) P.Taylor.
4th:
Corporal: (4762) F.A.Munnion.
5th:
Privates: (5598) A.J.Barnes, (4785) A.J.Packham.
7th:
Captain: (4856) D.C.Rutter.
9th:
Privates: (5916) F.E.Jakes, (6089) C.E.Pratt.
10th:
Private: (5569) T.H.L.Wyatt.

11th:
Private: (4350) P.Bish.
12th:
Second Lieutenants: (5873) R.M.Herron, (5465) F.W.Sheppard.
14th:
Privates: (5761) J.M.Dunning, (5166) E.J.Ellinor.
15th:
Company Sergeant Major: (4700) C.H.Lawson.
Private: (6294) G.F.Wells.
16th:
Privates: (4632) A.E.Holden, (6101) A.E.V.Read.
17th:
Privates: (5583) H.W.Attwater, (5763) A.Dyer, (6276) J.Wallis.
18th:
Private: (5698) C.H.Chapman.
19th:
Privates: (5966) W.Leach, (6246) F.Trower.
20th:
Private: (5928) N.Jillett.

Lowther's Lambs were destined next to return to the training grounds around St.Omer.

This time, on the 21st (11th and 13th Bns.) and 23rd June (12th Bn.), they travelled by train from Poperinghe to Watten and marched to the twin villages of Houlle (11th and 13th Bns.) and Moulle (12th Bn.). There they remained for almost a month undergoing intensive training of all kinds especially in 'The Attack' and 'Covering Fire in the Attack'. All this, again, was in preparation for the coming Ypres offensive.

JUNE:
21st:
Private: (5775) H.E.Ellis.
22nd:
Privates: (5607) H.J.Bastings, (6166) A.Snoxell.
28th:
Privates: (4338) G.H.Beale, (5243) A.Harding.
29th:
Sergeant: (6158) H.Smith.
Private: (5828) F.Goodasan.

CHAPTER 36
1917
JULY – DECEMBER

It was not until the 16th July that everyone returned by train to Poperinghe and marched into camp. Evidently the Germans were aware of British preparations because almost daily shelling, including gas, was received in the back areas. For the whole of one night, the noise was heard of shells exploding at a British dump set alight near Vlamertinghe. Towards the end of the month, extra bombs and small arms ammunition were drawn by all participating troops. As 'Z' Day drew near, a number of conferences were held for officers and N.C.O's to discuss final tactics. Lowther's Lambs moved up to their assembly trenches on the evening of the 28th July beneath the incessant British artillery barrage. Meals and hot tea were provided. Casualties had been taken already, particularly amongst 11th Battalion men.

JULY:
16th:
Private: (6224) W.H.Theoff.
20th:
Company Sergeant Major: (5622) W.H.Bignell.
Private: (4881) J.A.Smith.
22nd:
Privates: (4467) H.H.Davies, (5937) C.Julius.
23rd:
Privates: (5123) G.H.Coote, (6275) H.J.W.Waller.
24th:
Second Lieutenant: (5192) W.F.Fisher.
Lance Sergeant: (5053) T.H.Best.
Corporal: (5151) L.A.Davis.
Privates: (5321) T.King, (5554) W.E.Wickens.
25th:
Second Lieutenant: (5101) J.R.Carne.
Private: (4341) F.Bennett.
28th:
Privates: (4331) J.Barnes, (5436) A.Reed.
29th:
Corporals: (4417) G.Chamberlain, (4819) G.W.Porter.

Lance Corporals: (4795) C.F.Paul, (4944) J.Turner.
Privates: (4422) R.J.Charlish, (4549) H.W.Gibson, (4738) A.Millar, (4755) W.L.Moody, (4845) E.R.Roberts.

At 3.50am on the 31st July, with Lowther's Lambs in the forefront, began the Third Battle of Ypres, otherwise known as Passchendaele. The three Battalions went 'over the top' together from their front line assembly positions just to the right of Hill Top Farm about two miles north-north-east from the centre of Ypres. They headed north-east and soon took their objective 'Yellow', 'Red' and 'Blue' lines with relatively few casualties. However, resistance increased from enemy shell, trench mortar, machine gun and rifle fire, and losses multiplied. Despite this, the 13th Battalion had taken the village of St.Julien by 8.00am and consolidation on the 'Dotted Green Line' had been effected. The whole 39th Division assault had been successful on the first day and no enemy counter-attacks were made.

As the battle commenced, the rains came and continued, persistent in heavy downpours. The heaviest allied bombardment of the war to date quickly destroyed every semblance of the frail land drainage system and the whole battle area began to flood and disappear into an enormous, unimaginable quagmire. Edmund Blunden described how Company Headquarters was '. . . now under waterproof sheets stretched over shell holes, swiftly becoming swimming baths.'

Death came in many forms, bizarre and sudden. Edmund Blunden witnessed the death of a runner, Private A.Rackley: '. . . just as he set out . . . intercepted by a shrapnel bullet he fell on one knee, and his outstretched hand still clutched his message.' At another time a large shell penetrated 13th Battalion Headquarters killing and wounding 30 personnel.

JULY:

31st:

Second Lieutenants: (5580) B.J.W.Andrews, (5721) W.J.Colyer

Company Sergeant Major: (5145) A.E.Daniels.

Sergeants: (5248) H.A.Harper, (5464) C.Shelton.

Corporal: (5020) S.J.Apted.

Lance Corporals: (4307) R.Austin, (5586) B.G.Ayling, (4349) G.Bird, (4351) A.C.Bishop, (5660) R.W.Brown, (4453) W.G.Court, (5149) E.Davis, (5750) H.Dodd, (5837) C.Green, (5233) A.J.W.Groves, (4621) F.T.Hillary, (5380) A.Mills, (4790) V.A.Pannell, (5457) E.Scott, (6215) P.Tate, (6252) G.Turner, (4950) J.H.Vane, (4969) H.G.Waters, (6296) F.L.West.

Privates: (4286) J.Abbott, (5011) G.W.Adlard, (5036) C.J.Barnes, (5039) M.W.Barnet, (5041) A.W.Barton, (4335) C.H.Battersby, (5050) R.Bennett, (5659) F.A.Brown, (4387) W.Budd, (5668) W.Burchell, (5681) L.Cantor, (5685) J.E.Carter, (5690) M.Cass, (5115) H.G.Clibbon, (4440) W.Collins, (5144) J.T.Cunnington, (5753) H.E.Downes, (5784) C.W.Finch, (4532) J.H.Francis, (5205) A.Franklin, (4539) G.Froud, (5209) W.O.Fry, (5807) E.Gander, (5235) T.Gunn, (5854) E.Hardy, (5868) R.Helyer, (5869) A.T.Hendley, (5266) E.J.Herbert, (4616) A.Hercock, (5271) C.R.Hilton, (5884) A.Hodghton, (5894) A.W.Honour, (5287) W.C.Hoy, (4650) A.Hunt, (5293) P.A.Hurford, (5915) T.H.Jackson, (5942) C.Kemp, (5944) W.Kendall, (5316) A.J.Kewell, (5333) A.Large, (5335) C.Larkin, (5354) W.H.C.Lockwood, (5976) F.Long, (5980) P.F.Luget, (5981) G.C.Lusted, (5362) T.Mangan, (5997) G.A.Maslen, (5998) G.H.J.Maslin, (5384) C.W.G.Mitchell, (4753) J.A.Mockford, (6017) G.Morris, (5390) S.H.Munn, (4765) H.E.Muster, (6024) D.G.Newton, (5400) A.J.Oram, (5404) C.J.Paine, (4809) A.J.Phillips, (4823) S.Powdrill, (4827) S.E.Proctor, (4830) A.Rackley, (6102) H.A.Redman, (4837) G.E.Rhodes, (6118) E.Rode, (5452) C.Saunders, (6133) A.Scaife, (5467) G.C.Shrivell, (6148) L.W.Skilton, (4877) C.Smith, (6155) C.S.Smith, (6156) E.H.Smith, (5480) G.Smith, (6167) A.C.Soan, (6175) A.B.Squires, (4901) H.Sterk, (6186) C.E.Stevenson, (5498) J.Stevenson, (4907) R.S.Stock, (4908) J.Stone, (6218) W.Taylor, (5532) T.W.Verrall, (6263) R.Vigar, (6287) W.H.Watts, (6298) L.West, M.M., (6312) F.Willis, (5562) E.J.Wiltshire, (6329) A.Wright.

AUGUST:

1st:

Captain: (5359) R.B.Lupton.

Second Lieutenant: (5503) G.C.Syminton.

Corporal: (4709) R.W.Lower.

Lance Corporals: (4316) W.Baldwin, (5645) W.H.C.Bradbrook, (4812) H.F.G.Pigott, (6271) W.H.Waldron, M.M..

Privates: (4293) J.Allen, (5621) F.F.Berry, (5627) A.E.Bishop, (5634) A.P.Blann, (5754) C.L.Dudley, (5289) A.E.Hudson, (5901) V.Human, (5306) A.G.Jenkins, (5927) E.Jewell, (5952) E.H.King, (4829) A.Putland, (6206) L.T.Surridge, (6264) E.Vine.

2nd:

Sergeant: (6305) W.White.

Corporal: (5593) A.W.Ball.

Lance Corporals: (5718) T.Coles, (5481) H.Smith.

Privates: (5592) W.Baker, (5079) A.E.Breach, (5792) A.Flitney, (5814) A.H.Gibbons, (4581) J.O.Guildford, (5847) S.W.Hall, (5895) W.Hook, (4708) E.Long, (5989) F.Marchant, (6029) J.T.Nuttall, (6035) E.B.Orpin, (4799) T.Peck, (6070) G.B.Philpott, (4868) H.Sengelow, (4871) A.A.Simmons, (4887) H.T.Snow, (6194) J.T.N.Stokes, (4921) E.Tatnell, (6301) F.E.White.

Welcome relief came to Lowther's Lambs on the 3rd August allowing them to move back from the dreadful scene of fighting to the familiar canal bank dugouts for much-needed rest. From there they travelled by train to Poperinghe where they marched into the relative luxury of camp. They were still technically within reach of enemy long range guns so 'real' rest and relaxation was not theirs until the 8th when they moved by train from Hopoutre to Caestre and then by bus to completely safe billets at Meteren some 15 miles south-west from the recent theatre of fighting. The four days spent in relaxation at Meteren was the first time in a long while that the whole 39th Division had been together. During the evenings the whole Meteren area was thronged with officers and men of every Unit and with the bands of several battalions playing enthusiastically in the streets and outside Divisional Headquarters. The Battalions were inspected by General Sir H.Plumer, Officer Commanding the 2nd Army, who congratulated them on their recent fine work in the line.

AUGUST:

3rd:

Privates: (4312) H.Backshall, (5242) E.Hanmore, (5348) T.Light, (6022) W.Newnham.

4th:

Lance Corporal: (5815) A.Gibson, M.M.

Privates: (4642) G.Howard, (6149) T.V.Skinner.

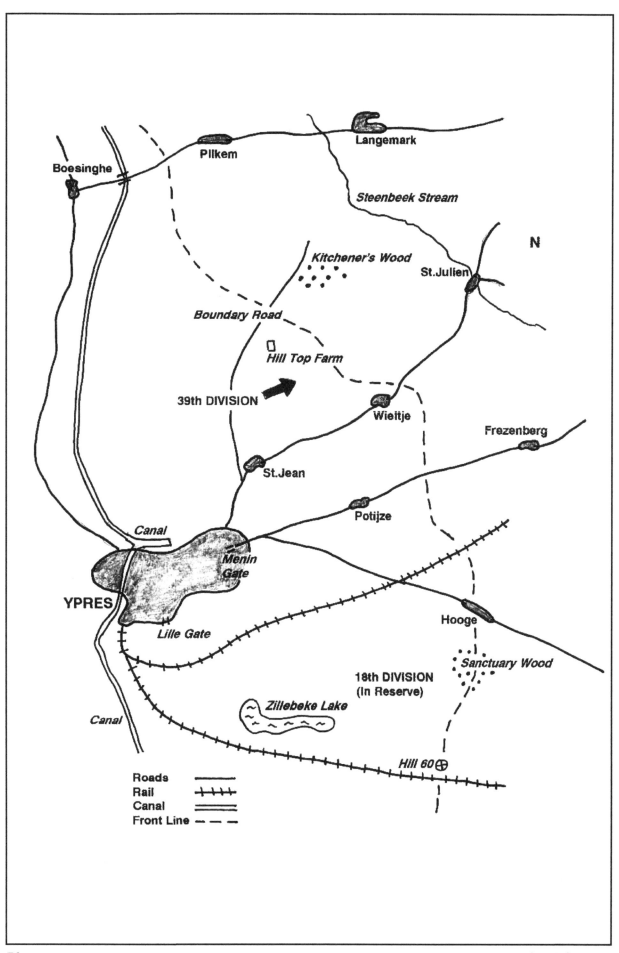

Boesinghe

Pilkem

Langemark

Steenbeek Stream

N

Kitchener's Wood

St.Julien

Boundary Road

Hill Top Farm

39th DIVISION

Wieltje

Frezenberg

St.Jean

Potijze

Canal

*Menin
Gate*

YPRES

Hooge

Lille Gate

Sanctuary Wood

18th DIVISION
(In Reserve)

Zillebeke Lake

Canal

Hill 60 ⊕

Roads
Rail
Canal
Front Line

5th:
Private: (6208) T.Swain.
6th:
Privates: (5366) R.J.Marsh, (4758) T.Mordle.

The days of relaxation passed all too quickly and a return towards the battle area, this time south-east of Ypres at Hollebeke, was made on the 12th August. The following night the enemy fired many shells, including gas, into the vicinity and almost everybody was affected to some extent and felt unwell due to the effects of gas. On the 14th a way was reconnoitred for bringing rations and water up to the line. Three succeeding nights were spent by parties of up to 100 men in preparing this mule track for use. The latter half of August was relatively quiet owing to the appalling ground conditions suffered by both sides. The artillery remained in action, however, causing disturbance, worry and occasional casualties. There was also some enemy aerial activity and Lewis Guns were mounted for anti-aircraft defence. The final three days of the month were very windy but this had the advantage of drying the ground considerably.

AUGUST:
13th:
Privates: (5579) N.B.Allery, (5581) H.W.Asbrey, (5014) F.Mc.N.Alesworth, (4408) W.F.Byford.
14th:
Lance Corporal: (4934) T.Thurtle.
Privates: (5641) F.E.Boulton, (4768) F.Nelson, (4959) A.Waller, (4962) W.Walpole.
15th:
Sergeant: (4943) E.E.Turner.
Corporals: (4506) F.Elms, (4960) H.Waller.
Private: (6003) T.Medhurst.
16th:
Private: (4323) H.G.Barker.
17th:
Second Lieutenant: (4325) C.A.Barlow.
Privates: (4358) J.G.W.Bonser, (4777) J.Nobbs, (4794) W.Partridge, (5005) A.J.Woolgar.
18th:
Second Lieutenant: (5693) J.E.G.Chaize.
22nd:
Private: (4327) A.Barnes.
27th:
Lance Corporal: (4724) S.J.Maugham.
28th:
Corporals: (5820) W.J.Glossop, (5567) C.Wright.

The three Battalions took their accustomed turns at rest, on working parties and in the line during the first part of September. Their sector of line was about Voormezele and Zwarteleen near the much-fought-over Hill 60. Rest periods were disturbed during some nights by haphazard bombing from enemy aircraft. On the 9th, while in the line at Shrewsbury Forest, the 13th Battalion launched an evening raid led by Second Lieutenant S.E.Knott, against two enemy dugouts. The Germans quickly vacated the dugouts and moved back to rear trenches. After holding the gained position for a while against enemy trench mortars and bombs, the raiding party had to retire without blowing up the dugouts because the Royal Engineer men with guncotton failed to arrive. This failure of planning or execution resulted in the death of Second Lieutenant Knott who was killed during the raid. During these days, 11th Battalion men found working parties to carry materials and rations for specialist tunnel digging Companies.

Similar working groups from the 12th Battalion spent their time at telephone cable burying, often a difficult and filthy task in the swamp-like conditions.

SEPTEMBER:
1st:
Private: (5365) F.C.Maple.
8th:
Private: (4517) H.J.Feist.
9th:
Second Lieutenant: (6027) S.E.Knott.

The 13th Battalion was inconvenienced by large quantities of mustard gas delivered by enemy shells on the 12th September; ten gassed men had to be evacuated. On the 18th, as one of the small advance parties from 11th Battalion Headquarters moved out on being relieved, a shell dropped amongst the group killing seven men. It was the turn of the 12th Battalion to become involved on the 20th, supporting and carrying materials during an attack by the 'sister' Infantry Brigade, the 117th.

SEPTEMBER:
16th:
Private: (5236) H.S.Guttridge.
17th:
Private: (6161) M.Smith.

18th:
Sergeants: (4420) H.J.Chandler, (4432) H.Clifford.
Lance Corporal: (4582) D.F.Gumbrill.
Privates: (4531) J.H.Clements, (4534) W.Francis, (4750) W.J.Mitchell, (4957) A.Walker.
20th:
Sergeant: (5423) C.E.Plank.
Privates: (5085) E.Brook, (5262) J.Heather, (5330) R.Lanceley, (5479) F.W.Smith, (5489) W.G.Southon, (5518) E.V.Townsend, (4418) R.Chambers

By the 24th September all three Battalions were in the line south of the Menin Road. During the early morning of the 25th the enemy launched an attack on a wide front. Shelling was very heavy and many casualties were sustained. A counter attack by the 11th, supported by the 12th Battalion, led by Captain Clarke, cleared the enemy from the Battalions' front and a dugout on the road.

The following day Lowther's Lambs launched their own combined attack and all limited objectives were taken. German heavy shelling had been almost continuous during this period and casualties were many amongst all Battalions.

SEPTEMBER:
21st:
Lance Corporal: (5094) C.E.Burt.
Privates: (4448) W.H.Cork, (5255) G.Hawkins.
23rd:
Corporal: (5435) J.H.Reading.
Lance Corporal: (5161) R.Dover.
Privates: (5165) F.G.Edwards, (5171) G.Essam, (5213) W.T.Gadd, (4556) L.Glover, (5226) F.L.Graysmark, (4731) P.Mepham, (5398) A.W.Odell, (6295) A.R.West.
24th:
Second Lieutenant: (4767) H.C.Naylor.
Sergeant: (4633) F.G.Holland.
Corporals: (4654) H.Ide, (4701) T.F.Leary.
Lance Corporals: (4554) G.E.Glinister, (4900) H.Stenning.
Privates: (4297) C.S.Amy, (4318) A.E.Banfield, (4333) L.B.Barrell, (4339) L.H.Beeley, (5647) W.Braybon, (4430) E.V.Claydon, (5116) E.V.Clissold, (5720) R.Collins, (4520) G.H.Field, (5786) H.A.Fish, (4548) C.T.George, (4563) H.Gower, (5938) J.Juniper, (4678) H.Jupp, (5956) J.Knight, (5353) G.W.Little, (4763) P.J.Murray, (6038) C.F.Owen, (6057) G.J.H.Pearce, (6111) U.C.Ridley, (4863) A.Scales, (6183) J.Stepney, (5511) W.Tester,

(6256) P.C.Upfold, (4974) G.V.Webster, (6310) F.T.Williams, (5560) A.Wilson.
25th:
Second Lieutenant: (4364) W.R.Botting.
Company Sergeant Majors; (5351) A.W.Linford, M.M., (4926) A.C.Terry.
Sergeants: (5139) C.Crowe, (5360) H.J.Lyons, (5437) A.F.Reed, (4882) N.L.G.Smith.
Lance Sergeant: (5381) G.A.Mills.
Corporals: (5193) D.Fitzpatrick, (5349) E.Lindeman, (4836) H.H.Renshaw, (4945) P.Turville.
Lance Corporals: (4359) R.W.Bootes, (4406) F.C.Buzwell, (5105) F.Casse, (5281) S.Hooker, (5309) C.W.Jesson, (5325) G.Knee, (5475) H.W.Smart, (4919) E.J.Swatton, (5536) W.Wakeford.
Privates: (4313) W.G.Bacon, (4319) A.H.Barber, (5599) A.Barnett, (5040) L.L.Bartlett, (5092) A.J.Bullen, (5093) C.V.Burden, (4421) J.W.Chapman, (5111) H.V.Chatterley, (5114) P.Claydon, (5148) A.Davey, (5163) C.R.Dudman, (5173) A.J.Everden, (5204) H.H.Francis, (5222) J.Goodwin, (4566) E.Graver, (4572) R.Grevitt, (5232) J.T.Grosse, (5256) S.T.Hayes, (5257) W.Haynes, (5259) J.I.Hayward, (5267) J.B.Hicks, (5291) N.Hull, (5322) W.G.Kingman, (4668) G.A.Johnson, (4681) J.Kemp, (4685) H.O.Knight, (4705) T.Little, (5392) T.O.Newell, (5415) S.G.Pearce, (4808) D.Pettigrew, (5421) G.Piper, (4817) R.J.Plaskitt, (5427) G.H.Pratt, (5430) C.Rae, (5471) H.Skates, (5477) A.Smith, (5478) F.P.Smith, (4899) H.V.Steel, (4930) F.Thomas, (5520) A.F.Tribe, (5529) F.G.Vail, (5546) H.Weller, (5550) B.White, (5570) L.Young.
26th:
Lieutenant: (5959) H.C.Langdale.
Second Lieutenants: (5818) R.G.W.Gillham, (5994) G.J.Martin, (6146) W.G.Sivewright.
Sergeant: (4985) A.Westwood.
Corporal: (5961) T.Lansdell.
Lance Corporals: (5625) A.Binstead, (4503) G.Ellis, (6192) A.J.Stillwell, (6196) H.Stratton, (6250) A.E.Turner.
Privates: (4305) H.Atkinson, M.M., (5626) S.Birt, (4357) F.Boden, (5643) R.Boyd, (5090) H.F.A.Brown, (5675) D.L.Butler, (5679) S.Cann, (4443) T.G.Conway, (5730) P.E.Corkish, (4471) R.Dawson, (4510) W.Evans, (5183) J.Fellowes, (4555) C.Glitheroe, (5831) L.Gough, (4571) H.T.Greenwood, (5861) S.A.Haves, (5936) R.W.Joyce, (5945) E.C.Kennard, (5960) A.C.Langford, (5986) W.Male, (6015) A.D.Moore, (4775) T.W.Nichol, (6033) G.H.Oram, (4802) R.Penfold, (6112) C.V.Roberts, (6126) J.Rowland, (6182) W.Stenning, (4903) F.Stevens, (4918)

J.R.Swan, (4920) W.Tait, (6255) J.B.Tyler,
(6290) F.Welch, (4978) S.T.G.Welling, (4986)
G.R.Wheatley, (5557) W.H.Wilkins, (6314)
G.W.Wilsher, (4999) A.Wood.
27th:
Captain: (4546) J.H.C.Gatchell.
Sergeants: (5725) R.D.Cooper, (6107) C.J.Richards.
Corporal: (4606) W.Harvey.
Lance Corporals: (4607) A.G.Haslett, (5943)
G.E.Kemp, (5496) A.Steels, (6237) S.Toogood, M.M.,
(4953) H.Vigor, (6300) C.R.White.
Privates: (4287) P.A.Adams, (5576) F.W.Alaway,
(5044) G.W.Baylis, (5051) W.H.Berry, (5624)
M.Bingham, (5663) H.A.Buckenham, (4396)
W.Burles, (5695) G.L.Challacombe, (5722)
E.E.Cook, (5735) H.E.Cudlipp, (4519) A.G.Field,
(4597) H.Harding, (5261) G.F.Heather, (5887)
A.Hole, (5890) S.Holman, (5899) G.Huggett, (4661)
A.E.James, (5919) W.F.James, (5939) D.T.Keat,
(5967) H.Lee, (6006) A.E.Meredith, (4797) J.Peach,
(6080) W.H.Plummer, (6087) A.Potter, (4825)
B.Price, (6125) E.Rowland, (6134) G.A.Scobell,
(6135) G.H.J.Scott, (6164) W.H.Smith, (4893)
H.A.Stacey, (6177) A.J.Standingford, (6232)
R.G.Tite, (6234) R.G.Todd, (6235) F.H.Tolhurst,
(6240) P.W.Toy, (6248) F.T.Tunstall, (4941)
C.W.Turbard, (4956) G.H.Vousden, (6286) W.Watts,
(6306) F.R.Whiteway.
28th:
Privates: (6115) G.Robinson, (6261) G.E.Verney,
(5541) G.A.Walton.

The 2nd October was the day for a parade and inspection by the General Officer Commanding 39th Division during which he presented decorations awarded to individuals for the 31st July operations at St.Julien, the most significant medal being the D.S.O. for Lt.Col. W.C.Millward commanding the 11th Battalion. The following two weeks were relatively quiet due, in part, to the continuing bad ground conditions. This was a time for which, later, Field Marshal Sir Douglas Haig was severely criticised for prolonging the Passchendaele battle and losing so many lives long after the original hope of a breakthrough had been shattered.

OCTOBER:
3rd:
Privates: (4714) F.S.Maidment, (4821) C.Potter.
4th:
Private: (5724) G.Cooper.

5th:
Sergeant: (5733) R.J.Crook.
9th:
Second Lieutenant: (6168) G.F.Sogno.
15th:
Lance Corporal: (5577) F.J.Allen.
Privates: (5729) A.Coote, (5745) G.L.Dedman, (5798)
F.Francis, (5973) P.F.Linfield, (6123) C.L.Roker.

By mid-October Lowther's Lambs were back in the relative security of Canada Street Tunnels at Zillebeke. From there, training, recreation and baths were organised. A three-day period was spent by the 13th Battalion in repairing trenches and in burials both of telephone cables and the dead. Before the end of the month all three Battalions had moved farther back, beyond Kemmel and Locre, to a camp of hutments and tents. Leave was approved at the low rate of four men per day which at least meant that the last men who had been granted no home leave since the Battalions arrived in France almost 20 months previously, were able to set out, thankfully and joyfully, for a break in England.

OCTOBER:
17th:
Privates: (5343) L.Lee, (5373) S.P.Matthews.
18th:
Lance Corporal: (5530) E.Veness.
Privates: (5924) A.E.Jenner, (5953) W.King, (6119)
E.Rodell, (6193) S.F.Stockwell, (6284) T.E.Watts,
(6328) E.Wrathmall.
19th:
Lance Corporal: (6245) C.E.Trott.
Privates: (4353) B.J.Blaber, (5632) F.Blackman.
20th:
Private: (5196) R.C.Fletcher.
21st:
Private: (5766) M.Easton.
22nd:
Privates: (5188) W.G.Figg, (5401) G.Osborne.
23rd:
Private: (5323) W.H.Kirby.
24th:
Private: (5744) S.J.Dear.
26th:
Private: (5030) A.H.Bailey.
29th:
Private: (5377) G.E.Message.
31st:
Privates: (4592) A.H.Hall, (4947) J.Unsworth.

By the end of the first week of November Lowther's Lambs were back in the line south of the Menin Road. The 11th Battalion provided a smoke barrage to mask the western side of Gheluvelt on the 6th in support of a general attack on the village of Passchendaele. Enemy shelling had been consistently heavy over this period, in the circumstances of which, casualties were remarkably light.

The weather was wet again and ground conditions dreadful. Thus, Lowther's Lambs were pleased to move out of the quagmire area for a period. They still had to provide working parties for various tasks but they were at least out of the direct firing line for the most part. However, the 13th Battalion was required to undertake a spell in the line and, while there on the 21st, they were raided by Germans in six pairs. Only two of the enemy managed to enter the British line and, for their pains, they were promptly taken prisoner. While out 'at rest' the same Battalion was made to send working parties into Ypres on the 30th but, the railway being so badly damaged, the delays were such that the men arrived too late to do any work and returned whence they came.

NOVEMBER:
2nd:
Private: (4320) A.J.Barber.
5th:
Private: (6331) J.Wright.
6th:
Lance Corporal: (5920) L.Jarvis.
Privates: (4716) T.B.March, (6109) A.A.Richardson, (4876) A.Smith, (4884) A.Smithers, (5008) E.C.Xerxes.
7th:
Second Lieutenant: (4605) G.L.G.Harrison.
Company Sergeant Major: (4917) G.W.Swain.
Corporal: (4404) W.M.P.Burton.
Private: (4683) W.W.Kent.
11th:
Private: (6200) H.J.Stride.
14th:
Major: (5604) C.Bartlett.
Lance Corporal: (5184) A.R.Felton.
Private: (5340) P.Lea.
15th:
Second Lieutenant: (4468) S.F.Davies.
20th:
Private: (5568) O.Wright.

21st:
Private: (5834) F.C.Gray.
23rd:
Lance Corporal: (5218) W.G.Gillham.
Privates: (5082) J.S.Bridgwater, (5292) W.Humphrey.
24th:
Private: (6074) A.Pierce.
28th:
Private: (4442) G.F.H.Colwell.

December began with parties of men working between Ypres and Potijze, mainly on road and camp improvements. Enemy planes dropped bombs on the 6th, one of which landed between 11th Battalion tents killing six men and wounding ten, of whom four died later. General duties of a pioneering nature continued as the weather turned much colder and the first snow of winter fell. Occasionally, enemy shelling caused work to be suspended and, on several more occasions, German planes dropped bombs nearby.

A move by all three Battalions brought them to St.Jean station on the 8th. From there, a train journey of an hour or so took them to Godewaersvelde, then they marched to billets in the area of Steenvoorde. New drafts of men arrived, 25 for the 11th Battalion and 33 for the 13th Battalion. Snow continued to fall as training and firing on the ranges got into full swing interspersed with various sports activities.

Intensive training continued right up to Christmas Eve. After Church Parade, Christmas Day was free with festive dinners and a concert being enjoyed. Time was also found for a morning football match between the officers and sergeants. Snow fell so heavily later in the day and through the night that organised snowball fights took place on Boxing Day afternoon. For several days thereafter the conditions of snow and ice made marching very difficult and hazardous. An attempt to move out by transport had to be abandoned because the vehicles could not cope with the conditions. However, by the 30th, movement was again possible and Lowther's Lambs travelled by train from Wizernes to Elverdinghe. Marching was still difficult and tiring and the transport, which had set out early, did not arrive until after midnight.

DECEMBER:

6th:

Privates: (4348) F.Billingham, (4376) H.C.Brooks, (1180) R.Divall, (1551) A.A.Gillam, (4552) E.R.Gilmore, (4553) J.Gleeson, (4859) S.D.Sands.

7th:

Lance Corporal: (5308) F.Jennings.

Privates: (4328) C.H.Barnes, (4419) F.Chandler, M.M., (4671) W.H.Jones.

10th: Private: (4409) F.Calder.

CHAPTER 37
1918
JANUARY – AUGUST

The New Year began frosty and with a very cold wind. Training was continued with outside activities aimed at keeping the men warm. Spirits were raised with indoor sports, the 11th Battalion winning six out of seven final bouts of the Boxing Tournament. By mid-January the familiar Irish Farm and Hill Top Farm were working areas again with particular attention being given to strengthening defences along the Steenbeek stream. A gale force wind and torrential rain storm on the 15th caused great difficulties for the 13th Battalion which was attempting to reach front line posts. Their crossing of usually small Paddebeek was hazardous. The stream was so flooded and in such spate that, during the difficult crossing, many men were swept off their feet and had to be helped from the freezing water by colleagues. Every man arrived at the destination drenched through and knee-deep in the quagmire. Everyone became exhausted over the five days tour of duty and, relief, on the 8th, was never more welcomed. As a result of the sodden conditions the problem of trench feet became serious; no less than 106 of the 13th Battalion men were evacuated 'sick' and unfit for duty.

JANUARY:
9th:
Privates: (5671) J.T.Burling, (5146) G.H.Daniels, (5402) G.Oxdale.
13th:
Private: (6222) H.Teesdale.
16th
Private: (5833) H.T.Grant.
18th:
Lance Corporal: (6001) A.J.Masser.
Private: (5200) F.D.Forde.
21st:
Privates: (5056) H.Bishop, (5264) E.J.Henden, (5285) G.Howe, (5418) L.R.Phillips, (5469) H.A.Simpson.

Having been engaged in and around Ypres for more than a year, with the exception of brief rest and training periods, Lowther's Lambs marched to Proven station on the 26th January for a protracted 13 hours train journey south and back to the area of the Somme battlefields. A welcome stop of 45 minutes was made during the journey when mugs of steaming hot tea were provided for the weary and uncomfortable travellers. Méricourt L'Abbé, east of Amiens, was the destination and the troops were glad of the change from the almost totally quagmired Ypres Salient. They did not know, at that stage, that the enemy, having withdrawn voluntarily east to the Hindenburg Line some 11 month earlier, were preparing to launch a major new offensive aimed at taking Amiens and breaking through to the channel ports. It was to help block that coming threat that Lowther's Lambs had been moved south. All three Battalions marched to Corbie on the 30th and travelled eastward from there to the town of Péronne. From Péronne they marched north to the hamlet of Haut Allaines and to accommodation in tents in bright, sunny but cold weather.

JANUARY:
29th:
Private: (4367) J.W.Bowman.

An interesting journey by battlefield light railway brought them, with some final marching, to the front line trenches facing the enemy's formidable Hindenburg Line on the 1st February. Much work was being done on the British defences which would have to withstand the first onslaught from German forces and all Battalions did their share.

A very sad day befell the Regiment on the 6th February when the 12th Battalion was disbanded. As a result of overall British troop

losses and a reluctance of the Prime Minister
to authorise the level of reinforcements
requested for the Western Front, the army was
re-organised by the reduction of brigades from
four to three battalions. Officers and men of the
many battalions chosen for disbandment were
scattered far and wide amongst remaining Units.
Fortunately for the 12th Battalion, almost all its
personnel were transferred to Units with The
Royal Sussex Regiment, namely the 7th, 8th,
9th, 11th and 13th Battalions. A bitter final blow
befell the 12th Battalion on the 16th when the
Transport, bombed from the air, had 19 faithful
horses killed and eight wounded. On the 22nd,
Lieutenant Edmund Blunden, M.C., whose varied
duties with the 11th Battalion since May, 1916,
had caused him much strain and stress, departed
for six months' rest and lighter duties in England.
The 11th and 13th Battalions continued with
duties in and out of the line around Revelon Farm
as this cold, snowy winter month drew to its
close.

FEBRUARY:
4th:
Private: (5168) H.C.Ellis.
5th:
Private: (4889) F.Spencer.
6th:
Corporal: (6077) J.L.Pitcher.
8th:
Lance Corporal: (6198) C.A.Street.
9th:
Captain: (5528) W.C.S.Uppleby.
Private: (5446) A.Robins.
17th:
Private: (4308) G.J.Avis.
20th:
Corporal: (4304) G.E.Atkins.
21st:
Private: (5174) W.J.Everett.
25th:
Private: (5176) H.St.J.Eyles.
26th:
Lance Corporal: (6030) A.Odell.
Private: (5955) M.J.Kitt.
28th:
Privates: (4584) G.Gunn, (6086) F.E.Porter.

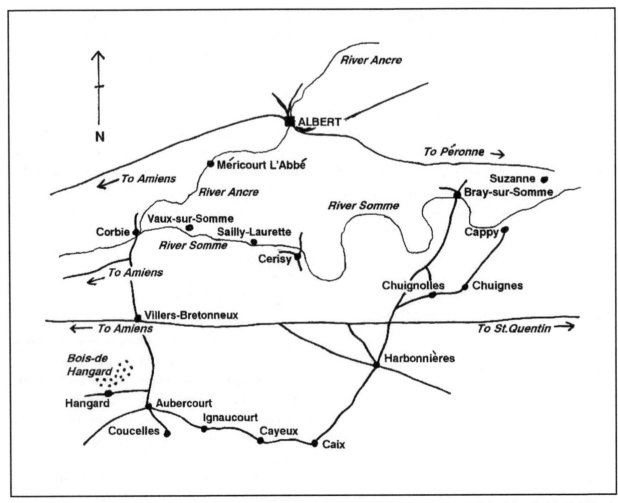

74.   *27th January to 31st March 1918 (West)*

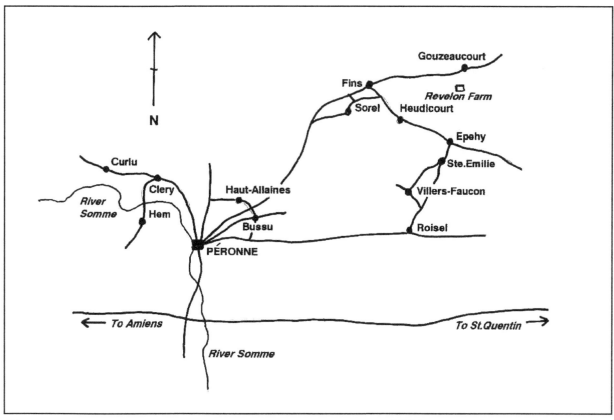

74.   *27th January to 31st March 1918 (East)*

The month of March began with clear, bright days and frost with snow at night. On the 6th, the enemy raided posts on both sides of the 11th Battalion. A certain amount of unease and jittery reaction to the threat of German attack was shown on the 10th when the 11th Battalion 'Stood To' at 4.00am in response to an 'S.O.S.' signal from the front line which later proved to be a false alarm.

MARCH:
3rd:
Captain: (5620) W.H.P.Bennett.
Private: (4602) P.Harmer.
8th:
Corporal: (5968) J.Lee.
Lance Corporal: (5974) C.A.Lisher, M.M.
Private: (5934) B.Jonson.
10th:
Corporals: (6092) A.Privett, (6281) H.E.C.Ward.
Lance Corporals: (5908) G.W.H.Hymus, (6059) J.Penfold.
Privates: (5732) E.Cosham, (5839) F.Green, (5958) J.W.Lane, (4979) J.L.Welsh.
16th:
Private: (6105) W.Reynolds.
19th:
Private: (6048) W.Parks.

On the 20th March, officers and 50 men went to Péronne to attend the military funeral of Brigadier Cape, C.M.G., the 39th Division Artillery Commander who had been killed by enemy shell fire on the 18th. In large part as a result of this senior officer's death, the 11th Battalion's Lieutenant Colonel W.C.Millward was called to Brigade temporarily as Acting Brigadier General.

The Big Crash came early in the misty morning of the 21st March. The German's great 'Spring Offensive' had begun along an extended front. Both the 11th and 13th Battalions were in the rear of the line and, during the day, they were moved forward, the 11th Battalion to Villers Faucon and the 13th Battalion to Ste.Emilie. The full measure of the enemy onslaught was felt on the 22nd when they attacked the 13th Battalion front at 7.00am. Although the attackers were driven back a short distance, the dye was cast with storm troopers infiltrating weak areas and leaving strong points to be cleared by their comrades following behind the initial assault. These new German tactics set the scene as British Units were outflanked forcing those on either side to fall back. 'A' Company and half of 'B' Company of the 13th Battalion were cut off and annihilated or taken prisoner in this way to a total of five officers and 150 other ranks. The 11th Battalion together with the remainder of the 13th Battalion, was quickly caught up in the general retreat which, holding up just short of a rout, was soon organised into a fighting withdrawal with one Unit standing fast, or fighting a rearguard action, while other battalions withdrew through them to take up, in turn, their own temporary stand. In this way, both the 11th and 13th Battalions were swept along in the withdrawal in a generally south-west direction, the 11th standing for a while at Villers-Faucon before falling back to Tincourt Wood on the 22nd.

MARCH:

21st:

Lance Corporals: (5129) R.H.Cosstick, (4543) R.Funnell.

Privates: (4459) W.H.Crouch, (5885) G.Holden, (4686) W.Knight, (4696) R.A.Langrish, (5992) W.J.Marsh, (4766) G.S.Nash, (6046) W.G.Parker, (6065) A.Perry, (6127) W.J.Rowlatt, (4897) D.M.Starkey, (4904) F.Stevens, (4966) J.Ward.

22nd:

Corporal: (4952) H.Verion.

Lance Corporals: (4410) H.J.Carter, (4455) A.G.Cox, (5979) T.Lucas, (4987) W.Whiston.

Privates: (5646) G.B.Branch, (5655) C.Brooks, (5674) H.J.Butcher, (4412) C.C.Castello, (4428) C.R.Circuit, (5708) W.A.Clarke, (5804) W.J.Funnell, (5826) J.Goldsmith, (5832) F.T.Grace, (5251) H.G.Harris, (5984) J.W.L.Mabey, (4828) E.Pusey, (6114) W.J.Roberts, (6117) J.Robinson, (6147) J.H.Skerry, (6230) H.H.Tinley. (4963) H.G.Walters.

The depleted 13th Battalion moved back to make a stand three miles east of Péronne on the 23rd but, because the enemy managed to get round both flanks, a stand was not possible so a withdrawal through the town itself was the only solution. In, and around, Péronne the bridges over the River Somme were held successfully until they could be blown up by sappers. Heavy casualties were again taken by the 13th Battalion.

That day, the 23rd March, the 11th Battalion which, to this point, had taken far less casualties than its sister Battalion, withdrew to high ground north of St.Denis, then to the rear of Mont St.Quentin before moving along the River Somme valley to cross at Buscourt. At 11.00pm

orders were received to re-cross the river at Frise and take up positions at Hem. There, on the next day, a stand was made to allow Units of the Leicestershire Regiment to pass through to the rear. Lieutenant Colonel Millward returned to the 11th Battalion that day when all officers and men collected together at Hérbecourt and then marched to Curlu. So depleted was the 13th Battalion by this time that its remnants were incorporated into a Composite Battalion of the 66th Division until rejoining its own 116th Infantry Brigade on the 26th.

MARCH:

23rd:

Lieutenant: (5875) H.C.Hickman.

Corporal: (6272) E.G.Walker.

Lance Corporals: (5964) H.W.Launder, (6180) W.G.Stebbings, (6316) J.Wilson, (6334) A.Yorke.

Privates: (5608) S.T.Batehup, (5610) R.A.Battle, (5642) W.Bowley, (4372) J.A.Brand, (5667) P.L.Burchell, (5683) F.C.Carter, (5838) E.Green, (5862) R.T.Hawkings, (5918) W.H.James, (5940) H.Keeley, (5949) A.J.Kidd, (5954) J.W.Kirby, (5999) G.S.F.Mason, (6144) F.G.Simpson, (6221) E.A.Teague, (6236) F.Tompkins, (6279) A.Walsh.

24th:

Captain: (5181) W.J.Fast.

Corporal: (4590) J.Haffenden.

Lance Corporals: (5714) E.R.Cobby, (5845) R.Guttridge.

Privates: (5644) J.Boys, (5699) T.Chapman, (5748) H.Diplock, (4712) W.Lumm, (6012) G.A.Millward, (6129) A.T.Saunders, (6253) H.C.Twitchett.

By route march on the 25th, the 11th Battalion withdrew through Suzanne and Cappy to Chuignolles where it re-organised itself. The Battalion stood fast the following day and a further withdrawal was made on the 28th by way of Harbonnieres and Caix to Cayeux where the whole 39th Division concentrated and took up position on the high ground facing enemy-occupied Wiencourt.

MARCH:

25th:

Lieutenant: (5559) P.D.Wilmot.

Lance Sergeant: (6315) E.T.Wilson.

Lance Corporals: (5791) B.Fletcher, (6110) S.J.Richardson.

Privates: (5669) E.G.Burgess, (5734) P.Cross, (5880) J.S.Hiron, (6154) C.F.Smith.

26th:
Second Lieutenants: (4585) A.H.E.Gunner, (4816) E.C.Piper.
Lance Sergeant: (5688) A.W.Cashin.
Privates: (5614) F.J.Behr, (5648) E.Bridger, (4378) C.H.Brown, (5678) A.Camp, (4424) E.E.Cheeseman, (5706) W.J.Clark, (4663) F.Jarman, (4669) A.Jolliffe, (4872) A.Simpson, (6322) L.Wiseman.

The 13th Battalion found, on the 27th March, that the Germans had crossed the Somme at Cérisy, more than a mile to their left rear. The Battalion was ordered to cut off the enemy at that point but arrived too late and, although a counter-attack pushed the Germans back a half mile, lack of ammunition and support forced the Battalion to fall back to a position about one mile east of Lamotte.

MARCH:
27th:
Second Lieutenant: (6220) W.E.E.Taylor.
Privates: (5636) J.Boaks, (4437) W.Coles, (5752) S.Dowling, (6247) F.Tugwell.

Because orders to withdraw were received late by the 13th Battalion on the 28th March, the Germans were almost upon them and a heavy engagement ensued. Only with great difficulties did the Battalion manage to retreat east of Marcelcave. The exhausted troops were able to remain in position there until the next evening.

The 11th Battalion, similarly exhausted, after eight days and nights of almost continual and harassed movement with very little sleep, fell into bivouacs in the wood at Ignaucourt late in the evening of the 28th March and were allowed to rest until dawn.

Next morning it was Good Friday and, as Lieutenant Colonel Millward stood outside his tent shaving, a stray German shell dropped into the wood and he fell severely wounded. His war and his command of the 11th Battalion were over. He was evacuated to a Base Hospital at Rouen where he stayed for eight months after his left leg was amputated.

Later on Good Friday morning, the 11th and 13th Battalions came together along a sunken road near Ignaucourt and south of Courcelles. When a battalion on the right was attacked by the enemy and forced to retire on the 30th, the 11th Battalion formed a defensive flank but

its own position was outflanked by the enemy and withdrawal to a line west of Aubercourt became necessary. Even there, the Battalion was fired upon in enfilade from both sides of the River L'Avre and had to drop back farther to the protection of the Aubercourt – Villers Bretonneux sunken road. The final move that day was rearwards, once more, to high ground in front of the Bois de Hangard. By this time, the 13th Battalion had moved in lorries to billets in Guignicourt.

MARCH:
28th:
Sergeant: (6000) S.R.V.C.Mason.
Privates: (5951) A.E.G.King, (4698) G.Larter.
29th:
Privates: (5972) E.Linfield, (5987) G.Mannering, (4728) F.T.Mead, (4732) A.S.Mercer, (6082) F.E.Pohl, (4824) A.A.Price, (6214) W.Tasker, (6258) T.Veasey, (6332) F.W.G.Yardley.
30th:
Second Lieutenant: (4401) F.Burton.
Lance Corporal: (5601) A.G.Barrett.
Private: (4774) W.A.Newnham.
31st:
Privates: (5629) W.T.Bishop, (4832) G.J.Redman.

April Fools Day was a day of rest for both Battalions and, slowly, it began to be realised that there was a welcome end to the continuous withdrawal of the last ten days and nights. At last, the German 'Spring Offensive' advance across the previously devastated Somme Battlefields and large areas which they themselves had laid waste during their February, 1917, withdrawal to the Hindenburg Line, was halted. With no railways, blown up bridges, very poor and damaged roads, the Germans found it more and more difficult to maintain adequate communications and to supply their fast-advancing troops. Such was the plight of the German economy that food and other necessities for the troops were at a very low and poor level. So when many of the soldiers came across undestroyed British dumps and stores of food, clothing and equipment of quality and quantity, they stopped to indulge themselves. These things, and large quantities of wine found in the town of Albert, persuaded the German rank and file that to take adavantage of such opportunities was preferable to taking further interest in the fighting. All these things, together, resulted in the enemy offensive being brought to a halt by the beginning of April.

It is clear from the 11th Battalion War Diary that the Battalion was finally relieved from active duty relating to the 'Spring Retreat' on the 31st March. However, records show that 50 men were killed in action on the 3rd April; that is certainly incorrect. Almost surely what happened was that, on the 3rd April, the names were recorded of 50 men who had been killed during that period of the German 'Spring Offensive' between 21st and 31st March. No doubt the Battalion, together with its War Diarist, had been so heavily pressed during that time that it had not been possible to keep perfectly accurate records, and so the dates of death for the men concerned were all recorded, incorrectly, as the 3rd April. The known burial cemeteries for some of those 50 men, for example at Ste.Emilie and Roisel, confirm that the men buried there had been killed early in the retreat, probably on the 22nd or 23rd March. The actual dates of death for nine of the 50 men have been established and they are recorded appropriately above; the records of the remaining 41 men follow:

MARCH:
21st – 31st (See paragraph above):
Sergeants: (4301) W.A.Ashford, (4324) L.Barker, M.M., (4805) C.A.Perry.
Lance Sergeant: (4865) C.E.Seall.
Lance Corporals: (4288) A.Ager, (4356) C.H.Blunden, (4647) G.J.Hughes, (4932) A.H.Thompsett, (4990) W.Whitelaw.
Privates: (4294) G.Allin, (4332) T.L.Barnes, (4355) A.C.Blanch, (4369) J.Bradbury, (4380) E.S.Brown, (4402) F.Burton, (4405) G.J.Bushell, (4435) H.E.Cockett, M.M., (4463) C.H.R.Damon, (4479) F.Divall, (4521) W.H.Finney, (4608) A.W.Hawkins, (4623) V.Hills, (4636) W.H.Honey, (4643) S.Howard, (4648) S.R.Hull, (4659) A.H.Jackson, (4660) S.Jacobs, (4693) A.W.H.Langham, (4697) W.Larcombe, (4704) W.A.Lingard, (4743) W.Millham, (4744) F.H.Minns, (4756) F.Moore, (4761) R.Munn, (4778) W.E.H.Nobes, (4784) J.W.Okey, (4811) H.M.Phillips, (4910) A.H.Storkey, (4954) G.Voice, (4968) E.C.Waterman, (5009) H.E.Youell.

Now, so confident were the British that they had stemmed the German tide, that some Units, including Lowther's Lambs, were moved away

from the area. Lowther's Lambs moved by long marches over four consecutive days until, on the 8th April, they arrived at Eu, boarded trains and set off north on a seven hour journey to Arques from where they marched to Tatinghem (11th Bn.) and Tilques (13th Bn.). On the 10th April both Battalions entrained at St.Omer. The recent intensive fighting retreat had reduced the overall strength which, even though the 11th Battalion received a new draft of 20 men, had fallen to six officers and 530 Other Ranks while the 13th Battalion consisted of only 14 officers and 336 Other Ranks. In these circumstances drastic reorganisational action was needed. The 13th Battalion was made up to reasonable strength by absorbing 13 officers and 368 men from the 13th Gloucestershires, which had been the Division's Pioneering Battalion, and by being re-named No.2 Composite Battalion. It was in this new formation that Lowther's Lambs arrived back in Belgium at Poperinghe and marched to camp at Vlamertinghe.

APRIL:
2nd:
Lance Sergeant: (5876) W.J.Hicks.
Privates: (4791) P.Parrott, (6088) L.Pouget.
3rd:
Private: (6311) J.T.Williams.
4th:
Lance Sergeant: (6323) A.V.Wood.
5th:
Lieutenant: (5120) J.S.Collins.
Private: (4675) W.A.Juden.
7th:
Private: (4340) T.W.Belshaw.
8th:
Private: (5851) F.D.Harding.
14th
Privates: (4593) C.W.Hall, (6128) R.W.Russell.
15th:
Privates: (5657) A.Brooman, (5773) H.G.E.Elliott.

During the middle of April enemy artillery and aircraft were very active. On the 16th, the 13th Battalion took part in a counter-attack during which its objectives of two farms and Wytschaete Wood were taken despite the failure of French troops to assist as planned. The 11th Battalion took casualties from enemy shelling on the 23rd, 24th and 25th. Then, on the 26th, both Battalions were hard hit, the 11th while holding up a

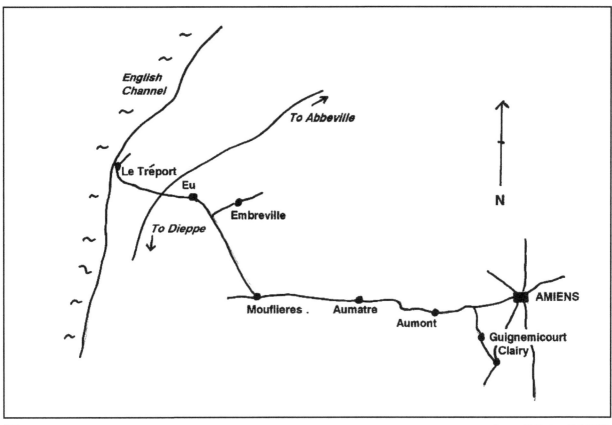

75.   *1st to 9th April 1918*

German attack and themselves counter-attacking later in the day, capturing two prisoners, two machine guns and inflicting many casualties on the enemy. In the mist, which refused to disperse that day, the Germans got into a position only 50 yards away from where they could bring intense machine gun and rifle fire to bear upon 13th Battalion Headquarters. Other Units of the Battalion were prevented, by the mist, from seeing or providing assistance, with the result that many Headquarters personnel became casualties, including the battalion Commander, Lieutenant Colonel H.T.K.Robinson and Regimental Sergeant Major B.A.Stone, D.C.M., both of whom were killed. New colleagues, formerly men from the Gloucestershires, held out gallantly but many became casualties or prisoners. This was the last action of the war for the 13th Battalion which, on the 27th, had been reduced in strength to 8 officers and 150 Other Ranks, of whom only 6 officers and 83 Other Ranks were combatants; these men were incorporated into No.3 Battalion Composite Brigade.

APRIL:
16th:
Second Lieutenant: (5836) C.J.Green.

Lance Corporal: (5762) W.A.Dutnall.
Privates: (5682) J.Carr, (5696) F.Chamberlain, (6028) G.Nurton, (6254) S.G.Tye, (6288) A.E.Weaver.
18th:
Second Lieutenant: (6039) R.S.Oxley.
Corporal: (5921) H.W.Jeffery.
Privates: (5653) A.Brooks, (5770) G.Elgar, (5812) J.Gemmell.
21st:
Privates: (5635) H.E.Blundell, (5821) A.Goacher, (4603) A.A.Harradine, (5877) W.Hill.
22nd:
Private: (6060) E.Percival.
23rd:
Sergeant: (6103) A.H.Reed.
Corporal: (4787) C.A.Page.
Private: (4973) G.Weaver.
24th:
Sergeant: (4559) A.W.Golden, D.C.M., M.M.
Privates: (4814) R.W.Pilsworth, (4842) C.Richardson.
25th:
Lance Corporals: (4334) T.Bassett, (5004) J.C.Woods.
Privates: (5751) J.F.Dorling, (4574) R.Grimes, (4796) T.P.Paynter.
26th:
Lieutenant Colonel: (6116) H.T.K.Robinson.
Regimental Sergeant Major: (6195) B.A.Stone, D.C.M.
Sergeant: (5904) H.D.Hunter.

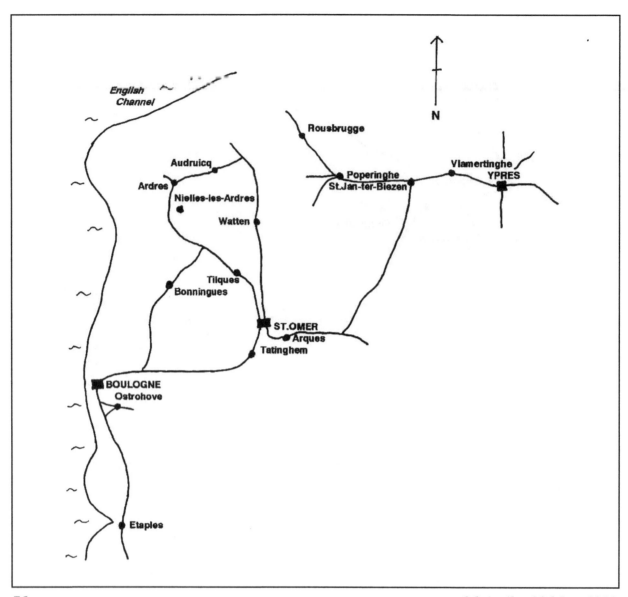

76.

Corporal: (5595) M.E.Banfield.

Lance Corporals: (5787) A.C.Fitch, (4604) E.J.Harris, (4653) J.Hutchison, (6201) G.S.Stringer.

Privates: (5656) W.G.Brooks, (5737) J.G.Cumbers, (5741) C.R.Daniels, (5767) F.E.Ede, (5796) P.T.Foster, (4622) J.E.Hillier, (5888) A.H.Hole, (5896) G.F.V.Hooper, (4772) C.Newick, (6025) L.A.Norman, (4793) H.Partridge, (6076) W.Piercy, (6157) G.S.Smith, (6178) R.G.Staplehurst, (6185) G.W.Stevens, (6191) W.G.Still, (6199) J.V.Streeter, (6231) E.Tite, (6257) W.Vansittart, (6262) S.E.Vick.

27th:

Sergeant: (4614) A.W.Heise, M.M.

Corporal: (4383) E.C.Browne.

Lance Corporal: (4393) F.B.Burgess.

Privates: (4757) G.W.Moore, (6283) R.K.Ware, (4997) C.H.Winter.

28th:

Sergeant: (4992) A.H.Wileman, M.M.

Private: (4515) C.R.Faulkner.

The 11th Battalion remained in position and took casualties from shell fire until relieved on the 29th April, its last active day of the war. A re-organisational and cleaning up period was then spent out of the line until a march was made to St.Jan-ter-Biezen on the 4th May. Next day, both Battalions went by train to Audricq and then aboard General Service Wagons and Limbers to welcome billets at Nielles-les-Ardres. On the 6th May the 13th Battalion was effectively re-formed with 11 Officers and 202 Other Ranks, made up of three officers and 32 men who had returned from the Salient, plus the arrival of a new draft.

APRIL:
29th:
Sergeant: (4925) G.F.Tee.
Privates: (4310) H.W.Ayling, (4322) H.J.Barker, (4389) S.Bull, (4398) J.E.Burnell, (5673) G.Butcher, (4458) V.A.Croft, (4475) E.G.Denman, (4492) A.J.Dunham, (4495) H.Durston, (4498) A.W.Edwards, (4500) W.J.Edwards, (4509) J.Etherington, (4545) J.C.Gamble, (4560) F.Goodman, (4976) E.A.Wellen, (4996) P.Williamson.

For the next three weeks both Battalions undertook training and re-fitting with time for relaxation at football matches and entertainment by the 'Divisional Follies'. Then, on the 23rd May, the life and service of Lowther's Lambs as a composite fighting Unit was brought to an end. Both the 11th and 13th Battalions were re-formed that day. Seven Officers and 394 Other Ranks (11th Bn.) and one Officer plus 44 Other Ranks (13th Bn.) were transferred to the Base at Étaples while the remainder stayed as potential training staff for newly-arriving Units of the American Army.

MAY:
3rd:
Private: (4912) A.Street.
5th:
Sergeant: (5618) O.Bennett.
6th:
Lance Corporal: (6050) J.H.G.Parsons.
8th:
Sergeant: (4874) L.W.Sims.
12th:
Private: (6083) C.Pollard.
15th:
Private: (4666) J.B.Jinman.
20th:
Lance Corporal: (4873) R.J.S.Simpson.
21st:
Lance Corporal: (5783) G.T.Field.

The Cadre 13th Battalion, a pale shadow of its former self, marched to Bonningues on the 25th May to be affiliated to the No. 1 and 3 Battalions of the 306th American Infantry Regiment. On the 1st June the 11th Battalion, at Licques, was similarly affiliated but to the 305th American Infantry Regiment and the 2nd Battalion of the 306th Infantry Regiment of the American Expeditionary Force. Intensive training of the Americans was carried out until they were ordered to move from the area on the

6th May. Cadre training personnel then carried out their own training exercises until the 17th when the 11th Battalion moved to Listergaux to be affiliated with, and to train, the 2nd Battalion, 120th Infantry Regiment, 60th American Brigade. For the same purpose, 13th Battalion personnel joined the same American Unit, also at Listergaux, on the 22nd.

MAY:
31st:
Private: (4400) F.G.Burt.
JUNE:
19th:
Private: (4806) G.J.Perry.
20th:
Private: (4991) G.A.Whyte.
25th:
Private: (6091) S.N.Prior.
28th:
Sergeant: (5778) P.Evershed.
31st:
Private: (5726) W.Cooper.

The end to service on the Western Front came quickly for what remained of the 11th Battalion. With just three days' notice that it was to proceed to England to re-constitute with the 25th Division, the Battalion left Audricq by train for Boulogne on the 29th June. Ironically, it was next day, the 30th June, two years to the day since its first severe mauling at the 'Boar's Head', that the Battalion re-crossed the channel from Boulogne to Folkestone and travelled by train to its new, and safe, home in barracks at Aldershot.

In France, the 13th Battalion took over the former duties of its sister Unit and continued to provide training and, above all, experience for the 'Doughboy' Americans. On the 25th July the Battalion made its final move to Licques and it was there, on the 14th August, that it was disbanded by all its remaining personnel being transferred to the 4th Battalion The Royal Sussex Regiment.

From that time until the Armistice a number of men continued to die from their wounds or from natural causes; their details are given below:

JUNE:
30th:
Private: (5846) W.Haffenden.
JULY:
5th:
Private: (5680) F.W.Cannon.

7th:
Private: (6141) A.Silvester.
19th:
Privates: (4329) F.Barnes, (6010) A.Miller
20th:
Private: (5863) G.A.Haycock.
26th:
Private: (5988) A.Mansfield.
28th:
Private: (6282) T.W.Ward.
29th:
Lance Corporal: (4896) A.E.Stannard.
AUGUST:
1st:
Lance Corporal: (5799) D.Fraser.
8th:
Private: (4536) C.H.Freed.
26th:
Private: (5677) J.H.Cammell.
SEPTEMBER:
4th:
Second Lieutenant: (5263) E.J.Hemsley.
28th:
Second Lieutenant: (4981) C.F.E.West.
OCTOBER:
3rd:
Private: (6293) F.W.Wells.
14th:
Private: (4707) T.E.Loader.
13th:
Private: (5995) W.Martin.
16th:
Private: (5764) W.H.Eager.
18th:
Private: (5707) G.H.Clarke.
24th:
Private: (5600) H.Barr.
29th:
Lance Corporal: (5062) W.Blann.
31st:
Private: (5975) G.C.Loades.
NOVEMBER:
6th:
Lance Corporal: (5957) W.Knights.

11th, 12th and 13th Battalions
Epilogue

Formed originally, from September, 1914, as 'South Down' Battalions by Colonel Claude Lowther, the three 'New Army' Battalions, later designated as the 11th, 12th and 13th Battalions,

The Royal Sussex Regiment, volunteers to a man, had stayed, trained, served, fought and died together. On the Western Front from March, 1916, until disbandment of the 12th Battalion in February, 1918, the 13th Battalion in August, 1918, and the return to England of the 11th Battalion at the end of June, 1918, they had interchanged their theatres of action between the Ypres Salient and the battlefields of the Somme. Major, set-piece engagements had been fought at the 'Boar's Head', Richebourg-L'Avoué, Pas-de-Calais, 30th June, 1916; on the River Ancre, Somme, 3rd September, 1916; at Stuff Trench, between Thiepval and Gommecourt, Somme, 21st October, 1916; and around Hill Top Farm and St.Julien, Ypres Salient, 31st July, 1917. Then they had also been involved heavily in the long, fighting retreat from the Hindenburg Line at the end of March, 1918, when, finally, they had helped to arrest the German's great 'Spring Offensive' thus preventing the enemy's breakthrough to Amiens and the channel ports.

By the time of the Armistice few of the original Lowther's Lambs remained; over 2,000 officers and men from the three battalions had lost their lives and many more than that number had been wounded. In a way similar to the 'Pals' Battalions', Lowther's Lambs had suffered dearly in the loss of no less than 26 sets of brothers (11th Battalion 6 sets, 12th Battalion 6 sets, 13th Battalion 14 sets) many of whom joined, served, fought and died together.

At home, in Herstmonceux Castle, their founder, Colonel Claude Lowther, prevented by his age from serving with them, had nonetheless followed their progress avidly throughout and, with his neighbours, the people of Sussex, was truly proud of their achievements. In particular, the gallantry of Company Sergeant Major Nelson Victor Carter, V.C. had brought the 'Lambs' their highest honour.

The affectionate sobriquet of 'Lowther's Lambs' was destined to be remembered with pride and would ring down the ages through future generations long after the passing, in the late 1920's, of both their founder, Colonel Lowther, and of Peter, the mascot Southdown lamb, from both of whom the nickname title was derived.

PART EIGHT

The 16th (Sussex Yeomanry) Battalion

CHAPTER 38
1918
MAY – THE ARMISTICE

This 'late' Battalion of the Western Front was formed from dismounted yeomanry troops at Mersa Matruh, in Egypt, on the 31st January, 1917, to form part of the 74th (Yeomanry) Division. The Battalion's service continued in the Middle-East until it sailed from Alexandria aboard His Majesty's Troopship 'Caledonia' on the 1st May, 1918. The next five days were spent upon the Mediterranean Sea before they arrived at Marseilles, on the southern French coast.

A long and tortuous train journey northward began on the 9th May. More than two days were spent in the train before arrival at Noyelle. Officers and men occupied billets in nearby Morlay, Hamel, and Ponthoile and, there, ten days of re-equipping and training began, particularly at bayonet fighting and defence against gas.

On the 22nd May the Battalion entrained at Rue and travelled to Ligny St.Flochel before billeting at Foufflin Ricametz and moving, two days later, to Manin. Training continued and it was noticable that, as a result of the significant change in climate, a number of men succumbed to colds or fever and one died. The Battalion, however, was up to good strength with 41 officers and 850 men.

MAY:
30th:
Private: (6428) W.G.Timlick.

The whole of the month of June, which included a move north to

Flechin on the 25th, was taken up by training with emphasis on 'open warfare'. Reinforcements were received bringing Battalion strength to 43 officers and 920 men. Cases of what had become known as 'three-day-fever' appeared to be on the increase.

After another move, this time to Guarbecque, on the 10th July, the Battalion entered the front line next day at Robecq where Private Bruce became the first Battalion fatality, dying later that day from wounds. The Battalion's first offensive enterprise took place on the night of the 21st – 22nd July when, with artillery support, a raid was carried out on a house known to be occupied by the enemy. The raid was successful with three prisoners being taken as an aid to German Unit identification. Relief on the 24th was apparently known to the enemy who shelled the area heavily with high explosive and gas. By the end of the month the outbreak of 'three-day-fever', having declined steadily over the previous two weeks, died out completely.

JULY:
12th:
Private: (6351) F.Bruce.
18th:
Private: (6420) T.A.S.Smith.
24th:
Lance Corporal: (6359) G.Clark.
Private: (6356) C.Chiles.

After a short period in Divisional Reserve, the Battalion was back in the line on the 4th August, this time at St.Floris. On the 7th it was realised that the enemy was withdrawing and the Division was ordered to advance to occupy vacated trenches. The advance began during the evening and great difficulty was experienced in attempting to cross the River Lys in the dark because all the bridges, except one which was covered by enemy machine gun fire, had been destroyed. One officer was mortally wounded during this time. However, by 4.15am on the 8th the leading Company was over the river, having used temporary bridges put across by the Royal Engineers.

AUGUST:
8th:
Second Lieutenant: (6424) A.J.Taylor.

Three more bridges were thrown across the river on the 9th enabling a bridgehead to be established. During the day an enemy machine gun team was spotted by Second Lieutenant R.Waugh moving towards a prepared emplacement. This officer, accompanied by Corporal Spickernell, crawled out unseen towards the gun emplacement. When within reach, they bombed and rushed the emplacement capturing two of the enemy and routing the remainder. For this brave action Second Lieutenant Waugh and Corporal Spickernell

were subsequently awarded the M.C. and M.M. respectively.

The Battalion came out of the line on the 16th August. From their accommodation at Hamet Billet, the men spent a happy week helping to bring in the local harvest. Training recommenced on the 24th and the whole Division was withdrawn from the line two days later, the Battalion taking billets at Bourecq. Another significant move, this time southward, was about to be made and, by the end of the month, the whole Division was on the old Somme Battlefields having taken a train journey of 18 hours from Lillers to Heilly.

An amusing but, at the same time, frustrating, occurrence took place on the 31st August when the Battalion had travelled by buses from Heilly to a point near Maricourt not far from the town of Péronne. A march was then made to rendezvous with a guide who was to take them to the support line north-west of Péronne. The guide was found and they set

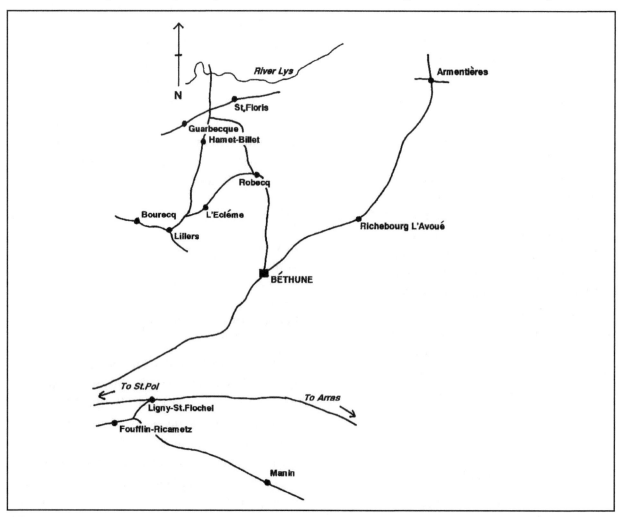

77. *May to 29th August 1918 and 28th September to 17th October 1918*

off for their destination. In the darkness of the night, however, the guide, much to his own embarrassment, could not find the way and, at 5.00am, now completely lost, a halt was called to await daylight ! The next morning, 1st September, the Battalion, exhausted after its night of futile and much-cursed wanderings, arrived at Hem Wood.

It was learned that a strong attack was to be carried out by the Division in conjunction with the Australians on the 2nd September. The role of the Division was to be in close support to the main attack and, to this end, assembly positions were taken up in lengths of old trench and shell holes by 5.45am. The allied barrage started at 5.30am and resulted in a prompt and heavy enemy reply with shells falling all around the Battalion's positions. News was received that the Australians were making good progress and had crossed the Canal du Nord. Consequently, the Battalion set off at 8.30am to follow-up their Australian colleagues. They were heavily shelled during this advance, particularly while crossing the Canal du Nord, but they pressed on to take up a position south-east of Haut-Allaines. A German counter-attack on neighbouring Units left a Battalion flank 'in the air' but a defensive flank was organised and the position was held for the rest of the day and through the night. Battalion casualties had been surprisingly light in the circumstances; in addition to those who lost their lives, three officers and 35 men had been wounded.

SEPTEMBER:
2nd:
Sergeant: (6355) H.D.Chatfield.
Corporals: (6361) A,G.Cozens, (6392) P.Hopkins.
Lance Corporals: (6346) F.C.Botting, (6347) V.J.Brace.
Privates: (6338) H.Baker, (6343) C.A.Blake, (6369) B.Eldridge, (6388) J.V.Hoadley, (6397) A.E.Klawier, (6399) B.Lake, (6402) S.Middleton, (6411) E.A.Ralph, (6430) F.Turner, (6447) W.Woodin.

Having waited through long hours expecting an enemy counter-attack, welcome news of a German retirement was received on the morning of the 3rd September. Patrols were sent forward to ascertain the enemy position but they were fired upon and had to withdraw bringing with them those of their colleagues, including Second Lieutenant Waugh, who had been wounded. A 5.9" shell burst in a Battalion dugout during the afternoon severely wounding two men and causing great shock to the others, including Captain Edwards. During the early hours of the 4th, the Battalion moved back to bivouacs and some rest.

SEPTEMBER:
3rd:
Private: (6337) T.A.Axtell.
4th:
Lance Corporal: (6391) H.E.Hopkins.
Privates: (6387) F.Hoad, (6405) H.C.Morton.

At 8.00pm on the 6th September the Battalion moved to the vicinity of Templeux-La-Fosse and took up a defensive position for the night. During the hours of darkness two men were badly

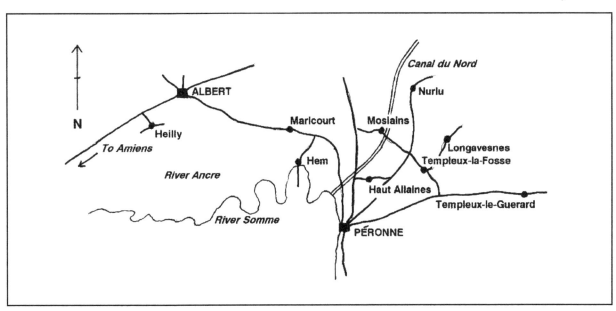

78.   *29th August to 28th September 1918*

wounded by the explosion of a booby-trap device in an old German trench. Progress was made through Longavesnes on the 7th amidst heavy shelling from the enemy.

SEPTEMBER:
8th:
Private: (6395) S.E.Johnson.

After two days welcome rest the Battalion moved into the front line during the evening of the 10th September. Positions were held through the next day but, during the following night, a trap was laid for a party of Germans suspected of using a night post in Bouleux Wood. At dusk Corporal Dowling and six men went out with a Lewis Gun to lay in wait. Very soon 20 enemy soldiers appeared and walked towards the ambush. Fire was opened with the Lewis Gun but it jammed irrevocably almost at once. The enemy then attempted to rush their ambushers but were fought off with bombs until Corporal Dowling and his men could retire safely to their own trench. Next day was quiet with little activity but men brought in from No-Man's-Land a badly wounded German airman who was seen to parachute down from his burning aircraft.

SEPTEMBER:
10th:
Lance Corporal: (6366) S.Dive.

A significant number of casualties were suffered over the next few days. On the 14th September a 5.9" shell fell amongst men of 'B' Company as they were getting into a railway cutting. Next day the enemy laid down a considerable bombardment and, on the 16th, a two hour barrage of mustard gas shells was received. There was no alternative but to remain in the gas-soaked area and several casualties resulted. The pressure eased on the 17th to allow preparations to be made for an attack scheduled for the following day.

SEPTEMBER:
14th:
Private: (6336) H.E.V.B.Apps.
15th:
Sergeant: (6383) A.V.Harvey.
Lance Corporal: (6381) E.V.Harborough.
Privates: (6341) W.J.Bell, (6362) C.W.Cross, (6432) R.Verrion.

16th:
Lance Corporal: (6436) H.Watson.
Privates: (6345) W.A.Boniface, (6378) W.Hall, (6406) W.H.Munday, (6407) E.Page, (6419) T.Scholes, (6422) W.R.Squires, (6446) E.H.C.Woodcock.
17th:
Private: (6415) G.H.Riley.

The Battalion was to be in the forefront of the attack on the 18th September. The barrage started at 5.20am and, three minutes later, began to creep forward followed closely by the Battalion's officers and men. In the early stages conditions were very dark and it was raining hard. Also, the smoke from the barrage reduced visibility to no more than five yards so that it was extremely difficult to maintain the correct line of advance. However, Captain Lascelles did a great job in keeping the right line and the men, staying very close behind the creeping barrage, were upon the enemy before they had time to organise any effective defence. The advance was across, and round, the huge chalk quarry spoil heaps at Templeux-le-Guerard. The total effort was a great success with relatively few casualties. Nine Other Ranks had been killed; two officers and 43 Other Ranks had been injured, of whom several died over the next two days, and one man was missing. On the other hand, the Battalion took its objectives and captured between 400 and 500 prisoners together with many machine guns. The Battalion consolidated and remained at its objective during the 19th and 20th September while other Units passed through to continue the advance.

SEPTEMBER:
18th:
Sergeants: (6404) T.J.Morgan, (6423) W.J.Sudds.
Lance Corporal: (6414) E.J.Ridley.
Privates: (6357) P.D.Clack, (6368) C.V.G.Edwards, (6377) F.Gaston, (6410) J.Preston, (6427) J.J.Thurlow, (6433) H.Wakeford.
19th:
Company Sergeant Major: (6425) T.W.H.Taylor.
Privates: (6354) J.Carrier, (6380) W.Hanson, (6390) B.Hook.
20th:
Lance Corporal: (6408) J.Penfold.
Privates: (6349) F.Bristow, (6429) A.E.V.Tottem.

No doubt as a result of the successful operation on the 18th September, a similar advance was planned, rather naively, for the 21st. Again, the attack was to follow closely behind a creeping barrage but, not suprisingly, this time the Germans were ready. They brought to bear a heavy machine gun and counter-artillery fire on the British assembly trenches even before zero hour. Things went wrong from the start; all telephone cables were severed and the 'runners' could not operate under such intense fire. The British artillery support was far less effective than previously. Troops to the left lost direction and swept across the Battalion's front. Only a few men reached the objective and they were forced to withdraw. Enemy machine guns had been passed by and they subsequently brought fire to bear from the rear. Inevitably, a withdrawal had to be ordered. All Company Commanders were casualties and survivors had to fight their way back. Clearly, the Battalion had committed too few men to this effort; only three officers and 31 men got back initially although more returned later.

SEPTEMBER:
21st:
Second Lieutenants: (6344) A.Boardman, (6426) W.E.Thomas.
Sergeant: (6340) A.E.Beal.
Lance Corporals: (6353) T.P.Butler, (6364) G.J.Daniels, (6440) T.A.Wiles.
Privates: (6339) E.J.Beacon, (6342) W.Blackman, (6348) P.Bridger, (6352) A.A.Burbridge, (6365) J.Dengate, (6372) P.F.Fieldwick, (6373) W.R.Flint, (6374) G.H.French, (6379) W.K.Hannant, (6384) R.Harvey, (6386) E.J.Hedger, (6389) J.Hogbin, (6393) C.W.Hunt, (6396) J.G.W.Jones, (6398) E.J.Knight, (6409) W.E.Potter, (6413) G.Reeves, (6416) A.Robinson, (6417) J.F.Rodgers, (6418) A.C.Saunders, (6437) C.E.Watts, (6443) W.R.Winterman, (6444) F.W.Wood, (6445) H.J.Wood.

Not until the 24th September was the Battalion relieved and able to march back to bivouac near Templeux-le-Fosse. This was the beginning of a move back to the north. By train, the Battalion travelled west to Villers-Bretonneux from Péronne on the 25th.

After two days' rest, came a longer train journey, this time from Heilly to Lillers. A march from Lillers station took the Battalion to billets in L'Ecleme on the 28th but next day, with no time to re-fit or re-organise, orders were received to take over the front line at Richebourg-L'Avoué ready for another attack.

The Battalion moved into position on the 1st October and the advance began on the 2nd at 7.30am. The objective for the day was taken successfully and without casualties. A further advance was achieved on the 3rd before the Battalion went into Brigade Reserve and collected together in huts within the remains of Châteux Wood on the 6th. Two or three quiet days were then experienced.

OCTOBER:
3rd:
Lance Corporal: (6376) H.Gardner, M.M.
5th
Lance Corporal: (6438) F.Whitewood.
6th
Private: (6400) C.R.C.J.Mare.
7th:
Private: (6403) J.W.Mills, M.M.
9th:
Private: (6412) T.E.Rathborn.

The front line was taken over once more on the 10th October along a stretch of railway. German artillery and trench mortars were troublesome but, on the 12th, a fighting patrol of one officer and 11 men attempted a raid on an enemy trench with the aim of securing a prisoner for Unit identification. Defensive machine gun fire from a concrete pill-box was so intense, however, that the raid was not successful. Next day, the Germans retaliated with a raid of their own which forced back from their post the 30 or 40 men of 'A' Company; although there was only one fatality, every remaining man in this group was wounded to a greater, or lesser, degree. The Battalion was ordered into Reserve that evening and the following days, devoted to cleaning and rest, were quiet.

OCTOBER:
10th:
Lance Corporal: (6385) F.Heather.
Private: (6363) H.J.Cummins.
12th:
Second Lieutenant: (6441) D.W.Wiley.
13th:
Private: (6401) W.P.McDonald.
14th:
Corporal: (6367) W.Duck.
Private: (6442) C.Winchester.

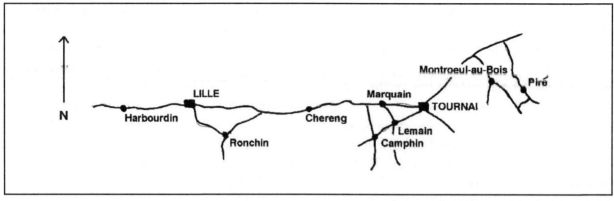

79.   *17th October to the Armistice 1918*

A report was received that the enemy were preparing to withdraw so, on the 15th October, the Battalion advanced by way of Santes and Harbourdin to billets in Flequieries. Such steady advances continued to Ronchin on the 18th, to Chereng next day and to Camphin on the 20th. A few quiet days at training were followed, on the 25th, by a return to the line and the receipt of 44 men as reinforcements. By the end of October the Battalion was in billets at Lemain.

OCTOBER:
18th:
Private: (6434) W.J.J.Wallis.
23rd:
Sergeant: (6350) F.T.Brookes.
27th:
Private: (6421) S.Spencer-Maynard.
31st:
Private: (6439) H.Wightman.

The early part of November was spent in generally cleaning up, mending uniforms and clothes, and attending to equipment. Training was undertaken but became of a less combatant nature concentrating on marching past and ceremonial drills. The last Battalion fatality during the war was Private Henry Tyler who, on the 2nd, died of wounds.

NOVEMBER:
1st:
Private: (6371) R.B.Ellis.
2nd:
Private: (6431) H.Tyler.

The Battalion's final wartime duty was to picquet the south and south-east entrances to the town of Tournai and this they did from the 8th

November. At 9.00am on the 11th, while still at Tournai, news of the signing of the Armistice at 11.00am that day was received. Initially, an order was received to 'stand fast' but, later in the day, with a light, relieved and happy step, the Battalion moved to the villages of Piré and Montroeul-au-Bois. The war was over.

16th Battalion Epilogue

The Battalion's involvement on the Western Front had been relatively short; just six months but its actions had been intensive. At first, many lessons had to be learned quickly, for France and Belgium were a far cry from the heat and form of action that everyone had been familiar with in the middle-east.

May, June and July, 1918, brought only minor contact and occasional skirmishes with the enemy but, as the Allied 'Advance to Victory', began in August and gained momentum, the Battalion was actively involved in pushing the Germans back steadily east of the old Somme Battlefields and near to the Hindenburg Line. The month of September was particularly active until, during the last few days, a move north and into Belgium took place. It was on the soil of 'neutral little Belgium' that the Battalion saw the end to the Great War.

Although the Battalion had been on the Western Front for only six months it had been involved in a number of hard-fought actions. Its fatality total of 111 officers and men may seem relatively low but the weight of its contribution should not be under-estimated. The 'Sussex Yeomanry' had more than proved their worth.

PART NINE

17th (Service) Battalion (originally 5th Garrison Guard Battalion)

CHAPTER 39
1918
MAY – THE ARMISTICE

This Battalion, recently formed in France as the '5th Garrison Guard Battalion', was re-designated as the '17th Battalion Royal Sussex Regiment' on 26th May, 1918. The Battalion formed part of the 176th Brigade, 59th Division.

On the 27th May, the day after becoming officially part of the Royal Sussex Regiment, the Battalion began digging trench lines near Robecq less than two miles south of the River Lys. The weather continued fine until the end of the month and this allowed work to proceed, intermingled with training. At this time the Battalion's strength was recorded as 33 officers and 923 other ranks.

The first half of June was spent in training and the continuation of trench digging. For the last two weeks of the month training was transferred to Beaumetz-les-Aire and, during that period, an outbreak of illness necessitated the isolation of 136 men.

Training programmes continued throughout July. On the 9th, the Battalion marched to Sains-les-Pérnes. After a journey by buses on the 20th, a two-day tour of duty in the front line at La Bassée was conducted without casualties.

After being relieved and returning to Sains-les-Pérnes on the 22nd July, the Battalion travelled by buses, next day, to Bellacourt. Movement into close support trenches took place on the 25th. During the night of the 28th / 29th a move into the front line was made. The change-over was wet and slow, however, and the Battalion's first fatal casualties were taken at that time.

JULY:
29th:
Company Sergeant Major: (6466) E.Pink, D.C.M.
Privates: (6455) W.Dalton, (6457) P.J.Furnell.
31st:
Private: (6456) J.Fraser.

The 3rd August brought welcome relief from the wet and very muddy trench conditions. Entraining at Blairville the Battalion travelled to Bavincourt and then marched to billets in Gouy-en-Artois. There, training re-commenced and a disposition into Brigade Reserve at Bretencourt occured on the 8th. On Sunday the 11th a Church Parade was followed by a nail and salvage hunt. Training, Reserve and support duties were carried out until a return to the front line on the 20th. Then, on the 23rd, the line was vacated and a march made to bivouac in a field beside the Arras – Doullens Road. That night, casualties were caused by enemy gas shelling; four officers and 61 other ranks were sent to hospital suffering from the effects of the gas.

AUGUST:
22nd:
Private: (6449) J.Austen.
23rd:
Private: (6452) J.Buchan.

A march was made to Labret Station on the 24th August. From there, the train journey north to Lillers took 20 hours in very hot conditions. An onward march to St.Hilarie next day and to Busnes on the 26th was somewhat less exhausting as the weather had turned showery and cooler. The end of August saw the Battalion in and around Robecq.

September began with days of training followed by a move into Divisional Support at outposts along the La Bassée – Estaires Road and then, on the 9th, into the front line. A succession of showery days made for wet and muddy conditions underfoot. Thus, relief was welcomed on the 13th with a move to Le Drumetz where they remained, technically, still in support.

The weather improved and became very hot for a couple of days which made the obligatory

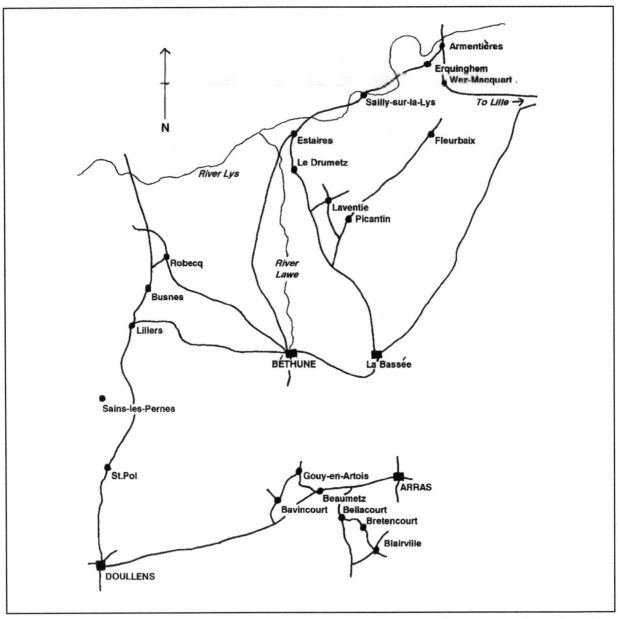

26th May to 17th October 1918

training uncomfortable and sweaty. The Battalion remained in, or close to, the front line which enabled wiring and trench improvements to be carried out. Another period of training was followed, by the end of the month, with a return to the front. Twenty-one other ranks had been returned to Base for re-classification on the 24th September so the strength on the 30th was down to 31 officers and 746 other ranks.

SEPTEMBER:
16th:
Private: (6462) G.Lumsden.
21st:
Second Lieutenant: (6472) W.L.Wright.
24th:
Second Lieutenant: (6461) W.Lathan.

A returning patrol reported, on the 1st October, that an enemy trench was unoccupied so a Lewis Gun post was pushed forward. Next day, the Battalion attacked the enemy positions and advanced to a depth of almost two miles. A halt was called only because battions forming part of the attack to the left and right had been unable to make such progress. Relief was effected on the 3rd with a march to Laventie and then a journey by buses to Sailly-sur-la-Lys. A move back to a support position at Fleurbaix was made next day.

OCTOBER:
3rd:
Private: (6460) W.Hardwick.

Another attack was ordered on the 5th October with the object of passing around the village of Wez Macquart. The advance began at 5.00pm and, at 5.15pm, a 15 minutes barrage over the troops' heads dropped on the village itself. The attack was held up in the early stages by enemy machine gun fire from houses in Wez Macquart and from the left flank down the old area of No-Man's-Land. By midnight the Battalion was halted, holding sections of the old British and German front lines. The Battalion remained in the front areas until relieved on the 11th. On the 9th, an enemy raiding party of 18 men attacked a Battalion post but was driven off. That day, too, a Battalion runner carrying messages between posts, was captured by the Germans.

OCTOBER:
5th:
Private: (6470) J.Wilson.
6th:
Privates: (6459) J.B.Graham, (6464) A.Parker.

The Battalion was at Erquinghem in Reserve for three days before returning to the front line at Wez Macquart for a good relief without casualties on the 15th October. Early in the morning of the 16th a report was received that the enemy had retired with the exception of a few snipers. Consequently an advance commenced at 10.00am with all troops proceeding cautiously due to suspected booby traps.

OCTOBER:
16th:
Private: (6458) J.Gee.

At dawn on the 17th, patrols realised that the Germans had continued their withdrawal. The advance was resumed and, as the day wore on, headway became so easy and straightforward that formations were abandoned and the troops marched on to Lommelet from which village civilians rushed forward with hearty greetings to meet their liberators.. Here, the canal bank was reached but the Germans had blown all bridges. The Battalion settled down in the comparative luxury of Lommelet billets, the first they had occupied for two months.

The next day was one of more advances with encouragement from civilian greetings all along the route through the northern suburbs of Lille. The troops were close on the heels of the Germans who blew up railway bridges across the River Marq shortly before the British arrived. The line of the river was held at day's end.

Unremitting advance continued on the 19th October, through the village of Sailly-les-Lannoy to an outpost line established just east of Trieu-du-Pâpe. The Tournai – Tourcoing railway line was reached on the morning of the 20th. A one-platoon patrol was sent forward to ascertain the situation and to see whether the River L'Escaut could be crossed at Havron. Although the enemy had been driven from the western bank, a crossing could not be effected for the time being due to the lack of suitable equipment and materials. For the same reason no progress could be made on the 21st but a detailed reconnaissance of the river bank was carried out. Second Lieutenant W.L.Wright was killed that day, the last man of the Battalion to lose his life in action, although Private J.W.Wildman died of wounds on the 2nd November.

On the 22nd October the Battalion was relieved and was able to move to billets at Toufflers. After time spent cleaning up, training was established and the Battalion was re-organised with only three platoons for each Company. Thus ended what was to be the last full month of the war.

OCTOBER:
21st:
Second Lieutenant: (6472) W.L.Wright.
25th:
Private: (6467) G.Rodd.
26th:
Company Sergeant Major: (6450) J.Bartlett.

After a period of days resting, cleaning and training, forward movement recommenced at only 15 minutes notice on the 9th November. The route passed through Bailleul and onward to the River L'Escaut. The roads were very congested with troop and transport movements because only one bridge was available to the Division for river crossing. To ease the situation the men crossed the river by a narrow and precarious footbridge which necessitated walking in single file with five yards between each man. By evening, arrival was achieved at billets in Quatre Vents on the east bank of the river.

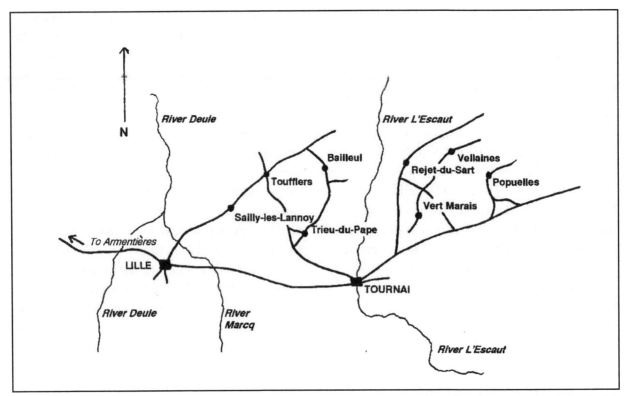

81.   *18th October to the Armistice 1918*

The line of march was resumed on the 10th November. Conditions were relatively easy and safe, the only concern being for the late arrival of rations ! Passing through Vert Marais and Rejet-du-Sart, the Battalion came to billets in Vellaines. Owing to the convergence of other army Units in pursuit of the enemy, the Battalion's forward impetus was halted much to the disappointment of all ranks.

So it was at Vellaines that the Battalion's war on the Western Front ended on the 11th November at 11.00am. News of the cessation of hostilities was received earlier that morning. At first, the news was received calmly and with gratitude. Later in the day, however, the atmosphere became more exciting. The local population retrieved from their hiding places a good selection of musical instruments and the village band paraded loudly and proudly up and down the streets.

NOVEMBER:
2nd:
Private: (6469) J.W.Wildman.
8th:
Sergeant: (6448) A.E.Ashton

17th Battalion Epilogue

It cannot be denied that the 17th was something of a 'cobbled-together' Battalion which operated through the 'rump' of the war on the Western Front. Many of its men were, for various reasons, of a relatively low physical fitness. Some were naturally not fully fit in the army's strict interpretation, and the condition of others had deteriorated as a result of wounds or illness sustained during the years of hostilities. From time to time the general condition of the men was reviewed as is evidenced by the fact that, on occasions, selected men were taken from Battalion strength and transferred to Base or Labour Battalions as being unfit to bear arms.

Nevertheless, the Battalion was brought into operations during those last months of the war and played a part particularly in the actions that hastened and harassed the German retreats. Only 24 officers and men of the Battalion lost their lives between May, 1918, and the Armistice and this, to some extent, in purely statistical terms, tends to give an undervalued impression of the Battalion's involvement and efforts. A part was required and a part was played without any sign of failure or dishonour; for that, the Battalion rightly stood proud.

Image 25: The Ypres Salient today. A German blockhouse surrounded by mine and shell craters at Hill 60.

Image 26: The Ypres Salient today. Preserved British trenches at Sanctuary Wood.

Image 27: Thiepval Memorial, Somme.

Image 28: Menin Gate Memorial, Ypres.

Image 29: The grave of 12th Battalion's Company Sergeant Major, Nelson Victor Carter V.C. at the Royal Irish Rifles Graveyard, Laventie.

Image 30: The war's never-ending requirements for ordnance, materials and supplies are seen being transported from a railhead station. Note there are no horse-drawn vehicles here. The motor lorries are relatively modern but all still have solid tyres.

Image 31: Summerdown Camp, Eastbourne, East Sussex. At that time the largest military convalescent camp in Europe.

Image 32: Pozières British Cemetery and Memorial to the Missing, Somme. At this cemetery an original Commission concept is maintained namely, that at some time during every sunny day, each gravestone should be touched by the shadow of an English rose.

Image 33: New recruits at the tented, later hutted, Cooden Mount Camp, Bexhill-on-Sea, East Sussex, probably September 1914. These Sussex men had been recruited at Colonel Claude Lowther's home, Herstmonceux Castle, and were destined to become known as "Lowther's Lambs". Note the medals worn by "old soldiers" and the attestation form held up proudly by one man.

Image 34: SD/1026 Private David Dunk of Bexhill-on-Sea. Shot by a sniper on 12th March, 1916. He was the first of "Lowther's Lambs" to be killed in action.

Image 35: William Colsey Millward D.S.O., Croix-de-Guerre, who enlisted as a Private in the 1st South Down Battalion, remained a "Lowther Lamb" throughout his service and rose to Lieutenant Colonel Commanding the 11th Battalion The Royal Sussex Regiment.

Image 36: At the 11th hour of the 11th day of the 11th month, succeeding generations place poppies on the grave of Lieutenant Colonel William Colsey Millward in St. Nicolas Churchyard, Pevensey, East Sussex, symbolically to remember him and all the Royal Sussex Regiment men who died, especially on the Western Front.

CEMETERIES AND MEMORIALS

A List of the Cemeteries containing Royal Sussex Regiment Graves
and of the
Memorials on which are inscribed the names of the missing.

Every man who lost his life on the Western Front has either an identifiable grave or, if he has no known grave, his name is inscribed upon one of the Commonwealth War Grave Commission's Memorials to the Missing.

**'At the going down of the sun,
and in the morning,
we will remember them'**

CEMETERIES

BELGIUM

Aeroplane
Artillery Wood
Ath Communal
Bard Cottage
Bedford House Enclosue No.2
Bedford House Enclosure No.4
Bedford House Enclosure No.6
Belgian Battery Corner
Belgrade
Berks Extension
Brandhoek Military
Brandhoek New Military
Brandhoek New Military No.3
Buffs Road, St.Jean-les-Ypres
Bus House
Cement House
Coxyde Military
Dadizeele
Dickebusch New Military
Dickebusch New Military Extension
Divisional Collecting Post
Dozinghem Military
Dranoutre Military
Duhallow A.D.S. (Advance Dressing Station)
Elzenwalle Brasserie
Essex Farm
Ferme-Oliver
Grootebeek British
Gwalia
Haringhe (Bandeghem) Military
Harlebeke New British
Ridge Wood Military

Hooge Crater
Hoogstaede Belgian Military
Hop Store
Irish House
Kemmel Château Military
Klein-Vierstraat British
La Brique Military No.2
La Clytte Military
La Laiterie Military
Larch Wood (Railway Cutting)
Lijssthenhoek Military
Locre Hospice
Maple Copse
Marcinelle New Communal
Mendinghem Military
Menin Road South Military
Minty Farm
New Irish Farm
Nine Elms British
Oak Dump
Oostaverne Wood
Oxford Road
Perth (China Wall)
Poelcapelle British
Poperinghe New Military
Poperinghe Old Military
Potijze Burial Ground
Railway Dugouts Burial Ground
Ramscapelle Road Military
Ration Farm (La Plus Douve) Annexe
Reninghelst New Military
Vlamertinghe New Military

Solferino Farm
Voormezeele Enclosures Nos.1 and 2
Spoilbank
Voormezeele Enclosure No.3
St.Julien Dressing Station
Westoutre Churchyard Extension
Tancrez Farm
White House,
The Huts
Wulverghem-Lindenhoek Road Military
Tournai Communal Allied Extension
Wytschaete Military
Track 'X'
Ypres Reservoir
Tyne Cot
Ypres Town Extension
Verviers Communal
Zantvoorde British
Vlamertinghe Military

FRANCE
(Listed by Departement, the French equivalent to
an English County)

AISNE:
Annois Communal
Montreuil-aux-Lions British
Béllicourt British
Moulins New Communal
Bérthaucourt Communal
Oulchy-le-Château Churchyard
Braine Communal
Paissy Churchyard
Chauny Communal British Extension
Prémont British
Fere-en-Tardenois Communal
Priez Communal
Grand Seraucourt British
Raperie British
Hargicourt British
St.Erme Communal
Hargicourt Communal Extension
Unicorn
Jeancourt Communal
Vadencourt British
La Capelle-en-Thierache Communal
Vauxbuin French National
La Vallée-Mulatre Communal Extension
Vendresse British
Marteville Communal

Villers-en-Prayeres Communal

ARDENNES:
Sedan (St.Charles) Communal

LOIRE-ATLANTIQUE:
Nantes (La Bouteillerie)
St.Nazaire (Tout Aides)

MARNE:
Jonchery-sur-Vesle

NORD:
Ascq Communal
Caudry Old Communal
Aubers Ridge British
Cité Bonjean Military
Awoingt British
Condé-sur-L'Escaut
Bailleul Communal Extension
Croix-du-Bac British, Steenwerck
Bérlaimont Communal
Cross Roads
Borre British
Don Communal
Brewery Orchard
Douai British
Busigny Communal Extension
Douai Communal
Cannone Farm British
Dunkirk Town
Esnes Communal
Maubeuge

Esquelbecq Military
Maurois Communal

Estaires Communal Extension
Mazinghien Communal
Fifteen Ravine British, Villers-Pluich
Outtersteene Communal Extension
Glageon Communal
Phalempin
Glageon Communal Extension
Pommereul British
Godeswaersvelde British
Pont-du-Hem Military
Gouzeaucourt British
Porte-de-Paris
Haumont Communal
Ration Farm Military

Hazebrouck Communal
Sains-du-Nord Communal
Highland, Le Cateâu
St.Aubert British
Honnechy British
St.Souplet British
Houplines Communal Extension
Valenciennes (St.Roch) Communal
Le Câteau Military
Villers Hill British
Le-Réjet-du-Beaulieu Communal
Villers-Pol Communal Extension
Lille Southern
Wargnies-le-Petit
Maroc British
Y Farm Military, Bois Grenier

OISE:
Noyon British
Verberie French National
Senlis French National

PAS-DE-CALAIS:
Achiet-le-Grand Communal Extension
Delsaux Farm

Agny Military
Dud Corner
Aire Communal
Duisans British
Aix-Noulette Communal
Dury Crucifix
Aix-Noulette Communal Extension
Étaples Military
Aubigny Communal Extension
Eterpigny British
Avesnes-le-Comte Communal Extension
Faubourg D'Amiens, Arras
Bancourt British
Feuchy Chapel British
Barlin Communal
Fosse No.10 Communal Extension
Bellacourt Military
Fouquieres Churchyard
Béthune Town
Gommecourt British No.2
Beuvry Communal
Gonnehem Churchyard
Boulogne Eastern
Gorre British and Indian
Brebières British

Gourock Trench, Tilloy-les-Moufflaines
Browns Road Military, Festubert
Grevillers British
Bucquoy Road
Guards (Cuinchy)
Bully-Grenay Communal British Extension
Habarcq Communal
Bully-Grenay Communal French Extension
Hébuterne Military
Cabaret-Rouge British
Houchin Military
Calais Southern
Houlle Churchyard
Cambrin Churchyard Extension
Labourse Communal
Cambrin Military
Lapugnoy Military
Canadian No.2
Le Touquet-Paris Plage Communal
Chocques Military
Le Touret Military
Couin British
Lebecquiere Communal
Cuinchy Communal
Les Baraques Military
Lievin Communal Extension
Sailly-sur-la-Lys Canadian
Ligny-St.Flochel British
St.Hilaire
Lillers Communal
St.Hilaire Extension
Longuenesse (St.Omer) Souvenir
St.Martin Calvaire British
Loos British
St.Mary's A.D.S. (Advanced Dressing Station)
Martinpuich British
St.Patrick's
Mazingarbe Communal Extension
St.Pol British
Monchy British
St.Vaast Post Military
Noeux-les-Mines Communal
St.Venant Communal
Noeux-les-Mines Communal Extension
St.Venant-Robecq Road British, Robecq
Orchard Dump
Ste. Catherine British
Pérnes British
Sucrerie, Ablain-St.Nazaire
Philosophe British, Mazingarbe
Sunken Road, Boislieux-St.Marc

Point-de-Jour Military
Tank
Post Office Rifles
Térlincthun British
Quarry (Vermelles)
Thilloy Road
Red Cross Corner
Tilloy British
Rimboval Churchyard
Vermelles British
Royal Irish Rifles Graveyard, Laventie
Verquin Communal
Rue David Military
Villers Station
Rue-des-Berceaux Military, Richebourg-L'Avoué
Warlencourt British
Rue-de-Bacquerot No.1 Military, Laventie
Warlincourt Halte British
Rue-de-Bois Military, Fleurbaix
Wimereux Communal
Rue-Petillon Military
Woburn Abbey
Sailly-le-Bourse Communal

RHONE:
St.Germain-au-Mont-d'Or Communal Extension

SEINE-ET-MARNE:
Pérreuse Château Franco-British National

SEINE-MARITIME:
Boisguillaume Communal
Mont Huon Military
Boisguillaume Communal Extension
St.Sever, Rouen
Étretat Churchyard
St.Sever Extension, Rouen
Étretat Churchyard Extension
Ste.Marie, Le Havre
Le Treport Military

SEINE-ST.DENIS:
City of Paris, Pantin

SOMME:
A.I.F. Burial Ground (Australian Imperial Force)
Adelaide, Villers Bretonneux
Abbeville Communal
Albert Communal Extension
Abbeville Communal Extension

Ancre British
Acheux British
Auchonvillers Military
Adanac British
Authuile Military
Aveluy Communal
Hem Farm Military
Aveluy Wood
Hérbecourt Communal
Bagneux British
Knightsbridge, Mesnil-Martinsart
Bapaume Post Military
La Chapelette British and Indian
Beacon
La Neuville British
Beauval Communal
London and Extension
Bécourt Military
Longueval Road
Bernafay Wood British
Lonsdale
Bértrancourt Military
Louvencourt Military
Blighty Valley
Mailly Wood
Bouzincourt Communal Extension
Mailly-Maillet Communal Extension
Bouzincourt Ridge
Méaulte Military
Boves West Extension
Méricourt L'Abbé Communal Extension
Bray Military
Mesnil Ridge
Bray Vale British
Mill Road
Brie British
Millencourt Communal Extension
Bronfay Farm Military
Montigny Communal
Bulls Road
Morlancourt British No.2
Carnoy Military
Namps-au-Val British
Caterpillar Valley
Ovillers Military
Cérisy-Gailly
Pargny British
Citadel New Military
Pérnois British
Combles Communal extension
Péronne Communal Extension, Ste.Radegonde

Connaught
Péronne Road, Maricourt
Contalmaison Châteux
Picquigny
Contay British
Puchevillers British
Corbie Communal
Querrieu British
Corbie Communal Extension
Regina Trench
Courcelette British
Ribémont Communal
Dantzig Alley British
Rocquigny-Equancourt Road British
Daours Communal Extension
Roisel Communal Extension
Dartmoor
Rosières British
Delville Wood
Rosières Communal Extension
Dernancourt Communal
Roye New British
Dernancourt Communal Extension
Soulcourt Churchyard
Dive Copse British
Senlis Communal Extension
Doingt Communal
Serre Road No.1
Doullens Communal Extension No.1
Serre Road No.2
Doullens Communal Extension No.2
St.Pierre, Amiens
Eclusier Communal
Ste.Emilie Valley, Villers-Faucon
Englebelmer Communal Extension
Stump Road
Epéhy Wood Farm
Sucrerie Military
Euston Road
Templeux-le-Guerard British
Fins New British
Templeux-le-Guerard Communal Extension
Flatiron Copse
Thistle Dump, High Wood, Longueval
Fouquescourt British
Tincourt New British
Guards (Lesboeufs)
Varennes Military
Guillemont Road
Vignacourt British
Hamel Military

Villers-Bocage Communal
Hancourt British
Villers-Bretonneux Military
Harponville Communal Extension
Villers-Faucon Communal Extension
Heath, Harbonnieres
Warloy-Baillon Communal Extension
Heilly Station, Méricourt L'Abbé

VAL-DE-MARNE:
Villeneuve-St.Georges Old Communal

YVELINE:
Les Gonards (Versailles)

GERMANY

(Men who died from wounds or natural causes
while Prisoners of War)

Berlin South-Western
Hamburg
Cologne Southern
Niederzwheren

GREAT BRITAIN

(Cemeteries and Churchyards (with church name
in brackets) containing graves of men who died
of wounds or natural causes 'at home' during the
time that their battalions served on the Western
Front)

Abney Park, London
Dover (St.James's), Kent
Aldingbourne (St.Mary), Sussex
Durrington, Wiltshire
Arlesley (St.Peter) , Bedfordshire
Eastbourne (Langney), Sussex
Balcombe (St.Mary), Sussex
Eastbourne (Ocklynge), Sussex
Battersea (Morden), London
East Wickham (St.Michael), Kent
Bedford
Elham (St.Mary), Kent
Bersted Roman Catholic, Sussex
Fairwarp (Christ Church), Sussex
Bexhill, Sussex
Felpham (St.Mary), Sussex
Blofield (SS. Andrew & Peter), Norfolk
Flamstead (St.Leonard), Hertfordshire
Bodle Street Green (St.John), Sussex
Folkestone Old, Kent
Bognor Regis, Sussex

Forest Row, Sussex

Bramshott (St.Mary), Hampshire

Framfield (St.Thomas-a-Becket), Sussex

Brighton (Bear Road), Sussex

Framsden (St.Mary), Suffolk

Brighton (Extra-Mural) Borough, Sussex

Golders Green Crematorium, Middlesex

Brighton (Lewes Road), Sussex

Great Stukeley (St.Bartholomew), Huntingdonshire

Brighton and Preston, Sussex

Greenstead (St.Andrew), Essex

Bristol (Arno's Vale)

Hadlow Down (St.Mark), Sussex

Brookwood, Surrey

Hailsham Cemetery, Sussex

Burgess Hill (St.Andrew), Sussex

Hammersmith, London

Burgess Hill (St.John), Sussex

Hampstead, London

Burwash (St.Bartholomew), Sussex

Handsworth (St.Mary), Warwickshire

Cambridge (Mill Road)

Hastings, Sussex

Cheshunt Burial Ground, Hertfordshire

Havant & Waterloo (Warblington), Hampshire

Chichester, Sussex

Heathfield (All Saints), Sussex

Chingford Mount, Essex

High Hurstwood (Holy Trinity), Sussex

Chobham (St.Lawrence), Surrey

Hollybrook, Hampshire

Clapham (St.Mary), Sussex

Hooe (St.Oswald), Sussex

Crawley (St.John the Baptist), Sussex

Hornchurch (St.Andrew), Essex

Crowborough Burial Ground

Horsham (Hills), Sussex

Crowhurst (St.George), Sussex

Hove Old, Sussex

Croydon (Queen's Road), Surrey

Hucclecote (SS.Philip & James), Gloucestershire

Danehill, Sussex

Hutton (All Saints), Essex

Ditchling (St.Margaret of Antioch), Sussex

Isfield (St.Margaret), Sussex

Kensal Green (All Souls), London

Southborough, Kent

Kingswinford (St.Mary), Staffordshire

Southover (St.John the Baptist), Sussex

Lewes, Sussex

Southwick (St.Michael), Sussex

Lewisham (Ladywell), London

St.Albans, Hertfordshire

Lincoln (Newport), Lincolnshire

St.Sampson Churchyard, Channel Islands

Lowestoft (Kirkley), Suffolk

Steyning (St.Andrew), Sussex

Loxwood (St.John the Baptist), Sussex

Stonegate (St.Peter), Sussex

Manchester Southern

Storrington (St.Mary), Sussex

Manor Park, Essex

Stoughton (St.Mary), Sussex

Mayfield (St.Dunstan), Sussex

Suffield (St.Margaret), Norfolk

Meonstoke (St.Andrew), Hampshire

Sunderland (Ryehope Road), County Durham

Moston (St.Joseph R.C.), Lancashire

Taunton (St.James), Somerset

Netley Military, Hampshire

Timperley (Christ Church), Cheshire

Norwich, Norfolk

Tooting (St.Nicholas), London

Nottingham General

Torquay, Devon

Nunhead, London

Tunbridge Wells, Kent

Oxford (Botley), Berkshire

Wadhurst (SS.Peter & Paul), Sussex

Patcham (All Saints), Sussex

Wandsworth (Earlsfield), London

Penhurst (St.Michael), Sussex

Westfield (St.Andrew), Norfolk

Pevensey (St.Nicolas), Sussex

Westham (St.Mary), Sussex

Portslade, Sussex

Westminster City, London

Rotherfield Burial Ground, Sussex

Whatlington (St.Mary Magdelene), Sussex

Rumboldswyke, Sussex

Widford (St.Mary), Essex

Ruston (All Saints), Northamptonshire

Willesden New, Middlesex

Seend (Holy Cross), Wiltshire

Withyham (St.Michael), Sussex

Shorncliffe Military, Kent

Woolwich (Plumstead), London

Siddlesham (St.Mary), Sussex

Worthing (Broadwater), Sussex

South Malling (St.Michael), Sussex

Yapton (St.Mary), Sussex.

MEMORIALS TO THE MISSING:

BELGIUM

Nieuport Memorial

Ploegsteert Memorial

Tyne Cot Memorial

Ypres (Menin Gate) Memorial.

FRANCE

Arras Memorial

Cambrai, Louverval Memorial

La Férte-sous-Jouarre Memorial

Le Touret Memorial

Loos Memorial

Pozières Memorial

Soissons Memorial

Thiepval Memorial

Vis-en-Artois, Haucourt Memorial.

Select Bibliography

BARNETT, Correlli, *The Great War*, Park Lane Press, 1979.

BLUNDEN, Edmund, *Undertones of War*, Penguin Books, 1928.

BRISTOW, Alan, *A Serious Disappointment*, Leo Cooper, 1995.

BROWN, Malcolm, *The Imperial War Museum Book of the Somme*, Sidgwick & Jackson, 1996.

CABLE, Boyd, *Between the Lines*, Smith, Elder & Co., 1916.

CAVE, Nigel, *Beaumont Hamel, Somme*, Leo Cooper, 1994.

CAVE, Nigel, *Hill 60*, Leo Cooper, 1998.

CAVE, Nigel, *Passchendaele*, Leo Cooper, 1997.

CAVE, Nigel, *Sanctuary Wood & Hooge*, Leo Cooper, 1993.

CLARK, Alan, *The Donkeys*, Pimlico, 1961.

COMMITTEE OF OFFICERS OF THE BATTALION, *The History of the 7th (Service) Battalion, The Royal Sussex Regiment 1914 – 1919*, The Times Publishing Co., Ltd., 1934.

COOMBS, Rose E.B., M.B.E., *Before Endeavours Fade*, Battle of Britain Prints International Ltd., 1976.

ELLIS, John, *Eye-Deep in Hell*, Purnell Book Services Ltd., 1976.

EVANS, Martin Marix, *The Battles of the Somme*, George Wiedenfeld & Nicholson Ltd., 1996.

FARRAR-HOCKLEY, Anthony, *Death of An Army*, Wordsworth Editions Ltd., 1998.

GARDNER, Brian, *The Big Push*, Cassell & Co., Ltd., 1961.

GLIDDON, Gerald, *When the Barrage Lifts*, Gliddon Books, 1987.

GROOM, W.H.A., *Poor Bloody Infantry – The Truth Untold*, Picardy Publishing Ltd., 1997.

HART, LIddell, *History of the First World War*, Faber & Faber Ltd., 1934.

HAY, Ian, *The First Hundred Thousand – K1*, William Blackwood & Son 1916.

HAYENS, Herbert, *Midst Shot and Shell In Flanders*, Collins Clear-Type Press.

HOLMES, Richard, *The Western Front*, B.B.C. Worldwide Ltd., 1999.

HOLMES, Richard, *Riding the Retreat*, Jonathan Cape, 1995.

HOLT, Major & Mrs., *Battlefield Guide to the Somme*, Leo Cooper, 1996.

HOLT, Toni & Valmai, *Battlefields of the First World War*, Parkgate Books Ltd., 1998.

JOHNSON, Hubert G., *Breakthrough*, Presidio Press, 1994.

JOHNSON, J.H., *Stalemate !*, Arms & Armour Press, 1995.

LAFFIN, John, *British Butchers and Bunglers of World War One*, Alan Sutton Publishing, 1998.

LAFFIN, John, *Panorama of the Western Front*, Sutton Publishing Ltd., 1994.

LIDDLE, Peter (Editor), *Passchendaele in Perspective*, Leo Cooper, 1997.

LIVESEY, Anthony, *Great Battles of World War I*, Marshall Editions Ltd., 1989.

LOMAS, David, *First Ypres 1914*, Osprey Publishing, 1999.

McCARTHY, Chris, *The Somme – The Day-by-Day Account*, Arms & Armour Press, 1993.

MIDDLEBROOK, Martin, *The Kaiser's Battle*, Penguin Books, 1978.

MIDDLEBROOK, Martin, *The Somme Battlefields*, Penguin Books, 1991.

MIDDLEBROOK, Martin, *Your Country Needs You*, Leo Cooper, 2000. 405

NICHOLLS, Jonathan, *Cheerful Sacrifice*, Leo Cooper, 1993.

PITT, Barrie, *1918 The Last Act*, (Macmillan Publishers Ltd., 1984.

POWELL-EDWARDS, H.I., Lt.Col., D.S.O., *The Sussex Yeomanry and 16th (Sussex Yeomanry) Battalion Royal Sussex Regiment 1914 – 1919*, Andrew Melrose Ltd.

SIMKINS, Peter, *World War I 1914-1918 – The Western Front*, Tiger Books International, 1994.

SIMPSON, Andy, *The Evolution of Victory*, Tom Donovan Publishing Ltd., 1995.

STEDMAN, Michael, *Great Battles of the Great War*, Leo Cooper, 1999.

STEDMAN, Michael, *La Boisselle, Ovillers, Contalmaison*, Leo Cooper, 1997.

TAYLOR, A.J.P., *The First World War*, Hamish Hamilton, 1963.

TUCHMAN, Barbara W., *The Guns of August*, Constable & Robinson Ltd., 2000.

WOLFF, Leon, *In Flanders Fields*, Penguin Books, 1958.

Serially Numbered
ALPHABETICAL LISTS
By Battalion of Men Who Died

Abbreviations used :

B   = Place of Birth
(Bel.) = Belgium
Brit. = British
Cem.   = Cemetery of interrment.
Com.   = Communal, meaning French
         village or parish.
D   = Died of natural causes.
E   = Place of Enlistment.
*   = Records discrepancy found; unless the author has strong reasons to the contrary, the
         Commonwealth War Graves Commission information is given precedence and is quoted here.

(G)   = Germany.
K   = Killed-in-Action.
Mem.   = Memorial to the missing
         where inscribed name
         may be found.
Mil.   = Military.
(UK)   = United Kingdom.
W   = Died of Wounds.

Notes :

(1) Unless marked '(Bel.)', Belgium, '(G)', Germany, or '(UK)', United Kingdom, all cemeteries and memorials are in France, for which the French Departement (an administrative area corresponding to an English County) is given.

(2) In some cases, birthplaces were recorded only as parishes e.g. 'St.Peter's, Sussex' rather than the town or village in which the parish was, or is, situated.

2nd Battalion

A

1. ABBOTT, Edward Ernest; B: Ipswich; E: St.Pancras; Pte. G 11175; K: 9.9.16; Thiepval Mem., Somme; Age 33; Son of Frederick William and Angela Abbott of 3, Little Wolsey Street, Ipswich.

2. ABBOTT, Peter; B: Blackburn; E: Blackburn; Pte. G 21985; K: 9.4.18; Cambrin Mil. Cem., Pas-de-Calais; Age 29; Son of Mrs.M.A.Abbott of 12, Curzon Street, Blackburn.

3. ADAMS, Frank; B: -; E: Great Saling; Pte. G 14647; K: 27.9.16; Thiepval Mem., Somme.

4. ADAMS, Frederick; B: Hastings; E: Hastings; Pte. L 10699; W: 13.10.15; Dud Corner Cem., Pas-de-Calais; Age 18; Son of Frederick and Milly Kate Adams of 6, Waterloo Passage, Hastings.

5. ADAMS, George; B: Chichester; E: Eastbourne; Pte. S 9988; K: 3.11.14; Ypres (Menin Gate) Mem., (Bel.); Age 50; Son of the late Mr. and Mrs. James Adams.

6. ADAMS, Joseph; 2nd Lt; K: 23.7.16; Thiepval Mem. Somme; Age 32; Son of the late Mr.J. and Mrs.K.Adams.

7. ADAMS, William; B: Portsmouth; E: Chichester; Pte. G 4575; K: 13.10.15; Loos Mem., Pas-de-Calais.

8. ADKIN, Frederick Edward; 2nd Lt; K: 24.9.18; Berthaucourt Com. Cem., Aisne; M.M.; Age 34; Son of Ada Mary Adkin of London and the late Frederick Adkin; Husband of Nellie Adkin of 134, Oxforn Road, Reading.

9. AIKMAN, James Byford; B: Leytonstone; E: Epping; L/Cpl. G 18965; W: 26.9.18; Brie Brit. Cem., Somme.

10. AINSWORTH, Philip; B: Paddington; E: Cockspur Street, London; Pte. G 4661; K: 9.5.15; Le Touret Mem., Pas-de-Calais; Age 20; Son of V.W.Ainsworth.

11. ALBERY, Richard; B: Petersfield, Hampshire; E: -; Pte. G 10455; Nieuport Mem. (Bel.); Son of Richard and Kate Albery of High Terse, East Liss, Petersfield. W: 18.7.17.

12. ALDRIDGE, Reginald John Petty Devenish; Capt; K: 7.10.14 at Troyon; Vendresse Brit. Cem. Aisne; Age 37; Son of the late Reginald Aldridge, J.P., and Mrs.Aldridge of Parkstone; Husband of Mabel Dulcibella Aldridge of Sausmarez Place, Les Gravees, Gurnsey.

13. ALEXANDER, Frederick Richard; B: Hove; E: Hove; L/Cpl. G 3075; W: 28.5.18; Cambrin Mil. Cem. Pas-de-Calais; Age 24; Son of Richard and Eliza Alexander of 18, Belfast Street, Hove.

14. ALEXANDER, Gordon Reuben; 2nd Lt; K: 24.4.17; Fifteen Ravine Brit. Cem., Villers-Plouich, Nord; Age 31; Son of James and Florence Alexander of 52, Redcliffe Square, South Kensington, London.

15. ALLEN, Frederick George; B: -; E: Manor Park, London; Pte. G 14558; W: 14.11.17; Oxford Road Cem. (Bel.); Husband of May E.Allen of 6, Lancaster Road, Westbourne Park, London.

16. ALLEN, Frederick John; B: Brighton; E: Brighton; Pte. L 10072; W: 3.10.15 from wound received at Loos; Boulogne Eastern Cem. Pas-de-Calais; Age 23; Son of John and Elizabeth Allen of 25, Paradise Street, Brighton.
17. ALLEN, Henry John; B: Fletching, Sussex; E: Uckfield, Sussex; Sgt. L 18479; W at Home; 15.7.16; Hastings Cem. (UK); Age 31; Husband of Mrs.G.Evershed, formerly Allen, of 11, Orford Street, Copper Cliff, Ontario, Canada.
18. ALLWRIGHT, William Arthur; B: Plumstead, London; E: Woolwich, London; Pte. G 11004; K: 27.9.16; Thiepval Mem. Somme; Age 19; Son of Miriam Allwright of 39, Ancona Road, Plumstead.
19. AMOS, Wilfred Weston; B: St.Leonards-on-Sea; E: Chichester; Pte. L 10282; K: 9.5.15; Le Touret Mem. Pas-de-Calais.
20. ANDREWS, Everard Ronald Theodious; B: Lowestoft; E: Lowestoft; Pte. G 5262; K: 25.9.15; Loos Mem. Pas-de-Calais; Age 18; Son of Frederick James and Rachel Jessie Andrews of 28, Salisbury Road, South Lowestoft.
21. ANNENBERG, Henry Bernard; B: City of London; E: Walthamstow; Pte. G 14751; K: 27.9.16; Warlencourt Brit. Cem. Pas-de-Calais.
22. ANNING, Charles; B: Borough; E: Chichester; L/Cpl. L 10031; K: 25.9.15; Loos Mem. Pas-de-Calais; Age 21; Son of Mrs.E.Anning of 68, Trevelyan Road, Tooting, London; His brother was also killed in the war.
23. ANSCOMBE, Edgar Stanley; B: Hurstpierpoint, Sussex; E: Chichester; Pte. G 1375; K: 26.1.15; Le Touret Mem. Pas-de-Calais; Age 19; Son of Arthur and Elizabeth Anscombe of Trubwick Villa, Sydney Road, Haywards Heath, Sussex.*
24. ANSELL, Frederick James; B: Angmering, Sussex; E: Lewes; L/Cpl. L 5928; W: 11.9.14; Priez Com. Cem. Aisne; Age 34; Son of Walter and Mary Ann Ansell of Angmering; Husband of Mildred Edith Ansell of 19, Sydney Terrace, Bridport Road, Dorchester.
25. APPLEGATE, Harold Edward; B: Ingleton; E: Sheffield; Pte. G 284; K: 27.3.15; Cabaret-Rouge Brit. Cem. Pas-de-Calais; Age 24; Son of Mrs. Harriet Applegate of School House, 26, Mansfield Street, Derby.
26. ARBEN, Walter; B: Poplar, London; E: Bognor Regis, Sussex; Pte. G 1151; K: 9.5.15; Le Touret Mem. Pas-de-Calais; Age 18; Son of Mrs.Ruth Shrubb, formerly Arben, of 8, Essex Road, Bognor Regis.
27. ARCHER, Charles; B: Portslade, Sussex; E: Hove; Pte. G 8625; K: 23.7.16; Thiepval Mem. Somme; Age 21; Son of George and Helen Archer of Mile Oak, Portslade.
28. ARNOLD, William George; B: St.John's, Sussex; E: Chichester; Pte. L 7961; W: 12.5.15; Lillers Com. Cem. Pas-de-Calais; Age 28; Son of William John and Millicent Arnold of 33, North Street, Lewes.
29. ARTHUR, Douglas; B: Brighton; E: Brighton; Pte. S 1056; K: 9.5.15; Le Touret Mem. Pas-de-Calais; Age 24; Son of Annie Arthur of 17, Southwell Street, Kingsdown, Bristol, and the late Richard Arthur; Husband of Emily Arthur of 6, Parchment Street, Chichester.
30. ASH, Henry Thomas; B: Houslow; E: Dover; Pte. L 6120; W: 30.10.14; Ypres Reservoir Cem. (Bel.).
31. ASH, William Joseph; B: Portsmouth; E: Acton, London; Pte. G 21177; K: 10.7.17; Ramscapelle Road Mil. Cem. (Bel.); Age 19; Son of Joseph Richard and Mary Jane Ash of 75, Brookfield Road, Bedford Park, Chiswick, London.
32. ASHDOWN, Willam; B: Peasmarsh, Sussex; E: Hastings; Pte. G 1392; K: 26.5.15; Le Touret Mem. Pas-de-Calais.
33. ASKEW, Joseph; B: Brighton; E: Chichester; Pte. L 9678; K: 7.10.14; Vendresse Brit. Cem. Aisne.
34. ATKINSON, Lewis de Burgh; Capt; K: 16.8.16; Thiepval Mem. Somme; Age 35; Son of Humphrey Alexander and Harriet Atkinson of 'Stoneville', Kings Road, Cheltemham; Husband of Louise Christine Atkinson of 9, Langley Road, Elmers End, Beckenham.
35. ATTREALL, Albert; B: Rodmell, Sussex; E: Lewes; Cpl. L 8032; K: 9.5.15; Le Touret Mem. Pas-de-Calais; Age 29; Son of the late Thomas and Jane Attreall of Rodmell.
36. ATTREE, Benjamin Rupert; B: Hove; E: Eastbourne; Pte. L 8745; W: 27.1.15; Le Touquet Paris-Plage Com. Cem. Pas-de-Calais; Son of Albert C. and Lucy A.Attree of Brighton.
37. ATTRIDGE, Leonard; B: Eastbourne; E: Eastbourne; Pte. G 7132; W: 15.5.16; St.Sever Cem., Rouen, Seine-Maritime.
38. AUCOCK, Herbert William; B: Brighton; E: Littlehampton, Sussex; Pte. L 10444; K: 9.9.16; Thiepval Mem. Somme; Age 20; Son of William and Harriet Emma Jane Aucock of 40, Gloucester Road, Littlehampton.
39. AUSTEN, Hubert; B: Hove; E: Hove; Pte. G 5672; K: 13.10.15; Loos Mem. Pas-de-Calais.
40. AUSTIN, Bertram; B: Hove; E: Hove; Pte. G 696; K: 30.6.16; Arras Mem. Pas-de-Calais.
41. AUSTIN, Oliver; 2nd Lt; K: 9.5.15; Le Touret Mem. Pas-de-Calais.
42. AWCOCK, George; B: Brighton; E: Brighton; Pte. L 10437; K: 9.5.15; Le Touret Mem. Pas-de-Calais; Age 20; Son of Matthias Edmund Awcock of 44, Arnold Street, Elm Park, Brighton.
43. AXELL, Sidney; B: Rye, Sussex; E: Brighton; Pte. G 4638; K: 9.5.15; Rue-du-Bois Mil. Cem. Fleurbaix, Pas-de-Calais; Son of John Axell of 57, Calvert Road, Greenwich, London.

B

44. BACON, Frederick; B: Yapton, Sussex; E: Arundel, Sussex; Pte. G 4629; K: 30.4.15; Le Touret Mem. Pas-de-Calais; Son of Frederick Bacon of Church Lane, Yapton.

45. BAILEY, Arthur; B: Tunbridge Wells; E: Eastbourne; Pte. S 1025; K: 16.2.15; Le Touret Mem. Pas-de-Calais.*

46. BAILEY, Francis John; B: Burton Latimer; E: Kettering; Pte. G 19908; D: 13.10.18; Vadencourt Brit. Cem. Aisne; Age 20; Son of Francis and Emma Bailey of Barrack Yard Cranford St.John, Kettering.

47. BAILEY, Francis John; B: Epsom; E: Kingston-upon-Thames; Pte. G 21240; K: 22.11.17; Tyne Cot Mem. (Bel.); Age 30; Son of Francis and Sarah Bailey; Husband of Christina Daisy Bailey of The Island, Downside, Cobham, Surrey.

48. BAILEY, Hector Charles; B: Colchester; E: Colchester; Pte. G 18966; W: 3.10.18; St.Sever Cem. Ext. Rouen, Seine=Maritime; Age 20; Son of Florence May Neville, formertly Bailey, 73, Mersea Road, Colchester and the late F.C.Bailey.

49. BAILEY, James; B: Cheadle, Staffordshire; E: Brighton; Pte. S 2203; K: 9.5.15; Le Touret Mem. Pas-de-Calais; Age 25; Son of Joseph and Harriett Bailey of Green Hill, Cheadle.

50. BAKER, Alfred; B: Brighton; E: Brighton; L/Cpl. S 554; K: 1.1.15; Le Touret Mem. Pas-de-Calais; Age 24; Son of Mrs.Charlotte Baker of 10, Sussex Terrace, Brighton; Husband of Charlotte Caroline Baker of 22, Nelson Row, Brighton.

51. BAKER, Arthur; B: Eaton Bray, Bedfordshire; E: Luton; Pte. G 17173; W: 5.11.18; Premont Brit. Cem. Aisne; Age 21; Son of Mr.J.G. and Mrs.M.A.Baker of High Street, Eaton Bray.

52. BAKER, Cecil Hubert; B: Brighton; E: Hove; Pte. G 1587; K: 9.5.15; Le Touret Mem. Pas-de-Calais; Age 19; Son of Austin A. and Harriet Baker of 47, Waldegrave Road, Brighton.

53. BAKER, Frank; B: Alfriston, Sussex; E: Eastbourne; Sgt. L 8710; K: 30.6.16; Arras Mem. Pas-de-Calais.

54. BAKER, Frederick; B: Folkestone; E: Eastbourne; Pte. L 7701; K: 30.10.14; Ypres (Menin Gate) Mem. (Bel.); Age 30; Son of Henry and Louisa Baker of 149, Upton Lane, Forest Gate, London.

55. BAKER, Frederick James; B: St.Matthew's, Sussex; E: Eastbourne; Pte. L 8227; K: 25.9.15; Ypres (Menin Gate) Mem. (Bel.).

56. BAKER, Frederick John, B: Salehurst, Sussex; E: Battle, Sussex; Cpl. L 10340; K: 25.9.15; Loos Mem. Pas-de-Calais; Age 21; Son of Mrs.E.Baker of Salehurst Fruit Farm.

57. BAKER, George Henry; B: Margate, Kent; E: Dover; Cpl. L 9387; K: 14.9.14; La Ferte-sous-Jouarre Mem. Seine-et-Marne.

58. BAKER, George Wilfred; B: -; E: -; Cpl. L 11483; K: 5.11.18; Premont Brit. Cem. Aisne; Son of Eli and Ellen Baker of Reed's Cottage, Frensham, Surrey.

59. BAKER, James; B: Billingshurst, Sussex; E: East Grinstead, Sussex; Pte. L 7751; K: 14.9.14; La Ferte-sous-Jouarre Mem. Seine-et-Marne; Age 31; Husband of Nora Baker of 146, Cromwell Road, Redhill, Surrey; Seven years service completed.

60. BAKER, James; B: Worthing; E: Worthing; Pte. L 10633; K: 13.12.15; Dud Corner Cem. Pas-de-Calais; Age 18; Son of Mr. and Mrs.William Baker of 34, Archibald Road, East Worthing.

61. BAKER, John William; B: Saffron Walden, Essex; E: Saffron Walden; Sgt. G 14552; K: 27.9.16; Thiepval Mem. Somme.

62. BAKER, William; B: Potten; E: Potten; Pte. G 14509; K: 16.12.16; Thiepval Mem. Somme.

63. BAKER, William; B: Brighton; E: Brighton; Pte. S 2066; K: 9.5.15; Le Touret Mem. Pas-de-Calais.

64. BAKER, William John; B: Galehampton; E: Shorncliffe, Kent; Pte. L 10174; K: 14.9.14; La Ferte-sous-Jouarre Mem. Seine-et-Marne.

65. BALCOMBE, William; B: Hove; E: Brighton; Sgt. L 8004; W: 18.9.14; Braine Com. Cem. Aisne.

66. BALDEY, Ernest Edward; B: Brighton; E: Hove; Pte. G 6590; K: 12.6.18; Cambrin Mil. Cem. Pas-de-Calais.

67. BALDOCK, Frederick; B: Rotherfield, Sussex; E: Uckfield, Sussex; L/Cpl. SD 282; K: 24.9.18; Bellicourt Brit. Cem Aisne.

68. BALDWIN, Albert Bart; B: Heathfield, Sussex; E: Dover; Pte. L 7632; K: 12.1.15; Le Touret Mem. Pas-de-Calais; Husband of Mrs.A.A.Jupe, formerly Baldwin, of 18, Portersbridge Street, Romsey, Hampshire.

69. BALDWIN, Henry; B: Marylebone, London; E: London; Pte. L 6074; K: 14.9.14; La Ferte-sous-Jouarre Mem. Seine-et-Marne; Age 38; Son of Frederick William Baldwin; Served in the South Africa campaign.

70. BALL, A.H.; Lt; K: 9.4.18; See also the list of those attached to, or from, Sussex Units. (Page 531).

71. BALLARD, James Frank; B: All Souls, Sussex; E: Hastings; Pte. L 8245; W: 14.9.14; La Ferte-sous-Jouarre Mem. Seine-et-Marne; Age 28; Son of William A.Ballard of 11, Grove Road, Ore, Hastings.

72. BANFIELD, Frederick Gerald; B: -; E: Sittingbourne, Kent; L/Cpl. G 17587; K: 9.9.16; Thiepval Mem. Somme.

73. BARBROOK, Alfred; B: Heybridge, Essex; E: Chelmsford, Essex; Pte. G 14857; K: 10.3.17; Hem Farm Mil. Cem. Somme; Son of Mrs. C.Barbrook of 131, Woodfield Cottages, Heybridge.

74. BARCOCK, Reuben; B: Custom House, Essex; E: West Ham, London; Pte. G 14775; K: 9.9.16; Thiepval Mem. Somme.

75. BARKER, Frederick; B: Chelsea, London; E: Southwark, London; Pte. G 5460; K: 29.5.16; Maroc Brit. Cem. Nord.

76. BARNARD, Edward Thomas; B: Nuthurst, Sussex; E: Hove; Pte. G 1185; W: 14.11.17; Dozinghem Mil. Cem. (Bel.); Age 33; Husband of Emma Barnard of 30, Canterbury Road, West Kilburn, London.

77. BARNARD, Henry William; B: Eastbourne; E: Eastbourne; Pte. GS 882; W: 16.5.16; Bethune Town Cem. Pas-de-Calais; Age 31; Son of Samuel and Mary Barnard; Husband of Edith Esther Barnard of 29, Channel View Road, Eastbourne.

78. BARNES, Albert; B: Croydon, Surrey; E: Croydon; Pte. G 5329; K: 24.4.17; Noeux-les-Mines Com. Cem. Pas-de-Calais; Age 26; Son of Mrs.R.Barnes of 19, Union Street, Old Town, Croydon.

79. BARNES, Hugh Cyril; Capt; K: 21.7.18; Loos Mem. Pas-de-Calais; M.C.; Age 21;*

80. BARNES, William; B: Birdham, Sussex; E: Chichester; Pte. G 1700; K: 25.9.15; Loos Mem. Pas-de-Calais; Age 20; Son of William and Clara Barnes of Rose Cottage, Court Lane, Birdham.

81. BARRAND, Herbert Beeson; B: Kings Cross, London; E: Brighton; Pte. GS 436; K: 25.9.15; Loos Mem. Pas-de-Calais; Age 37; Son of the late William Beeson Barrand and Mary Barrand of 27, Argyle Street, Kings Cross.

82. BARRY, James; B: Bermonsey, London; E: Southwark, London; Pte. G 5481; W: 24.3.16; Abbeville Com. Cem. Somme; Age 46; Husband of Elizabeth Barry of 78, Leroy Str

83. BARTHOLOMEW, Ernest Edward; B: Beddingham, Sussex; E: Newhaven, Sussex; Pte. G 1353; W: 7.3.16; Lapugnoy Mil. Cem. Pas-de-Calais.

84. BARTHOLOMEW, William Thomas; B: Lamberhurst, Kent; E: Hastings; L/Cpl. G 4353; K: 25.9.15; Dud Corner cem. Pas-de-Calais.

85. BARTHROPP, S.A.N.S.; 2nd Lt; K: 29.1.15.

86. BARTON, Reginald; B: Luton, Bedfordshire; E: Luton; L/Cpl. G 14510; K: 24.9.18; Vis-en-Artois Mem. Haucourt, Pas-de-Calais.

87. BARTON, William Henry; B: Chatham, Kent; E: Chatham; Pte. G 9065; W: 13.7.16; Heilly Station Cem., Mericourt-L'Abbé, Somme.

88. BASSETT, Robert; B: Southborough, Kent; E: Tunbridge Wells; Pte. L 8557; K: 9.5.15; Le Touret Mem. Pas-de-Calais; Age 27; Son of William Bassett of Southborough; Husband of Mary T.McDowell, formerly Bassett, of 1, Elm Sytreet, Belfast.

89. BASSFORD, John; B: Loughborough, Leicestershire; E: Nottingham; Pte. SD 654; K: 17.8.16; Thiepval Mem. Somme.

90. BATES, Arthur; B: Northiam, Sussex; E: Hastings; Pte. G 21010; K: 10.7.17; Ramscapelle Road Mil. Cem. (Bel.); Age 19; Son of John and Louisa Bates of 1, Orchard Terrace, Northiam.

91. BATT, Norman Harold; B: Hastings; E: Chichester; Pte. L 10140; K: 9.5.15; Le Touret Mem. Pas-de-Calais.

92. BATTLEY, Alfred William; B: Eye; E: Tollesbury; L/Cpl. G 14658; K: 9.4.18; Cambrin Mil. Cem. Pas-de-calais; Son of Alfred William Battley of Messing Street, Kelvedon, Essex.

93. BAXTER, Ralph Frederick; 2nd Lt; K: 29.5.15; Dud Corner Cem. Pas-de-Calais; Age 18; Son of John Henry and Ethel Louisa Baxter of Fryem, Pulborough, Sussex; Native of Gilston, Fife.

94. BEAL, Edgar; B: Lewes; E: Chichester; Pte. L 9964; K: 9.5.15; Le Touret Mem. Pas-de-Calais.

95. BEARD, William; B: Brighton; E: Chichester; Pte. L 10306; K: 14.11.17; Tyne Cot Mem. (Bel.); Age 23; Son of Frank and Harriett Beard of 10, Nelson Row, Brighton; Enlisted March, 1914.

96. BEARD, William; B: Chailey, Sussex; E: Brighton; Pte. G 21011; K: 19.9.18; Vis-en-Artois Mem. Haucourt, Pas de Calais; Age 41; Son of Harry Beard; Husband of Nellie Beard of Oakland Cottage, North Common, Chailey.

97. BEASLEY, Henry John; B: Greenwich, London; E: Greenwich; Pte. G 18548; W at Home: 29.10.18; Lewisham (Ladywell) Cem. (UK); Age 20; Son of Mr. and Mrs.J.H.Beasley of 55, Braxfield Road, Brockley, London.

98. BEATON, Harry; B: Headley; E: Littlehampton, Sussex; Pte. G 9068; K: 15.7.16; Thiepval Mem. Somme; Age 29; Son of Mary Ann Beaton of 22, Gloucester Place, Littlehampton.

99. BECK, George; B: Brighton; E: Brighton; Pte. L 7591; D: 5.5.17; Calais Southern Cem. Pas-de-Calais.

100. BEECHING, Henry Charles; B: Guestling, Sussex; E: Hastings; Pte. G 1716; K: 26.8.15; Vermelles Brit Cem. Pas-de-Calais; Age 26; Son of Luke and Ellen Beeching of Pett Road, Fairlight, Sussex.

101. BEER, Hugh Frank; B: Felpham, Sussex; E: Chichester; Pte. L 9064; K: 17.8.16; Thiepval Mem. Somme.

102. BEER, Thomas William; B: Herne Bay, Kent; E: Canterbury; Pte. G 17605; K: 9.9.16; Caterpillar Valley Cem. Somme; Age 19; Son of Frederick and Ellen Beer of Homestall Farm, Lynsted, Kent.

103. BEESLEY, Albert Victor; B: Bermondsey, London; E: Southwark, London; L/Cpl. G 5513; K: 2.3.16; Arras Mem. Pas-de-Calais.

104. BEESTON, Alfred Edward; B: Hastings; E: Brighton; Pte. G 4503; K: 13.10.15; Loos Mem. Pas-de-Calais.

105. BELL, Frederick John; B: Brighton; E: Chichester; Pte. L 10261; W: 9.5.15; Bethune Town Cem. Pas-de-Calais; Son of Mr.H.J.Bell of 57, Totland Road, Brighton.

106. BELLHAM, Robert Reginald; B: Fincham; E: King;s Lynn; Pte. G 9366; K: 15.7.16; Thiepval Mem. Somme.

107. BENISTON, Frank Percy; B: Swannington; E: Coalville; Pte. G 5214; K: 9.9.16; Thiepval Mem. Somme; Age 22; Son of John T. and Elizabeth Newbold Beniston of 18, Scotlands Road, Coalville.

108. BENNETT, Edward Henry; B: Portfield, Sussex; E: Chichester; L/Cpl. S 768; K: 9.5.15; Le Touret Mem. Pas-de-Calais.

109. BENNETT, George Frederick; B: Hellingly, Sussex; E: Eastbourne; Pte. G 1937; K: 1.3.17; Hem Farm Mil. Cem. Somme.

110. BENNETT, James; B: Godalming, Surrey; E: Guildford, Surrey; Pte. G 6078; K: 20.8.16; Thiepval Mem. Somme; Age 32; Son of George and Emily Bennett.

111. BERRY, Reginald John; B: Brighton; E: Chichester; Pte. L 10095; K: 24.4.16; Maroc Brit. Cem. Nord; Age 19; Son of John and Ada Berry of 23, Bampfield Street, Southcross, Portslade, Sussex.

112. BEVAN, George Edward; B: St.Luke's, Middlesex; E: London; Sgt. S 1849; W: 18.9.18; D.C.M.; Brie Brit. Cem. Somme.

113. BIGLAND, George; B: Hoxton; E: Dalston; Pte. L 6445; D: 19.9.15; Terlincthun Brit. Cem. Pas-de-Calais.

114. BIGNELL, Arthur Thomas; B: Eastbourne; E: Eastbourne; Pte. S 1809; K: 25.9.15; Loos Mem. Pas-de-Calais; Age 19; Son of Jabez and Elizabeth Bignell of 106, Firle Road, Eastbourne.

115. BIGNELL, Charles Albert; B: Kettering; E: Dalston; Pte. L 6736; W at Home: 18.5.15; Lincoln (Newport) Cem. (UK); Age 34; Son of John and Louisa Bignell of 19, Holmes Street, Shoreditch, London.

116. BILLINGS, Walter Thomas; B: West Hoathly, Sussex; E: Brighton; Pte. L 6177; W: 26.6.16; Maroc Brit. Cem. Nord; Age 36; Husband of Mary Isabel Billings of Birch Grove, East Grinstead, Sussex.

117. BILLINGTON, Joseph; B: Preston; E: Preston; Pte. G 6089; W: 13.10.15; Loos Mem. Pas-de-Calais; Son of Henry and Elizabeth Billington of 92, Wellington Street, Preston.

118. BINDOFF, Frank Ernest; B: Brighton; E: Brighton; Pte. G 9191; K: 2.9.16; Delville Wood Cem. Somme; Age 21; Son of Kate Bindoff of 76, Coventry Street, Brighton, and the late Frank Bindoff; Enlisted and killed together with his twin brother, Herbert Thomas (see 119).

119. BINDOFF, Herbert Thomas; B: Brighton; E: Brighton; Pte. G 9192; K: 2.9.16; Thiepval Mem. Somme; Son of Kate Bindoff of 76, Coventry Street, Brighton, and the late Frank Bindoff; Enlisted and killed together with his twin brother, Frank Ernest (see 118).

120. BIRCH, Sydney Joseph; B: KIngston-on-Thames; E: Kingston-on-Thames; L/Cpl. G 4044; K: 9.9.16; Thiepval Mem. Somme; Age 24; Son of Thomas A. and Ada Annie Birch of 23, Mill Place, Kingston-on-Thames.

121. BIRD, Allan; B: Walton; E: Whitehall, London; Pte. G 34523; W: 4.11.18; La Vallee-Mulatre Com. Cem. Ext. Aisne; Age 20; Son of Robert and Annie Bird of Nutty's Farm, Childerditch, Essex.

122. BISH, Edward Thomas; B: Dover; E: London; C.Q.M.S.; L 6774; W: 19.9.14; St.Nazaire (Toutes Aides) Cem. Loire-Atlantique; Age 20; Son of Thomas and Alice Bish of Dover; Husband of Lydia N.A.Bish of 137, Hartington Road, Brighton.

123. BISHOP, James; B: Burwash, Sussex; E: St.Leonards-on-Sea; Pte. L 8353; K: 17.8.16; Thiepval Mem. Somme; Age 28; Son of Thomas and Hannah Bishop of Palmer's Cottages, Dallington, Sussex.

124. BLACKMAN, Alexander John; B: Walworth, London; E: Camberwell, London; Pte. L 11876; W: 18.9.18; Brie Brit. Cem. Somme.

125. BLACKMAN, Arthur Harold; B: Emsworth, Hampshire; E: Hove; Sgt. L 10597; K: 26.6.16; Maroc Brit. Cem. Nord; Age 24; Son of Maurice and Emily Blackman of 17, Linden Road, Littlehampton, Sussex.

126. BLACKMAN, Ernest Charles; B: Hastings; E: Hastings; Pte. L 6890; K: 7.11.14; Ypres (Menin Gate) Mem. (Bel.).

127. BLACKMAN, George; B: Worthing; E: Chichester; Pte. L 8043; K: 14.9.14; Vendresse Brit. Cem. Aisne.

128. BLACKMAN, Jacob; B: Hampstead, London; E: KIlburn, London; Cpl. GS 583; K: 26.9.16; Thiepval Mem. Somme; Age 28; Son of Mrs.Emma Blackman of 37, Netherwood Street, Brondesbury, London; Husband of Rose Lilian Rowe Blackman of 313, Kilburn Lane, Willesden, London.

129. BLACKMAN, Maurice Henry; B: Cold Waltham; E: Chichester; Pte. G 4615; K: 9.5.15; Le Touret Mem. Pas-de-Calais.

130. BLACKMORE, Herbert Arthur; B: St.Peter's, Sussex; E: Chichester; L/Cpl. L 10056; K: 25.9.15; Dud Corner Cem. Pas-de-calais.

131. BLAKE, Frederick William; B: Cowfold, Sussex; E: Norwood; Pte. G 5447; K: 9.9.16; Thiepval Mem. Somme.

132. BLAKE, W.B.; B: -; E: -; Pte. L 7854; D at Home: 5.10.17; Croydon (Queen's Road) Cem. (UK); Age 33; Son of Albert Benjamin and Agnes Blake of 58, Jarvis Road, Croydon; Husband of Isabel Sarah Blake.

133. BUSS, Ernest; B: Hastings; E: Hastings; Pte. L 10129; K: 20.8.16; Thiepval Mem. Somme.

134. BLOORE, Fred; B: Leek, Staffordshire; E: Leek; Pte. G 1584; K: 9.5.15; Le Touret Mem. Pas-de-Calais.

135. BLUNDEN, Edward William; B: Midhurst, Sussex; E: Chichester; Cpl. L 10143; K: 26.1.15; Le Touret Mem. Pas-de-Calais; Age 21; Son of Mrs.Mary Fielder of Burnt House, Rowhook, Broadbridge Heath, Sussex.

136. BOARER, Charles; B: Withyham, Sussex; E: Tunbridge Wells; Pte. L 10393; K: 25.9.15; Loos Mem. Pas-de-Calais; Age 21; Son of William Henry and Mary Boarer of Tanyard New Cottages, Groombridge, Sussex.

137. BOLD, Edward; B: Yuisawdre, Glamorgan; E: Cowbridge; Pte. G 1119; W: 24.8.16; Dernancourt Com. Cem. Ext. Somme.

138. BOLT, Charles Henry; B: Worthing; E: Littlehampton, Sussex; Pte. G 1269; K: 25.9.15; Loos Mem. Pas-de-Calais; Age 21; Son of Mrs. Harriett Bolt of Beacon House, Watersfield, Pulborough, Sussex.

139. BONIFACE, Albert; B: East Dean, Sussex; E: Eastbourne; Pte. L 6996; W: 20.9.14; La Ferte-sous-Jouarre Mem. Seine-et-Marne.

140. BONIFACE, Charles William; B: Poling, Sussex; E: Worthing; Pte. GS 351; K: 25.9.15; Loos Mem. Pas-de-Calais; Age 37; Son of Steven and Harriett Boniface; Husband of Amy M.Boniface of 31, Penfold Road, Broadwater, Worthing, Sussex.

141. BONIFACE, Frederick Arthur; B: Pound Common, Sussex; E: Chichester; Pte. G 1139; K: 25.9.15; Loos Mem. Pas-de-Calais; Age 30; Son of George and

Charlotte Boniface of Terwick Mill Lane, Rogate, Sussex.

142. BONIFACE, Frederick George; B: Brighton; E: Brighton; Pte. G 4967; K: 23.6.16; Thiepval Mem. Somme; Age 24; Son of David and Amelia Letitia Boniface of 18, Mount Sion Place, Brighton.

143. BONIFACE, George Henry; B: Eastbourne; E: Hastings; Pte. L 7313; K: 20.1.15; Le Touret Mem. Pas-de-Calais; Age 30; Served in the South Africa Campaign and in India; Son of George Richard Boniface of 39, New Road, Eastbourne.

144. BONIFACE, Walter; B: St.Luke's, Middlesex; E: Wood Green; Pte. L 10560; K: 9.5.15; Le Touret Mem. Pas-de-Calais; Age 21; Son of Mr. and Mrs.B.Boniface of 96, Rathcoole Gardens, Hornsey, London.

145. BONNETT, Herbert; B: Great Waltham, Essex; E: Chelmsford, Essex; Pte. G 14660; K: 28.9.16; Thiepval Mem. Somme; Age 20; Son of John and Sarah Bonnett of Broad's Green, Great Waltham.

146. BOOTH, Charles Frederick; B: Dallington, Sussex; E: Battle, Sussex; L/Cpl. L 10339; K: 9.5.15; Cabaret-Rouge Brit. Cem. Pas-de-Calais; Age 18; Son of Frederick W. and Alice Booth of Manor Cottage, Brightling, Sussex.

147. BOOTY, William George; B: -; E: Colchester, Essex; Pte. G 14594; K: 14.11.17; Tyne Cot Mem. (Bel.); Age 20; Son of James William and Lucy Booty of 3, Sutton Court Drive, Rochford, Essex.

148. BOTTEN, John; B: Eltham; E: Woolwich; Pte. G 18541; K: 24.9.18; Berthaucourt Com. Cem. Aisne.

149. BOURN, Henry; B: Slaugham, Sussex; E: Brighton; Pte. G 4351; K: 25.9.15; Loos Mem. Pas-de-Calais; Age 32; Son of Henry Bourn; Husband of Louisa Streeter, formerly Bourn, of 4, London Road, Balcombe, Sussex.

150. BOURNE, Arthur Prince Wales; B: Canterbury; E: Canterbury; Pte. G 17532; K: 1.9.16; Thiepval Mem. Somme; Age 18; Son of Ernest Albert and Agnes Bourne of 2, Maypole Cottages, Sturry, Kent.*

151. BOURNE, Harold; B: Hastings; E: Hastings; Pte. S 2250; K: 17.8.16; Thiepval Mem. Somme.

152. BOURNE, Thomas Charles; B: Bolney, Sussex; E: Horsham, Sussex; Pte. S 414; K: 31.10.14; Ypres (Menin Gate) Mem. (Bel.).

153. BOURNE, William; B: Rye, Sussex; E: Rye; Pte. G 2142; K: 9.5.15; Le Touret Mem. Pas-de-Calais; Age 26; Son of Mrs.Harriett Smith of 12, Mermaid Street, Rye.

154. BOURNE, William Edward; B: Slaugham, Sussex; E: Haywards Heath, Sussex; Pte. G 1284; K: 27.1.15; Woburn Abbey Cem. Pas-de-Calais; Husband of M.Bourne of 6, Albert Cottages, Dante Avenue, Lindfield, Sussex.

155. BOWLEY, Bertram; B: Littlehampton, Sussex; E: Littlehampton; Pte. S 2078; K: 25.9.15; Loos Mem. Pas-de-Calais; Age 21; Son of Thomas Bowley of 2, Central Gardens, Littlehampton.

156. BOX, Sidney; B: Bristol; E: Bristol; Pte. G 17137; K: 23.10.18; St.Souplet Brit. Cem. Nord; Age 20; Son of Walter and Susan Ann Box of 17, Mildred Street, Barton Hill, Bristol.

157. BOXALL, Reginald Albert; B: Bedham; E: Horsham; Pte. SD 5343; K: 16.8.16; Thiepval Mem. Somme.

158. BOXALL, Sydney Charles; B: West Dean, Sussex; E: Chichester; Pte. G 8597; K: 18.4.18; Woburn Abbey Cem. Pas-de-Calais; Age 22; Son of Arthur and Charlotte Boxall of 84, The Warren, West Dean.

159. BOXALL, Walter Henry; B: Harting, Sussex; E: Chichester; Pte. G 11744; K: 10.7.17; Nieuport Mem. (Bel.).

160. BOYNE, William; B: Huswell; E: Sunderland; Pte. G 5118; K: 13.10.15; Loos Mem. Pas-de-Calais.*

161. BRACKPOOL, Sidney Edward; B: Worth, Sussex; E: East Grinstead, Sussex; Pte. G 4630; K: 9.5.15; Le Touret Mem. Pas-de-Calais.

162. BRADFORD, John; B: Broad Clyst; E: Hastings; Pte. L 7374; K: 12.10.14; La Ferte-sous-Jouarre Mem. Seine-et-Marne; Age 37; Son of John and mary Bradford.

163. BRADLEY, Ernest Arthur; B: Hastings; E: St.Leonards-on-Sea; L/Cpl. S 1547; K: 9.9.16; Thiepval Mem. Somme.

164. BRADLEY, William Alexander; B: Greenwich, London; E: Greenwich; Pte. G 10870; K: 27.9.16; Thiepval Mem. Somme; Age 20; Son of Mrs.Mary Bradley of 5, Rockfield Street, Greenwich.

165. BRADSHAW, John; B: Croydon; E: Eastbourne; Pte. S 8978; K: 25.9.15; Loos Mem. Pas-de-Calais.

166. BRANDOM, Ernest Samuel; B: Luton, Bedfordshire; E: Luton; Pte. G 14511; K: 9.9.16; Thiepval Mem. Somme; Age 21; Son of Frederick George and Sarah Ann Brandom of 38, Duke Street, Luton.

167. BRAZIL, George Thomas; B: Northiam, Sussex; E: Rye, Sussex; Pte. L 10159; W: 10.5.15; Bethune Town Cem. Pas-de-Calais; Age 21; Son of John and Rose Elizabeth Brazil of Dew Farm, Peasmarsh, Sussex.

168. BRECK, Alfred George; B: Bermondsey, London; E: Rotherhithe, London; Pte. G 14419; K: 18.9.18; Jeancourt Com. Cem. Aisne; Age 31; Son of George and Nance Breck of Rotherhithe; Husband of Lydia E.Breck of 16, Eden Road, Elmer's End, Beckenham.

169. BREED, George Henry; B: Woolwich, London; E: Southwark, London; Pte. G 5043; W: 29.9.15; Lillers Com. Cem. Pas-de-Calais.

170. BREEDS, George; B: Brighton; E: Brighton; Sgt. L 8977; K: 18.9.14; La Ferte-sous-Jouarre Mem. Seine-et-Marne.

171. BRETT, Charles; B: Hellingly, Sussex; E: Eastbourne; Pte. L 8548; K: 9.5.15; Le Touret Mem. Pas-de-Calais; Age 28; Son of Mrs.Rosana Brett of 65, King Edward's Road, Ponders End, London.

172. BRIDGER, Frank; B: Worthing; E: Worthing; Sgt. TF 201028; W: 18.9.18; Hancourt Brit. Cem.

Somme; Age 26; Son of Mrs. E.Bridger of 33, Gloucester Place, Worthing.

173. BRIDGER, William Albert; B: Newmarket; E: Chichester; L/Cpl. L 9082; W: 24.8.16; Heilly Station Cem., Mericourt L'Abbé, Somme.

174. BRIDGER, W.P.; B -; E: -; Pte. V 6832; D at Home; 13.8.18; Findon (St.John the Baptist) Churchyard (UK); Age 34; Husband of Mrs.F.M.Bridger of 4, Leigh Road, Broadwater, Worthing.*

175. BRIDGES, Frederick John; B: Hawkinge, Kent; E: Folkestone, Kent; Pte. G 17615; W: 24.1.18. Étaples Mil. Cem. Pas-de-Calais; Son of Albert William and Margaret Anne Bridges of Martello Hotel, Folkestone.

176. BRIGHT, John Leslie; 2nd Lt; K: 25.9.15; Loos Mem. Pas-de-Calais; Age 26.

177. BRISTOW, Percy; B: Hastings; E: Worthing; Pte. G 1518; K: 9.9.16; Thiepval Mem. Somme; Age 28; Son of Robert and Martha Bristow of 207, Harold Road, Hastings; Husband of Florence Matilda Harvey, formerly Bristow, of 80, All Saints Street, Hastings.

178. BRITT, Ralph; B: Bexhill-on-Sea; E: Bexhill-on-Sea; Pte. G 4358; K: 23.11.16; Thiepval Mem. Somme.

179. BRITTON, Arthur Henry; B: Ramsgate, Kent; E: Chelsea, London; Pte. G 14776; K: 27.9.16; Thiepval Mem. Somme; Age 21; Son of John and Matilda H.Britton of 182, High Street, Ramsgate.

180. BRITTON, Sidney George; B: Clacton-on-Sea, Essex; E: Colchester, Essex; Pte. G 14593; W: 6.6.18; Cambrin Mil. Cem. Pas-de-Calais; Age 25; Son of Fredrick and Elizabeth Britton of 2, Railway Cottages, Thorpe-le-Stoke, Essex.

181. BROAD, Clifford Newman; 2nd Lt; W: 9.4.16; Noeux-les-Mines Com. Cem. Pas-de-Calais; Age 21; Son of Nelson and Alice Sarah Broad of 3R, Gillespie Crescent, Edinburgh.

182. BROADBRIDGE, Alfred; B: St.Peter's, Kent; E: Canterbury; Pte. L 8101; K: 18.9.14; La Ferte-sous-Jouarre Mem. Seine-et-Marne; Age 29; Son of Mrs.Frances Broadbridge of 29, Notley Street, Canterbury.

183. BROMLEY, Ernest Gerald; B: Stamford Hill; E: Rye, Sussex; Pte. G 9232; K: 7.8.16; Thiepval Mem. Somme.

184. BROMLEY, Hugh Frederic; 2nd Lt; K: 25.9.15; Loos Mem. Pas-de-Calais; Age 19; Son of Richard and Edith Maud bromley of Carnedd, Rhyl.

185. BROOK, Charles Alfred; B: Burwash, Sussex; E: London; Cpl. G 4146; K: 20.8.16; Theipval Mem. Somme.

186. BROOK, Clifford; B: Warbleton, Sussex; E: Eastbourne; Pte. G 8246; K: 10.1.18; Duhallow A.D.S. Cem. (Bel.).

187. BROOK, Ernest Bertram; B: Eastbourne; E: Eastbourne; Pte. L 10266; K: 23.6.16; Theipval Mem. Somme; Age 20; Son of James and Susannah Brook of 1, Ocklynge Avenue, Eastbourne.*

188. BROOK, William; B: Ninfield, Sussex; E: Eastbourne; Pte. GS 819; K: 13.10.15; Loos Mem. Pas-de-Calais.

189. BROOK, William Henry; B: Lewes; E: Worthing; Pte. L 10490; K: 25.9.15; Loos Mem. Pas-de-Calais; Age 18; Son of James and Avis Brook of 474, Roundabouts, Storrington, Sussex.

190. BROOKER, Charles Frederick; B: Hove; E: East Grinstead, Sussex; Pte. L 10415; K: 1.1.15; Le Touret Mem. Pas-de-Calais.

191. BROOKER, Henry; B: Brighton; E: Brighton; Pte. G 1536; W: 30.1.15; Beuvry Com. Cem. Somme; Brother of Mr.J.G.Brooker of 'St.Marys', Broadwater, Worthing.

192. BROOKS, Aubrey; B: Newick, Sussex; E: Lewes; L/Cpl. G 1335; K: 9.5.15; Le Touret Mem. Pas-de-Calais; Age 26; Son of Mr.A.J.Brooks of Allington Road, Newick; Probably enlisted, and certainly served with, his brother, Jack, who was also killed on the same day and also has no known grave (see 193).

193. BROOKS, Jack; B: Newick, Sussex; E: Lewes; Pte. G 1320; K: 9.5.15; Le Touret Mem. Pas-de-Calais; Age 25; Son of Mr.J.A.Brooks of Allington Road, Newick; Probably enlisted, and certainly served with, his brother, Aubrey, who was also killed on the same day and also has no known grave (see 192). 194.

194. BROOKS, Samuel; B: Kew, London; E: Walthamstow, London; Pte. G 14743; K: 29.3.18; Buffs Road, Cem., St.Jean-les-Ypres (Bel.); Brother of Mr.E.P.Brooks of 15, Powell Road, Chiswick, London.

195. BROOM, Joseph; B: Hoxton, London; E: Epping, Essex; Pte. G 19899; K: 21.11.17; Tyne Cot Mem. (Bel.); Age 28; Son of Joseph Broom of 34, Allerton Street, New North Road, London; Husband of Jessica Ellen Broom of 18, Stanley Road, South Woodford, Essex.

196. BROWN, Albert Edward; B: Hastings; E: Hastings; Pte. G 9093; K: 2.9.16; Theipval Mem. Somme; Age 20; Son of William James and Emily Brown of 2, Oakfield Cottages, Cockfosters, London.

197. BROWN, Bert; B: Edenbridge; E: Lewes; Pte. G 8988; K: 20.8.16; Thiepval Mem. Somme.

198. BROWN, Bertie Frank; B: Leighton Buzzard, Bedfordshire; E: Dunstable, Bedfordshire; Pte. G 14503; K: 9.9.16; Thiepval Mem. Somme.

199. BROWN, Charles Edwin; B: Greenwich, London; E: Newport, Monmouthshire; Pte. G 7686; K: 15.8.16; Caterpillar Valley Cem. Somme; Age 18; Son of Mrs.Kate Brown of 45, Macclesfield Street, City Road, London.*

200. BROWN, Charles; B: Newick, Sussex; E: Lewes; Pte. G 4458; K: 25.9.15; Loos Mem. Pas-de-Calais; Age 26; Son of James and Eliza Brown of Font Hill, Newick.

201. BROWN, Frank; B: Buxted, Sussex; E: Lewes; Pte. L 6303; K: 30.10.14; Ypres (Menin Gate) Mem. (Bel.).

202. BROWN, George Allen; B: Barcombe, Sussex; E: Ditchling, Sussex; Pte. G 1141; K: 1.6.16; Maroc Brit. Cem. Nord; Age 31; Son of George and Ruth Brown of Tarring Neville, Sussex.*

203. BROWN, George William; B: Battersea, London;

E: Worthing; L/Cpl. G 1207; D: 3.2.15; Wimereux Com. Cem. Pas-de-Calais; Age 22; Son of Robert and Ellen Brown of Worthing; Died from enteric fever.

204. BROWN, Harold; B: Croydon; E: London; Pte. G 4648; W: 25.5.15; Boulogne Eastern Cem. Pas-de-Calais.

205. BROWN, Harry; B: St.Nicolas, Sussex; E: Eastbourne; Pte. L 8229; K: 17.9.14; La Ferte-sous-Jouarre Mem. Seine-et-Marne; Age 30; Brother of Mr.R.G.Brown of 222, High Street North, East Ham, London.*

206. BROWN, Henry Harry; B: Hastings; E: Hastings; Pte. S 1374; K: 31.12.14; Le Touret Mem. Pas-de-Calais; Son of Stephen Brown of 28, Fairlight Road, Hastings.

207. BROWN, John; B: Hurstwood, Sussex; E: Lewes; Pte. G 1644; K: 25.9.15; Loos Mem. Pas-de-Calais.

208. BROWN, Nathaniel Bertram; B: Saffron Walden, Essex; E: Brighton; Pte. G 1334; K: 26.5.15; Le Touret Mem. Pas-de-Calais.

209. BROWN, Sidney Edgar; B: South Bersted, Sussex; E: Bognor Regis, Sussex; Pte. G 6950; K: 23.7.16; Thiepval Mem. Somme; Age 23; Son of Charlotte Brown of 4, Franklin Terrace, Highfield, Bognor Regis.

210. BROWN, Thomas; B: Eastbourne; E: Eastbourne; Pte. L 10137; K: 30.10.14; Ypres (Menin Gate) Mem. (Bel.; Age 30; Son of Ezekiel and Elizabeth Brown.

211. BROWN, Walter George Charles; B: Eastbourne; E: Eastbourne; L/Cpl. S 813; W: 9.2.15; Boulogne Eastern Cem. Pas-de-Calais; Age 25; Son of Walter and Ellen Brown of 25, Western Road, Eastbourne.

212. BROWNE, Harry; B: London; E: Worthing; Pte. G 1506; W: 16.5.15; Longuenesse (St.Omer) Souvenir Cem. Pas-de-Calais; Age 24; Son of Mrs.G.Brown of 164, High Road, Tottenham, London.

213. BROWNING, Easter; B: Paddington, London; E: Dover; Pte. L 8205; K: 9.5.15; Le Touret Mem. Pas-de-Calais; Age 28; Son of Mrs.A.M.Browning of 120, London Road, Buckland, Dover.

214. BROWNING, John James; B: Southwick, Sussex; E: Hove; L/Cpl. G 8354; K: 27.11.16; Thiepval Mem. Somme; Age 32; Son of Eli and Elizabeth Martha Browning of 5, White Rock Place, Southwick.

215. BRYAN, Frederick Michael; B: Norwood, E: Chichester; Pte. L 6627; K: 25.1.15; Le Touret Mem. Pas-de-Calais.

216. BRYANT, George; B: Bexhill-on-Sea; E: Chichester; Pte. L 8193; W: 19.9.14; Montreuil-aux-Lions Brit. Cem. Aisne.

217. BUCKWELL, George Henry; B: Barcombe, Sussex; E: Brighton; Pte. G 1346; K: 30.6.16; Arras Mem. Pas-de-Calais; Age 21; Son of George and E,L. Buckwell of Slate Cottage, Barcombe.

218. BUDD, Henry Arthur; B: Worthing; E: Worthing; Pte. G 5541; K: 16.8.16; Thiepval Mem. Somme; Age 19; Son of George and Florence A.Budd of 27, West Street, Worthing.

219. BUGLER, Fredreick William; B: Redlanes; E: Ticehurst, Sussex; Pte. L 8162; K: 2.11.14; Tyne Cot Cem. (Bel.).

220. BULL, James; B: London; E: Manchester; L/Cpl. L 9252; K: 15.7.16; Thiepval Mem. Somme.

221. BULL, Thomas Richard; B: Chichester; E: Chichester; L/Cpl. L 8834; K: 9.5.15; Le Touret Mem. Pas-de-Calais; Age 27; Son of Thomas and Martha Bull of 118, St.Pancras, Chichester.

222. BULMAN, Charles; B: Denton, Sussex; E: Lewes; Sgt. L 8143; K: 9.5.15; Le Touret Mem. Pas-de-Calais.

223. BUNDY, Fred Graham; B: Hampstead, London; E: Mill Hill, London; Pte. G 2167; W: 15.11.17; Tyne Cot Mem. (Bel.).

224. BURBERRY, Lionel; B: Reigate, Surrey; E: Horsham, Sussex; Pte. TF 201032; K: 20.10.18; Cross Roads Cem. Nord.

225. BURCHELL, George; B: Horsham, Sussex; E: Horsham; Pte. S 416; K: 30.10.14; Ypres (Menin Gate) Mem. (Bel.).

226. BURDETT, Arthur James; B: Norwich; E: Norwich; Pte. G 19911; W at Home: 22.2.17; Norwich Cem. (UK); Age 19; Son of James and Emma Jane Burdett of 3, Quay Side, Wensum Street, Norwich.

227. BURDETT, George William; B: Blofield, Norfolk; E: Norwich; Pte. G 9339; W at Home: 25.9.16; Blofield (SS. Andrew and Peter) Churchyard (UK).

228. BURFORD, Frank; B: Brighton; E: Chichester; Pte. L 10210; K: 1.3.16; Dud Corner Cem. Pas-de-Calais.

229. BURGE, Russell; B: Hastings; E: Brighton; Pte. L 10070; K: 9.5.15; Le Touret Mem. Pas-de-Calais.

230. BURGESS, Walter; Capt; K: 13.10.15; Loos Mem. Pas-de-Calais.

231. BURR, Henry Rivers; B: Hadleigh; E: Southend-on-Sea, Essex; Pte. G 35431; W: 18.10.18; Vis-en-Artois Mem. Haucourt, Pas-de-Calais; Age 20; Son of John and Mary Burr of Cherry Gardens, Runsell Green, Danbury, Essex.

232. BURRELL, Frederick George; B: Brighton; E: Leeds; Pte. G 8548; K: 19.8.16; Thiepval Mem. Somme; Age 23; Son of George and Maud Burrell of 21, Allerton Terrace, Kirkstall Road, Leeds.

233. BURRELL, William Henry; B: Pulborough, Sussex; E: -; Pte. L 10414; K: 22.5.16; Mazingarbe Com. Cem. Ext. Pas-de-Calais; Age 21; Son of Charles Alfred and Fanny Burrell of Mill House, Fishbourne, Chichester; 'Shot at Dawn' following his second Courts Marshall conviction for desertion.

234. BURT, Alexander; B: Crossgate, Fife; E: Stepney, London; Sgt. G 5842; W: 14.9.16; Heilly Station Cem., Mericourt L'Abbé, Somme.

235. BURT, William Francis; B: Cuckfield, Sussex; E: Cuckfield; Pte. L 7569; K: 30.10.14; Ypres (Menin Gate) Mem. (Bel.).

236. BURT, William James; B: Eastbourne; E: Chichester; Pte. L 10146; K: 25.9.15; Loos Mem. Pas-de-Calais.

237. BURTON, Gilbert John; B: Tunstead, Norfolk; E: Norwich; Pte. G 14663; K: 13.11.17; Tyne Cot Mem. (Bel.); Age 22; Son of Benjamin George Burton of Mill Lane, Tunstead; Husband of Gertrude Louise Jane Woodhouse, formerly Burton, of Gunn's Corner, Smallburgh, Norfolk.

238. BURTON, Thomas James; B: Poplar, London; E: Stratford, London; Pte. L 9619; K: 30.10.14; Ypres (Menin Gate) Mem. (Bel.); Age 19; Son of Thomas and Julia Ann Burton of 22, Janet Street, Poplar.

239. BUSBY, Frank; B: Ramsgate, Kent; E: Brighton; Cpl. L 9843; K: 26.1.15; Le Touret Mem. Pas-de-Calais; Age 21; Son of Charles and Isabella Busby of 35, Shakespeare Road, Portsmouth.

240. BUSH, John; B: Cheshunt; E: Cheshunt; Pte. G 11201; W: 28.9.16; Dernancourt Com. Cem. Ext. Somme.

241. BUSH, Robert Stanley; B: Camden Town, London; E: Kilburn, London; Pte. G 5532; K: 23.7.16; Thiepval Mem. Somme; Age 22; Son of Robert and Alice Bush of 40, Maygrove Road, Brondesby, London; Husband of Matilda Bush of 17, Bolton Road, St.John's Wood, London.

242. BUSHBY, Frederick; B: Tarring, Sussex; E: Chichester; Pte. L 6622; K: 30.10.14; Ypres (Menin Gate) Mem. (Bel.).

243. BUSS, Alfred John; B: Croydon; E: Hastings; Pte. L 10934; K: 20.8.16; Thiepval Mem. Somme.

244. BUSSEY, Frederick George Alfred; B: Brighton; E: Brighton; Pte. G 9012; K: 18.12.16; Thiepval Mem. Somme.

245. BUTCHER, Percy; B: -; E: Brighton; Pte. G 17591; K: 24.9.18; Bellicourt Brit. Cem. Aisne.

246. BUTFOY, Thomas; B: Hackney, London; E: London; Sgt. L 6778; K: 14.9.14; La Ferte-sous-Jouarre Mem. Seine-et-Marne.

247. BUTLER, Arthur; B: Hailsham, Sussex; E: Brighton; Pte. S 2237; K: 9.5.15; Le Touret Mem. Pas-de-Calais.

248. BUTLER, Henry John; B: Fulham, London; E: Shepherd's Bush, London; Sgt. G 4387; K: 24.9.18; Vadencourt Brit. Cem. Aisne.

249. BUTT, Jesse Albert, B: West Tarring, Sussex; E: Chichester; L/Cpl. L 10136; W: 31.1.15; Lillers Com. Cem. Pas-de-Calais; Mortal wounds received at La Bassee; Age 20; Son of Frederick and Fanny Butt of The Bungalow, 14, Brougham Road, Worthing.

250. BUTT, William; B: Petworth, Sussex; E: Chichester; Pte. G 1694; K: 25.9.15; Loos Mem. Pas-de-Calais; Age 32; Son of Henry and Jane Butt of Hill Top Cottage, Tillington, Sussex.

251. BYFORD, Frederick; B: Brighton; E: Brighton; Pte. G 9189; K: 7.8.16; Brewery Orchard Cem. Nord.

252. BYFORD, Percy; B: Grays, Essex; E: Brighton; Pte. S 1807; K: 28.9.16; Thiepval Mem. Somme.

253. BYLES, John Henry; B: Dedham; E: Dedham; Pte. G 14665; K: 18.9.18; Vis-en-Artois Mem. Haucourt, Pas-de-Calais; Age 23; Son of Mrs.Emily Jane Byles of 2, Prine Cottages, High Street, Dedham.

C

254. CAESAR, Robert George; B: Puttenham, E: Guildford, Surrey; Pte. G 4635; K: 9.5.15; Le Touret Mem. Pas-de-Calais; Age 18; Son of S. and Lucy Caesar of Willow Cottage, Merstham, Surrey.

255. CAGER, Albert James; B: Brighton; E: Brighton; Pte. G 1342; K: 26.5.15; Le Touret Mem. Pas-de-Calais.

256. CAIN, Ernest; B: Brighton; E: Chichester; Pte. G 1148; K: 16.2.15; Le Touret Mem. Pas-de-Calais.

257. CAMP, Albert; B: Hastings; E: Lewes; L/Cpl. G 1649; K: 25.9.15; Loos Mem. Pas-de-Calais.

258. CAMPANY, William Charles Ernest; B: Hastings; E: Hastings; Pte. L 9556; K: 25.9.15 at Battle of Loos; St.Mary's A.D.S. Cem. Pas-de-Calais; Age 23; Son of Mr. and Mrs.Frank Campany of 30, Cambridge Gardens, Hastings.

259. CAMPBELL, Frederick Victor; B: London; E: Liverpool; Pte. G 4422; K: 9.5.15; Le Touret Mem. Pas-de-Calais; Age 19.

260. CAMPKIN, Edward; B: London; E: Chichester; Pte. L 5810; W: 12.5.15; Longuenesse (St.Omer) Souvenir Cem. Pas-de-Calais; Age 34; Son of Thomas and Emily Campkin of 122, Clarendon Road, Notting Hill, London; Husband of Alice Maud Campkin of 'St.Helens', Grove Road, Havant, Hampshire.

261. CANNON, Joseph Robert; B: -; E: Sittingbourne, Kent; Pte. G 17568; Caterpillar Valley Cem. Somme; Age 21; Son of Hannah Chadwick, formerly Cannon, of 3, Lamb Yard, Church Street, Chiswick, London, and the late Joseph Cannon. K: 9.9.16.

262. CAPELIN, Charles Frederick; B: Lewes; E: Newhaven, Sussex; Pte. G 5766; K: 16.12.16; Thiepval Mem. Somme; Age 20; Son of Henry and Margery Capelin of Swanborough, Lewes.

263. CAPLEN, George; B: Worthing; E: Chichester; Pte. G 1152; K: 9.5.15; Le Touret Mem. Pas-de-Calais; Age 21; Son of David Henry and Fanny Caplen of Nepcote, Findon, Sussex.

264. CAPLIN, Jack; B: Lindfield, Sussex; E: Chichester; Pte. L 10030; K: 9.5.15; Le Touret Mem. Pas-de-Calais; Age 18; Son of Thomas and Betty Caplin of 1, Blackhill Cottages, Lindfield.

265. CAPLIN, John; B: Brighton; E: Brighton; Pte. G 5120; K: 30.6.16; Arras Mem. Pas-de-Calais; Age 37; Husband of Ada Caplin of 42, Windmill Street, Brighton.

266. CARDEY, Francis Henry; B: -; E: Colchester, Essex; Pte. G 14595; W: 29.9.16; St.Sever Cem. Rouen, Seine-Maritime; Age 19; Son of Harry and Hannah cardey of Fingringhoe, Essex.

267. CARPENTER, Percy George; B: Chiddingfold, Sussex; E: Arundel, Sussex; Pte. S 2160; K: 9.5.15; Le Touret Mem. Pas-de-Calais.

268. CARR, William; B: Buxted, Sussex; E: Brighton; Pte. G 1563; K: 9.5.15; Le Touret Mem. Pas-de-Calais.

269. CARRINGTON, Arthur James; B: -; E: Bethnal Green, London; Pte. G 18566; W: 3.1.19; St.Sever Cem. Ext. Rouen, Seine-Maritime; Age 20.

270. CARTER, Charles; B: Eastbourne; E: Eastbourne;

Cpl. L 8430; K: 9.5.15; Le Touret Mem. Pas-de-Calais.

271. CARTER, Charles; B: Beckley, Sussex; E: Hastings; Pte. G 1386; K: 29.3.18; Buffs Road Cem., St.Jean-les-Ypres (Bel.); Age 24; Son of Jesse and Henrietta Carter of Clay Hill, Beckley.

272. CARTER, Charles Henry; B: Northiam, Sussex; E: Hastings; Pte. G 1389; K: 9.5.15 at Richebourg; Le Touret Mem. Pas-de-Calais; Age 20; Son of Thomas Reuben Carter of Godden's Farm, Northiam; Enlisted with his brother, William Thomas, who was also killed and also has no known grave (see 274).

273. CARTER, Leslie; B: Buxted, Sussex; E: Worthing; Pte. L 10469; K: 9.5.15; Le Touret Mem. Pas-de-calais; Age 19.

274. CARTER, William Thomas; B: Northiam, Sussex; E: Hastings; Pte. G 1388; K: 29.1.15; Le Touret Mem. Pas-de-Calais; Age 24; Son of Thomas Reuben Carter of Godden's Farm, Northiam; Enlisted with his brother, Charles Henry, who was also killed and also has no known grave (see 272).

275. CARTNER, Hubert William; B: Keswick; E: Haywards Heath, Sussex; Pte. G 1477; K: 9.9.16; Thiepval Mem. Somme; Age 20; Son of James and Dinah Cartner of 13, Loundes Square, Knightsbridge, London.*

276. CARVER, Wyndham; B: Lodsworth; E: Chichester; Pte. L 10463; K: 9.5.15. Le Touret Mem. Pas-de-Calais.

277. CATCHPOLE, Alfred George; B: Rotherhithe, London; E: Woolwich, London; Sgt. L 5420; K: 9.9.16; M.M.; Thiepval Mem. Somme.

278. CATO, Edward; B: St.Peter's, Sussex; E: Chichester; L.Cpl. L 8008; K: 10.9.14; Montreuil-aux-Lions Brit. Cem. Aisne.

279. CATTERMOLE, William George; B: Clacton-on-Sea, Essex; E: Colchester, Essex; Pte. G 30157; D: 13.10.18; Vadencourt Brit. Cem. Aisne.

280. CHAFFER, Ernest Albert; B: Chilgrove, Sussex; E: Chichester; Pte. L 10539; K: 9.5.15; Le Touret Mem. Pas-de-Calais; Age 17; Son of Thomas Chaffer of Chilgrove.

281. CHALTON, Herbert Henry; B: Horsham, Sussex; E: Horsham; Pte. G 5529; W: 6.12.17; Wimereux Com. Cem. Pas-de-Calais.

282. CHAMP, Raymond; B: Cowfold; E: Worthing; Pte. G 1241; D at Home: 4.7.15; Worthing (Broadwater) Cem. (UK).

283. CHANDLER, Ernest; B: Lichfold; E: Chichester; Pte. L 9556; K: 9.5.15; Le Touret Mem. Pas-de-Calais; Age 23; Son of John and Rosa Chandler of 272, Leggatt Hill, Lodsworth, Sussex.

284. CHAPMAN, Alfred John; B: All Souls, Sussex; E: Brighton; Sgt. GS 341; W: 18.5.16; Lillers Com. Cem. Pas-de-Calais; Age 33; Husband of Maud E.Chapman of Fox Cottage, Whitesmith, Sussex.

285. CHAPMAN, John; B: -; E: Brighton; L/Cpl. G 16585; W: 17.10.18; Busigny Com. Cem. Ext. Nord; Age 30; Son of Charles and Elizabeth Chapman of Audley End, Essex; Husband of Emily Chapman of 8, Trevor Gardens, Glynde, Sussex.

286. CHAPPELL, Sydney; B: St.Matthew, Sussex; E: Brighton; Pte. L 8314; K: 14.9.14; Chauny Com. Cem. Brit. Ext. Aisne.

287. CHAPPLE, Thomas George; B: Westham, Pevensey, Sussex; E: Eastbourne; Pte. SD 1287; W: 19.9.18; Brie Brit. Cem. Somme.

288. CHASE, William; B: St.Pancras, Sussex; E: Hastings; Pte. SD 3744; K: 16.12.16; Thiepval Mem. Somme.

289. CHATFIELD, Albert Edward; B: Hastings; E: Chichester; Pte. L 6835; K: 14.10.14; La Ferte-sous-Jouarre Mem. Seine-et-Marne.

290. CHATFIELD, Frank; B: Haywards Heath, Sussex; E: Haywards Heath; Pte. G 1475; K: 9.5.15; Le Touret Mem. Pas-de-Calais; Age 28; Son of George Richard and Clara Ellen Chatfield of Kent Street, Cowfold, Sussex.

291. CHATFIELD, Horace; B: Hove; E: Haywards Heath, Sussex; L/Cpl. L 8181; K: 14.9.14; Grand-Seraucourt Brit. Cem. Aisne.

292. CHEAL, William George; B: Bexhill-on-Sea; E: Bexhill-on-Sea; Pte. G 8605; K: 20.8.16; Thiepval Mem. Somme; Age 20; Son of W.Cheal of Pashley Farm, Ninfield, Sussex.

293. CHEESMAN, Arthur; B: Cold Waltham; E: Chichester; Pte. L 7992; K: 9.5.15 at Richebourg; Le Touret Mem. Pas-de-Calais; Age 31; Son of John and Fanny Cheesman of Lower Nash, Nutbourne, Sussex.

294. CHESSELL, Thomas Edward; B: Brighton; E: Brighton; Cpl. L 9929; K: 10.9.14; Montreuil-aux-Lions Brit. Cem. Aisne; Age 20; Son of Henry and Mary Jane Chessell of 32, Frederick Street, Brighton.

295. CHILD, Gilbert Richard Gregory; 2nd Lt; K: 9.5.15; Le Touret Mem. Pas-de-Calais; Age 18; Son of Stephen Ambrose and Mabel Child of The Crossways, Cobham, Surrey.

296. CHILDS, Charles William; B: Shere, Surrey; E: Guildford, Surrey; Pte. L 10401; K: 26.8.15; Vermelles Brit. Cem. Pas-de-Calais.

297. CHILDS, Henry; B: Brighton; E: Wakefield; Pte. GS 478; K: 25.4.15; Cararet-Rouge Brit. Cem. Pas-de-Calais.*

298. CHILDS, Percy George; B: Yalding, Kent; E: Haywards Heath, Sussex; Pte. G 1326; K: 9.5.15; Le Touret Mem. Pas-de-Calais; Age 19; Son of George and Ann Elizabeth Childs of Rose Cottage, Yalding.

299. CHILDS, Tom; B: Woking, Surrey; E: Brighton; L/Cpl. S 637; K: 25.9.15; Loos Mem. Pas-de-Calais; Age 26; Son of Thomas and Kate Childs; Husband of Florence Emily Childs of 67, Howard Street, Worthing.

300. CHOWNE, Edward; B: Henfield, Sussex; E: Horsham, Sussex; Pte. G 3939; K: 25.9.15; Loos Mem. Pas-de-Calais.

301. CHURCHER, Ernest Frederick; B: Brighton; E: Croydon; Pte. S 1857; W: 7.9.15; Fouquieres Churchyard Ext. Pas-de-Calais; Age 19; Son of Wilfred Ernest and Laura Rosetta Churcher of The Old Post Office, Beddington, Croydon.

302. CLARK, Ernest Edward; B: Heathfield, Sussex; E: Eastbourne; Pte. G 8682; K: 23.7.16; Thiepval Mem. Somme.

303. CLARK, Ernest Jonathon; B: Cambridge; E: Cambridge; Pte. G 19117; D: 13.10.18; Vadencourt Brit. Cem. Aisne.

304. CLARK, George; B: Wandsworth, London; E: Lewes; Pte. GS 49; W: 31.1.15; Lillers Com. Cem. Pas-de-Calais; Age 40; Son of Thomas and Annie Clarke of Spring Gardens, Lewes; Husband of Ellen M.Parrott, formerly Clark, of 1019, Carrier Road, Montreal, Canada; Served 12 years in the Regiment including the Chitral, Punjab Frontier and Tirah Campaigns.

305. CLARK, James; B: Hastings; E: Hastings; Pte. SL 1290; K: 17.8.16; Thiepval Mem. Somme.

306. CLARK, James Tony; 2nd Lt; K: 9.9.16; Thiepval Mem. Somme; Age 23; Son of Thomas and Jane Clark of Llanover, Monmouthshire.

307. CLARK, John George; B: Clerkenwell, London; E: Holborn, London; L/Cpl. G 5146; K: 17.8.16. Thiepval Mem. Somme.

308. CLARK, William; B: Walthamstow, London; E: Woolwich, London; Pte. G 18562; W: 10.4.18; Lillers Com. Cem. Pas-de-Calais.

309. CLARKE, Alfred Ernest; B: Brighton; E: Brighton; Sgt. L 8090; K: 14.9.14; La Ferte-sous-Jouarre Mem. Seine-et-Marne; Age 28; Son of Joseph and Sarah Clarke of 198, Elm Grove, Brighton.*

310. CLAY, Charles Percy Parker; B: Sutton Bridge; E: Rye, Sussex; Sgt. L 9157; K: 9.5.15; Le Touret Mem. Pas-de-Calais; D.C.M., Medaille Militaire (France) and Cross of St.George 3rd Class (Russia); Age 29; Son of Mrs.Mary Anne Redmile-Clay of Tweespruit, New Romney, Kent.

311. CLAYTON, Frank; B: Edgbaston; E: Birmingham; Pte. G 5956; K: 17.8.16; Caterpillar Valley cem. Somme; Age 40; Son of William and Caroline Clayton.*

312. CLEARE, Archibald Thomas; B: Chichester; E: London; Sgt. L 8672; K: 25.9.15 at the Battle of Loos; St.Mary's A.D.S. Cem. Pas-de-Calais; Age 22; Son of William and Harriet Louisa Cleare of 54, York Road, Chichester.

313. CLEARE, William; B: Secunderabad, India; E: Chichester; R.S.M. L 2946; K: 10.9.14; Montreuil-aux-Lions Brit. Cem. Aisne; Age 40; Husband of E.M.Cleare of 11, Malden Hill Gardens, New Malden.

314. CLEVETT, Herbert George; B: Angmering, Sussex; E: Chichester; Cpl. L 6816; W: 6.11.14; Ypres Town Cem. Ext. (Bel.).

315. CLEVETT, James; B: Selsey, Sussex; E: Brighton; Pte. G 4801; K: 25.9.15; Loos Mem. Pas-de-Calais.

316. CLIFFORD, William; B: Bath; E: Tring, Hertfordshire; Pte. G 15209; K: 24.9.18; Vis-en-Artois Mem Haucourt, Pas-de-Calais; Age 38; Brother of John Clifford of Young Fox, Holloway, Bath.

317. CLIFTON, William; B: Ticehurst, Sussex; E: Ticehurst; Pte. L 8323; K: 25.1.15; Le Touret Mem. Pas-de-Calais; Age 34; Son of James and Annie Clifton.

318. COATES, Charles Arthur; B: Brighton; E: Brighton; Pte. G 3430; W: 22.9.18; Ste.Marie Cem., Le Havre, Seine-Maritime; Age 24; Son of John Albert and May Coates of 17, Viaduct Road, Brighton.

319. COATSWORTH, Edgar; B: St.Faith's, Kent; E: Canterbury; Cpl. L 8058; K: 9.5.15; Le Touret Mem. Pas-de-Calais; Age 26; Son of Arthur Tom Coatsworth of 27, Coome Road, Tovil, Maidstone; Husband of E.G.Coatsworth of 49, Brewer Street, Maidstone.

320. COBBOLD, Reginald Louis; B: Holloway, London; E: Southwark, London; Pte. G 5582; K: 21.3.16; Maroc Brit. Cem. Nord; Age 17; Son of Clement Louis and Emma Bessie Cobbold of 1, Blythwood Road, Crouch End, London.

321. COBBY, William Richard; B: Worthing; E: Worthing; Pte. G 9067; W: 24.9.16; Étaples Mil. Cem. Pas-de-Calais; Age 27; Son of George and Charlotte Cobby of 47, Lyndhurst Road, Worthing.

322. COE, Arthur William; B: St.Barnabas, Kent; E: Tunbridge Wells; L/Cpl. G 8162; K: 18.9.18; Cerisy-Gailly Mil. Cem. Somme; Age 24; Son of Mr. and Mrs.J.Coe of 13, Dorking Road, Tunbridge Wells.

323. COLBEAR, John Henry; B: Heybridge; E: Heybridge; Pte. G 14596; K: 9.9.16; Thiepval Mem. Somme; Age 18; Son of David and Mary Ann Colbear of Briar Cottage, Purleigh, Mundon, Essex.

324. COLBRAN, Samuel George; B: Crowborough, Sussex; E: Crowborough; Pte. L 8876; K: 14.9.14; La Ferte-sous-Jouarre Mem. Seine-et-Marne.

325. COLBRAN, Thomas George; B: Hastings; E: Hastings; Pte. G 1520; K: 9.5.15; Le Touret Mem. Pas-de-Calais.

326. COLE, Ernest; B: Brighton; E: Brighton; Pte. L 8897; W: 10.5.15; Le Touret Mem. Pas-de-Calais; Age 24; Son of William and Louisa Cole 40, Scotland Street, Brighton.

327. COLE, William Albert; B: Hove; E: Hove; Pte. GS 744; K: 9.5.15; Le Touret Mem. Pas-de-Calais.

328. COLEMAN, George Thomas; B: Brighton; E: Brighton; Pte. G 1331; K: 23.11.17; Tyne Cot Mem. (Bel.); Son of Annie Maria Coleman of 35, Parklands Road, Hassocks, Sussex.

329. COLEMAN, Herbert Edward Evatt; 2nd Lt; K: 9.9.16; Thiepval Mem. Somme.

330. COLEMAN, Sidney Frank; B: Arlington, Sussex; E: Eastbourne; Pte. L 9923; K: 2.11.14; Ypres (Menin Gate) Mem. (Bel.).

331. COLEMAN, Thomas Henry; B: Brighton; E: Marylebone, London; Pte. G 4775; K: 25.9.15; Loos Mem. Pas-de-Calais.

332. COLEMAN, William Valentine; B: Ramsgate, Kent; E: Chelsea, London; Pte. G 4089; K: 25.9.15; Dud Corner Cem. Pas-de-Calais; Age 28; Son of Mrs. Martha Coleman of 36, Denmark Road, Lowestoft.

333. COLES, William John Thomas; B: Kensington, London; E: Worthing; Pte. L 10497; K: 25.9.15; Loos Mem. Pas-de-Calais.

334. COLES, William Thomas; B: Brighton; E: Brighton; Pte. S 2181; K: 25.9.15; Dud Corner Cem. Pas-de-

Calais; Age 21; Son of William and Rebecca Coles of 8, Newmarket Road, Brighton.

335. COLLINGS, Thomas Edward; B: Chichester; E: Chichester; Pte. L 8444; W: 2.11.14; Longuenesse (St.Omer) Souvenir Cem. Pas-de-Calais.

336. COLLINS, Charles Frank; B: Hastings; E: Chichester; Pte. L 10373; K: 25.1.15; Le Touret Mem. Pas-de-Calais; Age 19; Son of Ernest John and Ester Guy Collins of Duke Terrace, Silverhill, St.Leonards-on-Sea.

337. COLLINS, George William; B: Northiam, Sussex; E: Rye, Sussex; Pte. S 657; K: 26.1.15; Le Touret Mem. Pas-de-Calais.

338. COLLINS, John; B: Horsham, Sussex; E: Horsham; Pte. L 7331; W: 31.10.14; Ypres (Menin Gate) Mem. (Bel.); Age 32; Son of James and Fanny Collins.

339. COLLINS, Neville Lancelot; Lt; K: 15.8.16; Caterpillar Valley Cem. Somme; Age 22; Son of the Reverend Canon and Mrs.Percy H.Collins of The rectory, Lydd, Kent.

340. COLLINS, Sidney; B: Ashford, Kent; E: Canterbury; Pte. G 17550; K: 22.11.16; Theipval Mem. Somme.

341. COLWELL, Charles George; B: Brighton; E: Brighton; Pte. L 7704; W at Home: 1.3.15; Brighton (Bear Road) Cem. (UK); Age 28; Son of Mr.H.Colwell and husband of Harriett Colwell of 67a, Islington Street, Brighton.

342. COMBER, William Ephraim; B: West Hoathly, Sussex; E: East Grinstead, Sussex; Pte. GS 933; K: 9.5.15; Le Touret Mem. Pas-de-Calais; Age 42; Son of William and Elizabeth Comber of West Hoathly; Husband of Edith Constance Comber of 2, Bow Cottages, West Hoathly.

- - - COMPORO, Richard John Frederick; An alias surname; see PEARMAN (1176).

343. CONLON, Patrick; B: Cardiff; E: Hove; Pte. G 6801; K: 13.10.15; Loos Mem. Pas-de-Calais; Age 32; Son of Bernard and Catherine Conlon.

344. CONSTABLE, William; B: Findon, Sussex; E: Chichester; Sgt. L 9215; K: 25.9.15; Loos mem. Pas-de-Calais.

345. COOK, Albert; B: Brighton; E: Brighton; Pte. G 20693; W: 14.11.17; Lijssenthoek Mil. Cem. (Bel.); Age 20; Foster son of J.T.Upperton of 10, St.Leonards Avenue, Hove.

346. COOK, Charles Edwin James; B: Brixton, London; E: London; L/Cpl. L 6381; K: 4.9.15; Vermelles Brit. Cem. Pas-de-Calais; Age 31; Son of Charles Edwin and Esther Cook of Peckham, London; Husband of Lucy Ellen Cook of 50, Sydney Square, Latona Road, Peckham.

347. COOK, Cyril Edward; Lt. W: 8.7.16; Chocques Mil. Cem. Pas-de-Calais.

348. COOK, Thomas Henry; B: Rye, Sussex; E: Hastings; L/Cpl. G 5390; W: 24.8.16; Heilly Station Cem., Mericourt L'Abbé, Somme.

349. COOKE, Stanley; B: Hastings; E: Hastings; Pte. G 4916; K: 25.9.15; Loos Mem. Pas-de-Calais; Age 20; Son of James and Annie Cook of The Vines, Udimore, Sussex.

350. COOKE, William Edward; B: Tunbridge Wells; E: Choichester; Pte. S 2219; K: 25.9.15; Loos Mem. Pas-de-Calais.

351. COOKSON, Mostyn Eden; Maj; K: 14.9.14; La Ferte-sous-Jouarre Mem. Seine-et-Marne.

352. COOMBER, Edward; B: West Grinstead, Sussex; E: Steyning, Sussex; Pte. L 7832; K: 25.4.15; Cabaret-Rouge Brit. Cem. Pas-de-Calais.

353. COOMBER, Reginald; B: Hove; E: Brighton; Pte. L 10066; K: 13.11.14; Ypres (Menin Gate) Mem. (Bel.).

354. COOMBER, Walter Ebenezer; B: Worth, Sussex; E: East Grinstead; Pte. L 8412; K: 9.5.15; Le Touret Mem. Pas-de-Calais.

355. COOMBES, Frank George; B: Camberwell, London; E: Southwark, London; Pte. G 4695; K: 9 5 15; Le Touret Mem. Pas-de-Calais.

356. COOPER, George; B: Brighton; E: Brighton; Pte. GS 307; K: 25.9.15; Loos Mem. Pas-de-Calais; Age 41; Husband of Susan Cooper.

357. COOPER, Hubert; B: Henlow; E: Bedford; Pte. G 14518; K: 22.11.16; Thiepval Mem. Somme.

358. COOPER, Robert, Grain, Kent; B: – ; E: Canterbury; Pte. L 8079; K: 25.9.15; St.Mary's A.D.S. Cem. Pas-de-Calais.

359. COOPER, Thomas George; B: Stepney, London; E: Whitehall, London; Pte. G 18574; K: 18.9.18; Vis-en-Artois Mem., Haucourt, Pas-de-Calais.

360. COOPER, William Henry; B: -; E: Brighton; Pte. G 3885; K: 9.5.15; Le Touret Mem. Pas-de-Calais.

361. COOTE, William; B: Boxgrove; E: Chichester; Pte. S 1163; K: 9.5.15; Le Touret Mem. Pas-de-Calais; Age 27; Son of Joseph and Elisabeth Coote.

362. COPE, Samuel; B: Sandy, Bedfordshire; E: Sandy; Pte. G 14519; K: 28.9.16; Thiepval Mem. Somme.

363. COPELSTONE, Arthur Kennard; B: Notting Hill, London; E: Willesden, London; Pte. G 11208; K: 9.9.16; Caterpillar Valley Cem. Somme.

364. COPPARD, Albert; B: Brighton; E: Brighton; Pte. S 2165; W: 11.4.15; Bethune Town Cem. Pas-de-Calais; Age 28; Son of Joseph and Alice Coppard; Husband of Louisa Elizabeth Coppard of 13, Chapel Street, Brighton.

365. COPPARD, Stephen; B: Mountfield, Sussex; E: Eastbourne; Pte. S 124; K: 30.10.14; Ypres (Menin Gate) Mem. (Bel.).

366. COPPARD, Walter John; B: Dane Hill, Sussex; E: Lewes; L/Cpl. G 1646; K: 9.5.15; Le Touret Mem. Pas-de-Calais; Age 20; Son of Walter and Laura Coppard of 25, Westcote Road, Streatham, London.*

367. COPPARD, William Frederick; B: West Hoathly, Sussex; E: Horsham, Sussex; Pte. L 10386; W: 28.1.15; Le Touret Mem. Pas-de-Calais; Age 22; Son of Mrs.Mary Warburton of St.Andrew's Cottage Laundry, Ashurstwood, Sussex.

368. CORK, John James; B: Charlton, London; E: Dover; Pte. S 906; K: 25.1.15; Le Touret Mem. Pas-de-Calais.

369. CORK, Walter George; B: Hove; E: Brighton; Pte. S 2125; K: 9.9.16; Thiepval Mem. Somme; Age 20; Son of Walter George and Louisa Jane Cork of 20, Regent Street, Brighton.

370. CORNWELL, James; B: Eastbourne; E: Chichester; Pte. L 7838; K: 9.5.15; Le Touret Mem. Pas-de-Calais; Age 31; Son of Mrs.Caroline Cornwell of 12, Alma Road, Eastbourne.

371. COSHAM, Charles; B: Mayfield, Sussex; E: Eastbourne; Pte. SD 5353; K: 2.9.16; Caterpillar Valley Cem. Somme.

372. COSSON, Reginald Albert; B: Blackheath, London; E: Haywards Heath, Sussex; Pte. G 1363; K: 25.1.15 at Givenchy; Le Touret Mem. Pas-de-Calais; Age 26; Son of William James and Ellen Jane Cosson of 2, West Bank, Broad Way, Bournemouth.

373. COTTEN, Cecil John; B: Birdham, Sussex; E: Bognor Regis, Sussex; Pte. G 1159; K: 8.2.15; Le Touret Mem. Pas-de-Calais; Son of George Cotten of The Shrubbery, East Road, Selsey, Sussex.

374. COTTINGTON, George; B: -; E: -; Pte. GS 846; K: 9.5.15; Le Touret Mem. Pas-de-Calais.

375. COUCHMAN, Walter; B: Margate, Kent; E: Chichester; Sgt. L 9107; D.C.M.; K: 1.5.16; Maroc Brit. Cem. Nord; Age 25; Son of Walter and Sarah Couchman of 8, Moorcroft Cottages, William Street, Edgbaston, Birmingham.

376. COULDRY, Thomas Arthur; B: Dulwich, London; E: Brighton; Pte. G 5220; K: 17.8.16; Thiepval Mem. Somme.

377. COULSTOCK, Ernest; B: Redhill, Surrey; E: Tunbridge Wells; Pte. S 713; W: 30.1.15; Le Touquet-Paris Plage Com. Cem. Pas-de-Calais; Age 29; Son of Henry and Clara Coulstock of 1, Nelson Avenue, Tonbridge.

378. COVEY, Percy; B: Wisborough Green, Sussex; E: Haywards Heath, Sussex; Pte. G 1339; W at Home: 22.2.15; Dover (St.James's) Cem. (UK); Age 24; Son of Jane Strudwick, formerly Covey, of Wisborough Green, and the late Harvey Covey.

379. COWLING, Ernest Francis; B: Padstow; E: London; Cpl. G 4774; K: 9.9.16; Caterpillar Valley cem. Somme.

380. COX, James; B: Tolworth; E: Dublin; Pte. L 6424; K: 25.9.15; Loos Mem. Pas-de-Calais; Age 33; Husband of Ellen Cox of 31, Bullen Street, Battersea, London.

381. COX, Lionel John; B: Coldwaltham; E: Chichester; Pte. L 10385; K: 25.1.15; Le Touret Mem. Pas-de-Calais; Age 19; Son of Frank and Gertrude M.Cox of Watersfield, Pulborough, Sussex.*

382. COX, Robert Walter; B: Fulham, London; E: Borgnor Regis, Sussex; Pte. G 4727; K: 9.5.15; Le Touret Mem. Pas-de-Calais.

383. COX, Walter; B: Sevenoaks, Kent; E: Portsmouth; Pte. G 4645; K: 20.8.16; Thiepval Mem. Somme.

384. CRAIGHEAD, George; B: Bermondsey, London; E: Stratford, London; Pte. G 5261; K: 2.3.16; Arras Mem. Pas-de-Calais.

385. CRAMP, Leonard; B: Brede, Sussex; E: Hastings; Pte. G 9252; K: 7.8.16; Brewery Orchard Cem. Nord; Son of James and Frances Cramp of Brede.

386. CRANE, Sidney Earle; B: Portsmouth; E: Portsmouth; L/Cpl. L 10458; K: 20.8.16; Thiepval Mem. Somme.

387. CRANHAM, Edward Albert; B: Pulborough, Sussex; E: Arundel, Sussex; Pte. L 10347; W: 25.9.15; Verquin Com. Cem. Pas-de-Calais; Age 20; Son of Frederick and Caroline Cranham of Park Place, Arundel.

388. CRANMER, Oliver; B: Lapworth, Warwickshire; E: Warwick; Pte. G 22924; W: 23.10.18; Vadencourt Brit. Cem. Aisne; Age 19; Son of William and Jane Cranmer of Drawbridge Farm, Lapworth.

389. CRASSWELLER, Ernest; B: Worthing; E: Worthing; Pte. G 1135; K: 9.5.15; Rue-Petillon Mil. Cem. Pas-de-calais; Husband of Mrs.E.Crassweller of 12, Howard Street, Worthing.

390. CRAYTHORN, Harry Johnson; B: Crayland; E: Northampton; L/Cpl. G 18886; K: 10.7.18; Cambrin Mil. Cem. Pas-de-Calais; Age 20; Son of Robert J. and Florence Johnson Craythorn of 24, French Drove, Thorney, Peterborough.

391. CREASEY, Alexander William; B: Warbleton, Sussex; E: Battle, Sussex; W at Home: 4.10.16; Bodle Street Green (St.John's) Churchyard, Sussex (UK).

392. CREASEY, Frederick Leonard; B: Godstone, Surrey; E: Chichester; Pte. G 1494; K: 25.9.15; Loos Mem. Pas-de-Calais; Age 25; Son of Mrs.Fanny Creasey of 7, Model Cottages, Felbridge, Sussex.

393. CREED, Frank Alfred; B: -; E: Bexhill-on-Sea; Pte. L 8879; K: 31.10.14; Ypres (Menin Gate) Mem. (Bel.); Age 26; Son of William and Mrs.A.Creed of 52, Southwater Road, St.Leonards-on-Sea.*

394. CRIPPS, Reuben Frank; B: Hackney, London; E: Bognor Regis, Sussex; Pte. G 8595; K: 30.6.16; Maroc Brit. Cem. Nord; Age 19; Son of Reuben Charles and Katherine Annie Cripps of 'Downs View', Shripney, Bognor Regis.

395. CRISP, Albert; B: Trinity, Bedfordshire; E: Bedford; Pte. G 14520; K: 18.4.18; Woburn Abbey Cem. Pas-de-Calais; Age 21; Son of Thomas and Mary Jane Crisp of 69, Greyfriars Walk, Bedford.

396. CRISPIN, Hugh Trevor; Lt.Col.; K: 30.10.14; Ypres (Menin Gate) Mem. (Bel.); Age 46; Son of Alfred Trevor Crispin; Previously served 22 years with the Northumberland Fusiliers.

397. CRITTENDEN, Alfred Ernest; B: Tunbridge Wells; E: Tunbridge Wells; Pte. G 3962; K: 25.9.15; Loos Mem. Pas-de-Calais; Age 24.

398. CROCKET, Arthur; B: St.Luke's, Middlesex; E: Holloway, London; Pte. G 6052; D: 28.12.15; Le Treport Mil. Cem. Seine-Maritime; Age 24; Son of Thomas and Mary Ann Crockett of Islington, London.

399. CROFT, Leslie Robert; 2nd Lt; K: 30.10.14; Ypres (Menin Gate) Mem. (Bel.).

400. CROFT, Robert; B: Kensal Green, London; E: Chatham, Kent; Pte. L 7876; K: 27.9.14; La Ferte-sous-Jouarre Mem. Seine-et-Marne; Age 30; Son of M.A.Croft.

401. CROMPTON, Stephen; B: Birkenhead; E: Birkenhead; Pte. G 5888; K: 8.3.16; Arras Mem. Pas-de-Calais; Age 26; Son of James Crompton of 55, Payson Street, Birkenhead.

402. CROUCHER, Charles William; B: Bromley; E: East Grinstead, Sussex; Pte. G 4389; K: 25.9.15;

Loos Mem. Pas-de-Calais; Age 20; Son of Stanley Croucher of 55, Victoria Road, Bromley.

403. CROWLEY, Daniel; B: Brighton; E: Eastbourne; L/Cpl. S 9964; K: 30.10.14; Ypres (Menin Gate) Mem. (Bel.).*

404. CURD, Charles Thomas; B: Buxted, Sussex; E: Uckfield, Sussex; Pte. G 3984; K: 9.5.15 at Richebourg; Le Touret Mem. Pas-de-Calais; Son of Thomas William and Elizabeth Sarah Curd of Farm Cottage, Herons Ghyll, Sussex.

405. CUTTING, Weston; B: Beaumont Essex; E: Clacton-on-Sea, Essex; Pte. G 14669; D: 19.3.18; Longuenesse (St. Omer) Souvenir Cem. Pas-de-Calais; Age 29; Son of Samuel and Catharine Cutting of Chapel Road, Beaumont Weeley.

D

406. DACK, Ernest; B: Holt; E: Chelmsford, Essex; Pte. G 14677; K: 28.9.16; Thiepval Mem. Somme.

407. DADSWELL, Charles; B: Brighton; E: Chichester; Pte. L 7709; D: 17.11.17; Vevey (St.Martin's) Cem. Switzerland; Son of William James and Katherine Dadswell of Brighton; Husband of Ansley Hannah Dadswell of Roseir Gate Cottage, Billingshurst, Sussex; Agreements were made in 1916 between Britain, France and Germany for some wounded or ill Prisoners of War to be interred in Switzerland; This man was one of 61 to die there.

408. DALE, Edward Seldon; B: -; E: Canterbury; Cpl. G 17586; K: 9.9.16; Thiepval Mem. Somme; Age 23; Son of Edward and Elizabeth Dale of Ivy House, Stelling, Kent.

409. DAMERELL, John Edward; B: Fulham, London; E: London; L/Cpl. L 6106; K: 9.5.15; Le Touret Mem. Pas-de-Calais; Age 37; Son of Mr. and Mrs.J.Damerell of 52, Averill Street, Hammersmith, London.*

410. DANCY; Frederick Richard; B: Copthorne, Sussex; E: East Grinstead, East Sussex; Pte. L 7581; K: 9.5.15; Le Touret Mem. Pas-de-Calais; Age 31; Son of William Dancy of 3, Newtown, Copthorne.

411. DANN, Alfred George; B: Tunbridge Wells, E: Tunbridge Wells; L/Cpl. L 10750; K: 17.8.16; Thiepval Mem. Somme; Age 20; Son of George Dann.*

412. DAPP, Walter Edwin; B: Brighton; E: Hurstpierpoint, Sussex; Pte. L 8422; K: 25.9.15; Loos Mem. Pas-de-Calais; Age 29; Son of Trayton and Ellen Dapp of 19, Viaduct Road, Brighton.

413. DARREN, E.C.; Lt. K: 25.7.17; - - .

414. DARTNELL, James Charles; B: Portslade, Sussex; E: Hove; Pte. G 1189; K: 25.1.15; Le Touret Mem. Pas-de-Calais.

415. DATLEN, George Edward; B: Dover; E: Maidstone; L/Cpl. G 9046; K: 17.8.16; Thiepval Mem. Somme; Age 22; Son of Jessie Ann Denton, formerly, Datlen, of 2, Springdale Terrace, Nettlestead, Kent.

416. DAUN, Edward Charles; Lt; K: 14.9.14; La Ferte-sous-Jouarre Mem. Seine-et-Marne.

417. DAVEY, George William; B: Holy Trinity, Sussex; E: Chichester; L/Cpl. L 9676; W: 10.9.14; Priez Com. Cem. Aisne; Age 20; Son of Mr.G. and Mrs.M.J.Davey of 55, West Street, Worthing.*

418. DAVIES, Harry; B: Highgate, London; E: London; Pte. L 7767; K: 17.8.16; Caterpillar Valley Cem. Somme.

419. DAVIES, William Henry; B: Bradley, E: Wolverhampton; L/Cpl. G 5690; K: 2.3.18; Buffs Road Cem., St.Jean-les-Ypres (Bel.); Husband of Mrs.S.A.Davies of 3, Chapel Green, Willenshall, Staffordshire.*

420. DAVIS, Albert George; B: Brighton; E: Brighton; Pte. SD 5447; K: 16.8.16; Thiepval Mem. Somme; Age 19; Son of Mr.R.G.Davis of 23, Ditchling Road, Brighton.

421. DAVISON, Arthur Edward; B: Bermondsey, London; E: Southwark, London; Pte. G 4997; K: 25.9.15; Loos Me. Pas-de-Calais.

422. DAWES, Walter; B: West Wittering, Sussex; E: Chichester; Pte. G 8414; K: 9.9.16; Caterpillar Valley Cem. Somme; Age 34; Son of George and Emma Dawes of Webbs Farm, East Wittering.

423. DAY, George; B: Paddington, London; E: Chichester; Pte. L 9886; K: 27.9.14; La Ferte-sous-Jouarre Mem. Seine-et-Marne.

424. DEACON, Ernest Arthur; B: Eastbourne; E: Brighton; Pte. G 5428; K: 9.9.16; Caterpillar Valley Cem. Somme.

425. DEACON, George; B: Horsted Keynes, Sussex; E: Haywards Heath, Sussex; Pte. SD 5348; K: 17.8.16; Delville Wood Cem. Somme.

426. DEACON, John; B: Hastings; E: Hastings; Pte. S 762; K: 16.2.15; Le Touret Mem. Pas-de-Calais; Age 22; Husband of Harriett Cornelius, formerly Deacon, of 146, Church Street, Ore, Hastings.

427. DEACON, Robert St.John Pelham; B: Brighton; E: Brighton; Pte. G 7769; K: 14.7.17; Ramscapelle Road Mil. Cem. (Bel); Age 19; Son of Pelham Henry Russell and Henrietta Maud Deacon of 13, Ewhurst Road, Brighton.

428. DEACON, Thomas; B: Eastbourne; E: Eastbourne; Pte. L 7326; W: 14.9.14; St.Nazaire (Toutes-Aides) Cem. Loire-Atlantique.

429. DEADMAN, Alfred; B: Northfleet, Kent; E: Woolwich, London; Pte. G 10997; K: 9.9.16; Caterpillar Valley Cem. Somme; Age 42; Son of John Deadman of Northfleet.

430. DEAN, Frederick; B: Chelsea, London; E: London; Pte. S 690; K: 25.9.15; Loos Mem. Pas-de-Calais.

431. DEAN, Isaac George; B: Thakeham; E: Horsham; Pte. L 10409; K: 16.3.15; Browns Road Mil. Cem., Festubert, Pas-de-Calais.

432. DEDMAN, Alfred Charles; B: Blackheath, London; E: Lewes; Pte. L 4744; K: 14.9.14; La Ferte-sous-Jouarre Mem. Seine-et-Marne; Age 43; Son of John and Susan Dedman of 65, Star Road, Caversham, Berkshire.

433. DELANEY, Michael; B: Carlow, Ireland; E: Carlow; Sgt. L 9490; K: 30.10.14; Ypres (Menin Gate) Mem. (Bel.); Age 25; Son of William and Mary Delaney of Dublin Road, Carlow.

434. DELLAR, Arthur; B: Oakley Green; E: Dublin; L/Cpl. L 6422; K: 25.9.15; Loos Mem. Pas-de-Callais.

435. DELLOW, Frank Edward; B: Croydon; E: London; Pte. G 6433; K: 10.2.17; Fouquescourt Brit. Cem. Somme; Age 21; Son of Frank and Rosalie May Dellow of 18, Limes Grove, Lewisham, London.

436. DENNEY, Gabriel; B: Brighton; E: Chichester; L/Sgt. G 13364; K: 2.3.18; Buffs Road Cem., St.Jean-les-Ypres (Bel.); Age 26; Husband of Alice Lydia Denney of 35, Aronol Street, Elm Grove, Brighton.

437. DENYER, Albert; B: Angmering, Sussex; E: Chichester; Pte. L 8555; K: 14.9.14; Vendresse Brit. Cem. Aisne.

438. DENYER, George; B: Bersted, Sussex; E: Bognor Regis, Sussex; Pte. G 8128; K: 30.6.16; Maroc Brit. Cem. Nord.

439. DENYER, Hubert; B: Petworth, Sussex; E: Chichester; Pte. L 10010; K: 31.10.14; Ypres (Menin Gate) Mem. (Bel.).

440. DENYER, Percy Frederick; B: Farncombe; E: Hove; Pte. G 1172; K: 9.11.15; Lillers Com. Cem. Pas-de-Calais; Age 17; Son of George and Kate Ellen Denyer of 84, Albion Street, Southwick,Sussex.

441. DEVES, Arthur; B: -; E: -; Pte – 4807; D at Home: 11.6.18; Chichester Cem. (UK); Age 43; Husband of Mrs.M.Deves of 32, Westmorland Street, Pimlico, London; Served on the North West Frontier, India.

442. DICKINSON, John Malcolm; Lt; W: 12.6.18; Pernes Brit. Cem. Pas-de-Calais; Age 20; Son of the late Captain T.Malcolm Dickinson (Royal Artillery) and of Mrs.Paget Davies of 25, Brunswick Terrace, Hove; Educated at Marlborough and Sandhurst.

443. DINE, Henry; B: St.Margaret's, Sussex; E: Eastbourne; Pte. S 7768; K: 9.5.15; Royal Irish Rifles Graveyard, Laventie, Pas-de-Calais; Age 36; Son of Mr.H. and Mrs.S.E.Dine of 42, Sun Street, Brighton; Served in the South Africa Campaign.

444. DIPLOCK, Ernest; B: Rotherfield, Sussex; E: Chichester; Pte. S 2198; K: 9.5.15; Le Touret Mem. Pas-de-Calais; Age 25; Son of John and Philadelphia Diplock.

445. DIPLOCK, Thomas; B: Eastbourne; E: Eastbourne; C.Q.M.S. L 6868; W: 8.10.14; Villers-en-Prayeres Com. Cem. Aisne.

446. DIXON, Frederick Alfred; B: Newmarket; E: Newmarket; Pte. G 14524; K: 9.9.16; Thiepval Mem. Somme.

447. DOE, Alfred; B: Brighton; E: London; Pte. L 9525; K: 7.10.14; Vendresse Brit. Cem. Aisne.

448. DONOVAN, Alfred Burt; B: MInster, Kent; E: Chatham, Kent; L/Cpl. L 7906; K: 25.9.15; Dud Corner Cem. Pas-de-Calais.

449. DOO, Reginald Herbert; B: Brighton; E: Hove; Pte. L 10516; K: 9.5.15; Le Touret Mem. Pas-de-Calais.

450. DORSETT, James William; B: Eastbourne; E: Chichester; Pte. L 6810; W at Home: 12.10.15; Eastbourne (Langney) Cem. (UK); Age 31; Son of James William and Mary Ann Dorsett of 72, Beach Road, Eastbourne; Husband of Ruth Dorsett of 2, West Terrace, Herstmonceux, Sussex.*

451. DOWNER, Frank; B: Cuckfield, Sussex; E: Haywards Heath, Sussex; Pte. G 4294; K: 12.4.16; St.Patrick's Cem. Pas-de-Calais; Age 22; Son of G. and Rhoda Downer of 71, New England Road, Haywards Heath.

452. DOWNER, William; B: Hastings; E: Eastbourne; Pte. GS 230; K: 9.5.15; Le Touret Mem. Pas-de-Calais; Age 39; Husband of Alice Downer of 212, Chapel Street, Brighton.

453. DOWNES, Wilfred Harold; B: Chatham, Kent; E: Ramsgate, Kent; Pte. G 6053; D: 8.4.17; Bray Mil. Cem. Somme; Age 21.

454. DOWSON, William Henry; B: India; E: Ticehurst, Sussex; Pte. L 7617; W: 28.9.14; Fere-en-Tardenois Com. Cem. Aisne.

455. DRAY, Alfred; B: Crowborough, Sussex; E: Tunbridge Wells; Pte. L 5978; K: 13.1.15; Le Touret Mem. Pas-de-Calais; Age 33; Son of Alfred and Emily Dray of 6, Nevill Terrace, Crowborough; Husband of Alice Dray of Holly Cottage, Pilmer Road, Crowborough.

456. DRISCOLL, James; B: Southwark, London; E: London; Pte. L 6057; K: 9.5.15; Le Touret Mem. Pas-de-Calais; Age 33.

457. DUANE, Joseph Patrick; B: Woodford, County Galway, Ireland; E: London; Pte. G 3971; K: 9.8.15; Cambrin Churchyard Ext. Pas-de-Calais.*

458. DUDFIELD, Rupert; B: Brighton; E: Brighton; Pte. L 7484; K: 6.1.15; Guards Cem., Cuinchy, Pas-de-Calais.

459. DUFFIELD, James Richard; B: Tarring, Sussex; E: Worthing; Pte. G 1635; K: 25.9.15; Loos Mem. Pas-de-Calais; Age 23; Son of James and Mary Duffield of 'Ashleigh', St.Dunstan's Road, West Worthing.

460. DUGNOLLE, John Henry; 2nd Lt; K: 25.9.15; Dud Corner Cem. Pas-de-Calais; Age 39; Son of John and Emily Dugnolle of Brighton; Husband of Harriett Selina Dugnolle of 12, Montgomery Street, Hove.

461. DUKE, Barry Pevensey; Lt; K: 3.11.14; Ypres (Menin Gate) Mem. (Bel.); Age 27; Son of the late Colonel O.T.Duke and Blanche Duke of 84, Bouverie Road West, Folkestone.

462. DUMBRELL, George William; B: Hove; E: Brighton; Pte. S 2232; K: 16.2.15; Le Touret Mem. Pas-de-Calais; Age 19; Son of Alfred Ellis and Jane Dumbrell of 97, Shirley Street, Hove.

463. DUNCAN, Ernest Frederick; B: Battersea, London; E: Kingston-on-Thames; Pte, S 1836; W: 4.2.15; Le Touret Mem. Pas-de-Calais; Age 19; Son of Walter and Eliza Duncan of 3, St.John's Hill Grove, Clapham Junction, London.

464. DUNK, Thomas; B: Brighton; E: Brighton; Pte. L 5808; K: 1.1.15; Cabaret-Rouge Brit Cem. Pas-de-Calais.

465. DUNN, Sidney Ernest; B: St.James, Surrey; E: Croydon; L/Cpl. L 9873; W: 25.7.17; Duisans Brit. Cem. Pas-de-Calais; Age 23; Son of William John and Rose Dunn of 47, North Brook Road, West Croydon.*

466. DUNTON, John William; B: Soloy; E: Wroxham, Norfolk; Pte. G 9330; K: 7.8.16; Thiepval Mem.

Somme; Age 31; Son of Martin and Elizabeth Dunton of The Bungalow, Barton Turf; Norwich.

467. DYER, Aubrey; B: Putney, London; E: Littlehampton, Sussex; Pte. S 2077; K: 25.9.15; Loos Mem. Pas-de-Calais

468. DYER, Joshua; B: Flamstead, Hertfordshire; E: Luton; L/Cpl. G 15427; W at Home: 22.9.16; Flamstead (St.Leonard) New Churchyard (UK).*

469. DYER, William Seafield; B: Preston, Sussex; E: Hurstpierpoint, Sussex; Pte. G 986; K: 30.6.16; Arras Mem. Pas-de-Calais; Age 27; Son of Elizabeth and James Dyer; Husband of Edith Wadey Dyer of Stanley House, Hurstpierpoint.

E

470. EAGLE, William; B: Colchester, Essex; E: Colchester; Pte. G 11219; W: 28.9.16; Dernancourt Com. Cem. Ext. Somme.

471. EARL, Harry Walter; 2nd Lt; K: 18.9.18; Vis-en-Artois Mem., Haucourt, Pas-de-Calais.

472. EARL, Tom; B: West Malling, Kent; E: Chatham, Kent; Pte. S 593; K: 25.9.15; St.Mary's A.D.S., Cem. Pas-de-Calais.

473. EARTHEY, Percy; B: Shoreham, Sussex; E: Worthing; Pte. G 17812; K: 24.9.18; Berthaucourt Com. Cem. Aisne.

474. EASON, Thomas; B: Brighton; E: Hove; Pte. L 10598; K: 29.4.16; Noeux-les-Mines Com. Cem. Pas-de-Calais; Brother of Mr.W.T.Eason of 25, Essex Place, Brighton.

475. EAST, James John; B: Brighton; E: Brighton; Pte. G 6885; K: 13.10.15; Loos Mem. Pas-de-Calais; Age 23; Son of James Henry and Ann East.

476. EASTON, Ernest; B: Northiam, Sussex; E: Hastings; Pte. L 10263; K: 9.5.15; Le Touret Mem. Pas-de-Calais; Age 18; Son of Charles and Margaret Easton of Mill Corner, Northiam.

477. EASTWOOD, Charles Henry; B: Buxted, Sussex; E: Uckfield, Sussex; Pte. G 8267; K: 9.9.16; Thiepval Mem. Somme; Age 19; Son of George Henry and Sophia Margaret Eastwood of Eachon Wood, Buxted.

478. EASTWOOD, William; B: Bexhill-on-Sea; E: Chichester; Pte. G 14004; K: 19.11.17; Duhallow A.D.S. Cem. (Bel.).

479. EATON-RICHARDS, Julian David; 2nd Lt; K: 25.9.15; Loos Mem. Pas-de-Calais.

480. ECCLESTON, Charles Richard; B: Edgmond, E: Dover; Pte. G 28001; K: 6.9.18; Eterpigny Brit. Cem. Pas-de-Calais.

481. ECKERT, Joseph Frederick William; B: Brighton; E: Brighton; Pte. L 7504; K: 9.5.15; Le Touret Mem. Pas-de-Calais.

482. ECKERT, John Joseph George; B: Brighton; E: Brighton; Pte. L 7778; K: 1.11.14; Ypres (Menin Gate) Mem. (Bel.).

483. EDE, Sidney Arthur; B: Bersted, Sussex; E: Bognor Regis, Sussex; Pte. G 1210; W: 10.5.15; Chocques Mil. Cem. Pas-de-Calais; Age 20; Son of Charles and Kate Ede of Resort Cottages, Ivy Lane, South Bersted.

484. EDEN, Alfred Percy; B: Banbury, Oxfordshire; E: Bexhill-on-Sea; Pte. L 10538; W: 17.5.16; Lillers Com. Cem. Pas-de-Calais; Age 18; Son of Job and Elizabeth Eden of 9, Boxhedge Square, Banbury.

485. EDWARDS, Charles; B: Mancroft; E: Norwich; Pte. G 6892; K: 13.10.15; Loos Mem. Pas-de-Calais; Age 22; Son of Charles Slaughter Edwards.

486. EDWARDS, Frederick Sylvester; B: Hartfield, Sussex; E: Tunbridge Wells; Pte. G 1302; K: 9.5.15; Le Touret Mem. Pas-de-Calais.

487. EDWARDS, George; B: Brighton; E: Brighton; Pte. G 4134; K: 13.10.15; Loos Mem. Pas-de-Calais; Son of Mrs.Eliza Edwards.*

488. EDWARDS, Henry Harry; B: Barkham, Sussex; E: Chichester; Pte. L 7672; K: 14.9.14; La Ferte-sous-Jouarre Mem. Seine-et-Marne; Age 28; Son of Mr.Edwards of Barkham; Husband of Alice Edith Pellett, formerly Edwards, of 36, Lincoln Street, Brighton.

489. EDWARDS, James; B: Brighton; E: Brighton; Pte. S 2215; K: 25.1.15; Le Touret Mem. Pas-de-Calais; Son of Mrs.Elizabeth Edwards; Served in the South Africa Campaign.

490. EDWARDS, Reginald Bertie; B: Croydon; E: Chichester; Pte. G 5470; K: 13.10.15; Loos Mem. Pas-de-Calais; Age 23; Son of Mrs.Catherine Edwards of 4, Pentland Gardens, Haywards Heath, Sussex.

491. EDWARDS, William James; B: Barnham, Sussex; E: Chichester; Pte. G 8067; K: 9.9.16; Thiepval Mem. Somme; Age 26; Son of Mr. and Mrs.R.Edwards of Vine Cottage, North Bersted, Sussex.

492. ELDRIDGE, Edward Charles; B: Godalming, Surrey; E: Piccadilly, London; Pte. G 9202; K: 7.8.16; Brewery Orchard Cem. Nord; Age 20; Son of Edward and Emma Eldridge of 'Sunnyside', Partridge Green, Sussex.

493. ELDRIDGE, James; B: Chichester; E: Chichester; Pte. G 191; K: 7.9.16; Thiepval Mem. Somme;.

494. ELLIS, Charles William; B: Stoughton; E: Chichester; Pte. GS 509; K: 25.9.15; Philosophe Brit. Cem., Mazingarbe, Pas-de-Calais; Husband of Mrs.M.M.Ellis of 9, Buckler Street, Southern Cross, Portslade, Sussex.

495. ELLIS, William; B: St.Pancras; E: Holloway, London; Pte. G 19817; W: 15.11.17; Lijssenthoek Mil. Cem. (Bel.).

496. ELLIS, William Ernest; B: MIdhurst, Sussex; E: Chichester; Pte. 10092; W: 11.9.14; Priez Com. Cem. Aisne; Age 19; Son of John and Emily Frances Ellis of Perrott's Cottage, Grafham, Sussex.

497. ELMES, Bartlett Cecil; B: Holloway, London; E: Chichester; Pte. L 6315; K: 12.11.14; Ypres (Menin Gate) Mem. (Bel.).

498. ELMES, William Francis; B: Islington, London; E: Dover; Pte. L 6512; K: 9.5.15; Le Touret Mem. Pas-de-Calais; Age 34; Son of Frederick Lonsdale and Mary Rebecca Elmes; Served in the South Africa Campaign; His two brothers were also killed.

499. ELMS, Charles; B: Shoreditch, London; E: London;

Pte. L 5663; W: 17.5.15; Wimereux Com. Cem. Pas-de-Calais.

500. ELMS, Edward John; B: Portslade, Sussex; E: Worthing; Pte. G 7858; K: 22.11.16; Thiepval Mem. Somme.

501. ELPHICK, Ernest Alan; B: Westham, Pevensey, Sussex; E: Bexhill-on-Sea; Pte. G 1713; K: 9.5.15; Le Touret Mem. Pas-de-calais; Age 22; Son of Mr.J. and Mrs.L.Elphick of 13, Springfield Road, Bexhill-on-Sea.

502. ELWORTHY, Charles Ernest; B: Claygate, Sussex; E: Hammersmith, London; Pte. G 5349; W: 14.10.15; Noeux-les-Mines Com. Cem. Pas-de-Calais; Age 23; Son of Joseph and ElizabethElworthy.*

503. ENNALS, Charles George; B: -; E: Marks Tey, Essex; Pte. G 14680; W: 30.9.16; Dernancourt Com. Cem. Somme.

504. ENTICKNAPP, Frank; West Hoathly, Sussex; E: East Grinstead, Sussex; Pte. L 7908; K: 10.9.14; Montreuil-aux-Lions Brit. Cem. Aisne; Age 29; Son of Frederick and Sarah Enticknapp of Mill House, Selsfield, East Grinstead.

505. ETHERINGTON, Arthur James; B: Luggershall, Sussex; E: West Lavington, Sussex; Pte. G 8326; K: 21.7.18; Loos Mem. Pas-de-calais.

506. ETHERINGTON, Percy; B: Haslemere, Surrey; E: Chichester; Pte. S 1501; K: 9.5.15; Le Touret Mem. Pas-de-Calais; Age 22; Son of Mrs.Harriet Etherington of Sibb's Cottage, Windfulwood, Luggershall, Sussex.

507. ETHERINGTON, Walter George; B: Hove; E: Chichester; Pte. L 10238; K: 8.11.14; Ypres (Menin Gate) (Bel.); Age 21; Son of Letitia pelling of 108, Montgomery Street, Hove.

508. EUSTES, John Albert Frank; B: St.Leonards-on-Sea; E: Hastings; Pte. G 4691; K: 9.5.15; Le Touret Mem. Pas-de-Calais; Age 18; Son of William and Kate Eustes of 2, Star Cottages, Piltdown, Sussex.

509. EVANS, Harry John; B: Ringmer, Sussex; E: Lewes; Pte. G 1638; K: 30.6.16; Arras Mem. Pas-de-Calais; Son of Mr. and Mrs.J.Evans of Goat Cottage, Ringmer.

510. EVANS, Jesse; B: Lambeth, London; E: Cockspur Street, London; Pte. G 4462; K: 25.9.15; Loos Mem. Pas-de-Calais.

511. EWER, Frederick Edward; B: Brighton; E: Brighton; L/Cpl. S 2158; W: 13.9.16; Achiet-le-Grand Com. Cem. Pas-de-Calais.

F

512. FAIRBANK, Scott; B: Colne Engaine; E: Worthing; Pte. G 1278; K: 25.1.15; Woburn Abbey Cem. Pas-de-Calais; Age 21; Son of Mr. and Mrs.Alfred Fairbank of Halstead, Essex.*

513. FARLEY, Albert; B: East Hoathly, Sussex; E: Eastbourne; Pte. G 1417; K: 25.1.15; Le Touret Mem. Pas-de-Calais.

514. FARLEY, Charles Edward; B: Itchingfield; E: Colchester; Pte.L 10213; K: 3.11.14; Ypres (Menin Gate) Mem. (Bel.); Age 19; Son of Albert and Alice Farley of 15, Hayes Lane, Slinfold, Sussex.

515. FARMER, Alfred George; B: St.Mary's, Sussex; E: Chichester; Pte. L 10358; K: 9.5.15; Le Touret Mem. Pas-de-Calais.

516. FARMER, Charles Henry; B: Heathfield, Sussex; E: Eastbourne; Pte. G 1459; D at Home: 22.7.17; Portslade Cem., Sussex (UK).

517. FARMER, Isaac Henry; Heathfield, Sussex; E: Hastings; Sgt. SD 1883; W: 24.10.18; M.M.; St.Sever Cem. Ext., Rouen, Seine-Maritime; Age 32; Husband of Ethel Palmer of Wayside, Broad Oak, Sussex.

518. FARNES, Joseph; B: St.Barnabas, Kent; E: Tunbridge Wells; Pte. L 9859; K: 25.9.15; Loos mem. Pas-de-Calais.

519. FARRELL, William; B: Ashington, Sussex; E: Steyning, Sussex; C.S.M. L 8712; W at Home: 30.9.18; Brookwood Cem., Surrey (UK); Age 29; Son of W.Farrell of Ashington; Husband of Alice Lilian Farrell of 196, Ferguson Street, Palmerston North, New Zealand.

520. FELLINGHAM, William Ewart; B: Brighton; E: Brighton; Sgt. G 1558; W: 1.8.16; Mount Huon Mil. Cem., Seine-Maritime; Age 27; Son of William and Alice Fellingham of Brighton; Husband of Mrs.K.Fellingham of 101, St.Andrews Road, Portslade, Sussex.*

521. FELLOWS, George; B: Ewhurst, Sussex; E: Hastings; Pte. S 1499; W at Home: 13.7.16; Southover (St.John the Baptist) Churchyard, Sussex (UK); Age 41.

522. FELTON, George; B: Brighton; E: Chichester; Pte. L 7455; W: 15.11.14; Poperinghe Old Mil. Cem. (Bel.).

523. FENN, William; B: Bethnal Green, London; E: London; Pte. L 7802; D: 27.4.18; Mount Huon Mil. Cem., Seine-Maritime; Age 37; Husband of May Ann Fenn of 10, Wilman Grove; Hackney, London.

524. FIGG, William James; B: -; E: Worthing; Pte. G 7425; K: 17.8.16; Thiepval Mem. Somme.

525. FINCH, Edward; B: Kingston-on-Thames; E: Kingston-on-Thames; Pte. S 1858; K: 30.12.14; Le Touret Mem. Pas-de-Calais.

526. FINKE, Richard Fenwick; B: -; E: -; Capt; K: 9.5.15 at Richebourg-L'Avoué ; Le Touret Mem. Pas-de-Calais; Age 37; Son of William and Isabella Finke.

527. FISH, George William; B: Hove; E: Hove; Pte. G 1586; K: 9.5.15; Le Touret Mem. Pas-de-Calais; Age 17; Son of Thomas and Alice Fish of 114, Clarendon Road, Hove.

528. FISH, William Frederick; B: Heigham North; E: Norwich; Pte. G 14794; K: 9.9.16; Thiepval Mem. Somme.

529. FISHER, Albert Edward; B: Hoxton, London; E: Hackney, London; Pte. G 8276; Arras Mem. Pas-de-Calais; Age 26; Son of Henry Fisher of 21d, Beaconsfield Buildings, Bingfield Street, Islington, London; Husband of Matilda Ellen Fisher of 20, Peabody Buildings, Old Pye Street, Westminster, London. K: 30.6.16.

530. FISHER, William Ernest; B: Croydon; E: Wood Green; Pte. G 4669; K: 25.9.15; St.Mary's A.D.S. Cem. Pas-de-Calais.

531. FISSI, William John; B: Stoke Newington, London; E: London; Pte. G 6705; K: 27.9.14; La Ferte-sous-Jouarre Mem. Seine-et-Marne.*

532. FITSELL, Charles Richard; B: Hastings; E: Hastings; Pte. S 932; K: 25.9.15; Dud Corner Cem. Pas-de-Calais.*

533. FLEET, Alfred Edward; B: Brighton; E: Chichester; Pte. L 10334; K: 9.5.15; Le Touret Mem. Pas-de-Calais; Age 19; Son of Mr.W.Fleet of 39, Carlyle Street, Elm Grove, Brighton.

534. FLEET, Arthur James; B: Aldershot; E: Chichester; Pte. L 9677; D: 7.11.14; Ypres (Menin Gate) Mem. (Bel.); Age 21; Nephew of Mrs.L.K.Harrison of 32, Freemason's Road, Croydon.

535. FLESHER, Herbert; B: Haywards Heath, Sussex; E: Haywards Heath; Pte. G 1296; K: 29.1.15; Le Touret Mem. Pas-de-Calais; Age 22; Husband of Florence Flesher of 42, Darwin Road, Eastleigh, Hampshire.

536. FLETCHER, Harold; B: Brighton; E: Brighton; Pte. L 10199; K: 25.9.15; Loos Mem. Pas-de-Calais; Age 25; Son of Mrs. F.Fletcher of 1, Southampton Street, Brighton.

537. FLOWER, Edward Clark; B: -; E: Wandsworth, London; Pte. G 16422; K: 24.9.18; Vis-en-Artois Mem., Haucourt, Pas-de-Calais.

538. FOARD, William George; B: Bow, London; E: West Ham, London; Pte. G 14795; K: 9.9.16; Caterpillar Valley Cem. Somme; Age 25; Son of Nelson and Harriet Foard of Longborough, Moreton-in-the-Marsh.

539. FOLDS, Edwin; B: Breachwood Green; E: Hitchen, Hertfordshire; Pte. TF 202337; K: 4.11.18; Le Rejet-de-Beaulieu Com. Cem. Nord.

540. FOLEY, Alfred Montague; 2nd Lt; W: 9.9.16; Merville Com. Cem. Nord; Attached from 11th Battalion; Son of Alfred Edward and Alice Edith Foley of 7, Chambercombe Terrace, Ilfracombe, Devon.*

541. FOORD, Alfred; B: Alfriston, Sussex; E: Eastbourne; Pte. L 6210; K: 30.10.14; Ypres (Menin Gate) Mem. (Bel.); Age 35; Son of William and Matilda Foord of High Street, Alfriston.

542. FORBES, – ; Maj; W: 21.7.15; Attached from the 'New Army' for instruction.

543. FORD, Albert William; B: Hove; E: Chichester; Pte. G 9565; K: 23.11.17; Tyne Cot Mem. (Bel.); Age 24; Husband of Rose Evelene Ford of 20, Suffolk Street, Hove.*

544. FORD, Clement; B: Burwash Common, Sussex; E: Hastings; Pte. G 3980; K: 29.5.15; Dud Corner Cem. Pas-de-Calais.; Age 22; Son of Charles and Ann Ford of West End, Burwash Common.

545. FORD, Frederick John; B: Westcombe Park; E: London; Pte. G4686; K: 5.9.15; Woburn Abbey Cem. Pas-de-Calais.

546. FORD, Henry John; B: Hove; E: Brighton; Pte. S 1802; K: 20.12.14; Le Touret Mem. Pas-de-calais; Age 19; Son of George and Kate Ford of 68, Byron Street, Hove.

547. FORDER, Charles Frederick; 2nd Lt; K: 9.9.16; Thistle Dump Cem. Longueval, Somme; Age 34; Son of George and Margaret Forder of Plaisance, Bulwer, Natal, South Africa.

548. FOREMAN, George; B: Hampstead, London; E: Chichester; Pte. L 8134; K: 27.4.16; Bully-Grenay Com. Cem. French Ext. Pas-de-Calais; Age 31; Attached to 1st Division Headquarters; Son of Mr.J.E. and Mrs.P.Foreman of 1022, Montgomery Street, Hove.

549. FOREMAN, George William; B: Maidstone; E: Calcutta, India; L/Cpl. G 8091; K: 18.9.18; Vis-en-Artois Mem. Haucourt, Pas-de-Calais.

550. FOSSEY, Horace George; B: Husborne; E: Bedford; Pte. G 14534; K: 17.10.18; Busigny Com. Cem. Ext. Nord.

551. FOSTER, Edwin Charles; B: Brighton; E: Woolwich, London; Pte. G 4580; K: 9.5.15; Le Touret Mem. Pas-de-Calais.

552. FOSTER, William; B: Dunsfold; E: Chichester; Pte. G 6242; K: 18.9.18; Bellicourt Brit. Cem. Aisne; Age 34; Son of Harry and Charlotte Foster of North Street, Petworth, Sussex.

553. FOSTER, William Percy; B: Faversham, Kent; E: Canterbury; Pte. G 17538; W: 12.9.16; St.Sever Cem., Rouen, Seine-Maritime; Age 21; Son of William Henry and Harriet H.Foster of Church House, Oare, Faversham.

554. FOWLE, Frank; B: Brighton; E: Brighton; Pte. L 7300; W: 13.9.14; Moulins New Com. Cem. Aisne.

555. FOWLER, William Maurice; 2nd Lt; W: 26.9.18; Marteville Com. Cem. Aisne; Age 28; Son of Augustus and Sarah Fowler and husband of Ella Fowler, all of 37, Westfield Road, Caversham, Reading.

556. FRANCIS, Percy Jesse; B: Washington, Sussex; E: Hove; Pte. G 8619; K: 9.9.16; Thiepval Mem. Somme; Age 20; Son of George and Harriett Francis of Heath Common, Washington.

557. FRANCIS, William; B: Ampthill; E: Bedford; Pte. G 14532; K: 9.9.16; Thiepval Mem. Somme.

558. FRANKLIN, Harry; B: Bury, Lancashire; E: Accrington, Lancashire; Pte. G 6030; K: 13.10.15; Loos Mem. Pas-de-Calais; Age 33; Husband of Jane Franklin of 85, Burnley Road, Accrington.

559. FRAPE, William; B: Brighton; E: Brighton; Sgt. L 8074; K: 16.8.16; Thiepval Mem. Somme.

560. FRASER, James William; B: East Grinstead, Sussex; E: East Grinstead; Pte. L 6972; K: 14.9.14; Chauny Com. Cem. Brit. Ext. Aisne; Age 32; Son of John and Blanche Fraser of East Grinstead; Husband of Kate Mary Fraser of 188, Canterbury Road, West Croydon.

561. FREEGARD, Charles Henry; B: Llantrisant; E: Cowbridge; Pte. G 1118; K: 9.5.15; Le Touret Mem. Pas-de-Calais; Age 18; Son of Edward and Harriet Freegard of 23, Cowbridge Road, Brynsaddler, Pontyclun, Glamorgan.

562. FREEMAN, William Edward; B: Itchingfield; E: Horsham, Sussex; Pte. L 10405; K: 8.12.16; Thiepval Mem. Somme; Age 20; Son of Charles and Matilda M.Freeman of 22, Hayes Lane, Slinfold, Sussex.

563. FRENCH, Frederick James; B: Eastbourne; E: Hastings; Pte. SD 3820; K: 17.8.16; Thiepval Mem. Somme.

564. FRIEND, Edward; B: -; E: Canterbury; Pte, G 17606; W: 23.9.16; Étaples Mil. Cem. Pas-de-Calais; Age 24; Son of Mrs. Julia Friend of 9, Park Lane, Elham, Kent.

565. FRIEND, Frederick; B: Sarratt, Hertfordshire; E: Watford, Hertfordshire; Pte. TF 290313; K: 18.9.18; Vadencourt Brit. Cem. Aisne; Age 34; Brother of Miss E.Friend of Sarratt Post Office.

566. FRISCH, Geoffrey; B: Croydon; E: Littlehampton, Sussex; L/Cpl. G 1283; K: 25.1.15; Le Touret Mem. Pas-de-Calais; Age 25; Son of George and Gertrude Frisch of 3, Selbourne Place, Littlehampton.

567. FROST, Frank; B: Laughton, Sussex; E: Battle, Sussex; Pte. L 8560; K: 20.8.16; Delville Wood Cem. Somme.

568. FRY, Ernest; B: Crowborough, Sussex; E: Chichester; Pte. S 2199; K: 17.8.16; Thiepval Mem. Somme.

569. FRY, Frederick Samuel; B: Hartfield, Sussex; E: Chichester; C.S.M. L 5733; W: 25.9.15; Loos Mem. Pas-de-Calais; Age 35; Son of Albert Edward and Harriett Annie Fry of Hartfield; Husband of Alice Maud Fry of 4, Dromore Street, Cregagh, Belfast.

570. FRYER, Sydney Ernest; B: Thornton Heath, London; E: Midhurst, Sussex; Pte. G 596; K: 15.8.16; Flatiron Copse, Somme; Age 33; Son of William and Maria Fryer of Croydon.

571. FULLER, George; B: Lewes; E: Worthing; Pte. G 1228; K: 9.5.15; Le Touret Mem. Pas-de-Calais; Age 20; Son of William and Elizabeth Fuller.

572. FULLER, Thomas; B: St.Leonards-on-Sea, Sussex; E: Chichester; Pte. L 6408; K: 9.5.15; Le Touret Mem. Pas-de-Calais.

573. FUNNELL, Ernest; B: St.Barnabas, Kent; E: Crowborough, Sussex; Pte. L 8240; K: 14.9.14; La Ferte-sous-Jouarre Mem. Seine-et-Marne; Age 28; Son of James Funnell and Mary Heath, formerly Funnell, of 13, Aukland Road, Tunbridge Wells.

574. FUNNELL, Ernest Edward; B: Eastbourne; E: New Cross, London; Pte. L 6479; W: 4.10.14; Boisguillaume Com. Cem. Seine-et-Marne; Age 32; Son of Edward Richard and Carolina Hephzibah Funnell of Plumstead, London.

575. FUNNELL, Frederick; B: Lewes; E: Lewes; Pte. S 1705; K: 2.1.15; Le Touret Mem. Pas-de-Calais; Age 21; Son of James and Mary Ann Funnell of 9, Wellington Street, Lewes.

576. FUNNELL, Jack; B: Brighton; E: Brighton; Pte. L 10734; W: 2.5.16; Noeux-les-Mines Com. Cem. Pas-de-Calais; Age 19; Son of Richard Funnell of The Rosary, Blackstone, Sussex.

577. FUNNELL, Stephen Alfred; B: Southborough, Kent; E: Chichester; Pte. L 9872; K: 10.9.14; Montreuil-aux-Lions Brit. Cem. Aisne; Age 20; Son of Stephen and Emily Funnell of 18, Springfield Road, Southborough.

578. FURNESS, Robert; B: Bolton, Lancashire; E: Chichester; Pte. L 10392; D: 13.2.15; Wimereux Com. Cem. Pas-de-Calais; Age 28; Son of Mr. and Mrs.Furness of Bolton.

G

579. GADSDEN, Ernest Sidney; B: Hampstead, London; E: Shorncliffe, Kent; Cpl. L 7773; W: 26.1.15; Bethune Town Cem. Pas-de-Calais; Brother of Mrs.A.M.Ingram of 30, Winchester Road, Swiss Cottage, London.*

580. GALLARD, William Henry Edward; B: Eastbourne; E: Eastbourne; Pte. G 5435; K: 12.1.16; Dud Corner Cem. Pas-de-Calais.

581. GARBUTT, Alfred Henry William; B: Brighton; E: Brighton; Pte. L 6908; K: 9.5.15; Le Touret Mem. Pas-de-Calais; Age 32; Husband of Emily Garbutt of 27, Elder Street, Brighton.

582. GARDINER, Percy John; B: Ascot, Berkshire; E: Shepherd's Bush, London; L/Cpl . G 5946; K: 9.9.16; M.M.; Serre Road Cem. No.2, Somme; Age 22; Son of Percy and Gertrude Gardiner of Rose Cottage, Bowden Road, Sunninghill, Berkshire.

583. GARDNER, Thomas Henry; B: Harlington; E: Uxbridge, Middlesex; Pte. G 21175; K: 11.7.17; Ramscapelle Road Mil. Cem. (Bel.); Age 37; Son of James and Emily Gardner of Hayes; Husband of Ellen George, formerly Gardner, of 42, Clayton Road, Hayes.

584. GARTON, Arthur; 2nd Lt; K: 24.9.18; Bellicourt Brit. Cem. Aisne; Age 29; Husband of Annie Garton of 23, Cobden Road, Worthing.

585. GASSON, Lewis Victor; B: Crowhurst, Sussex; E: Chichester; Pte. G 1499; K: 30.1.15; Le Touret Mem. Pas-de-Calais; Age 24; Son of Clement E. and Esther Gasson of 161, London Road, East Grinstead, Sussex.

586. GASTON, George Henry; B: Newick, Sussex; E: Lewes; Pte. G 1323; K: 9.5.15; Le Touret Mem. Pas-de-Calais; Age 24; Son of W.Gaston of Bullfield Cottages, Newick Green.

587. GASTRELL, George Norton; B: Liverpool; E: Woolwich, London; L/Cpl. G 14801; W at Home: 8.10.16; Hucclecote (SS.Philip and James) Churchyard, Gloucestershire (UK); Age 26; Son of Edward I. and Susana Jane Gastrell of Dingle Holm, Hucclecote.

588. GATER, Edgar Allen; B: -; E: Stratford; Pte. G 15720; K: 24.9.18; Vis-en-Artois Mem., Haucourt, Pas-de-Calais; Age 29; Son of Charles J. and Caroline E.Gater of 39, Grosvenor Street, Cheltenham, Gloucestershire.

589. GATES, Frederick James; B: Chichester; E: Brighton; Pte. S 2075; K: 25.9.15; Loos Mem. Pas-de-Calais; Age 19; Son of Mr. and Mrs.F.Gates of 29, Lynton Street, Brighton.

590. GAUSDEN, Arthur Henry; B: Eastbourne; E: Eastbourne; Cpl. L 8247; K: 4.11.18; Le Rejet-de-Beaulieu Com. Cem. Nord; Age 35; Son of Mr. and Mrs.Charles Gausden of Eastbourne; Husband of Florence Emily Gausden of 11, Tower Street, Eastbourne.*

591. GEARING, Joseph; B: Eastbourne; E: Eastbourne; Pte. GS 769; K: 9.5.15; Le Touret Mem. Pas-de-Calais; Age 37; Son of Joseph and Annie Blackley Gearing of 12, Lunetree Terrace, Eastbourne; Husband of Mary Ann McLeod, formerly Gearing, of 57, St.Stephen Street, Edinburgh.

592. GEORGE, John; B: Llantwit Major; E: Cowbridge; L/Cpl. G 1031; K: 13.11.17; Tyne Cot Mem. (Bel.).

593. GIBBS, Frederick Cyril; B: -; E: Bury St.Edmunds, Suffolk; L/Cpl. G 14800; K: 28.9.16; Thiepval Mem. Somme.

594. GIBBS, Harry; B: Tunbridge Wells; E: Chichester; Pte. L 8545; K: 25.9.15; Loos Mem. Pas-de-Calais; Age 42; Son of William Gibbs of 24, Aukland Road, Tunbridge Wells.

595. GIBBS, Henry; B: Cudham; E: Dartford, Kent; Pte. G 10881; K: 27.9.16; Thiepval Mem. Somme; Age 32; Son of G. and Martha Gibbs of 22, Palmerstone Road, Farnborough, Kent.

596. GIBBS, Thomas; B: Redhill, Surrey; E: Croydon; Pte. L 10520; K: 25.9.15; Loos Mem. Pas-de-Calais; Age 25; Son of Mrs.Rosina M.Gibbs of 113, Lakehall Road, Thornton Heath, London.

597. GIBSON, Richard William; B: Hailsham, Sussex; E: Chichester; Cpl. L 8124; K: 6.9.16; Thiepval Mem. Somme.

598. GILBEY, Albert Victor; B: Lee, London; E: London; Pte. S 1843; K: 9.5.15; Y Farm Mil. Cem. Bois-Grenier, Nord; Age 20; Son of Henry Gilbey of 71, Eltham Road, Lee.

599. GILBEY, William; B: Fulham, London; E: Chichester; Pte. L 9937; K: 23.12.14; Le Touret Mem. Pas-de-Calais.

600. GILL, James; B: Lambeth, London; E: Tunbridge Wells; Pte. GS 914; K: 17.3.15; D.C.M.; Browns Road Mil. Cem., Festubert, Pas-de-Calais.

601. GLANFIELD, Charles; B: Chevening, Kent; E: London; Pte. S 1377; K: 25.9.15; Dud Corner Cem. Pas-de-Calais; Age 22; Son of Charles and Olive Glanfield of 8, East Milton, Gravesend, Kent.*

602. GLAYSHER, Frederick George; B: Tangmere, Sussex; E: Chichester; Pte. G 495; W: 10.7.17; Ramscapelle Road Mil. Cem. (Bel.); Age 22; Son of Frederick and Ellen Galysher of Tangmere.*

603. GLAZIER, Henry Stephen; B: Guestling, Sussex; E: Hastings; Pte. S 1268; K: 9.5.15; Le Touret Mem. Pas-de-Calais; Age 20; Son of Mr. and Mrs.H.Glazier of 18, Broadway Middle Road, Ore, Hastings.

604. GLENISTER, Arthur; B: Limbury; E: Leagrave; Pte. G 14539; K: 15.11.17; Tyne Cot Mem. (Bel.).

605. GLYNDE, Harold Ernest; B: St.Leonards-on-Sea, Sussex; E: Chichester; Pte. L 10288; K: 14.9.14; Grand-Seraucourt Brit. Cem. Aisne.

606. GODDARD, Frank; B: Cheesehill; E: Winchester, Hampshire; Pte. L 5854; K: 23.12.14; Le Touret Mem. Pas-de-Calais.

607. GODDARD, Frederick John; B: Brighton; E: Brighton; Pte. S 945; K: 22.1.15; Le Touret Mem. Pas-de-Calais; Age 24; Husband of Lily Batten, formerly Goddard, of 4, New Road, Hanworth, Middlesex.

608. GODDARD, Sydney George; 2nd Lt; K: 30.6.16; Arras Mem. Pas-de-Calais.

609. GODDARD, William Henry; B: Acton, London; E: London; Pte. G 4662; K: 23.5.15; Cambrin Churchyard Ext. Pas de Calais.

610. GODDEN, Arthur Thomas; B: Brighton; E: Bognor Regis, Sussex; Pte. G 1083; K: 9.5.15; Le Touret Mem. Pas-de-Calais.

611. GODDEN, Arthur William; B: Christchurch; E: Chichester; Sgt. L 8750; K: 9.5.15 at Richebourg; Le Touret Mem. Pas-de-Calais; Age 27; Son of Walter John Smith Godden; Husband of Mabel Lydia Sanders, formerly Godden, of 6, Roman Drive, Camelon, Falkirk.

612. GODDEN, George William; B: Hailsham, Sussex; E: Eastbourne; Pte. G 6923; W: 16.10.15; Bethune Town Cem. Pas-de-Calais; Age 27; Adopted son of William and Ellen Godden of Herstmonceux, Sussex; Husband of Mercy J.Keat, formerly Godden, of Little Gill Farm, Mersham, Kent.

613. GODFREY, Harry; B: Coggershall; E: Coggershall; L/Cpl. G 14556; K: 22.11.16; Thiepval Mem. Somme; Son of Mr. and Mrs.Godfrey of West Street, Coggershall.

614. GODWIN, Harold; B: -; E: -; Pte. – 63; W at Home: 5.8.15; Hammersmith Cem., London (UK); Age 38; Son of John and Mary Ann Godwin of Sevenoaks, Kent; Husband of Mary Ann Godwin of 2, Chancellor's Street, Hammersmith; Wounds received at La Bassee.

615. GODWIN, James Henry; B: Dublin, Ireland; E: East Grinstead, Sussex; Pte. G 7431; W: 17.10.15; Choques Mil. Cem. Pas-de-Calais.

616. GOLDING, Frank; B: Flimwell, Kent; E: Hastings; Pte. G 2526; W: 13.6.18; Cambrin Mil. Cem. Pas-de-Calais; Age 27; Son of Mr.C. and Mrs.F.Golding of Sunny Bank, Flimwell.

617. GOLDSMITH, Albert; B: Brighton; E: Brighton; Pte. S 2334; W: 29.9.16; Millencourt Com. Cem. Ext. Somme.

618. GOLDSMITH, Charles Ernest; B: Icklesham, Sussex; E: Rye, Sussex; Pte. L 10205; K: 9.5.15; Le Touret Mem. Pas-de-Calais; Age 23; Stepson of Mrs.H.M.Goldsmith of 'Stredwick's', Udimore, Sussex.

619. GOLDSMITH, Clement Jazeb; B: Wadhurst, Sussex; E: Tunbridge Wells; Pte. G 1079; K: 9.9.16; Thiepval Mem. Somme.

620. GOODACRE, Arthur Leslie; B: Whitchurch; E: Tunbridge Wells; Pte. G 1468; K: 25.9.15; Loos Mem. Pas-de-Calais.

621. GOODWIN, Charles Henry; B: Melton Mowbray; E: Newmarket; Pte. G 14542; K: 9.9.16; Thiepval Mem. Somme.

622. GOODWIN, Thomas Edwin; B: Hove; E: Brighton; Pte. G 4925; K: 25.9.15; Loos Mem. Pas-de-Calais.

623. GORDON, Ronald Granville; 2nd Lt; K: 18.9.18; Cerisy-Gailly Mil. Cem. Somme; Age 19; Son of Granville and Louise M.Gordon of 8, Scroop Terrace, Cambridge.

624. GORRINGE, Edgar; B: Marsh Green; E: East Grinstead; L/Cpl. L 8358; K: 30.10.14; Ypres (Menin Gate) Mem. (Bel.); Age 30; Son of John and Elizabeth Gorringe of 102, Ifield Road, Crawley, Sussex.

625. GOURD, William Charles; B: Paddington, London; E: Chelsea, London; Pte. G 4596; K: 9.5.15; Le Touret Mem. Pas-de-Calais; Age 20; Son of Mrs.Annie Jane Perry of 31, Stanley Road, Fulham, London.

626. GOWER, Albert Robert; B: Ramsgate, Kent; E: Bexhill-on-Sea; Pte. GS 799; K: 25.1.15; Le Touret Mem. Pas-de-Calais; Age 29; Son of Mrs. Jane Freemanof 10, Edinburgh Road, Bexhill-on-Sea; Husband of Mrs.A.Gower of 20, Salisbury Road, Bexhill-on-Sea; Served in the South Africa Campaign.

627. GRAMSHAW, Robert Wilfred Raleigh; 2nd Lt; W: 27.1.15 from wounds received on 25.1.15; Bethune Town Cem. Pas-de-Calais; Age 24; Son of the Reverend Robert Michael Oginski Gramshaw and Emily Gramshaw of Littlington Rectory, Sussex.*

628. GRANT, Albert James; B: Tunbridge Wells; E: Chichester; Pte. L 7382; K: 9.5.15; Le Touret Mem. Pas-de-Calais.

629. GRANT, Stephen John; B: Brighton; E: Hove; Pte. G 5402; K: 30.6.16; Arras Mem. Pas-de-Calais; Brother of Mrs.Alice Taylor of 87, Centurion Road, brighton.

630. GRAVETT, Edwin Thomas; B: Hove; E: Hove; Pte. L 10529; K: 9.5.15; Le Touret Mem. Pas-de-Calais.

631. GREAVES, Geoffrey Millett; B: Grahamstown, South Africa; E: London; Cpl. G 4659; K: 9.5.15; Le Touret Mem. Pas-de-Calais.

632. GREEN, Albert; B: Brighton; E: Brighton; Cpl. L 6780; W: 11.5.15; Le Touret Mem. Pas-de-Calais; Age 30; Son of Harry and Mary Green; Husband of H.P.Haskell, formerly Green, of 88, Gayford Road, Shepherd's Bush, London.

633. GREEN, Cyril; B: Norton; E: Eastbourne; L/Cpl. L 8230; K: 27.1.15; Le Touret Mem. Pas-de-Calais.

634. GREEN, Ernest Edward; B: Steyning, Sussex; E: Haywards Heath, Sussex; Pte. G 8616; K: 19.8.16; Thiepval Mem. Somme.

635. GREEN, Henry; B: Brighton; E: Chichester; Pte. L 10123; K: 30.10.14; Ypres (Menin Gate) Mem. (Bel); Age 21; Husband of Lucy Gertrude Florence Green of 'Sandley', 49, York Road, Woking, Surrey.

636. GREEN, John; B: Lancing, Sussex; E: Arundel, Sussex; L/Cpl. L 6927; K: 9.5.15; Le Touret Mem. Pas-de-Calais; Age 30; Husband of Mary E.Green of Myrtle Cottages, Lancing.

637. GREEN, William; B: Kensington, London; E: Horsham, Sussex; Pte. S 2270; K: 29.8.15; Vermelles Brit. Cem. Pas-de-Calais.

638. GREENFIELD, Albert; B: Horsham, Sussex; E: Eastbourne; Pte. L 10124; K: 14.9.14; La Ferte-sous-Jouare Mem., Seine-et-Marne; Age 18; Brother of John Greenfield of 2, Priory Bungalows, Eastbourne.

639. GREENFIELD, Walter Henry; B: St.George's, Sussex; E: Worthing; Pte. SD 519; K: 30.11.16; A.I.F. Burial Ground, Somme; Age 23; Son of Herbert and Ellen Greenfield of Worthing.

640. GREENING, Alfred; B: Wivelsfield, Sussex; E: Newhaven, Sussex; Pte. GS 935; K: 9.5.15; Le Touret Mem. Pas-de-Calais.

641. GREGORY, Frank; B: Frant, Sussex; E: Tunbridge Wells; Pte. G 1075; K: 10.7.17; Ramscapelle Road Mil. Cem. (Bel.); Age 32; Son of Albert and Ellen Gregory of Frant.

642. GREGORY, Sydney Percival; B: Manchester; E: Manchester; Pte. G 20064; K: 18.9.18; Vis-en-Artois Mem., Haucourt, Pas-de-Calais; Age 33; Son of Adam Doodson Gregory and Ann Gregory; Husband of Mary Gregory of 43, Buckley Street, Newton Heath, Manchester.

643. GRENDER, Ernest Herbert; B: Aldingbourne, Sussex; E: Chichester; Pte. L 10270; K: 14.11.14; Ypres (Menin Gate) Mem. (Bel.); Age 19; Son of Mr. and Mrs.Grender of Hook Lane, Aldingbourne.

644. GRIFFIN, Charles William; B: Mandam, Sussex; E: Eastbourne; Pte. G 19917; W: 14.3.17; Bray Mil. Cem. Somme.

645. GRIFFITH, Alfred; B: Epsom; E: Brighton; Pte. L 8254; W: 28.9.14; Vendresse Brit. Cem. Aisne.

646. GRIFFITHS, Archie; B: Northampton; E: Haverfordwest; Pte. G 5868; K: 30.6.16; Arras Mem. Pas-de-Calais; Age 20; Son of William and Maria Griffiths of 44, Dew Street, Haverfordwest.

647. GRINSTEAD, Solomon; B: Folkestone; E: Folkestone; Pte. G 17807; K: 24.9.18; Vis-en-Artois Mem., Haucourt, Pas-de-Calais; Age 30; Son of Alfred and Keziah Grinstead.

648. GROOMBRIDGE, Arthur John; B: St.Barnabas, Kent; E: Tunbridge Wells; Pte. L 10104; W: 10.5.15; Le Touret Mem. Pas-de-Calais.

649. GROSSMAN, Edward; B: Lambeth, London; E: Glasgow; Pte. G 4148; K: 16.6.15; Cambrin Churchyard Ext. Pas-de-Calais.

650. GUMBRILL, Walter; B: Hove; E: Brighton; Pte. L 8578; K: 4.10.14; La Ferte-sous-Jouarre Mem. Seine-et-Marne.

651. GUNFIELD, Walter William; B: St.Osyth, Essex; E: Colchester, Essex; Pte. G 11229; K: 9.9.16; London Cem. and Ext. Somme; Age 19; Son of George Dennis and Mary Ann Gunfield of 'Sunbeam', Weeley Heath, Essex.*

652. GURR, Albert; B: Catsfield, Sussex; E: Hastings; Pte. G 11230; K: 9.9.16; Thiepval Mem. Somme; Age 19; Son of David H. and Emma Gurr of Skinner's Lane, Catsfield.

653. GURR, Charles; B: Ifield, Sussex; E: Eastbourne; Pte. L 8391; K: 9.5.15; Le Touret Mem. Pas-de-Calais.

654. GUYMER, Joseph William; B: St.John's, Norfolk; E: Norwich; Pte. G 11601; D: 13.10.18; Vadencourt Brit. Cem. Aisne; M.M.; Age 20; Son of Mr. and Mrs.J.Guymer of 17, Russell Terrace, Trowse, Norwich.*

H

655. HAIGH, Walter; B: Brighton; E: Brighton; L/Cpl. G 5689; K: 9.9.16; Thiepval Mem. Somme.

656. HALFACRE, Frederick Thomas; B: Odiham,

Hampshire; E: Chichester; Pte. S 382; K: 9.5.15; Le Touret Mem. Pas-de-calais; Age 36; Son of William and Elizabeth Halfacre; Husband of Emma Halfacre of Peabody Cottages, Peabody Road, South Farnborough, Hampshire.

657. HALL, Alfred Henry; B: Winchester, Hampshire; E: Poole, Dorset; Pte. L 6601; K: 31.10.14; Ypres (Menin Gate) Mem. (Bel).

658. HALL, Frederick; B: Frocksfield; E: Chichester; Pte. S 2196; K: 9.5.15; Le Touret Mem. Pas-de-Calais; Age 33; Son of John Hall and Jouisa Vidler, formerly Hall, of The Home Farm, Stodham, Liss, Hampshire.

659. HALL, Jack; B: Mayfield, Sussex; E: Brighton; Pte. L 10089; K: 13.10.15; Phalempin Com. Cem. Nord.

660. HALL, John; B: Hastings; E: Hastings; Pte. S 1629; K: 9.5.15; Le Touret Mem. Pas-de-Calais;

661. Hall, Lewis; B: Brixton, London; E: West Ham, London; Pte. G 14837; K: 27.9.16; Thiepval Mem. Somme.*

662. HALLAM, John; B: Longton; E: Chichester; Pte. G 3829; K: 12.5.16; Arras Mem. Pas-de-Calais.

663. HAMMOND, Harry; B: Witham; E: Chelmsford; L/Cpl. G 14690; K: 20.6.18; Cambrin Mil. Cem. Pas-de-Calais.

664. HAMMOND, Thomas William; B: Chiswick; E: London; Pte. L 7760; K: 9.5.15; Le Touret Mem. Pas-de-Calais; Age 31; Son of Thomas and Lucy Hammond of Chiswick; Husband of Amelia Ethel Hammond of 109, Victoria Avenue, Cliftonville, Margate; Served in the South Africa campaign with the East Surrey Regiment.

665. HANCOCK, John; B: Hulme; E: Ashton-under-Lyne; Pte. L 9491; K: 10.9.14; Montreuil-aux-Lions Brit. Cem. Aisne; Age 17; Son of Amos and Edith Hancock of 9, Mill Street, Ancoats, Manchester.

666. HANDS, Robert Gilbert; B: Hove; E: Bognor Regis; Pte. G 9056; K: 7.8.16; Brewery Orchard Cem. Nord; Age 25; Son of Joseph and Annie Hands of 15, Blatchington Road, Hove.*

667. HANKS, Albert Edward; B: Cripplegate; E: London; Pte. S 1606; K: 29.1.15; Le Touret Mem. Pas-de-Calais; Age 19; Son of Mrs.Mary Hanks of 11, Bohemia Place, Hackney, London.*

668. HANKS, Frederick William; B: Brighton; E: Chichester; Pte. G 1503; K: 25.9.15; Loos Mem. Pas-de-Calais; Age 22; Son of William Henry Hanks and Kate Carter, formerly Hanks, of 4, Red House, West Hoathly, Sussex.

669. HANSFORD, Reginald John; B: Chiswick; E: Hove; Pte. L 10517; K: 9.5.15; Le Touret Mem. Pas-de-Calais; Age 22; Son of John Hugh and Emily Mary Hansford of 13, Wordsworth Street, Hove.

670. HANSON, Ernest; B: Parkinsville; E: Spennymoor; Pte. G 6005; K: 15.7.16; Thiepval Mem. Somme; Age 22; Son of Emanuel and Caroline Hanson of 24, Front Street, Croxdale Colliery, County Durham.

671. HANWELL, Thomas; B: London; E: London; Sgt. L 7812; K: 9.9.16; Thiepval Mem. Somme; Age 30; Husband of Alice Hanwell of 10, George Street, Euston Road, London.*

672. HARDEN, Arthur James Victor; 2nd Lt.; K: 25.9.15; Dud Corner Cem. Pas-de-Calais; Son of Lt.Col. George and Mrs.Mabel Elliott Harden.

673. HARDIMAN, William Charles; B: – ; E: Canterbury; Sgt. G 17583; W: 18.9.16; Porte-de-Paris Cem. Nord.

674. HARDING, Edward; B: Brighton; E: Brighton; Pte. L 8765; K: 9.5.15; Le Touret Mem. Pas-de-Calais.

675. HARGREAVES, James; B: Eastbourne; E: Eastbourne; Pte. G 1419; K: 9.5.15; Le Touret Mem. Pas-de-Calais.

676. HARLEN, Dennis; B: Brighton; E: Liverpool; Pte. G 4398; K: 25.9.15; Loos Mem. Pas-de-Calais.

677. HARMAN, George; B: Hastings; E: Hastings; Pte. G 3931; K: 25.9.15; Loos Mem. Pas-de-Calais.

678. HARPER, James; B: Kennington; E: Chichester; Pte. GS 7; K: 9.5.15; Le Touret Mem. Pas-de-Calais; Age 44; Husband of Elizabeth Harper of 4, East Walls, Chichester; Served in the South Africa campaign.

679. HARRINGTON, Walter George; B: Greenstead; E: Chelmsford; L/Cpl. G 14691; K: 18.9.18; Jeancourt Com. Cem. Aisne.

680. HARRIS, Alfred James; B: South Lambeth; E: Camberwell; Pte. G 18601; K: 17.10.18; Vadencourt Brit. Cem. Aisne; Age 19; Son of Mr. and Mrs.F.J.Harris of Clapham, London.

681. HARRIS, Frederick; B: – ; E: Law Courts, London 1915; Pte. TF 263163; K: 18.9.18; Vadencourt Brit. Cem. Aisne; Age 20; Son of Albert Isidore and Louise M.Harris of 14, Gordon Mansions, Gower Street, Bedford Square, London.

682. HARRISON, Cyril Arthur; B: St.Ives, Huntingdon; E: Haywards Heath; Pte. G 1374; K: 9.5.15; Le Touret Mem. Pas-de-Calais; Age 21; Son of Arthur James and Lizzie Harrison of "Iona", 8, Western Road, Haywards Heath.

683. HARRISON, Richard Henry; B: North Kensington; E: London; Pte. L 7867; K: 9.5.15; Le Touret Mem. Pas-de-Calais; Age 31; Son of Mr. and Mrs. Henry Harrison; Husband of Emily Harrison of 2, Pressland Street, Kensal Road, Westbourne Park, London.

684. HARRYMAN, Joseph; B: West Hartlepool; E: Durham; Pte. G 336; K: 24.11.16; Thiepval Mem. Somme; Age 24; Brother of Arthur Harriman of 6, Collingwood Street, Thornley, County Durham.

685. HART, John Walter; B: Sandgate; E: Brighton; Pte. GS 98; K: 9.5.15; Le Touret Mem. Pas-de-Calais; Age 42; Husband of Annie Hart of 75, New England Street, Brighton.

686. HARTT, Charles Edgar Whitby; B: Carbrook; E: Norwich; Pte. G 5552; K: 26.2.16; Arras Mem. Pas-de-Calais; Age 17; Son of James and Emma Hartt of Mount Pleasant, Barnham Broom, Norwich.

687. HARVEY, Rollo d'Aubigne; B: Eastbourne; Capt; K: 9.9.16; Caterpillar Valley Cem. Somme; Age 31; Son of Mrs. F.Clyde Harvey of Morel House, Mayfield and the late Prebendary F.Clyde Harvey vicar of Hailsham, Sussex.

688. HATCHER, John; B: Cranbrook; E: Tonbridge; Pte. G 20680; K: 23.11.17; Tyne Cot Mem. (Bel.); Age 22;

Son of Mr. and Mrs.G.Hatcher of Gammons Land, Hadlow Place, Tonbridge.

689. HAYDON, James; B: Swindon; E: Haywards Heath; Cpl. G 1362; K: 18.9.18; Roisel Com. Cem. Ext. Somme; Age 29; Son of Mrs.Robinson, formerly Haydon, of 66, Conway Street, Hove.

690. HAYES, Arthur James; B: Hounslow; E: Bognor Regis; L/Cpl. G 1222; K: 12.2.15; Le Touret Mem. Pas-de-Calais; Age 18; Son of James Evett and Annie Hayes of 69, London Road, Bognor Regis, Sussex.

691. HAYLOR, William; B: Slaugham, Sussex; E: Brighton; Pte. L 9478; K: 14.9.14; La Ferte-sous-Jouarre Mem. Seine-et-Marne.

692. HAYNES, George; B: Southwark; E: Southwark; L/Cpl. G 5123; W: 23.5.16; Bethune Town Cem. Pas-de-Calais; Age 28; Son of George and Mary Haynes; Husband of Mrs.E.Morris, formerly Haynes, of 152, Southwark Bridge Road, London.

693. HAYWARD, Charles George; B: Brighton; E: Brighton; Pte. S 2291; K: 9.5.15; Le Touret Mem. Pas-de-Calais; Age 17; Son of Charles Arthur Hayward of 24, Regent Street, Brighton.*

694. HAYWOOD, Henry Ridge Thomas; B: Peckham; E: Camberwell; Pte. G 18606; W: 26.9.18; Brie Brit. Cem. Somme; Age 19; Son of Henry Ridge Hayward of 59, Marmont Road, Peckham, London.*

695. HEAD, Arthur James; B: – ; E: Chelmsford; Pte. G 14696; K: 9.9.16; Serre Road No. 2 Cem. Somme; Age 20; Son of Mrs.I.Mayes, formerly Head, of Cookes Green, Little Clacton, Essex.

696. HEARN, James; B: Guildford; E: Chichester; Pte. L 10572; K: 25.9.15; Loos Mem. Pas-de-Calais.

697. HEASMAN, Frank Edward; B: Laughton, Sussex; E: Crowborough, Sussex; Pte. L 8356; K: 10.9.14; Montreuil-aux-Lions Brit. Cem. Aisne.

698. HEASTE, William James; B: Handsworth; E: Poole; Pte. L 6854; W: 14.9.14; St.Nazaire (Toutes-Aides) Cem. Loire-Atlantique; Age 28; Son of Mrs.W.Heaste of Winton; Husband of Beatrice Gamblin, formerly Heaste, of "Ivel Hurst", New Road, Norton-sub-Hamdon, Somerset.

699. HEATH, Herbert; B: Harwich; E: Dovercourt; Pte. G 14692; W: 16.11.17; Dozinghem Mil. Cem. (Bel.); Age 19; Son of Joseph and Clara Heath of 14, Coke Street, Harwich.

700. HEATHER, Robert James; B: Barlavington; E: Chichester; Cpl. L 7508; K: 30.10.14; Ypres (Menin Gate) Mem. (Bel.).

701. HEDGER, Frederick; B: Rudgwick, Sussex; E: Horsham, Sussex; Pte. L 5990; K: 16.2.15; Le Touret Mem. Pas-de-Calais.

702. HEMMINGS, James; B: Harrow; E: London; Pte. 5679; K: 31.10.14; Perth Cem. (China Wall) (Bel.).

703. HEMSLEY, Spencer Harold; B: Crowborough; E: Bostall Heath; L/Cpl. TF 202190; M.M., W: 28.9.18; Brie Brit. Cem. Somme; Age 20; Son of William James and Isabel Sarah Hemsley of 7, Gladstone Road, Crowborough, Sussex.

704. HEMSLEY, Thomas Cecil; B: Eastbourne; E: Eastbourne; Pte. G 11678; K: 23.10.18; Vis-en-Artois Mem., Haucourt, Pas-de-Calais; Age 23; Son of David and Mary Caroline Hemsley of 317, Seaside, Eastbourne.

705. HENDERSON, Gordon Murray; B: Greenwich; E: Chichester; L/Cpl. L 10197; W: 27.9.14; Nantes (La Bouteillerie) Cem. Loire-Atlantique; Age 19; Son of William and Eliza Henderson of 3, South View Gardens, Ilford.*

706. HENNESSY, Thomas; B: Bermondsey; E: London; Pte. S 2263; K: 9.5.15; Le Touret Mem. Pas-de-Calais.

707. HENRY, John; B: Aberdeen; E: St.Pancras; Pte. G 5982; W: 20.2.16; St.Patrick's Cem. Pas-de-Calais.

708. HENSHAW, Henry; B: Ticehurst, Sussex; E: Tunbridge Wells; Pte. L 6025; W: 7.2.15; Wimereux Com. Cem. Pas-de-Calais; Age 39; Husband of Agnes Eliza Henshaw of 176, Ashford Road, Eastbourne.

709. HENSON, George Robert; B: Hastings; E: Cork; L/Cpl. L 10432; K: 27.9.16; Thiepval Mem. Somme.

710. HENTY, Alfred; B: Hurstpierpoint, Sussex; E: Chichester; Pte. L 10073; K: 9.5.15; Le Touret Mem. Pas-de-Calais; Age 25; Son of Mr. and Mrs.W.Henty of 2, Marin Terrace, Junction Road, Worlds End, Sussex.

711. HENTY, Thomas; B: Uckfield, Sussex; E: Brighton; Pte. G 1543; W: 15.3.16; Calais Southern Cem. Pas-de-Calais; Age 24; Son of Albert and Harriet Henty of Ivy Cottage, Budletts, Uckfield, Sussex.

712. HERBERT, Albert William; B: Hove; E: Brighton; Pte. G 5266; K: 18.4.18; Woburn Abbey Cem. Pas-de-Calais.

713. HESELDEN, Seth Thomas; B: Burwash, Sussex; E: Hastings; Pte. G 1103; W: 31.5.15; Etretat Churchyard, Seine-Maritime; Age 28; Son of Thomas and Emma Heselden of 5, Victoria Terrace, Burwash, Sussex.

714. HESMER, George; B: Ore, Sussex; E: Hastings; Cpl. L 8178; K: 25.9.15; Loos Mem. Pas-de-Calais.

715. HEWETT, Percy Gordon; B: Herne Bay; E: Canterbury; Pte. G 17595; K: 27.9.16; Warlencourt Brit. Cem. Pas-de-Calais; Age 22; Son of Frederick and Sophia Hewett of 21, Guildford Road, Canterbury.

716. HEWETT, Thomas Elliott; B: Aberdeen; E: Worthing; L/Cpl. L 10277; K: 8.10.15; Loos Mem. Pas-de-Calais.

717. HEWITT, Richard Henry; B: Toronto, Canada; E: Liverpool; Pte. G 4400; K: 25.9.15; Loos Mem. Pas-de-Calais.

718. HEYES, John Arthur Manley; B: Jersey; E: Chichester; Pte. L 6999; K: 6.1.15; Le Touret Mem. Pas-de-Calais; Age 32 Son of George Manley and Mary Heyes; Husband of Annie Clara Heyes of 15, Lawn Street, Burnley.*

719. HICKMOTT, Stephen; B: Eastbourne; E: Eastbourne; Cpl. L 8827; K: 18.9.14; La Ferte-sous-Jouarre Mem. Seine-et-Marne; Age 22; Son of Stephen and Annie Hickmott of 315, Seaside, Eastbourne.

720. HIDE, Alfred William; B: Worthing; E: Worthing; Pte. GS 502; K: 25.9.15; Loos Mem. Pas-de-Calais.

721. HIDER, Henry William; B: Withyham, Sussex; E:

Tunbridge Wells; Cpl. L 9976; K: 14.9.14; La Ferte-sous-Jouarre Mem. Seine-et-Marne.

722. HIGGINS, James; B: Burnshope; E: Newcastle; Pte. G 373; K: 10.7.17; Ramscapelle Road Mil. Cem. (Bel.).*

723. HILDER, Roland Edward; B: Crawley, Sussex; E: Horsham, Sussex; Pte. L 7653; K: 23.12.14; Le Touret Mem. Pas-de-Calais.

724. HILL, Arthur; B: Brighton; E: Brighton; Pte. GS 306; K: 16.8.16; Thiepval Mem. Somme.

725. HILL, Percy James; B: Hammersmith; E: Shepherd's Bush; Pte. G 19883; W: 18.10.18; Vis-en-Artois Mem. Haucourt, Pas-de-Calais.

726. HILL, Robert; B: Harting, Sussex; E: Chichester; Pte. L 8365; K: 8.4.16; Arras Mem. Pas-de-Calais; Son of Mrs.G.B.Hughes of Yapton, Sussex.

727. HILL, William Cornelius; B: Brighton; E: Brighton; Pte. L 7338; K: 9.5.15; Le Touret Mem. Pas-de-Calais; Age 31; Son of William and Louisa Hill of 37, Elder Street, Brighton.

728. HILLMAN, William Norris; B: Southover, Sussex; E: Lewes; Pte. G 1488; K: 25.9.15; Loos Mem. Pas-de-Calais; Age 18; Son of W.A. and Beatrice Hillman of 8, Southover High Street, Lewes.

729. HILLS, Ernest Alfred; B: Broadwater, Sussex; E: Worthing; Pte. G 1235; K: 13.10.15; Loos Mem. Pas-de-Calais.

730. HILLS, Reginald; B: Walworth; E: Hammersmith; Pte. G 4709; K: 9.5.15; Le Touret Mem. Pas-de-Calais; Age 31; Son of Henry George and Louisa Hills of 19, Willingdon Road, Eastbourne

731. HILLSDON, William Robert; B: Finsbury; E: Wandsworth; Cpl. G 20721; K: 24.9.18; Berthaucourt Com. Cem. Aisne; Age 34; Son of Mr. and Mrs.George Hillsdon; Husband of Daisy May Hillsdon of 76c, The Chase, Clapham, London.

732. HILLYER, Horace George; B: Worthing; E: Worthing; Pte. L 8760; K: 1.1.15; Le Touret Mem. Pas-de-Calais; Age 23; Son of William Henry and Fanny Hillyer of 10, Anglesea Street, Worthing.

733. HILTON, Dennis Sydney; B: Emsworth; E: Chichester; Pte. L 7689; K: 14.9.14; La Ferte-sous-Jouarre Mem. Seine-et-Marne.

734. HILTON, George; B: Brighton; E: Brighton; Pte. S 528; K: 9.5.15; Royal Irish Rifles Graveyard, Laventie, Pas-de-Calais; Age 25; Husband of Annie Hilton of 48, Lynton Street, Brighton.

735. HILTON, George; B: Willingdon, Sussex; E: Eastbourne; L/Cpl. G 1964; K: 23.7.16; Thiepval Mem. Somme.

736. HISCOCK, Levi; B: Idsworth; E: Chichester; Pte. L 10484; K: 9.5.15; Le Touret Mem. Pas-de-Calais; Age 19; Son of Mrs.Mary Hiscock of "Fagg's Farm", Buriton, Sussex..

737. HOAD, Lawrence Wilfred; B: Eastbourne; E: Eastbourne; Pte. L 10292; K: 9.5.15; Le Touret Mem. Pas-de-Calais.

738. HOARE, William; B: Hunston; E: Chichester; Pte. G 4612; K: 13.12.15; Loos Mem. Pas-de-Calais; Age 17; Son of George and Ellen Hoare of New Cottages, Hunston, Sussex.

739. HOBBS, Frank Thomas; B: Rotherfield, Sussex; E: Eastbourne; Pte. S 2166; K: 25.9.15; Loos Mem. Pas-de-Calais.

740. HOBBS, Frederick; B: Chichester; E: Chichester; Pte. L 5907; K: 9.5.15; Le Touret Mem. Pas-de-Calais.

741. HODGE, John; B: Christ Church, Sussex; E: Crowborough; Pte. L 8511; K: 14.9.14; La Ferte-sous-Jouarre Mem. Seine-et-Marne; Delhi Durbar Medal; Age 24; Son of George Walter and Louisa Hodge of 2, Warwick Road, Tunbridge Wells.

742. HODGE, William Thomas; B: Fulham; E: London; Cpl. L 6073; K: 27.1.15; Le Touret Mem. Pas-de-Calais.

743. HODGES, Denis; B: Trotting; E: Rogate; Pte. G 1729; W: 13.7.17; Coxyde Mil. Cem. (Bel); Son of Mrs.L.Hodges of Terwick Common, Rogate, Hampshire.

744. HODGES, George; B: Rotherfield, Sussex; E: Chichester; Pte. L 7454; K: 9.5.15; Le Touret Mem. Pas-de-Calais.

745. HODGES, William Henry Joseph; B: Ditton; E: Maidstone; Pte. G 21181; W: 10.4.18; Lillers Com. Cem. Pas-de-Calais; Age 20; Son of William Henry and Jane Green of 26, High Street, Aylesford, Kent. *

746. HOGG, Arthur Joseph; B: Willesden; E: Arundel, Sussex; Pte. L 10353; K: 25.9.15; Loos Mem. Pas-de-Calais.

747. HOGWOOD, Thomas William; B: Lambeth; E: Southwark; Pte. G 5692; K: 17.5.16; St.Patrick's Cem. Pas-de-Calais.

748. HOKINGS, William Henry; B: Brighton; E: Brighton; Pte. S 2008; K: 9.5.15; Le Touret Mem. Pas-de-Calais.

749. HOLDEN, Charlie Francis; B: Godalming; E: Brighton; Pte. G 1349; W at Home 10.10.15; Godalming Old Cem. (U.K.); Age 25; Son of Francis and Julia Maria Holden of 36, Milton Road, Bournemouth. *

750. HOLDEN, Levi; B: Chichester; E: Brighton; Cpl. L 7518; K: 16.2.15; Le Touret Mem. Pas-de-Calais.

751. HOLDSTOCK, Frank; B: Rye, Sussex; E: Rye; Pte. G 2098; K: 25.9.15; Loos Mem. Pas-de-Calais; Age 25; Son of Edward and Ann Holdstock of 11, Richmond Villas, Rye.

752. HOLLAND, Frederick Curtis; B: Worthing; E: Chichester; Pte. L 6320; K: 30.10.14; Ypres (Menin Gate) Mem. (Bel); Age 30; Son of George and Harriett Holland of Newland Road, Worthing; Husband of Elizabeth Emma Rose Holland of 30, Cottenham Road, Worthing.*

753. HOLLAND, William; B: Standish; E: Wigan; Pte. G 5874; K: 17.8.16; Thiepval Mem. Somme.

754. HOLLEBONE, Charles James; B: Hailsham, Sussex; E: Eastbourne; Pte. G 4688; K: 9.5.15; Le Touret Mem. Pas-de-Calais; Age 20; Son of Mrs.Harriett Ellenor Hollebon of 12, Garfield Road, Hailsham.*

755. HOLLOWAY, James Thomas; B: Birmingham; E: Birmingham; Pte. G 7927; K: 23.7.16; Thiepval Mem. Somme.

756. HOLLOWAY, Robert Bruce; B: Eastbourne; E: Sheffield; Pte. G 4373; K: 25.9.15; Loos Mem. Pas-de-Calais.

757. HOLLOX, William Robert; B: Corpusty; E: Cromer; Pte. G 11915; K: 24.9.18; Berthaucourt Com. Cem. Aisne; Age 21; Son of Robert and Maria Hollox of Corpusty, Aylsham, Norfolk.

758. HOLMAN, Rupert Ernest; B: Brighton; E: Brighton; Pte. G 4363; K: 9.5.15; Le Touret Mem. Pas-de-Calais; Age 31; Son of John and Charlotte Holman of 70, Albion Hill, Brighton; Husband of Bessie Holman of 118, Sussex Street, Brighton; Served in the South Africa Campaign.

759. HOLMES, James Thomas; B: Stepney; E: Mill Hill; Pte. G 34600; K: 4.11.18; Le Rejet-de-Beaulieu Com. Cem. Nord.

760. HONEYBALL, Samuel; B: Newhaven; E: Newhaven; Pte. G 123; K: 24.9.18; Berthaucourt Com. Cem. Aisne; Age 32; Son of James and Edith Honeyball of 1, Oyster Pond Cottage, Newhaven. *

761. HONEYSETT, Frank Victor; B: Sidley, Sussex; E: Bexhill; Pte. G 1711; K: 25.9.15; Loos Mem. Pas-de-Calais; Age 26; Son of Mr.W. and Mrs.E.A.Honeysett of Kite Eye Farm, Sidley, Bexhill-on-Sea.

762. HONEYSETT, Thomas; B: Hartfield, Sussex; E: Tunbridge Wells; Pte. G 1306; K: 9.5.15; Le Touret Mem. Pas-de-Calais.

763. HONEYSETT, William; B: Sidley, Sussex; E: Bexhill-on-Sea; Pte. G 1099; K: 9.5.15; Le Touret Mem. Pas-de-Calais.

764. HOOK, Thomas George; B: Hethe, Oxfordshire; E: Brighton; Pte. G 6277; K: 28.11.16; Warlencourt Brit. Cem. Pas-de-Calais; Age 38; Husband of Emily J.Hook of 88, Mill Street, Wantage.

765. HOPKINS, Ivor Thomas; B: Llantwit; E: Cowbridge; Pte. G 1627; K: 25.9.15; Loos Mem. Pas-de-Calais.

766. HOPPER, William; B: Hastings; E: Hastings; Pte. S 2249; W: 10.5.15; -

767. HORE, Sidney Rowland; B: Stepney; E: Chichester; Pte. L 10579; K: 30.6.16; Arras Mem. Pas-de-Calais; Age 23; Son of Thomas and Emma Hore of 42, Engadine Street, Southfields, London.

768. HOUNSOM, Albert George; B: Eastbourne; E: Chichester; Sgt. L 5058; W: 12.5.15; Chocques Mil. Cem. Pas-de-Calais; Age 39; Son of William and Ann Hounsom; Husband of Ada Hounsom of 39, Foord Road, Folkestone.

769. HOUNSOME, Albert; B: Northiam, Sussex; E: Hastings; L/Cpl. G 4135; K: 25.9.15; Loos Mem. Pas-de-Calais.

770. HOUSE, Ernest Montague; B: Oxford; E: Willesden; Pte. GS 582; W: 27.9.15; Lapugnoy Mil. Cem. Pas-de-Calais.

771. HOUSE, Frederick Charles; B: Christchurch; E: Croydon; Pte. L 10016; W: 8.10.14; Villers-en-Prayeres Com. Cem. Aisne; Age 21; Husband of Lillian Rose Reid, formerly House, of 1, Raglan Road, Grahamstown, South Africa.

772. HOWARD, Henry Augustus; B: Dalston; E: London; Pte. L 7797; K: 13.10.14; La Ferte-sous-Jouarre Mem. Seine-et-Marne.

773. HOWARD, William; B: Hackney; E: Dalston; Cpl. L 6550; K: 9.5.15; Le Touret Mem. Pas-de-Calais.

774. HOWE, Frederick William; B: – ; E: Herne Hill; Pte. G 17551; K: 27.9.16; Thiepval Mem. Somme.

775. HOWE, Herbert; B: Stretham; E: Ely; L/Cpl. G 5862; K: 9.9.16; Caterpillar Valley Cem. Somme.

776. HOWELL, Edward Ernest; B: St.Leonards-on-Sea; E: Chichester; Pte. L 7750; W: 17.11.14; Boulogne Eastern Cem. Pas-de-Calais; Age 28; Husband of Jenny Howell of 286, Seaside, Eastbourne.

777. HOWES, Thomas Henry; B: Norwich; E: Norwich; L/Cpl. G 14697; K: 13.11.17; Tyne Cot Mem. (Bel.).

778. HOWLETT, Robert William; B: Paddington; E: London; Pte. G 18982; K: 23.10.18; M.M.; Highland Cem., Le Cateau, Nord; Age 19; Son of Mrs.S.E.Howlett of 10, Vallere Road, College Park, Harlesden, London.

779. HUDSON, Claude Gerald; B: Brighton; E: Haywards Heath, Sussex; Pte. S 2130; K: 23.12.14; Le Touret Mem. Pas-de-Calais; Age 20; Son of Mrs.Mary Jane Parsons of 1, Alma Villas, Hurstpeirpoint, Sussex.

780. HUGGETT, Matthew; B: Hastings; E: Hastings; Pte. G 4715; K: 19.8.16; Thiepval Mem. Somme.

781. HUGHES, Frederick Philip; B: Worthing; E: Worthing; Pte. G 1270; W: 10.2.15; Lillers Com. Cem. Pas-de-Calais; Age 18; Son of Frederick and Lauretta Hughes of 4, Oxford Terrace, Broadwater, Worthing.

782. HUGHES, Laurence Edward; B: Folkington, Sussex; E: Eastbourne; Pte. G 1412; K: 25.9.15; Loos Mem. Pas-de-Calais.

783. HUGHES, William; B: Birmingham; E: Birmingham; Pte. TF 203463; W: 9.4.18; Bethune Town Cem. Pas-de-Calais; Age 23; Son of William Hughes of 22, Court, 3, House, Sherlock Street, Birmingham.

784. HUGHES, William Sladen; Lt.; K: 14.9.14; La Ferte-sous-Jouarre Mem. Seine-et-Marne.

785. HULKES, Edward; B: Canterbury; E: Chichester; Sgt. L 9591; K: 4.8.16; Courcelette Brit. Cem. Somme; Husband of Hilda May Hulkes of 55, Wyke Road, Trowbridge.

786. HUMPHREY, Cornelius Coates; B: West Chiltington, Sussex; E: Petworth, Sussex; Pte. L 9867; K: 30.10.14; Ypres (Menin Gate) Mem. (Bel.); Age 19; Son of Harry and Rhoda A.Humphrey of 3, Islingword Street, Brighton.

787. HUMPHREYS, Ernest; B: Hemel Hempstead; E: Watford; Pte. G 23114; K: 4.11.18; Vis-en-Artois Mem. Haucourt, Pas-de-Calais.

788. HUMPHREYS, William George; 2nd Lt.; K: 9.9.16; Thiepval Mem. Somme.

789. HUMPHRIES, Charles William; B: – ; E: London; Pte. G 14611; K: 9.9.16;Thiepval Mem. Somme.

790. HUNT, Charles Robert; B: Gillingham; E: Brighton; Pte. G 1560; K: 9.5.15; Le Touret Mem. Pas-de-Calais; Age 19; Son of Mrs.E.L.Hunt.

791. HUNT, Frederick Horace; B: Canterbury; E: Canterbury; Pte. G 17599; K: 18.9.18; Cerisy-Gailly Mil. Cem. Somme; Age 21; Son of Thomas Henry and Alice Frances Hunt of 17, Best Lane, Canterbury.

792. HUNT, James William; B: Wolverhampton; E: Wolverhampton; Pte. G 6099; K: 13.10.15; Loos

335

Mem. Pas-de-Calais; Age 23 Son of Mrs.Eliza Emma Hunt of 6, Dartmouth Street, Wolverhampton.

793. HURLOCK, Frank; B: Bramley; E: Haywards Heath; Pte. L 10480; K: 9.9.16; Thiepval Mem. Somme.

794. HURMSON, William; B: Norton Canes; E: Wolverhampton; Cpl. G 6094; K: 9.9.16; Thiepval Mem. Somme; Age 38; Husband of Mary Hall, formerly Hurmson, of The Square, Norton Canes, Staffordshire.

795. HURST, Francis; B: Chichester; E: Chichester; L/Cpl. L 8030; K: 30.10.14; Ypres (Menin Gate) Mem. (Bel.).

796. HUSSEY, Henry George; B: Brighton; E: Brighton; L/Cpl. G 9011; W: 29.8.16; Étaples Mil. Cem. Pas-de-Calais; Age 24; Son of George Frederick Hussey of 4, George Street, Brighton.

797. HUTCHINGS, Edward Charles; B: Frencham; E: Chichester; Pte. L 10412; K: 9.5.15; Le Touret Mem. Pas-de-Calais.

798. HUTCHINS, Alfred John Avalon; B: Santa Catalina Island, California, U.S.A.; 2nd Lt; W: (in German hands) 22.3.18; Harlebeke New Brit. Cem. (Bel.); Age 20; Son of Alfred and Alice Maud Hutchins of East Looe House, Canford Cliffs, Bournemouth, Hampshire.*

799. HUTCHINSON, Thomas Horton; B: Hastings; E: Hastings; Pte. G 1106; K: 9.5.15; Le Touret Mem. Pas-de-Calais; Age 25; Son of Horten and Annie Maria Hutchinson of 65, St.George's Road, Hastings.

800. HUTSON, George William; B: Lewes; E: Chichester; Sgt. L 9097; K: 14.9.14; La Ferte-sous-Jouarre Mem. Seine-et-Marne; Age 25; Son of George William and Frances Hutson of Heathfield, Sussex; Husband of Kate Elizabeth Hutson of 19, Neville Road, St.Anne's, Lewes.

801. HUTT, Harold Vernon; 2nd Lt; K: 27.1.15; Cuinchy Com. Cem. Pas-de-Calais; Age 27; Son of Arthur William and Margaret Sarah Hutt of Tudor House, West Malling, Kent.*

802. HUTT, Richard Henry; B: – ; E: Stratford; Pte. G 14610; W: 27.11.16; Becourt Mil. Cem. Somme; Age 19; Son of Richard Henry and Matilda Hutt of 29, Tunmarsh Lane, Barking Road, Plaistow, London.

803. HYDE, George Henry; B: Stratford; E: London; Pte. G 6328; D: 16.7.17; Longuenesse (St. Omer) Souvenir Cem. Pas-de-Calais.

804. HYDE, Herbert William; 2nd Lt; K: 17.5.15 while attached to 2nd Battalion Royal Inniskillin Fusiliers; Le Touret Mem. Pas-de-Calais.

805. HYGHGATE, William; B: Brighton; E: Arundel; Pte. L 7942; K: 24.9.18; Bellicourt Brit. Cem. Aisne; Age 39; Son of Harriet Hyghgate of Brighton.

806. HYLAND, Alfred Charles; B: Walthamstow; E: Epping; Pte. SD 3897; K; 12.6.18; Cambrin Mil. Cem. Pas-de-Calais.

807. IDE, Benjamin Henry; B: Bognor Regis, Sussex; E: Bognor Regis; Pte. G 1150; K: 9.5.15; Le Touret Mem. Pas-de-Calais; Age 22; Son of Benjamin Albert and Charlotte Ide.

808. INGLETON, William George; B: St. John's, Kent; E: Margate; Pte. L 8073; K: 9.5.15; Le Touret Mem. Pas-de-Calais; Age 29; Son of Mr. and Mrs.W.C.Ingleton of Sea View Cottage, George Hill, Kingsgate, Kent.

809. INGRAM, James; B: Croydon; E: Hastings; Pte. L 10561; K: 14.12.15; Dud Corner Cem. Pas-de-Calais, Age 17; Son of William James and Ellen Ingram of 2, Pinders Road, Clive Vale, Hastings.

810. INKPEN, Percy; B: Brighton; E: Brighton; Pte. L 7628; W: 11.9.14; Priez Com. Cem. Aisne; Age 27; Son of Mrs.S.Inkpen of 45, Bernard Road, Brighton.

811. INSKIP, Bert William; B: Potten; E: Bedford; Pte. G 14547; K: 9.9.16; Caterpillar Valley Cem. Somme; Age 19; Son of George and Annie Inskip of Station Road, Potten, Bedfordshire.

812. INVARARITY, Alexander; B: St.Ninians; E: Mill Hill; Pte. G 20067; K: 5.7.17; Ramscapelle Road Mil. Cem. (Bel.).

813. IRISH, Gordon; B: Chichester; E: Chichester; Pte. L 9083; W at Home: 12.10.15; Rumboldswyke (or Old Wyke) (St.Rumbold) Sussex (U.K.); Age 22; Son of Walter and Fanny Irish of 14, The Hornet, Chichester; Brother, Leonard, also killed – see 814.

814. IRISH, Leonard; B: Wyke; E: Chichester; Pte. L 9755; K: 29.9.14; St.Erme Com. Cem; Aisne; Son of Walter and Fanny Irish of 14, The Hornet, Chichester; Brother, Gordon, also killed – see 813.

815. IRELAND, William; 2nd Lt; K: 25.9.15; Dud Corner Cem. Pas-de-Calais; Age 33; Son of William and Emily Ireland of Rudgwick, Sussex; Husband of Eva May Ireland of 54, London Road, Bognor Regis.

816. ISAACS, Henry; B: Salisbury; E: Horsham; Pte. L 6913; K: 10.9.14; Montreuil-aux-Lions Brit. Cem. Aisne.

817. ISDEN, Claud; B: Hastings; E: Hastings; Pte. S 1613; K: 30.1.15; Le Touret Mem. Pas-de-Calais; Age 19; Son of Richard Isden of 31, Fairlight Road, Ore, Hastings.

818. IZZARD, Ernest; B: Crowborough, Sussex; E: Brighton; Pte. G 4831; K: 25.9.15; Loos Mem. Pas-de-Calais; Age 33; Son of James Izzard and Mrs.D.Watson, formerly Izzard, of 2, Vine Cottages, Jarvis Brook, Sussex; Husband of Agnes Winifred Izzard of 39, Priory Street, Lewes.

819. IZZARD, William Henry; B: Blackboys, Sussex; E: Chichester; Pte. G 13401; D: 2.7.18; Pernes Brit. Cem. Pas-de-Calais; Age 20; Son of John and Mary Ann Izzard of Laughton, Sussex.

820. JACKSON, George James; B: Poplar; E: Littlehampton; Pte. G 4822; K: 25.9.15; Loos Mem. Pas-de-Calais.

821. JACKSON, George William; B: Bradford; E: Earlestown; Pte. G 7670; W: 7.9.16; St.Sever Cem. Rouen, Seine-Maritime; Age 42; Son of Charles and Sarah Jackson of Sowerby Bridge, Yorkshire; Husband of Ethel Ellen Frances Jackson of 61, Church Road, Haydock, St.Helens, Lancashire.

822. JACKSON, John Ellis; B: Brighton; E: Brighton; Pte. SD 5359; K: 23.11.17; Tyne Cot Mem. (Bel.); Age 25; Son of Milton John Jackson of 18, Winchester Street, Brighton.

823. JACKSON, Stanley Duncan; B: Brighton; E: Brighton; Pte. G 6884; K: 13.10.15; Loos Mem. Pas-de-Calais; Age 19; Son of Arthur and Rosina Jackson of 28, George Street Gardens, Brighton.

824. JAMES, Frank; B: Sandhurst, Kent; E: Tunbridge Wells; Sgt. L 4737; K: 8.11.14; Ypres (Menin Gate) Mem. (Bel.).

825. JAMES, Thomas; B: Horsted Keynes, Sussex; E: Haywards Heath; Pte. G 1347; K: 17.5.16; St.Patrick's Cem. Pas-de-Calais; Age 33; Son of Thomas and Jane James of Horsted Keynes; Brother, William, also killed- see 826.

826. JAMES, William; B: Horsted Keynes, Sussex; E: Haywards Heath; Pte. G 1341; K: 9.5.15; Le Touret Mem. Pas-de-Calais; Age 25; Son of Thomas and Jane James of Horsted Keynes, Sussex; Brother, Thomas, also killed – see 825.

827. JARDON, Albert; B: Brighton; E: Brighton; Pte. L 10438; K: 9.5.15; Le Touret Mem. Pas-de-Calais.

828. JARMAN, William; B: Northiam, Sussex; E: Rye, Sussex; Pte. L 10230; W: 25.9.15; Vermelles Brit. Cem. Pas-de-Calais; Age 20; Son of C. and Mrs. S.H.Jarman of Station Road, Northiam.

829. JARVIS, Henry; B: Hastings; E: Hastings; Pte. L 8382; K: 29.8.15; Vermelles Brit. Cem. Pas-de-Calais; Age 30; Son of James George and Emma Jarvis of Ore, Hastings; Husband of Daisy Jarvis of Iden Cottage, Station Road, Bexhill-on-Sea.

830. JARVIS, Owen; B: Waldron, Sussex; E: Eastbourne; Pte. G 1431; W: 30.4.15; Wimereux Com. Cem. Pas-de-Calais; Age 19; Son of Albert and Philadelphia Jarvis of Waldron, Sussex.

831. JAY, Ernest Alfred; B: Shoreham, Sussex; E: Hove; Pte. L 10755; K: 13.10.15; Loos Mem. Pas-de-Calais.*

832. JEFERY, Joe; B: Portslade, Sussex; E: Hove; Pte. G 1180; W: 26.4.15; Bethune Town Cem. Pas-de-Calais.

833. JEMMETT-BROWNE, Antony Edward; Capt; K: 10.9.14; Montreuil-aux-Lions Brit. Cem. Aisne. Age 32.*

834. JENNER, Thomas Joseph; B: Hastings; E: Chichester; Pte. L 8213; K: 9.5.15; Le Touret Mem. Pas-de-Calais; Age 30; Son of Thomas Jenner of 19a, South Terrace, Queen's Road, Hastings.

835. JENNINGS, Matthew John; B: Bury St.Edmunds; E: Haywards Heath; L/Cpl. G 236; K: 9.9.16; Thiepval Mem. Somme; Age 30; Son of Matthew and Annie Jennings of Cavenham, Suffolk; Husband of Annie Elizabeth Jennings of 23, Salop Street, Bridgnorth.

836. JEX, Alfred Henry; B: Islington; E: Dalston; L/Cpl. L 6500; K: 3.6.15; Cambrin Churchyard Ext. Pas-de-Calais.

837. JOHNSON, Charles Alfred; B: Bredhurst; E: Rainham; L/Cpl. G 17557; K: 9.9.16; Caterpillar Valley Cem. Somme; Age 25; Son of Henry and Sarah Johnson of 6, Naylor's Cottages, Bredhurst, Chatham.

838. JOHNSON, Frederick Shopland; B: Fulham; E: London; Pte. G 4815; K: 25.9.15; Loos Mem. Pas-de-Calais.

839. JOHNSTON, Thomas Roland; B: Lambeth; E: Chichester; Pte. L 10088; K: 30.6.16; Arras Mem. Pas-de-Calais; Age 23; Son of Thomas Rowland and Annie Johnston of 6, Crystall Terrace, Upper Norwood, London.*

840. JOHNSTON, William; B: Ruthven; E: Perth; L/Cpl. 18329; W: 5.11.18; Premont Brit. Cem. Aisne; Age 26; Son of William and Mary Mathers Johnston of Kinnaird, Lintrathen, Kirriemuir, Forfarshire.*

841. JOHNSTONE, Alfred; B: Luton; E: Luton; Pte. G 14550; K: 9.9.16; Thiepval Mem. Somme.

842. JOLLY, John; B: Chorley; E: Chorley; Pte. G 6006; W: 31.12.15; Chocques Mil. Cem. Pas-de-Calais; Age 22; Husband of Mary Jolly of Red Cat Lane, Burscough Bridge, Lancashire.*

843. JONES, Charles John; B: Poplar; E: Stratford; L/Cpl. L 7441; K: 23.9.14; La Ferte-sous-Jouarre Mem. Seine-et-Marne; Age 28; Son of Mrs.Elizabeth Jones of 1, Scarborough Road, Leytonstone, London; Student of the Military School of Music, Kneller Hall.

844. JONES, Frederick; B: Hastings; E: Chichester; Pte. L 10192; K: 10.1.18; Artillery Wood Cem. (Bel.); Son of Mrs.C.Jones of 10, Duke Street, Silverhill, St.Leonards-on-Sea.

845. JONES, Herbert Stanley Joseph; B: – ; E: London; L/Cpl. G 14613; W: 19.11.17; Mendingham Mil. Cem. (Bel.); Age 28; Son of Jessie Jones of 99, Shepperton Road, Islington, London.*

846. JONES, Walter William; B: Eastbourne; E: Eastbourne; Pte. G 1449; K: 9.5.15; Le Touret Mem. Pas-de-Calais; Age 20; Son of John Walter and Martha Jones of The Greys, Old Town, Eastbourne.

847. JONES, William Thomas; B: Chichester; E: Chichester; Pte. L 7487; K: 25.9.15; Loos Mem. Pas-de-Calais; Age 43; Son of William Thomas Jones of Toronto Terrace, Brighton; Husband of Annie Jones of 39, Southampton Street, Brighton.

848. JUCKES, Thomas Roland; Lt.; K: 9.5.15; Le Touret Mem. Pas-de-Calais.

849. JUDGE, Charles Edward; B: Hemel Hempstead; E: Chichester; L/Cpl. S 2292; K: 25.9.15; Dud Corner Cem. Pas-de-Calais; Age 17; Son of Edward and Kathleen Judge of 18, Clarendon Buildings, Balderton Street, London.*

850. JUPP, George Henry; B: Horsham; E: Horsham; Pte. G 4666; K: 9.5.15; Le Touret Mem. Pas-de-Calais.

851. JUPP, George James; B: Chichester; E: Chichester; Pte. L 8250; K: 28.2.17; Hem Farm Mil. Cem. Somme.

852. JUPP, Wilfred John; B: Brighton; E: Chichester; L/Cpl. L 10196; K: 7.11.14; Ypres (Menin Gate) Mem. (Bel.); Son of Charles and Caroline Jupp of 96, Elm Grove, Brighton.

K

853. KEATES, Ernest; B: Parham, Sussex; E: Chichester; Pte. L 9956; K: 14.9.14; La Ferte-sous-Jouarre Mem. Seine-et-Marne; Age 20; Son of Mr. and Mrs.Keates of Copy Hold Cottage, Lagness, Chichester.

854. KEEP, Albert; B: Wantage; E: Haywards Heath, Sussex; Pte. G 1286; K: 23.7.16; Thiepval Mem. Somme; Age 31; Son of Mr. and Mrs.J.Keep of Letcombe Regis, Berkshire; Husband of Mrs.M.E.Keep of Durnford House, Cuckfield, Sussex.

855. KELLAWAY-SMITH, G.F; B: – ; E: – ; Pte. G 8706; K: 16.8.16; Thiepval Mem. Somme; Age 21; Son of Mrs.Anne Kellaway-Smith of 27, Blatchington Road, Seaford, Sussex.

856. KELLY, Michael; B: Tuam, Co. Galway; E: Marylebone; Pte. G 5569; K: 9.9.16; Serre Road Cem. No.2. Somme.

857. KELSEY, Richard Cecil; B: Hove; E: Hove; Pte. SD 5003; K: 24.9.18; Vis-en-Artois Mem., Haucourt, Pas-de-Calais.

858. KEMBER, Frank; B: Haywards Heath, Sussex; E: Chichester; Pte. L 5982; K: 31.10.14; Ypres (Menin Gate) Mem. (Bel.).

859. KEMBER, John William; B: Walworth; E: Chichester; Pte. L 10294; K: 14.9.14; La Ferte-sous-Jouarre Mem. Seine-et-Marne; Age 22; Son of Arthur and Alice Maud Kember of 45, Castle Hill Road, Hastings.

860. KEMP. Charles Albert; B: Ticehurst, Sussex; E: Hastings; Pte. GS 699; K: 9.5.15; Le Touret Mem. Pas-de-Calais; Age 49; Son of Henry and Rebecca Kemp of Clarehurst Cottage, Flimwell, Kent.*

861. KEMP, Thomas; B: Hellingly, Sussex; E: Eastbourne; Cpl. L 9893; K: 25.9.15; Loos Mem. Pas-de-Calais; Age 18; Son of Caroline Mitchell of Frog Firle, Alfriston, Sussex.

862. KENNARD, Bernard; B: Wandsworth; E: Kingston-on-Thames; Pte. L 10020; W: 22.6.16; Bethune Town Cem. Pas-de-Calais; Age 21; Son of Marshall J. and Minnie M.Kennard of 24, Astonville Street, Southfields, London.

863. KENNARD, Edward; B: Brighton; E: Brighton; Pte. L 10360; W: 8.11.14; Ypres (Menin Gate) Mem. (Bel.); Age 22; Son of George Henry and Elizabeth Kennard.*

864. KENNARD, Frederick James; B: Brighton; E: Brighton; Pte. G 4922; W: 28.9.18; St.Sever Cem. Ext. Rouen, Seine-Maritime; Age 34; Son of Mrs. Ellen Kennard of 39, North Road, Brighton.

865. KENNAUGH, Gilbert Edward; B: Pontypool; E: Eastbourne; Pte. G 1400; K: 9.5.15; Le Touret Mem. Pas-de-Calais; Age 19; Son of the Reverend G.E. and Mrs.Sarah Kennaugh of 67, Victoria Drive, Eastbourne.

866. KENT, Frederick Harry; B: Littlehampton, Sussex; E: Worthing; L/Cpl. G 14027; W: 27.11.16; Dernancourt Com. Cem. Ext. Somme; Age 31; Husband of Lily Kent of 64, Broadwater Street West, Worthing.*

867. KENT, John Henry; B: Brighton; E: Chichester; Pte. L 10148; K: 8.9.16; Thiepval Mem. Somme.

868. KENT, Leo; B: Staffordshire; E: Dublin; L/Cpl. L 9137; D: 12.2.17; Bray Mil. Cem. Somme.

869. KENWARD, Conrad; B: Hastings; E: St.Leonards-on-Sea; Pte. L 9592; K: 21.9.14; Paissy Churchyard Aisne.

870. KENWARD, Ernest Henry; B: – ; E: – ; Pte. L 10151; W: 18.9.14; Nantes (La Bouteillerie) Cem. Loire-Atlantique; Age 20; Son of Albery Edwin and Harriet Kenward of Arundel.

871. KENWARD, James; B: Hever; E: Brighton; L/Cpl. L 8373; K: 25.9.15; Loos Mem. Pas-de-Calais.

872. KENWARD, Robert; 2nd Lt; K: 7.7.16; Thiepval Mem. Somme; Age 21; Son of Robert Kenward of Barkham Manor, Piltdown, Sussex.

873. KENWARD Robert Trillos; B: Hastings; E: Hastings; Pte. S 2157; K: 9.5.15; Le Touret Mem. Pas-de-Calais.*

874. KENWARD, Sidney; B: Lewes; E: Lewes; Pte. L 7474; K: 14.9.14; La Ferte-sous-Jouarre Mem. Seine-et-Marne.

875. KERSWILL, Arthur Herbert; B: London; E: London; Sgt. L 6581; K: 30.10.14; Ypres (Menin Gate) Mem. (Bel.); Age 30; Son of John Edward and Eliza Kerswill.

876. KETTLE, William Henry; B: Maidstone; E: Chichester; Sgt. L 9186; K: 10.9.14; Montreuil-aux-Lions Brit. Cem. Aisne.

877. KEY, Henry James; B: Islington; E: Hastings; Pte. G 558; K: 24.9.18; Berthaucourt Com. Cem. Aisne.

878. KINCH, George William; B: Fareham; E: Gosport; L/Cpl. L 6376; K: 1.1.15; Le Touret Mem. Pas-de-Calais.

879. KING, Alfred Henry; B: Brighton; E: Brighton; Pte. GS 309; K: 1.1.15; Le Touret Mem. Pas-de-Calais.

880. KING, Arthur; B: Fulham; E: Hammersmith; Pte. G 5277; K: 2.9.16; Thiepval Mem. Somme.

881. KING, George Herbert; B: Angmering, Sussex; E: Bognor; Pte. G 1469; K: 25.9.15; Loos Mem. Pas-de-Calais; Age 22; Son of Albert and Fanny King of 12, Gravits Lane, Bognor Regis, Sussex.

882. KING, Harry Arthur; B: West Hoathly, Sussex; E: Woolwich; Pte. L 7952; K: 14.9.14; Chauny Com. Cem. Brit. Ext. Aisne; Age 31; Husband of Agnes Florence King of Philpots Lodge, West Hoathly.

883. KING, Horace; B: Newport Pagnell; E: Maidstone; Pte. G 11977; W: 18.9.18; Vis-en-Artois, Mem. Haucourt, Pas-de-Calais.

884. KING, John Joseph; B: Jersey; E: Chichester; Sgt. L 4626; K: 14.9.14; La Ferte-sous-Jouarre Mem. Seine-et-Marne; Age 38; Son of Joseph King; Husband of Caroline King of 6, Westfield Square, Westfield, Surrey.*

885. KING, Philip Douglas Atwood; 2nd Lt; K: 18.12.16; A.I.F. Burial Ground, Somme.

886. KING, Stanley William; B: Battersey; E: Margate; Pte. G 21163; K: 14.11.17; Tyne Cot Mem. (Bel.).

887. KING, William; B: Hastings; E: Eastbourne; Pte. L 10215; K: 9.5.15; Le Touret Mem., Pas-de-Calais; Age 19.

888. KING, William Richard; B: Kingston-on-Thames; E: Chichester; L/Cpl. G 804; W: 27.9.16; Dernancourt Com. Cem. Ext. Somme; Age 30; Son of Mr. and Mrs.B.King of Kingston Hill, Surrey; Husband of Mrs.L.M.King of 2, Rosemary, Heath Road, Lake, Isle of Wight.

889. KINGETT, Henry; B: Lyndmere; E: Guildford; Pte. L 5954; K: 25.4.15; Le Touret Mem. Pas-de-Calais.

890. KINNARD, Walter Hews; B: Clapham, Sussex; E: Chichester; Pte. L 10150; K: 9.5.15; Le Touret Mem. Pas-de-Calais; Age 19; Son of Henry William Kinnard of 162, Clapham Street, Clapham.

891. KIRBY, Cyril Foers; B: Glapthorne; E: Perterborough; Pte. G 6059; K: 2.3.16; Dud Corner Cem. Pas-de-Calais; Age 31; Son of Alfred William and Mary Ann kirby of Glapthorne, Northamptonshire.

892. KNAPP, Charles; B: Shermanbury; E: Chichester; Pte. L 10374; K: 17.5.16; St.Patrick's Cem. Pas-de-Calais.

893. KNIFTON, Charles William McKinley; 2nd Lt; K: 23.11.17; Tyne Cot. Mem. (Bel.); Age 20; Son of John and Agnes Mary Knifton of 7, Vicarage Park, Plumstead, London; Served with the London Scottish October,1915, to August,1916, when he entered Sandhurst Military Academy; Commissioned April,1917; Brother, James, also killed – see 894.

894. KNIFTON, James McKinley; 2nd Lt; K: 21.7.18; Loos Mem. Pas-de-Calais; Brother also killed – see 893.

895. KNIGHT, George Edward; B: Chichester; E: Chichester; Cpl. G 4381; K: 9.9.16; Thiepval Mem. Somme.

896. KNIGHT, George Samuel; B: Henfield, Sussex; E: Chichester; L/Cpl. G 520; K: 17.8.16; Caterpillar Valley Cem. Somme.

897. KNIGHT, Louis James; B: Findon, Sussex; E: Worthing; Pte. G 1285; K: 9.5.15; Le Touret Mem. Pas-de-Calais; Age 34; Husband of Winifred Frances Knight of 114, Newland Road, Worthing.

898. KNIGHT, Percy Frederick; B: Roffey, Sussex; E: Chichester; Pte. L 10093; K: 9.5.15; Le Touret Mem. Pas-de-Calais; Age 20; Son of Mrs.J.Knight of York Cottages, 220, Crawley Road, Horsham, Sussex.*

899. KNIGHT, Richard; B: Midhurst, Sussex; E: Chichester; Pte. S 2147; K: 9.5.15; Le Touret Mem. Pas-de-Calais; Age 18; Son of Heber and Ellen Knight of 20, East Street, Wick, Sussex.

900. KNIGHT, Thomas Henry; B: Merton; E: Kingston-on-Thames; Pte. G 5194; W at Home: 4.5.16; Wandsworth (Earlsfield) Cem. (U.K.); Age 21; Son of Charles Knight of Tooting; Husband of Alice Elizabeth Smy, formerly Knight, of Springfield Farm, Garratt Green, Lower Tooting, London.

901. KNIGHT, Thomas James; B: – ; E: – ; Pte. G 4543; W: 9.11.16; Étaples Mil. Cem. Pas-de-Calais; Age 33; Husband of Kate Knight of 8, Freshbrooke Cottages, Salt Lake, Lancing, Sussex.*

902. KNIGHT, William; B: Brighton; E: Brighton; Pte. L 6951; K: 8.11.14; Ypres (Menin Gate) Mem. (Bel.).

903. KNOWLES, Harry; B: Crawley, Sussex; E: East Grinstead, Sussex; Pte. L 7316; K: 25.9.15; Loos Mem. Pas-de-Calais; Age 29; Son of Alfred and Mary Knowles; Husband of Elsie May Tame, formerly Knowles, of 13, Malthouse Road, Crawley, Sussex.

L

904. LAKER, Stephen; B: Esher; E: Chichester; Pte. G 3975; K: 3.6.15; Cambrin Churchyard Ext. Pas-de-Calais; Age 16; Son of Mrs.S.F.Spickemell of New Cottage, Shopewyke, Sussex.

905. LALLYETT, Joseph; B: Portslade, Sussex; E: Brighton; Pte. GS 312; K: 26.1.15; Le Touret Mem. Pas-de-Calais.

906. LAMBERT, Edward; B: Chichester; E: Chichester; Pte. L 10110; K: 25.9.15; Loos Mem. Pas-de-Calais.

907. LAMBERT, Edward; B: North Heigham; E: Norwich; Pte. G 14706; K: 24.9.18; Berthaucourt Com. Cem. Aisne.

908. LAMBERT, Harry James; B: Bognor Regis, Sussex; E: Chichester; Pte. G 6349; W: 9.12.16; Dernancourt Com. Cem. Ext. Somme; Age 29; Son of Eliza Humphrey, formerly Lambert; Stepson of Albert Humphrey; Husband of Charlotte Kate Short, formerly Lambert, of 46, Cavendish Street, Chichester.

909. LAMBOURNE, Ernest; B: Islington; E: London; Pte. L 7761; K: 30.10.14; Ypres (Menin Gate) Mem. (Bel.).

910. LANGFORD, Alfred; B: Brighton; E: Brighton; Pte. GS 167; K: 23.12.14; Le Touret Mem. Pas-de-Calais.

911. LARGE, William Edwin; B: Shaftesbury; E: Luton; Pte. G 11252; W: 10.9.16; Heilly Station Cem., Mericourt L'Abbé, Somme; Age 33; Son of Frederick William and Ellen Large of 22, Bell Street, Shaftesbury.

912. LARK, Arnold George; B: Melton; E: Cromer; Pte. TF 202342; K: 13.11.17; Tyne Cot Mem. (Bel.).

913. LA ROCHE, Frederick James Victor; B: London; E: Chichester; Pte. G 615; K: 30.6.16; Arras Mem. Pas-de-Calais; Age 21; Son of Frederick and Emily La Roche of 22, Borough High Street, London.

914. LASSETTER, Arthur James; B: Brighton; E: Brighton; Pte. L 7593; K: 14.9.14; La Ferte-sous-Jouarre Mem. Seine-et-Marne; Age 29; Son of James and Annie Lassetter of 30, Kingsley Road, Brighton.

915. LASSITER, Charles; B: Eastbourne; E: Chichester; Pte. G 4614; K: 25.9.15; St.Marys A.D.S. Cem. Pas-de-Calais.

916. LATTER, James; B: Uckfield, Sussex; E: Chelsea; Pte. G 4719; K: 9.5.15; Le Touret Mem. Pas-de-Calais; Age 38; Husband of Mrs.F.Latter of 126, Commonwealth Road, Caterham Valley, Surrey.

917. LAVENDER, Arthur; B: Hastings; E: Chichester; Sgt. L 9334; K: 9.5.15; Le Touret Mem. Pas-de-Calais.

918. LAVENDER, Asa; B: Heathfield, Sussex; E: Liverpool; L/Cpl. G 4248; K: 9.9.16; Caterpillar Valley Cem. Somme.

919. LAWRENCE, Leonard Ernest; B: Battersea; E: Brighton; Pte; Signaller; TF 202595; K: 23.11.17; Tyne Cot Mem. (Bel.); Age 26; Son of Harry and Emily Lawrence of 8, Aylesbury Street, Neasden, London.

920. LEDWORD, Charles; B: East Grinstead; E: East Grinstead; Pte. G 8834; W: 23.7.16; Albert Com. Cem. Ext. Somme.

921. LEE, Arthur Frederick; B: Flamstead; E: Hove; Pte. G 1181; K: 9.5.15; Le Touret Mem. Pas-de-Calais.

922. LEE, John; B: Shoreham, Sussex; E: Chichester; Pte. S 534; K: 25.9.15; Loos Mem. Pas-de-Calais.

923. LEE, John Herbert; B: Croydon; E: Kingston-on-Thames; Pte. G 4898; K: 13.10.15; Loos Mem. Pas-de-Calais; Age 36; Son of John Lee; Husband of Ellen Sarah Lee of 33, Lesley Street, Holloway, London.

924. LEGGATT, Albert; B: Petworth, Sussex; E: Chichester; Pte. L 8023; K: 20.8.16; Delville Wood Cem. Somme; Age 34; Son of George Leggatt of Sutton; Husband of Mrs.O.Leggatt of Sutton, Pulborough, Sussex.

925. LEGGATT, Ernest; B: West Tarring, Sussex; E: Worthing; Sgt. TF 200794; K: 24.9.18; Bellicourt Brit. Cem. Aisne.

926. LEIGHTON, Frederick James; B: Marylebone; E: Horsham, Sussex; Pte. SD 2031; W: 20.11.17; Dozinghem Mil. Cem. (Bel.).

927. LELLIOTT, Ernest Charles; B: Selsey, Sussex; E: Kingston-on-Thames; Pte. G 4587; K: 25.9.15; Loos Mem. Pas-de-Calais.

928. LENNARD, Arthur William; B: Hastings; E: Bexhill-on-Sea; Pte. G 4356; K: 9.5.15; Le Touret Mem. Pas-de-Calais; Age 31; Son of Henry and Jane Lennard; Husband of Minnie Lennard of 80, Bulverhithe Road, St.Leonards-on-Sea; Served 14 years as a volunteer with the Regiment.

929. LEONARD, Alfred Edward; B: Challock, Kent ; E: Eastbourne; Pte. G 11677; W: 17.11.17; Lijssenthoek Mil. Cem. (Bel.); Age 20; Son of Mrs.J.Leonard of Challock Lees, Kent.*

930. LEONARD, William John; B: Horsham, Sussex; E: Horsham; L/Cpl. L 7831; K: 25.9.15; Loos Mem. Pas-de-Calais.

931. LEPPER, Silas James; B: Hastings; E: Hastings; Pte. G 263; K: 18.9.18; Cerisy-Gailly Mil. Cem. Somme.

932. LETCHFORD, Victor Amos; B: Ash; E: Canterbury; Pte. L 9479; K: 14.9.14; La Ferte-sous-Jouarre Mem, Seine-et-Marne; Age 28; Son of Mr. and Mrs. Letchford of 7, Victoria Terrace, Ash, Kent; Husband of Lily Louisa Letchford of 26, Park Road, East Acton, London.

933. LEVERETT, Herbert John; B: Southsea; E: Bognor Regis, Sussex; L/Cpl. G 1225; K: 25.1.15; Vermelles Brit. Cem. Pas-de-Calais.

934. LEVETT, Charles Walter; B: Brighton; E: Brighton; Pte. L 8310; K: 12.1.15; Le Touret Mem. Pas-de-Calais; Age 29; Son of Frederick and Sarah Levett of 52, Toronto Terrace, Brighton.

935. LEVETT, James John; B: Battersea; E: Tunbridge Wells; Pte. S 1153; K: 25.9.15; Loos Mem. Pas-de-Calais; Age 23; Son of John James Levett of Polhearn, Brixham.

936. LEVICK, Edmund; B: Lambeth; E: Dublin; L/Cpl. L 6423; K: 25.9.15; Dud Corner Cem. Pas-de-Calais; Age 34; Son of Edward and Frances Levick of London; Husband of Frances Marie Levick of 78, Clapham Road, London; Served in the South Africa campaign.

937. LEWIN, Rex Richard; Lt; K: 25.9.15; Loos Mem. Pas-de-Calais; Age 21; Son of Charles John and Sarah Lewin of 10, Elmsleigh Road, Weston-super-Mare.

938. LEWRY, Frederick George; B: Brighton; E: Chichester; Cpl. L 8243, K. 9.5.15, Le Touret Mem. Pas-de-Calais.

939. LILLEY, Frederick Arthur; B: East Ham; E: Warley; Pte. G 14749; W: 4.10.16; Étaples Mil. Cem. Pas-de-Calais; Age 27; Son of Mrs.I.H.Lilley of 1, Oakley Cottages, Orsett Heath, Essex.

940. LIND, Thomas John; B: Shoreham, Sussex; E: Worthing; Pte. G 4837; K: 23.7.16; Thiepval Mem. Somme.

941. LINFIELD, Harold Frank; B: Worthing; E: Worthing; Pte. G 1295; K: 9.5.15; Rue- Petillon Mil. Cem. Pas-de-Calais; Age 21; Son of Arthur George and Edith Mary Linfield of The Laurels, Church Waltham, Worthing.

942. LINTOTT, William Richard; B: Brighton; E: Brighton; Pte. G 4384; K: 29.8.15; Vermelles Brit. Cem. Pas-de-Calais; Age 32; Husband of Lily E.Taylor, formerly Lintott, of 16, Melbourne Street, Brighton.

943. LITTLE, Christopher Stephen; B: Whitley Bay; E: Darlington; Pte. G 6062; K: 9.9.16; Thiepval Mem. Somme; Age 22; Son of Christopher and Eleanor Jane Little of 41, Linthorpe Avenue, Middlesborough.

944. LITTLE, Harry Ewart; 2nd Lt; K: 18.9.18; Vadencourt Brit. Cem. Aisne; Age 21; Son of Mr.H.Little of 84, Station Road, Redhill.

945. LLOYD, Arthur; B: Hastings; E: Hastings; Pte. G 1101; K: 9.5.15; Le Touret Mem. Pas-de-Calais; Age 23; Son of E.L. and Elizabeth Ann Lloyd of 22, Norman Road, St.Leonards-on-Sea.

946. LLOYD, Horace; B: Warrington; E: Oxford; Pte. G 20467; K: 25.1.17; Menin Road South Mil. Cem. (Bel.); Age 21; Son of Henry and Agnes Lloyd of West End, Epworth, Doncaster.

947. LLOYD, William George; B: Chelsea; E: Chelsea; Pte. G 18620; K: 24.9.18; Berthaucourt Com. Cem. Aisne; Age 20; Son of George and K.E.Lloyd of 14, Green Street, Draycott Avenue, Chelsea, London.

948. LOADER, Ernest Stanley; 2nd Lt; K: 4.11.18; Le Rejet-de-Beaulieu Com. Cem. Nord.

949. LOCK, Leslie John; B: Chichester; E: Chichester; Sgt. L 7717; K: 25.9.15; Dud Corner Cem. Pas-de-Calais; Age 30; Son of Frederick Henry and Annie Lock of 22, Earl Street, Hastings.

950. LONGLANDS, Thomas; B: Chichester; E: Chichester; Pte. S 2193; W: 10.5.15; Rue-des-Berceaux Mil. Cem., Richebourg-L'Avoué , Pas-de-Calais; Age 39; Son of Henry and Ann Longlands of Chichester.

951. LONGLEY, George; B: Rotherfield, Sussex; E: Tunbridge Wells; Pte. SD 438; K: 4.11.18; Le Rejet-de-Beaulieu Com. Cem. Nord.

952. LOUSADA, Edward Arthur; Lt; K: 30.10.14; Ypres (Menin Gate) Mem. (Bel.). *

953. LOVE, Albert Charles; B: Ryde I.O.W; E: Brighton; Pte. L 10112; K: 31.10.14; Ypres (Menin Gate)

Mem. (Bel.); Age 23; Son of Mrs.Jemima Love of 41, Shakespeare Street, Hove.

954. LOVELL, Arthur; B: Hove; E: Brighton; Pte. S 2231; K: 25.9.15; St.Marys A.D.S. Cem. Pas-de-Calais; Age 19; Son of Mr. and Mrs.W.Lovell of 2, Hove Place, Hove.

955. LOVELOCK, Albert Charles; B: – ; E: Tunbridge Wells; L/Cpl. G 3963; K: 25.9.15; St. Marys A..D.S. Cem. Pas-de-Calais.

956. LOWER, George; B: Newhaven, Sussex; E: Newhaven; Pte. G 5670; K: 27.9.16; Thiepval Mem. Somme.

957. LUCAS, James Edward; B: Fulking; E: Hove; Pte. G 9194; K: 7.8.16; Brewery Orchard Cem. Nord; Age 23; Son of Mr.O and Mrs.R.Lucas of Fulking, Sussex.

958. LUCK, John Ernest; B: Hawkhurst; E: Whileigh; Pte. L 10227; K: 25.9.15; Dud Corner Cem. Pas-de-Calais; Age 22; Son of Harriett Luck of Flimwell, Kent.

959. LUXFORD, Jesse; B: Billingshurst; E: Petworth; Pte. L 10179; K: 14.9.14; La Ferte-sous-Jouarre Mem. Seine-et-Marne.

960. LUXFORD, Percy Ernest George; B: Lingfield; E: East Grinstead; Pte. G 4678; K: 13.10.15; Loos Mem. Pas-de-Calais; Age 19; Son of Percy and Harriett Luxford.

M

961. MAC CABEE, William Ernest; B: Portsmouth; E: Chichester; Pte. L 7379; K: 7.10.14; Vendresse Brit. Cem. Aisne; Age 34; Husband of Mrs.A.E.Clark, formerly MacCabee, of 5, Richmond Road, Fisherton, Salisbury.

962. MAC GREGOR, Douglas Stewart; B: Gravesend; E: Lewisham; Pte. G 14815; K: 27.9.16; Thiepval Mem. Somme; Son of Mrs.Catherine MacGregor of 95, Halesworth Road, Lewisham, London.

963. MACKAY, James Macdonald Cathcart; B: Edinburgh; E: Glasgow; Pte. L 10041; K: 25.1.15; Le Touret Mem. Pas-de-Calais.

964. MALKOWSKI, William; B: – ; E: – ; Pte. G 5856; K: 3.3.16; Arras Mem. Pas-de-Calais; Age 29; Son of Mrs.Bessie Malkowski of 7, Harcourt House, Harcourt Street, Marylebone, London.

965. MANKTELOW, James; B: Wadhurst; E: Chichester; Pte. GS 850; K: 25.9.15; Loos Mem. Pas-de-Calais.

966. MANLEY, William; B: London; E: Woking; L/Cpl. L 8525; K in A at La Bassee on 1.1.15; Le Touret Mem. Pas-de-Calais; Age 24; Son of J.S. and Emily Manley.

967. MANN, Mark Percy; B: Brightlingsea; E: Huskurds; Pte. G 14619; K: 24.9.18; M.M., Vis-en-Artois Mem., Haucourt, Pas-de-Calais; Age 21; Son of George and Ellen Mann of 18, Council Houses, Ingatestone, Essex.

968. MANNERS, Douglas William; B: Grantham; E: Hove; Pte. G 6319; D: 27.11.16; Thiepval Mem. Somme; Age 20; Son of Frederick William John Manners Manners and Gertrude Susanna Manners.*

969. MANSBRIDGE, Arthur Ernest; B: Brighton; E:

Brighton; Pte. L 10369; K: 25.9.15; Loos Mem. Pas-de-Calais.

970. MANSER, Henry Frederick; B: Brighton; E: Brighton; Pte. L 8056; W: 10.11.14; Poperinghe Old Mil. Cem. (Bel.); Age 31; Husband of Ada Amelia Hoare, formerly Manser, of 25, Baxter Road, Brighton.*

971. MANVELL, William; B: Steyning; E: Hove; Pte. GS 784; K: 29.1.15; Le Touret Mem. Pas-de-Calais.

972. MANVILLE, Cecil; B: Chichester; E: London; Cpl. L 10014; W: 8.11.14; Ypres (Menin Gate) Mem. (Bel.); Age 20; Son of Joseph William and Elizabeth Ann Manville of 356, Merton Road, Southfields, London.

973. MANVILLE, Henry; B: Burgess Hill; E: Uckfield; Pte. L 8529; W: 20.11.14 Hazebrouck Com. Cem. Nord; Age 35; Son of John and Elizabeth Manville of Coxe's Cottage, Plumpton, Sussex.

974. MARCHANT, William; B: Netherfield; E: Hastings; Pte. GS 898; K: 18.9.18; Jeancourt Com. Cem. Aisne.

975. MARILLIER, Frederick Charles Jermens; 2nd Lt; K: 30.10.14; Ypres (Menin Gate) Mem. (Bel.).*

976. MARK, John; B: Tooting; E: Tooting; Pte. G 14836; K: 24.9.18; Berthaucourt Com. Cem. Aisne; Age 27; Son of John and Kesia Mark of Tooting; Husband of Elizabeth Watkinson Mark of 10, Trinity Road, Upper Tooting, London.

977. MARMENT, Henry; B: Paddington; E: Hammersmith; Pte. GS 701; K: 9.5.15; Le Touret Mem. Pas-de-Calais.

978 MARSH, Alfred; B: Hastings; E: Hastings; Pte. L 6501; K: 30.10.14; Ypres (Menin Gate) Mem. (Bel.).*

979. MARSH, Edward; B: Winchester; E: Chichester; Pte. L 10575; K: 9.5.15; Le Touret Mem. Pas-de-Calais.

980. MARSHALL, Edward; B: Liphook; E: Arundel; Pte. L 7939; K: 1.11.14; Ypres (Menin Gate) Mem. (Bel.); Age 29; Son of Mrs.Alice Eliza Marshall of 59, St.Pancras, Chichester.

981. MARTEN-SMITH, Cecil Eugene; 2nd Lt; K: 13.11.17; Tyne Cot Mem. (Bel.); Age 24; Son of William and Louise Marten-Smith of 14, Rastell Avenue, Streatham Hill, London.

982. MARTIN, Charles; B: Brighton; E: Brighton; Pte. L 8758; K: 30.10.14; Ypres (Menin Gate) Mem. (Bel.); Age 25; Son of Mr. and Mrs.Martin of 36, Islingword Street, Brighton; Husband of Mrs.Dunk, formerly Martin, of 65, Southampton Street, Brighton.

983. MARTIN, Edward Godfrey; B: East Grinstead; E: East Grinstead; Pte. L 8272; K: 9.5.15; Le Touret Mem. Pas-de-Calais.

984. MARTIN, George; B: Old Ford; E: Stratford; Pte. L 10296; K: 16.2.15; Le Touret Mem. Pas-de-Calais.

985. MARTIN, George; B: Brighton; E: Brighton; Pte. L 10398; K: 14.5.16; St.Patrick's Cem. Pas-de-Calais.

986. MARTIN, George Charles; B: Brighton; E: Brighton; Pte. G 8899; W: 24.8.16; Puchevillers Brit. Cem. Somme; Age 25; Son of Harriett Martin of 8, Bunkers Hill, Brighton.*

987. MARTIN, Harry Robert; B: Brighton; E: Marylebone; L/Cpl. G 5407; K: 20.8.16; Thiepval Mem. Somme.

988. MARTIN, Henry George; B: Millwall; E: Ramsgate;

Pte. G 287; K: 9.9.16; Caterpillar Valley Cem. Somme; Age 23; Son of Charles Edmund and Kate Martin; Husband of Elsie Rowena Mary Martin of Brighton Cottage, Newport, Essex.*

989. MARTIN, James; B: Eastbourne; E: Eastbourne; Pte. S 9957; K: 11.11.14; Ypres (Menin Gate) Mem. (Bel.).

990. MARTIN, John; B: Brighton; E: Brighton; Pte. L 7548; W: 11.9.14; Priez Com. Cem. Aisne.

991. MARTIN, Thomas Adams; B: Robertsbridge; E: Brighton; Pte. G 12131; Died in a railway collision 13.10.18; Vadencourt Brit. Cem. Aisne; Age 30; Son of Maurice and Ann Sophia Adams Martin of Robertsbridge, Sussex; Husband of Elizabeth Martin of 52, Havelock Road, Brighton.

992. MARTIN, William Thomas; B: Lewes; E: Lewes; Pte. G 1685; W: 27.8.16; St.Sever Cem., Rouen, Seine-Maritime; Age 19; Son of Thomas and Ruth Martin of Cliffe, Lewes.

993. MARYAN, Ernest; B: Hailsham; E: Eastbourne; Pte. L 7419; K: 1.11.14; Ypres (Menin Gate) Mem. (Bel.).

994. MASKELL, Gilbert Harry; B: Heathfield; E: Worthing; Pte. L 10522; K: 9.5.15; Le Touret Mem. Pas-de-Calais.

995. MASTERS, William; B: Guildford; E: Guildford; Pte. L 10402; D: 6.4.16; Lillers Com. Cem. Pas-de-Calais; Age 25; Son of Mr.A.Masters of 52, Bury Street, Guildford.

996. MATHIAS, Frederick; B: Fulham; E: Richmond; Pte. S 2348; W: 9.5.15; Le Touret Mil. Cem. Pas-de-Calais.

997. MATTHEWS, Charles; B: Newhaven; E: Shoreham; Pte. G 7009; K: 19.8.16; Thiepval Mem. Somme.

998. MATTHEWS, Henry; B: Hastings; E: Hastings; Pte. L 8190; K: 8.11.14; Ypres (Menin Gate) Mem. (Bel.); Age 31; Son of William and Mary Matthews of 242, 2nd Avenue East, Vancouver, Canada.

999. MATTHIAS, Thomas; B: Halcoy; E: Wrexham; Sgt. G 5865; K: 24.9.18; M.M., Vadencourt Brit. Cem. Aisne; Age 27; Son of William and Elizabeth Matthias of Oak Villas, Claytons Road, Brymbo, Wrexham, Denbighshire.

1000. MAYNARD, James; B: Walworth; E: St.Pancras; Pte. G 4729; W: 27.9.15; Nouex-les-Mines Com. Cem. Pas-de-Calais; Age 18; Son of Joseph and Amelia Andrews of 5, Kingston House, Camden Street, Camden Town, London.

1001. Mc CALL, John; B: Glasgow; E: Liverpool; Pte. G 4414; K: 25.9.15; Loos Mem. Pas-de-Calais.

1002. Mc COMAS, George Ernest; B: Bow; E: Stratford; Pte. G 18625; K: 28.4.18; Nouex-les-Mines Com. Cem. Ext. Pas-de-Calais; Age 19; Son of Frederick and Florence McComas of 35, Lefevre Road, Bow, London.

1003. Mc CREADY, George; B: Belfast; E: Glasgow; Pte. L 6353; K: 30.10.14; Ypres (Menin Gate) Mem. (Bel.).

1004. Mc DOUGALD, Eric; B: – ; E: Leyton; Pte. G 14623; K: 27.11.16; Thiepval Mem. Somme; Age 18; Son of John McDougald of 137, St.Mary's Road, Leyton, London.

1005. Mc GREGOR, Albert William; B: Keyhaven; E: Symington; Cpl. L 7814; K: 9.9.16; Caterpillar Valley Cem. Somme; Age 32; Son of Mrs.A.A.McGregor of 22, Hudson Road, Southsea, Hampshire.

1006. Mc GUINNESS, John; B: Leeds; E: Brighton; Pte. G 6806; W: 12.9.16; Heilly Station Cem., Mericourt L'Abbé, Somme; Age 23; Son of Patrick McGuinness.

1007. MEAD, Edward; B: Sible Hedingham; E: Halstead; Pte. G 14708; K: 9.9.16; Thiepval Mem. Somme.

1008. MEARING, John; B: Ash; E: Guildford; Pte. TF 201852; W: 4.3.18; Dozinghem Mil. Cem. (Bel.).

1009. MEEK, Ernest Albert; B: Atteborough; E: Norwich; Pte. G 14712; K: 24.9.18; Berthaucourt Com. Cem. Aisne; Age 31; Son of Harry and Clara Meek of Bridgham, Larling, Norfolk.

1010. MEEK, George Robert; B: Seaham Harbour; E: Newcastle-on-Tyne; Pte. G 16876; K: 9.4.18; Woburn Abbey Cem. Pas-de-Calais; Age 27; Son of Mr.W.Meek of 25, Single Row, Usworth Colliery, New Washington, County Durham.

1011. MEGNIN, William Francis; B: – ; E: Leyton; Pte. G 14570; K: 26.9.16; Thiepval Mem. Somme; Age 20; Son of William Robert Megnin of 49, Holloway Road, Leytonstone, London.

1012. MELLERSH, Frank William; B: Shepherd's Bush; E: Hammersmith; Pte. G 5670; K: 18.4.18; Woburn Abbey Cem. Pas-de-Calais; Age 33; Son of John and Eliza Mellersh of 20, Stanlake Road, Shepherd's Bush, London.

1013. MELTON, George; B: – ; E: Leyton; Pte. G 14622; K: 9.9.16; Thiepval Mem. Somme.

1014. MEREDITH, Frederick; B: Brighton; E: Brighton; Pte. S 2304; K: 29.1.15; Le Touret Mem. Pas-de-Calais; Age 30; Son of Charles and Ellen Meredith of Brighton.

1015. MESSAGE, Walter; B: Hither Green; E: Worthing; Pte. L 10330; W: 10.5.15; Bethune Town Cem. Pas-de-Calais; Age 19; Son of William and Caroline Message of 40, Cranworth Road, Worthing.

1016. MILES, David; B: Glamorgan; E: Cowbridge; Pte. G 1126; K: 9.5.15; Le Touret Mem. Pas-de-Calais; Age 17; Son of David and Angelina Miles of Malt House, Llamblethian, Glamorgan.

1017. MILES, Harold; B: Brighton; E: Brighton; Pte. S 2309; K: 25.9.15; Loos Mem. Pas-de-Calais.

1018. MILES, Jesse; B: Horsham; E: Horsham; Pte. G 14065; K: 18.9.18; Vis-en-Artois Mem., Haucourt, Pas-de-Calais.

1019. MILLER, Arthur Edward; B: Chichester; E: Chichester; Pte. L 9094; K; 9.5.15; Le Touret Mem. Pas-de-Calais; Age 24; Son of Fredreick and Eliza Jane Miller of Broomham, Guestling, Sussex.*

1020. MILLER, Charles Lambert; B: Brighton; E: Chichester; Sgt. L 5359; K: 30.10.14; Ypres (Menin Gate) Mem. (Bel.).

1021. MILLER, George; B: Buxted, Sussex; E: Lewes; Pte. L 10272; K: 25.1.15; Vermelles Brit. Cem. Pas-de-Calais; Age 19; Brother of Mr.C.H.Miller of 16, DeMontfort Road, St.Anne's, Lewes.

1022. MILLER, Myer; B: Spitalfields; E: Whitehall; Pte. G 10957; K: 10.7.17; Ramscapelle Road Mil. Cem. (Bel.).*

1023. MILLER, Peter; B: Fenton; E: London; Pte. G 14624; K: 9.9.16; Thiepval Mem. Somme; Age 20; Son of the Reverend Peter and Mrs.L.Miller of The Manse, Broughton, Northamptonshire.

1024. MILLER, William Harper; B: Farnham; E: Chichester; Pte. L 10622; K: 25.9.15; Loos Mem. Pas-de-Calais; Age 20; Son of Alfred and Eliza Miller of "Hurstland", The Haven, Horsham, Sussex.

1025. MILLINGTON, Cecil Walter; B: Bredgar; E: Sittingbourne; L/Cpl. G 17521; K: 27.9.16; Thiepval Mem. Somme; Age 25; Son of Henry William and Laura Millington of "Travers", Silver Street, Bredgar, Sittingbourne.

1026. MILLS, Edward Albert; B: – ; E: Colchester; Pte. G 14572; K: 12.9.16; Thiepval Mem. Somme.

1027. MILLS, Edward George; B: Littlehampton, Sussex; E: Worthing; Pte. L 10465; K: 25.9.15; Loos Mem. Pas-de-Calais; Age 19; Son of Mr.P. and Mrs.E.Mills of West Kingston Farm, East Preston, Sussex.*

1028. MILLS, Frank Allen; B: Peasmarsh, Sussex; E: Hastings; Pte. G 1387; K: 25.9.15; Loos Mem. Pas-de-Calais; Age 21; Son of George and Susan Mills.*

1029. MILLS, Thomas Henry; B: Sedlescombe, Sussex; E: Chichester; Pte. L 10348; K: 9.5.15; Le Touret Mem. Pas-de-Calais; Age 18; Son of Thomas and Kate Elizabeth Mills of Broomham, Guestling, Sussex.

1030. MILTON, Edgar; B: Brighton; E: Eastbourne; Sgt. L 8971; K: 28.12.14; Le Touret Mem. Pas-de-Calais; Age 26; Son of Mr.George Richard and Mrs.Jane Milton of 75, Dudley Road, Eastbourne; Brother, John, died of wounds – see 1032.

1031. MILTON, Edward; B: Brighton; E: Ashford; L/Cpl. L 10040; W at Home: 4.6.15; Eastbourne (Ocklynge) Cem. (U.K.).

1032. MILTON, John; B: Eastbourne; E: Eastbourne; Pte. G 8638; W: 12.9.16; Heilly Station Cem., Mericourt L'Abbé, Somme; Age 20; Son of George Richard and Jane Milton of 75, Dudley Road, Eastbourne; Brother, Edgar, killed in action – see 1030.

1033. MINNS, Walter Henry; B: Haywards Heath, Sussex; E: Chichester; L/Cpl. L 8149; K: 15.1.15; Le Touret Mem. Pas-de-Calais.

1034. MISSELBROOK, James; B: North Bursted; E: Chichester; Pte. G 4393; K: 25.9.15; Loos Mem. Pas-de-Calais; Age 35; Son of Charles and Eliza Misslebrook of 29, Essex Road, Bognor Regis, Sussex; Husband of Ada Misslebrook of 4, South Cottages, Wick, Sussex.

1035. MISSING, William Walter; B: Hinx Hill; E: Canterbury; Pte. G 17596; K: 30.11.16; A.I.F. Burial Ground, Somme.*

1036. MITCHELL, Henry David; B: Selscombe, Sussex; E: Eastbourne; Pte. L 9580; K: 29.9.14; La Ferte-sous-Jouarre Mem. Seine-et-Marne.

1037. MITCHELL, Reginald Alder; B: – ; E: – ; W at Home: 4.5.16; Steyning (St.Andrew) Churchyard, Sussex (UK); Son of Edwin L.Mitchell of 23, Charlton Street, Steyning.

1038. MITCHELL, Reginald James; B: Wylie; E: Hastings; Pte. SD 3633; K: 24.9.18; Berthaucourt Com. Cem. Aisne; Age 25; Son of James and Mary A.Mitchell of 24, Chapel Street, Chichester.

1039. MITCHELL, Sydney Edgar; B: Battersea; E: London; Pte. L 6886; K: 9.5.15; Le Touret Mem. Pas-de-Calais; Age 32; Son of Mr. and Mrs.William Mitchell; Husband of Caroline Elizabeth Mitchell of 34, Stewart's Road, Battersea, London.*

1040. MOCKETT, Albert Victor; B: Eastbourne; E: Eastbourne; Pte. L 10262; K: 9.5.16; Le Touret Mem. Pas-de-Calais; Age 18; Son of John and Susan M.Mockett of 5, Addingham Road, Eastbourne.

1041. MOCKETT, Arthur Henry Goldsmith; B: Arlington; E: Eastbourne; Pte. G 1458; K: 9.5.15; Le Touret Mem. Pas-de-Calais.

1042. MOCKFORD, William; B: Brighton; E: Brighton; Pte. GS 159; D at Home: 1.5.15; Brighton (Bear Road) Borough Cem. (U.K.).

1043. MOHR, John Carl Bernhard; B: New Cross; E: Eastbourne; Pte. G 1420; W: 4.2.15; Chocques Mil. Cem. Pas-de-Calais; Age 20; Son of Charles and Emma Mohr of 54, Upper Richmond Road, East Sheen, London.*

1044. MONERY, Owen Albert; B: Stoke Newington; E: Tottenham; Pte. G 4059; K: 1.6.16; Cambrin Churchyard Ext. Pas-de-Calais; Age 43; Son of Mr. and Mrs.Monery of Stoke Newington; Husband of Jane Louisa Monery of 12, Cressington Road, Stoke Newington, London.

1045. MONK, Henry; B: Beckley, Sussex; E: Hastings; Pte. G 1390; W: 26.1.15; Beuvry Com. Cem. Pas-de-Calais; Age 18; Son of Mrs.Annie Carman of Winchelsea Road, Rye.*

1046. MONK. William Charles; B: Knightsbridge; E: Haywards Heath, Sussex; Sgt. G 1337; K: 9.9.16; Caterpillar Valley Cem. Somme; Son of Mr.D.Monk of 102, Lumley Buildings, Pimlico Road, London.

1047. MONTAGUE, Archibald; B: Melbourne; E: Croydon; Pte. G 11260; K: 9.9.16; Thiepval Mem. Somme; Age 24; Son of Edward and Susanna Montague of 7, Manor Road, Hastings.

1048. MONTRESOR, Ernest Henry; Lt.-Col; K: 14.9.14; La Ferte-sous-Jouarre Mem. Seine-et-Marne; Age 50; Son of Charles F.Montressor; Served in Egypt (Nile 1884), India (Hazara 1888) and the South Africa campaign.

1049. MOODY, James Richard; B: Brinkworth; E: Newhaven, Sussex; Pte. L 9806; K: 25.9.15; Dud Corner Cem. Pas-de-Calais.

1050. MOORE, Gillachrist; 2nd Lt; K: 7.11.14; Ypres (Menin Gate) Mem.(Bel.); Age 20; Son of Norman (later Sir Norman, 1st Bart.) and Mrs.Moore.

1051. MOORE, Harry; B: Camberwell; E: London; Cpl. S 1939; K: 30.6.16; Maroc Brit. Cem. Nord; Age 20; Son of Charles Walter and Mary Moore of 139, Farmer's Road, Camberwell, London.

1052. MOORE, James; B: Brighton; E: Brighton; Pte. S 2170; K: 9.5.15; Le Touret Mem. Pas-de-Calais.

1053. MOORE, James; B: Welling; E: Woolwich; Pte. G 10285; K: 9.9.16; Caterpillar Valley Cem. Somme; Age 19; Son of Mr.C. and Mrs.E.Moore of 7, The Green, Welling, Kent.

1054. MOORE, Philip Herbert; B: Eastbourne; E: Eastbourne; Pte. S 8790; K: 25.1.15; Le Touret Mem. Pas-de-Calais; Brother of Maud Moore of 16, Jersey Street, Brighton.

1055. MOORE, William; B: West Chiltington, Sussex; E: Chichester; Pte. L 9756; K: 30.10.14; Ypres (Menin Gate) Mem. (Bel.); Age 22; Son of Harry Phillip and Elizabeth Moore of Ormonde House, Haslemere, Surrey.

1056. MOOREY, Archibald; B: Godalming; E: Chichester; Pte. G 11739; W at Home 19.5.18; Brighton (Bear Road) Borough Cem. (U.K.).

1057. MORFEE, Henry James; B: Hastings; E: Hastings; Pte. L 9831; K: 9.5.15; Le Touret Mem. Pas-de-Calais; Age 21; Son of Mrs.Fanny Hatch of The Violet Nurseries, St.Helens Wood, Hastings.

1058. MORLEY, Frank; B: Chichester; E: Chichester; Sgt. L 8035; K: 20.8.16; Thiepval Mem. Somme; Age 29; Son of Stanton and Mary Morley of 42, Franklin Street, Brighton; Husband of Elizabeth Jane Hards, formerly Morley, of 34, Donington Street, Grimsby.

1059. MORLEY, George; B: Brighton; E: Brighton; Pte. G 9045; K: 16.12.16; Thiepval Mem. Somme.

1060. MORRIS, William; B: Chichester; E: Chichester; Pte. S 781; K: 9.5.15; Le Touret Mem. Pas-de-Calais.

1061. MORTIMER, Herbert John; B: Lambeth; E: London; Pte. S 2265; K: 13.7.16; Thiepval Mem. Somme.

1062. MORTON, Hugh Goldie; B: Cape Town; E: Chichester; Pte. G 11412; K: 27.9.16; Thiepval Mem. Somme; Age 35; Son of Hugh Goldie and Frances Amelia Green Morton.

1063. MOSS, Arthur; B: Lawshall; E: Sudbury; Pte. G 11257; K: 9.9.16; Caterpillar Valley Cem. Somme; Age 39; Son of Mr. and Mrs.Thomas Moss of Lawshall Green, Bury St.Edmunds.

1064. MOTT, Louis; B: Hook; E: Gosport; Pte. L 5622; K: 9.5.15; Le Touret Mem. Pas-de-Calais; Age 33; Husband of Lottie Charlott Hurst, formerly Mott, of 1, Swanwick Lane, Lower Swanwick, Hampshire.

1065. MUGGERIDGE, William; B: Oakwood Hill; E: Hastings; L/Cpl. SD 2967; K: 24.9.18; Vis-en-Artois Mem., Haucourt, Pas-de-Calais; Age 26; Son of George and Ellen Muggeridge of Myrtle Cottage, Oakwood Hill, Surrey.

1066. MULLINS, Arthur James; B: Westminster; E: Chichester; Pte. L 7608; K: 30.10.14; Ypres (Menin Gate) Mem. (Bel.); Age 28; Son of William and Amelia Mullins of 10, Bedford Row, Worthing.

1067. MUNCEY, William Ernest; B: Plaistow; E: Bromley; Pte. G 14838; K: 9.9.16; Thiepval Mem. Somme; Age 26; Son of Ernest Muncey of 11, Croft Road, Bromley; Husband of Clara Ada Muncey of 44, Liddon Road, Bromley, Kent.

1068. MUNSON, Albert Edward; B: Chiswick; E: Worthing, L/Cpl. L 10578; K: 25.9.15; Loos Mem. Pas-de-Calais; Age 20; Son of Mr.B.J. and Mrs. E.A.Munson of 2, Chargable Lane, Plaistow, London.

1069. MUNSON, Walter Arthur; B: – ; E: Colchester; L/Cpl. G 14626; K: 18.9.18; Cerisy-Gailly Mil. Cem. Somme.

1070. MURPHY, Edward; B: London; E: Chichester; Pte. L 8530; K: 30.10.14; Ypres (Menin Gate) Mem. (Bel.).

1071. MURRAY, William; B: Paddington; E: Brighton; Pte. S 2183; K: 9.5.15; Le Touret Mem. Pas-de-Calais.

1072. MUSTCHIN, Joseph; B: Steyning, Sussex; E: Brighton; L/Cpl. L 8847; K: 7.10.14; Vendresse Brit. Cem. Aisne.

1073. MUZZALL, Frank; B: Henfield, Sussex; E: Chichester; Pte. L 7584; K: 13.11.14; Ypres (Menin Gate) Mem. (Bel.); Age 29; Son of Edward and Mary Muzzall of Adur Cottages, Henfield; Husband of Mrs.R.E.Muzzall of 66, Elder Street, Brighton.

1074. MUZZELL, Alfred; B: Hove; E: Worthing; Pte. G 1224; K: 9.5.15; Le Touret Mem. Pas-de-Calais; Son of Stephen and Amelia Muzzell of 47, Upper High Street, Worthing.

1075. MYERS, Edwin George Henry Ralph; B: Highbury; E: Hastings; Pte. G 1522; K: 25.9.15; Loos Mem. Pas-de-Calais; Age 23; Son of Edwin and Mary Ann Myers of 127, Balfour Road, Ilford, Essex.

N

1076. NEAL, William George;B: West Tarring, Sussex; E: Worthing; Pte. L 8068; K: 9.5.15; Le Touret Mem. Pas-de-Calais.

1077. NEALE, William Edward; B: Fittleworth, Sussex; E: Arundel, Sussex; Pte. L 8182; K: 25.9.15; St.Mary's A.D.S. Cem. Pas-de-Calais; Age 27; Son of Richard Edward and Annie A.B.Neale of 16, Old Hartford Turnpike, Whitneyville, Connecticut, U.S.A.

1078. NELSON, Arthur Horatio; B: Finsbury; E: Stratford; Pte. G 18632; K: 23.10.18; Vis-en-Artois Mem., Haucourt, Pas-de-Calais; Age 19; Son of Mr. and Mrs.H.Nelson of 22, Winchester Street, King's Cross, London.*

1079. NELSON, Charles William; B: Royston; E: Bedford; Pte. G 11270; K: 9.9.16; Caterpillar Valley Cem. Somme; Age 26; Son of Thomas and Emma Nelson.

1080. NETLEY, Edward; B: Worthing; E: Hove; Pte. L 10552; K: 9.5.15; Le Touret Mem. Pas-de-Calais; Age 17; Son of Mr.E.Netley of Chesswood Cottages, Ladydell Road, Worthing.*

1081. NEVE, George; B: Chelsea; E: Fulham; L/Cpl. GS 284; K: 25.9.15; Loos Mem. Pas-de-Calais; Age

35; Husband of Elizabeth Neve of 15, Wheatsheaf Terrace, Fulham, London.

1082. NEWBY, Ernest Arthur; B: Toxford; E: Saxmundham; Pte. G 11268; K: 9.9.16; Thiepval Mem. Pas-de-Calais; Age 29; Son of Arthur and Hannah Newby of Little Street, Yoxford, Suffolk.

1083. NEWMAN, Herbert Joseph; B: Eastbourne; E: Eastbourne; Pte. L 7730; K: 24.9.18; Berthaucourt Com. Cem. Aisne.

1084. NEWMAN. Michael Ernest; B: Balcombe, Sussex; E: Haywards Heath, Sussex; Pte. G 1474; K: 25.9.15; Loos Mem. Pas-de-Calais; Age 21; Brother of Mr.H.Newman of Malthouse Cottages, Cooksbridge, Sussex.

1085. NEWMAN, Percival Corney; B: East Preston, Sussex; E: Chichester; Cpl. L 10214; K: 9.5.15; Le Touret Mem. Pas-de-Calais.

1086. NEWMAN, Thomas; B: Brighton; E: Brighton; Pte. S 1624; K: 9.5.15; Le Touret Mem. Pas-de-Calais.

1087. NEWNHAM, Albert Edward Victor; B: Aldershot; E: Chichester; Pte. L 10100; W: 16.10.14; City of Paris Cem., Pantin, Seine-St.Denis; Age 20; Son of Jesse and Elizabeth Newman of "Erlemere", Compton Road, Lindfield, Sussex.

1088. NEWNHAM, George Vincent; B: Bury, Sussex; E: Horsham, Sussex; Pte. G 9560; K: 27.9.16; Thiepval Mem. Somme.

1089. NEWNHAM, Henry; B: South Malling, Sussex; E: Lewes; Sgt. L 6817; K: 10.3.16; Arras Mem. Pas-de-Calais; Age 31; Son of William and Amelia Newnham of Lewes; Husband of Annie Beatrice Guy, formerly Newnham, of Lywood Common, Ardingly, Sussex.*

1090. NEWSOME, Thomas Charles; B: Doncaster; E: Sheffield; Pte. G 5900; W: 5.11.18; Premont Brit. Cem. Aisne; Age 36; Husband of Mrs.B.Newsome of 19, Carlisle Road, Grimesthorpe, Sheffield.

1091. NEWSTEAD, Albert; B: Thorpe St.Andrew; E: Norwich; Pte. G 14716; W: 27.9.16; Millencourt Com. Cem. Ext. Somme.

1092. NEWTON, Benjamin Thomas; B: Bermondsey; E: Eastbourne; Pte. S 1878; K: 9.5.15; Le Touret Mem. Pas-de-Calais.

1093. NEWTON, William John; B: Newington; E: Southwark; L/Cpl. G 5583; K: 9.9.16; Thiepval Mem. Somme; Age 36; Husband of Clara Maud Nash, formerly Newton, of 15, Sandover Road, Camberwell, London.

1094. NICHOLLS, Bertie James; B: Dover; E: Eastbourne; Pte. G 4086; K: 25.9.15; Loos Mem. Pas-de-Calais.

1095. NICHOLLS, Ebeneezer; B: Hailsham, Sussex; E: Chichester; Pte. L 6990; K: 17.8.16; Combles Com. Cem. Ext. Somme; Age 29; Son of James and Ellen Nicholls of 6, Duke Street, Eastbourne; Husband of Mary Margaret Nicholls of The Rookery, Horsebridge, Hellingly, Sussex.*

1096. NICHOLLS, Sidney George; B: Thakeham; E: Worthing; Pte. G 1355; K: 9.5.15; Le Touret Mem. Pas-de-Calais.

1097. NICHOLLS, William Edward; B: Hackney; E: Whitehall; Pte. G 18628; K: 24.9.18; Berthaucourt Com. Cem. Aisne.

1098. NICHOLS, Lionel Walter; B: Leicester; E: Brighton; Pte. TF 202598; K: 5.7.17; Ramscapelle Road Mil. Cem. (Bel.); Age 21; Son of Walter E.C. and Florence Nichols of 15, Evington Road, Leicester.

1099. NICHOLSON, Ernest; B: Edburton, Sussex; E: Arundel, Sussex; Pte. L 10566; D: 6.5.17; Noeux-les-Mines Com. Cem. Pas-de-Calais; Age 26; Son of William and Elizabeth Nicholson of 61, Priory Cottages, Tortington, Arundel.

1100. NICKS, George Henry; B: Brighton; E: Brighton; Pte. G 1309; K: 9.5.15; Le Touret Mem. Pas-de-Calais.

1101. NORMAN, Frank; B: Uckfield, Sussex; E: Holborn; Pte. G 8547; K: 30.6.16; Arras Mem. Pas-de-Calais; Age 32; Son of Henry and Frances Norman of Gable Cottage, Fairwarp, Sussex.

1102. NORMAN, George; B: Pumpton, Sussex; E: Eastbourne; Pte. S 2117; K: 19.8.16; Thiepval Mem. Somme.

1103. NORMAN, Henry Lucas; B: West Grinstead, Sussex; E: Hove; Pte. G 1182; K: 25.9.15; Loos Mem. Pas-de-Calais; Age 26; Son of Thomas and Ruth Norman of Dean Cottage, Partridge Green, Sussex.

1104. NORRIS, Edward John; B: Tottenham; E: Stratford; Pte. L 6978; K: 9.5.15; Le Touret Mem. Pas-de-Calais.

1105. NORTH, John Henry; B: Fulham; E: London; Pte. G 18630; K: 9.4.18; Cambrin Mil. Cem. Pas-de-Calais; Age 19; Son of John Henry and Louisa Annie North of 10, Cumberland Crescent, North End Road, West Kensington, London.

1106. NORTON, Donald; B: Heigham; E: Norwich; Pte. G 14718; K: 5.7.17; Ramscapelle Road Mil. Cem. (Bel.).

1107. NOTT, Herbert Victor; B: Bethnal Green; E: Poplar; Pte. G 14818; K: 21.7.18; Loos Mem. Pas-de-Calais.

1108. NOVISS, Harry John; B: Hove; E: Hove; Pte. L 10951; K: 9.9.16; Thiepval Mem. Somme. *

1109. NOYCE, Frederick; B: Brighton; E: Brighton; Pte. S 1457; K: 9.5.15; Le Touret Mem. Pas-de-Calais; Age 20; Son of William George and Harriet Kate Noyce of 49, Upper Lewes Road, Brighton.

1110. NUTLEY, George; B: Brighton; E: Brighton; Pte. S 2169; K: 12.2.15; Le Touret Mem. Pas-de-Calais; Age 35; Husband of Lily Nutley of 64, Bentham Road, Brighton; Served in the South Africa campaign.

1111. NUTTMAN, George Robert; B: St.Leonards-on-Sea; E: Hastings; Pte. L 7928; K: 9.5.15; Le Touret Mem. Pas-de-Calais; Age 33; Son of William Richard and Ann Mawbury Nutman of 106, Bexhill Road, St.Leonards-on-Sea.*

O

1112. OAKLEY, George Frank; B: Hastings; E: Hastings; C.S.M. L 7411; K: 24.9.18; Bellicourt Brit. Cem. Aisne; Age 38; Son of Henry and

Amelia Oakley of Hastings; Husband of Louisa Oakley of 4, Hawthorne Cottages, Eaton Ford, Huntingdonshire.

1113. OAKMAN, Sidney; B: Hastings; E: Arundel, Sussex; Pte. L 7945; K: 18.8.16; Maroc Brit. Cem. Aisne; Husband of Phillis Oakman of 63, London Road, Bognor Regis, Sussex.

1114. OASGOOD, William George; B: Chatham; E: Chichester; Pte. L 10371; K: 25.9.15; Loos Mem. Pas-de-Calais; Age 22; Son of Harriett Holdom, formerly Oasgood, of 59, John Street, Ordnance Place, Chatham.*

1115. OCKENDEN, Ernest; B: Ashington, Sussex; E: Horsham, Sussex; Pte. G 8683; K: 23.7.16; Thiepval Mem. Somme; Age 21; Son of Charles and Harriett Ockenden of Fosters Cottage, West Grinstead, Sussex.

1116. OFFIN, William; B: Margate; E: Ramsgate; Pte. G 21159; K: 18.9.18; Vis-en-Artois Mem., Haucourt, Pas-de-Calais; Age 33; Son of Mrs.Alice Offin; Husband of Florance Alice Offin of Alloa House, High Street, Ash, Kent.*

1117. OLIVER, Albert John; B: Burwash, Sussex; E: Wadhurst, Sussex; Cpl. L 8772; W: 5.11.14; Boulogne Eastern Cem. Pas-de-Calais; Age 26; Son of Mrs.J.C.Oliver of Gloucester Place, Wadhurst, Sussex.

1118. OLIVER, John; B: Hamsey, Sussex; E: Lewes; Pte. G 1672; W: 25.9.15; Verquin Com. Cem. Pas-de-Calais; Age 26; Son of Mrs.Mercy Oliver of 17, St.John's Terrace, Lewes.

1119. OLIVER, Walter; B: Bexhill-on-Sea; E: Chichester; Cpl. L 10309; K: 13.8.18; Cambrin Mil. Cem. Pas-de-Calais; Son of W. and Emily Jane Oliver of 22, Cambridge Road, Bexhill-on-Sea.

1120. ORBELL, James; B: Denston; E: Canterbury; Pte. G 17575; K: 9.9.16; Caterpillar Valley Cem. Somme.

1121. ORFORD, Lancelot Edwin; B: Little Eaton; E: Norwich; Pte. G 5176; K: 13.10.15; Loos Mem. Pas-de-Calais; Age 28; Son of Edwin and Emily Kate Orford of School House, Marsham, Norfolk.

1122. ORME, Percy; B: London; E: Camberwell; Pte. G 18034; K: 24.9.18; Berthaucourt Com. Cem. Aisne.

1124. ORRIN, Albert Charles; B: Chelsea; E: London; L/Cpl. G 4579; K: 9.9.16; Thiepval Mem. Somme.

1125. ORTON, Robert; B: Leicester; E: Brighton; Pte. L 10628; K: 25.9.15; Loos Mem. Pas-de-Calais.

1126. OSBORNE, Albert; B: Staplecross; E: Rye; Pte. G 18221; K: 24.9.18; Bellicourt Brit. Cem. Aisne.

1127. OSBORNE, Sidney Dennis; B: Hastings; E: Eastbourne; L/Cpl. G 8705; K: 17.8.16; Caterpillar Valley Cem. Somme; Age 23; Son of Mrs.Mary Jane Osborne of 60, Vicarage Road, Hastings.*

1128. OVENDEN, Fred; B: Withyham, Sussex; E: Eastbourne; Pte. S 89; K: 31.10.14; Ypres (Menin Gate) Mem. (Bel.); Age 25; Son of Charles Henry and Annie Ovenden.

1129. OVENDEN, Walter; B: Withyham, Sussex; E: Tunbridge Wells; Pte. L 10287; K: 9.5.15; Le Touret Mem. Pas-de-Calais.

1130. OVERTON, Charles Henry; B: Brighton; E: Chichester; Pte. GS 795; K: 25.3.15; Le Touret Mem. Pas-de-Calais.

1131. OWEN, Harold Vincent; B: Perry Wood; E: Canterbury; Pte. G 17563; K: 27.9.16; Thiepval Mem. Somme.

P

1132. PACKETT, John Laurence; B: Eastbourne; E: Eastbourne; Sgt. L 8815; K: 20.8.16; London Cem. and Ext. Somme; Age 26; Son of Thomas and Catherine Packett of Eastbourne.

1133. PADBURY, William Thomas; B: Warwick; E: Midhurst, Sussex; Pte. G 579; K: 8.2.15; Le Touret Mem. Pas-de-Calais; Age 25; Son of Thomas and Mary Padbury.

1134. PADDON, Edward James; B: Hastings; E: Hastings; Pte. L 10319; K: 9.5.15; Le Touret Mem. Pas-de-Calais; Age 18; Son of Edward James Paddon of 3, High Wood Cottage, Whydown, Bexhill-on-Sea.*

1135. PADGHAM, Albert Edward; B: Chailey, Sussex; E: Brighton; Pte. L 10419; W: 24.8.16; Puchevillers Brit. Cem. Somme; Age.19; Son of John and Mary Ann Padgham of Chailey.*

1136. PADGHAM, Fred; B: Fletching, Sussex; E: Haywards Heath, Sussex; Pte. SD 5379; K: 18.4.18; Woburn Abbey Cem. Pas-de-Calais; Son of Mr.T.P.Padgham of Sheffield Green, Turner's Green, Sussex.

1137. PAGE. Charles; B: Eastbourne; E: Eastbourne; Cpl. L 8172; K: 9.5.15; Le Touret Mem. Pas-de-Calais.

1138. PAGE, Eli; B: South Malling, Sussex; E: Lewes; Pte. G 1642; K: 25.9.15; Loos Mem. Pas-de-Calais; Age 29; Son of Mr. and Mrs.Jesse Page of Toll Farm, Horney Common, Maresfield, Sussex.

1139. PAGE, Ernest; B: Harkstead; E: Ipswich; Pte. G 24363; K: 24.9.18; Berthaucourt Com. Cem. Aisne.

1140. PAGE, George; B: Brighton; E: Brighton; Pte. S 2081; K: 29.1.15; Le Touret Mem. Pas-de-Calais; Age 19; Son of James Amos and Emily Page of 18, Richmond Hill, Brighton.

1141. PAGE, Oliver; B: Clapton; E: Hove; Pte. G 8937; K: 23.7.16; Thiepval Mem. Somme.

1142. PAGE, William James; B: Shoreham; E: Worthing; Pte. G 1234; K: 9.5.15; Le Touret Mem. Pas-de-Calais; Son of Mr. G.A.Page of 61, High Street, Shoreham, Sussex.

— PAICE, Frank George – see PRICE, Frank George 1222.

1143 PAIN, Claude; B: Eastbourne; E: Eastbourne; Pte. SD 2270; K: 9.7.17; Ramscapelle Road Mil. Cem. (Bel.); Age 23; Son of W. and Mrs.E.Pain of Eastbourne; Husband of Mrs.H.Pain of 66, Green Street, Eastbourne.

1144. PALLETT, William Henry; B: Eastbourne; E: Eastbourne; Pte. L 8967; K: 9.5.15; Le Touret Mem. Pas-de-Calais; Age 25; Son of W. and Mary Pallett of 17, Brightland Road, Eastbourne.

1145. PANKHURST, Charles Henry; B: Tunbridge Wells;

E: Tunbridge Wells; L/Cpl. L 8518; K: 10.9.14; Montreuil-aux-Lions Brit. Cem. Aisne.*

1146. PANKHURST, Joseph; B: Pembury; E: Tunbridge Wells; Pte. L 7384; K: 23.12.14; Le Touret Mem. Pas-de-Calais.

1147. PANNIFER, Edward; B: West Ham, London; E: Eastbourne; Pte. L 7564; K: 31.10.14; Ypres (Menin Gate) Mem. (Bel.); Son of Mr. and Mrs.Pannifer of 59, Glasgow Street, Wanganui, New Zealand; Husband of Mrs.I.R.Wagstaff, formerly Pannifer, of The Police Station, Penn's Lane, Erdington, Birmingham.

1148. PARFECT, Thomas Barker; B: West Ham, London; E: West Ham, London; Pte. G 14819; W: 9.9.16; Thiepval Mem. Somme.

1149. PARK, Arthur; B: Brighton; E: Guildford; Pte. L 8267; W: 24.8.18; ——.

1150. PARKER, Richard; B: Hove; B: Brighton; Pte. L 6783; K: 30.10.14; Ypres (Menin Gate) Mem. (Bel.).*

1151. PARKS, John Leath; B: Hawkinge; E: Folkstone; Sgt. G 17584; K: 24.9.18; Berthaucourt Com. Cem. Aisne; Age 35; Son of George and Emma Parks of Maypole Farm, Hawkinge, Kent.*

1152. PARLETT, J. Arthur; B: Shoreham, Sussex; E: Brighton; Pte. S 2216; K: 9.5.15; Guards Cem. (Cuinchy) Pas-de-Calais.

1153. PARMENTER, George Thomas; B: – ; E: Colchester; Pte. G 14630; K: 30.11.16; A.I.F. Burial Ground, Somme; Age 27; Husband of Lily F.Parmenter of Fern Cottage, Kirby Cross, Essex.

1154. PARMENTER, William George; B: Brentwood; E: Warley; Pte. G 9322; K: 6.9.16; Thiepval Mem. Somme.

1155. PARROTT, William Edward Charles; B: St.Leonards-on-Sea; E: Hove; Pte. G 4689; K: 25.9.15; Loos Mem. Pas-de-Calais; Age 24; Husband of Ellen Elizabeth Parrott of 40, Scotland Street, Brighton.

1156. PARTRIDGE, Charles Herbert; B: Briston; E: Cromer; Pte. G 9277; K: 6.8.16; Brewery Orchard Cem. Nord.

1157. PARVIN, Leonard; B: Oving, Sussex; E: Arundel, Sussex; Pte. G 15957; K: 24.9.18; Vis-en-Artois Mem., Haucourt, Pas-de-Calais.

1158. PATCHEN, Thomas Sydney; B: Seaford, Sussex; E: Chichester; Pte. L 7512; K: 22.12.14; Ypres (Menin Gate) Mem. (Bel.); Age 29; Son of Mr. and Mrs. James Patchen of 27, Chichester Road, Seaford, Sussex; Husband of Rachel Rebecca Hocking, formerly Patchen, of 44, The Avenue, Bentley, Doncaster.*

1159. PATCHING, Albert William; B: Leighton; E: Chichester; Pte. L 10293; W: 13.7.16; Puchevillers Brit. Cem. Somme; Age 19; Son of Mary Patching of 14, White Rock Road, Southwick, Sussex,

1160. PATE, George; B: Brighton; E: Finsbury; Pte. G 5029; K: 9.5.15; Le Touret Mem. Pas-de-Calais.

1161. PATTEN, James; B: Compton; E: Chichester; Pte. G 1471; K: 9.5.15; Le Touret Mem. Pas-de-Calais; Age 32; Son of William and Lavinia Patten.

1162. PATTENDEN, Charles Thomas Henry; B: St.Saviour's, Middlesex; E: Southwark; L/Cpl. G 5494; K: 30.6.16; Arras Mem. Pas-de-Calais; Age 25; Husband of Elizabeth Pattenden of 9, "I" Block, Vine Street Buildings, Tooley Street, London.

1163. PATTENDEN, James; B: Burwash, Sussex; E: Bromley; Pte. G 4359; K: 25.9.15; Loos Mem. Pas-de-Calais; Age 28; Husband of Ada Marshall, formerly Pattenden, of Barn House, Burwash.

1164. PATTENDEN, William; B: Wadhurst, Sussex; E: Tunbridge Wells; Pte. L 7711; K: 31.10.14; Ypres (Menin Gate) Mem. (Bel.).

1165. PAVEY, John; B: Brighton; E: Brighton; Pte. L 10312; K: 13.10.15; Loos Mem. Pas-de-Calais; Age 23; Son of William Pavey of Elm Farm, Patcham, Sussex.

1166. PAXMAN, Harry Stanley; B: St.Margaret's, Suffolk; E: Chichester; Pte. 10153; K: 9.5.15; Le Touret Mem. Pas-de-Calais; Age 25; Son of Henry Edward and Alice Paxman of 19, Withipol Street, St.Margaret's, Ipswich.

1167. PAY, Charles; B: Harting, Sussex; E: Chichester; Pte. G 4610; K: 9.5.15; Le Touret Mem. Pas-de-Calais.

1168. PAYNE, Arthur; B: Whitstable; E: Hastings; Pte. G 9235; K: 7.8.16; Brewery Orchard Cem. Nord; Age 29; Son of William and Sarah Payne of 5, Nelson Road, Whitstable, Kent.

1169. PAYNE, Albert George; B: Oxted; E: London; Pte. L 6770; K: 26.9.14; Vendresse Brit. Cem. Aisne.

1170. PAYNE, Alfred Herbert; B: Paddington; E: London; Sgt. L 7714; K: 25.9.15; Loos Mem. Pas-de-Calais; Age 31; Son of William and Grace Payne; Husband of Mary Ann Alice Payne of 122, Carlton Vale, Kilburn, London.

1171. PAYNE, Christopher Charles; B: – ; E: Croydon; Pte. G 21146; K: 18.9.18; Cerisy-Gailly Mil. Cem. Somme; Age 20; Son of George and Fanny Payne of 41, Strathmore Road, Croydon.

1172. PAYNE, John James; B: Liss; E: Chichester; Cpl. S 2245; K: 9.5.15; Le Touret Mem. Pas-de-Calais; Age 33; Husband of Lydia J.Payne of "Ferndale", East Liss, Hampshire.

1173. PEACHY, Alfie; B: Littlehampton, Sussex; E: Worthing, Sussex; Pte. G 1598; K: 9.5.15; Le Touret Mem. Pas-de-Calais; Age 22; Son of Walter and Lavinia Peachy of 17, River Road, Littlehampton.

1174. PEACOCK, Albert; B: Petworth, Sussex; E: Petworth; Pte. G 15959; K: 23.10.18; Highland Cem., Le Cateau, Nord; Age 39; Son of George and Caroline Peacock of Petworth, Sussex.

1175. PEACOCK, Francis Joseph; B: Hammersmith; E: Chichester; Cpl. L 6909; W: 20.9.14; La Ferte-sous-Jouarre Mem. Seine-et-Marne; Age 35; Husband of Elizabeth Peacock of Temple Lodge, Queen Street, Hammersmith, London.

1176. PEARMAN, D; (served under the alias, Richard John Frederick Comporo); B: Peckham; E: Luton; Pte. G 14521; K: 23.11.17; Tyne Cot Mem. (Bel.).

1177. PEARSON, Albert Edward; B: Hastings; E:

Hastings; Pte. G 8954; K: 15.7.16; Thiepval Mem. Somme.

1178. PEARSON, William Forbert; B: Pateley Bridge; E: Barrow-in-Furness; Pte. G 5879; K: 20.8.16; Adanac Mil. Cem. Somme; Age 25; Son of James and Sophia E.Pearson of 7, Lustre Street, Keithley, Yorkshire.

1179. PEERLESS, Ernest Boon; B: Laughton, Sussex; E: Worthing; Pte. G 1232; K: 9.5.15; Le Touret Mem. Pas-de-Calais; Age 19; Son of Thomas Harry and Caroline Peerless.

1180. PELHAM, Hon. Herbert Lyttelton; B: Lambeth; Lt. K: 14.9.14; Cross of Legion of Honour; Vendresse Brit. Mil. Cem. Aisne; Age 30; Son of the 5th Earl of Chichester and the Countess of Chichester of Stanmer, Sussex.*

1181. PELLETT, Henry; B: Stone; E: Chichester; Pte. L 9782; K: 29.9.14; Vendresse Brit. Cem. Aisne.

1182. PELLING, Ernest Alfred; B: Hailsham, Sussex; E: Eastbourne; Pte. L 7327; K: 14.9.14; La Ferte-sous-Jouarre Mem. Seine-et-Marne.

1183. PELLING, William Henry; B: Worthing; E: Worthing; Pte. G 1380; W: 9.5.15; Rue-des-Berceaux Mil. Cem., Richebourg-L'Avoué , Pas-de-Calais.

1184. PENFOLD, John Berwick; B: Nutley, Sussex; E: Uckfield; Pte. SD 341; K: 18.9.18; Epehy Wood Farm Cem. Somme; Age 27; Son of Stephen Penfold of Hole Farm, Nutley; Husband of Mrs.M.E.Penfold of Havering, Surrey.

1185. PERKS-MORRIS, Arthur Bois; 2nd Lt; W: 14.11.17; Lijssenthoek Mil. Cem. (Bel.); Age 19; Son of Captain Arthur Edward and Edythe Perks-Morris of 28, Callow Street, Chelsea, London.

1186. PERRY, William Henry; B: Hastings; E: Hastings; Pte. S 2259; K: 9.9.16; Thiepval Mem. Somme.*

1187. PESCOTT, William James; B: Wick, Sussex; E: Chichester; Pte. S 1958; K: 9.5.15; Le Touret Mem. Pas-de-Calais.

1188. PESTEL, Arthur Robert; B: Holloway; E: Eastbourne; L/Cpl. G 1407; K: 26.1.15; Le Touret Mem. Pas-de-Calais; Age 21; Son of Arthur Pestel and Anne Lambkin, formerly Pestel, 49, Terminus Road, Eastbourne.

1189. PETERS, William; B: Newhaven, Sussex; E: Chichester; Sgt. L 8141; K: 14.9.14; La Ferte-sous-Jouarre Mem. Seine-et-Marne.

1190. PETTET, William; B: Dover; E: Canterbury; Pte. TF 260080; W: 25.10.18; Vadencourt Brit. Cem. Aisne.

1191. PETTY, Arthur; B: Bermondsey; E: London; L/Cpl. S 2127; K: 23.12.14; Le Touret Mem. Pas-de-Calais; Son of Mrs.L.J.Petty of 63, East Dulwich Grove, East Dulwich, London.

1192. PHILLIPS, Charles William; B: Eastbourne; E: Eastbourne; Pte. S 85; K: 9.5.15; Le Touret Mem. Pas-de-Calais.

1193. PHILLIPS, Percy Edwin; B: Lagness; E: Chichester; Pte. L 9896; K: 20.8.16; Thiepval Mem. Somme; Age 27; Son of Mr.B.Phillips of New Barn Cottages, Apuldram, Chichester.

1194. PHILP. Frederick Thomas Burdett; B: Hendon; E: Hastings; L/Cpl. G 1102; K: 9.5.15; Le Touret Mem. Pas-de-Calais.

1195. PHILPOTT, William James; B: Dover; E: Dover; Pte. L 8210; K: 27.1.15; Le Touret Mem. Pas-de-Calais.

1196. PHOENIX, Robert; B: Gwersylit; E: London; Pte. G 4594; W: 28.4.15; Chocques Mil. Cem. Pas-de-Calais.

1197. PIERCE, Arthur Edward; B: Ticehurst, Sussex; E: Hastings; Pte. G 8460; K: 23.7.16; Thiepval Mem. Somme; Age 21; Son of Thomas and Rose Pierce of 9, Church Street, Ticehurst, Sussex; Brother, Herbert, also killed – see 1199.

1198. PIERCE, Harry; B: Portslade, Sussex; E: Hove; Pte. G 1179; K: 9.5.15; Le Touret Mem. Pas-de-Calais.

1199. PIERCE, Herbert; B: Ticehurst, Sussex; E: Hastings; Pte. G 8459; K: 17.8.16; Thiepval Mem. Somme; Age 23; Son of Thomas and Rose Pierce of 9, Church Street, Ticehurst, Sussex; Brother, Arthur Edward, also killed – see 1197.

1200. PIKE, Leonard Charles; B: Lewisham; E: West Ham, London; Pte. G 1480; K: 9.9.16; Thiepval Mem. Somme; Age 20; Son of Charles and Marion Eliza Pike of 201, Murchison Road, Leyton, London.

1201. PILBEAM, Alfred Edmund; B: Brighton; E: Brighton; Pte. L 7627; K: 14.11.14; Ypres (Menin Gate) Mem. (Bel.); Age 29; Son of Alfred Edmund and Lydia Pilbeam of 32, Newhaven Street, Brighton; Husband of Christina Pilbeam of 8, Eastport Lane, Southover, Lewes. *

1202. PINYOUN, Henry; B: Hove; E: Brighton; Pte. G 1557; K: 26.6.16; Maroc Brit. Cem. Nord; Age 30; Son of Mr. and Mrs.Pinyoun of 16, Shirley Street, Hove.*

1203. PIPER, Edgar Sydney; B: Polegate, Sussex; E: Eastbourne; Pte. G 4989; K: 25.9.15; Loos Mem. Pas-de-Calais; Age 22; Son of John William and Florence Marie Annie Piper of 17, Junction Street, Polegate.*

1204. PIPER, George Norman; B: Peasmarsh, Sussex; E: Rye, Sussex; Pte. L 8140; K: 10.9.14; La Ferte-sous-Jouarre Mem. Seine-et-Marne.

1205. PIPER, Harry; B: Eastbourne; E: Eastbourne; Pte. G 1423; K: 25.1.15; Le Touret Mem. Pas-de-Calais.

1206. PITCHFORD, Albert Edward; B: – ; E: Colchester; L/Cpl. L 14553; K: 9.9.18; Thiepval Mem. Somme; Age 24; Son of Enoch and Catherine Pitchford of The Caledonian Hotel, 17, St.John's Green, Colchester.

1207. PLATER, Joseph; B: Brighton; E: Chichester; Pte. L 5874; K: 30.10.14; Ypres (Menin Gate) Mem. (Bel.); Age 30; Husband of Mrs.M.M.A.Plater of 7, De Montfort Road, Brighton.

1208. PLEDGE, Arthur; B: Brighton; E: Eastbourne; Cpl. L 8747; K: 19.8.18; Cambrin Mil. Cem. Pas-de-Calais.

1209. POLL, Edward John; B: East Dereham; E: Norwich; Pte. G 14721; K: 28.9.16; Bellicourt Brit. Cem. Aisne; Age 25; Son of James and Alice Poll of Norwich; Husband of May Jane Poll of 14, Arthur Street, Mariners Lane, Norwich.*

1210. POMFRETT, George Edward; B: Waltham Cross; E: Cheshunt; Pte. G 21559; W at Home: 8.10.18; Cheshunt Burial Ground (U.K.); Age 36.*

1211. POLLINGTON, John Edward; B: Crowborough, Sussex; E: Bexhill-on-Sea; Pte. G 6723; W: 13.5.18; Houchin Brit. Cem. Pas-de-Calais; Age 22; Son of Edward and Elizabeth Pollington.

1212. POOLE, Harry Walter; B: Sevenoaks; E: Hastings; Pte. L 7393; K: 4.10.14; La Ferte-sous-Jouarre Mem. Seine-et-Marne.

1213. POPE, George; B: Crowborough, Sussex; E: Uckfield, Sussex; Pte. SD 5347; K: 9.9.16; Thiepval Mem. Somme.

1214. POPPLEWELL, Charles Joseph; B: Romford; E: Romford; Pte. G 19890; W: 15.11.17; Vlamertinghe New Mil. Cem. (Bel.).

1215. PORTSMOUTH, Victor Charles Henry; B: Staines; E: Whitehall; Pte. G 20359; K: 23.11.17; Tyne Cot Mem. (Bel.); Age 20; Son of Charles and Emily Portsmouth of 25, Blays Lane, Englefield Green, Middlesex.

1216. POTTER, Albert Edward; B: Ide Hill; E: Maidstone; Pte. L 10746; K: 9.9.16; Caterpillar Valley Cem. Somme; Age 22; Son of John and Julia Potter of Scords Cottage, Toys Hill, Brasted, Kent.

1217. POTTER, Harry; B: Arundel, Sussex; E: Chichester; L/Cpl. G 824; K: 9.9.16; Thiepval Mem. Somme; Age 23; Son of Fred Potter of 10, Church Street, Uckfield, Sussex.

1218. POWELL, Charles; B: Rotherhithe; E: Southwark; Pte. G 4651; K: 9.5.15; Le Touret Mem. Pas-de-Calais.

1219. POWELL, Frederick Harry; B: Ticehurst, Sussex; E: Ticehurst; Pte. L 8413; K: 14.9.14; La Ferte-sous-Jouarre Mem. Seine-et-Marne; Age 28; Son of William and Emily Mary Powell of The Miner's Arms, Wadhurst, Sussex.

1220. PRATT, Charles; B: Southwark; E: Hurstpierpoint, Sussex; Pte. L 10044; K: 25.9.15; Loos Mem. Pas-de-Calais; Age 20; Son of George James and Sophia Pratt of The White Horse Inn, Ditchling, Sussex.

1221. PRATT, Thomas Richard; B: Uckfield, Sussex; E: Heathfield, Sussex; Pte. L 8946; K: 5.11.14; Ypres (Menin Gate) Mem. (Bel.); Age 24; Son of William Richard and Annie Pratt of 11, Commercial Road, Eastbourne.

1222. PRICE, Frank George; B: Brighton; E: Brighton; L/Cpl. L 10106; K: 14.9.14; La Ferte-sous-Jouarre Mem. Seine-et-Marne; Age 19; Son of William and Mary Ann Price.

1223. PRICE, Reginald; B: Benefield; E: Marylebone; Pte. G 6888; W: 12.5.16; St.Patrick's Cem. Pas-de-Calais; Age 24; Son of Benjamin Price of 11, Dorset Gardens, Brighton.

1224. PROCTOR Ralph William; B: Ipswich; E: Chelmsford; Pte. G 14720; K: 28.9.16; Thiepval Mem. Somme; Age 21; Son of James Thomas and Julia Sarah Proctor of 20, Dillwyn Street West, Ipswich.

1225. PULLEN, Arthur; B: Plumstead; E: Brighton; Pte. L 9840; K: 14.9.14; Vendresse Brit. Cem. Aisne.

1226. PULLEN, Hubert Lucas; B: Kirkford; E: Chichester; Pte. L 9643; K: 13.11.14; Ypres (Menin Gate) Mem. (Bel.); Age 20; Son of Mrs.A.Bromham of Crows Hall Farm, Binderton, Lavant, Sussex.

1227. PUMFREY, George; B: Portslade, Sussex; E: Brighton; Pte. S 1814; K: 23.7.16; Thiepval Mem. Somme; Son of Mr. and Mrs.Pumfrey of 19, George Street, Portslade.

1228. PURSER, Sidney Charles; B: Harefield; E: Harefield; Pte. G 17739; K: 11.3.17; Thiepval Mem. Somme.

1229. PUTTOCK, John; B: – ; E: Horsham, Sussex; Pte. TF 4656; D at Home: 4.7.16; Loxwood (St.John the Baptist) Churchyard, Sussex (U.K.).

Q

1230. QUAIFE, Alfred Charles; B: Hastings; E: Hastings; Pte. G 3858; W: 18.9.18; Brie Brit. Cem. Somme.

1231. QUINTON, Alfred Charles; B: Brighton; E: Brighton; Cpl. G 5655; K: 28.9.16; Flatiron Copse Cem. Somme.

R

1232. RADFORD, Walter Cyril Leigh; B: Brandon, I.O.W.; E: Whitehall; Pte. G 16826; W: 22.11.17; (attached to Royal West Surrey Regt.) Oxford Road Cem. (Bel.); Age 19; Son of S.C. and Mabel Ann Radford of Crosby, Liverpool.

1233. RALPH, William John; B: Holborn; E: Brighton; Pte. G 4623; K: 9.5.15; Le Touret Mem. Pas-de-Calais.

1234. RAMSAY, Duncan Gavin; Lt; K: 18.12.14; (attached to Royal West Surrey Regt.) Caberet-Rouge Brit. Cem. Pas-de-Calais. Age 21; Son of Alexander and Ada Ramsay of The Cedars, Upperton Road, Eastbourne.*

1235. RANGER, George R; B: Newhaven; E: Brighton; Pte. G 6362; M.M.; K: 17.10.18; Busigny Com. Cem. Ext. Nord.*

1236. RANGER, William Martin; B: East Grinstead, Sussex; E: East Grinstead; L/Cpl. G 3179; W: 13.8.18; Cambrin Mil. Cem. Pas-de-Calais; Age 23; Son of James E. and Mrs.M.A.Ranger of "The Nest", Frith Park, East Grinstead.

1237. RANSOM, William James; B: – ; E: Bexhill-on-Sea; Pte. G 8606; K: 16.8.16; Thiepval Mem. Somme.

1238. RANSON, Alfred William; B: Bexhill-on-Sea; E: Bexhill-on-Sea; Pte. G 8654; W: 28.11.16; St.Sever Cem. Ext., Rouen, Seine-Maritime; Age 21; Son of Alfred Ranson of 36, Beaconsfield Road, Bexhill-on-Sea.

1239. RAPLEY, Charles George; B: Chichester; E: Hove; Cpl. G 1193; K: 16.8.16; Thiepval Mem. Somme; Age 22; Son of Allen and Rose Rapley of Cairo Cottages, Southwater, Horsham, Sussex.

1240. RASEY, Albert Edward; B: Epsom; E: Croydon; Pte. G 4958; W: 20.6.18; Pernes Brit. Cem. Pas-de-Calais.

1241. RAWLINSON, Leonard Gordon; B: Camberwell; E: Chelsea; Pte. G 4091; K: 25.9.15; Loos Mem. Pas-de-Calais.

1242. RAWORTH, Alexander Harry; B: St.Pancras; E: Chichester; L/Cpl. L 10204; K: 20.6.16; Maroc Brit. Cem. Nord.

1243. RAYNSFORD, Arthur; B: Brighton; E: Brighton; Pte. G 13681; K: 24.9.18; Bellicourt Brit. Cem. Aisne.

1244. READ, Edwin; B: Hove; E: Chichester; Pte. L 6390; K: 31.10.14; Ypres (Menin Gate) Mem. (Bel.).

1245. READ, George Edward; B: Woodford; E: Woodford; Pte. G 34683; W: 5.11.18; Premont Brit. Cem. Aisne; Age 33; Son of James and Elizabeth Read of Woodford; Husband of Mrs.A.C.Marriott, formerly Read, of 121, Park Side, Woodford Green, Essex.

1246. READ, William Leonard; B: Southfleet; E: London; Pte. L 7784; K: 10.9.14; Montreuil-aux-Lions Brit. Cem. Aisne.

1247. READE, Charlton Leverton Ridout; 2nd Lt; K: 9.9.16; Thiepval Mem. Somme.

1248. READER, Jack; B: Hatfield, Sussex; E: Brighton; Pte. S 1061; K: 9.5.15; Le Touret Mem. Pas-de-Calais.

1249. REBBECK, William Alfred; B: Mayfield, Sussex; E: Eastbourne; Pte. G 8245; D at Home: 14.11.16; Mayfield (St.Dunstan) Churchyard, Sussex (U.K.); Age 19; Son of William Albert and Ellen Rebbeck of South Street, Mayfield, Sussex.

1250. REDFORD, Arthur; B: Horsham, Sussex; E: Brighton; Pte. L 7663; K: 9.5.15; Le Touret Mem. Pas-de-Calais; Age 34; Husband of Mildred Annie Bromley, formerly Redford, of 2, Zion Gardens, Brighton.

1251. REED, Charles; B: Billingshurst, Sussex; E: Chichester; Pte. L 7879; K: 9.5.15; Le Touret Mem. Pas-de-Calais; Age 28; Husband of Mrs.Emily Reed of 20, Queen Street, New Town, Stratford, London.

1252. REED, Ernest; B: Bedminster; E: Bristol; Cpl. L 7535; K: 29.1.15; Le Touret Mem. Pas-de-Calais.

1253. REED, William; B: Caterham; E: Chichester; Pte. G 851; W: 6.7.17; Coxyde Mil. Cem. (Bel.); Age 22; Son of Eliza Ruth Reed of 224, Bensham Lane, Thornton Heath, Surrey.

1254. REES, Daniel Spencer; B: Brecon; E: Hastings; Pte. G 28005; K: 18.9.18; Vis-en-Artois Mem., Haucourt, Pas-de-Calais; Age 27; Son of Thomas and Mary Rees of Besford, Worcester.

1255. REEVES, Ernest; B: Brighton; E: Chichester; Pte. L 9963; K: 24.9.18; Vis-en-Artois Mem., Haucourt, Pas-de-Calais; Age 23; Son of Mrs.Esther Reeves. *

1256. REEVES, George Charles; B: Hastings; E: Hastings; Sgt. L 7695; K: 17.8.16; Caterpillar Valley Cem. Somme; Age 35; Son of William and Ellen Reeves; Husband of Nellie Reeves of 24, Alma Villas, Silverhill, St.Leonards-on-Sea.

1257. REEVES, Oliver John; B: St.Ives, Hunts.; E: London; Sgt. L 7756; K: 9.5.15; Le Touret Mem. Pas-de-Calais.

1258. REGAN, Thomas; B: Brighton; E: Brighton; Pte. GS 6; K: 9.5.15; Le Touret Mem. Pas-de-Calais.

1259. RELF, Richard John; B: Bognor Regis, Sussex; E: London; Cpl. L 6494; K: 16.2.15; Le Touret Mem. Pas-de-Calais; Age 29; Son of Richard and Louisa Relf of East View, The Moor, Hawkhurst, Kent; Husband of Florence Amelia Relf of 21, Courtenay Road, Woking.

1260. RELF, Thomas William Asher; B: Heathfield, Sussex; E: Eastbourne; Pte. S 2351; K: 13.10.15; Loos Mem. Pas-de-Calais; Age 40; Son of Thomas Relf of Cross-in-Hand, Heathfield; Husband of Gertrude Relf of 51, Parsonage Road, Eastbourne.

1261. REMNANT, Percy; B: Northchapel, Sussex; E: Chichester; Pte. G 1149; D: 6.3.15; Wimereux Com. Cem. Pas-de-Calais.

1262. RENARD, Marshall V.; B: Bradford; E: Hove; Pte. L 10715; K: 20.8.16; Thiepval Mem. Somme.

1263. REYNOLDS, Bertram; B: Stockwell; E: Chichester; Cpl. L 9861; K: 26.9.16; Warlencourt Brit. Cem. Pas-de-Calais; Age 24; Son of William and Rose Reynolds of Brixton, London; Husband of Daisy Nellie Reynolds of 43, Westcote Road, Streatham, London.

1264. RICE, Albert; B: Brighton; E: Brighton; Pte. S 2123; K: 25.9.15; St.Mary's A.D.S. Cem. Pas-de-Calais.*

1265. RICE, Arthur; B: Lindfield, Sussex; E: Haywards Heath; Pte. G 1297; K: 25.9.15; Loos Mem. Pas-de-Calais; Age 27; Son of Mrs.A.Rice of "Lindfield", 5, Graham Cottages, Haywards Heath, Sussex.

1266. RICE, Ernest James; B: East Grinstead, Sussex; E: Poplar; Pte. G 4377; K: 25.9.15; Loos Mem. Pas-de-Calais.

1267. RICHARDS, C.; B: – ; E: – ; Pte. L 10248: D at Home: 3.11.18; Hampstead Cem. London (UK).

1268. RICHARDS, Edward Kelsey; B: Coldred; E: Dover; L/Sgt. G 17552; W: 11.9.16; Heilly Station Cem., Mericourt-L'Abbé, Somme; Age 31; Son of Frederick and Jane Richards of "Freecourt", Whitfield, Kent.

1269. RICHARDS, Harry; B: Portslade; E: Brighton; Pte. L 10308; K: 16.8.16; Thiepval Mem. Somme.

1270. RICHARDSON, Alfred Herbert; B: Chichester; E: Chichester; L/Cpl. L 7737; K: 28.9.16; Flatiron Copse Cem. Somme; Age 31; Son of Mr. and Mrs.G.A.Richardson of Brighton; Husband of Mrs.D.Congerton, formerly Richardson, of 10, Park Street, Brighton.

1271. RICHARDSON, David; B: Peckham; E: Lambeth; Pte. G 5405; K: 13.10.15; Loos Mem. Pas-de-Calais; Age 32; Son of William and Emily Richardson; Husband of Amelia Richardson of 84, Park Road, Eastleigh, Hampshire.

1272. RICHARDSON, Frederick; B: Firle, Sussex; E: Lewes; Pte. G 1687; K: 2.6.15; Cambrin Churchyard Ext. Pas-de-Calais; Age 19; Son of Edward and Elizabeth Richardson of 17, Malling Street, Lewes.

1273. RICHARDSON, Frederick; B: Bognor Regis, Sussex; E: Eastbourne; Pte. L 10133; K: 29.10.14; Ypres (Menin Gate) Mem. (Bel.).

1274. RICHARDSON, George Warwick; B: Cowfold, Sussex; E: Horsham, Sussex; Cpl. L 8248; K: 14.5.16; St.Patrick's Cem. Pas-de-Calais; Age 34; Son of Mr. and Mrs.W.Richardson of Manning's Heath, Horsham, Sussex.*

1275. RICHARDSON, Howard Curteis; B: Hanwell; E: Brighton; Pte. G 1534; K: 9.5.15; Le Touret Mem. Pas-de-Calais; Age 33; Son of Ernest Murray and Augustine Anna Maria Richardson of 44, Peel Street, Kensington, London. *

1276. RICHARDSON, Ivan Gordon; B: Mayfield, Sussex; E: Eastbourne; L/Cpl. G 5521; W: 10.3.16; Lillers Com. Cem. Pas-de-Calais; Age 21; Son of William Gordon and Rosa Harriett Richardson of "The Tryste", Rottingdean, Sussex.

1277. RICHARDSON, James; B: Pulborough, Sussex; E: Chichester; Sgt. L 8256; W: 29.1.15; Beuvry Com. Cem. Pas-de-Calais.

1278. RICHARDSON, Samuel; B: Brighton; E: Chichester; Drummer L 9584; K: 10.9.14; Montreuil-aux-Lions Brit. Cem. Aisne.

1279. RIDDLE, Edward; B: Hammersmith; E: London; Pte. L 7894; K: 8.11.14; Ypres (Menin Gate) Mem. (Bel.).

1280. RIDLEY, James Alfred John; B: Uckfield, Sussex; E: Chichester; Pte. L 10121; K: 9.5.15; Le Touret Mem. Pas-de-Calais.

1281. RIDLEY, Jesse; B: Iford, Sussex; E: Lewes; Pte. G 1635; K: 9.9.16; Thiepval Mem. Somme.

1282. ROBERE, Louis Anthony; B: – ; E: Colchester; Pte. G 14632; K: 9.9.16; Thiepval Mem. Somme.

1283. ROBERTS, William Rufus; B: Tarring, Sussex; E: Worthing; Pte. G 1376; K: 25.9.15; Dud Corner Cem. Pas-de-Calais; Age 24; Son of William Rufus Roberts of Worthing; Husband of Mary Joyce Roberts of 73, Cranworth Road, Worthing.

1284. ROBERTS, William Thomas; B: London; E: Chichester; L/Cpl. L 10426; W: 9.12.16; Dernancourt Com. Cem. Ext. Somme.

1285. ROBINS, Harry; B: Heathfield, Sussex; E: Eastbourne; Pte. S 2195; K: 1.1.15; Le Touret Mem. Pas-de-Calais; Age 22; Son of Robert James and Harriet Ann Robins of Foxhunt Lodge, Waldron, Sussex.

1286. ROBINSON, Eli; B: Kingston; E: Chichester; Pte. G 852; K; 9.9.16; Thiepval Mem. Somme.

1287. RODELL, Robert Frederick; B: Littlehampton, Sussex; E: Chichester; Pte. L 10324; K: 30.10.14; Ypres (Menin Gate) Mem. (Bel.); Age 18; Son of William Henry and Blanche Rodell of 82, Greyhound Lane, Streatham, London.

1288. ROGERS, Harry; B: Brighton; E: Hove; Pte. G 8944; K: 15.7.16; Thiepval Mem. Somme; Age 17; Son of George and Emily Lily Rogers of 40, Sutherland Road, Brighton.

1289. ROOKE, Alfred Francis; B: Newhaven, Sussex; E: Southwark; Pte. G 5069; K: 25.9.15; Loos Mem. Pas-de-Calais; Age 28; Husband of Violet Beatrice Rooke of 43, Claremont Road, Portsmouth.

1290. ROOKE, Ernest John; B: Chichester; E: Chichester; Pte. L 7866; K: 9.5.15; Le Touret Mem. Pas-de-Calais.

1291. ROOKS, Edgar Thomas; B: Eastbourne; E: Eastbourne; L/Cpl. G 1436; D: 4.2.15; Chocques Mil. Cem. Pas-de-Calais; Age 20; Son of Thomas Henry and Kate Rooks of 15, New Upperton Road, Eastbourne.

1292. ROPER, Herbert; B: Downham; E: Norwich; Pte. TF 202343; W: 5.11.18; Premont Brit. Cem. Aisne.

1293. ROSE, Thomas; B: West Orchard, Dorset; E: Pulborough; C.Q.M.S. L 8613; K: 15.5.18;Cambrin Mil. Cem. Pas-de-Calais; Age 30; Son of John and Emma Rose of Beacon Land Cottage, Warbleton, Sussex.

1294. ROSSITER, George; B: Chichester; E: Chichester; Pte. L 10502; K: 9.5.15; Le Touret Mem. Pas-de-Calais; Age 19; Son of George and Jane Rossiter of 22, St.Pancras, Chichester.

1295. ROTHWELL, Harry; B: Mottram, Cheshire; E: Ashton-under-Lyne; Pte. G 5904; K: 21.11.17; Tyne Cot Mem. (Bel.); Age 27; Son of Arnold and Annie Rothwell of 45, Pottingea Street, Ashton-under-Lyne.

1296. ROUTHAN, Alfred; B: Wellingborough; E: Brighton; Sgt. S 8892; K: 1.11.14; Ypres (Menin Gate) Mem. (Bel.).

1297. ROUTHAN, Mark; B: Bow; E: Eastbourne; Pte. S 9790; K: 16.2.15; Le Touret Mem. Pas-de-Calais.

1298. ROUTHAN, Thomas; B: Bow; E: Brighton; Pte. S 2331; K: 25.9.15; Dud Corner Cem. Pas-de-Calais; Father of Thomas Routhan of 74, Franklin Road, Brighton.

1299. ROWBERRY, Alfred Archibald; B: Sittingbourne; E: Chichester; L/Cpl. L 10028; K: at Vendresse: 14.9.14; Grand-Seraucourt Brit. Cem. Aisne; Age 20; Son of Alfred Rowberry.

1300. ROWE, Benjamin; B: East Grinstead, Sussex; E: East Grinstead; Pte. G 19680; K: 14.11.17; Tyne Cot Mem. (Bel.); Age 32; Son of Mr. and Mrs. A.A.Rowe of 49, Cantelupe Road, East Grinstead; Husband of Ellen Constance Rowe of 21, Rush Hill Road, Lavender Hill, London.

1301. ROWE, Percy Frank; B: Arundel, Sussex; E: Arundel; Pte. L 8239; K: 25.9.15; Dud Corner Cem. Pas-de-Calais; Age 28; Son of Alfred and Mary Rowe of 15, Wood View, Ford Road, Arundel.

1302. ROWLAND, Walter Horace; B: Brighton; E: Hove; Pte. L 10577; K: 3.12.15; Dud Corner Cem. Pas-de-Calais; Age 21; Son of Mr. and Mrs.J.Rowland of 2, Milton Terrace, Mill Road, Burgess Hill, Sussex.*

1303. RUFF, Ernest; B: Findon, Sussex; E: Worthing; Pte. L 10460; K: 9.5.15; Le Touret Mem. Pas-de-Calais.

1304. RUMMERY, Charles John; B: Tunbridge Wells; E: Herne; Pte. G 17530; W: 11.9.16; Achiet-le-Grand Com. Cem. Ext. Pas-de-Calais; Age 22; Son of Joseph John and Constance Lydia Rummery of 24, Western Road, Tunbridge Wells, Kent; Formerly of the East Kent Yeomanry.

1305. RUSHMORE, William; B: Poplar; E: London; Pte. L 6122; K: 9.5.15; Le Touret Mem. Pas-de-Calais.

1306. RUSSELL, Philip James Wensley; B: Fulham; E: Southwark; Pte. G 4701; K: 25.9.15; Loos

Mem. Pas-de-Calais; Age 20; Son of Laurence and Winifred Russell of "Ecclesfield", Ashford, Middlesex.*

1307. RUSTELL, George Bramwell; B: Llantrisant; E: Cowbridge; Pte. G 1117; K: 4.10.18; Berthaucourt Com. Cem. Aisne; Age 22; Son of J. and Martha Rustell of 34, Cowbridge Road, Pontyclun, Glamorgan.

1308. RUTHERFORD, Sidney; B: Hastings; E: Maidstone; Sgt. L 9611; K: 13.10.15; Loos Mem. Pas-de-Calais.

S

1309. SADLER, John; B: Lambeth; E: Lambeth; Pte. G 11091; K: 27.9.16; Thiepval Mem. Somme; Age 23; Son of John and Ellen Sadler of 14, Ward Street, Lambeth, London.

1310. SAGEMAN, George; B: Borden Wood; E: Chichester; Pte. L 8695; K: 14.9.14; La Ferte-sous-Jouarre Mem. Seine-et-Marne; Age 26; Son of Mrs. Ellen Sageman of The Tanyard, West Lavington, Sussex.

1311. SAINTON, Francis Charles; Capt. M.C., W: 18.4.18; Woburn Abbey Cem. Pas-de-Calais; Son of Mrs.A.Sainton of 5, Charleville Mansions, West Kensington, London; Died of wounds received on 17.4.18.

1312. SALISBURY, William Frederick; B: Harrow; E: Harrow; Pte. G 19329; K: 24.9.18; Vadencourt Brit.Cem. Aisne; Age 19; Son of Thomas and Ellen Salisbury of Valentine Cottage, Valentine Road, South Harrow, Middlesex.

1313. SALTMARSH, Albert; B: Brighton; E: Brighton; Pte. S 1796; W: 15.10.15; Lapugnoy Mil. Cem. Pas-de-Calais; Age 18; Son of Mr. and Mrs.Saltmarsh of 5, Albion Cottages, Brighton; Died of wounds received at Loos.

1314. SALVAGE, John; B: Brighton; E: Brighton; Pte. GS 131; K: 9.5.15; Le Touret Mem. Pas-de-Calais.

1315. SAMSON, Percy; B: Shoreham, Sussex; E: Hove; Pte. G 1168; K: 12.1.15; Le Touret Mem. Pas-de-Calais; Age 18; Son of William and Martha Samson of 35, Ham Road, Shoreham.

1316. SANDERS, Cyril John; B: Tiverton; E: Eastbourne; Pte. G 4143; K: 25.9.15; Loos Mem. Pas-de-Calais.*

1317. SANDERS, Frederick; B: Fernhurst; E: Midhurst, Sussex; Pte. L 10836; K: 22.11.17; Tyne Cot Mem. (Bel.); Age 28; Son of Ephraim and Eliza Sanders of Fernhurst, Haselmere, Surrey.

1318. SANDFORD, Henry Merton Way; B: Southwick, Sussex; E: Chichester; Pte. L 10471; K: 18.4.18; Woburn Abbey Cem. Pas-de-Calais; Son of Mrs.J.Sandford of 73, High Barn, Peppering, Arundel, Sussex.

1319. SANDS, George Henry; B: Worthing; E: Hastings; Pte. G 60; K: 25.9.15; Loos Mem. Pas-de-Calais; Age 33; Son of George William and Emily Sands of 22, Sandown Road, Ore, Hastings.

1320. SANDS, Moses David; B: Hastings; E: Eastbourne; Pte. GS 620; K: 9.5.15; Le Touret Mem. Pas-de-Calais; Age 42; Son of George and Margaret Sands; Husband of Elizabeth Ester Tutt, formerly Sands, of 15, Channel View Road, Eastbourne.

1321. SANGSTER, Edward George; B: Ipswich; E: East Grinstead, Sussex; Pte. L 10203; K: 6.11.14; Ypres (Menin Gate) Mem. (Bel.).

1322. SANSOME, William; B: Fareham; E: Gosport; Pte. L 6597; K: 27.9.14; Vendresse Brit. Cem. Aisne; Husband of Bridget Todd, formerly Sansome, of 5, Burke Street, Belfast.

1323. SARGENT, Robert; B: Eastbourne; E: Eastbourne; Pte. L 10050; K: 25.9.15; Loos Mem. Pas-de-Calais.*

1324. SAUNDERS, Charles Henry; B: Brighton; E: Brighton; L/Cpl. G 8174; K: 9.9.16; Caterpillar Valley Cem. Somme; Age 26; Husband of Alice Saunders of High Street, Rottingdean, Sussex.*

1325. SAUNDERS, Ernest; B: Hove; E: Brighton; Pte. L 10108; K: 14.9.14; La Ferte-sous-Jouarre Mem. Seine-et-Marne; Age 18; Son of the late John Henry Saunders and Louisa Kate Hearsey, formerly Saunders, of 67, Mount Zion, Tunbridge Wells, Kent.

1326. SAUNDERS, George; Sgt. L 8389; B: Barcombe, Sussex; E: Brighton; K: 17.8.16; Thiepval Mem. Somme.

1327. SAUNDERS, George Thomas; B: Hackney, London; E: Chichester; Pte. S 2188; K: 25.9.15; Loos Mem. Pas-de-Calais.

1328. SAUNDERS, Henry; B: Brighton; E: Brighton; Pte. G 8552; K: 17.8.16; Caterpillar Valley Cem. Somme; Age 37; Son of William Funnell Saunders; Returned from Canada to enlist.

1329. SAUNDERS, John William; B: Uckfield, Sussex; E: Lewes; Pte. G 1677; K: 25.9.15; Loos Mem. Pas-de-Calais; Age 21; Son of Alfred and Adelaide Saunders of Ringwood, Uckfield, Sussex.*

1330. SAUNDERS, William; B: St.Paul's, Sussex; E: Eastbourne; Pte. S 9848; K: 30.10.14; Ypres (Menin Gate) Mem. (Bel.).*

1331. SAWYERS, Herbert Harold; B: Haywards Heath, Sussex; E: Haywards Heath; Pte. G 1291; K: 25.1.15; Le Touret Mem. Pas-de-Calais; Age 21; Son of Charles Herbert and Annie Harriet Sawyers of "Silverlea", Silverlea Gardens, Horley, Surrey.*

1332. SCANDRETT, William Frederick; 2nd Lt; K: 27.6.16; Arras Mem. Pas-de-Calais; Age 20; Son of William Thomas and Ellen Mary Scandrett of Oak Lodge, Durlston Road, Kingston-on-Thames.

1333. SCOTT, Frederick George; B: North Stoke; E: Worthing; L/Cpl. G 1290; K: 9.5.15; Le Touret Mem. Pas-de-Calais; Age 23; Son of Albert and Edith Scott of The Hollies, Goring, Sussex.

1334. SCRASE, Frederick; B: Brighton; E: Brighton; Sgt. L 8699; K: 2.3.16; Arras Mem. Pas-de-Calais.

1335. SCRASE, Horace; B: Brighton; E: Camberwell; Pte. L 10641; K: 27.9.15; Loos Mem. Pas-de-Calais.

1336. SCRUBY, Harry; B – ; E: – ; Pte. G 24228; K: 20.7.16; Thiepval Mem. Somme; Age 22; Son of Henry William Scruby of 24, Hows Street, Kingsland Road, London.

1337. SCUTT, Alfred; B: Canning Town, London; E: Chichester; Pte. G 1036; K: 25.9.15; Loos Mem. Pas-de-Calais.

1338. SCUTT, Frank; B: Bury, Sussex; E: Hastings; L/Cpl. SD 2779; K: 23.7.16; Thiepval Mem. Somme; Age 33; Son of Thomas and Fanny Scutt of High Street, Amberley, Sussex; Husband of Kate Scutt of Jessamine Cottage, 198, Cocking Street, Midhurst, Sussex.

1339. SEACEY, William Henry; B: Toxteth; E: Glasgow; Pte. G 4150; K: 9.5.15; Le Touret Mem. Pas-de-Calais.

1340. SEALE, Sidney; B: Beckenham; E: Croydon; Pte. L 9989; K: 30.10.14; Ypres (Menin Gate) Mem. (Bel.).

1341. SEALEY, Sydney John; B: Sunbury; E: Brighton; Pte. GS 38; K: 29.1.15; Le Touret Mem. Pas-de-Calais.

1342. SEARLE, John; B: Wishaw; E: Uckfield, Sussex; Pte. G 8710; K: 30.6.16; Arras Mem. Pas-de-Calais.

1343. SECKER, Cecil; B: Homerton; E: Walthamstow; Pte. G 19886; K: 17.10.18; Busigny Com. Cem. Ext. Nord.*

1344. SELBY, William George; B: Cuckfield, Sussex; E: Chichester; Pte. L 8311; K: 30.10.14; Ypres (Menin Gate) Mem. (Bel.); Age 26; Son of Henry and Susan Selby of Brook Street, Cuckfield; Husband of Sarah Selby of 45, Sixth Street, Shankill Road, Belfast.

1345. SELLEN, Herbert Leonard; B: – ; E: Rainham; Pte. G 17562; K: 9.9.16; Caterpillar Valley Cem. Somme.

1346. SELLINGS, Amos John; B: Rusthall; E: Tunbridge Wells; L/Cpl. GS 847; K: 9.5.15; Le Touret Mem. Pas-de-Calais; Age 40; Son of Thomas and Elizabeth Sellings; Husband of Fanny Sellings of 1, Edward Street, Rustall, Sussex; Served in the South Africa campaign.

1347. SELMES, Herbert; B: Hastings; E: Hastings; Pte. L 10260; K in Action at Richebourg: 9.5.15; Le Touret Mem. Pas-de-Calais; Age 18; Son of William Selmes of 2, Cinque Ports Yard, Rye, Sussex.*

1348. SENDALL, Herbert Keith; B: Roffey, Sussex; E: Brighton; Pte. G 9015; K: 23.7.16; Adanac Mil. Cem. Somme; Age 27; Son of Ellen Sendall of 42, Trafalgar Road, Horsham, Sussex.

1349. SHAMBROOK, Charles Owen; B: Hanwell; E: Southwark; Pte. G 6807; K: 23.7.16; Thiepval Mem. Somme; Age 28; Son of Mrs.Matilda Shambrook of Lathroppe's Almshouses, Carter Street, Uttoxeter.

1350. SHARP, Walter; B: Brighton; E: Brighton; Pte. S 2222; K: 27.1.15; Le Touret Mem. Pas-de-Calais; Age 22; Son of Alexander and Jane Sharp of 62, Cobden Road, Brighton.

1351. SHATTOCK, George Edward; B: Cardiff; E: Northampton; Pte. G 11661; K: 15.11.17; Tyne Cot Mem. (Bel.); Age 19; Son of George and Mathilde Shattock of 6, Pembroke Road, Canton, Cardiff. *

1352. SHAW, Cuthbert Frank; 2nd Lt; K: 30.10.14; Ypres (Menin Gate) Mem. (Bel.); Age 20; Son of Frank Herbert and Fanny Mary Shaw of 60, London Road, St.Leonards-on-Sea, Sussex.

1353. SHAW, George James; B: Hastings; E: Hastings; L/Cpl. L 10195; K: 25.9.15; Loos Mem. Pas-de-Calais; Age 19; Son of Edward T. and Emma Shaw of East Hill Passage, Hastings.

1354. SHAW, Reginald Thomas; Lt; K: 9.5.15; Le Touret Mem. Pas-de-Calais; Age 22; Son of Lauriston E. and May H.Shaw of 4, Warrington Court, London.

1355. SHELLEY, George; B: Brighton; E: Brighton; Pte. G 9150; K: 6.9.16; Delville Wood Cem. Somme; Age 24; Son of Mr. and Mrs.James Shelley of 24, Cambridge Street, Brighton.

1356. SHELTON, Charles; B: Fulham; E: Newport; Pte. GS 881; K: 9.5.15; Le Touret Mem. Pas-de-Calais; Age 36; Husband of Mrs.B.Osborne, formerly Shelton, of 4, Bushey Park, Wainfelin, Pontypool, Glamorgan.

1357. SHEPPARD, Henry William; B: Eastbourne; E: Eastbourne; Sgt. L 9008; K: 9.5.15; Le Touret Mem. Pas-de-Calais; Age 23; Son of Alfred and Susannah Sheppard of 44, Duke Street, Eastbourne; Seven years' service.

1358. SHEPPARD, William James; B: Brighton; E: Brighton; Pte. L 10268; K: 31.12.14; Le Touret Mem. Pas-de-Calais.

1359. SHIFNER, Sir John Bridger, Bart.; 2nd Lt; K at Gricourt: 24.9.18; Bellicourt Brit. Cem. Aisne; Age 19; Son of Sir John, 5th Bart., and Lady Shifner of Combe Place, Lewes.

1360. SHIRLEY, Daniel; B: Crawley, Oxon.; E: Oxford; Pte. L 8887; K: 14.9.14; La Ferte-sous-Jouarre Mem. Seine-et-Marne; Age 27; Son of Christopher and Emma Shirley of 8, All Saints Street, Churchfield, West Bromwich; Husband of Agnes May Cross, formerly Shirley, of Grammar School Hill, Charlbury, Oxfordshire.

1361. SHOOSMITH, William Henry; B: Eastbourne; E: Eastbourne; Pte. L 9698; W: 16.9.14; St.Nazaire (Toutes-Aides) Cem. Loire-Atlantique.

1362. SHORT, Edwin Frank; B: Folkestone; E: Brighton; Pte. G 4672; K: 25.9.15; Loos Mem. Pas-de-Calais.

1363. SHORT, George Albert Victor; B: Southwick, Sussex; E: Hove; Pte. G 7595; K: 8.9.16; Thiepval Mem. Somme.

1364. SHORT, George William; B: Southwick, Sussex; E: Hove; Pte. G 1173; K: 25.9.15; Dud Corner Cem. Pas-de-Calais; Age 18; Son of Nathaniel and Martha Short of 9, Adur Terrace, Southwick.

1365. SHORT, John; B: Lewes; E: Brighton; Pte. L 8265; K: 31.12.14; Le Touret Mem. Pas-de-Calais.

1366. SHORT, Reginald; B: West Chiltington, Sussex; E: Chichester; Pte. L 10512; K: 25.9.15; Dud Corner Cem. Pas-de-Calais.

1367. SHORTER, Edward John; B: Paddington; E: Shepherd's Bush; Pte. GS 927; K: 25.9.15; St.Mary's A.D.S. Cem. Pas-de-Calais.

1368. SHUFFLEBOTTOM, William; B: Bootle; E: Manchester; L/Sgt. G 20076; K: 4.11.18; Le Rejet-de-Beaulieu Com. Cem. Nord.

1369. SILLIS, Harry; B: Great Massingham; E: King's Lynn; Pte. G 9303; K: 10.10.17; Tyne Cot Mem. (Bel.); Age 33; Son of Robert and Mary Sillis of 4, Church Lane, Great Massingham, Norfolk.

1370. SILVER, Humphrey William; B: Chiselhurst; 2nd. Lt; K: 8.6.18; Cambrin Mil. Cem. Pas-de-Calais; Age 34; Son of Col. Hugh Adams Silver and Ann Silver of 2, Michael's Place, Petersham, Surrey; Enlisted in the West Kent Yeomanry; Commission Gazetted 22.12.17. *

1371. SILVESTER, Anson Lloyd; B: Bath; 2nd. Lt; K: 31.12.14; Cuinchy Com. Cem. Pas-de-Calais; Age 26; Son of the Rev.James and Costance Silvester of The Vicarage, Great Clacton, Essex.*

1372. SIMMONDS, Frederick; B: Brighton; E: Hove; Pte. L 10760; K: 19.7.16; Thiepval Mem. Somme.

1373. SIMMONDS, William Charles; B: Burgess Hill, Brighton; E: Brighton; Pte. G 5231; W: 16.10.15; Lapugnoy Mil. Cem. Pas-de-Calais; Age 18; Son of William George Simmonds of 7, Newport Road, Burgess Hill, Sussex.

1374. SIMPSON, Percy William; B: – ; E: – ; Pte. – 15293; W: 12.11.18: Ste.Marie Cem., Le Havre; Seine-Maritime; Age 24; Son of W.T. and Louisa Simpson of 39, East Hill, Colchester; Previously wounded three times.

1375. SIMPSON, Sidney; B: Bury, Sussex; E: Chichester; Sgt. L 8696; K: 9.3.16; St.Patrick's Cem. Pas-de-Calais.

1376. SIMPSON, William; B: St.Martins-at-Oaks, Norfolk; E: Norwich; Pte. L 8521; K: 9.9.16; Thiepval Mem. Somme.

1377. SINGLETON, Thomas Henry; B: Boscombe; E: Poole; Cpl. L 6802; K: 9.5.15; Le Touret Mem. Pas-de-Calais. *

1378. SIVYER, George; B: Little Horsted, Sussex; E: Brighton; Pte. G 4920; K: 25.9.15; Loos Mem. Pas-de-Calais; Age 34; Son of Mr. and Mrs.Alfred Sivyer of Laburnham Cottage, Goring-by-Sea, Sussex; Husband of Emily Brown, formerly Sivyer, of 61a, Milner Road, Brighton.

1379. SIZELAND, Frederick Charles; B: Stansted; E: Saffron Walden; Pte. G 14576; W: 12.9.16; Heilly Station Cem. Mericourt-L'Abbé, Somme; Age 25; Son of Alfred and Mary Ann Sizeland of Stansted, Essex.

1380. SIZER, George Guy; B: Brighton; E: – ; D at Home: 23.10.18; Portslade Cem., Sussex (UK); Age 23; Son of Ernest H. and Louisa Sizer of 67, Wolesley Road, Portslade, Sussex.

1381. SJOQUIST, James Erskine; B: Slaugham, Sussex; E: Brighton; Pte. L 7848; W: 27.4.15; Bethune Town Cem. Pas-de-Calais; Age 30; Son of Charles Oscar and Emma Sjoquist of Handcross, Sussex; Husband of Rosa Allen, formerly Sjoquist, of Prince Rupert, British Columbia, Canada.

1382. SKEET, Alfred Lewis; B: Bungay; E: Great Yarmouth; Pte. G 5631; K: 23.7.16; Thiepval Mem. Somme.

1383. SKEGGS, William George; B: Brighton; E: Brighton; Pte. S 2140; K: 25.1.15; Le Touret Mem. Pas-de-Calais; Age 19; Son of Charles and Elizabeth Skeggs of 31, Fishergate Terrace, Portslade, Sussex.

1384. SKINNER, Arthur Edward; B: Herstmonceux, Sussex; E: Eastbourne; Pte. G 1454; K: 9.5.15; Le Touret Mem. Pas-de-Calais; Age 18; Son of Samuel and Eliza Mary Skinner of Chapel Row, Herstmonceux, Sussex.*

1385. SKINNER, Henry; B: Five Oaks; E: Chichester; Pte. G 14175; K: 29.3.18; Buffs Road Cem. St.Jean-les-Ypres (Bel.); Age 33; Husband of Mrs.E.Skinner of Hope Cottage, Belsham Lane, Yapton, Sussex.

1386. SKINNER, William; B: Lingfield; E: Tunbridge Wells; Pte. G 4130; K: 9.8.15; Cambrin Churchyard Ext. Pas-de-Calais; Age 23; Son of James William and Ann Skinner of High Street, Edenbridge, Kent.

1387. SKIPPER, James; B: Lewisham; E: London; L/Cpl. L 6035; K: 9.5.15; Guards Cem. (Cuinchy) Pas-de-Calais; Age 36; Husband of Mary and Elizabeth Skipper of 59, Golborne Road, North Kensington, London.

1388. SKUSE, George Percy; B: Guildford; E: Guildford; Pte. L 10535; K: 9.5.15; Le Touret Mem. Pas-de-Calais; Age 18; Son of George Percy Skuse of Edward Villa, Portsmouth Road, Cobham, Surrey.

1389. SLATER, Arthur Edwin; B: Storrington, Sussex; E: Brighton; Pte. GS 51; K: 16.2.15; Le Touret Mem. Pas-de-Calais; Age 39; Husband of Millicent Slater of 9, Aberdeen Road, Brighton.*

1390. SLATER, Leonard; Capt; K: 14.9.14; Vendresse Brit. Cem. Aisne; Age 38; Son of the Reverend F. and Mrs.Slater; Husband of Mrs.C.D.Durnford-Slater of Instow, Devonshire.

1391. SLATTER, Walter; B: – ; E: Crawley; Pte. G 17904; W at Home 6.6.18; Westminster City Cem. (U.K.).

1392. SLOAN, Robert Henry Stewart; B: Brighton; E: Chichester; Cpl. L 10094 D.C.M.; W: 24.7.16; Daours Com. Cem. Ext. Somme; Age 22; Son of the late Percival Sloan and Ellen Eliza Cullum, formerly Sloan, of 7, Dacre Gardens, Upper Beeding, Sussex.

1393. SMALE, Alfred Mark; B: Hastings; E: Hastings; Pte. L 10364; K: 9.5.15; Le Touret Mem. Pas-de-Calais; Son of Mrs.Eliza Smale of 63, Winchelsea Road, Ore, Hastings.

1394. SMART, Walter; B: Burton Latimer; E: Melton Mowbray; Pte. SD 1729; W: 24.9.18; Roisel Com. Cem. Ext. Somme.

1395. SMETHURST, John Vernon; B: Leek; E: Leek; Pte. G 4585; K: 9.5.15; Le Touret Mem. Pas-de-Calais; Age 20; Son of John and Harriet Smethurst of 21, Queen Street, Leek, Staffordshire.

1396. SMITH, Alexander Cooper; 2nd Lt; K: 23.7.16; Thiepval Mem. Somme; Age 26; Son of Mr. and Mrs.J.K.Smith of 4E, Hermitage Place, Leith, Edinburgh.

1397. SMITH, Alfred Ernest; B: Handcross, Sussex; E: Haywards Heath, Sussex; Pte. GS 297; K: 9.5.15; Le Touret Mem. Pas-de-Calais; Age 42; Son of Frederick and Mary Smith of 9, Highlands, Cuckfield, Sussex;

1398. SMITH, Andrew Harry; B: Hastings; E: Chichester; Cpl. L 7527; K: 18.9.14; La Ferte-sous-Jouarre Mem. Seine-et-Marne.

1399. SMITH, Charles; B: Brighton; E: Chichester; L/Cpl. L 10102; K: 25.9.15; Loos Mem. Pas-de-Calais.

1400. SMITH, Fred; B: Newick, Sussex; E: Lewes; Pte. G 1321; W: 27.9.15; Lillers Com. Cem. Pas-de-Calais; Age 19; Son of William and Frances Smith of Norris's Cottage, Newick.

1401. SMITH, George; B: Chiddingly, Sussex; E: Hailsham, Sussex; Pte. S 2146; K: 9.5.15; Le Touret Mem. Pas-de-Calais.

1402 SMITH, George; B: Rye, Sussex; E: Seaford, Sussex; Pte. G 8706; W: 16.8.16; Thiepval Mem. Somme.

1403 SMITH, George Frederick; B: Lee; E: Woolwich; Pte. G 11303; K: 9.9.16; Caterpillar Valley Cem. Somme.

1404. SMITH, Harry; B: Eastbourne; E: Eastbourne; Pte. G 4607; K: 9.5.15; Le Touret Mem. Pas-de-Calais.

1405. SMITH, John H; B: Cowes, I.O.W.; E: Arundel, Sussex; L/Cpl. L 10336; K: 12.6.18; Cambrin Mil. Cem. Pas-de-Calais; Foster-son of Eliza Smith of 3, Edinburgh Cottages, Western Row, Worthing.

1406. SMITH, Oswald; B: Worthing; E: Littlehampton, Sussex; Pte. G 1481; K: 12.2.15; Le Touret Mem. Pas-de-Calais; Age 19; Son of Oswald and Fannie E.Smith of 1, Gladstone Terrace, Wick, Sussex.

1407. SMITH, Percy William; B: Bradford-on-Avon; E: Rotherhithe; Pte. G 10165; K: 9.9.16; London Cem. and Ext. Somme; Age 21; Son of William and Rose Smith of Bradford-on-Avon, Wiltshire.

1408. SMITH, Sidney; B: Christchurch, Kent; E: Tunbridge Wells; Pte. S 1590; K: 20.8.16; Thiepval Mem. Somme; Age 19; Son of Philip and Fanny Smith of 20, North Farm Road, High Brooms, Tunbridge Wells.

1409. SMITH, Thomas Joseph; B: Dover; E: Dover; Pte. GS 371; K: 9.5.15; Le Touret Mem. Pas-de-Calais; Age 26; Son of Peter and Susannah Smith of 10, Woolcomber Lane, Dover.

1410. SMITH, William; B: Glasgow; E: Haddington; Pte. L 11534; M.M.; K: 4.11.18; Le Rejet-de-Beaulieu Com. Cem. Nord.

1411. SMITH, William; B: West Ewell; E: Kingston-on-Thames; Pte. G 4643; K: 13.10.15; Loos Mem. Pas-de-Calais; Age 18; Son of Mr. and Mrs. Richard Smith of 2, Chessington Road, West Ewell, Surrey.

1412. SMITH, William Charles; B: St.Luke's, Middx.; E: Stratford; Pte. L 7840; K: 9.5.15; Le Touret Mem. Pas-de-Calais; Age 28; Husband of Agnes Badham, formerly Smith, of 20, Peerless Street, City Road, London.

1413. SMITH, William Henry; B: Liverpool; E: Liverpool; Pte. G 4750; K: 9.9.16; Thiepval Mem. Somme.

1414. SMITH, William John; B: Newton Flotman; E: Norwich; Pte. G 9338; K: 7.8.16; Thiepval Mem. Somme.

1415. SMYTH, James Lawrence Hirst; B: Hassocks; E: Hove; L/Cpl. G 1582; K: 9.5.15; Le Touret Mem. Pas-de-Calais; Age 24; Son of Dr. J.D. and Mrs. Hirst Smyth.

—   SNELLINGS – see SELLINGS (1346).

1416. SOLE, Alfred Edgar; B: Littlebourne; E: Canterbury; Pte. G 17553; K: 24.9.18; Vadencourt Brit. Cem. Aisne; Age 24; Son of Alfred and Dinah S.J.Sole of Sawkinge Farm, Stodmarsh, Kent.

1417. SOMERS, William John Reeves; B: Chichester; E: Dover; Cpl. L 6660; K: 9.5.15; Le Touret Mem. Pas-de-Calais; Age 31; Son of Mr. and Mrs.Somers of Glenfarg Road, Catford, London; Husband of Kate Annie Somers of 4, Bridge Place, St.James' Road, Croydon.

1418. SPAIN, Edward; B: St.Laurence, Kent; E: Ramsgate; Pte. S 899; K: 25.9.15; Loos Mem. Pas-de-Calais.

1419. SPARKES, Frederick; B: Hampnel; E: Sittingbourne; Pte. G 17564; K: 29.12.16; Neiderzwehren Cem. (G).*

1420. SPARSHOTT, Reginald Thomas; B: Hermitage; E: Chichester; L/Cpl. SD 2790; K: 6.9.18; Eterpigny Brit. Cem,. Pas-de-Calais; Age 24; Son of Henry and Mary Sparshott of 30, Westhampnett, Sussex.*

1421. SPEED, Hugh James; B: – ; E: Canterbury; Pte. G 17534; K: 9.9.16; Thiepval Mem. Somme; Age 37; Son of Thomas Speed of Liverpool; Husband of Elizabeth Sarah Speed of Thatched Cottage, Mill Place, Ospringe, Kent.

1422. SPENCER, Charles; B: Tunbridge Wells; E: East Grinstead; Pte. 4295; K: 23.11.15; Loos Mem. Pas-de-Calais.

1423. SPENCER, Sydney; B: Bethnal Green; E: London; Pte. L 6556; K: 4.10.14; La Ferte-sous-Jouarre Mem. Seine-et-Marne.

1424. SPOONER, Alfred; B: – ; E: Colchester; Pte. G 14639; K: 9.9.16; Thiepval Mem. Somme.

1425. SPOONER, Charles; B: Chichester; E: Chichester; Pte. L 10554; W: 27.4.15; Bethune Town Cem. Pas-de-Calais.

1426. SPOONER, Joseph James; B: Lambeth; E: Chichester; Pte. L 10250; K: 27.9.16; Thiepval Mem. Somme; Age 20; Son of Mr. and Mrs.Spooner of 1, Redcar Cottage, Redcar Street, Camberwell, London.

1427. STACE, Frank; B: Guestling, Sussex; E: Hastings; Pte. G 9092; K: 5.8.16; Brewery Orchard Cem. Nord; Age 20; Son of Mr. and Mrs.J.F.Stace of Mount Pleasant, Guestling.

1428. STANDEN, Henry George; B: Wadhurst, Sussex; E: Hastings; Pte. G 4845; K: 25.9.15; Loos Mem. Pas-de-Calais; Age 30; Son of Mr. and Mrs.Walter Standen of "Durgates", Wadhurst, Sussex; Husband of Emily Francis Standen of The Platt, Frant, Sussex.

1429. STANDING. David Louis; B: Brighton; E: Brighton; Pte. G 3991; K: 22.3.18; Cement House Cem. (Bel.)

1430. STANFORD, Walter; B: Haggerston; E: Tottenham; Pte. G 4851; W: 8.10.15; Lillers Com. Cem. Pas-de-Calais; Husband of Gertrude Stanford of 5, Culvert Road, Seven Sisters Road, South Tottenham, London.

1431. STAPLEHURST, William Reginald; B: Maresfield, Sussex; E: Eastbourne; Pte. G 8708; K: 17.8.16; Serre Road Cem. No. 2, Somme; Age 23; Son of William and Annie Staplehurst of Langney Cemetery, Eastbourne.

1432. STAPLEY, Henry; B: – ; E: Hastings; Pte. S 2281; K: 25.9.15; Loos Mem. Pas-de-Calais; Age 19; Son of Henry and Elizabeth Stapley of 38, Essex Street, Kingsland Road, London.

1433. STEAD, Frederick Victor; B: St.Mary's, Middx.; E: Worthing; Pte. G 1253; K: 26.1.15; Le Touret Mem. Pas-de-Calais; Age 18; Son of William Stead and Ellen Frances Novell, formerly Stead, of "Ennismore", High Street, Worthing.

1434. STEADMAN, Frederick George; B: – ; E: Brighton; Pte. G 8622; K: 20.8.16; Thiepval Mem. Somme.

1435. STEED, H.A.L.; B: – ; E: – ; Pte. L 10226; K: 3.9.18; Esquelbecq Mil. Cem. Nord; Age 19; Son of Mr. and Mrs.E.J.Steed of St.Pancras, London.

1436. STEEL, Edward; B: Sidlesham;, Sussex E: Chichester; Pte. G 8062; W: 24.8.16; St.Sever Cem. Ext., Rouen, Seine-Maritime; Age 21; Son of George and Mary Ann Steel of 21, Norman Road, Southsea.

1437. STEELE, William Rufus; B: Brighton; E: Hove; Pte. G 7185; W: 9.9.16; Millencourt Com. Cem. Ext. Somme; Age 33; Son of Mr. R.Steele of 75, Park Crescent Road, Brighton; Husband of Mrs.M.Steele of 10, Rose Court, Daventry, Northants.*

1438. STEER, Frank; B: Hove; E: Southwark; Pte. G 4863; K: 25.9.15; Loos Mem. Pas-de-Calais.

1439. STEMP, Frederick Albert; B: Redhill; E: Arundel, Sussex; L/Cpl. L 8472; K: 30.6.16; Arras Mem. Pas-de-Calais; Age 32; Son of George and Charity Stemp of Jordans Cottage, Nutbourne, Sussex.

1440. STEMP, Jesse; B: Wisborough Green, Sussex; E: Petworth, Sussex; Pte. L 10113; K: 9.5.15; Le Touret Mem. Pas-de-Calais.

1441. STENNING, William; B: Hove; E: Brighton; Pte. G 5482; K: 9.10.15; Loos Mem. Pas-de-Calais; Age 18; Son of James Henry and Mary Ann Stenning of 9, Normanton Street, Brighton.

1442. STERNELL, Edwin James; B: Brighton; E: Brighton; Pte. S 1876; K: 25.9.15; St.Mary's A.D.S. Cem. Pas-de-Calais; also commemorated under the name STUNNELL at Loos Mem. Pas-de-Calais.*

1443. STEVENS, Edward; B: Kensington; E: Fulham; Pte. G 14825; W: 30.3.18; Haringhe (Bandeghem) Mil. Cem. (Bel.).

1444. STEVENS, Ernest William; B: Tarring, Sussex; E: Worthing; Pte. G 1249; W: 10.10.15; Bethune Town Cem. Pas-de-Calais; Age 20; Son of George Ernest and Annie Stevens of 23, Becket Road, Worthing.

1445. STEVENS, Frederick; B: Brighton; E: Brighton; Pte. L 10791; K: 23.11.17; Tyne Cot Mem. (Bel.).

1446. STEVENS, Frederick Thomas; B: Eastbourne; E: Eastbourne; Pte. G 1408; W: 13.10.15; Vermelles Brit. Cem. Pas-de-Calais.

1447. STEVENS, George Edward; B: Lambeth; E: Southwark; L/Cpl. G 5493; K: 20.8.16; Thiepval Mem. Somme.

1448. STEVENS, Harold; B: Southwick, Sussex; E: Hove; Pte. G 1164; W: 31.3.18; Haringhe (Bandeghem) Mil. Cem. (Bel.); Age 20; Son of Mr. and Mrs.G.W.Stevens of 4, White Rock Place, Southwick.

1449. STEVENS, Herbert Leslie; B: Plumpton, Sussex; E: Hurstpierpoint, Sussex; Cpl. L 8159; K: 30.10.14; Ypres (Menin Gate) Mem. (Bel.); Age 27; Brother of Miss E.K.Stevens of 134, Church Road, Burgess Hill, Sussex.*

1450. STEVENSON, Ernest Edgar; B: Danehill, Sussex; E: Haywards Heath, Sussex; L/Cpl. SD 3829; K: 9.9.16; Thiepval Mem. Somme.

1451. STILL, Thomas; B: Lindfield, Sussex; E: Hurstpierpoint, Sussex; Pte. L 10035; K: 14.9.14; La Ferte-sous-Jouarre Mem. Seine-et-Marne; Age 19; Son of Mr. and Mrs.H.Still.

1452. STOFFELL, Charles Ernest; B: Walworth; E: London; Pte. L 9719; K: 14.9.14; La Ferte-sous-Jouarre Mem. Seine-et-Marne.

1453. STOKES, William Robert; B: Poplar; E: Canning Town; Pte. G 1203; W: 16.8.16; Puchevillers Brit. Cem. Somme; Age 21; Son of John Thomas and Sarah Jane Stokes of Poplar, London.

1454. STONE, Alfred Lovell; B: Haywards Heath, Sussex; E: Haywards Heath; Pte. G 1482; K: 25.1.15; Le Touret Mem. Pas-de-Calais; Age 20; Son of Richard and Lucy Stone of 7, Gower Road, Haywards Heath.*

1455. STONE, D'Arcy Valentine Seymour; B: – ; E: Kingston-on-Thames; Pte. G 21248; K: 10.7.17; Ramscapelle Road Mil. Cem. (Bel.); Age 29; Husband of Mrs.E.A. Stone of Bramley Road, Snodland, Kent.*

1456. STONE, Percy; B: Rusper, Sussex; E: Horsham, Sussex; Pte. G 879; K: 22.11.17; Tyne Cot Mem. (Bel.); Age 23; Son of John and Olive Stone of Orlton's Cottage, Rusper.

1457. STONEHAM, James; B: Eastbourne; E: Eastbourne; Pte. S 2194; K: 9.5.15; Le Touret Mem. Pas-de-Calais; Age 31; Son of James and Mary Stoneham; Husband of Ellen Stoneham.

1458. STONER, Charles Henry; B: Eastbourne; E: Petworth, Sussex; Pte. G 3812; K: 27.9.16; Thiepval Mem. Somme; Age 21; Son of William and Eliza Stoner of Shepherds Lodge, Petworth Park, Petworth, Sussex.

1459. STONESTREET, Stanley; B: Heathfield, Sussex; E: Eastbourne; Pte. G 1418; K: 9.5.15; Le Touret Mem. Pas-de-Calais.

1460. STRANGE, Arthur; B: Portslade, Sussex; E: Brighton; Pte. L 10180; K: 9.5.15; Le Touret Mem. Pas-de-Calais.

1461. STRANGE, John; B: Portslade, Sussex; E: Brighton; Pte. L 10166; K: 28.9.16; Thiepval Mem, Somme.

1462. STRATFORD, Albert; B: Dublin; E: Hastings; Pte. L 10536; K: 25.9.15; Dud Corner Cem. Pas-de-Calais.

1463 STRATFORD, Arthur Reginald; B: Paddington; E: Tunbridge Wells; Pte. G 6129; W at Home: 16.10.18; Bristol (Arno's Vale) Cem. (U.K.).

1464. STREDWICK, Laurence James; B: Hastings; E: Mill Hill; Cpl. G 4944; K: 15.11.17; Tyne Cot Mem. (Bel.); Age 21; Son of George and Elizabeth Stredwick of 164, The Broadway, West Hendon, Middlesex.

1465. STREETER, Alfred; B: Brighton; E: Brighton; Pte. L 10183; K: 25.9.15; Loos Mem. Pas-de-Calais.

1466. STROUD, Albert; B: Thorpe St.Andrews; E: Lewisham; L.Cpl. G 5839; K: 10.1.18; Artillery Wood Cem. (Bel.); Age 20; Son of Albert George and Ellen Sarah Stroud of 6, Mendfield Street, Faversham, Kent.

-- STUNNELL, Edwin James – see STERNELL (1442).

1467. STURT, Frederick James; B: Bognor Regis, Sussex; E: Arundel, Sussex; Sgt. L 8164; W: 1.7.16; Bethune Town Cem. Pas-de-Calais; Age 30; Son of Frederick and Elizabeth Sturt of Tarrant Street, Arundel.

1468. STYLES, Arthur Henry; B: Battle, Sussex; E: Eastbourne; Pte. G 3843; K: 9.5.15; Le Touret Mem. Pas-de-Calais.

1469. SUGGITT, James Joseph; B: Hastings; E: Kingston-on-Thames; Pte. G 4897; K: 17.8.16; Thiepval Mem. Pas-de-Calais.

1470. SULLIVAN, Augustus; B: Lambeth; E: St.Paul's Churchyard, London; Pte. G 4640; K: 19.8.16; Delville Wood Cem. Somme.

1471. SUMNER, James; B: Sheldhurst; E: Tunbridge Wells; Pte. G 1305; K: 12.2.15; Le Touret Mem. Pas-de-Calais.

1472. SUNDERLAND, Geoffrey; Capt. K: 24.9.18; Berthaucourt Com. Cem. Aisne; Age 29; Son of John William and Agnes Henrietta Sunderland; Husband of Grace Lilian Sunderland of Amblets Cottage, Chithurst, Hampshire.

1473. SUTTON, John Wisdom Paige; B: St.Leonards-on-Sea; E: Hastings; Pte. G 1528; K: 9.5.15; Le Touret Mem. Pas-de-Calais; Age 20; Son of John and Phoebe Sutton of 43, Alma Terrace, Silverhill, St.Leonards-on-Sea, Sussex.

1474. SUTTON, Sidney; B: Little Cressingham; E: Norwich; Pte. G 11919; W: 30.9.16; Dernancourt Com. Cem. Ext. Somme.

1475. SWAIN, Ernest; B: Hastings; E: Hastings; Pte. G 9096; K: 17.8.16; Thiepval Mem. Pas-de-Calais.

1476. SWAINE, Thomas; B: Rye; E: Chichester; Pte. L 6991; K: 13.9.14; La Ferte-sous-Jouarre Mem. Seine-et-Marne.

1477. SWANNELL, Charles; B: London; E: Brighton; Pte. GS 439; W: 27.9.15; Noeux-le-Mines Com. Cem. Pas-de-Calais; Husband of Mrs.M.I.A.Ford, formerly, Swannell, of 3, Prospect Place, Burgess Hill, Sussex.

1478. SWIFT, George; B: Eastbourne; E: Eastbourne; Pte. S 2049; K: 17.8.16; Thiepval Mem. Somme.*

1479. SYGROVE, Charles William; B: Eastbourne; E: Eastbourne; Pte. L 7311; K: 14.9.14; Vendresse Brit. Cem. Aisne; Age 42 Son of Charles William Sygrove.

T

1480. TAPLIN, Leonard; B: Oving, Sussex; E: Chichester; Pte. G 5; K: 1.6.16; Maroc Brit. Cem. Nord.

1481. TAPNER, Arthur; B: Birdham, Sussex; E: Chichester; Pte. G 1701; W: 21.10.18; M.M.; Vadencourt Brit. Cem. Aisne; Age 22; Son of Thomas and Mary Ann Tapner of Birdham.

1482. TARLING, William; B: North Weald; E: Chichester; Pte. L 8451; K: 7.10.14; Vendresse Brit. Cem. Aisne; Age 27; Son of Frederick Hugh and Eliza Tarling.

1483. TASKER, Harry; B: Brighton; E: Brighton; Pte. G 7041; K: 23.10.18; Vis-en-Artois Mem., Haucourt, Pas-de-Calais.

1484. TAYLOR, Albert Frederick Randall; B: Woodhampton; E: Banstead; Pte. G 16458; K: 24.9.18; Tyne Cot Mem. (Bel.); Age 25; Son of Thomas G. Taylor of "Winkworth", High Street, Banstead, Surrey.*

1485. TAYLOR, Archibald; B: Kentish Town; E: London; Sgt. L 7919; K: 29.1.15; Le Touret Mem. Pas-de-Calais; Age 28; Son of Frederick and Gertrude Sarah Taylor of 22, Lark Avenue, Penwortham, Lancashire,

1486. TAYLOR, Ewart John; B: – ; E: – ; Pte. G 12651; K: 20.8.16; Thiepval Mem. Somme; Age 27; Son of Alfred and Mary E.Taylor of 8, High Road, East Finchley, London.

1487. TAYLOR, Frank Edwin; B: Westminster; E: Kilburn; Pte. G 5572; K: 17.5.16; St.Patrick's Cem. Pas-de-Calais.

1488. TAYLOR, James Harper; B: Caistor; E: Chichester; Pts. G 1132; W: 24.7.16; Puchevillers Brit. Cem. Somme; Husband of Lily C.Taylor of 120, Bognor Road, Chichester.

1489. TAYLOR, Walter Richard; B: Mile End; E: St.Paul's Churchyard, London; Pte. G. 5371; K: 13.10.15; Loos Mem. Pas-de-Calais.

1490. TEDBURY, Edwin Alfred; B: Marylebone; E: London; Pte. GS 808; K: 9.5.15; Le Touret Mem. Pas-de-Calais.

1491. TEE, Reginald Arthur; B: Worthing; E: Worthing; Pte. G 1254; K: 25.9.15; Loos Mem. Pas-de-Calais.

1492. TENNENT, Harry; B: Brighton; E: Brighton; Pte. S 215; K: 31.10.14; Ypres (Menin Gate) Mem. (Bel.); Age 32; Son of Mary Georgina Tennant of 11, Picton Street, Brighton; Husband of Mrs. Flora Lusted, formerly Tennant, of 7, Coronation Street, Brighton.

1493. TERRY, John; B: Eastbourne; E: Eastbourne; Pte. SD 4243; K: 10.7.17; Ramscapelle Road Mil. Cem. (Bel.).

1494. TERRY, Josiah; B: – ; E: Haywards Heath, Sussex; Pte. G 1570; K: 25.9.15; Loos Mem. Pas-de-Calais.

1495. TERRY, Robert Joseph Atkinson; Lt.Col. M.V.O., D.S.O.; W: 1.10.15; Noeux-les-Mines Com. Cem. Pas-de-Calais; Son of R. and Rose Terry of Greysmeade, Eastbourne; Husband of Kathleen A.Terry of "Kingslyn", Upper Norwood, London; Brigade Major; Died of wounds received 1.3.15;

Prior to the outbreak of war he was Provost Marshall at Aldershot, Commandant of the Military Mounted and Foot Police, and Officer in Charge of Records.*

1496. TESTER, John; B: Hadlow; E: Tunbridge Wells; L/Cpl. L 8513; M.M.; K: 20.8.16; Thiepval Mem. Somme.

1497. THEOBALD, Harry; B: Homerton; E: Dalston; Pte. L 6635; K: 4.10.14; La Ferte-sous-Jouarre Mem. Seine-et-Marne.

-- THOMAS, Albert Edward – see WATTS, Albert Edward (1600).

1498. THOMAS, Bernard Ernest; B: Westfield, Sussex; E: Hastings; Pte. L 7645; K: 25.9.15; Loos Mem. Pas-de-Calais.

1499. THOMPSON, Alec Charles; B: Lewes; E: Lewes; Pte. G 3339; K: 14.11.17; Tyne Cot Mem. (Bel.); Age 25; Son of Albert and Eliza Thompson of 42, Langton Avenue, East Ham, London.

1500. THOMPSON, Edward; B: Seaham; E: Seaham; L/Cpl. G 5995; K: 9.9.16; Thiepval Mem. Somme; Age 32; Husband of Elizabeth Thompson of 44, Longnewton Street, Dawdon, County Durham.

1501. THOMPSON, Percy; B: Horsham, Sussex; E: Horsham; Pte. S 424; K: 26.1.15; Le Touret Mem. Pas-de-Calais; Age 30; Son of Mr. and Mrs.Henry Thompson of Milton Road, Horsham.

1502. THOMPSON, Tom; B: – ; E: Stratford; Pte. G 9874; K: 14.11.17; Tyne Cot Mem. (Bel.) Age 26; Son of Mr.T.J. and Mrs.M.E.Thompson of 42, Langton Avenue, East Ham, London.

1503. THORNTON, Walter; B: London; E: London; L/Sgt. L 5889; W: 23.7.16; Contalmaison Chateau Cem. Somme; Age 32; Husband of Alice Emily Thornton of 57, Lonsdale Avenue, Hatherley Gardens, East Ham, London.

1504. THORPE, William Henry; B: Wadhurst, Sussex; E: Tunbridge Wells; Pte. L 10313; K: 9.5.15; Le Touret Mem. Pas-de-Calais.

1505. TIBBIT, Reginald Edward; B: – ; E: Hove; Pte. G 6832; W: 10.9.16; Millencourt Com. Cem. Ext. Somme; Age 19; Son of Edward John and Florence Tibbit of 19, Shaftesbury Road, Brighton.*

1506. TICEHURST, Alfred; B: Eastbourne; E: Eastbourne; Pte. G 1439; K: 9.5.15; Le Touret Mem. Pas-de-Calais; Age 19; Son of Richard and Mary Ticehurst of Church Farm, Litlington, Sussex.

1507. TICEHURST, Richard; B: Chichester; E: Southampton; Pte. G 5218; W: 13.10.15; Chocques Mil. Cem. Pas-de-Calais.

1508. TICKNER, James Frederick; B: Chobham; E: Chichester; Sgt. L 5471; W: 11.3.17; Barlin Com. Cem. Pas-de-Calais; Age 36; Son of William and Ellen Tickner of Eastbourne; Husband of Kate Maud Beatrice Tickner of 15, St.Anthony's Avenue, Eastbourne; Long Service and Good Conduct Medal; Served in the South Africa campaign.

1509. TILLER, James; B: Lambeth; E: London; Pte. L 6654; K: 21.8.15; Bethune Town Cem. Pas-de-Calais; Accidentally killed at bombing training.

1510. TILTMAN, Edward; B: Rye, Sussex; E: Hastings; Pte. G 5528; K: 24.9.18; Berthaucourt Com. Cem. Aisne; Age 21; Son of Mr. and Mrs.W.Tiltman of 3, West Cliff, Rye, Sussex.

1511. TIPPETT, Henry; B: St.Pancras, E. Bexhill on Sea; L/Cpl. G 1712; W: 29.1.15; Chocques Mil. Cem. Pas-de-Calais; Age 26; Son of John and Ellen Tippett.

1512. TITHERIDGE, Alfred James; B: Southwick, Sussex; E: Brighton; L/Cpl. L 9855; K: 25.9.15; Loos Mem. Pas-de-Calais; Age 22; Son of Albert James and Catherine Titheridge of 3, Cyprus Cottages, Southwick.

1513. TOBUTT, Alfred; B: Chiswick; E: London; Pte. G 5102; K: 12.5.16; St.Patrick's Cem. Pas-de-Calais.

1514. TODMAN, Henry William; B: Graffham, Sussex; E: Tillington, Sussex; Pte. L 7465; K: 9.5.15; Le Touret Mem. Pas-de-Calais.

1515. TOLLEY, Percival; B: Bermondsey; E: Rotherhithe; Pte. G 10859; W: 20.9.18; Brie Brit. Cem. Somme.

1516. TOMLIN, George; B: Chichester; E: Chichester; Pte. L 5591; K: 14.9.14; Terlincthun Brit. Cem. Pas-de-Calais.

1517. TOMPSETT, Alfred Edwin; B: Wadhurst, Sussex; E: Wadhurst; Pte. L 10259; K: 9.5.15; Le Touret Mem. Pas-de-Calais; Age 21; Son of Edward Tompsett of Mount Pleasant, Wadhurst.

1518. TOMPSETT, William; B: Lewes; E: Lewes; Pte. L 6847; K: 30.10.14; Tyne Cot Cem. (Bel.); Age 30; Son of George and Mary Tompsett of 11, Marshall's Row, Brighton; Husband of May McCutcheon Tompsett of Glen Road, Comber, County Down, Northern Ireland.

1519. TOMSETT, Thomas William; B: Brighton; E: Brighton; Pte. L 8259; K: 9.5.15; Le Touret Mem. Pas-de-Calais.

1520. TOOGOOD, Charles Frank; B: Hastings; E: Hastings; Pte. L 10708; K: 13.10.15; Loos Mem. Pas-de-Calais; Age 18; Son of Mr.F.N. and Mrs.M.J.Toogood of 44, Cornfield Terrace, St.Leonards-on-Sea, Sussex.*

1521. TOOLE, William; B: Marylebone; E: Cockspur Street, London; Pte. G 4494; K: 25.9.15; Loos Mem. Pas-de-Calais.

1522. TOON, Charles; B: Leicester; E: Northampton; Pte. TF 202408; K: 24.9.18; Vis-en-Artois Mem., Haucourt, Pas-de-Calais.

1523. TOPP, George William; B: Windsor; E: London; Pte. L 7875; K: 13.1.15; Le Touret Mem. Pas-de-Calais.

1524. TORRANCE, William Thomas; B: Hastings; E: Hastings; Sgt. L 9740; K: 8.9.16; Thiepval Mem. Somme.

1525. TOTTMAN, John; B: – ; E: Canterbury; Cpl. G 17754; W: 10.9.16; Flatiron Copse Cem. Somme.*

1526. TOWN, Frederick; B: East Sutton; E: Marylebone; Pte. G 3945; K: 25.9.15; Loos Mem. Pas-de-Calais.

1527. TOWNSEND, Frederick Edward; B: Islington; E: Holloway; L/Sgt. G 4785; K: 24.9.18; Berthaucourt Com. Cem. Aisne.

1528. TOWNSEND, William; B: Harrow; E: London; Pte. L 7745; K: 14.9.14; Grand-Seraucourt Brit. Cem. Aisne.

1529. TOYE, Hubert Clarence; 2nd Lt; W: 15.10.15; Lapugnoy Mil. Cem. Pas-de-Calais.

1530. TREE, Henry George; B: Ashford; E: Chichester; Pte. L 10026; K: 14.9.14; La Ferte-sous-Jouarre Mem. Seine-et-Marne; Age 19; Son of Mr. George Tree.

1531. TREHERNE, Henry; B: St.Giles, Middx.; E: Southwark; Pte. G 4864; K: 25.9.15; Loos Mem. Pas-de-Calais.

1532. TRIBE, Frederick; B: Brighton; E: Hove; Cpl. G 7383; K: 24.9.18; Vis-en-Artois Mem., Haucourt, Pas-de-Calais; Age 23; Son of W. and E, Tribe; Husband of Lily Maud Tribe of 10, Hercules Street, Mile End, Portsmouth.

1533. TRIMMER, Frederick; B: Ticehurst, Sussex; E: Rye, Sussex; Pte. TF 202264; K: 10.7.17; Ramscapelle Road Mil. Cem. (Bel.).

1534. TRINGHAM, Arthur Charles; B: Tooting; E: Kingston-on-Thames; Pte. L 10085; W at Home: 25.5.15; Tooting (St.Nicholas) Churchyard (U.K.); Age 21; Son of Francis Charles Tringham and Elenor Jane Coppard, formerly Tringham, of 65, Irevelyan Road, Tooting, London.

1535. TROW, Henry Charles; B: Manor Park; E: Ilford; Pte. G 14579; K: 27.9.16; Thiepval Mem. Somme.

1536. TRUSSLER, Alvah; B: Fernhurst; E: Chichester; Pte. L 7446; K: 14.9.14; La Ferte-sous-Jouarre Mem. Seine-et-Marne; Age 36; Son of John Trussler of Elm Grove, Easebourne, Sussex; His brother was also killed.

1537. TRUSSLER, Ferdinand; B: Bexley Hill; E: Chichester; Pte. G 4911; K: 17.8.16; Thiepval Mem. Somme.

1538. TUBB, Claude George; B: Eastbourne; E: London; Pte. G 4445; K: 29.8.15; Vermelles Brit. Cem. Pas-de-Calais; Age 21; Son of George and Mrs.Tubb of 29, Lumley Buildings, Sloan Square, London.

1539. TUCKNOTT, Frank; B: Ridgewood; E: Lewes; Cpl. G 1675; K: 17.8.16; Caterpillar Valley Cem. Somme.

1540. TUCKWELL, Archibald; B: Clerkenwell; E: Edmonton; Pte. G 21049; W: 13.7.17; Coxyde Mil. Cem. (Bel.); Age 21; Son of Mr. and Mrs.Tuckwell of 6, Ascot Road, Upper Edmonton, London.

1541. TUGNUTT, John; B: Brighton; E: Brighton; Pte. L 5866; W: 15.11.14; Lille Southern Cem. Nord; Age 33; Son of John and Jane Tugnutt of Brighton; Husband of Florence Tugnutt of 12, Sandown Road, Brighton.

1542. TUPPER, William George; B: Lavant, Sussex; E: Chichester; L/Cpl. G 4487; K: 30.6.16; Arras Mem. Pas-de-Calais; Age 23; Son of William and Elizabeth Tupper of Mid Lavant.

1543. TURNER, Charles; B: Lambeth; E: London; Pte. L 7725; K: 8.10.14; La Ferte-sous-Jouarre Mem. Seine-et-Marne; Age 29; Husband of Mary Jane Lock, formerly Turner, of 88, Carter Street, Walworth Road, London.

1544. TURNER, Charles Henry; B: Herstmonceux, Sussex; E: Eastbourne; Pte. G 1446; K: 25.9.15; Loos Mem. Pas-de-Calais; Age 21; Son of Clement and Sarah Turner of Acacia Cottage, Horham, Sussex.*

1545. TURNER, Ernest; B: Petersfield; E: Chichester; Pte. G 9186; W: 23.8.16; Puchevillers Brit. Cem. Somme; Age 20; Son of Albert and Emily Turner of The Hornet, Chichester.

1546. TURNER, George; B: Brighton; E: Brighton; Cpl. L 7343; K: 9.5.15; Caberet-Rouge Brit. Cem. Pas-de-Calais.

1547. TURNER, Henry John; B: Staple; E: Shorncliffe; Pte. L 8015; K: 25.9.15; Loos Mem. Pas-de-Calais.

1548. TURTON, Stanley Arthur; B: London; E: Eastbourne; Pte. G 19584; K: 19.8.18; Cambrin Mil. Cem. Pas-de-Calais; Age 36; Son of Arthur and Maria Turton of Eastbourne; Husband of Grace Victoria Lomas Turton of 19, Mayfield Place, Eastbourne.

1549. TWEEN, Ernest; B: Chelmsford; E: Chichester; Pte. L 10135; K: 14.9.14; La Ferte-sous-Jouarre Mem. Seine-et-Marne; Age 19; Son of Harry Tween of 203, Whitehorse Road, West Croydon.

1550. TWYMAN, John James; B: St.Mary's, Kent: E: Chatham; L/Cpl. L 7968; K: 30.10.14; Ypres (Menin Gate) Mem. (Bel.); Age 32; Son of James Twyman of 46, Northgate Street, Canterbury; Husband of Mrs.F.H.Webb, formerly Twyman, of 4, Baron Row, Lower Mitcham, Surrey.

U

1551. UMPLEBY, Edward John; B: Clayton, Sussex; E: Haywards Heath, Sussex; Pte. G 1274; K: 9.5.15; Le Touret Mem. Pas-de-Calais; Age 20; Son of Thomas and Emma Umpleby of 24, Western Road, Haywards Heath.

1552. UNICOMBE, William Ernest; B: Beckley, Sussex; E: Bexhill-on-Sea; Pte. G 5054; W: 12.2.16; St.Sever Cem. Rouen, Seine-Maritime; Age 20; Grandson of Mrs.E.Unicombe of 24, Sackville Road, Bexhill-on-Sea.

1553. URRY, John Thomas; B: Lewes; E: Lewes; Pte. G 1678; K: 20.8.16; Thiepval Mem. Somme.

1554 UWINS, Thomas; B: Fishergate, Sussex; E: Brighton; Pte. L 9573; W at Home: 29.9.14; Southwick (St.Michael) Churchyard (U.K.).

V

1555. VAUGHAN, John Muir; 2nd Lt; W: 18.9.18; Brie Brit. Cem. Somme; Age 19; Son of Major-General R.E.Vaughan, C.B., and Mrs.Amy Mountjoy Vaughan of The Hollies, West Tarring, Sussex.

1556. VENABLES, Herbert George; B: Wandsworth; E: West Ham; Pte. G 14829; W: 15.11.17; Dozinghem Mil. Cem. (Bel.); Age 20; Son of Thomas and Selina Venables of 14, Merton Road, Wandsworth, London.

1557. VENESS, John; B: Hastings; E: Aberavon; Pte. G 4571; K: 9.5.15; Le Touret Mem. Pas-de-Calais; Age 22; Son of Henry and Sarah Ann Veness of 1, Providence Row, Hastings.

1558. VENUS, Leonard; B: Custom House, Essex; E: Canning Town; Cpl. G 1201; K: 9.5.15; Le Touret Mem. Pas-de-Calais; Age 20; Son of Mrs.Emily Venus of 19, Chalk Road, Plaistow, London.

1559. VERRALL, Christopher Francis; Lt; K: 22.12.14; Le Touret Mem. Pas-de-Calais;.

1560. VINE, William; B: Eastbourne; E: Eastbourne; Pte. L 6171; K: 9.5.15; Le Touret Mem. Pas-de-Calais.

1561. VINCENT, Oswald Owen; B: Eastbourne; E: Eastbourne; Pte. L 10096; W at Home: 23.10.14; Netley Mil. Cem. (U.K.); Age 18; Son of Mrs.Maud E.Moore of 70, Grove Road, Eastbourne. *

1562. VIRGOE, S.; B: – ; E: – ; – 200373; K: 8.7.17; Ramscapelle Road Mil. Cem. (Bel.).*

1563. VINTER, Stephen; B: Wavering; E: Boston; Pte. G 15319; W: 23.3.18; Dozinghem Mil. Cem. (Bel.).

1564. VIVASH, Harry Austin; B: Brixton; E: Chichester; Pte. L 8749; K: 4.11.14; Ypres (Menin Gate) Mem. (Bel.); Age 25; Son of Edwin and Ellen Vivash; Husband of Ellen Farrell, formerly Vivash, of 9, Abbey Street, St.Vaas, County Kildare, Ireland.

W

1565. WAIN, Alfred; B: Lee; E: Woolwich; Pte. L 5984; K: 9.5.15; Le Touret Mem. Pas-de-Calais; Age 34; Husband of Mrs.M.Wain of 20, Portland Road, Mottingham, London.

1566. WAINWRIGHT, Geoffrey Lennox; 2nd Lt; K: 25.9.15 at Loos; Dud Corner Cem. Pas-de-Calais; Age 21; Son of Lennox and Edith Wainwright of 11, Upper Wimpole Street, London; Native of Folkestone, Kent.

1567. WAITE, Edwin Charles; B: Catsfield, Sussex; E: Hastings; Pte. L 8495; K: 13.11.14; Ypres (Menin Gate) Mem. (Bel.); Age 27; Son of James and Charlotte Waite of 14, North Road, Sidley, Bexhill-on-Sea.

1568. WAKEHAM, Alfred; B: Amberley, Sussex; E: Worthing; Pte. G 1277; K: 25.9.15; Loos Mem. Pas-de-Calais; Age 21; Brother of Ernest T.Wakeham of 5, St.Luke's Road, Brighton.

1569. WAKEHAM, Ernest; B: Hove; E: Brighton; Pte. L 6028; K: 9.5.15; Le Touret Mem. Pas-de-Calais; Age 33; Son of Thomas Wakeham of 92, Shirley Street, Hove; Husband of Caroline Charlotte Wakeham of 12, Mortimer Road, Hove.

1570. WAKELING, Frederick; B: Peckham; E: Camberwell; Pte. G 17503; K: 27.9.16; Thiepval Mem. Somme; Age 19; Son of William Valentine and Mary Ann Wakeling of 23, Leyton Square, Leyton, London; Formerly 3rd/1st West Kent Yeomanry.

1571. WALDER, Arthur; B: East Grinstead, Sussex; E: Horsham, Sussex; Pte. L 10388; K: 8.2.15; Le Touret Mem. Pas-de-Calais; Age 20; Son of Charles Walder of Hampton House, High Street, East Grinstead.

1572. WALDER, Charles; B: Rogate, Sussex; E: Chichester; Pte. G 5192; K: 25.9.15; Loos Mem. Pas-de-Calais.

1573. WALES, Cecil; B: Roffey, Sussex; E: Horsham, Sussex; Sgt. L 9345; K: 9.5.15; Le Touret Mem. Pas-de-Calais; Age 22; Son of Henry and Mary Wales of 31, Swindon Road, Horsham.

1574. WALKER, Charles Joseph; B: Malden; E: London; Pte. L 6828; W: 22.11.14; Le Touquet-Paris Plage Com. Cem. Pas-de-Calais; Age 39; Son of Charles and Harriet Walker of Westway, Upper Caterham, Surrey; Husband of Mrs.Walker of 6, Barden Cottages, Alexandra Road, Wallingham, Surrey.

1575. WALKER, James; B: Chichester; E: Chichester; Pte. L 8045; W: 15.9.14; St.Nazaire (Toutes-Aides) Cem. Loire-Atlantique.

1576. WALKER, William Edward; B: Foxhole; E: Chichester; Pte. L 10122; K: 9.5.15; Le Touret Mem. Pas-de-Calais.

1577. WALLER, Edwin; B: Horsham, Sussex; E: Horsham; Pte. S 1340; W: 28.9.15; Lillers Com. Cem. Pas-de-Calais; Age 20; Son of Mark and Fanny Waller of Ivy Cottage, Rudgwick, Sussex.*

1578. WALLIS, Frederick Albert; B: – ; E: Maidstone; Pte. G 17504; K: 9.9.16; Caterpillar Valley Cem. Somme; Age 25; Son of John and Mary Wallis of Medway Villas, Maidstone Road, Paddock Wood, Kent.

1579. WALTER, Edward; B: Tunbridge Wells; E: Chichester; Pte. L 9070; K: 14.9.14; La Ferte-sous-Jouarre Mem. Seine-et-Marne; Age 22; Son of Thomas and Emma Walter of 2, Market Road, Tunbridge Wells.

1580. WALTON, William Keep; B: Edmonton; E: Eastbourne; Pte. G 1448; D: 17.1.15; Ste.Marie Cem., Le Havre, Seine-Maritime; Age 19; Son of Albert and Sarah Walton of 17, Station Parade, Eastbourne.

1581. WANSTALL, Percy; B: Hastings; E: Chichester; Pte. L 7399; K: 8.11.14; Ypres (Menin Gate) Mem. (Bel.); Age 30; Son of E.S. and G.Wanstall.

1582. WARD, Albert Victor; B: North Wooton; E: Norwich; Pte. G 11964; W: 18.9.18; Brie Brit. Cem. Somme.*

1583. WARD, George Ernest; Capt; K: 25.9.15; Dud Corner Cem. Pas-de-Calais; Age 31; Brother of Mrs.A.O'Donovan of 152a, Cromwell Road, Kensington, London.

1584. WARD, John Benjamin; B: Shoreditch; E: London; Pte. L 7766; K: 30.10.14; Ypres (Menin Gate) Mem. (Bel.).

1585. WARD, Thomas Henry; B: Homerton; E: Dalston; Pte. L 6633; W: 8.10.14; Villers-en-Prayeres Com. Cem. Aisne; Age 31; Son of George Francis and Elizabeth Emma Ward.*

1586. WARD, William; B: Irthlingborough; E: Northampton; Pte. TF 202766; K: 18.9.18; Vis-en-Artois Mem., Haucourt, Pas-de-Calais.

1587. WAREHAM, John Harold Cortis; B: Portslade, Sussex; E: Brighton; Pte. S 2145; K: 9.5.15; Le Touret Mem. Pas-de-Calais; Age 18; Son of John and May Louise Wareham of 56, Trafalgar Road, Southern Cross, Portslade.*

1588. WARNER, Sydney; B: Eastbourne; E: Eastbourne; Pte. G 16001; K: 13.5.18; Cambrin Mil. Cem. Pas-de-Calais.*

1589. WARTON, Henry Proucy; B: Newick, Sussex; E: Lewes; Pte. GS 880; W: 1.2.15; Boulogne Eastern Cem. Pas-de-Calais; Age 40; Son of Mary Ann Martin of Gold Bridge Farm, Newick.*

1590. WATERMAN, John Edward; B: Balham; E: Wood Green; Pte. G 4668; K: 9.5.15; Le Touret Mem. Pas-de-Calais; Age 38; Son of George Waterman of 42, Hearnville Road, Balham, London; Husband of Edith May Waterman of 13, Warlborough Road, Wood Green, London.

1591. WATERS, Allen George; B: Hinderclay; E: Rickinghall; Pte. G 11318; W: 18.9.18; Brie Brit. Cem. Somme.*

1592. WATERS, Henry Arthur; B: Erith; E: Chichester; Pte. L 10003; K: 12.11.17; Tyne Cot Mem. (Bel.).

1593. WATERS, Montague Christopher; B: Brighton; E: Fulham; Pte. GS 121; K: 9.5.15; Rue- Petillon Mil. Cem. Pas-de-Calais.

1594. WATLING, George Victor; B: Lynn; E: Norwich; Pte. G 11965; W: 4.11.18; St.Souplet Brit. Cem. Nord; Age 21; Son of Frederick and Agnes Watling of 3, Hospital Walk, King's Lynn, Norfolk.

1595. WATSON, Albert; B: St.Giles, Middx.; E: Southwark; L/Cpl. G 4959; W: 25.3.16; Bethune Town Cem. Pas-de-Calais; Age 24; Son of Mr. and Mrs.W.Watson.

1596. WATSON, Albert Edward; B: Brighton; E: Chichester; Pte. L 10594; K: 9.5.15; Le Touret Mem. Pas-de-Calais; Age 17 Son of Mr.H. and Mrs.C.Watson of 1682, Northdown Road, Margate, Kent.

1597. WATSON, Frederick George; B: Leytonstone; E: West Ham, London; Pte. G 14832; W: 8.7.17; Coxyde Mil. Cem. (Bel.); Age 21; Son of Frederick and Sarah Jane Watson of 94, Carlyle Road, Manor Park, London.

1598. WATSON, Henry; B: Buxted, Sussex; E: Lewes; Pte. G 1491; K: 10.7.17; Ramscapelle Road Mil. Cem. (Bel.).

1599. WATSON, Lancelot Leopold; B: Buxted, Sussex; E: Uckfield, Sussex; Sgt. L 9744; W at Home: 6.9.16; High Hurstwood (Holy Trinity) Churchyard , Sussex (U.K.); Age 23; Son of Lambert Watson of Carrot's Farm, High Hurstwood, Sussex.

1600. WATTS, Albert Edward; B: Bath; E: Brighton; Pte. GS 9; W: At Home 2.3.15; Manchester Southern Cem. (U.K.); Husband of Mabel K.Lewis, formerly Watts, of 62, Lincoln Street, Brighton; Served under the alias surname, THOMAS; Served in the South Africa Campaign.

1601. WATTS, Henry; B: Southwark; E: Woodford; Pte. SD 5529; W: 21.11.17; Abbeville Com. Cem. Ext. Somme; Age 26; Son of Edward and Elizabeth Watts of South Woodford, Essex; Husband of Mrs.M.A.Watts of 53, Shernhall Street, Walthamstow, London.

1602. WATTS, Thomas Samuel; B: Walworth; E: Southwark; Pte. G 5495; K: 21.11.15; Loos Mem. Pas-de-Calais.

1603. WATTS, William; B: Tunbridge Wells; E: Tunbridge Wells; Pte. L 7588; K: 9.5.15; Le Touret Mem. Pas-de-Calais.

1604. WAY, Henry James; B: Shepherd's Bush; E: Brighton; Pte. S 1819; K: 25.9.15; Loos Mem. Pas-de-Calais; Age 23; Son of Mrs.Phoebe Way of 72, Coleridge Street, Hove.*

1605. WAYMARK, Bert Andrew; B: Eastbourne; E: Dover; Pte. L 7388; K: 9.5.15; Le Touret Mem. Pas-de-Calais.

1606. WEARING, Charles; B: Catford; E: Woolwich; Pte. L 7367; K: 25.9.15; Loos Mem. Pas-de-Calais; Age 36; Son of Edwin and Eliza Wearing of London; Husband of May Wearing of 5, Buttrells Estate, Barry, Cardiff; Served under the alias surname, WEBB.

1607. WEAVER, Albert Edward; B: Hastings; E: Hounslow; Pte. G 4891; K: 9.5.15; Le Touret Mem. Pas-de-Calais; Age 34; Son of Harry and Ellen Weaver; Husband of Susan Weaver of 31, Weatherstone Terrace, Southall, Middlesex.

1608. WEAVER, Jesse; B: Plumpton, Sussex; E: Eastbourne; Pte. SD 2815; W: 4.11.18; Premont Brit. Cem. Aisne; Age 36; Husband of Mrs.A.F.Weaver of 25, Springfield Road, Eastbourne.

1609. WEBB, Alfred William; B: Bristol; E: Horsham, Sussex; Pte. G 51; K: 9.5.15; Le Touret Mem. Pas-de-Calais.

1610. WEBB, Arthur Benjamin; B: Tottenham; E: Tottenham; Cpl. G 19821; D: 27.12.16; St.Sever Cem. Ext., Rouen, Seine-Maritime; Age 21; Son of Arthur William and Emily Webb of 52, Oxford Road, Banbury, Oxfordshire.

– – WEBB, Charles – see WEARING, Charles (1606).

1611. WEBB, George; B: Forton; E: Chichester; Pte. L 7729; K: 9.5.15 in action at Richebourg L'Avoué ; Le Touret Mem. Pas-de-Calais; Age 28; Son of Walter and Mary Webb of 9, Bedford Street, Gosport, Hampshire.

1612. WEBB, Samuel; B: Wimbish; E: Horsham, Sussex; Pte. G 11323; K: 8.6.18; Loos Mem. Pas-de-Calais.

1613. WEDGE, Albert Edward; B: Roorkee, India; E: Chichester; W: 25.1.15; Hazebrouck Com. Cem. Nord; Age 24; Son of Susannah Wedge of 39, Bognor Road, Chichester.

1614. WEEKES, Cecil Raymond; B: Stangate; E: Epsom; Pte. G 8408; W: 5.10.18; Etretat Churchyard, Seine-Maritime; Age 30; Son of Mrs.E.Weekes of Lower Gate, Ticehurst, Sussex.*

1615. WEEKLEY, John; B: Rottingdean, Sussex; E: Brighton; Pte. GS 809; K: 9.5.15; Le Touret Mem. Pas-de-Calais; Age 41; Son of Peter and Esther Weekley of 3, Vicarage Lane, Rottingdean.

1616. WELCH, Martin James Henry; B: Portslade, Sussex; E: Chichester; L/Cpl. L 10120; K: 9.5.15 in action ot Richebourg L'Avoué ; Le Touret Mem. Pas-de-Calais; Age 20;

1617. WELFARE, William; B: East Chiltington, Sussex; E: Lewes; Pte. G 1552; K: 13.10.15; Loos Mem. Pas-de-Calais; Son of Martin James and Nellie Welch of 7, St.Peter's Road, Portslade, Sussex.

1618. WELLARD, Arthur William; B: Chatham; E: Southwark; Pte. G 5603; W: 7.3.16; Calais Southern Cem. Pas-de-Calais.

1619. WELLEN, Reuben Frederick; B: Willesden; E: Midhurst, Sussex; L/Cpl. G 1610; K: 29.8.15; Vermelles Brit. Cem. Pas-de-Calais; Son of Mrs.E.Lindsey, formerly Wellen, of Station Road, Midhurst. *

1620. WELLER, Ernest; B: Holmwood; E: Bromley; Pte. G 11989; K: 4.11.18; Le Rejet -de-Beaulieu Com. Cem. Nord; Age 42; Son of Mark Weller and Mary Ann Gadd, formerly Weller, of Clark's Cottages, Newdigate, Dorking.

1621. WELLER, Reginald John; B: Dorchester; E: Worthing; Pte. G 1275; W: 29.1.15; Beuvry Com. Cem. Pas-de-Calais; Age 19; Son of Mrs.Ada L.Weller of Pump House, Coates, Fittleworth, Sussex.

1622. WELLS, Alfred William; B: Worthing; E: Worthing; Pte. G 1605; W: 13.8.15; Lillers Com. Cem. Pas-de-Calais; Age 23; Son of Alfred Edward Wells of 57, Newland Road, Worthing.

1623. WELLS, Archibald; B: Henfield, Sussex; E: Brighton; Pte. S 2154; K: 20.8.16; Thiepval Mem. Somme; Age 22; Son of Mrs.Ruth Wells of 14, Mount Pleasant, Henfield.

1624. WELLS, Fred; B: Tunbridge Wells; E: Tonbridge; Cpl. G 5293; K: 9.9.16; Caterpillar Valley Cem. Somme; Age 22; Son of Frederick and Arabella Mary Ann Wells of 36, Mount Sion, Tunbridge Wells.

1625. WELLS, Harry; B: Herne; E: Canterbury; Sgt. L 8088; **V.C.**; K: 25.9.15; Dud Corner Cem. Pas-de-Calais;

1626. WELLS, John George; B: Chalton; E: Lewes; Cpl. G 1676; K: 20.8.16; Thiepval Mem. Somme.

1627. WELLS, William; B: Egdean; E: Chichester; Pte. L 8041; K: 29.9.14; La Ferte-sous-Jouarre Mem. Seine-et-Marne.

1628. WERE, Leonard; B: Liverpool; E: Liverpool; Pte. G 5955; K: 30.6.16; Arras Mem. Pas-de-Calais.

1629. WEST, Alfred; B: Preston, Sussex; E: Hurstpierpoint, Sussex; Pte. L 9091; K: 4.10.14; La Ferte-sous-Jourre Mem. Seine-et-Marne.

1630. WEST, Charles Nelson; B: Haywards Heath, Sussex; E: Haywards Heath; Pte. GS 301; K: 8.9.16; Thiepval Mem. Somme; Age 33; Husband of Emily William West of 47, Newport Road, Burgess Hill, Sussex.

1631. WEST Clement Edward; B: – ; E: Hackney; Pte. G 9815; W: 15.11.17; Mendinghem Mil. Cem. (Bel.).

1632. WEST, Edward Alfred; B: Worthing; E: Worthing; Pte. G 3892; K: 22.11.17; Tyne Cot Mem. (Bel.); Age 26; Brother of Mrs.E.K.Marner of 17, Surrey Street, Worthing.

1633. WEST, Ernest Diamond; B: Arundel, Sussex; E: Arundel; Pte. G 7938; K: 9.5.15 at Richebourg L'Avoue ; Le Touret Mem. Pas-de-Calais, Age 33; Son of Mrs.Martha Jean West of 2, Rowalllan Road, Fulham, London.*

1634. WEST, Frederick; B: Lambourne; E: London; Pte. G 4447; K: 9.5.15 at Richebourg L'Avoué ; Le Touret Mem. Pas-de-Calais; Age 26; Son of Frederick William and Annie Elizabeth West of Bishops Hall, Romford, Essex.

1635. WEST, Gerald William; Lt; K: 25.9.15; Loos Mem. Pas-de-Calais;

1636. WEST. Lawrence; B: Norwood; E: Horsham, Sussex; Pte. G 4949; K: 25.9.15; Dud Corner Cem. Pas-de-Calais.

1637. WEST, William Robert; B: Chalvington, Sussex; E: Eastbourne; Pte. G 13442; K: 20.4.18; Woburn Abbey Cem. Pas-de-Calais; Age 19; Son of Mrs.J.West of Selmeston Croft, Chalvington.

1638. WESTALL, Ronald Cameron; Lt; K: 12.11.14; Ypres (Menin Gate) Mem. Pas-de-Calais.

1639. WESTON, William James; B: Wood Green; E: Wood Green; Pte. G 4848; K: 25.9.15; Loos Mem. Pas-de-Calais; Age 20; Son of Mr. and Mrs.D.J.Weston of 4, Truro Road, Wood Green, London.

1640. WHEATLEY, Doctor; B: Hartfield, Sussex; E: Brighton; Pte. S 260; K: 9.5.15; Le Touret Mem. Pas-de-Calais.

1641. WHEELER, Charles Edward; B: Epping; E: Christchurch, Sussex; Pte. L 8514; W: 10.19.14; Priez Com. Cem. Aisne.

1642. WHEELER, James Frederick; B: Holborn; E: London; Pte. S 1089; K: 20.8.16; Thiepval Mem. Somme; Age 27; Son of Mrs.Sarah Wheeler of 5, Wilmington Square, Rosebery Avenue, London.*

1643. WHEELER, William Francis Herbert; B: East Dulwich; E: Southwark; Pte. G 5152; K: 20.8.16; Thiepval Mem. Pas-de-Calais.

1644. WHITE, Albert; B: Chichester; E: Chichester; Pte. G 9057; K: 6.8.16; Brewery Orchard Cem. Nord.

1645. WHITE, Arthur Albert; B: Chichester; E: Bognor Regis, Sussex; Pte. G 1218; D at Home: 28.2.17; Bersted Roman Catholic Cem., Sussex (U.K.); Age 25; Son of Thomas and Minnie White of 26, Essex Road, Bognor Regis.

1646. WHITE, Douglas George; B: Shoreham, Sussex ; E: Hove; Pte. G 1171; K: 9.5.15; Le Touret Mem. Pas-de-Calais; Age 22; Grandson of Mrs.Martha F.White of 17, Surrey Street, Shoreham. *

1647. WHITE, Frederick Arthur; B: Bow; E: Chelsea; Pte. G 4090; K: 1.5.16; Maroc Brit. Cem. Nord; Age 23; Son of Mr. and Mrs.Arthur White of Stepney, London.

1648. WHITE, George Arthur; B: Brighton; E: Chichester; Pte. L 9086; K: 6.11.14; Tyne Cot Cem. (Bel.); Age 23; Son of Mrs.Caroline E.White of 108, Islingworth Road, Brighton.*

1649. WHITE, Herbert Moss; B: Rochester; E: London; Pte. G 8816; K: 15.7.16; Thiepval Mem; Somme; Brother of Mr.J.W.White of Chalvey Road, Slough.

1650. WHITE, John Stanley; 2nd Lt; K: 18.9.18; Cerisy-Gailly Mil. Cem. Somme; Age 28; Son of J.S. and Bertha White of 4, Bierton Hill, Aylesbury, Buckinghamshire.

1651. WHITE, William James; B: Hastings; E: Hastings; Pte. L 10082; K: 25.1.15; Le Touret Mem. Pas-de-Calais; Age 19; Son of Frederick George and Susan White of 17, Surrey Street, Shoreham, Sussex. *

1652. WHITING, George Cottingham; B: Lewes; E: Brighton; Pte. L 8355; D: 4.4.16; Calais Southern Cem. Pas-de-Calais; Age 28; Son of William and Jane Whiting of Henfield, Sussex.*

1653. WHITTAKER, Frank; B: Royston; E: Royston; Pte. G 20502; K: 10.7.17; Ramscapelle Road Mil. Cem. (Bel.); Age 27; Son of William Taylor and Fanny Whittaker of 309, Oldham Road, Long Sight, Lancashire.

1654. WHITTAKER, William; B: Great Bardfield; E: Chelmsford; Pte. G 14741; K: 28.9.16; Thiepval Mem. Somme.

1655. WHITTINGTON, George Benjamin; B: Wimbledon; E: Chichester; Drummer 9596; K: 10.9.14; Montreuil-aux-Lions Brit. Cem. Aisne; Age 20; Son of Alfred and Mary Whittington of Rock, Washington, Sussex.

1656. WICKENDEN, George; B: Chichester; E: Chichester; L/Cpl. G 1698; K: 25.9.15; Loos Mem. Pas-de-Calais; Age 23; Son of William and Alice Wickenden of 9, St.Martin's Street, Chichester.

1657. WICKENDEN, Thomas Henry; B: Chelsfield; E: Bromley; Pte. G 20745; K: 21.11.17; Tyne Cot Mem. (Bel.).

1658. WICKENS, Percy Alfred; B: Brighton; E: Croydon; L/Cpl. G 21150; W: 6.6.18; Houchin Brit. Cem. Pas-de-Calais; Age 20; Son of Alfred Frederick Wickens of 156, New Street, Horsham, Sussex.

1659. WICKS, James; B: Hastings; E: Chichester; Pte. L 9532; K: 3.10.14; Vendresse Brit. Cem. Aisne; Age 19; Son of George and Jane Wicks of 22, Park Field Road, Hollington, St.Leonards-on-Sea, Sussex.

1660. WILCOX, George Reginald; B: Hove; E: Hove; Pte. L 10518; K: 9.5.15; Woburn Abbey Cem. Pas-de-Calais; Age 18; Son of Harry and Elizabeth Wilcox of 114, Wandsworth Street, Hove.

1661. WILCOX, Sidney George; B: Tottenham; E: Chichester; L.Cpl. L 9875; W at Home: 19.8 16; Chichester Cem., Sussex (U.K.); Age 21; Son of George T. and C.M.Wilcox of Dorset Villa, Wood Grove, Edge Lane, Liverpool.*

1662. WILKINS, Bert; B: St.Paul's, Sussex; E: Eastbourne; Sgt. S 9851; K: 9.5.15; Le Touret Mem. Pas-de-Calais.

1663. WILLEY, Francis Henry Gibson; B: Cuckfield, Sussex; E: Chichester; Pte. L 10181; K: 14.9.14; La Ferte-sous-Jouarre Mem. Seine-et-Marne; Age 19; Son of Frank and Julia Willey of "Lorna Doone", 69, New England Road, Haywards Heath, Sussex.

1664. WILLIAMS, Charles Albert; B: Billingshurst, Sussex; E: Horsham, Sussex; Pte. L 8918; W: 30.9.14; Villers-en-Prayeres Com. Cem. Aisne; Age 24; Son of Mr. and Mrs.Williams of Gatefield Cottages, Billingshurst.

1665. WILLIAMS, Charles Edward; B: Brighton; E: Lewes; Pte. L 6487; K: 29.10.14; Ypres (Menin Gate) Mem. (Bel.).

1666. WILLIAMS, Ernest; B: – ; E: Wood Green; Cpl. G 4849; K: 23.7.16; Thiepval Mem. Somme.

1667. WILLIAMS, Frank; B: New York, U.S.A.; E: Haywards Heath, Sussex; Sgt. L 8597; K: 1.11.14; Ypres (Menin Gate) Mem. (Bel.); Age 26.

1668. WILLIAMS, Henry Edward; B: Cuckfield, Sussex; E: Haywards Heath, Sussex; Pte. L 10320; K: 25.9.15; Loos Mem. Pas-de-Calais; Age 19; Son of Henry and Ellen Williams of Old Thatch Cottage, Whiteman's Green, Cuckfield.

1669. WILLIAMS, Thomas Pilling; Lived: Wrexham; E: Galashiels; L/Cpl. G 11081; K: 9.9.16 at High Wood; Caterpillar Valley Cem. Somme; Age 26; Son of Frederick and Francis Williams of 31, Bradley Road, Wrexham.

1670. WILLINS, Arthur Thomas; B: Southwick, Sussex; E: Shoreham, Sussex; Pte. L 7339; W: 22.9.14; St.Nazaire (Toutes Aides) Cem. Loire-Atlantique; Age 35; Son of Mrs.Margaret Eames of 28, Ship Street, Shoreham.

1671. WILLIS, John. B: Dodford; E: Birmingham; Pte. G 5820; K: 6.4.16; Arras Mem. Pas-de-Calais; Age 22; Son of Mrs.E.Read of New Town, Belbroughton, Worcestershire.

1672. WILLMOTT, William; B: Llantwit-Major; E: Cowbridge; L/Cpl. G 1120; K: 25.9.15 at Hulluch; St.Mary's A.D.S. Cem. Pas-de-Calais; Age 27; Son of Fred and Margaret Willmott of Cowbridge, Glamorgan; Husband of Ethel May Firman Willmott of 67, Sugden Road, Lavender Hill, London.

1673. WILSON, George; B: St.Pancras; E: London; Pte. G 5850; K: 3.5.16; – – .

1674. WILSON, Richard; B: – ; E: Canterbury; Pte. G 17572; K: 17.3.18; Cement House Cem. (Bel.); Age 25; Son of Mrs.Emma Wilson of 1, Gosfield Road, Herne Bay, Kent.

1675. WINBORN, George Alfred; B: Hastings; E: Hastings; Pte. L 10088; K: 9.5.15; Le Touret Mem. Pas-de-Calais; Age 23; Son of Philip Winborn of 4, Claremont Terrace, High Bank, Ore, Hastings.

1676. WINCKLE, Jack Gibson; B: Leek; E: Leek; Pte. G 4583; W: 11.5.15; Chocques Mil. Cem. Pas-de-Calais; Age 23; Son of Sarah Winckle.*

1677. WINDMILL, Alfred William; B: Clerkenwell; E: Holborn; Pte. G 5860; K: 23.7.16; Thiepval Mem. Somme.

1678. WINSOR, Walter William; B: Brighton; E: Brighton; Pte. SD 5484; K: 16.8.16; Thiepval Mem. Somme.

1679. WINTER, Sydney Joseph; B: Great Berkhamstead; E: Hertford; Pte. G 15565; K: 23.10.18; Mazinghien

Com. Cem. Nord; Age 21; Son of Mr. and Mrs.
Winter of Berkhamstead, Hertfordshire.

1680. WINTON, Herbert Thomas; B: Littlehampton,
Sussex; E: Chichester; Pte. G 14001; D: 12.1.18 of
pneumonia; Les Baraques Mil. Cem. Pas-de-Calais;
Age 37; Son of G.N. and M.L.Winton of 36, Surrey
Street, Littlehampton; Served in the South Africa
campaign.

1681. WOOD, Henry James; B: Mile End; E: Poplar; Pte.
G 14835; W: 28.9.18; Brie Brit.Cem. Somme.

1682. WOOD, James; B: Rotherhithe; E: Kingston-on-
Thames; Cpl. G 19879; K: 24.9.18; Bellicourt
Brit. Cem. Aisne; Age 35; Son of James of Helen
Margaret Wood; Husband of Gordon Matlida
Fanny Wood of 23, Belmont Road, Woodside,
South Norwood, London.

1683. WOOD, Milton; B: Hastings; E: Hastings; Pte. L
7877; W: 26.8.16; Heilly Station Cem., Mericourt
L'Abbé, Somme; Age 27; Son of Mr. and Mrs.
Wood of Sidley, Bexhill-on-Sea, Sussex; Husband
of Rose Cartman, formerly Wood, of "Pinelands",
Beechwood Avenue, Weybridge, Surrey.

1684. WOOD, Samuel; B: Ringmer, Sussex; E: Chichester;
Pte. L 8186; W: 22.11.14; Wimereux Com. Cem.
Pas-de-Calais. Age 33.

1685. WOOD, William; B: Fletching, Sussex; E: Lewes;
Cpl. L 7344; K: 9.5.15; Le Touret Mem. Pas-de-
Calais; Age 36; Son of George and Annie Wood of
Freshfield Lane, Danehill, Sussex; Husband of Clara
Wood of 205, Neville Road, Forest Gate, London.

1686. WOODEN, Richard Charles; B: Great Yarmouth;
E: Norwich; Pte. G 14833; K: 9.9.16; Age 35;
Caterpillar Valley Cem. Somme.

1687. WOODHAMS, Frederick; B: Brighton; E:
Battersea; Pte. G 4722; W: 21.6.16; Bethune Town
Cem. Pas-de-Calais.

1688. WOODLEY, Henry John; B: Drayton; E: Hastings;
L/Cpl. L 10321; K: 26.1.15; Le Touret Mem. Pas-
de-Calais.

1689. WOOLFIT, John Edward; B: Pilkington; E: Holborn;
Pte. G 6115; W: 2.3.16; Bethune Town Cem. Pas-
de-Calais; Age 32; Husband of Mrs.A.C.Woolfitt of
154, Glengall Road, Peckham, London.

1690. WOOLLEY, Alfred; B: Hastings; E: Eastbourne;
Pte. S 2302; K: 11.5.15; Le Touret Mem. Pas-de-
Calais.

1691. WOOLNOUGH, Frank; B: Brighton; E: Hove; Pte.
G 6847; W: 1.10.16; Dernancourt Com. Cem. Ext.
Somme.

1692. WOOLVIN, William; B: Brighton; E: Chichester;
Sgt. L 9944; K: 3.10.15; Merville Com. Cem. Nord.

1693. WORSELL, Henry Edward; B: High Broome; E:
Chichester; Pte. L 10176; K: 7.11.14; Ypres (Menin
Gate) Mem. (Bel.); Age 19; Son of Mr. and Mrs.
James Worsell.

1694. WORSELL, John; B: Trinty, Sussex; E: Tunbridge
Wells; Pte. L 6342; K: 30.10.14; Ypres (Menin
Gate) Mem. (Bel.); Age 30; Husband of Frances
C.Howick, formerly Worsell, of 8, Red Row, Lower
Green, Pembury, Kent.

1695. WRAGG, Thomas; B: Brighton; E: Brighton; Pte. G
8676; K: 15.7.16; Thiepval Mem. Somme.*

1696. WREN, Ernest Edward John. B: Brighton; E:
Brighton; Pte. L 8689; K: 23.4.16; Noeux-les-Mines
Com. Cem. Pas-de-Calais; Age 25; Son of Ernest
and Eliza Wren of Portslade, Sussex; Husband of
Margaret E.Wren of 46, Albion Hill, Brighton.

1697. WRIGHT, Alfred; B: Brighton; E: Brighton; Pte. G
5498; K: 19.11.17; Duhallow A.D.S. Cem. (Bel.).

1698. WRIGHT, Basil Charles; Lt; M.C.; K: 24.9.18; Vis-
en-Artois Mem., Haucourt, Pas-de-Calais.

1699. WRIGHT, Isaac; B: Bilston; E: Bilston; Pte. G 6040;
K: 17.8.16; Thiepval Mem. Somme; Age 19; Brother
of Joseph Wright of 12, Union Street, Princess End,
Tipton, Staffordshire.

1700. WRIGHT, Robert; B: Hindringham; E: Hendon;
Pte. G 5092; W: 8.4.16; Bethune Town Cem. Pas-
de-Calais.

1701. WRIST, Norman; B: Shepherd's Buch; E: Whitehall;
Pte. G 34598; W: 4.11.18; Mazinghien Com.
Cem. Nord; Age 31; Husband of Amy Wrist of 9,
Crescent Lane, Clapham, London.

1702. WYATT, Charles Daniel George; B: Clerkenwell;
E: Dalston; Pte. L 6555; W: 30.9.14; Villeneuve-St.
George Old Com. Cem. Val-de-Marne.

Y

1703. YEATES, Frederick Charles; B: Islington; E:
Stratford; Pte. L 10285; K: 27.9.14; La Ferte-sous-
Jouarre Mem. Seine-et-Marne.

1704. YEATMAN, Albert Tom; B: Bognor Regis, Sussex;
E: Bognor Regis; Pte. L 8142; K: 14.9.14; La Ferte-
sous-Jouarre Mem. Seine-et-Marne; Age 30; Son
of William John and Hester Yeatman of 90, Grove
Road, Wyke, Chichester.*

1705. YOUNG, Arthur; B: Hurstpierpoint, Sussex; E:
Haywards Heath, Sussex; Sgt. G 1483; K: 9.9.16;
M.M.; Thiepval Mem. Somme; Age 23; Son of
George William Young.*

1706. YOUNG, Benjamin William; B: Godalming; E:
Dover; Pte. G 3779; K: 30.6.16; Maroc Brit. Cem.
Nord.*

1707. YOUNG, Bertie Charles; B: Branksome; E: Poole;
L/Cpl. L 6928; K: 9.5.15; Le Touret Mem. Pas-de-
Calais.

1708. YOUNG, Frederick George; B: Ramsgate; E:
Woolwich; Pte. G 21879; W: 30.3.18; Haringhe
(Bandeghem) Mil. Cem. (Bel.).

1709. YOUNG, Frederick John; B: Brighton; E: Brighton;
Pte. L 10172; K: 30.10.14; Ypres (Menin Gate)
Mem. (Bel.); Age 22; Son of George Footner Young
of 8, Kingsbury Road, Brighton.

1710. YOUNG, George; B: Bermondsey; E: Chichester;
Pte. L 7716; K: 16.7.16; St.Quentin Caberet Mil.
Cem. (Bel.); Age 36; Son of George Joseph and
Susannah Young of London.*

1711. YOUNG, George Thomas; B: Portslade, Sussex; E:
Worthing; Sgt. G 1599; M.M.; K: 9.9.16; Thiepval
Mem. Somme.

1712. YOUNG, James; B: Fontmell Magna; E: Midhurst, Sussex; Pte. G 8752; K: 20.8.16; Thiepval Mem. Somme.

1713. YOUNG, John Theobald; B: Shenton, Leicester; E: Swansea; Sgt. G 21465; W: 24.9.18; Roisel Com. Cem. Ext. Somme; Age 33; Husband of Florence Hilda Young of Inner Lodge, The Gnoll, Neath, Glamorgan.

1714. YOUNG, Nevill Lindsay; 2nd Lt; K: 20.8.16; Delville Wood Cem. Somme; Age 19; Son of Major-General J.C.Young, C.B., The Royal Sussex Regiment, and Mrs.M.M.Young of 7, Portland Court, Great Portland Street, London.

4th Battalion

A

1715. ASHBY, William John; B: Lower Beeding, Sussex; E: Horsham, Sussex; Pte. TF 200460; K: 9.10.18; Hooge Crater Cem. (Bel.); Age 22; Son of Mr. and Mrs.William Ashby of Faygate, Sussex.

1716 AUSTIN, Edgar William; 2nd Lt.; K: 23.7.18; Raperie Brit. Cem., Aisne; Age 23; Son of Mary Elizabeth Austin of 54, Umfreville Road, Harringay, London; Attached from 1st Battalion Cheshire Regiment; Died while travelling by train.

B

1717. BAILIE, Bernard; B: Westminster, London; E: Piccadilly, London; Pte. G 23840; K: 2.9.18; Tyne Cot Mem. (Bel.); Age 19.

1718. BENNETT, John; B: East Grinstead, Sussex; E: East Grinstead; Cpl. TF 200189; W: 27.9.18; Lijssenthoek Mil. Cem. (Bel.); Age 26; Son of John and Mary Elizabeth Bennett of East Grinstead.

1719. BENTLEY, Benjamin; B: Spitalfields, London; E: Whitehall, London; Pte. G 22145; K: 25.9.18; Wulverghem-Lindenhoek Road Mil. Cem. (Bel.).

1720. BIRD, Stanley Arthur; B: Ingrave, Essex; E: Warley, Essex; Pte. G 23931; K: 2.9.18; Tyne Cot Mem. (Bel.); Age 18; Son of Arthur and Emma Bird of 29, Warescote Road, Brentwood, Essex.

1721. BLACKMAN, Frederick; B: Angmering, Sussex; E: Chichester; Pte. G 11464; W: 2.9.18; St.Sever Cem. Ext., Rouen, Seine-Maritime.

1722 BLAGG, Sidney; 2nd Lt.; K: 29.7.18; Soissons Mem., Aisne; Age 37; Son of Thomas and Margaret E.Blagg of 25, Cartergate, Newark-on-Trent; Attached from Sherwood Foresters (Notts. and Derby Regiment); At the outbreak of war he was a Sergeant in the South Nottinghamshire Hussars and served with them as Regimental Quartermaster Sergeant for 3 years.

1723. BLEEZE, Frank James; B: Bromley, Kent; 2nd Lt.; K: 29.7.18; Raperie Brit. Cem., Aisne; Age 20; Son of Percy William and Edith Maud Bleeze of "Wellington", Swanley, Kent; Attached from Oxfordshire and Buckinghamshire Light Infantry.

1724. BOLTON, John; B: – ; E: Hastings; Pte. TF 202415; W: 6.9.18; Esquelbecq Mil. Cem., Nord; Age 22; Son of Charles and Charlotte Bolton of 42, William Street, Rainham, Kent; Served also in Palestine.

1725. BOND, Henry; B: Abingdon, Berkshire; E: Abingdon; Pte. G 21441; W: 24.7.18; Montreuil-aux-Lions Brit. Cem., Aisne; Age 25; Son of Mrs.S.Bond of 1, Bury Street, Abingdon.*

1726. BONIFACE, Francis Eli; B: Felpham, Sussex; E: Chichester; Pte. TF 201176; K: 29.7.18; Raperie Brit. Cem., Aisne; Age 27; Son of Frank and Ellen Boniface of 11, Guilden Road, Chichester.

1727. BOSTOCK, Edward Lyon; 2nd Lt.; W: 5.4.17; Bray Mil. Cem., Somme; Age 30; Son of Edward Ingram Bostock of Horsham, Sussex; Wounded while attached to another Unit.

1728. BRAKE, Frank Gilbert; B: Worthing, Sussex; E: Worthing; Pte. TF 200972; W: 27.7.18; Verberie French National Cem., Oise; Age 25; Son of Alfred Henry and Alice Brake of Newcastle House, Worthing.

1729. BRAND, Albert Victor; B: East Grinstead, Sussex; E: Horsham, Sussex; Pte. G 25693; W: 3.8.18; Ste. Marie Cem., Le Havre, Seine-Maritime; Age 26; Son of John and Mary Brand.

1730. BRANDI, Andrew; B: Walworth, London; E: Kingston-on-Thames; Pte. G 23938; K: 12.9.18; La Laiterie Mil. Cem. (Bel.); Age 18; Son of Antonio and Asunta Brandi of 67, Whitecross Street, London.

1731. BROW, James; B: Northampton; E: Northampton; Pte. 201708; K: 29.7.18; Soissons Mem., Aisne.*

1732. BROWN, Edward Clifton; B: Horsham, Sussex; E: Horsham; Pte. G 25455; K: 1.8.18; Oulchy-le-Chateau Churchyard, Aisne; Age 23; Son of Mrs. Agnes Brown of 184, Henly Road, Ilford, Essex.

1733. BRYANT, George Henry; B: Brighton; E: Brighton; Pte. TF 201394; K: 29.7.18; Raperie Brit. Cem., Aisne; Age 33; Son of William and Mary Grace Bryant of 72, Hanover Street, Brighton.

1734. BUDD, George William; B: Highgate, London; E: Mill Hill, London; Pte. G 22154; W: 31.7.18; Raperie Brit. Cem., Aisne; Age 20; Son of George and Lena Budd of 14, Yeatman Road, Highgate.

1735. BURCH, Arthur James; B: Arundel, Sussex; E: Horsham, Sussex; Pte. TF 200533; K: 29.7.18; Oulchy-le-Chateau Churchyard, Aisne.

1736. BUTLER, Arthur; B: Chichester; E: Chichester; Pte. TF 200468; W: 23.7.18; Montreuil-aux-Lions Brit. Cem., Aisne.

1737. BYRNE, – ; 2nd Lt.; D: 2.9.18; Voormezeele Enclosure No.3. (Bel.).*

C

1738. CAMPBELL, James; B: Eastbourne; E: Hove; L/ Cpl. TF 201274; K: 29.7.18; Soissons Mem., Aisne; Age 26; Son of Mrs.F.Campbell of 91, Coleridge Street, Hove.

1739. CHALCRAFT, Percy William; B: Steyning, Sussex;

E: Steyning; Pte. TF 200414; K: 29.7.18; Raperie Brit. Cem., Aisne; Age 25; Son of F. and Sarah Chalcraft of 30, Charlton Street, Steyning.

1740. CHAPLIN, Sidney Herbert Victor; B: West Norwood, London; E: New Barnet, Hertfordshire; Pte. G 25158; K: 1.8.18; Soissons Mem., Aisne; Age 25; Husband of Dorothy May Dales, formerly Chaplin, of 34, Farmstead Road, Bellingham Estate, Catford, London.

1741. CHARMAN, John Ewart; 2nd Lt.; W: 25.9.17; Harlebeke New Brit. Cem. (Bel.); Age 19; Son of John and Caroline Charman of 13, St.Leonards Road, Horsham, Sussex; Wounded while attached to another Unit.

1742. CHIPPER, Charles; B: Worthing, Sussex; E: Worthing; Pte. TF 201167; K: 23.7.18; Raperie Brit. Cem., Aisne; Age 23; Son of Mr.H.E.Chipper of 47, Cranworth Road, Worthing.

1743. CHITTY, Charles Frederick; B: Littlehampton, Sussex; E: Arundel, Sussex; Pte. TF 200329; W: 2.8.18; St.Sever Cem. Ext., Rouen, Seine-Maritime; Age 28; Son of William and Annie L.Chitty of 29, Duke Street, Littlehampton.*

1744. COMPTON, James; B: Southwater, Sussex; E: Haywards Heath, Sussex; Cpl. TF 200404; W: 16.10.18; Lijssenthoek Mil. Cem. (Bel.); Age 22; Son of James and Caroline Compton of 53, Gower Road, Haywards Heath.

1745. COOMBER, Gilbert; B: Horsham, Sussex; E: Horsham; Pte. TF 200698; K: 29.7.18; Soissons Mem., Aisne; Age 20; Son of George and Maria M.Coomber of 5, Mill Cottages, Dunning's Road, East Grinstead, Sussex.*

1746. COOPER, Edwin; B: -; E: Arundel, Sussex; Pte. TF 200851; K: 23.7.18; Raperie Brit. Cem., Aisne.

1747. COOPER, Thomas Edward; B: Hambrook, Sussex; E: Chichester; Pte. TF 201398; K: 29.7.18; Raperie Brit. Cem., Aisne; Husband of Mrs.M.Cooper of Oakshott Cottage, West Ashling, Sussex.

1748. CROSS, Frederick; B: Earl's Barton, Northamptonshire; E: Earl's Barton; Pte. TF 201761; K: 29.7.18; Oulchy-le-Chateau Churchyard, Aisne.

D

1749. DEADMAN, Joseph George; B: Broadwater, Sussex; E: Worthing, Sussex; Pte. TF 200378; D: 28.6.18; Les Gonards Cem. (Versailles), Yvelines; Age 37; Son of J.W. and M.Deadman of Worthing; Died from pneumonia.

1750. DENYER, Charles Dennis Daphne; B: Angmering, Sussex; E: Worthing, Sussex; Pte. SD 5031; W: 7.8.18; St.Sever Cem. Ext., Rouen, Seine-Maritime; Son of Mrs.E.Denyer of 69, Clarendon Road, Hove.

1751. DIXON, Leslie; B: Fulham, London; E: Fulham; Pte. G 25468; W: 1.8.18; Senlis French National Cem., Oise; Age 19; Son of Richard and Fanny Dixon of 1, Durrell Road, Fulham.

1752. DONNO, Charles Alfred William; B: Clapham,

London; E: Fulham, London; Pte. G 22162; K: 23.7.18; Raperie Brit. Cem., Aisne; Age 20; Son of Mr. and Mrs.I.Donno of 87, Burlington Road, Fulham.*

1753. DOWERS, Horace Elvery; B: Walworth, London; E: Southwark, London; Pte. G 22161; W: 29.7.18; Vauxbuin French National Cem., Aisne.

1754. DOWLING, Leo; B: Wimbledon, London; E: Wimbledon; D: 6.8.16; Glageon Com. Cem., Nord; Age 22; Son of Francis and Frances Dowling of 11, Southey Road, Wimbledon.*

1755. DOWMAN, Christopher Frederick Bertram; B: Tilbury, Essex; E: Warley, Essex; Pte. G 23960; K: 8.9.18; Tyne Cot Mem. (Bel.); Age 18; Son of William Henry and Elizabeth Emily Dowman of 2, Toronto Road, Tilbury Docks.*

1756. DURRANT, Alfred Ernest; B: Ball Cross, Sussex; E: Worthing, Sussex; Cpl. SD 3338; K: 4.9.18; Messines Ridge Brit. Cem. (Bel.); Brother, James Henry, who also had served with the 4th Battalion, died at home and buried at Northampton (Towcester Road) Cem. (UK).*

E

1757. ELLIS, George; B: Bexhill-on-Sea; E: Hastings; Pte. G 25422; K: 29.7.18; Raperie Brit. Cem., Aisne; Son of Mrs.M.J.Ellis of 11, Salisbury Road, Bexhill-on-Sea. *

1758. ELMS, Frederick; B: Storrington, Sussex; E: Storrington; Sgt. TF 200050; K: 1.8.18; Raperie Brit. Cem., Aisne; Brother of Miss B.Elms of Fern Villa, Storrington.

1759. EVEREST, Horace Henry; B: Wivelsfield, Sussex; E: Haywards Heath, Sussex; Pte. TF 200407; K: 29.7.18; Soissons Mem., Aisne; Age 21; Son of Frederick William and Harnett Esther Everest of Hole Cottages, Wivelsfield Green.*

1760. EVITT, Ernest Augustus; B: Wallington, Surrey; E: Hounslow, Middlesex; Pte. G 21650; K: 29.7.18; Oulchy-le-Chateau Churchyard, Aisne; Age 30; Son of Frederick and Minnie Evitt of Sutton, Surrey.*

F

1761. FEAST, Henry Alfred; B: St.Pancras, London; E: Brighton; Pte. G 25494; K: 1.8.18; Raperie Brit. Cem., Aisne; Age 38; Husband of May Feast of 27, Church Street, Brighton.

1762. FISHER, John William; B: Wimbledon, Cambridgeshire; E: Wisbech, Cambridgeshire; Pte. G 21769; K: 1.8.18; Oulchy-le-Chateau Churchyard, Aisne.

1763. FLECKNELL, Frank Albert Edward; B: Peckham, London; E: St.Paul's Churchyard, London; Pte. G 22166; K: 29.7.18; Soissons Mem., Aisne; Age 20; Son of Frank Albert Edward and Ada Lizzie Flecknell of 2, Alpha Villas, Belmont Road, Westgate-on-Sea, Kent.

1764. FRANCIS, Alfred John George; B: Hackney, London;

E: Statford, London; Pte. G 22169; K: 23.7.18; Raperie Brit. Cem., Aisne; Son of Mr.A.Francis of 7, De Beauvoir Road, Islington, London.*

1765. FRANCIS, Harold John; B: – ; E: Newport, Monmouthshire; Pte. G 21443; K: 29.7.18; Soissons Mem., Aisne; Age 20; Son of John Henry and Alice Francis of 19, Goodnich Crescent, Newport.

1766. FULLER, Frank; B: Colgate, Sussex; E: Horsham, Sussex; Pte. TF 201068; W: 15.10.18; Lijssenthoek Mil. Cem. (Bel.); Age 22; Son of John and E.Louise F.Fuller of 14, Caryll's Cottages, Horsham.

G

1767. GABBITAS, John William; B: Gainsborough, Lincolnshire; E: Gainsborough; Pte. TF 203218; K: 29.7.18; Raperie Brit. Cem., Aisne; Husband of Mrs.H.Smith, formerly Gabbitas, of 20, Providence Place, Trinity Street, Gainsborough.

1768. GENNERY, Cecil William; B: Peckham, London; E: Camberwell, London; Pte. G 22177; K: 2.9.18; Tyne Cot Mem. (Bel.); Age 21; Son of William H. and Elizabeth T.Gennery of 22, Nigel Road, Peckham Rye, London.*

1769. GERLISKY, Louis; B: Stepney, London; E: Whitehall, London; Pte. G 25435; W: 30.7.18; Vauxbuin French National Cem., Aisne; Age 20; Son of Daniel and Hannah Gerlisky of 43, Wentworth Buildings, Aldgate, London.

1770. GIDDINGS, Henry George; B: Hackney, London; E: Stratford, London; Pte. G 22179; D at Sea: 3.8.18; Hollybrook Mem., Hampshire (UK); Age 21; Son of Henry Giddings of 25, MacLaren Street, Clapton Park, London; Drowned at sea from the H.T. "Warilda".

1771. GILES, William Percy; B: Storrington, Sussex; E: Worthing, Sussex; Cpl. TF 203277; D at Home: 28.10.18; Worthing (Broadwater) Cem. (UK); Son of Mrs.Giles of 100, Becket Road, Worthing.

1772. GODDEN, Henry John; B: West Ham, London; E: Statford, London; Pte. G 22182; W: 1.8.18; Vauxbuin French National Cem., Aisne; Age 20; Son of William H.A. and Kate Godden of 41, Fredericks Road, Custom House, London.

1773. GOLBY, Arthur Hugh; 2nd Lt.; W: 13.8.17; Mendighem Mil. Cem.(Bel.); Age 30; Husband of Mrs.G.M.Golby of Villa Halois, Boulevard Degaune, Arachon, France; Wounded while attached to another Unit

1774. GOLDTHORPE, Frank; B: Wakefield; E: Ossett; Pte. G 25434; K: 11.10.18; Hooge Crater Cem. (Bel.).

1775. GRAHAM, Edwin George Mundell; B: Weybridge, Surrey; E: Chelmsford, Essex; Pte. G 25649; K: 29.7.18; Raperie Brit. Cem., Aisne; Son of Mrs.A.M.M.Graham of 6, Montgomery Street, Hove.

1776. GRANT, Eric Stuart; B: Streatham, London; E: Hove; Pte. TF 3878; K: 31.7.16; Browns Road Mil. Cem., Festubert, Pas-de-Calais; Age 22; Son of Reginald Stuart and Grace Eugenie Grant of

"Haselmere", 75, Hopton Road, Streatham; Killed while attached to the 12th Battalion.

1777. GRAY, Walter; B: Steyning, Sussex; E: Chichester; C.Q.M.S. TF 201553; K: 3.10.18; Oxford Road Cem. (Bel.); Age 36; Husband of Veta C.Gray of High Street, Steyning.

1778. GREEN, Richard John; B: – ; E: Stratford-on-Avon, Warwickshire; Pte. G 21442; K: 2.11.18; Harlebeke New Brit. Cem. (Bel.); Age 20; Nephew of Elixabeth S.Arnold of 88, Gordon Road, Peckham, London; Killed in enemy air raid.

H

1779. HALL, Frederick Arthur; B: Shoreditch, London; E: Hounslow, London; Pte. G 23980; K: 10.10.18; Lijssenthoek Mil. Cem. (Bel.); Age 18; Son of Henry and Emily Hall of 62, Mildmay Street, Islington, London.*

1780. HAMER, David Henry; B: Merthyr; E: Cardiff; Pte. G 23868; K; 29.9.18; Wytschaete Mil. Cem. (Bel.).

1781. HARPER, Albert; B: Eastbourne; E: Midhurst, Sussex; Pte. TF 201223; K: 31.7.18; Raperie Brit. Cem., Aisne.

1782. HARWOOD, James; B: Arundel, Sussex; E: Arundel; Sgt. TF 200236; Wulveringhem-Lindenhoek Road Mil. Cem. (Bel.); Age 22; Son of Henry and Sarah Harwood of Orchard Place, Arundel.* K: 25.9.18.

1783. HAZELL, Norman Wilfred; B: Ashford, Middlesex; E: Hounslow, Middlesex; Pte. G 23983; K: 14.9.18; Wulverghem-Lindenhoek Road Mil. Cem. (Bel.).

1784. HEDGECOCK, Arthur Archibald; B: – ; E: Chichester; Pte. TF 3074; W: 30.6.16; Rue-de-Bacquerot No.1 Mil. Cem., Laventie, Pas-de-Calais; Age 19; Son of Mrs.A.Hedgecock of 1, West Stoke, Chichester; Wounded while attached to the 6th Battalion, Royal Warwickshire Regiment.

1785. HILLS, Arthur Frederick; B: Kingston, Sussex; E: Littlehampton, Sussex; Pte. TF 200544; W: 11.8.18; Glageon Com. Cem., Nord; Age 30; Son of Thomas and Mary Hills of East Preston, Sussex; Husband of Charlotte Emily Skinner, formerly Hills, of 20a, Whitechapel Street, Old Basford, Nottingham.

1786. HISLOP, John; B: Lanark; E: Govan; Pte. G 21436; K: 29.7.18; Raperie Brit. Cem., Aisne; Husband of Mrs.C.Hislop of 258, Craig Street, Glasgow.

1787. HOLDER, Ernest Lightwood; B: Birmingham; E: Warwick; Pte. G 25466; K: 29.7.18; Soissons Mem., Aisne; Age 31; Son of Mrs.Louisa Holder of 21, Great King Street, Hockley, Birmingham.

1788. HOLDER, William Henry; B: Midhurst, Sussex; E: Horsham, Sussex; Pte. TF 200866; D: 1.7.18; Étaples Mil. Cem., Pas-de-Calais; Age 34; Son of Mrs.Holder of June Lane, Midhurst.

1789. HOLMAN, Frank; B: Marylebone, London; E: Whitehall, London; Pte. G 23987; K: 29.9.18; Tyne Cot Mem. (Bel.).

1790. HOLTON, Richard Hubert; B: Ifield, Sussex; E: Horsham, Sussex; Pte. TF 201234; K: 29.7.18; Jonchery-sur-Vesle Brit. Cem., Marne; Age 25; Son of Richard Henry and Sarah Holton of County Oak, Ifield.

1791. HUMPHREY, Edwin; B: Woodmancote, Sussex; E: Brighton; Pte. G 25312; W: 23.8.18; Niederzwehren Cem. (G); Age 27; Son of Frank and Christine Humphrey of Blackstone, Henfield, Sussex; Died while a Prisoner of War.

J

1792. JAY, Sidney Augustus; B: – ; E: Hastings; Pte. TF 202120; K: 2.9.18; Tyne Cot Mem. (Bel.) Age 21; Son of Mrs.Emma Jay of 40, Sackville Road, Bexhill-on-Sea.

1793. JOHNSON, George Henry; B: – ; E: Hove; Pte. TF 3950; D: 8.10.16; Étaples Mil. Cem., Pas-de-Calais; Age 33; Son of Victor Johnson; Husband of Mabel Florence Johnson of 17, Viaduct Road, Brighton; Died while attached to another Unit.

1794. JOHNSON, Sydney; B: Lodsworth, Sussex; E: East Grinstead, Sussex; Pte. TF 200239; K: 2.9.18; Tyne Cot Mem. (Bel.); Age 21; Son of Herbert and Kate Johnson of 11, Green Hedges Avenue, East Grinstead; Enlisted August,1914.

1795. JOLLY, Andrew Gordon; B: Duncannon Fort, County Waterford, Ireland; E: London; L/Cpl. G 4782; K: 29.7.18; Soissons Mem., Aisne; Age 30; Son of Andrew and Julia Jolly of "St.Leonards", 31, Beach Road, Southsea, Hampshire.

1796. JONES, Frank Kenneth; B: Cheam, Surrey; E: Hurstpierpoint, Sussex; Pte.TF 200281; K: 29.7.18; Raperie Brit. Cem., Aisne.

K

1797. KEMP, Albert Edward; B: Willesden, London; E: Mill Hill, London; Pte. G 22199; K: 1.8.18; Soissons Mem., Aisne; Age 19; Son of James and Sarah Jane Kemp of 11, Belton Road, Willesden Green.

1798. KENYON, Walter; B: Birmingham; E: Birmingham; Pte. G 22907; K: 23.7.18; Raperie Brit. Cem., Aiane; Son of Mrs.F.Kenyon of 53, Barrows Road, Sparkbrook, Birmingham.

1799. KERWOOD, Owen James Anthony ; B: Chichester; E: Chichester; Pte. TF 200474; K: 29.7.18; Raperie Brit. Cem., Aisne; Age 23; Son of Alfred James and Emma Kerwood of "Black Friars", 7, St.John's Street, Chichester.*

1800. KILDUFF, Harry Ignatius; B: Tottenham, London; E: Harrow, Middlesex; Pte. G 25446; K: 23.7.18; Raperie Brit. Cem., Aisne; Son of the Rev.Patrick Henry Kilduff.

1801. KING, Douglas Alfred; B: East Sutton, Kent; E: Maidstone; Pte. G 23992; W: 4.9.18; La Clytte Mil. Cem. (Bel.); Age 18; Son of Mrs.L.E.A.King of Friday Street, East Sutton.

1802. KIRBY, Ernest Frederick; B: Kensington, London; E: Kensington; Pte. G 10312; K: 23.7.18; Raperie Brit. Cem., Aisne; Age 35; Son of Mr. and Mrs. Kirby of 311, Kensal Road, North Kensington.

1803. KNAPP, Henry Thomas; B: Staplefield, Sussex; E: Haywards Heath, Sussex; Pte. TF 200853; K: 23.7.18; Raperie Brit. Cem., Aisne; Son of Mr.W.G.Knapp of 60, School House, Borde Hill, Cuckfield, Sussex.

L

1804. LEE, Albert Guy; B: St.Pancras, London; E: Camberwell, London; Pte. G 22200; K: 23.7.18; Raperie Brit. Cem., Aisne; Son of Mrs.E.Murphy of 153, Ossulston Street, Somers Town, London.*

1805. LEFTWICH, Percy James; B: Islington, London; E: Wembley, Middlesex; Pte. G 25437; K: 29.7.18; Soissons Mem., Aisne; Age 20; Son of James and Hannah Wiffin Leftwich of 35, Melbourne Avenue, West Ealing, London.

1806. LILLYWHITE, Archie Thomas; B: Horsham, Sussex; E: Horsham; L/Cpl. TF 200126; Oulchy-le-Chateau Churchyard, Aisne. K: 1.8.18.

M

1807. MACKLIN, Wilfred; B: Wivelsfield, Sussex; E: Haywards Heath, Sussex; Pte. TF 200405; W: 3.9.18; Esquelbecq Mil. Cem., Nord; Age 20; Son of George and Fanny Macklin of 68, Salcott Road, Northcote Road, Clapham Junction, London.

1808. MANWARING, Percy Frank; B: Wimbledon, London; E: Worthing, Sussex; Pte G 25426; K: 29.7.18; Soissons Mem., Aisne; Age 36; Son of Mr. and Mrs.F.Manwaring of "Queensmere", Broadwater, Worthing; Husband of Helen Tickner, formerly Manwaring, of "Kilindini", 71, Pavillion Road, Worthing.

1809. MARKWICK, Harry; B: – ; E: – ; Cpl. G 177540; K: 27.8.18; Beaulencourt Brit. Cem., Pas-de-Calais; Age 38; Son of Henry and Elizabeth Markwick of Brighton; Husband of Caroline May Markwick of 5, Luxford Road, Lindfield, Sussex; Killed while attached to the 7th Battalion Royal Fusiliers.

1810. MARTIN, George Edward; B: Chelsea, London; E: Hove; Pte. G 201020; W: 2.8.18; Senlis French National Cem., Oise.

1811. Mc INTYRE, George William; B: Camberwell, London; E: Kingston-on-Thames; Pte. G 24009; K: 25.9.18; Tyne Cot Mem. (Bel.); Age 18; Son of Frederic George Gustavus and Florence Nightingale McIntyre of 8, Sansom Street, Camberwell Green.*

1812. MEPHAM, Mark; B: Hastings; E: Hastings; Pte. TF 201401; K: 29.7.18; Soissons Mem., Aisne.

1813. MORPHEW, Albert; B: Maresfield, Sussex; E: Horham, Sussex; Pte. G 25695; W: 30.7.18; Senlis French National Cem., Oise; Age 27; Son of Owen and Catherine Brooker Morphew of 37, Meadow Road, Rusthall, Kent.*

N

1814. NEIGHBOUR, Henry Thomas; B: Purton Manor, Oxfordshire; E: Horsham, Sussex; Sgt. TF 200349; K: 29.7.18; Soissons Mem., Aisne.

1815. NORMAN, William; B: Hyde, Cheshire; E: Chester; Pte. G 23881; K: 28.9.18; Messines Ridge Brit. Cem., (Bel.); Age 18; Son of Edwin Norman of 7, Canal Street, Hyde.

1816. NUTLEY, George Albert Bernard; B: Lancing, Sussex; E: Horsham, Sussex; Pte. TF 201048; K: 1.8.18; Soissons Mem., Aisne; Age 20; Son of Charles and Mary Jane Nutley.

O

1817. OWEN, Ebenezer; B: Shepherd's Bush, London; E: Hammersmith, London; Pte. G 22220; K: 23.7.18; Raperie Brit. Cem., Aisne; Age 20; Son of Margaret Kandick Owen of 29, Alexandra Road, West Kensington Park, London.

P

1818. PARSONS, Wallace Percy; B: Shoreham, Sussex; E: Worthing, Sussex; Pte. G 1279; K: 23.7.18; Raperie Brit. Cem., Aisne; Husband of Mrs.E.M.Malone, formerly Parsons, of 6, Bishop's Road, Hanwell, London.

1819. PERRY, George; B: Chichester; E: Chichester; Pte. TF 200719; K: 29.7.18; Raperie Brit. Cem., Aisne; Age 23; Son of George and Maria Perry of 13, South Pallarst, Chichester.

1820. PETTIFER, Archibald Henry; B: Leigh, Surrey; E: East Grinstead, Sussex; Cpl. G 16058; K: 29.9.18; Tyne Cot Mem. (Bel.); Age 27; Son of Henry and Mercy Pettifer of Rose Cottage, Leigh; Husband of Elizabeth E.Pettifer of 3, Nechapel Road, Lingfield, Surrey.

1821. PHILLIPS, Herbert Edward; B: Hansey, Staffordshire; E: Grove Park, Kent; Pte. G 21450; K: 23.7.18; Raperie Brit. Cem., Aisne; Age 21; Son of Herbert and Gertrude F.Phillips of Hall Farm, Hulme, Longton, Staffordshire.

1822. PHILLIPS, Percival John; B: – ; E: Hove; Pte. TF 3721; K: 28.7.16; Brown's Road Mil. Cem., Festubert, Pas-de-Calais; Age 21; Son of Mr. and Mrs.Harry Phillips of 124, Ellen Street, Hove; Killed while attached to another Unit.*

1823. PIERSSENE, Frederick Andrew; Lt., W: 6.9.18; Esquelbecq Mil. Cem., Nord; Age 20; Son of Rene and Jane Pierssene of Chandler's Ford, Hampshire.

1824. PROCTOR, Charles; B: Marylebone, London; E: Whitehall, London; Pte. G 24027; K: 25.9.18; Wulverghem-Lindenhoek Road Mil. Cem. (Bel.); Age 18; Son of Joseph and Emily Proctor of 48, Enbrook Street, Queen's Park, London.

R

1825. REID, Stuart Keppel; Capt.; M.C.; W: 29.7.18; Vauxbuin French National Cem., Aisne; Age 30; Son of Percy T. and Florence Reid of Mill Hall, Cuckfield, Sussex.

1826. RICHARDSON, Ernest George; B: Streat, Sussex; E: Horsham, Sussex; Pte. TF 200374; K: 29.7.18; Soissons Mem., Aisne; Age 26; Son of George and Louisa Richardson of North Acres Cottage, Streat.

1827. RICHARDSON, Victor; Lt.; M.C.; W at Home: 9.6.17; Hove Old Cem., Sussex (UK); Age 22; Son of Frank Victor and Emily Caroline Richardson of 15, Cambridge Road, Hove; Wounded while attached to another Unit.

1828. RIST, William; B: Cuckfield, Sussex; E: Haywards Heath, Sussex; Pte. TF 200314; K: 29.7.18; Soissons Mem., Aisne.

1829. ROBERTS, Robert Harry; B: Blackfriars, London; E: Camberwell, London; Pte. G 22229; W: 7.8.18; St.Sever Cem. Ext., Rouen, Seine-Maritime.

1830. RODGERS, John Thomas; B: Ludleston, Shropshire; E: Shrewsbury; Pte. G 23861; K: 28.9.18; Tyne Cot Mem. (Bel.); Age 18; Son of John and Martha Rodgers of Bradenheath, Shropshire.

1831. ROSSITER, George Sheldrick; B: Wells, Somerset; EL Lewisham, London; Pte. TF 202627; D at Home: 17.7.18; Lewisham (Ladywell) Cem., London (UK) ; Son of Mr.R.G.Rossiter of 26, Rushford Road, Brockley, London.

1832. ROWLAND, William; B: Brighton; E: Brighton; Pte. L 11505; K: 29.7.18; Raperie Brit. Cem., Aisne; Age 23; Son of William and Lilian Rowland of 63, Wordsworth Street, Hove.

1833. RUDDERHAM, Edward Charles; B: Petersfield, Hampshire; E: Littlehampton, Sussex; Pte. TF 203206; K: 1.8.18; Raperie Brit. Cem., Aisne; Age 29; Son of Mrs.S.J.Rudderham of 18, Tilmore Terrace, Petersfield.

S

1834. SALES, Arthur Downs; B: Manchester; E: Manchester; Pte. G 19213; K: 2.9.18; Messines Ridge Brit. Cem. (Bel.); Age 19; Son of the late Seargent William D.Sales and Edith Ann Sales of 24, Langshaw Street, Old Trafford, Manchester; Father served with the Inniskillin Dragoons and was killed in the South Africa campaign.

1835. SAUNDERS, William John; B: Tillington, Sussex; E: Petworth, Sussex; Pte. TF 200032; K: 17.10.18; Dadizele New Brit. Cem. (Bel.); Age 35; Son of Henry and Priscilla Saunders of Upperton, Tillington; Husband of Harriet Saunders of 19, Terminus Road, Eastbourne.

1836. SHAW, Albert Philip; B: Peckham, London; E: Whitehall, London; Pte. G 22245; K: 29.7.18; Soissons Mem., Aisne; Age 20; Son of Frederick and Eunice Hannah Shaw of 40, Devonshire Street, Holborn, London.

1837. SHIER, Archibald Charles; B: – ; E: Chichester; L/Cpl. TF 200730; K: 29.7.18; Raperie Brit. Cem., Aisne; Age 29; Son of William John and Mary Shier of Chichester.

1838. SIMMONS, John; B: Hurstpierpoint, Sussex; E: Hurstpierpoint; R.S.M. TF 200287; D.C.M.; K: 29.7.18; Raperie Brit. Cem., Aisne; Age 28; Son of John and Mary Simmons of Sayers Common,

Sussex; Husband of Beatrice Simmons of 22, Windmill Street, Brighton.

1839. SMITH, David John; B: Shildon, County Durham; E: Whitby, Yorkshire; Pte. G 21641; K: 23.7.18; Raperie Brit. Cem., Aisne; Age 24; Son of Joseph and Mary A.Smith of 5, Elmfield Terrace, Shildon.

1840. SMITH, Edward Henry; B: Selsey, Sussex; E: Chichester; Cpl. TF 200558; K: 1.8.18; Raperie Brit. Cem., Aisne; Age 26; Son of Walter Amell Smith and Alice Smith of The New Inn, High Street, Selsey.

1841. SMITH, Francis Harold; B: West Meon, Hampshire; E: Horsham, Sussex; Pte. TF 200448; K: 29.7.18; Raperie Brit. Cem., Aisne; Son of Elizabeth Smith of Rose Cottage, West Meon.

1842. SMITH, Walter; B: Westhouses, Derbyshire; E: Nottingham; Pte. G 25469; K: 29.7.18; Soissons Mem., Aisne; Age 23; Son of Mr. and Mrs.J.Smith of 3, Allfort Terrace, Westhouses.

1843. SMITH, Wilfred; 2nd Lt., W: 9.5.17; Étaples Mil. Cem., Pas-de-Calais; Age 24; Son of Harry and Ann Elizabeth Smith of Goole; Husband of Helen Rebecca Smith of 6a, Woodsome Road, Highgate Road, London; Wounded at Arras while serving with another Unit.

1844. SPENCER, Oliver Neville; B: – ; E: Tottenham, London; Pte. TF 202922; K: 29.7.18; Soissons Mem., Aisne; Age 29; Husband of Amy Amelia Sweeney, formerly Spencer, of 14, Elmar Road, West Green, Tottenham.

1845. SQUIRES, Charles Thomas; 2nd Lt.; W: 30.3.18; Adelaide Cem., Villers-Bretonneux, Somme; Husband of Mrs.G.E.Squires of 80, Tressillian Road, Brockley, London; Wounded while attached to another Unit.

1846. STACE, Harry; B: Brighton; E: Hove; Pte. TF 201303; W: 17.8.18; St.Sever Cem. Ext., Rouen, Seine-Maritime.

1847. STANDING, Percy; B: Petworth, Sussex; E: Worthing, Sussex; Pte. TF 200988;K: 29.7.18; Soissons Mem., Aisne; Age 24; Son of James and Emily Standing of Nevells Wood, Fittleworth, Sussex.

1848. STEELE, George Maurice; B: Horsham, Sussex; E: Horsham; Pte. TF 200459; K: 29.7.18; Raperie Brit. Cem., Aisne; Age 22; Son of Samuel Walter and Florence Agnes Steele of 12a, Springfield Road, Horsham.*

1849. STEVENS, George Thomas; B: Brighton; E: Guildford; Pte. G 25392; K: 8.10.18; Tyne Cot Mem. (Bel.); Age 25; Son of George Thomas Stevens of 11, Bread Steet, Brighton.

1850. STONER, George Sharpe; B: Worthing, Sussex; E: Woolwich, London; Pte. G 25418; K: 29.7.18; Oulchy-le-Chateau Churchyard, Aisne; Age 33; Husband of Mary Jane Stoner of 31, Southfield Road, Worthing.

1851. STOUT, Christopher Thomas; B: Willesden, London; E: Paddington, London; Pte. G 22247; K: 31.7.18; Raperie Brit. Cem., Aisne; Son of Mrs.S.Stout of 83, Malvern Road, Kilburn, London.

1852. STYLES, William Joseph; B: Forest Row, Sussex; E: East Grinstead, Sussex; Pte. TF 200168; K: 29.7.18; Raperie Brit. Cem., Aisne; Age 23; Son of Joseph and Annie Styles of Tugela Villa, Hartfield Road, Forest Row.*

1853. SUMMERSELL, George Frederick; B: Petworth, Sussex; E: Petworth; Pte. TF 200811; W: 3.8.18; Senlis French National Cem., Oise; Age 21; Son of John and Elizabeth Mary Summersell of Upperton, Petworth.*

1854. SWAIN, George; B: – ; E: Littlehampton, Sussex; Pte. TF 201086; K: 29.7.18; Raperie Brit. Cem., Aisne; Age 34; Son of James and Fanny Swain of 11, Gratwicke Terrace, South Marshes, Arundel, Sussex.

T

1855. TABOUR, William; B: Worthing, Sussex; E: Chichester; L/Cpl. TF 200122; K: 29.7.18; Raperie Brit. Cem., Aisne; Husband of Mrs.E.Seagrave, formerly Tabour, of 2, Cleveland Cottages, Brighton Road, Horsham, Sussex.

1856. TARGETT, Percival Frank; B: Copthorne, Sussex; E: Horsham, Sussex; Pte. TF 200610; W: 7.8.18; St.Sever Cem. Ext., Rouen, Seine-Maritime; Age 21; Son of Henry and Letsie Targett of 1, Flora Villa, Charlesfield Road, Horley, Surrey.

1857. TICKNER, Arthur; B: Steyning, Sussex; E: Steyning; Pte. TF 2989; W: 3.9.18; Acheux Brit. Cem., Somme; Age 18; Son of Francis Charlwood Tickner and Alice Tickner of Adur House, Riverside, Beeding, Sussex.*

1858. TIZZARD, William Stanley; B: East Grinstead, Sussex; E: East Grinstead; Pte. TF 200181; K: 29.7.18; Raperie Brit. Cem., Aisne; Age 21; Son of G. and Mary Ann Tizzard of 77, Railway Aproach, East Grinstead.

1859. TREE, Arthur William; B: Pulborough, Sussex; E: Worthing, Sussex; L/Cpl. TF 201339; K: 29.7.18; Raperie Brit. Cem., Aisne; Age 48; Husband of Emily Tree of Arundel Road, Patching, Sussex.

1860. TUCKER, Arthur Haines; Lt.; K: 16.10.17; Hooge Crater Cem. (Bel.); Age 36; Son of Edward and E.Florence Tucker of "Belfort", Liverpool Gardens, Worthing, Sussex; Killed while attached to the 9th Battalion King's Royal Rifle Corps.

V

1861. VERRALL, John; B: Eastbourne; E: Eastbourne; Pte. G 12148; K: 29.7.18; Raperie Brit. Cem., Aisne; Age 30; Husband of Kate Verrall of 48, Melbourne Road, Eastbourne.

1862. VIDLER, Frank; B: Hastings; E: Hastings; Pte. G 25440; K: 29.7.18; Soissons Mem., Aisne.

W

1863. WALSHAM, William Terry; B: Brighton; E: Brighton; Sgt. TF 202544; W: 2.3.17; Étaples Mil. Cem., Pas-de-Calais; Age 21; Son of William Henry and Phoebe Ann Walsham of Brighton; Died of accidental injuries while attached to another Unit.*

1864. WARN, George Stanley; B: Colchester, Essex; E:

Maidstone, Kent; Pte. TF 290935; K: 2.9.18; Irish House Cem. (Bel.).

1865. WATSON, Albert; B: – ; E: Horsham, Sussex; Cpl. TF 200629; K: 23.7.18; Raperie Brit. Cem., Aisne; Age 20; Son of George Oliver and Fanny Watson of 3, Balaclava Road, Bittern, Southampton.

1866. WEEKES, Arthur Nelson Henry; Capt.; M.C.; K: 29.7.18; Raperie Brit. Cem., Aisne; Age 29; Son of Arthur and Jessie Weekes of The Mansion House, Hurstpierpoint, Sussex.

1867. WILKES, Ernest Arthur; B: London; E: Brighton; Pte. G 16778; K: 4.9.18; Tyne Cot Mem. (Bel.); Age 28; Son of Alfred Gilbert and Mary Ann Wilkes of 30, Denmark Road, Islington, London; Husband of Rosina Alma Wilkes of 66, Sparsholt Road, Upper Holloway, London.

1868. WILMSHURST, Cecil Arthur; 2nd Lt.; K: 5.4.18; Pozieres Mem., Somme; Age 29; Son of William and Sarah Jane Wilmshurst of Sissinghurst Castle, Kent; Killed while attached to the Royal Berkshire Regiment.

1869. WINDEBANK, Fred Harold; B: Brighton; E: Brighton; Pte. G 20117; K: 29.7.18; Soissons Mem., Aisnel Age 20; Son of Mr. and Mrs.Windebank of 19, Prince's Crescent, Brighton.

1870. WINKLE, Horace Frank; B: Kettering, Northamptonshire; E: Kettering; Pte. TF 201765; K: 29.7.18; Raperie Brit. Cem., Aisne; Husband of Mrs.G.W.Winkle of Church Street, Burton Latimer, Northamptonshire.

1871. WIXCEY, Herbert Frank; 2nd Lt.; K: 7.8.18; Beacon Cem., Somme; Age 33; Son of Richard and Phoebe Wixcey of London; Husband of Olive E.A.Wixcey of 30, Meteor Road, Westcliff-on-Sea, Essex.

1872. WOOLFORD, Thomas; B: Bepton, Sussex; E: Petworth, Sussex; Pte. TF 200531; W: 9.10.18; Lijssenthoek Mil. Cem. (Bel.); Age 25; Son of Thomas and Kate Woolford of Little Common, Tillington, Sussex.

1873. WOOLLVEN, Charles Morris; B: Cowfold, Sussex; E: Horsham, Sussex; Cpl. TF 200398; K: 29.7.18; Soissons Mem., Aisne.

1874. WYE, Stephen George; B: Highgate, London; E: Stratford, London; Pte. G 23839; W: 5.9.18; Terlincthun Brit. Cem., Pas-de-Calais.*

Y

1875. YEATES, Frederick Cecil; B: Haywards Heath, Sussex; E: Haywards Heath; Pte. TF 200632; K: 2.9.18; Tyne Cot Mem. (Bel.); Age 21; Son of Albert and Annie Weller Yeates of 18, Triangle Road, Haywards Heath.

5th Battalion

A

1876. ABRAHAM, Robert Horace; B: Brixton, London; E: Hastings; Q.M.S. TF 240004; D: 28.8.17; Lijssenthoek Mil. Cem. (Bel.); Age 32; Son of Robert and Annie Abraham of "St.Neots", 17, Old London Road, Hastings; Died from accidental injuries.

1877. ADAMS, Henry John; B: Buxted, Sussex; E: Hastings; Pte. TF 3303; W: 16.9.16; Warloy-Baillon Com. Cem. Ext., Somme.

1878. AKEHURST, Alexander James; B: Bellhurst, Sussex; E: Wadhurst, Sussex; Pte. TF 1539; K: 9.5.15; Le Touret Mem., Pas-de-Calais.

1879. AKEHURST, William Charles; B: Yalding, Kent; E: Hailsham, Sussex; L/Cpl. TF 1391; K: 16.9.16; Aveluy Com. Cem., Somme; Age 23; Son of Charles E.E.Akehurst of "South View", Hawkswood, Hailsham; Native of Hellingly, Sussex.

1880. ALCE, Harry Earl; B: Heathfield, Sussex; E: Hastings; L/Cpl. TF 1984; W at Home 8.6.15; Hadlow Down (St.Mark) Churchyard, Sussex (UK); Age 25; Son of Harry Earl Alce and Esther Alce of Bermuda Cottage, Hadlow Down.*

1881. ALINGTON, Geoffrey Hugh; 2nd Lt.; K: 9.8.16; Bouzincourt Com. Cem. Ext., Somme; Age 27; Son of Mr.E.H.Alington of Summer Fields, Oxford.

1882. ALLEN, George; B: – ; E: Wadhurst, Sussex; Pte. TF 2370; K: 9.5.15; Le Touret Mem., Pas-de-Calais; Age 25; Son of Emily Smith, formerly Allen, and the late Thomas Benjamin Allen of Gloucester Place, Wadhurst.

1883. ANDERSON, Bernard George; B: Battle, Sussex; E: Battle; Sgt. TF 1162; W: 21.8.16; St.Sever Cem., Rouen, Seine-Maritime; Age 24; Son of Bernard T. and Esther Anderson of 9, Mount Street, Battle.

1884. ANDREW, Clifford John; B: Ringmer, Sussex; E: Hastings; Pte. TF 2434; K: 9.5.15; Le Touret Mem., Pas-de-Calais; Age 20; Son of George Lovering Andrew and Constance Amelia Andrew of Southdown Avenue, Lewes, Sussex.*

1885. ANSCOMBE, Alfred Ernest; B: Rotherfield, Sussex; E: Hastings; Pte. TF 2232; K: 9.5.15; Le Touret Mem., Pas-de-Calais; Age 23; Son of Edward and Frances Anscombe of "Ivydean", Western Road, Wadhurst, Sussex.

1886. ARCHER, Fredreick John; B: Suffolk; E: – ; – 20170; D: 4.4.16; Lewes Cem., Sussex (UK); Accidentally while in UK.

1887. AVARD, Herbert William; B: – ; E: Hastings; Pte. TF 2463; K: 9.5.15; Le Touret Mem., Pas-de-Calais; Age 23; Son of William Joseph and Clara Avard of Great Bounds, Southborough, Kent.

1888. AXELL, William Henry; B: – ; E: Hastings; Pte. TF 240646; K: 7.8.17; Duhallow A.D.S. Cem. (Bel.); Age 20; Son of William and Jane Axell of Anchorlee, South Undercliff, Rye, Sussex.

B

1889. BAKER, Charles; B: Wadhurst; E: Hastings; Pte. TF 240433; W: 22.9.17; Dozinghem Mil. Cem. (Bel.).

1890. BAKER, George; B: – ; E: Hastings; Pte. TF 2799; K: 9.5.15; Le Touret Mem., Pas-de-Calais; Son of Mrs.H.Baker of 6, Watermill Lane, Guestling, Sussex.

1891. BAKER, Walter George; 2nd Lt.; K: 14.11.16;

Martinpuich Brit. Cem., Pas-de-Calais; Age 21; Son of George Edmund and Emily Martha Baker of 1, Churchill Road, South Croydon.

1892. BALCOMBE, Richard; B: Ticehurst, Sussex; E: Ticehurst; Sgt. TF 500; K: 9.5.15; Le Touret Mem., Pas-de-Calais; Age 25; Son of Richard and Sarah Balcombe of 10, Church Street, Ticehurst.

1893. BALDWIN, Sydney John; B: – ; E: Hastings; Pte. TF 2768; K: 9.5.15; Le Touret Mem., Pas-de-Calais; Age 22; Son of John and Harriet Baldwin of Durgates, Wadhurst, Sussex.

1894. BARKER, Alfred Lewin; B: – ; E: Hastings; Pte. TF 2619; W: 11.5.15; Bethune Town Cem., Pas-de-Calais; Age 24; Son of S.J. and E.Barker of 13, Caledon Terrace, Nunnery Fields, Canterbury, Kent; Died at No.1 Casualty Clearing Station.

1895. BARNES, Owen; B: Crowborough, Sussex; E: Hastings; Pte. TF 240885; W: 17.8.17; Brandhoek New Mil. Cem. No.3 (Bel.); Age 21; Son of George Barnes of Luxfords Lane, Crowborough.

1896. BARRETT, John Henry; B: Surbiton, Surrey; E: Hastings; Sgt. TF 1887; W: 10.5.15; Bethune Town Cem., Pas-de-Calais; Age 31; Son of Alfred and Lucy Margaret Barrett of Lammas, Cowes, Isle-of-Wight; Wounds received at Richebourg-L'Avoué 9.5.15.

1897. BARROW, Alfred Charles; B: – ; E: Wadhurst, Sussex; Pte. TF 2372; K: 9.5.15; Le Touret Mem., Pas-de-Calais; Age 20; Son of Alfred and Clara Barrow of 8, Gloster Road, Wadhurst.

1898. BARTLETT, Frank; B: Jersey, Channel Islands; E: Hastings; Pte. TF 1842; W at Home: 16.6.15; Widford (St.Mary) Churchyard, Essex (UK).

1899. BATES, Charles Edward; B: Hounslow, Middlesex; E: Crowborough, Sussex; Pte. TF 240151; W: 10.3.17; St.Sever Cem. Ext., Rouen, Seine-Maritime; Age 25; Son of Mrs.H.Bates of Station Road, Withyham, Sussex.

1900. BATEUP, Samuel Frederick; B: Brighton; E: Brighton; Pte. TF 3665; K: 31.7.16; Thiepval Mem., Somme; Age 19; Son of Stephen and Charlotte Bateup of 5, The Crescent, Keymer, Sussex.*

1901. BEALE, Albert; B: Hastings; E: Hastings; Pte. TF 1744; K: 9.5.15; Le Touret Mem., Pas-de-Calais; Age 18; Son of Mrs.Kate Frances Beale of Tanyard House, West Cross, Kent.

1902. BENEY, Ernest; B: – ; E: Hastings; Pte. TF 2550; K: 9.5.15; Le Touret Mem., Pas-de-Calais; Age 20; Son of James William and Eunice Beney of 4, St.Paul's Road, St.Leonards-on-Sea, Sussex.

1903. BENHAM, Frederick; B: Hastings; E: Hastings; Pte. TF 1809; K: 16.8.16; Thiepval Mem., Somme; Age 19; Son of Henry and Jemima Benham of 75, High Street, Hastings.

1904. BENNETT, William; B: Rye, Sussex; E: Hastings; L/Cpl. TF 240402; W: 12.10.17; Dozinghem Mil. Cem. (Bel.); Age 29; Son of Joseph Bayley Bennett and Hannah J.Bennett of Rye; Husband of Ann Bennett of Wish Ward, Rye.

1905. BERRY, Alfred John; B: Angmering, Sussex; E:

Worthing; Pte. TF 241308; K: 4.10.17; Tyne Cot Mem. (Bel.).

1906. BINGEN, Charles Adolph Max; Lt.; K: 10.2.16: Hebuterne Mil. Cem., Pas-de-Calais; Age 20; Son of Max N. and Leily Bingen of 14, Briardale Gardens, Hampstead, London; Killed instantly by 5.9" shell.*

1907. BISHOP, Albert; B: Worthing, Sussex; E: Littlehampton, Sussex; Pte. TF 241355; K: 22.9.17; Vlamertinghe New Mil. Cem. (Bel.).

1908. BISHOP, Henry George; B: – ; E: Hastings; Pte. TF 202730; K: 2.8.17; White House Cem. (Bel.).

1909. BISSENDEN, Charles Ernest; B: Holy Trinity, Sussex; E: Hastings; Pte. TF 1993; K: 9.5.15; Le Touret Mem., Pas-de-Calais; Age 22; Son of Mr.T.F. and Mrs. E.Bissenden of 103, Beaconsfield Road, Hastings.

1910. BLACKMAN, Hugh William; B: Hastings; E: Hastings; Pte. TF 2390; K: 21.9.15; Louvencourt Mil. Cem., Somme; Age 20; Son of William James and Florence Emily Blackman.*

1911. BLACKMAN, John Stephen George; B: Rye, Sussex; E: Rye; Pte. TF 240116; K: 7.8.17; Duhallow A.D.S. Cem. (Bel.); Age 22; Son of John and Margaret Blackman of Ferry Road, Rye.*

1912. BLAGROVE, Arthur John; B: – ; E: Hastings; Pte. TF 2338; K: 9.5.15; Le Touret Mem., Pas-de-Calais; Age 24; Son of Edwin and Jane Blagrove of 72, High Street, Lewes, Sussex.

1913. BLUNDELL, Robert; B: – ; E: Beckley, Sussex; Pte. TF 3642; W: 17.1.17; Dernancourt Com. Cem. Ext., Somme.

1914. BLUNDEN, Lewis; 2nd Lt.; K: 22.7.16; Bouzincourt Com. Cem. Ext., Somme; Son of Mr.G.Blunden of Mill House, East Malling, Kent.

1915. BOTTING, Alfred George; B: – ; E: Lewes; Pte. TF 3484; K: 28.6.16; Couin Brit. Cem., Pas-de-Calais; Age 25; Son of John Henry Botting of Beaks Cottage, Longford, Barcombe, Sussex.

1916. BOVIS, Albert Edward; B: Hurst Green, Sussex; E: Hurst Green; Sgt. TF 1061; K: 9.5.15; Le Touret Mem., Pas-de-Calais; Age 29; Son of Frank and Harriet Bovis; Husband of Alice Maud Bovis of Station Road, Hurst Green.

1917. BRAZIER, Frederick Owen; B: – ; E: Hastings; Pte. TF 3198; K: 9.5.15; Le Touret Mem., Pas-de-Calais; Age 18; Son of Frederick and Emily Brazier of 18, Calvert Road, Hastings.

1918. BRAZIL, John Henry; B: – ; E: Peasmarsh, Sussex; Pte. TF 3743; K: 14.11.16; Martinpuich Brit. Cem., Somme; Age 19; Son of Rose Edith Brazil of Hazel Grove, Dew Farm, Peasmarsh.

1919. BREACH, Harold Henry; B: South Malling, Sussex; E: Lewes, Sussex; Pte. TF 1672; K: 9.5.15; Le Touret Mem., Pas-de-Calais; Age 19; Son of Mrs.Harrriett Breach of 4, Daveys Lane, Lewes.

1920. BRETT, Thomas; B: – ; E: Hastings; Pte. TF 2726; K: 29.6.16; Hebuterne Mil. Cem., Pas-de-Calais.

1921. BRITT, Albert; B: Rye, Sussex; E: Rye; Pte. TF 1337; K: 9.5.15; Le Touret Mem., Pas-de-Calais; Age 21; Son of Mrs.Jane Britt of Wish Ward Street, Rye.

1922. BROOKS, Robert Henry; B: – ; E: Hastings; Pte. TF

2717; K: 9.5.15; Le Touret Mem., Pas-de-Calais; Age 21; Son of Mr.F.J.Brooks of 28, Canterbury Road, South Willesborough, Kent.

1923. BROWN, Frederick John; B: Lewes, Sussex; E: Lewes; Pte. TF 240015; K: 7.7.17; Gwalia Cem. (Bel.); Age 39; Son of Mrs.Lois Brown of Hampden Gardens, Glynde, Sussex.

1924. BULL, Edward Owen; B: Connington, Cambridgeshire; E: Bedford; Pte. TF 3962; W at Home: 8.10.16; Great Stukeley (St.Bartholomew) Churchyard, Huntingdonshire (UK); Age 28; Son of John Bull.

1925. BULL, Henry; B: Little Oakley, Essex; E: Hastings; C.S.M. L 3263; K: 1.5.15; Caberet-Rouge Brit. Cem., Pas-de-Calais.

1926. BYRNE, Hubert Corbett; 2nd Lt.; K: 2.9.18; Voormezeele Enclosure No.3 (Bel.).

C

1927. CANE. Leonard; B: Brighton; E: Brighton; Pte. TF 241390; W: 10.9.17; Divisional Collecting Post Cem. (Bel.); Age 26; Son of Edward and Ellen Cane of 33, Bear Road, Brighton.

1928. CARLEY, Montague Leonard; B: – ; E: Hastings; Pte. TF 2502; K: 9.5.15; Le Touret Mem., Pas-de-Calais.

1929. CARNAGHAN, Stanley; B: Hastings; E: Hastings; Cpl. TF 2153; K: 30.3.15; Cabaret-Rouge Brit. Cem., Pas-de-Calais.

1930. CATT, Bert; B: – ; E: Hastings; Pte. TF 2641; K: 20.3.15; Brown's Road Mil. Cem., Festubert, Pas-de-Calais.

1931. CHANDLER, Albert Henry; B: – ; E: Hastings; Pte. TF 1554; K: 9.5.15; Woburn Abbey Cem., Pas-de-Calais; Age 19; Son of George and Alice Chandler of Fontridge Lane, Etchingham, Sussex.

1932. CHAPMAN, Frank James Albert; Pte. TF 2856; K: 12.7.15; Cambrin Churchyard Ext., Pas-de-Calais.

1933. CHURCHER, Frederick William Thomas; B: Worthing, Sussex; E: Worthing; Pte. TF 241433; K: 2.8.17; White House Cem. (Bel.); Age 22; Son of Frederick and Clara Elizabeth Churcher of 51, Ham Road, Worthing.

1934. CLOUTING, Sidney; B: – ; E: Hastings; Pte. TF 2462; K: 9.5.15; Le Touret Mem., Pas-de-Calais.

1935. CLOVER, Herbert; B: – ; E: London; Pte. TF 240656; W: 5.10.17; Dozinghem Mil. Cem. (Bel.); Age 25; Son of Mr. and Mrs.William Clover; Husband of Dorothy Clover of 17, Rampayne Mews, Westminster, London.

1936. COCKERILL, Ernest; B: Gaydon, Northamptonshire; E: Northampton; Pte. TF 241147; W: 27.9.17; Dozinghem Mil. Cem. (Bel.).

1937. COLEMAN, Dick; B: Iden, Sussex; E: Rye, Sussex; Pte. TF 3576; K: 7.7.16; Knightsbridge Cem., Mesnil-Martinsart, Somme; Age 20; Son of William and E.Coleman of The Star Inn, Playden, Sussex.

1938. CONNOLLY, Thomas; B: Manchester; E: Maidstone; Pte. TF 241330; K: 30.9.17; Duhallow A.D.S. Cem. (Bel.).

1939. COPLAND, Maurice; B: Chelmsford, Essex; E: Hastings; Pte. TF 2363; D: 21.3.15; Wimereux Com. Cem., Pas-de-Calais; Age 38; Son of John Albert and Mary Copland of Chelmsford.*

1940. CORNWALL, Geoffrey; B: Hadlow Down, Sussex; E: Uckfield, Sussex; Pte. TF 1667; K: 9.5.15; Rue-du-Bois Mil. Cem., Fleurbaix, Pas-de-Calais.

1941. COWLEY, Harry Crichton; B: – ; E: Hastings; Pte. TF 2773; W at Home: 31.8.16; Hastings Cem., Sussex (UK).

1942. COX, George Leonard; B: Hastings; E: Hastings; Pte. TF 2362; K: 9.5.15; Le Touret Mem., Pas-de-Calais; Age 20; Son of Thomas G.R. and Lydia Mary Cox of 26, Stockleigh Road, St.Leonards-on-Sea.

1943. CRAMP, Albert St.Swithun; B: – ; E: Hastings; Pte. TF 202209; W: 10.9.17; Boulogne Eastern Cem., Pas-de-Calais.*

1944. CRAWFORD, Victor Thomas; B: Wisborough Green, Sussex; E: Brighton; L/Cpl. TF 241277; K: 25.4.17; Thiepval Mem., Somme; Age 20; Son of Felix and Ethel Crawford of "Beechurst", Frimley Green, Surrey.

1945. CREED, Harold; B: – ; E: Hastings; Pte. TF 202859; K: 16.8.17; Tyne Cot Mem. (Bel.); Age 20; Son of William and Annie Creed of Mornington Mansions, Wellington Square, Hastings.

1946. CROFT, Clement Bernard; B: Hastings; E: Ticehurst, Sussex; L/Cpl. TF 1957; K: 9.5.15; Le Touret Mem., Pas-de-Calais.

1947. CROUCH, James; B: – ; E: Lewes, Sussex; Pte. TF 240961; W: 7.10.17; Dozinghem Mil. Cem. (Bel.).

D

1948. DASH, John Lusby; B: St.Leonards-on-Sea; E: Hastings; L/Sgt. TF 1872; K: 14.11.16; Martinpuich Brit. Cem., Somme; Age 29; Son of Edward Lusby Dash and Jane Lavinia Dash of St.Leonard-on-Sea; Husband of Snowdrop Dash of 39, Salisbury Road, Bexhill-on-Sea.

1949. DEANE, Arthur Reginald; Lt.; W: 14.11.17; Dozinghem Mil. Cem. (Bel.); Age 22; Son of Frederick and Alice M.Deane.

1950. DENCE, Albert; B: – ; E: Wadhurst, Sussex; Pte. TF 2325; K: 9.5.15; Le Touret Mem., Pas-de-Calais.

1951. DENNISON, Ralph Edward McKie; 2nd Lt.; K: 9.5.15; Le Touret Mem., Pas-de-Calais; Age 37; Son of Ralph Abercrombie Dennison and Helen McTaffart Dennison of 90, Warrior Square, St.Leonards-on-Sea; Brother, Capt. Stuart Dennison, also fell.

1952. DEVELIN, Frank Henry; B: St.Leonards-on-Sea; E: Uckfield, Sussex; Pte. TF 1575; K: 9.5.15; Guards Cem. (Cuinchy) Pas-de-Calais; Age 18; Son of Francis Emery Develin and Caroline A.Develin of 7, Meadow Place, Uckfield.*

1953. DRAY, Charles; B: – ; E: Bostall Heath, Kent; Pte. TF 3308; K: 7.2.17; Eclusier Com. Cem., Somme.

1954. DRURY, James Edward; B: – ; E: Hastings; Pte. TF

2660; K: 16.8.16; Thiepval Mem., Somme; Age 34; Husband of Kate Drury of 3, Earl Buildings, Earl Street, Hastings.*

1955. DUDENEY, Percy James; B: – ; E: Hastings; Pte. TF 2818; W: 12.5.15; Bethune Town Cem., Pas-de-Calais; Age 19; Son of John and Kate Dudeney of 17a, Havelock Road, Hastings.*

1956. DUNSTER, Archibald Frank; B: Rye, Sussex; E: Hastings; Pte. TF 2070; W: 21.3.15; Bethune Town Cem., Pas-de-Calais; Age 25; Son of Frank Charles and Lottie Julia Dunster of Rye; Wounds received 20.3.15.*

E

1957. EDWARDS, Richard Frederick; B: – ; E: Wadhurst, Sussex; Pte. TF 2380; K: 9.5.15; Le Touret Mem., Pas-de-Calais.*

1958. ELLIS, Hubert James; B: – ; E: Tower of London; Pte. TF 2708; K: 9.5.15; Le Touret Mem., Pas-de-Calais; Age 18; Son of Frank and Kate Ellis of The Lodge, Comenden Manor, Cranbrook, Kent.

1959. ELPHICK, Sydney John; B: Hastings; E: Hastings; Pte.TF 1779; K: 1.5.15; Cabaret-Rouge Brit. Cem., Pas-de-Calais.

1960. EVENDEN, Charles William; B: Waldron, Sussex; E: Hastings; Pte. TF240367; K: 12.10.17; Vlamertinghe New Mil. Cem. (Bel.); Age 25; Son of George and Priscilla Evenden of Cross Ways, Waldron.

F

1961. FARRIER, Thomas Frederick; B: – ; E: Hastings; Pte TF 2586; K: 17.5.15; Bethune Town Cem., Pas-de-Calais; Son of Mrs.S.A.Shanks of 21, St.George Road, Hastings.

1962. FAZAN, Roy; 2nd Lt., K: 9.5.15; Le Touret Mem., Pas-de-Calais; Age 23; Son of Dr.Charles Herbert and Mrs.Fanny Fazan of "Boughton", 1, Amherst Road, Bexhill-on-Sea.

1963. FIELD, Thomas William; B: – ; E: Hastings; Pte. TF 3488; K: 19.8.16; Thiepval Mem., Somme; Age 19; Son of Henry and Eliza Mary Field of 208, Mount Pleasant Road, Hastings.*

1964. FILLERY, George; B: – ; E: Wadhurst, Sussex; K: 9.5.15; Le Touret Mem., Pas-de-Calais.

1965. FLETCHER, Thomas Samuel; B: Hertford Heath, Hertfordshire; E: Ticehurst, Sussex; Pte. TF 1976; W: 27.6.16; Couin Brit. Cem., Pas-de-Calais; Age 23; Son of Arthur and Jane Fletcher of London Road, Hertford Heath.*

1966. FOORD, Stephen J.; B: Hastings; E: Hastings; Sgt. TF 240013; W: 12.9.17; Wimereux Com. Cem., Pas-de-Calais.*

1967. FORD, Arthur; B: – ; E: Uckfield, Sussex; Pte. TF 2910; K: 14.11.16; Martinpuich Brit. Cem., Somme.

1968. FULLER, Ernest; B: – ; E: Hastings; Pte. TF 2859; K: 9.8.16; Aveluy Com. Cem., Somme.

1969. FUNNELL, Ernest David; B: West Hoathly, Sussex; E: London; Pte. TF 241339; K: 1.3.17; Herbecourt Brit. Cem., Somme; Age 40; Son of Isaac and Mary Funnell of Crawley Down, Sussex; Husband of Fanny M.Funnell of The Grange, Gresham Road, Staines, Middlesex.

1970. FUNNELL, Herbert George; B: Lewes; E: Lewes; Bugler TF 1709; K: 9.5.15; Le Touret Mem., Pas-de-Calais; Age 19; Son of James and Mary Ann Funnell of 9, Wellington Street, Lewes; Brother, Frederick, 2nd Battalion Royal Sussex Regiment killed 2.1.15.

1971. FUNNELL, William F.; B: – ; E: Hastings; Pte. TF 3490; K: 13.7.16; Knightsbridge Cem., Mesnil-Martinsart, Somme; Age 20; Son of Mrs.E.Funnell of Willitts Cottage, Muddles Green, Chiddingly, Sussex.

1972. FURNER, Albert Edward; B: – ; E: Buxted, Suhssex; Pte. TF 240876; W: 12.10.17; Dozinghem Mil. Ce. (Bel.); Age 18; Son of William J. and Emily J.Furner of High Beeches Cottages, Handcross, Sussex.*

G

1973. GANDER, Charles Edward; B: – ; E: Hastings; Pte. TF 2804; K: 9.5.15; Le Touret Mem., Pas-de-Calais.

1974. GANDER, Percy Albert; B: – ; E: Hastings; Pte. TF 1928; K: 31.5.15; Cambrin Churchyard Ext., Pas-de-Calais; Age 19; Son of Edwin Alfred and Annie Gander of 4, Hillside Cottage, White Hill Road, Crowborough, Sussex; Killed accidentally.*

1975. GARNER, William Walter; B: Hastings; E: Hastings; Pte. TF 2492; K: 28.3.15; Cabaret-Rouge Brit. Cem., Pas-de-Calais; Age 21; Son of William and Charlotte Ann Garner of 40, Maudslay Road, Well Hall, London.

1976. GARTON, Herbert; B: Tunbridge Wells; E: Hastings; Pte. TF 2152; K: 14.11.16; Martinpuich Brit. Cem., Somme; Age 21; Son of Walter ands Sarah Garton of Hadlow House, Hadlow Down, Sussex.

1977. GIBBS, William; B: Hastings; E: Hastings; Pte. TF 1003; W: 17.5.15; Bethune Town Cem., Pas-de-Calais.

1978. GILBERT, William Claude; B: East Wittering, Sussex; E: Hastings; Pte. TF 1588; K: 11.4.15; Le Touret Mem., Pas-de-Calais; Age 20; Son of James and Elizabeth Gilbert of 15, Peverall Park Road, Plymouth.

1979. GLADMAN, John Owen; B: – ; E: Hastings; Pte. TF 2874; K: 9.5.15; Le Touret Mem., Pas-de-Calais; Age 18; Son of John Owen and Elizabeth Ellen Gladman of 21, St.James' Road, Eastbourne.

1980. GOLDSMITH., Harold Edward; B: – ; E: Wadhurst, Sussex; Pte. TF 2328; K: 9.5.15; Le Touret Mem., Pas-de-Calais; Age 18; Son of Benjamin and Almena A.Goldsmith of 2, Fair View, Salisbury Road, Langton Green, Kent.

1981. GOODSELL, Percy; B: Robertsbridge, Sussex; E: Hastings; Cpl. TF 2233; W: 10.5.15; Longuenesse (St.Omer) Souvenir Cem., Pas-de-Calais: Age 21;

Son of Thomas and Annie Goodsell of "Streatley", Loose Road, Maidstone.

1982. GOODSELL, Thomas James; B: Hastings; E: Hastings; Pte. TF 1768; W: 29.9.16; Contay Brit. Cem., Somme; Age 20; Son of Mrs.E.Cooper of 23a, Calvert Road, Hastings.*

1983. GOULD, Reginald Thomas; B: – ; E: Abbey Wood, Kent; Pte. TF 3285; D: 20.5.16; Le Treport Mil. Cem., Seine -Maritime; Age 18; Son of Thomas Henry Treble and Ada Sophia Gould of Plumstead, London.

1984. GRABHAM, Richard John; B: Hastings; E: Hastings; Pte. TF 1888; W: 23.9.16: Warloy-Baillon Com. Ext., Somme.

1985. GRANT, Ferris Nelson; Capt.; K: 9.5.15; Le Touret Mem., Pas-de-Calais.

1986. GRANTHAM, Edward, B: Tring, Buckinghamshire; E: Tewksbury, Gloucestershire; Pte.TF 1524; W: 19.7.16; Warloy-Baillon Com. Cem. Ext., Somme; Age 26; Son of Rev.Herbert and Mrs.M.L.Grantham of Halton Rectory, Buckinghamshire.

1987. GREEN, Herbert William; 2nd Lt.; K: 16.8.17; Vlamertinghe New Mil. Cem. (Bel.); Age 34; Son of Mrs. Stanton, formerly Green, of The Cottage, Shenfoot Lane, Four Oaks and the late William Green.

1988. GRIFFEN, Percy; B: – ; E: Hastings; Pte. TF241015; K: 16.8.17; Tyne Cot Mem. (Bel.); Age 24; Son of George Richard and Eleanor Griffin of Danegate, Erridge Green, Kent.

1989. GRIFFIN, Robert; B: Winchelsea, Sussex; E: Rye, Sussex; Pte. TF 1103; W: 9.5.15; Rue-des-Berceaux Mil. Cem., Richebourg-L'Avoué , Pas-de-Calais; Age 21; Son of James and Fanny Griffin of 3, North Street, Winchelsea.*

1990. GRIFFITHS, William Thomas; B: – ; E: Hastings; Pte. TF 3190; K: 9.5.15; Le Touret Mem., Pas-de-Calais; Age 22; Son of Mrs.Jane Griffiths.

1991. GROOMBRIDGE, James Thomas; B: Blackham, Sussex; E: Hastings; Pte. TF 240785; W at Home: 12.6.17; Withyham (St.Michael) Churchyard, Sussex (UK); Age 22; Son of Mr. and Mrs. Groombridge; Husband of Mrs.N.R.Groombridge of 488, Hornsey Road, Holloway, London.*

1992. GURR, Albert Victor; B: Eastbourne; E: Uckfield, Sussex; Pte. TF 241037; K: 4.10.17; Duhallow A.D.S. Cem. (Bel.); Age 20; Son of David and Edith Gurr of Rose Cottage, Higher Cross, Framfield, Sussex.*

H

1993. HADAWAY, Percy; B: Elham, Kent; E: Folkestone, Kent; Pte. TF 3954; W at Home: 22.1.17; Elham (St.Mary) Churchyard, Kent (UK); Age 26; Son of James and Caroline Hadaway of High Street, Elham; Husband of Harriett E.Hadaway of 1, Pages Yard, Church Street, Chiswick, London.

1994. HARMAN, Ernest; B: – ; E: Hastings; Pte. TF 2725; W: 31.3.15; Chocques Mil. Cem., Pas-de-Calais;

Age 19; Son of Mary Foster of 41, Winchelsea Road, Hastings.*

1995. HARMAN, William; B: – ; E: Hastings; Pte. TF 240719; W: 18.8.17; Étaples Mil. Cem., Pas-de-Calais; Age 22; Son of Harry Harman of 12, Dalham Cottages, Guestling, Sussex.

1996. HARMER, Alfred; B: Ashburnham, Sussex; E: Hastings; Pte. TF 2108; K: 8.7.15; Cambrin Churchyard Ext., Pas-de-Calais; Age 21; Son of Mr. and Mrs.C.Harmer of Bay Cottage, The Forge, Ashburnham.

1997. HARMER, Sidney Herbert; B: Benenden, Kent; E: Ticehurst, Sussex; Pte. TF 1956; K: 9.5.15; Le Touret Mem., Pas-de-Calais.

1998. HART, William John; B: Hammersmith, London; E: Ticehurst, Sussex; C.S.M. TF 528; K: 27.6.16; Couin Brit. Cem., Pas-de-Calais.

1999. HASELGROVE, Alexander Basil; B: Lyminster, Sussex; E: Horsham, Sussex; Pte. TF 241449; K: 1.3.17; Herbecourt Brit. Cem., Somme; Age 21; Son of James and Fanny Haselgrove of 227, Poling, Arundel, Sussex.

2000. HAWKINS, Albert; B: – ; E: Wadhurst, Sussex; Pte. TF 2347; K: 9.5.15; Le Touret Mem., Pas-de-Calais; Age 20; Son of William and Sarah Jane Hawkins of 3, Balliol Cottages, Wadhurst; Brother, William, also killed in the same action on the same day and also has no known grave (see 2001).

2001. HAWKINS, William; B: – ; E: Wadhurst, Sussex; Pte. TF 2329; K: 9.5.15; Le Touret Mem., Pas-de-Calais; Age 24; Son of William and Sarh Jane Hawkins of 3, Balliol Cottages, Wadhurst; Brother, Albert, also killed in the same action on the same day and also has no known grave (see 2000).

2002. HAYDON, Lee; B: Lewes; E: Hastings; Pte. TF 2446; K: 9.5.15; Le Touret Mem., Pas-de-Calais; Age 28; Son of Flaxman and Anne Haydon of 76c, Stanlake Road, Shepherd's Bush, London.

2003. HAYWOOD, Albert; B: Mountfield, Sussex; E: Hastings; Pte. TF 2230; K: 28.3.15; Cabaret-Rouge Brit. Cem., Pas-de-Calais.

2004. HAZELDEN, William Henry Alfred; B: – ; E: Uckfield, Sussex; Pte. TF 2922; K: 9.5.15; Le Touret Mem., Pas-de-Calais; Age 22; Son of Frederick W. and Sally Hazelden of Pole House Common, Framfield, Sussex.*

2005. HICKS, James Thomas William; B: Rye, Sussex; E: Rye; Pte. TF 1849; W: 24.5.15; Bethune Town Cem., Pas-de-Calais; Age 20; Son of Albert and Emma Hicks of "Homelands", Cadborough Road, Rye.*

2006. HILL, Arthur; B: Jarvis Brook, Sussex; E: Hastings; Pte. TF 240958; K: 23.8.17; Bard Cottage Cem. (Bel.).

2007. HOAD, Percy Ewart; B: Wittersham, Sussex; E: Hastings; Pte. TF 2196; K: 28.7.15; Labourse Com. Cem., Pas-de-Calais; Age 17; Son of Mrs.Sarah Parsons of Ferry Road, Rye, Sussex.

2008. HOARE, Maurice; B: – ; E: Hastings; L/Cpl. TF 240473; K: 16.8.17; Tyne Cot Mem. (Bel.); Age

26; Son of Maurice and Matilda Hoare of 35, Canterbury Road, Pembury, Kent and formerly of 4, Huntingdon Terrace, Crowborough, Sussex.

2009. HOBART, Joseph Claude Anthony; 2nd Lt.; D at Home: 3.12.16; Kensal Green (St.Mary's) Cem., London (UK).*

2010. HODGES, James; B: – ; E: Hastings; Pte. TF 2810; K: 13.4.16; Hebuterne Mil. Cem., Pas-de-Calais; Age 20; Son of George Walter and Mary Hodges of St.John's Common, Crowborough, Sussex.

2011. HOLLEBON, William George; B: Seaford, Sussex; E: Hastings; L/Cpl. TF 240315; K: 7.7.17; Gwalia Cem. (Bel.); Age 22; Son of Charles James and Amy Elizabeth Hollebon of 59, Willowfield Road, Eastbourne.

2012. HOLMES, Albert Arundel; Capt.; D at Home: 19.5.15; Hornchurch (St.Andrew) Churchyard, Essex (UK); Husband of Ellen Holmes of "Sharigh", 122, London Road, St.Leonards-on-Sea, Sussex.

2013. HORNE, Reginald Harry; B: St.Martin's, Suffolk; E: Lewes, Sussex; Pte. TF 24106; K: 22.9.17; Vlamertinghe New Mil. Cem. (Bel.); Age 27; Son of Harry and Annie Horne of Stable Cottage, 24, High Street, Southover, Sussex; Killed during enemy air raid.

2014. HORSECROFT, Albert; B: – ; E: Uckfield, Sussex; Pte. TF 3071; W at Home: 15.8.16; Heathfield (All Saints) Churchyard, Sussex (UK); Age 30; Son of Spencer and Rhoda Horsecroft of 2, Bullseye Cottage, Heathfield.

2015. HORTON, Albert Edward; B: Maidstone; E: Maidstone; Pte. TF 241344; K: 29.7.17; Duhallow A.D.S. Cem. (Bel.); Age 30; Son of T.W.Horton of Maidstone; Husband of Mary Horton of 8, County Road, Maidstone.

2016. HOWELL, Frederick William; B: – ; E: Hastings; Pte. TF 3775; K: 28.7.16; Le Touret Mil. Cem., Pas-de-Calais; Age 21; Son of Frederick William and Susannah Howell of 2, Zariel Place, Hastings.

2017. HUGGETT, George; B: – ; E: Hastings; Pte. TF 2811; K: 9.5.15; Le Touret Mem., Pas-de-Calais.

2018. HUGGETT, Percy Stanley; B: – ; E: Hastings; Pte. TF 3183; W: 29.6.16; Warlincourt Halte Brit. Cem., Pas-de-Calais; Age 29; Son of Henry James and Emily Ann Huggett; Husband of Beatrice Alice Reed, formerly Huggett, of 45, Sidley Road, Eastbourne.

2019. HUMPHREY, Henry Joseph; B: – ; E: Hastings; Cpl. TF 240874; W: 24.8.17; Étaples Mil. Cem., Pas-de-Calais; Nephew of Charles Humphrey of 14, Windsor Road, Bexhill-on-Sea.

2020. HUNT, Frederick; B: Hastings; E: Hastings; Sgt. TF 240435; D: 31.8.17; Brandhoek Mil. Cem. No.3 (Bel.); Age 32; Husband of Marian Alice Hunt of 27, Plymouth Road, Barry Island, Glamorgan.

2021. HYLAND, Arthur; B: – ; E: Hastings; Pte. TF 3370; W: 18.8.16; Gezaincourt Com. Cem. Ext., Somme; Age 19; Son of Thomas and Rebecca Hyland of Mill Cottages, Whatlington, Sussex.

I

2022. IVES, Albert Edward; B: Gravesend, Kent; E: Gravesend; Pte. TF 6063; W: 8.11.16; Dernancourt Com. Cem. Ext., Somme.

J

2023. JARRETT, Alfred James; B: – ; E: Hastings; Pte. TF 2809; W: 19.10.16; Abbeville Com. Cem. Ext., Somme; Age 20; Son of James and Jane Jarrett of Crowborough, Sussex.

2024. JARRETT, Charles; B: Rye, Sussex; E: Hastings; Pte. TF 2185; K: 29.4.15; Cabaret-Rouge Brit. Cem., Pas-de-Calais.

2025. JARRETT, Frederick Henry; B: Rye, Sussex; E: Rye; Pte. TF 1439; W: 11.5.15; Longuenesse (St. Omer) Souvenir Cem., Pas-de-Calais; Age 20; Son of George and Jane Jarrett of The Mint, Rye.

2026. JOHNSON, George Edward; B: St.John's, Sussex; E: Lewes; Pte. TF 1639; W: 9.5.15; Bethune Town Cem., Pas-de-Calais.*

2027. JOY, Arthur; B: Rye, Sussex; E: Rye; Pte. TF 1771; D: 12.2.16; Villers-Bocage Com. Cem., Somme.

2028. JUDGE, William Lawson; B: – ; E: Hastings; Pte. TF 3029; K: 9.5.15; Le Touret Mem., Pas-de-Calais; Age 18; Son of Charles and Elizabeth Frances Judge of 3, Croft Road, Hastings.

K

2029. KENDALL, Hugh Lawrence; B: Bexhill-on-Sea; E: Bexhill-on-Sea; Pte. TF 2005; K: 9.5.15; Le Touret Mem., Pas-de-Calais.

2030. KENT, William Ernest; B: – ; E: Hastings; Pte. TF 2743; K: 16.8.16; Aveluy Com. Cem., Somme; Age 21; Son of William Henry and Mary Ellen Kent of 17, North Street, St.Leonards-on-Sea.

2031. KENWARD, George Albert; B: – ; E: Wadhurst, Sussex; Pte. TF 2379; K: 9.5.15; Le Touret Mem., Pas-de-Calais; Age 34; Son of Charles and Mary Jane Kenward; Husband of Elizabeth Kenward of 2a, Chester Avenue, Lancing, Sussex.

2032. KINNARD, Arthur Frederick; B: Worthing; E: Worthing; Pte. TF 260007; W: 26.8.17; Mendinghem Mil. Cem. (Bel.); Age 19; Son of Stephen and Julia Kinnard of Clapham Common, Worthing.

2033. KNIGHT, Alfred Howard; Capt., D at Home: 10.12.15; East Wickham (St.Michael) Churchyard, Kent (UK); Age 59; Husband of Mrs.Luna Lizzie Knight.

L

2034. LAKER, John William; B: Portslade, Sussex; E: Brighton; Pte. TF 241347; K: 29.7.17; Essex Farm Cem. (Bel.).

2035. LANCASTER, Henry William; B: Withyham, Sussex; E: Lewes; Pte. TF 1670; K: 9.5.15; Le Touret Mem., Pas-de-Calais.

2036. LANGHAM, Cecil Richard; Capt.; K: 16.8.17; Vlamertinghe New Mil. Cem., (Bel.); Age 26; Son of Col.F.G.Langham, C.M.G., and Frances Mary Langham of Valehurst, St.Helen's Park, Hastings.

2037. LANGRIDGE, Alfred Thomas; B: Lewes; E: Lewes; Pte. TF 1910; K: 9.5.15; Le Touret Mem., Pas-de-Calais.

2038. LANGRIDGE, Frederick Hansford; B: Newick, Sussex; E: Lewes; Pte. TF 240997; K: 7.7.17; Gwalia Cem. (Bel.); Age 26; Son of James and Eliza Langridge of Hadlow Down, Sussex; Previously wounded in August, 1916.*

2039. LARKIN, Philip; B: Hastings; E: Hastings; Pte. TF 3435; W: 16.9.16; Albert Com. Cem. Ext., Somme.

2040. LAUGHTON, George Granville Richard; B: Addiscombe, Surrey; E: Hastings; L/Cpl . TF 2386; K: 9.5.15; Le Touret Mem., Pas-de-Calais.

2041. LAVENDER, William James; B: – ; E: Hastings; Pte. TF 2470; K: 28.7.15; Labourse Com. Cem., Pas-de-Calais; Age 20; Son of William and Charlotte Lavender of 30, Horntye Road, St.Leonards-on-Sea.

2042. LEEVES, Wallace; B: Heathfield, Sussex; E: Hastings; Pte. TF 1987; K: 6.7.16; Knightsbridge Cem., Mesnil-Martinsart, Somme; Age 23; Son of Edward and Emily Maria Leeves of Spoods Farm, Hadlow Down, Sussex.

2043. LEGGATT, Albert Edward George; B: Petworth, Sussex; E: Horsham, Sussex; Pte. TF 6526; K: 14.11.16; Martinpuich Brit. Cem., Pas-de-Calais.

2044. LESTER, Harry William; B: Lavermarney, Essex; E: Hastings; Pte. TF 2426; W: 24.7.16; Puchevillers Brit. Cem., Somme; Age 28; Son of Charles and Emma Lester.

2045. LING, Isaac; B: – ; E: Bury St.Edmunds, Suffolk; Pte. TF 241130; K: 16.8.17; Tyne Cot Mem. (Bel.); Age 21; Son of Mr. and Mrs.James Ling of School Hill, Blaxhall, Suffolk.

2046. LYNCH, Percy Alexander; B: Hastings; E: Hastings; Pte. TF 240168; W: 30.9.17; Dozinghem Mil. Cem. (Bel.); Age 20; Son of Mr.E.C.J. and Mrs.A.C.Lynch of 95a, Hughenden Road, Hastings.

M

2047. MACKELLOW, Charles; B: Crowborough, Sussex; E: Crowborough; Pte. TF 1844; K: 16.8.16; Thiepval Mem., Somme; Son of Charles and Emily MacKellow of 2, Yew Tree House, Queen's Road, Crowborough.*

2048. MANKELOW, Charles; B: – ; E: Wadhurst, Sussex; Pte. TF 2331; K: 9.5.15; Le Touret Mem., Pas-de-Calais; Age 24; Son of Edwin Thomas and Harriet Ruth Mankelow of Cemetery Lodge, Bayham Road, Tunbridge Wells.

2049. MANKTELOW, Charles; B: – ; E: Wadhurst, Sussex; Pte. TF 2598; D at Home: 5.1.16; St.Albans Cem., Hertfordshire (UK).

2050. MANN, Herbert Victor; B: Hastings; E: Hastings; Pte. TF 2453; K: 9.5.15; Le Touret Mem., Pas-de-Calais.*

2051. MANNERS, William; B: Danehill, Sussex; E: Uckfield, Sussex; Pte. TF 241175; K: 12.10.17; Vlamertinghe New Mil. Cem. (Bel.).

2052. MANSER, Ernest; B: Hastings; E: Hastings; Pte. TF 1519; D at Home: 13.4.15; Hastings Cem., Sussex (UK); Age 18; Son of Mrs.Manser of 2, Rose Cottages, Winchelsea Row, Hastings.

2053. MARCH, William Henry; B: Worthing; E: Worthing; Pte. TF 6070; W: 11.11.16; St.Sever Cem. Ext., Rouen, Seine-Maritime; Son of Mrs. Ellen March of 39, Cobden Road, Worthing.

2054. MARCHANT, Albert Edward; B: – ; E: Hastings; Pte. TF 240736; K: 22.9.17; Vlamertinghe New Mil. Cem. (Bel.); Age 20; Son of Lillian B.Marchant of 3, Harts Cottages, Meads, Eastbourne.*

2055. MARKIE, Harold; B: Northampton; E: Northampton; Pte. TF 241131; K: 15.9.17; Vlamertinghe New Mil. Cem. (Bel.); Age 22; Son of Joseph and Amy Markie of 52, Perry Street, Northampton.

2056. MARRIOTT, Harold Deane; B: Hastings; E: Hastings; Pte. TF 2394; K: 9.5.15; Le Touret Mem., Pas-de-Calais; Son of Thomas Eustace and Emily Marriott.

2057. MARSHALL, Robert; B: Broomhill, Sussex; E: Rye, Sussex; Pte. TF 1851; D: 10.10.15; Étaples Mil. Cem., Pas-de-Calais; Age 20; Son of Samuel Arthur and Emma Jane Marshall of 46, Grove Road, Hastings.

2058. MARTIN, Alfred; B: Rotherfield, Sussex; E: Hastings; Pte. TF 240428; K: 25.4.17; Thiepval Mem., Somme.

2059. MARTIN, Ernest William; B: – ; E: Hastings; Cpl. TF 2348; K: 14.11.16; Martinpuich Brit. Cem., Pas-de-Calais; Age 24; Son of Harold T.J. and Louisa Martin of 49, Third Cross Road, Twickenham, Middlesex; This man's original battlefield timber Cross is preserved, with others, in the porch of St.Bartholomew's Church, Burwash, Sussex; the Crosses were brought back by Rudyard Kipling who lived at Burwash.

2060. MARTIN, Horatio Rodney; B: Brighton; E: Brighton; Pte. TF 3566; K: 16.8.16; Aveluy Com. Cem., Somme; Age 24; Husband of Mary Jesse Clews, formerly Martin, of 28, Artillery Street, Brighton.

2061. MESSAGE, Edgar; B: Warbleton, Sussex; E: Hastings; Pte. TF 2479; K: 9.5.15; Le Touret Mem., Pas-de-Calais; Age 22; Son of Herbert and Miriam Message of The Old School House, Rushlake Green, Sussex.

2062. MILLER, Charles; B: Udimore, Sussex; E: Chichester; Pte. TF 241350; W: 29.8.17; Dozinghem Mil. Cem. (Bel.).

2063. MILLER, George Henry; B: Warnham, Sussex; E: Warnham; Pte. TF 6527; K: 14.11.16; Martinpuich Brit. Cem., Pas-de-Calais; Age 19; Son of George and Louisa Miller of Friday House, Warnham.

2064. MOORE, Arthur; B: – ; E: Lewes; Pte. TF 3040; K: 9.5.15; Le Touret Mem., Pas-de-Calais; Age 20; Son of Mr.S.Moore of Wellingham Cottages, Ringmer, Sussex.

2065. MOORE, Arthur George; B: Hastings; E: Hastings; Sgt. TF 425; K: 9.5.15; Le Touret Mem., Pas-de-Calais.

2066. MORDAUNT, Arthur; B: St.Mary's, Surrey; E: Lewes; Pte. TF 240154; K: 22.9.17; Vlamertinghe New Mil. Cem. (Bel.).

2067. MORRIS, Henry James; B: Hastings; E: Hastings; Pte. TF 240201; K: 7.7.17; Gwalia Cem. (Bel.); Age 30; Husband of Mrs.H.E.Morris of 9a, 3rd Flat, Spring Street, St.Leonards-on-Sea.

2068. MOULDEN, John; B: Islington, London; E: Brighton; Pte. TF 260068; W: 22.7.17; Railway Dugouts Burial Ground (Bel.); Age 26; Son of William and Maria Moulden; Husband of Florence Mary Moulden of 12, Dresden Road, Highgate, London.

2069. MUSHETT, Frank; B: Rye, Sussex; E: Rye; Pte. TF 1730; W: 17.4.15; Boulogne Eastern Cem., Pas-de-Calais; Age 21; Son of Henry and Mary Mushett of Ferry Road, Rye.*

N

2070. NEVE, William John; B: Rye Foreign, Sussex; E: Rye; Sgt. TF 344; K: 9.5.15; Le Touret Mem., Pas-de-Calais; Age 28; Son of James and Emily Ellen Neve of Leasam Farm, Playden, Sussex.

2071. NEWNHAM, Herbert Belton; B: Warbleton, Sussex; E: Hastings; Pte. TF 2486; K: 27.6.16; Couin Brit. Cem., Pas-de-Calais; Son of Mrs.K.Newnham of Gardiner Street, Herstmonceux, Sussex.

O

2072. O'BEIRNE, Lawrence; B: Canning Town, London; E: Bostall Heath Camp, Kent; Pte. TF 3288; K: 19.8.16; Thiepval Mem., Somme; Age 21; Son of Vincent and Agnes O'Beirne of 87, Ravenscroft Road, Canning Town.

2073. OLIVER, Alfred; B: – ; E: Uckfield, Sussex; Pte. TF 2973; W: 16.11.16; Dernancourt Com. Cem. Ext., Somme.

2074. OLIVER, Sidney Arthur; B: – ; E: Hastings; Pte. TF 2532; K: 9.5.15; Le Touret Mem., Pas-de-Calais; Son of Edward Oliver of 1, Midland Terrace, Cricklewood, London.

2075. OSBORNE, Albert Vincent; B: Guestling, Sussex; E: Hastings; Pte. TF 1837; W at Home: 24.5.15; Manchester Southern Cem. (UK); Age 21; Son of Albert and Kate Osborne of Pickham, Guestling, Sussex.

P

2076. PAGE, Richard Frank; B: – ; E: Hastings; Pte. TF 2848; K: 21.8.16; Aveluy Com. Cem., Somme; Age 18; Son of Mr. and Mrs.R.T.Page of 4, St.Margaret's Terrace, Rye, Sussex.

2077. PAGE, William Henry; B:– ; E: Hastings; Pte. TF 3196; W: 17.8.16; Étaples Mil. Cem., Pas-de-Calais; Age 16; Son of Edward John and Emily Page of Rye.*

2078. PALING, Ira; B: Marchay, Derbyshire, E: Nottingham; Pte. TF 260025; K: 26.9.17; Tyne Cot Mem. (Bel.); Age 22; Son of George Thomas and Elizabeth Paling of Alfreton Road, Fulwood, Sutton in Ashfield, Nottinghamshire.

2079. PALMER, James; B: Westminster, London; E: Lewes, Sussex; Pte. TF 1805; K: 14.4.16; Hebuterne Mil. Cem., Pas-de-Calais; Age 18; Son of J.W. and Mary Frances Palmer of 8, St.Anns Crescent, Lewes.*

2080. PALMER, Samuel Edward; B: – ; E: Hastings; Pte. TF 3234; W: 2.1.16 Louvencourt Mil. Cem., Somme; Age 20; Son of William Owen and Mary Ann Palmer of Wadhurst, Sussex.

2081. PANTER, Claude; B:– ; E: Brighton; Pte. TF 6093; W: 5.12.16; St.Sever Cem. Ext., Rouen, Seine-Maritime.

2082. PARK, Thomas Allan; B: – ; E: Hastings; Pte. TF 240738; K: 15.9.17; Vlamertinghe New Mil. Cem. (Bel.); Son of Thomas Allan Park and Ann Elizabeth Park of Pay Gate, Burwash, Sussex; Also appears as 'PARKS, T.' on the Tyne Cot Mem. (Bel.); This man's original battlefield timber Cross is preserved, with others, in the porch of St.Bartholomew's Church, Burwash; the Crosses were brought back by Rudyard Kipling who lived at Burwash.

2083. PARKER, William Reuben; B: – ; E: Horsham, Sussex; Pte. TF 241371; K: 3.10.17; St.Julien Dressing Station Cem. (Bel.).

2084. PARKS, Edwin; B: Framfield, Sussex; E: Uckfield, Sussex; Pte. TF 1826; K: 23.7.16; Bouzincourt Com. Cem. Ext., Somme; Son of Mr.G.Parks of 4, Coburg Street, Portsmouth.

- - PARKS, Thomas; (see 2082).

2085. PARSONS, David; B: Hellingly, Sussex; E: Hailsham, Sussex; Pte.TF 240032; W: 12.10.17; Solferino Farm Cem. (Bel.); Age 24; Son of Aaron and Annie Parsons of 64, South Road, Hailsham.

2086. PAYNE, Henry John; B: – ; E: Hastings; Pte. TF 2553; W: 9.10.15; Beauval Com. Cem., Somme.*

2087. PEEL, George Ernest; B: – ; E: Lewes; L/Cpl. TF 2496; K: 9.5.15; Le Touret Mem., Pas-de-Calais; Age 24; Son of Mr. and Mrs.G.W.Peel of 10, St.Mary's Road, South Norwood, London.

2088 PHILLIPS, William George; B: – ; E: Hastings; Pte. TF 240718; K: 7.7.17; Gwalia Cem. (Bel.); Age 27; Son of Mr. and Mrs.Owen Phillips of Rye, Sussex; Husband of Mrs.Rowe, formerly Phillips, of 57, The Mint, Rye.

2089. PILBEAM, Arthur Jesse; B: – ; E: Wadhurst; Pte. TF 2333; K: 9.5.15; Le Touret Mem., Pas-de-Calais; Enlisted with brother, George Henry, who was also killed in the same action on the same day and also has no known grave (see 2090).

2090. PILBEAM, George Henry; B: – ; E: Wadhurst; Pte. TF 2334; K: 9.5.15; Le Touret Mem., Pas-de-Calais; Enlisted with brother, Arthur Jesse, who was also killed in the same action on the same day and also has no known grave (see 2089).

2091. PIPER, Harold Mark; B: – ; E: Uckfield, Sussex; Pte. TF 2966; K: 14.11.16; Martinpuich Brit. Cem.,

Pas-de-Calais; Age 21; Son of William Henry and Rhoda Piper of Greywood, East Hoathly, Sussex.*

2092. PLESTER, William Ernest; B: Hove; E: – ; Drummer TF 2653; D at Home: 16.7.15; Hooe (St. Oswald) Churchyard, Sussex (UK); Age 17; Son of Mrs.A.Bland, formerly Plester, of 41, Devonshire Road, Bexhill-on-Sea and the late William Plester.

2093. POOLE, Alfred, B: Sevenoaks, Kent; E: Hastings; Pte. TF 1876; D: 11.9.15; Terlincthun Brit. Cem., Pas-de-Calais.

2094. POOLE, Edward Bruce; B: – ; E: Hastings; Pte. TF 2262; K: 9.5.15; Le Touret Mem., Pas-de-Calais; Age 30; Son of Frederick and Frances Ann Poole of 9, Hill Street, Hastings.

2095. POPE, Henry James; B: – ; E: Hastings; Pte. TF 2292; K: 9.5.15; Le Touret Mem., Pas-de-Calais; Age 32; Son of Henry and Annie Pope of High Street, Burwash, Sussex; Husband of Alice Elizabeth Pope of "Sketrick", Etchingham, Sussex.

2096. POTTER, Fredric James; B: Guildford, Surrey; E: – ; Pte. – 2101; W at Home: 4.4.18; Whatlington (St.Mary Magdalene) Churchyard, Sussex (UK); Age 50; Husband of Jane Louise Potter of "Coulee Ridge", Whatlington Road, Battle, Sussex; Died of wounds received in France in 1915; Previously served 22 years with the Rifle Brigade; Served in the South Africa campaign.

2097. POWELL, Richard Henry; 2nd Lt.; K: 9.5.15; Le Touret Mem., Pas-de-Calais; Age 31; Son of Henry Pryor Powell and Helena M.Powell of The Rectory, Petworth, Sussex; Husband of Barbara Frances Powell of 17, Tite Street, Chelsea, London.

2098. PRICE, G.; B: – ; E: – ; Pte. TF 2166; D at Home: 6.3.15; Wadhurst (SS. Peter and Paul) Churchyard, Sussex (UK); Age 20; Son of James Price.

2099. PRICE, William Eric; 2nd Lt.; K: 2.5.15; Gonnehem Churchyard, Pas-de-Calais; Age 23; Son of William T. and Florence Price of Greenhill, Rotherfield, Sussex. K: 2.5.15.

R

2100. RANSOME, Arthur Frederick; B: – ; E: Hastings; Pte. TF 2896; K: 18.8.16; Aveluy Com. Cem., Somme; Son of Mrs.W.Ransome of Hope Cottage, London Road, Crowborough, Sussex.

2101. RAVEN, William George; B: Hastings; E: Hastings; Pte. TF 3355; K: 23.3.16; Hebuterne Mil. Cem., Pas-de-Calais; Age 19; Son of Mr. and Mrs.C.Raven of 190, Battle Road, St.Leonards-on-Sea.*

2102. REED, Selby; B: – ; E: Hastings; Pte. TF 2341; W: 2.5.15; Bethune Town Cem., Pas-de-Calais; Age 19; Son of Hector and Rose E.Reed of 5, Brunswick Terrace, Mount Sion, Tunbridge Wells.

2103. REED, Thomas William; B: – ; E: Wadhurst, Sussex; Pte. TF 240502; K: 12.10.17; Vlamertinghe New Mil. Cem. (Bel.); Age 25; Son of Henry George and Elizabeth H.Reed of 7, Turners Green, Wadhurst.

2104. RICHARDS, Percy; B: – ; E: Hastings; Pte. TF 240838; K: 25.8.17; Divisional Collecting Post Cem. (Bel.); Age 20; Son of Frederick and Annie Elizabeth Richards of Little Frankham Cottage, Mark Cross, Sussex.*

2105. RICHES, Thomas; B: Clerkenwell, London; E: Hastings; Cpl. TF 2117; K: 9.5.15; Le Touret Mem., Pas-de-Calais; Age 28; Son of Samuel and Louisa Riches of Norfolk Cottage, Waldron, Sussex.

2106. RICKARD, Frank; B: – ; E: Haywards Heath, Sussex; L/Cpl. TF 6078; W: 14.11.16; Becourt Mil. Cem., Somme; Age 32; Husband of Florence Rickard of 11, Bradstone Avenue, Folkestone, Kent.

2107. RIDDLE, Herbert James; B: – ; E: Rye, Sussex; Pte. TF 3647; W: 14.7.16; Doullens Com. Cem. Ext. No.1, Somme; Age 22; Son of William and Naomi Riddle of Rye.

2108. RIGELSFORD, Edgar; B: – ; E: Lewes; Pte. TF 2604; K: 9.5.15; Le Touret Mem., Pas-de-Calais; Age 23; Son of George and Frances Rigelsford of 42, Haringay Road, Haringay, London.

2109. ROBINSON, Frank; B: Salehurst, Sussex; E: Battle, Sussex; Sgt. TF 1362; W: 9.5.15; Chocques Mil. Cem., Pas-de-Calais; Age 20; Son of James and Alice Robinson of George Hill, Robertsbridge, Sussex.

2110. RUSSELL, Ernest Walter; B: – ; E: Hastings; Pte. TF 3184; K: 9.5.15; Le Touret Mem., Pas-de-Calais.

2111. RUSSELL, John Thomas; B: Penhurst, Sussex; E: Robertsbridge, Sussex; Pte.TF 1555; K: 16.8.16; Thiepval Mem., Somme.

S

2112. SALES, Alfred; B: – ; E: Hastings; Pte. TF 2907; K: 8.7.15; Cambrin Churchyard Ext., Pas-de-Calais; Age 20; Son of Amos and Jane Sales of 40, Sandown Road, Hastings.

2113. SAUNDERS, Frank; B: Heathfield, Sussex; E: Wadhurst, Sussex; L/Cpl. TF 1629; K: 9.5.15; Le Touret Mem., Pas-de-Calais; Age 26; Son of Trayton Saunders of Eastmount Cottages, Maidstone Road, Staplehurst, Kent.

2114. SAUNDERS, Oliver; B: Great Yarmouth; E: Norwich; Pte. TF 3998; W: 4.9.16; Gezaincourt Com. Cem. Ext., Somme; Age 20; Son of Henry Samuel and Louisa Saunders of 2, Greyhound Yard, Ber Street, Norwich.

2115. SCOTT, Gilbert; B: – ; E: Hastings; Pte. TF 3560; W: 6.7.16; Acheux Brit. Cem., Somme; Age 19; Son of Edward and Mary Scott of Punnetts Town, Sussex.

2116. SEDDON, Robert Joseph; B: Heath, Bedfordshire; E: Wandsworth, London; Pte. TF 4052; K: 14.11.16; Martinpuich Brit. Cem., Pas-de-Calais; Age 21; Son of Frederick and Elizabeth Seddon of Pear Tree Cottage, Southcott, Leighton Buzzard.

2117. SHANKS, Arthur Cain; B: – ; E: Hastings; Pte. TF 2732; K: 9.5.15; Le Touret Mem., Pas-de-Calais.

2118. SHEPHERD, James Harper; B: Leytonstone, London; E: Hastings; Pte. TF 2393; K: 9.5.15; Le Touret Mem., Pas-de-Calais; Age 18; Son of Charles and Mary Elizabeth Shepherd of 15, Alexander Road, Bexhill-on-Sea.*

2119. SHOESMITH, Edward Benjamin; B: –; E: Hastings; Pte. TF 2890; K: 8.7.15; Cambrin Churchyard Ext., Pas-de-Calais; Age 21; Son of Benjamin Shoesmith of 32, Collier Road, Hastings.*

2120. SHOESMITH, Frederick Herbert Walter; B: Upper Dicker, Sussex; E: Hastings; Pte. TF 3647; W: 5.9.16; Étaples Mil. Cem., Pas-de-calais; Age 19; Son of Ernest Edward and Sarah Jane Shoesmith of The Nurseries, Upper Dicker.*

2121. SIMMONDS, Robert Thomas; B: Uckfield, Sussex; E: Uckfield; Pte. TF 1579; K: 9.5.15; Le Touret Mem., Pas-de-Calais; Age 19; Son of George and Emma Simmonds of 2, Baker Street, Uckfield.*

2122. SIMMONS, Thomas; B: –; E: Hastings; Pte. TF 3060; K: 8.4.15; Le Touret Mem., Pas-de-Calais.

2123. SLARKS, George; B: Sittingbourne, Kent; E: Brighton; Pte. TF 3514; K: 14.11.16; Martinpuich Brit. Cem., Pas-de-Calais; Age 31; Son of Mr. and Mrs.C.E.Slarks of Tunstall, Sittingbourne.

2124. SMITH, Albert; B: Haywards Heath, Sussex; E: Haywards Heath; Pte. TF 241424; K: 30.9.17; Duhallow A.D.S. Cem. (Bel.); Age 19; Son of George and Annie Smith of 71, Queen's Road, Haywards Heath.

2125. SMITH, Charles; B: Hastings; E: Hastings; Pte. TF 1513; D at Home: 5.8.15; Hastings Cem., Sussex (UK).

2126. SMITH, Edward George; B: –; E: Lewes; Pte. TF 3469; W: 26.7.16; Puchevillers Brit. Cem., Somme; Age 25; Son of James and Emily Smith of Newick, Sussex; Husband of Alice Mabel Smith of 2, Sunnyside, Marlpit Hill, Edenbridge, Kent.

2127. SMITH, H.; B: –; E: –; Cpl. TF 414; D at Home: 24.10.15; Rotherfield Burial Ground, Sussex (UK); Age 34; Son of Frederic and Lydia Smith of Longcroft, Rotherfield.

2128. SMITH, J.; B: –; E: –; D at Home: 27.7.15; Stonegate (St.Peter) Churchyard, Sussex (UK).

2129. SPENCER, George; B: –; E: Hastings; Pte. TF 241083; K: 4.10.17; Duhallow A.D.S. Cem. (Bel.); Age 20; Son of Ann Spencer of 15, Coleman Street, Brighton.

2130. SPICE, Joseph William; B: Hastings; E: Hastings; Pte. TF240160; K: 16.9.17; Dozinghem Mil. Cem. (Bel.); Age 21; Son of James Henry and Caroline Spice of 22, Old Humphrey Avenue, Hastings.

2131. STARNES, William; B: Brighton; E: Hastings; Pte. TF 3051; K: 12.7.16; Mesnil Ridge Cem., Somme; Age 23; Son of Mr. and Mrs.G.H.Starnes of 82, Tivoli Crescent, Brighton.

2132. STEDMAN, William; B: Lewes, Sussex; E: Cranbrook, Kent; Pte. TF 3144; K: 9.5.15; Le Touret Mem., Pas-de-Calais.*

2133. STEPHENS, Hubert Stanley; B: Lewes; E: Lewes; Pte. TF 240511; K: 23.9.17; Dozinghem Mil. Cem. (Bel.); Age 22; Son of John and Elizabeth Stephens.*

2134. STEVENS, Alfred; B: Woking, Surrey; E: Hastings; Pte. TF 2485; K: 9.5.15; Woburn Abbey Cem., Pas-de-Calais; Brother of Mr.O.E.G.Stevens of 39, St.Peter's Road, Old Woking Village.

2135. STEWART-JONES, Thorold Arthur; Capt.; K: 9.5.15; Le Touret Mem., Pas-de-Calais.

2136. STONE, Thomas; B: –; E: Hastings; Pte. TF 2738; K: 9.5.15; Le Touret Mem., Pas-de-Calais.

2137. STRANGE, Arnold John; B: Watford, Hertfordshire; E: Crowborough, Sussex; Pte. TF 2190; W: 16.10.15; Louvencourt Mil. Cem., Somme; Age 19; Son of Charles J. and Mary Jane Strange of "Brackleigh", Crowborough.

2138. STRATFORD, John; B: –; E: Hastings; Pte. TF 240651; K: 16.8.17; Tyne Cot Mem. (Bel.).

2139. STUBBERFIELD, Frederick George; B: –; E: Hastings; Pte. TF 2611; K: 8.7.15; Cambrin Churchyard Ext., Pas-de-Calais; Age 17; Son of George and Sarah Stubberfield of Corner House, Ashburnham, Sussex.

2140. SWAIN, Joseph; B: –; E: Hastings; Pte. TF 2293; K: 28.3.15; Cabaret-Rouge Brit. Cem., Pas-de-Calais; Age 19; Son of Fredrick and Rose Swain of 2, Zion Cottage, Tackleway, Hastings.

2141. SWEATMAN, John Henry; B: Burwash, Sussex; E: Ticehurst, Sussex; Pte. TF 240309; K: 15.9.17; Vlamertinghe New Mil. Cem. (Bel.); Age 24; Son of William Sweatman of Station Road, Hurst Green, Sussex.

2142. SWEETMAN, Albert Edward; B: –; E: Hastings; Pte. TF 240680; W: 17.8.17; Brandhoek New Mil. Cem. No.3 (Bel.); Age 19; Son of Albert Edward and Charlotte Josephine Sweetman of Crowborough, Sussex.*

2143. SWEETMAN, Ernest Arthur; B: Rotherfield, Sussex; E: Crowborough, Sussex; L/Sgt. TF 417; K: 17.5.15; Bethune Town Cem., Pas-de-Calais; Age 34; Son of John and Mary Sweetman of Crowborough.*

2144. SYMONS, James Antony; 2nd Lt.; K: 18.7.16; Bouzincourt Com. Cem. Ext., Somme; Age 21; Son of William Christian and Cecilia Symons of 129, Beaufort Street, Chelsea, London.

T

2145. TAYLOR, Frank; B: Catsfield, Sussex; E: Bexhill-on-Sea; Pte. TF 1572; K: 28.3.15; Cabaret-Rouge Brit. Cem., Pas-de-Calais; Age 19; Son of Mrs.L.D.L.Taylor of Pond Cottage, Glovers Lane, Sidley, Bexhill-on-Sea.

2146. TAYLOR, Leslie Welfare; B: –; E: Rye, Sussex; Pte. TF 3246; K: 8.11.16; Martinpuich Brit. Cem., Pas-de-Calais; Age 18; Son of William Thomas and Mary Elizabeth Taylor of 4, King Street, Rye.

2147. TAYLOR, Stanley; B: Blackrod, Lancashire; E: Ticehurst, Sussex; Pte. TF 240292; K: 22.9.17; Vlamertinghe New Mil. Cem. (Bel.); Age 22; Son of George and Emma Taylor of 84, William Street, Heywood, Lancashire; This man's original battlefield timber Cross is preserved, with others, in the porch of St.Bartholomew's Church, Burwash, Sussex; the Crosses were brought back by Rudyard Kipling who lived at Burwash.

2148. TEAGUE, John Spencer; B: Uckfield, Sussex; E:

Uckfield; Pte. TF 202687; K: 15.9.17; Vlamertinghe New Mil. Cem. (Bel.); Age 31; Son of William and Eliza Teague of Ridgewood, Uckfield; Husband of Edith Teague of 19, Lewes Road, Ridgewood, Uckfield.

2149. TESTER, Arthur Ernest; B: – ; E: Hastings; Pte. TF 2819; K: 16.8.16; Thiepval Mem., Somme.

2150. TESTER, Christopher Charles; B: Maresfield, Sussex; E: Crowborough, Sussex; Pte. TF 1627; K: 30.3.15; Cabaret-Rouge Brit. Cem., Pas-de-Calais; Age 17; Son of Owen and Celinder Tester of 1, Hand and Sceptre Stables, London Road, Tunbridge Wells.*

2151. THORPE, John; B: Seaford, Sussex; E: Lewes; Drummer TF 1455; W at Home: 17.5.15; South Malling (St.Michael) Churchyard, Sussex (UK); Age 19; Son of Mrs.Annie Thorpe of 78a, South Street, Lewes; Rank also recorded as Bugler.*

2152. TILTMAN, Harry; B: Rye, Sussex; E: Rye; L/Cpl. TF 240870; K: 25.8.17; Track "X" Cem. (Bel.); Age 22; Son of William and Fanny Tiltman of 5, West Cliffe, Rye.

2153. TRIMMER, Reginald Charles; B: Farringdon; E: Wadhurst, Sussex; L/Cpl. TF 1674; K: 16.8.16; Thiepval Mem., Somme.

2154. TUCKER, Edward Richard; B: – ; E: Rye; Pte. TF 4055; K: 14.11.16; Martinpuich Brit. Cem., Pas-de-Calais; Age 24; Son of Mr.E.J. and Mrs.M.Tucker of 124, Luton Road, Chatham, Kent.*

2155. TURK, G.E.; B; – ; E: – ; Pte. TF 3648; K: 4.9.16; Acheux Brit. Cem., Somme; Age 22; Son of Mrs. and the late Mr.T.J.Turk of Old Hall Farm, Brookland, Kent.

2156. TURNER, George; B: Clapham, London; E: Hastings; Pte. TF 1963; K: 9.5.15; Le Touret Mem., Pas-de-Calais.

2157. TWICHETT, Arthur Clifford; B: – ; E: Uckfield, Sussex; Pte. TF 2506; W: 29.6.16; Merville Com. Cem., Nord; Wounded while attached to the 6th Battalion Royal Warwickshire Regiment.

V

2158. VIDLER, Reginald Walter; B: – ; E: Hastings; Pte. TF 2650; W: 7.7.16; Doullens Com. Cem. Ext. No.1, Somme; Age 19; Son of Charles and Elizabeth Ann Vidler of Northiam, Sussex.

2159. VIDLER, William; B: Wadhurst, Sussex; E: Hastings; Pte. TF 2163; K: 9.5.15; Le Touret Mem., Pas-de-Calais; Age 19; Son of Thomas and Mary Ann Vidler of 3, Dunstan Terrace, Sparrows Green, Sussex.

2160. VINCE, Percy William; B: – ; E: Wadhurst, Sussex; Pte. TF 2374; K: 19.3.15; Brown's Road Mil. Cem., Festubert, Pas-de-Calais; Age 20; Son of Walter Vince of Sparrows Green, Sussex.

2162. VINE, Bert; B: Hailsham, Sussex; E: Chichester; Pte. TF 202989; K: 12.10.17; Vlamertinghe New Mil. Cem. (Bel.); Age 25; Son of Mr. and Caroline Vine of 37, Station Road, Hailsham.

W

2162. WADEY, William Mark; B: Upperton, Sussex; E: Petworth, Sussex; Pte. TF 200499; W: 15.9.17; Dozinghem Mil. Cem. (Bel.).

2163. WALDER, Richard Down; B: – ; E: Uckfield, Sussex; Pte. TF 2873; W: 18.5.15; Boulogne Eastern Cem., Pas-de-Calais; Age 21; Son of George and Elizabeth Walder of Millside, Bolney, Sussex.

2164. WALLER, George; B: – ; E: Lewes; Pte. TF 3082; K: 9.5.15; Le Touret Mem., Pas-de-Calais; Age 19; Son of Mrs.Ann Waller of Uckfield Road, Ringmer, Sussex.

2165. WALLIS, Harry; B: Coursley Wood, Sussex; E: Ticehurst, Sussex; Pte. TF 2021; K: 9.5.15; Le Touret Mem., Pas-de-Calais; Age 35; Son of Thomas and Mary Wallis.

2166. WELLS, Thomas George; B: – ; E: Hastings; Pte. TF 2787; K: 9.5.15; Le Touret Mem., Pas-de-Calais; Age 19; Son of Thomas William and Mary A.Wells of Lidham Farm, Guestling, Sussex.

2167. WENHAM, William Herbert; B: Hailsham, Sussex; E: Hailsham; Pte. TF 202966; K: 25.8.17; Divisional Collecting Post Cem. (Bel.); Age 19; Adopted son of Rosa Mansell of 9, Woodseats House Road, Woodseats, Yorkshire.

2168. WEST, James Edwin; Pte. TF 3411; K: 24.8.16; Ovillers Mil. Cem., Somme; Age 19; Son of Charles James West.

2169. WEST, Robert Leslie; B: Catsfield, Sussex; E: Hastings; Pte. TF 241177; W at Home: 22.8.17; Crowhurst (St.George) Churchyard, Sussex (UK); Age 26; Son of Robert Alfred and Minnie Maria West of the Post Office, Crowhurst.

2170. WETTLE, Frank Alfred; B: Hastings; E: Hastings; Pte. TF 2008; K: 12.7.16; Mesnil Ridge Cem., Somme; Age 19; Son of Mr. and Mrs.Alfred James Wettle of 18, Alexandra Road, St.Leonards-on-Sea.

2171. WHILLOCK, Walter; B: Birmingham; E: Birmingham; Pte. TF 6502; W: 14.11.16; Becourt Mil. Cem., Somme; Age 21; Son of Mr. and Mrs.W.Whillock of 72, Witton Lane, Aston, Birmingham.

2172. WHITE, Wilfred James; B: East Grinstead, Sussex; E: East Grinstead; Pte. TF 260003; K: 26.2.17; Herbecourt Brit. Cem., Somme; Age 22; Son of Mr. and Mrs.White of 16, Glen Vue, East Grinstead; Husband of Harriett Clifton, formerly, White, of 26, Glen Vue, East Grinstead.

2173. WILKINSON, Arthur Benjamin; Lt.; W: 14.11.16; Becourt Mil. Cem., Somme; Age 29; Son of Benjamin Wilkinson of Windsor; Husband of Mrs.N.K.Wilkinson of 210, Station Road, Leigh-on-Sea, Essex.

2174. WILMSHURST, Frank Miles; B: Ringmer, Sussex; E: Brighton; Pte. TF 241181; W: 24.9.17; Dozinghem Mil. Cem. (Bel.).

2175. WINCHESTER, Robert; B: – ; E: Uckfield, Sussex; Pte. TF 2651; W: 9.4.15; Bethune Town Cem., Pas-de-Calais; Brother of Mrs.E.Richardson of 68, Longstone Road, Eastbourne.

2176. WOOD, James; B: South Malling, Sussex; E: Lewes; Pte. TF 240216; K: 15.9.17; Vlamertinghe New Mil. Cem. (Bel.).

2177. WOODS, Charles Edward; B: Woodbridge, Suffolk; E: Hastings; Pte. TF 1885; K: 9.5.15; Le Touret Mem., Pas-de-Calais.

2178. WRIGHT, Arthur E.; B: Uckfield, Sussex; E: Uckfield; Pte TF 1827; K: 6.7.16; Knightsbridge Cem., Mesnil-Martinsart, Somme; Age 21; Son of Mr. and Mrs.Ernest S.Wright of 8, Baker Street, Uckfield.*

2179. WRIGHT, Harold Wells; B: Lewes; E: Lewes; Pte. TF 1304; K: 9.5.15; Le Touret Mem., Pas-de-Calais.

2180. WRIGHT, John Leslie; B: – ; E: Hastings; Pte. TF 2477; W: 9.10.16; Aubigny Com. Cem. Ext., Pas-de-Calais; Age 19; Son of John and Lily Wright of 95, Milward Road, Hastings.

2181. WRIGHT, William John; B: – ; E: Hastings; Pte. TF 2266; K: 9.5.15; Le Touret Mem., Pas-de-Calais; Age 19; Son of Albert and Elizabeth Wright.*

7th Battalion

A

2182. ABEAR, Charles A.; B: – ; E: Chiswick, London; Pte. G 18039; W: 2.10.16; Heilly Station Cem., Mericourt L'Abbé, Somme.*

2183. ABRAMS, Herbert; B: Harpenden, Hertfordshire; E: Luton, Bedfordshire; Pte. G 14839; K: 18.9.18; Epehy Wood Farm Cem., Epehy, Somme.

2184. ADAMS, Albert; B: Bexhill-on-Sea; E: Bexhill-on-Sea; Pte. G 465; W: 15.10.15; Loos Mem., Pas-de-Calais.

2185. ADAMS, Charles; B: Bexhill-on-Sea; E: Hastings; Sgt. G 131; K: 25.7.17; Arras Mem., Pas-de-Calais; Age 27; Brother of Miss M.D.Adams of 18, Bradford Street, Eastbourne.

2186 ADAMS, Charles Emanuel; B: St.James, Northamptonshire; E: Nothampton; Pte. G 17143; K: 4.7.18; Harponville Com. Cem. Ext., Somme; Age 19; Son of William and Emma Adams of Northampton; Husband of Amy M.Adams of Nottingham.

2187. ADES, Bernard Henry; B: Waldron, Sussex; E: Chichester; Pte. G 13398; K: 3.5.17; Arras Mem., Pas-de-Calais; Age 19; Son of Henry Ades of Grove Cottage, Waldron.

2188. ADKIN, Stanley; B: Loughton, Leicestershire; E: Nottingham; Pte. G 1195; K: 2.8.16; Thiepval Mem., Somme; Age 24; Son of John and Sarah Adkin of Longdale Cottage, Woodhouse Eaves, Loughborough, Leicestershire.

2189. ADSETT, Arthur; B: Stopham, Sussex; E: Chichester; Pte. L 9151; K: 31.7.16; Thiepval Mem., Somme; Brother, Ernest, serving with the 8th Battalion was also killed, also has no known grave, and is also commemorated on the Thiepval Memorial (see 3250)

2190. AHERN, John; B: Tralee, Ireland; E: Cork, Ireland; Pte. G 4943; K: 7.7.16; Thiepval Mem., Somme.

2191. AITKEN, James Samuel; B: Hammersmith, London; E: Hastings; Pte. G 562; K: 3.5.17; Arras Mem., Pas-de-Calais, Age 29; Son of Robert and Cecilia Aitken of 5, Wellington Terrace, Rye, Sussex.*

2192. ALDERTON, James Alfred; B: Peshawr, India; E: East Grinstead, Sussex; L/Cpl. G 17766; K: 27.3.18; Pozieres Mem., Somme.

2193. ALDRIDGE, William Nathaniel; B: Stapleford, Hertfordshire; E: Tunbridge Wells; Pte. G 99; K: 7.7.16; Thiepval Mem., Somme; Age 24; Son of James and Sarah Aldgridge of Rose Cottage, Essendon, Hertfordshire.

2194. ALEXANDER, Edwin Albert; B: Kennington, London; E: Camberwell, London; Pte. TF 266383; K: 25.11.17; Cambrai Mem., Louverval, Nord.

2195. ALLCORN, Allan; B: Hailsham, Sussex; E: Hastings; Pte. G 18040; W: 18.10.16; Étaples Mil. Cem., Pas-de-Calais; Age 34; Son of Henry and Mary Allcorn of "The Chesnuts", Herstmonceux, Sussex.

2196. ALLEN, Reginald Gordon; B: Winchester; E: London; Pte. G 14772; K: 5.4.18; Bouzincourt Ridge Cem., Somme.

2197. ALLEN, William; B: Westbourne, Hampshire; E: Chichester; Pte. G 8815; K: 5.10.16; Thiepval Mem., Somme.

2198. AMES, Harman Herbert; B: St.James', Norfolk; E: Norwich; L/Cpl. G 20408; K: 3.5.17; Arras Mem., Pas-de-Calais;; Age 23; Son of Harman Herbert and Rosina Ames of 144, Marlborough Road, Norwich.

2199. ANDRESS, Arthur William; B: – ; E: Haywards Heath, Sussex; Pte. G 18041; K: 5.10.16; Thiepval Mem., Somme.

2200. ANSELL, Basil; B: Hampstead, London; E: East Grinstead, Sussex; Pte. G 8429; W: 26.7.16; St.Sever Cem., Rouen, Seine-Maritime; Age 20; Son of Frederick and Emily Ansell of West View Cottage, Turner's Hill Road, Crawley Down, Sussex.

2201. ANSELL, John William; B: Croydon; E: Croydon; Pte. G 23226; K: 26.3.18; Pozieres Mem., Somme.

2202. APPLEBY, Arthur Fenwick; B: Gateshead; E: Gateshead; Pte. G 22933; K: 5.4.18; Pozieres Mem., Somme; Age 19; Son of Joseph and Josephine Margaret Appleby of 55, Cross Keys Lane, Low Fell, Gateshead.

2203. ARNELL, Albert Colin; B: Hunstan, Sussex; E: Chichester; Sgt. G 978; K: 25.7.17; Monchy Brit. Cem., Pas-de-Calais; Age 27; Son of Henry Arnell of Donnington, Sussex.*

2204. ARNELL, Sidney John; B: Birdham, Sussex; E: Chichester; Pte. G 812; D at Home: 26.5.15; Sidlesham (St.Mary) Churchyard, Sussex (UK); Son of William and Elizabeth Jane Arnell of Mill Road, Sidlesham.*

2205. ARNOTT, Frederick; B: Roehampton, Surrey; E: Eastbourne; Pte. G 6936; W: 19.2.17; Avesnes-le-Comte Com. Cem. Ext., Pas-de-Calais.

2206. ARROWSMITH, Samuel; B: Accrington, Lancashire; E: Accrington; Pte. G 296; K: 16.4.16; Vermelles Brit. Cem., Pas-de-Calais; Age 26; Son of John and Martha Arrowsmith of Accrington.

2207. ASHBY, Thomas Philip; 2nd Lt.; K: 5.9.18; Peronne Com. Cem. Ext., Ste.Radegonde, Somme; Age 29; Son of Thomas H.Ashby of 37, Princes Road, Leicester.

2208. ASHDOWN, Thomas Charles; B: Peasmarsh, Sussex; E: Hastings; Pte. SD 2077; K: 16.10.18; Orchard Dump Cem., Pas-de-Calais; Age 21; Son of Richard and Elizabeth Ashdown of Bate's Farm, Wittersham, Kent.

2209. ASHENDEN, Archibald Herbert; B: Gillingham, Kent; E: Gravesend, Kent; Sgt. G 23693; K: 8.8.18; Beacon Cem., Somme; Age 26; Son of Herbert and Susan Ashenden; Husband of Eveline F.Ashenden of 23, Goss Lane East, Gravesend.*

2210. ASHMAN, George; B: Wickhambrook, Suffolk; E: Bury St.Edmunds, Suffolk; L/Cpl. G 11181; W: 27.3.18; Doullens Com. Cem. Ext. No.1, Somme; Age 22; Son of George and Mary Ann Ashman of Wickhambrook.

2211. ASLETT, Albert Edward; B: Storrington, Sussex; E: Brighton; Pte. G 14054; K: 5.7.17; Monchy Brit. Cem., Pas-de-Calais; Age 19; Son of Charles and Eliza Aslett of 4, North Street, Storrington.*

2212. ATKINSON, William Henry; B: Chichester; E: Chichester; L/Cpl. G 1056; K: 17.4.16; Vermelles Brit. Cem., Pas-de-Calais; Age 20; Son of William and Elizabeth Atkinson of 19, Chapel Street, Chichester.

2213. ATTWOOD, William Charles; B: Winchester; E: Brighton; Pte. SD 1862; K: 11.9.15; Houplines Com. Cem. Ext., Nord; Age 21; Son of Mr. and Mrs.C.Attwood of 10, Staple Gardens, Winchester.*

2214. AUBURTON, Gilbert William; B: Bulwick, Northamptonshire; E: Haywards Heath, Sussex; Cpl. G 238; K: 24.12.15; Loos Mem., Pas-de-Calais.

2215. AUKETT, Albert Edward; B:–; E: Portslade, Sussex; Pte. G 16641; W: 9.4.17; Faubourg d'Amiens Cem., Arras, Pas-de-Calais; Age 28; Son of Mr. Aukett of Newhaven, Sussex; Husband of Rose Aukett of 23, St.Nicholas Road, Portslade.

2216. AUKETT, Joseph Frederick; B: Eastbourne; E: Eastbourne; Pte. G 5378; K: 3.5.17; Arras Mem., Pas-de-Calais; Age 19; Son of Mr. and Mrs.Aukett of 28, East Street, Eastbourne.*

2217. AUSTIN, Harry James; B: Fishergate, Sussex; E: Hove; Sgt. G 772; K: 9.4.17; Arras Mem., Pas-de-Calais; Age 23; Husband of Emily Elizabeth Austin of 5, Freeman's Cottages, Portslade, Sussex.

2218. AVEY, Thomas; B: Cambridge; E: Chelmsford, Essex; Pte. G 14650; K: 19.5.18; Mailly Wood Cem., Somme; Son of Mrs.C.Avey of 69, Great Eastern Street, Cambridge.

2219. AVIS, Edward Arthur; B: Buxted, Sussex; E: Brighton; Pte. GS 216; K: 6.8.15; Houplines Com. Cem. Ext., Nord.*

2220. AVIS, George Henry; B: Bromley, Kent; E: Bromley; Pte. G 13048; W: 11.4.17; Arras Mem., Pas-de-Calais.

2221. AYLING, Alec Oliver; B: Barn Green, Hampshire; E: Chichester; Pte. L 10640; K: 7.7.16; Thiepval Mem., Somme.

B

2222. BACK, John Albert; B: Hove; E: Hove; Pte. L 10474; K: 7.7.16; Thiepval Mem., Somme.

2223. BACON, Edward; B: Yapton, Sussex; E: Arundel, Sussex; Pte. G 4628; K: 3.3.16; Loos Mem., Pas-de-Calais; Husband of Elizabeth Bacon of Rope Cottage, Yapton.

2224. BACON, Samuel Aubrey; B: Hastings; E: Rye, Sussex; Pte. G 188; W: 26.3.16; Bethune Town Cem., Pas-de-Calais; Age 21; Son of Mr. and Mrs. Alfred Samuel Bacon of Hastings; Died at No.33 Casualty Clearing Station.*

2225. BAGGETT, Edwin Victor; B: Lambeth, London; E: Lambeth; Pte. G 11078; W: 28.3.18; Doullens Com. Cem. Ext. No.1, Somme; Age 26; Son of James and Amy Baggett of London.

2226. BAILEY, Arthur Frederick; B: Hastings; E: Hastings; L/Cpl. S 2001; K: 7.7.16; Thiepval Mem., Somme.

2227. BAILEY, Arthur George; B: Haywards Heath, Sussex; E: Hastings; Pte. G 6443; K: 13.8.18; Vis-en-Artois Mem., Haucourt, Pas-de-Calais; Killed near Morlancourt, Somme.

2228. BAKER, Albert William; B: St.Paul's, Sussex; E: Guildford; Pte. S 386; K: 30.6.18; Harponville Com. Cem. Ext., Somme; Age 38; Son of Mrs.E.Baker of 158, Orchard Street, Chichester.*

2229. BAKER, Cecil; B: Mayfield, Sussex; E: Dallington, Sussex; Pte. G 441; K: 27.9.15; Cite Bonjean Mil. Cem., Nord.

2230. BAKER, Charles; B: Brighton; E: Chichester; Pte. L 10359; W: 30.3.18; Doullens Com. Cem. Ext. No.1, Somme.

2231. BAKER, George; B: Salford, Lancashire; E: Kilburn, London; Pte. G 4995; K: 7.7.16; Thiepval Mem., Somme; Age 27; Son of Jonathan and Alice Mary Baker of "Moorcot", Grange Lane, Didsbury, Manchester.

2232. BAKER, Louis James Henry; B: Hammersmith, London; E: Whitehall, London; Cpl. G 20398; K: 25.9.17; Arras Mem., Pas-de-Calais.*

2233. BAKER, Matthias; B: Chelwood, Sussex; E: Eastbourne; Pte. G 24225; K: 3.7.18; Harponville Com. Cem. Ext., Somme; Age 22; Son of Elias and Mary Baker of "Yew Tree House", Chelwood Gate, Sussex.

2234. BAKER, Ralph Dudley; B: Upton Park, London; E: Brighton; Pte. G 21351; K: 20.5.18; Mailly Wood Cem., Somme; Husband of Mrs.M.Baker of 14, Rose Hill, Brighton.

2235. BALCOMBE, George William; B: Hastings; E: Hastings; Pte. G 19997; K: 3.5.17; Arras Mem., Pas-de-Calais.

2236. BALDWIN, John Jackson; B: Barcombe, Sussex; E: Brighton; Sgt. G 12; Hollybrook Mem., Hampshire (UK); Age 27; Son of Francis James and Ann Baldwin of 12, Hornbeam Walk, Whiteley Village, Surrey; Drowned at sea from Hospital Ship Anglia.*

2237. BALLARD, Charles Willard; Capt.; M.C.; K: 25.11.17; Cambrai Mem., Louverval, Nord; Age 24; Son of Charles and Kate Ballard of 2, Norfolk Road, Brighton.

2238. BANGER, Charles; B: Battersea, London; E: Horsham, Sussex; Pte. G 16798; K: 5.4.18; Bouzincourt Ridge Cem., Somme; Age 32; Son of Henry and Eliza Banger; Husband of Lily Ella Banger of 8, Durkins Road, East Grinstead, Sussex.

2239. BARBER, Edward John; B: Hove; E: Hove; Pte. G 9085; K: 3.5.17; Arras Mem., Pas-de-Calais; Age 29; Son of Mr. and Mrs.E.J.Barber of 13, Molesworth Street, Hove.

2240. BARKER, Leslie Morris; B: Eastbourne; E: Lewes; L/Cpl. G 7323; W: 10.4.17; Duisans Brit. Cem., Pas-de-Calais; Son of Mrs.G.A.Barker of 41, South Road, Newhaven, Sussex.

2241. BARNES Edwin Richard; B: Ducklington, Oxfordshire; E: Oxford; Pte. G 20056; K: 3.5.17; Arras Mem., Pas-de-Calais; Husband of Mabel Eleanor Barnes of 115, Iffley Road, Cowley St.John, Oxford.

2242. BARNES, Ernest; B: Fulham, London; E: Worthing; Cpl. SD 1253; K: 3.5.17; Arras Mem., Pas-de-Calais; Age 30; Husband of Sybil Susie Barnes of 13, Nursery Road, Merton, London.

2243. BARNES, George; B: Cocking, Sussex; E: Chichester; Pte. G 4909; K: 7.7.16; Thiepval Mem., Somme.

2244. BARNES, Gilbert James; B: Charmouth, Dorset; E: West London; Pte. G 23696; K: 2.9.18; Guillemont Road Cem., Somme.

2245. BARNES, Hubert William; B: Rodmell, Sussex; E: Brighton; Pte. G 18046; W: 10.10.16; Heilly Station Cem., Mericourt L'Abbé, Somme; Age 20; Son of John S.Barnes of Rodmell, Sussex.

2246. BARNES, John Edward; B: – ; E: – ; Pte. G 4495; K: 4.7.17; Faubourg D'Amiens Cem., Arras, Pas-de-Calais; Age 24; Court Marshalled for desertion and sentenced to 15 years penal servitude; Sentence later suspended but he deserted a second time and was Court Marshalled again; 'Shot at Dawn'.

2247. BARRON, Harry; B: Murrow, Cambridgeshire; E: Chichester; L/Cpl. G 1049; W: 5.8.15; Cite Bonjean Cem., Nord.

2248. BARRS, Alec Richard; B: Loughborough, Leicestershire; E: Kettering, Northamptonshire; Pte. G 23252; D at Home:19.4.18; Rushton (All Saints) Churchyard, Northamptonshire (UK); Age 29; Son of John and Sarah Barrs of 57, Cobden Street, Kettering.

2249. BARTHOLOMEW, Harold; B: Heighton, Sussex; E: Newhaven, Sussex; Pte. G 950; K: 25.7.17; Arras Mem., Pas-de-Calais.

2250. BARTUP, George Albert; B: Brighton; E: Brighton; Pte. G 17671; K: 26.9.16; Agny Mil. Cem., Pas-de-Calais.

2251. BARWICK, William Rufus; B: Rushden, Northamptonshire; E: Leicester; L/Cpl. G 6016; M.M., K: 26.8.18; Peronne Road Cem., Maricourt, Somme; Age 23; Husband of Elsie N.Barwick of 39, Park Road, Wellingborough, Northamptonshire.

2252. BASSON, Albert John; B: St.Martin's, Kent; E: Chichester; Sgt. L 9287; K: 27.9.15; Cite Bonjean Mil. Cem., Nord; Age 24; Son of Mr.F.Basson of 64, Bridge Street, Wye, Kent.*

2253. BATCHELOR, John Thomas; B: Ide Hill, Kent; E: Gravesend, Kent; Pte. G 13125; K: 31.3.17; Arras Mem., Pas-de-Calais; Age 46; Husband of Eleanor Batchelor of 1, Mount View, Quakers Hall Lane, Sevenoaks, Kent; killed by shellfire while on digging duties at Arras.*

2254. BATEMAN, Sidney George; B: Cucklington, Dorset; E: Uckfield, Sussex; Pte. SD 2861; K: 25.7.17; Arras Mem., Pas-de-Calais.

2255. BATEMAN, William James; B: Brighton; E: Brighton; Pte. G 19925; K: 5.4.18; Bouzincourt Ridge Cem., Somme.

2256. BATTENSBY, Harry John Chase; B: Hove; E: Brighton; L/Cpl. G 17508; W: 9.8.18; Querrieu Brit. Cem., Somme; Age 22; Son of Robert Harry and Jane Elizabeth Battensby of 58, Torbay Road, Brondesbury, London.*

2257. BEALE, Alfred William; B: Bournemouth, Hampshire; E: Horsham, Sussex; Sgt. G 931; M.M., K: 9.4.17; Arras Mem., Pas-de-Calais.

2258. BEALE, Clifford William; Lt.; K: 3.3.16; Loos Mem., Pas-de-Calais; Age 24; Son of Dr. and Mrs. Clifford Beale of Allan Down, Rotherfield, Sussex; Attached to 36th Trench Mortar Battery.

2259. BEALL, Thomas Herman; B: Eastbourne; E: Eastbourne; Pte. G 648; M.M.; K: 27.3.18; Pozieres Mem., Somme; Age 31; Son of William and Hannah Beall.*

2260. BECK, George John Percy; B: Hove; E: Hove; Pte. L 10928; W: 24.9.17; Monchy Brit. Cem., Pas-de-Calais; Age 19; Son of John and Elizabeth Beck.*

2261. BECKETT, Arthur Samuel; B: Fulham, London; E: West London; Pte. G 14417; K: 25.11.17; Cambrin Mem., Nord.

2262. BEDFORD, William Henry; B: – ; E: Hounslow, London; Pte. G 23792; W: 10.8.18; Pernois Brit. Cem., Somme; Age 18; Son of Mr. and Mrs.W.Bedford of Thornton Heath, London.

2263. BEECHING, James Wallace; B: Ninfield, Sussex; E: Bexhill-on-Sea; Pte. G 18047; K: 9.4.17; Arras Mem., Pas-de-Calais.*

2264. BELFIELD, Percy; B: Leek, Staffordshire; E: Leek; Pte. G 15156; K: 13.8.18; Beacon Cem., Somme; Age 26; Son of George and Mary Ellen Belfield; Husband of Lizzie Belfield of 24, Union Street, Leek.

2265. BELL, Percy; B: Hamstead, London; E: Brighton; Pte. G 110; K: 7.7.16; Thiepval Mem., Somme.

2266. BELLAMY, David; B: Stockport; E:

Middlesborough; Pte. G 389; K: 4.8.16; Thiepval Mem., Somme.

2267. BENNETT, Albert Armand; B: Colwyn Bay; E: Chichester; Pte. GS 186; D: 17.10.18; Houchin Brit. Cem., Pas-de-Calais; Age 41; Husband of Flora Bennett of "Herondean", Lyon Street, Bognor Regis, Sussex.

2268. BENNETT, Frederick; B: Ashford, Middlesex; E: Hounslow, London; Pte. G 18048; K: 26.2.17; Faubourg D'Amiens Cem., Arras, Pas-de-Calais.

2269. BERRY, Alfred; B: Hammersmith, London; E: Hammersmith; Pte. G 24259; W: 22.4.18; Peronne Road Cem., Maricourt, Somme.

2270. BERRYMAN, Sidney; B: Woking, Surrey; E: Brighton; Pte. G 33; K: 28.8.15; Houplines Com. Cem. Ext., Nord.

2271. BIANCHI, Percy John; B: Edmonton, London; E: Camberwell, London; Pte. G 19413; W: 27.8.18; Daours Com. Cem. Ext., Somme; Age 19; Son of Mrs.B.Bianchi of 73, Manwood Road, Brockley, London.

2272. BIGGS, Sidney; B: Hastings; E: Hastings; Pte. G 228; W: 4.3.16; Bethune Town Cem., Pas-de-Calais; Age 21; Son of Ernest and Jane Caroline Biggs of 65, Bulverhythe Road, St.Leonards-on-Sea.

2273. BILLING, Cuthbert Stanley; B: Abingdon, Berkshire; E: Worthing, Sussex; Pte. G 20696; W: 21.4.18; St.Sever Cem. Ext., Rouen, Seine-Maritime; Age 19; Son of Herbert Osborn Billing and Adelaide Agnes Billing of 31, Linden Road, Littlehampton, Sussex.

2274. BILLINGS, Edward Victor; B: Abingdon, Berkshire; E: Worthing, Sussex; Sgt. G 18173; W: 22.8.18; Daours Com. Cem. Ext., Somme; Age 33; Son of James Billings of Underhill, Maresfield, Sussex.*

2275. BINSTEAD, Charles; B: Boxgrove, Sussex; E: Hove; Pte. G 8352; K: 7.7.16; Thiepval Mem., Somme; Age 26; Son of John Henry and Hannah Binstead of 14, Kingston Terrace, Kingston-by-Sea, Southwick, Sussex.

2276. BIRD, Arthur; B: Penge, London; E: Bromley, London; Pte. G 13058; K: 9.4.17; Arras Mem., Pas-de-Calais.

2277. BIRD, James; B: Holborn, London; E: London; Pte. S 2033; M.M.; K: 7.7.16; Thiepval Mem., Somme; Age 20; Son of Mrs.Annie Harrison of 74, Broadwall, Stamford Road, London.

2278. BISHOP, Sidney George Edmund; B: –; E: Uckfield, Sussex; L/Cpl. G 18037; K: 7.10.16; Thiepval Mem., Somme; Age 26; Son of Mr. and Mrs. Harry Bishop of Huggett's Farm, Buxted, Sussex; Husband of Edith F.Billings, formerly Bishop, of The Homestead, Maresfield, Sussex.

2279. BISHOPP, George; B: Nunhead, Surrey; E: Hastings; Pte. G 8658; K: 25.7.17; Arras Mem., Pas-de-Calais.

2280. BISSMIRE, Harry; B: Hoxton, London; E: Holborn, London; Pte. G 5458; K: 7.7.16; Thiepval Mem., Somme; Husband of Mrs.A.G.Chubb, formerly Bissmire, of 254, New North Road, Islington, London.

2281. BLACKHURST, Cecil; B: Kirkham, Lancashire; E: Hastings; Pte. G 567; K: 7.7.16; Thiepval Mem., Somme.

2282. BLAKE, Arthur William; B: Loddon, Norfolk; E: Lowestoft; L/Cpl. G 11192; K: 24.10.18; Valenciennes (St.Roch) Com. Cem., Nord; Age 22; Son of Arthur and Laura Blake of Park Hill Cottages, Corton, Lowestoft.

2283. BLENCOWE, Charles Edward; 2nd Lt.; K: 3.5.18; Tyne Cot Mem. (Bel.); Killed while attached to 1st Battalion Wiltshire Regiment.

2284. BOAKES, Frederick George; B: Hartfield, Sussex; E: Tunbridge Wells; Pte. G 786; K: 7.7.16; Thiepval Mem., Somme; Age 23; Son of Richard and Elizabeth Boakes of Hethe Place Cottage, Blackham, Langton Green, Kent.

2285. BOATER, James; B: St.George's, Middlesex; E: Guildford; Pte. L 10737; K: 27.3.18; Pozieres Mem., Somme.

2286. BONAS, George Frederick; B: Highgate, London; E: Hove; Pte. G 704; W: 10.4.17; Duisans Brit. Cem., Pas-de-Calais; Age 23; Son of James and Sarah Bonas of 63, Montgomery Street, Hove.

2287. BONE, Frederick John; B: Alton, Hampshire; E: Chichester; Pte. L 10807; K: 25.7.17; Arras Mem., Pas-de-Calais.

2288. BONIFACE, George; B: Eastbourne; E: Eastbourne; Pte. G 16483; K: 5.4.18; Pozieres Mem., Somme.

2289. BONIFACE, Martin John; B: Hailsham, Sussex; E: Herstmonceux, Sussex; Pte. SD 576; W: 27.4.17; Duisans Brit. Cem., Somme; Husband of Mrs.M.A.Boniface of 23, North Street, Hailsham.

2290. BOORMAN, Albert; B: Pembury, Kent; E: Tunbridge Wells; Pte. G 13153; K: 18.9.18; Epehy Wood Farm Cem., Epehy, Somme; Age 42; Son of Hannah Boorman of Pembury; Husband of Annie Rose Boorman.

2291. BORROW, Arthur; B: St.John's, Yorkshire; E: Hastings; L/Cpl. G 414; K: 24.10.15; Loos Mem., Pas-de-Calais.

2292. BOTTING, Jasper; B: Worth, Sussex; E: Brighton; Pte. G 4760; K: 31.7.15; Houplines Com. Cem. Ext., Nord; Killed by 4.9" shall fire.

2293. BOURNE, R.H.; 2nd Lt.; K: 25.10.18; Valenciennes (St.Roch) Com. Cem., Nord; Age 19: Son of Rowland Manlove Bourne J.P., and Gertrude Bourne of 26, Bath Road, Bedford Park, Chiswick, London; Attached from Army Service Corps.*

2294. BOWLEY, Charles; B: Chichester; E: Chichester; Pte. G 516; D at Home: 18.5.15; Aldingbourne (St. Mary) Churchyard, Sussex (UK).

2295. BOWLEY, Charles James; B: Brighton; E: Brighton; Pte. G 3287; K: 3.3.16; Loos Mem., Pas-de-Calais; Age 21; Son of Lawrence and Matilda Bowley of 80, Trafalgar Street, Brighton.

2296. BOWRA, Percy John; B: Hastings; E: Bexhill-on-Sea; Pte. G 8652; K: 7.7.16; Thiepval Mem., Somme.

2297. BOXALL, John; B: Luggashall, Sussex; E: West Lavington, Sussex; Pte. G 8328; K: 7.7.16; Thiepval Mem., Somme.

2298. BOYDE, Arthur; B: Sandhurst, Surrey; E: Bexhill-on-Sea; Pte. G 142; K: 7.7.16; Ovillers Mil. Cem., Somme; Age 20.

2299. BOYS, Sydney Charles; Lt.; K: 23.6.18; Harponville Com Cem. Ext., Somme; Age 28; Son of Mr. and Mrs.Charles Eveleigh Boys; Killed by machine gun fire.*

2300. BRABAN, George Thomas; B: Burwash, Sussex; E: Hastings; Pte. G 12135; K: 20.11.17; Cambrai Mem., Louverval, Nord.

2301. BRACE, Frank William; B: Little Barford, Huntingdonshire; E: Bedford; Pte. G 23789; K: 8.8.18; Beacon Cem., Somme; Age 18; Son of James Brace of Little Barford Road, Eynesbury, Huntingdonshire.

2302. BRACKSTONE, Albert Henry; B: Long Parish, Hampshire; E: Bexhill-on-Sea; Pte. SD 1004; K: 3.5.17; Arras Mem., Pas-de-Calais; Age 27; Son of Isaac Brackstone of Forton, Long Parish; Husband of Daisy Winifred Ireland, formerly Brackstone, of 65, Worthington Road, Tolworth, Surrey.

2303. BRADLEY, James; 2nd Lt.; W: 26.10.18; Duisans Brit. Cem., Pas-de-Calais; Age 21; Son of James and Elizabeth Florence Bradley of 19, Berkeley Road, Crouch End, London.

2304. BRAIN, Harry; B: Lee, Kent; E: London; L/Cpl. S 1872; K: 7.7.16; Serre Road Cem. No.2, Somme.

2305. BRAY, Frank; B: Northampton; E: Kingston-on-Thames; Pte. G 5103; K: 24.3.16; Vermelles Brit. Cem., Pas-de-Calais; Age 23; Son of Mrs.Harriet Bray of 12, Edmund's Street, Northampton.

2306. BRAZIER, Sidney; B: – ; E: Colchester, Essex; Pte. G 14587; K: 30.11.17; Cambrai Mem., Louverval, Nord; Age 42; Son of Isaac and Emma Brazier of Head Street, Halstead, Essex; Husband of Annie Brazier 16, Highbury Terrace, Halstead.

2307. BREED, Elijah; B: Hilton, Hampshire; E: Hove; Pte. G 9172; K: 3.10.16; Thiepval Mem., Somme.*

2308. BREWSTER, Richard; B: Hemmingstone, Suffolk; E: Colchester, Essex; Sgt. G 2075; K: 3.3.16; Loos Mem., Pas-de-Calais; Age 36; Son of Richard and Louisa Brewster; Served with the Northamptonshire Regiment in the 1897 – 1898 Tirah Campaign.

2309. BRIDGLAND, William Thomas; B: Hastings; E: Chichester; L/Cpl. TF 315363; K: 13.8.18; Vis-en-Artois Mem., Haucourt, Pas-de-Calais; Killed near Morlancourt, Somme; Probably killed by 'Friendly Fire'.

2310. BRIDGER, James; B: Lodsworth, Sussex; E: Midhurst, Sussex; Pte. G 8412; K: 5.10.16; Bancourt Brit. Cem., Pas-de-Calais.

2311. BRIDGER, Percy William; B: Hove; E: Brighton; Pte. G 4017; M.M.; K: 3.5.17; Arras Mem., Pas-de-Calais; Son of Mrs.Elizabeth Bridger of "Woodburn", Whytecliffe Road, Purley, Surrey.

2312. BRIDGSTOCK, Ralph; B: March, Cambridgeshire; E: March; Pte. SD 5640; K: 4.5.17; Arras Mem., Pas-de-Calais; Age 21; Son of William and Mary Ann Bridgstock of 98, Creek Road, March.

2313. BRIDLE, Walter Frank; B: Bournemouth; E: Chichester; Pte. G 13883; D: 13.4.18; Cabaret-Rouge Brit. Cem., Pas-de-Calais.

2314. BRIGHT, Henry James; B: Stratford, London; E: West Ham, London; Pte. G 14779; K: 5.4.18; Pozieres Mem., Somme; Age 20; Son of William J. and Ada E.Bright of 158, Cann Hall Road, Leytonstone, London.

2315. BRIND, Albert George; B: Sunbury-on-Thames; E: Sunbury-on-Thames; Pte. SD 5876; K: 24.8.18; Peronne Road Cem., Maricourt, Somme.

2316. BRISTOW, Frederick; B: West Ham, London; E: Stratford, London; Pte. G 22522; K: 29.6.18; Harponville Com. Cem. Ext., Somme; Age 20; Son of Sarah Jane Bristow of West Ham, London.

2317. BRITT, Harry William G.; B: Hove; E: Brighton; Pte. G 4921; W: 23.3.16; Calais Southern Cem., Pas-de-Calais; Age 34.*

2318. BROOKS, Jesse; B: Haywards Heath, Sussex; E: Worthing; Pte. L 10957; K: 7.7.16; Thiepval Mem., Somme; Age 20; Son of Mrs.Avis Brooks of Lane End, Cootham, Sussex.

2319. BROOKS, Samuel; B: Cinderford Bridge, Gloucestershire; E: Ealing, London; Pte. G 6044; K: 4.3.16; Loos Mem., Pas-de-Calais.

2320. BROOKS, William; B: – ; E: Horsham, Sussex; Pte. G 16112; D: 8.1.17; Habarcq Com. Cem., Pas-de-Calais.

2321. BROOMFIELD, Edward William; B: Ellingham, Hampshire; E: Chichester; L/Cpl. G 2674; K: 20.11.17; Cambrai Mem., Louverval, Nord; Age 31; Son of Harry Jesse and Fanny Broomfield of Melbury Abbas, Dorset.

2322. BROWN, Frederick; B: Brushfield, Hampshire; E: Chichester; Pte. G 492; K: 8.3.16; Lievin Com. Cem. Ext., Pas-de-Calais.

2323. BROWN, Frederick; B: – ; E: Tonbridge, Kent; Pte. G 12881; K: 3.5.17; Arras Mem., Pas-de-Calais; Age 37; Son of Mr.R.Brown of 4, Priory Street, Tonbridge; Husband of Mabel Mary Brown of 3, Rock Corner, Chiddingstone Hoath, Kent.

2324. BROWN, John; B: Rusthall, Sussex; E: Chichester; Pte. G 1042; K: 30.9.15; Dud Corner Cem., Pas-de-Calais; Age 37; Son of George and Esther Brown of Rusthall.

2325. BROWN, John Francis; B: Hanworth, Middlesex; E: Kingston-on-Thames; Pte. G 20350; K: 24.8.18; Daours Com. Cem. Ext., Somme; Age 24; Son of Frances Marden of 2, Barrack Road, Hounslow Heath, Middlesex.*

2326. BROWN, Leonard Marshall; B: Langley, Kent; E: Maidstone, Kent; Pte. G 18057; K: 9.4.17; Gourock Trench Cem., Tilloy-les-Mofflaines, Pas-de-Calais.

2327. BROWN, Samuel John; B: Lambeth, London; E: Rotherhithe, London; Pte. G 10187; W: 4.2.18; Croix-du-Bac Brit. Cem., Steenwerk, Nord.

2328. BROWNE, Alfred John; B: Portslade, Sussex; E:

Hove; L/Cpl. G 17780; K: 5.4.18; Bouzincourt Ridge Cem., Somme; Age 26; Son of Mr. and Mrs. Alfred Browne of The Plough, Steyning, Sussex.

2329. BROWNE, Edward Miller; B: Highbury, London; E: Hounslow, London; Pte. G 23797; K: 18.8.18; Vis-en-Artois Mem., Haucourt, Pas-de-Calais.

2330. BRYANT, James George; B: Camberwell, London; E: Southwark, London; Pte. G 5047; K: 7.7.16; Thiepval Mem., Somme; Age 24; Son of Emma Julia Deeks, formerly Bryant, of 11, Johnson Street, Euston Road, London and the late George Deeks, stepfather.

2331. BRYDER, William; B: Tillington, Sussex; E: Horsham, Sussex; Pte. TF 260042; K: 27.3.18; Pozieres Mem., Somme; Age 20; Son of William and Alice Kate Bryder of Tillington.

2332. BUCKMAN, Ernest George Charles; B: Peckham, London; E: Kingston-on-Thames; Pte. G 20201; W: 20.11.17; Tincourt New Brit. Cem., Somme; Age 25; Son of Ernest and Ellen Buckman; Husband of Amy Perry, formerly Buckman, of 26, St.John's Hill, Clapham Junction, London.

2333. BUCKWALTER, Harry; B: Stepney, London; E: Woolwich, London; Pte. G 19419; K: 5.9.18; Peronne Com. Cem. Ext., Ste.Radegonde, Somme; Age 19; Son of Mr. and Mrs.Buckwalter of 20, Spearman Street, Woolwich Common.

2334. BUDD, Thomas William; B: Chichester; E: Chichester; L/Cpl. G 778; K: 1.10.17; Monchy Brit. Cem., Pas-de-Calais; Age 20; Son of Mr. and Mrs.Budd of 43, Cavendish Street, Somerstown, Chichester.

2335. BUDGEN, George; B: East Grinstead, Sussex; E: Brighton; Pte. G 4759; W: 14.1.16; Chocques Mil. Cem., Pas-de-Calais; Age 27; Son of Mr. and Mrs. James Budgen; Husband of Alice M.M.Budgen of 352, Radford Road, Hyson Green, Nottingham; Died at No.1 Casualty Clearing Station.

2336. BUMSTEAD, Frank Henry; B: Hastings; E: Hastings; Pte. G 560; K: 7.7.16; Thiepval Mem., Somme; Age 34; Son of Mrs.M.F.Stretton, formerly Bumstead, of 6, Finsbury Grove, Hull and the late William G.Stretton, stepfather.

2337. BUMSTEAD, George William; B: Hastings; E: Chichester; Pte. G 13690; K: 25.11.17; Cambrai Mem., Louverval, Nord; Age 19; Son of Arthur and Peggy Elizabeth Bumstead of 7, Cornfield Terrace, St.Leonards-on-Sea.*

2338. BUNKER, Jesse; B: Boxmoor, Hertfordshire; E: Watford, Hertfordshire; Pte.G 14271; K: 19.5.18; Mailly Wood Cem., Somme; Age 19; Son of William and Frances Bunker of Bourne End, Hertfordshire.

2339. BUNNING, Robert Charles; B: Hammersmith, London; E: London; Pte. G 5920; K: 7.7.16; Ovillers Mil. Cem., Somme.

2340. BURCHELL, George; B: – ; E: – ; Pte. G 959; W at Home: 10.11.16; Hove Old Cem., Sussex (UK); Died of wounds received at Loos.

2341. BURDEN, Alfred William Percy; Pte. G 679; K: 7.7.16; Thiepval Mem., Somme; Age 21; Son of Richard and S.E.Burden of 98, Wordsworth Street, Hove.*

2342. BURGESS, Albert Henry; B: Peasmarsh, Sussex; E: Chichester; Pte. L 10271; K: 24.12.15; Loos Mem., Pas-de-Calais.

2343. BURGESS, Arthur; B: – ; E: Great Yarmouth; Pte. G 20220; K: 8.8.18; Villers-Bretonneux Mil. Cem., Somme; Age 22; Son of John T. and Mary Burgess; Husband of Emmeline M.Burgess of 7, Theatre Plain, Great Yarmouth.*

2344. BURGESS, John; B: Stoneham, Sussex; E: Lewes; Pte. SD 5458; K: 28.3.18; Pozieres Mem., Somme; Age 20; Son of Mrs.A.Miller, formerly Burgess, of 64, Five Ash Down, Sussex.

2345. BURGINS, Bertram Leonard; B: Thrapstone, Northamptonshire; E: Northampton; Pte. G 18058; W: 26.4.17; Boulogne Eastern Cem., Pas-de-Calais; Age 20.*

2346. BURLEY, Cyril Percy; 2nd Lt.; K: 9.8.18; Beacon Cem., Somme; Age 24; Son of Ernest and Sarah Ann Burley of 135, Mandeville Road, Enfield Wash, Middlesex.

2347. BURROUGH, Cyril George; B: Brighton; E: Brighton; Sgt. G 17661; K: 5.9.18; Peronne Com. Cem. Ext., Somme.

2348. BURT, James; B: Bloomsbury, London; E: Chelsea, London; Pte. G 5279; K: 7.7.16; Thiepval Mem., Somme.

2349. BUSHELL, Daniel; B: Wisbech, Cambridgeshire; E: Wisbech; Pte. G 11193; K: 25.4.18; Mailly Wood Cem., Somme; Age 25; Son of James and Ann E.Bushell of 4, Chapel Road, North Brink, Cambridgeshire.

2350. BUSS, Jesse; B: Brightling, Sussex; E: Hastings; Pte. S 2325; K: 2.3.16; Quarry Cem. (Vermelles) Pas-de-Calais; Age 18; Son of Charles Thomas Buss of 3, Longhouses, Brightling.

2351. BUSSELL, John Garrett; Capt.; K: 28.6.15; Tancrez Farm Cem. (Bel); Husband of Dorothea Bussell of Seven Stars, Marlborough.

2352. BUSWELL, Percy Bates; B: Sundridge, Kent; E: Mill Hill, London; Pte. G 5041; K: 5.10.16; Thiepval Mem., Somme; Age 35; Brother of Miss H.Buswell of 35, Kilburn Park Road, Kilburn, London.

2353. BUTCHER, Thomas Horeland; B: Battle, Sussex; E: Bromley, Kent; Pte. G 18881; K: 13.8.18; Vis-en-Artois Mem., Haucourt, Pas-de-Calais; Age 19; Son of James Butcher of 7, Lea Road, Beckenham, Kent; Killed near Morlancourt, Somme.

2354. BYLES, G.B.; Pte. – 45698; W at Home: 22.9.18; Chichester Cem., Sussex (U.K.) ; Son of Charles and Elizabeth Margaret Byles of 168, Orchard Street, Chichester.*

C

2355. CADDOW, Robert; B: Manchester; E: Manchester; Pte. G 18421; K: 18.9.18; Epehy Wood Farm Cem., Epehy, Somme; Age 26; Son of John and Beatrice Caddow; Husband of Sarah Ann Caddow of 23, Bedford Street, Moss Side, Manchester.

2356. CALLAGHAN, Daniel; B: Blantyre, Lanarkshire; E: Stirling; Pte. G 5871; K: 7.7.16; Thiepval Mem., Somme.

2357. CANE, Thomas Harry; B: Hove; E: Chichester; L/Cpl. L 10015; K: 20.11.17; Cambrai Mem., Louverval, Nord; Age 19; Son of Mrs.A.E.Cane of 63, Bates Road, Brighton.

2358. CANNON, Arthur; B: Newmarket, Cambridgeshire; E: Lambeth, London; L/Cpl. G 17675; W: 2.12.17; Rocquigny-Equancourt Road Brit. Cem., Somme; Son of Joseph Cannon of Lordship, Newmarket; Husband of Edith Wilbraham Cannon of 12, Trouville Road, Clapham Park, London.

2359. CANNONS, George Harry; B: Chelsea, London; E: Charlton Park, London; Pte. G 23798; K: 22.8.18; Meaulte Mil. Cem., Somme; Age 18; Son of Mrs. Minnie Cannons of 1, Burnaby Street, Chelsea.

2360. CANTON, George; B: Lambeth, London; E: Hastings; Pte. G 18024; K: 27.3.18; Aveluy Wood Cem., Somme.

2361. CARN, Charles Percy; B: North Chapel, Sussex; E: Chichester; Pte. G 661; W: 14.3.16; Bethune Town Cem., Pas-de-Calais; Son of Ellen Carn of Square House, North Chapel, Sussex.

2362. CARSON, William James; B: Stepney, London; E: Stepney; Pte. G 19420; D at Home: 1.11.18; Tunbridge Wells Cem., Kent (UK).

2363. CARSTAIRS, Philip Gordon; B: Westernhanger, Kent; E: Folkestone, Kent; Pte. G 18913; W: 9.8.18; Pernois Brit. Cem., Somme; Age 19; Son of James and Elizabeth Carstairs of Westernhanger.

2364. CARVER, Alfred William; B: – ; E: Chichester; Pte. G 15803; W: 7.9.18; Dernancourt Com. Cem. Ext., Somme; Age 35; Son of Walter and Caroline Carver of 15, Bond Street, Arundel, Sussex.

2365. CASS, Leonard Francis; Capt.; K: 13.12.15; Brown's Road, Mil. Cem., Festubert, Pas-de-Calais; 'A' Company Commander; killed by a sniper.

2366. CASSIDY, Albert; B: South Norwood, London; E: Bromley, Kent; Pte. G 12671; W: 29.11.17; Tincourt New Brit. Cem., Somme.

2367. CATE, John; B: West Witterington, Sussex; E: Chichester; Pte. SD 1768; K: 9.4.17; Arras Mem., Pas-de-Calais.

2368. CATT, William Nathan; B: Warbleton, Sussex; E: Haywards Heath, Sussex; Pte. G 4066; K: 7.7.16; Thiepval Mem., Somme.

2369. CAVE, Herbert Stanley; B: Acton, London; E: Fulham, London; L/Cpl. TF 266475; K: 26.3.18; Pozieres Mem., Somme.

2370. CHAFFEY, George; B: Battersea, London; E: Battersea; Pte. G 4408; K: 7.7.16; Thiepval Mem., Somme; Age 28; Son of John and Alice Chaffey.

2371. CHALK, William Edwin; B: Clerkenwell, London; E: Brighton; Sgt. S 4; K: 10.8.16; Thiepval Mem., Somme.

2372. CHAMBERS, Albert Edward; B: Paddington, London; E: Marylebone, London; Pte. G 20243; K: 9.4.17; Arras Mem., Pas-de-Calais; Age 18; Son of Henry and Catherine Chambers of 21, Chippenham Mews, Paddington.

2373. CHAPMAN, Ernest; B: Brighton; E: Brighton; Pte. G 4501; K: 13.8.18; Vis-en-Artois Mem., Haucourt, Pas-de-Calais; Killed near Morlancourt, Somme.

2374. CHAPMAN, Reginald George; B: Chichester; E: Chichester; Pte. G 817; W: 28.9.15; Bailleul Com. Cem. Ext., Nord.

2375. CHAPPELL, Ernest; B: Sawbridgeworth, Hertfordshire; E: Chichester; Pte. L 7824; W: 27.7.17; St.Sever Cem. Ext., Rouen, Seine-Maritime; Age 36; Son of William and Susan Chappell; Husband of Mrs.E.J.Chappell of 34, Cavendish Street, Chichester.

2376. CHAPPELL, George Richard; B: –; E: Camberwell, London; Pte. G 4429; K: 7.7.16; Thiepval Mem., Somme; Age 33; Son of Son of Henry and Mary A.Chappell of Peckham, London; Husband of Emma J.Chappell of 8, Chapel Road, West Norwood, London.

2377. CHARMAN, Arthur; B: Chichester; E: Chichester; Pte. G 1256; W: 6.3.16; Lapugnoy Mil. Cem., Pas-de-Calais; Age 23; Son of Henry and Emily Charman of Home Farm, Newdigate, Surrey.

2378. CHATFIELD, Frederick George; B: Wimbledon, London; E: Salisbury, Wiltshire; Pte. TF 266523; K: 5.9.18; Peronne Com. Cem. Ext., Ste.Radegonde, Somme; Age 33; Son of William H. and Louisa Chatfield of 39, George Street, Salisbury.

2379. CHEESEMAN, Reginald; B: Portslade, Sussex; E: Hove; Cpl. G 206; D.C.M.; W: 5.10.16; Heilly Station Cem., Mericourt-L'Abbé, Somme.

2380. CHEESMAN, William; B: Brighton; E: Brighton; Cpl. G 166; K: 7.7.16; Ovillers Mil. Cem., Somme; Age 22; Son of Francis and Sophia Cheeseman of 62, Chester Terrace, Brighton.

2381. CHEESMORE, Alfred T.; B: Rudgwick, Sussex; E: Horsham, Sussex; Pte. G 21012; W: 27.12.17; St.Sever Cem. Ext., Rouen, Seine-Maritime; Age 19; Son of Mr.T.Cheesmore of Bucks Green, Rudgwick.*

2382. CHERRIMAN, Edward Joseph; B: Ditchling, Sussex; E: Ditchling; Pte. G 213; K: 26.7.15; Houplines Com. Cem. Ext., Nord.

2383. CHERRYMAN, Alfred; B: Lower Beeding, Sussex; E: Horsham; Pte. G 903; K: 24.9.18; Epehy Wood Farm Cem., Epehy, Somme.

2384. CHEVIS, George Edwin; B: Easebourne, Sussex; E: Midhurst, Sussex; L/Cpl. G 583; W: 12.7.16; Étaples Mil. Cem., Pas-de-Calais; Age 23; Son of George and Emily Mary Chevis of 29, Easebourne Road, Midhurst; Brother, James Henry, also killed in action (see 2385)*

2385. CHEVIS, James Henry; B: Easebourne; E: Chichester; Cpl. G 655; K: 31.7.16; Thiepval Mem., Somme; Age 21; Son of George and Emily Mary Chevis of 29, Easebourne Road, Midhurst; Brother, George Edwin, also killed (see 2384)*

2386. CHILD, William Henry; B: Sutton, Surrey; E: Southampton; L/Cpl. G 6244; K: 5.4.18; Bouzincourt Ridge Cem., Somme.

2387. CHILDREN, Richard William; B: Finsbury,

London; E: Whitehall, London; Pte. G 19430; K: 8.8.18; Beacon Cem., Somme.

2388. CHIPPERFIELD, Stanley Cave; B: Tilbury, Essex; E: Warley, Essex; Pte. G 21572; W: 21.5.18; Acheux Brit. Cem., Somme; Age 20; Son of William and Emma Catherine Chipperfield of 2, Bryanstone Road, West Tilbury.*

2389. CHUNN, Erling Victor; B: Reading, E: Hastings; L/Cpl. SD 2646; K: 3.5.17; Arras Mem., Pas-de-Calais.

2390. CLARK, Edwin Arthur; B: Peckham, London; E: Worthing; Pte. G 23801; K: 26.8.18; Peronne Road Cem., Maricourt, Somme; Age 18; Son of William Henry and Edith J.Clark of 209, Tarring Road, Worthing.*

2391. CLARK, Lionel; B: St.Pancras, London; E: Brighton; Pte. GS 19; W: 3.11.15; St.Sever Cem., Rouen, Seine-Maritime; Mortally wounded when a Royal Engineer dump was struck by shell fire.

2392. CLARK, William; B: Brighton; E: Eastbourne; Pte. G 6900; K: 15.3.16; Vermelles Brit. Cem., Pas-de-Calais.

2393. CLARK, William Frank; B: Chichester; E: Chichester; Pte. G 1359; K: 26.8.18; Vis-en-Artois Mem., Haucourt, Pas-de-Calais; Age 21; Son of John William and Fanny F.Clark of 29, Cavendish Street, Chichester.

2394. CLARKSON, Charles Athelstan; B: Kingston-on-Thames; E: Kingston-on-Thames; Pte. G 25757; K: 18.9.18; Epehy Wood Farm Cem., Epehy, Somme; Age 19; Son of Robert James and Florence Julia Clarkson of 100, Shortlands Road, Kingston-on-Thames.*

2395. CLARKSON, William George Dunbar; B: Camberwell, London; E: Bromley, Kent; Pte. G 12650; K: 31.3.17; Arras Mem., Pas-de-Calais; Killed by shell fire while on digging duties at Arras.

2396. CLEMENTS, Reginald Francis; B: Oban, Argyle; Lt.; M.C.; K: 14.8.18; Morlancourt Brit. Cem. No.2, Somme; Age 26; Son of Henry and Agnes Clements of 9, The Woodlands, Long Park, Chesham Bois, Buckinghamshire.

2397. CLIFTON, George; B: Heathfield, Sussex; E: Liverpool; Pte. G 4247; K: 7.7.16; Thiepval Mem., Somme; Age 25, Son of George and Ellen Mercy Clifton of Wood View, Punnetts Town, Sussex; Served under the alias Holmes.

2398. CLUFF, George; B: Bethnal Green, London; E: Whitehall, London; Pte. G 23702; K: 18.9.18; Epehy Wood Farm Cem., Epehy, Somme.*

2399. COBB, George Edward; B: Isleworth, London; E: Hounslow, London; Pte. G 4871; K: 31.7.16; Thiepval Mem., Somme.

2400. COBBY, Benjamin James; B: Brighton; E: Camberwell, London; Pte. G 13044; K: 25.7.17; Arras Mem., Pas-de-Calais; Age 22; Son of Anthony and Elizabeth Cobby.*

2401. CODY, Alfred Henry; B: St.Pancras, London; E: St.Pancras; Pte. L 10675; W: 7.3.18; St.Pol Brit. Cem., Pas-de-Calais; Age 21; Son of Henry and Ellen Cody of 11, Newbury Mews, Kentish Town, London.*

2402. COE, Arthur George; B: St.John's, Middlesex; E: Canterbury; Pte. L 9425; W: 14.7.16; Boulogne Eastern Cem., Pas-de-Calais; Age 20; Son of Mr. and Mrs.A.Coe of 190, Orchard Street Estate, Westminster, London.

2403. COHEN, Dudley Trevor; 2nd Lt.; W: 20.11.17; Cambrai Mem., Louverval, Nord.

2404. COLBURN, George; B: Portslade, Sussex; E: Hove; Cpl. G 8164; W: 16.4.18; St.Sever Cem. Ext., Rouen, Seine-Maritime.

2405. COLBURN, William; B: Fishergate, Sussex; E: Hove; Pte. G 680; W: 8.12.17; Honnechy Brit. Cem., Nord; Age 23; Husband of Mrs.Colburn of 21, Crown Road, Portslade, Sussex.*

2406. COLEMAN, Bertram; B: Hargreave, Northamptonshire; E: Rushden, Northamptonshire; Pte. G 22637; K: 27.3.18; Serre Road Cem. No.2, Somme.

2407. COLEMAN, Percy; B: Woking, Surrey; E: Lewes; L/Cpl. G 1647; W: 5.3.16; Bethune Town Cem., Pas-de-Calais; Age 26; Son of Henry and Alice Coleman of Brock's House, Horton, Somerset.

2408. COLES, Albert Ernest; B: – ; E: Rushden, Northamptonshire; Pte. G 22650; K: 18.9.18; Epehy Wood Farm Cem., Epehy, Somme; Age 37; Husband of Beatrice Coles of 39, Pytchley Road, Rushden.*

2409. COLES, Ernest Walter; B: Cocking, Sussex; E: Chichester; Pte. L 9035; K: 18.9.18; Epehy Wood Farm Cem., Epehy, Somme; Son of Mr. and Mrs. Richard Coles of Cocking; Husband of Alice Ellen Coles of 3, Church Hill, Topcroft, Bungay, Suffolk.

2410. COLES, Reginald Joseph; B: Goring-on-Thames, Oxfordshire; E: Hamstead, London; Pte. G 19433; K: 9.8.18; Beacon Cem., Somme; Age 19; Son of John and Emily Sarah Coles of Rose Cottage, Croft Road, Goring-on-Thames.

2411. COLLIER, Walter Samuel; B: Walworth, London; E: Warminster, Wiltshire; Pte. G 22446; K: 27.3.18; Pozieres Mem., Somme.

2412. COLLINGS, James William; B: London; E: Brighton; Pte. L 10710; K: 7.7.16; Thiepval Mem., Somme; Age 18; Son of George and Jemima Collings of 65, Clarendon Road, Hove.

2413. COLTMAN, Victor Joseph; B: Croydon; E: Croydon; Pte. G 14120; K: 3.5.17; Arras Mem., Pas-de-Calais; Age 35; Son of James Josepf and Mrs.L.F.Coltman of 20, West Street, Croydon; Husband of Mrs.E.L.Coltman of 6, West Street, Croydon.

2414. COMBER, Bernard; B: Portslade, Sussex; E: Haywards Heath, Sussex; Pte. G 12081; W: 10.4.17; Duisans Brit. Cem., Pas-de-Calais; Husband of Mrs.C.J.Comber of 10, Field Row, Portland Road, Worthing.

2415. COMPER, Thomas James; B: Horsham, Sussex; E: Horsham; Pte. G 4832; K: 7.7.16; Thiepval Mem., Somme.*

2416. CONVOY, Bertie George; B: Strood, Kent; E: Ipswich, Suffolk; Pte. G 20913; K: 5.9.18; Peronne Com. Cem. Ext., Ste.Radegonde, Somme.

2417. COOK, Fred; B: Northfleet, Kent; E: Maidstone, Kent; Pte. G 20197; K: 5.4.18; Bouzincourt Ridge Cem., Somme; Age 21; Son of Arthur and Mary Cook of 13, Wood Street, Northfleet.

2418. COOK, Henry John Lewis; B: Frinsbury, Kent; E: Brighton; Pte. TF 26630; K: 23.9.18; Epehy Wood Farm Cem., Epehy, Somme.

2419. COOKE, Henry Frederick; 2nd Lt.; K: 4.8.16; Thiepval Mem., Somme; Age 31; Son of the late Rev.C.S.Cooke, Rector of Thurles, and Mrs.Cooke of Beakstown, Thurles, County Tipperary; Also served in German South-West Africa.

2420. COOKSEY, Leonard; B: Ashford, Middlesex; E: Rye, Sussex; Pte. G 18066; K: 17.8.17; Monchy Brit. Cem., Pas-de-Calais; Age 26; Son of John James and Elizabeth Cooksey of Oakfield House, Ashford.

2421. COOMBER, Percy George; B: Hove; E: Hove; Pte. G 697; K: 25.7.17; Arras Mem., Pas-de-Calais.

2422. COOMBES, Warren; B: – ; E: Hastings; Pte. G 18074; W: 8.10.16; Heilly Station Cem., Mericourt-L'Abbé, Somme; Age 16; Son of Mrs. Hannah Coombes of 65, Plynlimnon Road, Hastings.

2423. COOMBES, William George; B: Hammersmith, London; E: Hounslow, London; Pte. G 7341; K: 7.7.16; Thiepval Mem., Somme; Age 23; Son of William Coobes of 4, Garden Cottages, Cliffe, Lewes, Sussex; Served under alias surname Lewis.

2424. COOPER, Ashley James; B: Herstmonceux, Sussex; E: Eastbourne; Pte. G 404; D: 4.11.15; St.Sever Cem., Rouen, Seine-Maritime; Age 22; Son of Ashley and Ruth Cooper.

2425. COOPER, George; B: East Grinstead, Sussex; E: East Grinstead; Pte. G 4679; W: 11.8.16; Bouzincourt Com. Cem. Ext., Somme; Son of Mrs.M.A.Cooper of 4, Council House, East Grinstead.

2426. COOPER, Joseph; B: – ; E: Cambridge; L/Cpl. G 14926; K: 27.3.18; Pozieres Mem., Somme.

2427. COOTE, Charles; B: Shipley, Sussex; E: Worthing; Pte. G 12287; W: 10.4.17; Duisans Brit. Cem., Pas-de-Calais; Husband of Mrs.E.M.Coote of Bacons Farm, Dragons Green, Shipley.

2428. COPPING, Thomas Kenneth; B: Hammersmith, London; E: West London; Pte. G 14466; K: 20.11.17; Cambrai Mem., Louverval, Nord.

2429. CORBETT, Harold; B: Stanton Hill, Nottinghamshire; E: Mansfield, Nottinghamshire; Pte. TF 266511; K: 8.8.18; Villers-Bretonneux Mil. Cem., Somme; Age 21; Son of William Henry and Annie Maria Corbett.

2430. CORDER, Charles; B: Eastbourne; E: Eastbourne; Pte. G 3985; K: 5.4.18; Bouzincourt Ridge Cem., Somme.

2431. CORKE, William; B: Tonbridge, Kent; E: Tonbridge; Pte. G 13159; K: 20.11.17; Cambrai Mem., Louverval, Nord; Age 40; Husband of Caroline Corke of 117, Shipbourne Road, Tonbridge.

2432. CORNFORD, Charles Samuel Joseph; B: Mayfield, Sussex; E: Eastbourne; L/Cpl. G 6875; K: 25.7.17; Monchy Brit. Cem., Pas de Calais; Age 26; Son of David and Julia Cornford of 2, Beaconsfield Villas, Jarvis Brook, Sussex, formerly of Little Broad Reed, Hadlow Down, Sussex.

2433. CORNISH, Graham; B: Gloucester; E: Hastings; Pte. G 71; K: 28.3.16; Vermelles Brit. Cem., Pas-de-Calais.

2434. COTTERILL, Frederick; B: Brighton; E: Hove; Pte. G 709; W at Home: 27.9.15; Brighton (Bear Road) Borough Cem., Sussex (UK); Age 21; Son of Samuel and Adelaide Mary Cotterill; Wounds received at Armentieres.

2435. COURT, Frederick William; B: Chelsea, London; E: West London; Pte. G 24269; K: 8.8.16; Vis-en-Artois Mem., Haucourt, Pas-de-Calais; Killed near Morlancourt, Somme.

2436. COURT, Septimus; B: Lugashall, Sussex; E: Chichester; Drummer G 1059; K: 25.9.15; Houplines Com. Cem. Ext., Pas-de-Calais; Age 21; Son of George and Anna Court of Lugashall.*

2437. COVELL, Alfred John; B: Hastings; E: Hastings; Pte. G 9094; K: 9.4.17; Gourock Trench Cem., Tilloy-les-Mofflaines, Pas-de-Calais.

2438. COWDREY, Harry; B: Camden Town, London; E: Brighton; Pte. G 23805; K: 26.8.18; Meaulte Mil. Cem., Somme; Age 18; Son of William and Eliza Cowdrey of 3, Reigate Road, Brighton.

2439. COWTAN, Sydney Francis; B: – ; E: Mill Hill, London; Pte. G 22598; W at Home: 1.11.18; Orpington (All Saints) Churchyard Ext., Kent (UK).

2440. COX, George; B: Halton, Sussex; E: Hastings; Pte. S 1804; K: 2.3.16; Loos Mem., Pas-de-Calais.

2441. COX, Norman John; Lt.; K: 23.8.15; Houplines Com. Cem. Ext., Nord; Age 27; Son of Charles Henry and Harriet Mary Cox of London; Shot through the head by a chance bullet.

2442. COX, Sidney; B: Dunmow, Essex; E: Warley, Essex; Pte. G 23807; K: 13.8.18; Vis-en-Artois Mem., Haucourt, Pas-de-Calais; Age 18; Son of Mrs.C.E.Cox of 7, The Broadway, Great Dunmow; Killed near Morlancourt, Somme, probably by 'friendly fire'.

2443. CRABB, Albert Edward; B: Black Horse Drove, Cambridgeshire; E: Bury St.Edmunds, Suffolk; Pte. G 18067; W: 17.5.17; Étaples Mil. Cem., Pas-de-Calais; Age 20; Son of William and Eliza Crabb of Black Horse Drove, Littleport, Cambridgeshire.*

2444. CRACKNELL, Arthur; B: Alfriston, Sussex; E: Eastbourne; Pte. G 10754; W: 27.4.17; Étaples Mil. Cem., Pas-de-Calais; Age 32; Son of Alfred Heber Cracknell and Emily Cracknell; Husband of Annie Cracknell of 4, Phoenix Terrace, Ashurstwood, Sussex.

2445. CRAMPHORN, Thomas Howard; B: Colnbrook, Buckinghamshire; E: Hounslow, London; Pte. G

11336; K: 4.8.16; Thiepval Mem., Somme; Age 19; Son of Mrs.Ada Cramphorn of Park Street, Colnbrook.*

2446. CRAWLEY, Frederick James; B: St.Andrew's, Sussex; E: Brighton; Cpl. L 10397; K: 7.7.16; Thiepval Mem., Somme; Age 21; Son of Mrs. Susie Hamilton Crawley of 46, Lavender Sweep, Clapham Junction, London.*

2447. CREIGHTON, William Thomas; B: Brixton, London; E: Eastbourne; Pte. SD 166; K: 8.8.18; Beacon Cem., Somme; Age 26; Son of William Thomas Creighton of Eastbourne; Husband of Hild Mary Creighton of 39, Willoughby Crescent, Eastbourne.

2448. CRIPPS, John Henry; B: Chalfont, Essex; E: Bromley, Kent; Pte. G 12679; K: 31.3.17; Faubourg D'Amiens Cem., Arras, Pas-de-Calais; Killed by shell fire on digging duties at Arras.

2449. CRITTENDEN, Harry Albert; B: Rusthall, Sussex; E: Tunbridge Wells; Pte. G 4019; K: 7.7.16; Thiepval Mem., Somme.*

2450. CROFT, Ernest Frank; B: Westbourne, Sussex; E: Chichester; Pte. L 10404; K: 7.7.16; Thiepval Mem., Somme; Age 22; Son of Frank and Caroline Croft of 6, Dukes Cottages, Tangmere, Sussex.

2451. CROFT, Horace Guy; B: Bournemouth; E: Hounslow, London; Pte. G 23800; K: 8.8.18; Beacon Cem., Somme; Age 18; Son of Edmund John and Bessie Croft of Bournemouth.

2452. CROOKE, Moses John; B: Cowbridge, Glamorgan; E: Cowbridge; Pte. G 1017; K: 7.7.16; Thiepval Mem., Somme; Age 28; Son of Jenkin and Sarah Crooke of St.Mary Church, Glamorgan.*

2453. CROUCH, Douglas; B: Chelsea, London; E: Hastings; Pte. G 132; K: 31.7.15; Houplines Com. Cem. Ext., Nord; Killed by 4.5" shell fire.

2454. CROUCH, William Charles; B: Catsfield, Sussex; E: Hastings; Pte. G 4160; K: 4.7.17; Monchy Brit. Cem., Pas-de-Calais.

2455. CROUCHER, James Frederick; B: Tottenham, London; E: Woolwich, London; Pte. G 13027; W at Home: 26.6.17; Chingford Mount Cem., Essex (UK); Age 32; Son of James F.Croucher; Husband of Mary Ann Croucher of 68, Dunloe Avenue, South Tottenham.

2456. CRUTTENDEN, Henry John; B: St.Leonards-on-Sea; E: Hastings; Sgt. G 6428; K: 26.8.18; Peronne Road Cem., Maricourt, Somme.

2457. CUNDELL, Arthur; B: Wilburton, Cambridgeshire; E: Southwark, London; Pte. G 5222; K: 4.8.16; Thiepval Mem., Somme.

2458. CURD, Henry; B: – ; E: Eastbourne; L/Cpl. L 14377; K: 18.9.18; Epehy Wood Farm Cem., Epehy, Somme; Age 41; Son of Edwin and Elizabeth Curd of Buxted, Sussex.

2459. CURTIS, Percy; B: East Grinstead, Sussex; E: Guildford, Surrey; Pte. G 7659; W: 6.2.18; Estaires Com. Cem. Ext., Nord; Age 19; Son of William and Lucy Curtis of 16, De La Warr Road, East Grinstead.

2460. CUSACK, John; B: Brighton; E: Hove; Pte. G 5409; W at Home: 13.8.16; Brighton (Bear Road) Borough Cem., Sussex (UK); Age 32; Son of James and Mary Cusack of 19, Rochester Street, Brighton.

D

2461. DABORN, William Henry; B: Knaphill, Surrey; E: Guildford; Pte. G 5788; K: 7.7.16; Thiepval Mem., Somme.

2462. DADSWELL, Charles; B: Laughton, Sussex; E: St.Pancras, London; Pte. G 7375; K: 23.3.16; Vermelles Brit. Cem., Pas-de-Calais.*

2463. DADSWELL, Clifford Irwin; 2nd Lt.; K: 7.7.16; Serre Road Cem. No.2, Somme; Age 23; Son of James Thomas and Elizabeth Dadswell of 35, Victoria Road, Surbiton, Surrey.

2464. DANIELS, Joe; B: Scudamore, Wiltshire; E: Hurstpierpoint, Sussex; Pte. G 550; W at Home: 29.7.16; Bramshott (St.Mary) Churchyard, Hampshire (UK); Age 39; Son of John and Eliza Daniels of Upton Scudamore.

2465. DANN, John; B: Brighton; E: Brighton; Pte. G 261; W: 5.11.15; Sailly-Labourse Com. Cem., Pas-de-Calais; Brother of Mr.H.Dann of 19, Richmond Hill, Brighton.

2466. DAUNT, Barry; 2nd Lt.; K: 21.9.18; Epehy Wood Farm Cem, Epehy, Somme.*

2467. DAVIDSON, Thomas Blackburn; B: Riding Mills, Northumberland; E: Sunderland; Pte. G 289; K: 15.10.15; Loos Mem., Pas-de-Calais; Age 21; Son of Thomas and Jane Davidson.*

2468. DAVIS, Ernest; B: Selsey, Sussex; E: Chichester; Pte. G 424; K: 4.8.15; Cite Bonjean Mil. Cem., Nord.

2469. DAVIS, Thomas Stephen; B: Marylebone, London; E: Herne Bay, Kent; Pte. G 3966; K: 25.7.17; Arras Mem., Pas-de-Calais.

2470. DAWES, Bert; B: Framfield, Sussex; E: Lewes; Pte. G 1645; W: 18.8.17; Duisans Brit. Cem., Pas-de-Calais; Age 21; Son of Mrs.C.E.Dawes of 25, Pale House Common, Framfield.

2471. DAWSON, Leonard; B: Ewhurst, Sussex; E: Eastbourne; L/Sgt. GS 2283; W: 9.8.18; Pernois Brit. Cem., Somme; Age 22; Son of Caleb and Louisa Dawson of Ewhurst.

2472. DAY, Frank Gilbert; B: High Broome, Kent; E: Tunbridge Wells; Pte. G 3964; W: 14.8.18; Pernois Brit. Cem., Somme.*

2473. DAY, George; B: Ifold, Sussex; E: Horsham, Sussex; Cpl. G 15808; K: 2.9.18; Guillemont Road Cem., Somme.

-- DEADMAN, James (see Winter 3233).

2474. DEADMAN, Sidney Herbert; B: Buckingham; E: Uckfield, Sussex; Pte. G 8369; K: 3.5.17; Arras Mem., Pas-de-Calais.

2475. DEADMAN, William Walter; B: Portslade, Sussex; E: Brighton; Pte. TF 315172; K: 22.8.16; Meaulte Mil. Cem., Somme; Age 24; Son of George and Kate Deadman of 29, Coleridge Street, Hove.

2476. DEAN, Arthur Castle Gordon; B: Hove; E: Hove;

Pte. L 10927; W: 3.5.17; Étaples Mil. Cem., Pas-de-Calais; Age 19; Son of George and Annie Dean of 58, Montgomery Street, Hove,

2477. DEAN, Joseph; B: Brighton; E: Hove; Pte. L 10650; K: 14.2.16; Quarry Cem., (Vermelles), Pas-de-Calais; Age 18; Son of Joseph and A.Dean of 37, Essex Street, Brighton.

2478. DEAN, Wesley William; B: Dagnell, Berkshire; E: Eastbourne; Pte. G 7610; K: 4.8.16; Thiepval Mem., Somme.

2479. DEANE, Thomas Henry James; B: Upper Holloway, London; E: Upper Holloway; Pte. G 20200; W: 5.5.17; Duisans Brit. Cem., Pas-de-Calais; Age 33; Husband of Elizabeth Matilda Deane of 2, Moray Road, Finsbury Park, London.*

2480. DEARLING, Alonzo Robert; B: Wick, Sussex; E: Rye, Sussex; Pte. G 18078; K: 5.4.18; Pozieres Mem., Somme; Age 23; Son of Alonzo Dearling of 7, Purbeck Place, Littlehampton, Sussex.

2481. DEBENHAM, Herbert; B: Sudbury, Suffolk; E: Ipswich, Suffolk; Pte. G 23810; K: 13.8.18; Vis-en-Artois Mem., Haucourt, Pas-de-Calais; Age 18; Son of Herbert and Eliza Debenham of 22, Queen's Terrace, Suffolk Road, Sudbury; Killed near Morlancourt, Somme.

2482. DE GRUCHY, George Henry; B: Fulham, London; E: London; Pte. G 5255; W: 18.7.16; Étaples Mil. Cem., Pas-de-Calais; Age 33; Husband of Mrs.M.De Gruchy of 6, Haywood Villa, Collingwood Road, Sutton, Surrey.

2483. DELL, Henry; B: Dawley, Middlesex; E: Shepherd's Bush, London; Pte. G 4413; K: 7.10.16; Thiepval Mem., Somme.

2484. DENNIS, Alfred Orton; B: Worthing; E: Worthing; Pte. G 814; W: 3.5.16; Calais Southern Cem., Pas-de-Calais; Age 20; Son of Henry John and Eliza Agnes Dennis of 3, Stanley Road, Worthing.

2485. DENTON, Walter; B: Rushden, Northamptonshire; E: Kettering, Northamptonshire; Pte. G 23137; K: 28.3.18; Pozieres Mem., Somme; Husband of Elizabeth Emily Denton of 76, Gold Street, Wellingborough, Northamptonshire.

2486. DENYER, Charles George; B: Arundel, Sussex; E: Arundel; L/Cpl. G 1142; K: 25.7.17; Arras Mem., Pas-de-Calais; Age 25; Son of George and Annie Denyer of Eagle House, Maltravers Road, Arundel; Husband of Lilian Denyer of South Hill Park, Bagshot Road, Bracknell, Berkshire.

2487. DENYER, George Charles; B: Farncombe, Surrey; E: Hove; Pte. G 1165; K: 7.7.16; Thiepval Mem., Somme; Age 20; Son of George and Kate Ellen Denyer of 84, Albion Street, Southwick, Sussex.

2488. DE STE. CROIX, Arthur Nicholas; B: Stoke Newington, London; E: London; Cpl. G 273; K: 23.10.15; Loos Mem., Pas-de-Calais; Age 26; Son of the Rev.H.M. and Mrs.De Ste.Croix of St.Saviour's Rectory, Gurnsey, Channel Islands.

2489. DEWAR, George Nash; B: Rotherhithe, Kent; E: Rotherhithe; Pte. G 9661; W: 2.10.18; St.Sever Cem. Ext., Rouen, Seine-Maritime.

2490. DEWLEY, William George; B: Woodburn Green, Buckinghamshire; E: Sevenoaks, Kent; Pte. G 13149; K: 9.5.17; Arras Mem., Pas-de-Calais.

2491. DICKINSON, John George; B: Brighton; E: Hove; Pte. L 10618; K: 7.7.16; Thiepval Mem., Somme, Age 19; Son of George Dickinson of 11, London Street, Brighton.*

2492. DINMORE, John James; B: Woolwich, London; E: Grove Park, London; Pte. G 22936; K: 8.8.18; Beacon Cem., Somme; Age 19; Son of Mrs.E.J.Dinmore of 31, Robert Street, Plumstead, London.

2493. DIXON, Albert Ernest; B: Plaistow, London; E: Canning Town, London; Pte. G 4005; W: 11.7.16; Heilly Station Cem., Mericourt-L'Abbe, Somme.

2494. DIXON, Peter Sydenham; Lt.; K: 7.8.18; Ribemont Com. Cem. Ext., Somme; Age 35; Son of Francis Peter and Jane Dixon of "Wood View", Carlisle.

2495. DOLLERY, Sidney Thomas; B: Barnham, Sussex; E: Chichester; L/Cpl. G 429; W: 2.10.15; Bethune Town Cem., Pas-de-Calais; Died at No.33 Casualty Clearing Station.

2496. DORSET, Albert; B: Frimley, Surrey; E: Camberley, Surrey; Pte. L 10941; K: 4.8.16; Courcelette Brit. Cem., Somme; Son of Alfred and Tamar Dorset of 8, Council Houses, Sandhurst, Berkshire.

2497. DOWN, James Frederick; B: Hove; E: Brighton; Pte. S 2126; K: 9.4.16; Vermelles Brit. Cem., Pas-de-Calais; Killed by trench mortar fire.

2498. DOWNHAM, Leonard James; B: – ; E: Colchester, Essex; Pte. G 14597; K: 8.8.18; Vis-en-Artois Mem., Haucourt, Pas-de-Calais; Killed near Morlancourt, Somme.

2499. DOYLE, Alexander William; B: Hove; E: Hove; Pte. SD 3563; K: 21.9.18; Vis-en-Artois Mem., Haucourt, Pas-de-Calais.

2500. DRAKE, Samuel; B: – ; E: Hammersmith, London; L/Cpl. G 10314; W: 4.12.17; Boisguillaume Com. Cem. Ext., Seine-Maritime; Age 36; Son of Samuel and Louisa Mary Drake of Cambridge.

2501. DRISCOLL, Jerry; B: St.John's, Sussex; E: Worthing; Pte. L 8279; W: 19.3.16; Vermelles Brit. Cem., Pas-de-Calais; Son of John and Ellen Driscoll of Brighton.

2502. DUDMAN, Ernest; B: Easebourne, Sussex ; E: – ; L/Cpl. – 31017; M.M.; K: 27.9.18; Gouzeaucourt New Brit. Cem., Nord; Son of John and Harriet Dudman of Upper Vining, Lodsworth, Sussex; Native of Easebourne; Killed while attached to the 1st Queens Own (Royal West Kent Regiment).

2503. DUFFIELD, Oscar Sydney; B: Tarring, Sussex; E: Worthing; L/Cpl. G 3252; K: 3.5.17; Arras Mem., Pas-de-Calais; Age 22; Son of James and Mary Duffield of 10, St.Dunstans Road, West Worthing.

2504. DUKE, Alfred William; B: Amberley, Sussex; E: Petworth, Sussex; Pte. G 8384; K: 7.7.16; Serre Road Cem. No.2, Somme.

2505. DUMSDAY, Frederick; B: Crawley Down, Sussex; E: Rye, Sussex; Pte. G 18079; K: 5.4.18; Bouzincourt Ridge Cem., Somme; Age 28; Son of

Henry Dumsday of Holmans Cottage, Copthorne, Sussex; Husband of Sarah Jane Dumsday.

2506. DYKES, Willaim Albert; B: – ; E: Worthing; Pte. G 7784; K: 10.7.16; Thiepval Mem., Somme.

E

2507. EADE, William John; B: Bognor Regis, Sussex; E: Chichester; Pte. SD 1180; K: 20.5.18; Mailly Wood Cem., Somme; Age 38; Son of John and Mary Ann Eade; Husband of Jane Selina Eade of St.John's Links Avenue, Felpham, Sussex.

2508. EALDEN, John; B: Benenden, Kent; E: Hastings; Pte. G 3965; K: 23.10.18; Auberchicourt Brit. Cem., Nord.

2509. EARL, Arthur Bernard; B: – ; E: – ; Pte. G 69297; K: 10.8.18; Morlancourt Brit. Cem. No.2, Somme; Killed while attached to The Queens (Royal West Surrey Regiment).

2510. EARL, Tom; B: – ; E: – ; Pte. S 593; K: 25.9.15; St.Mary's A.D.S.Cem., Pas-de-Calais.*

2511. EASON, Henry; B: Horsham, Sussex; E: Horsham; Pte. G 940; D at Home: 6.10.15; Horsham (Hills) Cem., Sussex (UK).

2512. EAST, Frank Bernard; B: Deptford, London; E: Brighton; Pte. G 3432; W: 24.9.18; Doingt Com. Cem., Somme; Age 33; Son of Frank and Charlotte East of Brighton; Husband of Edith Mary East of 5a, Totland Road, Brighton.

2513. EATON, John; B: Crewe, E: Warrington; Pte. G 20478; W: 5.12.18; Les Baraques Mil. Cem., Pas-de-Calais.*

2514. EDMONDS, George Thomas; B: Earls Barton, Northamptonshire; E: Earls Barton; L/Cpl. G 11348; K: 13.4.17; Tank Cem., Pas-de-Calais.*

2515. EDWARDS, Albert William; B: – ; E: Horsham, Sussex; Pte. G 16688; K: 25.11.17; Villers Hill Brit. Cem., Nord.

2516. EELLS, Richard Walter Robert; B: Battersea, London; E: Tooting, London; Pte. G 14121; K: 9.4.17; Gourock Trench Cem., Tilloy-les-Mofflaines, Pas-de-Calais; Age 40; Son of Henry Eells; Husband of Ada Mary Eells of 44, Gassiot Road, Tooting.

2517. EGGLETON, Benjamin; B: Crawley, Sussex; E: Horsham, Sussex; Pte. L 7652; K: 4.7.17; Arras Mem., Pas-de-Calais; Age 30; Son of Charles and Ellen Eggleton of 146, Brookwood Road, Southfields, London; An original 'Old Contemptible' with the 2nd Battalion, finally killed while attacking a range of shell holes near Monchy-le-Preux.

2518. ELLIOTT, Stanley John; B: Hastings; E: Hastings; Pte. G 18195; K: 25.11.17; Cambrai Mem., Louverval, Nord.

2519. ELLIS, Percy; B: Tangmere, Sussex; E: Chichester; Pte. G 619; K: 6.8.15; Houplines Com. Cem. Ext., Nord.

2520. ELLIS, Richard; B: Bishops Cleve, Goucestershire; E: Lewes; Pte. SD 917; K: 5.4.18; Bouzincourt Ridge Cem., Somme.

2521. ELMS, Gordon William; B: Brighton; E: Hove; Pte. L 10772; K: 7.7.16; Thiepval Mem., Somme.

2522. ELPHICK, Walter; B: Hailsham, Sussex; E: Hastings; Pte. G 6354; K: 18.9.18; Epehy Wood Farm Cem., Epehy, Somme; Age 27; Son of Caleb and Rhoda Elphick of Vicarage Cottage, Hailsham.

2523. ELSEY, Frederick James; B: Balcombe, Sussex; E: Chichester; Pte. G 182; W: 23.3.16; Vermelles Brit. Cem., Pas-de-Calais; Age 20; Son of Mr. and Mrs. Alfred Elsey of The Alley, Balcombe.

2524. EMBLEN, Albert; B: Ardington, Berkshire; E: Brighton; Pte. TF 201565; K: 25.11.17; Cambrai Mem., Louverval, Nord; Husband of Emma Isabel Emblen of 1, Orford Villas, Heath Road, Hillingdon, Middlesex.

2525. EMERY, Walter; B: Walton-on-the-Hill, Surrey; E: Rye, Sussex; Pte. G 18083; W: 24.8.18; Daours Com. Cem. Ext., Somme; Age 25; Son of William and S.Emery of Walton-on-the-Hill.

2526. ERICSON, Eric Charles; B: Surrey; 2nd Lt.; M.M.; K: 18.9.18; Epehy Wood Farm Cem., Epehy, Somme; Age 27; Son of Eric and Louisa Ericson; Husband of Julia Catherine Ericson of 75, St.Luke's Avenue, Ramsgate, Kent.

2527. EVANS, Arthur James; B: Brighton; E: Hove; Sgt. G 764; M.M.; K: 7.7.16; Serre Road Cem. No.2, Somme; Also commemorated at Ovillers Mil. Cem., Somme, as having been buried originally at the nearby Mash Valley Cem., Somme, from which bodies were removed after the war.

2528. EVANS, Cecil James; B: Brighton; E: Hove; Pte. G 4188; K: 2.11.15; Loos Mem., Pas-de-Calais.

2529. EVANS, Owen; B: Llancarfan, Glamorgan; B: Cowbridge, Glamorgan; Pte. G 1025; K: 7.7.16; Ovillers Mil. Cem., Somme; Age 24; Son of the Rev.W.E. and Mary Evans of The Manse, Llanbethery, Cowbridge.*

2530. EVANS, Sidney Charles; B: Rickmansworth, Hertfordshire; E: Watford; Pte. G 17369; K: 18.9.18; Epehy Wood Farm Cem., Epehy, Somme.

2531. EVENDEN, George; B: Eastbourne; E: Chichester; Pte. G 14380; W at Home: 25.4.17; Kensal Green (All Souls) Cem., London (UK); Age 29; Son of Curly and Delia Evenden of Little Common Road, Bexhill-on-Sea, Sussex; Husband of Rose Davis, formerly Evenden, of 24, Salisbury Road, Bexhill-on-Sea.

2532. EVERETT, Ernest William; B: Charlton Huntingdonshire; E: Bognor Regis, Sussex; L/Cpl. G 733; K: 1.8.16; Thiepval Mem., Somme; Age 26; Husand of Mary Agnes Everett of 1, Bellvue Cottage, Westergate, Sussex.

2533. EYLES, Charles; B: Catsfield, Sussex; E: Eastbourne; Pte. G 18085; W: 10.4.17; Duisans Brit. Cem., Pas-de-Calais.

F

2534. FAIRCLOTH, Henry Latham; B: St.John's, Sussex; E: Chichester; C.Q.M.S. L 9149; K: 28.12.15; Guards Cem. (Cuinchy) Pas-de-Calais. Killed accidentally in the trenches when a rifle grenade pin was removed to early.*

2535. FAIRHALL, Frederick Charles; B: Brighton; E: Chichester; Sgt. L 10228; K: 25.11.17; Cambrai Mem., Louverval, Nord; Age 20; Son of Mrs. Caroline Fairhall of 6, Arnold Street, Brighton.

2536. FAULKNER, Thomas Edward; B: – ; E: Brighton; Pte. G 16635; K: 14.5.17; Dury Crucifix Cem., Pas-de-Calais.

2537. FEARNLEY, Joseph Henry; B: Acton, London; E: Piccadilly, London; L/Cpl. G 20331; W: 24.11.17; Abbeville Com. Cem. Ext., Somme; Age 30; Son of William and Sarah Fearnley of Acton; Husband of Ethel M.Fearnley of 10, Lettice Street, Fulham, London.*

2538. FEIST, John Thomas; B: Hastings; E: Hastings; L/Cpl. G 8856; W: 3.5.17; Faubourg d'Amiens Cem., Arras, Pas-de-Calais; Age 22; Son of William and Harriet Feist of 8, Courthouse Street, Hastings.

2539. FICKLING, Walter; B: Clerkenwell, London; E: Camberwell, London; Pte. G 10705; K: 27.3.18; Pozieres Mem., Somme.

2540. FIELD, John Morton; 2nd Lt.; K: 11.4.16; Vermelles Brit. Cem., Pas-de-Calais; Age 24; Son of Mr. and Mrs.Charles Edward Field of 98, Christchurch Road, Tulse Hill, London; Killed by piece of debris.

2541. FILTNESS, Frank; B: East Grinstead, Sussex; E: Eastbourne; Pte. G 13455; K: 6.4.18; Bouzincourt Ridge Cem., Somme; Age 20; Son of Edward Filtness of Home Farm Buildings, Rowfant, Sussex.

2542. FINCH, Leonard; B: Walsham-le-Willows, Suffolk; E: Norwich; Pte. G 18087; K: 30.11.17; Cambrai Mem., Louverval, Nord; Age 23; Son of John and Emily Finch of Walsham-le-Willows.

2543. FINNIMORE, Henry James; 2nd Lt.; W: 27.3.18; Soissons Mem., Aisne; Age 21; Son of James and Jane Finnimore of 83, Park Road, Plumstead, London; Attached to Royal Flying Corps

2544. FISH, Frederick Charles; B: Small Dole, Sussex; E: Chichester; Pte. G 23816; K: 18.9.18; Epehy Wood Farm Cem., Epehy, Somme; Age 18; Son of James and Mary Ann Fish of The Rosary, Upper Beeding, Sussex.

2545. FISHER, Ernest; B: Kinsale, County Cork, Ireland; E: Eastbourne; Pte. G 8158; K: 24.9.18; Epehy Wood Farm Cem., Epehy, Somme; Age 24; Son of George and Charlotte Fisher of 20, Sidley Road, Eastbourne.

2546. FITCH, Frederick William; B: Turlow, Cambridgeshire; E: Hove; Pte. G 688;K: 7.7.16; Thiepval Mem., Somme.

2547. FITT, Thomas; B: Reading, Berkshire; E: Warley, Essex; Pte. G 18088; K: 9.4.17; Arras Mem., Pas-de-Calais.

2548. FITZELL, Herbert; B: Chiddligly, Sussex; E: Hastings; Pte. G 4104; K: 27.3.18; Pozieres Mem., Somme.

2549. FITZPATRICK, Lawrence Valentine; B: Finchley, London; E: Whitehall, London; L/Cpl. G 19454; W: 30.6.18; Gezaincourt Com. Cem. Ext., Somme; Age 19; Son of Edward and Marie Fitzpatrick of 14, Yerbury Road, Tufnell Park, London.*

2550. FITZSIMONS, Terrance; 2nd Lt.; K: 4.4.16; Loos Mem., Pas-de-Calais.

2551. FLECKNOE, Frederick George Carrick; B: Fairlight, Sussex; E: Hastings; L/Cpl. G 18026; K: 3.5.17; Arras Mem., Pas-de-Calais; Age 20; Son of William and Margaret Flecknoe of 15, Prospect Place, Hastings.*

2552. FLOWERS, John Arthur; 2nd Lt.; K: 1.9.16; Arras Mem., Pas-de-Calais; Age 20; Son of Arthur Flowers of 18, Hove Park Villas, Hove.

2553. FOORD, George Fred; B: Ilford, Essex; E: Chichester; L/Cpl. G 798; W: 19.7.16; Boulogne Eastern Cem., Pas-de-Calais; Age 21; Son of Fred and Emma Foord of Tickeridge Cottage, Blackboys, Sussex.

2554. FOSTER, Alfred; B: Battle, Sussex; E: Hastings; Pte. L 7596; K: 8.4.16; Vermelles Brit. Cem., Pas-de-Calais.

2555. FOSTER, Percy George; 2nd Lt.; W at Home: 2.4.16; Hastings Cem., Sussex (UK); Age 23; Son of Mrs.Ada Foster of 1, Alexandra Road, St.Leonards-on-Sea.

2556. FOSTER, William Henry; B: Loxwood, Sussex; E: Horsham; Pte. SD1928; K: 24.9.18; Epehy Wood Farm Cem., Epehy, Somme; Son of Mr.W.Foster of "Hillside", Alford, Sussex.*

2557. FRAMP, Eric William John; B: Sherborne, Dorset; E: Camberwell, London; Pte. G 11112; K: 9.2.17; Faubourg d'Amiens Cem., Arras, Pas-de-Calais.

2558. FRANKS, Frank William; B: St.Leonards-on-Sea; E: Hastings; Pte. G 62; K: 2.1.16; Bethune Town Cem., Pas-de-Calais; Age 26; Son of Frank Gilbert and Sarah Franks of 9, Dorset Place, Hastings.

2559. FREELAND, William Charles; B: – ; E: Hove; Cpl. G 6827; K: 4.2.18; Croix-du-Bac Brit. Cem., Steenwerck, Nord.

2560. FRENCH, Ernest William; B: Worthing; E: Worthing; Cpl. G 1406; K: 3.5.17; Arras Mem., Pas-de-Calais.

2561. FROST, Archibald; B: St.Pancras, London; E: Chichester; Pte. G 547; K: 7.7.16; Thiepval Mem., Somme.

2562. FROST, Joseph Alfred; B: Barnes, Surrey; E: Mortlake, Surrey; Pte. G 18089; K: 25.4.18; Mailly Wood Cem., Somme; Age 22; Son of Henry and Harriett S.Frost of 30, Railway Street, Barnes.

2563. FULLER, Charles; B: Tunbridge Wells; E: Maidstone; Pte. G 23821; K: 9.8.18; Beacon Cem., Somme; Age 18; Son of Jonathan and Harriet Fuller of 172, Goods Station Road, Tunbridge Wells.

2564. FUNNELL, Albert; B: – ; E: Uckfield, Sussex; Pte. G 18091; K: 3.5.17; Feuchy Chapel Brit. Cem., Pas-de-Calais; Age 40; Son of Stephen and Lucy Funnell; Husband of Alice Emma Funnell of 13, Hempstead Gardens, Uckfield.

2565. FUNNELL, Douglas; B: Dallington, Sussex; E: Dallington; L/Sgt. G 406; K: 25.11.17; Cambrai Mem., Louverval, Nord.

2566. FURNER, Charlie; B: Buxted, Sussex; E: Eastbourne; Pte. G 22656; W: 18.7.18; Bagneux Brit. Cem., Somme; Age 28; Son of Mrs.E.E.Furner of 13, Greenfield Road, Eastbourne.

G

2567. GALE, Harold William; 2nd Lt.; K: 8.8.16; Dive Copse Brit. Cem., Somme; Age 24; Son of William Willson Gale and Kate Gale of 145, Milton Avenue, East Ham, London; Killed while attached to the 5th Battalion Royal Berkshire Regiment.

2568. GALE, Joseph; B: South Hetton, Durham; E: Gateshead; Pte. G 5959; K: 31.3.16; Loos Mem., Pas-de-Calais.*

2569. GALLARD, Henry; B: Notting Hill, London; E: Eastbourne; Pte. G 21684; K: 5.4.18; Bouzincourt Ridge Cem., Somme.

2570. GANDER, Thomas; B: Brighton; E: Bexhill-on-Sea; Pte. SD 2092; W: 6.4.18; St.Hilaire Cem. Ext., Pas-de-Calais.

2571. GATES, George; B: Knebworth, Hertfordshire; E: Hitchin, Hertfordshire; Pte. G 20049; K: 10.4.17; Faubourg-d'Amiens Cem., Arras, Pas-de-Calais; Age 43; Son of George Gates of Knebworth; Husband of Martha Elixabeth Gates of Diddington, Huntingdonshire.

2572. GAUNT, William; B: Collyhurst, Lancashire; E: Manchester; Pte. TF 260222; K: 18.9.18; Epehy Wood Farm Cem., Epehy, Somme; Age 20, Son of Alfred and Emma Gaunt of 56, Ryder Street, Collyhurst.

2573. GEALL, Samuel George; B: Brighton; E: Brighton; L/Cpl. G 3488; W: 26.8.18; St.Sever Cem. Ext., Rouen, Seine-Maritime.

2574. GEARING, John Ambrose; B: Beddingham, Sussex; E: Hurstpierpoint, Sussex; Pte. G 1085; K: 4.3.16; Loos Mem., Pas-de-Calais.

2575. GEARING, Sidney; B: Beddingham, Sussex; E: Eastbourne; Pte. SD 1338; K: 18.9.18; Epehy Wood Farm Cem., Somme; Age 28; Son of Mr.C. and Mrs.A.L.M.Gearings of 9, Wannock Road, Eastbourne.*

2576. GEER, Frederick; B: Eastbourne; E: Eastbourne; L/Cpl. G 3747; K: 30.6.18; Harponville Com. Cem. Ext., Somme.

2577. GELL, Walter Henry; B: – ; E: Hastings; Pte. SD 3577; K: 3.5.17; Arras Mem., Pas-de-Calais.*

2578. GEORGE, Albert William; B: Worcester; E: Hove; Pte. G 713; D at Home: 28.1.15; Shorncliffe Mil. Cem., Kent (UK); Age 33; Son of Edwin George; Husband of Ellen Page, formerly George, of 22, Ivory Place, Brighton.

2579. GEORGE, Edward; B: Titchfield, Hampshire; E: Chichester; Pte. GS 180; K: 6.11.15; Loos Mem., Pas-de-Calais; Age 30; Son of Thomas George of 81, Kingsley Road, Milton, Hampshire.

2580. GEORGE, William; B: Southwick, Sussex; E: Chichester; Pte. GS 177; K: 3.5.17; Arras Mem., Pas-de-Calais; Age 34; Son of Thomas and Emily George; Husband of Elizabeth George of 2, War Memorial Cottages, Felpham, Sussex.

2581. GIBBS, Charles Arthur; B: Eastbourne; E: Eastbourne; Pte. S 1799; K: 14.5.17; Arras Mem., Pas-de-Calais; Age 22; Son of Arthur and Alice Emily Gibbs of 85, Dennis Road, Eastbourne.*

2582. GIBBY, Albert William; B: Reigate, Surrey; E: Horsham, Sussex; Pte. G 16127; K: 24.9.18; Epehy Wood Farm Cem., Epehy, Somme; Age 25; Son of Benjamin and Matilda Gibby of Copthorne, Sussex.

2583. GIBSON, Sidney James; B: Horsham, Sussex; E: Horsham; L/Cpl. G 16657; K: 18.9.18; Epehy Wood Farm Cem., Epehy, Somme; Age 28; Son of James and Emily Gibson of Horsham; Husband of Emily Ann Gibson of 76, Spencer's Road, Horsham.

2584. GIBSON-LEE, William Charles; B: – ; E: Woking, Surrey; Pte. G 17387; K: 18.9.18; Epehy Wood Farm Cem., Somme; Age 20; Son of Frederick William and Louisa Gibson-Lee of 171, Boundary Road, Woking.

2585. GILLHAM, Frederick Stephen Michael; B: Little Common, Sussex; E: Hastings; Sgt. GS 127; W: 4.3.16; Bethune Town Cem., Pas-de-Calais; Age 25; Son of Stephen and Ellen Gillham; Husband of Ellen J.Gillham of Peach Cottage, Little Common.

2586. GLADWISH, William; B: Hastings; E: Hastings; L/Cpl. G 116; K: 4.8.16; Thiepval Mem., Somme.

2587. GLUE, Charles Richard; B: East Ashington, Sussex; E: Chichester; Pte. G 994; D at Home: 22.1.15; Stoughton (St.Mary) Churchyard, Sussex (UK); Age 20; Son of George and Florence M.Glue of East Marden, Sussex; Died of Pneumonia.

2588. GOBLE, George William; B: Aldingbourne, Sussex; E: Bognor Regis, Sussex; Cpl. G 1055; K: 3.7.17; Monchy Brit. Cem., Pas-de-Calais; Age 22; Son of George William and Ellen Goble of Hungerdown, Fontwell, Sussex.

2589. GOBLE, John; B: Brighton; E: Brighton; Pte. G 17292; K: 4.8.16; Thiepval Mem., Somme.

2590. GOCHER, Aubrey Cyril; B: Brighton; E: Brighton; Pte. G 4824; K: 7.7.16; Ovillers Mil. Cem., Somme.

2591. GODDARD, John; B: Brighton; E: Hove; Pte. G 5420; W: 29.7.17; Cabaret-Rouge Brit. Cem., Pas-de-Calais.

2592. GODDARD, Percy William; B: Aldershot, E: Norwich; Pte. G 5404; K: 7.7.16; Thiepval Mem., Somme.

2593. GODDEN, Charles Tower Rayson; B: – ; E: Bognor Regis, Sussex; Pte. G 16656; K: 14.5.17; Arras Mem., Pas-de-Calais; Age 41; Son of Charles and Hepzibah Godden of "Silver Dale", Gordon Avenue, Bognor Regis; Husband of Mary Jane Godden of 101, Victoria Road, Chichester.

2594. GODDEN, E.; B: – ; E: – ; L/Cpl. G 583; D at Home: 22.12.17; Worthing (Broadwater) Cem., Sussex (UK); Son of John Godden of "Chiswick", Tarring Road, West Worthing.

2595. GODDEN, George; B: Margate, Kent; E: Hastings; Pte. G 466; K: 4.3.16; Loos Mem., Pas-de-Calais; Age 26; Son of Mrs.S.H.Godden of 1, Carn Brae, Bath Road, Margate.

2596. GODDEN, George Henry; B: Rottingdean, Sussex; E: Brighton; Pte. G 3509; K: 3.5.17; Arras Mem., Pas-de-Calais; Age 23; Son of Mrs.M.Godden of Northgate Cottages, Rottingdean.

2597. GODFREE, Henry; B: Brighton; E: Brighton; Pte. G 3944; K: 15.4.16; Vermelles Brit. Cem., Pas-de-Calais.

2598. GODFREE, Richard; B: Brighton; E: Brighton; Pte. L 10333; K: 7.7.16; Thiepval Mem., Somme; Age 20; Son of Mrs.Caroline Godfree of 50, Jersey Street, Brighton.

2599. GODWIN, John Charles Raymond; 2nd Lt.; K: 7.7.16; Thiepval Mem., Somme.

2600. GOLDS, Frank; 2nd Lt.; K: 5.10.16; Guards Cem. (Lesboeufs) Somme; Age 37; Son of Hugh William and Ellen Golds of Littlehampton, Sussex; Killed at Flers while attached to the East Surrey Regiment.

2601. GOLDSMITH, George Thomas; B: Waldron, Sussex; E: Eastbourne; Pte. G 6217; K: 9.4.17; Faubourg d'Amiens Cem., Arras, Pas-de-Calais; Age 39; Husband of Mrs.E.H.Goldsmith of Ivy Cottage, Mill Lane, East Hoathly, Sussex.

2602. GOODERSON, Harry; B: Nutley, Sussex; E: Brighton; Pte. G 262; K: 8.4.16; Loos Mem., Pas-de-Calais.

2603. GORDON, Henry Bernard; Lt.; K: 7.7.16; Thiepval Mem., Somme; Bombing Officer; Killed by a 'Whiz Bang'.

2604. GORRINGE, Edward Clifton; Capt.; M.C.; K: 5.9.18; Peronne Com. Cem. Ext., Ste. Radegonde, Somme; Age 32; Son of Frank and Mary Gorringe of "Rowfant", Hampden Park, Eastbourne.

2605. GOUGH, John; B: Brackley, Northamptonshire; E: Hinkley, Leicestershire; Pte. G 18281; D: 8.3.18; Tournai Com. Cem. Allied Ext., (Bel.); Age 45; Son of Mrs.Mary Barber of Church Row, Greatworth, Oxfordshire.

2606. GOULD, James; B: Dorset; E: Chichester; Pte. G 848; W: 10.8.16; Boulogne Eastern Cem., Pas-de-Calais.

2607. GOWER, Charles Henry; B: Hastings; E: Tooting, London; Pte. G 14099; W: 25.7.17; Monchy Brit. Cem., Pas-de-Calais; Age 41; Husband of Mrs.E.S.Gower of Renmuir House, 25, Renmuir Street, Tooting Junction, London.*

2608. GRAHAM, Harry; B: Brighton; E: Brighton; Pte. L 10796; W: 10.4.17; Faubourg d'Amiens Cem., Arras, Pas-de-Calais; Age 19; Son of Frederick and Edith May Graham of 2, Yew Tree Cottages, Mill Road, Burgess Hill, Sussex.

2609. GRANT, Charles; B: Ticehurst, Sussex; E: Hastings; Pte. G 5173; K: 4.8.16; Thiepval Mem., Somme.

2610. GRANT, William Christian George; B: Great Yarmouth; E: Brighton; Pte. G 17513; K: 9.4.17; Feuchy Chapel Brit. Cem., Pas-de-Calais.

2611. GRATWICKE, Frederick; B: Shipley, Sussex; E: Horsham, Sussex; L/Cpl. SD 676; K: 9.4.17; Faubourg d'Amiens Cem., Arras, Pas-de-Calais; Age 21; Son of Harry and Fanny Gratwicke of Chivers Cottage, Shipley *

2612. GRAY, Henry Justus; B: Littlehampton, Sussex; E: Worthing; L/Cpl. G 3268; W: 25.7.17; Monchy Brit. Cem., Pas-de-Calais; Age 21; Son of Margaret Gray of 22a, Blithdale Road, Plumstead, London.*

2613. GREENFIELD, Harry; B: Lugashall, Sussex; E: Chichester; Pte. G 600; K: 7.7.16; Thiepval Mem., Somme; Age 23; Son of William and Rhoda Ellen Greenfield of Windfall Wood, Lugashall.

2614. GREENWAY, William James; B: Brighton; E: Brighton; Pte. SD 5412; W: 10.4.17; Duisans Brit. Cem., Pas-de-Calais; Son of W.J.Greenway of 2, Brewer Street, Brighton.

2615. GREGORY, Harry; B: Long Marston, Hertfordshire; E: Tring, Hertfordshire; Pte. G 5914; W: 28.8.18; St.Sever Cem. Ext., Rouen, Seine-Maritime; Age 36; Son of James and Elizabeth Gregory of Little Farm, Long Marston; Husband of Mary Pond, formerly Gregory, of Cheddington Road, Long Marston.

2616. GRENDER, Sidney; B: Aldingbourne, Sussex; E: Bognor Regis, Sussex; Pte. G 727; W: 4.3.16; Vermelles Brit. Cem., Pas-de-Calais; Son of John and Annie Grender of Hook Lane, Aldingbourne.

2617. GRIFFITHS, Victor; B: St.Patrick's, Middlesex; E: Whitehall, London; Pte. G 18370; K: 26.8.18; Vis-en-Artois Mem., Haucourt, Pas-de-Calais; Age 19; Son of Benjamin and Annie Griffiths of 26, Georgiana Street, Camden Town, London.

2618. GROVER, Albert Henry; B: Hurstpierpoint, Sussex; E: Hurstpierpoint; Pte. G 2723; K: 6.8.15; Houplines Com. Cem. Ext., Nord.

2619. GROVER, Reginald; B: Dunsfold, Surrey; E: Petworth, Sussex; Pte. G 17830; K: 5.9.18; Peronne Com. Cem. Ext., Ste. Radegonde, Somme.

2620. GROVER, Walter John; B: Hurstpierpoint, Sussex; E: Hurstpierpoint; Pte. G 526; K: 15.2.16; Quarry Cem. (Vermelles) Pas-de-Calais; Son of Mr.J.Grover of Bramberwells Cottages, Hurstpierpoint.

2621. GUNTON, Harry Victor; B: Kelvedon, Essex; E: Colchester, Essex; L/Cpl. G 14689; W: 15.5.18; St.Sever Cem. Ext., Rouen, Seine-Maritime.

2622. GUTSELL, George; B: Brede, Sussex; E: Hastings; Pte. G 15821; K: 5.4.18; Bouzincourt Ridge Cem., Somme.

H

2623. HACK, Roland; B: Eastbourne; E: Eastbourne; Pte. G 18097; K: 19.10.16; Thiepval Mem., Somme; Age 20; Son of Arthur and Elizabeth Hack of Eakington House, Ripe, Sussex.

2624. HALE, George James; B: Pagham, Sussex; E: Chichester; L/Cpl. G 990; K: 24.6.18; Harponville Com. Cem. Ext., Somme; Age 24; Son of James and Ellen Hale of Pagham.*

2625. HALL, Harry Francis; B: Portfield, Sussex; E: Chichester; Cpl. G 452; W: 24.5.18; St.Sever Cem. Ext., Rouen, Seine-Maritime; Age 25; Son of Mr. and Mrs.H.W.Hall of 6, St.James Road, Chichester; Attached to the 36th Trench Mortar Battery, Royal Sussex Regiment.

2626. HALL, Robert; B: Eastbourne; E: Eastbourne; L/Cpl. L 10130; K: 25.11.17; Cambrai Mem., Louverval, Pas-de-Calais; Age 22; Son of John and Annie Hall of 5, Waterworks Cottages, Friston, Sussex.

2627. HALL, William John; B: Goudhurst, Kent; E: Tunbridge Wells; L/Cpl. G 88; K: 31.3.17; Faubourg d'Amiens Cem., Arras, Pas-de-Calais; Killed by shell fire while on digging duties at Arras.

2628. HALLAM, William; B: Sutton Bonnington, Leicestershire; E: Loughborough, Leicestershire; Pte. G 15078; K: 18.9.18; Epehy Wood Farm Cem. Epehy, Somme.*

2629. HAMMOCKS, Frederick Francis; B: Parsons Green, Middlesex; E: Fulham, London; Pte. G 18603; W: 29.10.18; Brebieres Brit. Cem., Pas-de-Calais; Died at No.23 Casualty Clearing Station.

2630. HAMPTON, William Montague; B: St.Erith, Cornwall; E: Camborne; Pte. G 5234; K: 12.4.17; Arras Mem., Pas-de-Calais.

2631. HAMSON, Thomas; B: Scaldwell, Northamptonshire; E: Northampton; Pte. G 22544; K: 8.8.18; Beacon Cem., Somme.

2632. HAND, Herbert; B: Audlem, Cheshire; E: Sittingbourne, Kent; Pte. G 367; K: 24.8.16; Vermelles Brit. Cem., Pas-de-Calais; Age 23; Grandson of George and Mary Hand of Green Lane, Audlem; Killed while attached to 130th Company Royal Engineers.*

2633. HARBOUR, Harry; B: Worth, Sussex; E: East Grinstead, Sussex; Pte. G 7674; K: 16.5.18; Mailly Wood Cem., Somme; Son of Mrs.E.Harbour of West Hoathly, Sussex.

2634. HARBOUR, Thomas; B: Ditchling, Sussex; E: Hurstpierpoint, Sussex; Pte. G 635; K: 4.3.16; Loos Mem., Pas-de-Calais; Age 26; Son of Thomas and Annie Caroline Harbour of Forge Cottage, East End Lane, Ditchling.

2635. HARDHAM, George; B: Brighton; E: Brighton; Sgt. L 6245; K: 18.9.18; Epehy Wood Farm Cem., Somme.

2636. HARDING, Victor Bertram; B: Brighton; E: Hove; Pte. L 10635; W: 20.10.16; Étaples Mil. Cem., Pas-de-Calais; Age 19; Son of Elizabeth Harding of 40, Richmond Street, Brighton.*

2637. HARDY, William Albert; B: Luton; E: Hertford; Pte. G 15578; K: 13.10.18; Point-de-Jour Mil. Cem., Pas-de-Calais.

2638. HARE, Percy Herbert; B: Sevenoaks, Kent; E: Sevenoaks; Pte. G 13030; K: 3.5.17; Arras Mem., Pas-de-Calais; Age 42; Son of Francis George and Margaret Hare; Husband of Mary Hare of 2, Lyndhurst Cottage, Dunton Green, Kent.

2639. HARPER, Thomas William; B: Petworth, Sussex; E: Horsham, Sussex; Pte. G 8823; K: 5.4.18; Bouzincourt Ridge Cem., Somme; Son of William Harper of 371, Bynorth, Petworth.

2640. HARRIS, Ernest Albert; B: Small Heath, Warwickshire; E: Law Courts, London; Pte. G 20050; D: 1.11.18; Douai Brit. Cem., Nord; Age 40; Husband of Florence Jessie Harris of 45, Preston Road, Brighton.

2641. HARRIS, Ernest Alfred Cecil; B: Newhaven, Sussex; E: Eastbourne; Pte. G 657; K: 27.9.15; Cite Bonjean Mil. Cem., Nord; Age 22; Son of Mr.R.A. and Annie Harris of 5, Meeching Road, Newhaven.

2642. HARRIS, John; B: Epping, Essex; E: Petworth, Sussex; SD 5339; K: 14.11.16; Agny Mil. Cem., Pas-de-Calais.*

2643. HARRISON, Harry Oscar; B: Little Hay, Staffordshire; E: Litchfield, Staffordshire; Pte. G 5876; K: 7.7.16; Thiepval Mem., Somme; Age 34; Son of Mr. and Mrs.Henry Harrison of Little Hay; Husband of Fanny Harrison of Queslett Road, Great Barr, Birmingham.

2644. HARVEY, Alec; B: Lewes; E: Eastbourne; Pte. G 4336; D.C.M.; K: 18.9.18; Epehy Wood Farm Cem., Somme; Age 23; Son of Owen and Sarah Anne Harvey of 112, Western Road, Lewes.*

2645. HARWOOD, George; B: – ; E: Horsham, Sussex; Pte. G 17846; K: 22.8.18; Vis-en-Artois Mem., Haucourt, Pas-de-Calais.

2646. HASSALL, James; B: Shavington, Shropshire; E: Bognor Regis, Sussex; L/Cpl. G 498; K: 29.3.16; Loos Mem., Pas-de-Calais; Age 21; Son of James and Martha Hassall of 11, Shavington Park.*

2647. HAWKINS, Thomas Frederick; B: Camberwell, London; E: Lambeth, London; Pte. G 13393; K: 3.5.17; Arras Mem., Pas-de-Calais.

2648. HAWORTH, William; B: Blackburn, Lancashire; E: Burnley, Lancashire; Pte. G 22988; K: 24.8.18; Meaulte Mil. Cem., Somme; Age 19; Son of John and Mary Ellen Haworth of 24, Manchester Road, Burnley.*

2649. HAYDOCK, Frederick Bernard; B: Spitalfields, London; E: Bromley, Kent; Pte. G 12660; K: 25.11.17; Cambrai Mem., Louverval, Nord.

2650. HAYES, Harry; B: Westminster, London; E: Whitehall, London; Pte. G 19479; K: 3.7.18; Harponville Com. Cem. Ext., Somme; Age 19; Son of Harry and Charlotte Hayes of Westminster.

2651. HAYLOR, Allan; B: Matfield, Kent; E: Tunbridge Wells; Pte. G 258; K: 8.4.16; Quarry Cem. (Vermelles) Pas-de-Calais; Son of Mr.G. and Mrs.S.Haylor of Beech Hill, Matfield.

2652. HAZELDINE, Frederick; B: Hove; E: Hove; Pte. G 961; K: 7.7.16; Thiepval Mem., Somme.

2653. HEAD, Arthur Henry; B: Lewes; E: Brighton; Cpl. S 1667; K: 7.10.16; Thiepval Mem., Somme.

2654. HEARSAY, William; B: Hailsham, Sussex; E: Eastbourne; Pte. G 345; K: 4.3.16; Loos Mem., Pas-de-Calais.

2655. HEASMAN, James; B: Rotherfield, Sussex; E: Hove; Pte. G 4798; K: 25.11.17; Cambrai Mem., Louverval, Nord.

2656. HEASMAN, William George; B: Brighton; E: Brighton; Pte. G 14048; K: 5.4.18; Pozieres Mem., Somme.

2657. HEASMER, Edgar; B: Hastings; E: Hastings; Pte. G 16659; K: 9.4.17; Arras Mem., Pas-de-Calais.

2658. HEATH, James George; B: Hove; E: Hove; Pte. L 10583; K: 18.9.18; Epehy Wood Farm Cem., Epehy, Somme; Age 20; Son of James and Mary F.J.Heath of 92, Clarendon Road, Hove.

2659. HEDGER, William James; B: Upton Park, London; E: East Ham, London; Pte. G 9781; W: 5.5.17; Duisans Brit. Cem., Pas-de-Calais; Age 38; Son of William Hedger of 79, Stamford Road, East Ham.

2660. HEMSLEY, Robert; B: Brighton; E: Brighton; Pte. G 7693; W: 28.4.18; Valenciennes (St.Roch) Com. Cem., Nord.

2661. HENDRY, William; B: Wallsend, Northumberland; E: Jarrow, County Durham; Pte. G 350; M.M.; K: 2.11.16; Agny Mil. Cem., Pas-de-Calais.

2662. HENSON, James; B: Winchester; E: Hove; L/Cpl. G 745; K: 20.11.17; Cambrai Mem., Louverval, Nord.

2663. HEYDON, Archibald John; B: Assington, Essex; E: Midhurst, Sussex; L/Sgt. G 1632; K: 27.3.18; Pozieres Mem., Somme; Age 23; Son of William and Harriet Heydon of 336F, Grove Street, Petworth, Sussex.

2664. HILL, Harry; B: –; E: Aldershot; L/Cpl. G 5243; K: 25.11.17; Cambrai Mem., Louverval, Nord; Age 25; Son of Samuel and Annie Hill of 43, Thames Street, Belfast, Northern Ireland.

2665. HILL, Herbert Henry; B: Boxmoor, Hertfordshire; E: Watford; Pte. G 14272; K: 20.11.17; Cambrai Mem., Louverval, Nord.

2666. HILL, John; B: North Chapel, Sussex; E: Brighton; Pte. G 9635; D: 1.2.17; Étaples Mil. Cem., Pas-de-Calais.

2667. HILTON, Fred; B: Ifield, Sussex; E: Horsham, Sussex; Pte. L 10275; K: 24.3.16; Vermelles Brit. Cem., Pas-de-Calais; Age 19; Son of Frederick Hilton of "Tushmoor", London Road, Crawley, Sussex.

2668. HISCOCK, Harry Albert; B: Northam, Hampshire; E: Southampton; Pte. G 11352; K: 1.11.17; Cambrai Mem., Louverval, Nord; Age 23; Son of George Henry Hiscock of 21, Princes Street, Northam.

2669. HOADLEY, William Lewis; B: Langley, Sussex; E: Hastings; L/Cpl. G 32; W: 19.10.15; Bethune Town Cem., Pas-de-Calais; Age 19; Son of William and Hagar Hoadley of 5, Stonefield Road, Hastings.*

2670. HODGES, Frederick George; B: Angmering, Sussex; E: Chichester; L/Cpl. G 13; K: 29.8.18; Vis-en-Artois Mem., Haucourt, Pas-de-Calais.

2671. HODKINSON, James Bradley; B: St.James, Lancashire; E: Worthing; L/Cpl. G 613; K: 4.3.16; Loos Mem., Pas-de-Calais; Age 20; Son of Mrs. Alice Elizabeth Patmore of 29, St.John's Road, Margate, Kent.

2672. HOGAN, James Henry; B: Jarrow; E: Jarrow; Pte. G 351; K: 11.9.15; Houplines Com. Cem. Ext., Nord; Killed by shell fire while at Battalion Headquarters.

2673. HOLDEN, Charles; B: Wisborough Green, Sussex; E: Horsham, Sussex; Cpl.G 3676; K: 5.10.16; Thiepval Mem., Somme.

2674. HOLDEN, Frank William; B: Hermitage, Sussex; E: Chichester; Pte. G 806; K: 7.7.16; Thiepval Mem., Somme; Age 33; Son of Charles and Sarah Holden of 50, Victoria Road, Chichester.

2675. HOLLAND, Henry; B: Cransley, Northamptonshire; E: Hove; Pte. G 753; K: 30.6.15; Ploegsteert Mem. (Bel.); Shot by a sniper.

2676. HOLLINGDALE, Leslie Herbert; B: Brighton; E: Eastbourne; Pte. G 8410; K: 7.7.16; Thiepval Mem., Somme; Age 19; Son of Herbert and Mary E.Hollingdale of 89, Upper Lewes Road, Brighton.

2677. HOLLINGSWORTH, George; B: Islington, London; E: Brighton; Pte. G 7480; K: 19.3.16; Vermelles Brit. Cem., Pas-de-Calais.

2678. HOLLIS, Harry Lee; B: Bracknell, Berkshire; E: Bognor Regis, Sussex; Pte. G 7237; K: 20.11.17; Cambrai Mem., Louverval, Nord.

2679. HOLLMAN, Thomas; B: Brighton; E: Brighton; Pte. GS 146; W: 18.3.16; Bethune Town Cem., Pas-de-Calais.

2680. HOLLOWAY, Percy Leonard; B: Eastbourne; E: Chichester; L/Cpl. L 10256; K: 8.9.15; Houplines Com. Cem. Ext., Nord; Shot by machine gun fire while at a listening post.*

-- HOLMES, George (an alias, see Clifton 2397).

2681. HOOK, Ernest; B: Clerkenwell, London; E: Hastings; Pte. G 18111; K: 9.4.17; Faubourg d'Amiens Cem., Arras, Pas-de-Calais.

2682. HOOK, Frederick Charles; B: Tottenham, London; E: Horsham, Sussex; L/Cpl. G 30; W: 8.11.15; Sailly-Labourse Com. Cem., Pas-de-Calais; Age 24; Son of Frederick and Eliza Alice Hook of 33, Swindon Road, Horsham.*

2683. HOOPER, Sydney Mark; B: Fairlight, Sussex; E: Hove; Pte. G 968; K: 5.3.16; Loos Mem., Pas-de-Calais; Age 19; Son of Mortimer and Ellen Henrietta Hooper of The White Cottage, Falmer, Sussex.

2684. HOPKINS, Alfred George; B: Uckfield, Sussex; E: Eastbourne; Pte. G 2263; K: 5.9.17; Duhallow A.D.S. Cem. (Bel.).

2685. HOPKINS, Percy; B: Brighton; E: Hove; Pte. G 962; K: 25.9.15; Houplines Com. Cem. Ext., Nord.

2686. HOPKINS, William Charles; B: Ringwood, Hampshire; E: Maidstone, Kent; Pte. G 21545; K: 25.11.17; Cambrai Mem., Louverval, Nord.

2687. HORN, John Felix; B: Walgrave, Northamptonshire; E: Kettering, Northamptonshire; Pte. G 11805; W: 11.7.18; Gezaincourt Com. Cem. Ext., Somme; Age 20; Son of William and Elizabeth Ann Horn of Sion Hill, Walgrave; Twice previously wounded.

2688. HORNEY, Robert; B: Ditchling, Sussex; E: Hurstpierpoint, Sussex; L/Sgt. G 504; K: 6.4.18; Pozieres Mem., Somme.

2689. HOSIER, Christopher Arthur; B: St.George's, Sussex; E: Worthing; Pte. SD 1699; K: 20.11.17; Cambrai Mem., Louverval, Nord.

2690. HOUGHTON, Frank; B: Croft, Lancashire; E: London; Pte. G 5386; D: 10.5.17; Gorre Brit. and Indian Cem., Pas-de-Calais; Age 34; Son of Mr. and Mrs.John Houghton of Warrington, Lancashire; Husband of Zillah Houghton of The Hall, Leighton, Shrewsbury.

2691. HOWARD, John; B: Rowhook, Sussex; E: Horsham, Sussex; Pte. G 873; K: 7.7.16; Ovillers Mil. Cem., Somme; Age 29; Son of Edward William and Mary Howard of Picks Cottage, Cowfold, Sussex.

2692. HOWARD, William Alfred; B: Bethnal Green, London; E: Mill Hill, London; Pte. G 18105; W: 8.10.16; Heilly Station Cem., Mericourt-L'Abbé, Somme; Age 21; Son of John and Alice Howard of 9, Bernard Road, South Tottenham, London.*

2693. HOWDEN, Samuel Charles; B: Lambeth, London; E: Lambeth; Pte. G 23011; K: 5.4.18; Bouzincourt Ridge Cem., Somme; Age 19; Son of Samuel Charles and Emily Howden of 44, Grenville Place, Brighton.

2694. HOWELL, Wilfred; B: Hastings; E: Hastings; Pte. G 16308; K: 25.11.17; Cambrai Mem., Louverval, Nord; Age 27; Son of George and Sarah Howell of Silverhill, St.Leonards-on-Sea; Husband of Maggie Howell of 8, Holding, Crowhurst, Sussex.

2695. HOWETT, William; 2nd Lt.; K: 18.9.18; Epehy Wood Farm Cem., Epehy, Somme; Age 20; Son of George and Darah Howett of 43, Macdonald Road, Friern Barnett, London.

2696. HUBBOLD, John Thomas; B: Barrow-in-Furness, Lancashire; E: Liverpool; Pte. G 5896; K: 7.7.16; Thiepval Mem., Somme; Age 25; Son of John Thomas and Rachel Shaw Hubbold of 9c, Walney Road, Barrow-in-Furness.

2697. HUDSON, George Ernest; B: Lynn, Norfolk; E: Norwich; L/Cpl. G 19904; K: 13.8.18; Vis-en-Artois Mem., Haucourt, Pas-de-Calais.

2698. HUGGETT, George; B: Early, Sussex; E: Tunbridge Wells; Pte. SD 5827; K: 5.4.18; Bouzincourt Ridge Cem., Somme.

2699. HUGGETT, Sydney George; 2nd Lt.; K: 18.9.18; Epehy Wood Farm Cem., Somme; Age 31; Son of Sydney James and Emily Emma Huggett of East Grinstead, Sussex; Husband of Bessie Huggett of 120, Tilehurst Road, Reading.

2700. HUGHES, Charlie; B: Firle, Sussex; E: Lewes; Pte. G 20630; W: 28.8.18; Daours Com. Cem. Ext., Somme; Age 20; Son of Charles Edward and Annie Hughes of 37, West Firle, Sussex.

2701. HULKES, Edward; B: Canterbury; E: Chichester; Sgt. L 9591; K: 4.8.16; Courcelette Brit. Cem., Somme; Husband of Hilda May Hulkes of 55, Wyke Road, Trowbridge, Wiltshire.

2702. HULME, Joseph Arthur; B: Leek, Staffordshire; E: Leek; Cpl. G 4581; K: 3.10.16; Thiepval Mem., Somme.

2703. HUMBERSTONE, Edward Owen Bray; B: Boston, Lincolnshire; E: Brighton; Pte. G 16363; K: 3.5.17; Feuchy Chapel Brit. Cem., Pas-de-Calais.*

2704. HUMPHREY, James Thomas; B: Greatham, Sussex; E: Chichester; Pte. G 224; K: 28.3.18; Pozieres Mem., Somme.

2705. HUMPHREYS, George Frederick; B: Lambeth, London; E: Kingston-on-Thames; Pte. G 22447; K: 27.3.18; Pozieres Mem., Somme.

2706. HUMPHREYS, Harry Bob; B: Shoreditch, London; E: London; Pte. L 7765; W: 9.2.17; Faubourg d'Amiens Cem., Arras, Pas-de-Calais; Age 20; Husband of Charlotte Humphreys of 52, Lambert Road, Canning Town, London.*

2707. HUTCHISON, William Sylvester; B: Stepney, London; E: Walthamstow, London; Pte. G 19475; K: 18.9.18; Epehy Wood Farm Cem., Epehy, Somme; Age 20; Son of Peter Joseph and Florence Caroline Hutchison of 81, Gosport Road, Walthamstow.

2708. HUTESON, Thomas Edward; B: Hull; E: Hull; Pte. G 6045; K: 6.7.16; Thiepval Mem., Somme; Age 37; Son of Thomas King Huteson and Fanny Huteson of 3, Beechcrofts Terrace, Bean Street, Hull; Husband of Sarah Ann Huteson of 52, White Street, Hawthorn Avenue, Hull.

2709. HYDE, George; B: Cowfold, Sussex; E: Haywards Heath, Sussex; Pte. G 19592; K: 3.5.17; Arras Mem., Pas-de-Calais.

2710. HYGATE, Harold Philip; B: Slaugham, Sussex; E: Crawley, Sussex; L/Sgt. SD 2105; W: 23.9.18; Doingt Com. Cem., Somme; Age 31; Husband of Annie Hygate of 119, High Street, Crawley.

2711. HYLAND, George; B: Brighton; E: Brighton; Pte. G 19961; K: 25.11.17; Villers Hill Brit. Cem., Nord.

2712. HYLANDS, Albert; B: Firle, Sussex; E: Chichester; Pte. G 19531; K: 29.9.18; Vis-en-Artois Mem., Haucourt, Pas-de-Calais; Age 32; Son of Mrs. Louisa Goldsmith, formerly Hylands, and the late Joseph Hylands; Husband of Emily Hylands of The Arlington Arms, 480, Seaside, Eastbourne.

I

2713. IRESON, Alfred; B: Headless Cross, Worcestershire; E: Coventry; Pte. G 20482; W: 1.12.17; Le Cateau Mil. Cem., Nord.*

2714. ISTED, David Frederick; B: Lewes; E: Lowestoft, Suffolk; L/Sgt. GS 207; K: 9.4.16; Vermelles Brit. Cem., Pas-de-Calais; Killed by trench mortar fire.

2715. IVES, Albert Edward; B: Carnbourne, Dorset; E: Eastbourne; Pte. G 1947; W: 21,8,18; Mont Huon Cem., Seine-Maritime; Age 22; Son of Frederick D. and Mary A.Ives of Holly Bank, Pilford, Dorset.

J

2716. JACKMAN, Hubert George; B: Devonport; E: Fulham, London; Pte. G 19484; D: 17.11.18; Douai Brit. Cem., Nord; Age 19; Son of the Rev. George H.F. and Mrs.Emily S.Jackson of The Manse, Clipston, Leicestershire.

2717. JACKSON, Frederick William; B: Derby; E: Hove; Pte. G 419; K: 7.7.16; London Cem. and Ext., Somme; Age 22; Son of Charles and Harriet Charlotte Jackson of Derby.

2718. JACKSON, Richard James; B: Walthamstow, London; E: Walthamstow; Pte. G 19398; K: 16.10.18; Orchard Dump Cem., Pas-de-Calais.

2719. JACOBS, Charles Edmund; B: Brighton; E: Hove; Pte. G 964; K: 1.8.16; Thiepval Mem., Somme.

2720. JAMES, Ernest Alfred; B: Brighton; E: Brighton; Pte. SD 2451; W: 10.5.18; Valenciennes (St.Roch) Com. Cem., Nord; Age 42; Husband of Ellen James of 23, Frederick Gardens, Brighton.

2721. JAMES, George; B: Sileby, Leicestershire; E: Leicester; Pte. G 18286; K: 27.3.18; Pozieres Mem., Somme.

2722. JARMAN, Thomas; B: Stratford, London; E: Brighton; Sgt. GS 298; K: 7.7.16; Thiepval Mem., Somme.*

2723. JARRETT, William; B: Rye, Sussex; E: Grimsby; Pte. G 15448; K: 27.3.18; Pozieres Mem., Somme.

2724. JARVIS, Charles; B: Hamerton, Huntingdonshire; E: Bedford; Pte. G 18112; W at Home: 21.1.17; Hamerton (All Souls) Churchyard (UK); Age 20; Son of Frederick and Charlotte Jarvis.

2725. JEFFERY, Frank; B: – ; E: Hastings; L/Cpl. G 18114; K: 9.4.17; Faubourg d'Amiens Cem., Arras, Pas-de-Calais.

2726. JEFFERY, Eardley Robert Preston; B: Bath; E: Coventry; Pte. G 20508; K: 30.11.17; Cambrai Mem., Louverval, Nord.*

2727. JENNER, Douglas; B: Brightling, Sussex; E: Hastings; Pte. S 2326; K: 4.10.15; Loos Mem., Pas-de-Calais; Age 19; Son of Harry and Caroline Jane Jenner of Chestnut Lodge, Boreham Street, Sussex.

2728. JENNER, Edward; B: Hastings; E: Hastings; L/Cpl. G 16294; W: 28.3.18; Varrennes Mil. Cem., Somme.

2729. JENNER, George Alfred; B: Portsmouth; E: Hove; Pte. L 10886; W: 18.7.16; Étaples Mil. Cem., Pas-de-Calais; Age 18; Son of Alfred James and Emily Charlotte Jenner of Yew Tree Cottage, Bramber, Sussex.

2730. JENNER, Gordon William Alfred John; B: Plumstead, London; E: Woolwich, London; Pte. G 19486; K: 9.8.18; Beacon Cem., Somme; Age 19; Son of William Alfred and Emily Mary Pierce Jenner of 59, Sladedale Road, Plumstead Common; Killed at Morlancourt, Somme.

2731. JEROME, Reginald Frederick; B: Croydon; E: Chichester; Pte. G 776; K: 7.7.16; Thiepval Mem., Somme; Age 19; Son of Fred and Kate Jerome of 200, Parchmore Road, Thornton Heath, London.

2732. JINKS, Charles; B: Hastings; E: Hastings; Pte. SD 1064; K: 7.10.16; Thiepval Mem., Somme.

2733. JOHNSON, George; B: St.Luke's, Lancashire; E: Bolton, Lancashire; Pte. G 5897; K: 28.12.15; Guards Cem. (Cuinchy) Pas-de-Calais; Age 19; Nephew of Amelia Johnson of 68, John Brown Street, Bolton.

2734. JOHNSON, Walter James; B: Eastergate, Sussex; E: Bognor Regis, Sussex; Pte. G 1054; K: 25.7.15; Houplines Com. Cem. Ext., Nord; Age 18; Son of Henry and Martha Johnson of The Villa, Eastergate.

2735. JOHNSTONE, Edward; B: Kenton, Northumberland; E: Newcastle-on-Tyne; Pte. G 355; K: 5.11.15; Loos Mem., Pas-de-Calais; Age 19; Son of Edward J. and Hannah Mary Johnstone of 52, Portland Road, Shieldfield, Northumberland.

2736. JONES, Alfred John Joseph; B: Waltham Cross, Hertfordshire; E: Cheshunt, Hertfordshire; Pte. G 19953; K: 5.4.18; Pozieres Mem., Somme.

2737. JONES, Henry Cornelius; B: Finsbury, London; E: Holloway, London; Pte. G 19481; K: 24.8.18; Meaulte Mil. Cem., Somme; Age 19; Son of Mr.G.H. and Mrs.M.A.E.Jones of 181, Barnsbury Road, Islington, London.

2738. JOY, Benjamin Henry; B: Brenchley, Kent; E: Tunbridge Wells; Pte. G 103; K: 18.10.15; Loos Mem., Pas-de-Calais; Age 23; Son of Henry Benjamin and Martha Jane Joy of 5, Brecon Terrace, Church Road, Rotherfield, Sussex.

2739. JUKES, Louis; B: Gillingham, Dorset; E: Brighton; Pte. G 17703; W: 3.5.17; Duisans Brit. Cem., Pas-de-Calais; Age 42; Son of John and Elizabeth Jukes of Railway Terrace, Gillingham, Dorset.*

2740. JUPP, George William; B: Brighton; E: Redhill, Surrey; Pte. G 8769; K: 18.9.18; Epehy Wood Farm Cem., Epehy, Somme; Age 32; Husband of Edith Agnes Jupp of 29, Mill Road, Three Bridges, Sussex.

K

2741. KAY, Andrew; B: Pennington, Wigtown; E: Newton Stewart, Galloway; Pte. G 23013; K: 8.8.18; Beacon Cem., Somme.

2742. KAYE, William Fairlie; B: Glasgow; E: Hackney, London; Pte. TF 266466; K: 20.11.17; Cambrai Mem., Louverval, Nord; Son of John Kaye of 14, King's Road, Finsbury Park, London.*

2743. KEATING, Joseph; B: Canning Town, London; E: London; Pte. SD 3925; K: 27.3.18; Aveluy Wood Cem., Somme; Son of Mrs.Alice Christine Steele of 90, Hollybush Street, Plaistow, London.

2744. KEEGAN, James; B: – ; E: Chichester; Sgt. L 10187; D.C.M.; K: 4.3.16; Loos Mem., Pas-de-Calais; Age 20; Son of Henry and Harriett A. Keegan of 47, Bates Road, Brighton; Served under the alias 'King'.*

2745. KEHLBACHER, George Walter; B: Brighton; E: Chichester; Pte. G 20210; K: 25.7.17; Arras Mem., Pas-de-Calais; Age 23; Son of Otto August and Emily Minnie Kehlbacher of 17, Upper North Street, Brighton.*

2746. KEIGWIN, Sydney; B: Llandudno; E: Leeds; L/Cpl. TF 266067; W: 17.8.18; St.Sever Cem. Ext., Rouen, Seine-Maritime; Age 28; Son of George and Alice Keigwin of The Rock, Llandudno; Husband of Florence M.Keigwin of 384, Great Clowes Street, Higher Broughton, Manchester.

2747. KELLY, Albert Alfred; B: Camberwell, London; E: Southwark, London; Pte. L 10725; K: 27.3.18; Pozieres Mem., Somme.

2748. KEMPTON, Jabez; B: Hammersmith, London; E: London; Pte. G 21456; K: 17.8.17; Monchy Brit. Cem., Pas-de-Calais.

2749. KENNABY, James Charles; B: Notting Hill, London; E: West London; Pte. G 18376; K: 13.8.18; Vis-en-Artois Mem., Haucourt, Pas-de-Calais; Age 19; Son of Frederick W. and Clara Kennaby of 21,

Lancaster Road, Westbourne Park, London; Killed near Morlancourt, Somme.

2750. KENNARD, Robert; B: Sompting, Sussex; E: Worthing; Pte. G 1505; W: 21.10.16; Arras Mem., Pas-de-Calais.

2751. KENNEDY, Herbert; B: Manchester; E: Ardwick; Pte. TF 260233; K: 18.9.18; Epehy Wood Farm Cem., Epehy, Somme: Age 36; Son of M.E. and Philomena Kennedy of Manchester.

2752. KENSETT, George; B: Clayton, Sussex; E: Haywards Heath, Sussex; Pte. G 208; W: 8.10.15; Noeux-les-Mines Com. Cem., Pas-de-Calais; Age 30; Son of William and Mary Kensett of 23, St.Mary's Terrace, Burgess Hill, Sussex; Husband of Ellen Edith Thompson, formerly, Kensett, of 5, Pitt Street, Southern Cross, Portslade, Sussex.

2753. KENT, George Alfred John; B: Portslade, Sussex; E: Hove; Pte. L 10931; K: 5.8.16; Thiepval Mem., Somme.

2754. KENT, Herbert; B: Hastings; E: Hastings; Pte. G 6389; K: 25.11.17; Cambrai Mem., Louverval, Nord.

2755. KENT, Joseph Charles; B: Tillington, Norfolk; E: Chichester; Sgt. G 637; K: 7.7.16; Thiepval Mem., Somme; Age 24; Son of Mr. and Mrs.J.W.Kent of 405, Station Road, Petworth, Sussex.

2756. KERSWILL, Alfred Leslie; B: Plymouth; E: Plymouth; Pte. G 17096; K: 9.8.18; Beacon Cem., Somme; Killed near Morlancourt, Somme.

2757. KEWELL, Harry; B: Bosham, Sussex; E: Chichester; Pte. G 4350; K: 7.7.16; Thiepval Mem., Somme; Age 30; Grandson of Mrs.Hannah Kewell of 19, Gifford Road, Bosham.

2758. KEWELL, Walter; B: West Wittering, Sussex; E: Chichester; Cpl. G 1752; K: 4.2.18; Croix-du-Bac Brit. Cem., Steenwerke, Nord.

2759. KING, Charles James; B: Hackney, London; E: Whitehall, London; Pte. G 19493; K: 9.8.18; Beacon Cem., Somme; Age 19; Son of Charles Alfred and Alice King of 9, Aden Grove, Stoke Newington, London; Killed near Morlancourt, Somme.

2760. KING, George; B: East Grinstead, Sussex; E: Bexhill-on-Sea; Pte. G 571; K: 13.6.15; Houplines Com. Cem. Ext., Nord.

-- KING, James (an alias, see KEEGAN 2744).

2761. KINGSHOTT, Frederick; B: South Stoke, Sussex; E: Chichester; Pte. G 4742; K: 24.3.16; Vermelles Brit. Cem., Pas-de-Calais; Son of Mrs.Annie Kingshott of Raygate Cottage, Cootham, Sussex.*

2762. KINGSLAND, Albert; B: Hadlow Down, Sussex; E: Sevenoaks, Kent; Pte. G 18117; W: 3.5.17; Duisans Brit. Cem., Pas-de-Calais; Age 36; Son of David and Frances Kingsland of Hadlow Down; Husband of Nellie Kingsland of 96, Stephen's Road, Tunbridge Wells.

2763. KIRBY, Alfred Harold; B: Brighton; E: Brighton; Pte. G 17705; K: 9.4.17; Gourock Trench Cem., Tilloy-les-Mofflaines, Pas-de-calais; Age 26; Son of John Thomas and Fanny Kirby of 74a, Hanover Street, Brighton.

2764. KIRK, George Stanley; B: Lewes; E: Hove; Pte. G 8674; K: 25.11.17; Cambrai Mem., Louverval, Nord.

2765. KNIGHT, Archibald; B: St.Peter's, Sussex; E: Haywards Heath, Sussex; Pte. G 1340; K: 6.3.16; Loos Mem., Pas-de-Calais.

2766. KNIGHT, Thomas; B: St.Martin's, Sussex; E: Brighton; Pte. G 1540; K:5.4.18; Bouzincourt Ridge Cem., Somme.

2767. KNIGHT, William Harold; B: Shepshed, Leicestershire; E: Coalville, Leicestershire; Pte. G 18262; K: 8.8.18; Beacon Cem., Somme; Killed near Morlancourt, Somme.

2768. KNOWLES, Arthur Herbert; B: Plumstead, London; E: Woolwich, London; Pte. G 4026; W at Home: 4.9.16; Woolwich (Plumstead) Cem., London (UK); Age 29; Son of Herbert William and Elizabeth L.Knowles of Plumstead.

2769. KNOWLES, Charles William; B: Ramsgate, Kent; E: Newhaven, Sussex; Pte. G 4193; W: 15.10.16; Heilly Station Cem., Mericourt-L'Abbé, Somme; Age 37; Son of Mrs.E.A.Gardner of Ramsgate.*

2770. KNOWLES, Herbert; B: Kensington, London; E: Kensington; Pte. G 14809; W: 8.4.18; Gezaincourt Com. Cem. Ext., Somme; Age 28; Son of Charles and Emily Knowles.

2771. KNOX, John Lawrence; 2nd Lt.; K: 20.11.17; Cambrai Mem., Louverval, Nord.

2772. KOHLER, Roland; B: Brighton; E: Brighton; Pte. G 17706; K: 5.10.16; Thiepval Mem., Somme.

L

2773. LAKE, John Henry; B: Outwell, Cambridgeshire; E: Norwich; Pte. G 11951; D: 18.3.18; Cologne Southern Cem. (G); Died while a prisoner of war.

2774. LAKE, Percy Albert; B: Brighton; E: Chichester; Pte. G 695; K: 30.11.17; Cambrai Mem., Louverval, Nord; Age 31; Son of Eli and Clara Lake of 103, Wordsworth Street, Hove.

2775. LAMBERT, Harry; B: Brighton; E: Chichester; Sgt. GS 1761; K: 27.3.18; Pozieres Mem., Somme.*

2776. LANAWAY, Francis Charlton; 2nd Lt.; K: 21.8.18; Achiet-le-Grand Com. Cem. Ext., Pas-de-Calais; Age 36; Son of Hugh and Mrs.E.M.Lanaway; Husband of Frances Grace Lanaway of "Bouveret", Borstal Road, Rochester, Kent; Killed while attached to the 7th Battalion, Royal Fusiliers.

2777. LATHAM, William; B: Brighton; E: Brighton; Pte. L 7641; K: 7.7.16; Thiepval Mem., Somme.

2778. LAVENDER, Harry Richard; 2nd Lt.; K: 26.8.18; Peronne Com. Cem. Ext., Ste. Radegonde, Somme; Killed by machine gun fire.

2779. LAWES, Ernest Alexander; B: Eastbourne; E: Eastbourne; Pte. G 9710; W: 29.3.18; Doullens Com. Cem. Ext., Somme; Age 21; Son of Mr. and Mrs.H.Lawes of Eastbourne.

2780. LAWES, James Percy; B: Edgware, London; E: Edgware; Cpl. G 20254; K: 5.4.18; Bouzincourt Ridge Cem., Somme; Age 22; Son of Mrs.Lear Lawes of 34, Chandos Crescent, Edgware.

2781. LAWRENCE, Thomas Edward; 2nd Lt.; W: 24.9.18; Doingt Com. Cem., Somme; Age 19; Son of Henry Lakin Lawrence and Emma Lawrence; Died at No.20 or No. 55 Casualty Clearing Station.

2782. LAWSON, Frank; B: Thakeham, Sussex; E: Worthing; Pte. G 816; K: 4.8.16; Thiepval Mem., Somme.

2783. LAWSON, Thomas Arthur; B: West Ham, London; E: Woolwich, London; Pte. G 19496; K: 13.8.18; Bray Vale Brit. Cem., Somme.

2784. LEA, Henry Thomas; B: All Saints, Sussex; E: Chichester; Cpl. G 6184; W: 23.7.15; Houplines Com. Cem. Ext., Nord; Age 34; Son of Edward Gillam Lea and Elizabeth Lea of 31, High Street, Seaford, Sussex.

2785. LE CHEVALIER, Albert John; B: – ; E: Manchester; L/Sgt/ TF 260241; W: 26.9.18; Doingt Com. Cem., Somme; Age 36; Son of Mr.M. and Mrs.D.Le Chevalier of Lavender Villa, Grouville, Jersey, Channel Islands.*

2786. LEDGER, Robert John; 2nd Lt.; W: 11.3.17; Avesne-le-Comte Com. Cem. Ext., Pas-de-Calais; Age 26; Son of Frederic and Julia Ann Ledger of Epsom, Surrey; Mortally wounded by a bomb at practise on 9.3.17.

2787. LE DOUX VEITCH, Dallas Gerard; 2nd Lt.; K: 4.8.16; Thiepval Mem., Somme.

2788. LEE, Percy; B: Bury, Sussex; E: Worthing; Pte. GS 55; K: 10.2.17; Avesne-le-Comte Com. Cem. Ext., Pas-de-Calais; Age 35; Husband of Mrs.A.K.Lee of The Forge, Charing Heath, Kent.

2789. LEE, Thomas George; B: London; E: Bedford; Pte. G 18371; K: 24.8.18; Vis-en-Artois Mem., Haucourt, Pas-de-Calais; Age 18; Son of Thomas Henry and Grace Elizabeth Lee of 31, Chesnut Road, Tottenham, London.

2790. LEVETT, Jesse; B: Arlington, Sussex; E: Bexhill-on-Sea; Pte. G 6424; K: 9.4.18; Pozieres Mem., Somme; Age 20; Son of Harry and Mary Levett of Cane Heath, Arlington.

2791. LEWCOCK, Horace; B: Hampton Hill, Middlesex; E: Twickenham, Middlesex; Pte. G 18120; K: 5.10.16; Thiepval Mem., Somme.

2792. LEWIS, Arthur John; B: Craddock, Staffordshire; E: Willesden, London; Pte. G 14014; K: 3.7.17; Monchy Brit. Cem., Pas-de-Calais; Age 40; Son of William and Hannah Lewis of Willesden; Husband of Emily Florence Lewis of 78, Hampden Street, Paddington, London.*

2793. LEWINGTON, Ernest Victor; B: – ; E: Horsham, Sussex; Pte. G 16730; K: 18.9.18; Epehy Wood Farm Cem., Epehy, Somme.

2794. LEWIS, James; B: Hammesrmith, London; E: Hounslow, London; Pte. G 4023; K: 7.7.16; Thiepval Mem., Somme.

-- LEWIS, William George (an alias – see Coombes 2423).

2795. LIGHT, William John; B: Tangmere, Sussex; E: Bognor Regis, Sussex; L/Cpl G 998; K: 7.7.16; Thiepval Mem., Somme; Age 19; Son of Edward and Fanny Agnes Light of Pack Lane, Oakley, Hampshire.

2796. LILLYWHITE, Edwin; B: Storrington, Sussex; E: Petworth, Sussex; L/Cpl. G 4578; K: 7.7.16; Thiepval Mem., Somme; Age 36; Son of Lewis Lillywhite; Husband of Sarah Grace Tolman, formerly Lillywhite, of Leggatt Farm, Blackdown, Surrey.

2797. LINDEN, Walter; B: Brighton; E: Hove; Cpl. G 128; K: 1.8.16; Thiepval Mem., Somme; Age 30; Son of James Frederick and Ann Linden of 2, St.John's Cottages, Leylands Road, Burgess Hill, Sussex.

2798. LINFIELD, William Denn; B: Stroud, Gloucestershire; E: Worthing; Pte. SD 1164; K: 5.4.18; Pozieres Mem., Somme.

2799. LITTLE, John Robert; B: Arlecdon, Cumberland; E: Chichester; Pte. G 591; K: 28.12.15; Guards Cem. (Cuinchy) Pas-de-Calais; Age 33; Son of David and Hannah Little of Arlecdon.

2800. LITTLECHILD, George Edward; B: Bognor Regis, Sussex; E: Chichester; Pte. G 17962; K: 30.11.17; Cambrai Mem., Louverval, Nord; Age 30; Son of Mrs.Eliza Littlechild of 3, Victoria Cottages, South Bersted, Sussex.

2801. LLOYD, Gerald Burton; B: Hampton Hill, Middlesex; E: Hitchin, Hertfordshire; Pte. G 18722; K: 18.9.18; Epehy Wood Farm Cem., Epehy, Somme; Age 19; Son of Frederick David Lloyd of "Linden", Western Road, Guildford.

2802. LLOYD, William; B: Canarvon; E: Chichester; Pte. L 10454; K: 9.4.17; Arras Mem., Pas-de-Calais.

2803. LONG, Clarence Sidney; B: Brent Eleigh, Suffolk; E: Warley, Essex; Pte. G 18122; K: 25.11.17; Cambrai Mem., Louverval, Nord; Age 21; Son of William Frederick and Maria Elizabeth Long of 7, Black Cottages, Broad Street Green, Heybridge, Essex; Late of Grapnell Farm Cottage, Wood Lane, Heybridge.

2804. LONGBOTTOM, John; B: Wakefield; E: Lowestoft; L/Cpl. L 11256; K: 24.8.18; Meaulte Mil. Cem., Somme; Age 26; Son of Thomas and Ellen Longbottom of 8, Stafford Terrace, Wakefield.

2805. LONGHURST, William John; B: Brighton; E: Brighton; Pte. G 4962; W: 10.7.16; Heilly Station Cem., Mericourt-L'Abbé, Somme; Age 20; Son of Mrs.Martha J.Longhurst of 26, Frederick Gardens, Brighton; Died at Casualty Clearing Station.

2806. LUCAS, Albert James; B: Freezywater, Middlesex; E: Mill Hill, London; Pte. G 22423; K: 18.9.18; Epehy Wood Farm Cem., Epehy, Somme; Age 21; Son of James Lucas of 53a, St.Loy's Road, Tottenham, London.

2807. LUCAS, Frederick George; B: Brighton; E: Chichester; Pte. L 10141; K: 3.5.17; Arras Mem., Pas-de-Calais.

2808. LUCK, Herbert Edward; B: Hastings; E: Hastings; Pte. G 18124; K: 31.3.17; Arras Mem., Pas-de-Calais; Age 33; Son of Geroge and Mrs.J.E.Luck of The Post Office, Baldslow, St.Leonards-on-Sea; Killed by shell fire while on digging duties at Arras.

2809. LUXFORD, Arthur Ernest; B: Horsham, Sussex; E: Epsom, Surrey; Cpl. G 20229; W: 6.5.17; Étaples Mil. Cem., Pas-de-Calais; Age 35; Brother of F.A.Luxford of 14, Park Street, Horsham.

2810. LUXFORD, Percy; B: Kirdford, Sussex; E: Guildford; Pte. G 5031; K: 7.7.16; Thiepval Mem., Somme.

2811. LYDDALL, Herbert Percy Sydney; B: Chichester; E: Chichester; L/Cpl. L 8635; K: 25.11.17; Cambrai Mem., Louverval, Nord; Age 28; Son of George William and Alice Lyddall of 91, Sugden Road, Clapham Common, London; Husband of Jeanie Lyddall of 59, Lavinia Street, Belfast.

M

2812. MACE, Robert Sidney; B: Hove; E: Brighton; Pte. G 17709; K: 5.10.16; Thiepval Mem., Somme; Age 19; Son of Wallace J. and Fanny Mace of 75, Springfield Road, Brighton.

2813. MACKEY, Arthur; B: Fulham, London; E: London; Pte. G 5258; K: 12.4.17; Arras Mem., Pas-de-Calais.

2814. MACKEY, John; B: Brighton; E: Brighton; Pte. G 4738; K: 5.10.16; Thiepval Mem., Somme.

2815. MADGE, William; B: Oxted, Surrey; E: Aldershot; Sgt. G 5241; K: 7.7.16; Thiepval Mem., Somme; Age 29; Husband of Bessie Kenney, formerly Madge, of Rose Bank, Gloucester County, New Brunswick, Canada.*

2816. MAHER, Frank; B: Thurles, County Tipperary, Ireland; E: London; Pte. G 18128; K: 7.10.16; Thiepval Mem., Somme.

2817. MAIN, Thomas George; B: Hambleton, Hampshire; E: Horsham, Sussex; Pte. K: 7.7.16; Thiepval Mem., Somme.

2818. MALCHER, James Denis; B: Hertford; E: London; Pte. G 8209; K: 1.8.16; Thiepval Mem., Somme; Age 19; Son of Denis and Ethel Malcher of 39, Edward Road, Addiscombe, Surrey.

2819. MAN, Reginald Herbert Richard; B: Eastbourne; E: Brighton; Pte. G 1771; K: 5.10.16; Thiepval Mem., Somme; Age 21; Son of George and Alice Man of Bedeford House, Tideswell Road, Eastbourne; Husband of Jennie Man of 77, Firle Road, Eastbourne.

2820. MANKTELOW, George William; B: Tunbridge Wells; E: Eastbourne; Pte. G 5484; K: 4.8.16; Thiepval Mem., Somme.

2821. . MANLEY, Hamilton Douglas; 2nd Lt.; K: 27.3.18; Pozieres Mem., Somme.

2822. MANSBRIDGE, William; B: Cuckfield, Sussex; E: Haywards Heath, Sussex; Pte. G 1578; K: 20.11.17; Cambrai Mem., Louverval, Nord.

2823. MARCH, Charles William; B: Brighton; E: Portslade, Sussex; Pte. G 17712; D at Home: 7.4.18; Portslade Cem., Sussex (UK).

2824. MARCHANT, Frederick; B: Brunthouse, Sussex; E: Eastbourne; Pte. G 8976; K: 5.4.18; Bouzincourt Ridge Cem., Somme; Age 29; Son of Mr. and Mrs.H.Marchant of Lullington, Sussex.

2825. MARCHANT, James Henry; B: Brighton; E: Brighton; Pte. G 16668; K: 9.4.17; Arras Mem., Pas-de-Calais; Husband of Mary A.Marchant of 38, Montreal Road, Brighton.

2826. MARCHANT, Philip Henry; B: Woodchurch, Kent; E: Ashford, Kent; Pte. G 1812; K: 9.4.18; Senlis Com. Cem. Ext., Somme.

2827. MARDLE, Ernest; B: Hatfield, Hertfordshire; E: Hertford; Pte. G 15596; K: 4.2.18; Croix-du-Bac Brit. Cem., Steenwerke, Nord; Age 29; Son of Henry and Elizabeth Mardle of Cromer Hyde, Hatfield.*

2828. MARKS, Harry; B: Nuneham Courtenay, Oxfordshire; E: Horsham, Sussex; Pte. G 456; K: 7.7.16; Thiepval Mem., Somme.

2829. MARSH, Robert Samuel; B: Malvern, Worcestershire; E: Nottingham; Pte. G 278; K: 1.10.15; Dud Corner Cem., Pas-de-Calais; Age 22; Son of William and Mary Marsh of Hill View Cottage, Malvern Wells.

2830. MARSH, Tom; B: – ; E: Hastings; Pte. G 18130; K: 5.4.18; Bouzincourt Ridge Cem., Somme.

2831. MARSHALL, Frank; B: – ; E: – ; Pte. SR 822; D at Home: 17.2.17; Folkestone Old Cem., Kent (UK); Age 32; Son of Stephen and Julia M.Marshall of 110, Guildhall Street, Folkestone.*

2832. MARTIN, Amos; B: Tunbridge Wells; E: Tunbridge Wells; L/Cpl. G 8371; W at Home: 1.11.18; Tunbridge Wells Cem., Kent (UK); Age 22; Son of Richard and Violet Bertha Martin of The Bungalow, Galley Hill, Bexhill-on-Sea.

2833. MARTIN, Harold Sales; B: St.Matthew's, Surrey; E: Croydon; Pte. L 9982; K: 4.3.16; Loos Mem., Pas-de-Calais; Age 21; Son of George Sales Martin of 3, Bridge Terrace, Cross Road, East Croydon.

2834. MARTIN, John; B: Yalding, Kent; E: Maidstone; Pte. G 12530; W: 10.4.17; Duisans Brit. Cem., Pas-de-Calais; Age 34; Son of Richard and Caroline Martin; Husband of Annie Martin of Gidds Pond, Bexley, Kent.

2835. MARTIN, Joseph; B: Coleorton, Leicestershire; E: Portsmouth; L/Cpl. G 605; K: 3.3.16; Loos Mem., Pas-de-Calais.

2836. MASCALL, Victor Edward; B: Balham, London; E: Wandsworth, London; Pte. G 18379; W: 13.9.18; Dernancourt Com. Cem. Ext., Somme; Age 20; Son of Arthur and Sarah Mascall of 156, Mantilla Road, Upper Tooting, London; Gassed.

2837. MASKELL, Frederick Charles; B: Brighton; E: Brighton; Pte. G 4208; K: 26.8.18; Peronne Road Com. Cem., Maricourt, Somme.

2838. MASKELL, Harry; B: Mayfield, Sussex; E: Eastbourne; Pte. G 607; K: 1.8.16; Thiepval Mem., Somme.

2839. MASLIN, George; B: Linch, Sussex; E: Midhurst, Sussex; L/Cpl. G 551; W: 26.11.17; Cambrai Mem., Louverval, Nord; Age 33; Son of Emma Jane Maslin of Ivy Cottages, Terwick Common, Rogate, Sussex.

2840. MATTHEWS, Frederick George Alexander; B: Brighton; E: Chichester; Pte. G 8591; K: 5.10.16; Thiepval Mem., Somme.

2841. MATTHEWS, J.L.; Lt.; K: 29.12.17; Aire Com. Cem., Pas-de-Calais; Killed while attached to Divisional Signals Royal Engineers.

2842. MAUGHAN, Henry; B: Croxdale, Count Durham; E: South Shields; L/Cpl. G 266; M.M.; K: 25.11.17; Cambrai Mem., Louverval, Nord.

2843. MAXWELL, George Ernest; B: Brighton; E: Brighton; Pte. G 9204; W: 6.4.18; Varennes Mil. Cem., Somme; Age 32; Son of Mr. and Mrs.G.Maxwell of Brighton.

2844. MAY, Harry; B: – ; E: Worthing; Pte. G 17871; K: 11.8.18; Vis-en-Artois Mem., Haucourt, Pas-de-Calais; Age 22; Son of John and Martha S.May of Hurst Cottage, Dial Post, Sussex.

2845. MAY, Richard Trelawny; Capt.; K: 7.7.16; Thiepval Mem., Somme; Age 26; Son of Charles Gibbons May and Katherine Frances May of 49, Lincolns Inns Fields and Pine Lodge, Weighbridge, Surrey; Killed attacking Ovillers, Somme.

2846. MAYNARD, Samuel Charles; B: Watton, Hertfordshire; E: Mansion House, London; Pte. G 13439; K: 25.11.17; Cambrai Mem., Louverval, Nord.

2847. Mc CALL, Lawrence; B: Fareham, Hampshire; E: Chichester; Pte. G 8387; K: 7.7.16; Theipval Mem., Somme; Age 37; Son of Lawrence and Ellen E.Mc Caul of 147, Orchard Street, Chichester; Served in the South Africa Campaign.

2848. MEASOR, Frederick; B: Brighton; E: Brighton; Pte. L 10648; W: 12.4.16; Bethune Town Cem., Pas-de-Calais.*

2849. MEEKINGS, Horace Jacob; B: Islington, London; E: Whitehall, London; Pte. G 23611; K: 18.9.18; Epehy Wood Farm Cem., Epehy, Somme.

2850. MEETEN, George; B: Wiston, Sussex; E: Hove; Pte. G 718; K: 17.10.15; Loos Mem., Pas-de-Calais; Son of Alice Meeten of Wiston; Brother, Harry, also killed (see 2851).

2851. MEETEN, Harry; B: Wiston, Sussex; E: Hove; L/Cpl. G 775; W: 10.7.16; Warloy-Baillon Com. Cem. Ext., Somme; Age 32; Son of Alice Meeton of Wiston; Brother, George, also killed (see 2850).

2852. MEIN, William James; B: Lewisham, London; E: Lewisham; Pte. G 11425; K: 25.7.17; Arras Mem., Pas-de-Calais.

2853. MENNIE, James; 2nd Lt.; K: 18.9.18; Epehy Wood Farm Cem., Somme; Age 19; Son of James Gilchrist Mennie and Caroline Overy Mennie of 63, Mayfield Road, Moseley, Birmingham.

2854. MERCER, Harry; B: Ashurst, Kent; E: Eastbourne; Pte. G 16833; K: 21.9.18; Epehy Wood Farm Cem., Somme.

2855. MERRITT, George Thomas; B: Felpham, Sussex; E: Chichester; Pte. G 426; W: 3.7.15; Bailleul Com. Cem. Ext., Nord; Died at Casualty Clearing Station.

2856. MERRITT, Samuel George; B: Washington, Sussex; E: Dover; L/Cpl. L 10239; K: 28.8.18; Becourt Mil. Cem., Somme.

2857. MIDDLETON, Walter; B: Walthamstow, London; E: Hertford; Pte. G 20252; K: 20.11.17; Cambrai Mem., Louverval, Nord; Age 33; Son of Mrs.Stotter of 99, Geere Road, West Ham Park, London; Husband of Grace Middleton of 3, Jesmond Cottage,Hertford Heath, Hertfordshire.

2858. MIDMORE, Albert Ernest; B: Eastbourne; E: Eastbourne; Pte. G 4172; K: 7.7.16; Thiepval Mem., Somme.*

2859. MILES, Alfred Edward; B: Dane Hill, Sussex; E: Hove; Pte. G 8433; K: 5.10.16; Thiepval Mem., Somme; Age 19; Son of Caleb and Ann Miles of Laurel Cottage, Chelwood Gate, Sussex; Enlisted with brother, Arthur John, who was also killed, who also has no known grave and who is also commemorated on the Thiepval Memorial. (see 2860).

2860. MILES, Arthur John; B: Dane Hill, Sussex; E: Hove; Pte. G 8434; K: 4.8.16; Thiepval Mem., Somme; Age 32; Son of Caleb and Ann Miles of Laurel Cottage, Chelwood Gate, Sussex; Enlisted with brother, Alfred Edward, who was also killed, who also has no known grave and who is also commemorated on the Thiepval Memorial (see 2859).*

2861. MILLARD, Frederick William; B: Guildford; E: London; Pte. G 5076; K: 7.7.16; Serre Road Cem. No.2, Somme; Age 22; Son of Frederick William and Louisa Millard of 3, Clinton Terrace, Sutton, Surrey.*

2862. MILLER, Alfred; B: Blackfriars, London; E: Southwark, London; Pte. G 5108; K: 13.3.16; Loos Mem., Pas-de-Calais.

2863. MILLER, Arthur John; B: Pevensey, Sussex; E: Hastings; Pte. SD 1199; K: 13.8.18; Vis-en-Artois Mem., Haucourt, Pas-de-Calais; Age 28; Son of Stephen Lawrence and Bertha Miller of 3, Castle Terrace, Pevensey, Sussex; Enlisted in the 11th Battalion, wounded twice at the 'Boar's Head', Artois on 30.6.16 and returned to hospital in England; After convalescence and rehabilitation at Summerdown Camp, Eastbourne, returned to France to join the 7th Battalion; Killed near Morlancourt, probably by short-fall friendly fire; Brother, Wilfred, also killed (see 4742); Brother Stephen died at home after discharge (see 4740); Brothers Frederick George and Robert Randolph, both of The Royal Sussex Regiment, survived.

2864. MILLS, Ernest Richard; B: Easebourne, Sussex; E: Midhurst, Sussex; Pte. G 16670; W: 25.7.17; Monchy Brit. Cem., Pas-de-Calais; Age 40; Son of Arthur and Sarah Mills of Easebourne; Husband of Mrs.E.J.Mills of 22, Lutner Road, Easebourne.*

2865. MILLS, Frank; B: Washington, U.S.A.; E: Brighton; Pte. G 16770; K: 9.4.17; Arras Mem., Pas-de-Calais.

2866. MILLS, George; B: Bognor Regis, Sussex; E: Chichester; Pte. G 819; W: 31.12.15; Bethune Town Cem., Pas-de-Calais; Age 19; Son of Jesse and Janet Mills of 45, Chapel Street, Bognor Regis; Died at No.33 Casualty Clearing Station, Bethune.

2867. MILLS, John Robert; B: Walton-le-Dale, Lancashire; E: Bury, Lancashire; Pte. G 5933; W: 4.10.15; Bethune Town Cem., Pas-de-Calais; Son of Mrs.Mary Mills of 2506, Caithness Place, Denver,

Colorado, U.S.A.; Died at No.33 Casualty Clearing Station, Bethune.

2868. MILSTED, William Walter; B: Tooting, Surrey; E: Kingston-on-Thames; L/Cpl. G 20213; K: 3.5.17; Arras Mem., Pas-de-Calais; Age 28; Husband of Mary Milsted of 17, Grange Road, Thornton Heath, London.

2869. MINALL, Edward George; B: Hove; E: Hove; Sgt. L 10459; K: 27.3.18; Pozieres Mem., Somme; Son of Elizabeth Kate Sharp, formerly Minall, and Walter Sharp, stepfather, of 48, Ingram Crescent, Hove.

2870. MINNIS, James; B: Sheffield; E: Sheffield; Pte. G 22968; K: 3.7.18; Pozieres Mem., Somme.

2871. MISSELBROOK, Stephen; B: Pagham, Sussex; E: Bognor Regis, Sussex; Pte. G 7240; K: 18.9.18; Epehy Wood Farm Cem., Epehy, Somme.

2872. MITCHELL, Frank; B: Nottingham; E: Loughborough, Leicestershire; Pte. G 15092; K: 18.9.18; Epehy Wood Farm Cem., Epehy, Somme.

2873. MITCHELL, Frederick; B: Manchester; E: Hove; Sgt. G 153; K: 9.4.17; Feuchy Chapel Brit. Cem., Pas-de-Calais.

2874. MITCHELL, Frederick George; B: Worthing; E: Chichester; Pte. G 29; K: 19.10.15; Sailly-Labourse Com. Cem., Pas-de-Calais; Son of Mr.G.F.Mitchell of 14, London Street, Worthing.

2875. MITCHELL, Henry John; B: –; E: –; Pte. G 16053; K: 5.4.18; Pozieres Mem., Somme; Age 21; Son of James Thomas and Alice Emma Mitchell of 2, Vine's Passage, Bourne Walk, Hastings.

2876. MITCHELL, James Frederick; B: Hastings; E: Hastings; Pte. G 16053; K: 5.4.18; – – -.

2877. MOCKFORD, Nathaniel; B: Brighton; E: Brighton; Pte.TF 260046; K: 31.3.17; Faubourg d'Amiens Cem., Arras, Pas-de-Calais; Age 24; Son of Mr. and Mrs. N. Mockford of 7, Dane Hill Grove, Margate, Kent; Killed by shell fire while on digging duties at Arras.*

2878. MONTESOLE, Eric Alfred; 2nd Lt.; K: 4.3.16; Loos Mem., Pas-de-Calais; Age 28; Son of Max and Ellen Montesole of 270, Wightman Road, Hornsey, London; Husband of Liena Constance Montesole of 8, Shipstone Road, Norwich; Lewis Gun Officer; Brother, Herbert Sarif Roy, also killed (see 2879).

2879. MONTESOLE, Herbert Sarif Roy; Lt.; K: 17.5.15; Guards Cem., Cuinchy, Pas-de-Calais; Age 22; Son of Max and Emma Montesole of Hornsey, London; Killed at Festubert while attached to 2nd Battalion Yorkshire Regiment; Brother, Eric Alfred, also killed (see 2878).

2880. MOORE, Arthur; B: Kentish Town, London; E: Whitehall, London; Pte. G 23602; W: 4.9.18; Dernancourt Com. Cem. Ext., Somme.*

2881. MOORE, Sidney; B: Itchingfield, Sussex; E: Horsham, Sussex; Pte. G 11432; K: 5.5.17; Arras Mem., Pas-de-Calais; Age 26; Son of Charles and Jane Moore of The Ark Cottage, Barnes Green, Sussex; Husband of Mrs.E.M.Moore.*

2882. MOORE, Wilfred Oswald; B: Banbury,

Oxfordshire; E: Banbury; Pte. G 6063; K: 29.7.17; Monchy Brit. Cem., Pas-de-Calais; Age 22; Son of Mr. and Mrs.W.B.Moore of 37a, Queen Street, Banbury.*

2883. MORGAN, Aubrey Lloyd; B: Cowbridge, Glamorgan; E: Cowbridge; Pte. G 1028; K: 21.10.15; Loos Mem., Pas-de-Calais; Age 21; Son of Thomas Henry and Emily Anne Morgan of "Cusop", Llanblethian, Glamorgan.

2884. MORGAN, Alfred Thomas; B: Bath; E: Hounslow, London; Pte. G 13903; K: 20.11.17; Cambrai Mem., Louverval, Nord; Age 32; Son of Alfred and Jane Morgan; Husband of Lucy Morgan of Press Forward Lodge, Mickleham, Surrey.

2885. MORLEY, William Leonard; B: Hove; E: Hove; Sgt. G 693; K: 5.9.18; Peronne Com. Cem. Ext., Ste. Radegonde, Somme; Age 25; Son of Martin S. and Louisa Morley of 60, Western Road, Hove.

2886. MORRIS, Andrew George Warder; B: Newport, Isle of Wight; E: Fernhurst; Pte. G 17718; D: 15.3.17; St.Hilaire Cem., Pas-de-Calais; Age 21; Son of James Andrew and A.A.Morris of Chillerton Farm, Newport; Died of pneumonia.

2887. MORRIS, Edward Frederick; B: Chichester; E: Chichester; Pte. G 181; K: 4.8.16; Thiepval Mem., Somme.

2888. MORRIS, Owen Corby; B: St.Paul's, Northampton-shire; E: Northampton; Pte. G 17388; M.M.; K: 26.8.18; Peronne Road Cem., Maricourt, Somme.

2889. MOUNTSTEPHENS, Arthur; B: Hornsey, London; E: Mill Hill, London; Pte. G 18135; W: 14.8.18; Pernois Brit. Cem., Somme; Age 23; Son of Mrs. Mountstephens of 20, Yeatman Road, Highgate; Died at Casualty Clearing Station, Pernois.

2890. MUIR, Charles; B: Bengeo, Hertfordshire; E: London; Pte. G 4783; K: 8.4.16; Vermelles Brit. Cem., Pas-de-Calais; Age 44; Son of Mrs. Leatherdale of Beamish Road, Lower Edmonton, London; Husband of Mrs.Muir of 79, Besley Street, Streatham, London.

2891. MUIRHEAD, William Charles Read; B: Dulwich, London; E: London; Pte. S 1738; K: 4.8.16; Thiepval Mem., Somme.

2892. MUNNS, William; B: Chatteris, Cambridgeshire; E: March, Cambridgeshire; Pte. G 14981; W: 27.9.18; Peronne Com. Cem. Ext., Ste.Radegonde, Somme; Age 24; Son of William and Eliza Munns of 3, Bridge Street, Chatteris.

2893. MURRAY, Arthur; 2nd Lt.; K: 7.8.18; Villers-Bretonneux Mil. Cem., Somme; Age 25; Foster son of Mrs.Helen Uphoff of 27, Richmond Road, Bayswater, London.*

2894. MURRAY, John George; B: Bishopwearmouth, County Durham, E: Sunderland; Pte. G 268; K: 7.7.16; Ovillers Mil. Cem., Somme; Son of Mrs. Murray of 23, Rockingham Street, Leeds.

2895. MURRELL, William Edward; B: Warburton, Sussex; E: Chichester; Pte. L 8206; K: 3.5.17; Arras Mem., Pas-de-Calais.

N

2896. NAGLE, Gilbert; Capt. and Adjutant: K: 5.7.17; Faubourg d'Amiens Cem., Arras, Pas-de-Calais; Killed by a shell falling in Shrapnel Trench near Battalion H.Q.; Buried at Arras 6.30pm. 8.7.17. (See also Sansom 3045).

2897. NAISBITT, John; B: Hebburn Colliery, County Durham; E: Jarrow; Pte. G 317; W: 5.10.15; Chocques Mil. Cem., Pas-de-Calais; Died at No.1 Casualty Clearing Station, Chocques.

2898. NAPPER, Maurice Edward; B: Rudgwick, Sussex; E: Hurstpierpoint, Sussex; Pte. G 1060; K: 17.3.16; Vermelles Brit. Cem., Pas-de-Calais; Age 29; Son of Mrs.James Napper of Tismans Common, Sussex; Husband of Edith Annie Napper of West Park Cottages, Newchapel, Surrey.*

2899. NEW, Ernest Reginald; B: Croydon; E: Kingston-on-Thames; Pte. G 23265; W: 30.3.18; Delville Wood Cem., Somme.

2900. NEW, John Edward; B: Felpham, Sussex; E: Bognor Regis, Sussex; L/Cpl. G 617; K: 7.7.16; Thiepval Mem., Somme.

2901. NEWINGTON, Percy; B: Wadhurst, Sussex; E: Hastings; Pte. G 12170; K: 23.2.17; Faubourg d'Amiens Cem., Arras, Pas-de-Calais; Age 28; Son of William Horace and Jane Newington of Sparrows Green, Sussex; Husband of Eva Newington.

2902. NEWMAN, William Joshua; B: Brighton; E: Brighton; Pte. G 1308; K: 25.9.15; Ploegsteert Mem. (Bel.).

2903. NEWTON, Frank; B: – ; E: Oldham, Lancashire; Cpl. TF 260199; K: 18.9.18; Epehy Wood Farm Cem., Epehy, Somme.

2904. NEWTON, William; B: Brighton; E: Chichester; Pte. L 10316; K: 22.7.15; Houplines Com. Cem. Ext., Nord.

2905. NICHOLLS, Charles Herbert; B: Worthing; E: Worthing; Pte. G 6516; K: 3.5.17; Arras Mem., Pas-de-Calais.

2906. NICHOLS, Frank Victor; B: Kensington, London; E: Bexhill-on-Sea; Pte. G 124; M.M.; K: 4.8.16; Thiepval Mem., Somme.

2907. NICHOLSON, Samuel; B: Brighton; E: Brighton; Pte. GS 911; W: 13.7.16; Wimereux Com. Cem., Pas-de-Calais; Age 27; Husband fo Kate E.Nicholson of 15a, Grove Street, Brighton; Died in Military Hospital.

2908. NICKLESS, Thomas Alfred; B: Brighton; E: Brighton; Pte. G 8333; K: 8.8.18; Beacon Cem., Somme; Age 26; Son of Mrs.Alice Wray of 4, Albion Cottages, Brighton; Killed near Morlancourt, Somme.*

2909. NIEDERALLER, Albert; B: Hastings; E: Hastings; Pte. G 163; W: 27.9.15; Cite Bonjean Mil. Cem., Nord.*

2910. NIGHTINGALE, Leonard; B: Brighton; E: Brighton; Pte. G 6858; K: 9.4.17; Ste. Catherine Brit. Cem., Pas-de-Calais.

2911. NOBLE, James; B: Hastings; E: Hastings; Pte. G 18141; K: 3.5.17; Arras Mem., Pas-de-Calais.

2912. NORMAN, John Cecil; B: Brighton; E: Brighton; Cpl. G 539; K: 5.10.16; Thiepval Mem., Somme.

2913. NORRIS, William Edward; B: Boughton Monchelsea, Kent; E: Maidstone; Pte. G 12738; K: 9.4.17; Arras Mem., Pas-de-Calais; Age 34; Son of William Norris; Husband of Alice Norris of Prospect Place, Boughton Monchelsea.

2914. NORTH, George; B: Nutborne, Sussex; E: Horsham, Sussex; Pte. G 918; K: 24.3.16; Vermelles Brit. Cem., Pas-de-Calais.

2915. NORTON, Alfred; B: Chiswick, London; E: Hammersmith, London; Pte. G 4039; K: 28.2.17; Faubourg d'Amiens Cem., Arras, Pas-de-Calais.

2916. NURDEN, Charles; B: Chipping Norton; E: Tunbridge Wells; Pte. G 12031; K: 9.4.17; Arras Mem., Pas-de-Calais; Age 39; Son of Stephen and Eliza Nurden; Husband of Maud M.Nurden of 6, Park View, Pembury, Kent.

O

2917. OAKLEY, William Edwin; B: Birmingham, E: Brighton; Pte. G 4828; K: 1.8.16; Thiepval Mem., Somme.

2918. OLLEY, John George Gregory; B: New Buckingham, Norfolk; E: Norwich; Pte. G 24088; W: 6.9.18; Dernancourt Com. Cem. Ext., Somme; Age 20; Son of John and Hannah Olley of Buckenham Road, Banham, Norfolk; Gassed.*

2919. ONSLOW, Albert George William; B: Brighton; E: Brighton; Pte. G 21013; K: 9.4.18; Senlis Com. Cem. Ext., Somme.*

2920. ORAM, Leonard; B: Brighton; E: Hove; Pte. G 4159; K: 7.7.16; Thiepval Mem., Somme.

2921. OSBORN, Harry Cecil; B: Watford, Hertfordshire; E: Warley, Essex; Pte.G 18143; K: 9.4.18; Senlis Com. Cem. Ext., Somme; Age 23; Son of Charles Edward and Elizabeth Helen Osborn of 344, Westborough Road, Westcliff-on-Sea, Essex.

2922. OSBORNE, Harry; B: Robertsbridge, Sussex; E: Hastings; Pte. GS 113; K: 25.9.15; Houplines Com. Cem. Ext., Nord.

2923. OSBORNE, Walter Jesse; B: Hawkhurst, Kent; E: Hastings; Sgt. G 415; M.M.; W: 21.11.17; Tincourt New Brit. Cem., Somme; Age 26; Son of Walter Jesse and Emma Osborne of 5, Howe's Cottages, The Moor, Hawkhurst.*

2924. OSBORNE, William James; B: Robertsbridge, Sussex; E: Hastings; Pte. G 4167; K: 13.10.16; Thiepval Mem., Somme; Age 23; Son of Mr. and Mrs.Spencer Osborne of Stone Cottage, Salehurst Fruit Farm, Salehurst, Sussex.

2925. OWEN, Thomas; B: Bedford; E: Horsham, Sussex; Pte. G 49; D at Home: 30.5.15; Bedford Cem. (UK).

P

2926. PACK, George Robert; B: East Harting, Hampshire; E: Harting; Pte. G 834; K: 7.7.16; Thiepval Mem., Somme; Age 23; Son of George and Emma Pack of East Harting.

2927. PACKHAM, Reuben; B: Burgess Hill, Sussex; E: Hitchin, Hertfordshire; Pte. G 4674; K: 8.8.18; Beacon Cem., Somme; Killed near Morlancourt, Somme.

2928. PADFIELD, Herbert George; B: Dorset; E: Chichester; Pte. G 481; K: 4.8.16; Thiepval Mem., Somme.

2929. PAGE, Albert; B: Lewes; E: Lewes; Pte. G 20119; K: 1.10.17; Monchy Brit. Cem., Pas-de-Calais; Age 19; Son of Frank and Alice Page of 14, Friars Walk, Lewes.

2930. PAGE-MITCHELL, Sidney William; B: Jarvis Brook, Sussex; E: Tunbridge Wells; Pte. TF 203407; K: 26.8.18; Vis-en-Artois Mem., Haucourt, Pas-de-Calais; Age 24; Son of William James and Clara Jane Page-Mitchell of Western Road, Jarvis Brook.

2931. PAICE, Arthur Edward; B: Brighton; E: Brighton; Sgt. L 10418; K: 25.11.17; Cambrai Mem., Louverval, Nord; Age 24; Son of William and Mary Ann Paice; Husband of Pouie Paice of 5, Bute Street, Brighton.*

2932. PAICE, Edgar William; B: Portfield, Sussex; E: Chichester; L/Cpl. G 984; K: 5.10.16; Thiepval Mem., Somme; Age 24; Son of Thomas and Emily Paice of 26, Grove Road, Wick, Sussex.*

2933. PAIN, George Montague; B: Eastbourne; E: Brighton; Pte. G 17724; W: 10.4.17; Duisans Brit. Cem., Pas-de-Calais; Age 20; Son of Charles and Henrietta Pain of 118, Ashford Road, Eastbourne.

2934. PALMER, Horace John; 2nd Lt.; K: 8.8.18; Beacon Cem., Somme; Age 25; Son of William and Mary Palmer of Foxcombe, Devon; Killed near Morlancourt, Somme.

2935. PALMER, Maurice William; B: Shepherd's Bush, London; E: Littlehampton, Sussex; L/Cpl. G 1266; K: 7.7.16; Ovillers Mil. Cem., Somme.

2936. PALMER, Percy Alexander; B: Peckham, London; E: Tooting, London; L/Cpl. G 17517; K: 3.5.17; Arras Mem., Pas-de-Calais.*

2937. PALMER, Sydney Abel; B: Kensington, London; E: Worthing; Pte. SD 2397; W at Home: 2.10.18; Brookwood

2938. PANNELL, Frederick Lawrence; B: Portsmouth; E: Hove; L/Sgt. L 17664; K: 1.10.17; Monchy Brit. Cem., Pas-de-Calais; Age 29; Husband of Mrs.E.J.Pannell of 16, Molesworth Street, Hove,

2939. PAPWORTH, Frederick; B: Brampton, Hampshire; E: Bedford; Pte. SD 5736; K: 8.8.18; Villers-Bretonneux Mil. Cem., Somme.

2940. PAPWORTH, Leonard; B: St.Peter's, Cambridgeshire; E: Whittlesea; Pte. G 14994; K: 3.7.18; Pozieres Mem., Somme.

2941. PARK, Colin Archibald Mungo; B: Arundle, Hampshire; E: Maidstone, Kent; L/Cpl. G 21544; K: 24.10.18; Valenciennes (St.Roch) Com. Cem., Nord; Age 31; Son of the Rev.Mungo Park; Husband of Marion Alexander Park of 23, Precot Street, New Brighton, Cheshire.

2942. PARKINSON, William James Frederick; B: Chelsea, London; E: Piccadilly, London; Pte. G 23623; K: 20.5.18; Mailly Wood Cem., Somme; Age 19; Son of William and Alice Parkinson of 11, Cumberland Street, South Belgravia, London.

2943. PARTINGTON, Edward Horace; B: Bethnal Green, London; E: Cockspur Street, London; Pte. G 4460; W: 3.8.17; Duisans Brit. Cem., Pas-de-Calais.*

2944. PATTEN, Maurice; B: Thorney, Somerset; E: Chichester; Pte. G 483; W: 13.1.16; Bethune Town Cem., Pas-de-Calais; Age 24; Son of William Walter and Sarah Patten of Eartham, Sussex.

2945. PAYNE, Frank Henry; B: Hadlow, Kent; E: Tonbridge; Pte. G 13189; D: 12.12.16; Mont Huon Mil. Cem., Seine-Maritime; Husband of Kate Payne of 3, Castle Terrace, Hadlow.*

2946. PEARSON, Herbert; B: Rampside, Lancashire; E: Barrow-in-Furness; Pte. G 5901; W: 25.9.15; Cite Bonjean Mil. Cem., Nord; Age 21; Son of Thomas and Agnes Alma Pearson of Waver Farm, Rampside.

2947. PEART, Thomas; B: Peckham, London; E: Camberwell, London; Pte. G 11114; W: 15.4.17; Duisans Brit. Cem., Pas-de-Calais.*

2948. PECKHAM, Charles William; B: Barcombe, Sussex; E: Newmarket, Cambridgeshire; Pte. G 8556; W at Home: 11.7.18; Torquay Cem. and Ext., Devonshire (UK); Age 25; Son of Joseph and Florence Peckham of High Street, Barcombe; Husband of Alice M.Peckham of 100, Hartop Road, St.Mary Church, Devonshire.*

2949. PEEN, John Robert; B: Ulcombe, Kent; E: Maidstone; Pte. G 21023; K: 20.11.17; Cambrai Mem., Louverval, Nord; Age 28; Son of William John Peen of East Wood, Ulcombe.

2950. PEGRAM, Edgar George; B: Enfield, London; E: Tottenham, London; Pte. G 18739; K: 5.9.18; Peronne Com. Cem. Ext., Ste.Radegonde, Somme; Age 19; Son of Joel and Emma Louisa Pegram of 34, Down Road, Enfield.

2951. PELLING, Ernest Alfred; B: Horsham, Sussex; E: Horsham; Pte. G 922; K: 25.7.17; Arras Mem., Pas-de-Calais.

2952. PENFOLD, Henry Leonard James; B: Reigate, Surrey; E: Chichester; Pte. G 15; K: 9.11.15; Sailly-Labourse Com. Cem., Pas-de-Calais; Son of Mrs.R.E.Woods of 30, Adelaide Road, Chichester.

2953. PENNELL, Charles; B: Swanscombe, Kent; E: Gravesend, Kent; Pte. G 13088; W: 7.5.17; Faubourg d'Amiens Cem., Arras, Pas-de-Calais; Age 40; Son of George Pennell of Swanscombe; Husband of Alice Maud Pennell of "Haywood", St.James's Avenue, Gravesend.

2954. PENRITH, James; B: Toxteth Park, Lancashire; E: Liverpool; Pte. G 5823; K: 13.4.17; Feuchy Chapel Brit. Cem., Pas-de-Calais; Age 36.

2955. PEPPER, Leonard Lionel; B: Peasenhall, Suffolk; E: Battersea, London; Pte. G 5141; K: 7.7.16; Thiepval Mem., Somme.

2956. PERRY, Ernest; B: Ramsgate, Kent; E: Bexhill-on-Sea; Pte. G 144; W: 9.10.15; Bethune Town Cem., Pas-de-Calais; Son of Mr.W. and Mrs.F.Perry of

14, Suffolk Street, Bexhill-on-Sea; Died at No.33 Casualty Clearing Station, Bethune.

2957. PETERS, Henry William; B: – ; E: Rye, Sussex; Pte. G 18224; K: 18.9.18; Epehy Wood Farm Cem., Epehy, Somme; Age 21; Son of Mr.C.W. and Mrs.E.Peters of 22, Bridge Street, Folkestone, Kent.

2958. PHILCOX, Thomas William; B: Hastings; E: Hastings; Cpl. S 1232; K: 8.8.18; Vis-en-Artois Mem., Haucourt, Pas-de-Calais; Killed near Morlancourt, Somme.

2959. PHILLIPS, Arthur; B: Hereford; E: Haringay, London; Pte. L 10993; K: 31.7.16; Thiepval Mem., Somme; Age 17; Son of Aban William and Annie E.Phillips of 18, Scudamore Street, Hereford.

2960. PHILLIPS, Richard Charles; B: Newcastle-on-Tyne; E: Lowestoft, Suffolk; Pte. G 11271; K: 9.9.16; London Cem. and Ext., Somme; Age 22; Son of Margaret H.C.Taylor of 11, Norfolk Street, Lowestoft.

2961. PHILLIPS, Stephen; B: Hastings; E: Hastings; Pte. G 43; K: 2.10.15; Lapugnoy Mil. Cem., Pas-de-Calais.

2962. PICKERING, Edward; B: – ; E: – ; Pte. G 357; D at Home: 19.11.17; Sunderland (Ryhope Road) Cem., County Durham; Labour Corps.

2963. PINK, William J.; B: Kingston-on-Thames; E: Chichester; Pte. G 17888; K: 18.9.18; Epehy Wood Farm Cem., Epehy, Somme; Age 22; Son of Robert and Ellen Pink of 49, Stanhope Road, Littlehampton, Sussex.*

2964. PIRIE, Ernest; B: Brighton; E: Brighton; Pte. G 4931; K: 7.7.16; Ovillers Mil. Cem., Somme; Age 33; Husband of Florence Marguerite Pirie of 49, Exeter Street, Brighton.

2965. PLAYFORD, Harry; B: Hastings; E: Hastings; Pte. GS 128; K: 7.7.16; Thiepval Mem., Somme.

2966. PLUMMER, Frank; B: Marylebone, London; E: Cockspur Street, London; Pte. G 5463; W: 27.5.18; St.Sever Cem. Ext., Rouen, Seine-Maritime.

2967. PLUMMER, John Robert; B: Hickling, Norfolk; E: Wroxham, Norfolk; Pte. G 14283; K: 18.9.18; Epehy Wood Farm Cem., Epehy, Somme; Age 31; Son of John William and Elizabeth Plummer of Brumstead, Norfolk; Husband of Louisa Plummer of The Common, Happisburgh, Norfolk.

2968. POCKNEY, Ernest James; B: Hove; E: Hove; Pte. G 250; W: 7.10.15; Wimereux Com. Cem., Pas-de-Calais; Age 18; Son of James H. and Sarah Ann Pockney of Hove; Died in Military Hospital, Wimereux.

2969. POCOCK, Amos; B: – ; E: Hastings; Pte. G 18153; K: 9.4.17; Faubourg d'Amiens Cem., Arras, Pas-de-Calais; Age 30; Husband of Elizabeth Duale of 20, Earl Street, Hastings.

2970. POOLE, Henry George; B: Mile End, London; E: Finsbury Barracks, London; Pte. G 11280; K: 5.8.16; Thiepval Mem., Somme; Age 37; Son of Sarah Ann Poole of 2a, South Grove, Bow, London.

2971. POPE, Edward George; B: Hanworth, Middlesex; E: Hove; L/Cpl. G 121; K: 7.7.16; Thiepval Mem., Somme.

2972. PORTEOUS, Dennis Reid; B: Bolton, Lancashire; E: Bolton; Pte. G 22923; M.M.; K: 28.3.18; Pozieres Mem., Somme.

2973. POTTER, Frederick; B: Chapel-en-le-Frith, Derbyshire; E: Rusholme, Manchester; Pte. G 18417; W: 7.9.18; St.Sever Cem. Ext., Rouen, Seine-Maritime; Age 28; Son of Mr. and Mrs. William Potter of 2, Marlboro' Street, Higher Openshaw, Manchester; Husband of Edith Potter of 9, Lincoln Street, Rusholme.*

2974. POWELL, Arthur Henry; B: Wandsworth, London; E: Hastings; Pte. G 17969; W: 3.5.18; Étaples Mil. Cem., Pas-de-Calais; Age 25; Son of James F. and Lavinia Powell of 4, Balvernie Grove, Wandsworth; Died at Military Hospital, Étaples.*

2975. PRATT, Joseph Walter; B: Canvey Isalnd, Essex; E: Law Courts, London; Pte. G 19865; W: 8.8.18; Villers-Bretonneux Mil. Cem., Somme; Age 34; Son of Joseph and Fanny Pratt of Canvey Island; Husband of Susie Winifred Pratt of 13a, Midmore Road, Balham, London.

2976. PRATT, William; B: Merston, Sussex; E: Arundel, Sussex; Pte. G 4178; W: 13.3.16; Bethune Town Cem., Pas-de-Calais; Age 26; Son of William and Mary Pratt of Tillington Cottage, Yapton, Sussex; Died at No.33 Casualty Clearing Station, Bethune.

2977. PRATT, William George; B: East Meon, Hampshire; E: Chichester; Pte. G 4908; K: 3.5.17; Arras Mem., Pas-de-Calais; Age 34; Husband of Harriett Pratt of East Ashling, Sussex.

2978. PREATER, George Montague; B: Harmondsworth, Middlesex; E: Uxbridge, Middlesex; Pte. G 6046; K: 4.8.16; Thiepval Mem., Somme.

2979. PREECE, Stanley; B: Cardiff; E: Cardiff; Pte. G 22967; K: 5.4.18; Pozieres Mem., Somme; Age 20; Son of Thomas Preece of 3, Oxford Street, Cardiff.

2980. PRESTON, George William; B: Merton, Surrey; E: Hove; Cpl. G 684; M.M.; K: 20.11.17; Cambrai Mem., Louverval, Nord; Age 26; Son of Edith Collins, formerly Preston, of 1, Drove Cottages, Patcham, Brighton, and the late Thomas Preston.

2981. PREVETT, Robert; B: Ardingly, Sussex; E: Brighton; Sgt. G 541; D.C.M.; W: 6.10.16; Dartmoor Cem., Somme; Age 26; Son of Robert and Emma Prevett of Horncombe, Ardingly.

2982. PREVOST, Arthur George; B: Hackney, London; E: Stratford, London; Pte. G 23635; K: 18.9.18; Vis-en-Artois Mem., Haucourt, Pas-de-Calais; Age 19; Son of Mrs.Matilda Miller of 50a, Chatham Place, Hackney.

2983. PRIOR, William James; B: St.Pancras, London; E: Brighton; Pte. L 10447; K: 7.7.16; Thiepval Mem., Somme.

2984. PULLEN, Gerald Cliff; B: North Chapel, Sussex; E: Chichester; L/Cpl. G 580; K: 7.7.16; Thiepval Mem., Somme; Age 22; Son of George and Madeline Pullen of Post Office, North Chapel; Husband of Edith F.Pullen of "Clifton", Western Road, Liss, Hampshire.*

2985. PULLEN, William Robert; B: Worthing; E: Rye, Sussex; Pte. G 18151; K: 1.10.16; Thiepval Mem., Somme; Age 26; Son of William Robert and Agnes Matilda Pullen of The Cottage, Manor Road, Worthing.

2986. PUMPHREY, George; B: Brighton; E: Brighton; Pte. G 17622; K: 3.5.17; Arras Mem., Pas-de-Calais.

2987. PURCHASE, Charles; B: Chichester; E: Chichester; Pte. G 13496; D: 26.4.18; Conde-sur-L'Escaut Com. Cem., Nord.

2988. PUTMAN, Wilfred; B: Eastbourne; E: – ; Pte. G 20149; D: 25.12.17; Étaples Mil. Cem., Pas-de-Calais; Age 19; Son of Mr.H. and Mrs.E.Putman of 36, Terminus Place, Eastbourne; Labour Corps; Died at Military Hospital, Étaples.

Q

2989. QUAIFE, George Henry; B: Bexhill-on-Sea; E: Hove; L/Cpl. G 712; K: 7.10.16; Thiepval Mem., Somme.

2990. QUELCH, Arthur Leslie; B: Brighton; E: Brighton; Pte. G 7763; K: 7.7.16; Thiepval Mem., Somme; Age 23; Son of Alfred Christopher and Emma Quelch of 44, Wigmore Road, Broadwater, Sussex.

2991. QUESTED, Alec William; B: Willesden, London; E: Brighton; Pte. G 20031; K: 24.9.18; Epehy Wood Farm Cem., Epehy, Somme.

2992. QUINN, John; B: Newcastle-on-Tyne; E: Newcastle-on-Tyne; L/Cpl. G 20490; K: 5.4.18; Bouzincourt Com. Cem. Ext., Somme.

R

2993. RALPH, Albert Edward; B: Lewes; E: Brighton; Pte. G 8341; K: 7.7.16; Thiepval Mem., Somme; Age 27; Husband of Mrs.N.Bashford, formerly Ralph, of 32, Apollo Terrace, Brighton.

2994. RAND, James; B: Barking, London; E: Stratford, London; Pte. G 23636; K: 8.8.18; Dive Copse Brit. Cem., Somme; Age 19; Son of Mrs.J.Rand of 21, Howard's Road, Barking.

2995. RANDALL, Leonard Victor; B: Shepherd's Bush, London; E: Whitehall, London; Pte. G 22921; K: 27.3.18; Pozieres Mem., Somme; Age 20; Son of James and Isabella Maria Randall of 11, Avenue Road, Hammersmith, London.

2996. RANSOM, Edward Alfred; B: Newhaven, Sussex; E: Lewes; Pte. L 6855; K: 3.3.16; – .

2997. RANSOM, Frederick James; B: Bexhill-on-Sea; E: Bexhill-on-Sea; Sgt. G 574; D.C.M., M.M., Croix de Guerre; W: 7.10.18; St.Sever Cem. Ext., Rouen, Seine-Maritime; Age 27; Son of Frederick and Caroline Ransom of 9, North Road, Bexhill-on-Sea.*

2998. RATCLIFFE, Albert; B: Worcester; E: Kidderminster, Worcestershire; Pte. G 5905; K: 3.5.17; Arras Mem., Pas-de-Calais; Age 26; Brother of Mrs.A.L.Jackson of 74, Slaney Street, Birmingham.

2999. RAVEN, William; B: Brompton Hill, Northampton-shire; E: Brighton; Pte. G 82; K: 7.7.16; Ovillers Mil. Cem., Somme.

3000. RAWLING, Leonard John; B: Herne Hill, London; E: London; Pte. G 20553; K: 12.4.17; Arras Mem., Pas-de-Calais; Age 29; Son of Charles Hewes Rawling and Emma J.Rawling of 38, Lancaster Road, West Norwood, London.

3001. RAY, Joseph; B: – ; E: Canterbury; L/Cpl. G 17547; K: 6.4.18; Bouzincourt Ridge Cem., Somme.

3002. RAYMENT, John William; B: Wood Green, London; E: Whitehall, London; Pte. G 24033; W: 18.9.18; La Chapelette Brit. and Indian Cem., Somme; Age 18; Son of Ambrose and Ethel Rose Elizabeth Rayment of 84, Rathcoole Gardens, Hornsey, London; Died at No.53 Casualty Clearing Station (known as North Midland Casualty Clearing Station) La Chapelette, Somme.

3003. REED, Richard; B: Alfriston, Sussex; E: Seaford, Sussex; Pte. G 9132; W: 23.9.18; St. Sever Cem. Ext., Rouen, Seine-Maritime; Age 33; Son of Charles and Ellen Reed of 3, West Street, Alfriston.

3004. REED, Thomas John; B: – ; E: Hastings; Pte. G 16679; K: 9.4.17; Faubourg d'Amiens Cem., Arras, Pas-de-Calais; Age 34; Son of Thomas John and Jane Reed of Hastings; Husband of Bessie Maud Reed of 15, School Road, Hastings.

3005. REED, William George; B: Brighton; E: Southwark, London; L/Cpl. G 4960; K: 4.8.16; Thiepval Mem., Somme.

3006. REES, Alexander Armstrong; Capt.; W: 4.2.17; Wanquentin Com. Cem. Ext., Pas-de-Calais; Age 32; Son of Robert L. and Gertrude A.Rees of Liverpool; Attached from Royal Army Medical Corps.; Died at No.41 Casualty Clearing Station.

3007. REEVE, Frederick Joseph; B: Great Bursted, Essex; E: Warley, Essex; Pte. G 18752; K: 24.8.18; Meaulte Mil. Cem., Somme; Age 19; Son of James and Clara M.Reeve of High Street, Billericay, Essex.

3008. REICKIE, William Herbert; B: St.Pancras, London; E: Finsbury Barracks,, London; Pte. G 23642; K: 9.8.18; Vis-en-Artois Mem., Haucourt, Pas-de-Calais; Killed near Morlancourt, Somme.

3009. RELF, Henry; B: Hawkhurst, Kent; E: Eastbourne; Pte. GS 695; K: 25.7.17; Arras Mem., Pas-de-Calais; Age 41; Husband of Florence R.H.Relf of 8, Fairlight Road, Eastbourne.

3010. RELFE, Percival Edward; B: Hastings; E: Hastings; Pte. G 2179; K: 21.9.18; Epehy Wood Farm Cem., Epehy, Somme; Age 22; Son of Mr. and Mrs. George Relfe of School Hill, Sedlescombe, Sussex.

3011. RICH, Frederick Arthur; B: Cambridge; E: Bury St.Edmunds, Suffolk; Pte. G 24034; K: 18.9.18; Epehy Wood Farm Cem., Epehy, Somme; Age 18; Son of Frederick Robert and Charlotte Jane Rich of 84, Castle Street, Cambridge.

3012. RICHARDSON, Charles; B: Hornsey, London; E: Harringay, London; Pte. G 5732; K: 7.7.16; Thiepval Mem., Somme.

3013. RICHARDSON, Harold Thomas Burchett; B:

Portfield, Sussex; E: Chichester; L/Cpl. L 8832; K: 7.7.16; Thiepval Mem., Somme.

3014. RICHARDSON, William Henry; B: Bognor Regis, Sussex; E: Bognor Regis; L/Cpl. G 8138; K: 3.5.17; Arras Mem., Pas-de-Calais.

3015. RIDLEY, James Frank; B: East Chiltington, Sussex; E: Lewes; Pte. G 18154; K: 9.4.17; Arras Mem., Pas-de-Calais; Husband of Margaret Ethel Yeat, formerly Richardson, of Hapstead, Farm, Ardingly, Sussex.

3016. ROBBINS, William; B: Chichester; E: Chichester; C.Q.M.S. L 5857; K: 25.11.17; Cambrai Mem., Louverval, Nord; Age 32; Husband of Margaret Robbins of 29, Sandymount Street, Belfast, Northern Ireland; Long Service and Good Conduct Medal.

3017. ROBERTS, Roy Alfred; B: Normandy, Surrey; E: Grove Park, London; L/Cpl. G 23020; K: 26.8.18; Dantzig Alley Brit. Cem., Somme; Age 19; Son of Ernest Henry and Mary Roberts of Pirbright Road, Normandy.

3018. ROBERTS, William Alfred; B: Slindon, Sussex; E: Chichester; Pte. G 431; K: 18.12.15; Loos Mem., Pas-de-Calais; Age 22; Son of Charles and Emily Kate Roberts of 58, Slindon Common, Sussex.

3019. ROBIN, Ernest; B: Walworth, London; E: Camberwell, London; Pte. G 11113; W: 8.10.16; Heilly Station Cem., Mericourt-L'-Abbe, Somme; Died at Casulty Clearing Station, Mericourt-L'-Abbe.

3020. ROBINSON, Alfred; B: Hove; E: Hove; Pte. G 749; K: 7.7.16; Thiepval Mem., Somme.

3021. RODGERS, William; B: Grimley, Worcestershire; E: Arundel, Sussex; Pte. G 4195; K: 4.3.16; Loos Mem., Pas-de-Calais; Age 21; Son of Mr.W.Rodgers of 4, Disraeli Terrace, Ladywood, Birmingham.

3022. ROGERS, Edward Thomas; B: Brighton; E: Chichester; L/Cpl. L 10244; K: 4.3.16; Loos Mem., Pas-de-Calais.

3023. ROGERS, James Vincent; B: Croydon; E: London; Pte. G 4942; W: 9.7.16; Warloy-Baillon Com. Cem. Ext., Somme; Age 20; Son of James Henry and Julia Rogers; Probably died at the Operating Centre, Warloy-Baillon.

3024. ROGERS, John; B: Chatham, Kent; E: Bromley, Kent; Pte. G 12972; K: 20.11.17; Cambrai Mem., Louverval, Nord; Age 37; Husband of Lucy Ellen Rogers of New House, Wellington Road, St.Mary Cray, Kent.

3025. ROUSELL, William Stephen; Lt.; K: 8.8.18; Beacon Cem., Somme.*

3026. ROUTLEDGE, Ernest Gordon; B: Stretham, Cambridgeshire; E: Newmarket, Cambridgeshire; Pte. G 14267; K: 30.11.17; Cambrai Mem., Louverval, Nord; Age 19; Son of Alfred R. and Emily J.Routledge of The Manse, Stretham.

3027. ROWE, George; B: Portsea, Hampshire; E: Southampton; Pte. G 7603; K: 7.7.16; Serre Road Cem. No.2, Somme.

3028. ROXBEE, Charles Frederick; B: Brighton; E:

Brighton; Pte. L 10075; W: 6.10.16; Dartmoor Cem., Somme; Son of Mr.L.S.Roxbee of 3, Devonshire Street, Brighton.

3029. RUSSELL, Alfred; B: Marylebone, London; E: St.Pancras, London; Pte. G 25788; K: 25.10.18; Vis-en-Artois Mem., Haucourt, Pas-de-Calais; Age 19; Son of Mr. and Mrs.I.Rosenbaum 2, Maple Street, Tottenham Court Road, London.

3030. RUSSELL, Frederick John; B: Portslade, Sussex; E: Hove; Sgt. G 190; K: 3.10.16; Thiepval Mem., Somme.

3031. RUSSELL, Frederick William; B: Hastings; E: Hastings; Pte. S 2253; K: 27.3.18; Pozieres Mem., Somme; Age 28; Son of William and Eleen Russell; Husband of Gertrude Alice Atkinson, formerly Russell, of Denzil, Saskatchewan, Canada.

3032. RUSSELL, William Arthur; B: Whissonsett, Norfolk; E: East Dereham, Norfolk; Pte. G 11893; K: 5.7.17; Monchy Brit. Cem., Pas-de-Calais; Age 20; Son of Mrs.E.N.Russell of Mileham, Norfolk.*

3033. RUTLAND, George William; B: Titchwell, Norfolk; E: Elswick, Rutland; Pte. G 11292; K: 27.3.18; Pozieres Mem., Somme; Age 30; Son of William and Charlotte Rutland of Titchwell.

S

3034. SADLER, Alfred James; B: North Chapel, Sussex; E: Chichester; Pte. G 1146; K: 3.3.16; Loos Mem., Pas-de-Calais; Age 20; Son of James and Edith Sadler of Valentine's Hill, North Chapel.

3035. SADLER, Stanley Victor; B: Mortlake, Surrey; E: Hastings; L/Cpl. SD 2335; W: 28.8.18; St.Sever Cem. Ext., Rouen, Seine-Maritime; Age 22; Son of Mrs.A.Sadler of Gloucester House, Richmond Hill, Surrey.

3036. SALES, Frederick Charles; B: Tunbridge Wells; E: St.Swithin's Lane; Pte. G 13057; K: 8.5.17; Arras Mem., Pas-de-Calais; Age 40; Son of Samuel and Ruth Sales of 89, Brunswick Street, Reading; Husband of Edith Mary Sales of 63, Arol Road, Beckenham, Kent.

3037. SALVAGE, Henry; B: St.Margaret's, Sussex; E: Brighton; Pte. G 1908; D: 14.7.18; St.Sever Cem. Ext., Rouen, Seine-Maritime; Age 29; Son of Henry James and Grace Salvage of 52, Balfour Road, Brighton.*

3038. SALVAGE, John Albert; B: – ; E: Lewes; Pte. G 18164; W: 9.4.17; Duisans Brit. Cem., Pas-de-Calais; Age 36; Son of George and Mary Salvage of Newick, Sussex; Husband of Mary Ann Salvage of Bullfield Cottage, Newick.

3039. SAMBROOK, George Frederick; B: Isleworth, London; E: Wood Green, London; Pte. G 20051; W: 29.7.17; Duisans Brit. Cem., Pas-de-Calais; Age 39; Husband of Rhoda Sambrook of 2, Warlborough Road, Wood Green.

3040. SAMMONDS, John Edward; B: Fulham, London; E: Whitehall, London; L/Cpl. G 11386; K: 5.4.18; Bouzincourt Ridge Cem., Somme.

3041. SANDERS, Albert George; B: Heston, Middlesex;

E: Hounslow, London; Pte. TF 290767; K: 22.8.18; Vis-en-Artois Mem., Haucourt, Pas-de-Calais.

3042. SANDS, John; B: Eastbourne; E: Eastbourne; Pte. SD 1615; W: 26.11.17; Tincourt New Brit. Cem., Somme; Husband of Mrs.Irene M.Novis, formerly Sands, of 1, Artillery Cottages, Seaside, Eastbourne.*

3043. SANDS, Walter; B: Buxted, Sussex; E: Uckfield, Sussex; Cpl. SD 1090; K: 29.8.18; Vis-en-Artois Mem., Haucourt, Pas-de-Calais; Age 30; Son of Walter and Sarah Ann Sands of 28, Cambridge Street, Tunbridge Wells.

3044. SANDS, William; B: Eastbourne; E: Eastbourne; Pte. G 3849; K: 29.9.18; Vis-en-Artois Mem., Haucourt, Pas-de-Calais; Age 34; Son of George and Emily Sands of 22, Sandown Road, Hastings.

3045. SANSOM, Alfred John; Lt. Col.; K: 5.7.17; Faubourg d'Amiens Cem., Arras, Pas-de-Calais; Age 50; Son of James and Phebe Sansom; Husband of Ivy Sansom of 5, Brassey Road, Bexhill-on-Sea; Killed by a shell falling in Shrapnel Trench near Battalion H.Q.; Buried at Arras 6.30pm. 8.7.17. (See also Nagle 2896).

3046. SAVAGE, Charles Robert; B: Langton, Dorset; E: Horsham, Sussex; L/Cpl. G 5114; K: 3.5.17; Arras Mem., Pas-de-Calais.

3047. SAWYER, Arthur Douglas Henderson; B: Seven-oaks, Kent; E: Ashford, Kent; Pte. G 23961; W: 30.4.18; Doullens Com. Cem. Ext. No.2, Somme; Age 19; Son of James and Sophia Sawyer of 3, Burnett Buildings, High Street, Ashford, Kent.*

3048. SAWYER, George Harry; B: Hampton, Middlesex; E: Hounslow, London; Pte. G 20419; K: 5.4.18; Bouzincourt Ridge Cem., Somme.

3049. SAYERS, Harold Theodore; B: Worthing; E: Worthing; Pte. G 1268; W: 11.7.16; Warloy-Baillon Com. Cem. Ext., Somme; Age 29; Son of William and Catherine Sayers of Worthing; Probably died at the Operating Centre, Warloy-Baillon.

3050. SAYERS, Henry; B: Cowfold, Sussex; E: Horsham, Sussex; L/Sgt. G 1850; W: 9.8.18; Querrieu Brit. Cem., Somme; Age 22; Son of George and Ellen Sayers of Little Brook, Cowfold.

3051. SAYERS, William Richard; B: Southwater, Sussex; E: Horsham, Sussex; L/Cpl. G 6741; K: 26.8.18; Peronne Road Cem., Maricourt, Somme; Age 29; Son of Stephen and Mary Sayers of Southwater; Husband of Harriett Elizabeth Sayers of Southwater.

3052. SCARCE, Ernest William; B: Blaxhall, Suffolk; E: Bury St.Edmunds, Suffolk; Pte. G 18157; K: 8.10.16; Thiepval Mem., Somme.

3053. SCOPES, George Lewis; B: Camberwell, London; E: Southwark, London; Pte. L 10742; K: 5.10.16; Thiepval Mem., Somme.

3054. SCOTT, Leonard Randall; B: Christchurch, New Zealand; E: London; Pte. G 386; K: 30.7.16; Bapaume Post Mil. Cem., Somme; Age 24; Son of George and Betsy Scott of "Compton", Opawa Road, Christchurch, New Zealand.

3055. SCRIVENS, William Frederick; B: Kingsdown, Kent; E: Chichester; Pte. G 5767; K: 27.3.18; Pozieres Mem., Somme; Age 24; Son of Alfred and S.L.Scrivens of 2, Mill Cottages, Chidham, Nutborne, Hampshire.

3056. SCUTT, Frederick; B: Petworth, Sussex; E: Petworth; Pte. G 17757; K: 18.9.18; Epehy Wood Farm Cem., Epehy, Somme; Age 19; Son of John and Emma Jane Scutt of Sandrock Cottage, Fittleworth, Sussex.

3057. SCUTT, Thomas William; B: Lancing, Sussex; E: Worthing; Pte. G 3304; K: 4.8.16; Thiepval Mem., Somme.

3058. SEAMARK, Joseph Samuel; B: Walthamstow, London; E: Walthamstow; Pte. G 23647; K: 9.8.18; Vis-en-Artois Mem., Haucourt, Pas-de-Calais.

3059. SEARS, Henry George; B: Chatham, Kent; E: Chatham; Pte. G 13196; D: 10.2.17; Étaples Mil. Cem., Pas-de-Calais; Age 40; Son of G. and Frances Sears; Husband of Mrs.A.Sears of 15, St.John Street, Chatham.

3060. SECKER, George; B: Dereham, Norfolk; E: Kingston-on-Thames; Pte. G 24040; K: 29.9.18; Epehy Wood Farm, Epehy, Somme; Age 18; Son of Bessie Secker of 41, Prince Street, Deptford, London.

3061. SECKER, William; B: St.Martin's, Norfolk; E: Norwich; Pte. G 18755; W: 25.8.18; Daours Com. Cem. Ext., Somme; Age 19; Son of William and Mary Secker of School Lane, Earith St.Ives, Huntingdonshire.

- - SECKHAM, Gerald (An alias – see Tozer 3167).

3062. SELBY, Albert Edward; B: Cuckfield, Sussex; E: Haywards Heath, Sussex; Sgt. G 111; M.M.; K: 8.8.18; Beacon Cem., Somme; Age 24; Son of Edward and Caroline Selby of Longacre, Cuckfield.

3063. SELDEN, Herbert Alfred; B: Hastings; E: Hastings; Pte. G 6509; K: 9.4.17; Ste.Catherine Brit. Cem., Pas-de-Calais; Age 33; Son of George and Ellen Selden of 115, Stonefield Terrace, Hastings; Husband of Mrs.N.Selden of 220, Harold Road, Hastings.

3064. SEWELL, Herbert Charles; B: Clapham, London; E: Bromley, Kent; Pte. G 12987; W: 16.4.17; Étaples Mil. Cem., Pas-de-Calais; Age 40; Son of William Alfred and Rose Sewell; Husband of Emily J.Sewell of "Retreat", Taxey Road, Green Street Green, Kent.

3065. SEYMOUR, William Henry Stephens; B: Stepney, London; E: Stratford, London; Pte. G 23661; K: 16.5.18; Mailly Wood Cem., Somme; Age 19; Son of Henry and Mary Anne Seymour of 10, Morley Road, Barking, Essex.*

3066. SHAWYER, Ernest Henry; B: Bognor Regis, Sussex; E: Chichester; Pte. GS 182; K: 1.8.16; Thiepval Mem., Somme; Age 36; Son of Mr. and Mrs.Shawyer of Meka Cottage, Bersted, Sussex.

3067. SHEPPARD, Frederick; B: Bermondsey, London; E: Camberwell, London; Pte. G 24041; K: 18.9.18; Epehy Wood Farm Cem., Epehy, Somme; Age 18;

Son of George Sheppard of 320, Lynton Road, Bermondsey.

3068. SHEPPARD, William John; B: Wimborne, Dorset; E: Chichester; L/Cpl. G 1073; K: 4.3.16; Loos Mem., Pas-de-Calais.

3069. SHERMAN, Laurence Shuster; B: Fredericton, New Brunswick, Canada; E: St.Paul's Churchyard, London; L/Cpl. G 7933; W: 5.8.16; Boulogne Eastern Cem., Pas-de-Calais; Age 31; Son of Louis Walsh Sherman and Alice Maxwell Sherman of Fredericton; Died at a Military Hospital, Boulogne.

3070. SHOESMITH, David William; B: Bexhill-on-Sea; E: Hastings; Pte. G 16070; K: 28.3.18; Pozieres Mem., Somme.

3071. SHORT, Herbert; B: Hurst Green, Sussex; E: Worthing; Pte. G 9072; W: 29.3.18; Tincourt New Brit. Cem., Somme; Age 28; Son of Mr. and Mrs. Charles Short of Worthing; Husband of Beatrice Short of 11, Baycliff Road, Pye Hill, Dorset; Died while a Prisoner of War.*

3072. SHORTEN, John Daniel; B: St.Mary's, Norfolk; E: Norwich; Pte. G 11304; K: 3.5.17; Arras Mem., Pas-de-Calais.

3073. SHORTER, Aaron; B: Whitechurch, Kent; E: Canterbury; Pte. G 21588; D: 1.5.18; Niederz-wehren Cem. (G); Died while a Prisoner of War.

3074. SICKLEMORE, Charles Stanley; B: Preston, Sussex; E: Chichester; Cpl. G 540; K: 30.11.17; Cambrai Mem., Louverval, Nord; Age 22; Son of Charles Ernest and Margaret Sicklemore of 15, Upper Hamilton Road, Brighton; Attached to 36th Infantry Brigade and in charge of Brigade Observation Post.

3075. SILSBY, Charles; B: Twineham, Sussex; E: Brighton; Pte. G 4833; W: 16.4.16; Bethune Town Cem., Pas-de-Calais; Age 35; Father of Ivy Christine Silsby of Furzefield House, Cowfold, Sussex.

3076. SILSBY, Frederick; B: – ; E: Guildford; Pte. G 7803; W: 5.10.16; Longueval Road Cem., Somme.

3077. SIMMONDS, Frank; B: Crawley Down, Sussex; E: East Grinstead, Sussex; Pte. G 8430; K: 7.7.16; Thiepval Mem., Somme; Age 19; Son of Edward and Emily S.Simmonds of 10, Bowers Place, Crawley Down.

3078. SIMMONS, Charles; B: Seaford, Sussex; E: Eastbourne; Pte. SD 357; W: 27.8.18; Daours Com. Cem. Ext., Somme.

3079. SIMMONS, Harry; B: – ; E: Rye, Sussex; Pte. G 18158; K: 5.7.17; Monchy Brit. Cem., Pas-de-Calais.

3080. SIMMONS, Hugh; B: Rotherfield, Sussex; E: Horsham, Sussex; Pte. G 905; K: 31.7.15; Houplines Com. Cem. Ext., Nord; Killed by a 4.5" shell.

3081. SIMMONS, Sidney John; B: Barking, Essex; E: Barking; Pte. G 23662; K: 18.9.18; Epehy Wood Farm Cem., Epehy, Somme; Age 19; Son of Thomas and Caroline Simmons of 31, Orchard Avenue, Barking.

3082. SIMONS, Ambrose Ernest; B: Colchester, Essex; E: Colchester; Pte. G 20233; K: 9.4.17; Fenchy Chapel Brit. Cem., Pas-de-Calais; Age 22; Son of Charles and Annie Simons of Station Road, Ardleigh, Essex.*

3083. SIMS, Harry; B: Chichester; E: Chichester; Pte. G 779; W: 6.8.15; Cite Bonjean Mil. Cem., Nord; Age 22; Son of Mr.W. and Mrs.S.A.Sims of 69, North Street, Chichester.

3084. SINCLAIR, Daniel; B: Southwark, London; E: Southwark; Pte. G 5098; K: 7.7.16; Ovillers Mil. Cem., Somme; Age 21; Son of Mr. and Mrs.C.Sinclair of 32, Albert House, Blendon Row, East Street, Walworth, London.

3085. SINCLAIR, John; B: Buckhaven, Fifeshire; E: Cowdenbeath; Pte. G 5851; K: 20.1.16; Guards Cem. (Cuinchy) Pas-de-Calais.

3086. SING, Charles Millington; 2nd Lt.; W: 7.7.16; Serre Road Cem. No.2, Somme; Age 27; Son of Edward Joshua and Sarah Synge (late Sing) of Rotherfield, Dorset.

3087. SISLEY, Charles Lawrence; B: Slinfold, Sussex; E: Cardiff; Cpl. TF 202556; K: 9.7.18; Harponville Com. Cem. Ext., Somme; Age 27; Son of Charles and Mary Sisley of Brighton; Husband of Isabel Sarah Sisley of 3, Orchard Place, Canton, Cardiff.

3088. SKERRETT, Arthur; B: Barkham, Sussex; E: Chichester; Sgt . G 850; W: 14.4.16; Lillers Com. Cem., Pas-de-Calais.

3089. SKINNER, Frank; B: Mayfield, Sussex; E: Tunbridge Wells; Pte. G 104; K: 4.3.16; Loos Mem., Pas-de-Calais; Age 23; Son of Charity Ann Skinner of Colkin's Mill, Mayfield.

3090. SLADE, James; B: Marylebone, London; E: Kingston-on-Thames; Pte. G 13939; D: 3.2.17; Warlincourt Halte Brit. Cem., Pas-de-Calais; Age 37; Husband of Sarah Jane Slade of 14, Bourtonville, Buckinghamshire; Died of bronchitis.

3091. SMALL, Frank Mitchell; B: Rye, Sussex; E: Chatham, Kent; Pte. G 12924; K: 3.5.17; Arras Mem., Pas-de-Calais.

3092. SMISSEN, George Franklin; B: Mountfield, Sussex; E: Hastings; Pte. G 76; K: 31.3.17; Faubourg d'Amiens Cem., Arras, Pas-de-Calais; Age 24; Son of Franklin and Sarah Smissen of Darwell Road, Netherfield, Sussex; Killed by shell fire while on digging duties at Arras*

3093. SMITH, Alfred; B: Frant, Sussex; E: Tunbridge Wells; Pte. G 1092; K: 20.11.17; Cambrai Mem., Louverval, Nord.

3094. SMITH, Arthur; B: Denston, Suffolk; E: Lowestoft; Pte. G 11301; K: 3.7.17; Monchy Brit. Cem., Pas-de-Calais; Age 23; Son of William Smith of Stradishall, Suffolk.

3095. SMITH, Arthur Henry Thomas; B: Freefolk, Hampshire; E: Hove; Pte. G 8679; K: 7.7.16; Thiepval Mem., Somme.

3096. SMITH, Arthur William; B: Limehouse, London; E: London; Cpl. G 381; W: 24.10.15; Lapugnoy Mil. Cem., Pas-de-Calais; Age 21; Son of George and Anne Smith of 178, Leander Road, Brixton Hill, London.

3097. SMITH, Bertram Frank; B: Eastbourne; E: Eastbourne; Pte. G 14363; K: 18.9.18; Epehy Wood Farm Cem., Epehy, Somme; Age 20; Son of Frank C.A.Smith of 13, Church Street, Eastbourne.

3098. SMITH, Harry; B: Leeds; E: Leeds; L/Cpl. G 24072; W: 20.9.18; Doingt Com. Cem., Somme; Son of Mrs.L.M.Smith of "The Twelve Bells", Hunslet, Leeds.

3099. SMITH, Henry; B: – ; E: Brighton; Pte. G 16681; K: 14.5.17; Arras Mem., Pas-de-Calais.

3100. SMITH, Walter William; B: Warwick; E: Walthamstow, London; Pte. G 23651; W: 24.8.18; Daours Com. Cem. Ext., Somme; Age 19; Son of Mr. and Mrs.W.W.Smith of 1, Luton Road, Walthamstow.

3101. SMITH, William; B: Brighton; E: Newhaven, Sussex; Pte. G 35; K: 19.10.15; Lillers Com. Cem., Pas-de-Calais; Age 31; Husband of May Smith of 67, Islingword Road, Brighton.

3102. SMITHERS, Frederick James; B: Sunningdale, Berkshire; E: Guildford; Pte. G 8359; D at Home: 8.8.16; Chobham (St.Lawrence) Church Cem., Surrey (UK); Age 20; Son of Frederick James and Annie Smithers of Burrow Hill, Chobham.

3103. SNELL, Frederick; B: Roydon, Essex; E: Epping, Essex; Pte. G 16944; K: 21.9.18; Epehy Wood Farm Cem., Epehy, Somme; Age 20; Son of William and Julia Snell of Nazeing Upper Gate, Waltham Cross, Essex.

3104. SOAL, Arthur; B: Ryefield, Sussex; E: Nyewood, Hampshire; Pte. G 1128; K: 9.11.15; Quarry Cem. (Vermelles) Pas-de-Calais; Killed by shell fire.

3105. SOFFE, Gabriel; B: – ; E: Storrington, Sussex; Pte. G 16683; W: 10.4.17; Duisans Com. Cem., Pas-de-Calais; Husband of Mrs.C.J.Soffe of Pulborough, Sussex.

3106. SOUCH, Frederick Harry; B: Brighton; E: Brighton; L/Cpl. GS 107; W: 10.8.17; Tilloy Brit. Cem., Pas-de-Calais; Age 35; Husband of Florence Deanes, formerly Souch, of 18, Kensington Place, Brighton; Served in the South Africa Campaign.*

3107. SOUTHON, Jesse; B: Rotherfield, Sussex; E: Uckfield, Sussex; SD 1099; K: 5.4.18; Bouzincourt Ridge Cem., Somme; Age 24; Son of Mrs.E.Warnett of Sunnyside Cottage, Pound Gate, Buxted, Sussex.

3108. SOUTHON, Robert; B: St.Margaret's, Sussex; E: Brighton; L/Cpl. G 174; K: 7.7.16; Loos Mem., Pas-de-Calais.*

3109. SPENCELEY, John Henry; B: Newport, Buckinghamshire; E: Holloway, London; Pte. G 23654; K: 11.8.18; Beacon Cem., Somme; Age 19; Son of Edwin and Rose Jane Spenceley of 500, Hornsey Road, Upper Holloway.*

3110. SPRINGETT, Frederick Richard; B: – ; E: Hertford; Pte. G 15645; K: 25.11.17; Cambrai Mem., Louverval, Nord.

3111. SQUIRES, Arthur Edwin; B: Chichester; E: Chichester; Pte. L 10989; K: 5.3.18; Croix-du-Bac Brit. Cem., Somme; Age 21; Son of Mr. and Mrs.W.Squires of 1, White House, Shripney, Bognor Regis, Sussex; Brother, James Edward, also killed (see 3113).*

3112. SQUIRES, David; B: Aldingbourne, Sussex; E: Arundel, Sussex; Pte. G 14176; K: 9.4.17; Arras Mem., Pas-de-Calais; Age 38; Husband of Edith Mabel Squires of Walberton, Sussex.

3113. SQUIRES, James Edward; B: Chichester; E: Chichester; Pte. G 623; K: 21.10.15; Loos Mem., Pas-de-Calais; Age 19; Son of Mr. and Mrs.W.Squires of 1, White House, Shripney, Bognor Regis, Sussex; Brother, Arthur Edwin, also killed (see 3111).

3114. STAMPE, Herbert William; B: Llamon, Cardiganshire; E: London; Pte. G 7374; K: 7.7.16; Thiepval Mem., Somme.

3115. STANLEY, John; B: Aycliffe, County Durham; E: Sevenoaks, Kent; Pte. G 12917; K: 5.4.18; Bouzincourt Ridge Cem., Somme.

3116. STAPLEHURST, Ernest; B: Framfield, Sussex; E: Lewes; Pte. SD 964; W: 19.9.18; Doingt Com. Cem., Somme; Son of Mrs.R.Staplehurst of Palehouse Common, Sussex; Died at Casualty Clearing Station, Doingt.

3117. STAPLEHURST, George; B: Fletching, Sussex; E: Uckfield, Sussex; Pte. G 3580; W: 6.8.16; Varennes Mil. Cem., Somme; Age 23; Son of Ross and Louisa Staplehurst of Rose Cottage, Piltdown, Sussex.

3118. STARLING, Frederick Charles; B: Chingford, Essex; E: Hastings; Pte. G 4049; K: 7.7.16; Serre Road Cem. No.2, Somme.

3119. STEADMAN, Charles; B: Dane Hill, Sussex; E: East Grinstead, Sussex; Pte. G 8421; K: 7.7.16; Serre Road Cem. No.2, Somme.

3120. STEAR, Gilbert; B: Bosham, Sussex; E: Chichester; L/Cpl. G 802; K: 8.4.16; Loos Mem., Pas-de-Calais; Age 23; Son of George and Julia Stear of 3, Myrtle Cottages, Old Fishbourne, Sussex.

3121. STEBBINGS, Walter Henry; B: Stowupland, Suffolk; E: Bury St.Edmunds, Suffolk; Pte. G 18161; K: 9.4.17; Gourock Trench Cem., Tilloy-les-Mofflaines, Pas-de-Calais.

3122. STEDMAN, Arthur George; B: Cobham, Surrey; E: Guildford; Pte. G 5496; K: 8.10.16; Thiepval Mem., Somme; Age 19; Son of C.G. and Flora Stedman of Providence Cottage, Street, Surrey.

3123. STEEDMAN, Cyril Alfred; B: Brighton; E: Brighton; Pte. S 2336; K: 7.7.16; Thiepval Mem., Somme; Age 17; Son of Simeon Duncan and Eleanor Jane Steedman of 52, Southampton Street, Brighton.*

3124. STENNER, William George; B: Mitcham, Surrey; E: Horsham, Sussex; L/Cpl. G 904; K: 17.3.16; Vermelles Brit. Cem., Pas-de-Calais; Age 26; Son of James and Emma Stenner of Binfield Heath, Surrey.

3125. STEPHENSON, Mossetse; B: Chorley, Lancashire; E: Chorley; Pte. G 23025; K: 26.8.18; Vis-en-Artois Mem., Haucourt, Pas-de-Calais; Age 27; Husband of Annie Stephenson of 22, Northgate, Chorley.

3126. STEVENS, Harry; B: Horsell, Surrey; E: Guildford; Pte. G 7678; K: 1.8.16; Thiepval Mem., Somme; Age 30; Son of Mrs.S.Courtney.

3127. STONE, Frederick Edward; B: Holloway, London; E: Holloway; Pte. G 21657; K: 20.5.18; Mailly Wood Cem., Somme; Age 19; Son of James and Rebecca Stone of 15, Market Street, Barnsbury, London.

3128. STONE, Richard William; B: Brighton; E: Hove; L/Cpl. L 10653; K: 7.10.16; Thiepval Mem., Somme; Age 20; Son of Richard and Emily Stone of 23, Richmond Hill, Brighton.

3129. STONER, Edward; B: Hove; E: Hove; Sgt. G 748; K: 9.4.17; Feuchy Chapel Brit. Cem., Pas-de-Calais.

3130. STRUDWICK, William; B: – ; E: Brighton; Pte. G 16684; K: 25.7.17; Arras Mem., Pas-de-Calais.

3131. STUBBS, Thomas; B: Buddington, Sussex; E: West Lavington, Sussex; Pte. G 8329; K: 7.7.16; Ovillers Mil. Cem., Somme.

3132. STURT, Harry James; B: Littlehampton, Sussex; E: Chichester; L.Cpl. G 535; K: 7.7.16; Thiepval Mem., Somme.

3133. SUMMERFIELD, Henry; B: Horsham, Sussex; E: Horsham; Pte. G 877; W: 15.4.16; Vermelles Brit. Cem., Pas-de-calais; Age 28; Son of Mrs.Emma Fillery of 7, Milton Road, Horsham.

3134. SUMMERS, Harold; B: St.Peter's, Kent; E: Eastbourne; Pte. G 2314; K: 18.9.18; Epehy Wood Farm Cem., Epehy, Somme.

3135. SUMMONS, Arthur Stephen; B: Benacre, Suffolk; E: Lowestoft; Pte. G 11300; K: 5.8.16; Thiepval Mem., Somme; Age 19; Son of Robert Stephen and Emma Louisa Summons of Benacre Street, Wrentham, Suffolk.

3136. SUTTON, Eric Guy; Lt.; M.C.; K: 8.4.16; Vermelles Brit. Cem., Pas-de-Calais; Age 21; Son of Leonard Goodheart Sutton and Mrs.M.C.A.Sutton of Hillside, Reading; Killed while climbing over a filled-in crater at the Hohenzollern Redoubt.

3137. SWAIN, Edward Alfred; B: Hastings; E: Brighton; Pte. G 24050; W: 19.9.18; Doingt Com. Cem., Somme; Died at Casualty Clearing Station, Doingt.*

3138. SWAYNE, Albert Dennis; B: Sherrington, Wiltshire; E: Chichester; Pte. L 8133; W: 11.7.16; Boulogne Eastern Cem., Pas-de-Calais; Age 28; Son of Francis and Anna Swayne of 19, St.Johns Road, Magdalen Hill, Winchester; Died at a Military Hospital, Boulogne.

3139. SWIFT, Frederick; B: Sheffield; E: Sheffield; Pte. G 24074; K: 18.9.18; Epehy Wood Farm Cem., Epehy, Somme.

3140. SYLVESTER, Samuel; B: Nether Edge, Yorkshire; E: Sheffield; Pte. G 5054; K: 7.7.16; Thiepval Mem. Somme.

T

3141. TAYLOR, Alfred Edward; B: Hammersmith, London; E: White City, London; Pte. G 24052; W: 16.10.18; Vis-en-Artois Mem., Haucourt, Pas-de-Calais.*

3142. TAYLOR, Arthur Hines; B: Maidenhead, Berkshire; E: Brighton; Pte. G 13622; W: 28.3.18; St.Hilaire Cem., Pas-de-Calais; Age 28; Son of Arthur and Ruth M.Taylor of "Wesdeigh", Alwyn Road, Maidenhead.

3143. TAYLOR. Frederick; B: Newport, Monmouthshire; E: Eastbourne; Pte. G 2335; K: 7.7.16; Ovillers Mil. Cem., Somme; Age 19; Son of Richard Taylor.*

3144. TAYLOR, George; B: St.Pancras, London; E: Kingston-on-Thames; Pte. G 24053; W at Home: 18.10.18; Croydon (Queen's Road) Cem., Surrey (UK); Age 18; Son of Mr. and Mrs.William Taylor of 21, Harrington Road, South Norwood, London.

3145. TAYLOR, George Edward; B: Wolverhampton; E: Wolverhampton; Pte. G 5965; K: 18.3.16; Vermelles Brit. Cem., Pas-de-Calais; Age 27; Son of Jane Smith, formerly Taylor, of 55, Maxwell Road, Wolverhampton, and the late James Taylor.

3146. TAYLOR, George Henry; B: Lewisham, London; E: Lambeth, London; Pte. G 9610; K: 3.5.15; Arras Mem., Pas-de-Calais; Age 26; Son of George and Jane Taylor of 13, Burnhill Road, Beckenham, Kent; Husband of Amy Agnes Taylor of 4, Windmill Lane, East Grinstead, Sussex.

3147. TAYLOR, George William Edward; B: Malling, Sussex; E: Lewes; Sgt. S 1701; K: 4.7.17; Arras Mem., Pas-de-Calais; Age 24; Son of Henry and Mary Ann Taylor of 103, South Street, Lewes.*

3148. TEAGUE, Jonathan Eric; B: Burgess Hill, Sussex; E: Brighton; Pte. G 24058; W: 26.9.18; Doingt Com. Cem., Somme; Age 17; Son of Mr. and Mrs.J.Teague of Burgess Hill; Died at Casualty Clearing Station, Doingt.*

3149. TEE, James Edward; B: Worthing; E: Worthing; L/Cpl. G 856; K: 7.7.16; Ovillers Mil. Cem., Somme.

3150. TEGERDINE, John Oscar; B: Wisbech, Cambridgeshire; E: Wisbech; Pte. G 15014; K: 26.8.18; Peronne Road Com. Cem., Maricourt, Somme.

3151. TESTER, Harry; B: St.John's, Sussex; E: Lewes; Pte. S 1806; K: 30.7.17; Monchy Brit. Cem., Pas-de-Calais.

3152. THACKER, Robert George; B: Southwark, London; E: Southwark; Pte. G 5000; W: 9.10.16; Heilly Station Cem., Mericourt-l'Abbé, Somme; Age 25; Son of Mr. and Mrs.Thacker of 45, Russell Street, Brixton, London.

3153. THAKE, Ernest; B: Haverhill, Suffolk; E: Sudbury, Suffolk; Pte. G 17016; K: 18.9.18; Epehy Wood Farm Cem., Epehy, Somme; Son of Mr. and Mrs. James Thake of 3, Down's Place, Haverhill.

3154. THIRST, William; B: Suffield, Norfolk; E: Cromer, Norfolk; Pte. G 9353; M.M.; W at Home: 4.10.18; Suffield (St.Margaret) Churchyard, Norfolk (UK); Age 30; Son of James and Mary Ann Thirst of Suffield.

3155. THOMSON, Alfred Maurice; Capt.; K: 7.7.16; Thiepval Mem., Somme; Age 30; Son of Alfred and Florence C.Thomson of 9, Osborne Mansions, Northumberland Street, London; Attached from Royal Army Medical Corp; Having treated the wounded on the battlefield all morning, he returned to an injured officer and, while dragging him to safety, was himself shot and died instantly.

3156. THOMPSON, Arthur James; B: Horsham, Sussex; E: Chichester; Pte. G 490; K: 8.7.15; Tancrez Farm Cem. (Bel.).*

3157. TIFFIN, Fred Baxter; B: Christchurch, Sussex; E: Christchurch; Pte. G 197; K: 26.7.15; Houplines Com. Cem. Ext., Nord.

3158. TILL, Ernest George; B: Ford, Sussex; E: Worthing; L/Cpl. G 17665; K: 5.10.16; Thiepval Mem., Somme.

3159. TIMMINS, John Caswell; B: Cheltenham, Gloucestershire; E: Arundel, Sussex; Pte. G 8727; K: 7.7.16; Thiepval Mem., Somme.

3160. TINDELL, John Harold; B: Ringaskiddy, County Cork, Ireland; E: Hove; Pte. SD 3476; W: 16.10.16; Heilly Station Cem., Mericourt-l'Abbé, Somme; Age 24; Son of Francis and Hannah Tindell.

3161. TINGLEY, George Arthur; B: Cowfold, Sussex; E: Worthing; Pte. G 1153; K: 7.7.16; Ovillers Mil. Cem., Somme; Age 22; Son of Thomas and Emily Tingley of 17, Parklands Road, Hassocks, Sussex.

3162. TINSLEY, Edward; B: Rochester, Kent; E: Lewes; Pte. G 5703; K: 31.3.17; Faubourg d'Amiens Cem., Arras, Pas-de-Calais; killed by shell fire while on digging duties at Arras.

3163. TITMAN, Lewis; B: – ; E: Oundle, Northamptonshire; Pte. G 11774; K: 18.9.18; Epehy Wood Farm Cem., Epehy, Somme; Age 21; Son of Alfred and Amy Titman of Polebroke, Northamptonshire.

3164. TOOKE, Albert Edward; B: –; E: Cambridgeshire; Pte. G 14886; W: 14.12.17; Abbeville Com. Cem. Ext., Somme; Age 20; Son of William and Alice Elizabeth Tooke of 30, Mount Terrace, Wisbech, Cambridgeshire.*

3165. TOOMS, Frederick John; B: Rotherhithe, London; E: Camberwell, London; L/Sgt. G 5070; M.M.; K: 22.8.18; Vis-en-Artois Mem., Haucourt, Pas-de-Calais; Age 22; Son of George Henry and Rosina Tooms of 3, Bryant's Court, Rotherhithe.

3166. TOWNSEND, Charles Arthur; B: Clerkenwell, London; E: Walthamstow, London; Pte. G 23670; K: 28.4.18; Mailly Wood Cem., Somme; Son of Mrs.C.C.Townsend of 3, Claremont Road, Walthamstow.

3167. TOZER, Geoffrey Goodall; B: – ; E: – ; L/Sgt. G 5430; K: 4.8.16; Thiepval Mem., Somme; Age 23; Son of Soloman and Helenora Adair Tozer of Ashburton, Devonshire; Served under the alias Gerald SECKHAM.

3168. TRILL, Charles Tower; B: Newick, Sussex; E: Hove; L/Cpl. G 759; K: 7.7.16; Ovillers Mil. Cem., Somme.*

3169. TROTMAN, Alfred John; B: King's Cross, London; E: Shoreditch, London; Pte. G 20240; K: 9.4.17; Arras Mem., Pas-de-Calais; Age 19; Son of James and Annie Alexandra Trotman of 80, Grosvenor Road, Highbury, London.

3170. TULLY, Arthur; B: Ardingly, Sussex; E: Brighton; Pte. S 2295; W: 23.6.18; Varennes Mil. Cem., Somme; Age 20; Brother of Mary Tully of 50, Hewins Cottage, Cooksbridge, Sussex.

3171. TURNER, Frederick Thomas; B: Croydon; E: Whitehall, London; Pte. G 25305; W: 8.8.18; Vis-en-Artois Mem., Haucourt, Pas-de-Calais; Age 18; Son of Thomas John and Nellie Turner of 2, Latimer Road, Croydon; Killed near Morlancourt, Somme.

3172. TWIBILL, Reginald; B: Bursted, Sussex; E: Bognor Regis, Sussex; L/Cpl. G 6739; K: 28.7.17; Arras Mem., Pas-de-Calais; Age 20; Son of Eliza Letitia Waight of Elm Villa, London Road, Bognor Regis.*

3173. TWINE, Harold John; B: Littlehampton, Sussex; E: Littlehampton; Pte. G 4951; K: 7.7.16; Thiepval Mem., Somme; Age 20; Son of Harry and Alice Mary Twine of 37, Western Road, Littlehampton.

3174. TWINN, Walter Wallace; B: Glumstead, Suffolk; E: Wokingham, Berkshire; Pte. G 11310; K: 22.8.18; Vis-en-Artois Mem., Haucourt, Pas-de-Calais; Age 24; Son of Wallace W. and Alice Elizabeth Twinn of Tye Green, Glemsford, Suffolk.

3175. TYRELL, George Warden; B: Balcombe, Sussex; E: Chichester; Sgt. G 4; K: 1.8.16; Thiepval Mem., Somme; Killed west of Pozieres by an enemy shell burst.

U

3176. UNSTEAD, William; B: Firle, Sussex; E: Hove; Sgt. G 692; K: 7.7.16; Thiepval Mem., Somme; Age 34; Son of Harry and Jane Unstead.

3177. UTTING, Edward; B: Martham, Norfolk; E: Wroxham, Norfolk; Pte. G 18528; K: 18.9.18; Epehy Wood Farm Cem., Epehy, Somme; Age 20; Son of Mr.D. and Mrs.M.A.Utting of Black Street, Martham.

V

3178. VENN, Edward Noah; B: St.Mary's, Sussex; E: Chichester; C.S.M.; L 9049; K: 9.8.18; Vis-en-Artois Mem., Haucourt, Pas-de-Calais; Killed near Morlancourt, Somme.

3179. VINCENT, James; B: Charlton, London; E: Woolwich, London; Pte. G 10589; K: 5.4.18; Bouzincourt Ridge Cem., Somme; Age 22; Son of Henry and Louisa Vincent.*

3180. VOAK, Harry; B: Brighton; E: Brighton; L/Cpl. G 19691; K: 25.7.17; Monchy Brit. Cem., Pas-de-Calais.

3181. VOICE, Arthur; B: Newhaven, Sussex; E: Brighton; Pte. G 4926; K: 8.4.16; Loos Mem., Pas-de-Calais.

W

3182. WADE, Arthur; B: Coggeshall, Essex; E: Chelmsford, Essex; Pte. G 14740; K: 5.4.18; Bouzincourt Ridge Cem., Somme.

3183. WADY, Edward; B: Broadwater, Sussex; E:

Worthing; Cpl. G 130; K: 7.7.16; Thiepval Mem., Somme.

3184. WAKEFORD, Harry; B: Emsworth, Hampshire; E: Chichester; Pte, TF 315283; K: 8.8.18; Beacon Cem., Somme; Son of Jane Wakeford of North Street, Westbourne, Hampshire; Killed near Morlancourt, Somme.

3185. WAKEHAM, Peter; B: Amberley, Sussex; E: Horsham, Sussex; Pte. G 934; K: 28.3.18; Pozieres Mem., Somme; Age 32; Son of Peter and Sarah Wakeham of 4, Cross Gates, Amberley.

3186. WALDER, Percy; B: Hickstead, Sussex; E: Brighton; Pte. G 11392; K: 12.9.16; Agny Mil. Cem., Pas-de-Calais; Age 22; Son of Mr. and Mrs.M.E.Walder of 17, Windsor Road, Hailsham, Sussex.

3187. WALKER, Frederick Charles; B: – ; E: Hastings; Pte. G 18034; K: 5.10.16; Thiepval Mem., Somme.

3188. WALKER, George Edwin; B: Aldingbourne, Sussex; E: Chichester; Pte. G 841; K: 7.7.16; Thiepval Mem., Somme.

3189. WALL, Percy Charles; B: Brighton; E: Brighton; Pte. G 8469; K: 7.7.16; Thiepval Mem., Somme; Age 26; Husband of Elizabeth Catherine Wall of Ingleside, Wroxall, Isle of Wight.

3190. WALLER, Charles William; B: Ditchling, Sussex; E: Brighton; Pte. G 5033; K: 7.7.16; Thiepval Mem., Somme.

3191. WALLER, Frank; B: Worthing; E: Hove; Pte. L 10849; K: 9.4.17; Ste.Catherine Brit. Cem., Pas-de-Calais.

3192. WALLER, Charles Henry; B: B: Portslade, Sussex; E: Worthing; L/Cpl. SD 1750; D: 14.11.18; – - .

3193. WALLS, James; B: Sudbury, Middlesex; E: Chichester; Pte. G 820; W: 28.3.16; Sailly-Labourse Com. Cem., Pas-de-Calais; Son of Mr.W.Walls of 3, South View, East Road, Selsey, Sussex.

3194. WALLS, John; B: Harrow, Middlesex; E: Chichester; Pte. G 586; K: 7.7.16; Mash Valley Mem., Ovillers Mil. Cem., Somme; Age 21; Son of Mr.W. and Mrs.F.Walls of "Elmcroft", East Road, Selsey, Sussex; Originally buried at Mash Valley Cem. from which those bodies that could be found there were moved to the nearby Ovillers Mil. Cem. after the war; Men whose bodies could not be traced were each given a memorial headstone at Ovillers Mil. Cem.

3195. WARE, Thomas William; B: Sydney, New South Wales, Australia; E: Newhaven, Sussex; Pte. G 8096; W: 4.5.17; Duisans Brit Cem., Pas-de-Calais; Age 33; Son of Nathaniel Robert and Elizabeth Emma Ware; Husband of Maud Ellen Ware of 63, Brisbane Street, Waverley, Sydney.

3196. WARING, Frederick Royden; 2nd Lt.; K: 7.7.16; Thiepval Mem., Somme; Age 20; Son of Frederick J. and Dorothy Ann Waring of 20, Morley's Hill, Burton-on-Trent.

3197. WARRINGTON, Fred; B: Ramsey, Huntingdon-shire; E: Huntingdon; Pte. G 16831; W: 24.9.18; Saulcourt Churchyard, Somme.

3198. WASHER, George; B: Hove; E: Hove; L/Cpl. SD 3720; K: 3.7.18; Harponville Com. Cem. Ext., Somme; Age 20; Son of William and Elizabeth Washer of 26, Cowper Street, Hove.

3199. WATSON, Alfred; B: Eastbourne; E: Eastbourne; Pte. G 4031; K: 16.10.15; Loos Mem., Pas-de-Calais; Age 17; Son of William Alfred and Bessie Watson of 94, Susans Road, Eastbourne.

3200. WATSON, Charles John; B: Felpham, Sussex; E: Chichester; Pte. G 434; W: 2.3.16; Bethune Town Cem., Pas-de-Calais; Age 30; Son of Mrs.Fanny Watson of 3, Gordon Terrace, Felpham.

3201. WATSON, Edwin; B: Leatherhead, Surrey; E: London; Pte. G 20588; K: 25.11.17; Cambrai Mem., Louverval, Nord; Age 29; Son of Alfred and Arm Watson of "Carol", 217, Kingston Road, Leatherhead; Husband of Eliza Watson of 2, Bradford Cottages, Elm Road, Leatherhead.*

3202. WATTS, Andrew George; B: Petersfield, Hampshire; E: Hastings; Pte. G 660; K: 4.3.16; Vermelles Brit. Cem., Pas-de-Calais; Age 27; Son of Henry and Agnes Watts of High Street, Buriton, Hampshire.

3203. WATTS, George Frederick; B: Haywards Heath, Sussex; E: Hove; Pte. G 968; W: 28.9.15; Bailleul Com. Cem. Ext., Nord.

3204. WEATHERLEY, William; B: Arkley, Hertfordshire; E: Edmonton, London; Pte. G 20053; W: 30.8.17; Faubourg d'Amiens Cem., Arras, Pas-de-Calais.

3205. WEBB, Bertie Frank; B: Kentish Town, London; E: Walthamstow, London; Pte. G 23677; K: 24.8.18; Vis-en-artois Mem., Haucourt, Pas-de-Calais; Age 19; Son of Sharwood James Webb of 5, King Edward Road, Walthamstow.

3206. WEBBER, Frederick Percy; B: East Grinstead, Sussex; E: East Grinstead; Pte. G 8448; K: 4.7.17; Monchy Brit. Cem., Pas-de-calais; Age 19; Son of Alfred and Florence Catherine Webber of Queensburg Cottage, Forest Row, Sussex.

3207. WEBBER, Thomas; B: Hoxton, London; E: Holloway, London; Pte. G 20503; W: 11.4.17; Duisans Brit. Cem., Pas-de-Calais; Husband of Mrs.L.F.Webber of 97, Duncombe Road, Upper Holloway.

3208. WEBSTER, Thomas; B: Southwark, London; E: London; Cpl. G 20283; K: 31.7.17; Arras Mem., Pas-de-Calais.

3209. WEEDEN, Robert George; B: Kennington, London; E: Clapham, London; Pte.SD 5759; K: 30.11.17; Cambrai Mem., Louverval, Pas-de-Calais; Age 25; Son of Mr. and Mrs. Weeden of 20, Rossiter Road, Balham, London Husband of Florence L.Everest, formerly Weeden, of 59, Gladstone Road, Wimbledon, London.

3210. WELLS, Ronald Graham; Lt.; K: 4.3.16; Loos Mem., Pas-de-Calais.

3211. WEST, Henry Edward; B: Iver, Buckinghamshire; E: Watford, Hertfordshire; Pte. G 21620; W: 23.11.17; Rocquigny-Equancourt Road Brit. Cem., Somme; Age 31; Husband of Mary Caroline West of Treadgold Street, Notting Hill, London.

3212. WEST, William; B: Westfield, Sussex; E: Chichester; Pte. L 5740; K: 7.7.16; Thiepval Mem., Somme.

3213. WESTGATE, James William George; B: Belvedere, Kent; E: Woolwich, London; Pte. G 23680; W: 18.9.18; Peronne Com. Cem. Ext., Ste. Radegonde, Somme; Age 19; Son of George and Charlotte Westgate of The Nest, Kentish Road, Belvedere.

3214. WESTGATE, William; B: Hurstpierpoint, Sussex; E: Haywards Heath, Sussex; Pte. G 9562; W: 5.5.17; Duisans Brit. Cem., Pas-de-Calais; Son of Mr.W.Westgate of 1, Pretoria Road, Burgess Hill, Sussex.

3215. WESTON, Albert George; B: Brighton; E: Brighton; Pte. G 240; K: 7.7.16; Thiepval Mem., Somme; Age 32; Son of Stephen and Alice Weston of 5, Carlton Row, Brighton; Husband of Celia Weston of 22, Trinity Street, Islington, London.

3216. WHARTON, David; B: – ; E: Wigan, Lancashire; Pte. TF 260172; K: 24.9.18; Epehy Wood Farm Cem., Epehy, Somme.

3217. WHITE, Arthur Thomas; B: – ; E: Chichester; Pte. G 16285; W: 9.8.18; Pernois Brit. Cem., Somme; Age 23; Son of Mr. and Mrs.White of Pear Tree Cottages, Donnington, Sussex; Died at Casualty Clearing Station, Pernois.

3218. WHITEMAN, James; B: Warbleton, Sussex; E: Hastings; L/Cpl. G 1112; W: 7.7.16; Albert Com. Cem. Ext., Somme.

3219. WHITENSTALL, Albert; B: Dymchurch, Kent; E: Chichester; L/Cpl. G 1062; K: 7.7.16; Thiepval Mem., Somme.

3220. WHITTEMORE, Frederick Arthur; B: Campton, Bedfordshire; E: Bedford; Pte. G 14877; M.M.; K: 26.8.18; Carnoy Mil. Cem., Somme; Age 21; Son of Arthur and Annie Whittemore of 21, Rectory Road, Campton.

3221. WICKHAM, Ernest Humphrey; B: Dover; E: Hastings; Pte. SD 5151; K: 25.7.17; Arras Mem., Pas-de-Calais.

3222. WIGHTWICK, Edwin Bert; B: Maidstone; E: Maidstone; Pte. G 12992; K: 9.4.17; Arras Mem., Pas-de-Calais; Age 39; Son of Edwin and Emily Wightwick of Park View, Loose, Kent.

3223. WILD, George; B: Knapton, Norfolk; E: Wroxham, Norfolk; Pte. G 14284; K: 9.8.18; Vis-en-Artois Mem., Haucourt, Pas-de-Calais; Killed near Morlancourt, Somme.

3224. WILDMAN, Ernest Vaughan; B: Hampstead, London; E: Kilburn, London; Pte. G 5065; K: 5.7.16; Thiepval Mem., Somme; Age 45; Husband of Emily Wildman of 38a, Oak Grove, Cricklewood, London.

3225. WILKINS, Edward J.F.; B: Lewes; E: Lewes; Pte. G 17507; K: 25.7.17; Monchy Brit. Cem., Pas-de-Calais.*

3226. WILLARD, Albert Ellis; Lt.; K: 4.7.17; Arras Mem., Pas-de-Calais; Age 25; Son of Albert and Mary Willard of "La Roseraie", 59, Summerheath Road, Hailsham, Sussex.

3227. WILLIAMS, John; B: – ; E: Wigan, Lancashire; L/Cpl/ TF 260204; K: 18.9.18; Epehy Wood Farm Cem., Epehy, Somme; Age 30; Son of Mr. and Mrs. Evan Williams; Husband of Maria Williams of 406, Woodhouse Lane, Wigan.

3228. WILLS, William Henry; B: Exeter, Devonshire; E: London; Pte. G 8115; W: 20.4.17; Boulogne Eastern Cem., Pas-de-Calais; Age 30; Son of Joseph and Ellen Agnes Wills; Husband of Beatrice Hilda Wills of 6, Winchester Street, Clyde Road, Brighton; Died at a Military Hospital.*

3229. WILSON, Frederick William; B: Putney, London; E: Newhaven, Sussex; Pte. G 20238; W: 26.11.17; Tincourt New Brit. Cem., Somme; Age 22; Son of William and Amelia Wilson of "Preswylfa", Maswell Park, Hounslow, London; Died at Casualty Clearing Station, Tincourt, from wounds received the previous day.

3230. WINGFIELD, John; B: Worthing; E: Worthing; Pte. SD 1742; K: 24.5.18; Mailly Wood Cem., Somme; Age 29; Son of Edmund and Jane Wingfield of 2, Brickfield Cottages, Durrington, Sussex.

3231. WINKWORTH, Victor Charles; B: St.Pancras, London; E: St.Pancras; Pte. G 6013; K: 8.4.16; Loos Mem., Pas-de-Calais; Age 21; Son of Walter Thomas and Rhoda Winkworth of 21, Willes Road, Kentish Town, London.

3232. WINTER, Henry Horace; B: – ; E: Brighton; Pte. TF 266438; W: 12.8.18; Terlincthun Brit. Cem., Pas-de-Calais.

3233. WINTER, James; B: – ; E: – ; Pte. SR 1207; K: 3.5.17; Arras Mem., Pas-de-Calais; Age 26; Son of Mrs.C.Winter; Husband of Elsie Victoria Carey, formerly Winter, of 4, East Street, Hastings; Served under the alias surname Deadman.

3234. WINTER, Robert Ernest; B: Shoreham, Sussex; E: Hove; Pte. G 11517; K: 8.8.16; Thiepval Mem., Somme; Age 21; Son of Alfred John and Louisa Winter of 3, St.John's Terrace, Shoreham.

3235. WISE, Edward Hilary; B: Staines, Middlesex; E: Richmond, Surrey; Cpl. S 2349; K: 8.8.18; Villers-Bretonneux Mil. Cem., Somme; Age 24; Son of Edward and May Emily Wise of Staines; Husband of Florence May Emily Wise of 10, Sheendale Road, Richmond.*

3236. WOOD, Albert; B: Hove; E: Hove; Pte. L 10950; W: 18.3.16; Vermelles Brit. Cem., Pas-de-calais; Age 17; Son of Harry and Caroline Wood of Hove.*

3237. WOOD, Alexander; Maj.; W: 12.4.17; Faubourg d'Amiens Cem., Arras, Pas-de-Calais; Age 37; Son of Maj. Gen. Edward and Mrs.E.Wood of Hampton Court Palace; Husband of Doris Margaret Wood of The Old Gables, Warfield, Berkshire.

3238. WOOD, Leonard Daniel; B: Arundel, Sussex; E: Woking, Surrey; Pte. G 8948; K: 9.4.17; Ste. Catherine Brit. Cem., Pas-de-Calais; Son of Edwin and Jane Wood of 17, Bond Street, Arundel.

3239. WOOD, Thomas Victor; 2nd Lt.; K: 4.8.16; Thiepval Mem., Somme.

3240. WOODHAMS, Geoffrey; Capt.; K: 19.3.16;

Vermelles Brit. Cem., Pas-de-Calais; Age 24; Son of Albert Woodhams of "Sundvolden", Littlehampton, Sussex; Killed while bringing in a wounded man.

3241. WOOFF, Ernest George; B: Ecchinswell, Berkshire; E: Maidstone; Pte. G 12894; K: 9.4.17; Arras Mem., Pas-de-Calais; Age 37; Son of Mr. and Mrs.G.Wooff of Bracknell, Berkshire; Husband of Ethel S.Wooff of Offham Road, West Malling, Kent.*

3242. WOOLER, Albert Stanley; B: Clayton, Sussex; E: Hurstpierpoint, Sussex; Pte. G 1078; K: 7.7.16; Thiepval Mem., Somme; Age 21; Son of Mrs. Abigail Wooler of Whitelands Cottage, Keymer, Sussex.

3243. WORTH, Lewes Peter; B: Brighton; E: Hove; Cpl. G 152; K: 4.8.15; Houplines Com. Cem. Ext., Nord; Age 24; Son of Mr. and Mrs.Worth of 42, Mighell Street, Brighton.*

3244. WRAPSON, William; B: Brighton; E: Brighton; Pte. G 8617; K: 8.7.16; Thiepval Mem., Somme.

3245. WRIGHT, Ernest Victor; B: Brighton; E: Chichester; Pte. L 10046; W: 10.8.15; Bailleul Com. Cem. Ext., Nord; Age 20; Son of John Owen and Frances Caroline Wright of 50, Elder Street, Brighton.*

3246. WRIGHT, George Henry; B: Barnacle, Warwickshire; E: Coventry; Pte. G 20498; K: 3.5.17; Arras Mem., Pas-de-Calais; Age 25; Son of George and Mary Ann Wright of Top Road, Barnacle.

3247. WRIGHT, John Armer; Lt.; M.C.; K: 18.9.18; Epehy Wood Farm Cem., Epehy, Somme; Age 24; Son of Mr.I and Mary Bessie Tomalin of "Peverell", Mill Road, Worthing; Shot as a result of German treachery (see page 231).

8th Battalion

A

3248. ABLEY, John Thomas; B: Bethnal Green, London; E: Bethnal Green; Pte. G 23753; K: 14.5.18; Ribemont Com. Cem. Ext., Somme; Age 19; Son of Benjamin and Sarah Abley of 15, Wennington Road, Bow, London; Killed while improving a trench.

3249. ADDISON, Frank; 2nd Lt.; W: 22.3.16; Corbie Com. Cem., Somme; Age 23; Son of Richard James and Anne Addison of 85, Ramsden Street, Barrow-in-Furness; Died at No.1 Casualty Clearing Station.*

3250. ADSETT, Ernest; B: Stopham, Sussex; E: Petworth, Sussex; Pte. G 4287; K: 14.7.16; Thiepval Mem., Somme; Brother, Arthur, serving with the 7th Battalion was also killed, also has no known grave, and is also commemorated on the Thiepval Memorial (see 2189).

3251. ALLEN, Albert John; B: Brighton; E: Brighton; Pte. G 17668; K: 13.8.18; Vis-en-Artois Mem., Haucourt, Pas-de-Calais.

3252. ALLEN, Frederick Charles; B: Wiston, Sussex; E:

Brighton; Pte. G 522; K: 9.5.18; Warloy-Baillon Com. Cem. Ext., Somme; Son of Thomas Allen of Hole Street, Wiston.

3253. ALLWRIGHT, Albert Edward; B: Bexley Heath, London; E: Hove; Pte. G 1986; W: 15.7.16, La Neuville Brit. Cem., Somme; Age 19; Son of Ernest and Emily Allwright of 15, Vale Road, Portslade, Sussex.

3254. ANDREWS, George John; B: Bitterne, Hampshire; E: Hove; Pte. G 2056; K: 14.7.16; Thiepval Mem., Somme.

3255. ARMSTRONG, Thomas; B: Bridgeton, Lanarkshire; E: Bridgeton; Pte. G 7275; W: 12.5.18; Pernois Brit. Cem., Somme; Age 24; Son of Thomas and Elizabeth Armstrong of Bridgeton; Died at Casualty Clearing Station, Pernois.*

B

3256. BAILEY, Horace; B: Hackney, London; E: London; L/Cpl. G 2491; W: 23.10.17; Mendinghem Mil. Cem. (Bel.); Age 20; Son of T.R. and Mary Bailey of 38, Leswin Road, Stoke Newington, London.

3257. BAINES, Frederick; B: Pirton, Hertfordshire; E: Pirton; Pte. G 15609; K: 23.10.18; Highland Cem., Le Cateau, Nord.

3258. BAKER, Frederick; B: Poplar, London; E: London; Pte. G 2327; W: 31.10.18; Maurois Com. Cem., Nord; Age 21; Son of Mr. and Mrs.N.M.Baker of 14, Swanscombe Street, Canning Town, London.

3259. BAKER, Henry James; B: Southease, Sussex; E: Lewes; Pte. G 2243; K: 21.3.18; Pozieres Mem., Somme; Age 24; Son of Henry and Mary E.Baker of The Post Office, Rodmell, Sussex.

3260. BANKS, William Henry; B: Preston, Sussex; E: Lewes; Pte. G 2228; K: 7.2.16; Albert Com. Cem. Ext., Somme; Son of John and Sarah Banks of Barcombe, Sussex; Husband of Eleanor Banks of 30, Brunswick Place, Hove.*

3261. BANNISTER, William; B: East Grinstead, Sussex; E: Chichester; L/Cpl. G 1600; D: 16.7.17; Étaples Mil. Cem., Pas-de-Calais; Age 30; Son of Edward and Martha Rhoda Bannister of Forest Row, Sussex; Husband of Helen Emily Maria Bannister of 57, St. Mark's Street, Heaton, Newcastle-on-Tyne; Died at Military Hospital, Étaples.

3262. BAYTON, Belcher; B: Kingston-on-Thames; E: Kingston-on-Thames; Pte. G 1740; K: 1.7.16; Dive Copse Brit. Cem., Somme.

3263. BERRY, William John; B: East Grinstead, Sussex; E: Brighton; Pte. G 6820; W: 20.2.17; Dernancourt Com. Cem. Ext., Somme; Age 25; Son of William John and Emily Berry of 162, London Road, East Grinstead.

3264. BISH, Walter; B: Blackheath, London; E: Brighton; Pte. G 2843; K: 1.10.16; Blighty Valley Cem., Somme; Age 27; Son of Mrs.Sarah Howick of Langham Lane, Godalming, Surrey.

3265. BISHOP, George William; B: Brighton; E: Brighton; Pte. G 1903; W at Home: 3.8.16; Brighton (Extra-

Mural) Borough Cem., Sussex (UK); Age 20; Son of Matthew and Elizabeth Bishop of 32, George Street, Brighton.

3266. BLEACH, Percy Andrew; B: Nuthurst, Sussex; E: Hove; Pte. G 1985; K: 8.9.17; Duhallow A.D.S. Cem. (Bel.); Son of James Bleach of Mid Lavant, Sussex.

3267. BOND, Harry George; B: Chichester; E: Southampton; Pte. G 14296; W: 12.12.17; Dozinghem Mil. Cem (Bel.); Son of Mary Ann Bond of 34, High Street, Chichester.*

3268. BOURNE, Alfred Henry; B: Nuthurst, Sussex; E: Horsham, Sussex; Pte. G 1822; K: 13.5.17; St.Martin Calvaire Brit. Cem., Pas-de-Calais; Killed while sleeping in the Hindenburg Line.

3269. BOWLES, Frederick; B: Hastings; E: Hastings; L/ Sgt. G 1722; K: 22.9.17; Duhallow A.D.S. Cem. (Bel.); Age 27; Son of Mr. and Mrs.Bowles of 57, Paynton Road, St.Leonards-on-Sea, Sussex.

3270. BOWLING, Thomas Frederick; B: Poplar, London; E: Eastbourne; Sgt. GS 2275; Dickebusch New Mil. Cem. Ext. (Bel.); Age 23; Husband of Charlotte Mary Greenhill King, formerly Bowling, of 27, Beechy Avenue, Eastbourne.* W: 29.6.17.

3271. BOXALL, Frederick Edward; B: Hastings; E: Hastings; Pte. G 2081; K: 1.7.16; Thiepval Mem., Somme.

3272. BOXALL, John; B: Hove; E: Hove; L/Cpl. G 2367; K: 14.10.17; Minty Farm Cem. (Bel.); Son of Mrs.M.A.Boxall of 10, Malvern Street, Hove.

3273. BREACH, William; B: St.John's, Sussex; E: Lewes; Pte. G 2227; W: 25.3.18; Roye New Brit. Cem., Somme; Died at No.50 Casualty Clearing Station, Roye.

3274. BROWN, Alfred James; B: Poplar, London; E: Woolwich, London; Pte. G 23771; D: 24.6.18; Pernois Brit. Cem., Somme; Age 19; Son of Mr. and Mrs.Brown of 77, Royal Hill, Greenwich, London.

3275. BROWN, Cyril Edward; B: Eastbourne; E: Eastbourne; Pte. G 2316; K: 13.9.17; Mendinghem Mil. Cem. (Bel.); Age 22; Son of Mrs.M.J.Saxby of 127, Mount Pleasant Road, Hastings.*

3276. BRYANT, Ernest; B: Rye, Sussex; E: Hastings; Pte. SD 1872; K: 30.3.18; Pozieres Mem., Somme.

3277. BURCHELL, David; B: Nutbourne, Sussex; E: Hove; C.S.M. GS 280; K: 11.9.16; Blighty Valley Cem., Somme.

3278. BURRIDGE, Charles Edward; B: St.Albans, Hertfordshire; E: Hastings; Pte. G 1127; K: 9.5.18; Warloy-Baillon Com. Cem. Ext., Somme; Age 34; Husband of Mrs.M.M.Burridge of 6, Lower Dagnanall Street, St.Albans.

3279. BURTENSHAW, Harold George; B: Wick, Sussex; E: Littlehampton, Sussex; Pte. G 2149; W: 22.4.17; Boulogne Eastern Cem., Pas-de-Calais; Age 25; Son of John and Annie Burtenshaw of 2, May Cottages, Wick.

3280. BUSS, Cyril Victor; B: Dallington, Sussex; E: Eastbourne; Pte. G 2274; W: 30.9.16; Puchevillers Brit. Cem., Somme; Died at Casualty Clearing Station, Puchevillers.

C

3281. CADE, Walter; B: Newcastle-on-Tyne; E: Hurstpierpoint, Sussex; Cpl. G 2682; K: 26.11.17; Duhallow A.D.S. Cem. (Bel.); Age 34; Son of Walter and Alice Cade.

3282. CAESAR, George; B: Farncombe, Surrey; E: Guildford; Sgt. G 2379; M.M.; M.S.M.; K: 7.8.18; Ribemont Com. Cem. Ext., Somme; Age 35; Son of George and Annie Caesar of, 65, Farncombe Street, Farncombe; Husband of Amy J.Caesar of 16, North Street, Farncombe.

3283. CAIGER, Charles; B: Newhaven, Sussex; E: Worthing; L/Cpl. G 1954; K: 13.7.16; Thiepval Mem., Somme; Age 28; Son of Alfred and Ellen R.Caiger of Bersted House, South Bersted, Sussex.

3284. CALVERT, Eric Ruegg; 2nd Lt.; K: 8.8.17; Dickebusch New Mil. Cem. Ext. (Bel.); Age 27; Son of Maud H.Calvert of Whitehall, Nailsworth, Gloucestershire.

3285. CAMPBELL, Islay MacKinnon; Lt.; W: 4.4.18; St.Sever Cem., Rouen, Seine-Maritime; Age 23; Son of Duncan Macalpine Campbell and Anna Graham Campbell of Aberdeen; Served in France with the 1st Battalion London Scottish 1914-1915 and in Egypt with the 1st/1st Sussex Yeomanry 1916-1917.

3286. CARE, Albert William; B: Brookland, Kent; E: Dover; Pte. G 14487; W: 30.4.18; Sains-du-Nord Com. Cem., Nord; Age 25; Son of William and Ellen Care of Brook House, Fairfield, Brookland.

3287. CASTLE, Christopher Stephen; B: St.Matthew's, Sussex; E: Hastings; Pte. G 2187; K: 13.9.17; Duhallow A.D.S. Cem. (Bel.); Age 22; Son of James and Edith Castle of 64, Alexandra Road, St.Leonards-on-Sea.*

3288. CATER, Walter Henry; B: Ashford, Middlesex; 2nd Lt.; W: 16.8.18; St.Sever Cem., Rouen, Seine-Maritime; Age 23; Son of Walter and Lavenia Maud Cater of Bridge Street, St.Ives, Huntingdonshire; Accidentally wounded.*

3289. CHALLEN, Arthur George; B: Angmering, Sussex; E: Chichester; L/Cpl. G 2438; K: 18.6.16; Bronfay Farm Mil. Cem., Somme.

3290. CHANDLER, James; B: West Wittering, Sussex; E: Chichester; Pte. G 1750; W: 25.8.15; Mericourt-L'Abbé Com. Cem. Ext., Somme; Age 21; Son of J. W. and Sarah Chandler of West Wittering; Wounded 24.8.15 and the Battalion's first casualty.

3291. CHANT, Harry; B: Angmering, Sussex; E: Chichester; Pte. G 1745; K: 6.4.18; Boves West Com. Cem. Ext., Somme; Age 23; Son of George and Charlone Rebecca Chant of 22, Chalk's Cottages, Angmering; Killed during enemy air raid.

3292. CHASE, A.A.; Lt. Col.; D.S.O.; W: 11.3.17; Aveluy Com. Cem., Somme; Wounded by shell fire in the front line at 5.00pm on 10.3.17; Brought back but died next day at No.45 Casualty Clearing Station; Buried at 5.30pm on 11.3.17 with full military honours.*

3293. COBBY, Joseph; B: Pulborough, Sussex; E: Worthing; Pte. G 5693; W: 13.5.17; Warlincourt Halte Brit. Cem., Pas-de-Calais.

3294. COLES, Frank Cecil; B: West Chiltington, Sussex; E: Worthing; Pte. G 2422; K: 23.10.18; Highland Cem., Le Cateau, Nord.

3295. COLLINS, Henry; B: Terwick Common, Sussex; E: Rogate, Sussex; Pte. G 1739; W: 31.7.17; Bedford House Cem. No.2 (Bel.).

3296. COMBER, Frederick John; B: West Hoathly, Sussex; E: Chichester; Pte. G 2713; W: 30.6.16; St.Pierre Cem., Amiens, Somme.

3297. COOMBS, Henry; B: Finsbury, London; E: London; Pte. G 2050; K: 14.7.16; Thiepval Mem., Somme; Age 19; Son of Henry and Annie Coombs of 25, Allen's Buildings, Leonard Street, Finsbury.

3298. CORNWALL, Alfred; B: Warbleton, Sussex; E: Eastbourne; L/Cpl. G 2281; K: 9.5.18; Warloy-Baillon Com. Cem. Ext., Somme; Age 29; Son of John and Harriett A.Cornwall of Heathfield, Sussex.

3299. CORNWALL, Percy; B: Heathfiled, Sussex; E: Eastbourne; L/Cpl. G 2259; K: 6.9.17; Duhallow A.D.S. Cem. (Bel.); Age 24; Son of William H. and Ruth Cornwall of Down Oaks Cottage, Westfield, Sussex.

3300. COTTINGHAM, Frederick Samuel; B: Chorley, Sussex; E: Chichester; Pte. G 2521; K: 1.7.16; Thiepval Mem., Somme; Age 25; Son of Mr. and Mrs.W.Cottingham of The Potteries, South Common, Chailey, Sussex.*

3301. COURT, Percy John; B: Burgess Hill, Sussex; E: Hurstpierpoint, Sussex; Cpl. G 2701; K: 1.7.16; Thiepval Mem., Somme; Age 24; Son of Percy and Catherine Louise Court of 145, London Road, Burgess Hill.

3302. COUSINS, Frederick Thomas; B: Nash, Surrey; E: Haywards Heath, Sussex; Pte. G 2753; K: 23.3.18; Chauny Com. Cem. Brit. Ext., Aisne.

3303. COWSTICK, Frederick; B: Hove; E: Hove; Pte. G 2369; W: 23.9.17; Dozinghem Mil. Cem. (Bel.); Age 20; Son of Samuel and Elizabeth Cowstick of 124, Cowper Street, Hove.

3304. CROUCHER, Albert; B: Cuckfield, Sussex; E: Cuckfield; Pte. G 2664; K: 14.7.16; Thiepval Mem., Somme.

D

3305. DARAGON, William; B: Mitcham, Surrey; E: Croydon; L/Cpl. G 20328; K: 5.9.17; Tyne Cot Mem. (Bel.).

3306. DAUGHTRY, John; B: Storrington, Sussex; E: Worthing; L/Cpl. G 2424; M.M.; K: 1.10.16; Thiepval Mem., Somme.

3307. DAVEY, Ernest; B: Wineham, Sussex; E: Horsham, Sussex; Pte. G 2398; K: 12.4.17; Arras Mem., Pas-de-Calais; Age 28; Son of Edwin and Clara Davey of Jessop's Cottages, Ashurst, Sussex.*

— DELANEY, William (an Alias – see Dunn (3312).

3308. DIPLOCK, Horace Reginald; B: Hove; E: Brighton; Sgt. L 9685; M.M. K: 8.9.17; Duhallow A.D.S. Cem.

(Bel.); Age 23; Son of Alfred and Annie Diplock of 8, Connaught Road, Hove.

3309. DOBSON, George William; B: Peterborough; E: London; Pte. G 4658; W: 31.7.17; Bouzincourt Ridge Cem., Somme; Age 22; Son of William and Annie Dobson of 15, Charles Street, Peterborough.

3310. DOIDGE, George Charles; B: Eastbourne; E: Eastbourne; Pte. G 2258; K: 5.5.17; St.Martin Calvaire Brit. Cem., Pas-de-Calais.

3311. DUDMAN, Frank; B: Easebourne, Sussex; E: Midhurst, Sussex; Cpl. G 2738; K: 22.9.17; Duhallow A.D.S. Cem. (Bel.); Age 22; Son of John and Harriet Dudman of Upper Vining, Easebourne.*

3312. DUNN, William M.; B: Busby, Lanarkshire; E: Glasgow; Cpl. G 2738; K: 1.6.17; Sunken Road Cem., Boisleux-St.Marc., Pas-de-Calais; Age 26; Son of Dennis and Mary McLaughlin Dunn of 122, Main Street, Bridgetori, Glasgow; Served under the alias Delaney.

3313. DUNSTER, Reginald Ernest; B: Woodchurch, Kent; E: Tunbridge Wells; Pte. G 8160; W: 29.11.16; St.Sever Cem. Ext., Rouen, Seine-Maritime; Age 30; Son of John A. and Jane Dunster of The Green, Woodchurch.

3314. DURRANT, Arthur Reginald; B: Eastbourne; E: Eastbourne; Pte. G 2282; K: 14.7.16; Thiepval Mem., Somme; Age 20; Son of William and Carlione Durrant of 8, St.Leonards Palace, Eastbourne.

3315. DUTTON, Geoffrey; 2nd Lt.; W: 8.9.17; Dozinghem Mil. Cem. (Bel.); Age 22; Son of Alfred Henry and Annie Alice Dutton of "Alpha", Llanishen, Cardiff; Previously served with the 3rd/5th Queens in Galipoli.

3316. DYER, Albert Henry; B: Stratford, London; E: London; L/Cpl. G 2513; K: 1.7.16; Dantzig Alley Brit. Cem., Somme; Age 23; Son of Charles E. and Harriet Dyer of 123, Ridge Street, Watford, Hertfordshire.

E

3317. EDGAR, William; B: Glasgow; E: Glasgow; Pte. G 7258; K: 23.12.15; Albert Com. Cem. Ext., Somme; Age 42; Son of William Edgar of 22, Carstait Street, Bridgeton, Glasgow; Husband of Susan Edgar of 15, McDougall Street, Parkhead, Glasgow.

3318. EDWARDS, Charles; B: Rudgwick, Sussex; E: Petworth, Sussex; Pte. G 2774; W: 31.7.17; Lijssenthoek Mil. Cem. (Bel.).

3319. EDWARDS, Sidney Arthur; B: Kingsland, Suffolk; E: Lowestoft; Pte. G 11216; K: 24.9.18; Vis-en-Artois Mem., Haucourt, Pas-de-Calais.

3320. ELSEY, Harry; B: Horsted Keynes, Sussex; E: Brighton; Pte. G 16019; W: 1.6.18; Ribemont Com. Cem. Ext., Somme.

F

3321. FARRANT, Percy Luther; B: Framfield, Sussex; E: Eastbourne; Pte. SD 1590; W: 9.5.18; Montigny Com. Cem., Somme; Age 23; Son of Luther and

Alice Elizabeth Farrant of 8, Junction Street, Polegate, Sussex.*

3322. FIELD, John; B: Wick, Sussex; E: Worthing; Pte. G 2168; W: 13.5.17; Mont Huon Mil. Cem., Seine-Maritime; Age 26; Son of John and Ellen Field of Wick.*

3323. FORD, Charles Edward; B: Lindfield, Sussex; E: Horsham, Sussex; Pte. G 2390; K: 13.7.16; Thiepval Mem., Somme; Age 31; Son of Mrs.Emily Ford of 12, Albert Cottages, Sunte Avenue, Haywards Heath, Sussex; Husband of Daisy Ford. *

3324. FORD, Walter David; B: Alciston, Sussex; E: Lewes; Pte. G 2592; W: 26.1.16; Meulte Mil. Cem., Somme; Age 28; Son of Daniel and Louisa Ford of 18, Swingate Cottages, West Firle, Sussex.

3325. FORSTER; P.J.; B: –; E: –; Pte. – 36668; K: 17.8.18; Glageon Com. Cem., Nord.

3326. FOSTER, Alfred David; 2nd Lt.; M.C.; K: 5.5.17; St.Martin Calvaire Brit. Cem., Pas-de-Calais; Age 24; Son of Mrs.Magdalena Foster, formerly Wolffenstein, of 1a, Neville Park, Tunbridge Wells, and the late Leopold Wolffenstein.

3327. FOWLER, Harold; B: Rawtenstall, Lancashire; E: Chatham, Kent; Pte. G 23432; W: 20.10.17; Mendinghem Mil. Cem. (Bel.); Age 19; Son of John and Alice Fowler of 7, St.Paul's Road, Blackpool.

3328. FREEMAN, William Percy; B: Winchelsea, Sussex; E: Rye, Sussex; Pte. G 2096; K: 1.7.16; Thiepval Mem., Somme.

G

3329. GABELL, Leonard; B: Battersea, London; E: London; Pte. G 2027; K: 14.7.16; Thiepval Mem., Somme.

3330. GANE, Edwin Gordon; B: Limehouse, London; E: London; Pte. G 2034; K: 21.3.18; Pozieres Mem., Somme.

3331. GASSON, Charles Alfred; B: – ; E: Horsham, Sussex; Pte. G 893; K: 1.7.16; Thiepval Mem., Somme; Age 19; Son of Mrs.Sarah Annie Gasson of 58, High Street, Rusthall, Tunbridge Wells.

3332. GAULT, Harry William; B: Bradfield Combust, Suffolk; E: Bury St.Edmunds, Suffolk; Pte. G 14266; K: 25.9.17; Duhallow A.D.S. Cem. (Bel.).

3333. GIBSON, George; B: Cuckfield, Sussex; E: Haywards Heath, Sussex; Pte. G 2779; W: 14.7.16; Peronne Road Cem., Maricourt, Somme.

3334. GODLEY, Charles Henry; B: Burwash, Sussex; E: Hurst Green, Sussex; Pte. G 6367; K: 16.10.17; Minty Farm Cem. (Bel.).

3335. GOODSELL, Frederick; B: Ewhurst, Sussex; E: Hastings; Pte. G 2202; K: 14.7.16; Thiepval Mem., Somme.*

3336. GOODSELL, Richard; B: Westfield, Sussex; E: Rye, Sussex; Pte. G 2531; K: 31.7.17; Ypres (Menin Gate) Mem. (Bel.).

3337. GORE, Sidney George; B: Sittingbourne, Kent; E: London; Pte. G 2029; W: 10.10.18; Roisel Com. Cem. Ext., Somme.

3338. GOVER, Robert John; B: Leytonstone, London; E: Leytonstone; Pte. G 23735; K: 23.10.18; Highland Cem., Le Cateau, Nord; Age 19; Son of Mary Ann Elizabeth Gover of 4, Leyton High Road, Stratford, London.

3339. GREENSHIELDS, Archibald; B: Portsmouth; E: Chichester; L/Cpl. G 4496; K: 8.9.17; Duhallow A.D.S. Cem. (Bel.).

H

3340. HALFORD, Henry; B: Oxton, Nottinghamshire; E: Nottingham; L/Cpl. G 374; K: 6.9.17; Track "X" Cem. (Bel.).

3341. HAMMER, George Conrad; B: Hornsey, London; E: London; Pte. G 20401; K: 25.9.17; Tyne Cot Mem. (Bel.).

3342. HARBOUR, George Albert Richard; B: Stanmer, Sussex; E: Hurstpierpoint, Sussex; D: 1.4.18; St.Sever Cem. Ext., Rouen, Seine-Maritime.

3343. HART, John; B: Sydney, New Brunswick, Canada; E: Glasgow; Pte. G 7064; K: 14.7.16; Thiepval Mem., Somme.

3344. HATCHETT, Ernest; B: Clerkenwell, London; E: London; L/Cpl. G 2338; W: 22.9.15; Becourt Mil. Cem., Somme; Age 21; Son of Leonard John and Louisa Hatchett of Town Road, Lower Edmonton, London; Bullet wound.

3345. HAYWARD, John Edward Thomas; B: Cuckfield, Sussex; E: Cuckfield; Pte. G 2448; K: 23.10.18; Pommereuil Brit. Cem., Nord; Age 32; Son of John Edward and Eliza Hayward of Cuckfield.

3346. HEAP, John; B: Cloughfold, Lancashire; E: Bacup; Pte. G 5947; K: 4.11.16; Thiepval Mem., Somme; Age 19; Son of Mr. and Mrs.A.A.Heap of 3, Baron Street, Cloughfold.

3347. HENLEY, Charles Frederick; B: Bromley-by-Bow, London; E: Hove; Sgt. G 2000; D: 24.11.15; Ste.Marie Cem., Le Havre, Seine-Maritime; Age 23; Son of Charles William and Annie Henley of Portslade, Sussex; Died of erysipelas.

3348. HILL, Alfred James; B: East Grinstead, Sussex; E: Chichester; Cpl. G 2669; K: 1.6.17; Sunken Road Cem., Boisleux-St.Marc, Pas-depCalais; Age 23; Son of James and Jane Hill of Acacia Cottage, Felbridge, Sussex.

3349. HILL, Edward Arundel; Maj.; K: 26.10.18; Villers-Bretonneux Mil. Cem., Somme.

3350. HODGES, Alfred James; B: Newick, Sussex; E: Eastbourne; Pte. G 1924; K: 23.10.18; Highland Cem., Le Cateau, Nord.

3351. HUMPHREY, Albert George; B: Hadlow Down, Sussex; E: Eastbourne; Pte. G 6412; K: 5.9.17; Duhallow A.D.S. Cem. (Bel.); Age 21; Son of Jabez and Mary Jane Humphrey of Summer Hill Lodge, Five Ashes, Sussex.

3352. HURN, Percy; B: Battersea, London; E: London; Pte. G 2016; K: 14.7.16; Ovillers Mil. Cem., Somme.

J

3353. JAMES, William James; B: Bethnal Green, London; E: East Ham, London; Pte. G 20081; K: 8.9.17; Duhallow A.D.S. Cem. (Bel.).

3354. JEAL, Harry; B: Upper Beabush, Sussex; E: Horsham, Sussex; Pte. G 1776; K: 14.7.16; Thiepval Mem., Somme; Age 22; Son of Mrs.Jane Jeal of Tilgate Row, Crawley, Sussex.

K

3355. KEEBLE, Philip John; B: Bethnal Green, London; E: London; Cpl. G 2511; K: 5.5.17; St.Martin Calvaire Brit. Cem., Pas-de-Calais; Age 21; Son of Mrs.E.Keeble of 7, New Street, Hackney, London.

3356. KEELEY, James William; B: Heathfield, Sussex; E: Hastings; Pte. G 2535; K: 25.2.17; Aveluy Com. Cem., Somme; Age 21; Son of Mr. and Mrs.J.Keeley of Sparks Cottage, Northiam, Sussex.*

3357. KEEN, James Raglan; Lt.; W: 19.10.17; Duhallow A.D.S. Cem. (Bel.).

3358. KEMP, Horace Douglas; 2nd Lt.; W at Home: 31.8.16; Oxford (Botley) Cem., Berkshire, (UK); Age 20; Son of Mr. and Mrs.Frederick Kemp of The Laurels, Haywards Heath, Sussex.

3359. KENWARD, Henry John Noel; B: Eastbourne; E: Eastbourne; Cpl. G 2298; K: 14.7.16; Thiepval Mem., Somme; Husband of Annie Louisa Kenward of 7, Cornfield Terrace, Eastbourne.*

3360. KETCHER, Charles Edward; B: Loxwood, Sussex; E: Petworth, Sussex; Pte. G 2756; W: 19.9.16; Puchevillers Brit. Cem., Somme; Age 24; Son of William and Sarah Ann Ketcher of Loxwood; Wounded as a result of a premature shell burst; Died at Casualty Clearing Station, Puchevillers.*

3361. KNAGGS, Frank; B: Dalston, London; E: London; Pte. G 2052; K: 14.7.16; Thiepval Mem., Somme.

3362. KNIGHT, Archibald Ernest; B: Slaugham, Sussex; E: Chichester; Pte. G 832; K: 21.3.18; Pozieres Mem., Somme.

3363. KNIGHT, Charles George; B: Slinfold, Sussex; E: Horsham, Sussex; Pte. G 1794; D at Home: 16.6.17; Horsham (Hills) Cem., Sussex (UK); Age 21; Son of Mrs.Rose Knight.

3364. KNIGHT, Stanley Albert; B: Tarring, Sussex; E: Worthing; Pte. G 2767; K: 14.1.16; Meaulte Mil. Cem., Somme; Age 19; Son of Mrs.Harriet Standing of 2, South View, Durrington, Sussex.*

L

3365. LAKER, Frederick James; B: Southwater, Sussex; E: Horsham, Sussex; Pte. G 1805; K: 12.7.17; Dickebusch New Mil. Cem. Ext. (Bel.); Age 21; Son of James and Elizabeth Laker of 2, Bonfire Hill, Southwater.

3366. LANGRIDGE, Henry James; B: Holloway, London; E: London; Pte. G 2515; W: 17.7.16; St.Sever Cem., Rouen, Seine-Maritime; Age 24; Son of Frederick Charles and Louisa Ellen Langridge of 59, Rensburg Road, Walthamstow, London.*

3367. LEE, Alfred; B: Slaugham, Sussex; E: Horsham; Pte. G 1781; K: 29.10.17; Minty Farm Cem. (Bel.).

3368. LEE, Richard; B: Fishbourne, Sussex; E: Chichester; Pte. G 1763; W: 7.7.16; Daours Com. Cem. Ext., Somme; Age 33; Son of Mary Feast of Clay Lane, Fishbourne; Died at No.34 Casualty Clearing Station.

3369. LELLIOTT, Herbert; B: Ashurst, Sussex; E: Horsham, Sussex; Pte. G 878; K: 1.7.16; Thiepval Mem., Somme.*

3370. LEWIS, George Frederick; B: Fairwarp, Sussex; E: Lewes; Pte. G 2229; W: 22.10.17; Dozinghem Mil. Cem. (Bel.).*

3371. LONGLAND, Charles Henry; B: Brighton; E: Hove; Pte. G 2059; K: 5.7.17; Dickebusch New Mil. Cem. Ext. (Bel.); Son of Mrs.C.H.Longland of 29, Claremont Place, Brighton.

3372. LORD, Norman; B: – ; E: Accrington, Lancashire; Pte. TF 260061; K: 12.7.17; Dickebusch New Mil. Cem. Ext. (Bel.); Age 23; Son of John and Annie Lord of 39, Stanley Terrace, Lion Street, Church, Accrington.*

3373. LOWER, John Henry; B: Eastbourne; E: Eastbourne; Pte. TF 291084; W: 30.3.18; St.Sever Cem. Ext., Rouen, Seine-Maritime; Age 35; Son of John and Eliza Lower of 7, Star Road, Eastbourne.

3374. LYLE, James Cochran; B: – ; E: Glasgow; Pte. G 23317; W: 14.11.17; Dozinghem Mil. Cem. (Bel.).

M

3375. MAC INTYRE, John; B: – ; E: West Street, Glasgow; Pte. G 7270; K: 21.7.17; Dickebusch New Mil. Cem. Ext. (Bel.).*

3376. MANVELL, Ernest James; B: Haywards Heath, Sussex; E: Haywards Heath; Sgt. G 2519; M.M.; K: 23.3.18; Chauny Com. Cem. Brit. Ext., Aisne.

3377. MARSLAND, John; Lt.; K: 23.7.17; Dickebusch New Mil. Cem. Ext. (Bel.).

3378. MARTIN, Luther; B: Ewhurst, Sussex; E: Hastings; Sgt. G 9061; K: 20.11.16; Stump Road Cem., Somme; Age 30; Son of William and Eliza Martin of Ewhurst.

3379. MARTIN, Walter; B: East Grinstead, Sussex; E: Guildford; Pte. G 2380; K: 22.3.18; Pozieres Mem., Somme.

3380. MASKREY, Edward Lewes; B: Shalford, Surrey; E: Kingston-on-Thames; Pte. G 21941; W: 7.4.18; Picquigny Brit. Cem., Somme; Age 40; Son of William and Ann Maskrey of Shalford; Husband of Olive E.Maskrey of 93, Douglas Road, Surbiton, Surrey; Died at No.5 Casualty Clearing Station, Picquigny.

3381. MEADE, Horace Waren; Capt.; K: 13 – 14.7.16; Peronne Road Cem., Maricourt, Somme.

3382. MELLISH, Roland John; B: Hackney, London; E: Stratford, London; Pte. G 23708; W: 24.6.18; Ribemont Com. Cem. Ext., Somme; Age 19; Son of George Ernest and Edith Sarah Mellish of 65, Sophia Road, Leyton, London.

3383. MERRYWEATHER, Ernest John; B: Battersea, London; E: London; Pte. G 2033; W: 14.7.16; Dive Copse Brit. Cem., Somme.

3384. MIDDLETON, Arthur Henry; B: Acton, London; E: Lewes; Pte. G 2251; K: 5.7.17; Dickebusch New Mil. Cem. Ext. (Bel.); Age 21; Son of Richard and

Sarah Middleton of "Lyndhurst", Plumpton Green, Sussex.

3385. MILES, George William; B: Somerby, Leicestershire; E: London; Pte. G 18274; Pozieres Mem., Somme. K: 21.3.18.

3386. MILLER, Henry Harold; B: Walthamstow, London; E: Hastings; Pte. G 18032; W: 24.9.17; Duhallow A.D.S. Cem. (Bel.); Bullet wound to the head.

3387. MILLER, Herbert Thomas; B: Walthamstow, London; E: Walthamstow; Cpl. GS 355; K: 29.1.16; Meaulte Mil. Cem., Somme; Age 39; Son of William and Ellen Martha Miller of Walthamstow; Served in India 1895-98.*

3388. MITCHELL, Arthur; B: Horsham, Sussex; E: Horsham; Pte. G 1786; D: 24.11.18; St.Sever Cem. Ext., Rouen, Seine-Maritime; Age 24; Son of Herbert and Mary King of 24, Burford Road, Horsham.

3389. MOON, Charles Daniel; B: Burwash, Sussex; E: Hastings; Pte. G 2212; K: 20.9.16; Aveluy Com. Cem., Somme; Age 31; Son of Samson and Ellen Moon of Burwash Common; Killed in camp by enemy shelling.

3390. MUIR, John; B: Glasgow; E: Cockspur Street, London; Pte. G 4283; W: 19.11.16; Albert Com. Cem. Ext., Somme; Age 21; Son of John and Marion Muir of 31, Penge Road, Upton Park, London.

3391. MURRAY, Robinson; B: Walker, Northumberland; E: Ashington, Northumberland; L/Cpl. SD 710; W: 18.12.17; Duhallow A.D.S. Cem. (Bel.); Age 33; Husband of Elizabeth Murray of 14, Downies Buildings, Newbiggin-by-the-Sea, Northumberland.*

N

3392. NEWMAN, Henry; B: Billinshurst, Sussex; E: Horsham, Sussex; Pte. G 1783; W: 15.7.16; Corbie Com. Cem. Ext., Somme; Age 23; Son of John Charles and Mary Ann Newman of Oak Villas, Lower Station Road, Billingshurst.

3393. NEWMAN, Richard James; B: Kirkford, Sussex; E: Worthing; Pte. G 2633; K: 5.9.17; Duhallow A.D.S. Cem. (Bel); Age 24; Son of Frederick and Rosina Newman of Gunters Bridge, Petworth, Sussex.

3394. NEWNHAM, Leonard; B: Ditchling, Sussex; E: Hurstpierpoint, Sussex; L/Cpl. G 2670; K: 14.7.16; Bernafay Wood Brit. Cem., Somme.

3395. NORMAN, Percy Harry; B: Tottenham, London; E: London; Pte. G 2492; K: 23.10.18; Highland Cem., Le Cateau, Nord.

3396. NYE, John Edwin; B: Burgess Hill, Sussex; E: Hurstpierpoint, Sussex; L/Cpl. G 2702; W at Home: 6.8.16; Burgess Hill (St.Andrew) Chucrchyard, Sussex (UK); Age 30; Son of Walter and Mary Nye of Burgess Hill; Husband of Anna Greer Penfold, formerly Nye, of Pollard's Farm, Burgess Hill.

O

3397. OSBORN, Walter; B: Shadwell, London; E: Stratford, London; Pte. G 23710; K: 10.5.18;

Ribemont Com. Cem. Ext., Somme; Age 19; Son of J.W. and Caroline Osborn of 12, Coleman Street, Shadwell, London.*

P

3398. PAISH, Alfred Victor; B: Hove; E: Horsham, Sussex; Pte. G 1798; K: 5.5.17; St.Martin Calvaire Brit. Cem., Pas-de-Calais; Age 19; Son of Henry and Mary Ann Paish of 38, Belfast Street, Hove.

3399. PALMER, William Frederick; B: Pyecombe, Sussex; E: Brighton; Pte. GS 338; K: 14.7.16; Thiepval Mem., Somme.*

3400. PARKER, Bertram; B: Woolwich, London; E: Woolwich; Pte. G 10519; W: 15.5.18; Vignacourt Brit. Cem., Somme; Age 21; Son of Elsie Cora Parker of 239, Queen's Road, Peckham, London; Died at No.61 (known as South Midland) Casualty Clearing Station, Vignacourt.

3401. PARKER, Francis Lionel Frank; B: Eastbourne; E: Hove; Pte. G 4004; W: 30.6.17; Lijssenthoek Mil. Cem. (Bel.); Age 28; Son of George and Sarah Jane Parker of 63, Frederick Street, Brighton.

3402. PARKES, Horace; B: Hailsham, Sussex; E: Rye, Sussex; L/Cpl. G 2547; K: 1.7.16; Dantzig Alley Brit. Cem., Somme.*

3403. PARSONS, Arthur James; B: Angmering, Sussex; E: Worthing; Pte. G 5683; K: 14.12.15; Dernancourt Com. Cem., Somme; Age 19; Son of James and Marion Parsons of 23, Chalk's Cottages, Angmering.

3404. PARSONS, George Henry; B: Hove; E: Brighton; Pte. G 6986; W: 13.9.15; Citadel New Mil. Cem., Somme; Died from wounds to right hip and left thigh.

3405. PARSONS, William; B: Hurstpierpoint, Sussex; E: Hurstpierpoint; Pte. G 2650; K: 1.7.16; Thiepval Mem., Somme.

3406. PAVEY, Reginald William; B: Wimbledon, London; E: London; Pte. G 6709; K: 5.7.17; Dickebusch New Mil. Cem. Ext. (Bel.); Son of Mrs.J.M.Pavey of 34, Oxford Street, Putney, London.

3407. PEAKE, Arthur Walter; B: – ; E: Ipswich, Suffolk; Pte. G 14259; W: 10.5.18; Pernois Brit. Cem., Somme; Died at Casulty Clearing Station, Pernois.

3408. PEARSON, Henry Thomas; B: Kennington, London; E: Leyton, London; Pte. G 23725; K: 23.10.18; Highland Cem., Le Cateau, Nord; Age 19; Son of Annie Lee, formerly Pearson, 39, Theobald Road, Leyton, and of Frederick Lee, step-father.

3409. PEERLESS, Cuthbert Henry; 2nd Lt.; D at Home: 12.5.18; Brighton (Extra-Mural) Borough Cem., Sussex (UK); Son of Henry Heathfield Peerless and Amelia Sarah Peerless of 12, Saint James Avenue, Brighton.

3410. PENFOLD, Edgar Thomas; B: Adisham, Kent; E: Bexhill-on-Sea; Pte. G 2548; K: 31.7.17; Ypres (Menin Gate) Mem. (Bel.); Age 23; Son of Isaac and Eliza Penfold of Blooden, Adisham.

3411. PERKINS, James Philip; B: Croydon; E: Croydon; L/Cpl. G 20582; M.M.; K: 23.2.18; Highland Cem., Le Cateau, Nord; Age 21; Son of Henry James and

Annie Alice Perkins of 95, Stanley Road, Croydon; Killed at Le Cateau.

3412. PETTITT, Percy Edward; B: Fairlight, Sussex; E: Hastings; Pte. G 2123; K: 23.10.18; Highland Cem., Le Cateau, Nord; Age 28; Son of Mrs.C.Holland of The Moor, Westfield, Sussex.

3413. POILE, William; B: Northiam, Sussex; E: Hastings; Pte. G 2184; M.M.; W: 12.4.18; St.Sever Com. Ext., Rouen, Seine-Maritime; Age 39; Son of Charles and Georgiana Poile of Well House, Northiam.

3414. PUNNETT, Egbert James; B: Heathfield, Sussex; E: Eastbourne; Pte. G 2269; W: 24.3.18; Noyon New Brit. Cem., Oise; Age 24; Son of Albert and Mary Ann Punnett of Luck's Farm, Punnetts Town Sussex; Died at No.46 Casualty Clearing Station, Noyon.

3415. PUTLAND, Albert; B: Polegate, Sussex; E: Eastbourne; Cpl. G 1930; W at Home: 14.7.16; Hailsham Cem., Sussex (UK; Age 26; Son of Mrs. Caroline Putland of 26, Brook Street, Polegate.

R

3416. REES, Roland; B: Bedfont, Middlesex; E: Eastbourne; Pte. G 1933; K: 14.7.16; Thiepval Mem., Somme; Age 21; Son of Mrs.Olive Susan Rees of 3, Callow Hill, Virginia Water, Surrey.

3417. RICE, Frederick William; B: Slaugham, Sussex; E: Haywards Heath, Sussex; Pte. G 2447; W: 12.5.18; Contay Brit. Cem., Somme; Age 28; Son of Stephen and Mary Rice of Peas Pottage, Sussex.

3418. RICE, William; B: Slaugham, Sussex; E: Haywards Heath, Sussex; G 2444; W: 1.11.16; St.Sever Cem. Ext., Rouen, Seine-Maritime; Age 19; Son of Mr. and Mrs.Richard Rice of 6, Horsham Road, Peas Pottage, Sussex.

3419. RICHARDS, David; B: Nursling, Hampshire; E: Cuckfield, Sussex; Pte. G 2615; W: 13.10.15; Dernancourt Com. Cem., Somme; Bullet wound to the head.

3420. RICHARDS, William; B: Haslemere, Surrey; E: Hinkley. Leicestershire; Pte. G 18275; W: 28.10.16; Contay Brit. Cem., Somme.

3421. RIDGWAY, Herbert; B: Regent's Park, London; E: London; Pte. G 2454; K: 16.7.16; Thiepval Mem., Somme.

3422. ROBERSON, George Lewis; 2nd Lt.; W: 21.3.18; Noyon Brit. Cem., Oise.

3423. ROTHWELL, Charles; B: Portslade, Sussex; E: Hove; Pte. G 2063; K: 14.7.16; Thiepval Mem., Somme.

3424. RUSSELL, David; B: East Hoathly, Sussex; E: Eastbourne; L/Cpl. G 1416; K: 22.9.17; Duhallow A.D.S. Cem. (Bel.); Age 28; Son of George and Emily Russell.*

S

3425. SCOTT, Charles Walter; B: Fairwarp, Sussex; E: Brighton; Pte. G 4078; W: 11.6.17; Étaples Mil. Cem., Pas-de-Calais; Age 22; Son of Mr. and Mrs.H.Scott of Coffe Hall, Duddleswell, Sussex.*

3426. SCOTT, Sydney; B: Uckfield, Sussex; E: Haywards Heath, Sussex; Pte. G 2429; D: 6.6.18; Annois Com. Cem., Aisne.

3427. SCUTT, William George; B: Ifield, Sussex; E: Horsham, Sussex; Pte. G 2389; K: 13.7.16; Thiepval Mem., Somme; Age 21; Son of William and Jane Scutt of County Oak, Crawley, Sussex.

3428. SEAMAN, James William; B: Andover, Hampshire; E: Hurstpierpoint, Sussex; Pte. G 2689; K: 14.7.16; Thiepval Mem., Somme.

3429. SHIPTON, Frederick William; B: Camberwell, London; E: Lambeth, London; Pte. G 10790; K: 8.9.17; Duhallow A.D.S. Cem. (Bel.).

2430. SIMCOX, Enoch; B: Hanley, Staffordshire; E: Brighton; Pte. GS 335; K: 29.1.17; Aveluy Com. Cem., Somme.*

3431. SLATER, John Mackenzie; B: Brockley, Kent; E: Chichester; Pte. L 10589; K: 8.9.17; Duhallow A.D.S. Cem. (Bel.); Age 20; Son of John McKenzie of London.

3432. SMART, Alexander; B: Wisborough Green, Sussex; E: Chichester; Pte. G 2644; K: 13.5.17; St.Martin Calvaire Brit. Cem., Pas-de-Calais; Age 22; Son of George Smart of Wisborough Green; Killed while sleeping in the Hindenburg Line. *

3433. SMITH, Cyril Ralph; B: Cuckfield, Sussex; E: Cuckfield; Pte. G 2663; K: 17.5.16; Carnoy Mil. Cem., Somme; Age 26; Son of Samuel Lewis Smith; Grandson of Mary Smith of 9, Highlands, Cuckfield.

3434. SMITH, James; B: Punnetts Town, Sussex; E: Eastbourne; Pte. G 2297; W: 30.6.16; Daours Com. Cem. Ext., Somme; Died at No.34 Casualty Clearing Station, Daours.

3435. SMITH, Walter; B: Swadlincote, Derbyshire; E: Lewes; Pte. G 1969; W: 2.7.16; Thiepval Mem., Somme.

3436. SPARROW, John; B: Willesden, London; E: Guildford; Pte. G 24880; W: 23.3.18; Noyon New Brit. Cem., Oise; Died at No.46 Casualty Clearing Station, Noyon.

3437. SPARSHOTT, Cyril George; B: Felpham, Sussex; E: Bognor Regis, Sussex; Pte. G 8325; W: 6.8.17; Calais Southern Cem., Pas-de-Calais; Age 29; Son of Joseph and Eliza Kate Sparshott of Compton House, Golf Links Avenue, Felpham; Died at Military Hospital, Calais.

3438. SPENCER, George; B: Derby; E: Leicester; Pte. G 18287; W: 23.10.16; Contay Brit. Cem., Somme; Age 38; Died at Casualty Clearing Station, Contay.

3439. STACEY, Sydney; B: Stedham, Sussex; E: Chichester; L/Cpl. G 1611; W: 14.7.16; La Neuville Brit. Cem., Somme; Age 26; Son of Charles and Edith Stacey of Stedham.*

3440. STANDING, Frederick Peter; B: Petworth, Sussex; E: Chichester; Pte. G 2857; K: 29.10.17; Cement House Cem. (Bel.); Age 22; Son of Mrs.E.Bridgewater, formerly Standing, of Rock

Cottage, Pulborough, Sussex, and the late James Standing.

3441. STEVENS, Charles; B: Hellingly, Sussex; E: Eastbourne; Pte. G 2304; K: 14.7.16; Delville Wood, Cem., Somme.

3442. STEVENS, Harry; B: Tillington, Sussex; E: Hastings; L/Cpl. G 2131; K: 14.7.16; Thiepval Mem., Somme; Age 30; Son of Mrs.S.Courtney.

3443. STEWART, Henry Edward; Capt.; K: 1.6.17; Sunken Road Cem., Boisleux-St.Marc, Pas-de-Calais.

3444. STRAINES, Charles Theodore; B: Hastings; E: Hastings; Pte. G 11381; K: 14.11.17; Minty Farm Cem. (Bel.).*

3445. STRATFORD, Joseph; B: Nettlebed, Oxfordshire; E: Hove; Pte. G 1580; K: 5.9.17; Duhallow A.D.S. Cem. (Bel.); Age 32; Son of Joseph and Hannah Stratford.

3446. STREVENS, Frederick John; B: Portslade, Sussex; E: Hove; Pte. G 2362; K: 5.9.17; Duhallow A.D.S. Cem. (Bel.).*

3447. STRINGER, Ernest; B: Coat, Sussex; E: Horsham, Sussex; Sgt. G 1834; M.M.; K: 14.5.18; Ribemont Com. Cem. Ext., Somme; Age 31; Son of Fredrick Henry and Martha Stringer of Easebourne Road, Midhurst, Sussex.

3448. STRINGER, William; B: Birmingham; E: Birmingham; Pte. G 24184; W at Home: 6.4.18; Handsworth (St.Mary) Churchyard, Warwickshire (UK); Age 41; Husband of Ida Mary Jane Stringer of 8, Church Vale, Handsworth.

3449. STROUD, Thomas; B: Midhurst, Sussex; E: Midhurst; Cpl. G 1635; K: 6.9.17; Tyne Cot Mem. (Bel.).

3450. STUNT, Ernest John; B: Westfield, Sussex; E: Westfield; Pte. G 2105; K: 22.11.16; Bapaume Post Mil. Cem., Somme; Age 22; Son of Lester William and Mary Ann Stunt of Westfield; Husband of Alice Maud May Stunt of 104, Sedlescombe Road North, St.Leonards-on-Sea.

3451. STUNT, Henry; B: Hastings; E: Chichester; L/Cpl. L 11064; K: 14.7.16; Ovillers Mil. Cem., Somme.*

T

2452. TAYLOR, William George; B: Beckenham, Kent; E: Chichester; Pte. G 91; K: 20.9.16; Aveluy Com. Cem., Somme; Killed in camp by enemy shelling.*

3453. THOMPSON, Raymond; B: Crawley, Sussex; E: Horsham, Sussex; Pte. G 1804; K: 5.7.17; Dickebusch New Mil. Cem. Ext. (Bel.); Brother of Mr.P.H.Thompson of 24, Observatory Road, Redhill, Surrey.

3454. TITHERIDGE, Joseph; B: Stoke Newington, London; E: London; Pte. G 4379; K: 31.7.17; Ypres (Menin Gate) Mem. (Bel.).

3455. TOWN, John; B: Worthing; E: Worthing; L/Cpl. G 2152; K: 23.10.18; Highland Cem., Le Cateau, Nord; Age 28; Husband of Ada Louisa Street, formerly Town, of 35, Clifton Road, Worthing.

3456. TRAYHURN, Charles Victor; B: Thornbury, Gloucestershire; E: London; L/Cpl. G 2032; W: 21.7.16; Étaples Mil. Cem., Pas-de-Calais; Age 27; Son of George and Elizabeth Trayburn of The Plain, Thornbury.

3457. TULETT, Frederick; B: Hayes, Kent; E: Hove; Pte. G 1983; W: 16.7.16; Dickebusch New Mil. Cem. Ext. (Bel.); Age 34; Son of Albel and Harriet Tulett of 28, Wolesley Road, Portslade, Sussex.

3458. TURNER, Arthur; B: Little Horsted, Sussex; E: Lewes; Pte. G 21022; W: 27.11.17; Dozingham Mil. Cem. (Bel.); Age 24; Son of Henry and Elizabeth Turner of White Lodge, Roeheath, Chailey, Sussex.

3459. TURNER, John Frank; B: – ; E: Kingston-on-Thames; Sgt. G 20296; M.M.; K: 21.3.18; Pozieres Mem., Somme; Age 26; Son of Mr. and Mrs.J.Turner of 6, Butts Road, Woking, Surrey.

3460. TYLER, Frank; B: Poynings, Sussex; E: Worthing; Cpl. G 2170; W: 9.5.18; Franvillers Com. Cem. Ext., Somme; Age 32; Son of Henry Walter and Caroline Tyler.

V

3461. VENESS, Frederick William; B: Vinehall, Sussex; E: Hastings; Pte. G 2127; K: 8.9.16; Thiepval Mem., Somme.

3462. VENN, William Edward; B: Wisborough Green, Sussex; E: Horsham, Sussex; Pte. G 1780; W: 5.7.17; Bailleul Com. Cem. Ext., Nord; Died at Casualty Clearing Station, Bailleul.

3463. VINCENT, Gideon James; B: Eastbourne; E: Eastbourne; Pte. G 7277; W: 16.7.16; La Neuville Brit. Cem., Somme; Age 21; Son of James Vincent of 119, Whelly Road, Eastbourne.

W

3464. WALKER, William Arthur; B: Leicester; E: Leicester; Pte. G 18283; K: 27.9.16; Thiepval Mem., Somme; Age 24; Son of Mrs.Mary Walker of 14, Victoria Road North, Belgrave, Leicester.*

3465. WARD, Thomas William; B: Dalston, London; E: London; L/Cpl. G 2025; K: 14.7.16; Thiepval Mem., Somme.

3466. WATSON, Joseph; B: Dartford, Kent; E: Eastbourne; Pte. G 2272; K: 1.7.16; Thiepval Mem., Somme.

3467. WEBB, George; B: Bosham, Sussex; E: Worthing; Pte. G 1617; K: 13.7.16; Thiepval Mem., Somme.

3468. WENHAM, Walter Henry; B: Hastings; E: Hastings; Pte. G 3907; K: 1.7.16; Thiepval Mem., Somme; Age 32; Husband of Mary Wenham of 19, The Broadway, Hastings.

3469. WERE, Henry Hawes; B: Birmingham; E: Southport; Pte. G 10092; K: 4.10.16; Authuille Mil. Cem., Somme; Age 32; Son of Henry and Kate Were; Husband of Jennie S.Were of 17, Grosvenor Road, Skegness, Lincolnshire.

3470. WEST, Alfred Thomas; B: Fishergate, Sussex; E: Hove; Pte. G 1993; K: 31.7.17; Ypres (Menin Gate)

Mem. (Bel.); Age 21; Son of Albert Henry West of 11, The Terrace, Fishergate Terrace, Portslade, Sussex.

3471. WHEELER, Leonard Pearl; B: Winchester; E: Westfield, Sussex; Pte. G 2611; W: 21.3.18; Noyon New Brit. Cem., Oise; Age 28; Son of James Albert and Mary Agnes Wheeler of Vale Brook Lodge, Ore, Hastings.

3472. WHIMHURST, Charles William; B: Halton, Sussex; E: Hastings; Pte. G 2210; K: 10.4.16; Carnoy Mil. Cem., Somme; Killed by a rifle bullet.

3473. WHITEHEAD, Frederick Walter; B: Deptford, London; E: Deptford; Pte. G 10241; W: at Home: 5.2.17; Netley Mil. Cem., Hampshire (UK); Age 26; Son of George and Harriett Whitehead of 313, Lower Road, Deptford; Died at Military Hospital, Netley.

3474. WHITTINGTON, Arthur; B: Petworth, Sussex; E: Petworth; L/Cpl. G 9181; K: 20.7.17; Dickebusch New Mil. Cem. Ext. (Bel.); Age 31; Son of Edwin and Jane Whittington of Egremont Terrace, Petworth.

3475. WHITTINGTON, George; B: Ringmer, Sussex; E: Hurstpierpoint, Sussex; Pte. G 2748; K: 21.3.18; Pozieres Mem., Somme.

3476. WHYTE, John Dudley; Capt.; K: 13 – 14.7.16; Peronne Road Com. Cem., Maricourt, Somme.

3477. WILLIAMS, Thomas; B: Ardingly, Sussex; E: Brighton; Pte. G 1902; W: 25.11.16; Warloy-Baillon Com. Cem. Ext., Somme; Age 22; Son of James and Mary Williams of Ardingly.

3478. WILLIS, Edgar Reginald; Lt.; K: 13.-.14.7.16; Peronne Road Com. Cem., Maricourt, Somme.

3479. WILSON, Nicholas John; B: – ; E: Hammersmith, London; Pte. G 23737; K: 23.10.18; Highland Cem., Le Cateau, Nord; Age 19; Son of George H. and Sarah Wilson of 31, Coedcae Street, Grangetown, Cardiff.

3480. WOOD, Richard David; B: Greenwich, London; E: Coventry; Pte. G 18292; W: 1.6.17; Sunken Road Cem., Boisleaux-St.Marc, Pas-de-Calais; Age 29; Son of Richard Abraham and Annie Louise Wood.*

3481. WOODS, Horace; B: Wellingborough, Northamptonshire; E: Northampton; Pte. G 11393; K: 24.4.17; Bully-Grenay Com. Cem. Brit. Ext., Pas-de-Calais.

3482. WORCESTER, Sydney Arthur; B: Nuthurst, Sussex; E: Horsham, Sussex; Pte. G 1813; K: 13.5.17; St.Martin Calvaire Brit. Cem., Pas-de-Calais; Age 28; Son of Walter and Mary Ann Worcester of 8, Thrift Cottages, Monk's Gate, Sussex; Killed while sleeping in the Hindenburg Line.

9th Battalion

A

3483. ADDLINGTON, A.James Walter; B: Camberwell, London; E: Battersea, London; Pte. G 9950; K:

26.8.17; Voormezeele Enclosures No.1 and 2, (Bel.).*

3484. ADSETT, William; B: North Chapel, Sussex; E: Petworth, Sussex; Pte. G 15878; K: 3.4.18; Pozieres Mem., Somme.

3485. AGATE, Arthur; B: East Grinstead, Sussex; E: East Grinstead; G 8182; K: 13.4.17; Arras Mem., Pas-de-Calais; Age 32; Son of James William and Millicent Agate of Council Terrace, East Grinstead; Husband of Elizabeth Mary Agate of Gasson's Cottages, Baldwin's Hill, East Grinstead.

3486. AGATE, James; B: Brighton; E: Brighton; Pte. L 9983; K: 10.10.18; St.Aubert Brit. Cem., Nord; Age 25; Son of George and Lois Ann Agate of 65, Newmarket Road, Brighton.*

3487. ALLFREY, Charles; B: Brighton; E: Brighton; Pte. G 3226; K: 18.8.16; Thiepval Mem., Somme.

3488. ALMOND, George Edward; B: Enfield, London; E: Hastings; Pte. G 18170; K: 20.6.17; Oxford Road Cem. (Bel.); Age 22; Son of Frederick John and Emma Almond of 5, The Willows, Sedlescombe Road North, St.Leonards-on-Sea.*

3489. AMBROSE, George Edward; B: Hackney, London; E: Putney, London; Pte. G 16544; K: 4.11.18; Villers-Pol Com. Cem. Ext., Nord; Age 21; Son of Mr. and Mrs.E.J.Ambrose of 67, Mercers Road, Tufnell Park, London.

3490. ANDREWS, William James; B: Lambeth, London; E: London; Pte. G 7885; K: 28.9.15; Loos Mem., Pas-de-Calais.

3491. ANSON, Percival A; B: Liverpool; E: Liverpool; Pte. G 19253; K: 31.5.18; Bully-Grenay Com. Cem. Brit. Ext., Pas-de-Calais; Age 19; Son of Henry and Jessie Anson of 55, Main Street, Buffalo, U.S.A.

3492. ARMITAGE, Douglas William; 2nd Lt.; K: 25.9.15; Loos Mem., Pas-de-Calais; Son of Mr. and Mrs.J.Amiel Armitage of "Netherwood", St.Helens Park, Hastings.

3493. ARNOLD, Stephen Edwin Arthur; B: Earlsfield, Surrey; E: Wandsworth, London; Pte. G 24373; K: 4.11.18; Villers-Pol Com. Cem. Ext., Nord; Age 19; Son of Stephen John and Harriet Elizabeth Arnold of 9, Groton Road, Earlsfield.

3495. ARUNDEL, James Edward; B: Eastbourne; E: Brighton; Pte. G 16616; K: 13.4.17; Ypres (Menin Gate) Mem. (Bel.).

3496. ASHBURNER, Henry; B: Liverpool; E: Liverpool; Pte. G 19257; K: 4.11.18; Cross Roads Cem., Nord.

3497. ASHENDEN, Frank; B: – ; E: Hastings; Pte. G 16494; W: 8.6.17; Mendinghem Mil. Cem. (Bel.); Age 41; Husband of Ellen Frances Ashenden of 6, Tillingham Villas, Rye, Sussex.

3498. ASHFORD, Sidney Patrick; B: Manchester; E: Manchester; Pte. G 19258; W: 1.6.18; Pernes Brit. Cem., Pas-de-Calais; Age 19; Son of Frank and Letitia Ashford of Manchester; Gassed.*

3499. ATFIELD, G.J; B: – ; E: – ; Pte. G 5177; W at Home: 25.10.18; Storrington (St.Mary) Churchyard, Sussex (UK); Age 36; Son of George James Atfield;

Husband of Sarah Atfield of 1, Elder Tree Cottage, Durrington, Sussex.

3500. ATHERALL, Percy; B: Withyham, Sussex; E: Tunbridge Wells; Pte. S 2129; W: 18.6.16; Bailleul Com. Cem. Ext., Nord; Died at Casualty Clearing Station, Bailleul.

3501. ATTWOOD, James; B: Hoxton, London; E: Brighton; Pte. G 16206; K: 15.2.18; Hargicourt Brit. Cem., Aisne; Age 23; Son of William and Julia Alice Attwood of 18, Balmes Road, Southgate Road, London.*

3502. AVIS, David; B: Rottingdean, Sussex; E: Brighton; Pte. G 3634; K: 25.9.15; Loos Mem., Pas-de-Calais.

3503. AYLARD, Percy Frederick; B: Ticehurst, Sussex; E: Warley, Essex; Pte. G 12938; K: 11.6.17; Ypres (Menin Gate) Mem. (Bel.); Age 22; Son of Mrs.H.E.Aylard of Church Street, Ticehurst.

B

3504. BAILEY, Ernest Spencer; B: Stanton, Suffolk; E: Bury St.Edmunds, Suffolk; Pte. G 19095; K: 4.11.18; Vis-en-Artois Mem., Haucourt, Pas-de-Calais.

3505. BAILEY, William Bridger; B: – ; E: Chichester; Sgt. G 6339; M.M.; K: 23.3.18; Pozieres Mem., Somme.

3506. BAKER, Archibald John; B: Brondesbury, London; E: Hove; Pte. G 16548; K: 12.4.17; Ypres (Menin Gate) Mem. (Bel.); Age 39; Son of Amelia H.Baker; Husband of Caroline Ann Nightingale Baker.

3507. BAKER, Ernest; B: Danehill, Sussex; E: Haywards Heath, Sussex; Pte. SD 3830; W: 13.4.17; Bethune Town Cem., Pas-de-Calais; Age 20; Son of Walter and Mary Baker of Brook Cottage Danehill.

3508. BAKER, Henry; B: Brighton; E: Brighton; Pte. G 3491; K: 25.9.15; Loos Mem., Pas-de-Calais.

3509. BAKER, Wallace James; B: Maidstone; E: Fulham, London; Pte. G 5970; K: 28.9.15; Loos Mem., Pas-de-Calais.

3510. BALCOMBE, Edward John William; B: Hastings; E: Haywards Heath, Sussex; Pte. L 10727; K: 13.4.17; Canadian Cem. No.2, Pas-de-Calais.

3511. BALDOCK, Charles; B: Purley, Surrey; E: Haywards Heath, Sussex; Pte. G 3258; K: 25.9.15; Loos Mem., Pas-de-Calais; Age 20; Son of Edward and Annie Baldock of 15, West View, Lindfield, Sussex.

3512. BALDOCK, Lewis John; B: Penshurst, Kent; E: Uckfield, Sussex; Pte. G 3571; K: 25.9.15; Loos Mem., Pas-de-Calais.

3513. BALDWIN, Reuben; B: Ticehurst, Sussex; E: Hastings; Pte. G 4136; K: 3.4.18; Pozieres Mem., Somme.

3514. BANHAM, Joseph John; Maj; K: 27.3.18; Pozieres Mem., Somme; Age 31; Son of Joseph John and Julia Banham of The Meadows, Crawley, Sussex; Killed near Meharicourt.

3515. BANKS, Joseph Ernest; B: Bromley, Kent; E: Bromley; Pte. G 12611; K: 27.3.17; Aix-Noulette Com. Cem. Ext., Pas-de-Calais; Age 36; Son of Joseph Banks of 13, Palace Road, Bromley; Husband of Sarah Ann Banks of 27, Palace Road, Bromley.

3516. BANKS, Robert Frank; B: Hampstead, London; E: Brighton; Pte. G 3603; W: 20.2.16; Lijssenthoek Mil. Cem. (Bel.); Age 22; Son of T.Banks of 40, Church Road, Hove.

3517. BARBER, Harry; B: Leek, Staffordshire; E: Leek; Pte. G 15150; K: 26.3.18; Pozieres Mem., Somme.

3518. BARKER, Frederick Ernest; B: Bexhill-on-Sea; E: Hastings; Pte. SD 4806; K: 4.11.18; Vis-en-Artois Mem., Haucourt, Pas-de-Calais.

3519. BARLOW, James; B: Birkenhead; E: Liverpool; Pte. G 9425; K: 16.7.16; St.Quentin Cabaret Mil. Cem. (Bel.).

3520. BARNARD, Frederick; B: Christcurch, Sussex; E: Chichester; C.S.M. L 10145; D.C.M.; K: 13.4.17; Arras Mem., Pas-de-Calais.

3521. BARNES, Oswald Spice; B: Battersea, London; E: Westminster; L/Sgt. G 2944; K: 28.9.15; Loos Mem., Pas-de-Calais; Age 21; Son of Thomas and Elizabeth Barnes of "Eastdale", Chapel Lane, Swanage, Dorset; A chorister at Westminster Abbey.

3522. BARRATT, Victor; B: St.James, London; E: Lambeth, London; L/Cpl. G 4115; K: 19.8.16; Thiepval Mem., Somme.

3523. BARRETT, George; B: Oldham, Lancashire; E: Oldham; Pte. G 15259; W: 31.5.18; Bully-Grenay Com. Cem. Brit. Ext., Pas-de-Calais; Age 19; Son of William and Elizabeth Hannah Barrett of 7, Church Street, Lees, Lancashire; Gassed.*

2524. BARTLETT, Austin George Henry; B: Compton, Devon; E: Petworth, Sussex; Pte. G 1369; K: 13.2.16; Menin Road South Mil. Cem. (Bel.); Age 21; Son of John Austin and Emily Jane Bartlett of Blandford House, Lower Compton; Killed during front line trench duty at Hooge.

3525. BASSETT, Alfred Thomas; B: Pluckley, Kent; E: Pluckley; Pte. TF 260093; W: 7.8.17; Étaples Mil. Cem., Pas-de-Calais; Age 27; Son of Mr.J. and Mrs.M.Bassett of Brickfield Cottages, Pluckley.

3526. BATEHUP, Henry Stephen; B: Ewhurst, Sussex; E: Hastings; L/Cpl. G 16350; K: 22.3.18; Pozieres Mem., Somme; Age 24; Son of Amos and Frances Batehup of Knight's Cottage, Pett, Sussex; Husband of Nellie Rosabel Batehup of 16, Grove Road, Hastings.*

3527. BAXENDALE, Ernest; B: Farnworth, Lancashire; E: Bolton, Lancashire; Pte. G 19260; W: 7.6.18; Pernes Brit. Cem., Pas-de-Calais; Age 19; Son of William and Elizabeth Baxendale of Farnworth.

3528. BAZELEY, Roland Arthur; 2nd Lt,; K: 28.1.16; Ypres (Menin Gate) Mem. (Bel.); Killed in the front line by a sniper at Zouave Wood, Ypres Salient.

3529. BECK, Harold Richard; B: Lower Kingswood, Surrey; E: Brighton; Pte. G 3047; K: 27.3.17; Aix-Noulette Com. Cem. Ext., Pas-de-Calais; Age 24; Son of Richard and Isabella Beck of 77, Brockley Rise, Forest Hill, London.*

3530. BEDFORD, Sydney; B: Worthing; E: London;

Pte. G 7927; K: 31.8.16; London Cem. and Ext., Somme.

3531. BEECHING, Walter Ernest; B: Littlehampton, Sussex; E: Littlehampton; Pte. G 3787; W: 7.10.15; St.Sever Cem., Rouen, Seine-Maritime; Age 19; Son of Walter and Minnie Beeching of 28, Gloucester Road, Littlehampton.*

3532. BEETON, Maurice Henry Reginald; B: Wandsworth, London; E: Bognor Regis, Sussex; Pte. G 7233; K: 18.8.16; Thiepval Mem., Somme; Age 20; Son of Walter and Luise Beeton.*

3533. BELL, Henry William; B: Paddington, London; E: Kilburn, London; Pte. G 4187; K: 28.9.15; Loos Mem., Pas-de-Calais.

3534. BENNETT, Charles Leonard; B: Woolwich, London; E: Woolwich; Pte. G 14393; K: 13.4.17; Aix-Noulette Com. Cem. Ext., Pas-de-Calais; Age 19; Son of Samuel James and Mary Elizabeth Bennett of 16, Prospect Row, Woolwich.

3535. BERRIMAN, Frederick; B: Chichester; E: Chichester; Pte. S 2306; K: 17.5.16; Ration Farm (La Plus Douve) Annexe (Bel.); Son of Mrs.P.Berriman of 14, St.Pancras Place, Chichester.

3536. BERWICK, Edward; B: Irthlingborough, Northamptonshire; E: Wellingborough, Northamptonshire; Pte. G 18181; W: 21.6.17; Dickebusch New Mil. Cem. Ext. (Bel.); Age 20; Son of Arthur and Martha Ann Berwick of Northampton Road, Yardley-Hastings, Northamptonshire.

3537. BETTS, Reginald Crane; B: Paston, Norfolk; E: Petworth, Sussex; Pte. G 4213; K: 28.6.16; Kemmel Chateau Mil. Cem. (Bel.); Age 20; Son of William and Esther Betts of Paston.

3538. BIGG, Edward Samuel; B: – ; E: Hove; L/Cpl. G 3055; K: 28.9.15; Loos Mem., Pas-de-Calais; Age 27; Son of Edward James and Emma Elizabeth Bigg of 81, Whippingham Road, Brighton.

3539. BILLINGTON, Roy Hemer; B: Liverpool; E: Liverpool; Pte. G 19363; W: 10.6.18; Pernes Brit. Cem., Pas-de-Calais; Age 19; Son of Thomas Herbert and Sarah Maud Billington of 12, Ronald Street, Old Swan, Liverpool; Died at Casualty Clearing Station, Pernes.

3540. BIRCHMORE, George James; B: Wimbledon, London; E: Horsham, Sussex; Pte. G 3108; W: 24.4.16; Bailleul Com. Cem. Ext., Nord; Age 21; Son of William and Sarah Birchmore of "The Haven", Billingshurst, Sussex; Died at Casualty Clearing Station, Bailleul.

3541. BIRD, William James; B: Bromley, Kent; E: Bromley; Cpl. GS 540; K: 13.4.17; Arras Mem., Pas-de-Calais.

3542. BIRTLE, John James; B: Pyecombe, Sussex; E: Brighton; Pte. G 3451; W: 18.6.16; Bailleul Com. Cem. Ext., Nord; Died at Casualty Clearing Station, Bailleul, Nord.*

3543. BISHOP, Alexander; B: Burwash, Sussex; E: Battle, Sussex; Pte. G 3380; K: 25.9.15; Loos Mem., Pas-de-Calais; Age 25; Son of Thomas and Hannah Bishop of Coombero Farm, Dallington, Sussex

3544. BISHOP, Arthur Walter; 2nd Lt.; K: 21.3.1918; Roisel Com. Cem. Ext., Somme.

3545. BLACKWELL, Ernest Albert; B: Crudwell, Wiltshire; E: Midhurst, Sussex; Pte. G 1620; K: 14.3.16; White House Cem. (Bel.).

3546. BLADES, William; B: Yarwell, Northamptonshire; E: Northampton; Pte. G 7834; K: 25.9.15; Loos Mem., Pas-de-Calais.

3547. BLATTMAN, Horace Charles; B: Kentish Town, London; E: St.Paul's Churchyard, London; Pte. G 4231; K: 28.9.15; Loos Mem., Pas-de-Calais; Age 23; Son of Mr.A.Z. and Mrs.J.Blattman of 50, Mileard Crescent, Hastings.

3548. BLEACH, Charles; B: Cowfold, Sussex; E: Chichester; Pte. G 9590; W: 5.2.17; Étaples Mil. Cem., Pas-de-Calais; Died at Miliary Hospital, Étaples.

3549. BLISS, Charles James; Sgt. G 5427; M.M.; K: 4.11.18; Cross Roads Cem., Nord.

3550. BLUNDEN, Ernest William; B: Sompting, Sussex; E: Worthing; Pte. G 7021; W: 18.6.16; Bailleul Com. Cem. Ext., Nord; Age 28; Son of Edwin and Mary Jane Blunden of 82, Broadwater Street, Broadwater, Sussex; Died at Casualty Clearing Station, Bailleul.

3551. BLUNT, Ernest; B: Thakenham, Sussex; E: Worthing; Pte. G 3697; K: 28.9.15; Loos Mem., Pas-de-Calais; Age 27; Brother of Albert Blunt of Railway Stables, Haywards Heath, Sussex.

3552. BOND, William Charles Henry; B: Eastbourne; E: Eastbourne; Pte. G 5739; K: 18.8.16; London Cem. and Ext., Somme; Age 26; Son of William and Katherine Bond of 125, Ashford Road, Eastbourne.

3553. BONES, Harold William; B: Crowborough, Sussex; E: Brighton; Pte. G 5669; K: 18.8.16; Thiepval Mem., Somme.

3554. BONIFACE, Harry; B: Brighton; E: Brighton; L/Cpl. G 3228; W: 10.8.17; Calais Eastern Cem., Pas-de-Calais; Age 41; Died at Military Hospital, Calais.*

3555. BONIFACE, John Charles; B: Chichester; E: Bognor Regis, Sussex; Pte. G 3245; K: 28.9.15; Loos Mem., Pas-de-Calais; Age 17; Son of John and Ada Amy Boniface of 2, Chermside Villas, The Broadway, Summersdale, Sussex.

3556. BONIFACE, Murray James; B: Brighton; E: Brighton; L/Sgt. G 1545; K: 18.8.16; Thiepval Mem., Somme; Age 28; Son of Mr. and Mrs.G.Boniface of 19, Kingsbury Road, Brighton; Husband of Rosanna Boniface of 23, Spring Gardens, Brighton.

3557. BOOTHBY, Sydney Edmund; B: Whaley Bridge, Cheshire; E: Stockport, Cheshire; Pte. G 19089; K: 3.6.18; Bully-Grenay Com. Cem. Brit. Ext., Pas-de-Calais; Age 19; Son of Mark and Margaret Boothby of 72, Richardson Street, Stockport.*

3558. BOTTOMS, Robert; B: Hetton-le-Hole, County Durham; E: South Shields, County Durham; Pte. G 6086; K: 13.4.17; Arras Mem., Pas-de-Calais; Age 26; Son of Robert and Catherine Bottoms of 14, Eccleston Road, South Shields; His brother, Thomas, also fell.

3559. BOUCHER, James William; B: Fulham, London; E: Southwark, London; Pte. G 8021; K: 31.8.16; Thiepval Mem., Somme.

3560. BOURNE, Charles William; B: Islington, London; E: London; Sgt. G 19945; K: 11.6.17; Ypres (Menin Gate) Mem. (Bel.).

3561. BOWDEN, Charles Herbert; B: Erith, Kent; E: Maidstone; Pte. G 12994; K: 13.9.18; Maroc Brit. Cem., Nord.

3562. BOWDEN, Harry Victor; B: Eastbourne; E: Eastbourne; Pte. G 8497; W: 2.2.17; Bethune Town Cem., Pas-de-Calais; Age 21; Son of John and Alma H.Bowden of 39, Green Street, Eastbourne; Died at No.33 Casualty Clearing Station, Bethune.

3563. BOWLER, Frank Hubert; B: Henfield, Sussex; E: Hove; Pte. G 5238; K: 28.6.16; Kemmel Chateau Mil. Cem. (Bel.); Age 24; Son of Frank and Charlotte Bowler of 3, Croft Villas, Henfield.*

3564. BOWLEY, William Charles; B: West Grinstead, Sussex; E: Haywards Heath; Pte. G 3391; K: 28.9.15; Loos Mem., Pas-de-Calais; Age 20; Son of Charlie and Elizabeth Bowley of Church Street, Cuckfield, Sussex.

3565. BRACEGIRDLE, Thomas; B: Stockport, Cheshire; E: Manchester; Pte. G 19264; K: 9.10.18; Vis-en-Artois Mem., Haucourt, Pas-de-Calais.

3566. BRACKPOOL, Oliver; B: Worth, Sussex; E: East Grinstead, Sussex; L/Sgt. G 3200; K: 27.7.17; Ypres (Menin Gate) Mem. (Bel.); Age 20; Son of Isable Brackpool of 17, Albert Road, Southwick, Sussex.

3567. BRADLEY, William Henry; B: Armley, Yorkshire; E: Hastings; Pte. G 7398; K: 13.4.17; Ypres (Menin Gate) Mem. (Bel.).

3568. BRADSHAW, James; B: Battersea, London; E: Brighton; Pte. G 4251; K: 18.8.16; Thiepval Mem., Somme; Age 33; Son of Frank Bradshaw of Sheffield; Husband of Mary Bradshaw of "Croftcot", Bellingdon, Buckinghamshire.

3569. BRAY, Frank Hugh; 2nd Lt.; K: 28.5.18; Maroc Brit. Cem, Nord; Age 19; Son of Frank Douglas and Sybil Bray of King Street, Hammersmith, London; Accidentally killed while on patrol.

3570. BRICE, Reginald; B: Spalding, Lincolnshire; E: Brighton; Sgt. G 3478; K: 14.2.16; Menin Road South Mil. Cem. (Bel.); Killed in the front line at Hooge.

3571. BRIDGER, Ernest James; B: St.Paul's, Sussex; E: Guildford; Pte. G 3342; K: 14.2.16; Menin Road South Mil. Cem. (Bel.); Age 24; Son of Ernest J. and Sarah Bridger of 3, Russell Street, Chichester.

3572. BRIDGER, George; B: East Grinstead, Sussex; E: Chichester; Pte. G 4214; K: 17.6.16; Ration Farm (La Plus Douve) Annexe (Bel.); Son of Mrs.E.Bridger of 4, Manor Cottages, Felpham, Sussex.

3573. BRIGHT, Kenneth Coldwell; 2nd Lt.; K: 18.8.16; Thiepval Mem., Somme; Killed by machine gun fire while leading his men across No-Man's-Land to reinforce an attack at Guillemont.

3574. BRISTOW, Charles; B: Chailey, Sussex; E: Lewes; Pte. G 1654; K: 3.9.17; La Clytte Mil. Cem. (Bel.); Age 25; Son of Henry and Emma Bristow of Chailey; Husband of Emily Kate Bristow of Ashleigh Grange, The Leas, Westcliff-on-Sea, Essex.

3575. BROMLEY, Laurence Frederick William; B: Croydon; E: Croydon; Pte. G 8113; W: 7.6.17; Brandhoek Mil. Cem. (Bel.); Age 20; Son of Mrs.L.K.Bromley of Crown Inn, Wickham Road, Shirley, Surrey; Gassed.

3576. BROOKER, Ernest; B: West Grinstead, Sussex; E: Worthing; Pte. G 3235; K: 25.9.15; Loos Mem., Pas-de-Calais; Age 19; Son of Harry and Fanny Brooker of Pict's Cottages, Cowfold, Sussex.

3577. BROOKFIELD, Joseph Henry; B: – ; E: Woolwich, London; Pte. G 4221; W: 30.6.16; Bailleul Com. Cem. Ext., Nord; Age 22; Son of Jane Elizabeth Wells, formerly, Brookfield.*

3578. BROOMAN, James; B: Crowborough, Sussex; E: Warley, Essex; Pte. G 12748; K: 11.3.17; Aix-Noulette Com. Cem., Pas-de-Calais; Age 22; Son of Thomas and Emily Brooman of 7, Pleasant View Cottages, Crowborough. .

3579. BROWN, Albert; B: Croydon; E: Brighton; Pte. S 2241; W: 28.1.16; Lijssenthoek Mil. Cem. (Bel.); Age 18; Son of Charles and Clara Brown of 24, Essex Street, Brighton.*

3580. BROWN, Benjamin; B: St.John's, Surrey; E: Brighton; Pte. SD 3013; K: 5.6.16; Ration Farm (La Plus Douve) Annexe (Bel.); Age 21; Son of Mr. and Mrs.Brown of 24, Grove Street, Brighton.

3581. BROWN, Frank; B: Pembury, Kent; E: Tunbridge Wells; Pte. G 12432; D at Home: 23.6.18; Southborough Cem., Kent (UK); Age 32; Husband of Florence V.Brown of 46, Nursery Road, High Brooms, Kent; Died from influenza.

3582. BROWN, Henry; B: Walworth, London; E: Southwark, London; Pte. G 5086; K: 18.8.16; Thiepval Mem., Somme; Age 37; Son of Mrs.Sarah Brown of 365, Earlsfield Road, Earlsfield, Surrey.

3583. BROWN, Robert Robinson; B: Richmond, Yorkshire; E: Brighton; Pte. G 7578; K: 12.2.16; Menin Road South Mil. Cem. (Bel.); Age 36; Son of Anna Brown of Richmond; Killed during front line trench duty at Hooge.*

3584. BROWNING, Charles; B: Horsted Keynes, Sussex; E: Haywards Heath, Sussex; Pte . G 3592; K: 26.9.15; Loos Mem., Pas-de-Calais; Age 22; Son of Albert and Eliza Browning of Ash Grove Cottage, Horsted Keynes.

3585. BRUNTON, Robert; B: Hove; E: Hove; Pte. SD 5215; K: 13.4.17; Ypres (Menin Gate) Mem. (Bel.).

3586. BRYANT, Harry; B: Hastings; E: Hastings; Pte. G 16486; K: 3.8.17; Ypres Reservoir Cem. (Bel.).*

3587. BRYANT, James; B: Marylebone, London; E: Marylebone; Pte. G 14416; K: 3.8.17; Ypres (Menin Gate) Mem. (Bel.).

3588. BUCK, Ernest; B: Widcombe, Somerset; E: Cardiff; Pte. G 16816; K: 4.8.17; Hooge Crater Cem. (Bel.).

3589. BUCKLAND, Alfred John; B: Wick, Sussex; E: Arundel, Sussex; L/Cpl. L 8049; K: 13.4.17; Ypres (Menin Gate) Mem. (Bel.).

3590. BULLETT, Harry; B: Hessett, Suffolk; E: Bury St.Edmunds, Suffolk; Pte. G 15089; K: 4.11.18; Cross Roads Cem., Nord.

3591. BURCHETT, Sidney; B: East Grinstead, Sussex; E: Tunbridge Wells; Pte. G 5411; K: 8.8.17; Ypres (Menin Gate) Mem. (Bel.).

3592. BURDEN, Percy George; B: Brighton; E: Hove; Pte. G 16497; K: 11.6.17; Ypres (Menin Gate) Mem. (Bel.).

3593. BURGESS, William John; B: Hove; E: Hove; Pte. L 10740; K: 1.1.17; Philosophe Brit. Cem., Mazingarbe, Pas-de-Calais; Son of Mrs.S.Burgess of 101, Shirley Street, Hove.

3594. BURNIER, Richard; Lt.; W: 21.2.18; Tincourt New Brit. Cem., Somme; Age 20; Son of Mrs.C.H.Burnier of 18, Hurst Road, Eastbourne; Died at Casualty Clearing Station, Tincourt, from wounds received at Hargicourt while acting as Brigade Intelligence Officer.

3595. BURRELL, Ernest; B: Worthing; E: Brighton; Pte. G 3517; K: 6.3.16; Menin Road South Mil. Cem. (Bel.); Age 19; Son of Charles Alfred Burrell of Mill House, Fishbourne, Sussex.

3596. BURT, Albert Harry; B: Hastings; E: Woolwich, London; Pte. G 12883; K: 28.3.17; Aix-Noulette Com. Cem. Ext., Pas-de-Calais; Age 21; Son of Thomas Henry and Mary Ann Burt of 83, Winchelsea Road, Hastings.*

3597. BURTENSHAW, Charles Edward; B: Eastbourne; E: Eastbourne; Pte. G 24457; K: 22.3.18; Pozieres Mem., Somme; Age 20; Son of Mrs.Minnie Burtenshaw.

3598. BURTON, Herbert; B: Herne Hill, London; E: Steeple Morden, Hertfordshire; Pte. G 11191; K: 29.8.16; Thiepval Mem., Somme.

3599. BURTON, William; B: Preston, Sussex; E: Brighton; Pte. GS 542; K: 25.9.15; Loos Mem., Pas-de-Calais.

3600. BUTCHER, William Henry Ashby; B: Stone, Kent; E: Woolwich, London; Pte. G 6001; K: 8.3.16; Ypres (Menin Gate) Mem. (Bel.); Age 22; Son of Daniel and Emily Esther Butcher of Hedge Place, Stone.

3601. BUTLER, George; B: Larkfield, Kent; E: Guildford; Sgt. G 3728; K: 31.8.16; Thiepval Mem., Somme.

3602. BUTTON, Stanley; B: Coddenham, Suffolk; E: Ipswich, Suffolk; Pte. SD 5562; K: 11.6.17; Ypres (Menin Gate) Mem. (Bel.); Age 23; Son of George Button of Coddenham; Husband of Mary May Abbott, formerly Button, of Bridge Street, Needham Market, Suffolk.

C

3603. CADMAN, Stanley Charles; B: East Ham, London; E: Putney, London; Pte. G 16559; W: 15.4.17; Aix-Noulette Com. Cem. Ext., Pas-de-Calais; Age 20; Son of Mr. and Mrs.F.S.Cadman of 274, Shrewsbury Road, East Ham.

3604. CALLCUT, Thomas George; B: Plaistow, London; E: Southwark, London; Pte. G 5792; W: 18.6.16; Bailleul Com. Cem. Ext., Nord; Son of Thomas and Mrs.E.B.Callcut of 58, Walker Street, Limehouse, London; Died at Casualty Clearing Station, Bailleul, from the effects of gas.

3605. CALLOW, Albert Edward; B: Hove; E: Brighton; Pte. G 3633; K: 25.9.15; Loos Mem., Pas-de-Calais.

3606. CALWAY, Frederick; B: Gloucester; E: Brighton; Pte. G 3421; K: 14.2.16; Menin Road South Mil. Cem. (Bel.); Age 21; Son of Mr. and Mrs.Calway of 4, Newmarket Terrace, Brighton; Killed during front line trench durty at Hooge.

3607. CANNON, Frank; B: Mitcham, Surrey; E: Croydon; Pte. G 5330; K: 24.4.17; Menin Road South Mil. Cem. (Bel.).*

3608. CARD, Charles; B: Brighton; E: Brighton; Pte. SD 5357; K: 10.12.16; Philosophe Brit. Cem., Mazingarbe, Pas-de-Calais; Age 25; Son of Mrs. Card of 35, Lewes Street, Brighton.

3609. CARELESS, Reginald; B: Tunbridge Wells; E: Tonbridge; Pte. G 19120; W: 1.7.18; Pernes Brit Cem., Pas-de-Calais; Age 19; Son of John and Elizabeth C.Careless of Tunbridge Wells; His father, John Careless, Pte. 5101 Royal West Kent Regiment, was killed-in-action 22.7.16.

3610. CARPENTER, Arthur Bourne; B: Woodchurch, Kent; E: Brighton; Pte. G 3714; K: 28.9.15; Loos Mem., Pas-de-Calais; Age 25; Son of G.E. and Fanny Carpenter of The Limes, Cranbrook, Kent.

3611. CARPENTER, James Samuel; B: Brighton; E: Brighton; Pte. G 16567; W: 4.8.17; The Huts Cem. (Bel.); Age 21; Son of W.A. and A.Carpenter of 54, Southampton Street, Brighton.

3612. CARR, Edgar Arthur; B: Melvin, Worcestershire; E: Horsham, Sussex; Pte. G 3113; K: 4.9.16; Thiepval Mem., Somme.

3613. CARTER, Albert; 2nd Lt.; K: 12.4.17; Arras Mem., Pas-de-Calais; Age 27; Husband of Ellen Carter of 43, Lansdown Road, Dalston, London.

3614. CARTER, Percival Charles; B: – ; E: Elswick, Northumberland; Pte. G 18820; W: 15.10.18; Étaples Mil. Cem., Pas-de-Calais; Age 38; Son of Mrs.A.Tompkins, formerly Carter, of 36, Colls Road, Peckham, London; Died at Military Hospital, Étaples.

3615. CASTELL, Alfred; B: Liverpool; E: Liverpool; Pte. G 19112; W: 6.11.18; Awoingt Brit. Cem., Nord; Died at Casualty Clearing Station, Awoingt.

3616. CHAMBERS, Alfred Henry; B: Grantham, Lincolnshire; E: Wisbech, Cambridgeshire; Pte. G 20561; K: 25.3.18; Pozieres Mem., Somme.

3617. CHANDLER, William Thomas; B: Brighton; E: Brighton; Pte. G 3280; K: 25.9.15; Loos Mem., Pas-de-Calais; Age 24; Son of Charles T. and Priscilla Chandler of 21, Loder Road, Brighton.

3618. CHANNING, Lionel; B: Hove; E: Hove; Pte. G 3262; K: 25.9.15; Loos Mem., Pas-de-Calais.

3619. CHARLTON, Frank; B: Tunbridge Wells; E: Eastbourne; Pte. G 16555; Died at Home: 16.8.17; Tunbridge Wells Cem., Kent (UK).*

3620. CHEESEMAN, Edmund; B: East Peckham, Kent; E: Tonbridge; Pte. G 11945; W: 28.3.18; Le Cateau Mil. Cem., Nord; Age 21; Son of Amos and Mercy Cheeseman of The Freehold, East Peckham.

3621. CHEESMAN, Jonathan; B: Brighton; E: Hastings; Pte. SD 3552; K: 15.2.17; Philosophe Brit. Cem., Mazingarbe, Pas-de-Calais; Age 39; Son of Edwin and Harriet Cheesman of Brighton; Husband of Blanche L.Parker, formerly Cheesman ,of Errington, Vancouver Island, British Columbia, Canada.*

3622. CHEPMELL, William Dobree; Lt.; K: 12.4.17; Aix-Noulette Com. Cem. Ext., Pas-de-Calais; Age 21; Son of Charles and Mary Chepmell.

3623. CHILDS, Frank; B: Hertford Heath, Hertfordshire; E: Hertford; Pte. G 19111; K: 29.7.18; Bully-Grenay Com. Cem. Brit. Ext., Pas-de-Calais; Age 20; Son of Frank and Emily Childs of Hertford Heath.

3624. CHRISTIAN, Arthur James; B: Eastbourne; E: Brighton; Pte. G 16591; K: 13.4.17; Arras Mem., Pas-de-Calais.

3625. CHURCHER, William John; B: St.Mary's, Glamorgan; E: Cardiff; L/Cpl. G 3500; K: 21.2.16; New Irish Farm Cem. (Bel.); Age 25; Son of Mr.J.C. and Mrs.E.Churcher of Cardiff; Husband of Mary Evans, formerly Churcher, of 10, Stafford Road, Grangetown, Cardiff.

3626. CLARK, George Henry; B: All Saints, Hampshire; E: Shepherd's Bush, London; Pte. GS 687; K: 13.2.16; Tyne Cot Cem. (Bel.); Age 35; Son of George Henry Clark; Killed during front line trench duty at Hooge.

3627. CLARKE, Herbert George; B: Ilford, Essex; E: Eastbourne; Pte. G 6449; K: 24.10.17; Roisel Com. Cem. Ext., Somme; Age 23; Son of Herbert and Elizabeth Mary Clarke of 102, Longstone Road, Eastbourne.

3628. CLARKE, J. Gay; Capt.; K: 27.9.15; Loos Mem., Pas-de-Calais.

3629. CLEMENTS, Alfred; B: Desborough, Northamptonshire; E: Market Harborough, Leicestershire; Pte. G 7835; K: 25.9.15; Loos Mem., Pas-de-Calais.

3630. CLIFT, Alber Oliver; B: Wimbledon, London; E: Hounslow, London; Pte. G 16089; K: 21.3.18; London Cem. and Ext., Somme; Son of Mary Ellen Clift.

3631. CLYBOUW, Reginald Mordant; B: Leytonstone, London; E: Brighton; Cpl. TF 265162; K: 28.3.18; Pozieres Mem., Somme. *

3632. COLDMAN, James; B: Preston, Sussex; E: Brighton; Pte. SD 3168; K: 25.9.15; Loos Mem., Pas-de-Calais; Age 17; Son of Arthur and Rose Coldman of 43, Arnold Street, Brighton.

3633. COLE, Frederick James; B: Hove; E: Brighton; Pte. G 17681; K: 23.8.18; Hesbecourt Com. Cem., Somme; Age 26; Son of Mr.J.Cole of 58, Westbourne Street, Hove.

3634. COLEMAN, John; B: Uckfield, Sussex; E: Uckfield; Pte. G 12327; K: 12.8.17; Hooge Crater Cem. (Bel.); Age 32; Son of John and Annie Coleman of Uckfield; Husband of Emily Coleman of 22, Mayfield Grove, Long Eaton, Nottinghamshire.*

3635. COLEMAN, Sidney Charles; B: Hastings; E: Hastings; Sgt. G 4105; W: 10.6.17; Mendinghem Mil. Cem. (Bel.); Age 21; Son of Mr. and Mrs.Cole of Tidleway, Hastings; Husband of Mabel Elsie Coleman of 13, Old Church Road, Hastings.*

3636. COLLINS, John Charles; B: Hastings; E: Hastings; Cpl. G 16476; K: 13.4.17; Ypres (Menin Gate) Mem. (Bel.); Age 33; Son of John Collins of 95, Bohemia Road, Hastings; Husband of Alice C.Collins of Pashley Farm, Ninfield, Sussex.

3637. COLVIN, Leonard; B: Hastings; E: Warley, Essex; Pte. G 12936; K: 13.4.17; Arras Mem., Pas-de-Calais.

3638. COMBER, Charles Fredrick; B: Brighton; E: Hove; Pte. G 3151; W: 22.8.16; La Neuville Brit. Cem., Somme; Son of Alice and George Comber of 12, Temple Street, Brighton.

3639. COMPTON, Guy; 2nd Lt.; K: 26.7.17; Ypres (Menin Gate) Mem. (Bel.).*

3640. CONSTABLE, Robert George; B: Brighton; E: Brighton; Pte. G 2980; W: 18.6.16; Bailleul Com. Cem. Ext., Nord; Age 28; Son of Mr. and Mrs. Robert Constable of Brighton; Husband of Dorothy E.Constable of 2, Ewhurst Road, Brighton; Died at Casualty Clearing Station, Bailleul.

3641. COOK, Charles Albert; B: Worth, Sussex; E: Horsham, Sussex; Pte. G 8886; K: 18.8.16; Thiepval Mem., Somme.

3642. COOK, Henry; B: Edenbridge, Kent; E: Horsham, Sussex; Pte. G 3734; K: 25.9.15; Loos Mem., Pas-de-Calais.

3643. COOK, James; B: Shoreditch, London; E: Camberwell, London; Pte. G 18803; K: 21.3.18; Pozieres Mem., Somme.

3644. COOTE, Frank; B: Dial Post, Sussex; E: Horsham, Sussex; Pte. G 17800; K: 27.3.18; Pozieres Mem., Somme; Age 23; Son of William and Eliza Coote of 59, Worthing Road, West Grinstead, Sussex.

3645. COPPARD, Arthur Richard; B: Patcham, Sussex; E: Hove; Pte. SD 3545; W: 3.5.18; Berlin South-Western Cem. (G); Age 21; Son of Frederick and Ruth J.Coppard of 5, Drove Cottages, Patcham; Died while Prisoner of War.

3646. COPPARD, Frederick; B: Horsham, Sussex; E: Horsham; Pte. G 17796; K: 4.11.18; Villers-Pol Com. Cem. Ext., Nord; Husband of Mrs.A.E.Coppard of 5, Upper Market Street, Hove.

3647. CORNFORD, James William; B: Patcham, Sussex; E: Hove; Pte. SD 3545; K: 18.8.16; Thiepval Mem., Somme.*

3648. CORNOCK, Arthur Henry; B: Hove; E: Hove; Pte. G 16102; K: 13.4.17; Lievin Com. Cem. Ext., Pas-de-Calais; Age 34; Son of John Capel Cornock and Charlotte Johnson Cornock of Hove.

3649. CORNWALL, George; B: Walberton, Sussex; E: Brighton; L/Cpl. G 18185; K: 3.8.17; Ypres Reservoir Cem. (Bel.); Age 20; Son of John and

Harriett A.Cornwall of 2, Fir Tree Cottage, Punnnett's Town, Sussex.

3650. COTTAM, Christopher; B: Barton-on-Irwell, Lancashire; E: Manchester; Pte. G 9575; W: 22.4.16; Bailleul Com. Cem. Ext., Nord; Died at Casualty Clearing Station, Bailleul.

3651. COWDREY, George Edward; B: Portslade, Sussex; E: Brighton; Pte. G 5007; K: 14.2.16; Menin Road South Mil. Cem. (Bel.).

3652. COZENS, William Henry; B: Fulham, London; E: Harrow, Middlesex; Pte. G 19948; K: 21.3.18; Pozieres Mem., Somme.

3653. COZENS, William James; B: Beeding, Sussex; E: Worthing; L/Cpl. G 3306; W: 9.10.16; Barlin Com. Cem., Pas-de-Calais.

3654. CRONSHAW, Joseph Allan; B: Accrington, Lancashire; E: Manchester; Pte. G 19272; W: 3.11.18; Awoingt Brit. Cem., Nord.

3655. CROSS, William; B: Rock Ferry, Cheshire; E: Birkenhead; Pte. G 5803; K: 11.6.17; Ypres (Menin Gate) Mem. (Bel.); Son of John and Mary Cross of Lunar Street, Rock Ferry.

3656. CROWHURST, Charles James; B: Brighton; E: Chichester; Pte. G 16500; W: 11.12.17; Tincourt New Brit. Cem., Somme; Age 31; Son of James and Mary Crowhurst of Brighton; Husband of Mary Crowhurst of 22, Grantham Road, Brighton.

3657. CUDDINGTON, George Walter; B: Battersea, London; E: Horsham, Sussex; Pte. G 8826; K: 18.8.16; Thiepval Mem., Somme.

3658. CUDDON, Francis Avondale; B: Kensal Rise, London; E: Kilburn, London; Sgt. G 3544; W: 24.6.17; Lijssenthoek Mil. Cem. (Bel.); Age 25; Son of George and Mary Anne Cuddon of 42, Felixstowe Road, Kensal Rise.*

3659. CURTIS, George Edward; B: Angmering, Sussex; E: Chichester; Pte. L 10406; K: 18.8.16; Delville Wood Cem., Somme; Son of William Curtis of Bittlesham Cottage, North Chapel, Sussex.*

D

3660. DACEY, Thomas; B: Brighton; E: Brighton; Pte. G 4830; K: 31.8.16; Thiepval Mem., Somme; Age 34; Son of Michael and Julia Dacey.

3661. DADSWELL, James Edward; B: Hurstpierpoint, Sussex; E: Hurstpierpoint; Pte. G 1161; K: 14.2.16; Menin Road South Mil. Cem. (Bel.).

3662. DALE, George Thomas; B: Eastbourne; E: Eastbourne; Pte. G 14364; K: 2.8.17; Ypres (Menin Gate) Mem. (Bel.); Age 19; Son of Mr.G.T. and Eliza Jane Dale of 58a, Tideswell Road, Eastbourne.

3663. DANCER, Leonard Arthur William; B: Chichester; E: Hastings; Cpl. SD 3333; K: 3.4.18; Rosieres Com. Cem. Ext., Somme; Age 26; Son of Sarah Dancer.

3664. DANN, Arthur George; B: Heathfield, Sussex; E: East Grinstead, Sussex; Pte. G 8225; K: 17.6.16; Ration Farm (La Plus Douve) Annexe (Bel.); Age 20; Son of Mr. and Mrs.H.Dann of Prospect Cottages, Ashurstwood, Sussex.

3665. DANN, Frederick John Edward; B: Burwash, Sussex; E: Hastings; Pte. G 3904; K: 3.6.16; Ration Farm (La Plus Douve) Annexe (Bel.); Son of Mrs.E.Dann of Morden Cottages, Burwash.

3666. DAVID, Alfred; B: Croydon; E: Croydon; Pte. G 20578; K: 25.3.18; Fouquescourt Brit. Cem., Somme; Age 20; Son of Mrs.M.David of 22, Boston Road, Croydon.

3667. DAVID, Thomas; B: Brighton; E: Brighton; Pte. G 5467; K: 25.9.15; Loos Mem., Pas-de-calais; Age 24; Husband of Louisa David of 5, Wellington Place, Brighton.

3668. DAVIS, Charles Henry; B: Oxford Street, London; E: Southwark, London; Pte. G 5344; D: 3.11.18; Berlin South-Western Cem. (G); Age 18; Son of A.R. and Ellen Davis of 19, Empress Street, Walworth, London; Died while a Prisoner of War.

3669. DAWSON, Charles; B: Heywood, Lancashire; E: Bury, Lancashire; Pte. G 19126; K: 4.11.18; Villers-Pol Com Cem. Ext., Nord; Age 19; Son of Charles and Mary Dawson of 43, Agincourt Street, Heywood.

3670. DAWSON, Claude William Little; B: Bootham, Yorkshire; E: Hove; Pte. G 2527; K: 25.9.15; Loos Mem., Pas-de-Calais; Age 20; Son of William Dawson of 26, Keere Street, Lewes, Sussex.

3671. DAWSON, Ernest Thomas; B: Berwick, Sussex; E: Brighton; Pte. G 3481; W: 5.5.16; Dranoutre Mil. Cem. (Bel.).

3672. DAWTREY, William; B: Rogate, Hampshire; E: Chichester; Pte. G 4065; K: 1.10.15; Phalempin Com. Cem., Nord.

3673. DAY, John; B: All Souls, Sussex; E: Brighton; Pte. L 7683; K: 17.8.16; Peronne Road Com. Cem., Maricourt, Somme.

3674. DAY, William George; B: Fyzabad, India; E: Chichester; L/Cpl. L 10315; K: 15.5.16; Ration Farm (La Plus Douve) Annexe (Bel.); Age 19; Son of John Thomas and Sally Day of 20, New Road, Ridgewood, Uckfield, Sussex.

3675. DEAKIN, Edward Henry Major; B: Northfleet, Kent; Gravesend, Kent; Pte. G 13087; W: 31.3.18; St.Sever Cem. Ext., Rouen, Seine-Maritime.

3676. DELL, Alfred James; B: Finsbury, London; E: Kingsway, London; L/Cpl. L 10537; D.C.M.; W: 24.3.18; Pozieres Mem., Somme; Age 21; Son of Walter Henry and Grace Dell of 38, Ormond Yard, Bloomsbury, London.

3677. DENNIS, John; B: Eastbourne; E: Eastbourne; Pte. SD 53; K: 6.6.17; Ypres (Menin Gate) Mem. (Bel.); Age 23; Son of Mrs.Dennis of 33, Dudley Road, Eastbourne.

3678. DENTON, Charles George; B: Paddington, London; E: Ealing, London; Sgt. G 20392; K: 4.11.18; Cross Roads Cem., Nord.

3679. DENYER, Frederick Thomas; B: Godalming, Surrey; E: Godalming; L/Cpl. G 3778; K: 13.4.17; Arras Mem., Pas-de-Calais; Age 23; Son of Mrs. Alice Denyer of 39, Manor Road, Farncombe, Surrey.

3680. DE WOLF, George Le Blanch; Lt.; K: 14.2.16; Menin Road South Mil. Cem. (Bel.); Age 36; Son of William Henry and Constance De Wolf of Oxton, Cheshire.

3681. DEXTER, Horace John; B: – ; E: Kettering, Northamptonshire; Pte. G 23259; K: 22.3.18; Pozieres Mem., Somme.

3682. DICKERSON, John William; B: Rye Harbour, Sussex; E: Hastings; Pte. G 6651; D: 26.6.18; Étaples Mil. Cem., Pas-de-calais; Age 27; Son of Frederick and Maria Dickerson; Husband of Mrs.M.Dickerson of 1, South Road, Newhaven; Died at Military Hospital, Étaples.

3683. DICKINSON, William Maurice; B: Wood Green, London; E: Watford, Hertfordshire; Pte. G 19121; K: 4.6.18; Bully-Grenay Com. Cem. Brit. Ext., Pas-de-Calais; Age 19; Son of Thomas James and Alice Dickinson of "Ivor", Station Road, Pinner, Middlesex.

3684. DIMES, Harry; B: – ; E: Andover, Hampshire; Pte. TF 260166; K: 4.11.18 at Wargnies-le-Petit: Villers-Pol Com. Cem. Ext., Nord; Son of Mr.G.Dimes of "Esmeralda", Clarence Road, Fleet, Hampshire.

3685. DIVALL, Charles; B: Brighton; E: Hove; Pte. G 5789; W: 3.10.16; Niederzwehren Cem. (G); Died while a Prisoner of War.

3686. DIVALL, Edward; B: – ; E: Hastings;L/Cpl. G 21713; K: 4.11.18; Cross Roads Cem., Nord; Age 30; Husband of Lilian May Dival of Elphick's Cottage, Burwash, Sussex; This man's original battlefield timber cross is preserved, with others, in the porch of St. Bartholomew's Church, Burwash; The crosses were brought back by Rudyard Kipling who lived at Burwash.

3687. DIX, Sidney Charles; B: Norwich; E: Norwich; Pte. G 11611; K: 3.8.17; Ypres (Menin Gate) Mem. (Bel.).

3688. DODMAN, Albert Richard; B: Worthing; E: Worthing; Pte. G 1513; K: 31.5.18; Bully-Grenay Com. Cem. Brit. Ext., Pas-de-Calais.

3689. DOGGETT, Edward Albert; B: Cossey, Norfolk; E: Norwich; L/Sgt. G 4417; K: 27.3.17; Aix-Noulette Com. Cem. Ext., Pas-de-Calais; Age 34; Son of Edward Doggett of Costessey, Norfolk; Husband of Ellen Susan Doggett of 6, View Terrace, Horn's Lane, Norwich.*

3690. DOWNARD, Frank; B: Burgess Hill, Sussex; E: Brighton; Pte. G 16622; W: 4.2.17; Bethune Town Cem., Pas-de-Calais; Age 16; Son of George W. and Emmaline Downard of 46, West Street, Burgess Hill; Died at No.33 Casualty Clearing Station, Bethune.

3691. DRAY, Archibald Arthur; B: Guildford; E: Guildford; Pte. G 3732; K: 14.2.16; Menin Road South Mil. Cem. (Bel.).*

3692. DRIVER, Benjamin; B: Manchester; E: Manchester; Pte. G 19125; W: 8.11.18; St.Sever Cem. Ext., Rouen, Seine-Maritime; Age 19; Son of John H. and Mary Driver of 45, Windsor Road, Manchester.

3693. DRIVER, William; B: – ; E: Brighton; Pte. G 3621; K: 29.7.17; Ypres (Menin Gate) Mem. (Bel.); Age 34; Son of Mr.C and Mrs.E.Driver of 185, Bear Road, Brighton.

3694. DUNKERLEY, Vernon Arnold; B: Temperley, Cheshire; E: Altrincham, Cheshire; Pte. G 16807; W at Home: 10.5.18; Timperley (Christ Church) Churchyard, Cheshire (UK); Age 29; Son of Zacchaeus and Louisa Dunkerley; Husband of Lilian Ella Dunkerley of 86, Darnley Street, Brook's Bar, Manchester.*

3695. DUNKLEY, William John; B: Camberwell, London; E: Hammersmith, London; L/Cpl. G 3899; K: 11.2.16; Menin Road South Mil. Cem. (Bel.); Age 24; Son of William and Rosetta Dunkley of 60, Jubilee Road, Southsea, Hampshire.

3696. DUNN, John; B: Oldham, Lancashire; E: Oldham; Pte. G 19369; W: 1.6.18; Fosse No.10 Com. Cem. Ext., Pas-de-Calais; Age 19; Son of James and Mary A.Dunn of 15, Overens Street, Oldham.

3697. DUXBURY, William James; B: Colne, Lancashire; E: Nelson, Lancashire; Pte. G 19280; W: 1.6.18; Pernes Brit. Cem., Pas-de-Calais; Age 19; Son of Pickles and Margaret Ann Duxbury of Colne; Gassed.

3698. DYE, Frank Eugene; B: Milcham, Norfolk; E: East Dereham, Norfolk; Pte. G 11952; K: 22.3.18; Pozieres Mem., Somme.

E

3699. EAMES, Joseph; B: Lewes; E: Brighton; Pte. G K: 17.6.16; Ration Farm (La Plus Douve) Annexe (Bel.); Age 19; Son of Joseph and Emily Edith Eames of 47, Ewhurst Road, Brighton.

3700. EASTMAN, Robert John; B: Upper Rodmersham, Kent; E: Sittingbourne, Kent; Pte. G 18847; D: 18.10.18; Hautmont Com. Cem., Nord; Age 20; Son of Charles and Mary Elizabeth Eastman of 4a, Shakespeare Road, Sittingbourne.

3701. EASTWOOD, Horace; B: West Hoathly, Sussex; E: Uckfield, Sussex; Pte. L 7676; W: 29.4.16; Boulogne Eastern Cem., Pas-de-Calais; Died at Military Hospital, Boulogne.

3702. EDWARDS, Harry; B: Hurtmore, Surrey; E: Guildford; Pte. G 3222; K: 25.9.15; Loos Mem., Pas-de-Calais.

3703. ELDRIDGE, Frank; B: Peasmarsh, Sussex; E: Hastings; Pte. G 5437; K: 31.8.16; Thiepval Mem., Somme; Age 24; Husband of Elizabeth H.Glazier, formerly Eldridge, of White Hart Cottage, Guestling, Sussex.

3704. ELLIS, Charles George Payne; B: Somerton, Norfolk; E: Lowestoft; Pte. G 9328; W: 22.6.17; Railway Dugouts Burial Ground (Bel.).

3705. ELLIS, Frank; B: Brighton; E: Brighton; L/Cpl. G 8809; K: 27.3.18; Pozieres Mem., Somme; Age 37; Son of George and Emma Ellis of 8, Exeter Street, Brighton.

3706. EMERY, William; B: Beckham, Norfolk; E: Cromer, Norfolk; Pte. G 9386; K: 4.11.18; Cross Roads Cem., Nord.

3707. ETHERIDGE, Albert James; B: Holmwood, Surrey; E: Haywards Heath, Sussex; Pte. G 3568; W: 7.6.17; Belgian Battery Corner Cem. (Bel.); Age 30; Son of James and Hannah Etheridge of Tudor Cottage, Westcott, Surrey.

3708. EVANS, Laban; B: Netherton, Worcestershire; E: Brighton; Sgt. G 16363; W at Home: 5.5.17; Kingswinford (St.Mary) Churchyard, Staffordshire (UK).

F

3709. FARRANT, John Edwin; B: Camberwell, London; E: Southwark, London; Pte. G 5187; K: 14.2.16; Menin Road South Mil. Cem. (Bel.); Age 31; Son of Nathaniel and Elizabeth Farrant of Folkestone; Husband of Blanche Farrant of 3, Avondale Square, Old Kent Road, London.*

3710. FAULKNER, John Edward; B: Hove; E: Chichester; Pte. TF 203181; W: 12.10.18; Delsaux Farm Cem., Pas-de-Calais; Age 22; Son of Walter and Sarah Faulkner of 18, Byron Street, Hove.

3711. FENNELOW, William; B: Gorefield, Cambridgeshire; E: Norwich; Cpl. G 6684; Ypres (Menin Gate) Mem. (Bel.); Age 21; Son of Mrs.Jane Hutchinson of Fitton End, Gorefield. K: 23.6.17.

3712. FERGUS, James; B: Glasgow; E: Horsham, Sussex; Pte. G 1608; K: 14.2.16; Menin Road South Mil. Cem. (Bel.); Age 20; Son of James Fergus of 51, Holland Park Mews, Holland Park, London.

3713. FIELDWICK, William James; B: Burwash, Sussex; E: Brighton; Pte. G 1344; K: 26.9.15; Loos Mem., Pas-de-Calais; Age 23; Son of William and Martha Fieldwick of Horspits, Burwash.

3714. FINCH, William Lionel; B: Leatherhead, Surrey; E: Worthing; Pte. SD 1683; K: 21.3.18; Pozieres Mem., Somme; Age 21; Son of William Henry and Hannah Finch of 24, Harrow Road, West Worthing.

3715. FINDLAY, Walter; B: Glasgow; E: London; Pte. G 4262; K: 25.9.15; Loos Mem., Pas-de-Calais; Age 31; Son of James and Isabella Morris Findlay of 86, St.Andrew's Drive, Maxwell Park, Glasgow.

3716. FISHER, Harry Albert; B: Aldershot; E: Guildford; Pte. G 4683; K: 30.7.16; Ypres (Menin Gate) Mem. (Bel.); Age 20; Son of James Edward and Annie Fisher of 28, George Road, Farncombe, Surrey.

3717. FISHER, Harrison Henry; B: Frilsham, Berkshire; E: East Grinstead, Sussex; Pte. G 16351; K: 11.6.17; Ypres (Menin Gate) Mem. (Bel.).

3718. FLECKNEY, Frederick George; B: Mangrove, Bedfordshire; E: Bedford; Pte. G 14538; K: 21.3.18; Pozieres mem., Somme; Age 22; Son of George and Hannah Fleckney.*

3719. FLEET, William Leeson; B: Helidon, Northamptonshire; E: Paddington, London; Pte. G 18811; K: 21.3.18; Pozieres Mem., Somme; Age 39; Son of William and Sarah Fleet of Dunsmore Terrace, Rugby; Husband of Florence Eliza Fleet of 76, Elgin Avenue, Maida Vale, London.

3720. FOLLETT, William Walter; B: Stoke-sub-Hambden, Somerset; E: South Petherton, Somerset; Pte. G 8035; K: 21.3.18; Pozieres Mem., Somme; Age 20; Son of Walter and Elizabeth Follet of 18, New Town, Martock, Somerset.

3721. FORD, Henry Edwin; B: Brighton; E: Brighton; Pte. G 3641; W: 2.10.15; Wimereux Com. Cem., Pas-de-Calais.*

3722. FORD, John; B: – ; E: Brighton; Pte. G 8238; K: 17.6.16; Ration Farm (La Plus Douve) Annexe (Bel.); Son of Mr.H.Ford of 25, Richmond Hill, Brighton.

3723. FORRYAN, John Owen; B: Wigston, Leicestershire; E: Brighton; Cpl. G 4252; K: 4.11.18; Cross Roads Cem., Nord; Age 24; Son of John George and Elizabeth Forryan of 33, Noel Street, Forest Side, Nottingham.

3724. FOSTER, Walter; B: Dover, Kent; E: Bolton, Lancashire; Pte. G 5923; K: 17.6.16; Ration Farm (La Plus Douve) Annexe (Bel.); Age 33; Son of Walter and Bridget Foster; Husband of Catherine Foster of 24, Bath Street, Hulme, Manchester.

3725. FOWLER, David; B: Brighton; E: Brighton; Pte. SD 2348; K: 29.11.17; Roisel Com. Cem. Ext., Somme.

3726. FOX, Herbert William; B: Dane Hill, Sussex; E: Brighton; Pte. G 19136; K: 10.10.18; St.Aubert Brit. Cem., Nord; Nephew of Miss M.Fox of 1, West View, Lindfield, Sussex.

3727. FOX, William; B: Woodhead, Cheshire; E: Chester; Pte. G 19137; K: 4.11.18; Cross Roads Cem., Nord; Age 19; Son of Mary Teasdale, formerly Fox, of Newfield Terrace, Helsby, Warrington, Lancashie and the late Vincent Fox.

3728. FRANKS, William; B: Helpston, Northamptonshire; E: Peterborough; Pte. G 7888; K: 25.9.15; Loos Mem., Pas-de-Calais; Age 23; Son of William and Martha Franks.

3729. FREELAND, Henry John; B: St.Leonards-on-Sea; E: Eastbourne; Pte. G 7995; K: 17.5.16; Ration Farm (La Plus Douve) Annexe (Bel.); Husband of Mrs.M.L.Harris, formerly Freeland, of 52, Newton Road, Faversham, Kent.

3730. FREEMAN, Noel Herbert; B: Eaton, Norfolk; E: Norwich; Pte. G 11715; W: 23.6.17; Lijssenthoek Mil. Cem. (Bel.); Age 19; Son of Herbert George and Alice Freeman of 33, Onley Street, Unthank Road, Norwich.

3731. FROST, Wilfrid; B: – ; E: Ashton-under-Lyne; Pte. G 19134; K: 3.6.18; Bully-Grenay Com. Cem. Brit. Ext., Pas-de-Calais; Age 19; Son of Margaret F.H.Frost of 117, Manchester Road, Higher Ince, Lancashire.

3732. FULLER, John Arthur; B: Stetchworth, Cambridgeshire; E: Newmarket, Cambridgeshire; Pte. G 18813; K: 21.3.18; Pozieres Mem., Somme; Age 20; Son of John and Ellen Fuller of Stetchworth.

3733. FULLER, Theodore Beresford; B: Worth, Sussex; E: East Grinstead, Sussex; Pte. G 3198; W: 6.8.16; Heilly Station Cem., Mericourt-L'Abbé, Somme; Age 20; Son of Thomas Edward and Emily Fuller of 4, Builders Inn Cottage, Copthorne, Sussex; Died at Casualty Clearing Station, Mericourt-L'Abbé;

Accidentally and mortally wounded on 4.8.16 by a hand grenade while visiting former German trenches.

3734. FUNNELL, Harry John; B: Crawley, Sussex; E: Brighton; L/Cpl. G 3440; K: 14.2.16; Menin Road South Mil. Cem. (Bel.); Age 26; Son of Harry Funnell of "The Garage", Buchan Hill, Crawley.

G

3735. GARDNER, Frederick; B: Farnham, Surrey; E: Horsham, Sussex; Pte. G 8881; K: 22.3.18; Pozieres Mem., Somme; Age 29; Son of Alfred and Elizabeth Gardner of Ivy Cottage, The Sands, Farnham.

3736. GARDNER, George; B: Dunks Green, Sussex; E: Chichester; Pte. G 506; K: 31.8.16; Thiepval Mem., Somme; Age 27; Son of George Gardner.*

3737. GARDNER, Jack Copestake; B: High Wycombe, Buckinghamshire; E: Arundel, Sussex; L/Cpl. G 5752; K: 14.2.16; Menin Road South Mil. Cem. (Bel.); Age 21; Son of John Martin and Matilda Axten Gardner of "Ellwood", 21, Roberts Road, High Wycombe; Killed while on front line duty at Hooge.

3738. GARROD, Arthur; B: Ipswich, Suffolk; E: East Dereham, Norfolk; Pte. G 11916; K: 12.4.17; Lievin Com Cem. Ext., Pas-de-Calais.

3739. GEARING, Harry; B: Brighton; E: Hove; Pte. G 4859; K: 31.8.16; Thiepval Mem., Somme.

3740. GEORGE, John Lewis; B: Chiselhurst, Kent; E: Holborn, London; Pte. G 5355; K: 13.2.16; Menin Road South Mil. Cem. (Bel.); Age 23; Son of David and Emma George of Chiselhurst; Husband of Ivy Annie George of 54, Melford Road, Walthamstow, London; Killed during front line trench duty at Hooge.

3741. GILBERT, William; B: Ripe, Sussex; E: Lewes; Pte. G 2921; K: 13.4.17; Ypres (Menin Gate) Mem. (Bel.); Age 25; Son of John and Alice Gilbert of Church Road, Ripe.

3742. GLAYSHER, William George; B: Horsham, Sussex; E: Horsham; Pte. TF 201445; K: 6.6.17; Ypres (Menin Gate) Mem. (Bel.); Age 26; Son of William and Lucy Glaysher of The Dunn Horse Inn, Manning's Heath, Sussex.

3743. GLEW, William Nevil; B: Peterborough; E: Lambeth, London; Pte. G 8399; W: 11.10.18; Vis-en-Artois Mem., Haucourt, Pas-de-Calais; Son of R. and M.E.Glew of 27, North End, Wisbech, Cambridgeshire.

3744. GODDARD, Arthur Reginald; B: Horndean, Hampshire; E: Chichester; Pte. G 14172; W: 17.11.18; St.Sever Cem. Ext., Rouen, Seine-Maritime; Age 20; Son of Mrs.F.Goddard of North Marden, Chilgrove, Sussex.

3745. GODDEN, Frederick William; B: Hastings; E: Hastings; Pte. G 11942; K: 24.1.17; Philosophe Brit. Cem., Mazingarbe, Pas-de-Calais.

3746. GODMAN, Frederick Tyrell; Capt.; D: 12.10.17; Niederzwehren Cem. (G); Age 42; Son of General Richard Temple Godman; Husband of Josephine Eleanor Godman of Victoria, British Columbia, Canada; Wounded and taken Prisoner of War at Loos on 25th September,1915; Died in captivity; Native of Sussex.

3747. GOLDEN, Alfred William; 2nd Lt.; K: 25.3.18; Pozieres Mem., Somme; Age 30; Son of Frank and Bessie Golden of 86, High Street, Rye, Sussex.

3748. GOLDING, Frederick; B: Flimwell, Kent; E: Cranbrook, Kent; L/Cpl. G 8089; K: 18.4.16; Ration Farm (La Plus Douve) Annexe (Bel.); Age 22; Son of Mrs.C.W.Golding of The Mount, Flimwell; Husband of Isabel Jefferis, formerly Golding, of 10, Lomax Buildings, Bradshaw Gate, Bolton, Lancashire.

3749. GOLDRING, Alfred Ernest; B: Southwick, Sussex; E: Hove; Pte. G 14153; K: 20.6.17; Ypres (Menin Gate) Mem. (Bel.).

3750. GOLDSMITH, Edward Henty; B: Willingdon, Sussex; E: Haywards Heath, Sussex; Cpl. G 3257; K: 11.6.17; Ypres (Menin Gate) Mem. (Bel.); Age 20; Son of Tom and Emily Goldsmith of 2, Ivy Cottages, Wannock, Sussex.*

3751. GOODERHAM, John Charles; B: Great Yarmouth; E: Great Yarmouth; Pte. G 11630; W: 6.11.18; Awoingt Brit. Cem., Nord; Age 21; Son of Walter and Minnie Gooderham of 4, Stanley Terrace, Middle Market Road, Great Yarmouth; Died at Casualty Clearing Station, Awoingt.

3752. GOODWIN, Frederick George; B: – ; E: Dover; L/Cpl. TF 260089; W: 1.6.18; Pernes Brit. Cem., Pas-de-Calais; Age 29; Son of Henry Holtum Goodwin and Clara Eliza Goodwin of Dover; Died at Casualty Clearing Station, Pernes.

3753. GOODWIN, William Henry; B: Clerkenwell, London; E: Woolwich, London; Pte. G 17748; K: 13.4.17; Lievin Com. Cem. Ext., Pas-de-Calais.

3754. GORDON, Leslie; B: Brighton; E: Westminster, London; Sgt. GS 572; K: 14.2.16; Menin Road South Mil. Cem. (Bel.); Killed while on front line trench duty at Hooge.

3755. GORRINGE, Ethelbert; B: Lingfield, Surrey; E: Haywards Heath, Sussex; Pte. SD 3134; K: 23.6.16; Ration Farm (La Plus Douve) Annexe (Bel.); Age 23; Son of George and Annie Maria Gorringe of 2, Council Cottages, Merstham, Surrey.

3756. GRANT, Ralph; B: Maresfield, Sussex; E: Eastbourne; Pte. G 4109; W: 23.8.16; Abbeville Com. Cem., Somme.

3757. GRAVETT, James; B: Horsham, Sussex; E: Horsham; L/Cpl. G 17841; K: 4.11.18; Cross Roads Cem., Nord; Age 21; Son of Mr. and Mrs. John Gravett of 30, Denne Parade, Horsham.

3758. GRAY, George Frederick; B: Brighton; E: Croydon; Cpl. L 10697; K: 26.11.16; Philosophe Brit. Cem., Mazingarbe, Pas-de-Calais; Age 19; Son of Harry and Florence Gray of Croydon.*

3759. GRAY, William Charles; B: Hove; E: Brighton; Pte. G 16604; K: 11.6.17; Voormezele Enclosure No.3 (Bel.).

3760. GREEN, William; B: New Lakenham, Norfolk; E: Norwich; Pte. G 11692; D: 18.7.18; Cologne Southern Cem. (G); Died while a Prisoner of War.

3761. GREENGRASS, Laurence William; B: Oulton Broad, Suffolk; E: Lowestoft, Suffolk; Pte. G 19140; K: 9.10.18; Awoingt Brit. Cem., Nord; Age 19; Son of Robert and Mary Greengrass of Victoria Road, Oulton Broad.

3762. GRIFFIN, William George; B: Southampton; E: Sevenoaks, Kent; Pte. G 12406; K: 28.1.18; Hargicourt Brit. Cem., Aisne; Age 33; Son of William and Annie Griffin of Rownham's, Southampton; Husband of Beatrice Griffin of Young Cottage, Victoria Road, Sevenoaks.*

3763. GRIFFIN, Stanley Jack; B: Highgate, London; E: Wood Green, London; Pte. G 19285; K: 4.11.18; Villers-Pol Com. Cem. Ext., Nord; Age 19; Son of T.Bennett Griffin and Ellen Sarah Griffin of Stanley Villa, High Road, East Finchley, London.*

3764. GRIFFITHS, Andrew Owen; B: Herne Hill, London; E: Westminster, London; Cpl. G 2953; K: 28.9.15; Loos Mem., Pas-de-Calais; Age 21; Son of Evan and Minnie Emily Griffiths of 24, Brockwell Park Gardens, Herne Hill.*

3765. GRIFFITHS, Frederick Charles; B: Preston, Sussex; E: Brighton; Pte. G 2981; W: 12.4.17; Choques Mil. Cem., Pas-de-Calais; Age 20; Son of Mr. and Mrs.C.R.Griffiths of 21, Exeter Street, Brighton; Died at No.1 Casualty Clearing Station, Choques.

3766. GRIFFITHS, Harold; B: Kilburn, London; E: Portslade, Sussex; Pte. G 5050; K: 28.9.15; Loos Mem., Pas-de-Calais.

3767. GRIFFITHS, William John; B: Nyneddgarig, Carmarthenshire; E: Llanelly; Pte. G 5825; K: 25.9.15; Loos Mem., Pas-de-Calais.

3768. GRIST, Joseph; B: Chichester; E: Chichester; Pte. G 7947; K: 31.8.16; Bulls Road Cem., Flers, Somme.

3769. GROVER, Henry; B: Laughton, Sussex; E: Brighton; Pte. G 4945; K: 23.2.16; Ypres (Menin Gate) Mem. (Bel.).

3770. GROVER, Wallace Joseph; B: Brighton; E: Brighton; Pte. G 5270; K: 28.9.15; St.Mary's A.D.S. Cem., Pas-de-Calais.

3771. GUMBRELL, Alfred George; B: Southwick, Sussex; E: Hove; Pte. G 3072; K: 25.9.15; Loos Mem., Pas-de-Calais.

3772. GURNEY, Charles Frederick; B: Eastbourne; E: Eastbourne; Pte. G 16031; K: 22.3.18; Pozieres Mem., Somme; Age 26; Son of Amos and Fanny Gurney of 48, Cavendish Place, Eastbourne.

H

3773. HADDINGTON, Robert Edmund; B: Brighton; E: Brighton; Pte. L 8371; K: 14.2.16; Menin Road South Mil. Cem. (Bel.); Killed while on front line trench duty at Hooge.

3774. HADLEY, Walter Hammands; B: – ; E: Watford, Hertfordshire; Sgt. G 20295; M.M.; K: 4.11.18; Villers-Pol Com. Cem. Ext., Nord; Age 35; Son of Harry Hadley of East Haddon, Northampton.*

3775. HADLOW, William Thomas; B: Vange, Essex; E: Sittingbourne, Kent; Pte. TF 260261; W: 27.3.18; St.Sever Cem. Ext., Rouen, Seine-Maritime.

3776. HAIGH, John William; B: Colton, Yorkshire; E: Worthing; Pte. G 16588; W: 26.4.17; Lillers Com. Cem., Pas-de-Calais; Husband of Frances Louise Haigh of 2, Eastern Cottages, Broadwater, Sussex; Died at Casualty Clearing Station, Lillers.

3777. HALL, Edward Lionel; 2nd Lt.; K: 27.3.18; Pozieres Mem., Somme; Age 21; Son of Samuel Richard Hall and Annie Hall (stepmother) of 6, Franklin Place, Chichester.

3778. HALL, Frank; B: Chester; E: Littlehampton, Sussex; Pte. G 529; K: 28.9.15; Loos Mem., Pas-de-Calais; Age 33; Son of Mrs.Emma Wright of Ashton, Cheshire.

3779. HALL, William Frank; B: Fernhurst, Sussex; E: West Lavington, Sussex; Pte. G 8330; K: 24.7.17; Ypres (Menin Gate) Mem. (Bel.); Age 27; Son of Mrs.F.Hall of Tillington, Sussex; Husband of Fanny Andrews, formerly Hall, of Midhurst Road, Fernhurst.*

3780. HALL, William Henry; B: Elstead, Sussex; E: West Lavington, Sussex; Pte. G 14180; W: 6.8.17; Aeroplane Cem. (Bel.).

3781. HALLEY, William Alfred; B: Bow, London; E: Stratford, London; Pte. G 18983; W: 5.7.18; Ligny-St.Flochel Brit. Cem., Pas-de-Calais; Age 19; Son of Richard William and Susannah Halley of 39, Herbert Road, Forest Gate, London.

3782. HAMES, Reginald Arthur; B: Richmond, London; E: Fulham, London; Pte. G 8086; K: 31.8.16; Thiepval Mem., Somme.

3783. HAMMOND, Albert; B: Guildford; E: Guildford; Pte. G 3718; K: 14.2.16; Menin Road South Mil. Cem. (Bel.); Killed while on front line trench duty at Hooge.

3784. HAMMOND, Frank; B: Darsham, Suffolk; E: Norwich; Pte. G 14698; K: 31.5.18; Bully-Grenay Com. Cem. Brit. Ext., Pas-de-Calais; Age 36; Son of Henry John and Sophia Hammond.

3785. HAMPSON, John; B: Cropwell Bishop, Nottinghamshire; E: Newark, Nottinghamshire; Pte. G 18428; W: 13.11.18; St.Sever Cem. Ext., Rouen, Seine-Maritime.

3786. HARDING, Alfred; B: Seaford, Sussex; E: East Grinstead, Sussex; Pte. G 3180; K: 10.5.16; Ration Farm (La Plus Douve) Annexe (Bel.); Age 20; Son of Alfred and Louisa C.Harding of 2, Warren Cottages, Tadworth, Surrey.

3787. HARMAN, Harry Mark; B: Brighton; E: Brighton; Pte. G 2390; K: 25.9.15; Loos Mem., Pas-de-Calais; Age 20; Son of George and Mary Jane Harman of 3, Blackman Street, Brighton.*

3788. HARRIS, George Samuel; B: Brighton; E: Brighton; Pte. G 7039; K: 14.2.16; Menin Road South Mil. Cem. (Bel.); Killed while on front line trench duty at Hooge.

3789. HARRIS, Richard; B: Bow, London; E: Stratford, London; Pte. G 9772; K: 11.6.17; Ypres (Menin Gate) Mem. (Bel.); Son of James Harris of 4, Earl Street, Stratford, London.

3790. HARRISON, Albert Edward; B: Plumstead, London; E: Woolwich, London; Pte. G 18805; K: 22.6.18; Bully-Grenay Com. Cem. Brit. Ext., Pas-de-Calais; Age 19; Son of Richard John and Letitia Marie Harrison of 12, Palmerston Road, Plumstead.

3791. HARROD, Peter James; B: Hastings; E: Hastings; Pte. G 7743; K: 18.8.16; Delville Wood Cem., Somme; Age 22; Son of Benjamin and Martha Harrod of 45, Middle Road, Hastings.*

3792. HARVEY, Charles William; B: Henfield, Sussex; E: Henfield; Pte. G 16506; K: 21.11.17; Hargicourt Brit. Cem., Aisne; Age 20; Son of Ernest George and Isabella Burgess Harvey of 8, Westgate Street, Lewes, Sussex.

3793. HARVEY, Edgar Moore; B: Islington, London; E: Chelmsford, Essex; L/Cpl. G 14695; K: 25.3.18; Pozieres Mem., Somme; Age 21; Son of Alfred and Elizabeth M.Harvey of 30, Bunyan Road, Walthamstow, London.

3794. HARWOOD, Leslie Herbert; B: Fulham, London; E: Harrow, Middlesex; Pte. G 19156; W: 1.6.18; Pernes Brit. Cem., Pas-de-Calais; Age 19; Son of Herbert Edward and Hilda Gertrude Harwood of "Pernes", Bellfield Avenue, Harrow Weald; Gassed; Died at Casualty Clearing Station, Pernes.

3795. HAVELL, Eric Tunbridge; B: Lee, Kent; E: London; Pte. G 3959; K: 28.9.15; Loos Mem., Pas-de-Calais; Age 22; Son of Frederick Henry and Louisa Emma Havell of 40, Wheturangi Road, Auckland, New Zealand.*

3796. HAWKINS, Ernest William; B: Petworth, Sussex; E: Petworth; Pte. G 16507; K: 13.1.17; Philosophe Brit. Cem., Maricourt, Pas-de-Calais; Age 19; Son of Ernest and Annie Hawkins of Golf House, Burton Park, Petworth.

3797. HAWKRIDGE, J.A.; B: Sydenham; 2nd Lt.; W: 6.11.16; Barlin Com Cem Ext., Pas-de-Calais; Son of Joseph and Mary Louisa Hawkridge; Attached from Royal Fusiliers; Mortally wounded on 5.11.16 while out with a wiring party.

3798. HAYLER, Alfred Henry; B: Storrington, Sussex; E: Chichester; L/Cpl. L 10573; W at Home: 15.8.17; Brighton and Preston Cem., Sussex (UK); Age 27; Son of Mr. and Mrs.A.Hayler of Pulborough.

3799. HAYLER, Henry; B: Alfriston, Sussex; E: Hastings; Pte. SD 5196; K: 31.8.16; Thiepval Mem., Somme.

3800. HAYWARD, Albert Henry; B: Salehurst, Sussex; E: Etchingham, Sussex; Pte. S 2307; K: 28.1.16; Ypres (Menin Gate) Mem. (Bel.); Age 19; Son of John and Harriett Hayward of Yew Tree Cottage, Etchingham.

3801. HAZELL, Reginald Stanley; B: Devizes, Wiltshire; E: Worthing; Sgt. G 3623; K: 26.9.15; Loos Mem., Pas-de-Calais; Age 30; Husband of Mrs.Violet M.Goldspink, formerly Hazell, of 29, Cunliffe Road, Streatham, London.

3802. HEARN, Frank; B: Byfleet, Surrey; E: Uckfield, Sussex; Pte. G 3582; K: 11.6.17; Voormezele Enclosure No.3 (Bel.).*

3803. HEATHER, Arthur; B: Crawley, Sussex; E: Brighton; Pte. G 19692; K: 21.3.18; Pozieres Mem., Somme.

3804. HEATHER, Stanley George; B: Worthing; E: Worthing; Pte. G 1595; K: 14.2.16; Menin Road South Mil. Cem. (Bel.); Age 26; Husband of Elsie Harriett Heather of 56, London Street, Worthing; Killed while on front line trench duty at Hooge.

3805. HELDMAN, Harry Randolph; Lt.; K: 27.9.15; Loos Mem., Pas-de-Calais; Age 27; Son of Richard Bernard Heldman (Richard Marsh, Novelist) and Ada Kate Heldman of 27, Holland Road, Hove.

3806. HELME, Alfred; B: Bradford, E: Manchester; Pte. G 5981; K: 28.9.15; Loos Mem., Pas-de-Calais.

3807. HEMSLEY, Charles; B: Brighton; E: Brighton; Pte. G 7667; K: 31.8.16; Thiepval Mem., Somme; Age 19; Son of Robert and Ellen Helmsley of 34, Carlton Row, Brighton.*

3808. HENLEY, Ernest; B: Cuckfield, Sussex; E: Haywards Heath, Sussex; Pte. G 3583; K: 25.9.15; Loos Mem., Pas-de-Calais; Son of Mrs.Edith Caroline Hemsley of 4, Lavender Cottage, Anstye Lane, Cuckfield.

3809. HENNESSEY, Henry; B: Westminster, London; E: Southwark, London; Pte. G 8022; W: 14.7.17; Boulogne Eastern Cem., Pas-de-Calais; Died at Military General Hospital, Boulogne.

3810. HENNIKER, Ernest Edward; B: Smarden, Kent; E: Tonbridge, Kent; Pte. G 24433; W: 21.2.18; Tincourt New Brit. Cem., Somme; Age 19; Son of Edward and Jane Henniker of The Hurst, West Peckham, Maidstone; Died at Casualty Clearing Station, Tincourt.

3811. HENSON, Ernest William; B: Shoreham, Sussex; E: Hove; Pte. SD 5446; K: 22.3.18; Pozieres Mem., Somme; Age 21; Son of William and Ellen Henson of 17, Linton Road, Hove.*

3812. HEPDEN, Charles; B: Burwash, Sussex; E: Hastings; Pte. G 6703; K: 11.3.17; Aix-Noulette Com. Cem., Pas-de-Calais; Age 20; Son of Elizabeth Hepden of Paygate, Burwash.

3813. HERRINGTON, Albert Ernest; B: Paistow, London; E: Petworth, Sussex; Pte. G 4791; K: 15.2.16; Menin Road South Mil. Cem. (Bel.); Killed while on front line trench duty at Hooge.

3814. HEWSON, Frederick George; B: Chichester; E: Chichester; Pte. G 7503; K: 6.6.17; Ypres (Menin Gate) Mem. (Bel.); Age 21; Son of George and Agnes Hewson of 144, Whyke Road, Chichester.*

3815. HILL, Charles Douglas Lucas; 2nd Lt.; K: 14.2.16; Menin Road South Mil. Cem. (Bel.); Age 22; Son of William John and Susannah Maria Hill of "Ashburnham", Royston Park Road, Hatch End, Middlesex; Buried alive by the blowing of a German mine at Hooge but his body was subsequently recovered for military re-burial.

3816. HILL, Edward Albert; B: Guildford; E: Brighton; Pte. SD 942; W: 15.6.17; Mendingham Mil. Cem.

(Bel.); Age 21; Son of Mrs.F.Wase of 15, Lanfranc Road, Worthing.

3817. HILLMAN, Frank; B: Slaugham, Sussex; E: Brighton; Pte. G 3013; K: 25.9.15; Loos Mem., Pas de-Calais.

3818. HINCH, Thomas; B: –; E: Grimsby; Pte. G 15438; K: 21.3.18; Pozieres Mem., Somme; Age 23; Son of Elizabeth Hinch of North Kelsey, Lincolnshire.

3819. HINGSTON, George; B: Louisville, U.S.A.; E: Westminster, London; Sgt. G 2952; K: 31.8.16; Thiepval Mem., Somme; Age 23; Son of Alice Tadman, formerly Hingston, of "Merrymount", West Hall Road, Wallingham, Surrey, and the late George Henry Hingston.

3820. HINTON, Frank Edwin; B: Bournemouth; E: Brighton; Pte. G 3643; K: 29.10.15; Elzenwalle Brasserie Cem. (Bel.); Age 17; Son of Jospeh H. and Mrs.E.Hinton of 73, Bonchurch Road, Brighton.

3821. HOBBS, Robert John; B: Dalston, London; E: Hove; L/Cpl. G 3061; K: 25.9.15; Loos Mem., Pas-de-Calais; Age 22; Son of Robert and Lilah Hobbs of 13, Edbrooke Road, Paddington, London.

3822. HODGE, Frederick Joseph; B: Fulham, London; E: London; C.S.M.; GS 464; K: 5.5.16; Ration Farm (La Plus Douve) Annexe (Bel.); Age 38; Son of Joseph and Caroline Hodge; Husband of Nellie Albina Hodge of 7, Lion Street, Walworth, London.

3823. HOLCOMBE, Albert William; B: Forest Row, Sussex; E: East Grinstead, Sussex; Pte. G 8014; W: 15.9.16; St.Sever Cem., Rouen, Seine-Maritime.

3824. HOLDING, Archie; B: East Hoathly, Sussex; E: Uckfield, Sussex; Pte. G 3567; K: 28.9.15; Loos Mem., Pas-de-Calais; Age 20; Son of Mrs.Dinah Cornford of P.C. Cottage, Hadlow Down, Sussex.

3825. HOLLAND, Albert; B: Netherfield, Sussex; E: Hastings; Pte. G 6696; K: 27.3.18; Pozieres Mem., Somme; Age 36; Husband of Annie Maria Holland of 3, Council Cottages, Netherfield Hill.

3826. HOLLAND, Reginald; B: Horsted Keynes, Sussex; E: Lewes; Pte. G 3122; K: 27.9.15; Loos Mem., Pas-de-Calais.

3827. HOLLEBON, William; B: Milwaukee, Wisconsin, U.S.A.; E: Brighton; Sgt. G 3017; W: 5.6.18; Pernes Brit. Cem., Pas-de-Calais; Age 27; Son of Mr. and Mrs.G.Hollebon of Milwaukee; Husband of Margaret Hollebon of Brighton; Died at Casualty Clearing Station, Pernes.

3828. HOLLOWAY, Arthur; B: Brighton; E: Brighton; Pte. G 7649; K: 31.8.16; Thiepval Mem., Somme; Age 18; Son of Mr.G.H.Holloway of 71, Toronto Terrace, Brighton.

3829. HOLLOWAY, Bernard Henry; Capt.; K: 27.9.15; Loos Mem., Pas-de-Calais; Age 27; Son of Sir Henry and Lady Holloway of Draxmont, Wimbledon Hill, London.

3830. HOLMAN, Jesse; B: Ardingly, Sussex; E: Brighton; Pte. G 4209; K: 24.3.16; Ration Farm (La Plus Douve) Annexe (Bel.); Age 23; Son of Mr.Jesse Holman of 2, Carter's Cottages, Ardingly.

3831. HOLMES, Thomas; B: Cardiff; E: Cardiff; L/Cpl. GS 403; K: 18.8.16; Thiepval Mem., Somme; Age 38; Son of Joseph and Sarah Holmes; Served on the Punjab Frontier and in the Tirah Campagn 1897-98.

3832. HOMEWOOD, Percy Edward; B: Headcorn, Kent; E: Tunbridge Wells; Pte. SD 1371; K: 22.3.18; Jeancourt Com. Cem., Aisne.

3833. HOPE, George Thomas; B: Leatherhead, Surrey; E: Newhaven, Sussex; L/Cpl. G 8214; K: 18.8.16; Delville Wood Cem., Somme; Age 25; Son of Mr. and Mrs.G.Hope of 17, Church Walk, Leatherhead.

3834. HOPE, George Victor; B: Brighton; E: Brighton; Pte. G 16575; W: 1.4.18; Roye New Brit. Cem., Somme.

3835. HOPE, Jack Ernest; B: Newhaven, Sussex; E: Brighton; Pte. G 16510; K: 17.6.18; Arras Mem., Pas-de-Calais.

3836. HOPKINS, Felix James; B: Brighton; E: Brighton; Pte. G 6864; W: 31.8.16; Dernancourt Com. Cem. Ext., Somme; Age 26; Son of Felix James and Harriet Hopkins of Brighton; Husband of Constance Annie Hopkins of 3, Buller Road, Brighton.

3837. HORSLEY, Joseph; B: Kineton, Warwickshire; E: Arundel, Sussex; L/Cpl. G 4198; K: 21.6.17; Oxford Road Cem. (Bel.).

3838. HOSKINS, James; B: Sutton, Surrey; E: Kingston-on-Thames; Pte. G 17192; K: 5.6.18; Loos Brit. Cem., Pas-de-Calais.

3849. HOUGH, Arthur David Thomas; B: Hampstead, London; E: Kilburn, London; Pte. G 3548; K: 30.6.16; Kemmel Chateau Mil. Cem. (Bel.).

3840. HOWARD, Edwin; B: Wingfield, Suffolk; E: Harleston, Norfolk; Pte. G 15245; K: 23.6.17; Ypres (Menin Gate) Mem. (Bel.); Age 19; Son of George and Eleanor Howard of Upper Weybread, Norfolk.

3841. HOWES, Albert; B: Brighton; E: Brighton; Pte. G 3048; W: 7.10.15; Valenciennes (St.Roch) Com. Cem., Nord.

3842. HOWLETT, William; B: Higham, Norfolk; E: Norwich; Pte. TF 290450; K: 21.3.18; Pargny Brit. Cem., Somme.

3843. HOY, Jack; B: Charlwood, Surrey; E: Horsham, Sussex; Cpl. G 3407; K: 28.9.15; Loos Mem., Pas-de-Calais.

3844. HUGHES, Arthur Walter; B: East Ham, London; E: Brighton; Pte. G 16564; W: 11.6.17; Abbeville Com. Cem. Ext., Somme; Age 25; Son of Charles John and Rosetta Eliza Hughes.

3845. HUGHES, James; B: Rochester, Kent; B: Maidstone; Pte. G 12307; K: 28.7.17; Perth Cem. (China Wall), (Bel.).

3846. HUGHES, William Charles; B: St.Paul's, Sussex; E: Hove; Sgt. G 3058; D.C.M.; K: 18.8.16; Thiepval Mem., Somme; Age 24; Son of Mr. and Mrs.H.Hughes of 10, Upper Russell Street, Brighton.*

3847. HUMFRESS, Stanley Allen; B: Camden Town London; E: London; Cpl. G 9104; W: 22.3.18; Peronne Com. Cem. Ext., Ste. Radegonde, Somme.

3848. HUNT, Patrick; B: Liverpool; E: Liverpool; Pte. G 19293; W: 10.10.18; St.Aubert Brit. Cem., Nord;

Age 19; Son of William and Mary Hunt of 3, William Terrace, Liverpool.

3849. HURRELL, Ernest; B: Brighton; E: Hove; L/Cpl. G 6689; K: 22.3.18; Pozieres Mem., Somme; Age 22; Son of Frederick and Catherine Hurrell of 9, Islingword Road, Brighton.

3850. HUTCHINGS, Arthur; B: Hastings; E: Eastbourne; Pte. SD 1601; W: 4.8.17; Lijssenthoek Mil. Cem. (Bel.); Age 22; Son of William and Phoebe Hutchings of 18, Tower Street, Eastbourne.

3851. HYDER, Jack H.; B: – ; E: Hastings; Cpl. G 17647; W: 22.3.18; Roye New Brit. Cem., Somme.

3852. ISSAACSON, Abraham; B: Manchester; E: Manchester; Pte. G 19161; K: 13.9.18; Maroc Brit. Cem., Nord; Age 19; Son of Solomon and Emily Issaacson of 12, Cornwall Buildings, Cheetham, Manchester.*

J

3853. JACKSON, Joseph; B: Littlehampton, Sussex; E: Worthing; Pte. L 10801; K: 11.6.17; Ypres (Menin Gate) Mem. (Bel.); Age 21; Son of Henry and Fanny Jackson of 6, Central Gardens, Littlehampton.

3854. JACOB, Sidney Goodwin; B: Bermondsey, London; E: Wandsworth, London; L/Cpl. G 20290; K: 4.11.18; Villers-Pol Com. Cem. Ext., Nord; Age 23; Son of Arthur and M.Jacob of 30, Pretoria Road, Streatham, London.*

3855. JAMES, John; B: Cardiff; E: Cardiff; Pte. G 3537; K: 18.8.16; Thiepval Mem., Somme.

3856. JAMIESON, Mercer; B: Salehurst, Sussex; E: Hastings; Pte. G 8959; K: 13.4.17; Arras Mem., Pas-de-Calais; Age 27; Son of William and Ellen Jamieson of Fuchsia Cottage, Bodiam, Sussex.

3857. JARVIS, Bertram; B: Worthing; E: Herstmonceux; Pte. SD 604; K: 11.6.17; Ypres (Menin Gate) Mem. (Bel.).

3858. JARVIS, Herbert Robert; B: Eastbourne; E: Eastbourne; Pte. G 7620; K: 23.6.17; Ypres (Menin Gate) Mem. (Bel.); Age 20; Son of Mr. and Mrs. Jarvis of 9, East Street, Eastbourne.

3859. JEPSON, Charles Herbert; B: Kensal Rise, London; E: Northampton; Pte. G 7889; K: 25.9.15; Loos Mem., Pas-de-Calais; Age 25; Husband of Jane Carpenter, formerly Jepson, of Manor Road, Brackley, Northamptonshire.

3860. JERMY, George William; B: Hayes, Middlesex; E: Uxbridge, Middlesex; Pte. G 19295; K: 31.5.18; Bully-Grenay Com. Cem. Brit. Ext., Pas-de-calais; Age 19; Son of Mr.J.H. and Mrs.E.M.Jermy of 4, Angel Lane, Hayes End.

3861. JERROLD, George; B: West Hampstead, London; E: Worthing; Sgt. G 3216; K: 18.8.16; Thiepval Mem., Somme; Son of Henry William and Mary Lucy Jerrold of 1, Foxholt Gardens, Stonebridge Park, London.

3862. JERVIS, John Frederick; B: Worthing; E: Worthing; Pte. G 3780; K: 25.9.15; Loos Mem., Pas-de-Calais; Age 24; Son of John Henry and Flora Jervis of 116, Becket Road, Tarring, Sussex.

3863. JESTICO, Frank William; B: Brighton; E: Brighton; Sgt. L 9263; K: 3.8.17; Ypres Reservoir Cem. (Bel.); Age 29; Son of Issac and Annie Jestico of 132, Ellen Street, Hove; Husband of Mrs.L.M.Jestico of 121, Westbourne Street, Hove.

3864. JEWELL, Arthur William; B: Brighton; E: Brighton; Pte. G 6913; W: 6.8.17; Aeroplane Cem. (Bel.); Age 19; Son of William Henry and Sarah Elizabeth Jewell of 9, Jersey Street, Brighton.

3865. JEWERS, Charles Cyril; B: – ; E: – ; Pte. – 43566; K: 18.7.17; Arras Mem., Pas-de-Calais.

3866. JOHNSON, Charles; B: – ; E: Brighton; Pte. G 7342; K: 28.10.17; Hargicourt Brit. Cem., Aisne.

3867. JOHNSON, Frederick Arthur; B: Fittleworth, Sussex; E: Chichester; Pte. G 4987; K: 23.6.17; Ypres (Menin Gate) Mem. (Bel.).

3868. JOHNSON, Harry; B: Waldersham, Kent; E: Canterbury; Pte. G 20575; W: 25.7.17; Larch Wood (Railway Cutting) Cem. (Bel.).

3869. JONES, Albert Victor; B: St.Luke's, Sussex; E: Brighton; Pte. G 3278; K: 25.9.15; Loos Mem., Pas-de-calais; Age 19; Son of Mrs.Georgina Annetta Fowler, formerly Jones, of 37, Caledonian Road, Brighton.

3870. JONES, Alfred; B: Brighton; E: Eastbourne; Pte. G 4990; K: 31.8.16; Thiepval Mem., Somme; Age 17; Son of Albert and Maria Jones of 17, Robertson Road, Brighton.

3871. JONES, Frank; B: Birmingham; E: Birmingham; Pte. G 5702; K: 25.9.17; Tyne Cot Mem. (Bel.).

3872. JONES, William John; B: Pagham, Sussex; E: Bognor Regis, Sussex; Pte. G 7752; K: 18.8.16; Thiepval Mem., Somme; Age 20; Son of F. and Ruth Jones of Flansham Lane, Bognor Regis.

3873. JOSEPH, Albert Edward; B: Guildford; E: East Grinstead, Sussex; L/Cpl. G 3540; K: 27.3.18; Pozieres Mem., Somme.

3874. JOSEPH, Archibald; B: Guildford; E: East Grinstead, Sussex; Pte. G 3399; W: 17.6.16; Bailleul Com. Cem. Ext., Nord; Age 21; Son of Frederick John and Mary Jane Joseph of The Manse, Harpole, Northamptonshire; Died at Casualty Clearing Station, Bailleul.

3875. JOYES, Jack; B: Tarring, Sussex; E: Worthing; Pte. G 3648; W: 29.6.16; Bailleul Com. Cem. Ext., Nord; Died at Casualty Clearing Station, Bailleul.

3876. JUPP, Mervyn George Crisp; B: Burgess Hill, Sussex; E: Hurstpierpoint, Sussex; Sgt. G 3238; D.C.M.; K: 31.8.16; Thiepval Mem., Somme; Age 22; Son of George W. and Selina A.Jupp of Friars Oak, Hassocks, Sussex.

K

3877. KELLY, Alfred George; B: Southwark, London; E: Southwark; L/Cpl. G 5256; K: 9.9.16; Thiepval Mem., Somme.

3878. KENNEDY, Henry; B: Blackburn, Lancashire; E: Blackburn; Pte. G 19297; K: 17.6.18; Arras Mem., Pas-de-Calais.

3879. KENNELLY, Leslie William; Lt.; W: 9.10.15; Longuenesse (St.Omer) Souvenir Cem., Pas-de-Calais; Age 20; Son of the Rev. Canon W. and Mrs. Kennelly of 95, Arundel Road, Littlehampton, Sussex.

3880. KENNETT, Herbert George Philpott; B: St.Peter's, Kent; E: Herne Bay, Kent; Pte. G 18842; K: 31.5.18; Bully-Grenay Com. Cem. Brit. Ext., Pas-de-calais.

3881. KENT, Stanley Gordon; B: Stoke Newington, London; E: Cockspur Street, London; Pte. G 4275; K: 18.8.16; Thiepval Mem., Somme; Age 30; Son of Alfred Tamar Kent of The Nook, 31, Derwent Road, Palmers Green, London.

3882. KING, Albert William; B: Lewisham, London; E: Bromley, London; L/Cpl. G 12670; K: 13.4.17; Ypres (Menin Gate) Mem. (Bel.); Age 24; Son of Thomas King; Husband of Alice Caroline King of 98, Wiggin Street, Ladywood, Birmingham.

3883. KING, Frederick; B: Barcombe, Sussex; E: Lewes; L/Cpl. G 3346; K: 24.2.16; Ypres (Menin Gate) Mem. (Bel.).

3884. KING, John; B: – ; E: Cranbrook, Kent; Pte. TF 260165; K: 21.3.18; Pozières Mem., Somme; Age 19; Son of John and Sarah King of Hancocks, Cranbrook.

3885. KINGHAM, John; B: Marylebone, London; E: Paddington, London; Pte. G 18990; K: 4.11.18; Cross Roads Cem., Nord.

3886. KIPLING, John; B: Cotherstone, County Durham; E: Barnard Castle, County Durham; Pte. G 20466; K: 3.4.18; Pozières Mem., Somme.

3887. KNIGHT, Ernest; B: – ; E: Cambridge; Pte. G 14972; D: 18.5.18; Pernes Brit. Cem., Pas-de-Calais; Age 22; Son of John Thomas and Miriam Knight of Cambridge; Died of disease at Casualty Clearing Station, Pernes.

3888. KNIGHT, Harold John; B: Plumstead, London; E: Woolwich, London; Pte. G 18993; K: 4.11.18; Cross Roads Cem., Nord.*

3889. KNIGHT, Harry; B: Duncton, Sussex; E: Petworth, Sussex; Pte. G 3710; K: 25.9.15; Loos mem., Pas-de-Calais; Age 21; Son of Richard and Fanny Knight.

3890. KNIGHT, John; B: Horsham, Sussex; E: Horsham; Sgt. G 3461; W: 12.4.17; Fosse No.10 Com. Cem. Ext., Pas-de-calais; Age 27; Son of John and Mary Knight of Horsham; Husband of May Knight.

3891. KNIGHT, Sidney; B: Worthing; E: Worthing; Pte. G 1034; K: 27.3.17; Aix-Noulette Com. Cem. Ext., Pas-de-Calais; Son of Mrs.E.Knight.

3892. KNOWLES, William; B: Roose, Lancashire; E: Ulverston, Lancashire; Pte. G19301; K: 4.11.18; Villers-Pol Com. Cem. Ext., Nord.

L

3893. LAKE, Sydney; B: Croydon; E: Worthing; Cpl. G 16608; K: 13.4.17; Ypres (Menin Gate) Mem. (Bel.); Age 26; Husband of Elsie Kathleen Lake of 21, Shelley Road, Worthing; Former Musketery Instructor, Sussex Imperial Yeomanry, joined 1909.*

3894. LAKER, Harold; B: Dial Post, Sussex; E: Worthing; Pte. G 3699; K: 25.9.15; Loos Mem., Pas-de-Calais; Age 20; Son of Mr. and Mrs.H.Laker of New House Farm, Warminghurst, Storrington, Sussex.

3895. LANCASTER, John Henry; B: Hastings, E: Battersea, London; Pte. G 4239; K: 10.5.16; Berks Cem. Ext. (Bel.); Age 20; Son of William George and Lucy Lancaster of 19, Falcon Terrace, Battersea.

3896. LANGLEY, Robert; B: Brighton; E: Brighton; Pte. G 16566; K: 12.8.17; Hooge Crater Cem. (Bel); Age 20; Son of William and Clara Langley of 47, Cobden Road, Brighton.*

3897. LANGRIDGE, Willie; B: Copthorne, Sussex; E: Hastings; Pte. SD 2956; K: 11.6.17; Ypres (Menin Gate) Mem. (Bel.); Age 25; Son of Mr. and Mrs. David Langridge of "Heath View", Copthorne.

3898. LAWRENCE, Arthur; B: Portsmouth; E: Croydon; Pte. G 22955; K: 27.8.18; Bully-Grenay Com. Cem. Brit. Ext., Pas-de-Calais; Age 28; Husband of C.G.Lawrence of 39, Ferress Road, Streatham, London.

3899. LEE, Henry; B: St.Albans, Hertfordshire; E: London; Pte. G 5288; K: 25.9.15; Loos Mem., Pas-de-Calais; Age 21; Son of Mr. and Mrs.H.A.Lee of 46, Parker Street, Watford, Hertfordshire.

3900. LEE, James William; B: North Hill, Bedfordshire; E: Arundel, Sussex; Pte. G 3132; K: 14.2.16; Menin Road South Mil. Cem. (Bel.); Age 26; Son of James and Eden Lee of "The Slade", Claphill, Bedfordshire; Killed while on front line trench duty at Hooge.

3901. LEEK, John William; B: Scarborough, Yorkshire; E: Southwark, London; Pte. G 5212; W: 16.11.15; Lijssenthoek Mil. Cem. (Bel.); Age 38; Husband of Gertrude Maud Leek of 1, West Dock Street, Hull.

3902. LEEVES, Joseph; B: Buxted, Sussex; E: Worthing; Pte. SD 4942; K: 22.3.18; Pozières Mem., Somme; Age 24; Son of Joseph and Rhoda Leeves of 5, New Road, Buxted; Served under the alias surname, Lewes.*

3903. LEGG, Harold; B: Selsey, Sussex; E: Warley, Essex; Pte. G 12969; W: 8.6.17; Lijssenthoek Mil. Cem. (Bel.); Age 21; Son of Mr. and Mrs.W.Legg of Selsey.

3904. LEPPARD, Herbert; B: Dane Hill, Sussex; E: Haywards Heath, Sussex; Pte. G 3385; K: 25.9.15; Loos Mem., Pas-de-Calais.

- - -. LEWES, Joseph (an alias surname – see LEEVES, Joseph 3902).

3905. LIAS, Ronald John Mortlock; Lt.; K: 23.2.16; Menin Road South Mil. Cem. (Bel.); Age 26; Son of the Rev.J.J.Lias, Chancellor of Llandaff Cathedral, and Mrs.M.B.Lias of The Lodge, Abington, Cambridgeshire.

3906. LINCOLN, Percy William; B: – ; E: Peterborough, Northamptonshire; Pte. G 7846; K: 23.6.17; Ypres (Menin Gate) Mem. (Bel.); Age 23; Son of William and Martha Lincoln of 30, London Road, Peterborough.

3907. LINES, John Henry; B: Wimbledon, London; E:

Woolwich, London; Pte. G 12867; K: 13.4.17; Canadian Cem. No.2, Pas-de-Calais.

3908. LINTOTT, Frederick; B: Capel, Surrey; E: Horsham, Sussex; Pte. G 3106; W: 8.4.16; Bailleul Com. Cem. Ext., Nord; Died at Casualty Clearing Station, Bailleul.

3909. LOCK, Percy Owen; B: Deptford, London; E: Cockspur Street, London; Sgt. G 20423; W: 15.4.17; Calais Southern Cem., Pas-de-Calais; Age 31; Husband of Annie Lock of 5, Morden Grove, Lewisham, London; Died at Military Hospital, Calais.

3910. LONG, William James; B: Sutton, Sussex; E: Worthing; Pte. G 6304; K: 28.7.17; Ypres (Menin Gate) Mem. (Bel.).

3911. LONGHURST, George; B: Weybridge, Surrey; E: Horsham, Sussex; Pte. G 8184; K: 18.8.16; Thiepval Mem., Somme; Age 18; Son of Mr.L.W.Longhurst of The Vicarage, Wisborough Green, Sussex.

3912. LOOP, Reginald Thomas; B: Northampton; E: Brighton; Pte. G 16606; K: 13.4.17; Ypres (Menin Gate) Mem. (Bel.); Age 29; Son of Thomas Loop; Husband of Florence Loop of 12, Grena Road. Richmond, Surrey.

3913. LOWN, Thomas Gordon; B: Colby, Norfolk; E: Warley, Essex; Pte. G 12952; W: 23.2.17; Étaples Mil. Cem., Pas-de-Calais; Age 18; Son of Mrs.N.Harwood of King's Cottage, Mare Hill, Pulborough, Sussex; Died at Military Hospital, Étaples.*

3914. LUCK, Leonard George; B: –; E: Piccadilly, London; Pte. G 17653; K: 31.3.17; Aix-Noulette Com. Cem. Ext., Pas-de-Calais; Age 31; Son of George and Jane Elizabeth Luck of St.Leonards-on-Sea, Sussex.

3915. LUSCOMBE, Sydney; B: Islington, London; E: St.Paul's Churchyard, London; Pte. G 5372; W: 17.6.16; Bailleul Com. Cem. Ext., Nord; Age 20; Son of William Henry and Louisa Luscombe of 63, Norfolk Road, Islington; Died at Casualty Clearing Station, Bailleul.*

3916. LYNN, Alfred; B: Seaton Sluice, Northumberland; E: Newcastle-on-Tyne; Pte. G 16818; K: 22.6.17; Ypres (Menin Gate) Mem. (Bel.); Age 33; Son of John Reed Lynn and Margaret Lynn of 17, Avenue Road, Seaton Delaval.

3917. LYTHARBY, William; B: Brighton; E: Brighton; Pte. G 16602; K: 13.4.17; Ypres (Menin Gate) Mem. (Bel.); Age 34; Husband of Nellie Brook Lytharby of 65, Landor Road, Clapham, London.

M

3918. MACDONALD, Alfred Alexander; B: Graffham, Sussex; E: Warley, Essex; Pte. G 12970; K: 24.1.17; Philosophe Brit. Cem., Mazingarbe, Pas-de-Calais; Age 26; Son of James and Minnie Macdonald of 23, Linden Road, Littlehampton, Sussex; Struck in the head while operating his Lewis Gun; His brother, Tom, was a member of the same Lewis Gun team. (see text). *

3919. MAFFRET, Alfred; B: Stepney, London; E: London; Pte. G 19387; K: 11.10.18; St.Aubert Brit. Cem., Nord; Age 18; Son of Mr. and Mrs.Paul Maffret.

3920. MAHY, William Blandfield; B: St.Sampson, Guernsey, Channel Islands; E: Guernsey; Pte. G 3362; W at Home: 26.11.15; St.Sampson Churchyard, Guernsey.

3921. MALCOLM, Alfred Livingstone; B: Tunbridge Wells; E: Tunbridge Wells; Pte. G 7905; W: 17.6.16; Ration Farm (La Plus Douve) Annexe (Bel.); Age 20; Son of Alexander and Sarah Ann Malcolm of Tunbridge Wells.*

3922. MALLOWS, Thomas; B: Westminster, London; E: Brighton; Pte. G 4552; K: 14.2.16; Menin Road South Mil. Cem. (Bel.); Killed while on front line trench duty at Hooge.

3923. MANSFIELD, Bertie; B: Impington, Cambridge-shire; E: Bury St.Edmunds, Suffolk; Pte. G 17657; K: 11.6.17; Ypres (Menin Gate) Mem. (Bel.).

3924. MANT, Henry George; B: Westergate, Sussex; E: Bexhill-on-Sea; Pte. G 6272; K: 13.4.17; Lievin Com. Cem. Ext., Pas-de-Calais.

3925. MANVILLE, Alfred; B: Lewes; E: Brighton; Pte. G 5766; K: 20.8.16; Thiepval Mem., Somme,*

3926. MARCHANT, James; B: Fletching, Sussex; E: Chichester; L/Cpl. GS 413; D at Home: 6.5.18; Felpham (St.Mary) Churchyard, Sussex (UK).

3927. MARCHANT, James; B: Alfriston, Sussex; E: Lewes; Pte. G 3345; K: 14.2.16; Menin Road South Mil. Cem. (Bel.); Age 27; Son of Mr. and Mrs.James Marchant of 10, West Street, Alfriston; Killed while on front line trench duty at Hooge.

3928. MARCHANT, Walter; B: Brighton; E: Brighton; Pte. S 2321; W: 17.8.17; Étaples Mil. Cem., Pas-de-Calais; Age 21; Son of Mr. and Mrs.A.F.Marchant of 33, Mount Pleasant, Brighton.; Died at Military Hospital, Étaples.

3929. MARDEN, Harold John G.; B: Lingfield, Surrey; E: East Grinstead, Sussex; Pte. G 8186; W: 20.8.16; Dive Copse Brit. Cem., Somme; Age 20; Son of Mr.G.Marden of Baldwin's Hill, East Grinstead.

3930. MARSH, Rufus Sidney Herbert; B: Bournemouth; E: Brighton; Pte. G 3638; K: 28.9.15; Loos Mem., Pas-de-Calais; Age 21; Son of Charles and Bessie Marsh of 17, Camelford Street, Brighton.

3931. MARSHALL, David Samuel; B: Haggerston, London; E: Shoreditch, London; Pte. G 19020; W: 6.11.18; Canonne Farm Brit. Cem., Sommaing, Nord; Age 19; Son of Mr.H.W. and Mrs.E.J.Marshall of 35, Holms Street, Hackney Road, London.

3932. MARSHALL, John; B: Bosham, Sussex; E: Bognor Regis, Sussex; Pte. SD 823; K: 23.6.17; Ypres (Menin Gate) Mem. (Bel.); Age 21; Son of Richard Marshall of The Bungalow, Woodgate, Aldingbourne, Sussex.

3933. MARTIN, Harry; B: Tonbridge, Kent; E: Bromley, Kent; Pte. G 8259; W: 10.4.18; La Capelle-en-Thierache Com. Cem., Aisne; Age 39; Son of Alfred Martin of Heathfield Terrace, Swanley, Kent.

3934. MARTIN, Herbert Lockyer; B: Brighton; E:

Brighton; Pte. G 6690; K: 22.3.18; Pozieres Mem., Somme.

3935. MARTIN, James; B: Brighton; E: Brighton; Cpl. G 16543; K: 11.6.17; Ypres (Menin Gate) Mem. (Bel.).

3936. MARTIN, John; B: Wivelsfield, Sussex; E: Lewes; Pte. G 3376; K: 18.8.16; Thiepval Mem., Somme; Age 21; Son of Jesse and Martha Jane Martin of Wivelsfield Green.

3937. MARTIN, Richard; B: Brentford, London; E: Hounslow, London; Pte. G 4206; K: 14.2.16; Menin Road South Mil. Cem. (Bel.) Killed while on front line trench duty at Hooge.

3938. MASKELL, Alfred Cyril; B: Groombridge, Sussex; E: Deptford, London; Pte. G 6659; W: 11.3.17; Lapugnoy Mil. Cem., Pas-de-Calais; Died at No.18 Casualty Clearing Station, Lapugnoy.

3939. MASKELL, George; B: Heathfield, Sussex; E: Tunbridge Wells; Pte. G 5679; K: 25.9.15; Loos Mem., Pas-de-Calais.

3940. MASON, Alfred; B: Aldershot; E: Aldershot; Pte. G 6028; K: 25.9.15; Loos Mem., Pas-de-Calais.

3941. MASON, William; B: Aston, Warwickshire; E: Birmingham; Pte. G 5832; K: 18.8.16; Thiepval Mem., Somme.

3942. MATHEW, George Henry; B: Chalk Farm, London; E: Holloway, London; Pte. G 19010; W: 5.11.18; Awoingt Brit. Cem., Nord; Age 19; Son of Thomas William Shave Mathew and Amy Mathew of 2, Bovay Place, Holloway Road, London; Died at Casualty Clearing Station, Awoingt, from wounds received the previous day.

3943. MATON, Ernest John; B: Winchester; E: Chichester; Pte. G 4936; K: 31.8.16; Bulls Road Cem., Flers, Somme; Age 35; Son of George and Laura Maton of New House Farm, The Grange, Alresford, Hampshire; Husband of Harriet Smith, formerly Maton, of South Farm Cottages, East Meon, Hampshire.

3944. MATTHEWS, George Oliver; B: Clerkenwell, London; E: Harringay, London; Sgt. G 3671; K: 28.9.15; Loos Mem., Pas-de-Calais; Age 30; Son of Mr. and Mrs.G.Matthews of 45, Effingham Road, Harringay; Husband of Florence Ellen Green, formerly Matthews, of 8, Marquis Road, Bowes Park, Wood Green, London.

3945. MAY, Ernest William; B: Catsfield, Sussex; E: Eastbourne; L/Cpl. G 3753; K: 18.8.16; Thiepval Mem., Somme; Age 26; Son of Harry and Maria Markis May of 1, Rupert Villas, London Road, Bracknell, Berkshire.

3946. McARTHUR, James; B: Dumbarton; E: Brighton; Pte. G 3678; K: 19.6.17; Ypres (Menin Gate) Mem. (Bel.); Age 30; Son of James and Jane McArthur of 57, McLean Street, Plantation, Glasgow.

3947. McDERMOTT, Michael; B: Helton, County Durham; E: Newcastle-on-Tyne; Pte.G 16874; K: 17.6.18; Arras Mem., Pas-de-Calais.

3948. MC GREGOR,, James; B: Westminster, London; E: West London; Cpl. G 19021; K: 4.11.18; Cross Roads Cem., Nord; Age 19; Son of James and Isabella McGregor of 19, Hugon Road, Fulham, London.*

3949. McNAIR, Eric Archibald; Capt.; V.C..; D: 12.8.16; Died while serving with another Unit in Italy; V.C. won at Hooge 14.2.16. (see text).

3950. MEREDITH, James; B: Roffey, Sussex; E: Horsham, Sussex; Pte. G 8378; K: 31.8.16; Thiepval Mem., Somme; Age 31; Husband of Alice Meredith of 164, Crawley Road, Horsham.

3951. MERTON, Charles Frederick G.; B: – ; E: Maidstone; Pte. G 13509; K: 30.12.16; Philosophe Brit. Cem., Mazingarbe, Pas-de-Calais; Husband of Mrs .E.J.Fletcher, formerly Merton, of Borough Green, Kent.*

3952. MIDGLEY, Robert; B: Kelloe, County Durham; E: Kelloe; Pte. G 16873; W: 5.11.18; Awoingt Brit. Cem., Nord; Age 21; Son of Samuel and Sarah Midgley of Green Street, Kelloe; Died at Casualty Clearing Station, Awoingt.

3953. MILES, Frank; B: Fishergate, Sussex; E: Hove; Pte. G 4508; K: 9.11.15; Elzenwalle Brasserie Cem. (Bel.); Age 24; Son of William and Sarah Miles of 44, Laylands Road, Fishergate.

3954. MILHAM, Charles; B: Hellingly, Sussex; E: Hove; Pte. G 3460; K: 25.9.15; Loos Mem., Pas-de-Calais; Age 32; Son of William and Emma Milham of Mill Farm Chiddingly, Sussex; Husband of Eunice Elizabeth Barber, formerly Milham, of Nash Street, Hellingly.

3955. MILLER, William; B: Sunderland; E: Sunderland; Pte. G 363; K: 18.6.18; Vervieres Com. Cem. (Bel.); Age 27.

3956. MILWARD, Edward; B: Liverpool; E: Seaforth; Pte. G 19316; K: 10.10.18; St.Aubert Brit. Cem., Nord; Nephew of Miss A.Milward of 291, Upper Parliament Street, Liverpool.

3957. MITCHELL, Francis Sidney; Lt.; K: 15.2.16; Menin Road South Mil. Cem. (Bel.); Age 26; Son of George and Anne Mitchell of Ardlin, Blackrock, County Dublin, Ireland; Attached from Royal Army Medical Corps; Killed during front line trench duty at Hooge.

3958. MITCHELL, Herbert T.; B: Croydon; E: Chichester; Pte. G 1493; K: 13.2.16; Menin Road South Mil. Cem. (Bel.); Age 25; Son of William and Elizabeth Annn Mitchell of 54, Pawson's Road, Croydon; Killed during front line trench duty at Hooge.

3959. MITTELL, Walter John; B: Tenterden, Kent; E: Chichester; Sgt. GS 489; K: 18.8.16; Thiepval Mem., Somme.

3960. MITTEN, Ernest John; B: Hastings; E: Hurstpierpoint, Sussex; Pte. G 3393; K: 3.8.17; Ypres (Menin Gate) Mem. (Bel.).

3961. MOORE, Charles; B: Llangeinor, Glamorgan; E: Bridgend, Glamorgan; Pte. G 3116; K: 18.4.16; Ration Farm (La Plus Douve) Annexe (Bel.); Age 23; Son of Fanny Moore of Ffrud Villa, Llangeinor.

3962. MORLEY, Frank George; B: Fishergate, Sussex; E: Brighton; Pte. G 4226;K: 19.7.16; St.Quentin

Cabaret Mil. Cem. (Bel.); Age 23; Son of William and Ellen Maria Morley of 63, Buller Road, Brighton.

3963. MORTIMER, William James; B: Southwark, London; E: Southwark; Pte. G 20347; K: 4.11.18; Villers-Pol Com. Cem. Ext., Nord; Age 21; Son of Mrs.Emma Jane Dixon of 187, Brook Street, Kennington, London.*

3964. MOSS, William George; B: Redhill, Surrey; E: Haywards Heath, Sussex; L/Cpl. G 3564; K: 25.9.15; Loos Mem., Pas-de-Calais.

3965. MOTTRAM, Arthur; B: Longton, Staffordshire; E: Longton; Pte. G 5385; K: 1.1.17; Philosophe Brit. Cem., Mazingarbe, Pas-de-Calais; Husband of Mrs.E.J.Sprout, formerly Mottram, of 10, Oldgate Street, Morpeth, Northumberland.

3966. MOYLAND, Patrick John; B: – ; E: Wandsworth, London; Pte. G 22978; W: 11.10.18; Delsaux Farm Cem., Pas-de-Calais; Age 38; Husband of Mrs.B.E.Moyland of 4, Ravensbury Terrace, Wandsworth.*

3967. MURRELL, William George; B: Farnborough, Hampshire; E: Worthing; Pte. G 3244; K: 28.9.15; Loos Mem., Pas-de-Calais.

3968. MUSTCHIN, Robert; B: Sompting, Sussex; E: Brighton; Pte. G 3190; K: 25.9.15; Loos Mem., Pas-de-Calais.

N

3969. NALLY, Thomas; B: Bala, County Mayo, Ireland; E: Brighton; Pte. G 4371; W: 6.6.16; Baillleul Com. Cem. Ext., Nord; Died at Casualty Clearing Station, Bailleul.

3970. NEAL, Harry Edward; B: Exning, Suffolk; E: Newmarket, Cambridgeshire; Pte. G 19185; K: 30.5.18; Bully-Grenay Com. Cem. Brit. Ext., Pas-de-Calais; Age 19; Son of Mr. and Sarah A.Neal of Mill Hill, Exning.*

3971. NEIL, Horace; B: Shablington, Buckinghamshire; E: London; Pte. G 18829; D: 12.7.18; Hautmont Com. Cem., Nord; Age 27; Son of Thomas Neil of Oxford; Husband of Lillie Elsie Prettyman, formerly Neil, of 124, Hamilton Crescent, South Harrow, Middlesex.

3972. NEWBERY, Joseph James; B: Brighton; E: Brighton; Pte. G 6802; K: 14.2.16; Menin Road South Mil. Cem. (Bel.); Age 34; Son of Joseph Nathaniel and Kathleen Newbery of Brighton; Husband of Mary E.Newbery of Pendrells, Nep Town, Henfield, Sussex; Killed during front line trench duty at Hooge.

3973. NEWELL, Leonard C.; B: Eastbourne; E: Midhurst, Sussex; Pte. G 3610; W: 11.10.18; Delsaux Farm Cem., Pas-de-Calais.

3974. NEWELL, Walter; B: Eastbourne; E: Eastbourne; Pte. G 1403; K: 6.11.18; Wargnies-le-Petit Com. Cem., Nord; Age 34; Son of Mr. and Mrs. M.Newell of 2, Railway Terrace, Eastbourne.

3975. NEWMAN, Lawrence; B: Hurstpierpoint, Sussex; E: Hurstpierpoint; L/Cpl. G 428; W: 19.8.16; Dive Copse Brit. Cem., Somme; Age 31; Husband of Harriett Jane Newman of West Cottage, Fairfield Road, Burgess Hill, Sussex.

3976. NEWTON, Edward George; B: Upton Park, London; E: Stratford, London; Cpl.G 19024; K: 10.11.18; Maubeuge Centre Cem., Nord.

3977. NICHOLLS, Frederick Edward; B: Lodsworth, Sussex; E: West Lavington, Sussex; Pte. G 8134; K: 21.3.18; Jeancourt Com. Cem., Aisne; Husband of Beatrice Agnes Nicholls of 49, Talbot Road, Southsea, Hampshire.

3978. NOAKES, Percy; B: Hailsham, Sussex; E: Hastings; Pte. SD 2978; K: 11.6.17; Ypres (Menin Gate) Mem. (Bel.); Age 24; Son of Mr. and Mrs.Alfred John Noakes of 1, Eastwell Place, Hailsham.

3979. NORRIS, Ernest Henry; B: Handcross, Sussex; E: Haywards Heath, Sussex; L/Cpl. G 16349; K: 22.3.18; Pozieres Mem., Somme.

3980. NOTTAGE, Arthur William; B: Shoreham, Sussex; E: Worthing; Pte. G 15501; K: 13.4.17; Aix-Noulette Com. Cem. Ext., Pas-de-Calais; Age 19; Son of Mrs.Alice Nottage of 58, Tweedy Road, Bromley, Kent.

O

3981. OLIVER, Charles Valentine; B: Ratcliffe, Middlesex; E: Southwark, London; Pte. G 5557; K: 20.2.16; Ypres (Menin Gate) Mem. (Bel.).

3982. OLIVER, William George; B: Shoreham, Sussex; E: Worthing; Pte. G 1230; K: 31.8.16; Thiepval Mem., Somme.

3983. ORAM, Albert Thomas; B: Ashford, Kent; E: Tonbridge, Kent; Pte. G 24362; W: 22.2.18; Tincourt Brit. Cem., Somme; Age 19; Son of Thomas and Sarah Oram of Rectory Farm, Sevenoaks, Kent; Died at Casualty Clearing Station, Tincourt.

3984. ORCHIN, Frederick James A.; B: Putney, London; E: Putney; Sgt. G 6066; K: 13.2.16; Menin Road South Mil. Cem. (Bel.); Killed during front line trench duty at Hooge.

3985. OSBORNE, George Henry; B: Salehurst, Sussex; E: Hastings; Pte. G 3085; W: 6.9.17; Lijssenthoek Mil. Cem. (Bel.); Age 36; Son of James and Ellen Osborne; Husband of Mrs.G.A.M.M.Osborne of 18, High Street, Robertsbridge, Sussex.

3986. OVERY, Hubert John; B: Hellingly, Sussex; E: Eastbourne; Pte. G 8357; K: 13.4.17; Ypres (Menin Gate) Mem. (Bel.); Age 19; Son of Mr.R.P.L. and Mrs.F.Overy of Lewhurst, Hellingly.

3987. OVERY, John Henry; B: – ; E: Worthing; Pte. G 6975; K: 31.8.16; Thiepval mem., Somme; Age 43; Son of Mr.J.H.Overy; Husband of Mrs.A.V.Overy of 157, West Street, Deal, Kent.

3988. OWEN, Ernest Clarence; B: Forest Gate, London; E: Brighton; Pte. G 3457; K: 8.8.16; Thiepval Mem., Somme; Age 21; Son of Mr. and Mrs.J.Owen of "Peacehaven", Linden Avenue, Bognor Regis, Sussex.

P

3989. PACKHAM, George; B: Brighton; E: Brighton; Pte. G 16595; K: 11.6.17; Ypres (Menin Gate) Mem. (Bel.); Age 30; Husband of Elizabeth Packham of 123, Loder Road, Brighton.

3990. PADGHAM, William; B: Forest Row, Sussex; E: Horsham, Sussex; Pte. SD 3199; K: 3.9.17; La Clytte Mil. Cem. (Bel.); Age 31; Son of Alfred and Mary Agnes Jane Padgham of 1, Medway Cottages, Forest Row.

3991. PADWICK, Sydney; B: Milford, Surrey; E: Guildford; Pte. G 8914; W: 17.7.16; Dranoutre Mil. Cem. (Bel.); Age 32; Son of William and Martha Padwick of Hurtmore, Surrey; Husband of Annie Padwick.

3992. PAGE, Charles Henry; B: Brighton; E: Brighton; Pte. SD 5473; K: 22.3.18; Pozieres Mem. Somme.

3993. PAGE, Henry; B: St.Mary's, Sussex; E: Brighton; Pte. G 3273; K: 28.5.17; Hop Store Cem. (Bel.); Age 20; Son of Mrs.H.Page of 153, Edward Street, Brighton.

3994. PARKER, Joshua E.; B: Dover; E: Southwark, London; Pte. G 4954; K: 14.2.16; Menin Road South Mil. Cem. (Bel.); Age 26; Son of Charles Arthur and Ellen Rose Parker of 8, Winchester Cottages, Orange Street, Southwark; Killed during front line trench duty at Hooge.

3995. PARKER, Percy William Frank; B: Alkham, Kent; E: Dover; Pte. G 16804; K: 23.6.17; Ypres (Menin Gate) Mem. (Bel.); Age 21; Son of Alfred Charles and Edith Laura Parker of "Carlile", London Road, Deal, Kent.

3996. PARKER, Walter; B: – ; E: Bury St.Edmunds, Suffolk; Pte. TF 260085; K: 25.3.18; Pozieres Mem., Somme.

3997. PARRIS, Richard William; B: Eastbourne; E: Maidstone; Cpl. G 8402; K: 18.8.16; Thiepval Mem., Somme.

3998. PARSONS, Benifold Warren; B: Keymer, Sussex; E: Haywards Heath, Sussex; Pte. G 3310; W: 12.4.17; Fosse No.10 Com. Cem. Ext., Pas-de-Calais; Age 20; Son of James and Harriett Parsons of Lodge Farm Cottage, Keymer.*

3999. PARTRIDGE, Francis George; B: Notty Green, Buckinghamshire; E: Portsmouth; Pte. G 13290; W: 30.3.17; Fosse No.10 Com. Cem. Ext., Pas-de-Calais; Age 32; Husband of Rose Partridge of 30, Kensington Road, Reading, Berkshire.

4000. PATERSON, James Cochrane; B: Hampstead, London; E: Westminster, London; Pte. G 2950; W: 21.10.15; Cologne Southern Cem. (G); Age 25; Son of James and Hannah Paterson of Kirkliston, Prince's Road, Felixstowe, Suffolk; Died of wounds while a Prisoner of War.

4001. PAYNE, Frederick Albert; B: Eastbourne; E: Eastbourne; L/Cpl. G 3757; K: 29.9.15; Loos Mem., Pas-de-Calais; Age 20; Son of Walter and Caroline Payne of 15, Motcombe Road, Eastbourne.*

4002. PAYNE, George Alfred; B: Fulham, London; E: Shepherd's Bush, London; Pte. G 4386; W: 17.6.16; Dranoutre Mil. Cem. (Bel.); Age 37; Son of William and Sarah Payne; Husband of Sarah Payne of 63, Dieppe Street, West Kensington, London.

4003. PEARCE, Frederick James; B: Hambledon, Hampshire; E: Brighton; Pte. G 3009; K: 25.9.15; Loos Mem., Pas-de-Calais; Age 25; Son of Frederick and Jane Annie Pearce of "Stroods", Brook Street, Cuckfield, Sussex.

4004. PEARCE, Robert William; B: Boldre, Hampshire; E: Arundel, Sussex; Pte. G 4197; K: 28.9.16; Arras Mem., Pas-de-Calais.

4005. PEARCY, William Richard; B: Forest Gate, London; E: Hove; Pte. G 3368; W: 22.3.18; Bellicourt Brit. Cem., Aisne; Age 35; Son of Elizabeth Pearcy of Selway Farm, Uplime, Devonshire; Husband of Phoebe Howard, formerly Pearcy, of 41, King Street, Worthing.*

4006. PEAT, John; B: Westminster, London; E: Southwark, London; Pte. G 5305; K: 25.9.15; Loos Mem., Pas-de-Calais.

4007. PECK, William Edward; B: Hackney, London; E: Hastings; Pte. G 5696; W: 18.6.16; Bailleul Com. Cem. Ext., Nord; Age 19; Son of William and Elizabeth Peck of 93, Blurton Road, Clapton, London; Died at Casualty Clearing Station, Bailleul, from the effects of gas.

4008. PEER, Alfred John; B: Romford, Essex; E: Romford; Pte. G 24382; K: 4.11.18; Cross Roads Cem., Nord.

4009. PELLING, Ernest John Richard; B: Framfield, Sussex; E: Newhaven, Sussex; Sgt. G 9343; W at Home: 13.7.16; Lewes Cem., Sussex (U.K.); Son of James Pelling of 5, Bull Lane, Lewes.

4010. PENNINGTON, Harold Evelyn; 2nd Lt.; K: 27.9.15; Loos Mem., Pas-de-Calais.

4011. PEPPER, Alfred John; B: Brighton; E: Brighton; Pte. G 3188; K: 17.5.16; Ration Farm (La Plus Douve) Annexe (Bel.); Age 35; Son of Alfred and Ann Pepper of Brighton.

4012. PERKINS, John William; B: Rawal Pindi, India; E: Westminster, London; Pte. G 8987; K: 18.8.16; Thiepval Mem., Somme; Age 27; Son of Henry and Caroline Eliza Perkins of 4, Clarke Road, Richards Town, Bangalore, Southern India.

4013. PETTINGILL, William Alfred; B: Plumstead, London; E: Woolwich, London; Pte. G 19052; K: 4.11.18; Villers-Pol Com. Cem. Ext., Nord; Age 19; Son of William and Eva Pettingill of 1a, Bartletts Terrace, Plumstead.

4014. PETTITT, Arthur Charles; B: Hove; E: Portslade, Sussex; Pte. G 4956; K: 18.8.16; Thiepval Mem., Somme; Age 26; Son of Mrs.E.J.Pettitt of 2, Westbourne Street, Hove.

4015. PETTITT, Frederick John; B: Rottingdean, Sussex; E: Brighton; Pte. G 3016; K: 25.9.15; Loos Mem., Pas-de-Calais; Age 27; Son of Frederick John and Mary Ann Pettitt of 20, Rifle Butt Road, Brighton.

4016. PHILLIPS, James; B: Heathfield, Sussex; E: Marylebone, London; Pte. G 4556; K: 14.2.16; Menin Road South Mil. Cem. (Bel.); Age 24; Son of G.W. and Kate Phillips of 39, Mannett Road, Hastings.

4017. PHILLIPS, Leonard; B: Sompting, Sussex; E: Worthing; Pte. G 3175; K: 16.1.16; Dickebusch New Mil. Cem. (Bel.); Age 21; Son of Herbert and Louisa Phillips; Husband of Daisy Phillips of 69, The Drive, West Worthing; Killed while attached to the 172nd Company, Royal Engineers.

4018. PIKE, Alfred; B: Bridgwater, Somerset; E: Littlehampton, Sussex; Sgt. G 3383; W: 10.5.16; Bailleul Com. Cem. Ext., Nord; Died at Casualty Clearing Station, Bailleul.

4019. PIKE, Herbert Joseph; B: Great Waltham, Essex; E: Kensington, London; Pte. G 16598; K: 13.4.17; Ypres (Menin Gate) Mem. (Bel.).

4020. PILCHER, Henry; B: Ashford, Kent; E: Bexhill-on-Sea; Pte. G 6678; D: 12.2.17; Boulogne Eastern Cem., Pas-de-Calais; Died at Military Hospital, Calais.

4021. PITMAN, Charles George; B: Brighton; E: Brighton; Pte. G 9004; K: 19.7.16; St.Quentin Cabaret Mil. Cem. (Bel.); Age 27; Son of Robert Henry Pitman of 16, Shanklin Road, Brighton.

4022. PITMAN, Ernest; B: Brighton; E: Brighton; Pte. G 6912; K: 28.9.15; Loos Mem., Pas-de-Calais; Age 15; Son of Robert C.C. and Ruth Kate Pitman of 8, Blackman Street, Brighton; One of the youngest soldiers to be killed during the war.*

4023. PLAYFORD, John Frederick; B: King's Lynn, Norfolk; E: King's Lynn, Norfolk; Pte. G 24364; K: 21.3.18; Pozieres Mem., Somme.

4024. PONT, James Robert; B: Brighton; E: Brighton; Pte. G 4982; D: 31.8.18; Cologne Southern Cem. (G); Died while a Prisoner of War.

4025. POPE, Charles Oliver Thomas; B: Pulborough, Sussex; E: Horsham, Sussex; Pte. 17890; K: 15.8.17; Ypres (Menin Gate) Mem. (Bel.); Age 22; Son of Mr.C.A. and Mrs.L.Pope of Cray Lane Crossing, Codmore Hill, Sussex.

4026. POPE, Joseph William; B: Much Marcle, Herefordshire; E: Eastbourne; Pte. G 8124; W: 4.8.17; Lijssenthoek Mil. Cem. (Bel.); Age 35; Son of Joseph William and Katherine Mary Pope of Hall Court, Much Marcle.*

4027. POULTER, Christopher; B: Hanover Square, London; E: Uckfield, Sussex; Cpl. G 3575; K: 14.2.16; Tyne Cot Cem. (Bel.); Age 20; Son of James Poulter of Fern Cottage, Camp Road, Freshwater, Isle of Wight.

4028. POWELL, Frank John; B: Bursted, Sussex; E: Bognor Regis, Sussex; Pte. SD 1204; W: 13.8.17; The Huts Cem. (Bel.); Age 30; Husband of Nellie Blanche Barnes, formerly Powell, of 128, St.Pancras, Chichester.

4029. PRATT, Archibald; B: Homerton, London; E: London; Pte. G 5308; K: 17.6.16; Ration Farm (La Plus Douve) Annexe (Bel.); Age 22; Husband of Jessie Sophia Gilhies, formerly Pratt, of 2, Coolege Lane, Homerton.

4030. PRINCE, Claude Melnotte; 2nd Lt.; K: 18.8.16; Thiepval Mem., Somme; Age 20; Son of Mr. and Mrs.F.Prince of Thornton Heath, London; Husband of Edith Marian Prince of 4, Colebrook Road, Southwick, Sussex; Killed by the enemy bombardment while attacking Guillemont.*

4031. PRING, Francis Raleigh; Lt.; K: 25.9.15; Loos Mem., Pas-de-Calais; Age 27; Son of Mr.F.G. and Mrs.G.Pring of Calceto, Lyminster, Littlehampton, Sussex.

4032. PRINGLE, Charles John; B: St.Leonards-on-Sea; E: Hastings; Pte. G 3872; K: 9.3.16; Menin Road South Mil. Cem. (Bel.); Husband of Mrs.B.A.Parris, formerly Pringle, of 12, Gilbert Road, Belvedere, Kent.

4033. PROWSE, Gerald Maurice Warren; 2nd Lt.; K: 12.4.17; Arras Mem., Pas-de-Calais; Age 24; Son of T.W. and Clara Warren Prowse of Darley Road, Eastbourne.

4034. PRYOR, Hubert Cyril; B: Burgess Hill, Sussex; E: Brighton; Pte. SD 3170; W: 19.8.16; La Neuville Brit. Cem., Somme; Age 19; Son of William and Ada Pryor of Burgess Hill.

4035. PULL, Charles Henry; B: – ; E: – ; Cpl. G 3301; W: 26.8.17; Mendingham Mil. Cem. (Bel.); Age 24; Edwin Walter and Sarah Ann Pull of The Gardens, Petworth Park, Petworth, Sussex; Wounded while attached to the 73rd. Light Trench Mortar Battery, The Royal Sussex Regiment.

4036. PULLEN, William; B: Brighton; E: Hove; Cpl. G 3664; K: 14.2.16; Menin Road South Mil. Cem. (Bel.); Killed during duty in the front line trenches at Hooge.

4037. PURDY, Frederick Charles; B: Brighton; E: Brighton; Pte. G 3534; K: 13.4.17; Ypres (Menin Gate) Mem. (Bel.).

4038. PUTMAN, Thomas Graham; B: Terwick, Sussex; E: Midhurst, Sussex; Pte. G 3372; K: 25.9.15; Loos Mem., Pas-de-Calais; Age 22; Son of William and Elizabeth Putman of Fern Bank, Trotton, Hampshire.*

4039. PUTTOCK, Frank; B: Loxwood, Sussex; E: Horsham, Sussex; Pte. G 6225; K: 4.11.18; Villers-Pol Com. Cem. Ext., Nord; Son of Mr.J.Puttock of Gunshot Common, Wisborough Green, Sussex.

4040. PUTTOCK, James; B: Wisborough Green, Sussex; E: Horsham, Sussex; Pte. G 6658; K: 28.6.17; Ypres (Menin Gate) Mem. (Bel.).

Q

4041. QUAIFE, Stanley; B: St.Leonards-on-Sea; E: Haywards Heath, Sussex; Sgt. G 3335; K: 28.9.15; Loos Mem., Pas-de-Calais.

4042. QUIGLEY, Daniel; B: Dublin, Ireland; E: Southwark, London; Pte. G 5326; K: 25.9.15; Loos Mem., Pas-de-Calais; Age 37; Husband of Fanny Sophia Ann Quigley of 61, St.Hugh's Road, Anerley, London.

R

4043. RADFORD, Charles; B: – ; E: Aberdare; Pte. G 5462; K: 21.3.18; Pozieres Mem., Somme; Age 20; Son of William and Elizabeth Radford.

4044. RADFORD, Frederick Alexander; B: Ramsgate, Kent; E: Portslade, Sussex; L/Cpl. G 4894; K: 18.8.16; Thiepval Mem., Somme; Age 21; Son of Stanley A.G. and Laura E.Radford of 49, Erroll Road, Hove; Enlisted with his brother, Harold Stanley, who was also killed serving with this Battalion (see 4045).

4045. RADFORD, Harold Stanley; B: Ramsgate, Kent; E: Portslade, Sussex; Pte. G 4895; K: 28.6.16; Kemmel Chateau Mil. Cem. (Bel.); Age 19; Son of Stanley S.G. and Laura E.Radford of 49, Erroll Road, Hove; Enlisted with his brother, Frederick Alexander, who was also killed serving with this Battalion (see 4044). *

4046. RAFFLE, James; B: Cramlington, Northumberland; E: North Shields, Northumberland; Pte. G 5914; W: 27.3.16; Ration Farm (La Plus Douve) Annexe (Bel.); Age 23; Son of Edward and Jane Raffle of 34, Camden Lane, North Shields.

4047. RANDALL, George Henry; B: Camberwell, London; E: Camberwell; Pte. G 7843; K: 18.8.16; Thiepval Mem., Somme.

4048. RANDALL, Harold; B: Walthamstow, London; E: Camberwell, London; Pte. G 18653; K: 21.3.18; Pozieres Mem., Somme; Age 19; Son of William Edward and Catherine G.Randall of Church Road, Binstead, Isle of Wight.

4049. READ, John; B: Shrivenham, Berkshire; E: Swindon, Wiltshire; Pte. SD 3877; W: 15.6.17; Boulogne Eastern Cem., Pas-de-Calais; Age 28; Died at Military Hospital, Boulogne.

4050. REEVES, Arthur John; B: Wareham, Sussex; E: Chichester; Pte. L 10519; K: 21.2.16; Ypres (Menin Gate) Mem. (Bel.); Age 26; Brother of Miss Ellen Mary Reeves of 226, Portland Road, South Norwood, London.*

4051. REEVES, Herbert; B: Uckfield, Sussex; E: Croydon; Sgt. G 3330; K: 14.2.16; Menin Road South Mil. Cem. (Bel.); Age 25; Son of Abraham and Thirza Reeves of 262, Kennington Road, London; Killed while on duty in the front line trench at Hooge.

4052. REGAN, Ernest Charles; 2nd Lt.; K: 21.3.18; Jeancourt Com. Cem., Aisne; Age 20; Son of William James and Antoinette Regan of 9, Queen Anne's Gate, London.

4053. REMNANT, Edwin; B: Plaistow, London; E: Guildford; Pte. G 3666; K: 29.1.16; Ypres (Menin Gate) Mem. (Bel.).

4054. REMNANT, George Ernest; B: Plaistow, London; E: Petworth, Sussex; Pte. G 4813; K: 25.9.15; Loos Mem., Pas-de-Calais.

4055. REYNOLDS, John; B: Beddington, Surrey; E: Croydon; Pte. G 5439; K: 28.9.15; Loos Mem., Pas-de-Calais; Age 35; Son of John and Elizabeth Reynolds of Dawson's Cottage, Beddington; His brother, Frederick James, also fell.

4056. REYNOLDS, John Edmond; B: Hereford; E: Fishguard; Pte. G 19196; K: 4.11.18; Wargnies-le-Petit Com. Cem., Nord; Age 18; Son of John and Hannah Reynolds of 11, Plasygamil Road, Goodwick, Pembrokeshire.*

4057. RICHARDSON, Ewart Blake; B: Tonbridge, Kent; E: Tonbridge; Pte. G 18799; D: 22.10.18; Berlin South-Western Cem. (G); Died while a Prisoner of War.

4058. RICHARDSON, M.; B: - ; E. - ; Pte. G 3544; D at Home: 23.8.16; Lewes Cem., Sussex (UK); Age 24; Son of Mark and Harriet Richardson of 2, Walwers Lane, Lewes.

4059. RICHARDSON, Ridley Gordon; B: Bognor Regis, Sussex; E: Bognor Regis; Pte. G 17624; K: 11.6.17; Ypres (Menin Gate) Mem. (Bel.); Age 20; Son of John Richardson of 30, West Street, Bognor Regis.

4060. RICHARDSON, William George; B: Brighton; E: Guildford; Pte. G 6220; W: 23.6.17; Lijssenthoek Mil. Cem. (Bel.); Age 39; Son of Samuel and Harriet Richardson of Rodmell, Sussex; Husband of Mrs.R.M.Richardson of 95, St.George's Road, Brighton.

4061. RICHES, Reginald; B: North Waltham, Norfolk; E: Wroxham, Norfolk; Pte. G 18797; K: 21.3.18; Pozieres Mem., Somme; Age 19; Son of William and Mary Ann Riches of Mill Road, Shepdham, Norfolk.

4062. RICKETTS, Robert; B: Pentonville, London; E: Holborn, London; Pte. G 5963; W: 9.6.16; Bailleul Com. Cem. Ext., Nord; Age 20; Son of Robert and Emma Ricketts of 11, Risinghill, Pentonville; Died at Casualty Clearing Station, Bailleul.

4063. RIDDLE, Harold; B: Hastings; E: Cardigan; Pte. G 4557; K: 25.9.15; Loos Mem., Pas-de-Calais.

4064. RIDDLES, Percy Edgar; B: Brighton; E: Eastbourne; Pte. G 5736; W: 21.8.16; La Neuville Brit. Cem., Somme; Age 32; Son of Richard and Helen Riddles of 4, Park Road, Crowborough, Sussex.

4065. RIDLEY, Eric Samuel; B: Eastbourne; E: Hove; Pte. G 5763; K: 23.6.16; Kemmel Chateau Mil. Cem. (Bel.); Age 19; Son of Frederick Rowland Spencer Ridley of Oak Lodge, Green Lane, Crowborough, Sussex.

4066. ROBBINS, John Henry William; B: Brighton; E: London; Pte. G 5226; K: 14.2.16; Menin Road South Mil. Cem. (Bel.); Age 19; Son of Sarah Ann Louisa Robbins of 40, Elder Street, Brighton; Killed while on duty in the front line trench at Hooge.

4067. ROBINS, George; B: Warbleton, Sussex; E: Eastbourne; Pte. G 1396; K: 27.3.18; Pozieres Mem., Somme; Age 26; Son of George and Rhoda Robins of Church Cottages, Warbleton.

4068. ROBINSON, Richard Francis; B: Portsmouth; E: Portsmouth; Pte. G 5264; K: 25.9.15; Loos Mem., Pas-de-Calais; Age 20.

4069. ROBINSON, Robert; B: Belfast; E: Hove; Pte. GS 471; D: 27.5.16; La Clytte Mil. Cem. (Bel.).

4070. ROBSON, Robert; B: Gateshead; E: Newcastle-on-Tyne; L/Cpl. G 5883; K: 3.10.16; Villers Station Cem., Pas-de-Calais; Age 29; Son of Mathew and Margaret Robson of Gateshead; Husband of Frances Ann Robson of 68, Queen's Street, Gateshead.

4071. ROGERS, James Albert; B: Brighton; E: Hove;

Pte. G 5135; K: 21.11.17; Hargicourt Brit. Cem., Aisne; Son of Mr.G.Rogers of 40, Sutherland Road, Brighton.

4072. ROGERSON, Ernest Sidney; Capt.; K: 19.8.16; Thiepval Mem., Somme; Age 28; Son of Arthur William and Elizabeth Rogerson of "Denton", The Avenue, Lewes; Killed while on duty in the front line trench at Hooge.

4073. ROLLING, Philip Ernest; B: Woking, Surrey; E: Guildford; Pte. G 18852; W: 17.5.18; Pernes Brit. Cem., Pas-de-Calais; Age 18; Son of Mrs.A.Rolling of 6, Lye Cottages, St.John's, Woking; Died at Casualty Clearing Station, Pernes.

4074. ROSS, Leonard; B: Exeter; E: Pontypridd; Pte. G 3660; W: 29.9.15; Bethune Town Cem., Pas-de-Calais; Died at No.33 Casualty Clearing Station, Bethune.

4075. ROUS, Arthur; B: Brighton; E: Brighton; L/Cpl. G 8342; K: 3.4.18; Pozieres Mem., Somme.

4076. ROUSE, Albert James; B: Shoreham, Sussex; E: Brighton; Pte. G 3520; K: 18.8.16; Thiepval Mem., Somme.

4077. RUBIDGE, Ernest William; B: Portslade, Sussex; E: Brighton; Cpl. G 2979; K: 14.2.16; Menin Road South Mil. Cem. (Bel.); Killed while on duty in the front line trenc at Hooge.

4078. RUSSELL, John Alfred; B: Chiddingly, Sussex; E: Lewes; Pte. GS 3343; W: 29.3.18; Namps-au-Val Brit. Cem., Somme; Son of Mr.D.Russell of 164, Price's Cottages, Whitesmith, Sussex; Died at Casualty Clearing Station, Namps-au-Val.

S

4079. SADLER, Alfred; B: Colchester, Essex; E: Colchester; Pte, G 7895; K: 28.9.15; Loos Mem., Pas-de-Calais; Age 19; Son of Mr.S.R.W. and Mrs.Z.H.Sadler of 72, Winchester Road, Colchester.

4080. SAGE, Henry; B: – ; E: Chichester; Sgt. L 5946; W: 13.12.16; Barlin Com. Cem., Pas-de-Calais; Age 34; Son of Mary Sage of 4, Romney Street, Seaside, Eastbourne; Husband of Mrs.Maggie Sage of Woodgrange, Ballydugan, County Down, Northern Ireland.

4081. SAGE, John William; B: Hucking, Kent; E: Sittingbourne, Kent; Pte. SD 5681; K: 31.8.16; Thiepval Mem., Somme.

4082. SAGEMAN, Benjamin; B: Littlehampton, Sussex; E: Bognor Regis, Sussex; Pte. G 7234; D: 13.6.18; Premont Brit. Cem., Aisne.

4083. SALVAGE, George; B: Brighton; E: Brighton; Pte. G 3281; K: 28.6.16; Kemmel Chateau Mil. Cem. (Bel.); Age 23; Son of Henry James and Grace Salvage of 52, Balfour Road, Brighton.

4084. SANDALLS, Alfred; B: Barcombe, Sussex; E: Lewes; Pte. G 3336; K: 7.10.15; Potijze Burial Ground Cem. (Bel.); Age 37; Son of Albert and Harriett Sandalls of Lewes; Husband of Ellen Sandalls of 56, Barden Road, Tonbridge, Kent.

4085. SANDERS, Edward William; B: Rottingdean, Sussex; E: Brighton; Pte. G 3414; K: 18.8.16; Delville Wood Cem., Somme; Age 28; Son of Edward William and Mary Sanders of 19, Redvers Road, Brighton.

4086. SANTER, William Aubrey; B: Battle, Sussex; E: Hastings; Pte. G 12141; K: 21.3.18; Pozieres Mem., Somme; Age 30; Son of William and Annie Santer of 9, Upper Lake, Battle.

4087. SARGENT, Thomas William; B: Hastings; E: Chichester; Pte. G 6228; K: 23.6.17; Ypres (Menin Gate) Mem. (Bel.); Age 30; Son of Frederick and Emily Sargent of 10, High Street, Hastings; Husband of Agnes Anna Sargent of The Bungalow, Stunts Green, Sussex.

4088. SAUNDERS, Leonard Charles; B: Brighton; E: Brighton; Pte. G 12201; K: 15.1.17; Philosophe Brit. Cem., Mazingarbe, Pas-de-Calais; Age 31; Son of Charles and Elizabeth Phoebe Saunders; Husband of Olive Saunders of 13, Seville Street, Brighton.

4089. SAWYER, Richard John; B: Maidstone; E: Hove; Pte. G 8120; K: 27.3.17; Aix-Noulette Com. Cem. Ext., Pas-de-calais; Son of Mr.R.Sawyer.

4090. SAYER, Ernest Edward; B: Margate; E: Guildford; L/Sgt. G 3727; K: 17.6.16; Ration Farm (La Plus Douve) Annexe (Bel.); Son of Mrs.E.Sayer of 5, Victoria Avenue, Cliftonville, Kent.

4091. SCOTT, William; B: Glasgow; E: Shoreham, Sussex; Pte. G 6919; K: 24.1.17; Philosophe Brit. Cem., Mazingarbe, Pas-de-Calais.

4092. SCRIVENER, Frederick John; B: St.Mary-at-the-Elms, Suffolk; E: Tunbridge Wells; Cpl. SD 470; K: 4.11.18; Cross Roads Cem., Nord; Age 24; Son of Frederick William and Maria Scrivener of Alexandra Ward, Heathfields, Ipswich, Suffolk.

4093. SEAL, Robert David James; B: Deptford, London; E: Brighton; Cpl. G 16492; K: 25.3.18; Pozieres Mem., Somme; Age 25; Son of David and Anne Maria seal of 26, Brookdale Road, Catford, London.

4094. SEARLE, Charles; B: Fernhurst, Surrey; E: Horsham, Sussex; L/Cpl. G 925; K: 13.4.17; Lievin Com. Cem. Ext.,, Pas-de-Calais; Age 21; Son of Mr.C. and Mrs.E.Searle of Dora Cottages, Greatham, Sussex.

4095. SEARLE, Charles Caleb; B: Broadwater, Sussex; E: Brighton; Pte. G 16577; K: 28.7.17; Ypres (Menin Gate) Mem. (Bel.); Age 35; Husband of Edith Kate Searle of 63, Bates Road, Brighton.

4096. SECRETAN, Ivan Archer; B: Staines, Middlesex; E: Hove; Pte. G 1998; W: 10.3.18; Pernois Brit Cem., Somme; Age 21; Son of Archer Jeston Secretan and Kate Amelia Secretan of Brighton; Died at Casualty Clearing Station, Pernois.

4097. SEELEY, Stanley John; B: New Cross, London; E: Woolwich, London; Pte. G 18664; K: 21.3.18; Pozieres mem., Somme; Age 19; Son of Harry and Jessie Annie Seeley of 106, Dumbreck Road, Eltham, London.

4098. SEPHTON, George; B: Tyldesley, Lancashire; E: Leigh, Lancashire; Pte. G 6096; W: 20.11.17; Tincourt New Brit. Cem., Somme; Age 37; Husband of Maria Sephton of 7, Alfred Street, Tyldesley; Died at Casualty Clearing Station, Tincourt.

4099. SEYMOUR, James Frederick; B: Harlow, Essex; E: Bury St.Edmunds, Suffolk; Pte. SD 5608; K: 22.6.17; Ypres (Menin Gate) Mem. (Bel.); Age 25; Son of William and Alice Jane seymour of Harlow Tye.

4100. SHARP, Ernest; B: Brighton; E: Hove; Pte. L 10877; K: 13.4.17; Canadian Cem. No.2, Pas-de-Calais.*

4101. SHARP, Frederick; B: Hove; E: Hove; Pte. L 10721; K: 13.4.17; Ypres (Menin Gate) Mem. (Bel.).

4102. SHAW, William Bernard; Lt.; K: 12.4.17; Arras Mem., Pas-de-Calais; Age 23; Son of William Lingsdon Shaw and Martha Fletcher Shaw of "Longstone", Bristol Gardens, Brighton.

4103. SHERIFF, Joseph; B: Clent, Worcestershire; E: Stourbridge, Worcestershire; Pte. G 6074; K: 23.6.17; Ypres (Menin Gate) Mem. (Bel.); Age 23; Son of Mary Sheriff of Clent.

4104. SHERWOOD, Thomas; B: Aylesford, Kent; E: Maidstone; Pte. SD 5683; W: 1.9.16; Dantzig Alley Brit. Cem., Somme.

4105. SHOESMITH, William George; B: Whitstable, Kent; E: Fulham, London; Pte. G 5783; W: 25.11.15; Lijssenthoek Mil. Cem. (Bel.).

4106. SILVERTON, John Henry; B: Hammersmith, London; E: Hove; Pte. G 7656; W: 5.5.16; Bailleul Com. Cem. Ext., Nord; Died at Casualty Clearing Station, Bailleul.

4107. SIMMONDS, Frederick Albert; B: Shoreham, Sussex; E: Worthing; Pte. G 3307; K: 25.9.15; Loos Mem., Pas-de-Calais.

4108. SIMMONS, Bertie Arthur; B: Uckfield, Sussex; E: Eastbourne; Pte. G 19533; K: 3.4.18; Pozieres Mem., Somme; Age 20; Son of George and Annie Elizabeth Simmons of 14, Alexandra Road, Uckfield.*

4109 SIMMONS, Newton; B: Winfield, Sussex; E: Tonbridge, Kent; Pte. G 12953; W: 7.12.16; Barlin Com. Cem., Pas-de-Calais; Age 25; Son of William and Sarah Simmons of Sidley, Bexhill-on-Sea.*

4110. SKEITES, William James; B: Plansham, Sussex; E: Bognor Regis; Pte. G 7230; K: 2.7.16; Dranoutre Mil. Cem. (Bel.); Age 22; Son of James and Annie E.Skeites of Plansham, Sussex.

4111. SKINNER, Ernest Arthur; B: Camden Town, London; E: Maidstone; Pte. G 22607; K: 22.3.18; Pozieres mem., Somme.

4112. SKINNER, Harry Herbert; B: West Norwood, London; E: Brighton; L/Cpl. G 17631; K: 11.3.17; Aix-Noulette Com. Cem., Pas-de-calais.

4113. SKINNER, James; B: Hildenborough, Kent; E: Tonbridge; Pte. G 18841; W: 24.3.18; Rosieres Brit. Cem., Somme.

4114. SKINNER, William; B: Storrington, Sussex; E: Worthing; Pte. G 3692; W: 1.10.15; Le Treport Mil. Cem., Seine-Maritime; Age 20; Son of Albert and Jane Skinner of 7, North Lane, Storrington; Died at Military Hospital, Le Treport.

4115. SKIPWORTH, Bernard William; Lt.; K: 25.4.18; Tyne Cot Mem. (Bel.); Age 28; Son of William Green Skipworth and Emily Skipworth of Brookhurst, Broadbridge Heath, Sussex; Attached from 3rd Battalion Royal Sussex regiment to the 9th Battalion Machine Gun Corps (Infantry).

4116. SLATER, Walter; B: Brighton; E: Brighton; Pte. G 3606; D: 11.12.15; Houlle Churchyard, Pas-de-Calais; Age 38; Son of Thomas and Elizabeth Slater.

4117. SMETHURST, James; B: Walshaw, Lancashire; E: Bury, Lancashire; Pte. G 19335; W: 5.11.18; Awoingt Brit. Cem., Nord; Age 19; Son of John and Elizabeth Alice Smethurst of 85, Church Street, Walshaw; Died at Casualty Clearing Station, Awoingt.

4118. SMITH, Charles; B: Burton-on-Trent; E: Cannock, Staffordshire; Pte. G 6073; W: 1.6.16; Bailleul Com. Cem. Ext., Nord; Age 19; Son of Frank and Elizabeth Smith of 186, Stafford Road, Cannock.

4119. SMITH, Ernest; B: Heathfield, Sussex; E: Hove; Pte. L 10852; K: 11.6.17; Ypres (Menin Gate) Mem. (Bel.).

4120. SMITH, Fred; B: Radcliffe, Lancashire; E: Bury, Lancashire; Pte. G 19334; W: 2.6.18; Pernes Brit. Cem., Pas-de-calais; Died at Casualty Clearing Station, Pernes.

4121. SMITH, George Ernest; B: Tower of London; E: Colchester; L/Cpl. G 14637; K: 31.5.18; Bully-Grenay Com. Cem. Brit. Ext., Pas-de-Calais; Age 21; Son of Joseph Smith, Colour Sergeant, 1st Bn. Grenadier Guards, and Harriett Smith of 62, Brookdale Road, Walthamstow, London.

4122. SMITH, George William; B: Brighton; E: Redhill, Surrey; Pte. G 4671; K: 25.9.15; Loos Mem., Pas-de-Calais.

4123. SMITH, Harry; B: Eastbourne; E: Eastbourne; Pte. G 5759; K: 9.6.16; Berks Cem. Ext. (Bel.); Age 19; Son of George and Emma Smith of 1, Parkes Terrace, Hampden Park, Eastbourne.

4124. SMITH, Harry George; B: Brighton; E: Brighton; Pte. G 11909; W: 26.8.17; Lijssenthoek Mil. Cem. (Bel.); Age 21; Son of Henry and Mary Ann Smith of 2, Ditchling Road, Brighton.*

4125. SMITH, Herbert Stanley; B: Grays, Essex; E: Grays; Pte. SD 5520; K: 29.11.16; Philosophe Com. Cem., Nord; Husband of Mrs.E.R.Wright, formerly Smith, of 17, Florence Cottages, Grays.

4126. SMITH, Herbert Stephen; B: –; E: Steyning, Sussex; Sgt. G 4183; W: 17.5.16; Bailleul Com. Cem. Ext., Nord; Age 27; Husband of Ethel Alice Smith of Buckwish, Henfield, Sussex; Died at Casualty Clearing Station, Bailleul.

4127. SMITH, Jack; B: Hadlow Down, Sussex; E: Uckfield, Sussex; Pte. G 3579; K: 25.9.15; Loos Mem., Pas-de-Calais.

4128. SMITH, James; B: Bathgate, Linlithgow; E: Grove Park; Pte. G 16822; K: 25.3.18; Pozieres Mem., Somme; Age 34; Son of Mr.John and Mrs.S.C.Smith of 118, Beechwood Cottages, Uphall, Linlithgow.

4129. SMITH, John; B: High Hurstwood, Sussex; E: Lewes; Pte. G 1663; K: 18.8.16; Thiepval Mem., Somme.

4130. SMITH, John; B: Stapleton, Gloucestershire; E: Haywards Heath, Sussex; Pte. G 3612; K: 27.9.15; Loos mem., Pas-de-Calais; Age 25; Son of Mrs.E.Smith of 2, Foots Hill, Hanham, Bristol.

4131. SMITH, William Charles; B: Eastbourne; E: Eastbourne; Pte. G 1453; W: 17.6.16; Dranoutre Mil. Cem. (Bel.); Age 31; Husband of Lilian Smith of 39, Avondale Road, Eastbourne.

4132. SMITH, William John; B: Buxted, Sussex; E: Uckfield, Sussex; Pte. SD 1818; W: 4.8.17; Lijssenthoek Mil. Cem. (Bel.); Age 21; Son of William Henry and Kate Smith of Buxted.

4133. SMITHERMAN, Albert; B: Rusthall, Kent; E: Bristol; Pte. L 11459; K: 27.1.18; Hargicourt Brit. Cem., Aisne; Son of Mr.A.Smitherman of 21, Erskine Park Road, Rusthall Common.

4134. SOMERVILLE, Francis Leslie Ferdinand; B: Windsor; E: Brighton; Pte. SD 4092; K: 4.11.18; Villers-Pol Com. Cem. Ext., Nord; Age 21; Son of Alfred H. and Emmeline Somerville of 136a, Western Road, Brighton.

4135. SOPER, John Gilbert; B: Guildford; E: Hammersmith, London; L/Cpl. G 11970; D: 25.9.17; Étaples Mil. Cem., Pas-de-Calais; Age 38; Son of Thomas Rundle Soper and Annie Soper; Husband of Florence Soper of 91, Cheyne Walk, Chelsea, London; Died of nephritis at Military Hospital, Étaples.

4136. SOPP, Herbert Archer; B: Petworth, Sussex; E: Petworth; Pte. G 3775; K: 18.8.16; London Cem. and Ext., Somme.

4137. SPENCER, Henry; B: Marylebone, London; E: Whitehall, London; Pte. G 18823; W: 28.3.18; Abbeville Com. Cem. Ext., Somme; Age 36; Husband of Mary Spencer of 10, Grantbridge Street, Islington, London.

4138. SPICKNELL, Charles Alfred; B: Aldgate, London; E: Whitehall, London; Pte. G 18659; W: 31.3.18; Premont Brit. Cem., Aisne; Age 19; Son of James A. and Eliza Isabella Spicknell of 2, Hope Cottages, Feltham Hill Road, Ashford, Middlesex.

4139. SPRIGGS, Richard; B: Whittlesea, Cambridgeshire; E: Peterborough; Pte. G 7831; K: 28.9.15; Loos Mem., Pas-de-Calais; Age 33; Husband of Ann Follows, formerly Spriggs, of 21, Jarrom Street, Leicester.

4140. SPURGIN, Harold Jerrold; B: Croydon; E: Croydon; Cpl. G 3311; K: 15.7.16; St.Quentin Cabaret Mil. Cem. (Bel.); Age 21; Son of Frederic and Emma Spurgin of Fairlie Estate, Ringwood, Hampshire.*

4141. SQUELCH, Leonard; B: West Hampstead, London; E: Bognor Regis, Sussex; Pte. G 1216; K: 25.9.15; Loos Mem., Pas-de-Calais.

4142. STAGLES, Arthur; B: Stanninglley, Yorkshire; E: Wisbech, Cambridgeshire; Pte. SD 5614; W: 4.9.16; Heilly Station Cem., Mericourt-L'Abbé, Somme; Son of Harry and Hannah Stagles of Wisbech; Husband of Florence May Hibbert, formerly Stagles, of 12, Firhill Road, Bellingham, London.

4143. STAKER, Francis William; B: Ryde, Isle of Wight; E: Guildford; Pte. G 4069; K: 28.9.15; Loos Mem., Pas-de-Calais.

4144. STANDEN, James Philip; B: Hastings; E: Hastings; Pte. G 8598; K: 31.8.16; Thiepval Mem., Somme; Age 20; Son of Edwin William and Frances Hannah Standen of 36, Harold Road, Hastings.

4145. STANLEY, Frederick Charles; B: Hastings; E: Hastings; Pte. G 5437; W: 21.8.16; Dive Copse Brit. Cem., Somme; Age 19; Son of Mrs.M.J.Stanley of 7, New Road, Hastings.

4146. STEDMAN, Frederick George; B: Salfords, Surrey; E: East Grinstead, Sussex; Pte. G 3261; K: 31.8.16; Thiepval Mem., Somme.

4147. STEED, James William; B: King's Lynn, Norfolk; E: Norwich; Pte. G 9350; W: 23.6.17; Lijssenthoek Mil. Cem. (Bel.); Son-in-Law of George Worthington of 111, Waterloo Road, Norwich.

4148. STEPHENS, George; B: Hellingly, Sussex; E: Tunbridge Wells; Pte. G 6635; W: 14.4.17; Lillers Com. Cem., Pas-de-Calais; Age 23; Son of George and Annie Stephens of 4, Carlton Terrace, Crowborough, Sussex; Died at Casualty Clearing Station, Lillers.

4149. STEVENS, Arthur; B: Horsebridge, Sussex; E: Lewes; Pte. G 3130; K: 25.9.15; Loos Mem., Pas-de-Calais; Son of Phineas Stevens.

4150. STEVENS, Frederick; B: Eastbourne; E: Guildford; Cpl. G 5019; K: 22.3.18; Pozieres Mem., Somme.

4151. STEVENS, Henry James; B: Ridgewood, Sussex; E: Haywards Heath, Sussex; Pte. G 3321; W: 18.6.16; Bailleul Com. Cem. Ext., Nord; Age 31; Son of George and Sarah Stevens of Ringmer, Sussex; Died at Casualty Clearing Station, Bailleul, from the results of gas.*

4152. STEVENSON, Arthur Lionel; B: – ; E: Maidstone; L/Cpl. G 16346; K: 23.6.17; Oxford Road Cem. (Bel.); Age 21; Son of Frederick John and Harriet Stevenson of "Tristella", Loose, Kent.

4153. STEWART, Alan Dundas; 2nd Lt.; K: 19.9.15; Rimboval Churchyard, Pas-de-Calais; Age 21; Son of Dr.Howard Douglas Stewart and Helen Stewart of 98, Redcliffe Gardens, West Brompton, London; Accidentally killed by the explosion of a bomb at a training school at Quilen.

4154. STILL, Charles Albert; B: Shoreham, Sussex; E: Brighton; L/Cpl. G 19357; K: 4.11.18; Cross Roads Cem., Nord; Age 19; Son of Harry Still of 33, Ship Street, Shoreham.

4155. STILL, Walter Edward; B: Norwich; E: Hove; Cpl. G 3076; K: 25.9.15; Loos Mem., Pas-de-Calais; Age 26; Son of Mrs.Louisa Still of 80, Coleridge Street, Hove.

4156. STILWELL, James; B: Littlehampton, Sussex; E: Littlehampton; Pte. G 3207; K: 31.8.16; Thiepval Mem., Somme.

4157. STOCKER, Patrick Walter; B: Stratford, London; E: Stratford; Pte. G 19073; K: 4.11.18; Cross Roads Cem., Nord; Age 19; Son of Charles and Ada Stocker of 22, Priscilla Road, Bow, London.

4158. STOCKFORD, William James; B: Tingwick, Buckinghamshire; E: Willesden, London; Pte. G 3673; W: 20.8.16; La Neuville Brit. Cem., Somme; Age 21; Son of William and Mary Stockford of Rayleigh, Essex.

4159. STOFER, Arthur Percival; B: Eastbourne; E: Hove; Pte. G 3150; K: 27.9.15; Loos Mem., Pas-de-Calais; Age 17; Son of Charles and Priscilla Stofer of 52, Ashford Road, Eastbourne.

4160. STONE, Charles Herbert; B: Chichester; E: Bognor Regis, Sussex; Pte. G 16594; K: 27.3.17; Aix-Noulette Com. Cem. Ext., Pas-de-Calais; Age 29; Son of Arthur and Nellie Stone; Husband of Ada Kathleen Stone of North Lodge, North Gate, Chichester.*

4161. STONE, Frank Robert; B: Stubbington, Hampshire; E: Bexhill-on-Sea; Pte. G 6646; K: 11.3.17; Aix-Noulette Com. Cem., Pas-de-Calais.

4162. STONER, Frank; B: Bolney, Sussex; E: Horsham, Sussex; Pte. G 8143; K: 17.6.16; Ration Farm (La Plus Douve) Annexe (Bel.); Age 25; Son of Edmund and Darah Jane Stoner of 12, Colwood Hill, Warninglid, Sussex.

4163. STONER, William; B: Ditchling, Sussex; E: Haywards Heath, Sussex; Pte. GS 462; D: 13.3.16; Hazebrouck Com. Cem., Nord; Age 41; Son of George and Anne Stoner of Keymer, Sussex; Died of nephritis at Casualty Clearing Station, Hazebrouck.

4164. STOPPS, Edwin Thomas; B: Moreton Pinkney, Northamptonshire; E: Burton Latimer, Northamptonshire; Pte. G 11751; W: 2.6.18; Pernes Brit. Cem., Pas-de-Calais; Age 20; Son of William Thomas and Mary Stopps of Barton Seagrave, Northamptonshire; Died at Casualty Clearing Station, Pernes.

4165. STREET, Thomas; B: Blackstone, Sussex; E: Hove; Sgt. G 3066; K: 31.8.16; Bulls Road Cem., Flers, Somme; Age 22; Son of Mr.T. and Mrs.L.Street of 75, Park Avenue, East Ham, London.

4166. STRICKETT, John; B: Deptford, London; E: Deptford; Pte. G 5099; K: 25.9.15; Loos Mem., Pas-de-Calais; Age 29; Son of Ben W. and Elizabeth Strickett of 24, Goodrich Road, East Dulwich, London.

4167. STRIKE, John William; B: – ; E: Hertford; Pte. G 5646; K: 29.9.17; Hargicourt Brit. Cem., Aisne.*

4168. STRINGER, Walter Samuel; B: Storrington, Sussex; E: Worthing; Pte. G 66; K: 11.3.16; Ypres (Menin Gate) Mem. (Bel.); Age 36; Son of Mrs.E.Stringer of 4, Bartlett's Cottages, Broadwater, Sussex; Husband of Rosa Stringer of 1, Bartlett's Cottages, Broadwater.

4169. STRINGER, William Henry; B: Southwick, Sussex; E: Worthing; Pte. G 17903; K: 3.8.17; Ypres (Menin Gate) Mem. (Bel.); Age 18; Son of William and Margaret Stringer of Dancton, Lychpool, Sompting, Sussex.

4170. STRONG, William James; B: Brighton; E: Brighton; Pte. G 8192; W: 23.3.18; Roye New Brit. Cem., Somme; Died at No.50 Casualty Clearing Station, Roye.

4171. STRUDWICK, Harry; B: Bermondsey, London; E: Southwark, London; Pte. G 5345; K: 26.9.15; Loos Mem., Pas-de-Calais; Age 18; Son of Mr. and Mrs.T.Strudwick of 281, New Kent Road, London.*

4172. STUBBS, John Edward; B: St.Helens, Lancashire; E: Grove Park; Pte. G 16821; W: 21.6.17; Étaples Mil. Cem., Pas-de-Calais; Age 21; Son of John and Rose Ann Stubbs of Haydock, Lancashire; Husband of Ellen Stubbs of 107, Clipsley Lane, Haydock; Died at Military Hospital, Étaples.

4173. STUNELL, Ernest; B: Brighton; E: Brighton; Cpl. G 3639; K: 18.8.16; Serre Road Cem. No.2, Somme; Age 18; Son of Mr. and Mrs.Stunell of 34, Cambridge Street, Brighton; Husband of Daisy Patching, formerly Stunell, of 2, The Rise, Crayford, Kent.

4174. STURMEY, Frederick Stephen; B: Thames Ditton; E: Uckfield, Sussex; Pte. G 8269; W: 20.8.16; Abbeville Com. Cem., Somme; Son of Frederick William and Alice Sturmey of 11, Springfield Gardens, Beacon Street, Lichfield, Staffordshire.

4175. SWAN, Andrew; B: Seacombe, Cheshire; E: Liverpool; Pte. G 5907; W: 9.4.18; Le Cateau Mil. Cem., Nord.

4176. SYMONDS, Benjamin Charles; B: Brighton; E: Brighton; Cpl. G 16539; K: 21.3.18; Pozieres Mem., Somme.

T

4177. TANN, Thomas Henry; B: Kilburn, London; E: Harrow, Middlesex; Pte. G 3988; K: 14.2.16; Menin Road South Mil. Cem. (Bel.); Age 33; Son of Mr. and Mrs.Frederick William Tann of 31, Palmerston Road, Wealdstone, Middlesex; Killed while on duty in the front line trench at Hooge.

4178. TAPPER, William Goss; B: Peckham, London; E: Camberwell, London; Pte. G 5556; K: 20.8.16; Theipval Mem., Somme; Age 24; Son of James and Elizabeth Tapper of 2, Princes Terrace, Peckham Rye.

4179. TAPSELL, George; B: Rotherfield, Sussex; E: Hastings; Pte. G 9024; W: 29.3.17; Barlin Com. Cem., Pas-de-Calais; Age 23; Son of Isaac Samuel and Mary Ann Tapsell of Rotherfield.

4180. TAYLOR, Alfred; B: Battersea, London; E: Camberwell, London; Pte. G 19043; K: 4.11.18; Villers-Pol Com. Cem. Ext., Nord; Age 19; Son of Mrs.Ada Ann Taylor of 45, Landseer Street, Battersea Park Road, London.

4181. TAYLOR, Arthur Gerard; B: Dundee; E: Barrow-in-Furness; Pte. G 10340; K: 31.5.18; Bully-Grenay Com. Cem. Brit. Ext., Pas-de-Calais; Age 19; Son of William and Mary Taylor of 50, Walney Road, Barrow-in-Furness.

4182. TERRY, Stanley; B: Worth, Sussex; E: East Grinstead, Sussex; Pte. G 3320; K: 12.11.16

Philosophe Com. Cem., Nord; Age 24; Son of James and Emma Terry of Brickworks, Rowfant, Sussex.

4183. THATCHER, Frederick; B: Brighton; E: Brighton; Pte. G 4253; K: 25.9.15; Loos Mem., Pas-de-Calais.

4184. THEOBALD, George; B: Mundford, Norfolk; E: Norwich; Pte. G 11721; K: 5.2.18; Gouzeaucourt New Brit. Cem., Nord; Age 21; Son of Bircham and Selina Theobald of Buckenham, Norfolk.*

4185. THOMPSON, Oliver; B: Broughton, Northamptonshire; E: Kettering, Northamptonshire; Pte. G 7839; K: 28.9.15; Loos Mem., Pas-de-Calais; Age 35; Son of George and Lizzie Thompson; Husband of Mary Lizzie Thompson of Cransley, Northamptonshire.

4186. THOMPSON, William Eli; B: Brighton; E: Lewes; Pte. G 3337; K: 28.9.15; Loos Mem., Pas-de-Calais; Age 24; Son of William Eli and Annie Thompson of 52, Islingwood Street, Brighton; Husband of Mary Winifred Thompson of 43, Ewart Street, Brighton.

4187. THOMPSON, William George; B: East Grinstead, Sussex; E: East Grinstead; Sgt. G 3707; W: 12.4.17; Choques Mil. Cem., Pas-de-Calais; Age 30; Son of George and Annie Thompson of East Grinstead; Died at No.1 Casualty Clearing Station, Choques.

4188. THORPE, George Nicholas; B: Norwich; E: Norwich; Pte. G 11312; K: 11.6.17; Ypres (Menin Gate) Mem. (Bel.); Age 20; Son of George and Phoebe Thorpe of 38, St. Olave's Road, Norwich.*

4189. THURLOW, Albert; B: Bow, London; E: Bedford; Pte. G 11314; K: 23.6.17; Ypres (Menin Gate) Mem. (Bel.); Age 39; Son of Mrs.Sarah Thurlow of 34, Rye Road, Hoddesdon, Hertfordshire.

4190. TISDALL, Charles Henry; 2nd Lt.; K: 13.2.16; Menin Road South Mil. Cem. (Bel.); Age 18; Son of Archibald Walter and Elizabeth Amy Tisdall of 26, Baskerville Road, Wandsworth Common, London; Killed at Hooge during an enemy bombardment while attempting to dig out a man who had been buried alive by a shell explosion.

4191. TODMAN, Daniel; B: East Grinstead, Sussex; E: Lewes; Pte. G 5738; W: 18.2.16; Brandhoek Mil. Cem. (Bel.).

4192. TOMLINSON, Harry; B: Pinchbeck, Lincolnshire; E: Norwich; Pte. SD 5594; M.M.; W: 6.4.18; Le Cateau Mil. Cem., Nord.*

4193. TOPLIS, Sidney Alfred; B: High Wycombe, Buckinghamshire; E: Arundel, Sussex; Sgt. G 5750; K: 13.4.17; Ypres (Menin Gate) Mem. (Bel.); Age 23; Son of Charles and Hillary A.Toplis of 18, New Upperton Road, Eastbourne.

4194. TOWLER, Edgar Frederick; B: Stepney, London; E: Brighton; L/Cpl. G 7630; K: 25.3.18; Pozieres Mem., Somme.

4195. TOWNSEND, Thomas; B: Brighton; E: Brighton; Pte. G 5342; K: 23.6.17; Ypres (Menin Gate) Mem. (Bel.); Age 34; Son of Thomas and Sarah Townsend of 12, Chapel Street, Newhaven, Sussex; Husband of Edith Emily Townsend of 35, Cuthbert Road, Brighton.

4196. TRATT, Thomas James Philip; B: – ; E: Horsham, Sussex; Pte. G 19574; D: 8.3.18; Ste.Marie Cem., Le Havre, Seine-Maritime; Age 28; Son of Thomas James and Theresa Mary Tratt of 1, The Retreat, Cranleigh, Surrey; Died of syncope.

4197. TREVETT, Tom; B: Lancing, Sussex; E: Worthing; Pte. G 7366; W: 6.4.18; Abbeville Com. Cem. Ext., Somme; Age 23; Son of Louisa Trevett of Rose Cottage, Penthill Road, Lancing.

4198. TRILL, John; B: Ditchling, Sussex; E: Brighton; Pte. GS 628; K: 28.9.15; Loos mem., Pas-de-calais; Age 32; Son of Mr. and Mrs.John Trill of Bank Cottages, Westmeston, Sussex; Husband of Florence Martha trill of 20, Sussex Road, Tonbridge, Kent.

4199. TRODD, William; B: Havant, Hampshire; E: Warley, Essex; Pte. G 12946; W: 21.11.16; Barlin Com. Cem., Pas-de-Calais; Age 18; Son of E.G. and C.Trodd of 1, Grove Road, Chichester.

4200. TRUSLER, William; B: Pulborough, Sussex; E: Worthing; Pte. G 19215; K: 4.11.18; Cross Roads Cem., Nord; Age 19; Son of Mr.H.Trusler of 463, Cokeham, Sompting, Sussex.

4201. TUESLEY, Bertram; B: Sheet, Hampshire; E: Chichester; Pte. G 8887; K: 11.6.17; Ypres (Menin Gate) Mem. (Bel.); Age 26; Son of Luke and Caroline Tuesley.

4202. TURKINGTON, Frederick Edgar; B: Calcutta, India; E: Woolwich, London; Pte. G 4259; K: 28.9.15; Loos mem., Pas-de-Calais; Age 20; Son of William Horatio and Emma Turkington of 178, Wickham Lane, Plumstead, London.*

4203. TURNER, Alfred Stephen; B: Hastings; E: Hastings; Pte. G 16313; K: 22.3.18; Jeancourt Com. Cem., Aisne.

4204. TURNER, George; B: Lewes; E: Brighton; Pte. L 10749; W: 23.8.16; Corbie Com. Cem. Ext., Somme; Age 19; Son of Mr. and Mrs.T.Turner of 19, Stoneham Road, Hove but late of Chailey, Sussex.*

4205. TURNER, William Edwin; B: Chichester; E: Chichester; Pte. G 19582; K: 7.4.17; Aix-Noulette Com. Cem. Ext., Pas-de-Calais; Age 24; Son of George and Ellen Turner of 8, Tower Street, Chichester.*

4206. TWINE, William Edward; B: Emsworth, Hampshire; E: Chichester; Pte. G 16523; K: 3.1.17; Philosophe Com. Cem., Nord; Age 20; Son of Mrs.A.Twine of 2, Raglan Terrace, Lumby Road, Emsworth.

4207. TYRRELL, Albert Edward; B: Woodham Ferrers, Essex; E: Tottenham, London; Cpl. SD 5510; K: 12.4.17; Arras Mem., Pas-de-Calais; Age 25; Husband of Mrs.Ada Mary Tyrrell of 14, Dawlish Road, Tottenham.*

U

4208. UPTON, Gaius; B: Eastbourne; E: Croydon; Pte. GS 433; W: 17.6.16; Boulogne Eastern Cem., Pas-de-Calais; Age 37; Husband of Minnie Miller Upton of 21, Nicholson Square, Edinburgh; Served in the South Africa Campaign; Died at Military Hospital, Boulogne.*

4209. UPTON, George Alfred; B: Slaugham, Sussex; E: Haywards Heath, Sussex; Pte. G 3254; K: 25.9.15; Loos Mem., Pas-de-Calais.

4210. USHER, Herbert; B: Hythe, Kent; E: Canterbury; L/Cpl. TF 260163; W: 10.11.18; Cambrai East Mil. Cem., Nord; Died at Casualty Clearing Station, Cambrai.

V

4111. VERION, George William Pratt; B: Bersted, Sussex; E: Bognor Regis, Sussex; Pte. G 1211; K: 28.3.16; Ration Farm (La Plus Douve) Annexe (Bel.); Son of Mrs.S.Verion of "South View", North Bersted.

4212. VERRALL, George; B: Eastbourne; E: Eastbourne; Pte. G 3986; K: 11.6.17; Voormezele Enclosure No.3 (Bel.).

4213. VIDLER, Bertram Hall; B: Victoria, British Columbia, Canada; 2nd Lt.; K: 12.4.17; Aix-Noulette Com. Cem. Ext., Pas-de-Calais; Age 23; Son of Percy Alexander Vidler and Edith Vidler of 40, Berkeley Road, Crouch End, London; Mentioned in 'Undertones of War' by Edmund Blunden.*

4214. VINE, Stephen James; B: Jamaica, British West Indies; E: Falmouth, Devonshire; Pte. SD 4246; W: 2.6.18; Pernes Brit. Cem., Pas-de-Calais; Age 24; Son of James Alfred and Susannah Vine of Kingston, Jamaica; Died at Casualty Clearing Station, Pernes.

4215. VIRGO, Arthur; B: Portslade, Sussex; E: Steyning, Sussex; Pte. G 4486; W: 20.1.16; Lijssenthoek Mil. Cem. (Bel.); Age 37; Husband of Louisa Winifred Kennard, formerly Virgo, of 47, Fishergate Terrace, Brighton.

4216. VOGEL, George Henry; B: St.Pancras, London; E: Cockspur Street, London; Pte. G 5403; K: 28.9.15; Loos Mem., Pas-de-Calais.

W

4217. WADEY, Percy David; B: Eastbourne; E: Eastbourne; L/Cpl. G 3756; K: 25.9.15; Loos Mem., Pas-de-Calais; Age 22; Son of Isaac and Sarah Wadey of "Fernlea", Littlehampton Road, West Worthing.

4218. WAITE, Albert; B: Brighton; E: Brighton; Pte. G 7647; K: 25.9.15; Loos Mem., Pas-de-Calais; Age 18; Son of James and Rosetta Waite of 29, Carlyle Street, Brighton.

4219. WAKLEY, Frank Charles; B: Compton, Hampshire; E: Steyning, Sussex; Pte. G 2153; K: 28.9.15; Loos Mem., Pas-de-Calais.

4220. WALKER, Albert; B: Manchester; E: Manchester; Pte. G 19224; K: 4.11.18; Villers-Pol Com. Cem. Ext., Nord; Son of Mrs.H.Walker of 66, Lord Street, Gorton, Manchester.

4221. WALLIS, Stephen, B: Hoo, Kent; E: Gravesend, Kent; Pte. G 12872; W: 6.12.16; Philosophe Brit. Cem., Mazingarbe, Pas-de-Calais; Age 38; Son of Henry and Susan Wallis of Northfleet, Kent; Husband of Mary A.S.Wallis of 40, Toronto Road, Tilbury Docks, Essex.

4222. WALTER, Walter George; B: Maresfield, Sussex; E: Uckfield, Sussex; L/Cpl. L 9124; W at Home: 6.9.16; Fairwarp (Christ Church) Churchyard, Sussex (UK).*

4223. WALTERS, John; B: Liverpool; E: Liverpool; Pte. G 6038; K: 29.10.15; Elzenwalle Brasserie Cem. (Bel.); Age 37; Son of John Walters; Husband of Elizabeth Walters 54, Priory Street, Liverpool.

4224. WARD, Ernest; B: Leicester; E: Leicester; Pte. G 15028; K: 22.3.18; Pozieres Mem., Somme.

4225. WARD, Frederick Joseph; B: Chalk Farm, London; E: St.Pancras, London; Pte.G 18685; K: 22.3.18; Honnechy Brit. Cem., Nord; Age 19; Son of William and Mary Ann Ellen Ward of 9, Kirkwood Road, Chalk Farm.

4226. WARD, Henry Seymour; B: Brighton; E: Chichester; Pte. G 16538; W: 28.3.18; St.Sever Cem. Ext., Rouen, Seine-Maritime; Age 35; Son of John S. and Maggie Ward of Brighton; Husband of Nellie Smith, formerly Ward, of 124, Ditchling Road, Brighton.

4227. WARDLAW, A.P.M.; Maj.; D at Home: 14.5.17; Golders Green Crematorium, London.

4228. WARREN, Edward Frank; B: Newnham, Gloucestershire; E: London; Pte. G 4981; K: 12.8.17; Hooge Crater Cem. (Bel.).

4229. WARRINER, Albert; B: Blindley Heath, Surrey; E: East Grinstead, Sussex; L/Sgt. L 6201; W: 17.6.16; Bailleul Com. Cem. Ext., Nord; Died at Casualty Clearing Station, Bailleul.

4230. WATERS, Arthur George; B: Hailsham, Sussex; E: Hove; Pte. G 3408; K: 28.6.16; Kemmel Chateau Mil. Cem. (Bel.); Age 21; Son of Eliza Waters of Rutland Road, Hove.

4231. WATKINS, Alfred Mornington; B: Marylebone, London; E: Woolwich, London; Pte. G 18680; K: 23.3.18; Pozieres Mem., Somme; Age 20; Son of Joseph and Lilian Watkins of 32, Barnfield Road, Plumstead, London.

4232. WATSON, Reginald; B: Salehurst, Sussex; E: Hastings; Pte. G 15874; W: 12.4.18; Le Cateau Mil. Cem., Nord; Age 24; Son of George and Mary Jane Watson of 18, East Street, Robertsbridge, Sussex.

4233. WATSON, Stanley John; B: Camberwell, London; E: Camberwell; Pte. G 10683; K: 4.11.18; Villers-Pol Com. Cem. Ext., Nord; Age 19; Son of Mrs.Lauro Watson of 54, Rugby Street, Peckham, London.

4234. WEBB, Charles Henry; B: Brighton; E: Brighton; Pte. G 4228; K: 25.9.15; Loos Mem., Pas-de-Calais.

4235. WEBBER, Bertie; B: Brighton; E: Brighton; Pte. G 3196; K: 14.2.16; Menin Road South Mil. Cem. (Bel.); Age 31; Son of Thomas and Alice Webber of Brighton; Killed while on duty in the front line trench at Hooge.

4236. WELCH, Charles William; B: Herne Bay, Kent; E: Herne Bay; Pte. G 19351; K: 4.11.18; Cross Roads Cem., Nord; Age 19; Son of Alfred and Ellen Welch of 7, The Grove, Herne Bay.

4237. WELHAM, Harry George; Lt.; M.C.; K: 4.11.18; Wargnies-Le-Petit Com. Cem., Nord; Age 27; Son of Frank and Ellen Welham of Mountnessing Road, Billericay, Essex.

4238. WELLAND, George Frederick; B: Woldingham, Surrey; E: Canterbury; Pte. G 22400; W: 8.9.18; Terlincthun Brit. Cem., Pas-de-Calais; Age 32; Son of George and Susan Welland of Woldingham; Husband of Florence Elizabeth Welland of 51, Norwood Street, Hull.

4239. WELLER, Charles C.; B: Lewes; E: Lewes; Pte. G 17655; K: 28.3.17; Aix-Noulette Com. Cem. Ext., Pas-de-Calais; Son of Mr.C.C.Weller.*

4240. WELLER, Frederick George; B: Maresfield, Sussex; E: Eastbourne; Pte. G 5776; W: 13.2.16; Lijssenthoek Mil. Cem. (Bel.); Killed while on duty in the front line trench at Hooge.

4241. WENBAN, Walter Alfred Stephen; B: Hastings; E: Hastings; Pte. G 9099; K: 11.6.17; Ypres (Menin Gate) Mem. (Bel.); Age 25; Son of Alfred and Elizabeth Wenban of 92, Alexandra Road, St.Leonards-on-Sea.

4242. WENHAM, Frederick Peter; B: Eastbourne; E: Eastbourne; Pte. SD 261; W: 30.7.17; Lijssenthoek Mil. Cem. (Bel.); Age 21; Son of Mr. and Mrs.H.S.Wenham of 9, Northcote Parade, Southall, Middlesex.

4243. WEST, Edward; B: Worthing; E: Worthing; Pte. G 3325; K: 28.9.15; Loos Mem., Pas-de-Calais; Age 30; Son of Edward and S.B.West of 34, Orme Road, Worthing.

4244. WESTON, Albert John; B: Rotherfield, Sussex; E: Tunbridge Wells; Pte. G 5377; K: 17.1.17; Philosophe Brit. Cem., Mazingarbe, Pas-de-Calais; Age 20; Son of James and Elizabeth Weston of 5, Springfield Cottage, New Road, Rotherfield.

4245. WESTON, Frank; B: – ; E: Hastings; Pte. G 17656; K: 13.4.17; K: 13.4.17; Arras Mem., Pas-de-Calais; Age 20; Son of Mr. and Mrs.C.S.Weston of Sandrock House, Croft Road, Crowborough, Sussex.

4246. WHITE, Arthur James; B: Lingfield, Surrey; E: East Grinstead, Sussex; L/Cpl. G 7319; K: 18.8.16; Serre Road No.2 Cem., Somme.

4247. WHITE, Francis; B: Stockland, Devonshire; E: Shepherd's Bush, London; Pte. G 5726; K: 31.8.16; Thiepval Mem., Somme; Age 20; Son of George and Elizabeth White of Woodleigh Farm, Wivelsfield Green, Sussex.

4248. WHITE, Frederick Stephen; B: Newhaven, Sussex; E: Newhaven; Pte. G 860; K: 11.6.17; Ypres (Menin Gate) Mem. (Bel.); Age 27; Son of Alfred and Sarah Jane White of 1, Lewes Cottage, Denton, Sussex.

4249. WHITE, George Charles David; B: Whitton, Middlesex; E: Brighton; L/Cpl. G 3298; K: 21.3.18; Pozieres Mem., Somme; Age 22; Husband of Emily Rhoder Collins, formerly White, of 96, Montgomery Street, Hove.*

4250. WHITE, George; B: Funtington, Sussex; E: Chichester; Pte. G 8217; K: 31.8.16; Thiepval Mem., Somme.

4251. WHITE, Horace; B: Hastings; E: Hastings; L/Cpl. G 3445; K: 19.11.15; Duhallow A.D.S. Cem. (Bel.).

4252. WHITE, Jack; B: Redhill, Surrey; E: Warley, Essex; Pte. G 12935; K: 17.11.16; Philosophe Brit. Cem., Mazingarbe, Pas-de-Calais; Age 25; Son of Alma Mary White of 10, West Parade, Horsham, Sussex.

4253. WHITE, William; B: Hastings; E: Hastings; Pte. G 5014; K: 25.9.15; Loos Mem., Pas-de-Calais; Age 38; Husband of Caroline White of 6, School Road, Hastings.

4254. WHITEHEAD, John; B: Bolton, Lancashire; E: Bolton; Pte. G 5911; K: 24.3.16; Ration Farm (La Plus Douve) Annexe (Bel.); Age 23; Son of Thomas and Bessie Whitehead of 49, Oxford Grove, Bolton.

4255. WHITEHOUSE, Herbert Percy; B: Epsom, Surrey; E: Brighton; Pte. G 5354; K: 20.2.16; Ypres (Menin Gate) Mem. (Bel.).

4256. WHITLOCK, Arthur Ernest; B: Camberwell, London; E: Sheerness, Kent; Sgt. G 5943; M.M.; W: 4.11.18; Canonne Farm Brit. Cem., Sommaing, Nord; Age 26; Son of Arthur John and Lydia Martha Whitlock.

4257. WHITNER, Frederick William; B: Southwater, Sussex; E: Horsham, Sussex; Sgt. TF 200889; K: 21.3.18; Pozieres Mem., Somme; Age 26; Son of F. and R.Whitner; Husband of Gertrude Randell, formerly Whitner, of 92, Tarring Road, Worthing.

4258. WHITSEY, Harry William Baring; B: St.Lawrence, Northamptonshire; E: Northampton; Pte. G 19230; K: 5.6.18; Bully-Grenay Com. Cem. Brit. Ext., Pas-de-Calais.

4259. WHITTAKER, George; B: Stockbridge, Warwickshire; E: Sheffield; Pte. G 19234; K: 4.11.18; Villers-Pol Com. Cem. Ext., Nord; Age 19; Son of Alfred and Ruth Whittaker of 5, Manchester Road, Old Haywoods, Deepcar, Yorkshire.

4260. WHITTOME, John Daniel; B: Southwark, London; E: Southwark; Pte. G 5800; K: 14.2.16; Menin Road South Mil. Cem. (Bel.); Killed while on duty in the front line trench at Hooge.

4261. WICKERSHAM, Henry Thomas; B: Horsham, Sussex; E: Chichester; L/Sgt. GS 599; K: 25.9.15; Loos Mem., Pas-de-Calais; Age 47; Husband of Kate Wickersham of 6, Wellington Terrace, Military Road, Rye, Sussex.

4262. WILES, Walter; B: Claygate, Surrey; E: Camberwell, London; Cpl. G 4566; W: 24.6.17; Lijssenthoek Mil. Cem. (Bel.); Age 24; Son of George and Polly Wiles of Commercial Road, Paddock Wood, Kent.

4263. WILKIN, Robert; B: Godmanchester, Huntingdonshire; E: Peterborough, Northamptonshire; Pte. G 7849; K: 25.9.15; Loos Mem., Pas-de-Calais.

4264. WILKINSON, Alfred; B: Hertford; E: Bedford; Pte. G 15199; K: 4.11.18; Villers-Pol Com. Cem. Ext., Nord; Brother of Mr.J.E.Wilkinson of 15, Chameleon Road, Tottenham, London.

4265. WILLEY, George Alfred; B: Lindfield, Sussex; E: Haywards Heath; Pte. G 3596; K: 25.9.15; Loos Mem., Pas-de-Calais; Age 30, Son of Alfred and Elizabeth Willey of South Lodge, Paxhill Park, Lindfield.

4266. WILLIAMS, David; B: Wolverhampton; E: Wolverhampton; Pte. TF 260134; W: 8.8.17; Lijssenthoek Mil. Cem. (Bel.).

4267. WILLIE, William John; B: Haywards Heath, Sussex; E: East Grinstead, Sussex; Pte. G 7745; K: 13.4.17; Lievin Com. Cem. Ext., Pas-de-Calais.

4268. WILLSON, H.Laurence; B: Dalston, London; E: Brighton; L/Cpl. G 3683; W: 25.8.16; La Neuville Brit. Cem., Somme; Age 20; Son of William and Ann Amelia Willson of "Oaklands", Baldwin's Hill, Surrey.*

4269. WILTSHIRE, Edward George; B: Croydon; E: Croydon; Pte. G 20583; K: 18.9.18; Vis-en-Artois Mem., Haucourt, Pas-de-Calais.

4270. WINCH, Charles; B: Tunbridge Wells; E: Petworth, Sussex; Pte. G 8003; K: 31.8.16; Thiepval Mem., Somme.

4271. WINCHESTER, James; B: Brighton; E: Brighton; Cpl. G 3677; K: 31.8.16; Thiepval Mem., Somme.

4272. WINK, Alfred Joseph; B: Walworth, London; E: Camberwell, London; Pte. G 18686; W: 30.8.18; Aubigny Com. Cem. Ext., Pas-de-Calais; Age 19; Son of Alfred henry and Frances Elizabeth Wink of 30, Azenby Road, Peckham, London.

4273. WINTER, Fred; B: Rotherfield, Sussex; E: Bexhill-on-Sea; Pte. SD 1504; K: 28.5.18; Arras Mem., Pas-de-Calais; Age 21; Son of Harriett Winter of 3, Rotherview Villas, Poundfield, Sussex.

4274. WINYARD, William; B: Brighton; E: Brighton; Pte. G 9042; W: 1.10.16; Abbeville Com. Cem. Ext., Somme.

4275. WOOD, Ernest Charles; BL Smarden, Kent; E: Chelsea, London; L/Cpl. G 20566; K: 3.8.17; Ypres (Menin Gate) Mem. (Bel.); Age 23; Son of James and Elizabeth Rebecca Wood of Forge Hill, Pluckley, Kent.

4276. WOOD, Stanley; B: Liverpool; E: Seaforth, Lancashire; Pte. G 19223; K: 4.11.18; Cross Roads Cem., Nord; Age 19; Son of Harry and Mary Jane Wood of Liverpool.

4277. WOODHAMS, Thomas Henry; B: Hartfield, Sussex; E: Tunbridge Wells; Sgt. G 1307; K: 13.4.17; Arras Mem., Pas-de-Calais; Age 24; Son of Henry Thomas and Sophia Catherine Woodhams of New Cottages, Colchford Farm, Hartfield.

4278. WOODHOUSE, William Henry; B: Bethnal Green, London; E:Poplar, London; Pte. G 18684; W at Home: 5.4.18; Manor Park Cem., London (UK); Age 19; Son of Mr.J. and Mrs.M.A.Woodhouse of 29, Lamprell Street, Old Ford, London.

4279. WOOLER, Henry; B: Willingdon, Sussex; E: Eastbourne; L/Cpl. G 651; K: 17.6.18; Arras Mem., Pas-de-Calais; Age 26; Son of Mr. and Mrs.David Wooler of 4, Rose Bank Cottages, Willingdon.

4280. WOOLVEN, William Thomas; B: Horsham, Sussex; E: Horsham; Pte. G 870; K: 25.9.15; Loos Mem., Pas-de-Calais; Age 19; Son of Alfred and Midiam Mary Woolven of 12. Little Haven Lane, Roffey, Sussex.

4281. WORSFOLD, Frederick Henry; B: Camden Town, London; E: London; L/Cpl. G 14891; W: 4.11.18; Awoingt Brit. Cem., Nord; Age 33; Son of Mr.E. and Mrs.A.J.Worsfold of 21, Moray Road, Finsbury Park, London; Died at Casualty Clearing Station, Awoingt.

4282. WREN, Albert Edward; B: Buxted, Sussex; E: Brighton; Pte. G 4969; K: 14.2.16; Menin Road South Mil. Cem. (Bel.); Killed while on duty in the front line trench at Hooge.

4283. WRIGHTON, Josiah Garland; B: Ilfracombe, Devonshire; E: Horsham, Sussex; Pte. TF 200628; K: 24.3.18; Pozieres Mem., Somme; Age 23; Son of Alfred and Martha Wrighton of 3, Florence Villas, Torrs Park, Ilfracombe.*

4284. WYNNE, Thomas; B: Brixton, London; E: Brighton; Cpl. G 3433; K: 13,8,16; Carnoy Mil. Cem., Somme; Killed near Carnoy by the explosion of an enemy heavy shell.

Y

4285. YOUNG, Jeremiah; B: Rampton, Cambridgeshire; E: Huntingdon; Pte. G 11327; K: 3.9.17; Voormezeele Enclosures No.1 and No.2 (Bel.).*

11th Battalion

A

4286. ABBOTT, James; B: Brighton; E: Brighton; Pte. G 11518; K: 31.7.17; – – .

4287. ADAMS, Percy Albert; B: – ; E: Brighton; Pte. TF 241487; K: 27.9.17; Tyne Cot Mem. (Bel.).

4288. AGER, Allen; B: Wetheringsett, Suffolk; E: Hurstpierpoint; L/Cpl. G 16265; K: 3.4.18; Pozieres Mem. Somme; Age 24; Son of Charles Ager and Kate Wilden, formerly Ager, of Old Street, Haughley, Suffolk.

4289. AGNEW, William Alfred; B: Battersea; E: London; Pte. SD 3935; K: 3.9.16; Thiepval Mem. Somme; Age 27; Son of Archibald and Fanny Agnew.

4290. AITKEN, Herbert Richard; B: Bermondsey; E: London; Pte. SD 3934; K: 3.9.16; Thiepval Mem. Somme; Age 21; Son of James and Caroline Aitken of 26, Hillside Drive, Edgware.

4291. AKEHURST, Sidney Ware; B: Eastbourne; E: Eastbourne; Sgt. SD 388; W: 10.7.16; Bethune Town Cem. Pas-de-Calais.

4292. ALCOCK, Uriah; B: Leek; E: Leek; Pte. G 13134; K: 21.10.16; Thiepval Mem. Somme.

4293. ALLEN, John; B: – ; E: Loughborough; Pte. G 15030; K; 1.8.17; Divisional Collecting Post Cem, Ext. (Bel.); Age 26; Husband of Edith Rose Allen of 10, New Street, Barrow-on-Soar, Leicestershire.*

4294. ALLIN, George; B: Midhurst, Sussex; E: Midhurst;

Pte. TF 290013; K: 3.4.18; Pozieres Mem. Somme; Age 36; Son of Frederick and Elizabeth Allin of Curch Street, Midhurst; Husband of Daisy Bailey, formerly Allin.

4295. ALVIS, Frank George; B: Bicknoller, Somerset; E: Hastings; Pte. G 16479; K: 21.10.16; Thiepval Mem. Somme; Age 33; Son of William and Louisa Alvis of Higher Weacombe, Bicknoller, Somerset.

4296. AMOS, Henry William; B: Brixton; E: London; Pte. SD 3883; K: 30.6.16; St.Vaast Post Mil. Cem. Pas-de-Calais.*

4297. AMY, Charles Stanley; B: Newhaven, Sussex; E: Newhaven; Pte. TF 241477; K: 24.9.17; Tyne Cot Mem. (Bel.); Age 21; Son of Philip J. and Ellen Amy of Newfield Road, Newhaven.

4298. —ANDREWS, Frederick Leopold; B: Leytonstone; E: Stepney, London; Pte. SD 3886; K: 29.8.16; Thiepval Mem. Somme; Age 30; Husband of Ethel Ada Andrews of 8, Bute Road, Barkingside, Essex.

4299. ARNOLD, Herbert; B: Alresford, Essex; E: Colchester; Pte. SD 5872; K: 21.10.16; Thiepval Mem. Somme.

4300. ASHDOWN, Alfred; B: Mayfield, Sussex; E: Eastbourne; Pte. SD 277; K: 28.4.16; Guards Cem. (Cuinchy), Pas-de-Calais; Age 24; Son of Mr. and Mrs.G.Ashdown of Colkin's Mill, Mayfield, Sussex.

4301. ASHFORD, Walter Augustus; B: – ; E: Eastbourne; Sgt. SD 138; M.M.; K: 3.4.18; Pozieres Mem. Somme; Age 30; Son of Mr. and Mrs.H.W.Ashford of 66, Queen's Road, Wimbledon.*

4302. ASTLEY, Edwin Chappell; B: Stoke-on-Trent, Staffordshire; E: Longton; Cpl. G 15131; K: 21.10.16; Grandcourt Road Cem. Somme.

4303. ATKINS, Ernest William; B: Hailsham, Sussex; E: Eastbourne; L/Sgt. SD 274; K: 3.9.16; Thiepval Mem. Somme.

4304. ATKINS, George Edward; B: Downham Market, Norfolk; E: East Dereham, Norfolk; Cpl. G 15273; K: 20.2.18; Gouzeaucourt New Brit. Cem. Nord.

4305. ATKINSON, Horace; B: Sheerness, Kent; E: London; Pte. G 5966; M.M.; K: 26.9.17; Tyne Cot Mem. (Bel.).

4306. AUSTIN, Frederick Nelson; B: All Souls, Sussex; E: Bexhill; L/Sgt. SD 1160; K: 25.9.16; La Clytte Mil. Cem. (Bel.); Killed on his birthday.*

4307. AUSTIN, Robert; B: St.Miles, Norfolk; E: Norwich; L/Cpl. G 11619; K: 31.7.17; Ypres (Menin Gate) Mem. (Bel.); Age 20; Son of Ephraim and Elizabeth Austin of 23, Napier Street, Norwich.

4308. AVIS, Gordon John; B: Sneldhurst, Sussex; E: Bognor Regis, Sussex; Pte. SD 773; M.M.; K: 17.2.18; Gouzeaucourt New Brit. Cem. Nord; Age 25; Son of John and Emily Avis of Old Town, Groombridge, Sussex.

4309. AVIS, William; B: Rodmell, Sussex; E: Hove; L/Cpl. SD 3852; K: 3.9.16; Ancre Brit. Cem. Somme.

4310. AYLING, Harry Walter; B: Chichester; E: Chichester; Pte. G 11451; K: 29.4.18; Voormezeele Enclosure No. 3 (Bel.).

4311. AYNSWORTH, Charles Henry; B: Bermondsey; E: London; L/Cpl. SD 3942; K: 30.6.16; St.Vaast Post Mil. Cem. Pas-de-Calais; Age 21; Son of Henry F.H. and Ellen Alice Aynsworth of 27, Calverton Road, Barking Road, East Ham, London.

B

4312. BACKSHALL, Harry; B: Cuckfield, Sussex; E: Eastbourne; Pte. SD 290; W: 3.8.17; Brandhoek New Mil. Cem. (Bel.); Age 33; Son of William and Jane Backshall.

4313. BACON, William George; B: Bethnal Green, London; E: Holborn, London; Pte. G 17319; K: 25.9.17; Tyne Cot Mem. (Bel.); Age 19; Son of Henry William and Elizabeth Martha Bacon of 31, Avenue Terrace, Southend-on-Sea.*

4314. BAILEY, Harry Walter; B: Flimwell, Sussex; E: Hastings; Pte. SD 1002; K: 3.9.16; Thiepval Mem. Somme; Age 26; Son of Mrs.A.Bailey of Flimwell.

4315. BAKER, Alfred; B: Dane Hill, Sussex; E: Haywards Heath; Pte. SD 3828; K: 4.6.16; Cambrin Churchyard Ext. Pas-de-Calais; Age 19; Son of Mrs. Mary Baker of Brook Cottage, Dane Hill, Sussex.

4316. BALDWIN, William; B: Ticehurst, Sussex; E: Ticehurst; L/Cpl. G 20438; K: 1.8.17; New Irish Farm Cem. (Bel.); Age 21; Son of George and Mary Baldwin of The Village, Ticehurst.

4317. BALLARD, Charles James; B: St.Matthew's, Sussex; E: Hastings; Pte. SD 1001; W: 3.9.16; Acheux Brit. Cem. Somme; Age 26; Son of Charles and Caroline Ballard of Shornden Cottage, Silverhill, St.Leonards-on-Sea.*

4318. BANFIELD, Albert Ernest; B: Hankham, Pevensey, Sussex; E: Eastbourne; Pte. SD 67; K: 24.9.17; Tyne Cot Mem. (Bel.).

4319. BARBER, Albert Henry; B: Hove; E: Brighton; Pte. L 9916; K: 25.9.17; Tyne Cot Mem. (Bel.).

4320. BARBER, Alfred John; B: Stone Cross, Pevensey, Sussex; E: Eastbourne; Pte. G 16488; K: 2.11.17; Lijssenthoek Mil. Cem. (Bel.).Age 23; Son of Mr. and Mrs.A.Barber of Stone Cross.

4321. BARHAM, David; B: Poplar, London; E: Eastbourne; Sgt. SD 2; K: 3.9.16; Thiepval Mem. Somme; Age 37; Husband of Emma Louisa Barham of 50, Cobbold Road, Leytonstone.

4322. BARKER, Henry John; B: Somerleyton, Suffolk; E: Great Yarmouth; Pte. G 11705; K: 29.4.18; Tyne Cot Mem. (Bel.).

4323. BARKER, Herbert George; B: Brondesbury, London; E: Worthing; Pte. SD 501; K: 16.8.17; Bus House Cem. (Bel.); Age 29; Son of William James and Mary Ann Barker of "Withersdale", Wyke Avenue, Worthing.

4324. BARKER, Lawrence; B: Henfield, Sussex; E: Worthing; Sgt. G 5743; M.M.; K: 3.4.18; Roisel Com. Cem. Ext. Somme; The date of death was recorded at the end of the 'Spring Retreat' and is incorrect; Death would have been during the period 21 – 31.3.18, probably the 23rd.

4325. BARLOW, Charles Alfred; 2nd Lt.; W: 17.8.17;

Lijssenthoek Mil. Cem. (Bel.); Age 22; Son of Charles Bird Barlow and Florence Arabella Barlow of 4, Abbey Road, Brighton; Attached 4th Squadron Royal Flying Corps.

4326. BARNARD, Tom; B: Eastbourne; E: Eastbourne; Pte. SD 41; K: 3.9.16; Thiepval Mem. Somme.

4327. BARNES, Albert; B: Brighton; E: Hove; Pte. G 6470; W: 22.8.17; Voormezeele Enclosure No. 2 (Bel.).

4328. BARNES, Charles Henry; B: – ; E: East Dereham, Norfolk; Pte. G 15274; W: 7.12.17; Nine Elms Brit. Cem. (Bel.); Age 29; Son of George and Harriett Barnes of Hardwick, Norfolk; Mortally wounded in camp by a bomb dropped during an air raid.

4329. BARNES, Frederick; B: Norwich; E: Lowestoft; Pte. G 21971; W: 19.7.18; Cologne Southern Cem. (G); Age 20; Son of Frederick and Lucy Barnes of 68, Howard Street Central, Great Yarmouth; Died while a prisoner of war.

4330. BARNES, George Albert Elliott; B: Westham, Pevensey, Sussex; E: Eastbourne; Pte. SD 148; K: 12.7.16; Cambrin Churchyard Ext. Pas-de-Calais; Age 22; Son of Albert and Jane Barnes of Horseye, Pevensey, Sussex.*

4331. BARNES, John; B: Winchester; E: Lewes; Pte. SD 886; W: 28.7.17; Lijssenthoek Mil. Cem. (Bel.); Age 40; Son of Edwin and Emily Barnes of Ovington Down, Alresford, Hampshire.

4332. BARNES, Thomas Leonard; B: Putney; E: Wandsworth; Pte. G 16691; K: 3.4.18; Ste.Emilie Valley Cem., Villers-Faucon, Somme; Age 19; Son of Thomas Barnes of 36, Bendon Valley, Earlsfield, London;

The date of death was recorded at the end of the 'Spring Retreat' and is incorrect; Death would have been during the period 21 – 31.3.18, probably the 22nd.

4333. BARRELL, Leonard Barton; B: – ; E: Birmingham; Pte. G 17278; K: 24.9.17; Tyne Cot Mem. (Bel.).

4334. BASSETT, Thomas; B: Brighton; E: Brighton; L/Cpl. SD 888; K: 25.4.18; Brandhoek New Mil. Cem. (Bel.); Age 29; Son of Thomas and Catherine S.Bassett of 14, Spring Gardens, Brighton.

4335. BATTERSBY, Charles Henry; B: Wapping; E: Stepney; Pte. G 15692; K: 31.7.17; Duhallow A.D.S., Cem. (Bel.); Age 27; Son of Charles Henry Battersby of Stepney, London; Husband of Emily E.Battersby of 173, Oxford Street, Stepney.

4336. BATTLEY, Frederick Walter, B: Camberwell, London; 2nd Lt.; K: 21.4.16; Guards Cem. (Cuinchy), Pas-de-Calais; Age 21; Son of Ernest F. and Frances Battley of 21, Old Kent Road, London; Killed by a rifle grenade at the 'Duck's Bill', Givenchy; Buried by the Church of England Chaplain.

4337. BEAL, Horace Edward; B: Chalvington, Sussex; E: Eastbourne; Pte. SD 65; K: 3.9.16; Serre Road Cem. No. 2, Somme; Age 22; Son of Mrs.Fanny Beal of Novington Cottages, Plumpton, Sussex.

4338. BEALE, George Henry; B: Manor Park, London; E: Croydon; Pte. G 19832; K: 28.6.17; Brandhoek Mil. Cem. (Bel.); Son of George and Catherine Beale of Manor Park.

4339. BEELEY, Leslie Henry; B: Lewisham; E: Lewisham; Pte. G 17304; K: 24.9.17; Tyne Cot Mem. (Bel.); Age 19; Son of John Henry and Rose Christina Beeley of 120, Court Hill Road, Lewisham, London; His brother, John Edward, also fell.

4340. BELSHAW, Thomas William; B: St.Stephen's, Hertfordshire; E: Hertford; Pte. G 15516; W: 7.4.18; Premont Brit. Cem. Aisne; Son of Ada Emily Cooper, formerly, Belshaw, and the late George Belshaw.

4341. BENNETT, Francis; B: Warbleton, Sussex; E: Hastings; Pte. SD 3735; W: 25.7.17; Lijssenthoek Mil. Cem. (Bel.).

4342. BENTON, Alfred; B: Hastings; E: Hastings; Pte. SD 4979; K: 3.9.16; Ancre Brit. Cem. Somme.

4343. BERRESFORD, Leonard; B: Ashover, Derbyshire; E: Derby; Pte. G 15151; K: 28.2.17; – .

4344. BEST, Peter Metcalfe; B: Holy Trinity, Yorkshire; E: Hull; SD 3910; K: 3.9.16; Thiepval Mem. Somme; Age 28; Son of John Joseph and Sarah Jane Best.

4345. BEYNON, Herbert John; B: Llanelly; E: Warley, Essex; Pte. 15694; K: 8.10.16; Auchonvillers Mil. Cem. Somme; Age 39; Husband of Helen Beynon of 48, Park Avenue, Whitley Bay, Northumberland.

4346. BIGNELL, Charles Henry; B: Eastbourne; E: Eastbourne; Pte. SD 5033; W: 3.9.16; Acheux Brit. Cem. Somme.

4347. BILBIE, George Ernest; B: Nottingham; E: Beeston; Pte. G 15141; K: 21.10.16; Mill Road Cem. Somme.

4348. BILLINGHAM, Frederick; B: Kislingbury, Northamptonshire; E: Northampton; Pte. G 17344; K: 6.12.17; White House Cem. (Bel.); Age 19; Son of Frank and Elizabeth Billingham of The Green, Kislingbury; Killed in camp by a bomb dropped during an air raid.

4349. BIRD, George; B: Breckles, Norfolk; E: East Dereham, Norfolk; L/Cpl. G 15277; K: 31.7.17; New Irish Farm Cem. (Bel.).

4350. BISH, Percy; B: Blackheath; E: Brighton; Pte. G 6081; K: 11.6.17; Ypres (Menin Gate) Mem. (Bel.); Age 23; Son of Mrs.Sarah Howick of Cattershall Lane, Godalming, Surrey.*

4351. BISHOP, Arthur Charles; B: Loughborough; E: Loughborough; L/Cpl. G 15037; K: 31.7.17; Track "X" Cem. (Bel.).

4352. BISHOP, James; B: Cross-in-Hand, Sussex; E: Eastbourne; Pte. SD 405; M.M.; W: 23.10.16; Contay Brit. Cem. Somme; Age 28; Son of Mr. and Mrs. Owen Bishop.*

4353. BLABER, Bernard John; B: Hove; E: Brighton; Pte. TF 260121; K: 19.10.17; Hooge Crater Cem. (Bel.); Age 20; Son of Stephen and Martha Phylis Blaber of 102, Wordsworth Street, Hove.

4354. BLACKFORD, Percy Robert; B: Isfield, Sussex; E: Uckfield, Sussex; Pte. SD 1262; K: 3.9.16; Thiepval Mem. Somme; Age 21; Son of Mr. and Mrs.G.Blackford of Old Mill, Isfield, Sussex.

4355. BLANCH, Alfred Charles; B: Beckley, Sussex; E: Hastings; Pte. SD 1868; K: 3.4.18; Ste.Emilie Valley Cem. Somme; The date of death was recorded at the end of the 'Spring Retreat' and is incorrect; Death would have been during the period 21 – 31.3.18, probably the 23rd.

4356. BLUNDEN, Charles Henry; B: Arundel, Sussex; E: Portsmouth; L/Cpl. G 15882; M.M.; K: 21.3.18; Pozieres Mem. Somme.*

4357. BODEN, Frederick; B: Walworth, London; E: Southwark, London; Pte. G 5798; K: 26.9.17; Tyne Cot Mem. (Bel.); Age 34; Husband of Catherine Boden of 29, Miniver Street, Southwark.

4358. BONSER, John George William; B: Hinkley, Leicestershire; E: Hinkley; Pte. G 15031; K: 17.8.17; Oak Dump Cem. (Bel.); Age 23; Son of Thomas and Bertha Jane Bonser of 12, Tollington Place, Tollington Park, Holloway, London.

4359. BOOTES, Robert Walter; B: Newcastle-on-Tyne; E: Newcastle-on-Tyne; L/Cpl. G 17164; K: 25.9.17; Tyne Cot Mem. (Bel.); Age 20; Son of Frederick B. and Elizabeth Bootes of Philip, Newcastle-on-Tyne.

4360. BOOTH, Matthew Frank; B: Westham, Pevensey, Sussex; E: Eastbourne; Cpl. SD 391; K: 3.9.16; Thiepval Mem. Somme.

4361. BOSWELL, William; B: Midhurst, Sussex; E: Horsham; Pte. SD 5628; K: 21.10.16; Thiepval Mem. Somme.

4362. BOSWORTH, Charles Thomas; B: Ladywood, Warwickshire; E: Oakham, Leicestershire; Pte. G 15035; K: 23.9.16; Auchonvillers Mil. Cem. Somme.

4363. BOTTING, Archibald; B: Worthing; E: Bexhill-on-Sea; L/Cpl. G 776; K: 30.6.16; Cabaret-Rouge Brit. Cem. Pas-de-Calais; Age 26; Son of Frederick and Kate Botting of "Bayou", James Lane, Burgess Hill, Sussex.

4364. BOTTING, William Rolph; 2nd Lt.; K: 25.9.17; Tyne Cot Mem. (Bel.); Age 22; Son of Dr.Herbert William and Mrs.Botting of Brighton.

4365. BOWER, Herbert; B: Golcar, Yorkshire; E: Worcester; Pte. SD 3889; K: 21.10.16; Thiepval Mem. Somme.

4366. BOWERS, George; B: Putney, London; E: Streatham, London; Pte. SD 5777; K: 21.10.16; Thiepval Mem. Somme.

4367. BOWMAN, James William; B: Harewood, Yorkshire; E: Manchester; Pte. G 17265; D at Home; 29.1.18; Manchester Southern Cem. (UK).

4368. BRACKPOOL, Alfred George; B: Lowestoft; E: Hastings; Pte. SD 1007; K: 23.7.16; St.Vaast Post Mil. Cem. Pas-de-Calais; Age 26; Son of Alfred and Susannah Brackpool of 7, Western Place, Rye, Sussex; Killed while returning from a night time raid on enemy trenches.*

4369. BRADBURY, John; B: Lambeth, London; E: Battersea, London; Pte. G 13724; K: 3.4.18; Ste. Emilie Valley Cem., Villers-Faucon, Somme; The date of death vwas recorded at the end of the 'Spring Retreat' and is incorrect; Death would have been during the period 21 – 31.3.18, probably the 23rd.*

4370. BRADBURY, William George; B: Loggerheads, Staffordshire; E: Market Drayton; Pte. G 15142; K: 21.10.16; Thiepval Mem. Somme; Son of Joseph Bradbury of Loggerheads.

4371. BRAIDEN, George; B: Brighton; E: Eastbourne; Pte. SD 25; K: 3.9.16; Thiepval Mem. Somme; Son of John Braiden of 53, Queen Park Road, Brighton.

4372. BRAND, James Andrew; B: Shanghai, China; E: Brighton; Pte. TF 241479; K: 23.4.18; Pozieres Mem. Somme; The date of death was recorded at the end of the 'Spring Retreat' and is incorrect; Death would have been during the period 21 – 31.3.18.*

4373. BRAY, Frank; B: Eastbourne; E: Eastbourne; Pte. SD 35; K: 3.9.16; Thiepval Mem. Somme.

4374. BROMLEY, Albert Stephen; B: Eastbourne; E: Eastbourne; Pte. SD 389; K: 3.9.16; Thiepval Mem. Somme; Age 20; Son of Mr.A.Bromley of 2, Prospect Gardens, Old Town, Eastbourne.

4375. BROOKES, Robert; B: Burslem, Staffordshire; E: Stoke-on-Trent; L/Cpl. G 15147; W: 12.11.16; Warloy-Baillon Com. Cem. Ext. Somme; Age 21; Son of John and Ann Brookes of Tunstall, Staffordshire.

4376. BROOKS, Herbert Cecil; B: Wisbech, Cambridgeshire; E: Wisbech; Pte. G 11333; K: 6.12.17; White House Cem. (Bel.); Age 32; Son of George and Elizabeth M.Brooks of 55, Albert Street, Wisbech; Killed in camp by a bomb dropped during an air raid.

4377. BROWN, Arthur William; B: Westmeston, Sussex; E: Brighton; Pte. SD 4950; K: 30.6.16; St.Vaast Post Mil. Cem. Pas-de-Calais; Age 33; Son of James Arthur and Mary Anne Brown.

4378. BROWN, Charles Hubert; B: Tewkesbury; E: Kingston-upon-Thames; Pte. TF 290133; W: 26.3.18; Dernancourt Com. Cem. Ext. Somme; Son of Hubert George and Elizabeth Alice Brown of Jarvis Street, Eckington, Worcestershire.*

4379. BROWN, Don Owen; B: Deptford, London; E: London; Pte. SD 3885; K: 30.6.16; St.Vaast Post Mil. Cem. Pas-de-Calais; Age 20; Son of William Owen and Jane Brown of 12, Carlton Villas, Welling, Kent.*

4380. BROWN, Edwin Samuel; B: Fulham; E: Paddington; Pte. TF 203118; K: 3.4.18; Pozieres Mem. Somme; Age 31; Son of Mr. and Mrs.S.H.Brown of 28, Hestercombe Avenue, Fulham; Husband of Mrs.B.M.Brown of 19, Greenford Avenue, Southall; The date of death was recorded at the end of the 'Spring Retreat' and is incorrect; Death would have been during the period 21 – 31.3.18.

4381. BROWN, Ernest James; B: Bexhill-on-Sea; E: Bexhill-on-Sea; L/Cpl. SD 1157; M.M.; K: 12.10.16; at Schwarben Redoubt; Hamel Mil. Cem. Somme; Age 27; Son of William and Emily Brown of 20, Emmanuel Road, Hastings; Husband of Annie B.Brown of 4, Portland Terrace, Burwash, Sussex; This man's original battlefield timber cross is preserved in the porch of St. Bartholomew's Church, Burwash; The cross was brought back by Rudyard Kipling who lived at Burwash.

4382. BROWN, Thomas Henry; B: Hurst Wood, Sussex; E: Brighton; Pte. SD 894; K: 21.10.16; Villers Bretonneux Mil. Cem. Somme.

4383. BROWNE, Edgar Cosset; B: St.Leonards-on-Sea; E: Hastings; Cpl. SD 1871; K: 27.4.18; Tyne Cot Mem. (Bel.); Age 21; Son of Elizabeth Jane Cosset Browne; Husband of Frances Evelyn Cosset Browne of 23, Wellington Gardens, Battle, Sussex.*

4384. BRULEY, William Richard; B: – ; E: Stratford, London; Pte. G 15697; W: 26.1.17; Lijssenthoek Mil. Cem. (Bel.); Age 20; Son of Mrs.E.Bruley of 13, Swinburne Avenue, Manor Park, London.

4385. BRUNIGE, Edward Thomas; B: Barnsbury, London; E: London; Pte. SD 3900; K: 3.9.16; Ancre Brit. Cem. Somme; Brother of W.G.H.Brunige of 37, Ridge Road, Stroud Green, London.

4386. BUDD, Robert; B: Heathfield, Sussex; E: Eastbourne; Sgt. SD 270; D.C.M.; K: 3.9.16; Villers-Bretonneux Mil. Cem. Somme; Age 30; Son of Robert Budd of Horam, Sussex; Husband of Florence Ada Botterill, formerly, Budd, of 10, Alma Road, Eastbourne.

4387. BUDD, Wilfred; B: Arundel, Sussex; E: Arundel; Pte. G 15885; K: 31.7.17; Buffs Road Cem. St.Jean-les-Ypres (Bel.); Age 28; Son of Mrs.M.Budd of 67, Maltravers Street, Arundel.

4388. BUDGEN, John Henry; B: Aldershot; E: Brighton; Pte. SD 890; W: 30.6.16; St.Vaast Post Mil. Cem. Pas-de-Calais; Age 28; Son of John and Hannah Budgen of 32, Artillery Street, Brighton.

4389. BULL, Spencer; B: Walsham-le-Willows, Suffolk; E: Bury St.Edmunds, Suffolk; Pte. G 16896; K: 29.4.18; Voormezele Enclosue No.3 (Bel.).

4390. BUNN, Arthur; B: Audley, Staffordshire; E: Stoke-on-Trent; L/Cpl. G 15158; K: 23.9.16; Auchonvillers Mil. Cem. Somme; Age 25; Son of Arthur and Agnes Bunn of Talke, Staffordshire; Husband of Mary Bunn of 2, Cop Houses, Canal Side, Tunstall, Staffordshire.

4391. BURCH, Louis Albert; B: Aldbury, Hertfordshire; E: Tring, Hertfordshire; Pte. G 15207; K: 21.10.16; Thiepval Mem. Somme; Age 23; Son of George and Eliza Burch of Aldbury.

4392. BURCHETT, William; B: Herstmonceux, Sussex; E: Eastbourne; Pte. SD 143; K: 3.9.16; Ancre Mil. Cem. Somme.

4393. BURGESS, Frederick Bonsey; B: Polegate, Sussex; E: Hitchin, Hertfordshire; L/Cpl. G 15206; K: 27.4.18; Tyne Cot Mem. (Bel.).

4394. BURGESS, John Charles David; B: Fulham, London; E: Eastbourne; Pte. SD 294; K: 3.9.16; Thiepval Mem. Somme.

4395. BURGESS, William Henry; B: St.Thomas, Staffordshire; E: Stoke-on-Trent; Pte. G 15148; K: 21.10.16; Thiepval Mem. Somme.

4396. BURLES, William; B: Gravesend, Kent; E: Gravesend; Pte. TF 241467; K: 27.9.17; Tyne Cot Mem. (Bel.); Age 19; Son of Emma Burles of 71, Clarence Street, Gravesend.

4397. BURNARD, Sydney Frederick; B: – ; E: Prittlewell, Essex; Pte. G 15699; K: 27.10.16; Thiepval Mem. Somme.

4398. BURNELL, Joseph Edward; B: Islington, London; E: Tottenham, London; Pte. TF 202781; K: 29.4.18; Tyne Cot Mem. (Bel.); Age 20; Son of Joseph Edward and Emma Burnell of 7, Montague Road, Broad Lane, South Tottenham, London.*

4399. BURR, Ernest William; B: Old Ford, London; E: London; Pte. SD 3936; K: 3.9.16; Thiepval Mem. Somme; Age 18; Son of James and Marian Alice Burr of 16, Coopersdale Road, Homerton, London.

4400. BURT, Frederick George; B: Bulverhythe, Sussex; E: Hastings; Pte. SD 1839; K: 31.5.18; Étaples Mil. Cem. Pas-de-Calais; Age 40; Son of Mr. and Mrs. Burt of St.Leonards-on-Sea; Killed during an air raid at Étaples.

4401. BURTON, Frank; 2nd Lt.; W: 30.3.18; Pozieres Mem., Somme; Age 28; Son of John Francis and Annie Burton of 7, Riseldene Road, Honor Oak Park, London.*

4402. BURTON, Frederick; B: Oulton, Norfolk; E: Norwich; Pte. G 15233; K: 3.4.18; Ste.Emilie Valley Cem. Villers-Faucon, Somme; Son of Mr.C.W.Burton of Bloick Hall Cottage, Fundenhall, Norfolk; The date of death was recorded at the end of the 'Spring Retreat' and is incorrect; Death would have been during the period 21 – 31.3.18, probably the 23rd.*

4403. BURTON, Hedley John; B: St.Leonards-on-Sea; E: Hastings; Cpl. SD 1006; K: 3.9.16; Ancre Brit. Cem. Somme; Age 24; Son of John B. and Mary Burton of Merriment's Farm, Hurst Green, Sussex.*

4404. BURTON, William Myles Pascoe; B: Accrington, Lancashire; E: Chichester; Cpl. G 20409; K: 7.11.17; Tyne Cot Mem. (Bel.).

4405. BUSHELL, George Jesse; B: Burgess Hill, Sussex; E: Croydon; Pte. G 20718; K: 3.4.18; Pozieres Mem. Somme; The date of death was recorded at the end of the 'Spring Retreat' and is incorrect; Death would have been during the period 21 – 31.3.18.*

4406. BUZWELL, Frederick Charles; B: Malden, Surrey; E: Tooting; L/Cpl. SD 5760; K: 25.9.17; Tyne Cot Mem. (Bel.); Age 25; Son of Frederick Heney and Ada Buzwell of 46, Grafton Road, New Malden, Surrey; Husband of Ellen Florence Streeter, formerly Buzwell, of Church Lodge, Crawley Down, Sussex.*

4407. BYE, Albert Edward; B: Enfield, Middlesex; E: Mill Hill, London; Pte. G 20305; K: 28.2.17; Railway Dugouts Burial Ground, (Bel.); Age 22; Son of Ellen Hasselgren, formerly Bye, of 363, Hertford Road, Enfield Highway, Middlesex and the late Ernest William Bye.*

4408. BYFORD, William Frederick; B: Widmore, Kent; E: Bromley; Pte. G 13378; W: 13.8.17; Boulogne Eastern Cem. Pas-de-Calais; Age 24; Son of Mr. and Mrs.A.Byford of Bromley, Kent; Husband of

Minnie Byford of "Woodbank", Nightingale Lane, Bromley.

C

4409. CALDER, Frederick; B: Hayes, Kent; E: – ; Pte. G 19984; K: 10.12.17; Bucquoy Cem., Flers, Somme; Age 28; Son of Mr. and Mrs. William Calder of "Springfield", Woodlea Road, Worthing; Labour Corps.

4410. CARTER, Henry James; B: – ; E: Stratford, London; L/Cpl. G 15703; K: 22.3.18; Pozieres Mem. Somme.

4411. CARTER, Willam Thomas; B: Fareham, Hampshire; E: Bognor Regis, Sussex; Pte. SD 782; K: 24.5.16; Gorre Brit. and Indian Cem. Pas-de-Calais; Age 21; Son of William and Elizabeth Carter of M.T.Cottage, 29, Crescent Road, Bognor Regis.

4412. CASTELLO, Claude Cecil; B: Cheshunt, Hertfordshire; E: Cheshunt; Pte. G 6343; W: 22.3.18; Pozieres Mem. Somme; Age 20; Son of Captain W. and Mrs. W.Costello of 45, Turners Hill, Cheshunt; Signaller.

4413. CATT, Arthur George; B: Warbleton, Sussex; E: Hastings; L/Cpl. SD 909; K: 3.9.16; Thiepval Mem. Somme.

4414. CATT, Frederick James; B: Westfield, Sussex; E: Hastings; Pte. SD 4957; W: 14.3.16; Sailly-sur-La-Lys Canadian Cem. Pas-de-Calais; Age 18; Son of Francis Catt of Sandycroft, Westfield.

4415. CAWLEY, Jack; B: Eastbourne; E: Eastbourne; Pte. G 15797; K: 21.10.16; Thiepval Mem. Somme.

4416. CEENEY, Thomas Alfred; B: Clerkenwell, London; E: Shoreditch, London; Pte. SD 3932; K: 3.9.16; Thiepval Mem. Somme; Age 17; Son of Henry and Emily M.Ceeney of 80, Haggerston Road, Dalston, London.

4417. CHAMBERLAIN, George; B: Hanwell, London; E: Fulham, London; Cpl. G 20391; K: 29.7.17; Ypres (Menin Gate) Mem., (Bel.); Age 22; Son of Ambrose and Alice Chamberlain of "The Stables", Brent Lodge, Hanwell.

4418. CHAMBERS, Robert; B: Sunderland; E: Sunderland; Pte. G 17741; K: 20.9.17; Tyne Cot Mem. (Bel.).

4419. CHANDLER, Frederick; B: Lichfold, Sussex; E: Gentilshurst, Sussex; Pte. G 15802; M.M.; W: 7.12.17; Nine Elms Brit. Cem. (Bel.); Age 28; Son of John and Rosa Chandler; Husband of Agnes A.S.Chandler of Woolhurst, Lodsworth, Sussex; Mortally wounded in camp on 6.12.17 by a bomb dropped during an enemy air raid.

4420. CHANDLER, Harold James; B: Rotherfield, Sussex; E: Herstmonceux, Sussex; Sgt. SD 578; K: 18.9.17; La Clytte Mil. Cem. (Bel.); Age 25; Son of Charles and Elizabeth Chandler of Eastbourne; Husband of Maud Elizabeth Mary Chandler of 107, Langney Road, Eastbourne.

4421. CHAPMAN, James William; B: Bermondsey, London; E: Bermondsey; Pte. TF 260148; K: 25.9.17; Tyne Cot Mem. (Bel.).

4422. CHARLISH, Robert James; B: Rockheath, Norfolk; E: Norwich; Pte. G 11632; W: 29.7.17; Vlamertinghe New Mil. Cem. (Bel.); Age 20; Son of James H.C. and Lydia Charlish of 8, Rackheath, Norfolk.

4423. CHEAL, Edward Richard; B: Herstmonceux, Sussex; E: Eastbourne; Pte. SD 159; K: 3.9.16; Thiepval Mem. Somme; Age 21; Son of Edward and Hannah Cheal of Foords Lane, Hankham, Pevensey, Sussex.

4424. CHEESEMAN, Ernest Edward; B: Deptford; E: Kingston-on-Thames; Pte. G 18532; W: 26.3.18; Cerisy-Gailly Mil. Cem. Somme.

4425. CHRISTIE, Denis Halstead; 2nd Lt.; K: 21.9.18; Vis-en-Artois Mem., Haucourt, Pas-de-Calais.

4426. CHURCHILL, Daniel; B: Stockton-on-Tees; E: Burslem, Staffordshire; Pte. G 15115; W: 23.10.16; Puchevillers Brit. Cem. Somme; Age 38; Husband of Bridget Churchill of 14, Peakes Top Row, Tunstall, Staffordshire.*

4427. CHUTER, George Andrew Frederick; B: Guidford; E: Guildford; Pte. G 6332; K: 3.6.17; Vlamertinghe Mil. Cem. (Bel.); Age 20; Son of Andrew Frederick and Mary Jane Chuter of 23, Latimer Road, Godalming, Surrey.

4428. CIRCUIT, Charles Reginald; B: Eastbourne; E: Eastbourne; Pte. SD 151; K: 22.3.18; Villers-Faucon Com. Cem. Ext. Somme; Age 28.*

4429. CLARK, John; B: Ninfield, Sussex; E: Bexhill-on-Sea; Pte. SD 1013; K: 3.9.16; Thiepval Mem. Somme; Age 36; Husband of Hannah H.Clark of 7, Claremont Road, Sidley, Bexhill-on-Sea.

4430. CLAYDON, Ernest Victor; B: Harlow, Essex; E: Epping, Essex; Pte. G 16901; K: 24.9.17; Tyne Cot Mem. (Bel.).

4431. CLEMENTS, George Herbert; B: Braughing, Hertfordshire; E: Hertford; Pte. G 15496; K: 18.9.17; Larch Wood (Railway Cutting) Cem. (Bel.); Age 22; Son of Albert Clements of "Edenagreena", Poncroft, Hertfordshire.

4432. CLIFFORD, Harold; B: Battersea, London; E: Southend-on-Sea; Sgt. G 15706; K: 18.9.17; Tyne Cot Mem. (Bel.); Age 34; Son of Frederick Clifford; Husband of Florence Winifred Clifford of "Arnewood", Rectory Road, Hadleigh, Essex; Mentioned in 'Undertones of War' by Edmund Blunden.

4433. CLIFFORD, William; B: Finmere, Buckinghamshire; E: Willesden, London; Pte. SD 659; K: 3.9.16; Thiepval Mem. Somme; Age 26; Son of Thomas and Margaret Clifford of Finmere.*

4434. CLIFTON, Thomas; B: Heathfield, Sussex; E: Eastbourne; Pte. SD 303; K: 28.4.16; Guards Cem. (Cuinchy), Pas-de-Calais; Age 23; Son of Ellen Mercy Clifton (known as Holmes) of "Woodview", Punnetts Town, Sussex, and the late George Clifton.

4435. COCKETT, Horace Edward; B: St.Mary's, Sussex; E: Hastings; Pte. SD 1017; M.M. and Bar; K: 3.4.18; Pozieres Mem. Somme; Age 28; Son of Mrs.Sophia Lily Cockett of 45a, High Street, Battle, Sussex; The date of death was recorded at the end of the 'Spring Retreat' and is incorrect; Death would have been during the period 21 – 31.3.18 *

4436. COLEMAN, Ernest Edmund; B: Hailsham, Sussex; E: Eastbourne; Pte. SD 157; K: 3.9.16; Thiepval Mem. Somme.

4437. COLES, Walter; B: Leicester; E: Leicester; Pte. G 15068; K: 27.3.18; Peronne Com. Cem. Ext., Ste.Radegonde, Somme; The date of death was redorded at the end of the 'Spring Retreat' and is incorrect; Death would have been during the period 21 – 31.3.18, probably the 23rd.*

4438. COLEY, Leonard; B: Benenden, Kent; E: Cranbrook, Kent; Pte. SD 5795; K: 21.10.16; Thiepval Mem. Somme.

4439. COLLINS, Charles; B: Worthing; E: Worthing; Pte. SD 505; W: 18.3.16; Merville Com. Cem. Nord; Age 20; Son of Mrs.Annie Chaplin of Beverley Park Road, Worthing.

4440. COLLINS, William; B: Eastbourne; E: Hitchin; Pte. SD 5740; K: 31.7.17; Buffs Road Cem., St.Jean-les-Ypres (Bel.); Son of Mr.G.Collins of "Princess of Wales", Weston, Hertfordshire.

4441. COLLISON, James Ambrose; B: Ifield, Sussex; E: Cooden, Sussex; Pte. SD 1153; K: 4.6.16; Cambrin Churchyard Ext. Pas-de-Calais; Age 26; Son of James and Ada Amelia Collison of Swiss Cottage, 46, Alpha Road, Crawley, Sussex.

4442. COLWELL, George Francis Henry; B: Brixton, London; E: Hammersmith, London; Pte. G 20451; W at Home: 28.11.17; Brighton (Bear Road) Borough Cem. (UK).*

4443. CONWAY, Thomas George; B: Hatfield, Derbyshire; E: Northampton; Pte. G 16904; K: 26.9.17; Tyne Cot Mem. (Bel.).

4444. COOK, Albert; B: – ; E: Stratford, London; Pte. G 15708; K: 21.10.16; Grandcourt Road Cem. Somme; Age 19; Son of Mr. and Mrs.Edward Cook of 51, Paul Steet, West Ham, London.

4445. COOK, James; B: Eastbourne; E: Eastbourne; Pte. SD 406; K: 21.10.16; Grandcourt Road Cem. Somme; Age 24; Son of Mr. and Mrs.J.Cook of 20, Tower Street, Eastbourne; Husband of Mrs.G.F.Guilt, formerly Cook, of 8, South Close, Cemetery Road, Shrewsbury.

4446. COOK, Cyril Joseph; B: Melton Mowbray; E: Loughborough; Pte. G 15043; W: 16.9.16; Doullens Com. Cem. Ext. No.1, Somme.

4447. COOPER, William Thomas; B: King's Sutton, Northamptonshire; E: Banbury; Oxfordshire; Pte. G 11792; W: 3.1.17; Ferme-Olivier Cem. (Bel.).*

4448. CORK, William Henry; B: Meopham, Kent; E: Canterbury; Pte. G 6475; W: 21.9.17; Godewaersvelde Brit. Cem. Nord; Husband of L.M.Anderson of 61, High Street, Queenborough, Kent.*

4449. CORNISH, John Arthur; B: – ; E: Brentwood, Essex; Pte. G 15709; K: 20.9.16; Auchonvillers Mil. Cem. Somme; Age 26; Son of Robert and Annie Amelia Cornish of Warley, Essex; Killed by trench mortar fire at Auchonvillers; His brother, Tom, was very badly wounded at the same time by the same explosion.

4450. COSSTICK, Cyril Norman; B: Seaford, Sussex; E: Eastbourne; Sgt. SD 302; K: 20.9.16; Auchonvillers Mil. Cem. Somme; Age 23; Son of Mr. and Mrs. Cosstick of Seaford; Killed by trench mortar fire at Auchonvillers; Enlisted with brother, Frederick, who was also killed (see 4451).

4451. COSSTICK, Frederick; B: Seaford, Sussex; E: Eastbourne; Cpl. SD 300; K: 3.9.16; Thiepval Mem. Somme; Age 27; Son of Mr. and Mrs.William Cosstick of 14, Church Road, Seaford; Enlisted with brother, Cyril Norman, who was also killed (see 4450).

4452. COUCHMAN, Frank; B: Sittingbourne; E: Hastings; Sgt. SD 1015; K: 20.9.16; Auchonvillers Mil. Cem. Somme; Age 21; Son of George and Caroline Couchman of Sittingbourne, Kent; Killed by trench mortar fire at Auchonvillers.

4453. COURT, William George; B: Aldingbourne, Sussex; E: Bognor Regis, Sussex; L/Cpl. SD 780; K: 31.7.17; Ypres (Memin Gate) Mem. (Bel.).

4454. COWARD, Walter; B: Barrow-in-Furness; E: Ulverston; Pte. SD 3895; K: 3.9.16; Ancre Brit. Cem. Somme.

4455. COX, Arthur George; B: Bermondsey, London; E: Horsham, Sussex; L/Cpl. G 16727; K: 22.3.18; Pozieres Mem. Somme; Age 22; Son of Arthur Herbert and Ada Cox of 23, Devonshire Road, Horsham; Also served with the 4th Battalion at Gallipoli. *

4456. CREASEY, Ernest Stanley; B: Godstone, Surrey; E: East Grinstead, Sussex; L/Cpl. SD 4899; K: 3.9.16; Thiepval Mem. Somme; Son of John and Fanny Creasey of 7, Model Cottages, Felbridge, Sussex; His brother, Frederick Leonard, also fell.

4457. CREASEY, Sidney; B: Eastbourne; E: Eastbourne; Pte. SD 47; K: 3.6.16; Cambrin Churchyard Ext. Pas-de-Calais; Age 21; Son of J. and Alice Creasey of 8, Upwich Cottages, East Dean Road, Eastbourne.

4458. CROFT, Victor Albert; B: Brightling, Sussex; E: Hastings; Pte. SD 2267; K: 29.4.18; Wytschaete Mil. Cem. (Bel.).

4459. CROUCH, William Henry; B: Brightling, Sussex; E: Hastings; Pte. SD 1877; K: 21.3.18; Pozieres Mem. Somme; Age 33; Husband of Florence Kate Crouch of 27, Gensing Road, St.Leonards-on-Sea.

4460. CURREY, Arthur William; B: Little Cressingham, Norfolk; E: Norwich; Pte. G 15236; K: 21.10.16; Thiepval Mem. Somme.

4461. CUSHEN, Aylett Cameron; 2nd Lt.; K: 30.6.16; Loos Mem. Pas-de-Calais.

D

4462. DADSWELL, Sydney Hanbury; B: Paddock Wood, Kent; E: Herstmonceux, Sussex; Pte. SD 586; K: 30.6.16; St.Vaast Post Mil. Cem. Pas-de-Calais.

4463. DAMON, Charles Henry Robert; B: Waddon,

Surrey; E: Frome, Somerset; Pte. G 17076; K: 3.4.18; Pozieres Mem. Somme; Age 19; Son of Henry and Jane Damon of Farleigh Castle, Somerset; The date of death was recorded at the end of the 'Spring Retreat' and is incorrect; Death would have been during the period 21 – 31.3.18. *

4464. DANIELS, John; B: Mayfield, Sussex; E: Horsham; Pte. G 15805; K: 1.10.16; Auchonvillers Mil. Cem. Somme; Age 35; Son of Walter and Ann Daniels of Chilthurst, Bodle Street, Sussex.

4465. DANIELS, John William; B: Loughton, Essex; E: Eastbourne; R.S.M. SD 169; W: 2.3.17; Vlamertinghe Mil. Cem. (Bel.); Age 32; Son of Mr. and Mrs.Daniels of Eastbourne; Husband of Ada Daniels of 55a, Sydney Road, St.Margarets, Middlesex; Mentioned in 'Undertones of War' by Edmund Blunden.

4466. DAVEY, Hamlet; B: Sainthorpe, Lincolnshire; E: Middlesborough; L/Sgt. 3930; K: 9.8.16; Gorre Brit. and Indian Cem. Pas-de-Calais; Son of Mrs.L.Davey of 24, Dover Street, Cargo Fleet, Middlesborough.

4467. DAVIES, Harold Harper; B: Stockwell, London; E: Purley, Surrey, Pte. G 6156; K: 22.7.17; Essex Farm Cem. (Bel.); Age 26; Son of Samuel and Mary Ann Davies of 11, Churchill Road, South Croydon; Husband of Ida L.Davies of "Romala", Purley Oaks Road, Sanderstead, Surrey.

4468 DAVIES, Sidney Francis; 2nd Lt.; W: 15.11.17; Hooge Crater Cem. (Bel.); Age 24; Son of Jessie Thomas, formerly Davies, of 10, Rose Hill Terrace, Swansea and the late John Francis Davies.

4469. DAVISON, Edmund; 2nd Lt.; K: 24.9.17; Tyne Cot Mem. (Bel.).

4470. DAWES, James Charles; B: Worthing; E: Herstmonceux, Sussex; Pte. SD 587; K: 3.9.16; Thiepval Mem. Somme.

4471. DAWSON, Reginald; B: West Wratting, Cambridgeshire; E: Hastings; Pte. G 16905; K: 26.9.17; Tyne Cot Mem. (Bel.); Age 18; Son of Rebecca Dawson of Barrack Cottage, Sedlescombe, Sussex.

4472. DAY, Albert Edward; B: Pulborough, Sussex; E: Brighton; Pte. L 10955; K: 21.10.16; Thiepval Mem. Somme.

4473. DEAN, Thomas; B: Halmer End, Staffordshire; E: Stoke-on-Trent; Pte. G 15117; K: 21.10.16; Mill Road, Cem. Somme.

4474. DELPHINE, Sydney Victor; B: Holborn, London; E: Holborn; Pte. SD 3753; K: 3.9.16; Ancre Brit. Cem. Somme.*

4475. DENMAN, Edwin George; B: Wandsworth, London; E: Guildford; Pte. G 8094; K: 29.4.18; Tyne Cot Mem. (Bel.); Age 25; Son of Edwin and Annie Denman of Bridge Cottage, Hammer Lane, Haslemere, Surrey.

4476. DENNIS, Lionel; B: Willingdon, Sussex; E: Eastbourne; Pte. SD 409; W: 11.7.16; Bethune Town Cem. Pas-de-Calais; Age 36; Son of Thomas and Lucy Dennis of Willingdon.

4477. DIPLOCK, Harry; B: Eastbourne; E: Eastbourne; Pte. SD 51; K: 21.4.16; Guards Cem. (Cuinchy), Pas-de-Calais; Age 20; Son of Harry and Caroline Diplock of 35, The Village, Meads, Eastbourne; Killed by a rifle grenade at the 'Duck's Bill', Givenchy.

4478. DIVAL. Frank; B: Buxted, Sussex; E: Uckfield, Sussex; Pte. SD 1028; K: 3.9.16; Thiepval Mem. Somme; Age 23; Son of Stephen and Ellen Dival.

4479. DIVAL, Frederick; B: Withyham, Sussex; E: Croydon; Pte. G 23261; K: 3.4.18; Pozieres Mem. Somme; The date of death was recorded at the end of the 'Spring Offensive' and is incorrect; Death would have been during the period 21 – 31.3.18.*

4480. DIVALL, Reginald; B: Colemans Hatch, Sussex; E: Tonbridge; Pte. SD 4882; K: 6.12.17; White House Cem. (Bel.); Age 26; Son of Leonard and Hannah Dival of Colemans Hatch; Husband of Sarah Divall; Killed in camp by a bomb during an air raid.

4481. DODDS, Sidney Frank; B: Kneeton, Nottinghamshire; E: Coalville, Leicestershire; Pte. G 15044; K: 21.10.16; Regina Trench Cem. Somme; Age 20; Son of John and Sarah Dodds of 9, Berrisford Street, Coalville.

4482. DOOGAN, George William; Lt.; K: 21.10.16; Thiepval Mem. Somme; Age 19; Son of John and Jane Eliza Doogan of 4, Claremont Road, Leamington Spa; Mentioned in 'Undertones of War' by Edmund Blunden.

4483. DORLING, Ernest; B: Croxton, Norfolk; E: Lewes; Pte. SD 914; K: 3.6.16; Cambrin Churchyard Ext. Pas-de-Calais; Son of George and Susan Dorling of The Street, Chiddingly, Sussex; Enlisted with brother, George, who was also killed (see 4484).

4484. DORLING, George; B: Somerton, Norfolk; E: Lewes; L/Cpl. SD 913; K: 30.6.16; Loos Mem. Pas-de-Calais; Son of George and Susan Dorling of The Street, Chiddingly, Sussex; Enlisted with brother, Ernest, who was also killed (see 4483).

4485. DORRINGTON, Albert; B: Spalbrook, Essex; E: Chelsea, London; Pte. SD 3875; K: 3.9.16; Thiepval Mem. Somme; Age 21; Son of Daniel S. and Alice Dorrington of Waddesdon Cottage, Little Hallingbury, Hertfordshire.

4486. DOWEN, George James; B: Sneinton, Nottinghamshire; E: Derby; Pte. G 15116; K: 31.10.16; Thiepval Mem. Somme.

4487. DRIVER, Ambrose; B: Framfield, Sussex; E: Lewes; Pte. SD 912; W: 1.7.16; Bethune Town Cem. Pas-de-Calais; Age 30; Son of Thomas and Ellen Driver of Hawkhurst Gate, Blackboys, Sussex.

4488. DUFFIELD, Alfred Robert; B: Hindringham, Norfolk; E: Wymondham; Pte. G 15237; K: 4.11.16; Boulogne Eastern Cem. Pas-de-Calais; Age 31; Son of Robert and Charlotte Duffield of Kimberly, Wymondham.*

4489. DUKE, Herbert; B: Hastings; E: Hastings; Pte. SD 5193; K: 30.6.16; St.Vaast Post Mil. Cem. Pas-de-Calais; Age 19; Son of George Duke of 2, Cromwell Street, Elm Grove, Brighton.

4490. DUKE, William Henry; B: Eastbourne; E: Eastbourne; Pte. SD 170; K: 3.9.16; Thiepval Mem. Somme.

4491. DUMMER, Percy; B: Eastbourne; E: Hove; L/Cpl. SD 297; K: 3.9.16; Serre Road No.2 Cem. Somme.

4492. DUNHAM, Albert James; B: Bedford; E: Bedford; Pte. G 17408; K: 29.4.18; Ste. Emilie Valley Cem., Villers-Faucon, Somme.

4493. DUNK, David Thomas; St.Andrew's, Sussex; E: Hastings; Pte. SD 1026; K: 12.3.16; Rue-David Mil. Cem. Pas-de-Calais; Shot by a sniper; The first of 'Lowther's Lambs' to be killed in action.*

4494. DUNNING, James; B: Guisborough, Yorkshire; E: Middlesborough; Pte. SD 3876; K: 3.9.16; Ancre Brit. Cem. Somme,

4495. DURSTON, Harold; B: – ; E: Chichester; Pte. G 12670; K: 29.4.18; Tyne Cot Mem. (Bel.); Age 23; Son of James Rouse and Harriett Durston of 12, Basin Road, Chichester.

4496. DYER, William; B: Battle, Sussex; E: Herstmonceux, Sussex; Pte. SD 585; K: 30.8.17; Englebelmer Com. Cem. Ext. Mem. Somme; Brother of George Dyer of Reeves Cottages, Northiam, Sussex; Killed by shellfire at Mailly-Maillet Wood; Originally buried at Beaussart, Somme, where the graves were disturbed by shelling later in the war. After the war the remains, excluding two that could not be found, were removed from Beaussart and re-intered at Englebelmer. The remains of this man could not be found and he is commemorated on a special stone at Englebelmer. (see also 4860).

E

4497. EARL, Thomas James; B: Eastbourne; E: Eastbourne; L/Cpl. SD 410; W: 13.7.16; Bethune Town Cem. Pas-de-Calais; Age 22; Son of Charles and Mary Ann Earl of Eastbourne.

4498. EDWARDS, Aundry William; B: Ditchling, Sussex; E: Hove; Pte. G 17813; K: 29.4.18; Tyne Cot Mem. (Bel.); Age 25; Son of William and Herphibah Edwards of Mile End Cottages, Patcham, Brighton.

4499. EDWARDS, George; B: East Grinstead, Sussex; E: Brighton; Pte. SD 4916; W at Home: 11.7.16; Staplefield (St.Mark) Churchyard, Sussex (UK).

4500. EDWARDS, William James; B: Charlwood, Surrey; E: Redhill, Surrey; Pte. G 16910; K: 29.4.18; Tyne Cot Mem. (Bel.); Age 19; Son of Emily Elizabeth Edwards of Glovers Road, Charlwood.

4501. EKE, Frederick William; B: Hindolvestone, Norfolk; E: East Dereham, Norfolk; L/Cpl. G 15265; K: 21.10.16; Thiepval Mem. Somme; Age 20; Son of William John and Martha Ann Eke of Ivy Cottage, Hindolvestone.*

4502. ELLIOTT, Ernest William; B; Rye, Sussex; E: Hastings; Pte. SD 5055; K: 3.9.16; Thiepval Mem. Somme.

4503. ELLIS, George; B: Lingfield, Surrey; E: Chichester; L/Cpl. G 3687; K: 26.9.17; Tyne Cot Mem. (Bel.); Age 24; Son of Mr. W.H. and Caroline Ellis of 4, Mill Cottages, Dunning Road, East Grinstead, Sussex.

4504. ELLIS, Richard; B: Ipswich; E: Westminster; Pte. SD 788; K: 3.9.16; Ancre Brit. Cem. Somme; Age 25; Son of George and Jane Ellis of Woodside Villa, Laughton, Sussex.*

4505. ELLIS, Victor Richard; 2nd Lt.; M.C.; K: 28.4.18; Tyne Cot Mem. (Bel.).*

4506. ELMS, Frederick; B: Eastbourne; E: Eastbourne; Cpl. SD 15; K: 15.8.17; Bus House Cem. (Bel.).

4507. ELPHICK, Walter; B: Herstmonceux, Sussex; E: Herstmonceux; Pte. SD 569; K: 10.7.16; Cambrin Churchyard Ext. Pas-de-Calais.*

4508. EMERY, Arthur; B: Steyning, Sussex; E: Hove; Pte. SD 5500; W: 18.9.16; Doullens Com. Cem. Ext. No.1, Somme.

4509. ETHERINGTON, Jesse; B: Merston, Sussex; E: Worthing; Pte. G 16907; K: 29.4.18; Tyne Cot Mem. (Bel.); Age 19; Son of Mrs.E.Etherington of 54, Southfield Road, Broadwater, Worthing.

4510. EVANS, William J.; B: Malmesbury, Wiltshire; E: Eastbourne; Pte. TF 290264; K: 26.9.17; Hooge Crater Cem. (Bel.).

4511. EVENDEN, Ernest; B: Bexhill-on-Sea; E: Hastings; Pte. SD 5129; D at Netley Military Hospital, Hampshire: 1.9.16; Netley Mil. Cem., Hampshire (UK).*

F

4512. FAIRES, Wilfred George; B: Shipley, Sussex; E: Horsham; L/Cpl. SD 672; W: 18.10.16; Étaples Mil. Cem. Pas-de-Calais; Age 19; Son of Edmund and Emily Charlotte Faires of Ivy Cottage, Coolham, Sussex.*

4513. FARMER, Owen F.; B: Frittenden, Kent; E: Wadhurst, Sussex; Pte. SD 1033; K: 3.9.16; Hamel Mil. Cem. Somme; Age 28; Son of Edwin and Mary Farmer of "Sweetlands", Staplehurst, Kent; Husband of Dora Farmer of 10, Northcote Road, Tonbridge.*

4514. FARNES, William Robert; B: Hurstwood, Sussex; E: Eastbourne; Pte. SD 308; K: 3.9.16; Thiepval Mem. Somme.

4515. FAULKNER, Charles Richard; B: Bolney, Sussex; E: Haywards Heath; Pte. SD 5904; W: 28.4.18; Berlin South-Western Cem. (G); Age 27; Son of C.R. and Sarah Ann Faulkner of Tithe Cottage, Bolney, Sussex; Died while a Prisoner of War.

4516. FAYERS, Thomas Robert; B: King's Lynn, Norfolk; E: East Dereham, Norfolk; Pte. G 15279; W: 12.10.16; Contay Brit. Cem. Somme; Age 19; Son of R.H.Fayers of 3, Marshall Street, King's Lynn.

4517. FEIST, Harold James; B: Brighton; E: Brighton; Pte. G 11539; W at Home: 8.9.17; Brighton (Lewes Road) Borough Cem. (UK); Age 20; Son of James Andrew and Louise Ada Feist of 34, Viaduct Road, Brighton.

4518. FENN, George Isaac; B: Seething, Norfolk; E: East Dereham, Norfolk; Pte. G 15280; K: 21.10.16; Thiepval Mem. Somme.

4519. FIELD, Alfred George; B: Chalk, Kent; E: Maidstone, Kent; Pte. G 17302; K: 7.9.17; Tyne Cot Mem. (Bel.).*

4520. FIELD, George Henry; B: Crowthorne, Berkshire; E: Hove; Pte. TF 241488; K: 24.9.17; Zantvoorde Brit. Cem. (Bel.); Age 34; Son of George and Charlotte Field; Husband of Mabel Louisa Field of 55, The Drive, West Worthing.

4521. FINNEY, William Henry; B: Knossington, Leicestershire; E: Melton Mowbray, Leicestershire; Pte. SD 1684; K: 3.4.18; Ste.Emilie Valley Cem., Villers-Faucon, Somme; Age 22; Son of William and Catherine Finney of Greystones, Sunningdale; The date of death was recorded at the end of the 'Spring Retreat' and is incorrect; Death would have been during the period 21 – 31.3.18, probably the 23rd.*

4522. FISH, Barrow Edmondson; B: Burton-on-Trent; 2nd Lt.; K: 3.9.16; Ancre Brit. Cem. Somme; Son of Barrow and Frances Ellen Fish of 19, Warner Road, Hornsey, London.

4523. FISHER, Herbert Henry Andrews; B: Langham, Rutland; E: Oakham, Rutland; Pte. G 15046; W: 30.10.16; Boulogne Eastern Cem. Pas-de-Calais; Age 19; Son of Frank and Mary Ann Fisher of 41, Dean Street, Oakham.

4524. FISHER, Leslie; B: East Runton, Norfolk; E: Brighton; Pte. SD 7959; K: 21.10.16; Mill Road Cem. Somme.*

4525. FLEET, Albert Benjamin; B: Brighton; E: Hove; Pte. G 16710; K: 13.2.17; Vlamertinghe Mil. Cem. (Bel.); Son of Alfred and Edith Fleet of Brighton.

4526. FOAT, William Thomas; B: Brighton; E: Brighton; Pte. SD 5026; K: 30.6.16; St.Vaast Post Mil. Cem. Pas-de-Calais.

4527. FOLKARD, Frank Middleton; B: St.Julian's, Norfolk; E: Norwich; Pte. G 15246; K: 21.10.16; Thiepval Mem. Somme.

4528. FOORD, William Albert; B: East Dean, Sussex; E: Eastbourne; Pte. SD 178; W: 25.6.16; Boulogne Eastern Cem. Pas-de-Calais; Age 20; Son of Albert and Mary Jane Foord of Ocklynge Cottages, Willingdon, Sussex.

4529. FOSTER, Alfred Jim; B: Brighton; E: Brighton; Pte. SD 926; K: 30.6.16; St.Vaast Post Mil. Cem. Pas-de-Calais; Son of Mrs.Foster of 3, Albion Place, Brighton.

4530. FOULKES, Edward Frederick; B: Chichester; E: Worthing; Pte. SD 515; K: 2.6.16; Cambrin Churchyard Ext. Pas-de-Calais; Age 24; Son of Frederick and Emma Charlotte Foulkes of 1, City Cottages, Ditchling Common, Sussex.

4531. FOWLER, Charles; B: Framfield, Sussex; E: Lewes; Pte. SD 923; W at Home: 22.9.16; Framfield (St. Thomas-a-Becket) Churchyard, Sussex (UK).

4532. FRANCIS, John Henry; B: Thakeham, Sussex; E: Worthing; Pte. SD 5053; K: 31.7.17; Ypres (Menin Gate) Mem. (Bel.).

4533. FRANCIS, Reginald Graham; B: Eastbourne; E: Eastbourne; Pte. SD 309; K: 24.7.16; Loos Mem. Pas-de-Calais; Age 21; Son of Richard and Alice Francis of "Angleside", Hailsham Road, Heathfield, Sussex.

4534. FRANCIS, William; B: Henfield, Sussex; E: Tunbridge Wells; Pte. G 8508; K: 18.9.17; Tyne Cot Mem. (Bel.).

4535. FREDMAN, Arthur Edward; B: – ; E: Stratford, London; Pte. G 15717; K: 21.10.16; Regina Trench Cem. Somme; Age 19; Son of Mr.W.J. and Mrs.F.E.Fredman of 27, South Esk Road, Forest Gate, London.

4536. FREED, Charles Henry; B: Maidstone; E: Woolwich; Pte. G 17495; W: 8.8.18; Berlin South-Western Cem. (G); Age 28; Husband of Alice Maud Freed of 26, Skinner Street, Chatham; Died while a Prisoner of War.

4537. FREELAND, Edwin Tunstall; B: Balham, London; E: Eastbourne; Pte. SD 57; K: 3.9.16; Thiepval Mem. Somme.

4538. FRENCH, Albert Anthony; 2nd Lt.; K: 3.9.16; Thiepval Mem. Somme; Age 20; Son of Mr. P. and Mrs.S.P.French of School Hill, Storrington, Sussex.

4539. FROUD, George; B: Compton, Hampshire; E: Chichester; Pte. SD 794; K: 31.7.17; Ypres (Menin Gate) Mem. (Bel.); Age 20; Son of Sam and Fanny Froud of 10, Manor Villas, Wickham, Hampshire.

4540. FULLER, James; B: Willingdon, Sussex; E: Hastings; L/Cpl. SD 922; W: 30.6.16; Cabaret-Rouge Brit. Cem. Pas-de-Calais.

4541. FUNNELL, Edwin George; B: Eastbourne; E: Eastbourne; L/Cpl. SD 58; K: 30.6.16; St.Vaast Post Mil. Cem. Pas-de-Calais; Age 22; Son of Edwin and Frances Funnell of 427, Seaside, Eastbourne.

4542. FUNNELL, Frederick William; B: Hayes, Middlesex; E: Willesden, London; Pte. G 17420; K: 27.9.16; Thiepval Mem. Somme.*

4543. FUNNELL, Robert; B: Brighton; E: Brighton; L/Cpl. SD 3842; K: 21.3.18; Pozieres Mem. Somme; Age 29; Son of Robert and Jemima Funnell of 28, Newtown Road, Hove.*

G

4544. GALLUP, Alfred; B: Wadhurst, Sussex; E: Wadhurst; Pte. SD 5411; K: 21.10.16; Grandcourt Road Cem. Somme; Age 24; Son of Edwin Gallup of The Forge, Best Beech Hill, Wadhurst.

4545. GAMBLE, Joseph Charles; B: Little Baddow, Essex; E: Chelmsford; Pte. G 24369; K: 29.4.18; Voormezele Enclosure No.3 (Bel.); Age 19; Son of Mrs.Alice Eliza Cottee of 2, View Cottages, Little Baddow.

4546. GATCHELL, J.H.C.; B: Earl's Gift, Donemana, County Tyrone, Ireland; Capt.; M.C.; K: 27.9.17; Bedford House Cem. Enclosure No.4 (Bel.); Son of the Revd.J.H. and Louisa J.Gatchell of 30, Cliftonville Avenue, Belfast; R.A.M.C. attached 11th Battalion; Mentioned in 'Undertones of War' by Edmund Blunden.

4547. GEORGE, Arthur James; B: Hove; E: Brighton; Pte. SD 4863; K: 3.9.16; Thiepval Mem. Somme.

4548. GEORGE, Charles Thomas; B: Islington; E: Chelsea; Pte. G 19847; K: 24.9.17; Tyne Cot Mem. (Bel.); Age 27; Husband of Maria George of 67, Blantyre Street, King's Road, Chelsea, London.

4549. GIBSON, Harold William; B:Kettering, Northamptonshire; E: Northampton; Pte. G 11659; K: 29.7.17; Ypres (Menin Gate) Mem. (Bel.).

4550. GILBERT, Charles Oliver; B: Hassocks, Sussex; E: Worthing; Pte. SD 518; K: 3.9.16; Thiepval Mem. Somme; Age 25; Son of Oliver and Matilda Gilbert of 101, Cranworth Road, Worthing.*

4551. GILLAM, Alfred Abram; B: Brighton; E: Brighton; Pte. S 962; K: 6.12.17; White House Cem. (Bel.); Killed in camp by a bomb dropped during an enemy air raid.

4552. GILMORE, Edwin Reginald; B: Totton, Hampshire; E: Brighton; Pte. G 17322; K: 6.12.17; White House Cem. (Bel.); Killed in camp by a bomb dropped during an enemy air raid.

4553. GLEESON, John; B: – ; E: Bradford; Pte. G 17281; W: 6.12.17; Nine Elms Brit. Cem. (Bel.); Age 19; Son of Jeremiah and Maria Gleeson of Bradford; Mortally wounded in camp by a bomb dropped during an enemy air raid.

4554. GLINISTER, George Edmund; B: Manor Park, London; E: Worthing; L/Cpl. SD 3818; K: 24.9.17; Tyne Cot Mem. (Bel.); Age 24; Son of George and Alice Glinister of "Garfield", 64, Ashdown Road, Worthing.*

4555. GLITHEROE, Charles; B: Marylebone, London; E: Hove; Pte. G 6342; K: 26.9.17; Tyne Cot Mem. (Bel.); Age 22; Son of Charles and Mary Elizabeth Glitheroe.

4556. GLOVER, Leonard; B: Stepney, London; E: Hove; Pte. L 10556; K: 23.9.17; Tyne Cot Mem. (Bel.); Son of Frank Francis and Elizabeth Glover.

4557. GODDEN, Charles Vere; B: Worthing; E: Worthing; Cpl. SD 520; K: 13.11.16; Thiepval Mem. Somme; Age 21; Son of John Newell and Alice Godden of "Chiswick", Tarring Road, Worthing.

4558. GODDEN, William; B: Ewhurst, Sussex; E: Hastings; Pte. SD 930; D: 1.10.16; Caudry Old Com. Cem. Nord.

4559. GOLDEN, Arthur Wilfred; B: Devonport; E: East Grinstead; Sgt. SD 1766; D.C.M., M.M.; W: 24.4.18; St.Sever Cem. Ext., Rouen, Seine-Maritime; Age 26; Son of William S.G. and Hannah Golden of 33, Longfellow Road, Worcester Park, Surrey.

4560. GOODMAN, Frank; B: Boston, Linclonshire; E: Lincoln; Pte. G 15422; W: 29.4.18; Valenciennes (St.Roch) Com. Cem. Nord; Age 23; Son of Arthur and Mary Ann Goodman of Boston.

4561. GOODRICH, Herbert; B: St.Martin's, Sussex; E: Eastbourne; Pte. SD 310; W: 20.9.16; Couin Brit. Cem. Pas-de-Calais; Son of Mrs.H.Goodrich of 23, Church Road, Seaford, Sussex.

4562. GOSLING, Frederick Stanley; B: Chelmsford; E: Warley; L/Cpl. G 15723; K: 21.10.16; Thiepval Mem. Somme.

4563. GOWER, Herbert; B; Weybread, Suffolk; E: Harleston; Pte. G 15247; K: 24.9.17; Tyne Cot Mem. (Bel.).

4564. GRATWICKE, Albert; B: Shipley, Sussex; E: Horsham; Pte. SD 675; K: 2.6.16; Cambrin Churchyard Ext. Pas-de-Calais; Age 31; Son of Harry and Fanny Gratwicke of Chivers Cottage, Shipley, Sussex.*

4565. GRATWICKE, Peter; B: Itchingfield, Sussex; E: Horsham; Pte. SD 677; Le Touret Mil. Cem. Pas-de-Calais; Age 34; Son of Mrs.C.Gratwicke of Swaine's Cottage, Southwater, Sussex. K: 25.7.16.

4566. GRAVER, Edward; B: Gorleston, Suffolk; E: Great Yarmouth; Pte. G 9360; K: 25.9.17; Tyne Cot Mem. (Bel.); Age 33; Son of Eliza Graver of 142, Oddfellows Hall Passage, High Street, Gorleston.

4567. GRAY, Charles; B: Sheffield Park, Sussex; E: Brighton; Pte. SD 501; W: 6.9.16; Étaples Mil. Cem. Pas-de-Calais.*

4568. GREEN, Edwin James; B: St.Stephen's, Surrey; E: Hastings; C.S.M.; SD 874; D.C.M.; K: 21.10.16; Regina Trench Cem. Somme; Age 21; Son of Mr. J.F. and Mrs.A,L,Green of 48, Solon New Road, Clapham, London.*

4569. GREEN, Henry Percival; B: Horland Common, Yorkshire; E: Brighton; Sgt. SD 876; K: 30.6.16; Cabaret-Rouge Brit. Cem. Pas-de-Calais; Age 24; Son of Henry and Louisa Green of 21, Trench Street, Alveston, Derbyshire.

4570. GREEN, Thomas John; B: Bethnal Green, London; E: Walthamstow, London; L/Cpl. G 15724; K: 21.10.16; Mill Road Cem. Somme; Age 24; Son of Thomas John and Jane Green of 5, Ritching's Avenue, Walthamstow.

4571. GREENWOOD, Henry Thomas; B: Watford; E: Watford; Pte. G 17308; K: 26.9.17; Tyne Cot Mem. (Bel.); Age 19; Son of Henry Thomas and Annie Elizabeth Greenwood of 66, Neal Street, Watford.

4572. GREVITT, Richard; B: Whitley, Surrey; E: Chichester; Pte. G 3973; W: 25.9.17; Lijssenthoek Mil. Cem. (Bel.); Age 35; Son of Robert and Ellen Grevitt of Thursley, Surrey.

4573. GRIFFITHS, George; B: Vauxhall, London; E: London; Pte. SD 3896; K: 3.9.16; Thiepval Mem. Somme.

4574. GRIMES, Robert; B: Crawley, Sussex; E: Wakefield; Pte. G 17283; K: 25.4.18; Hoogstaede Belgian Mil. Cem. (Bel.); Age 19; Son of Albert and Sarah Ann Grimes of Boyds Cottage, Lepton, Yorkshire.

4575. GRIMLEY, Harold; B: Codsall, Staffordshire; E: Hertford; Sgt. G 15550; K: 21.10.16; Thiepval Mem. Somme.

4576. GRIMSEY, Arthur; B: – ; E: Stratford, London; Pte. G 15725; K: 28.2.17; Railway Dugouts Burial Ground (Bel.); Age 25; Son of James William and Dinah Grimsey of 75, Harvey Road, Ilford, Essex.

4577. GRISEWOOD, Francis; 2nd Lt.; K: 30.6.16; Loos Mem. Pas-de-Calais.

4578. GRISEWOOD, George Maria Joseph Alphonsus; Capt.; D: 27.3.16; Merville Com. Cem. Nord; Son of Mrs.Grisewood of 39, Cadogan Street, Chelsea, London; Died in hospital.

4579. GROOM, Frederick Robert; B: Croxley Green, Hertfordshire; E: Hertford; Pte. G 15551; W: 3.11.16; Boisguillaume Com. Cem. Seine-Maritime.*

4580. GROVES, Leonard Alloway; Lt.; K: 3.9.16; Serre Road Cem. No.2, Somme.*

4581. GUILDFORD, John Otho; B: Brighton; E: Brighton; Pte. G 19559; K: 2.8.17; Buffs Road Cem., St.Jean-les-Ypres (Bel.); Son of Mr.J.O.Guildford of 2, Jersey Street, Brighton.

4582. GUMBRILL, David Frederick; B: Stoneham, Sussex; E: Eastbourne; L/Cpl. G 4800; W: 20.9.17; Tyne Cot Mem. (Bel.).

4583. GUNN, Charles; B: Brighton; E: Newhaven; Pte. SD 3774; K: 3.9.16; Thiepval Mem. Somme; Age 19; Son of Mrs.Abbey Gunn of 67, Milner Road, Brighton.

4584. GUNN, George; B: Tring; E: Watford; Pte. G 18702; K: 28.2.18; Gouzeaucourt New Brit. Cem. Nord; Age 18; Son of Mr.B. and Mrs.S.A.Gunn of New Road, New Mill, Tring, Hertfordshire.

4585. GUNNER, Arthur Henry Edmund; 2nd Lt.; K: 26.3.18; Delville Wood Cem. Somme; Age 28; Son of Mr. and Mrs.W. H. Gunner of Arundel; Husband of Emily May Gunner of "Meadowcroft", Arundel, Sussex.*

4586. GURR, Arthur; B: Isfield, Sussex; E: Brighton; Pte. SD 799; W at Home: 4.7.16; Isfield (St.Margaret) Churchyard (UK); Son of Moses and Mary A.Gurr of Deepdene Cottage, Buckham Hill, Isfield; Died from wounds received 1.7.16.*

4587. GURR, George David; B: Eastbourne; E: Lewes; Pte. SD 929; K: 13.11.16; Thiepval Mem. Somme; Age 22; Son of David and Edith Gurr of Rose Cottage, Higher Cross, Framfield, Sussex.

H

4588. HABGOOD, William Roy; B: Worth, Sussex; E: Crawley, Sussex; Sgt. SD 2931; K: 21.10.16; Thiepval Mem. Somme.

4589. HAFFENDEN, Ernest Arthur; B: Hailsham, Sussex; E: Herstmonceux, Sussex; Drummer SD 596; W: 8.7.16; Cambrin Churchyard Ext. Pas-de-Calais; Age 22; Son of Daniel and Emily Haffenden of 2, Beech Villas, Ghyll Road, Heathfield, Sussex.*

4590. HAFFENDEN, James; B: Boreham Street, Sussex; E: Herstmonceux, Sussex; Cpl. SD 595; K: 24.3.18; Heath Cem. Harbonnieres, Somme.

4591. HAGGAR, John; Hankham, Pevensey, Sussex; E: Eastbourne; Pte. SD 72; K: 3.9.16; Thiepval Mem. Somme; Age 20; Son of Mrs.John Haggar of 421, Seaside, Eastbourne.

4592. HALL, Alfred Henry; B: Ossett, Yorkshire; E: Cambridge; Pte. G 17374; K: 31.10.17; Bedford House Cem. Enclosure No.2 (Bel.); Age 19; Son of Mrs.L.Hall of 9, Clement Place, Park Street, Cambridge.

4593. HALL, Charles William; B: Lambeth, London; E: Lambeth; Pte. G 10772; K: 14.4.18; St.Venant-Robecq Road Brit. Cem., Robecq, Pas-de-Calais.

4594. HALL, Percy; B: Uckfield, Sussex; E: Eastbourne; Pte. SD 322; K: 9.7.16; Cambrin Churchyard Ext. Pas-de-Calais; Age 23; Son of George and Mary Ann Hall.

4595. HAMBROOK, Albert George; B: Hove; E: Hove; Pte. SD 3591; K: 3.9.16; Thiepval Mem. Somme.

4596. HARBOUR, Frederick Thomas; B: St.Leonards-on-Sea; E: Hastings; Pte. SD 4885; K: 30.6.16; St.Vaast Post Mil. Cem. Pas-de-Calais.

4597. HARDING, Harry; B: Battersea, London; E: Wandsworth, London; Pte. G 17334; K: 27.9.17; Tyne Cot Mem. (Bel.); Age 19; Son of George and Emily Harding of 49, Selverton Road, Battersea.

4598. HARE, Albert; B: Lewes; E: Brighton; Pte. G 16787; W: 9.3.17; Lijssenthoek Mil. Cem. (Bel.); Age 22; Son of Mrs.A.Constable, formerly Hare, of 29, Newtown Road, Hove.

4599. HARMAN, Arthur; B: Halton, Sussex; E: Hastings; Pte. SD 1048; K: 3.9.16; Thiepval Mem. Somme; Age 19; Son of George Richard and Alice Harman of 271, Mount Pleasant Road, Hastings.

4600. HARMER, Frank Riley; B: Eastbourne; E: Eastbourne; Sgt. SD 386; K: 6.8.16; Gorre Brit. and Indian Cem. Pas-de-Calais; Age 31; Son of Charles and Sarah Ann Harmer of 29, Leaf Road, Eastbourne.

4601. HARMER, Harold Edwin; B: Burwash, Sussex; E: Hastings; Pte. G 15823; K: 21.10.16; Grandcourt Road Cem. Somme; Age 33; Son of Henry Harmer of Shop Cottage, Crowhurst, Sussex.

4602. HARMER, Percy; B: Dallington, Sussex; E: Hastings; Pte. G 24434; W: 3.3.18; Tincourt New Brit. Cem. Somme.

4603. HARRADINE, Albert Arthur; B: Royston, Hertfordshire; E: Hitchin, Hertfordshire; Pte. G 18711; W: 21.4.18; Wimereux Com. Cem. Pas-de-Calais; Age 19; Son of Arthur Albert and Mrs.E.A.Harradine of Kenilworth Cottage, Morton Street, Royston.

4604. HARRIS, Edward John; B: Guestling, Sussex; E: Hastings; L/Cpl. G 15929; K: 26.4.18; Tyne Cot Mem. (Bel.).

4605. HARRISON, George Launcelot Godwin; 2nd Lt.; K: 7.11.17; Tyne Cot Mem. (Bel.); Age 34; Son of Annie Louise and W.Launcelot Harrison of Kent Villa, Boundary Road, Hove.

4606. HARVEY, Walter; B: Lewes; E: Eastbourne; Cpl. SD 318; W at Home: 27.9.17; Ditchling (St. Margaret of Antioch) Churchyard, Sussex (UK); Age 25; Son of Owen and Annie Harvey of 112, Western Road, Lewes.

4607. HASLETT, Alfred George; B: Eastbourne; E: Eastbourne; L/Cpl. SD 70; K: 27.9.17; Hooge Crater Cem. (Bel.); Son of Alfred George and Mary Jane Haslett of 7, Gilbert Road, Eastbourne;

4608. HAWKINS, Arthur William; B: Deptford, London; E: London; Pte. L 7705; K: 3.4.18; Pozieres Mem.

Somme; The date of death was recorded at the end of the 'Spring Retreat' and is incorrect; Death would have been during the period 21 – 31.3.18. *

4609. HAYLER, Alfred; B: Worthing; E: Worthing; Pte. SD 525; W: 21.7.16; St.Vaast Post Mil. Cem. Pas-de-Calais; Age 36; Son of William and Fanny Hayler of 9, Winton Place, Worthing.

4610. HEASMAN, Edgar; B: Shipley, Sussex; E: Horsham; Pte. SD 689; K: 3.9.16; Thiepval Mem. Somme; Son of Harry and Susan Heasman of White Hall, Shipley; Enlisted with brother, Thomas, who was also killed in the same major attack on the same day (see 4611).

4611. HEASMAN, Thomas; B: Shipley, Sussex; E: Horsham; Pte. SD 687; K: 3.9.16; Serre Road Cem. No.1, Pas-de-Calais; Age 32; Son of Harry and Susan Heasman of White Hall, Shipley; Enlisted with brother, Edgar, who was also killed in the same major attack on the same day (see 4610).

4612. HEATHER, Percy; B: Hascombe, Surrey; E: Guildford; Pte. SD 940; K: 3.9.16; Thiepval Mem. Somme.

4613. HEFFORD, George Edward; B: Bermondsey, London; E: Brighton; Pte. TF 266322; W: 5.8.17; Mont Huon Mil. Cem. Seine-Maritime; Age 25; Son of George Edward and Martha Hefford of 62, Beatrice Road, Bermondsey; Husband of Hettie Hefford of 4a, Elm Grove, Rye Lane, Peckham, London.

4614. HEISE, Albert William; B: Brighton; E: Brighton; Sgt. G 3186; M.M.; K: 27.4.18; Tyne Cot Mem. (Bel.); Age 25; Son of Fred Heise of 44, Wichelo Place, Brighton; Husband of Grace Heise of 18, Bentham Road, Brighton.

4615. HENTY, John Robert; B: Warbleton, Sussex; E: Eastbourne; Pte. SD 321; K: 3.9.16; Thiepval Mem. Somme.

4616. HERCOCK, Alfred; B: – ; E: Stamford, Northamptonshire; Pte. G 17750; K: 31.7.17; Ypres (Menin Gate) Mem. (Bel.); Age 18; Grandson of Daniel Hercock of 7, Blatherwycke, Peterborough.

4617. HIDE, Charles Arthur; B: Goring-by-Sea, Sussex;; E: Hove; Pte. L 10576; W at Home: 26.3.17; Clapham (St.Mary) Churchyard, Sussex (UK); Age 19; Son of Mrs. E. Daniels of 161, Clapham, Worthing.*

4618. HIDE. Edwin Beckett; B: Eastbourne; E: Eastbourne; Pte. SD 430; W: 6.9.16; Doullens Com. Cem. Ext. No.1, Somme.

4619. HILL, Harold; B: Crowborough, Sussex; E: Tunbridge Wells, Kent; Pte. SD 428; K: 20.6.16; St.Vaast Post Mil. Cem. Pas-de-Calais.*

4620. HILL, Richard; B: Upton-on-Severn, Worcestershire; E: Worcester; Sgt. SD 3904; K: 3.9.16; Thiepval Mem. Somme.

4621. HILLARY, Frederick Thomas; B: New Cross, London; E: Bexhill-on-Sea; L/Cpl. SD 1120; K: 31.7.17; Buffs Road Cem., St.Jean-les-Ypres, (Bel.); Son of Mr. J.R.Hillary of 2, Dupree Road, Charlton, London.*

4622. HILLIER, John Ernest; B: St.Margaret's, Middlesex; E: Hounslow, Middlesex; Pte. L 5993; W: 26.3.18; Cerisy-Gailly Mil. Cem. Somme; Age 36; Son of Mrs.Louisa Hillier of Twickenham; Husband of Frances Amelia Hillier of 62, Second Cross Road, Twickenham.

4623. HILLS, Victor; B: Dane Hill, Sussex; E: Uckfield, Sussex; Pte. G 11561; K: 3.4.18; Ste.Emilie Valley Cem. Villers-Faucon, Somme; The date of death was recorded at the end of the 'Spring Retreat' and is incorrect; Death would have been during the period 21 – 31.3.18, probably the 23rd.*

4624. HILTON, Aubrey Frank; B: Stoughton, Sussex; E: Chichester; Pte. SD 3588; W: 4.9.16; Étaples Mil. Cem. Pas-de-Calais; Son of Henry and Kezia Hilton of 3, Brookland Cottages, Emsworth, Hampshire.

4625. HISCOCK, Albert; B: – ; E: Brentwood, Essex; Sgt. G 15773; K: 21.10.16; Thiepval Mem. Somme.

4626. HITCHMAN, Walter John; B: Walthamstow, London; E: Horsham, Sussex; Sgt. SD 682; K: 13.3.16; Rue-David Mil. Cem. Pas-de-Calais; Age 24; Son of Walter and Susan Hitchman of Walthamstow; Mortally wounded when an enemy 5.9" shell struck his billet in Fleurbaix.

4627. HOAD, Frank Albert; B: Battle, Sussex; E: Eastbourne; Sgt. SD 429; K: 3.9.16; Thiepval Mem. Somme; Age 28; Son of Mr.N. and Mrs.M.A.Hoad of Ripe, Sussex.

4628. HOBBS, Frank; B: Woodford, Essex; E: Worthing; Pte. SD 1156; W: 13.3.16; Sailly-sur-La-Lys Canadian Cem. Pas-de-Calais; Mortally wounded when an enemy 5.9" shell struck his billet in Fleurbaix.

4629. HOBBS, Herbert Henry; B: St.Matthew's, Sussex; E: Hastings; Pte. SD 1051; K: 29.6.16; St.Vaast Post Mil. Cem. Pas-de-Calais; Age 21; Son of Mary Ann Hobbs of 83, Bexhill Road, West St.Leonards, Sussex.

4630. HOBDAY, George Henry; B: Penhurst, Sussex; E: Hastings; Pte. SD 5159; K: 21.10.16; Grandcourt Road Cem. Somme; Age 20; Son of William and Mary Ann Hobday of Battle Lodge, Battle, Sussex.

4631. HODGINS, Francis Edward; B: – ; E: Brighton; Pte. G 9255; K: 13.2.17; Vlamertinghe Mil. Cem. (Bel.).

4632. HOLDEN, Arthur Edward; B: Cuckfield, Sussex; E: Haywards Heath; Pte. G 9592; D: 16.6.17; Longuenesse (St.Omer) Souvenir Cem. Pas-de-Calais; Age 33; Son of William and Augusta Martha Holden of 11, Glebe Road, Cuckfield.

4633. HOLLAND, Franklin Gilbert; B: Netherfield, Sussex; E: Hastings; Sgt. SD 806; M.M.; K: 24.9.17; Tyne Cot Mem. (Bel.); Age 23; Son of William and Mary Ann Holland of "Sea View", Netherfield.

4634. HOLMAN, Albert Edward; B: Worth, Sussex; E: Horsham; Pte. SD 680; K: 3.9.16; Thiepval Mem. Somme; Age 23; Son of John and Matilda Holman of Mount Noddy, Worth.

4635. HOLMWOOD, Owen Ernest; B: Rotherfield, Sussex; E: Tunbridge Wells; Pte. SD 425; K: 21.10.16; Bouzincourt Ridge Cem. Somme; Age

25; Son of Frank and Mary Jane Holmwood of 2, Church Road, Rotherfield.*

4636. HONEY, William Henry; B: Ashford, Middlesex; E: Staines, Middlesex; Pte. G 17348; K: 3.4.18; Pozieres Mem. Somme; The date of death was recorded at the end of the 'Spring Retreat' and is incorrect; Death would have been during the period 21 – 31.3.18.*

4637. HONEYSETT, Robert; B: Herstmonceux, Sussex; E: Herstmonceux; L/Cpl. SD 599; K: 3.9.16; Thiepval Mem. Somme; Age 24; Son of Mrs. Harriett Honeysett of 6, Sea View, Harebeating, Hailsham, Sussex.

4638. HOOD, Oswald, Lt.; K: 1.9.16; Englebelmer Com. Cem. Ext. Somme; Son of the Rev.E.P. and Eleanor Hood of 12, College Terrace, Brighton; Probably killed in billet by shell fire. *

4639. HOOK, Albert Henry; B: Tonbridge; E: Hastings; Pte. SD 1052; K: 3.9.16; Thiepval Mem. Somme; Age 28; Son of George H. and Mary Ann Hook; Husband of Emma Elizabeth Hook of 9, Sackville Road, Bexhill-on-Sea.; Enlisted with, and was killed in the same major attack as, his brother Frederick (see 4640).

4640. HOOK, Frederick; B: Hastings; E: Hastings; Pte. SD 1053; K: 3.9.16; Thiepval Mem. Somme; Son of George H. and Mary Ann Hook; Enlisted with, and was killed in the same major attack as, his brother Albert Henry (see 4639).

4641. HOSKINS, Albert Arthur; B: Eastbourne; E: Eastbourne; Pte. SD 75; K: 3.9.16; Ancre Brit. Cem. Somme.

4642. HOWARD, George; B: Stotford, Bedfordshire; E: Bedford; Pte. G 15217; W: 4.8.17; Étaples Mil. Cem. Pas-de-Calais; Age 28; Son of Mr. and Mrs. Alfred Howard of Brook Street, Stotfold; Husband of Mrs.Howard of 5, Henshall Street, Islington, London.*

4643. HOWARD, Sidney; B: Norwich; E: Norwich; Pte. G 24416; K: 3.4.18; Pozieres Mem. Somme; The date of death was recorded at the end of the 'Spring Retreat' and is incorrect; Death would have been during the period 21 – 31.3.18.*

4644. HUCKSTEPP, Albert; B: Peasmarsh, Sussex; E: Hastings; Pte. SD 5175; K: 22.3.16; Le Touret Mil. Cem. Pas-de-Calais.

4645. HUDSON, George; B: March, Cambridgeshire; E: March; Pte. SD 3906; K: 3.9.16; Thiepval Mem. Somme; Age 20; Son of Mrs.Frances M.Hudson of 208, Times Villas, Station Road, March.

4646. HUGGETT, James; B: Brenzett, Kent; E: Hastings; Pte. SD 5135; K: 11.5.16; Le Touret Mil. Cem. Pas-de-Calais.

4647. HUGHES, George James; B: Uppington, Berkshire; E: Swindon; L/Cpl. G 24845; K: 3.4.18; Pozieres Mem. Somme; The date of death was recorded at the end of the 'Spring Retreat' and is incorrect; Death would have been during the period 21 – 31.3.18.*

4648. HULL, Stanley Richard; B: Ascot, Berkshire; E: Bedford; Pte. G 18709; K: 3.4.18; Pozieres Mem. Somme; The date of death was recorded at the end of the 'Spring Retreat' and is incorrect; Death would have been during the period 21 – 31.3.18.*

4649. HULME, Harry; B: Leek, Staffordshire; E: Leek; Pte. G 15741;; K: 22.4.17; Vlamertinghe Mil. Cem. (Bel.); Age 19; Son of George and Harriett Hulme of 49, Burton Street, Rochdale Road, Manchester.*

4650. HUNT, Alfred; B: Hardingham, Norfolk; E: Norwich; Pte. G 11689; K: 31.7.17; Ypres (Menin Gate) Mem. (Bel.); Age 20; Son of Alfred and Ellen Hunt of 70, Montague Road, Clarendon Park, Leicester.

4651. HUNT, Alfred Frank; B: Petworth, Sussex; E: Petworth; Pte. SD 5629; K: 18.10.16; Bouzincourt Com. Cem. Ext. Somme; Age 23; Son of Alfred and C.M.Hunt of Hoad's Common Lodge, Petworth.

4652. HUNT, Sydney John; B: Haywards Heath; E: Haywards Heath; Pte. G 15827; W: 22.10.16; Blighty Valley Cem. Somme; Age 35; Son of the late John Hunt and Louisa White, formerly Hunt, of 2, Lyndhurst Cottages, Kents Road, Haywards Heath., Sussex.*

4653. HUTCHISON, John; B: Bexhill-on-Sea; E: Hastings; L/Cpl. SD 1059; W: 26.4.18; Lijssenthoek Mil. Cem. (Bel.); Age 30; Son of Stephen and Ellen Hutchison of Staplecross, Sussex.

I

4654. IDE, Harry; B: Bognor Regis, Sussex; E: Bognor Regis; Cpl. SD 809; K: 24.9.17; Tyne Cot Mem. (Bel.).*

4655. IRWIN, Marcus; B: Birkenhead; E: Wallasey; Pte. SD 3901; K: 3.9.16; Thiepval Mem. Somme.

4656. ISTED, James Henry; B: Herstmonceux, Sussex; E: Herstmonceux; Pte. SD 603; K: 11.7.16; Cambrin Churchyard Ext, Pas-de-Calais; Age 20; Son of Henry and Jane Isted of "Fairseat", Herstmonceux.

4657. ISTED, Sydney John; B: Sidley, Bexhill-on-Sea, Sussex; E: Bexhill-on-Sea; Pte. SD 1077; K: 24.7.16; St.Vaast Post Mil. Cem. Pas-de-Calais; Age 21; Son of George and Charlotte N.Isted of 1, Laburnum Cottages, Sidley, Bexhill-on-Sea.*

4658. IVENS, Frank Harold Howe; Capt.; K: 21.10.16; Thiepval Mem. Somme; Age 29; Son of John William Howe Ivens of Dunstable, Bedfordshire; Mentioned in 'Undertones of War' by Edmund Blunden.

J

4659. JACKSON, Arthur Henry; B: Grimston, Norfolk; E: Norwich; Pte. G 18713; K: 3.4.18; Pozieres Mem. Somme; The date of death was recorded at the end of the 'Spring Retreat' and is incorrect; Death would have been during the period 21 – 31.3.18.*

4660. JACOBS, Stewart; B: Bolsham, Cambridgeshire; E: Grays, Essex; Pte. SD 5519; K: 3.4.18; Pozieres Mem. Somme; The date of death was recorded at the end of the 'Spring Retreat' and is incorrect;

Death would have been during the period 21 – 31.3.18.*

4661. JAMES, Albert Edward; B: Norwood, London; E: Guildford; Pte. G 18503; K: 27.9.17; Hooge Crater Cem. (Bel.); Age 19; Son of Samuel Charles and Elizabeth James of 6, West Road, Teddington, Middlesex.

4662. JAMES, Harry Bond; B: Frant, Sussex; E: Tunbridge Wells; Pte. SD 433; K: 3.9.16; Thiepval Mem. Somme; Age 23; Son of Walter and Emily James of High Street, Frant.

4663. JARMAN, Frederick; B: Northiam, Sussex; E: Hastings; Pte. G 15835; W: 26.3.18; Roisel Com. Cem. Ext. Somme.

4664. JARRETT, John; B: Hadlow Down, Sussex; E: Tonbridge; Pte. G 15834; K: 21.10.16; Thiepval Mem. Somme; Age 27; Son of Mrs.Ellen Cook of Woodgates, Hadlow Down.

4665. JARVIS, Charles John; B: Heathfield, Sussex; E: Brighton; Pte. SD 5146; K: 3.9.16; Thiepval Mem. Somme; Age 24; Son of Edward and Sophia Jarvis of Fir Tree Cottage, Tilsmore, Heathfield.

4666. JINMAN, John Bedford; B: Eastbourne; E: Chichester; Pte. G 11498; W: 15.5.18; Boulogne Eastern Cem. Pas-de-Calais; Age 20; Son of John and Alice Jinman of 95, Whitley Road, Eastbourne.

4667. JOCELYN, Herbert; B: Little Hallenbury, Hertfordshire; E: Eastbourne; Pte. SD 323; K: 3.9.16; Thiepval Mem. Somme.

4668. JOHNSON, George Avis; B: Havant, Hampshire; E: Horsham, Sussex; Pte. G 16143; K: 25.9.17; Tyne Cot Mem. (Bel.).

4669. JOLLIFFE, Augustine; B: Swindon, Wiltshire; E: Worthing; Pte. SD 2419; K: 26.3.18; Pozieres Mem. Somme.

4670. JONES, Ernest Alfred; B: Worthing; E: Chichester; Pte. L 11063; K: 21.10.16; Thiepval Mem. Somme; Age 20; Brother of Mrs.Walker of 75, Sugden Road Flat, Worthing.

4671. JONES, William Henry; B: Monmouth; E: Warley, Essex; Pte. G 17326; W: 7.12.16; Nine Elms Brit. Cem. (Bel.); Age 19; Son of William and S.H.Jones of Seven Kings, Essex; Mortally wounded in camp on 6.12.16 by a bomb dropped during an enemy air raid.*

4672. JONES, William James; B: Hailsham, Sussex; E: Herstmonceux, Sussex; Pte. SD 607; K: 3.9.16; Ancre Brit. Cem. Somme; Age 22; Son of William Jones of 11, Gordon Place, Hailsham.*

4673. JORDON, Archibald; B: Worthing; E: Worthing; Pte. SD 526; K: 3.9.16; Hamel Mil. Cem. Somme; Age 21; Son of James Theophilus and Ellen Jordon of Worthing.

4674. JOYCE, Stanley Charles; B: Mile End, London; E: London; Pte. SD 3926; D: 27.1.17; Lijssenthoek Mil. Cem. (Bel.); Son of Henry Joyce of 9, Norfolk Street, Globe Road, Mile End, London.*

4675. JUDEN, William Arthur; B: Shoreham, Sussex; E: Brighton; Pte. SD 811; W: 5.4.18; St.Sever Com. Cem. Ext., Rouen, Seine-Maritime; Age 29; Son of William Arthur and Agnes Grace Juden of 14, Railway Street, Brighton.*

4676. JUDGE, Henry Thomas; B: Maidstone, Kent; E: Hastings; Pte. SD 5131; W: 5.9.16; Couin Brit. Cem. Pas-de-Calais; Age 25; Son of George and Fanny Judge.

4677. JUPP, Charles William; B: Brighton; E: Brighton; Pte. G 6541; K: 25.1.17; Vlamertinghe Mil. Cem. (Bel.); Age 32.

4678. JUPP, Herbert; B: Brighton; E: Hove; Pte. SD 2416; K: 24.9.17; Bedford House Cem. Enclosure No.4 (Bel.); Killed defending a trench against an enemy raid at Potijze.*

4679. JUSTICE, James William; B: Sowerby Bridge, Yorkshire; E: Halifax; L/Cpl. SD 3954; K: 3.9.16; Thiepval Mem. Somme; Age 27; Son of Henry and Eliza Ann Justice of 19, Rhondda Place, West End, Halifax; Husband of Gertrude Justice of Dean Cottage, Skircoat Green, Yorkshire.

K

4680. KEATES, William Russell; B: Bersted, Sussex; E: Chichester; Pte. SD 2724; K: 21.10.16; Thiepval Mem. Somme; Age 22; Son of William George Keates of Rosegreen, Pagham, Sussex.

4681. KEMP, Jabez; B: Heathfield, Sussex; E: Eastbourne; Pte. TF 241492; K: 25.9.17; Hooge Crater Cem. (Bel.); Age 19; Son of William James and Emily Kemp of Bigknowle Farm, Heathfield.

4682. KENSETT, Sydney; B: Shipley, Sussex; E: Horsham; Pte. SD 699; K: 3.9.16; Thiepval Mem. Somme; Age 28; Son of the late Reuben Kensett and Rose Laker, formerly Kensett, of Trawlers Farm, Southwater, Sussex.

4683. KENT, William Worsley; B: Manchester; E: Manchester; Pte. G 17268; W: 7.11.17; Lijssenthoek Mil. Cem. (Bel.); Age 19; Son of William Worsley and Margaret Kent of Chorlton-cum-Hardy, Lancashire; Formerly served in the 20th Bn. Royal Fusiliers.

4684. KING, William; B: Leeds; E: Breary Banks, Yorkshire; L/Cpl. SD 700; W: 16.5.16; Bethune Town Cem. Pas-de-Calais; Age 19; Son of Albert and Emily King of 10, Marsh Road, Bulwark, Monmouthshire.

4685. KNIGHT, Herbert Oliver; B: Sidcup, Kent; E: Maidstone; Pte. G 18505; K: 25.9.17; Hooge Crater Cem. (Bel.); Age 25; Son of William C. and Ida C.Knight of 67, Loose Road, Maidstone.

4686. KNIGHT, William; B: Cuckfield, Sussex; E: Haywards Heath; Pte. G 6198; K: 21.3.18; Heath Cem., Harbonnieres, Somme.

L

4687. LAKER, William James Cuthbert; B: Lindfield, Sussex; E: Horsham; Pte. G 15839; K: 25.1.17; Vlamertinghe Mil. Cem. (Bel.); Age 18; Son of William Laker of "King's Head", Rudgwick, Sussex; Killed defending a trench against an enemy raid at Potijze.*

4688. LAMBERT, Edward; B: Eastbourne; E: Eastbourne; L/Cpl. SD 82; K: 3.9.16; Thiepval Mem. Somme; Age 21; Son of Edward and Lily Lambert of 3, Channel View Road, Eastbourne.

4689. LAMBERT, Robert Charles Alfred; B: James Town, St.Helena; E: Eastbourne; Pte. G 15841; W: 3.11.16; Puchevillers Brit. Cem. Somme; Age 36; Son of the Rev.Joseph Christopher and Johanna Mary Lambert.

4690. LANDER, Fred; B: Petworth, Sussex; E: Eastbourne; L/Cpl. SD 203; K: 3.9.16; Thiepval Mem. Somme.

4691. LANE, Ernest William; B: Melton Constable, Norfolk; E: Great Yarmouth; Pte. G 15287; K: 13.2.17; Vlamertinghe Mil. Cem. (Bel.); Age 19, Son of A.C. and J.W.Lane of Great Yarmouth.

4692. LANGFORD, Henry; B: Watford; E: Horsham; Pte. SD 705; K: 30.6.16; St.Vaast Post Mil. Cem. Pas-de-Calais; Age 21; Son of Frederick Bailey Langford and Rosina Langford of Boddington, Buckinghamshire.

4693. LANGHAM, Arthur William Herbert; B: Hanworth, Middlesex; E: Staines; Pte. G 17364; K: 3.4.18; Ste.Emilie Valley Cem. Villers-Faucon, Somme; The date of death was recorded at the end of the 'Spring Retreat' and is incorrect; Death would have been during the period 21 – 31.3.18, probably the 23rd. *

4694. LANGLEY, Charles J.; B: Beckenham, Kent; E: Bromley, Kent; Pte. G 6563; W: 30.1.17; Lijssenthoek Mil. Cem. (Bel.).*

4695. LANGMAID, Albert Thomas; B: Bexhill-on-Sea; E: Hastings; Pte. SD 5156; K: 12.5.16; Le Touret Mil. Cem. Pas-de-Calais; Age 22; Son of Albert and Maud Langmaid of 24, Cornwall Road, Bexhill-on-Sea.*

4696. LANGRISH, Reginald Albert; B: Huntingford, Hertfordshire; E: Hertford; Pte. G 15581; K: 21.3.18; Pozieres Mem. Somme; Age 20; Son of Albert Thomas and Florence Fanny Langrish of 4, Pegs Lane, Hertford.

4697. LARCOMBE, William; B: Watford; E: Watford; Pte. G 18716; K: 3.4.18; Pozieres Mem. Somme; The date of death was recorded at the end of the 'Spring Retreat' and is incorrect; Death would have been during the period 21 – 31.3.18.*

4698. LARTER, George; B: Fressingfield, Norfolk; E: Harleston; Pte. G 15252; W: 28.3.18; Namps-au-Val Brit. Cem. Somme.*

4699. LAWRENCE, George Edward; B: – ; E: Stratford, London; L/Cpl. G 15746; K: 21.10.16; Mill Road Cem. Somme.

4700. LAWSON, Charles Henry; B: Worthing; E: Worthing; C.S.M. L 5936; K: 15.6.17; Vlamertinghe New Mil. Cem. (Bel.); Age 35; Son of Charles and Sophia Lawson; Husband of Alice Maud Lawson.*

4701. LEARY, Thomas Frederick; B: Felpham, Sussex; E: Bognor Regis, Sussex; Cpl. SD 815; K: 24.9.17; Tyne Cot Cem. (Bel.); Age 20; Son of the late George William Leary and Edith Ellen Ridgers, formerly Leary, of 7, Retort Cottages, Ivy Lane, South Bersted, Sussex.

4702. LEE, Charles; B: – ; E: Kenley, Surrey; Pte. G 6565; K: 3.6.17; Vlamertinghe Mil. Cem. (Bel.); Age 31; Husband of Florence Lee of Chailey, Sussex.

4703. LEE, John James; B: Blackburn; E: Blackburn; Pte. SD 3917; W: 28.7.16; Merville Com. Cem. Nord; Age 25; Son of William and Mary Alice Lee of 3, Wensley Street, Blackburn.

4704. LINGARD, William Alfred; B: Rushden, Northamptonshire; E: Kettering; Pte. G 18721; K: 3.4.18; Pozieres Mem. Somme; Age 19; Son of Mr.W. and Mrs.G.E.Lingard of 21, King's Road, Rushden; The date of death was recorded at the end of the 'Spring Retreat' and is incorrect; Death would have been during the period 21 – 31.3.18.*

4705. LITTLE, Tom; B: Fulham, London; E: Chichester; Pte. G 14171; K: 25.9.17; Tyne Cot Mem. (Bel.); Age 19; Son of Isaac and Jane Elizabeth Little of Butterfly Lodge, Salt Hill, Chichester.

4706. LIVINGS, Frederick Percy; B: – ; E: Brentwood, Essex; Pte. G 15770; D at Home; 2.12.16; Hutton (All Saints) Churchyard, Leicestershire (UK); Age 20; Son of Walter and Milicent Livings.

4707. LOADER, T.E.; B: – ; E: – ; Pte. SD 706; W or D at Home: 14.10.18; Framsden (St.Mary) Churchyard, Suffolk (UK); Age 27.

4708. LONG, Ernest; B: New Cross, London; E: Bexhill-on-Sea; Pte. SD 1071; W: 2.8.17; Brandhoek New Mil. Cem. (Bel.); Age 28; Son of Mr. and Mrs.A.Long of London.

4709. LOWER, Roy William; B: Seaford, Sussex; E: Eastbourne; Cpl. SD 81; K: 1.8.17; Ypres (Menin Gate) Mem. (Bel.); Age 25; Son of Mrs.H.A.Green of 2, Gloster Place, Dane Road, Seaford.*

4710. LOWNDES, Joseph; B: Tillington, Staffordshire; E: Hastings; Pte. SD 2429; K: 14.5.16; Le Touret Mil. Cem. Pas-de-Calais; Age 28; Son of the late Daniel Lowndes and Emily Boydon, formerly Lowndes, of 133, Eccleshall Road, Stafford; Killed during 'Stand To'.*

4711. LUCAS, William; B: Shipley, Sussex; E: Hastings; Pte. SD 4040; K: 3.9.16; Thiepval Mem. Somme.

4712. LUMM, William; B: – ; E: Watford; Pte. G 18724; K: 24.3.18; Pozieres Mem., Somme.

M

4713. MAC FARLANE, James; B: Greenock, Renfrewshire; E: London; Pte. SD 3878; W: 13.6.16; Étaples Mil. Cem. Pas-de-Calais; Age 27; Son of John and Jessie MacFarlane of 31, Bank Street, Greenock.

4714. MAIDMENT, Francis Samuel; B: Salisbury, Wiltshire; E: Worthing; Pte. L 9344; W: 3.10.17; Étaples Mil. Cem. Pas-de-Calais; Age 29; Husband of Mrs.M.Maidment of Coombe Cottages, Littleham, Devonshire.

4715. MANSELL, Ernest; B: Brighton; E: Hove; Pte. SD 2343; K: 21.10.16; Thiepval Mem. Somme.

4716. MARCH, Thomas Bertie; B: Worthing; E: Chichester; Pte. G 15850; K: 6.11.17; Tyne Cot Mem. (Bel.); Age 25; Son of William Thomas and Ellen March of 39, Cobden Road, Worthing.

4717. MARKER, Frank Edwin; B: Hackney, London; E: Tottenham, London; Pte. SD 5730; K: 4.10.16; Auchonvillers Mil. Cem. Somme; Age 27; Son of Frederick and Maria Marker of 11, Swiss Cottages, Lauriston Road, South Hackney; Killed by an enemy shell during relief from trenches at Auchonvillers.*

4718. MARTIN, Charles Claude; B: Lambeth, London; E: Worthing; Pte. SD 531; K: 13.3.16; Rue-David Mil. Cem. Pas-de-Calais; Age 29; Son of Jessie Martin of "Weston Dene", Lyndhurst Road, Worthing; Killed when an enemy 5.9" shell struck his billet at Fleurbaix.

4719. MARTIN, Ernest Percival; B: Willingdon, Sussex; E: Eastbourne; L/Cpl. SD 209; K: 3.9.16; Thiepval Mem. Somme; Enlisted with brother, Thomas, who was also killed in the same major attack on the same day (see 4721).

4720. MARTIN, Reginald Norfolk; B: Brighton; E: Brighton; Pte. SD 4913; K: 4.6.16; Cambrin Churchyard Ext. Pas-de-Calais; Age 19; Son of Eleanor Jane Martin of 14, Caledonian Road, Brighton.

4721. MARTIN, Thomas; B: Willingdon, Sussex; E: Eastbourne; Pte. SD 208; K: 3.9.16; Thiepval Mem. Somme; Enlisted with brother, Ernest Percival, who was also killed in the same major attack on the same day (see 4719).

4722. MATTHEWS, David; B: Hailsham, Sussex; E: Herstmonceux, Sussex; Pte. SD 616; K: 21.10.16; Grandcourt Road Cem. Somme; Age 23; Son of Mrs.Mary Ann Matthews of 8, Windsor Road, Hailsham.

4723. MATTIN, Amos; B: Colchester; E: Colchester; Pte. SD 5870; K: 21.10.16; Thiepval Mem. Somme; Age 32; Son of Police Constable and Ellen Mattin of 60, Mile End, Colchester.

4724. MAUGHAM, Sidney John; B: Clapham, London; E: Battersea, London; L/Cpl. G 3875; W at Home: 27.8.17; Battersea (Morden) Cem. London (UK).

4725. MAY, Charles; B: Withyham, Sussex; E: Tunbridge Wells; L/Cpl. SD 443; W: 24.5.16; Bethune Town Cem. Pas-de-Calais; Age 35; Son of Daniel and Sophia May of 3, Horse Grove, Rotherfield, Sussex; Husband of Elizabeth Rose May of 2, Ferndale Villa, Jarvis Brook, Sussex.

4726. MAY, George Edward; B: Kis, India; E: Bognor Regis, Sussex; L/Sgt. SD 769; K: 30.6.16; St.Vaast Post Mil. Cem. Pas-de-Calais; Age 20; Son of Mrs. Sophia May of "Alverton", Linden Avenue, Bognor Regis.

4727. MAY, Walter; B: – ; E: Brentwood, Essex; Pte. G 15747; K: 25.1.17; Vlamertinghe Mil. Cem. (Bel.); Age 20; Son of Alfred and Clara May of 12, Gough Road, Stratford, London; Killed defending a trench against an enemy raid at Potijze.

4728. MEAD, Frederick Thomas; B: – ; E: Hove; Pte. G 17880; K: 29.4.18; Tyne Cot Mem. (Bel.).

4729. MEADWELL, Bert; B: – ; E: Brentwood, Essex; Pte. G 15771; K: 25.1.17; Vlamertinghe Mil. Cem. (Bel.); Killed while defending a trench against an enemy raid at Potijze.

4730. MEEKINGS, James Henry; B: Fordham, Cambridgeshire; E: Croydon; Pte. SD 5647; K: 21.10.16; Mill Road Cem. Somme; Age 25; Son of Mr.Meekings of Thornton Heath, London; Husband of Mary Meekings of 60, Winterbourne Road, Thornton Heath.*

4731. MEPHAM, Percy; B: Frant, Sussex; E: Chichester; Pte. G 20440; W:23.9.17; Voormezeele Enclosures Nos.1 and 2 (Bel.); Age 21; Son of Ellen and James Mepham of Bridge Farm, Frant, Sussex.*

4732. MERCER, Alfred Sidney; B: Farnham, Surrey; E: Guildford; Pte. G 18728; K: 29.4.18; Tyne Cot Mem. (Bel.); Age 19; Son of Alfred Robert and Anna Maria Mercer of 12, The Cottages, Weybourne, Surrey.

4733. MERCER, Harry; B: Bexhill-on-Sea; E: Hastings; Pte. SD 4810; K: 30.6.16; St.Vaast Post Mil. Cem. Pas-de-Calais; Age 18; Son of Charles and Caroline Mercer of Steer's Green, Battle, Sussex.

4734. MERRICKS, Bert William; B: Portsmouth; E: Hastings; Pte. SD 1075; K: 21.10.16; Grandcourt Road Cem. Somme.

4735. MERRITT, George Edward; B: Penge, London; E: Brighton; Pte. G 16383; K: 15.3.17; Railway Dugouts Burial Ground (Bel.).

4736. MESSER, Thomas Frank; B: Peas Pottage, Sussex; E: Horsham; Pte. G 15848; W: 25.10.16; Contay Brit. Cem. Somme.

4737. MIDDLETON, Frank Arthur; B: Rotherfield, Sussex; E: Tunbridge Wells; Pte. SD 444; K: 30.6.16; St.Vaast Post Mil. Cem. Pas-de-Calais.

4738. MILLAR, Arthur; B: Seaford, Sussex; E: Eastbourne; Pte. SD 329; K: 29.7.17; Ypres (Menin Gate) Mem. (Bel.).

4739. MILLER, Enoch, B: Nether Broughton, Lincolnshire; E: Melton Mowbray, Leicestershire; Pte. SD 2243; K: 30.6.16; St.Vaast Post Mil. Cem. Pas-de-Calais.*

4740. MILLER, Stephen; B: Pevensey, Sussex; E: Herstmonceux, Sussex; Pte; SD 615; Died at Home: 22.11.16; Age 23; Son of Stephen Lawrence and Bertha Miller of 3, Castle Terrace, Pevensey; Died of tuberculosis; Of his brothers who all served in The Royal Sussex Regiment, Wilfred Lawrence (11th Battalion – see 4742) and Arthur John (7th Battalion – see 2863) were killed in action, while Robert Randolph (Butcher) and Frederick George (Groom) survived.

4741. MILLER, Tom; B: Warrington; E: Beary Banks, Yorkshire; Pte. SD 712; K: 3.9.16; Thiepval Mem. Somme.

4742. MILLER, Wilfred Lawrence; B: Pevensey, Sussex; E: Herstmonceux; Pte. SD 614; K: 30.8.16; Age 21; Englebelmer Com. Cem. Ext. Somme; Son of Stephen Lawrence and Bertha Susan Miller of 3, Castle Terrace, Pevensey; Killed during shrapnel shelling of Mailly-Maillet Wood; Originally buried at Beaussart, Somme, but the graves there were disturbed by shelling later in the war. After the war the remains were removed from Beaussart and re-intered at Englebelmer. Of his brothers who all served in The Royal Sussex Regiment, Stephen died (see 4740), Arthur John (twice wounded in the 11th Battalion and subsequently transferred to the 7th Battalion – (see 2863) was killed in action, while Robert Randolph (Butcher) and Frederick George (Groom) survived.

4743. MILLHAM, William; B: – ; E: Horsham; Pte. TF 200758; K: 3.4.18; Pozieres Mem. Somme; Age 19; Son of William and Alice Jane Millham of 2, Firle Cottage, South Street, Partridge Green, Sussex; The date of death was recorded at the end of the 'Spring Retreat' and is incorrect; Death would have been during the period 21 – 31.3.18.*

4744. MINNS, Frederick Henry; B: Buxted, Sussex; E: Uckfield, Sussex; Pte. SD 5239; K: 3.4.18; Ste.Emilie Valley Cem. Villers-Faucon, Somme; The date of death was recorded at the end of the 'Spring Retreat' and is incorrect; Death would have been during the period 21 – 31.3.18, probably 23rd.*

4745. MINNS, George; B: Rotherfield, Sussex; E: Tunbridge Wells; Cpl. SD 448; K: 3.9.16; Thiepval Mem. Somme.

4746. MITCHELL, Arthur Thomas; B: Bognor Regis, Sussex; E: Bognor Regis; Pte. SD 819; K: 30.6.16; Loos Mem. Pas-de-Calais.

4747. MITCHELL, Benjamin; B: Ore, Sussex; E: Hastings; L/Cpl. SD 1076; D: at Home: 24.7.15; Hastings Cem. Sussex (UK); Age 24; Son of Benjamin and Elizabeth A.Mitchell of 288, Priory Road, Hastings.

4748. MITCHELL, Charles Kenneth; B: Ifield, Sussex; E: Crawley, Sussex; Pte. SD 1148; D at Home: 5.2.15; Crawley (St.John the Baptist) Churchyard, Sussex (UK); Age 25; Son of Charles James and Sarah Blanche Mitchell of Oak Lodge, Crawley.

4749. MITCHELL, Richard; B: Rotherfield, Sussex; E: Tunbridge Wells; Pte. SD 441; K: 17.8.16; Loos Mem. Pas-de-Cal;ais; Age 26; Son of Mr. R.Mitchell of 46, South Road, Hailsham, Sussex.

4750. MITCHELL, William James; B: Bognor Regis, Sussex; E: Bognor Regis; Pte. SD 820; K: 18.9.17; La Clytte Mil. Cem. (Bel.); Age 19; Son of George and Annie Mitchell of 37, Clifford Road, South Norwood, London; Native of Bersted, Sussex.

4751. MITCHELL, William Thomas; B: Worth, Sussex; E: Bexhill-on-Sea; Pte. SD 1136; K: 21.10.16; Mill Road Cem. Somme; Age 20; Son of William and Jane Mitchell of Bruce Cottage, Copthorne, Sussex; Native of Crawley Down, Sussex.

4752. MOATES, William James; B: Sprowston, Norfolk; E: Norwich; Pte. G 15168; K: 23.10.16; Puchevillers Brit. Cem. Somme; Age 48; Son of Benjamin and Agnes Moates of Norwich; Husband of Elizabeth Moates of 4, Boston Street, Norwich.*

4753. MOCKFORD, Jesse Allen; B: Notting Hill, London; E: Herstmonceux, Sussex; Pte. SD 612; K: 31.7.17; Duhallow A.D.S. Cem. (Bel.); Age 19; Son of William and Rosina Elizabeth Mockford of 21, Carlton Road, Eastbourne.*

4754. MOLE, Harold Pearce; 2nd Lt.; K: 3.9.16; Thiepval Mem. Somme; Age 22; Son of Chamberlain and Katherine Berners May Mole of Woodthorpe, Surrey.

4755. MOODY, Wilfred Lewin; B: – ; E: Witcomb Street, London; Pte. G 14625; W: 29.7.17; Lijssenthoek Mil. Cem. (Bel.); Age 20; Son of Tyrell and Elizabeth Moody of 87, Tantallon Road, Balham, London

4756. MOORE, Frederick; B: Great Deekering, Essex; E: Southend-on-Sea; Pte. G 17198; K: 3.4.18; Pozieres Mem. Somme; Age 19; Son of Frederick Moore of "Elmsville", Millfield Road, Rochford, Essex; The date of death was recorded at the end of the 'Spring Retreat' and is incorrect; Death would have been during the period 21 – 31.3.18. *

4757. MOORE, George Walter; B: Lewes; E: Lewes; Pte. G 15790; K: 27.4.18; Tyne Cot Mem. (Bel.); Age 31; Son of Harry and Mary Ann Moore of 20, Eastport Lane, Southover, Lewes.

4758. MORDLE, Thomas; B: Midhurst, Sussex; E: Midhurst; Pte. TF 201436; W: 6.8.17; Dozinghem Mil. Cem. (Bel.); Age 28; Husband of Rose Lewis, formerly Mordle, of Little Common, Tillington, Petworth, Sussex.

4759. MORLING, Thomas Brown; B: Maresfield, Sussex; E: Uckfield, Sussex; L/Cpl. SD 1078; D at Home: 11.5.16; Fletching Burial Ground, Sussex (UK); Age 21; Son of Mr. and Mrs.George Morling of The Homestead, Horney Common, Sussex.*

4760. MUDDLE, Willam Benjamin George; Pte. G 15849; K: 2.3.17; Railway Dugouts Burial Ground (Bel).

4761. MUNN, Reginald; B: Hastings; E: Bexhill-on-Sea; Pte. G 8653; K: 3.4.18; Poziers Mem. Somme.

4762. MUNNION, Frederick Arthur; B: Ardingly, Sussex; E: Brighton; Cpl. G 821; W: 4.6.17; Boulogne Eastern Cem. Pas-de-Calais; Age 35; Son of Henry and Maria Munnion of Ardingly; Husband of Mrs.M.Munnion of Rolvenden, Kent.

4763. MURRAY, Patrick Joseph; B: Ballymena, County Antrim, Northern Ireland; E: Belfast; Pte. G 18524; K: 24.9.17; Tyne Cot Mem. (Bel.); Age 16; Son of Mrs.Mary Murray of 12, Colin Street, Falls Road, Belfast.

4764. MURRELL, Frederick William; B: Preston, Sussex; E: Eastbourne; L/Cpl. SD 215; K: 30.6.16; Loos Mem. Pas-de-Calais.

4765. MUSTER, Henry Eustace; B: Bromley-by-Bow, London; E: Brighton; Pte. G 16774; K: 31.7.17; Ypres (Menin Gate) Mem. (Bel.).

N

4766. NASH, George Stanley; B: – ; E: Chichester; Pte. TF 203438; W: 21.3.18; Ste.Emilie Valley Cem., Villers-Faucon, Somme; Age 19; Son of Thomas and Eliza Nash of River Road, Arundel, Sussex.*

4767. NAYLOR, Henry Charles; 2nd Lt.; W: 24.9.17; Voormezeele Enclosures Nos.1 and 2 (Bel.); Age 25; Son of John Naylor of Fulham, London; Husband of Marian Elizabeth Naylor of "Fairholme", Drove Road, Swindon; Mentioned in 'Undertones of War' by Edmund Blunden.

4768. NELSON, Frank; B: –; E: Leek, Staffordshire; Pte. G 15122; W: 14.8.17; Dozinghem Mil. Cem. (Bel.).

4769. NEVILLE, Henry; B: Beckenham, Kent; E: Bognor Regis, Sussex; L/Cpl. SD 764; K: 3.9.16; Ancre Brit. Cem. Somme; Age 19; Son of Henry William and Jane Neville of 28, Lansdowne Place, Lewes.

4770. NEVILLE, Percy; B: Hove; E: Uckfield, Sussex; Pte. SD 1079; K: 21.10.16; Bouzincourt Com. Cem. Ext. Somme.

4771. NEWELL, Henry Charles; B: Eastbourne; E: Eastbourne; L/Cpl. SD 216; K: 25.6.16; St.Vaast Post Mil. Cem. Pas-de-Calais.

4772. NEWICK, Charles; B: Mayfield, Sussex; E: Brighton; Pte. G 19861; K: 26.4.18; Tyne Cot Mem. (Bel.); Age 34; Son of Henry and Emily Newick of Darbys Cottage, Wadhurst, Sussex; Husband of Emily Newick of 22, Dale Road, Tonbridge.

4773. NEWMAN, Arthur Thomas; B: Worthing; E: Worthing; Pte. SD 535; K: 13.3.16; Rue-David Cem. Pas-de-Calais; Age 32; Son of Mrs.Charlotte Newman of 7, West Buildings, Worthing; Killed when an enemy 5.9" shell struck his billet at Fleurbaix.

4774. NEWNHAM, William Albert; B: Haywards Heath; E: Brighton; Pte. L 11019; W: 30.3.18; St.Sever Cem. Ext., Rouen, Seine-Maritime.

4775. NICHOL, Thomas William; B: Gateshead; E: Newcastle-on-Tyne; Pte. G 17289; K: 26.9.17; Tyne Cot Mem. (Bel.).*

4776. NICHOLLS, Herbert Charles; B: Eastbourne; E: Eastbourne; Pte. SD 90; K: 3.9.16; Thiepval Mem. Somme.

4777. NOBBS, John; B: Woodston, Suffolk; E: Norwich; Pte. G 15170; W: 17.8.17; Oak Dump Cem. (Bel.).

4778. NOBES, Wilfred Edgar Harry; B: Hanworth, Middlesex; E: Staines, Middlesex; Pte. G 18734; K: 3.4.18; Roisel Com. Cem. Ext. Somme; Age 18; Son of William and Emily Nobes of Lime Villas, Staines Road, Hanworth; The date of death was recorded at the end of the 'Spring Retreat' and is incorrect; Death would have been during the period 21 – 31.3.18, probably the 22nd or 23rd.*

4779. NORHCOTE, Edward Stafford; Capt.; K: 3.9.16; Thiepval Mem. Somme; Mentioned in 'Undertones of War' by Edmund Blunden; During the major attack on 3.9.16 he led some men so far as the German second line and remained holding that precarious position all day despite the great odds; they were forced to withdraw at 6.30pm and he was killed while leading his men back across No-Man's-Land to their own lines.

4780. NUNN, Arthur; B: Ardingly, Sussex; E: Brighton; Pte. SD 827; K: 31.10.16; Thiepval Mem. Somme; Age 22; Son of Harry and Flora Nunn of Holland Cottage, Ardingly.

4781. NUNNE, Ernest William; B: Battersea, London; E: Hove; Pte. SD 4939; K: 30.6.16; Rue-des-Berceaux Mil. Cem. Pas-de-Calais.

O

4782. OFFILER, John William; B: Herne Hill, London; E: Brighton; Pte. S 2205; M.M.; K: 31.7.17; New Irish Farm Cem. (Bel.); Age 20; Son of John William and Elizabeth Offiler of London.*

4783. OLIVER, Percy John; B: Erith, Kent; E: Hastings; Pte. SD 956; W: 21.5.16; Bethune Town Cem. Pas-de-Calais; Age 22; Son of Mr. and Mrs.H.J.Oliver of 49, High Street, Battle, Sussex.*

4784. OKEY, John William; B: Northampton; E: Rushden, Northamptonshire; Pte. G 22679; K: 3.4.18; Ste. Emilie Valley Cem., Villers-Faucon, Somme; Son of Mrs.K.Okey of 26, Albion Place, Rushden; The date of death was recorded at the end of the 'Spring Retreat' and is incorrect; Death would have been during the period 21 – 31.3.18, probably the 23rd.

P

4785. PACKHAM, Alfred James; B: Brighton; E: Eastbourne; Pte. G 6515; K: 5.6.17; Ypres (Menin Gate) Mem. (Bel.).

4786. PADGHAM, Spencer; B: Forest Row, Sussex; E: Horsham. Sussex; Pte. SD 3823; K: 3.9.16; Serre Road Cem. No.2, Somme.

4787. PAGE, Charles Alfred; B: Lancing, Sussex; E: Worthing; Cpl. SD 1145; K: 23.4.18; Tyne Cot Mem. (Bel.).

4788. PAGET, A.Harold; B: –; E: Brentwood, Essex; Pte. G 15750; K: 21.10.16; Grandcourt Road Cem. Somme; Husband of Annie Paget of Prospect Place, Cookham Rise, Cookham, Berkshire.*

4789. PAIGE, Thomas; B: Rotherfield, Sussex; E: Tonbridge; L/Cpl. SD 454; K: 22.4.17; Vlamertinghe Mil. Cem. (Bel.).

4790. PANNELL, Valentine Arthur; B: –; E: Brentwood, Essex; L/Cpl. G 15774; K: 31.7.17; Duhallow A.D.S. Cem. (Bel.); Age 23; Son of Mr.W.Pannell of Stoke, Suffolk.

4791. PARROTT, Percy; B: –; E: –; Pte. G 8872; W or D at Home: 2.4.18; Penhurst Churchyard, Sussex (UK); Age 26; Son of Mrs.M.Parrott of Brays Hill, Ashburnham, Sussex.

4792. PARSONS, Harry Frank; B: –; E: –; Pte. SD 139; D at Home: 28.1.16; Age 22; Son of Mrs.Annie Parsons of 19, Eldon Road, Worthing.

4793. PARTRIDGE, Herbert; B: Great Yarmouth; E: Great Yarmouth; Pte. G 15291; W: 26.4.18; Haringhe (Bandeghem) Mil. Cem. (Bel.); Age 23; Son of Edward and Amelia Partridge of 11, Granville Road, Cobholme Island, Great Yarmouth.

4794. PARTRIDGE, William; B: Sherringham, Norfolk; E: Cromer, Norfolk; Pte. G 15171; W: 17.8.17;

Godewaersvelde Com. Cem. Ext. Nord; Son of Mr.G.Partridge of Craymere Beck, Briston, Norfolk.

4795. PAUL, Cedric Franklin; B: Killenule, Ireland; E: Eastbourne; L/Cpl. G 20442; K: 29.7.17; Ypres (Menin Gate) Mem. (Bel.); Age 27; Son of the Rev. Henry and Mrs.Maud Paul of 23, Morehampton Road, Dublin.*

4796. PAYNTER, Thomas Percy; B: Brighton; E: Eastbourne; Pte. SD 3661; W: 25.3.18; St.Sever Cem. Ext., Rouen, Seine-Maritime.

4797. PEACH, Jack; B: Old Hill, Staffordshire; E: Northampton; Pte. G 17382; K: 27.9.17; Tyne Cot Mem. (Bel.).

4798. PEARCE, Samuel; B: Starston, Norfolk; E: Norwich; Cpl. G 15231; K: 21.10.16; Thiepval Mem. Somme.

4799. PECK, Thomas; B: Barnsbury, Middlesex; E: Holloway, London; Pte. G 5810; W: 2.8.17; Mendinghem Mil. Cem. (Bel.); Age 22; Son of Samuel and Sarah Peck of 60, Roman Road, Barnsbury.

4800. PECKHAM, Cecil Hugh; B: Barcombe, Sussex; E: Worthing; Pte. SD 538; W: 19.3.16; Calais Southern Cem. Pas-de-Calais; Age 20; Son of Joseph and Florence Mary Peckham of Fern Cottage, High Street, Barcombe.

4801. PELLING, Alfred Walter; B: Westfield, Sussex; E: Hastings; Pte. G 6569; W: 27.1.17; Lijssenthoek Mil. Cem. (Bel.); Age 33; Son of Walter and Elizabeth Pelling of Brede, Sussex; Husband of Mrs.A.W.Pelling of 2, Sunflower Cottages, High Street, Brede, Sussex.

4802. PENFOLD, Ralph; B: Newdigate, Sussex; E: Horsham; Pte. L 10408; K: 26.9.17; Tyne Cot Mem. (Bel.); Age 24; Son of Joseph and Elizabeth Penfold of Stumbleholme Farm, Ifield, Sussex.

4803. PENRUDDOCKE, Cyril Powys; Capt.; K: 3.9.16; Serre Road Cem. No.2, Somme; Age 20; Son of J. and Clara A.Penruddocke of Winchester House School, Meads, Eastbourne; Mentioned in 'Undertones of War' by Edmund Blunden.

4804. PERHAM, Robert Charles; B: Yeovil, Somerset; E: Worthing; Pte. SD 2991; K: 21.10.16; Thiepval Mem. Somme; Age 19; Son of Henry William and Elizabeth Mary Perham of Home Farm, Charlwood Park, Horley, Surrey.

4805. PERRY, Charles Alfred; B: Welwyn, Hertfordshire; E: Hertford; Sgt. G 15557; K: 3.4.18; Pozieres Mem. Somme; The date of death was recorded at the end of the 'Spring Retreat' and is incorrect; Death would have been during the period 21 – 31.3.18. *

4806. PERRY, George John; B: Hampstead, London; E: Ealing, London; Pte. G 18741; D: 19.6.18; Hamburg Cem. (G); Age 19; Son of Walter Francis and Phoebe Anne Perry of 7, St.Helen's Road, West Ealing; Died while a Prisoner of War.

4807. PERRY, Kenneth George; 2nd Lt.; W: 1.11.16; Puchevillers Brit. Cem Somme; Age 33; Son of

Charles A. and Caroline Perry of Hazelglen, Horley, Surrey; Husband of Dorothy Perry of Harraton Lodge, Exning, Suffolk.

4808. PETTIGREW, Donald; B: Horton-cum-Studley, Oxfordshire; E: Bedford; Pte. TF 241498; K: 25.9.17; Hooge Crater Cem. (Bel.); Age 25; Son of John and Alice Pettigrew of Horton-cum-Studley.

4809. PHILLIPS, Alexander James; B: – ; E: Brighton; Pte. TF 266367; K: 31.7.17; Bedford House Cem. Enclosure No.6 (Bel.); Age 19.

4810. PHILLIPS, Charles Ernest; B: Steyning, Sussex; E: Brighton; Pte. SD 961; K: 3.9.16; Thiepval Mem. Somme; Age 21; Son of George Henry and Kate Phillips of Fern Cottage, Church Lane, Steyning.

4811. PHILLIPS, Harold Morley; B: Putney, London; E: London; Pte. TF 266376; K: 3.4.18; Pozieres Mem. Somme; Age 33; Son of the late Walter Phillips and Elizabeth Louisa Norris, formerly Phillips, of "St. David's", Warwick Par, Tunbridge Wells, Kent; The date of death was recorded at the end of the 'Spring Retreat' and is incorrect; Death would have been during the period 21 – 31.3.18. *

4812. PIGOTT, Harry Frederick Gard; B: Brighton; E: Brighton; L/Cpl. G 16369; K: 1.8.17; New Irish Farm Cem. (Bel.).

4813. PILBEAM, Frank; B: Ditchling, Sussex; E: Haywards Heath; Pte. G 15858; K: 21.10.16; Grandcourt Road Cem. Somme; Husband of Mrs.R.A.Pilbeam of 16, Buckingham Place, Brighton.

4814. PILSWORTH, Reginald Walter; B: Cambridge; E: Cambridge; Pte. G 24450; K: 24.4.18; Tyne Cot Mem. (Bel.); Age 20; Son of Samuel and Eliza Frances Pilsworth of 77, Burnside, Brookfields, Cambridge.

4815. PIPER, Charles Alfred; B: Ticehurst, Sussex; E: Hastings; Pte. SD 1093; W: 8.7.16; Cambrin Churchyard Ext. Pas-de-Calais; Age 23; Son of Thomas and Harriett Piper of Ward Brooke, Ticehurst.*

4816. PIPER, E.C.; 2nd Lt.; K: 26.3.18; – – .

4817. PLASKITT, Robert James; B: Irby, Lincolnshire; E: Grimsby; Pte. G 17290; K: 25.9.17; Hooge Crater Cem. (Bel.).

4818. PLUMMER, Frederick Henry; B: Framfield, Sussex; E: Eastbourne; Pte. SD 3662; K: 3.9.16; Ancre Brit. Cem. Somme; Age 30; Son of Frank and Rose Plummer of 77, South Street, Dorking, Surrey; Husband of Anslie Elizabeth Plummer of 11, Ghyll Road, Heathfield, Sussex.

4819. PORTER, George William; B: Brighton; E: Horsham; Cpl. SD 718; W: 29.7.17; Lijssenthoek Mil. Cem. (Bel.); Age 25; Son of Richard and Mary Alice Porter of Brighton; Husband of Daisy Harriet Porter of 20, Sutherland Road, Brighton.

4820. POTTER, Albert William; B: Ardleigh, Essex; E: Colchester; Pte. G 15775; K: 21.10.16; Thiepval Mem. Somme.

4821. POTTER, C; B: – ; E: – ; Pte. – – 457; W or D at Home: 3.10.17; Rotherfield Burial Ground, Sussex (UK); Son of Walter Potter.

4822. POVEY, Willam Alfred; B: Eastbourne; E: Eastbourne; Pte. SD 223; W: 13.9.16; Beauval Com. Cem. Somme; Age 26; Son of William and Adelaide Povey of "Grovebridge", 23, Gore Park Road, Eastbourne.

4823. POWDRILL, Samuel; B: Wilson, Leicestershire; E: Loughborough; Pte. G 15053; K: 31.7.17; Buffs Road Cem., St.Jean-les-Ypres (Bel.); Age 28; Son of Mrs.A.J.Powdrill of Breedon-on-the-Hill, Derbyshire.

4824. PRICE, Arthur Augustus; B: – ; E: Brighton; Pte. TF 266364; K: 29.3.18; Pozieres Mem. Somme; Age 28; Son of Henry and Mary Ann Sophia Price.

4825. PRICE, Bernard; B: Middlesborough; E: Middlesborough; Pte. G 17291; W: 27.9.17; Mendinghem Mil. Cem. (Bel.).

4826. PRIOR, Harry James; B: Nyewood, Hampshire; E: Chichester; Pte. SD 831; K: 21.10.16; Thiepval Mem. Somme; Age 23; Husband of Mary Charlotte Graver, formerly Prior, of Marden Cottage, East Harting, Sussex.

4827. PROCTOR, Stanley Ernest; B: – ; E: Brighton; Pte. G 3800; K: 31.7.17; Ypres (Menin Gate) Mem. (Bel.); Age 21; Son of George and Emily Sarah Proctor of 91, Compton Road, Brighton; Twice previously wounded.

4828. PUSEY, Edward; B: Hounslow, Middlesex; E: Hounslow; Pte. G 18749; K: 22.3.18; Ste.Emilie Valley Cem. Villers-Faucon, Somme; Age 19; Son of William and Charlotte Pusey of 87, Wellington Road, South Hounslow.*

4829. PUTLAND, Alec; B: Godalming, Surrey; E: Eastbourne; Pte. G 6506; K: 1.8.17; Ypres (Menin Gate) Mem. (Bel.); Age 35; Son of Charles Frederick and Amelia Putland; Husband of Emily Ivy Putland of 66, Susans Road, Eastbourne.

R

4830. RACKLEY, Albert; B: Watford; E: Hertford; Pte. G 15530; K: 31.7.17; New Irish Farm Cem. (Bel.); His death as a 'runner' is graphically described in 'Undertones of War' by Edmund Blunden. (See text).

4831. RALPH, William Thomas; B: Fernhurst, Surrey; E: Horsham; Pte. SD 3844; W: 18.7.16; Calais Southern Cem Pas-de-Calais; Age 25; Son of Henry and Kate Ralph of Hawksfold Cottage, Fernhurst.

4832. REDMAN, George Joseph; B: Brighton; E: Brighton; Pte. TF 265087; K: 21 – 31.3.18; Ste. Emilie Cem., Villers-Faucon, Somme; Age 38; Husband of Alice Lydia Redman of 62, Carlton Hill, Brighton.*

4833. REED, Frederick Stanford Ernest; B: Brighton; E: Hove; Pte. SD 4835; W: 6.9.16; Achiet-le-Grand Com. Cem. Ext. Pas-de-Calais; Age 19; Son of Emma Bertha Norman of 93, Coleman Street, Brighton.*

4834. RELF, Henry; B: Burwash, Sussex; E: Hastings; L/Cpl. SD 3666; K: 21.10.16; Thiepval Mem. Somme.

4835. RELF, Robert; B: Hawkhurst, Kent; E: Hastings; Sgt. SD 1152; K: 4.6.16; Cambrin Churchyard Ext. Pas-de-Calais.

4836. RENSHAW, Herbert Henry; B: – ; E: Brentwood, Essex; Cpl. G 15777; K: 25.9.17; Hooge Crater Cem. (Bel.); Age 38; Son of John George Renshaw of Colchester.

4837. RHODES, George Ernest; B: Shipley, Sussex; E: Horsham; Pte. G 12145; K: 31.7.17; New Irish Farm Cem. (Bel.); Age 30; Son of Henry and Charlotte Rhodes of Ifield, Sussex; Husband of Alice Martha Rhodes of "Sunnyview", 43, Greenside Road, West Croydon.

4838. RICE, Alfred; B: Crawley, Sussex; E: Crawley; Pte. SD 2118; K: 21.10.16; Thiepval Mem. Somme; Age 22; Son of John and Eliza Rice of 80, Ifield Road, Crawley.

4839. RICHARDS, Elmo Leslie; B: Bristol; E: Eastbourne; Pte. G 15860; K: 21.10.16; Grandcourt Road Cem. Somme; Age 34; Son of the late William Richards and Lily M.D.Corbett, formerly Richards, of 51, Keppoch Street, Cardiff.*

4840. RICHARDS, George Edward; B: Rotherfield, Sussex; E: Tunbridge Wells; L/Cpl. SD 467; K: 4.6.16; Cambrin Churchyard Ext. Pas-de-Calais; Age 22; Son of Amos and Eva Richards of Newlyn, Jarvis Brook, Sussex.

4841. RICHARDS, Ronald Henry; 2nd Lt.; K: 2.6.16; Cambrin Churchyard Ext. Pas-de-Calais.

4842. RICHARDSON, Charles; B: Braham, Sussex; E: Chichester; Pte. L 10638; D: 24.4.18; Longuenesse (St.Omer) Souvenir Cem. Pas-de-Calais; Age 21; Son of Charles and stepmother Ada Richardson of Old Fishbourne, Sussex.

4843. ROACH, MIchael; B: Stockton, County Durham; E: Stockton; Pte. SD 728; K: 3.9.16; Thiepval Mem. Somme.

4844. ROBERTS, Charles David; B: Three Bridges, Sussex; E: Hastings; Pte. SD 1177; K: 3.9.16; Mill Road Cem. Somme.

4845. ROBERTS, Ernest Richard; B: Bow, London; E: Whitehall, London; Pte. G 16789; K: 29.7.17; Ypres (Menin Gate) Mem. (Bel.); Age 33; Son of William and Ellen Roberts; Husband of Ethel May Roberts of 82, Greyhound Lane, Streatham, London.

4846. ROBERTS, Robert Charles; B: Welshpool, Montgomeryshire; E: Eastbourne; Cpl. SD 343; K: 3.9.16; Thiepval Mem. Somme; Age 33; Son of Mrs. Jane Ellis, formerly Roberts, of 24, Berriew Road, Welshpool.

4847. ROBERTS, Robert Hugh; B: Carnarvon; E: Eastbourne; Sgt. SD 271; K: 22.4.16; Guards Cem. (Cuinchy) Pas-de-Calais; Age 35; Son of Robert and Elizabeth Roberts of Hellingly, Sussex; Husband of Jane Beatrice Roberts of Sunnyside, Hawkswood, Hailsham, Sussex.*

4848. ROBEY, Albert; B: – ; E: Loughborough; Pte. G 15055; K: 21.10.16; Thiepval Mem. Somme; Age 23; Son of Mr. and Mrs.Jack Robey; Husband of Mrs.Clara B.Robey of 8, Buckhom Square, Loughborough.

4849. ROGERS, Leonard; B: – ; E: Brentwood, Essex; Pte. G 15754; K: 21.10.16; Grandcourt Road Cem. Somme; Age 19; Son of Mrs. Ellen Elizabeth Rogers of 3, High Street, Brentwood; Native of Braintree, Essex.

4850. ROSS, Francis; B: Watford; E: Watford; Pte. SD 5752; K: 21.10.16; Thiepval Mem. Somme.

4851. ROUSE, Bertram; B: Soham, Cambridgeshire; E: Eastbourne; L/Cpl. SD 103; K: 21.4.16; Guards Cem. (Cuinchy) Pas-de-Calais; Killed by a rifle grenade at the 'Duck's Bill', Givenchy.

4852. ROWE, William Charles; B: King's Lynn, Norfolk; E: King's Lynn; Pte. G 15175; W: 31.10.16; Connaught Cem. Somme.

4853. ROWLAND, Geoffrey Ellis; B: Horsham, Sussex; E: Worthing; L/Cpl. SD 725; K: 3.9.16; Thiepval Mem. Somme; Age 22; Son of Ellis and Alice Rowland of 18, Madeira Avenue, Horsham.

4854. RUSH, John Herbert; B: Atteborough, Norfolk; E: Wymondham Norfolk; Pte. G 15242; K: 21.10.16; Grandcourt Road Cem. Somme; Age 21; Son of John and Sarah Ann Rush of Norwich Common, Wymondham.*

4855. RUSSELL, Reginald; B: Shipley, Sussex; E: Horsham, Sussex; L/Cpl. SD 726; K: 30.6.16; St.Vaast Post Mil. Cem. Pas-de-Calais; Age 24; Son of Walter and Elizabeth Russell of South Lodge, Knepp Castle, Shipley.

4856. RUTTER, Donald Campbell; Capt.; M.C.; K: 7.6.17; Tyne Cot Cem. (Bel.); Age 20; Son of Hugh and Hilda Rutter of White House, Piltdown, Sussex; Native of Morden, Surrey.

S

4857. SALTER, Francis Henry; 2nd Lt.; K: 21.10.16; Grandcourt Road Cem. Somme; This man was probably the "brother" mentioned as having been buried by Geoffrey Salter in Chapter XI of 'Undertones of War' by Edward Blunden.

4858. SAMBUCCI, Albert; B: Brighton; E: Hove; L/Cpl. SD 3144; K: 3.6.16; Cambrin Churchyard Ext. Pas-de-Calais.

4859. SANDS, Stanley David; B: Hastings; E: Hastings; Pte. G 14366; K: 6.12.17; White House Cem. (Bel.); Killed in camp by a bomb dropped during an air raid.

4860. SAUNDERS, Harold George; B: Icklesham, Sussex; E: Hastings; Pte. SD 2120; K: 30.8.16; Englebelmer Com. Cem. Ext. Mem. Somme; Age 18; Son of Frederick William and Elizabeth Saunders of Inkerman Cottages, Rye Harbour, Sussex; Killed during shrapnel shelling at Mailly-Maillet Wood; Originally buried at Beaussart, Somme, where the burial ground was disturbed by shelling later in the war; After the war, the bodies were removed from Beaussart and re-interred at Englebelmer with the exception of two whose remains could not be found; this man was one of the two whose bodies could not be found and for whom a special memorial stone has been placed at Englebelmer. (see also 4496).*

4861. SAUNDERS, Percy Alfred Thomas; B: Salvington, Sussex; E: Worthing; Pte. SD 3817; K: 3.9.16; Thiepval Mem. Somme.

4862. SAXBY, Frederick John; B: Yapton, Sussex; E: Chichester; Sgt. SD 3008; W at Home: 13.12.16; Yapton (St.Mary) Churchyard, Sussex (UK).

4863. SCALES, Arthur; B: Essendon, Hertfordshire; E: Hertford; Pte. G 15539; K: 24.9.17; Tyne Cot Mem. (Bel.); Age 23; Son of Mrs. A. Scales of Essendon.

4864. SCARTERFIELD, James; B: Falmer, Sussex; E: Eastbourne; Pte. G 15864; K: 21.10.16; Mill Road Cem. Somme.

4865. SEALL, Charles Edward; B: Worthing; E: Worthing; L/Sgt. SD 547; K: 3.4.18; Villers-Faucon Com. Cem. Ext. Somme; Age 27; Son of William and Caroline Seall of 88, Portland Road, Worthing; Mentioned in 'Undertones of War' by Edward Blunden; The date of death was recorded at the end of the 'Spring Retreat' and is incorrect; Death would have been during the period 21 – 31.3.18, probably the 21st; Enlisted with brother, William Samuel, who was also killed (see 4866).

4866. SEALL, William Samuel; B: Worthing; E: Worthing; SD 548; K: 13.3.16; Rue-David Mil Cem. Pas-de-Calais; Son of William and Caroline Seall of 88, Portland Road, Worthing; Killed when an enemy 5.9" shell struck his billet in Fleurbaix; Enlisted with brother, Charles Edward, who was also killed (see 4865).

4867. SEAMER, Alfred George; B: Framfield, Sussex; E: Eastbourne; Sgt. SD 348; K: 21.10.16; Grandcourt Road Cem. Somme; Age 35; Husband of Agnes Sophia Seamer of 6, Baker's Cross Avenue, Cranbrook, Kent.

4868. SENGELOW, Harold; B: West Hartlepool; E: West Hartlepool; Pte. SD 3912; K: 2.8.17; New Irish Farm Cem. (Bel.).

4869. SHARPE, James; B: Eastbourne; E: Uckfield, Sussex; Pte. SD 1095; K: 3.9.16; Ancre Brit. Cem. Somme.

4870. SHIRLEY, Frederick Edward; B: – ; E: Stratford, London; Pte. G 15756; M.M.; K: 21.10.16; Thiepval Mem. Somme; Age 19; Son of Richard Henry and Charlotte Mary Shirley of 333, Higham Hill Road, Walthamstow, London.*

4871. SIMMONS, Alfred Arthur; B: Newhaven, Sussex; E: Lewes; Pte. SD 2271; K: 2.8.17; Bedford House Cem. Enclosure No.4 (Bel.).

4872. SIMPSON, Arthur; B: Lower Beeding, Sussex; E: Horsham; Pte. G 17406; K: 26.3.18; Pozieres Mem. Somme; Age 19; Son of William F. and Emily Simpson of Nuthurst, Sussex.*

4873. SIMPSON, Reginald Jack Sydney; B: Briston, Norfolk; E: Melton Constable, Norfolk; L/Cpl. G 15270; W at Home: 20.5.18; Lowestoft (Kirkley) Cem. Suffolk; Age 21; Son of John and Mary Ann Simpson of 6, Trafalgar Terrace, Norwich Road, North Walsham, Norfolk.*

4874. SIMS, Lionel Wesley; B: Eastbourne; E: Eastbourne; Sgt. SD 115; W at Home: 8.5.18;

Eastbourne (Ocklynge) Cem., Sussex (UK); Age 25; Son of Mr.F.F.W. and Mrs.F.Sims of 45, New Road, Eastbourne.*

4875. SLOMAN, Harold; B: Hampstead, London; E: Eastbourne; Pte. SD 362; W: 27.7.16; Bethune Town Cem. Pas-de-Calais.

4876. SMITH, Amos; B: Eastbourne; E: Eastbourne; Pte. G 15867; W at Home: 6.11.16; Eastbourne (Langney) Cem., Sussex (UK); Age 23; Son of David and Alice Smith of 202, Southbourne Road, Eastbourne.

4877. SMITH, Charles; B: Waldron, Sussex; E: Horsham; Pte. SD 732; K: 31.7.17; Buffs Road Cem., St.Jean-les-Ypres (Bel.); Age 27; Son of John and Harriett Smith of Tanyard Cottage, Waldron.*

4878. SMITH, Ernest Edward; B: – ; E: East Dereham, Norfolk; L/Cpl. G 15271; K: 21.10.16; Thiepval Mem. Somme.

4879. SMITH, George Robert; B: Dovercourt, Essex; E: Oakley, Essex; Pte. SD 5848; W: 22.10.16; Puchevillers Brit. Cem. Somme; Age 21; Son of Joseph and Emily Smith of Dovercourt.*

4880. SMITH, Henry; Burwash, Sussex; E: Hastings; Pte. SD 4872; K: 3.9.16; Ancre Brit. Cem. Somme; Age 20; Son of Mrs.Olive Smith of Burwash; This man's original battlefield timber Cross is preserved, with others, in the porch of St.Bartholomew's Church, Burwash; the Crosses of these Burwash men were brought back from the Western Front by Rudyard Kipling.

4881. SMITH, Joseph Allen; B: Worthing; E: Worthing; Pte. G 6679; K: 20.7.17; Cite Bonjean Mil. Cem., Nord; Attached to 53rd Anti-Aircraft Section.

4882. SMITH, Norman Leslie George; B: Walthamstow; E: Bromley; Sgt. G 17301; K: 25.9.17; Tyne Cot Mem. (Bel.); Age 22; Son of Henry George and Minnie Smith of 17, Westbury Road, Penge, London.

4883. SMITHER, Reginald Ernest; B: Maidenhead; E: Brighton; Sgt. SD 4816; K: 3.9.16; Thiepval Mem. Somme.

4884. SMITHERS, Albert; B: – : E: Chichester; Pte. G 16700; K: 6.11.17; La Clytte Mil. Cem. (Bel.); Age 27; Son of George and Elizabeth Smithers of 18, St.Paul's Road, Chichester.

4885. SNELLING, Reginald Guy; B: Tivershall, Norfolk; E: East Dereham, Norfolk; Pte. G 15295; K: 21.10.16; Thiepval Mem. Somme.

4886. SNOOK, Bryon; B: Brighton; E: Bognor Regis, Sussex; Pte. SD 847; D at Home: 29.12.15; Felpham (St.Mary) Churchyard, Sussex (UK); Age 28; Son of Henry Thomas and Emma Snook of The Mill, Felpham.

4887. SNOW, Henry Thomas; B: Furneux, Hertfordshire; E: Bishop's Stortford; Pte. G 15541; K: 2.8.17; Ypres (Menin Gate) Mem. (Bel.); Age 21; Son of Thomas Henry and Annie Snow of The Willows, Stocking Pelham, Hertfordshire.

4888. SOFTLEY, Frank Gurr; B: Godalming, Surrey; E: Guildford; Pte. SD 3956; W: 3.7.16; Merville Com.

Cem., Nord; Age 38; Son of Mr. and Mrs.Softley of Godalming; Husband of Margaret Darby Softley of 28, Whitton Road, Hounslow.

4889. SPENCER, Ernest; B: Silesden, Yorkshire; E: Keighley; Pte. G 17293; K: 5.2.18; Gouzeaucourt New Brit. Cem., Nord; Age 19; Son of Herbert and Mrs.A.J.Spencer of Laurel Bank, Sheriff Lane, Gilshead, Yorkshire; Killed by shell fire in the front line at Revelon Farm.*

4890. SPURGE, Thomas William; B: – ; E: – ; L/Sgt. SD 111; K: 30.6.16; St.Vaast Post Mil. Cem., Pas-de-Calais; Age 22; Son of Charles and Nellie Spurge of 21, Windhill, Bishop's Stortford, Hertfordshire.

4891. SQUIRES, Ernest; B: Aldingbourne, Sussex; E: Horsham; Sgt. SD 639; K: 3.9.16; Serre Road Cem. No.2, Somme.

4892. STACE, Herbert; B: East Dean, Sussex; E: Brighton; Pte. SD 856; Age 22; Thiepval Mem., Somme; Age 22; Son of David and Florence Stace of 26, Barbette Avenue, Well Hall, Eltham, Middlesex. K: 21.10.16.

4893. STACEY, Herbert Arthur; B: Kingston-on-Thames; E: Kingston-on-Thames; Pte.G 17339; K: 27.9.17; Tyne Cot Mem. (Bel.).

4994. STANDEN, Sidney Herbert; B: Hastings; E: Hastings; Pte. SD 2324; W: 12.6.16; Bethune Town Cem. Pas-de-Calais; Husband of Elsie M.Hughes, formerly Standen, of 146, Beaconsfield Road, Hastings.

4895. STANFORD, Jesse; B: Ringmer, Sussex; E: Eastbourne; Pte. SD 364; K: 3.9.16; Thiepval Mem. Somme; Age 31; Son of Henry and Sarah Stanford of 30, Brightland Road, Eastbourne; Husband of Kathleen Higgs.

4896. STANNARD, Albert Ernest; B: – ; E: East Dereham, Norfolk; L/Cpl. G 15296; D: 29.7.18; Valenciennes (St.Roch) Com. Cem. Nord.

4897. STARKEY, Digby Mounteney; B: – ; E: Lincoln's Inn, London; Pte. G 16735; K: 21.3.18; Pozieres Mem. Somme; Age 31; Son of Frederick St.John and Isabella Sybil Starkey of 20, Perry Rise, Forest Hill, London.

4898. STEBBINGS, William; B: Grimston, Norfolk; E: King's Lynn, Norfolk; Pte. G 15192; K: 15.3.17; Railway Dugouts Burial Ground (Bel.); Age 33; Son of William Stebbings of Church Hill, Grimston.

4899. STEEL, Horace Victor; B: Spalding, Lincolnshire; E: Peterborough; Pte. G 17349; K: 25.9.17; Tyne Cot Mem. (Bel.); Age 19; Son of Mr. and Mrs.W.Steel of 23, Whalley Street, Peterborough.

4900. STENNING, Harold; B: Uckfield, Sussex; E: Eastbourne; L/Cpl. SD 238; K: 24.9.17; Tyne Cot Cem. (Bel.).

4901. STERK, Harry; B: Camberwell, London; E: Bognor Regis, Sussex; Pte. SD 849; K: 31.7.17; Ypres (Menin Gate) Mem. (Bel.); Age 25; Son of Albert and Rachel Esther Sterk of "Glendale", Aldwick Road, West Bognor.

4902. STEVENS, Edward; B: Brompton, London; E: Hove; C.S.M. SD 640; K: 3.9.16; Thiepval Mem. Somme.

4903. STEVENS, Frederick; B: Luton; E: Luton; Pte. G 17371; K: 26.9.17; Tyne Cot Mem. (Bel.).*

4904. STEVENS, Frank; B: Marylebone, London; E: Hove; Pte. TF 203188; K: 21.3.18; Pozieres Mem. Somme.

4905. STEVENS, William Thomas; B: Willingdon, Sussex; E: Eastbourne; Pte. SD 231; K: 3.9.16; Ancre Brit. Cem. Somme; Age 28; Brother of Miss M.Stevens of 123, Foxley Lane, Purley, Surrey.

4906. STEVENSON, Thomas Norton; B: Eastbourne; E: Eastbourne; Cpl. SD 239; K: 4.6.16; Cambrin Churchyard Ext. Pas-de-Calais; Age 32; Son of Norton Luther and Elizabeth Stevenson of 12, Bedfordwell Road, Eastbourne.*

4907. STOCK, Reginald Stephen; B: Carlton, Bedfordshire; E: Bedford; Pte. G 15182; K: 31.7.17; Track "X" Cem. (Bel.); Age 35; Son of William and Elizabeth Stock of The Causeway, Carlton.

4908. STONE, John; B: Haywards Heath; E: Haywards Heath; Pte. G 16721; K: 31.7.17; New Irish Farm Cem. (Bel.).

4909. STONER, James; B: – ; E: Eastbourne; Pte. SD 240; W: 1.11.16; Warloy-Baillon Com. Cem. Ext. Somme.*

4910. STORKEY, Arthur Henry; B: Anerley, Surrey; E: Croydon; Pte. G 18531; K: 3.4.18; Pozieres Mem. Somme; Age 19; Son of William and Emily Hadden Storkey of 2, Sutherland Road, Croydon; The date of death was recorded at the end of the 'Spring Retreat' and is incorrect; Death would have been during the period 21 – 31.3.18.*

4911. STREET, Albert; B: St.Albans; E: Hertford; Pte. G 15537; K: 21.10.16; Mill Road Cem. Somme; Age 23; Son of Mr. and Mrs.G.Street of 34, Portland Road, St.Albans.

4912. STREET, Alfred; B: Arlesey, Bedfordshire; E: Hitchin, Hertfordshire; Pte. G 18762; W at Home: 3.5.18; Arlesey (St.Peter) Churchyard (UK); Age 19; Son of William and Mary Ann Street of Church End, Arlesey.

4913. SULLIVAN, Charles; B: Kensington, London; E: Mill Hill, London; Pte. G 15012; K: 21.10.16; Thiepval Mem. Somme.

4914. SUTTON, Herbert George; B: Rye, Sussex; E: Eastbourne; L/Cpl. SD 112; K: 3.9.16; Thiepval Mem. Somme; Age 27; Son of Alfred G. and Lydia J.Sutton of Alexandra Cottage, Ypres Steps, Rye.

4915. SUTTON, William Robert; B: Upton, Norfolk; E: Norwich; Pte. G 11585; W: 17.3.17; Lijssenthoek Mil. Cem. (Bel.); Age 19; Son of Walter and Louisa Sutton of Marsh Road, Upton.

4916. SWAIN, Basil Fitzroy; Lt. and Quartermaster; W: 22.3.18; Pozieres Mem. Somme.

4917. SWAIN, George William; B: Worthing; E: Worthing; C.S.M. SD 1175; K: 7.11.17; Tyne Cot Mem. (Bel.).

4918. SWAN, John Robert; B: Sutton, Surrey; E: Kingston-upon-Thames; Pte. G 17370; Tyne Cot Mem. (Bel.). K: 26.9.17.

4919. SWATTON, Edwin John; B: Paddington, London; E: Harlesden, Middlesex; L/Cpl. G 18507; K: 25.9.17; Tyne Cot Mem. (Bel.); Age 30; Son of William and Annie Swatton of Queen's Park, London; Husband of Edith Annie Swatton of 66, Minet Avenue, Harlesden.

T

4920. TAIT, Wilfred; B: Hull; E: Grove Park, London; Pte. G 17367; K: 26.9.17; Tyne Cot Mem. (Bel.); Age 19; Son of John William and Ann Eliza Tait of 46, Melrose Street, Anlaby Road, Hull.

4921. TATNELL, Edward; B: – ; E: Brighton; Pte. TF 266455; K: 2.8.17; Ypres (Menin Gate) Mem. (Bel.).

4922. TAYLOR, Archibald Francis Edward; B: Wadligton, Sussex; E: Horsham; Pte. SD 744; K: 21.10.16; Thiepval Mem. Somme; Age 21; Son of Edward Charles and Mary Ann Taylor of 1, Hucks Cottage, 5, Gravel Hill, Leatherhead, Surrey.*

4923. TAYLOR, Charles Herbert; B: Forest Hill, London; E: Worthing; L/Cpl. SD 551; K: 3.9.16; Thiepval Mem. Somme; Age 19; Son of William and Jessie Taylor of 1, Southview Terrace, Rowlands Road, Worthing.

4924. TAYLOR, Edward Charles; B: St. Pancras, London; E: Bexhill-on-Sea; Pte. SD 864; W: 1.7.16; Merville Com. Cem. Nord.

4925. TEE, George Frederick; B: Worthing; E: Chichester; Sgt. TF 201543; K: 29.4.18; Voormezele Enclosure No.3 (Bel.).

4926. TERRY, Albert Charles; B: Eastbourne; E: Eastbourne; C.S.M. SD 120; K: 25.9.17; Tyne Cot Mem. (Bel.).

4927. TESTER, Edward William; B: Ardingly, Sussex; E: Brighton; L/Cpl. SD 976; K: 30.6.16; St.Vaast Post Mil. Cem. Pas-de-Calais; Age 30; Son of John Henry and Mary Humphrey Tester of Brickyard Cottage, Ardingly.*

4928. THOMAS, Arthur Jack; B: Eastbourne; E: Eastbourne; L/Cpl. SD 3031; D: 13.8.16; Étaples Mil. Cem. Pas-de-Calais; Age 19; Son of William Henry and Eliza Thomas of Eastbourne; Died following an operation for appendicitis, probably at No.6 B.R.C.S. Hospital, known as Liverpool Merchants Hospital, at Étaples Military Base.

4929. THOMAS, Ernest Christopher Percival; B: Eastbourne; E: Eastbourne; Pte. SD 248; K: 10.6.16; Cambrin Churchyard Ext. Pas-de-Calais.

4930. THOMAS, Frederick; B: Bow, London; E: Chiswick, London; Pte. G 17340; Tyne Cot Mem. (Bel.); Age 19; Son of Mrs.E.Thomas of 23, Swanscombe Road, Chiswick. K: 25.9.17.

4931. THOMAS, George Francis; B: Brighton; E: Hove; Pte. G 8578; K: 11.11.16; Connaught Cem. Somme; Age 27; Husband of Gertrude Thomas of 23, St.Nicholas Road, Brighton.

4932. THOMPSETT, Albert Henry; B: – ; E: Haywards Heath, Sussex; L/Cpl. G 17915; K: 3.4.18; Pozieres Mem. Somme; The date of death was recorded at the end of the 'Spring Retreat' and is incorrect; Death would have been during the period 21 – 31.3.18.*

4933. THORPE, William; B: – ; E: Leicester; Pte. G 15017; K: 21.10.16; Thiepval Mem. Somme; Son of Mrs.A.Stovell of Langham, Rutland.

4934. THURTLE, Thomas; B: Winterton, Norfolk; E: Norwich; L/Cpl. G 9314; K: 14.8.17; Bus House Cem. (Bel.).

4935. TICE, Ernest Wilfred; 2nd Lt.; W: 1.8.17; Brandhoek New Mil. Cem. (Bel.); Son of Alfred and Elizabeth Tice of Ockham, Surrey; Mentioned in 'Undertones of War' by Edmund Blunden.

4936. TILBURY, Arthur William; B: Meonstoke, Hampshire; E: Steyning, Sussex; Pte. SD 742; D at Home: 14.6.16; Meonstoke (St.Andrew) Churchyard (UK); Son of James and Margaret E.M.Tilbury of "Hillside", Meonstoke.

4937. TIVEY, Berkeley Thomas; B: Willesden Green, London; E: Worthing; Cpl. SD 741; D at Home: 16.2.15; Willesden New Cem. Middlesex (UK); Age 21; Son of Mrs.D.Tivey of 308, Chapter Road, Willesden Green.

4938. TOMPSETT, Edwin William Henry; B: Willigdon, Sussex; E: Eastbourne; L/Cpl. SD 367; K: 3.6.16; Cambrin Churchyard Ext. Pas-de-Calais; Age 22; Son of Albert Edward and Hannah R.Thompsett of 1, Langney Fort Villas, Eastbourne.

4939. TOPPING, Robert; B: Abram, Lancashire; E: Atherton; Pte. SD 3944, K: 30.6.16; St.Vaast Post Mil. Cem. Pas-de-Calais.

4940. TULLY, Robert Tait; B: Newbiggin-by-the-Sea, Northumberland; E: Ashington, Lancashire; Pte. SD 747; K: 30.6.16; St.Vaast Post Mil. Cem. Pas-de-Calais; Age 24; Son of James and Jane Tully of 18, Gibson Street, Newbiggin-by-the-Sea.

4941. TURBARD, Charles William; B: Stanborne, Essex; E: Tottenham, London; Pte. G 20052; K: 27.9.17; Tyne Cot Mem. (Bel.).*

4942. TURNER, Alfred R.; B: Rotherfield, Sussex; E: Tunbridge Wells; Pte. SD 479; K: 23.6.16; St.Vaast Post Mil. Cem. Pas-de-Calais; Age 28; Son of Mrs.Mary J.Turner of Horam Flat Farm, Horam, Sussex.*

4943. TURNER, Ernest Edward; B: Heathfield, Sussex; E: Eastbourne; Sgt. SD 3478; K: 15.8.17; Bus House Cem. (Bel.); Age 24; Son of Clement and Sarah Turner of Acacia Cottage, Horam, Sussex.*

4944. TURNER, James; B: Binenden, Kent; E: 29.7.17 at Hastings; L/Cpl. SD 1105; K: 29.7.17; Ypres (Menin Gate) Mem. (Bel.); Age 22; Son of Mrs. Elizabeth Turner of "Sunny View", Flimwell, Kent.

4945. TURVILLE, Percy; B: Haywards Heath; E: Brighton; Cpl. SD 2020; K: 25.9.17; Tyne Cot Mem. (Bel.).

4946. TYLER, Charles Thomas; B: – ; E: Brentwood, Essex; L/Cpl. G 15784; K: 21.10.16; Mill Road Cem. Somme.

U

4947. UNSWORTH, Joseph; B: Shankhill, Belfast, Northern Ireland; E: Grove Park, London; Pte.

G 23131; K: 31.10.17; Bedford House Cem. Enclosure No.2 (Bel.); Age 19; Son of Joseph and Ellen Unsworth of 945, Tennent Street, Belfast.*

4948. UPPERTON, Edwin Payne; B: Southwick, Sussex; E: Worthing; L/Cpl. SD 749; K: 3.9.16; Ancre Brit. Cem. Somme; Age 24; Son of Mr. and Mrs.J.Upperton of 3, The Gardens, Southwick.

4949. UPTON, Frederick Edward; B: Brighton; E: Hove; Pte. SD 4973; K: 3.9.16; Hamel Mil. Cem. Somme.

V

4950. VANE, John Henry; B: Biddenden, Kent; E: Southwark, London; L/Cpl. G 8949; K: 31.7.17; Ypres (Menin Gate) Mem. (Bel.); Age 22; Son of John and Grace E.A.Vane of Standen Cottage, Biddenden.

4951. VENESS, George Gains; B: Herstmonceux, Sussex; E: Herstmonceux; Pte. SD 632; W: 22.5.16; Le Touret Mil. Cem. Pas-de-Calais; Age 26; Son of Thomas Herbert and Mrs.P.F.Veness of Oak Cottage, Gardner Street, Herstmonceux.*

4952. VERION, Horace; B: Angmering, Sussex; E: Chichester; Cpl. SD 1784; K: 22.3..18; Roisel Com. Cem. Ext., Somme.

4953. VIGOR, Henry; B: Flimwell, Sussex; E: Hastings; L/Cpl. SD 1106; K: 27.9.17; Tyne Cot Mem. (Bel.); Age 25; Son of Mr.H. and Mrs.F.Vigor of 130, High Street, Tooting, London.

4954. VOICE, George; B: Worthing; E: Chichester; Pte. TF 266666; K: 3.4.18; Pozieres Mem. Somme; The date of death was recorded at the end of the 'Spring Retreat' and is incorrect; Death would have been during the period 21 – 31.3.18.*

4955. VORLEY, Charles Archibald; Lt.; W: 13.9.16; Caudry Old Com. Cem. Nord; Age 24; Son of Joseph and Elizabeth Vorley of 12, Marshalls Road, Raunds, Northamptonshire; Died while a Prisoner of War.*

4956. VOUSDEN, George Henry; B: Goudhurst, Kent; E: Canterbury; Pte. G 17318; Spoilbank Cem. (Bel.); Age 19; Son of James and Ruth Vousden of North Road, Goudhurst.

W

4957. WALKER, Arthur; B: Polegate, Sussex; E: Eastbourne; Pte. SD 3812; W: 18.9.17; Larch Wood (Railway Cutting) Cem. (Bel.).

4958. WALKER, Percy Edward; B: Eastbourne; E: Eastbourne; Pte. SD 255; K: 8.10.16; Auchonvillers Mil. Cem. Somme; Age 27; Son of Jonathan Walker of Sandbank Cottages, Hailsham, Sussex.

4959. WALLER, Alfred; B: Ditchling, Sussex; E: Bexhill-on-Sea; Pte. SD 2129; K: 14.8.17; Bus House Cem. (Bel.).

4960. WALLER, Henry; B: Eastbourne; E: Eastbourne; Cpl. SD 130; K: 15.8.17; Bus House Cem. (Bel.); Age 23; Son of Harry and Mary Waller of 2, Norman Cottages, Worthing Road, Eastbourne.

4961. WALLER, William James; B: Hascombe, Surrey; E: Guildford; Sgt. SD 983; K: 30.10.16; Thiepval

Mem. Somme; Age 25; Son of Mrs.Emily Parsons of Labourne Lane, Hascombe.

4962. WALPOLE, William; B: St.Finharr's, Co.Cork, Ireland; E: Chichester; Pte. G 16705; K: 14.8.17; Bus House Cem. (Bel.).

4963. WALTERS, Herbert Gregory; B: Selston, Nottinghamshire; E: Hucknall; Pte. G 17299; K: 22.3.18; Roisel Com. Cem. Ext. Somme.*

4964. WARD, Charles Albert; B: Bures, Suffolk; E: Eastbourne; L/Cpl. SD 128; W: 30.4.16; St.Vevant Com. Cem. Pas-de-Calais.

4965. WARD, Edward; B: Southwark, London; E: Herstmonceux, Sussex; Pte. SD 633; K: 3.9.16; Thiepval Mem. Somme.

4966. WARD, John; B: Islington, London; E: London; Pte. L 7909; K: 21.3.18; Ste.Emilie Valley Cem., Villers-Faucon, Somme.

4967. WARNER, Stanley Thomas; B: Halstead, Essex; E: Bedford; Pte. G 15027; K: 21.10.16; Regina Trench Cem. Somme; Age 28; Son of William Horne Warner and Elizabeth Warner of 143, Station Street East, Coventry.

4968. WATERMAN, Edward Charles; B: Brighton; E: Haywards Heath; Pte. SD 5492; K: 3.4.18; Heath Cem., Harbonnieres, Somme; The date of death was recorded at the end of the 'Spring Retreat' and is incorrect; Death would have been during the period 21 – 31.3.18, probably the 25th.*

4969. WATERS, Harold George; B: Ewhurst, Sussex; E: Hastings; L/Cpl. SD 2002; K: 31.7.17; Buffs Road Cem., St.Jean-les-Ypres (Bel.); Age 25; Son of Charles and Martha Mary Waters of Virginia Cottage, Peasmarsh, Sussex.

4970. WATLING, George Edward; B: St.George's-in-the-East, London; E: Eastbourne; Sgt. SD 264; K: 13.7.16; Cambrin Churchyard Ext. Pas-de-Calais; Age 21; Son of George and Sarah Alice Watling of 20, Grosvenor Terrace, Camberwell, London.

4971. WATSON, George William Frederick; B: Eastbourne; E: Eastbourne; L/Cpl. SD 127; K: 3.9.16; Bouzincourt Ridge Cem. Somme; Age 23; Son of George and Georgina Watson of 8, St.George's Road, Eastbourne.

4972. WAYMARK, Benjamin; B: Westham, Pevensey, Sussex; E: Bexhill-on-Sea; Pte. SD 488; D: 24.3.17; Lijssenthoek Mil. Cem. (Bel.); Age 46; Son of James Waymark of Westham, Pevensey, Sussex; Husband of Frances Mary Ann Waymark of 21, St.James' Road, Bexhill-on-Sea; Served in the South Africa Campaign.

4973. WEAVER, George; B: Framfield, Sussex; E: Brighton; Pte. G 19509; K: 23.4.18; Tyne Cot Mem. (Bel.); Age 22; Son of Jarvis and Caroline Weaver of Downlands Cottage, Uckfield, Sussex.

4974. WEBSTER, George Victor; B: Attleborough, Norfolk; E: King's Lynn; Pte. G 15272; K: 24.9.17; Tyne Cot Cem. (Bel.); Age 19; Son of Mrs.Angelina Webster of 12, Wellington Street, King's Lynn.

4975. WELCHMAN, Robert Stanley, B: Belper, Derbyshire; E: Eastbourne; Sgt. SD 131; W: 13.9.16; Achiet-le-Grand Com. Cem. Ext. Pas-de-Calais; Age 21; Son of Stanley and Lucy Welchman of West Lydford, Somerset.

4976. WELLEN, Edward Arthur; B: Lower Launch, Surrey; E: Chichester; Pte. G 19510; K: 29.4.18; Voormezele Enclosure No.3 (Bel.).

4977. WELLER, Albert Edward; B: Hastings;; E: Hastings; Pte. SD 1108; W: 4.9.16; Couin Brit. Cem. Pas-de-Calais; Son of Mr.J.Weller of 122, Mount Pleasant Road, Hastings.

4978. WELLING, Sidney Thomas George; B: Brighton; E: Hove; Pte. TF 241506; K: 26.9.17; Tyne Cot Mem. (Bel.); Age 32; Son of Sydney William Welling of 30, Lansdowne Street, Hove; Husband of Evelyn Mary Denniss, formerly Welling, of "St.Neots", Langdale Road, Hove.

4979. WELSH, John Leslie; B: Chalk Farm, London; E: Willesden, London; Pte. G 18770; K: 10.3.18; Thiepval Mem. Somme; Reported missing during a night raid at Revelon Farm and later confirmed as killed.

4980. WEST, Charles Fossey; B: Worthing; E: Worthing; L/Cpl. SD 561; K: 3.9.16; Thiepval Mem. Somme; Age 34; Son of Edward West of 34, Orme Road, Worthing; Husband of Mabel West of 3, Paragon Cottages, Worthing.

4981. WEST, Cyril Frederick Ernest; 2nd Lt.; K at St.Eloi: 28.9.18; Perth Cem. (China Wall) (Bel.); Age 19; Son of George Frederick and Lucritia Gertrude West of Ebor Lodge, West Byfleet, Surrey.*

4982. WEST, Percival; B: Fernhurst, Surrey; E: Midhurst, Sussex; Pte. SD 3848; K: 3.9.16; Thiepval Mem. Somme; Age 29; Son of Mrs.Elizabeth West of The Cylinders, Fernhurst.

4983. WEST, Thomas Harvey; B: Tunbridge Wells; E: Eastbourne; Pte. SD 484; K: 3.9.16; Thiepval Mem. Somme; Age 23; Son of Harvey Head Mathew West and Emma West of 52, Beach Road, Eastbourne.

4984. WEST, William Henry; B: Lewes; E: Brighton; Pte. G 16377; K: 13.2.17; Vlamertinghe Mil. Cem. (Bel.).

4985. WESTWOOD, Albert; B: Brierley Hill, Staffordshire; E: Stoke-on-Trent; Sgt. G 15129; K: 26.9.17; Tyne Cot Mem. (Bel.).

4986. WHEATLEY, George Robert; B: Southwark, London; E: Camberwell, London; Pte. G 21300; K: 26.9.17; New Irish Farm Cem. (Bel.).

4987. WHISTON, William; B: St.Giles, London; E: Brighton; L/Cpl. G 5627; K: 22.3.18; Ste.Emilie Valley Cem., Villers-Faucon, Somme; Age 33; Husband of Agnes C.E.Whiston of 45, St.Paul's Street, Lewes Road, Brighton. *

4988. WHITE, Arthur; B: Willigdon, Sussex; E: Eastbourne; Pte. SD 490; K: 30.6.16; Loos Mem. Pas-de-Calais; Age 25; Brother of Charles White of Ivy Cottage, The Dicker, Hellingly, Sussex.

4989. WHITE, William George Alfred; B: – ; E: Stratford, London; Pte. G 15762; K: 21.10.16; Grandcourt Road Cem. Somme; Son of Mrs.W.S.White of 51, Thorpe Road, Forest Gate, London.

4990. WHITELAW, William; B: Wrestlingworth, Bedfordshire; E: Hastings; L/Cpl. SD 1923; K: 3.4.18; Pozieres Mem. Somme; The date of death was recorded at the end of the 'Spring Retreat' and is incorrect; Death would have been during the period 21 – 31.3.18.*

4991. WHYTE, George Albert; B: Bungay, Suffolk; E: Lowestoft; Pte. G 18769; W: 20.6.18; Cologne Southern Cem. (G); Age 19; Son of Robert and Ellen Whyte of 7, Earsham Street, Bungay; Died while a Prisoner of War.

4992. WILEMAN, Arthur Harold; B: – ; E: Kingsway, London; Sgt. G 19825; M.M., K: 28.4.18; Tyne Cot Mem. (Bel.); Age 36; Husband of Blanche Wileman of 34, Temple Street, Keynsham, Bristol.

4993. WILKINS, Percy; B: Holloway, London; E: Hertford; Pte. G 15564; K: 21.10.16; Grandcourt Road Cem. Somme; Son of Mr.E.Wilkins of Kingsland Terrace, Ashwell, Hertfordshire.

4994. WILKINSON, Henry Sydney; B: Marylebone, London; E: Worthing; Sgt. SD 751; M.M., K: 30.10.16; Grandcourt Road Cem. Somme; Age 23; Son of Henry and Florence Wilkinson of London.

4995. WILLIAMS, Charles Henry; B: Brighton; E: Brighton; Pte. SD 978; K: 3.9.16; Thiepval Mem. Somme.

4996. WILLIAMSON, Percy; B: Brancaster, Norfolk; E: King's Lynn, Norfolk; Pte. G 18773; K: 29.4.18; Tyne Cot Mem. (Bel.).

4997. WINTER, Charles Herbert; B: Shoreham, Sussex; E: Worthing; Pte. SD 556; K: 27.4.18; Borre Brit. Cem. Nord; Age 27; Son of Charles Andrew and Susan Winter of 38, Portland Road, Worthing.

4998. WISKER, Robert William; B: East Bilney, Norfolk; E: Leicester; Pte. G 15025; K: 22.10.16; Thiepval Mem. Somme; Age 40; Son of Mrs.C.Wisker of 5, Eastwood Street, Streatham, London.

4999. WOOD, Albert; B: – ; E: Horsham; Pte. G 16740; K: 26.9.17; Tyne Cot Mem. (Bel.).

5000. WOOD, Edward; B: Brighton; E: Brighton; Pte. SD 965; K: 3.6.16; Cambrin Churchyard Ext. Pas-de-Calais.*

5001. WOOD, Ernest; B: Framfield, Sussex; E: Uckfield, Sussex; Pte. SD 253; D: 19.4.16; St.Sever Cem. Rouen, Seine-Maritime; Age 26; Brother of Mr.W.Wood of High Common Cottage, Buxted, Sussex; Died of meningitis.

5002. WOOD, Sidney; B: Leicester; E: Leiceste; Pte. G 15020; K: 21.10.16; Thiepval Mem. Somme; Age 20; Son of Joseph and Rose Wood of 8, All Saints' Place, Leicester.

5003. WOOD, Sidney Arthur; B: Chichester; E: Worthing; Pte. SD 553; W: 26.6.16; Merville Com. Cem. Nord; Age 29; Son of Mrs.E.Wood of 8, Corsehill Street, Streatham, London.

5004. WOODS, John Charles; B: Campsea Ash, Suffolk; E: Finsbury Barracks, London; L/Cpl. SD 755; K: 25.4.18; Brandhoek New Mil. Cem. No.3 (Bel.).

5005. WOOLGAR, Albert John; B: Newhaven, Sussex; E: Tunbridge Wells; Pte. SD 1509; K: 17.8.17; Oak Dump Cem. (Bel.); Age 27; Son of Mrs.Mancel Woolgar of Bedford Lodge, Tunbridge Wells, Kent.

5006. WORTLEY, Dudley Charles Arthur; B: Norwich; E: Norwich; Pte. G 15230; K: 28.9.16; Auchonvillers Mil. Cem. Somme; Age 20; Son of W.A. and Sarah J.Wortley of 33, Old Palace Road, Norwich.*

5007. WRIGHT, Robert; B: Hempton, Norfolk; E: East Dereham, Norfolk; Pte. G 15298; K: 16.9.16; Auchonvillers Mil. Cem. Somme; Son of Albert and Blanche Wright of Hempton Green, Norfolk.

X

5008. XERXES, Edwin Charles; B: Bermondsey, London; E: Hertford; G 15566; K: 6.11.16; Tyne Cot Mem. (Bel.); Age 20; Son of Edwin Charles Xerxes of 38, Camp View Road, St.Albans, Hertfordshire.

Y

5009. YOUELL, Herbert Ernest; B: Ketteringham, Norfolk; E: Norwich; Pte. G 14742; K: 3.4.18; Pozieres Mem. Somme; Age 26; Son of Harry Thomas and Minnie Youell of Station House, Cromer, Norfolk; The date of death was recorded at the end of the 'Spring Retreat' and is incorrect; Death would have been during the period 21 – 31.3.18.*

12th Battalion

A

5010. ADDY, Alfred George; B: Beckley, Sussex; E: Hastings; Pte. SD 1947; K: 9.9.16; Thiepval Mem. Somme.

5011. ADLARD, George William; B: Lincoln; E: Lincoln; Pte. G 15345; K: 31.7.17; Buffs Road Cem., St.Jean-les-Ypres (Bel.); Age 24; Son of Mr. and Mrs.G.Adlard of Corporation House, Harvey Street, Lincoln.

5012. AKEHURST, James Stephen; B: Heathfield, Sussex; E: Eastbourne; Pte. SD 4824; K: 30.6.16; Loos Mem. Pas-de-Calais; Age 20; Son of Stephen James and Esther Akehurst of 3, Roselands Terrace, Eastbourne.

5013. ALDRIDGE, John Frederick; B: Eastbourne; E: Hastings; Pte. SD 2391; K: 30.3.16; Loos Mem. Pas-de-Calais; Age 19; Son of Mr. and Mrs.W.Aldridge of 95, Dennis Road, Eastbourne.

5014. ALESWORTH, Frank McNaughton; B: Portsmouth; E: Bexhill-on-Sea; Pte. SD 1860; K: 13.8.17; Ypres (Menin Gate) Mem. (Bel.); Age 23; Son of Mrs.Agnes Alesworth of 1305, Queen's Road, Hastings.

5015. ALFORD, Percy; B: Tonbridge; E: London; Pte. SD 2035; K: 30.6.16; Loos Mem. Pas-de-Calais.

5016. ANDREWS, Alfred Frederick; B: New Cross, London; E: Brighton; Pte. G 16204; K: 17.10.16; Thiepval Mem. Somme; Enlisted with brother,

Clement Charles, who was also killed on the same day and also has no known grave (see 5018).

5017. ANDREWS, Charles Cyril; B: Hunstanton, Norfolk; E: London; Pte. SD 1948; K: 30.6.16; St.Vaast Post Mil. Cem. Pas-de-Calais; Age 26; Son of Charles and Caroline Andrews of Hunstanton.

5018. ANDREWS, Clement Charles; B: Woodford Wells, Essex; E: Brighton; Pte. G 16205; K: 17.10.16; Thiepval Mem. Somme; Enlisted with brother, Alfred Frederick, who was also killed on the same day and also has no known grave. (see 5016).

5019. APPS, Percy David Baldock; B: Robertsbridge, Sussex; E: Hastings; Pte. SD 2075; K: 2.3.17; Maple Copse Cem. (Bel.).*

5020. APTED, Sidney Joseph; B: Chiswick, London; E: Croydon; Cpl. G 15569; K: 31.7.17; Buffs Road Cem., St.Jean-les-Ypres (Bel.); Age 33; Brother of Miss S.Apted of Grayswood Stores, Haslemere, Surrey.

5021. ARBON, Sidney James; B: Elvedon, Suffolk; E: Bury St.Edmunds, Suffolk; Pte. G 15344; K: 31.10.16; Thiepval Mem. Somme; Killed at Auchonvillers by shell fire.

5022. ARKCOLL, Frederick Thomas; 2nd Lt.; K: 30.6.16; Loos Mem. Pas-de-Calais; Age 27; Son of Mr. and Mrs.Herbert Arkcoll of 35, St.Germans Road, Forest Hill, London; Attached from 10th Battalion; Formerly 20th Battalion London Regiment; Also served in Egypt.

5023. ARNOLD, David; B: St.John's, Sussex; E: Lewes; Pte. G 15786; K: 12.11.16; Lonsdale Cem. Somme; Age 25; Son of Edward Arnold of 24, North Street, Lewes.

5024. ASHTON, Frederick; B: West Ham, London; E: Doncaster; Pte. G 16315; W: 17.10.16; Varennes Mil. Cem. Somme.

5025. AUSTIN, Albert Edward; B: Herstmonceux, Sussex; E: Bexhill-on-Sea; Cpl. SD 3269; K: 3.9.16; Thiepval Mem. Somme

5026. AYLING, Albert; B: Pulborough, Sussex; E: Worthing; Pte. G 17768; K: 11.9.16; Hamel Mil. Cem. Somme; Age 18; Son of Mrs.Louisa Adsett of Codmore Farm, Pulborough.

5027. AYLING, Rodwell Thomas; B: St.Andrew's, Sussex; E: Worthing; Cpl. SD 1249; K: 28.2.17; Railway Dugouts Burial Ground (Bel.).

5028. AYLWARD, William; B: Sundridge, Kent; E: Horsham; Pte. SD 2292; K: 30.6.16; Cabaret-Rouge Brit. Cem. Pas-de-Calais.

B

5029. BAGLEY, Charles Edward; B: Kirdford, Sussex; E: Chichester; Pte. G 19512; K: 13.4.17; Vlamertinghe Mil. Cem. (Bel.); Age 24; Son of Charles and Ada Bagley of Chestnut Road, Billingshurst, Sussex.*

5030. BAILEY, Albert Henry; B: Chichester; E: Petworth, Sussex; Pte. G 17779; K: 26.9.17; Tyne Cot Cem. (Bel.); Age 22; Son of Henry and Mary Bailey of 3, Osbrook Cottages, Kempshott Road, Horsham, Sussex.

5031. BAINES, George Edmund; B: Wanstead, Essex; E: London; Cpl. SD 2143; W: 2.7.16; Boulogne Eastern Cem. Pas-de-Calais; Age 23; Son of the Revd. and Mrs.J.Baines of Baden Villas, Fordingbridge, Hampshire.

5032. BAKER, Samuel; B: Portslade, Sussex; E: Worthing; Pte. G 16288; K: 22.10.16; Connaught Cem. Somme; Husband of Mrs.S.Baker of Stable Cottage, Allbourne Street, Hassocks, Sussex.

5033. BAKER, William George; B: Beckenham, Kent; E: Horsham, Sussex; L/Sgt. SD 1758; W: 22.4.16; Bethune Town Cem. Pas-de-Calais; Son of Mrs. Sarah Arm Baker of 9, Dempster Road, East Hill, Wandsworth, London.

5034. BALDWIN, Edwin; B: Eastbourne; E: Eastbourne; Pte. SD 1252; W at Home 3.11.16; Age 21; Son of David and Emily Baldwin of Rodmill Lime Works, Willingdon Road, Eastbourne; Eastbourne (Ocklynge) Cem. Sussex (UK); In the same grave is also buried his brother, Thomas (see 5035).

5035. BALDWIN, Thomas; B: Eastbourne; E: Eastbourne; Pte. G 7747; W or D at Home: 17.7.16 Eastbourne (Ocklynge) Cem. Sussex (UK); Son of David and Emily Baldwin of Rodmill Lime Works, Willingdon Road, Eastbourne; In the same grave is buried also his brother, Edwin, (see 5034).

5036. BARNES, Charles Jesse; B: Fernhurst, Sussex; E: Chichester; Pte. G 19521; K: 31.7.17; Ypres (Menin Gate) Mem. (Bel.).

5037. BARNES, John Edward; B: Hastings; E: Hastings; Pte. G 14189; K: 3.2.17; Ypres (Menin Gate) Mem. (Bel.); Age 32; Son of John and Julia Annie Barnes of 188, Queen's Road, Hastings; Husband of Emily Jane Barnes of 1 Flat, 5, Quarry Crescent, Hastings.

5038. BARNETT, Benjamin Thomas; B: Loxwood, Sussex; E: Horsham, Sussex; Pte.G 16300; K: 14.12.16; New Irish Farm Cem. (Bel.).

5039. BARNETT, Maurice Walter; B: Watersfield, Sussex; E: Petworth, Sussex; Pte. G 16108; K: 31.7.16; Buffs Road Cem., St.Jean-les-Ypres (Bel.).

5040. BARTLETT, Leslie Leonard; B: Handsworth, Warwickshire; E: Birmingham; Pte.G 17062; K: 25.9.17; Hooge Crater Cem. (Bel.); Age 19; Son of Joseph Henry and Minnie Elizabeth Bartlett of 154, Heathfield Road, Handsworth.*

5041. BARTON, Alfred Walter; B: Rochester, Kent; E: Whitstable, Kent; Pte. G 16850; K: 31.7.17; Ypres (Menin Gate) Mem. (Bel.); Age 19; Son of Albert Barton of 31, Victoria Street, Whitstable.

5042. BARTON, Karl; B: East Croydon; E: Eastbourne; Pte. SD 1256; W: 30.6.16; Royal Irish Rifles Graveyard, Laventie, Pas-de-Calais; Age 24; Son of George and Emily Barton of 64, Clifton Terrace, Brook Street, Polegate, Sussex.

5043. BAYLESS, William Henry; B: Hoxton, London; E: St.Paul's Churchyard, London; L/Cpl. SD 1952; K: 30.6.16; St.Vaast Post Mil. Cem. Pas-de-Calais.

5044. BAYLISS, Geoffrey William; B: Evesham, Worcestershire; E: Worcester; Pte. G 17063; K: 27.9.17; Tyne Cot Mem. (Bel.).

5045. BEAGLEY, Frank; B: – ; E: Eastbourne; Pte. SD 2058; K: 30.6.16; Loos Mem. Pas-de-Calais; Age 30; Son of Annie Tunks, formerly Beagley, of 58, Kay Road, Stockwell, London and the late George Beagley.

5046. BEALE, Frank Thomas; B: Beckley, Sussex; E: Eastbourne; Cpl. SD 1259; K: 29.4.16; Guards Cem. (Cuinchy) Pas-de-Calais.

5047. BEATON, Leonard; B: Eastbourne; E: Eastbourne; Pte. SD 1938; K: 30.6.16; Guards Cem. (Cuinchy) Pas-de-Calais.

5048. BEDDING, William Francis; B: Oxford; E: Hastings; Pte. SD 2078; K: 30.6.16; St.Vaast Post Mil. Cem. Pas-de-Calais; Age 20; Son of James and Abigail Annie Bedding.

5049. BENNETT, Arthur Ernest; B: Eastbourne; E: Eastbourne; Pte. SD 2252; K: 30.6.16; Loos Mem. Pas-de-Calais; Age 24; Son of Charles Henry and Martha Bennett of 99, Bradford Street, Eastbourne.

5050. BENNETT, Reginald; B: Dane Hill, Sussex; E: Haywards Heath, Sussex; Pte. G 3402; K: 31.7.17; New Irish Farm Cem. (Bel.); Age 28; Son of Caesar and Charlotte Bennett of "Fieldview", Chelwood Gate, Sussex.

5051. BERRY, William Henry; B: Long Handborough, Oxfordshire; E: Oxford; Pte. G 17056; K: 27.9.17; Hooge Crater Cem. (Bel.); Son of Mr.W.Berry of Ivy Cottage, Long Handborough.

5052. BERWICK, William Robert; B: Rotherfield, Sussex; E: Tunbridge Wells; Pte. SD 1261; D at Home: 15.3.15; Crowborough Burial Ground, Sussex (UK); Age 23; Son of Benjamin and Mrs.R.J.Berwick of Newlands Farm, Boar's Head, Tunbridge Wells, Kent.

5053. BEST, Thomas Harold; B: Brighton; E: Brighton; L/Sgt. G 9002; K: 24.7.17; Essex Farm Cem. (Bel.).

5054. BINGHAM, Alec Henry; B: Horsham, Sussex; E: Horsham; Pte. G 17787; W: 19.4.17; Lijssenthoek Mil. Cem. (Bel.); Age 21; Son of A.W. and E.H.Bingham of Chestnut Cottage, Felbridge, Sussex.

5055. BISHOP, Harold Epton; B: Grimsby; E: Grimsby; Pte. G 15370; K: 21.10.16; Thiepval Mem. Somme; Age 22; Son of Joseph and Elizabeth Bishop of 18, Taylor Street, New Cleethorpes, Linclolnshire.

5056. BISHOP, Harold; B: – ; E: Turner's Hill, Sussex; Pte. G 22653; K: 21.1.18; Tyne Cot Mem. (Bel.).

5057. BISHOP, Iden Claud Murdoch; B: Rotherfield, Sussex; E: Bexhill-on-Sea; Sgt. SD 1517; K: 30.6.16; Loos Mem. Pas-de-Calais; Age 24; Son of John and Sarah Bishop of High Street, Rotherfield; Husband of Dorothy Lilie Bishop of Eden Cottages, Broadmoor Road, Crowthorne, Berkshire.

5058. BISSENDEN, Francis James; B: Holy Trinity, Sussex; E: Hastings; Sgt. SD 1867; K: 17.10.16; Thiepval Mem. Somme.

5059. BLACKFORD, Horace Reader; B: – ; E: Tunbridge Wells; Pte. G 15787; K: 17.10.16; Thiepval Mem. Somme; Age 28; Son of Albert and Frances Fanny Blackford; Husband of Emily Blackford.

5060. BLACKMAN, Charles; B: Waldron, Sussex; E: Eastbourne; L/Sgt. SD 1263; K: 30.6.16; Loos Mem. Pas-de-Calais; Age 33; Son of Thomas Blackman; Husband of Daisy Lillian Blackman of Swiffe Farm, Heathfield, Sussex.

5061. BLAKER, Frank; B: Worthing; E: Worthing; Pte. SD 1659; K: 30.6.16; Loos Mem. Pas-de-Calais; Age 27; Son of Benjamin Barrack Blaker and Lucy Blaker of 12, Richmond Road, Worthing; Brother, Leonard, 13th Battalion, also killed (see 5633).

5062. BLANN, William; B: Worthing; E: Worthing; L/Cpl. SD 1265; D: 29.10.18; Niederzwehren Cem. (G); Age 26; Son of Mr. and Mrs.William Blann of 15, Buckingham Road, Worthing; Died while Prisoner of War.

5063. BLIGHT, Edwin; B: St.Mary's, Kent; E: Worthing; Pte. SD 1660; K: 30.6.16; Cabaret-Rouge Brit. Cem. Pas-de-Calais.

5064. BLUNDEN, Leonard; B: Worthing; E: Worthing; Pte. SD 1266; K: 3.9.16; Thiepval Mem. Somme; Age 17; Son of Mrs.C.L.Blunden of Bedford Cottage, Bedford Row, Worthing.

5065. BLURTON, Eric Brian; B: Highgate, London; E: Hastings; Pte. SD 2403; K: 30.6.16; Cabaret-Rouge Cem. Pas-de-Calais; Age 19; Son of Tom Blackford Burton and Florence Alice Burton of 13, Fitzwarren Gardens, Highgate; Brother, Tom Pain, was killed in the same action on the same day (see 5066).

5066. BLURTON, Tom Pain; B: Tufnell Park, London; E: London; L/Sgt. SD 1955; K: 30.6.16; Loos Mem. Pas-de-Calais; Age 20; Son of Tom Blackford Burton and Florence Alice Burton of 13, Fitzwarren Gardens, Highgate; Brother, Eric Brian, was killed in the same action on the same day (see 5065).

5067. BONAS, William; B: Holloway, London; E: Hove; Pte. SD 1268; K: 30.6.16; Loos Mem. Pas-de-Calais.

5068. BOOLES, Alfred Percy; B: Ewerby, Lincolnshire; E: Grantham, Linclonshire; Pte. G 15352; K: 21.10.16; Thiepval Mem. Somme; Age 29; Son of James and Elizabeth Booles of 31, Ewerby; Husband of Mima Booles.

5069. BOTTERILL, John Thomas; B: Rothersthorpe, Northamptonshire; E: Bugbrooke; Pte. G 15372; W: 18.10.16; Varennes Mil. Cem. Somme; Age 36; Son of Francis and Emma Botterill of Rothersthorpe.

5070. BOURNER, Walter Ernest; B: Vines Cross, Sussex; E: Eastbourne; Pte. SD 1795; K: 19.3.16; 'Y' Farm Mil. Cem., Bois-Genier, Nord.

5071. BOUD, Alexander Charles; 2nd Lt.; K: 5.6.16; Cambrin Churchyard Ext. Pas-de-Calais.*

5072. BRACHER, Charles Edward; B: Plummers Plain, Horsham, Sussex; E: – ; Pte. – 4142; W: 2.2.17; Bethune Town Cem. Pas-de-Calais; Age 29; Son of Samuel and M.Annie Bracher of 43, George Road, Farncombe, Surrey.*

5073. BRACKELL, Stanley; B: Homerton, London; E: Bexhill-on-Sea; L/Sgt. SD 1519; K: 30.6.16; Cabaret-Rouge Brit. Cem. Pas-de-Calais.*

5074. BRACKENBURY, John; B: Gayton-le-Marsh, Lincolnshire; E: Lincoln; Pte. G 15359; K: 31.10.16;

Connaught Cem. Somme; Killed at Auchonvillers by shell fire.

5075. BRADFORD, Frederick; B: Eastbourne; E: Eastbourne; Pte. SD 1796; K: 30.6.16; St.Vaast Post Mil. Cem. Pas-de-Calais; Age 32; Son of Alfred Bradford of 70, Beach Road, Eastbourne; Brother, George, also killed in the same action on the same day (see 5076).

5076. BRADFORD, George; B: Eastbourne; E: Eastbourne; Pte. SD 1267; K: 30.6.16; Guards Cem. (Cuinchy) Pas-de-Calais; Age 23; Son of Alfred and Constance Rebecca Bradford of 70, Beach Road, Eastbourne; Brother, Frederick, also killed in the same action on the same day (see 5075).

5077. BRADLEY, Ernest James; B: Marylebone, London; E: Marylebone; Pte. G 14920; W: 3.3.17; Lijssenthoek Mil. Cem. (Bel.); Age 34; Son of C.Bradley of 17, Henstridge Place, St.John's Wood, London.

5078. BRADLEY, Wilfred James; B: Cirencester, Gloucestershire; E: Eastbourne; Pte. SD 4971; K: 30.6.16; Loos Mem. Pas-de-Calais; Age 26; Son of Eliza Rogers, formerly Bradley, and the late James Bradley of 100, Watermoor Road, Cirencester.

5079. BREACH, Albert Edward; B: Wilmington, Sussex; E: Eastbourne; Pte. SD 397; W: 2.8.17; Dozinghem Mil. Cem. (Bel.); Age 32; Son of Frederick and Miriam Ruth Breach of Hankham, Pevensey, Sussex; Attached 116th Brigade Royal Engineers.

5080. BRETT, Albert Edward; B: West Horsley, Surrey; E: Crawley, Sussex; Pte. SD 2081; K: 30.6.16; Loos Mem. Pas-de-Calais.

5081. BRETT, William Charles; B: Hastings; E: Hastings; Sgt. SD 996; K: 3.2.17; Vlamertinghe Mil. Cem. (Bel.); Age 37; Son of William and Elizabeth Brett of St.Leonards-on-Sea; Husband of Florence Jane Brett of 40, Western Road, St.Leonards.

5082. BRIDGWATER, John Sydney; B: Bishopston, Gloucestershire; E: Bristol; Pte. G 16075; K: 23.11.17; Tyne Cot Mem. (Bel.).

5083. BRINGLOE, Edward John; B: West Dereham, Norfolk; E: Maidstone, Kent; Pte. G 15106; K: 28.2.17; Railway Dugouts Burial Ground (Bel.); Age 31; Son of George and Eliza Bringloe; Husband of Rose Ellen Bringloe of 14, Melville Road, Maidstone; Native of West Farleigh.*

5084. BROMWICH, Charles Martin; B: Andover, Hampshire; E: Worthing; Cpl. SD 1273; W: 30.6.16; St.Vaast Post Mil. Cem. Pas-de-Calais.

5085. BROOK, Ernest; B: Brighton; E: Brighton; Pte. G 13635; W: 20.9.17; Reninghelst Mil. Cem. (Bel.).

5086. BROOKS, Sydney; B: Newick, Sussex; E: Brighton; Pte. SD 1632; K: 30.6.16; Loos Mem. Pas-de-Calais.

5087. BROWN, Cecil James; B: Littlehampton, Sussex; E: Littlehampton; Pte. SD 1275; K: 30.6.16; St.Vaast Post Mil. Cem. Pas-de-Calais; Age 20; Son of James L. and Eliza Brown of 27, Norfolk Road, Littlehampton.

5088. BROWN, Frederick; B: Nutley, Sussex; E: Arundel, Sussex; Pte. SD 3301; K: 20.8.16; Thiepval Mem.

Somme; Age 25; Son of George Joseph Brown of Passal's Farm, Blackboys, Sussex.

5089. BROWN, George; B: Marylebone, London; E: London; Sgt. SD 1957; K: 29.4.16; Loos Mem. Pas-de-Calais.*

5090. BROWN, Harry Frederick Arthur; B: Ryde, Isle-of-Wight; E: Newport, Isle-of-Wight; Pte. G 17067; K: 26.9.17; Tyne Cot Cem. (Bel.); Age 20; Son of Charles and Fannie Brown of 59, Bettesworth Road, Ryde.

5091. BUCKWELL, Reginald; B: Eastbourne; E: Eastbourne; Pte. SD 1578; W at Home: 11.6.16; Eastbourne (Ocklynge) Cem., Sussex (UK); Son of Mrs.Catherine Chapman of 11, Marine Road, Eastbourne.

5092. BULLEN, Albert James; B: Great Walsingham, Norfolk; E: Norwich; Pte. G 17176; K: 25.9.17; Hooge Crater Cem. (Bel.).

5093. BURDEN, Clement Victor; B: St.Helens, Isle-of-Wight; E: Newport, Isle-of-Wight; Pte. G 17068; K: 25.9.17; Tyne Cot Mem. (Bel.); Age 19; Son of Lewis and Emily Ada Burden of Imogene, Newlands, St.Helens.

5094. BURT, Cecil Ernest; B: Worthing; E: Worthing; L/Cpl. G 16267; W: 21.9.17; Godewaersvelde Brit. Cem. Nord; Age 33; Husband of Margaret Burt of Heathercrest, Fern Road, Storrington, Sussex.

5095. BUTLER, Arthur; B: Beckley, Sussex; E: Hastings; Pte. SD 1280; K: 30.6.16; Loos Mem. Pas-de-Calais; Age 20; Son of Mrs.Fanny Eldridge of 96, Old Lane, Hollington, Hastings.

5096. BUTLER, John Herbert; B: Oxford; E: Eastbourne; L/Cpl. SD 1581; K: 3.6.16; Cambrin Churchyard Ext. Pas-de-Calais; Age 23; Son of John and Annie Butler of 18, Magdelen Road, Oxford.

5097. BUTTERS, Arthur James; B: Brightling, Sussex; E: Hastings; Pte. G 18100; K: 21.10.16; Mill Road, Cem. Somme.*

C

5098. CALLINGHAM, Harry; B: Brighton; E: Newhaven; Pte. SD 2326; D: 30.6.16; Cabaret-Rouge Brit.Cem. Pas-de-Calais; Age 21; Son of William Henry and Martha Callingham of 9, South Road, Newhaven, Sussex.

5099. CANNING, Walter Robert Frank; B: Strood, Kent; E: Hastings; L/Sgt. SD 1850; W: 14.11.16; Contay Brit. Cem. Somme; Age 25; Son of Robert Montague and Harriett Sophia Canning; Husband of Minnie Canning of 14, Egremont Place, Brighton.*

5100. CARLIN, William Thomas; B: Myton-on-Swale, Yorkshire; E: Eastbourne; Sgt. SD 1926; K: 30.6.16; Cabaret-Rouge Brit. Cem. Pas-de-Calais.

5101. CARNE, John Reeves; 2nd Lt.; W: 25.7.17; Lijssenthoek Mil. Cem. (Bel.); Age 27; Son of William and Elizabeth Carne of 26, Terrace Road, South Hackney, London.

5102. CARTER, Nelson Victor; B: Hailsham, Sussex; E: Eastbourne; C.S.M. SD4; **V.C;** K: 30.6.16; Royal

Irish Rifles Graveyard, Laventie, Pas-de-Calais; Age 29; Son of Richard Carter of Harebeating, Battle Road, Hailsham, Sussex; Husband of Kathleen Carter of 33, Guys Road, Eastbourne – see text.

5103. CARVER, William; B: Hailsham, Sussex; E: Eastbourne; Pte. SD 1799; K: 30.6.16; Loos Mem. Pas-de-Calais; Age 33; Son of William and Phoebe Carver of Hailsham; Husband of Mary J.R.Carver of 20, Winter Road, Eastbourne.

5104. CASEY, Frank; B: Walton-on-Thames; E: London; Sgt. SD 2145; K: 30.6.16; Loos Mem. Pas-de-Calais.

5105. CASSE, Frederick; B: Kingston-on-Thames; E: Bognor Regis, Sussex; L/Cpl. SD 1282; K: 25.9.17; Ypres Reservoir Cem. (Bel.).

5106. CATTON, Frederick; B: Battle, Sussex; E: Hastings; Pte. SD 2879; K: 30.6.16; Loos Mem. Pas-de-Calais.

5107. CAWTE, Frederick James; B: St.George's, Sussex; E: Worthing; Pte. SD 1284; K: 30.6.16; Cabaret-Rouge Brit. Cem. Pas-de-Calais.

5108. CHANDLER, Frederick William; B: Eastbourne; E: Eastbourne; L/Cpl. SD 1583; K: 30.6.16; St.Vaast Post Mil. Cem. Pas-de-Calais.

5109. CHAPMAN, Walter; B:Hayes, London; E: Oxford; Pte. G 17071; K: 25.9.17; Hooge Crater Cem. (Bel.); Age 19; Son of Frank and Eliza Chapman of The Red Lion, Longwick, Buckinghamshire.

5110. CHAPMAN, William Henry; B: Grimsby; E: Grimsby; Pte. G 15378; W: 30.9.16; Gezaincourt Com. Cem. Ext. Somme; Age 22; Son of Levi and Lavinia Ann Chapman of Chapman Hotel, Central Market Place, Grimsby.

5111. CHATTERLEY, Horace Victor; B: Reditch, Warwickshire; E: Warwick; Pte. G 17032; K: 25.9.17; Hooge Crater Cem. (Bel.); Age 19; Son of Victor and Annie Chatterley of Wesley Villas, Crabb's Cross, Worcestershire.

5112. CLARKE, Harry; B: Kettering, Northamptonshire; E: Kettering; Pte. SD 5937; K: 30.10.16; Lonsdale Cem. Somme; Age 22; Son of George and Sarah Clarke of 66, Edmund Street, Kettering.

5113. CLARKE, William Henry; B: Heathfield, Sussex; E: Hastings; Pte. SD 3746; K: 30.6.16; Loos Mem. Pas-de-Calais; Age 29; Son of William Clarke; Husband of Sarah Ann Clarke of Rushlake Green, Sussex.

5114. CLAYDON, Percy; B: Maldon, Essex; E: Maldon; Pte. G 17181; K: 25.9.17; Tyne Cot Mem. (Bel.); Age 19; Son of Mrs.A.G.Claydon of 5, North Street, Maldon.

5115. CLIBBON, Herbert George; B: - ; E: Hertford; Pte. G 15567; K: 31.7.17; La Brique Mil. Cem. No.2 (Bel.); Age 25; Son of Elizabeth Clibbon of 4, Redan Road, Ware, Hertfordshire.

5116. CLISSOLD, Edward Victor; B: Thornbury, Gloucestershire; E: Stroud, Gloucestershire; Pte. G 17073; K: 24.9.17; Tyne Cot Mem. (Bel.); Age 29; Son of Edward and Alice Clissold of Ludgate Hill, Wotton-under-Edge, Gloucestershire.

5117. COLEMAN, William Thomas; B: Hailsham, Sussex; E: Herstmonceux, Sussex; C.S.M. SD 568; K: 3.9.16; Thiepval Mem. Somme; Age 40; Son of Charles and Harriet Coleman; Husband of Charlotte Head, formerly Coleman, of 4, Rockland Cottages, Victoria Road, Herstmonceux.*

5118. COLLINS, Ernest George; B: Worthing; E: Worthing; Pte. SD 1670; K: 30.6.16; St.Vaast Post Mil. Cem. Pas-de-Calais; Age 20; Son of Mr. and Mrs.Collins of "Simla", Park Road, Worthing.

5119. COLLINS, John; B: Brighton; E: Brighton; Pte. SD 2237; W: 30.4.16; Bethune Town Cem. Pas-de-Calais; Age 22; Son of John and Emily Collins of 31, Mount Zion Place, Queen's Road, Brighton.

5120. COLLINS, John Stratford; Lt.; K: 5.4.18; Bouzincourt Ridge Cem. Somme.

5121. COOMBE, Edward; B: Eastbourne; E: Eastbourne; Cpl. SD 1585; K: at Thiepval 31.10.16; Serre Road Cem. No.2 Somme; Age 40; Son of Mr. and Mrs. Joseph Coombe; Husband of Laura Jane Coombe of 20, Bradford Street, Eastbourne; Killed at Auchonvillers by shell fire.

5122. COOMBS, Francis Marshall; B: Lee, Kent; E: Eastbourne; Pte. SD 1293; K: 30.6.16; Cabaret-Rouge Brit. Cem. Pas-de-Calais; Age 21; Son of Mrs.Rosina Elizabeth Mockford, formerly Coombs, of 21, Carlton Road, Eastbourne and the late Marshall James Coombs.

5123. COOTE, George Herbert; B: Bankside, London; E: Croydon; Pte. G 16841; K: 23.7.17; Essex Farm Cem. (Bel.); Age 19; Son of Mr. and Mrs.G.Coote of 28, Sandown Road, South Norwood, London.*

5124. COPELAND, Richard; B: Eastbourne; E: Eastbourne; L/Cpl. SD 1586; K: 21.10.16; Thiepval Mem. Somme.

5125. COPPARD, Ernest James; B: Brighton; E: Hove; Pte. SD 2268; K: 30.6.16; St.Vaast Post Mil. Cem. Pas-de-Calais; Age 29; Son of Albert and Sarah Coppard of Brighton; Husband of Alice Emily Coppard of 26, Seaville Street, Brighton.

5126. CORKE, Alfred Harry; B: East Hoathly, Sussex; E: Worthing; Pte. SD 1675; K: 30.6.16; St.Vaast Post Mil. Cem. Pas-de-Calais; Age 25; Son of Sam Corke of Middle Road, Kingston-by-Sea, Southwick, Sussex.

5127. CORKE, Reginald; B: Hove; E: Bexhill-on-Sea; Pte. SD 1875; K: 30.6.16; Loos Mem. Pas-de-Calais.

5128. CORNFORD, Ernest Thomas; B: Rotherfield, Sussex; E: Tunbridge Wells; Pte. SD 1299; W: 5.9.16; Acheux Brit. Cem. Somme; Age 18; Son of Charles and Ann Cornford of Floral Cottage, Beeches Estate, Crowborough, Sussex.

5129. COSSTICK, Reginald Harold; B: Seaford, Sussex; E: Eastbourne; L/Cpl. SD 301; K: 21.3.18; Jeancourt Com. Cem. Aisne; Age 23; Son of Mr. and Mrs.W.Cosstick of 22, Chichester Road, Seaford.

5130. COTTON, Aubrey Nightingale; B: London; Capt.; K: 30.6.16; St.Vaast Post Mil. Cem. Pas-de-Calais; Age 37; Son of James Robert and Eliza Ellen Cotton; Formerly Honorary Artillery Company.

5131. COUSINS, Sydney Arthur; B: Southwark, London;

E: St.Paul's Churchyard, London; L/Cpl. SD 2158; K: 30.6.16; Cabaret-Rouge Brit. Cem Pas-de-Calais; Age 20; Son of George S. and Annie Cousins of 26, Temple Street, Southwark.

5132. COWLEY, Alfred William; B: St.Nicholas, Sussex; E: Eastbourne; Pte. SD 1737; K: 30.6.16; Loos Mem. Pas-de-Calais.

5133. COX, Clarence Rupert; Capt.; K: 13.4.17; Attached to Royal Flying Corps

5134. COXON, Lawrence Frederick; 2nd Lt.; K: 17.10.16; Mill Road Cem. Somme; Age 18.

5135. CREASEY, Frederick William; B: Eastbourne; E: Eastbourne; L/Cpl. SD 1303; K: 30.6.16; Loos Mem. Pas-de-Calais; Age 22; Son of Mrs,Creasey of 2, Summerdown Road, Eastbourne.*

5136. CRITTENDEN, Alfred Charles; B: Tunbridge Wells; E: Tunbridge Wells; Pte. SD 4011; K: 30.6.16; Loos Mem. Pas-de-Calais.

5137. CROFT, Gilbert; B: Brightling, Sussex; E: Hastings; Pte. SD 2266; K: 30.6.16; St.Vaast Post Mil. Cem. Pas-de-Calais.

5138. CROSS, Harry Ralph; B: New Hackleton, Northamptonshire; E: Northampton; Pte. G 15382; K: 17.10.16; Thiepval Mem. Somme.

5139. CROWE, Charles; B: Castle Rising, Norfolk; E: Guildford; Sgt. G 20302; K: 25.9.17; Tyne Cot Mem. (Bel.); Age 40; Son of Edward Crowe of Castle Rising; Husband of Eleanor Crowe of 12, Crescent Road, Worthing.

5140. CROXON, Ivor Robert; B: – ; E: Paddington, London; Pte. G 14931; K: 17.10.16; Mill Road Cem. Somme; Age 26; Son of George Willsmer Croxon and Charlotte M. Croxon of 63, Ashmore Road, Paddington.

5141. CULPIN, Richard Benjamin; B: – ; E: Cambridge; Pte. G 14939; W at Home: 16.12.18; Cambridge (Mill Road) Cem. (UK); Age 20; Son of John and Elizabeth Culpin of 17, Malta Road, Mill Road, Cambridge.

5142. CULVER, George Stephen; B: Ramsgate, Kent; E: Bexhill-on-Sea; Pte. SD 1878; K: 22.4.16; Guards Cem. (Cuinchy) Pas-de-Calais; Age 27; Husband of Mary A.Culver of 3, Camperdown Street, Bexhill-on-Sea.

5143. CULVER, Sidney; B: Wadhurst, Sussex; E: Tunbridge Wells; Pte. SD 1302; W: 30.6.16; Merville Com. Cem. Nord; Son of Mrs.H.Culver of 3, Derwent Cottages, Wadhurst.

5144. CUNNINGTON, John Thomas; B: Bolderton, Nottinghamshire; E: Grantham, Lincolnshire; Pte. G 15376; K: 31.7.17; Ypres (Menin Gate) Mem. (Bel.); Age 26; Son of George Cunnington of Easton, Lincolnshire.

D

5145. DANIELS, Arthur Edward; B: Lambeth, London; E: Kingston-on-Thames; C.S.M. G 20276; K: 31.7.17; Buffs Road Cem., St.Jean-les-Ypres (Bel.); Age 35; Son of Fred and Emma Daniels of Brixton, London.

5146. DANIELS, George Herbert; B: March, Cambridge-shire; E: Sleaford, Lincolnshire; Pte. G 15401;K: 9.1.18; New Irish Farm Cem. (Bel.).

5147. DAUGHTREY, Percy; B: Goring-by-Sea, Sussex; E: Worthing; Pte. SD 1676; K: 30.8.16; Thiepval Mem. Somme.

5148. DAVEY, Arthur; B: Nuthurst, Sussex; E: Horsham, Sussex; Pte. G 3148; K: 25.9.17; Bedford House Cem. Enclosure No.4 (Bel.); Age 25; Son of Charles and Fanny Davey of Nuthurst Street, Horsham.

5149. DAVIS, Ernest; B: Seaford, Sussex; E: Bexhill-on-Sea; L/Cpl. SD 1306; K: 31.7.17; Buffs Road Cem. St.Jean-les-Ypres, (Bel.); Age 23; Son of Ernest and Charlotte Davis of Hampden Park, Eastbourne; Husband of Dorothy Maud Davis of 3, Railway Road, Hampden Park.

5150. DAVIS, Laurence; B: – ; E: Brighton; Pte. SD 1636; K: 30.6.16; Loos Mem. Pas-de-Calais; Age 20; Son of Alfred Forbes Davis and Laura Marie Monica Davis of 7, Goldstone Road, Hove.

5151. DAVIS, Louis Augustus; B: Mile End, London; E: Stepney, London; Cpl. G 16219; K: 24.7.17; Essex Farm Cem. (Bel.).

5152. DAWES, Spencer; B: Maidstone; E: Bexhill-on-Sea; Pte. SD 2087; K: 17.10.16; Thiepval Mem. Somme.

5153. DAY, Alfred Walter; B: Plaistow, Sussex; E: Petworth, Sussex; Pte. G 16301; K: 21.10.16; Serre Road Cem. No.2, Somme; Age 21; Son of George and Margaret Day; Husband of Beatrice Ellen Scott, formerly Day, of 2, Council Houses, Lambourn Woodlands, Berkshire.

5154. DEADMAN, Arthur; B: Eastbourne; E: Eastbourne; Pte. SD 1927; K: 17.10.16; Thiepval Mem. Somme.*

5155. DEAN, Herbert; B: Slindon, Sussex; E: Horsham, Sussex; Pte. G 17811; K: 3.9.16; Hamel Mil. Cem. Somme; Age 26; Son of Mr. and Mrs.James Dean of 47, Park Lane, Slindon.

5156. DE BOO, Albert Ephraim; B: – ; E: Hastings; Pte. SD 2284; K: 3.9.16; Thiepval Mem. Somme.

5157. DEEPROSE, Ernest William; B: St.Andrews, Sussex; E: Hastings; Pte. SD 1879; K: 3.9.16; Thiepval Mem. Somme.*

5158. DEWEY, Frank; B: Hose, Leicestershire; E: Melton Mowbray, Leicestershire; Pte. SD 1679; W: 22.7.16; Étaples Mil. Cem. Pas-de-Calais; Age 22; Son of George and Ada Emma Dewey of Glen House, Hose.

5159. DIGGENS, Bert; B: Hastings; E: Hastings; Pte. SD 1881; K: 30.6.16; Loos Mem. Pas-de-Calais; Age 21; Son of Mrs.Jane Jeffrey Diggens of 1, Halton Crescent, Hastings.

5160. DIXON, William; B: Ashington, Northumberland; E: Newcastle-upon-Tyne; Pte. SD 2072; K: 10.5.16; Loos Mem. Pas-de-Calais; Age 37; Son of Thomas and Margaret Dixon; Husband of Mrs.Sarah Dixon of 22, Katherine Street, Ashington.

5161. DOVER, Ralph; B: – ; E: Hertford; L/Cpl. G 15568; K: 23.9.17; Tyne Cot Mem. (Bel.).

5162. DOYLE, Herbert James; B: Hove; E: Hove; Pte. SD 4966; K: 30.6.16; Loos Mem. Pas-de-Calais.

5163. DUDMAN, Charles Robert; B: Eastbourne; E: Chichester; Pte. G 19527; K: 25.9.17; Hooge Crater Cem. (Bel.); Age 25; Son of John and Harriet Dudman of Upper Vining, Easebourne, Sussex.

E

5164. EASTON, Charles Alfred; B: St.Andrew's, Sussex; E: Hastings; Pte. SD 2088; K: 16.10.16; Connaught Cem. Somme.

5165. EDWARDS, Frederick George; B: Horsham; E: Horsham; Pte. G 17943; K: 23.9.17; Tyne Cot Cem. (Bel.).

5166. ELLINOR, Ernest James; B: Gislingham, Suffolk; E: Eye, Cambridgeshire; Pte. G 20461; W: 14.6.17; Lijssenthoek Mil. Cem. (Bel.).

5167. ELLIS, Ernest George; B: Geat Missenden, Buckinghamshire; E: East Grinstead, Sussex; Pte. G 16319; K: 8.10.16; Auchonvillers Mil. Cem. Somme; Age 26; Son of Mr. and Mrs.T.Ellis of Great Missenden; Husband of Mrs.E.Ellis of 24, Dormans Park Road, East Grinstead.

5168. ELLIS, Herbert Charles; B: Great Yarmouth; E: Great Yarmouth; Pte. G 16986; D: 4.2.18; Gouzeaucourt New Brit. Cem., Nord; Age 19; Son of Herbert and Emma E.Ellis of 6, Ordnance Road, Great Yarmouth.

5169. ELSEY, Ernest Gordon; B: Kirdford, Sussex; E: Kirdford; Pte. G 16290; W: 23.10.16; Boulogne Eastern Cem. Pas-de-Calais; Age 25; Son of Mr. and Mrs.Elsey of Kirdford.

5170. EMPHRINGHAM, George; B: –; E: Lincoln; Pte. G 15405; K: 17.10.16; Pargny Brit. Cem. Somme.

5171. ESSAM, George; B: Northmpton; E: Northampton; Pte. G 17184; K: 23.9.17; Ypres Reservoir Cem. (Bel.).

5172. ETHERTON, Hugh; B: Worthing; E: Worthing; L/Cpl. SD 1680; K: 30.6.16; Cabaret-Rouge Brit. Cem. Pas-de-Calais; Age 29; Son of Harvey Etherton of Worthing; Husband of Lilian Etherton of 27, King Street, Worthing.

5173. EVERDEN, Albert John; B: Slaugham, Sussex; E: Horsham; Pte. G 19540; K: 25.9.17; Tyne Cot Mem. (Bel.).

5174. EVERETT, William John; B: Cheshunt, Hertfordshire; E: Hertford; Pte. G 15521; K: 21.1.18; Tyne Cot Mem. (Bel.); Age 23; Son of George and Elizabeth Everett of Lucas End, Goff's Oak, Hertfordshire.

5175. EVERSHED, Richard Alfred Ichabod; B: Brighton; E: Hove; Pte. SD 2327; K: 10.4.16; Loos Mem. Pas-de-Calais.

5176. EYLES, Henry St.John; B: Brighton; E: Brighton; Pte. TF 290281; W: 25.2.18; Roye New Brit. Cem. Somme; Age 34; Son of Frank Eyles; Husband of Alice Maud Eyles of 3, Park Crescent, Brighton.

F

5177. FAIRMAN, Percy Gordon; B: Bromley Common, Kent; E: Bexhill-on-Sea; L/Cpl. SD 1032; K: 2.3.17; Ypres (Menin Gate) Mem. (Bel.).

5178. FAIRS, Henry Evan; B: Alborne, Sussex; E: Worthing; L/Cpl.; SD 1682; D: 15.7.16; Choques Mil. Cem. Pas-de-Calais; Age 21; Son of George and Marie Annie Fairs of Shoreham, Sussex; Died of pneumonia.

5179. FARLEY, Arthur Frederick; B: Bognor Regis, Sussex; E: Bognor Regis; Pte. SD 1210; W: 20.9.16; Doullens Com. Cem. Ext. Somme; Age 26; Husband of Angelina M.Farley of 36, Church Cottages, Stedham, Midhurst, Sussex.*

5180. FARLEY, George; B: Bognor Regis, Sussex; E: Bognor Regis; Cpl. SD 1225; W: 25.8.16; Couin Brit. Cem. Somme.*

5181. FAST, William Jack; Capt.; K: 24.3.18; Pozieres Mem. Somme.

5182. FEARN, Charles; B: Swadlincote, Derbyshire; E: Woking, Surrey; Pte, G 15413; D: 16.12.16; Mendingham Mil. Cem. (Bel.).

5183. FELLOWS, Jesse; B: Mountfield, Sussex; E: Hastings; Pte. SD 2291; K: 26.9.17; Voormezeele Enclosures No.1 and No.2 (Bel.).*

5184. FELTON, Arthur Robert; B: Hollingbourne, Kent; E: Bexhill-on-Sea; L/Cpl. SD 1317; K: 14.11.17; Tyne Cot Mem., (Bel.); Age 21; Son of Arthur James and Caroline Frances Felton of 54, Cornwall Road, Bexhill-on-Sea.

5185. FENCHELLE, George John; 2nd Lt.; W: 30.6.16; Cabaret-Rouge Brit. Cem. Pas-de-Calais.

5186. FIELDWICK, Charlie; B: Turner's Hill, Sussex; E: East Grinstead; Pte. G 17825; K: 3.9.16; Hamel Mil. Cem. Somme; Age 19; Son of William and Florence Fieldwick of Little Miswells, Turner's Hill.*

5187. FIFIELD, Harry Christopher; B: Hove; E: Brighton; Pte. G 16096; W: 27.10.16; Wimereux Com. Cem. Pas-de-Calais; Age 18; Son of William and Kate Fifield of Hove.*

5188. FIGG, Walter George; B: Haywards Heath, Sussex; E: Haywards Heath; Pte. G 17817; K: 22.10.17; Tyne Cot Mem. (Bel.); Age 20; Son of Albert Edward and Emily A.Figg of 28, Western Road, Haywards Heath.

5189. FINBOW, Benjamin James; B: Hindringham, Norfolk; E: Bury St.Edmunds, Suffolk; Pte. G 15412; W at Home: 18.4.17; Nunhead (All Saints) Cem. London (UK); Age 26; Son of David and Hannah Finbow of Otley, Suffolk.

5190. FISHER, Ernest Frederick; B: Eastbourne; E: Bexhill-on-Sea; Pte. SD 1851; K: 21.10.16; Thiepval Mem. Somme.

5191. FISHER, Fred; B: Bexhill-on-Sea; E: Bexhill-on-Sea; Sgt. SD 1852; K: 30.6.16; Loos Mem. Pas-de-Calais.

5192. FISHER Wilfrid Frederick; 2nd Lt.; K: 24.7.17; Ypres (Menin Gate) Mem. (Bel.).

5193. FITZPATRICK, David; B: Marylebone, London; E: Marylebone; Cpl. G 20286; K: 25.9.17; Tyne Cot Mem. (Bel.); Age 25;

5194. FLETCHER, Harold; B: Worthing; E: Worthing; Pte. SD 2176; K: 30.6.16; Cabaret-Rouge Brit. Cem. Pas-de-Calais.*

5195. FLETCHER, Henry; B: Bermondsey, London; E: Chichester; Pte. G 17822; W: 26.4.17; Wimereux Com. Cem. Pas-de-Calais.

5196. FLETCHER, Ralph Cecil; B: – ; E: Cheltenham; Pte. G 17078; W: 20.10.17; Outtersteene Com. Cem. Ext., Bailleul, Nord; Age 19; Son of Philip and Rebecca C.Fletcher of Hob Nails, Little Washbourne, Gloucestershire; Wounds sustained on 16.10.17.

5197. FOLLETT, William Cecil; B: – ; E: Chichester; Pte. G 16273; K: 17.10.16; Thiepval Mem. Somme; Age 24; Son of William and Louisa Follett of 7, Broyle Road, Chichester.*

5198. FOORD, Albert; B: Alfriston, Sussex; E: Eastbourne; Pte. SD 1591; K: 30.6.16; Royal Irish Rifles Graveyard, Laventie, Pas-de-Calais; Age 35; Husband of Ettie Julia Foord of 5, New Cottages, Beachy Head Road, Eastbourne.

5199. FOORD, William Charles; B: Hailsham, Sussex; E: Eastbourne; Pte. SD 1323; K: 30.6.16; Loos Mem. Pas-de-Calais.

5200. FORDE, Frank Duncan; B: Dorking, Surrey; E: Dorking; Pte. G 16987; W: 18.1.18; Mendingham Mil. Cem. (Bel.); Age 19; Son of Frank D.Forde of 78, Orchard Road, Dorking.

5201. FOSTER, Alfred; B: Ewhurst, Sussex; E: Hastings; Pte. SD 2277; K: 20.9.16; Sucrerie Mil. Cem. Somme; Age 36; Son of Mr. and Mrs.Alfred Foster of Snaggs Hall, Ewhurst.

5202. FOSTER, Charles; B: Burpham, Sussex; E: Horsham, Sussex; Sgt. G 17824; W: 11.12.16; Lijssenthoek Mil. Cem. (Bel.); Age 23; Son of Charles and Alice Foster of Welpham Green, Burpham.*

5203. FOWLER, Arthur James; B: Eastbourne; E: Eastbourne; Pte. SD 1326; K: 30.6.16; Loos Mem. Pas-de-Calais; Age 21; Son of George Fowler of 31, Cavendish Place, Eastbourne.

5204. FRANCIS, Henry Herbert; B: Bruton, Somerset; E: Taunton, Somerset; Pte. G 17035; K: 25.9.17; Tyne Cot Mem. (Bel.); Age 19; Son of John and Elizabeth Ann Francis of 65, High Street, Bruton.

5205. FRANKLIN, Albert; B: – ; E: Doddington, Cambridgeshire; Pte. G 14947; K: 31.7.17; New Irish Farm Cem. (Bel.); Age 28; Son of Mrs. Susannah Canham of High Street, Doddington.

5206. FRAPE, Reginald David; B: Burgess Hill, Sussex; E: Worthing; L/Cpl. SD 1685; K: 30.6.16; Cabaret-Rouge Brit. Cem. Pas-de-Calais; Age 32; Son of Henry David and Katherine Jane Frape of "Normandy", Crescent Road, Burgess Hill.

5207. FRENCH, Walter John; B: Ware, Hertfordshire; E: Hertford; Pte. G 15591; K: 21.10.16; Connaught Cem. Somme.

5208. FRY, Richard; B: Hellingly, Sussex; E: Bexhill-on-Sea; Pte. SD 1330; K: 30.6.16; St.Vaast Post Mil. Cem. Pas-de-Calais; Age 23; Son of Jesse and Mary Ann Fry.

5209. FRY, William Osborne; B: Bristol; E: Brighton; Pte. SD 2312; K: 31.7.17; Track 'X' Cem. (Bel.).

5210. FULCHER, Henry; B: – ; E: Wisbech, Cambridgeshire; Pte. G 14949; K: 5.11.16; Puchevillers Brit. Cem. Somme.*

5211. FULLER, Peter; B: Ferring, Sussex; E: Bognor Regis, Sussex; Pte. SD 1331; K: 30.6.16; Cabaret-Rouge Brit. Cem. Pas-de-Calais; Age 26; Son of Mr. and Mrs.G.Fuller of 1, Memorial Cottages, Flamsham Lane, Felpham, Sussex.

5212. FUNNELL, Ernest George; B: Westham, Pevensey, Sussex; E: Eastbourne; Pte. SD 1333; K: 30.6.16; Loos Mem. Pas-de-Calais; Age 23; Son of William George Funnell of 3, Aylesbury Cottages, Langney, Eastbourne.

G

5213. GADD, William Thomas; B: Yeovil, Somerset; E: Guildford; Pte. G 19950; K: 23.9.17; Tyne Cot Mem. (Bel.); Age 37; Son of Henry and Jane Gadd of 27, Vincent Street, Yeovil; Husband of Nellie Gadd.

5214. GALE, George; B: Hambledon, Surrey; E: Guildford; Pte. G 20349; W: 26.12.16; Mendinghem Mil. Cem. (Bel.); Age 22; Son of Harry and Mary Gale of Stone Cottages, Church Lane, Whitley, Surrey.

5215. GAUT, Percy Bernard Johnson; B: Westham, Pevensey, Sussex; E: Bexhill-on-Sea; Pte. SD 1227; K: 30.6.16; Loos Mem. Pas-de-Calais; Age 27; Son of Henry Gaut of 55, Droop Street, Paddington, London; Husband of Kate Gaut of High Street, Sidbury, Devon.

5216. GEARING, Jack; B: Eastbourne; E: Hastings; Pte. SD 2093; K: 30.6.16; Loos Mem. Pas-de-Calais.

5217. GILES, Edward; B: – ; E: Loughborough, Leicestershire; Pte. G 15072; K: 26.2.17; Railway Dugouts Burial Ground (Bel.); Age 24; Son of Thomas and Susan Giles of Walton-le-Wolds, Leicestershire.

5218. GILLHAM, William George; B: – ; E: Brighton; L/Cpl. TF 320543; K: 23.11.17; Perth Cem. (China Wall) (Bel.).

5219. GODDARD, Frank; B: Finchhampstead, Berkshire; E: Eastbourne; Pte. SD 2251; K: 30.6.16; Loos Mem. Pas-de-Calais; Age 20; Son of Jerry and Henrietta Goddard of 2, Luckley Path, Wokingham, Berkshire.

5220. GODDARD, John William; B: Grimsby; E: Lincoln; Pte. G 15418; W: 5.11.16; St.Sever Cem. Ext., Rouen, Seine-Maritime.

5221. GOODBURN, Edward Charles; B: Dover; E: Grimsby; Pte. G 15415; K: 15.10.16; Thiepval Mem. Somme.

5222. GOODWIN, John; B: Manchester; E: Wisbech, Cambridgeshire; Pte. G 14957; K: 25.9.17; Tyne Cot Mem. (Bel.); Age 36; Son of John and Annie Goodwin of Manchester.

5223. GORE, Frederick Edwin; B: Faversham, Kent; E: Canterbury; Pte. SD 5940; K: 12.10.16; Euston Road Cem. Somme; Age 27; Son of Edwin and Rose Ann Gore of Faversham.

5224. GRAINGER, Albert John; B: Hove; E: Worthing; Pte – 2373; W: 23.7.16. Bethune Town Cem., Pas-de-Calais.*

5225. GRANT, James Horace; B: Eastbourne; E: Eastbourne; Pte. SD 2260; K: 3.9.16; Hamel Mil. Cem. Somme; Age 24; Son of Mr.T.D. and Mrs.S.E.Grant of 107, Whitley Road, Eastbourne.

5226. GRAYSMARK, Francis Leopold; B: Brighton; E: Brighton; Pte. G 17839; K: 23.9.17; Tyne Cot Mem. (Bel.); Son of Thomas and Sarah Graysmark of 34, Over Street, Brighton.

5227. GREGORY, Albert Henry; B: Nether Broughton, Leicestershire; E: Melton Mowbray, Leicestershire; Pte. SD 1648; K: 30.6.16; Loos Mem. Pas-de-Calais; Age 19; Son of Edmund and Charlotte Anne Gregory of Nether Broughton.*

5228. GRENYER, Albert Charles; B: Worthing; E: Worthing; Pte. SD 1690; K: 30.6.16; Loos Mem. Pas-de-Calais; Age 24; Son of Charles and Ellen Grenyer of Pem Villas, 29, Sompting Road, Broadwater, Worthing.

5229. GRIFFITHS, Harold; B: Southsea, Hampshire; E: Horsham; Pte. SD 2287; W: 30.6.16; Cabaret-Rouge Brit. Cem. Pas-de-Calais; Age 21; Son of Frank and Alice Jane Griffiths of 30, Linacre Road, Cricklewood, London.*

5230. GRIFFITHS, Henry Charles; B: Eastbourne; E: Eastbourne; Pte. SD 1350; K: 16.5.16; Brown's Road Mil. Cem., Festubert, Pas-de-Calais.

5231. GRINSTEAD, William; B: Petworth, Sussex; E: Petworth; Pte. SD 2346; K: 3.9.16; Ancre Brit. Cem. Somme.

5232. GROSSE, Joseph Thomas; B: Camberwell, London; E: Camberwell; Pte. G 17059; K: 25.9.17; Tyne Cot Mem. (Bel.); Age 20; Husband of Mrs.C.Wynn, formerly Grosse.

5233. GROVES, Archibald James William; B: Worthing; E: Worthing; L/Cpl. SD 1692; K: 31.7.17; Buffs Road Cem., St.Jean-les-Ypres (Bel.); Son of Mr.J.W.Groves of 16, Surrey Street, Worthing.*

5234. GRUNNELL, Webster; B: Grimsby; E: Grimsby; Pte. G 15417; K: 17.10.16; Thiepval Mem. Somme.

5235. GUNN, Thomas; B: St.George's-in-the-East, London; E: Canning Town, London; Pte. G 20353; K: 31.7.17; Buffs Road Cem, St.Jean-les-Ypres (Bel.).

5236. GUTTRIDGE, Harold Stanley; B: Brixton, London; E: Wandsworth, London; Pte. G 16917; W: 16.9.17; Voormezeele Enclosures No.1 and No.2. (Bel.); Age 19; Son of William and John Guttridge; Husband of Ellen Louise Guttridge of 117, Gassiot Road, Tooting, London.

H

5237. HABBERJAM, William; B: Wakefield, Yorkshire; E: Ashington, Northumberland; Pte. SD 2070; K: 10.5.16; Loos Mem. Pas-de-Calais; Age 34; Son of Charles and Jane Habberjam of 125, Pont Street, Ashington; Husband of Anna Habberjam of 46, South Villas, Ashington.

5238. HAKE, Alfred James; B: Greenwich, London; E: Hastings; Pte. SD 2289; K: 12.7.16; Cambrin Churchyard Ext. Pas-de-Calais; Age 27; Son of Mrs.C.M.Hake of 5, Tyler Street, East Greenwich.

5239. HALE, John; B: Nazeing, Essex; E: Warley, Essex; Pte. G 15442; W: 13.11.16; Puchevillers Brit. Cem. Somme; Age 30; Son of William and Caroline Hale of Long Green, Nazeing.

5240. HAMPSHIRE, Arthur; B: Pulborough, Sussex; E: Petworth, Sussex; Pte. SD 2283; K: 30.6.16; Loos Mem. Pas-de-Calais.

5241. HANBY, Francis James; 2nd Lt.; K: 30.6.16; Loos Mem. Pas-de-Calais; Age 28; Son of the Rev.James and Harriett Alicia Hanby of 12, Ellesmere Avenue, Sutton Ings, Yorkshire.

5242. HANMORE, Ernest; B: Speldhurst, Kent; E: Tunbridge Wells; Pte. G 12871; K: 3.8.17; Duhallow A.D.S. Cem. (Bel.).

5243. HARDING, Alfred; B: Tunbridge Wells; E: Brighton; Pte. G 16195; W: 28.6.17; Brandhoek Mil. Cem. (Bel.); Age 28; Son of James and Mary Ann Harding of Withyham, Sussex.*

5244. HARDS, Arthur; B: Horsham, Sussex; E: Horsham; Pte. G 17844; K: 10.10.16; Auchonvillers Mil. Cem. Somme; Age 26; Son of Eldred and Jane Hards of Warnham, Sussex.*

5245. HARDS, William Thomas; B: Brighton; E: Hove; Pte. SD 2394; K: 30.6.16; Loos Mem. Pas-de-Calais; Son of William Hards of 3, Hastings Road, Brighton.*

5246. HARLAND, William; B: Portslade, Sussex; E: Hove; Pte. G 17849; K: 17.10.16; Mill Road Cem. Somme.

5247. HARLOTT, Thomas; B: Hastings; E: Hastings; Pte. SD 1886; K: 30.6.16; Loos Mem. Pas-de-Calais; Son of Thomas Harlott of 18, Geat Fenchurch Street, Folkestone.

5248. HARPER, Horace Andrew; B: Brighton; E: Camberwell, Surrey; Sgt. G. 20107; K: 31.7.17; White House Cem. (Bel.).

5249. HARRINGTON, John; B: Liptree, Essex; E: Grimsby; Pte. G 15431; K: 18.9.17; Larch Wood (Railway Cutting) Cem. (Bel.).

5250. HARRIS, Alfred Thomas; B: Salehurst, Sussex; E: Bexhill-on-Sea; Sgt. SD 1887; K: 30.6.16; Loos Mem. Pas-de-Calais; Age 32; Son of John and Elizabeth Ann Harris of Herstmonceux, Sussex; Husband of Lilian Maria Harris.

5251. HARRIS, Harry Glossop; B: High Wycombe, Buckinghamshire; E: Brighton; Pte. TF 207231; K: 22.3.18; Arras Mem. Pas-de-Calais.*

5252. HARTWELL, Charles; B: Leicester; E: Leicester; Pte. G 15077; K: 21.10.16; Thiepval Mem. Somme.

5253. HAULKHAM, Sidney George; B: – ; E: Worthing; Pte. SD 2027; W: 18.10.16; Varennes Mil. Cem. Somme; Age 29; Son of Mrs.Ann Haulkham of Worthing.*

5254. HAWES, Ernest William; B: Willingdon, Sussex; E: Eastbourne; Pte. SD 1956; K: 30.6.16; Loos Mem. Pas-de-Calais; Age 25; Son of Robert Hawes of 59, Grey's Road, Eastbourne.

5255. HAWKINS, George E.A.; B: Worthing; E: Worthing; Pte. SD 1693; W: 21.9.17; Godewaersvelde Brit. Cem., Nord; Husband of Jane Belton, formerly Hawkins, of 58, Park Road, Worthing.*

5256. HAYES, Sidney Theodore; B: Camberwell, London; E: Wandsworth, London; Pte. SD 5781; K: 25.9.17; Tyne Cot Mem. (Bel.); Age 25; Son of Mr. and Mrs.I.Hayes of 33, Chaffinch Road, Beckenham, Kent; Husband of Daisy May West, formerly Hayes, of 89, Railton Road, Herne Hill, London.

5257. HAYNES, William; B: St.Ives, Huntingdonshire; E: Cambridge; Pte. G 14905; K: 25.9.17; Hooge Crater Cem. (Bel.); Age 21; Son of Mr. and Mrs.J.Haynes.

5258. HAYTER, Henry George; B: – ; E: Horsham, Sussex; Pte. G 16130; K: 12.9.17; Voormezeele Enclosures No.1 and No.2 (Bel.).

5259. HAYWARD, James Isaac; B: St.Andrew's, Kent; E: Deal, Kent; Pte. G 293; K: 25.9.17; Zantvoorde Brit. Cem. (Bel.); Age 29; Son of Mrs.Susan Hayward of 6, Brewer Street, Deal.*

5260. HEADEY, Maurice Alfred; B: Dunstable, Bedfordshire; E: Luton; Pte. G 16922; W: 18.9.17; Godewaesvelde Brit. Cem., Nord; Age 19; Son of Alfred and Maud Headey of "Westleigh", West Street, Dunstable.*

5261. HEATHER, George Frederick; B: Uxbridge, Middlesex; E: Uxbridge; Pte. G 17190; K: 27.9.17; Hooge Crater Cem. (Bel.); Age 18; Son of Mr.G. and Mrs.C.Heather of 1, The Dell, Laundry Road, Uxbridge.*

5262. HEATHER, James; B: Petworth, Sussex; E: Chichester; Pte. G 995; K: 20.9.17; Tyne Cot Mem. (Bel.); Age 21; Son of Henry William and Margaret Winifred Heather of 24, Essex Road, Bognor Regis, Sussex.

5263. HEMSLEY, Ernest James; 2nd Lt; M.C.; K: 4.9.18; Grootebeek Brit. Cem. (Bel.); Age 29; Son of Thomas and Martha Hemsley of Tunbridge Wells.

5264. HENDEN, Edward John; B: Streatham, London; E: Kingston-on-Thames; Pte. TF 200441; K: 21.1.18; Tyne Cot Mem. (Bel.).

5265. HENTY, Herbert Alfred; B: Eastbourne; E: Bexhill-on-Sea; Pte. SD 1360; W at Home: 10.7.16; Eastbourne (Ocklynge) Cem., Sussex (UK); Age 19; Son of Mr. and Mrs.Herbert Henty of Hampden Park Lodge, Eastbourne.*

5266. HERBERT, Edward John; B: Eastbourne; E: Eastbourne; Pte. SD 4219; K: 31.7.17; White House Cem. (Bel.); Age 26; Son of Charles Seaward Herbert and Rebecca Herbert.

5267. HICKS, John Bernard; B: Birmingham; E: Birmingham; Pte. G 17087; K: 25.9.17; Tyne Cot Mem. (Bel.).

5268. HICKS, Thomas; B: Burwash, Sussex; E: Bexhill-on-Sea; Pte. SD 2102; K: 30.6.16; Loos Mem. Pas-de-Calais.

5269. HIDE, Walter Becket; B: Eastbourne; E: Eastbourne; Pte. SD 1808; K: 30.6.16; Loos Mem. Pas-de-Calais.

5270. HILLS, Frederick George; B: Portslade, Sussex; E: Hove; Pte. SD 2395; W: 6.9.16; Étaples Mil. Cem. Pas-de-Calais; Age 22; Son of William and Georgina Hills of 9, Camden Street, Portslade.

5271. HILTON, Charles Robert; B: Eastbourne, Sussex; E: Bexhill-on-Sea; Pte. SD 1815; K: 31.7.17; Buffs Road Cem., St.Jean-les-Ypres (Bel.); Brother of Mr.A.Hilton of New Road, Eastbourne.

5272. HODGES, Charles; B: Newick, Sussex; E: Lewes; Pte. SD 1637; K: 30.6.16; Loos Mem. Pas-de-Calais; Age 20; Son of George Hodges.

5273. HODGES, James; B: Hammersmith, London; E: Worthing; Pte. SD 1698; K: 3.6.16; Cambrin Churchyard Ext., Pas-de-Calais.

5274. HOLCOMBE, Frank; B: South Norwood, London; E: Horsham, Sussex; Pte. SD 1971; D at Home: 28.5.16; Oxford (Botley) Cem. (UK).

5275. HOLLAND, Archibald; B: Nottingham; E: Hove; Pte. G 17934; K: 10.10.16; Euston Road Cem Somme; Foster son of Mrs.H.Wood of 88, Cowper Street, Hove.

5276. HOLLAND, George; B: Battle, Sussex; E: Hastings; Pte. SD 2103; K: 30.6.16; Loos Mem. Pas-de-Calais; Age 22; Son of Walter and Harriet Holland of Stoney Wood Cottage, Netherfield, Sussex.

5277. HOLLOBONE, James Frederick George; B: Eastbourne; E: Eastbourne; L/Cpl. SD 1366; K: 1.5.16; Guards Cem. (Cuinchy) Pas-de-Calais; Age 23; Son of Mr. and Mrs.R.Hollobone of Eastbourne; Husband of Edith M.A.Hollobone of 67, Tideswell Road, Eastbourne.

5278. HOLTER, Charles; B: Eastbourne; E: Bexhill-on-Sea; Pte. SD 1370; K: 3.9.16; Thiepval Mem. Somme; Age 27; Son of Mrs.Agnes Holter of 206, Whitley Road, Eastbourne.

5279. HOMEWOOD, Alfred William; B: – ; E: Tonbridge; Pte. G 15427; W: 10.10.16; Puchevillers Brit. Cem. Somme.

5280. HONEYBUN, Ernest James; B: Sidlesham, Sussex; E: Hastings; Pte. SD 3785; K: 30.6.16; Loos Mem. Pas-de-Calais.

5281. HOOKER, Stanley; B: Burstow, Surrey; E: Horsham, Sussex; L/Cpl. SD 1931; K: 25.9.17; Bedford House Cem. Enclosure No.4 (Bel.); Age 23; Son of Charles and Annie E.Hooker of "Henley", Shelley Park, Horsham.

5282. HORTON, William; B: Boston, Lincolnshire; E: Boston; Pte. G 15433; W: 20.12.16; Étaples Mil. Cem. Pas-de-Calais; Son of Charles and Sarah Ann Horton.

5283. HOWARD, Harold; B: Margate, Kent; E: Canterbury; Pte. G 16920; K: 18.9.17; Perth Cem. (China Wall) (Bel.); Age 19; Son of Mrs.Emma Howard of 5, Charlotte Square, Margate.

5284. HOWARD, Harry; B: Loughborough, Leicestershire; E: Loughborough; Pte. G 15074; K: 17.10.16; Thiepval Mem. Somme.

5285. HOWE, George; B: Chisel Green, Hertfordshire; E: Watford; Pte. TF 290990; K: 21.1.18; Tyne Cot Mem. (Bel.); Age 28; Son of Joseph and Elizabeth

Howe of Cobden Hill Cottages, Radlett; Husband of Ruth Howe of 6, Scrubbitts Square, Radlett, Hertfodshire.

5286. HOWLETT, Charles Albert; B: Twyford, Leicestershire; E: Melton Mowbray, Leicestershire; Pte. SD 1653; K: 30.6.16; St.Vaast Post Mil. Cem. Pas-de-Calais.

5287. HOY, William Charles; B: Harlow, Essex; E: Epping, Essex; Pte. G 6163; K: 31.7.17; New Irish Farm Cem. (Bel.); Age 26; Son of John and Harriett Hoy of Housham, Tye, Essex.

5288. HUBBARD, Walter Ernest; B: Eastbourne; E: Eastbourne; Pte. SD 1598; K: 30.6.16; Loos Mem. Pas-de-Calais; Age 20; Son of Joseph Thomas and Annie Mercy Thomas of 113, Whitley Road, Eastbourne.

5289. HUDSON, Arthur Ernest; B: Hornsey, London; E: Brighton; Pte. G 16228; K: 1.8.17; Ypres (Menin Gate) Mem. (Bel.).*

5290. HUGHES, William Thomas; B: Watford; E: Hampstead, London; Pte. SD 5812; K: 12.10.16; Euston Road Cem. Somme.

5291. HULL, Noah; B: Farnham, Surrey; E: Chichester; Pte. SD 3126; K: 25.9.17; Tyne Cot Mem. (Bel.); Age 32; Son of Mr.G. and Mrs.M.K.Hull of 10, Commonside, Westbourne, Hampshire.

5292. HUMPHREY, William; B: – ; E: Brighton; Pte. G 14164; K: 23.11.17; Tyne Cot Mem. (Bel.).

5293. HURFORD, Percy Albert; B: – ; E: Brighton; Pte. SD 1834; K: 31.7.17; Ypres (Menin Gate) Mem. (Bel.); Age 22; Husband of May Thurza Hurford of 2, Faith Cottages, Dibden, Southampton.

5294. HUTCHINSON, Robert; B: Waterloo, London; E: Croydon; Pte. G 19851; K: 3.2.17; Ypres (Menin Gate) Mem. (Bel.); Age 34; Son of Henry March Hutchinson of Torrington Cottage, Minster, Kent; Husband of Nellie Warner, formerly Hutchinson, of 50, Dalmally Road, Addiscombe, Surrey.

5295. HUTLEY, Frederick; B: Great Wigborough, Essex; E: Beccles, Suffolk; Pte. SD 1972; K: 30.6.16; Loos Mem. Pas-de-Calais; Age 34; Son of Mr. and Mrs. Charles Hutley of Great Wigborough.

5296. HUTSON, Alfred James; B: Eastbourne; E: Eastbourne; Pte. SD 1373; K: 30.6.16; Loos Mem. Pas-de-Calais.

I

5297. IRONS, William; B: Willingdon, Sussex; E: Bexhill-on-Sea; Pte. SD 1377; K: 1.7.16; Loos Mem. Pas-de-Calais; Age 24; Son of William Charles and Agnes Irons of The Stables, Hampden Park, Eastbourne.

5298. ISTED, Alfred; B: Burwash, Sussex; E: Hastings; L/Cpl. SD 1894; K: 30.6.16; Loos Mem. Pas-de-Calais; Age 19; Son of James and Sophie Isted of Rock Cottages, Burwash.

J

5299. JACKSON, George Henry; B: Lindsey, Lincolnshire; E: Hastings; Cpl. SD 1895; K: 30.6.16; Cabaret-Rouge Brit. Cem. Pas-de-Calais.

5300. JAMES, Harry; B: Enderby, Leicestershire; E: Huckley; Pte. G 15081; K: 17.10.16; Thiepval Mem. Pas-de-Calais; Age 23; Son of William and Annie James of 3, Bulls Lane, Burbage, Leicestershire.

5301. JAMES, Henry; B: St.Luke's, Kent; E: Bexhill-on-Sea; Pte. SD 1230; K: 30.6.16; St.Vaast Post Mil. Cem. Pas-de-Calais.

5302. JARMAN, Albert William; B: Upper Norwood, London; E: Hastings; Pte. SD 1845; K: 30.6.16; St.Vaast Post Mil. Cem. Pas-de-Calais.

5303. JARROLD, George Frederick; B: Ipswich, Suffolk; E: Bury St.Edmunds, Suffolk; Pte. G 19855; K: 3.2.17; Ypres (Menin Gate) Mem. (Bel.); Age 22; Son of Mr.A.J. and Emma Alice Jarrold of Cavendish Park House, Thorpe-le-Soken, Essex.

5305. JEFFERY, George William; B: Salehurst, Sussex; E: Hastings; Pte. SD 2107; K: 3.2.17; Vlamertinghe Mil. Cem. (Bel.)); Age 31; Husband of Edith Miriam Jeffery of Lime Tree House, Burwash, Sussex.

5306. JENKINS, Arthur George; B: Preston, Hertfordshire; E: Eastbourne; Pte. G 14342; K: 1.8.17; Duhallow A.D.S. Cem. (Bel.); Age 19; Son of Mr.G.Jenkins of 17, Stanley Road, Eastbourne.

5307. JENNER, William; B: Washington, Sussex; E: Worthing; Pte. SD 2329; K: 30.6.16; Loos Mem. Pas-de-Calais; Age 18; Son of Alfred Thomas and Emily Jenner of Heath Common, Washington.

5308. JENNINGS, Frederick; B: Harpenden, Hertfordshire; E: Hertford; L/Cpl. G 15553; W: 7.12.17; St.Sever Cem. Ext., Rouen, Seine-Maritime.

5309. JESSON, Charles William; B: Leicester; E: Leicester; L/Cpl. SD 2136; K: 25.9.17; Tyne Cot Mem. (Bel.); Age 27; Son of William and Annie Jesson of 15, Stanley Street, Leicester; Husband of Alice Jesson of 52, Upperton Road, Leicester.

5310. JOHNS, Arthur Hugh; Lt.; K: 1.9.16; Mailly-Maillet Com. Cem. Ext. Somme; Age 23; Son of Rev.R.O. and Mrs.Jessie Marianne Johns of The Vicarage, Billingshurst, Sussex.

5311. JOHNSON, William; B: Brighton; E: Brighton; Pte. G 17861; K: 3.2.17; Vlamertinghe Mil. Cem. (Bel.); Age 30; Son of James and Sarah Johnson of Brighton.

5312. JOHNSTON, William; B: Ashington, Northumberland; E: Newcastle-upon-Tyne; Pte. SD 2073; K: 10.5.16; Loos Mem. Pas-de-Calais; Age 20; Son of John T. and Margaret Jane Johnston of 26, Third Row, Ashington.

5313. JONES, Frederick Cyril; B: – ; E: Cambridge; Pte. G 14970; K: 17.10.16; Connaught Cem. Somme; Age 22; Son of Frederick and Emma Jones of 9, Eden Street, Cambridge.

5314. JONES, Percy Stephen Charles; B: Chiddingly, Sussex; E: Uckfield, Sussex; L/Cpl. SD 2443; K: 8.10.16; Euston Road Cem. Somme; Age 21; Son of Mr. and Mrs.William John Jones.

K

5315. KENNEDY, Walter Louis; 2nd Lt.; K: 3.9.16; Ancre Brit. Cem. Somme; Age 19; Son of Mrs.A.Kennedy of 133, Dorchester Road, Weymouth.

5316. KEWELL, Albert John; B: West Wittering, Sussex; E: Chichester; Pte. G 14369; K: 31.7.17; Ypres (MeninGate) Mem. (Bel.); Age 18; Son of William Kewell.

5317. KEWELL, Charles Henry; B: West Wittering, Sussex; E: Bexhill-on-Sea; Cpl. SD 2207; K: 21.10.16; Thiepval Mem. Somme; Age 30; Grandson of Mrs.Hannah Kewell of 19, Gifford Road, Bosham, Sussex.

5318. KIFF, Herbert; B: Grimsby; E: Grimsby; Pte. G 15454; W: 29.1.17; Lijssenthoek Mil. Cem. (Bel.); Age 20; Son of John and Frances Kiff of 71, Rendel Street, West March, Grimsby.

5319. KILLICK, William; B: Hartfield, Sussex; E: Maidstone; Pte. G 15455; K: 17.10.16; Mill Road Cem. Somme.

5320. KING, Frederick; B: Hackney, London; E: Mill Hill, London; Pte. G 19858; K: 3.2.17; Ypres (Menin Gate) Mem. (Bel.); Age 29; Husband of Florence Simkins, formerly King, of 13, Halefield Road, Tottenham, London.

5321. KING, Thomas; B: St.James', Kent; E: Tunbridge Wells; Pte. SD 1603; K: 24.7.17; Essex Farm Cem. (Bel.); Age 27; Son of Mrs.Emma King of 3, North Farm Road, High Brooms, Kent.

5322. KINGMAN, Wesley George; B: Paulton, Somerset; E: Taunton; Pte. G 17044; K: 25.9.17; Tyne Cot Mem. (Bel.); Age 19; Son of George and Kate Kingman of 112, West Street, Bedminster, Bristol.

5323. KIRBY, William Henry; B: Wood Green, London; E: Wood Green; Pte. SD 5816; K: 24.9.17; Tyne Cot Mem. (Bel.).

5324. KIRK, Frederick; B: Walworth, London; E: London; Pte. SD 813; K: 30.6.16; Cabaret-Rouge Brit. Cem. Pas-de-Calais.

5325. KNEE, George; B: Brighton; E: Hove; L/Cpl. G 9165; K: 25.9.17; Tyne Cot Mem. (Bel.).

5326. KNIGHT, Alfred Denis; B: – ; E: Horsham, Sussex; Pte. G 16278; K: 13.11.16; Mill Road Cem. Somme.

5327. KNIGHT, John Edward; B: Shoreham, Sussex; E: Hove; Pte. G 19856; K: 3.2.17; Ypres (Menin Gate) Mem. (Bel.); Age 22; Son of Mrs.A.A.Cullum of 31, Cork Cottages, New Road, Shoreham.

L

5328. LAKER, Albert John; B: Sundridge, Kent; E: Hove; C.S.M. SD 2364; D: 28.11.16; Mendighem Mil. Cem. (Bel.); Age 27; Husband of Rose Bentley, formerly Laker, of 48, Goldstone Road, Hove.

5329. LAMBERT, George; B: Chichester; E: Chichester; Pte. SD 1387; K: 30.8.16; Thiepval Mem. Somme.

5330. LANCELEY, Reuben; B: St.George's, Middlesex; E: Brighton; Pte. G 16238; K: 20.8.17; Tyne Cot Mem. (Bel.).

5331. LANGTON, Patrick Francis; B: Teddington; E: Hove; Pte. SD 2379; K: 30.6.16; Loos Mem. Pas-de-Calais; Age 19; Son of John and Ada Langton of 6, Hove Street, Hove.

5332. LAPWOOD, Harry; B: Hatfield Peveral, Essex; E: Hammersmith; Pte. G 14977; K: 21.10.16; Thiepval Mem. Somme.

5333. LARGE, Alfred; B: Luton; E: Luton; Pte. G 14842; K: 31.7.17; Ypres (Menin Gate) Mem. (Bel.); Age 27; Son of Mrs.Susan Large of 43, Chobham Street, Luton.

5334. LARGE, George Jewson; B: – ; E: Wisbech, Cambridgeshire; Pte. G 14976; W: 8.10.16; Couin Brit. Cem. Pas-de-Calais; Age 16; Son of John Harrison Large and Ann Maria Large of Fence Bank, Walpole, Highway, Cambridgeshire.*

5335. LARKIN, Cyril; B: Horsmonden, Kent; E: Tonbridge; Pte. G 13656; K: 31.7.17; Ypres (Menin Gate) Mem. (Bel.); Age 22; Son of Samuel Frederick and Annie Larkin of Palmer's Farm, Pembury, Kent.*

5336. LARKIN, Ernest; B: Herstmonceux; E: Lewes; Pte. SD 1638; K: 2.6.17; Hop Store Cem. (Bel.); Age 26; Son of Emma Larkin of 5, Union Place, South Street, Lewes.

5337. LARKIN, William John; B: Shoreham, Sussex; E: Brighton; Pte. G 16237; K: 10.10.16; Euston Road Cem. Somme; Age 26; Son of William George and Agnes Larkin.*

5338. LAWRANCE, Maurice Theodore; B: Seaford, Sussex; E: Bexhill-on-Sea; Pte. SD 2110; K: 3.9.16; Thiepval Mem. Somme; Age 18; Son of the Rev. George William Augustus Lawrance and Catherine Elizabeth Lawrance of West Dene Rectory, Seaford; Attached to 116th Coy. Machine Gun Corps.

5339. LAWRENCE, George Thomas; B: Eastbourne; E: Eastbourne; L/Cpl. SD 1389; K: 30.6.16; Loos Mem. Pas-de-Calais; Age 33; Husband of Fanny Kate Lawrence of 145, Seaside, Eastbourne.

5340. LEA, Percy; B: Halesowen, Warwickshire; E: Worcester; Pte. G 17045; K: 14.11.17; Tyne Cot Mem. (Bel.); Age 19; Son of Mr. and Mrs.Harry Lea of 29, Blackberry Lane, Halesowen.

5341. LEANEY, John; B: Seaford, Sussex; E: Eastbourne; Pte. SD 1392; K: 3.9.16; Aveluy Wood Cem Somme; Age 26; Son of William and Ruth Leaney of Plumpton, Sussex; Husband of Mrs.N,H,Levett, formerly Leaney, of Married Quarters, The Barracks, Chichester.

5342. LE BLANCQ, Edgar Arthur; B: St.Saviour's, Jersey; E: Worthing; Pte. G 17949; K: 17.10.16; Thiepval Mem. Somme.

5343. LEE, Louis; B: Fulham, London; E: Hertford; Pte. G 17195; K: 17.10.17; Tyne Cot Mem. (Bel.).

5344. LEEKE, Sidney; B: – ; E: Cambridge; Pte. G 14974; K: 21.10.16; Thiepval Mem. Somme; Age 24; Son of John and Jane Lucas Leeke of 11, Natal Road, Mill Road, Cambridge.

5345. LEVY, Edward Herbert; B: Newhaven, Sussex; E: Brighton; Pte. G 16317; W: 17.10.16; Contay Brit. Cem. Somme; Age 25; Son of Mr. and Mrs.Levy of Brighton; Husband of Mrs.A.Levy of 87, Brading Road, Brighton.

5346. LEWIS, Horace; B: St.George's, Sussex; E: Worthing; Pte. SD 1707; W: 16.5.16; Gorre

Brit. and Indian Cem. Pas-de-Calais; Husband of Mrs.C.M.Lewis of 19, London Street, Worthing.

5347. LEWIS, Laurence Percival; B: Midhurst, Sussex; E: Chichester; Pte. G 19547; W: 3.2.17; Vlamertinghe Mil. Cem. (Bel.).

5348. LIGHT, Thomas; B: Roffey, Sussex; E: Horsham, Sussex; Pte. G 17866; W: 3.8.17; Mendinghem Mil. Cem. (Bel.); Son of Thomas and Jane Light of 132, Crawley Road, Horsham.

5349. LINDEMAN, Edward; B: Stepney, London; E: Whitehall, London; Cpl. G 20299; K: 25.9.17; Tyne Cot Mem. (Bel.).

5350. LINFIELD, William Ernest; B: Thakeham, Sussex; E: Worthing; Pte. SD 5183; K: 30.6.16; Loos Mem. Pas-de-Calais; Age 20; Son of Mrs. Harriett Linfield of 2, Spring Villas, Lyminster, Sussex.

5351. LINFORD, Alfred William; B: Potton, Bedfordshire; E: Hertford; C.S.M. G 20279 M.M.; K: 25.9.17; Tyne Cot Mem. (Bel.).

5352. LINGHAM, Albert; B: Maidstone; E: Maidstone; Pte. G 15464; K: 26.9.16; Sucrerie Mil. Cem. Somme.

5353. LITTLE, George William; B: Brighton; E: Brighton; Pte. G 4947; K: 24.9.17; Tyne Cot Mem. (Bel.)); Age 23; Son of George James and Charlotte Jane Little of 4, Wellington Street, Brighton.

5354. LOCKWOOD, William Henry Charles; B: Bagworth, Leicestershire; E: Coalville, Leicestershire; Pte. G 15086; K: 31.7.17; Ypres (Menin Gate) Mem. (Bel.); Age 24; Husband of Frances Harriett Lockwood of 8, Station Road, Bagworth.

5355. LONG, Bernard Henry Willmot; B: Brighton; E: Brighton; Pte. SD 4830; W: 23.4.17; Vlamertinghe Mil. Cem. (Bel.); Age 20; Son of Henry David and Ruth Long of Brighton.*

5356. LUCAS, Robert Henry; B: Brighton; E: Bognor Regis, Sussex; Pte. SD 1772; W: 1.7.16; Merville Com. Cem., Nord; Age 23; Son of Robert and Mary Lucas of Brighton; Husband of Lily May Lucas of Laburnum Cottage, North Bersted, Sussex.

5357. LUCAS, William Edward; B: Brighton; E: Hove; Pte. SD 2351; K: 30.6.16; Cabaret-Rouge Brit. Cem. Pas-de-Calais.

5358. LUCK, William; B; Hastings; E: Hastings; C.S.M. TF 202289; K: 14.3.17; Railway Dugouts Burial Ground (Bel.); Age 39; Husband of Annie Luck of 7, Hurrell Road, Hastings.

5359. LUPTON, Reginald Bannister; Capt.; K: 1.8.17; Duhallow A.D.S. Cem. (Bel.).

5360. LYONS, Herbert Joseph; B: Bethnal Green, London; E: St.Paul's Churchyard, London; Sgt. G 20277; K: 25.9.17; Ypres Reservoir Cem. (Bel.).

M

5361. MACE, Joe; B: Seaford, Sussex; E: Bexhill-on-Sea; Pte. SD 2112; K: 30.6.16; Loos Mem. Pas-de-Calais.

5362. MANGAN, Timothy; B: Hanley, Staffordshire; E: Stoke-on-Trent; Pte. S 2360; K: 31.7.17; Buffs Road Cem., St.Jean-les-Ypres; Husband of Mrs.H.A.Mangan of 42, Sydney Street, Hanley.

5363. MANLEY, Alfred; B: Borrowash, Derbyshire; E: Loughborough, Leicestershire; Pte. G 15091; K: 21.10.16; Thiepval Mem. Somme.

5364. MANWARING, Reginald Charles; B: Worthing; E: Worthing; Pte. SD 1711; K: 30.6.16; Loos Mem. Pas-de-Calais; Age 18; Son of Charles and Elizabeth Manwaring of 97, Broadwater Street East, Worthing.

5365. MAPLE, Frederick Charles; B: Wiston, Sussex; E: Hove; Pte. SD 1639; K: 1.9.17; Tyne Cot Mem. (Bel.); Age 27; Son of Mrs.Jane Maple of 26, Dunvegan Gardens, Eltham, London.

5366. MARSH, Ronald John; B: Eastbourne; E: Eastbourne; Pte. G 19552; W: 6.8.17; Dozinghem Mil. Cem. (Bel.).

5367. MARSHALL, John; B: Eastbourne; E: Hastings; Pte. SD 1837; K: 16.10.16; Grandcourt Road Cem. Somme; Age 20; Son of Othniel John and Mary Jane Marshall of Eastbourne.

5368. MARTIN, August William; B: St.Pancras, London; E: Piccadilly, London; Pte. G 14980; W: 11.9.16; Auchonvillers Mil. Cem. Somme; Age 26; Son of Mr.A.E.Martin of 22, Talbot Road, Bayswater, London.

5369. MARTIN, Lewis John; B: Wickham Skeith, Suffolk; E: Bury St.Edmunds, Suffolk; Pte. G 19859; K: 13.4.17; Vlamertinghe Mil. Cem. (Bel.).

5370. MARTIN, Walter; B: Forest Row, Sussex; E: Horsham, Sussex; Pte. G 17882; K: 17.10.16; Thiepval Mem. Somme.

5371. MASON, Ernest George; B: St.Paul's, Sussex; E: Brighton; Cpl. SD 1404; K: 30.6.16; Cabaret-Rouge Brit. Cem. Pas-de-Calais.

5372. MATTHEWS, Albert Aston; B: Eastbourne; E: Eastbourne; Pte. SD 1609; K: 30.6.16; St.Vaast Post Mil. Cem. Pas-de-Calais.

5373. MATTHEWS, Sydney Philip; B: Paddington, London; E: Acton, London; Pte. G 16934; W: 17.10.17; Voormezeele Enclosures No.1 and No.2, (Bel.).

5374. MAWER, John Henry; B: Coalville, Leicestershire; E: Loughborough, Leicestershire; Pte. G 15088; K: 17.10.16; Thiepval Mem. Somme.

5375. MEPHAM, Ernest Leonard; B: Hastings; E: Hastings; Pte. SD 4975; K: 30.6.16; Cabaret-Rouge Brit. Cem. Pas-de-Calais; Age 19; Son of Edwin and Sylvia Catherine Mepham of 91, St.Thomas's Road, Hastings.*

5376. MERCER, Walter George; B: Chiddingly, Sussex; E: Eastbourne; Pte. SD 1406; K: 30.6.16; Loos Mem. Pas-de-Calais.

5377. MESSAGE, George Ernest; B: – ; E: Chichester; Pte. G 16186; W: 29.10.17; Lijssenthoek Mil. Cem. (Bel.).

5378. MEWETT, Alexander George; B: Wannock, Sussex; E: Eastbourne; Pte. SD 1407; K: 30.6.16; Guards Cem. (Cuinchy) Pas-de-Calais.

5379. MILLARD, Robert Stanley; B: Littlehampton, Sussex; E: Littlehampton; Sgt. SD 1408; W: 20.11.16; Etretat Churchyard, Seine-Maritime; Age

20; Son of Robert and Jane Millard of 40, East Ham Road, Littlehampton.

5380. MILLS, Albert; B: – ; E: Horsham, Sussex; L/Cpl. G 17879; K: 31.7.17; New Irish Farm Cem. (Bel.); Age 20; Son of James and Sarah Ann Mills of Felbridge Park, Sussex.

5381. MILLS, George Arthur; B: Arundel, Sussex; E: Horsham, Sussex; L/Sgt. G 17873; K: 25.9.17; Tyne Cot Mem. (Bel.); Age 24; Son of Mrs.Matilda Mary Gilbert of 2, Queen's Lane, Arundel.

5382. MILLS, Reginald Robert; B: Eastbourne; E: Hastings; Pte. SD 2272; W: 1.7.16; St.Vaast Post Mil. Cem. Pas-de-Calais; Age 22; Son of Mr. and Mrs.Harry Ernest Mills of 26, Firle Road, Eastbourne.

5383. MINGAY, George Henry; B: Bury St.Edmunds, Suffolk; E: Bury St.Edmunds; Pte. G 19860; K: 3.2.17; Ypres (Menin Gate) Mem. Bel.); Age 31; Son of Mrs. Emma Amelia Mingay of 73, Chalk Lane, Bury St.Edmunds.

5384. MITCHELL, Charles William George; B: Brixton, London; E: Horsham, Sussex; Pte. G 16154; K: 31.7.17; Poelcapelle Brit. Cem. (Bel.).

5385. MONCUR, Cecil Alexander John Alfred; B: Bournemouth; E: Brighton; Pte. SD 2236; W: 4.7.16; Longuenesse (St.Omer) Souvenir Cem. Pas-de-Calais; Age 22; Son of Capt. Alfred Brown Moncur and Mrs.A.Moncur of 1, Hampton Terrace, Brighton; Author of "The Charge", "When the Fleet Pass By" and "The Old Brier Pipe".

5386. MOODY, Leonard Leighton; 2nd Lt.; K: 30.6.16; Loos Mem. Pas-de-Calais; Age 21; Son of Thomas and Sarah Moody of Cleeve House, Barton, Hampshire.

5387. MOON, Bertram; B: Hurstwood, Sussex; E: Hurstwood; Pte. 15789; K: 17.10.16; Connaught Cem. Somme.

5388. MORLEY, Alfred David; B: Pyecombe, Sussex; E: Brighton; Pte. SD 1412; K: 30.6.16; Cabaret-Rouge Brit. Cem. Pas-de-Calais; Age 22; Son of David and Catherine Morley of 5, Nye Road, Burgess Hill, Sussex.*

5389. MUGGRIDGE, Stanley Thomas; B: Billingshurst, Sussex; E: Horsham, Sussex; Pte. SD 1774; W: 21.4.16; Bethune Town Cem. Pas-de-Calais; Age 31; Son of Thomas and Ann Muggridge of 2, Daux Road, Billingshurst.

5390. MUNN, Stephen Henry; B: Ninfield, Sussex; E: Bexhill-on-Sea; Pte. G 15847; K: 31.7.17; New Irish Farm Cem. (Bel.); Age 34; Son of Samuel and Ann Munn of Lower Street, Ninfield; Husband of Annie Elizabeth Evernden, formerly Munn, of 2, Crommere Avenue, Bexhill-on-Sea.

N

5391. NEVELL, Charles Arthur; B: Brighton; E: Hove; Pte. SD 4869; K: 30.6.16; Loos Mem. Pas-de-Calais; Age 24; Son of Charles and Maria Amelia Nevell of 2, Shanklin Road, Brighton.

5392. NEWELL, Thomas Oliver; B: Worth, Sussex; E: Chichester; Pte. G 8224; K: 25.9.17; Tyne Cot Mem. (Bel.); Age 25; Son of George and Rosina Newell of Dyke Cottages, The Dyke, Small Dole, Sussex.

5393. NEWMAN, Alfred Frederick James; B: Eastbourne; E: Hastings; Pte. SD 2398; W: 6.9.16; Étaples Mil. Cem. Pas-de-Calais; Age 32; Husband of J.Newman of 96, Winter Road, Eastbourne; Probably died at No.6 B.R.C.S. Hospital (known as Liverpool Merchants Hospital) at Étaples Military Camp.

5394. NEWMAN, Charles; B: Billingshurst, Sussex; E: Horsham, Sussex; L/Cpl. SD 1775; K: 17.10.16; Thiepval Mem. Somme.

5395. NICHOLAS, Gerald Arthur; B: Brighton; E: Hove; C.S.M. SD 1418; K: 30.6.16; Cabaret-Rouge Brit. Cem. Pas-de-Calais; Age 25; Son of Arthur and Adelaide Mary Nicholas.

5396. NORRIS, Maurice Edwin; B: Broadwater, Sussex; E: Arundel, Sussex; Pte. G 17886; K: 3.9.16; Thiepval Mem. Somme.

O

5397. OAKLEY, Thomas; B: Weston, Hertfordshire; E: Hitchin, Hertfordshire; Pte. SD 5742; W: 22.10.16; Abbeville Com. Cem. Ext. Somme; Age 21; Son of Sarah Oakley of Damask Green, Weston.

5398. ODELL, Albert William; B: Wheathampstead, Hertfordshire; E: Hertford; Pte. G 15582; K: 23.9.17; Aeroplane Cem. (Bel.); Age 21; Son of William John and Cicely Jane Odell of "The Folly", Wheathampstead.

5399. OLDHAM, John George; B: Hinkley, Leicestershire; E: Hinkley; Pte. G 15095; W: 14.10.16; Étaples Mil. Cem. Pas-de-Calais; Age 23; Son of George and Eliza Arm Oldham of 67, Rugby Road, Hinkley; Probably died at No.6 B.R.C.S. Hospital (known as Liverpool Merchants Hospital) at Étaples Military Camp.

5400. ORAM, Albert James; B: Hove; E: Hove; Pte. G 14303; K: 31.7.17; New Irish Farm Cem. (Bel.).

5401. OSBORNE, George; B: – ; E: Chichester; Pte. G 17887; K: 22.10.17; Tyne Cot Mem. (Bel.).

5402. OXLADE, George; B: West Wycombe, Buckinghamshire; E: High Wycombe; Pte. G 17061; K: 9.1.18; New Irish Farm Cem. (Bel.).*

P

5403. PACKHAM, Benjamin; B: Burgess Hill, Sussex; E: Burgess Hill; Pte. G 16157; K: 17.10.16; Thiepval Mem. Somme; Age 26; Son of Reuben Packham of Brewery House, London Road, Burgess Hill; Husband of Beatrice Annie Saunders, formerly Packham, of 5, St.George's Terrace, Burgess Hill.

5404. PAINE, Charles James; B: Eridge, Sussex; E: Tunbridge Wells; Pte. G 19518; K: 31.7.17; Buffs Road Cem. St.Jean-les-Ypres, (Bel.); Husband of Mrs.L.Paine of 4, Louth Street, Rotherfield, Sussex.

5405. PALMER, Charles Henry; B: Halton, Sussex; E: Hastings; Pte. SD 1857; K: 30.6.16; Loos Mem. Pas-de-Calais.

5406. PANNELL, William; B: Lodworth, Sussex; E: Worthing; Pte. SD 5108; K: 30.6.16; Loos Mem. Pas-de-Calais.

5407. PARKER, Arthur Ernest; B: Pulborough, Sussex; E: Petworth, Sussex; Pte. SD 2282; W: 13.2.17; Wimereux Com. Cem. Pas-de-Calais; Age 29; Son of Charlotte Parker of Pulborough.

5408. PARKER, Arthur William; B: Hackney, London; E: Holloway, London; Pte. G 14990; K: 11.9.16; Auchonvillers Mil. Cem. Somme;Son of Charles Amos Parker of 96, Wilberforce Road, Finsbury Park, London.

5409. PARKER, Henry Charles; B: Shoreham, Sussex; E: Petworth, Sussex; Pte. G 16307; K: 8.10.16; Auchonvillers Mil. Cem. Somme; Age 24; Son of George and Matilda Parker of Byworth, Sussex; Husband of Annie Hilda Parker of 2, Riverside, Pixham, Surrey.*

5410. PARNELL, Bertram Eric; B: Bromley, London; E: Brighton; Pte. G 12644; K: 12.10.16; Euston Road Cem. Somme.

5411. PARSONS, David; B: Hailsham, Sussex; E: Eastbourne; Pte. SD 1427; K: 30.6.16; Loos Mem. Pas-de-Calais.

5412. PARSONS, Ernest; B: – ; E: Haywards Heath, Sussex; Pte. G 16159; K: 3.2.17; Vlamertinghe Mil. Cem. (Bel.).

5413. PATTENDEN, Herbert; B: Eastbourne; E: Eastbourne; Sgt. SD 1429; W: 6.7.16; Longuenesse (St.Omer) Souvenir Cem. Pas-de-Calais; Age 23; Son of Thomas and Mary Pattenden of 52, Longstone Road, Eastbourne; Enlisted with brother, William George, who also fell while serving with the Battalion (see 5414).

5414. PATTENDEN, William George; B: Eastbourne; E: Bexhill-on-Sea; Pte. SD 1430; W: 9.6.16; Bethune Town Cem. Pas-de-Calais; Age 19; Son of George and Ann Pattenden of 19, Station Road, Hampden Park, Eastbourne; Enlisted with brother, Herbert, who also fell while serving with the Battalion (see 5413).*

5415. PEARCE, Sidney George; B: Sevenoaks, Kent; E: Maidstone; Pte. G 11685; K: 25.9.17; Hooge Crater Cem. (Bel.).

5416. PELLING, William Wickens; B: Brightling, Sussex; E: Hastings; Pte. SD 2248; K: 30.6.16; Loos Mem. Pas-de-Calais.

5417. PEREGOE, Herbert; B: Hastings; E: Hastings; Pte. SD 1846; K: 30.6.16; Cabaret-Rouge Brit. Cem. Pas-de-Calais.

5418. PHILLIPS, Louis Reginald; B: Grimsby; E: Grimsby; Pte. TF 266567; K: 21.1.18; Tyne Cot Mem. (Bel.).

5419. PHIPPS, Edwin Benjamin; B: Iden, Sussex; E: Hastings; Pte. SD 1434; W: 3.7.16; Longuenesse (St.Omer) Souvenir Cem. Pas-de-Calais; Age 18; Son of Benjamin and Annie L.Phipps of Bowlers Town, Playden, Sussex.*

5420. PHYPERS, William Anthony; B: Cambridge; E: Eastbourne; Sgt. SD 2057; W: 17.7.16; St.Venant Com. Cem. Pas-de-Calais; Age 31; Son of William and Mary Phypers of Cambridge; Husband of Audrey Phypers.

5421. PIPER, George; B: – ; E: East Grinstead, Sussex; Pte. G 1/891; K: 25.9.17; Tyne Cot Mem. (Bel.); Age 20; Son of William and Ellen Mary Piper of Hoskins Cottage, East Grinstead.

5422. PITCHER, George Henry; B: Eastbourne; E: Eastbourne; Pte. SD 1435; W: 20.6.16; Merville Com. Cem., Nord; Brother of John A.E.Pitcher of 95, Bourne Street, Eastbourne.

5423. PLANK, Charles Edgar; B: Putney, London; E: Worthing; Sgt. G 20308; K: 20.9.17; Tyne Cot Mem. (Bel.); Age 28; Son of William Charles and Eliza Ann Plank of 42, Hazelwell Road, Putney.

5424. PLUMMER, Ernest William; B: Ringmer, Sussex; E: Lewes; L/Cpl. SD 1643; W: 3.9.16; Couin Brit. Cem. Pas-de-Calais; Husband of Mrs.J.Blackman, formerly Plummer, of 6 Row, South Street, Chailey, Sussex.

5425. POINEY, Herbert Frederick; B: Brighton; E: Hove; Pte. SD 2269; K: 28.4.16; Guards Cem. (Cuinchy) Pas-de-Calais.

5426. POPE, Ernest George; B: Dunton, Bedfordshire; E: Bedford; Pte. G 15795; K: 8.10.16; Auchonvillers Mil. Cem. Somme; Age 20; Son of Walter Francis and Sarah Pope of Dunton.*

5427. PRATT, George Henry; B: Paddington, London; E: Ipswich, Suffolk; Pte. G 19864; K: 25.9.17; Tyne Cot Mem. (Bel.).

5428. PUMPHREY, Walter Nathaniel; B: Brighton; E: Hove; Pte. SD 2212; K: 30.6.16; St.Vaast Post Mil. Cem. Pas-de-Calais; Age 19; Son of William Thomas and Ellen Bertha Pumphrey of 3, Wakfield Road, Brighton.

R

5429. RABSON, Charles; B: Wadhurst, Sussex; E: Hastings; Pte. SD 3671; W: 2.7.16; Merville Com. Cem., Nord.

5430. RAE, Colin; B: Cambridge; E: Mill Hill ; Pte. G 20304; K: 25.9.17; Tyne Cot Mem. (Bel.); Age 39; Son of James and Mary Ann Rae.

5431. RANDELL, Albert Victor; B: Brighton; E: Hove; L/Cpl. SD 1778; K: 30.6.16; Cabaret-Rouge Brit. Cem. Pas-de-Calais; Age 24; Husband of Mrs.H.White, formerly Randell, of 12, Glynde Road, Brighton.

5432. RAWLINGS, Tom; B: Harby, Leicestershire; E: Melton Mowbray, Leicestershire; L/Cpl. SD 1722; K: 17.10.16; Thiepval Mem. Somme; Age 32; Son of William and Phoebe Rawlings of Sandy Lane, Harby.

5433. RAY, Frederick William; B: Brighton; E: Bexhill-on-Sea; Pte. SD 1443; K: 30.6.16; Loos Mem. Pas-de-Calais.

5434. READING, George; B: St.Martin's, Sussex; E: Lewes; Sgt. S 222; K: 3.2.17; Ypres (Menin Gate) Mem. (Bel.).

5435. READING, John Henry; B: Westminster, London;

E: Kingston-on-Thames; Cpl. G 20310; K: 23.9.17; Tyne Cot Mem. (Bel.); Age 26; Son of Thomas and S.E.J.Reading of 99, Florence Road, Wimbledon, London.

5436. REED, Albert; B: Bishops Stortford, Hertfordshire; E: Bishops Stortford; Pte. G 15604; K: 28.7.17; Ypres (Menin Gate) Mem. (Bel.).

5437. REED, Arthur Frederick; B: Bethnal Green, London; E: Brighton; Sgt. G 16200; K: 25.9.17; Tyne Cot Mem. (Bel.); Age 27; Son of Mrs.E.S.Reed of 12, Hollybush Place, Bethnal Green Road, London.

5438. REED, Nelson John; B: Eastbourne; E: Bexhill-on-Sea; Pte. SD 1906; K: 30.6.16; Loos Mem. Pas-de-Calais; Age 19; Son of John Thomas and Emily Mary Reed of 10, Eshton Road, Eastbourne.

5439. REED, William; B: Fletching, Sussex; E: Hove; Pte. SD 4938; W: 1.7.16; Merville Com. Cem., Nord; Age 29; Son of James and Julia Reed of Fletching; Husband of Alice Annie Reed of Bank Passage, Steyning, Sussex.

5440. REEVES, Albert Bert; B: Brighton; E: Brighton; Pte. SD 2386; W: 3.7.16; Longuenesse (St.Omer) Souvenir Cem. Pas-de-Calais.

5441. REEVES, Ernest; B: Wadhurst, Sussex; E: Hastings; Pte. SD 5059; K: 27.4.16; Guards Cem. (Cuinchy) Pas-de-Calais.

5442. RICHARDS, Frank; B: Eastbourne; E: Eastbourne; Pte. SD 1614; K: 30.6.16; Loos Mem. Pas-de-Calais; Age 20; Son of Mrs.Betsy Richards of 27, Watts Lane, Eastbourne.

5443. RICHFORD, Arthur Edgar; B: Hastings; E: Hastings; Cpl. SD 2210; K: 5.6.16; Cambrin Churchyard Ext. Pas-de-Calais.

5444. RICHFORD, Frederick George; B: St.Lawrence, Kent; E: Hastings; Pte. SD 1858; K: 30.6.16; Loos Mem. Pas-de-Calais.

5445. RIPLEY, Joseph; B: Hastings; E; Hastings; Pte. SD 1547; M.M.; W: 4.11.16; Contay Brit. Cem. Somme.

5446. ROBINS, Alfred; B: Radwinter, Essex; E: Saffron Walden, Essex; Pte. G 16840; K: 9.2.18; Gouzeaucourt New Brit. Cem., Nord; Age 23; Son of Harry and Harriett Robins of Potah Farm, Radwinter.

5447. ROPER, Arthur William; B: Worthing; E: Littlehampton; Pte. SD 4969; W: 18.3.16; Sailly-sur-la Lys Canadian Cem. Pas-de-Calais; Age 19; Son of Florence Annie Gates of Church Farm Cottage, Rustington, Sussex.

5448. RUFF; Ralph Samuel; Brighton; E: Brighton; Pte. G 16198; W: 18.10.16; Varennes Mil. Cem. Somme; Age 23; Son of Rolf and Lizzie Ruff of Henfield, Sussex.

5449. RUMBELOW, Frederick Francis; B: Lambeth, London; E: Worthing; Cpl. SD 4937; W: 11.9.16; Étaples Mil. Cem. Pas-de-Calais; Age 24; Son of John Quantick Rumbelow and Emily Rumbelow of 17, West Street, Worthing.

5450. RUSSELL, Frederick; B: Islington, London; E: Bexhill-on-Sea; Pte. SD 1546; K: 30.6.16; Loos Mem. Pas-de-Calais.

S

5451. SALBERG, John Beaumont; 2nd Lt.; D: 30.6.16; Age 21; Cabaret-Rouge Brit. Cem. Pas-de-Calais; Son of Salis Ernest and Fanny Salberg of Lee, Kent.*

5452. SAUNDERS, Charles; B: Midhurst, Sussex; E: Worthing; Pte. G 14370; K: 31.7.17; New Irish Farm Cem. (Bel.); Son of George and Alice Saunders of Water Lane, Albury, Surrey.

5453. SAUNDERS, William James; B: Hastings; E: Eastbourne; Cpl. SD 2246; K: 30.6.16; Loos Mem. Pas-de-Calais.

5454. SAVAGE, Walter William; B: Walkern, Hertfordshire; E: Hertford; Pte. G 15595; K: 17.10.16; Gommecourt Brit. Cem. No.2., Pas-de-Calais.

5455. SAVILLE, George Sheriff; B: Balham, London; E: Worthing; Pte. SD 1454; K: 30.6.16; Cabaret-Rouge Brit. Cem. Pas-de-Calais; Age 20; Son of Sheriff and Elizabeth J.Saville of 57, Malvern Road, Surbiton, Surrey.*

5456. SAWYER, Frank Walter; B: Brighton; E: Petworth, Sussex; Pte. G 16322; K: 17.10.16; Connaught Cem. Somme; Age 23; Son of William Walter and Jane Frances Saker Sawyer of 16, Fairfield Street, Wandsworth, London.*

5457. SCOTT, Edwin; B: Horsham, Sussex; E: Chichester; L/Cpl. G 16172; K: 31.7.17; New Irish Farm Cem. (Bel.); Age 25; Son of Harry and Sarah Scott of 19, New Street, Horsham.

5458. SCOTT, Ernest James; B: Regent's Park, London; E: Hastings; Sgt. SD 1910; W: 11.7.16; Longuenesse (St.Omer) Souvenir Cem. Pas-de-Calais.

5459. SEARLE, Frederick W.; B: Clavering, Essex; E: Hertford; Pte. G 15588; K: 21.10.16; Connaught Cem. Somme.*

5460. SEARLE, John; B: Clapham, London; E: Worthing; Pte. SD 2389; K: 30.6.16; Loos Mem. Pas-de-Calais.

5461. SELSBY, Alfred; B: –; E: Haywards Heath, Sussex; Pte. G 16166; K: 21.10.16; Serre Road Cem. No.2., Somme; Age 31; Husband of Mary A.Selsby of 105, Church Road, Burgess Hill, Sussex.

5462. SETTATREE, Isaac; B: Westwell, Kent; E: Hastings; Pte. SD 2410; W: 21.5.16; Bethune Town Cem. Pas-de-Calais; Age 23; Son of George and Margaret Settatree of 88, Canterbury Road, South Willesborough, Kent.

5463. SEXTON, Frederick William; B: Bayswater, London; E: Hastings; Pte. SD 5132; K: 30.6.16; Loos Mem. Pas-de-Calais.

5464. SHELTON, Cecil; B: Upper Broughton, Leicestershire; E: Melton Mowbray, Leicestershire; Sgt. SD 1649; K: 31.7.17; Buffs Road Cem. St.Jean-les-Ypres (Bel.); Age 24; Son of Robert and Sarah Shelton.

5465. SHEPPARD, Frederick William; 2nd Lt.; K: 12.6.17; Poelcapelle Brit. Cem. (Bel.).

5466. SHORE, George; B: Linton, Cambridgeshire; E: Hastings; Pte. SD 3022; W: 2.7.16; Merville Com. Cem., Nord; Age 24; Son of Walter and Annie Shaw of Six Mile Bottom, Cambridgeshire; Ambushed while visiting an advanced listening post; could not be found by a search party so, at the time, he was wrongly assumed to have been taken prisoner.

5467. SHRIVELL, George Clarence; B: Brighton; E: Croydon; Pte. G 5290; K: 31.7.17; Buffs Road Cem. St.Jean-les-Ypres (Bel.).

5468. SIMMONS, Herbert Arthur; B: London; E: Hove; Pte. SD 1457; K: 30.6.16; St.Vaast Post Mil. Cem. Pas-de-Calais; Age 18; Son of Mr.H.A. and Mrs.M.Simmons.

5469. SIMPSON, Henry Arthur; B: – ; E: Louth, Lincolnshire; Pte. G 15309; K: 21.1.18; Tyne Cot Mem. (Bel.); Age 29; Son of Robert and Maria Simpson.

5470. SIPPETS, Albert James; B: – ; E: East Grinstead, Sussex; Pte. G 16332; K: 21.10.16; Thiepval Mem. Somme; Age 21; Son of Frank and Annie Sippets of 27, Freshfield Street, Brighton; Husband of Bertha Ann Jones, formerly Sippets, of St.Lina, Alberta, Canada.

5471. SKATES, Harry; B: Hammersmith, London; E: East Grinstead, Sussex; Pte. G 19629; K: 25.9.17; Zantvoorde Brit. Cem. (Bel.).

5472. SLATER, George Ernest; B: Burgess Hill, Sussex; E: Brighton; Pte. SD 4853; K: 30.6.16; Cabaret-Rouge Brit. Cem. Pas-de-Calais.*

5473. SLOMAN, Herbert; B: Sydney, Australia; E: Brighton; Pte. G 16249; K: 12.10.16; Euston Road Cem. Somme; Age 26; Son of John and Mrs.A.L.Sloman of 22, St.Mary's Road, Canonbury, London.

5474. SMART, Charles Reginald; B: Shoreham, Sussex; E: Hove; Pte. SD 2018; K: 30.6.16; Loos Mem. Pas-de-Calais.

5475. SMART, Henry Walter; B: Pycombe, Sussex; E: Horsham, Sussex; L/Cpl. G 17910; K: 25.9.17; Tyne Cot Mem. (Bel.); Age 25; Son of Mrs.Ellen Smart of 5, Lodge Road, Keymer, Sussex.

5476. SMITH, Albert Edward; B: Peasmarsh, Sussex; E: Hastings; Pte. SD 1847; K: 2.3.17; Maple Copse Cem. (Bel.); Son of Jeremiah Smith of Winton's Cottage, Peasmarsh.

5477. SMITH, Albert; B: Freemantle, Hampshire; E: Bexhill-on-Sea; Pte. G 1549; K: 25.9.17; Zantvoorde Brit. Cem. (Bel.).

5478. SMITH, Frank Percy; B: Great Yarmouth; E: Great Yarmouth; Pte. G 9283; K: 25.9.17; Tyne Cot Mem. (Bel.).

5479. SMITH, Frederick William; B: Wandsworth, London; E: Tooting, London; Pte. G 19873; K: 20.9.17; Tyne Cot Mem. (Bel.).

5480. SMITH, George; B: Eastbourne; E: Eastbourne; Pte. G 8659; K: 31.7.17; Buffs Road Cem. St.Jean-les-Ypres (Bel.); Son of Mrs.R.V.Smith of 36, Leslie Street, Eastbourne.

5481. SMITH, Harry; B: Ipswich, Suffolk; E: Brighton; L/Cpl. G 5023; W: 2.8.17; Dozinghem Mil. Cem. (Bel.).

5482. SMITH, James Vernon; B: Storrington, Sussex; E: Hove; Pte. G 16311; K: 17.10.16; Connaught Cem. Somme; Age 24; Husband of Mary Matilda Smith of 31, Chapel Road, Fishergate, Sussex.

5483. SMITH, Jeremiah; B: Peasmarsh, Sussex; E: Hastings; Pte. SD 1550; W: 13.7.16; Wimereux Com. Cem. Pas-de-Calais; Age 27; Son of Jeremiah and Caroline Smith of Peasmarsh.

5484. SMITH, W.; B: – ; E: – ; Pte. SD 2284; K: 3.9.16; Hamel Mil. Cem. Somme

5485. SMITH, Walter; B: Framfield, Sussex; E: Uckfield, Sussex; Pte. SD 473; K: 25.5.16; Guards Cem. (Cuinchy) Pas-de-Calais; Age 33; Son of Walter Smith of High Cross Cottage, Little Horsted, Sussex.

5486. SMITH, William Frederick; B: Westminster, London; E: Bexhill-on-Sea; Pte. SD 1203; K: 2.7.16; Merville Com. Cem., Nord; Age 36; Husband of Beatrice Alice Smith of 111, Tachbrook Street, Westminster.

5487. SMITH, William Hiram; B: Brede, Sussex; E: Hastings; Pte. SD 1911; W at Home: 27.9.16; Hastings Cem., Sussex (UK); Age 31.*

5488. SMITH-HOWARD, Kenneth Overend Howard; 2nd Lt.; K: 18.10.16; Thiepval Mem. Somme; Age 23; Son of G. and Laura Smith-Howard of 33, Macaulay Road, Clapham Common, London.*

5489. SOUTHON, William George; B: Rotherfield, Sussex; E: Eastbourne; Pte. SD 3689; K: 20.9.17; Tyne Cot Mem. (Bel.); Age 28; Son of Mrs.Warnett; Husband of Elice Southon.

5490. SPARKS, Clive; Lt.; K: 30.6.16 at Richebourg-St. Vaast; Cabaret-Rouge Brit. Cem. Pas-de-Calais; Age 25; Son of Arthur and Rose Sparks of 16, Great Dover Street, Southwark, London.*

5491. SPRANGE, Alfred; B: Eastbourne; E: Bexhill-on-Sea; Pte. SD 1551; W: 4.7.16; Boulogne Eastern Cem. Pas-de-Calais; Age 32; Husband of Eva Sprange of 5, Neville Road, Eastbourne.

5492. STACE, William Alfred; B: Hastings; E: Hastings; Pte. SD 2122; K: 30.6.16; Loos Mem. Pas-de-Calais.

5493. STRANGEMORE, Frederick Joseph; B: Newhaven, Sussex; E: Eastbourne; Pte. SD 1944; K: 30.6.16; Loos Mem. Pas-de-Calais.

5494. STAPLEHURST, Herbert Jenner; B: Seaford, Sussex; E: Eastbourne; Pte. SD 1467; K: 30.6.16; Loos Mem. Pas-de-Calais; Age 21; Son of James and Susan Staplehurst of 2, St.James Terrace, Polegate, Sussex.

5495. STEEL, Cecil James; B: Parkstone, Dorset; E: Eastbourne; Pte. G 16104; W: 20.10.16; Lonsdale Cem. Somme.

5496. STEELS, Albert; B: Peterborough; E: Peterborough; L/Cpl. G 17172; K: 27.9.17; Hooge Crater Cem. (Bel.).

5497. STEERE, Jesse; B: Billingshurst, Sussex; E: Horsham, Sussex; Pte. SD 2029; K: 17.5.16; Le Touret Mil. Cem. Pas-de-Calais.

5498. STEVENSON, John; B: Nutley, Sussex; E: Horsham, Sussex; Pte. G 16170; K: 31.7.17; Ypres (Menin Gate) Mem. (Bel.); Age 24; Son of John and Addie Stevenson of 1, East Street, Crowborough, Sussex.

5499. STONE, Walter Henry; B: West Kensington, London; E: St.Paul's Churchyard, London; Pte. SD 2169; K: 3.9.16; Thiepval Mem. Somme; Age 28; Son of Charles Louis and Selina Stone of 32, Stafford Road, Brighton; Husband of Ada Stone of 10, Oxford Place, Plymouth.

5500. STONE, William George; B: Little Common, Sussex; E: Bexhill-on-Sea; Pte. SD 1471; K: 3.9.16; Hamel Mil. Cem. Somme.

5501. STOVOLD, Alan George; B: – ; E: Haywards Heath, Sussex; Pte. TF 2761; W: 7.8.16; Choques Mil. Cem., Pas-de-Calais; Age 19; Son of Thomas and Jane Stovold of The Old Vicarage, North Street, Midhurst, Sussex; Died at No.1 Casualty Clearing Station, Choques.

5502. SUMNER, John George; B: Three Bridges, Sussex; E: Crawley, Sussex; L/Sgt. SD 1859; W: 30.6.16; Cabaret-Rouge Brit. Cem. Pas-de-Calais; Age 19; Son of Ellen Bramwell, formerly Sumner, of "Glen View", Dunscar, Lancashire and the late John Sumner.

5503. SYMINTON, George Charles; 2nd Lt.; W: 1.8.17; Dozinghem Mil. Cem. (Bel.); Age 19; Son of Maud Syminton of Valparaiso, Chile and London, and the late Thomas Syminton of Kirkcudbright, Scotland.*

T

5504. TADD, Frederick Harry; B: Selsey, Sussex; E: Chichester; Pte. SD 1474; W: 4.9.16; Gezaincourt Com. Cem. Ext. Somme; Age 29; Son of Stephen and Eliza Tadd of "Fern Cliff", Manor Road, Selsey.*

5505. TATE, Tom Campbell; 2nd Lt.; W: 2.9.16; Couin Brit. Cem. Pas-de-Calais; Age 23; Son of William Tate of 47, Salisbury Road, Southsea, Hampshire.

5506. TAYLERSON, Ronald; B: Hastings; E: Eastbourne; Pte. G 19919; K: 11.6.16; Essex Farm Cem. (Bel.); Age 19; Son of George and Alice Taylerson of 29, Tideswell Road, Eastbourne.*

5507. TAYLOR, Albert; B: East Ham, London; E: Brighton; L/Cpl. G 16201; K: 13.11.16 during the Battle of the Ancre; Authuile Mil. Cem. Somme; Age 17; Son of Ada Mary Schneider and the late James Joseph Taylor of East Ham.

5508. TAYLOR, Patrick Joseph; B: Drumlion, Co. Leitrim, Ireland; E: Brighton; Pte. G 16254; K: 13.11.16; Thiepval Mem. Somme; Age 19; Son of William and Eleanor Taylor of Drumod, Co. Leitrim.

5509. TEALE, Walter William; B: Tunbridge Wells; E: Brighton; Pte. G 16252; K: 12.10.16; Euston Road Cem. Somme; Age 30; Son of Mr. and Mrs.F.W.Teale of 66, Upper Grosvenor Road, Tunbrdige Wells.

5510. TESTER, Arthur; B: Hurstpierpoint, Sussex; E: Crawley, Sussex; Pte. SD 2125; K: 3.9.16; Thiepval Mem. Somme; Age 19; Son of Thomas and Elizabeth Tester.

5511. TESTER, William; B: Forest Row, Sussex; E: East Grinstead, Sussex; Pte. G 4534; K: 24.9.17; Tyne Cot Mem. (Bel.).

5512. THOMAS, John; B: Hastings; E: Hastings; Pte. SD 2601; K: 3.9.16; Hamel Mil. Cem. Somme; Age 22; Son of Mr. and Mrs.Z.Thomas of Hastings; Husband of Ellen Louisa Buchanan, formerly Thomas, of Cross Creek, York County, New Brunswick, Canada.*

5513. THORNCROFT, Frank; B: Tunbridge Wells; E: Eastbourne; Pte. SD 1478; K: 3.6.16; Cambrin Churchyard Ext. Pas-de-Calais; Age 22; Son of Frank and Carrie Thorncroft of 57, Elm Grove, Brighton.

5514. TIDY, Thomas; B: Chichester; E: Worthing; Pte. G 16297; K: 3.2.17; Vlamertinghe Mil. Cem. (Bel.).

5515. TIER, Harry; B: Worthing; E: Worthing; L/Cpl. SD 1734; W: 21.3.16; Sailly-sur-la-Lys Canadian Cem. Pas-de-Calais; Age 24; Son of Harry and Matilda Tier of 26, Stanley Road, Worthing.

5516. TINGLEY, Arthur; B: Eastbourne; E: Bexhill-on-Sea; Pte. SD 1912; K: 30.6.16; Loos Mem. Pas-de-Calais.

5517. TITCHENER, Harold; B: Hastings; E: Hastings; L/Cpl. SD 1913; W: at Home 9.3.16; Hollington (St. Leonards) Churchyard, Sussex (UK); Age 19; Son of Frederick and Harriett Titchener of 4, Wilting Cottages, Hollington.

5518. TOWNSEND, Ernest Victor; B: Camberwell, London; E: Brighton; Pte. G 19662; K: 20.9.17; Tyne Cot Mem. (Bel.); Age 22; Son of William Henry and Florence Ellen Townsend of 30, Coleridge Street, Hove.

5519. TOYNBEE, Charles Robert; B: Brighton; E: Brighton; Pte. G 16177; K: 17.10.16; Gommecourt Brit. Cem. No.2., Pas-de-Calais

5520. TRIBE, Albert Frederick; B: Tooting, London; E: Wimbledon, London; Pte. G 14489; K: 25.9.17; Tyne Cot Mem. (Bel.).

5521. TRITTON, Joseph Francis; B: Bermondsey, London; E: Wood Green, London; Pte. SD 5856; K: 19.10.16; Thiepval Mem. Somme.

5522. TUGWELL, William George; B: Willingdon, Sussex; E: Bexhill-on-Sea; Pte. SD 1481; K: 30.6.16; St.Vaast Post Mil. Cem. Pas-de-Calais; Age 18; Son of William and Eliza Tugwell of 7, Brodrick Road, Hampden Park, Eastbourne. *

5523. TUPPEN, James; B: Eastbourne; E: Eastbourne; Pte. SD 1569; K: 30.6.16; Loos Mem. Pas-de-Calais; Age 21; Son of George Albert Tuppen of 13, Dudley Road, Eastbourne.*

5524. TURNER, Charles Norton; B: Eastbourne; E: Eastbourne; Pte. SD 1620; W: 2.7.16; Étaples Mil. Cem. Pas-de-Calais; Age 20; Son of Charles and Kate Turner of 120, Hurst Road, Eastbourne.

5525. TURNER, Francis; B: Ashburnham, Sussex; E: Hastings; Pte. SD 2362; K: 30.6.16; Loos Mem. Pas-de-Calais; Age 37; Brother of Mrs.Mercy Parrott of Bray's Hill, Ashburnham.

5526. TURNER, Richard Radford; 2nd Lt.; K: 3.2.17; Vlamertinghe Mil. Cem. (Bel.); Age 20; Son of Rev. Richard Turner, former Vicar of Barnstable, and Mrs,L.Turner of 2, St.Germans, Exeter.

5527. TUTTIET, Laurence William; Capt.; K: 2.9.16; Thiepval Mem. Somme; Age 26; Son of Laurence Rayner Tuttiet; Husband of Frances Alice Tuttiet of 89, The Avenue, West Ealing, London.*

U

5528. UPPLEBY, Wyvill Charles Spinola; Capt.; W: 9.2.18; Croix-du-Bac Brit. Cem., Steenwerk, Nord; Age 35; Son of Colonel J.G. and Louise Uppleby of Liverpool.

V

5529. VAIL, Frederick George; B: Rodford, Essex; E: Hertford; Pte. G 15598; K: 25.9.17; Ypres Reservoir Cem. (Bel.).

5530. VENESS, Edgar; B: Tunbridge Wells; E: Brighton; L/Cpl. L 10381; K: 18.10.17; Tyne Cot Mem. (Bel.); Age 25; Son of William and Ellen Veness of Pound Street, Petworth, Sussex.

5531. VENIS, Edwin; B: Southwark, London; E: Brighton; Pte. G 16255; W: 18.11.16; Boulogne Eastern Cem. Pas-de-Calais; Age 19; Son of James and Ann E.Venis of 27, West Buildings, Worthing.

5532. VERRALL, Thomas William; B: Eastbourne; E: Eastbourne; Pte. G 14345; K: 31.7.17; Ypres (Menin Gate) Mem. (Bel.); Age 26; Son of George Verrall of 4, St.Leonard's Place, Eastbourne.

5533. VINE, Albert John; B: Eastbourne; E: Eastbourne; Pte. SD 1822; K: 12.7.16; Loos Mem. Pas-de-Calais.

5534. VIRGO, Arthur Edgar; B: Portslade, Sussex; E: Eastbourne; Pte. SD 1623; K: 30.6.16; Loos Mem. Pas-de-Calais.

W

5535. WAGSTAFF, Frederick George; B: Eastbourne; E: Eastbourne; Pte. SD 1486; W: 15.5.16; Bethune Town Cem. Pas-de-Calais; Age 26; Son of Emily Wagstaff of 2, Artillery Cottages, Eastbourne.*

5536. WAKEFORD, William; B: Petworth, Sussex; E: Horsham, Sussex; L/Cpl. G 18297; K: 25.9.17; Hooge Crater Cem. (Bel.).

5537. WALKER, Sidney H.; B: Brighton; E: Hove; Pte. SD 1487; K: 30.6.16; Cabaret-Rouge Brit. Cem. Pas-de-Calais.*

5538. WALKER, William Randolph; B: Hastings; E: Hastings; Pte. SD 3040; K: 30.6.16; Cabaret-Rouge Brit. Cem. Pas-de-Calais; Age 31; Son of James and Jane Walker of Hastings.*

5539. WALLER, Frank; B: Walthamstow, London; E: Brighton; Pte. G 16257; K: 13.11.16; Mill Road Cem. Somme; Age 20; Son of Mrs.E.Waller of 188, Queen's Road, Walthamstow.

5540. WALLS, George Edward; B: Lewisham, London; E: Bexhill-on-Sea; Pte. SD 2199; W: 30.6.16; Cabaret-Rouge Brit. Cem. Pas-de-Calais; Age 39; Son of Frederick John and Maria Elizabeth Walls.

5541. WALTON, George Alfred; B: Brighton; E: Brighton; Pte. G 16263; K: 28.9.17; Tyne Cot Mem. (Bel.).*

5542. WARD, Joseph Richard; B: Ellistown, Leicestershire; E: Coalville, Leicestershire; Pte. G 15098; K: 13.11.16; Authuile Mil. Cem. Somme.

5543. WATSON, Ernest; B: Catsfield, Sussex; E: Hastings; Pte. G 16333; K: 16.10.16; Thiepval Mem. Somme.*

5544. WATTS, Charles; B: Frant, Sussex; E: Hastings; Pte. SD 1496; K: 30.6.16; Loos Mem. Pas-de-Calais; Age 27; Son of Frederick and Emma Watts of Thatched Cottages, Bells Yew Green, Kent.

5545. WEBB, Thomas; B: Chichester; E: Horsham; Pte. G 17919; K: 3.9.16; Thiepval Mem. Somme.

5546. WELLER, Henry; B: Forest Row, Sussex; E: East Grinstead, Sussex; Pte. SD 2425; K: 25.9.17; Tyne Cot Mem. (Bel.); Age 28; Husband of Bertha Kate A.Weller of 6, West Street, East Grinstead.

5547. WENTWORTH, Cyril John; 2nd Lt.; W: 3.2.17; Lijssenthoek Mil. Cem. (Bel.).

5548. WEST, John Thomas; B: Barwell, Leicestershire; E: Hinkley, Leicestershire; Pte.G 15100; K: 21.9.16; Sucrerie Mil. Cem. Somme; Age 22; Husband of Lillian E.West of 5, Ten Foot, Factory Road, Hinkley.

5549. WESTGATE, Frederick; B: East Grinstead, Sussex; E: East Grinstead; Pte. G 16183; W: 26.11.16; St.Sever Cem. Ext., Rouen, Seine-Maritime; Age 21; Son of Mrs.E.M.Westgate of 24, Stockwell Road, East Grinstead.

5550. WHITE, Bertie; B: Briston, Norfolk; E: Cromer, Norfolk; Pte. G 17208; K: 25.9.17; Tyne Cot Cem. (Bel.).

5551. WHITE, Walter; B: Cobham, Surrey; E: Guildford; Pte. G 20352; W: 24.12.16; Mendinghem Mil. Cem. (Bel.); Age 21; Son of William and Eliza White of 3, Arch Cottages, Lower Tilt, Surrey.

5552. WHITING, Albert Henry; B: Falmer, Sussex; E: Steyning, Sussex; Pte. G 17927; K: 3.9.16; Aveluy Wood Cem. Somme.

5553. WICKENS, Walter John; B: Tunbridge Wells; E: Hastings; Pte. SD 5204; K: 30.6.16; St.Vaast Post Mil. Cem. Pas-de-Calais; Age 19; Son of Walter and Harriett Wickens of 15, Gladstone Terrace, Hastings.

5554. WICKENS, William Ernest; B: Putney, London; E: Kingston-on-Thames; Pte. G 20579; K: 24.7.17; Essex Farm Cem. (Bel.).*

5555. WICKER, Raymond; B: Mayfield, Sussex; E: Eastbourne; Pte. SD 5829; K: 14.3.17; Railway Dugouts Burial Ground (Bel.).

5556. WIDGERY, William; B: Chelsea; E: Cockspur Street, London; Pte. SD 2004; K: 20.4.16; Guards Cem. (Cuinchy) Pas-de-Calais.

5557. WILKINS, William Henry; B: Brighton; E: Brighton; Pte. G 17923; K: 26.9.17; Tyne Cot Mem. (Bel.); Age 39; Husband of Grace Smaysland, formerly Wilkins, of 4, Portland Street, Brighton.

5558. WILLIAMS, Henry; B: Brighton; E: East Grinstead, Sussex; Pte. G 2442; K: 30.6.16; Loos Mem. Pas-de-Calais; Age 21; Son of Owen and Florence Williams of Brighton.

5559. WILMOT, Paul Dominie; Lt.; K: 25.3.18; Pozieres Mem. Somme.

5560. WILSON, Alfred; B: Mitcham, Surrey; E: Mitcham; Pte. G 19896; K: 24.9.17; Tyne Cot Mem. (Bel.).

5561. WILSON, Gilbert Hermann Royce; B: St.Mary Abbott's, London; E: Eastbourne; Pte. SD 5260; K: 30.6.16; Loos Mem. Pas-de-Calais; Age 23; Son of Mr. and Mrs.Hermann Wilson of 59, Rayleigh Road, West Kensington, London.

5562. WILTSHIRE, Edward John; B: Broughton, Hampshire; E: Chichester; Pte. G 17925; K: 31.7.17; Buffs Road Cem. St.Jean-les-Ypres (Bel.).

5563. WINTON, Harry; B: Worthing; E: Worthing; Pte. SD 2141; K: 17.5.16; Browns Road Mil. Cem., Festubert, Pas-de-Calais.

5564. WOODFORD, Leslie; B: – ; E: Loughborough, Leicestershire; Pte. G 15097; K: 21.9.16; Sucrerie Mil. Cem. Somme; Age 23; Son of Mrs.Hannah Woodford of Harby, Leicestershire.

5565. WOODHOUSE, Rev. Disney Charles; W or D : 6.10.16; Boulogne Eastern Cem. Pas-de-Calais; Age 32; Son of Rev.A.C. and Mrs. Woodhouse of Pampisford Vicarage, Cambridge; Serving with the Army Chaplains' Department attached to 12th Battalion.

5566. WOOLER, Ernest; B: Willingdon, Sussex; E: Bexhill-on-Sea; Pte. SD 2223; K: 30.6.16; St.Vaast Post Mil. Cem. Pas-de-Calais; Son of David and Emily Wooler of 4, Rosebank Cottages, Lower Willingdon.

5567. WRIGHT, Charles; B: – ; E: Hastings; Cpl. L 8233; D: 28.8.17; Red Cross Corner Cem. Pas-de-Calais.

5568. WRIGHT, Owen; B: Peterborough; E: Peterborough; Pte. G 19875; K: 20.11.17; Tyne Cot Mem. (Bel.); Age 20; Son of Thomas and Isabella Wright of 204, Bellsize Avenue; Woodstone, Northamptonshire.

5569. WYATT, Thomas Henry Lavender; B: – ; E: Littlehampton, Sussex; Pte. G 16182; K: 10.6.17; Vlamertinghe New Mil. Cem. (Bel.); Age 28; Husband of Mabel M.Wyatt of 33, Gratwicke Terrace, Arundel, Sussex.

Y

5570. YOUNG, Lawrence; B: Croydon; E: Horsham, Sussex; Pte. G 17929; K: 25.9.17; Tyne Cot Mem. (Bel.));Age 19; Son of Mr.W.D. and Mrs.J.A.Young of 62, Regent Street, Watford.

13th Battalion

A

5571. ADAMS, Ernest Arthur; B: Peckham, London; E: St.Paul's Churchyard, London; Pte. SD 2607; K: 30.6.16; Cabaret-Rouge Brit. Cem. Pas-de-Calais; Age 23; Son of Ernest and Auguste Adams of 78, Charnwood Road, South Norwood, London.*

5572. ADAMS, Sidney Hugh; B: Withyham, Sussex; E: Eastbourne; Pte. G 16002; W: 1.10.16; Euston Road Cem. Somme.

5573. ADE, Edwin Stapley; B: Lewes; E: Lewes; L/Cpl. G 16386; W at Home: 21.3.17; Lewes Cem., Sussex (UK); Age 39; Son of George Stapley Ade; Husband of Mrs.L. L. Ade of 17, St.Swithin's Terrace, Lewes.

5574. AGATE, Robert; B: Thakenham, Sussex; E: Chichester; L/Cpl. SD 3509; K: 30.6.16; Loos Mem. Pas-de-Calais.

5575. AKEHURST, James; B: Cowfold, Sussex; E: Horsham, Sussex; L/Cpl. SD 2834; K: 1.3.17; Railway Dugouts Burial Ground (Bel.); Age 39; Husband of Ann Akehurst of 65, Trafalgar Road, Horsham.

5576. ALAWAY, Frank William; B: Holloway, London; E: Mill Hill, London; Pte. G 17422; K: 27.9.17; Tyne Cot Mem. (Bel.); Age 19; Son of John and E.A.Alaway of 18, Eastbourne Road, South Tottenham, London.

5577. ALLEN, Frederick James; B: Lewes; E: Eastbourne; L/Cpl. G 7286; K: 15.10.17; Kemmel Chateau Mil. Cem. (Bel.); Son of George and Maria Allen of 3, Thorpe's Cottages, South Street, Lewes.

5578. ALLEN, William Farquhar; B: Milton, Kent; E: St.Paul's Churchyard, London; Pte. SD 2604; W: 20.9.16; Bertrancourt Mil. Cem. Somme; Age 24; Son of Mr.E.J. and Mrs.J.M.Allen of 10, The Avenue, Gravesend, Kent.

5579. ALLERY, Nelson Barrett; B: Newhaven, Sussex; E: Brighton; Pte. SD 3268; K: 13.8.17; Klein-Vierstraat Brit. Cem. (Bel.); Age 26; Son of Robert and Ellen Allery of Newhaven.

5580. ANDREWS, Bertram John William; 2nd Lt.; W: 31.7.17; Dozinghem Mil. Cem. (Bel.); Age 22; Son of W.E. and C.J.Andrews of 41, Coxwell Road, Plumstead, London.

5581. ASBERY, Harold Wilfred; B: Kettering; E: Kettering; Pte. G 15683; K: 13.8.17; Klein-Vierstraat Brit. Cem. (Bel.); Age 20; Son of William and Bertha Asbery of 75, Montagu Street, Kettering.*

5582. ASCOTT, Victor Charles; B: Hastings; E: Hastings; Pte. G 18169; K: 3.9.16; Hamel Mil. Cem. Somme.

5583. ATTWATER, Harry William; B: Horsham, Sussex; E: Greys, Essex; Pte. TF 201834; K: 17.6.17; Vlamertinghe New Mil. Cem. (Bel.).

5584. AUSTIN, Frederick; B: Cokeham, Sussex; E: Worthing; Pte. SD 5109; K: 19.7.16; Le Touret Mil. Cem. Pas-de-Calais.

5585. AWCOCK, William Vince; B: Rotherfield, Sussex; E: Tunbridge Wells; Pte. SD 5106; K: 30.6.16; Loos Mem. Pas-de-Calais; Age 22; Son of Emmie Jessop, formerly Awcock, of Hammond's Cottage, Hammond's Lane, Scaynes Hill, Sussex, and the late Vince Awcock.

5586. AYLING, Benjamin George; B: – ; E: Horsham, Sussex; L/Cpl. G 16389; K: 31.7.17; White House

Cem (Bel.); Age 32; Son of Benjamin and Ann Ayling of 54, Offam, Arundel, Sussex; Husband of Minnie Gladys Ayling of 7, Wood View, Ford Road, Arundel.

5587. AYLING, Norman; B: Pulborough, Sussex; E: Worthing; Pte. SD 5027; K: 30.6.16; Loos Mem. Pas-de-Calais; Age 22; Son of Alfred and Naomi Ayling of Lintotts, West Chiltington, Sussex.

B

5588. BAGOT, Frederick Spencer Wellesley; B: – ; E: Hastings; Pte. G 18180; K: 21.10.16; Grandcourt Road Cem. Somme; Age 26; Son of Arthur Greville Bagot and Lily Bagot (stepmother) of Old Croft Cottage, Brimpsfield, Gloucestershire.*

5589. BAILEY, Charles; B: Rye, Sussex; E: Putney, London; Pte. G 13955; K: 30.1.17; Ypres (Menin Gate) Mem. (Bel.); Age 38; Son of Mr. and Mrs. Bailey of Rye; Husband of Ethel Florence Bailey of 7, Merivale Road, Putney.

5590. BAILEY, Charles Frederick; B: Langton Herring, Dorset; E: Hampton Hill, London; Pte. SD 5878; D at Home: 7.3.17; Leicester (Welford Road) Cem. (UK); Age 25; Son of Mrs.Bailey of Langton Herring; Husband of Elizabeth Bailey of 3, Beards Hill, Middlesex.

5591. BAILEY, Walter William; B: Tangmere, Sussex; E: Bognor Regis, Sussex; Pte. G 16401; K: 3.11.16; Thiepval Mem. Somme; Age 41; Husband of Alice Bailey of 2, Gordon Terrace, Sea Road, Felpham, Sussex.

5592. BAKER, William; B: St.John's, Sussex; E: Brighton; Pte. G 3044; W: 2.8.17; Dozinghem Mil. Cem. (Bel.).

5593. BALL, Albert William; B: Brighton; E: Hove; Cpl. G 2616; K: 2.8.17; Ypres (Menin Gate) Mem. (Bel.); Age 22; Son of Mr. and Mrs.V.A.Ball of 222, London Road, Bognor Regis, Sussex.

5594. BALL, Charles Edward; B: Brighton; E: Brighton; L/Sgt. SD 3521; M.M.; K: 3.9.16; Hamel Mil. Cem. Somme.

5595. BANFIELD, Marcus Ebenezer; B: Brighton; E: Hove; Cpl. G 6667; W: 26.4.18; Haringhe (Bandaghem) Mil. Cem. (Bel.); Age 24; Son of Joseph and Emma Banfield of 1, Chanctonbury Road, Hove.

5596. BANKS, Joseph; B: Hove; E: Brighton; Pte. SD 2865; K: 30.6.16; St.Vaast Post Mil. Cem. Pas-de-Calais; Age 37; Son of John and Sarah Banks of Hove; Husband of Louise E.Banks of 55, Cowper Street, Hove.

5597. BARBER, Edward Frederick; B: – ; E: Hove; Pte. G 16003; K: 23.9.16; Euston Road Cem. Somme; Age 35; Son of Edward and Adnie K.E.Barber of 172, Sackville Road, Hove; Killed with eight others in a Redan Ridge trench by an enemy trench mortar explosion.

5598. BARNES, Arthur John; B: Westfield, Sussex; E: Bexhill-on-Sea; Pte. G 16004; K: 5.6.17; Vlamertinghe Mil. Cem. (Bel.); Served as a sniper.

5599. BARNETT, Alfred; B: Hanley, Staffordshire; E: Hanley; Pte. S 2358; K: 25.9.17; Larch Wood (Railway Cutting) Cem. (Bel.); Age 31; Husband of Jane Bossons, formerly Barnett, of 81, Hope Street, Hanley.

5600. BARR, Harry; B: Ingatestone, Essex; E: Colchester, Essex; Pte. G 14655; W: 24.10.18; Hamburg Cem. (G); Age 21; Son of Frederick William and Ellen Barr of Hyde Cottage, Ingatestone; Died while Prisoner of War.*

5601. BARRETT, Albert George; B: Chichester; E: Hastings; L/Cpl. SD 4002; W: 30.3.18; Roisel Com. Cem. Ext. Somme.

5602. BARROW, Frederick William; B: Woking, Surrey; 2nd Lt.; K: 3.9.16; Ancre Brit. Cem. Somme; Attached from 14th Battalion; Age 31; Son of William and Emma Barrow of 50, Hollingbury Park Avenue, Brighton;

5603. BARROW, Tom; B: Manchester; E: Eastbourne; Pte. G 3283; K: 30.6.16; Loos Mem. Pas-de-Calais; Age 26; Son of Mrs.Christina Barrow of Tabley Brook, Over Tabley, Cheshire.

5604. BARTLETT, Cyril; Maj.; W: 14.11.17; Outersteene Com. Cem. Ext., Bailleul, Nord; Mentioned in 'Undertones of War' by Edmund Blunden.

5605. BASHFORD, Reuben; B: Worthing; E: Worthing; Pte. SD 3071; K: 30.6.16; Loos Mem. Pas-de-Calais.

5606. BASSETT, William; B: Frant, Sussex; E: Hastings; Sgt. SD 2838; K: 30.6.16; Loos Mem. Pas-de-Calais.

5607. BASTINGS, Henry John; B: Peckham, London; E: Southwark, London; Pte. G 4999; K: 22.6.17; Bard Cottage Cem. (Bel.).

5608. BATEHUP, Stephen Thomas; B: Ewhurst, Sussex; E: Hastings; Pte. SD 837; K: 23.3.18; Ste.Emilie Valley Cem., Villers-Faucon, Somme; Age 25; Son of Bertram and Ellen Batehup of Ewhurst; Husband of Alice Batehup of 21, Herne Hill, London.*

5609. BATES, Albert John; B: Ebony, Kent; E: Hastings; Pte. G 18003; K: 3.9.16; Thiepval Mem. Somme.

5610. BATTLE, Robert Arthur; B: Westminster, London; E: Cricklewood, London; Pte.G 13914; K: 23.3.18; Pozieres Mem. Somme.

5611. BEACHER, John Ezra Bryant; B: Cowfold, Sussex; E: Horsham, Sussex; Pte. SD 2866; K: 21.6.16; St.Vaast Post Mil. Cem. Pas-de-Calais; Age 21; Son of Charley E. and Alice E.Beacher of The Haven, Billigshurst, Sussex.

5612. BEALE, George; B: Icomb, Gloucestershire; E: Hastings; Pte. SD 4004; K: 30.6.16; Loos Mem. Pas-de-Calais; Age 19; Son of John and Emma Beale of Icomb.

5613. BEESLEY, Charles; B: Brighton; E: Brighton; Pte. SD 3289; K: 30.6.16; Cabaret-Rouge Brit. Cem. Pas-de-Calais.

5614. BEHR, Francis Joseph; B: Brighton; E: Brighton; Pte. G 16391; K: 26.3.18; Pozieres Mem. Somme.

5615. BELCHER, Percy John; B: St.Neots, Huntingdonshire; E: Brighton; Pte. SD 3734; K: 30.6.16; Loos Mem. Pas-de-Calais; Age 18; Son of

John Robert and Janet Belcher of 7, Station Road, Southwold, Suffolk.

5616. BENNETT Frederick Charles; B: Brighton; E: Hove; Pte. SD 3290; W: 18.3.16; Sailly-sur-la-Lys Canadian Cem. Pas-de-Calais; Age 19; Son of Frederick and A.Bennett of 66, Newhaven Street, Brighton.

5617. BENNETT, Harry; B: Worthing; E: Worthing; Sgt. SD 2196; K: 31.7.16; Le Touret Mil. Cem. Pas-de-Calais.

5618. BENNETT, Ormonde; B: Worthing; E: Worthing; Sgt. G 16388; W: 5.5.18; Boulogne Eastern Cem. Pas-de-Calais; Age 32; Son of Harry and Augusta Bennett of Gordon House, Pond Lane, Durrington, Sussex.

5619. BENNETT, William Alfred; B: Steyning, Sussex; E: Hove; Pte. SD 3288; W: 30.6.16; Merville Com. Cem., Nord; Son of Alfred Bennett of 15, St.George's Place, Steyning.

5620. BENNETT, William Henry Pope; Capt.; M.C.; K: 3.3.18; Thiepval Mem. Somme.

5621. BERRY, Ernest Frank; B: Furrell, Sussex; E: Chichester; Pte. G 13466; K: 1.8.17; Ypres (Menin Gate) Mem. (Bel.); Age 19; Son of Alfred Ernest and Mary Berry of Ruckford, Sussex.

5622. BIGNELL, William Henry; B: St.Leonards-on-Sea, Sussex; E: Chichester; C.S.M. SD 2611; D: 20.7.17; Dernancourt Com. Cem. Ext. Somme; Age 47; Son of William and Maria Bignell of Hastings; Husband of Mary Bignell of 1, Chermside Villas, Summersdale, Chichester.

5623. BILLINGHURST, Henry Thornton; B: Barcombe, Sussex; E: Hastings; Pte. SD 3296; K: 30.6.16; Loos Mem. Pas-de-Calais.

5624. BINGHAM, Moses; B: Frittenden, Kent; E: Tunbridge Wells; Pte. TF 260100; K: 27.9.17; Tyne Cot Mem. (Bel.); Age 35; Son of Thomas and Frances Bingham; Husband of Beatrice Emily Bingham of Hare Plain, Biddenden, Kent.

5625. BINSTEAD, Arthur; B: Odiham, Hampshire; E: Hastings; L/Cpl. G 810; K: 26.9.17; Tyne Cot Mem. (Bel.); Age 23; Son of Walter and Sarah Ann Bibstead of Church Street, Odiham.

5626. BIRT, Sidney; Littlemore, Oxfordshire; E: Oxford; Pte. G 17136; K: 26.9.17; Tyne Cot Mem. (Bel.); Age 19; Son of Mrs.R.Birt of Colledge Lane, Littlemore.

5627. BISHOP, Albon Edward; B: Hastings; E: Brighton; Pte. G 16469; K: 1.8.17; Ypres (Menin Gate) Mem. (Bel.); Age 31; Son of William and Alice Bishop of 19, Paynton Road, St.Leonards-on-Sea, Sussex.

2628. BISHOP, Jack; B: Crouch End, Middlesex; E: Hastings; Cpl. SD 2845; K: 30.6.16; St.Vaast Post Mil. Cem. Pas-de-Calais.

5629. BISHOP, Walter Thomas; B: Willesden, London; E: Chichester; Pte. G 13701; W: 31.3.18; Le Cateau Mil. Cem., Nord.

5630. BLACKFORD, William James; B: Frant, Sussex; E: Hastings; L/Cpl. SD 4163; K: 30.6.16; Loos Mem. Pas-de-Calais; Age 23; Son of Albert and Frances Blackford.

5631. BLACKMAN, Ernest; B: Newhaven, Sussex; E: Worthing; Pte. SD 5066; K: 31.7.16; Le Touret Mil. Cem. Pas-de-Calais; Killed by 'friendly' artillery fire during a night raid (See text).

5632. BLACKMAN, Frederick; B: Battle, Sussex; E: Chichester; Pte. G 16405; K: 19.10.17; Tyne Cot Mem. (Bel.); Age 27; Son of Thomas Charles Blackman of 66, High Street, Battle.

5633. BLAKER, Leonard; B: Worthing; E: Worthing; Pte. SD 3525; K: 30.6.16; St.Vaast Post Mil. Cem. Pas-de-Calais; Age 29; Son of Benjamin Barrack Blaker of 12, Richmond Road, Worthing; Brother, Frank, 12th Battalion, also killed (see 5061).

5634. BLANN, Alfred Percy; B: Worthing; E: Hove; Pte. SD 3067; K: 1.8.17; Ypres (Menin Gate) Mem. (Bel.).*

5635. BLUNDELL, Herbert Edward; B: Kentish Town, London; E: Brighton; Pte. G 16208; K: 21.4.18; Tyne Cot Mem. (Bel.); Age 31; Son of Edward Harry and Emma S.Blundell; Husband of Lilian A.Blundell of 53, Commerce Road, Wood Green, London.

5636. BOAKS, Joseph; B: Ide Hill, Kent; E: Sevenoaks, Kent; Pte. G 13171; K: 27.3.18; Pozieres Mem. Somme.

5637. BOND, Albert James; B: Gillingham, Kent; E: Hastings; Pte. SD 4135; K: 30.6.16; Cabaret-Rouge Brit. Cem. Pas-de-Calais.*

5638. BOOKER, John William; B: Rotherfield, Sussex; E: Hastings; Pte. G 18183; W: 23.10.16; Puchevillers Brit. Cem. Somme.*

5639. BOTTING, Jesse; B: Haywards Heath, Sussex; E: Horsham, Sussex; Pte. SD 2858; W: 30.6.16; Loos Mem. Pas-de-Calais; Enlisted with brother, Robert, who was killed in the same action on the same day (see 5640).

5640. BOTTING, Robert; B: Balcombe, Sussex; E: Horsham, Sussex; Pte. SD 2857; W: 30.6.16; Bethune Town Cem. Pas-de-Calais; Enlisted with brother, Jesse, who was killed in the same action on the same day (see 5639).

5641. BOULTON, Francis Edward; B: Walworth, London; E: Hounslow, London; Pte. G 13905; W: 14.8.17; Mont Huon Mil. Cem., Seine-Maritime; Age 33; Husband of Emily Boulton of 29, Gravel Road, Twickenham, Middlesex.

5642. BOWLEY, William; B: Aldingbourne, Sussex; E: Chichester; Pte. SD 4006; K: 23.3.18; Pozieres Mem. Somme; Age 23; Son of Charles E. and Mary Bowley of Limmer Pond, Aldingbourne.

5643. BOYD, Robert; B: Westminster, London; E: Tooting, London; Pte. G 13960; K: 26.9.17; Tyne Cot Mem. (Bel.); Age 35; Son of Henry and Ellen Boyd; Husband of Beatrice Harbord, formerly Boyd, of 90, Mortimer Road, Kingsland, London.

5644. BOYS, John; B: Godmersham, Kent; E: Tunbridge Wells; Pte. TF241322; K: 24.3.18; Heath Cem., Harbonnieres, Somme; Age 36; Husband of Maud F.Boys of 2, Park Terrance, Hildenborough, Kent.

5645. BRADBROOK, William Herbert Claude; B:

501

Pimlico, London; E: Piccadilly, London; L/Cpl. G 15569; K: 1.8.17; Ypres (Menin Gate) Mem. (Bel.).

5646. BRANCH, George Benjamin; B: Felixstowe, Suffolk; E: Brighton; Pte. SD 3063; K: 22.3.18; St.Pierre Cem., Amiens, Somme; Husband of Mrs.A.G.Branch of 21, Pevensey Road, Eastbourne.*

5647. BRAYBON, Walter; B: Brighton; E: Hastings; Pte. G 18007; K: 24.9.17; Tyne Cot Mem. (Bel.); Age 21; Son of Mr.F.W.Braybon of 27, Arundel Street, Brighton.

5648. BRIDGER, Edward; B: Worthing; E: Worthing; Pte. G 16396; K: 26.3.18; Pozieres Mem. Somme; Age 27; Son of Edward and Mary Bridger; Husband of Annie Blake, formerly Bridger, of 3, Hampshire Terrace, Southsea, Hampshire.

5649. BRIDGEWATER, Thomas George; B: Tillington, Sussex; E: Petworth, Sussex; Pte. G 17765; K: 21.10.16; Grandcourt Road Cem. Somme; Age 19; Son of William and Fanny Bridgewater of New Barn Cottages, Midhurst Road, Tillington.

5650 BRISTOW, Edward; B: Wiston, Sussex; E: Hove; Pte. SD 3300; K: 30.6.16; Loos Mem. Pas-de-Calais; Enlisted with his brother, Frederick, who was killed in the same action on the same day and also has no known grave (see 5651).

5651. BRISTOW, Frederick; B: Wiston, Sussex; E: Hove; L/Cpl. SD 3299; K: 30.6.16; Loos Mem. Pas-de-Calais; Enlisted with his brother, Edward, who was killed in the same action on the same day and also has no known grave (see 5650).

5652. BROOKER, Thomas Edwin; B: Ditchling, Sussex; E: Brighton; Pte. G 16303; W: 6.11.16; Puchevillers Brit. Cem. Somme; Age 37; Son of George and Emma Brooker of Hassocks, Sussex; Husband of Florence Martha Brooker of 30, Barklands Road, Hassocks.*

5653. BROOKS, Alfred; B: Ringmer; E: Lewes; Pte. G 1667; K: 18.4.18; Tyne Cot Mem. (Bel.); Age 26; Son of Mr.C. and Mrs.S.F.Brooks.

5654. BROOKS, Alfred Edward; B: Brighton; E: Brighton; Pte. SD 3738; K: 11.5.16; Pont-de-Hem Mil. Cem., Nord.

5655. BROOKS, Charles; B: – ; E: Lewes; Pte. SD 5825; K: 22.3.18; Pozieres Mem. Somme.

5656. BROOKS, William George; B: Clapton, London; E: Southend-on-Sea; Pte. G 17242; K: 26.4.18; Tyne Cot Mem. (Bel.); Age 20; Son of William and Elizabeth Brooks.

5657. BROOMAN, Arthur; B: Rotherfield, Sussex; E: Tunbridge Wells; Pte. G 16008; K: 15.4.18; Tyne Cot Mem. (Bel.).

5658. BROWN, Alfred Ernest; B: Lincoln; E: Bexhill-on-Sea; Pte. SD 1870; K: 4.6.16; Cambrin Churchyard Ext. Pas-de-Calais; Age 37; Son of George and Ellen Brown; Husband of Ellen Brown of 7, Bertram Street, Cardiff.

5659. BROWN, Frederick Arthur; B: Trotton, Sussex; E: Petersfield, Hampshire; Pte. G 8663; K: 31.7.17; Ypres (Menin Gate) Mem. (Bel.).

5660. BROWN, Robert Walter; B: Tunbridge Wells; E: Tunbridge Wells; L/Cpl. L 11051; K: 31.7.17; Buffs Road Cem., St.Jean-les-Ypres (Bel.); Age 20; Son of Jesse and Emma Brown of 9, Avon Street, Tunbridge Wells.*

5661. BROWNING, Frederick William; B: Barnstable, Devon; E: Bonor Regis, Sussex; Pte. SD 4200; K: 30.6.16; Loos Mem. Pas-de-Calais.

5662. BRUNNING, Albert; B: Swallowfield, Berkshire; E: Hastings; Pte. SD 2839; K: 30.6.16; Loos Mem. Pas-de-Calais.

5663. BUCKENHAM, Herbert Augustus; B: Burnham, Norfolk; E: Norwich; Pte. G 17425; K: 27.9.17; Tyne Cot Mem. (Bel.); Age 19; Son of John and Christina Buckenham of Hall Cottages, Marham, Norfolk.*

5664. BUCKLAND, Frank Herbert; B: Tottenham, London; E: St.Paul's Churchyard, London; L/Cpl. SD 2637; K: 16.4.16; Post Office Rifles Cem. Pas-de-Calais; Age 29; Son of George and Jessie Buckland of 102, Derby Road, Ponders End, Middlesex.

5665. BULBECK, John; B: Hurstpierpoint, Sussex; E: Haywards Heath, Sussex; Pte. G 4219; K: 14.1.17; Artillery Wood Cem. (Bel.).

5666. BURCHELL, Charles Henry; B: Burgess Hill, Sussex; E: Brighton; Pte. SD 3529; K: 30.6.16; Loos Mem. Pas-de-Calais; Age 22; Son of Thomas and Harriett Burchell of Mate's Nest, Balcombe, Sussex.

5667. BURCHELL, Percy Ludley; B: Hove; E: Brighton; Pte. G 17786; K: 23.3.18; Pozieres Mem. Somme.*

5668. BURCHELL, William; B: Horsham, Sussex; E: Horsham; Pte. SD 2843; K: 31.7.17; New Irish Farm Cem. (Bel.).

5669. BURGESS, Edward George; B: London; E: Warminster, Wiltshire; Pte. G 17069; K: 25.3.18; Pozieres Mem. Somme.

5670. BURGESS, Henry Thomas; B: Westham, Pevensey, Sussex; E: Hastings; Pte. SD 2864; K: 30.6.16; Loos Mem. Pas-de-Calais; Age 25; Son of Edward and Sarah Burgess.

5671. BURLING, John Thomas; B: Bovinger Mill, Essex; E: Epping, Essex; Pte. G 22435; D: 9.1.18; Mendinghem Mil. Cem. (Bel.); Age 33; Son of George and Mary Burling of Bovinger; Husband of Alice May Pavitt, formerly Burling, of 31, Bovinger Green, Essex.

5672. BURNS, William Speir; B: Kilbarchan, Renfrewshire; E: Arundel; Sgt. SD 3304; K: 30.6.16; Loos Mem. Pas-de-Calais; Age 35; Son of Mr. and Mrs.John Burns of Tibbers, Thornhill, Dumfrieshire; Husband of Edith Burns of Singleton, Sussex.

5673. BUTCHER, George; B: Brighton; E: Brighton; Pte. G 16114; W: 29.4.18; Oostaverne Wood Cem. (Bel.).

5674. BUTCHER, Henry Joseph; B: Brighton; E: Bexhill-on-Sea; Pte. G 6597; K: 22.3.18; Villers-Faucon Com. Cem. Ext. Somme; Age 26; Son of Henry Joseph Butcher of Orchard Street, Chichester;

Husband of Ellen Moon, formerly Butcher, 10, Hallsworth Avenue, Hemmingfield, Yorkshire.

5675 BUTLER, David Lee; B: West Croydon; E: Guildford; Pte. G 17437; K: 26.9.17; Tyne Cot Mem. (Bel.).

C

5676. CALVER, Ernest Edwin; B: Swaffham, Norfolk; E: London; L/Cpl. G 4075; K: 21.10.16; Thiepval Mem. Somme; Age 23; Son of Edgar and Maria Calver of Gooderstone, Norfolk; Husband of Margaret Calver of Globe Hill, Swaffham.

5677. CAMMELL, James Harvey; B: Wellingborough; E: Kettering; Pte. G 18937; D: 26.8.18; Hautmont Com. Cem. Nord; Son of Robert Charles and Annie Cammell.*

5678. CAMP, Albert; B: Looe, Cornwall; E: Lewisham, London; Pte. G 16216; K: 26.3.18; Pozieres Mem. Somme.

5679. CANN, Samuel; B: South Tawton, Devon; E: Okehampton, Devon; Pte. G 17156; K: 26.9.17; Tyne Cot Mem. (Bel.); Age 19; Son of Robert and Mrs.R.Cann of South Tawton.

5680. CANNON, Frederick Wilbur; B: Bexhill-on-Sea; E: Hastings; Pte. G 18011; D: 5.7.18; Sedan (St. Charles) Com. Cem., Ardennes; Age 29; Son of Mrs.Mary Ann Cannon of 37, Station Road, Bexhill-on-Sea.*

5681. CANTOR, Louis; B: Hackney, London; E: Hackney; Pte. G 9807; K: 31.7.17; New Irish Farm Cem. (Bel.); Age 20; Son of Samuel and Annie Cantor of 77, Middlesex Wharf, Lea Bridge, London.

5682. CARR, James; B: Christ Church, Sussex; E: Chichester; Pte. L 10370; K: 16.4.18; Tyne Cot Mem. (Bel.).

5683. CARTER, Frederick Charles; B: Horsham, Sussex; E: Horsham; Pte. G 17806; K: 23.3.18; Villers-Faucon Com. Cem. Ext. Somme; Age 30; Son of Henry John Carter of Garden Cottages, Wimblehurst, Sussex.

5684. CARTER, Fritz; B: Uckfield, Sussex; E: Horsham, Sussex; L/Sgt. SD 3551; W: 2.7.16; Merville Com. Cem., Nord; Age 19; Son of Sarah Carter of Nursery Farm, Chelwood Gate, Sussex.

5685. CARTER, John Edward; B: – ; E: Hastings; Pte. TF 202994; K: 31.7.17; Buffs Road Cem., St.Jean-les-Ypres (Bel.); Age 26; Son of Colour Sergeant E.M. and Mrs.H.Carter of Hastings.

5686. CARTER, Norman Cecil; B: Oxford; 2nd Lt.; W: 22.7.16; Bethune Town Cem. Pas-de-Calais; Age 22; Son of W.C. and Lucy Carter of 46, Claverton Street, Pimlico, London.

5687. CARVER, James; B: Easebourne, Sussex; E: Chichester; Pte. SD 4209; K: 5.10.16; Thiepval Mem. Somme.; Age 36; Son of Charles and Emily Carver of Easebourne; Husband of Mary Annie Carver of 17, Stedham, Midhurst, Sussex.*

5688. CASHIN, Albert William; B: Fulham, London; E: Fulham; L/Sgt. SD 4207; K: 26.3.18; Pozieres Mem. Somme.

5689. CASLEDEN, Fred; B: Woolwich, London; E: Bostall Heath; Pte. G 18186; K: 3.9.16; Hamel Mil. Cem. Somme.

5690. CASS, Montague; B: Sutton, Surrey; E: Worthing; Pte. SD 504; K: 31.7.17; Ypres (Menin Gate) Mem. (Bel.); Age 22; Son of Charles and Mrs.M.E.Cass of 7, Eastcourt Road, Worthing.

5691. CATHERWOOD, Frederick Adolphus; B: Crawley, Sussex; E: Horsham, Sussex; Pte. G 18012; W: 23.10.16; Contay Brit. Cem. Somme; Age 28; Son of Lilian Gibson of 26, Highbury Grange, London.

5692. CATT, Reginald; B: Herstmonceux, Sussex; E: Hastings; Sgt. SD 3073; K: 21.10.16; Thiepval Mem. Somme; Age 20; Son of James Catt of Woodbine Cottages, Victoria Road, Herstmonceux.

5693. CHAIZE, Jean Edward Gabriel; 2nd Lt.; W: 18.8.17; Boulogne Eastern Cem. Pas-de-Calais; Age 23; Husband of Mrs.R.Chaize of 91, Stormont Road, Lavender Hill, London; Mortal wounds received on 31.7.17.

5694. CHALCRAFT, Walter Stanley; B: St.James', Kent; E: Bexhill-on-Sea; Pte. SD 2640; K: 30.6.16; Loos Mem. Pas-de-Calais; Age 25; Son of Louisa Jane Packham, formerly Chalcraft, of 2, Railway Cottages, Falmer, Sussex and the late Walter William Chalcraft.*

5695. CHALLACOMBE, George Leslie; B: Ilfracombe, Devon; E: Devizes, Wiltshire; Pte. G 17134; K: 27.9.17; Tyne Cot Mem. (Bel.); Age 19; Son of Edgar George and Ellen Elizabeth Challacombe of 22, Belmont Road, Ilfracombe.

5696. CHAMBERLAIN, Frederick; B: Mortimer, Berkshire; E: Reading; Pte. TF 241490; K: 16.4.18; Tyne Cot Cem. (Bel).

5697. CHAMBERS, Percy William; B: Paddington, London; E: Harrow, Middlesex; Pte. G 15670; K: 21.10.16; Grandcourt Road Cem. Somme; Age 21; Husband of Ada Amelia Thomas, formerly Chambers, of 28, Great Western Road, Westbourne Park, London.

5698. CHAPMAN, Charles Herbert; B: Penge, London; E: Bromley, Kent; Pte. TF 201702; K: 18.6.17; Vlamertinghe New Mil. Cem. (Bel.); Age 31; Son of W.Chapman; Husband of Alice Maud Chapman of 81, Lyvden Road, Tooting, London.

5699. CHAPMAN, Thomas; B: Brighton; E: Hove; Pte. SD 3075; K: 24.3.18; Ste.Emilie Valley Cem., Villers-Faucon, Somme; Son of Mrs.E.Chapman of 40, Essex Street, Brighton.

5700. CHARMAN, Samuel Ernest Mitchell; B: Goring-by-Sea, Sussex; E: Worthing; L/Cpl. SD 3313; K: 30.6.16; Loos Mem. Pas-de-Calais.

5701. CHATFIELD, William Charles; B: Uckfield, Sussex; E: Uckfield; Pte. G 18013; W: 8.9.16; Couin Brit. Cem. Pas-de-Calais; Age 30; Brother of Mrs.A.E.Wickens of 122, Framfield Road, Uckfield.

5702. CHEAPE, John de Carrich; Lt.; K: 3.9.16; Hamel Mil. Cem. Somme; Age 22; Son of Antoinette Ann Cheape of Great Streele, Framfield, Sussex; Attached from 8th Battalion; Shot by a sniper while bringing in a wounded man from No-Man's-Land by stretcher.*

5703. CHEESEMAN, William Edward; B: Sutton, Surrey; E: Horsham, Sussex; Pte. SD 3555; K: 30.6.16; Loos Mem. Pas-de-Calais.

5704. CLANFORD, Albert Thomas; B: – ; E: Hertford; Pte. G 15632; K: 27.10.16; Connaught Cem. Somme; Age 24; Son of William and Fanny Clanford of 5, New Road, Sheering, Essex.

5705. CLARK, George William; B: Herne, Kent; E: Rye, Sussex; Pte. G 18188; K: 21.10.16; Thiepval Mem. Somme.

5706. CLARK, Walter John; B: Cambridge; E: Eastbourne; Pte. G 16011; K: 26.3.18; Pozieres Mem. Somme.

5707. CLARKE, George Herbert; B: Brighton; E: Brighton; Pte. TF 241483; M.M.; K: 18.10.18; Tyne Cot Mem. (Bel.); Age 23; Son of George and Emma L.Clarke of 187, Queen's Road, Brighton.*

5708. CLARKE, Walter Amos; B: Lambeth, London; E: Croydon; Pte. G 13946; K: 22.3.18; Pozieres Mem. Somme; Age 40; Husband of Kate Emily Clarke of 84, Belmont Road, South Norwood, London.

5709. CLAYTON, Charles; B: New York, U.S.A.; E: Hastings; L/Cpl. SD 4144; W: 2.7.16; Merville Com. Cem., Nord; Age 22; Son of Robert and Rose Clayton.

5710. CLOAKE, George; B: St.Leonards-on-Sea, Sussex; E: Hastings; Pte. SD 2875; K: 30.6.16; St.Vaast Post Mil. Cem. Pas-de-Calais; Husband of Esther Cloake of 19, Cornfield Terrace, Bohemia Place, St.Leonards-on-Sea.

5711. CLOUT, Edward Albert; B: Brighton; E: Hove; Pte. SD 3547; K: 30.6.16; Cabaret-Rouge Brit. Cem. Pas-de-Calais; Age 19; Son of Harry and Mary Clout of 29, Arnold Street, Brighton.

5712. COATES, George Rupert; Brixton, London; E: Bexhill-on-Sea; Pte. SD 1127; K: 30.6.16; Loos Mem. Pas-de-Calais; Age 23; Son of William J.Coates of 22a, Wingford Road, Brixton Hill; Husband of Charlotte Coates.

5713. COATES, Walter; B: Hove; E: Hove; Pte. SD 2649; K: 30.6.16; Loos Mem. Pas-de-Calais; Age 19; Son of Frederick and Ellen Coates of 69, Shirley Street, Hove.

5714. COBBY, Ebenezer Richard; B: Hastings; E: Hastings; L/Cpl. G 9243; K: 24.3.18; Ste.Emilie Valley Cem., Villers-Faucon, Somme.

5715. COLBOURNE, Bernard Barton; B: Lancing, Sussex; E: Worthing; L/Cpl. G 7083; K: 19.10.16; Thiepval Mem. Somme.

5716. COLEMAN, Ernest Henry; B: – ; E: Iden, Sussex; Pte. G 18015; K: 26.10.16; Thiepval Mem. Somme.

5717. COLEMAN, Sydney; B: Brighton; E: Brighton; Pte. SD 5906; K: 6.11.16; Thiepval Mem. Somme; Age 25; Son of Lawrence Holtham and Eliza Maria Coleman of 24, St.Luke's Road, Brighton.

5718. COLES, Thomas; B: Alperton, Middlesex; E: Woolwich, London; L/Cpl. G 13909; K: 2.8.17; La Brique Mil. Cem. No.2; (Bel.); Husband of Ellen Haynes, formerly Coles, of 7, Burns Road, Alperton.

5719. COLLINS, Herbert; B: Bognor Regis, Sussex; E: Chichester; L.Cpl. G 2653; W: 20.5.16; Bethune Town Cem. Pas-de-Calais; Age 34; Son of George and Eliza Collins of The Cottage, Eastergate, Sussex.

5720. COLLINS, Reginald; B: Chard, Somerset; E: Chard; Pte. SD 4210; K: 24.9.17; Tyne Cot Mem. (Bel.).

5721. COLYER, William James; 2nd Lt.; K: 31.7.17; Ypres (Menin Gate) Mem. (Bel.); Mentioned in 'Undertones of War' by Edmund Blunden.

5722. COOK, Ernest Ewart; B: Banbury, Oxfordshire; E: Devizes, Wiltshire; Pte. G 17152; K: 27.9.17; Tyne Cot Mem. (Bel.).

5723. COOMBS, Samuel Howard; B: Dulwich, London; E: Eastbourne; L/Cpl. SD 2654; W: 12.7.16; Longuenesse (St.Omer) Souvenir Cem. Pas-de-Calais; Son of Samuel and Sarah Mary Coombs of 163, New Park Road, Streatham Hill, London.

5724. COOPER, George; B: Spalding, Lincolnshire; E: King's Lynn, Norfolk; Pte. SD 5587; W: 4.10.17; Godewaersvelde Brit. Cem., Nord; Husband of Mrs.F.E.Pocock, formerly Cooper, of Calthorpe Cottages, Barton-on-Humber, Lincolnshire.

5725. COOPER, Ronald Douglas; B: Burgess Hill, Sussex; E: Lewes; Sgt. SD 3077; K: 27.9.17; Tyne Cot Mem. (Bel.); Age 23; Son of John and Frances Cooper of 1, Waterloo Place, Lewes.

5726. COOPER, Walter; B: Portsmouth; E: Bognor Regis, Sussex; Pte. G 14356; K: 31.5.18; Étaples Mil. Cem. Pas-de-Calais; Son of Walter and Sabina Cooper of 106, Victoria Road North, Southsea, Hampshire; Killed during an enemy air raid.

5727. COOPER, William; B: St.Osyth, Essex; E: Newhaven, Sussex; L/Cpl. SD 3326; K: 26.10.16; Thiepval Mem. Pas-de-Calais.

5728. COOPER, William Richard; B: Hove; E: Hove; L/Cpl. SD 3080; K: 30.6.16; Guards Cem. (Cuinchy) Pas-de-Calais; Age 21; Son of Arthur and Esther Cooper of 54, Rutland Road, Hove.

5729. COOTE, Alfred; B: – ; E: Chichester; Pte. G 15861; K: 15.10.17; Kemmel Chateau Mil. Cem. (Bel.); Age 24; Son of George and Alice Coote of 12, Grove Farm, Colworth, Oving, Sussex.

5730. CORKISH, Philip Edward; B: Ramsey, Isle-of-Man; E: Birmingham; Pte. G 17147; K: 26.9.17; Tyne Cot Mem. (Bel.).

5731. CORNWELL, Joseph; 2nd Lt.; W: 29.5.16; Bethune Town Cem. Pas-de-Calais.

5732. COSHAM, Edward; B: Horsham, Sussex; E: Staines, Middlesex; Pte. G 17448; K: 10.3.18; Fins New Brit. Cem. Somme; Age 19; Son of Thomas and Alice Cosham of "Brackley", Queen's Road, Weybridge, Surrey.

5733. CROOK, Roger Joseph; B: Ardwick, Lancashire; E: Hastings; Sgt. G 6432; W at Home: 5.10.17; Moston (St.Joseph's) Roman Catholic Cem. Lancashire (UK); Age 28; Son of James and Lavina Crook of 245, Peel Green Road, Manchester.

5734. CROSS, Percy; B: Mountnessing, Essex; E: Warley, Essex; Pte. G 18068; K: 25.3.18; Pozieres Mem. Somme.

5735. CUDLIPP, Harold Edward; B: Plymouth; E: Plymouth; Pte. G 17151; K: 27.9.17; Tyne Cot Mem. (Bel.); Age 19; Son of Edwin and Louisa J.Cudlipp of 214, Beaumont Road, Plymouth.

5736. CULLEN, Sydney Thomas; B: – ; E: Horsham, Sussex; Pte. G 15889; K: 21.10.16; Thiepval Mem. Somme; Age 18; Son of Thomas and Emma Cullen of 20, Clifton Road, Worthing.

5737. CUMBERS, James George; B: Brentwood, Essex; E: Warley, Essex; Pte. G 18941; K: 26.4.18; Tyne Cot Mem. (Bel.).

5738. CUTLER, Albert Edward; B: South Stoke, Sussex; E: Horsham, Sussex; Sgt. SD 657; K: 30.6.16; Loos Mem. Pas-de-Calais.

D

5739. DABBS, Sidney Arthur; B: Chichester; E: Hastings; Pte. SD 2657; K: 16.4.16; Post Office Rifles Cem. Pas-de-Calais; Age 28; Son of Mr.G. and Mrs.Ann Dabbs of 14, Broyle Road, Chichester.*

5740. DADSWELL, David John; B: Crowborough, Sussex; E: Eastbourne; L/Cpl. SD 3328; K: 3.9.16; Thiepval Mem. Somme.

5741. DANIELS, Claude Robert; B: Swanton Abbott, Norfolk; E: Wrexham; Pte. G 18944; K: 26.4.18; Tyne Cot Mem. (Bel.).

5742. DANN, Frederick Walter; B: Crowhurst, Sussex; E: Hastings; Pte. SD 4013; K: 30.6.16; Loos Mem. Pas-de-Calais; Age 17; Son of Mr. and Mrs. George Dann of New Coghurst Farm Cottage, Ore, Hastings.*

5743. DAWS, George William; B: Croydon; E: Horsham, Sussex; L/Sgt. SD 3093; K: 30.5.16; Cambrin Churchyard Ext. Pas-de-Calais; Age 39; Son of George Daws of Croydon; Husband of Rebecca Muggridge, formerly Daws, of 5, Chestnut Road, Billingshurst, Sussex; Captured and dragged from the front line trench by an enemy raiding party at Cuinchy; His body was found and brought in during the following night*

5744. DEAR, Sidney James; B: Stotfold, Bedfordshire; E: Hitchin, Hertfordshire; Pte. G 17252; W: 24.7.17; Godewaersvelde Brit. Cem., Nord; Age 19; Son of George and Eliza Dear of Common Road, Stotfold.*

5745. DEDMAN, George Levi; B: King's Cross, London; E: Kingston-on-Thames; Pte. G 14943; K: 15.10.17; Kemmel Chateau Mil. Cem. (Bel.).

5746. DENYER, James; B: Alford, Surrey; E: Angmering, Sussex; Pte. G 15976; W: 26.10.16; Warloy-Baillon Com. Cem. Ext., Somme.

5747. DIGGENS, Martin Charles; Capt.; K: 30.6.16; Cabaret-Rouge Brit. Cem. Pas-de-Calais.*

5748. DIPLOCK, Harry; B: Lewes; E: Chichester; Pte. G 13869; K: 24.3.18; Pozieres Mem. Somme.

5749. DOBLE, Charles; B: – ; E: Deal, Kent; Pte. G 15672; W at Home: 13.12.16; Taunton (St.James's) Cem. Somerset (UK).

5750. DODD, Harry; B: Hammersmith, London; E: Fulham, London; L/Cpl. G 8084; K: 31.7.17; Ypres (Menin Gate) Mem. (Bel.).

5751. DORLING, John Francis; B: Walthamstow, London; E: Watford; Pte. G 18952; K: 25.4.18; Tyne Cot Mem. (Bel.); Age 19; Son of John Henry and Emma Matilda Dorling of 55, Boundary Road, St.Albans, Hertfordshire.*

5752. DOWLING, Sidney; B: Wadhurst, Sussex; E: Rye, Sussex; Pte. TF 202263; K: 27.3.18; Pozieres Mem. Somme.*

5753. DOWNES, Herbert Eugene; B: Thorpe Hamlet, Norfolk; E: Norwich; Pte. G 11609; K: 31.7.17; Buffs Road Cem., St.Jean-les-Ypres (Bel.); Age 20; Son of William and Hannah Downes of 11, Weeds Square; Thorpe Hamlet.

5754. DUDLEY, Cecil Lawrence; B: Weedon, Northmptonshire; E: Daventry, Warwickshire; Pte. TF 201883; K: 1.8.17; Ypres (Menin Gate) Mem. (Bel.); Age 21; Son of Richard and Margaret Dudley of 6, West Street, Weedon.

5755. DUDLEY, Eric Whittington; 2nd Lt.; K: 30.6.16; Loos Mem. Pas-de-Calais.

5756. DUKE, George Wilfred; B: Eastbourne; E: Eastbourne; Pte. SD 3560; K: 21.10.16; Thiepval Mem. Somme; Age 21; Brother of A.B.John James Duke.

5757. DUKE, Victor George; B: Brighton; E: Hastings; Pte. SD 2667; K: 30.6.16; St.Vaast Post Mil. Cem. Pas-de-Calais; Age 19; Son of George Duke of 2, Cromwell Street, Brighton.

5758. DULY, William Charles; B: Herstmonceux, Sussex; E: Eastbourne; Sgt. SD 3090; K: 30.6.16; Loos Mem. Pas-de-Calais; Age 36; Son of William and Esther Duly of "Eversley", Herstmonceaux; Husband of Alma Elizabeth Duly of Fairlight Bungalow, Herstmonceux.

5759. DUMMER, George; B: West Mardon, Sussex; E: Chichester; Pte. SD 2891; K: 30.6.16; Cabaret-Rouge Brit. Cem. Pas-de-Calais.

5760. DUNK, Arthur Edward; B: Hove; E: Hove; Pte. SD 3559; K: 30.6.16; St.Vaast Post Mil. Cem. Pas-de-Calais; Age 23; Husband of Amy Louisa Tutt, formerly Dunk, of 37, Ingram Crescent, Hove.

5761. DUNNING, John Montague; B: Nantwich, Cheshire; E: Lewes; Cpl. G 16392; K: 14.6.17; Vlamertinghe New Mil. Cem. (Bel.); Age 30; Son of John and Mary E.Dunning of Norbury House, Gobowen, Shropshire.

5762. DUTNALL, William Archibald; B: – ; E: Sittingbourne, Kent; L/Cpl. G 21157; K: 16.4.18; Tyne Cot Mem. (Bel.); Age 20; Son of Frederick John and Clara Dutnall of Swanton Street, Bredgar, Kent.

5763. DYER, Albert; B: Brighton; E: Hove; Pte. TF 202309; K: 17.6.17; Vlamertinghe New Mil. Cem. (Bel.).

E

5764. EAGER, William Henry; B: Eastbourne; E: Eastbourne; Pte. G 18948; D: 16.10.18; Perreuse

Chateau Franco-British National Cem., Seine-et-Marne; Age 20; Son of Mrs.Ellen Mary Eager of 6, Avondale Road, Eastbourne.

5765. EAST, Alfred John; B: Guestling, Sussex; E: Newhaven, Sussex; Pte. G 18019; K: 21.10.16; Thiepval Mem. Somme.*

5766. EASTON, Maurice; B: Eastbourne; E: Hove; Pte. SD 2902; W: 21.10.17; Kemmel Chateau Mil. Cem. (Bel.); Age 19; Son of Sidney and Alice Easton of 56, Royal Parade, Eastbourne.

5767. EDE, Frank Ernest; B: Christchurch, Sussex; E: Worthing; Pte. SD 1312; K: 26.4.18; Tyne Cot Mem. (Bel.); Age 20; Son of Frank Edward and Lily Eliza Ede of 11, South Farm Road, Worthing.

5768. EDWARDS, Frederick Robert; B: Tunbridge Wells; E: Tunbridge Wells; Pte. SD 2668; K: 26.10.16; Thiepval Mem. Somme.

5769. EDWARDS, William; B: East Grinstead, Sussex; E: Brighton; Pte. G 4210; K: 3.4.17; Railway Dugouts Burial Ground (Bel.).

5770. ELGAR, George; B: – ; E: Grimsby; Pte. G 15407; K: 18.4.18; Tyne Cot Mem. (Bel.).

5771. ELLIOTT, Arthur; B: Parham, Sussex; E: Bexhill-on-Sea; Cpl. SD 3095; K: 30.6.16; Cabaret-Rouge Brit. Cem. Pas-de-Calais; Age 23; Son of Mrs.Emily Jane Elliott of 6, Kerrsland Cottages, Hurtmore, Surrey.

5772. ELLIOTT, George Edward; 2nd Lt.; W: 20.5.16; Bethune Town Cem. Pas-de-Calais; Age 20; Son of Rev. W. Hayward Elliott, Vicar of Bramhope, Leeds.

5773. ELLIOTT, Harry George Ernest; B: Rye, Sussex; E: Dover; Pte. G 10820; K: 15.4.18; Ridge Wood Mil. Cem. (Bel.).

5774. ELLIS, Frank; B: Slaugham, Sussex; E: Brighton; Pte. SD 3103; K: 30.6.16; Cabaret-Rouge Brit. Cem. Pas-de-Calais; Age 21; Son of W.H. and Isabella Ellis of Stone Delph, Warninglid, Sussex.

5775. ELLIS, Harry Edward; B: Brettenham, Suffolk; E: Romford, Essex; Pte. TF 201839; K: 21.6.17; Vlamertinghe New Mil. Cem. (Bel.).

5776. ELLIS, John; B: Framfield, Sussex; E: Eastbourne; Pte. SD 172; K: 21.10.16 Thiepval Mem. Somme; Son of Horace and Naomi Ellis of The Bungalow, Fletching, Sussex.

5777. ENTICKNAP, John; B: Kirdford, Sussex; E: Petworth, Sussex; L/Cpl. G 4539; W: 14.3.17; Lijssenthoek Mil. Cem. (Bel.); Age 21; Son of Charles and Elizabeth Enticknap of Clark's Farm, Wisborough Green, Sussex.

5778. EVERSHED, Percy; B: Washington, Sussex; E: Hitchin, Hertfordshire; Sgt. G 4673; D: 28.5.18; Age 34; Peronne Com. Cem. Ext., Ste.Radegonde, Somme; Son of Daniel and Sarah Jane Evershed; Husband of Kate Evershed of Ashington, Sussex.

F

5779. FABIAN, Arthur Stanley; Capt.; K: 3.9.16; Hamel Mil. Cem. Somme; Age 23; Son of James W.Fabian of 6, Daleham Gardens, Hampstead, London;

Attached from 8th Battalion; Following an attack, and when men were retiring in confusion, he rallied them with the cry, 'Come on 'A' Company 13th' and led them back towards the enemy lines. About 70 yards short of the enemy, he had two fingers blown from his right hand but he pressed on until shot through the head and killed instantly.

5780. FARMINER, Richard Victor; B: Fernhurst, Sussex; E: Hastings; L/Cpl. SD 3104; K: 30.6.16; Loos Mem. Pas-de-Calais; Age 26; Son of Richard and Ann Farminer of Tanyard, Fernhurst, Sussex.

5781. FARNDEN, Edward Leslie; B: Friern Barnet, London; E: Wimbledon, London; Sgt. SD 3106; K: 30.6.16; Cabaret-Rouge Brit. Cem. Pas-de-Calais; Age 34; Son of Noel and Frances Farnden of Southgate, London; Husband of Edith Lucy Farnden of Christ Church School House, Worthing.

5782. FAULKNER, William; B: Fairwarp, Sussex; E: Bexhill-on-Sea; Pte. SD 3108; K: 30.6.16; Loos Mem. Pas-de-Calais.

5783. FIELD, George Tilt; B: Eastbourne; E: Eastbourne; L/Cpl. SD 1321; D: 21.5.18; Hautmont Com. Cem., Nord; Age 34; Son of George and Matilda Field of 353, Seaside, Eastbourne.

5784. FINCH, Charles William; B: Swanscombe, Kent; E: Gravesend, Kent; Pte. TF 202672; K: 31.7.17; New Irish Farm Cem. (Bel.).

5785. FIRRELL, Frank Jabez; B: Hailsham, Sussex; E: Eastbourne; L/Cpl. SD 306; K: 3.6.16; Cambrin Churchyard Ext. Pas-de-Calais.*

5786. FISH, Henry Alfred; B: Sawbridgeworth, Hertfordshire; E: Hertford; Pte. G 15664; K: 24.9.17; Tyne Cot Mem. (Bel.); Age 21; Son of Josiah and Mary Fish (stepmother) of 11, Springhall Road, Sawbridgeworth.*

5787. FITCH, Arthur Clifford; B: Hove; E: Hove; L/Cpl. G 14000; K: 26.4.18; Tyne Cot Mem. (Bel.); Age 20; Son of Joseph and Alice Harriett Fitch of 23, Townsend Road, Southall, Middlesex.

5788. FITZHERBERT, Harold Lancelot; Lt.; K: 30.6.16; Cabaret-Rouge Brit. Cem. Pas-de-Calais; Age 23; Son of Fanny Fitzherbert of New Zealand and the late William Alfred Fitzherbert; Brother, Wyndham Waterhouse Fitzherbert, also killed (see 5789).

5789. FITZHERBERT, Wyndham Waterhouse; Capt.; K: 7.7.16; Arras Mem. Pas-de-Calais; Age 25; Son of Fanny Fitzherbert of New Zealand and the late William Alfred Fitzherbert; Brother, Harold Lancelot Fitzherbert, also killed (see 5788).

5790. FLEET, Frank Arthur; B: – ; E: Chichester; Pte. G 15891; K: 30.6.16; St.Vaast Post Mil. Cem. Pas-de-Calais; Age 22; Son of Mr. and Mrs.Frank Fleet of Portsmouth.

5791. FLETCHER, Beaumont; B: Bardsea, Lancashire; E: Worthing; L/Cpl. TF 290298; K: 25.3.18; Pozieres Mem. Somme; Age 43; Son of A.E.Fletcher (former Editor of the Daily Chronicle) and Mrs.R.Fletcher of 79, Gordon Road, Ealing, London; Husband of Mrs.F.K.Fletcher of 348, Kennington Green, London.

5792. FLITNEY, Abel; B: Ellesborough, Buckinghamshire; E: Sevenoaks, Kent; Pte. G 12022; K: 2.8.17; La Brique Mil. Cem. No.2 (Bel.); Age 39; Son of Ellie and Ellen Flitney of Ellesborough; Husband of Matilda Flitney of 3, Hill Cottages, Chipstead, Kent.

5793. FOGDEN, Charles Henry; B: Chichester; E: Hastings; Sgt. SD 3099; K: 30.6.16; Cabaret-Rouge Brit. Cem. Pas-de-Calais.

5794. FOORD, Ernest; B: Brighton; E: Brighton; Pte. G 16026; K: 21.10.16; Thiepval Mem. Somme.

5795. FORD, Alfred Samuel; B: Newhaven, Sussex; E: Newhaven; Pte. SD 3101; M.M.; K: 30.6.16; Loos Mem. Pas-de-Calais; Age 32; Son of Mrs.A.Mockford of 32, Lewes Road, Newhaven.

5796. FOSTER, Peter Thomas; B: Brighton; E: Hove; Pte. SD 3347; K: 26.4.18; Tyne Cot Mem. (Bel.); Age 22; Son of Mr.P.T.Foster of 19, Essex Place, Brighton.

5797. FRANCIS, Charles Arthur; B: Ifield, Sussex; E: Hastings; Pte. SD 3765; K: 21.10.16; Thiepval Mem. Somme.

5798. FRANCIS, Frederick; B: Teignmouth, Devon; E: Horsham, Sussex; Pte. G 927; K: 15.10.17; Kemmel Chateau Mil. Cem. (Bel.).

5799. FRASER, Donald; B: South Norwood, London; E: Croydon; L/Cpl. G 13947; D: 1.8.18; Tincourt New Brit. Cem. Somme.

5800. FRENCH, John; B: Purbright, Surrey; E: Worthing; Sgt. SD 2677; K: 30.6.16; St.Vaast Post Mil. Cem. Pas-de-Calais; Age 24; Son of Mr.P. and Mrs.S.French of Storrington, Sussex.

5801. FROST, Charles; B: Lewes; E: Lewes; Pte. SD 3349; W at Home: 6.8.16; Lewes Cem., Sussex (UK).

5802. FUNNELL, Charles Henry; B: Etchingham, Sussex; E: Hastings; L/Cpl. SD 3768; K: 30.6.16; Loos Mem. Pas-de-Calais; Age 32; Son of James and Silvie Funnell of Coldharbour, Sussex; Husband of Charlotte Funnell of Brand's Cottage, Frontridge, Etchingham.

5803. FUNNELL, John Edward; B: Brighton; E: Hove; Pte. SD 2672; K: 30.6.16; Loos Mem. Pas-de-Calais.

5804. FUNNELL, William John; B: Hellingly, Sussex; E: Eastbourne; Pte. G 7287; K: 22.3.18; Ste.Emilie Valley Cem., Villers-Faucon, Somme; Son of Mr.A.Funnell of The Mount, Lower Dicker, Sussex.

G

5805. GADD, James George; B: Goudhurst, Sussex; E: London; Pte. SD 4213; K: 30.6.16; Loos Mem. Pas-de-Calais.

5806. GADD, William Edward; B: Purley, Surrey; E: Norwood, London; Pte. SD 5678; K: 21.10.16; Thiepval Mem. Somme; Age 26; Son of John and Maud Gadd of 9, Cambridge Grove; Husband of Rose Emma Gadd of 10, Cambridge Grove, Anerley, London.

5807. GANDER, Ernest; B: Framfield, Sussex; E: Chichester; Pte. G 13805; K: 31.7.17; Ypres (Menin Gate) Mem. (Bel.); Age 19; Son of Edwin Alfred and Annie Gander of 4, Hillside Cottages, White Hill Road, Crowborough, Sussex.

5808. GARBETT, Hubert Eustace King; B: Hassocks, Sussex; E: Worthing; Pte. SD 3113; K: 30.6.16; St.Vaast Post Mil. Cem. Pas-de-Calais; Age 28; Youngest twin son of Francis and Mary M.Garbett of North Court Lodge, Stanford Avenue, Keymer, Sussex.

5809. GARRETT, Stephen Alfred; B: Lewes; E: Lewes; Pte. SD 3110; K: 30.6.16; Cabaret-Rouge Brit. Cem. Pas-de-Calais.

5810. GEALL, Thomas Walter; B: Bognor Regis, Sussex; E: Southwark, London; Pte. G 16028; K: 21.10.16; Thiepval Mem. Somme.

5811. GELL, Charles; B: Pevensey Bay, Sussex; E: Hastings; L/Cpl. SD 2920; K: 30.6.16; Loos Mem. Pas-de-Calais.

5812. GEMMELL, John; B: Lanark; E: Aberdeen; Pte. G 24860; W: 18.4.18; Haringhe (Bandaghem) Mil. Cem. (Bel.); Age 24; Son of Susan Gemmell of 152, Garngad Hill, Townshead, Glasgow.

5813. GENT, Edward; B: Dublin, Ireland; E: Worthing; Pte. SD 5004; K: 30.6.16; Loos Mem. Pas-de-Calais.

5814. GIBBONS, Albert Henry; B: Billesdon, Leicestershire; E: Northampton; Pte. TF 201886; K: 2.8.17; Ypres (Menin Gate) Mem. (Bel.); Age 23; Son of Mr. and Mrs.R.Gibbons of Rugby, Leicestershire.

5815. GIBSON, Arthur; B: Islington, London; E: Harlesdon, London; L/Cpl. SD 5509; M.M.; W: 4.8.17; Étaples Mil. Cem. Pas-de-Calais; Age 26; Son of David and Emily Gibson of Harlesdon.

5816. GILLESPIE, Francis Sydney; Capt.; W: 18.6.16; Merville Com. Cem., Nord; Son of John and Eleanor A.Gillespie of 102, West Hill, Sydenham, London; Mortally wounded near Ferme du Bois, Richebourg L'Avoué , while leading a night time patrol.

5817. GILLETT, Charles Walter; B: Charlbury, Oxfordshire; E: Lewes; Drummer G 18199; K: 3.9.16; Hamel Mil. Cem. Somme; Age 19; Son of George John and Fanny Charlotte Gillett of Sydney House, 199, High Street, Lewes, Sussex.*

5818. GILLHAM, Reginald George William; 2nd Lt.; K: 26.9.17; Tyne Cot Mem. (Bel.); Age 22; Son of Mr.G.H. and Mrs.J.Gillham of The Laurels, South Leigh Road, Emsworth, Hampshire.

5819. GILLMAN, Ernest Francis Henry; B: Brighton; E: Hove; Pte. SD 3351; K: 30.6.16; Loos Mem. Pas-de-Calais.

5820. GLOSSOP, Walter Joseph; B: Arundel, Sussex; E: Arundel; Cpl. SD 2082; K: 28.8.17; Tyne Cot Mem. (Bel.); Age 29; Grandson of Mr. and Mrs.W.E.Glossop of Old Ship, Tring Street, Arundel.

5821. GOACHER, Arthur; B: West Grinstead, Sussex; E: Chichester; Pte. TF 203011; K: 21.4.18; Tyne Cot Mem. (Bel.); Age 38; Son of Henry and Mary Goacher; Husband of Lizzie Goacher of 8, North Gardens, Horsham, Sussex.

5822. GOBLE, William; B: – ; E: Littlehampton, Sussex; Pte. G 15913; K: 21.10.16; Thiepval Mem. Somme.

5823. GODDEN, Thomas Henry; B: Bexhill-on-Sea; E: Hastings; Pte. G 18023; K: 8.1.17; Artillery Wood Cem. (Bel.); Age 25; Son of Mr. and Mrs.Godden of 71, Bexhill Road, St.Leonards-on-Sea, Sussex; Husband of Dorothy A.Godden of 20, Gladstone Terrace, Hastings.

5824. GODIN, Ralph Edward; B: Loughton, Essex; E: St.Paul's Churchyard, London; Pte. SD 2681; W: 1.7.16; Cabaret-Rouge Brit. Cem. Pas-de-Calais; Age 26; Son of Ralph and Florence Godin of 20, Hurst Road, Buckhurst Hill, Essex.

5825. GODSON, Cecil Frederick; B: Chichester; E: Chelsea; Pte. G 15674; W: 3.11.16; Puchevillers Brit. Cem. Somme; Age 19; Son of Jane Rhoda Godson of 29, Dartney Road, Chlsea, London.

5826. GOLDSMITH, Jack; B: Hastings; E: Eastbourne; Pte. SD 1594; K: 22.3.18; Pozieres Mem. Somme; Age 21; Son of Mrs.Kate Goldsmith of 17, Western Road, Eastbourne.

5827. GOLDSMITH, John Edward; B: Headcorn, Kent; E: Hove; L/Cpl. SD 3772; K: 30.6.16; Loos Mem. Pas-de-Calais; Age 21; Son of John Edward and Eliza Goldsmith of Upper Chaneton, Washington, Sussex.

5828. GOODASAN, Frederick; B: Luton, Bedfordshire; E: Luton; Pte. G 14840; W: 29.6.17; Mendinghem Mil. Cem. (Bel.).*

5829. GOODFELLOW, Charles Edwin; B: Chiswick, London; E: Mill Hill, London; Pte. G 13924; W: 1.4.17; Lijssenthoek Mil. Cem. (Bel.); Age 22; Son of Walter and Sarah Alice Goodfellow of 49, Lincoln Road, Ponders End, Middlesex.

5830. GOODMAN, Alfred; B: – ; E: Hastings; Pte. SD 4020; K: 21.3.17; Railway Dugouts Burial Ground (Bel.); Killed when he was the only man inside a Battalion cookhouse in Sanctuary Wood when it was struck by an enemy 4.2" shell.

5831. GOUGH, Leonard; B: Highbury, London; E: St.Pancras, London; Pte G 2684; K: 26.9.17; Tyne Cot Mem. (Bel.).

5832. GRACE, Frederick Thomas; B: Littlehampton, Sussex; E: Horsham, Sussex; Pte. G 15910; K: 22.3.18; Pozieres Mem. Somme; Age 38; Son of Mr. and Mrs.M.Grace of Littlehampton.

5833. GRANT, Henry Tylor; B: Beckenham, Kent; E: Bromley, Kent; Pte. TF 201694; W: 16.1.18; Mendinghem Mil. Cem. (Bel.); Age 40; Son of Amos and Mary Grant of Beckenham; Husband of Emily Ada Grant of 26, Faversham Road, Beckenham.*

5834. GRAY, Frederick Charles; B: Tottenham, London; E: Shoreditch, London; Pte. TF 202783; K: 21.11.17; Menin Road South Mil. Cem. (Bel.)).

5835. GRAY, George; B: Hastings; E: Bexhill-on-Sea; Pte. SD 3575; K: 30.3.16; St.Vaast Post Mil. Cem. Pas-de-Calais; Son of Gertrude Charlotte Gray of 31, Duke Street, St.Leonards-on-Sea, Sussex.*

5836. GREEN, Charles James; 2nd Lt.; K: 16.4.18; La Clytte Mil. Cem. (Bel.); Age 31; Son of John and Mary Green of London.*

5837. GREEN, Claud; B: Chertsey, Surrey; E: Rye, Sussex; L/Cpl. G 17984; K: 31.7.17; Ypres (Menin Gate) Mem. (Bel.); Age 28; Son of Henry and Julia E.Green of Addlestone Hill, Addlestone, Surrey.

5838. GREEN, Edward; B: Upper Norwood, London; E: Romford, Essex; Pte. TF 201842; K: 23.3.18; Pozieres Mem. Somme; Age 30; Husband of Lavinia Maud Stokes, formerly Green, of 3, Archibald Road, Harold Wood, Essex.

5839. GREEN, Frank; B: Lewes; E: London; Pte. G 4766; K: 10.3.18; Fins New Brit. Cem. Somme; Age 36; Son of Henry and Mary Green of St.James Street, Lewes; Husband of Harriet L.Green of Sea Lane, Ferring, Sussex.

5840. GREENAWAY, Alfred; B: East Grinstead, Sussex; E: Hastings; Pte. SD 2692; K: 30.6.16; Cabaret-Rouge Brit. Cem. Pas-de-Calais; Age 24; Son of William George and Emma Greenaway of 25, Glen Vue Road, East Grinstead.

5841. GREENFIELD, Frederick Henry; B: Storrington, Sussex; E: Chichester; Pte. SD 3358; K: 30.6.16; Loos Mem. Pas-de-Calais.

5842. GRISBROOK, Llewellyn Alfred; B: Forest Row, Sussex; E: East Grinstead, Sussex; Cpl. G 15919; K: 21.12.16; Essex Farm Cem. (Bel.); Husband of Mrs.E.Rowcliffe, formerly Grisbrook, of 19, Knox Road, Stamshaw, Portsmouth.

5843. GROUT, Walter; B: – ; E: Hove; Pte. G 17952; K: 21.10.16; Thiepval Mem. Somme; Age 30; Son of John Ashwell Grout and Emily Grout of Stirling Place, Hove.

5844. GUMBRELL, Ernest Samuel; B: Brighton; E: Brighton; Pte. SD 3770; K: 30.6.16; Cabaret-Rouge Brit. Cem. Pas-de-Calais.

5845. GUTTRIDGE, Richard; B: Hastings; E: Hastings; L/Cpl. SD 2691; M.M.; W: 24.3.18; Abbeville Com. Cem. Ext., Somme; Age 38; Husband of Mrs.E.Guttridge of 35, Percy Road, Hastings.

H

5846. HAFFENDEN, William; B: Eastbourne; E: Eastbourne; Pte. SD 73; K: 30.6.16; Ploegsteert Mem. (Bel.); Age 24; Son of P.S.Haffenden of 4, Wartling Road, Eastbourne.*

5847. HALL, Sidney William; B: Surbiton, Surrey; E: Kingston-on-Thames; Pte. G 15685; K: 2.8.17; Ypres (Menin Gate) Mem. (Bel.); Age 27; Son of Mrs.Louisa Hall of Alpha Road, Surbiton Hill; Husband of Mary Louise Hall of 6, Smith Street, Surbiton Hill.

5848. HAMILTON, Edward; B: Petworth, Sussex; E: Chichester; L/Cpl. SD 3144; W: 11.5.16; Bethune Town Cem. Pas-de-Calais; Husband of Mrs.S.A.Hamilton of The Square, Westbourne, Hampshire.

5849. HAMPER, Robert; B: Lewes; E: Brighton; Pte. SD 3604; K: 30.6.16; Loos Mem. Pas-de-Calais.

5850. HAND, Herbert; B: Plungar, Nottinghamshire; E: Nottingham; L/Cpl. SD 3145; K: 30.6.16; Loos Mem. Pas-de-Calais; Age 24; Husband of Sarah Ellen Hand of 1, Union Square, Leicester.

5851. HARDING, Frederick Donald; B: Brighton; E: Redhill, Surrey; Pte. G 16375; W: 8.4.18; Ste.Marie Cem., Le Havre, Seine-Maritime.

5852. HARDING, Willie James; B: Selsey, Sussex; E: Chichester; L/Sgt. SD 3129; K: 30.6.16; Cabaret-Rouge Brit. Cem. Pas-de-Calais.

5853. HARDS, Albert; B: Rustington, Sussex; E: Rustington; L/Cpl. SD 5000; K: 3.9.16; Knightsbridge Cem., Mesnil-Martinsart, Somme; Age 18; Son of Robert Henry and Kate Hards of Worthing Road, Rustington.

5854. HARDY, Ernest; B: – ; E: Hastings; Pte. G 17953; K: 31.7.17; Buffs Road Cem., St.Jean-les-Ypres (Bel.); Age 24; Son of Henry Edward and Eugene Hardy.

5855. HARGREAVES, Robert; B: Leeds; E: Hove; Pte. SD 3364; K: 30.6.16; Loos Mem. Pas-de-Calais; Age 42; Husband of Rhoda Hargreaves of 99, Wordsworth Street, Hove.

5856. HARMAN, Arthur George; B: Ripley, Surrey; E: Edmonton, London; L/Cpl. SD 4215; K: 21.6.16; St.Vaast Post Mil. Cem. Pas-de-Calais.

5857. HARRIOTT, Gilbert; B: Pumpton, Sussex; E: Lewes; L/Sgt. SD 3363; K: 11.5.16; Le Touret Mil. Cem. Pas-de-Calais; Age 23; Son of Gilbert and Mrs.A.Harriott of 106, Littell Wales Cottage, Plumpton; Battalion Sniping Sergeant, himself killed by a sniper.

5858. HARRIS, Ernest Charles; B: Selsey, Sussex; E: Chichester; Pte. SD 4216; K: 30.6.16; Loos Mem. Pas-de-Calais; Age 24; Son of Albert and Mary Agnes Harris of West Street, Selsey.

5859. HARROLD, Walter Philip Gordon; L/Sgt. SD 2698; M.M.; K: 3.9.16; Thiepval Mem. Somme; Age 18; Son of Charles Henry Harrold of 55, Heene Road, Worthing.*

5860. HARTLEY, Ernest; B: Warbleton, Sussex; E: Chichester; Pte. SD 3121; K: 30.6.16; Loos Mem. Pas-de-Calais; Age 33; Husband of Ella Beatrice Hartley of 1, Prospect Cottages, West Barnham, Sussex.

5861. HAVES, Stanley Alfred; B: West Ham, London; E: East Ham, London; Pte. G 17254; K: 26.9.17; Tyne Cot Mem. (Bel.); Age 19; Son of Alfred Henry and Amy Martha Haves of "Hawthorn", 41, Sandleigh Road, Leigh-on-Sea, Essex.

5862. HAWKINGS, Richard Thomas; B: Deptford, London; E: Greenwich, London; Pte. G 15658; K: 23.3.18; Pozieres Mem. Somme.*

5863. HAYCOCK, George Alfred; B: Witheybrook, Warwickshire; E: Coventry; Pte. G 17124; D: 20.7.18; Tincourt New Brit. Cem. Somme.

5864. HAYES, Harold Ingersoll; B: Ponders End, Middlesex; E: Horsham, Sussex; Cpl. SD 2699; K: 30.6.16; Loos Mem. Pas-de-Calais.

5865. HAYLAR, William Reginald; B: Birmingham; E: Brighton; Pte. SD 5121; K: 30.6.16; Loos Mem. Pas-de-Calais; Age 24; Son of Emmiline Beatrice Longstreeth, formerly Haylar, of 40, Lansdowne Street, Hove and the late William Charles Haylar.

5866. HEAGERTY, William Thomas; Maj.; K: 31.1.17; Lijssenthoek Mil. Cem. (Bel.);.

5867. HEASMAN, Leonard; B: Forest Row, Sussex; E: Horsham, Sussex; Pte; SD 686; K: 30.6.16; Loos Mem. Pas-de-Calais; Age 25; Son of John and Alice Olive Heasman of Park, Slinfold, Sussex.

5868. HELYER, Richard; B: Chagford, Devon; E: Horsham, Sussex; Pte. G 16035; K: 31.7.17; Ypres (Menin Gate) Mem. (Bel.); Age 26; Son of John and Elizabeth Down Helyer of The Farm, Littlehampton, Sussex.

5869. HENDLEY, Albert Thomas; B: Tunbridge Wells, E: Eastbourne; Pte. SD 1357; K: 31.7.17; Buffs Road Cem., St.Jean-les-Ypres (Bel.); Son of Mr.W.R.Hendley of "Sea View", Willingdon, Sussex.

5870. HENLEY, Thomas; B: Anstey, Sussex; E: Brighton; Pte. SD 3142; K: 30.6.16; Cabaret-Rouge Brit. Cem. Pas-de-Calais; Age 40; Son of Charles William and Edith Caroline Henley of Anstey; Husband of Alice Jane Henley of Hazeldene, Anstey.

5871. HENRYS, Robert; B: Sheffield; E: Hastings; Pte. G 16037; K: 23.9.16; Euston Road Cem. Somme; Killed with eight others in a Redan Ridge trench by an enemy trench mortar explosion.

5872. HENSHAW, George Harry; B: – ; E: Worthing; Pte. SD 2701; K: 30.6.16; St.Vaast Post Mil. Cem. Pas-de-Calais.*

5873. HERRON, Reginald Maurice; 2nd Lt.; W: 12.6.17; Lijssenthoek Mil. Cem. (Bel.); Age 31; Son of Dr.James and Mrs. Sarah Elizabeth Herron of 24, Prince of Wales Mansions, Battersea Park, London; Mortally wounded when with a night time working party and died at No.2 Canadian Casualty Clearing Station, Poperinghe.

5874. HEWITT, Ernest; B: Tunbridge Wells; E: Eastbourne; Pte. SD 3146; K: 30.6.16; Loos Mem. Pas-de-Calais.

5875. HICKMAN, Harry Claude; Lt.; K: 23.3.18; Ste. Emilie Valley Cem., Villers-Faucon, Somme; Age 33; Son of Alfred Joseph and Ellen Harriet Hickman of 92, Leonard Street, Finsbury, London.

5876. HICKS, William John; B: – ; E: Hertford; L/Sgt. G 15618; W: 2.4.18; St.Sever Cem. Ext., Rouen, Seine-Maritime.

5877. HILL, William; B: Oakley, Oxfordshire; E: Horsham, Sussex; Pte. G 15923; K: 21.4.18; Tyne Cot Mem. (Bel.).

5878. HILLS, Charles William; B: Burpham, Sussex; E: Arundel, Sussex; Pte. G 15926; K: 21.10.16; Grandcourt Road Cem. Somme; Age 31;Son of Albert John and Sarah Arm Hills of 78, Malt House, Burpham, Sussex.

5879. HILLS, Frederick Chater; B: Brighton; E: Brighton; Pte. G 17998; K: 21.10.16; Thiepval Mem. Somme.

5880. HIRON, John Samuel; B: Rugby; E: Warwick; Pte. G 17140; K: 25.3.18; Villers-Faucon Com. Cem. Ext. Somme; Age 19; Son of Charles S. and Hannah Hiron of 14, Victoria Street, Leamington Spa, Warwickshire.

5881. HOATH, Frank; B: Hadlow Down, Sussex; E: Uckfield, Sussex; Pte. SD 315; D at Home: 31.1.17; Hadlow Down (St.Mark) Churchyard, Sussex (UK); Son of James and Mary Ann Hoath of Hastingsford Farm, Hadlow Down.

5882. HOBDAY, Harry; B: Ashburnham, Sussex; E: Eastbourne; Pte. SD 3370; K: 30.6.16; Loos Mem. Pas-de-Calais.

5883. HOBDEN, Arthur Alfred Thomas; B: Brighton; E: Brighton; Pte. G 17955; K: 24.12.16; Essex Farm Cem. (Bel.); Age 21; Son of Arthur Austin Hobden and Martha Hobden of 11g, Burchington Road, Brighton; Killed by shell fire at Hill Top Farm.

5884. HODGHTON, Alfred; B: Woolwich, London; E: Woolwich; L/Cpl. G 15690; K: 31.7.17; Ypres (Menin Gate) Mem. (Bel.); Age 20; Son of Alfred and Emma Charlotte Hodghton of 4a, Red Lion Lane, Shooter's Hill, London.

5885. HOLDEN, George; B: Lambeth, London; E: Chichester; Pte. G 487; K: 21.3.18; Pozieres Mem. Somme; Age 20; Nephew of Elizabeth Burch of Pine View, Slindon Common, Sussex.

5886. HOLDEN, Harry William; B: Steyning, Sussex; E: Steyning; Pte. G 16432; K: 30.1.17; Vlamertinghe Mil. Cem. (Bel.); Age 24; Son of Mr. and Mrs.H.Holden of 3, Hill Side Terrace, Steyning.

5887. HOLE, Albert; B: Ifield, Sussex; E: Chichester; Pte. G 13885; K: 27.9.17; Tyne Cot Mem. (Bel.); Lived at Flint Cottage, Tilgate, Sussex; Painter.

5888. HOLE, Albert Henry; B: Haywards Heath, Sussex; E: Maidstone; Pte. G 17946; K: 26.4.18; Tyne Cot Mem. (Bel.).

5889. HOLLAND, George William; B: Goring-by-Sea, Sussex; E: Worthing; Pte. G 13068; W: 31.10.16; Contay Brit. Cem. Somme; Husband of Mrs.E.D.J.Holland of 18, Becket Road, Worthing.*

5890. HOLMAN, Spencer; B: Ardingly, Sussex; E: Brighton; Pte. G 3284; K: 27.9.17; Tyne Cot Mem. (Bel.).

5891. HOMER, Percy; B: Selsey, Sussex; E: Chichester; Cpl. SD 2928; K: 29.7.16; Le Touret Mil. Cem. Pas-de-Calais.

5892. HONEYSETT, Cecil; B: Brightling, Sussex; E: Bexhill-on-Sea; Pte. SD 2706; K: 30.6.16; Loos Mem. Pas-de-Calais; Age 29; Son of Edward and Clara Honeysett of 5, Beaconsfield Road, Bexhill-on-Sea; Enlisted with brother, James George, also killed in the same action on the same day (see 5893).

5893. HONEYSETT, James George; B: Brightling, Sussex; E: Bexhill-on-Sea; Pte. SD 2707; K: 30.6.16; St.Vaast Post Mil. Cem. Pas-de-Calais; Age 36; Husband of Alice Ethel May Abbott, formerly Honeysett, of 2, Laburnum Cottages, Sidley, Bexhill-on-Sea; Enlisted with brother, Cecil, also killed in the same action on the same day (see 5892).

5894. HONOUR, Alfred William; B: Lincoln; E: Woolwich, London; Pte. G 16855; K: 31.7.17; Buffs Road Cem., St.Jean-les-Ypres (Bel.); Age 18; Brother of Mr.H.T.Honour of 8, Barleycom Street, Eltham, London.

5895. HOOK, William; B: Rye, Sussex; E: Hastings; Pte. G 16431; K: 2.8.17; Ypres (Menin Gate) Mem. (Bel.); Age 24; Husband of Lily Hook of 2, Cadborough Road, Rye.*

5896. HOOPER, George Frederick Victor; B: Exeter, Devon; E: Littlehampton, Sussex; Pte. G 16135; K: 26.4.18; Tyne Cot Mem. (Bel.); Age 21; Son of Mrs. Elizabeth Ann Field of 31, East Street, Wick, Sussex.

5897. HOPWOOD, Marcus; 2nd Lt.; K: 3.9.16; Thiepval Mem. Somme.

5898. HORTON, George Lancaster; B: Angmering, Sussex; E: Worthing; Pte. SD 5048; K: 30.6.16; Loos Mem. Pas-de-Calais; Age 19; Son of Jesse and Annie Horton of Bylfeet Cottages, Angmering.

5899. HUGGETT, George; B: St.John's, Sussex; E: Eastbourne; Pte. G 7045; W: 27.9.17; Godewaersvelde Brit. Cem., Nord; Son of Charles and Esther Huggett of Eastbourne; Husband of Florence Maud Huggett of 95, Toronto Road, Portsmouth.

5900. HULL, Thomas; B: Battersea, London; E: Wandsworth, London; Pte. SD 5761; K: 21.10.16; Thiepval Mem. Somme; Age 24; Son of William Hull of 9, Stonnell's Road, Battersea; Husband of Lily Fisk, formerly Hull, of 52, Zenor Road, Balham, London.

5901. HUMAN, Victor; B: Isleham, Cambridgeshire; E: Bury St.Edmunds, Suffolk; Pte. G 11236; K: 1.8.17; Buffs Road Cem., St.Jean-les-Ypres (Bel.); Son of Mrs.A.M.Human of 2, Field Terrace, Exnung Road, Newmarket, Cambridgeshire.

5902. HUMBLE-CROFTS, Cyril Mitford; Capt.; K: 30.6.16; Loos Mem. Pas-de-Calais; Age 34; Son of Rev.W.T. and Mrs.Bridget Humble-Crofts of Waldron, Sussex.

5903. HUNT, Alfred; B: Canterbury; E: Kingston-on-Thames; Pte. G 13941; D: 22.3.17; Lijssenthoek Mil. Cem. (Bel.).

5904. HUNTER, Herbert Douglas; B: Leicester; E: Coventry; Sgt. G 17094; K: 26.4.18; Tyne Cot Mem. (Bel.); Age 32; Brother of William A.Hunter of 122, Clarendon Street, Leicester.*

5905. HYDE, Frank Harold; B: – ; E: Hertford; Pte. G 15637; K: 21.10.16; Grandcourt Road Cem. Somme; Age 23; Son of Mrs.Rosa Hyde of 10, Queen's Road, Waltham Cross, Hertfordshire; Husband of Lily Hyde of 8, White's Cottages, Lancaster Road, Enfield, Middlesex.

5906. HYDER, Frank; B: Tonbridge; E: Hastings; Pte. SD 2934; K: 16.4.16; Post Office Rifles Cem. Pas-de-Calais; Husband of Mrs.M.E.Hyder of "The Rough", Colman's Hatch, Sussex.

5907. HYLAND, David; B: Whatlington, Sussex; E: Hastings; Pte SD 3140; W: 6.9.16; Étaples Mil. Cem. Pas-de-Calais; Age 20; Son of Thomas and Rebecca Hyland of 20, St.Andrew's Square, Queen's Road, Hastings.

5908. HYMUS, George William Henry; B: – ; E: Wimbledon, London; L/Cpl. TF 290408; W: 10.3.18; Tincourt New Brit. Cem. Somme; Age

23; Son of Samuel Bailey Hymus and Jane Hymus; Husband of Ethel Kathleen Hayward, formerly Hymus, of 8, Bloomhall Road, Upper Norwood, London; Died of multiple wounds.

I

5909. IDE, Albert; B: Westergate, Sussex; E: Hastings; Pte. SD 3786; K: 30.6.16; Loos Mem. Pas-de-Calais.

5910. IRELAND, Charles; B: – ; E: Hove; Pte. SD 3147; K: 30.6.16; St.Vaast Post Mil. Cem. Pas-de-Calais; Age 29; Son of John and Elizabeth Ireland.

5911. ISARD, Percy John; B: Newick, Sussex; E: Lewes; Pte. SD 2940; K: 30.6.16; Cabaret-Rouge Brit. Cem. Pas-de-Calais; Age 23; Son of Mrs.Ellen M.Isard of The Firs, Newick.

5912. IVERMEE, Robert; B: Kilburn, London; E: Brighton; Cpl. SD 3375; W: 14.7.16; Longuenesse (St.Omer) Souvenir Cem. Pas-de-Calais; Age 28; Husband of Alice D.Lacey, formerly Ivermee, of 7, Brighton Place, Brighton.

J

5913. JACKSON, Ralph; B: Amberley, Sussex; E: Chichester; Pte. SD 3150; W: 3.7.16; Cabaret-Rouge Brit. Cem. Pas-de-Calais; Son of John and Esther Jackson of Amberley; Enlisted with brother, Reginald Henry, and mortally wounded, probably in the same action and at the same time, most likely on 30.6.16. (see 5914).

5914. JACKSON, Reginald Henry; B: Amberley, Sussex; E: Chichester; Pte. SD 3151; W: 3.7.16; Wimereux Com. Cem. Pas-de-Calais; Age 29; Son of John and Esther Jackson of Amberley; Enlisted with brother, Ralph, and mortally wounded probably at the same time and in the same action, most likely on 30.6.16. (see 5913).

5915. JACKSON, Thomas Henry; B: Seagrave, Leicestershire; E: Northampton; Pte.TF 201799; K: 31.7.17; Ypres (Menin Gate) Mem. (Bel.).

5916. JAKES, Frank Ernest; B: Bedford; E: Bedford; Pte. SD 5750; W: 9.6.17; Mendinghem Mil. Cem. (Bel.); Age 20; Son of Mr.G. and Mrs.R.Jakes of 28, Grosvenor Street, Bedford.

5917. JAMES, Edward; B: Sandhurst, Kent; E: Hastings; C.S.M. SD 3790; W at Home: 7.7.16; Chichester Cem., Sussex (UK); Husband of Jane Taylor, formerly James, of 108, Windsor Road, Bexhill-on-Sea; Served in the Sudan and South Africa campaigns.

5918. JAMES, Wilfred Harold; B: Yiewsley, Middlesex; E: Uxbridge, Middlesex; Pte. G 21511; K: 23.3.18; Pozieres Mem. Somme; Age 19; Son of Henry and Fanny G.James of 32, Edgar Road, Yiewsley.

5919. JAMES, William Frank; B: Rottingdean, Sussex; E: Brighton; Pte. G 3265; K: 27.9.17; Tyne Cot Mem. (Bel.).

5920. JARVIS, Leonard; B: Waldron, Sussex; E: Warley, Essex; L/Cpl. G 12932; K: 6.11.17; Tyne Cot Mem. (Bel.); Age 20; Son of Albert and Philadelphia Jarvis of Spring Bank, Waldron.

5921. JEFFERY, Henry William; B: – ; E: Hastings; Cpl. G 16435; W: 18.4.18; Mendighem Mil. Cem. (Bel.); Age 20; Son of William and Rhoda Jeffery of Poundfield Farm, Crowborough, Sussex.

5922. JEMPSON, Bertram; B: Fairlight, Sussex; E: Bexhill-on-Sea; Pte. SD 2717; K: 30.6.16; Loos Mem. Pas-de-Calais; Age 19; Son of Charles Vidion Jempson and Flora Beatrice Jempson of 75, Battle Road, St.Leonards-on-Sea, Sussex; Brother, Charles Stapley, also killed in the same action on the same day (see 5923).

5923. JEMPSON, Charles Stapley; B: Battle, Sussex; E: Hastings; Pte. SD 3611; K: 30.6.16; Cabaret-Rouge Brit. Cem. Pas-de-Calais; Age 22; Son of Charles Vidion Jempson and Flora Beatrice Jempson of 75, Battle Road, St.Leonards-on-Sea, Sussex; Brother, Bertram, also killed in the same action on the same day (see 5922).

5924. JENNER, Albert Edward; B: Hailsham, Sussex; E: Lewes; Pte. SD 1379; K: 18.10.17; Tyne Cot Mem. (Bel.).

5925. JENNER, Albert Ernest; B: Ticehurst, Sussex; E: Hastings; Pte. SD 3608; W: 3.7.16; Douai Com. Cem., Nord; Age 29; Son of Mrs.Mercy Jenner of Three Legged Cross, Ticehurst.

5926. JENNER, James Curtis; B: East Grinstead, Sussex; E: Hastings; Pte. SD 4029; K: 30.6.16; St.Vaast Post Mil. Cem. Pas-de-Calais; Age 19; Son of Mr. and Mrs.W.Jenner of 12, Council Terrace, East Grinstead.

5927. JEWELL, Edmund; B: Brighton; E: Brighton; Pte. G 16042; K: 1.8.17; Ypres (Menin Gate) Mem. Pas-de-Calais; Age 35; Son of John Gilliam Jewell and Elizabeth Jewell of 122, Sussex Street, Brighton.

5928. JILLETT, Nelson; B: Emsworth, Hampshire; E: Worthing; Pte. G 15935; K: 20.6.17; Vlamertinghe New Mil. Cem. (Bel.).

5929. JINKERSON, Albert Victor; B: Great Yarmouth; E: Great Yarmouth; Pte. G 15286; K: 28.9.16; Auchonvillers Mil Cem. Somme; Age 18; Son of Mrs.M.A.Jinkerson of 30, St.Mary's Lane, Southtown, Great Yarmouth.*

5930. JOHNSON, George; B: Billingshurst, Sussex; E: Hastings; Pte. SD 4030; K: 30.6.16; Guards Cem. (Cuinchy) Pas-de-Calais; Age 21; Son of George and Harriett Johnson of 35, Park Street, Horsham, Sussex.

5931. JOHNSON, Walter; B: Bridgewater, Somerset; E: Chichester; Pte. L 7607; K: 3.9.16; Thiepval Mem. Somme.

5932. JONES, Barney; B: Emsworth, Hampshire; E: Chichester; Pte. SD 3610; K: 24.4.16; Guards Cem. (Cuinchy) Pas-de-Calais.

5933. JONES, William Charles; B: Roxton, Bedfordshire; E: Biggleswade, Bedfordshire; Pte. G 14841; W: 19.10.16; Varennes Mil. Cem. Somme; Died at Casualty Clearing Station, Varennes.

5934. JONSON, Ben; B: Dulwich, London; E: Wandsworth, London; Pte. G 14488; K: 8.3.18; Fins New Brit. Cem. Somme.

5935. JOY, Percival Douglas; B: Capel, Kent; E: Hastings; Pte. SD 2942; W at Home: 9.7.16; Kensal Green (All Souls') Cem., London (UK); Age 37; Son of Henry Benjamin and Martha Jane Joy.*

5936. JOYCE, Robert William; B: Bow, London; E: New Court, London; Pte. TF 260104; K: 26.9.17; Tyne Cot Mem. (Bel.); Age 19; Son of Robert John and Alice Joyce of 7, Lockhart Street, Mile End, London.

5937. JULIUS, Charles; B: Stepney, London; E: Whitehall, London; Pte. G 10749; K: 22.7.17; Essex Farm Cem. (Bel.); Age 19; Son of Samuel and Annie Julius of 40, Cable Street, Stepney, London; Killed while in a party carrying trench mortar ammunition up to the front line.

5938. JUNIPER, James; B: Hassocks, Sussex; E: Ditchling, Sussex; Pte. G 15938; K: 24.9.17; Tyne Cot Mem. (Bel.).

K

5939. KEET, David Thomas; B: Bournemouth; E: Hove; Pte. SD 2432; K: 27.9.17; Tyne Cot Mem. (Bel.); Age 21; Son of Elizabeth Keet of 24, Carlton Hill, Brighton. *

5940. KEELEY, Herbert; B: Burwash, Sussex; E: Hastings; Pte. SD 3798; K: 23.3.18; Pozieres Mem. Somme; Age 21; Son of Henry Edwin and Annia Maria Keeley of Borough Hill, Burwash Weald, Sussex.

5941. KELLY, Charles; B: Brighton; E: Brighton; L/Cpl. SD 5029; K: 30.6.16; Loos Mem. Pas-de-Calais.

5942. KEMP, Charles; B: Hastings; E: Hastings; Pte. G 17960; K: 31.7.17; Buffs Road Cem., St.Jean-les-Ypres (Bel.); Age 34; Son of Charles and Kerzia Kemp of Fairlight, Sussex.

5943. KEMP, George Edward S.; B: Brede, Sussex; E: Hastings; L/Cpl. G 16436; W: 27.9.17; Godewaersvelde Brit. Cem., Nord; Son of Mr.J.Kemp of Brede Hill, Brede, Sussex.*

5944. KENDALL, William; B: Margate, Kent; E: Colchester, Essex; Pte. TF 260115; K: 31.7.17; Track "X" Cem. (Bel.).

5945. KENNARD, Edwin Charles; B: Wadhurst, Sussex; E: Tunbridge Wells; Pte. G 6454; K: 26.9.17; Perth Cem. (China Wall), (Bel.); Age 25; Son of Edwin and Rhoda Kennard of The Angel, Sparrows Green, Wadhurst.

5946. KENT, Edgar; B: Woodford, Essex; E: Enfield, Middlesex; Pte. SD 5885; W: 8.10.16; Thiepval Mem. Somme; Age 19; Son of Mr. and Mrs.G.Kent of 6, Dewhurst Road, Cheshunt, Hertfordshire.*

5947. KENT, James; B: Hastings; E: Hastings; L/Cpl. SD 3154; K: 30.6.16; Cabaret-Rouge Brit. Cem. Pas-de-Calais; Age 27; Son of James and Elizabeth Kent of Hastings; Husband of Annie Baylis, formerly Kent, of 73, Coupland Street, Chorlton-on-Medlock, Manchester.*

5948. KEOGH, Henry Claude; B: Farnham, Surrey; 2nd Lt.; K: 4.4.17; Railway Dugouts Burial Ground (Bel.); Age 20; Son of Claude E.A. and Elizabeth Keogh of Southsea, Hampshire; Shot through the head by an enemy sniper when he climbed onto the firing step of the trench in order to direct retaliatory fire.

5949. KIDD, Arthur John; B: Fletching, Sussex; E: Twickenham; Pte. G 13908; W: 23.3.18; Pozieres Mem. Somme.

5950. KILLICK, John; B: Crawley, Sussex; E: Horsham, Sussex; Pte. G 15940; K: 26.10.16; Thiepval Mem. Somme; Age 23; Son of Francis and Maria Killick; Husband of Maud M.A.Killick of South View, County Oak, Crawley.

5951. KING, Arthur Ernest Gromett; B: Salter's Lodge, Norfolk; E: Norwich; Pte. TF 202353; K: 28.3.18; Villers-Faucon Com. Cem. Ext. Somme.*

5952. KING, Edward Harry; B: Petworth, Sussex; E: Croydon; Pte. TF 201870; K: 1.8.17; White House Cem. (Bel.).

5953. KING, William; B: Eastbourne; E: Cooden Camp, Bexhill-on-Sea; Pte. SD 4886; K: 18.10.17; Bedford House Cem. Enclosure No.4 (Bel.).

5954. KIRBY, John William; B: Cromer, Norfolk; E: Cromer; Pte. G 14703; K: 23.3.18; Pozieres Mem. Somme; Age 22; Son of Mr.J.H. and Mrs.E.Kirby of 12, Meadow Cottages, West Street, Cromer.

5955. KITT, Martin James; B: St.Stephen's-by-Saltash, Cornwall; E: Saltash; Pte. G 17098; K: 26.2.18; Villers Hill Brit. Cem., Nord.

5956. KNIGHT, James; B: St.Stephen's, Worcester; E: Worcester; Pte. G 17099; K: 24.9.17; Tyne Cot Mem. (Bel.).

5957. KNIGHTS, Walter; B: Kensington, London; E: Hastings; L/Cpl. SD 4158; D: 6.11.18; Tournai Com. Cem. Allied Ext. (Bel.); Age 20; Son of Walter and Catherine Knights of 144, Inderwick Road, Hornsey, London; Died while a Prisoner of War.

L

5958. LANE, John William; B: Brighton; E: Brighton; Pte. G 14421; K: 10.3.18; Thiepval Mem. Somme.

5959. LANGDALE, Harold Carthew; Lt.; K: 26.9.17; Tyne Cot Mem. (Bel.); Age 25; Son of Arthur Carthew Langdale and Annie Susan Langdale of Heathfield House, Heathfield Tower, Heathfield, Sussex.

5960. LANGFORD, Alfred Charles; B: Banstead, Surrey; E: Caversham, Surrey; Pte. G 17132; K: 26.9.17; Tyne Cot Mem. (Bel.); Age 19; Son of Alfred and Edith Langford of The Lodge, Watcombe Park, Torquay, Devon; Formerly of Thamesfield Farm, Henley-on-Thames.

5961. LANSDELL, Thomas; B: Brighton; E: Hove; Cpl. SD 2955; K: 26.9.17; Tyne Cot Mem. (Bel.).

5962. LATTER, Walter; B: Wadhurst, Sussex; E: Wadhurst; Pte. G 17963; W: 5.9.16; Couin Brit. Cem. Pas-de-Calais; Son of Mrs.A.Latter of 9, Fair Glen Cottages; Best Beech Hill, Wadhurst.

5963. LATTER, William; B: Crowborough, Sussex; E: Eastbourne; Pte. SD 4220; W: 3.9.16; Acheux Brit. Cem. Somme.

5964. LAUNDER, Herbert William; B: Petworth, Sussex; E: Chichester; L/Cpl. SD 3157; W: 23.3.18; Roye

New Brit. Cem. Somme; Died at No.50 Casualty Clearing Station, Roye.

5965. LAWS, George Henry; B: Hove; E: Hove; Pte. G 17755; W: 22.10.16; Puchevillers Brit. Cem. Somme.

5966. LEACH, William; B: Hunston, Sussex; E: Hastings; Pte. SD 3163; K: 19.6.17; Poperinghe New Mil. Cem. (Bel.); Age 41; Son of Mr. and Mrs.Beedon of Chichester; Husband of Mrs.E.Leach of 93, Cleveland Road, Chichester.

5967. LEE, Harry; B: Brighton; E: Hove; Pte. SD 3622; K: 27.9.17; Tyne Cot Mem. (Bel.).

5968. LEE, Jack; B: Watford, Hertfordshire; E: Eastbourne; Cpl. G 6617; K: 8.3.18; Fins New Brit. Cem. Somme; Age 23; Son of John and Alice Lee of 2, Romney Street, Eastbourne.

5969. LEGGE, Harry Herbert; B: St.John's, Sussex; E: Eastbourne; Pte. SD 4222; K: 30.6.16; St.Vaast Post Mil. Cem. Pas-de-Calais.

5970. LEVERTON, Henry; B: Barnham, Sussex; E: Barnham; Pte. G 15943; K: 23.9.16; Euston Road Cem. Somme; Age 31; Son of Joseph Levington; Killed with eight others in the front line trench on the Redan Ridge by an enemy trench mortar explosion.

5971. LIGHTFOOT, Robert Chrishop; B: – ; E: – ; L/Cpl. SD 2735; W at Home: 29.5.17; Abney Park Cem., London (UK); Age 21; Son of John and Margaret A.Lightfoot of 73, Frampton Park Road, Hackney, London.

5972. LINFIELD, Edwin; B: Ifield, Sussex; E: Horsham, Sussex; Pte. G 15944; K: 29.3.18; Villers-Bretonneux Mil. Cem. Somme.

5973. LINFIELD, Percy Frank; B: – ; E: East Grinstead; Pte. G 16044; K: 15.10.17; Kemmel Chateau Mil. Cem. (Bel.); Age 31; Son of John and Friend Linfield of Storrington, Sussex; Husband of Esther Barbara Linfield of White Horse Yard, Storrington; Killed in enemy air raid.

5974. LISHER, Charles Alfred; B: St.Matthew's, Sussex; E: Worthing; L/Cpl. SD 2137; M.M.; K: 8.3.18; Fins New Brit. Cem. Somme; Son of Frederick George and Amelia Lisher of 48, Orme Road, Worthing.

5975. LOADES, Gordon Charles; B: Kelling, Norfolk; E: Cromer, Norfolk; Pte. G 17456; D: 31.10.18; Hamburg Cem. (G); Age 20; Son of William and Emily Loades of "Brookside", The Avenue, Sherringham, Norfolk; Died while a Prisoner of War.

5976. LONG, Frank; B: Brighton; E: Tottenham, London; Pte. G 13925; K: 31.7.17; Buffs Road Cem., St.Jean-les-Ypres (Bel.); Husband of Mrs.J.Long of 121, St.Loys Road, Tottenham.

5977. LONG, Walter Harold; B: Wick, Sussex; E: Hove; Pte. SD 2951; K: 30.6.16; Loos Mem. Pas-de-Calais; Age 20; Son of James and Annie Long of 1, The Butts, Littlehampton, Sussex.

5978. LONGHURST, Mark; B: Cuckfield, Sussex; E: Haywards Heath, Sussex; Pte. SD 2958; W: 1.7.16; Merville Com. Cem., Nord.

5979. LUCAS, Thomas; B: Capel, Surrey, E: Brighton; L/Cpl. G 16046; M.M.; K: 22.3.18; Pozieres Mem. Somme.

5980. LUGET, Percy Follett; B: Exeter, Devon; E: Battersea, London; Pte. G 3999; K: 31.7.17; Ypres (Menin Gate) Mem. (Bel.); Age 31; Son of John and Louisa Luget of 28, Illminster Gardens, Clapham Common, London; Husband of Amelia Sophia Luget of 32, Hydethorpe Road, Balham, London.

5981. LUSTED, George Catton; B: Wimbledon, London; E: Hastings; Pte. G 10778; K: 31.7.17; Buffs Road Cem., St.Jean-les-Ypres (Bel.); Age 20; Son of Mrs.J.Simmonds of 107, Meadrow, Farnham, Surrey.

5982. LYDFORD, Alfred James; B: Brighton; E: Hove; L/Cpl. SD 4150; K: 3.9.16; Englebelmer Com. Cem. Ext. Somme; Age 27; Son of James and Clara Ellen Lydford of 124, Boundaries Road, Balham, London; Brother, Arthur William, also killed (see 5983). *

5983. LYDFORD, Arthur William; B: Brighton; E: Hove; Pte. SD 3159; K: 30.6.16; Loos Mem. Pas-de-Calais; Age 24; Son of James and Clara Ellen Lydford of 124, Boundaries Road, Balham, London; Brother, Alfred James, also killed (see 5982). *

M

5984. MABEY, Joseph William Lloyd; B: Newchurch, Isle of Wight; E: Mill Hill, London; Pte. G 5113; K: 22.3.18; Ste.Emilie Valley Cem., Villers-Faucon, Somme; Age 25; Son of John and Jane Mabey of Branstone, Isle of Wight.

5985. MACNAGHTEN, Arthur Edward Hay; 2nd Lt.; K: 31.7.16; Le Touret Mil. Cem. Pas-de-Calais; Age 29; Son of Col. William Hay Macnaghten; Killed by 'friendly' machine gun fire while leading a night time patrol (See text).*

5986. MALE, William; B: Bridgewater, Somerset; E: Yeovil, Somerset; Pte. G 17101; K: 26.9.17; Tyne Cot Mem. (Bel.); Age 19; Son of William and Bessie Male of High Street, Stoke-under-Ham, Somerset.

5987. MANNERING, George; B: Hastings; E: Hastings; Pte. G 1113; K: 29.3.18; Pozieres Mem. Somme; Age 21; Son of Harry and Bertha Mannering of 42, Old Church Road, Hastings.

5988. MANSFIELD, Alfred; B: Guildford; E: Brighton; Pte. G 16472; K: 26.7.18; Vendresse Brit. Cem., Aisne.

5989. MARCHANT, Fred; B: Hastings; E: Hastings; Pte. G 6213; K: 2.8.17; Ypres (Menin Gate) Mem. (Bel.); Age 28; Son of Mr. and Mrs.J.Marchant of Pear Tree Cottage, Northiam, Sussex.

5990. MARDELL, Cecil; B: Islington, London; E: London; Pte. SD 4245; K: 30.6.16; Loos Mem. Pas-de-Calais; Age 17; Son of Ernest S. and Beatrice P.Mardell of 31, Compton Road, Canonbury, London.

5991. MARSH, Albert Victor; B: Westbourne, Sussex; E: Chichester; Pte. SD 2975; K: 30.6.16; Loos Mem. Pas-de-Calais; Age 23; Son of Mrs.Elizabeth E.Marsh of White Horse Lane, Westbourne.

5992. MARSH, William James; B: Hollingbourne, Kent;

E: Eastbourne; Pte. SD 3387; K: 21.3.18; Pozieres Mem. Somme.

5993. MARTIN, John William; B: Luton; E: Luton; Pte. G 14844; K: 21.10.16; Grandcourt Road Cem. Somme; Age 18; Son of Francis Joseph and Anna Susannah Martin of 198, North Street, Luton.

5994. MARTIN, George Johnston; 2nd Lt.; K: 26.9.17; Tyne Cot Mem. (Bel.).

5995. MARTIN, William; B: – ; E: Maidstone, Kent; Pte. G 13518; D at Home: 13.10.18; Tunbridge Wells Cem., Kent (UK); Age 33; Husband of Mrs.C.M.Martin of Romford Farm Cottage, Pembury, Kent.

5996. MASKELL, Herbert; B: Barcombe, Sussex; E: Lewes; Pte. SD 2963; K: 30.6.16; Loos Mem. Pas-de-Calais.

5997. MASLEN, George Alfred; B: Hove; E: Haywards Heath, Sussex; Pte. G 9419; K: 31.7.17; Buffs Road Cem., St.Jean-les-Ypres (Bel.); Age 23; Son of George William and Ellen Maslen of 76, Livingstone Road, Hove.

5998. MASLIN, George Henry John; B: Hove; E: Hove; Pte. G 10771; K: 31.7.17; Ypres (Menin Gate) Mem. (Bel.); Age 18; Son of George and Alice Maslin of 119, Wordsworth Street, Hove.

5999. MASON, George Stuart Frederick; B: Hackney, London; E: Stratford, London; Pte. L 11464; K: 23.3.18; Villers-Faucon Com. Cem. Ext. Somme.

6000. MASON, Sidney Richard Victor Clous; B: Lindfield, Sussex; E: Worthing; Sgt. G 11950; K: 28.3.18; Pozieres Mem. Somme.*

6001. MASSER, Arthur Joseph; B: Cowes, Isle of Wight; E: Guildford, Surrey; L/Cpl. G 17130; K: 18.1.18; Tyne Cot Mem. (Bel.); Age 19; Son of Mrs.Eliza Masser of 27, Stockwell Road, East Grinstead, Sussex.

6002. MEAD, Ernest; B: – ; E: Hertford; L/Sgt. G 15620; W: 23.10.16; Puchevillers Brit. Cem. Somme; Age 19; Son of William and Elizabeth Mead of 13, St.Margaret's, Hemel Hempstead, Hertfordshire.

6003. MEDHURST, Thomas; B: Bognor Regis, Sussex; E: Horsham, Sussex; Pte. G 15947; W: 15.8.17; Wimereux Com. Cem. Pas-de-Calais.

6004. MEEK, Albert Benjamin; B: Norwich; E: Lowestoft; Pte. SD 5645; W: 15.3.17; Ypres (Menin Gate) Mem. (Bel.).*

6005. MEPHAM, Tom; B: Eastbourne; E: Eastbourne; Pte. G 16049; K: 21.10.16; Thiepval Mem. Somme.

6006. MEREDITH, Albert Edward; B: Wimbledon, London; E: Camberwell, London; Pte. G 11125; K: 27.9.17; Tyne Cot Mem. (Bel.); Age 27; Son of Joseph Edward and Elizabeth Jane Meredith of 83, Crown Street, Camberwell.

6007. MERRICKS, George Henry; B: Hastings; E: Eastbourne; Pte. SD 3167; K: 30.6.16; Loos Mem. Pas-de-Calais.

6008. MERRYDEW, Harry; B: – ; E: Arundel, Sussex; Pte. G 16411; K: 13.4.17; Vlamertinghe Mil. Cem. (Bel.); Age 19; Son of Charles and Jane Merrydew of Arundel.

6009. MILES, Leonard; B: Rusper, Sussex; E: Cranleigh, Surrey; Pte. SD 4048; K: 30.6.16; St.Vaast Post Mil. Cem. Pas-de-Calais; Age 20; Son of Mrs.Mary Miles of Rose Cottage, Rusper.

6010. MILLER, Alfred; B: Hankham, Pevensey, Sussex; E: Bexhill-on-Sea; Pte. SD 2309; W at Home: 19.7.18; Westham (St.Mary) Churchyard, Sussex (UK); Son of James Nelson Miller and Sally Miller of Peelings Farm Cottages, Hankham.

6011. MILLER, Sidney; B: King's Langley, Hertfordshire; E: Hastings; Pte. SD 3174; K: 30.6.16; Loos Mem. Pas-de-Calais; Age 28; Son of Thomas and Annie Miller of Stoughton, Hampshire.

6012. MILLWARD, Gilbert Abraham; B: Birmingham; E: Birmingham; Pte. G 17155; K: 24.3.18; Peronne Com. Cem. Ext., Ste.Radegonde, Somme.

6013. MITCHELL, Alfred James; B: Eastbourne; E: Brighton; Pte. G 16052; K: 20.3.17; Railway Dugouts Burial Ground (Bel.); Age 34; Son of Mrs.F.M.Mitchell of Brighton.

6014. MOON, William; B: Heathfield, Sussex; E: Chichester; Pte. SD 3404; W: 15.7.16; Cabaret-Rouge Brit. Cem. Pas-de-Calais.

6015. MOORE, Alfred Donald; B: Brighton; E: London; Pte. TF 266362; K: 26.9.17; Tyne Cot Mem. (Bel.); Age 23; Son of Ernest and Winifred Moore of 52, Florence Road, Brighton.

6016. MORGAN, Douglas Noel; 2nd Lt.; K: 30.6.16; Loos Mem. Pas-de-Calais; Age 26; Son of Thomas Henry and Bessie Morgan of Barn House, Eltham, London.

6017. MORRIS, George; B: Willesden, London; E: Cricklewood, London; Pte. G 20730; K: 31.7.17; Buffs Road Cem., St.Jean-les-Ypres (Bel.); Son of Mr.W.Morris of 21, Douglas Road, Kilburn, London.

6018. MORRISS, John Abel; B: Lewes; E: Hastings; Pte. SD 3403; K: 30.6.16; St.Vaast Post Mil. Cem. Pas-de-Calais.

6019. MOSELEY, George; B: Minstead, Sussex; E: Chichester; Pte. G 4224; K: 3.9.16; Knightsbridge Cem., Mesnil-Martinsart, Somme.

6020. MUSTCHIN, John; B: Yapham, Sussex; E: Hastings; Pte. SD 3623; K: 30.6.16; Loos Mem. Pas-de-Calais; Age 18; Son of George Mustchin of Yewtree Cottage, West Chiltington, Sussex.

N

6021. NEWNHAM, George Frederick; B: Battersea, London; E: Brighton; Pte. G 16471; K: 3.11.16; Thiepval Mem. Somme; Age 20; Son of William and Elizabeth Newnham of 14, Marmion Road, North Side, Clapham Common, London; Enlisted with brother, William James, who was also killed in the same action on the same day and also has no known grave (see 6023).

6022. NEWNHAM, William; B: Bury, Sussex; E: Horsham, Sussex; Pte. SD 4230; W: 3.8.17; Dozingham Mil. Cem. (Bel.); Age 28; Son of Henry and Esther Newnham of Broadford Bridge, Billingshurst, Sussex.

6023. NEWNHAM, William James; B: Brighton; E: Brighton; Pte. G 16470; K: 3.11.16; Thiepval Mem. Somme; Age 27; Son of William and Elizabeth Newnham of 14, Marmion Road, North Side, Clapham Common, London; Enlisted with brother, George Frederick, who was also killed in the same action on the same day and also has no known grave (see 6021).

6024. NEWTON, David George; B: Hemel Hempstead, Hertfordshire; E: Watford; Pte. G 14274; K: 31.7.17; Buffs Road Cem., St.Jean-les-Ypres (Bel.); Age 31; Son of Emily Newton of 9, Grosvenor Terrace, Boxmoor, Hertfordshire.

6025. NORMAN, Leslie Alfred; B: Acton, London; E: Hounslow, London; Pte. G 17002; K: 26.4.18; Tyne Cot Mem. (Bel.).

6026. NORRIS, Alfred; B: Pagham, Sussex; E: Chichester; Pte. G 15954; K: 21.10.16; Thiepval Mem. Somme; Age 40; Son of George Norris.

6027. NOTT, Saumarez Ewen; 2nd Lt.; K: 9.9.17; Tyne Cot Mem. (Bel.); Killed when leading a raiding party and upon reaching the objective.

6028. NURTON, George; B: Blackburn; E: Blackburn; Pte. G 22965; K: 16.4.18; Tyne Cot Mem. (Bel.); Age 18; Son of George and Jessey Nurton of 193, Branch Road, Ewood, Lancashire.

6029. NUTTALL, James Thomas; B: Bacup, Lancashire; E: Newmarket, Cambridgeshire; Pte. G 11983; K: 2.8.17; New Irish Farm Cem. (Bel.); Age 26; Son of Joseph Nuttall of 13, Ross Cottage, Bacup.

O

6030. ODELL, Arthur; B: Pirton, Hertfordshire; E: Pirton; L/Cpl. G 15640; K: 26.2.18; Fins New Brit. Cem. Somme; Age 21; Son of Mrs.M.Odell of 2, Royal Oak Lane, Pirton.

6031. OLIVER, Harry Percy Greenwood; 2nd Lt.; K: 30.6.16; Loos Mem. Pas-de-Calais.

6032. OLIVER, James William; B: Sutton Bridge, Lincolnshire; E: King's Lynn, Norfolk; L/Cpl. G 9323; W: 29.3.16; Abbeville Com. Cem. Ext. Somme; Age 30; Son of James and Alice Oliver of Sutton Bridge.*

6033. ORAM, George Henry; B: Hove; E: Hove; Pte. G 1583; K: 26.9.17; Tyne Cot Mem. (Bel.); Age 21; Son of Elizabeth Oram of 13, Molesworth Street, Hove.

6034. ORMSBY, Francis James; 2nd Lt.; K: 3.9.16; Hamel Mil. Cem. Somme; Age 32; Son of Col. John Betcher Ormsby.

6035. ORPIN, Ernest Barrett; B: Long Ditton, Surrey; E: Kingston-on-Thames; Pte. G 13942; K: 2.8.17; New Irish Farm Cem. (Bel.); Age 38; Son of Joseph and Mary Orpin of Long Ditton; Husband of Emily Anne Orpin of Blake's Cottage, The Rushet, Long Ditton.*

6036. OSBORNE, Frederick; B: Staplecross, Sussex; E: Hastings; Pte. SD 3643; W: 14.7.16; Longuenesse (St.Omer) Souvenir Cem. Pas-de-Calais; Age 34; Son of Anthony and Matilda Osborne of Ewhurst, Sussex; Husband of Alice Osborne of Old Coast Guard Cottages, Pett Level, Sussex.

6037. OSBORNE, Herbert; B: Brighton; E: Brighton; Pte. SD 3641; K: 30.6.16; Loos Mem. Pas-de-Calais; Age 21; Son of Mrs.Sarah Ann Osborne of 3, White Street, Brighton.

6038. OWEN, Cecil Frederick; B: Acton, London; E: London; Pte. SD 5052; K: 24.9.17; Tyne Cot Mem. (Bel.).

6039. OXLEY, Richard Stephen; 2nd Lt.; K: 18.4.18; Tyne Cot Mem. (Bel.).

P

6040. PAGE, Edward; B: Bexhill-on-Sea; E: Canterbury; L/Cpl. SD 3417; K: 30.6.16; Loos Mem. Pas-de-Calais; Age 24; Son of Daniel and Nellie Yates Page of 56, Gore Park Road, Eastbourne.

6041. PAIGE, Albert Frederick; B: Bognor Regis, Sussex; E: Bognor Regis; Pte. SD 4233; K: 30.6.16; St.Vaast Post Mil. Cem. Pas-de-Calais; Age 28; Son of Stephen James Paige; Husband of Alice E.M.Keattes, formerly Paige, of 2, Royal Oak Cottages, Lagness, Sussex.

6042. PAIN, William Tyler; B: Eastbourne; E: Eastbourne; Pte. SD 1424; K: 21.10.16; Thiepval Mem. Somme; Age 36; Husband of Ada Ruth Pain of 25, Oxford Road, Eastbourne.*

6043. PALMER, Moses; B: Billingshurst, Sussex; E: Horsham, Sussex; Pte. G 15956; D: 31.12.16; Mendinghem Mil. Cem. (Bel.); Age 32; Son of George and Mary Palmer of Windmill Cottage, Pulborough, Sussex.

6044. PANNELL, Alfred; B: Lodsworth, Sussex; E: Worthing; Pte. SD 5107; K: 30.6.16; Loos Mem. Pas-de-Calais; Son of John Pannell of The Drive, West Worthing; Brother, Charles John, also killed in the same action on the same day and also has no known grave (see 6045). *

6045. PANNELL, Charles John; B: Lodsworth, Sussex; E: Worthing; Pte. SD 4063; K: 30.6.16; Loos Mem. Pas-de-Calais; Age 39; Son of Charles Pannell of The Drive, West Worthing; Husband of Kate Ann Pannell of 47, London Street, Worthing; Brother, Arthur, also killed in the same action on the same day and also has no known grave (see 6044).

6046. PARKER, William George; B: Crowborough, Sussex; E: Hastings; Pte. SD 2986; K: 21.3.18; Pozieres Mem. Somme; Age 20; Son of Arnos and Alice Mary Parker of Capesthorn Villa, Sidlesham, Sussex.*

6047. PARKHOUSE, James Harold; B: Taunton, Somerset; E: Brighton; L/Cpl. SD 2760; K: 30.6.16; Loos Mem. Pas-de-Calais; Age 19; Son of Mr.J.G. and Mrs.E.C.Parkhouse of 2, Rugby Road, Brighton.

6048. PARKS, Walter; B: Ticehurst, Sussex; E: Hastings; Pte. G 4428; W: 19.3.18; Tincourt New Brit. Cem. Somme; Age 23; Brother of George Parks of Lower Hazelhurst Farm, Wallcrouch, Wadhurst, Sussex.

6049. PARSONS, Alfred; B: Hailsham, Sussex; E: Eastbourne; Pte. G 15960; K: 21.10.16; Grandcourt Road Cem. Somme; Husband of Mrs.M.A.Cook, formerly, Parsons, of 68, Summer Street, Stroud, Gloucestershire.

6050. PARSONS, James Henry George; B: Horsham, Sussex; E: Brighton; L/Cpl. G 17726; W: 6.5.18; Harlebeke Brit. Cem. (Bel.); Age 20; Son of Thomas and Emily Matilda Parsons of 19, Kempshott Road, Horsham.

6051. PARSONS, Percy; B: Litlington, Sussex; E: Eastbourne; Cpl. SD 2761; K: 30.6.16; Cabaret-Rouge Brit. Cem. Pas-de-Calais; Age 37; Husband of Susanna Parsons of 20, Lower Road, Eastbourne.

6052. PARTRIDGE, Ernest Sidney; B: Clare, Suffolk; E: Colchester, Essex; Pte. SD 5865; K: 30.1.17; Vlamertinghe Mil. Cem. (Bel.); Age 24; Son of Dennis and Ellen Partridge of Church Street, Sible Heddingham, Essex; Husband of Mrs.E.Partridge of 1, Riding Street, Werneth, Lancashire.

6053. PATCHING, Richard George; B: Hove; E: Hove; Pte. SD 4065; K: 30.6.16; St.Vaast Post Mil. Cem. Pas-de-Calais.*

6054. PATCHING, Walter Mark; B: Portslade, Sussex; E: Hove; Sgt. SD 2993; K: 3.9.16; Thiepval Mem. Somme.

6055. PAVEY, Harold Herbert; B: Whitechapel, London; E: Shoreditch, London; Pte. SD 4231; K: 30.6.16; Loos Mem. Pas-de-Calais; Age 19; Son of John William and Nellie Pavey of 66, Regent's Row, Haggerston, London.

6056. PEACHAM, Sidney Arthur; B: Hastings; E: Hastings; L/Cpl. SD 4067; K: 30.6.16; Loos Mem. Pas-de-Calais; Age 20; Son of Oliver Albert and Alice Edith Pearham of 395, Battle Road, St.Leonards-on-Sea, Sussex.*

6057. PEARCE, George James Hunneikin; B: Plymouth; E: Plymouth; Pte. G 17107; K: 24.9.17; Tyne Cot Mem. (Bel.); Age 19; Son of Mr.J.J.R. and Mrs.A.Pearce of 7, Quarry Park Road, Peverell, Devon.*

6058. PELLETT, Joseph Frank; B: Brighton; E: Hove; Pte. SD 2762; W: 1.7.16; Bethune Town Cem. Pas-de-Calais; Age 22; Son of Mr. and Mrs.Pellett of 14, Holland Street, Brighton.*

6059. PENFOLD, Jack; B: Fernhurst, Sussex; E: Midhurst, Sussex; L/Cpl. G 16309; K: 10.3.18; Fins New Brit. Cem. Somme.

6060. PERCIVAL, Enos; B: Wellingborough, Northamptonshire; Kettering, Northamptonshire; Pte. G 22640; K: 22.4.18; Epehy Wood Farm Cem., Epehy, Somme; Husband of Mrs.E.Percival of 86, Robinson Road, Rushden, Northamptonshire.

6061. PERIGOE, Harold Sydney; B: Hastings; E: Hastings; Pte. G 16057; K: 21.10.16; Grandcourt Road Cem. Somme; Son of Mr.J.Perigoe of 130, Mount Pleasant Road, Hastings.

6062. PERKINS, Frederick; B: Cavan; E: Worthing; L/Cpl. SD 4175; K: 30.6.16; Loos Mem. Pas-de-Calais; Age 40; Son of George and Emily Perkins; Husband of Gertrude Perkins of 8, Arminger Road, Shepherds Bush, London

6063. PERKINS, John Henry; B: Hove; E: Brighton; Pte. SD 3423; W: 4.11.16; Boulogne Eastern Cem. Pas-de-Calais; Age 19; Son of Roland Harry and Gertrude Perkins of 38, Payne Avenue, Hove.

6064. PERRIN, Percival Philip; B: Liss, Hampshire; E: Chichester; Pte. SD 3188; W: 30.6.16; Bethune Town Cem. Pas-de-Calais; Age 35; Son of Alfred and Matilda Perrin of Rake, Hampshire.

6065. PERRY, Arthur; B: –; E: Hertford; Pte. G 15641; K: 21.3.18; Pozieres Mem. Somme; Age 28; Brother of John William Perry of Bromley's Farm, Harlow, Essex.

6066. PETTITT, Charles Henry; B: Mayfield, Sussex; E: Eastbourne; Pte. G 16059; K: 23.9.16; Euston Road Cem. Somme; Age 25; Husband of Alice Ruth Pettitt of Argos Hill, Mayfield; Killed with eight others in the front line trench on the Redan Ridge by an enemy trench mortar explosion.*

6067. PETTITT, Henry; B: Millwall, London; E: Hove; L/Cpl. SD 2998; W: 7.7.16; Merville Com. Cem., Nord.

6068. PHILBY, John; B: Upper Marden, Sussex; E: Chichester; Pte. SD 3189; K: 22.7.16; St.Vaast Post Mil. Cem. Pas-de-Calais; Age 29; Son of Robert and Elizabeth Philby of Hill Cottage, Houghton Bridge, Amberley, Sussex.*

6069. PHILLIPS, Albert Gordon; B: Brighton; E: Hove; Pte. SD 3184; K: 30.6.16; Loos Mem. Pas-de-Calais; Age 18; Son of Albert and Cicely Jane Phillips of 22, Stoneham Road, Hove.

6070. PHILPOTT, George Boyer; B: Great Sampford, Essex; E: Great Bardfield, Essex; Pte. TF 260113; K: 2.8.17; New Irish Farm Cem. (Bel.); Age 38.

6071. PHILPOTT, Henry George; B: St.Leonards-on-Sea; E: Hastings; Pte. SD 2983; K: 21.10.16; Grandcourt Road Cem. Somme; Son of Mr.H.Philpott of 6, Mount Pleasant, St.Leonards-on-Sea, Sussex.

6072. PHIPPEN, Sidney; B: Chard, Somerset; E: Chard; Pte. SD 4234; K: 30.6.16; Loos Mem. Pas-de-Calais; Age 20; Son of Mr.G. and Mrs.E.J.Phippen of 25, Coombe Street, Chard.

6073. PIERCE, Albert; B: Steyning, Sussex; E: Hove; Pte. SD 3428; K: 16.8.16; Flatiron Copse Cem. Somme; Age 22; Son of Marchant and Rosettta Pierce of 17, Charlton Street, Steyning.

6074. PIERCE, Alfred; B: Rye, Sussex; E: Chichester; Pte. G 19523; W: 24.11.17; Lijssenthoek Mil. Cem. (Bel.); Son of Mrs.A.Pierce of 5, South-under-Cliff, Rye.*

6075. PIERCE, Leonard; B: Shipley, Sussex; E: Worthing; L/Cpl. SD 5008; K: 30.6.16; Loos Mem. Pas-de-Calais; Age 30; Son of Harry and Sarah Ann Pierce of 4, Daux Road, Billingshurst, Sussex.

6076. PIERCY, William; B: Brighton; E: Portsmouth; Pte. G 16306; K: 26.4.18; Tyne Cot Mem. (Bel.).

6077. PITCHER, James Luther; B: Jevington, Sussex; E: Eastbourne; Cpl. G 13806; K: 6.2.18; Gouzeaucourt New Brit. Cem., Nord; Age 40; Husband of Emily Pitcher of 58, Brook Street, Polegate, Sussex.

6078. PLAYFORD, Harry; B: Northiam, Sussex; E: Hastings; Pte. SD 5039; K: 30.6.16; Loos Mem. Pas-de-Calais; Age 21; Husband of Daisy Emily Playford of 22, Sandown Road, Hastings.

6079. PLUMMER, Albert; B: Chailey, Sussex; E: Eastbourne; L/Cpl. SD 3427; W: 2.7.16; Cabaret-Rouge Brit. Cem. Pas-de-Calais; Age 36; Son of Charles and Caroline Plummer; Husband of Esther Plummer of 3, Andros Close, South Common, Lewes, Sussex.

6080. PLUMMER, William Henry; B: Fareham, Hampshire; E: Worthing; Pte. G 16061; K: 27.9.17; Tyne Cot Mem. (Bel.); Age 20; Son of Eliza Goldsmith, formerly Plummer, of 2, Dolphin Terrace, Kingston-by-Sea, Brighton, and the late Henry Plummer.

6081. POCOCK, Henry Peter; B: Angmering, Sussex; E: Lewes; Pte. SD 3200; K: 30.6.16; Loos Mem. Pas-de-Calasi; Age 22; Son of Simeon and Kate Pocock of Blaber Cottage, Angmering.

6082. POHL, Frederick Ernest; B: – ; E: Birkenhead; Pte. TF 203446; W: 29.3.18; Namps-au-Val Brit. Cem., Somme; Died at Casualty Clearing Station, Namps-au-Val.

6083. POLLARD, Charles; B: Singleton, Sussex; E: Hastings; Pte. SD 4073; W: 12.5.18; Hamburg Cem. (G); Grandson of George Pollard of Bepton, Sussex; Died while a Prisoner of War from the effects of gass.

6084. POLLARD, Sydney Samuel; B: Eastbourne; E: Eastbourne; Pte. SD 3191; W: 31.3.16; Merville Com. Cem., Nord; Age 24; Son of John and Annie Pollard of 50, Melbourne Road, Eastbourne; Died at Casulaty Clearing Station, Merville.*

6085. POPE, Henry James; B: Heathfield, Sussex; E: Eastbourne; Pte. SD 3654; W: 29.9.16; Euston Road Cem. Somme.

6086. PORTER, Frank Ernest; B: Bow, London; E: High Wycombe, Buckinghamshire; Pte. G 17129; W: 28.2.18; Tincourt New Brit. Cem. Somme; Died at Casualty Clearing Station, Tincourt.

6087. POTTER, Arthur; B: Lancing; E: Worthing; Pte. G 16063; K: 27.9.17; Tyne Cot Mem. (Bel.); Age 31.

6088. POUGET, Louis; B: Brighton; E: Hove; Pte. SD 3186; W: 2.4.18; St.Sever Cem. Ext., Rouen, Seine-Maritime.

6089. PRATT, Claude Ernest; B: Luton; E: Luton; Pte. G 14855; W: 9.6.17; Mendinghem Mil. Cem. (Bel.); Age 26; Son of Mr. and Mrs.James Pratt of 21, Peach Street, Luton.

6090. PRIOR, Lewis Atkins; 2nd Lt.; K: 30.6.16; Loos Mem. Pas-de-Calais.

6091. PRIOR, Scott Noel; B: Tittlesham, Norfolk; E: Norwich; Pte. G 17009; W at Home: 25.5.18; Westfield (St.Andrew) Churchyard, Norfolk (UK); Age 19; Son of Robert James and Mary Ann Prior.

6092. PRIVETT, Alfred; B: Wareham, Dorset; E: Brighton; Cpl. G 16473; K: 10.3.18; Fins New Brit. Cem. Somme; Age 30; Son of Edward and Ellen Privett of 8, Milton Avenue, Croydon.

6093. PULLEN, Frank; B: Brighton; E: Hove; Pte. SD 3190; W: 30.6.16; Loos Mem. Pas-de-Calais.

6094. PULLEN, William Henry; B: Rudgwick, Sussex; E: Horsham, Sussex; L/Cpl. SD 2981; K: 21.10.16; Thiepval Mem. Somme; Age 37; Husband of Jane Pullen of Pounds Cottage, Okehurst, Sussex.

6095. PUNCH, Edward; B: – ; E: Worthing; Pte. SD 3182; K: 29.5.16; Cambrin Churchyard Ext. Pas-de-Calais.

Q

6096. QUINNELL, Ernest; B: Eastbourne; E: Hastings; Pte. SD 2999; D at Home: 22.1.16; Bramshott (St. Mary) Churchyard, Hampshire (UK).

R

6097. RANSLEY, J.W.R.; B: – ; E: – ; Pte. SD 3667; W or D at Home: 30.4.17; Brighton (Bear Road) Cem. Sussex (UK).

6098. RATCLIFF, Cyril; B: Brighton; E: Arundel; L/Cpl. G 7297; W: 4.4.17; Lijssenthoek Mil. Cem. (Bel.); Age 19; Son of William and Lily C.Ratcliff of The Laurels, Lyminster, Sussex.

6099. RAYNER, L.K.; 2nd Lt.; K: 18.4.17; Vlamertinghe Mil. Cem. (Bel.); Age 27; Son of Arthur Leopold and Charlotte Annie Rayner of 17, Dryburgh Road, Putney; London; Attached to 116th Trench Mortar Battery; Killed by shell fire while reconnoittering.*

6100. RAYNSFORD, Thomas James; B: Brighton; E: Brighton; Pte. SD 2765; K: 30.6.16; Loos Mem. Pas-de-Calais; Age 41; Husband of Annie Raynsford of 29, Southampton Street, Brighton.

6101. READ, Albert Edward Victor; B: Littlehampton, Sussex; E: Littlehampton; Pte. G 15966; K: 16.6.17; Mendinghem Mil. Cem. (Bel.); Age 20; Son of Albert and Mary S.Read of 11, Surrey Street, Littlehampton.*

6102. REDMAN, Harold Arthur; B: Wick, Sussex; E: Warley, Essex; Pte. G 12942; K: 31.7.17; Ypres (Menin Gate) Mem. (Bel.).

6103. REED, Albert Henry; B: Sidlesham, Sussex; E: Chichester; Sgt. G 6430; K: 23.4.18; Villers-Faucon Com. Cem. Ext. Somme; Age 31; Son of Frank and Emma Reed of Chalder Farm, Sidlesham; Husband of Elsie Reed of Old Fishbourne, Sussex.

6104. REED, Ernest Thomas; B: Wick, Sussex; E: Worthing; Pte. SD 5075; W: 12.7.16; Cabaret-Rouge Brit. Cem. Pas-de-Calais.

6105. REYNOLDS, Walter; B: Peterborough; E: Peterborough; Pte. G 24302; K: 16.3.18; Thiepval Mem. Somme; Age 19; Son of Walter and Mary Ann Reynolds of 209, Great Northern Railway Cottages, New England, Northamptonshire.

6106. RICE, Charles Henry James; B: Hounslow, London; E: Kingston-on-Thames; Pte. SD 5665; K: 21.10.16; Thiepval Mem. Somme.

6107. RICHARDS, Charles James; B: Brianants Puddle, Dorset; E: Chichester; Sgt. SD 2766; W: 27.9.17; Locre Hospice Cem. (Bel.); Age 27; Husband of Alice Mary Richards of Milton End, Whitechurch, Dorset.

6108. RICHARDSON, Albert Ernest; B: Wick, Sussex; E: Littlehampton, Sussex; Pte. G 15962; K: 21.10.16; Grandcourt Road Cem. Somme; Age 30; Son of Mr. and Mrs.G.J.Richardson of Baffalo Cottage, Wick.

6109. RICHARDSON, Arthur Amos; B: Bethnal Green, London; E: Stratford, London; Pte. G 17125; K: 6.11.17; Hooge Crater Cem. (Bel.); Age 19; Son of Mrs.Alice E.Richardson of 31, Scotts Road, Leyton, London.

6110. RICHARDSON, Stanley John; B: Hastings; E: Hastings; L/Cpl. G 20447; W: 25.3.18; Roisel Com. Cem. Ext. Somme; Age 21; Son of John and Josephine Richardson of 54, All Saints' Street, Hastings.

6111. RIDLEY, Urban Charles; B: Maresfield, Sussex; E: Uckfield, Sussex; Pte. G 17224; W: 24.9.17; Tyne Cot Mem. (Bel.).

6112. ROBERTS, Cecil Vincer; B: Brighton; E: Brighton; Pte. TF 241501; K: 26.9.17; Tyne Cot Mem. (Bel.); Age 21; Son of William Thomas and Elizabeth Ann Roberts of 13, Preston Road, Brighton.*

6113. ROBERTS, Frederick; B: –; E: Lewes; Pte. G 17970; W: 2.4.17; Vlamertinghe Mil. Cem. (Bel.).

6114. ROBERTS, William John; B: Wellingborough, Northamptonshire; E: Kettering, Northamptonshire; Pte. G 22639; K: 22.3.18; Pozieres Mem. Somme.*

6115. ROBINSON, George; B: Clapham, Bedfordshire; E: Bedford; Pte. G 17429; K: 28.9.17; Tyne Cot Mem. (Bel.); Age 18; Son of Joseph and Emma Robinson of 2, Preservine Cottages, Clapham.

6116. ROBINSON, Hugh Thomas Kay; Lt. Col., D.S.O.; K: 26.4.18; Tyne Cot Mem. (Bel.); Son of Rev. William Kay Robinson, Rector of Walwyn's Castle, Pembrokeshire; Husband of Mrs.Evelyn R.Kay Robinson of 1, Cecil Court, Tunbridge Wells; Killed while Officer Commanding 13th Battalion.

6117. ROBINSON, John; B: Shalton, County Durham; E: West Hartlepool, County Durham; Pte. G 5936; K: 22.3.18; Pozieres Mem. Somme; Age 29; Husband of Sarah Robinson of 8, Alexandra Terrace, Wheatley Hill, County Durham.

6118. RODE, Edward; B: Finsbury, London; E: Mill Hill, London; Pte. TF 202778; K: 31.7.17; New Irish Farm Cem. (Bel.); Age 20; Son of Josephine Rode of 26, Ritches Road, Harringay, London.

6119. RODELL, Ernest; B: St.Paul's, Bedfordshire; E: Luton; Pte. G 14864; K: 18.10.17; Tyne Cot Mem. (Bel.).

6120. ROE, John Sidney; B: Bramshott, Hampshire; E: Guildford; Pte. SD 4237; W: 13.6.17; Cambrin Churchyard Ext. Pas-de-Calais.

6121. ROGERS, Benjamin; B: Brighton; E: Hove; Pte. SD 3673; K: 30.6.16; Loos Mem. Pas-de-Calais; Age 18; Son of Mr.W.Rogers of 25, New Dorset Street, Brighton; His brother, John Fredrick, also fell.

6122. ROGERS, Charles; B: Richmond, Surrey; E: Richmond; Pte. G 13953; W: 17.2.17; Boulogne Eastern Cem. Pas-de-Calais; Age 43; Son of Charles and Emily Rogers; Husband of Alice Elizabeth Rogers of 55, Stanley Road, East Sheen, London; Died of blood poisoning; Served in the South African Campaign.*

6123. ROKER, Clive Leslie; B: Kingston-on-Thames; E: Kingston-on-Thames; Pte.TF 201861; K: 15.10.17; Kemmel Chateau Mil. Cem. (Bel.); Age 19; Son of Mrs.Kate Roker of 188, Elm Road, Kingston-on-Thames.

6124. ROLFE, Lionel Thomas; B: Worthing; E: Worthing; Pte. SD 3002; K: 30.6.16; St.Vaast Post Mil. Cem. Pas-de-Calais.

6125. ROWLAND, Edward C; B: Aldingbourne, Sussex; E: Chichester; Pte. G 15963; K: 27.9.17; Perth Cem. (China Wall) (Bel.).*

6126. ROWLAND, James; B: Cuckfield, Sussex; E: Haywards Heath; Pte. G 1463; K: 26.9.17; Perth Cem. (China Wall) (Bel.).

6127. ROWLATT, William John; B: Corby, Northamptonshire; E: Kettering, Northamptonshire; Pte. TF 201788; K: 21.3.18; Pozieres Mem. Somme.

6128. RUSSELL, Ralph William; B: Horsham, Sussex; E: Chichester; Pte. TF 203197; D at Home: 14.4.18; Horsham (Deane Road) Cem., Sussex (UK); Age 34; Son of William Smart Russell and Caroline Russell; Husband of Ethel Russell of 15, Albion Terrace, Horsham.

S

6129. SAUNDERS, Alfred Thomas; B: Ongar, Essex; E: Epping, Essex; Pte. G 17245; K: 24.3.18; Pozieres Mem. Somme.

6130. SAXBY, Walter; B: Hastings; E: Hastings; Pte. SD 5007; K: 30.6.16; St.Vaast Post Mil. Cem. Pas-de-Calais.

6131. SAYERS, Arthur Barnett; B: Nutley, Sussex; E: Uckfield, Sussex; Pte. G 15974; K: 14.10.16; Euston Road Cem. Somme; Age 25; Son of Charles and Harriett Sayers; Husband of Maud Frances Sayers of Nursery Cottage, Nutley.

6132. SAYERS, John; B: Hurstpierpoint, Sussex; E: Hurstpierpoint; Pte. G 3394; K: 3.9.16; Ancre Brit. Cem. Somme.

6133. SCAIFE, Arthur; B: Darlington, County Durham; E: Kingston-on-Thames; Pte. G 13945; K: 31.7.17; Buffs Road Cem., St.Jean-les-Ypres (Bel.); Husband of Mrs.F.E.Scaife of 7, Bedford Row, Worthing.

6134. SCOBELL, George Alfred; B: Streatham, London; E: St.Paul's Churchyard, London; Pte. G 17237; K: 27.9.17; Tyne Cot Mem. (Bel.).

6135. SCOTT, George Harold James; B: Horley, Surrey; E: Chiswick, London; Pte. G 17431; K: 27.9.17; Tyne Cot Mem. (Bel.); Age 19; Son of George and Edith Annie Scott of 4, Powis Road North, Bromley-by-Bow, London.

6136. SCOTT, Henry Charles; B: Bognor Regis, Sussex; E: Bognor Regis; Pte. SD 3225; M.M.; K: 30.6.16; St.Vaast Post Mil. Cem. Pas-de-Calais.

6137. SCUTT, Leonard; B: Cowfold, Sussex; E: East

Grinstead, Sussex; Pte. SD 5270; K: 21.10.16; Thiepval Mem. Somme; Age 20; Son of Alice Page, formerly Scutt, Broomlye Farm House, Newick, Sussex, and the late Leonard Scutt.

6138. SHEARING, Robert John Edward; B: Homerton, London; E: Eastbourne; Pte. SD 3451; W: 30.6.16; Cabaret-Rouge Brit. Cem. Pas-de-Calais; Age 25; Son of Mr. and Mrs.C.Shearing of London.

6139. SHEPHERD, William Thomas; B: Hove; E: Eastbourne; Pte. SD 356; K: 30.6.16; Cabaret-Rouge Brit. Cem. Pas-de-Calais; Age 30; Son of John Shepherd of Old Mill House, Henfield, Sussex.

6140. SHOESMITH, John; B: Leeds; E: Brighton; Pte. G 16474; K: 3.11.16; Thiepval Mem. Somme.

6141. SILVESTER, Arthur; B: Littlehampton, Sussex; E: Chichester; Pte. G 19524; D: 7.7.18; Tincourt New Brit. Cem. Somme.

6142. SIMMONDS, Albert Edward; B: Handcross, Sussex; E: Maidstone, Kent; Pte. SD 2433; K: 30.6.16; Loos Mem. Pas-de-Calais; Age 18; Son of Henry and Agnes Simmonds of 12, St.Mary's Cottages, Church Street, Eastbourne.*

6143. SIMPSON, Ernest George; B: – ; E: Petworth, Sussex; Pte. G 16071; K: 21.10.16; Grandcourt Road Cem. Somme; Age 29; Son of George and Mary Simpson of East Horsley, Surrey.

6144. SIMPSON, Frank George; B: Brighton; E: Hove; Pte. SD 3217; K: 23.3.18; Pozieres Mem. Somme; Age 22; Son of Alfred Simpson of 4, Trafalgar Terrace, Brighton.

6145. SINNOCK, George Arthur; B: Brighton; E: Brighton; Pte. SD 3025; K: 30.6.16; Cabaret-Rouge Brit. Cem. Pas-de-Calais; Age 26; Son of Alfred and Mary Ann Sinnock of 54, Leicester Road, Lewes.

6146. SIVEWRIGHT, William George; 2nd Lt.; K: 26.9.17; Tyne Cot Mem. (Bel.).

6147. SKERRY, John Henry; B: Astcote, Northamptonshire; E: Northampton; Pte. G 23136; K: 22.3.18; Pozieres Mem. Somme.

6148. SKILTON, Leonard Walter; B: Hornchurch, Essex; E: Romford, Essex; L/Cpl. G 20228; K: 31.7.17; Buffs Road Cem., St.Jean-les-Ypres (Bel.); Age 27; Son of George and Annie Skilton of Romford; Husband of Agnes Skilton of Joslyns Lodge, Corbets Tey, Essex.

6149. SKINNER, Thomas Valentine; B: Salvington, Sussex; E: Brighton; Pte. G 16072; W: 4.8.17; Dozinghem Mil. Cem. (Bel.); Age 24; Son of W.Skinner of Middle Road, Kingston-by-Sea, Brighton.

6150. SKIPP, Ernest James; B: – ; E: Hertford; Pte. G 15628; K: 21.10.16; Thiepval Mem. Somme; Age 28; Son of Samuel and Katherine Skipp of 61, New Road, Ware, Hertfordshire.

6151. SLAUGHTER, Leonard; B: Worthing; E: Worthing; Sgt. SD 4087; W at Home: 7.7.16; Worthing (Broadwater) Cem., Sussex (UK); Son of Cunetia A.Slaughter of 474, Home Street, Winnipeg, Canada, and the late W.H.Slaughter.

6152. SMITH, Albert; B: Bognor Regis, Sussex; E: Chichester; Pte. SD 3015; K: 30.6.16; Cabaret-Rouge Brit. Cem. Pas-de-Calais.

6153. SMITH, Arthur; B: Eastbourne; E: Eastbourne; Pte. G 16074; K: 23.9.16; Euston Road Cem. Somme; Enlisted with brother, Walter, and both were killed by the same Minnenwerfer, both having only just arrived in the trenches with a new draft of men; Both buried side by side in the same cemetery (see 6163).

6154. SMITH, Charles Francis; B: Lee, Kent; E: Croydon; Pte. G 21862; K: 25.3.18; Epehy Wood Farm Cem., Epehy, Somme; .

6155. SMITH, Colin Stanley; B: – ; E: Lincoln; Pte. G 15310; K: 31.7.17; Buffs Road Cem., St.Jean-les-Ypres (Bel.); Brother of Mr.F.J.Smith of 14, Rawmarsh Hill, Parkgate, Rotherham.*

6156. SMITH, Edward Henry; B: Old Hall Green, Hertfordshire; E: Hertford; Pte, G 14275; K: 31.7.17; Ypres (Menin Gate) Mem. (Bel.).

6157. SMITH, George Spencer; B: Cooksbridge, Sussex; E: Chichester; Pte. G 9591; K: 26.4.18; Tyne Cot Mem. (Bel.); Age 32; Son of James and Margaret Emma Smith of Yew Tree Cottage, Colonels Bank, Chailey, Sussex.*

6158. SMITH, Harold; B: Westbury, Buckinghamshire; E: Chichester; Sgt. G 6444; W: 29.6.17; Étaples Mil. Cem. Pas-de-Calais; Age 30; Son of Albert Smith of Shalstone, Buckinghamshire.

6159. SMITH, Harold Harry; B: Irthlingborough, Northamptonshire; Arlesey, Bedfordshire; Pte. G 14871; K: 21.10.16; Grandcourt Road Cem. Somme; Age 19; Son of Mrs.A.H.Rook of 24, Newtown, Arlesey.*

6160. SMITH Herbert Whitworth; B: Norwich; E: Brighton; Sgt. SD 3457; K: 7.6.16; Cambrin Churchyard Ext. Pas-de-Calais.*

6161. SMITH, Matthew; B: Heathfield, Sussex; E: Hastings; Pte. G 5165; K: 17.9.17; Voormezeele Enclosures No.1 and 2 (Bel.).

6162. SMITH, Thomas; B: Chiddingly, Sussex; E: Worthing; Pte. SD 3009; W: 30.6.16; Loos Mem. Pas-de-Calais.

6163. SMITH, Walter; B: Mayfield, Sussex; E: Eastbourne; Pte. G 16073; K: 23.9.16; Euston Road Cem. Somme; Age 25; Son of Mr. and Mrs.Horace Smith of Toronto, Canada; Husband of Agnes Mary Wansbon, formerly Smith, of Stonehouse, Bassetts, Mark Cross, Sussex; Enlisted with brother, Arthur, and both were killed by the same Minnenwerfer, both having only just arrived in the trenches with a new draft of men; both buried side by side in the same cemetery (see 6153).

6164. SMITH, William Henry; B: Faversham, Kent; E: Canterbury; Pte. G 16859; K: 27.9.17; Zantvoorde Brit. Cem. (Bel.); Age 33; Son of William Walter and Annie Smith of Faversham; Husband of Priscilla Jane Smith of 33, Wincheap Grove, Canterbury.

6165. SMITH, Willam Stephen; B: Herstmonceux, Sussex; E: Hastings; Pte. SD 3692; K: 30.6.16; Loos Mem. Pas-de-Calais; Age 39; Son of George Henry Smith of Gardner Street, Herstmonceux; Husband of Caroline Annie Hide, formerly Smith, of 3, Elm Cottage, Upper Dicker, Sussex.

6166. SNOXELL, Arthur; B: –; E: Hertford; Pte. G 15644; K: 22.6.17; Vlamertinghe New Mil. Cem. (Bel.).

6167. SOAN, Albert Clarence; B: Sedlescombe, Sussex; E: Hastings; Pte. G 17973; K: 31.7.17; Buffs Road Cem., St.Jean-les-Ypres (Bel.); Age 21; Son of Mrs.F.Soan of Sedlescombe.

6168. SOGNO, George Frank; 2nd Lt.; W: 9.10.17; Mendinghem Mil. Cem. (Bel.); Age 21; Son of Frank and Alice Sogno of 38, Upper Avenue, Eastbourne.

6169. SOUTH, Henry Samuel; B: Brighton; E: Hove; Pte. SD 4093; K: 30.6.16; Loos Mem. Pas-de-Calais.

6170. SPALDING, Bertram Hubert; B: Hornsey, London; E: Luton; Pte. G 14865; K: 27.10.16; Thiepval Mem. Somme; Age 19; Son of Bertram and Emma Spalding of 206, Hitchin Road, Luton.*

6171. SPARKES, W.T.; B: Brighton; E: Hove; Pte. SD 3681; K: 30.6.16; St.Vaast Post Mil. Cem. Pas-de-Calais.*

6172. SPARKS, Adolphus; B: Hove; E: Brighton; L/Cpl. SD 3687; K: 30.6.16; St.Vaast Post Mil. Cem. Pas-de-Calais.*

6173. SPINK, Bert; B: Brighton; E: Hove; Pte. SD 3680; W: 18.4.16; Bethune Town Cem. Pas-de-Calais; Age 19; Son of George Ransom Spink and Caroline Spink of Brighton.

6174. SPRING, Albert; B: Brighton; E: Brighton; Pte. SD 3026; W: 21.5.16; Bethune Town Cem. Pas-de-Calais; Age 25; Son of Mrs. Emily Laura Spring of 9, Windsor Buildings, Brighton.*

6175. SQUIRES, Alfred Benjamin; B: Felpham, Sussex; E: Bognor Regis, Sussex; Pte. G 8133; K: 31.7.17; Buffs Road Cem., St.Jean-les-Ypres (Bel.); Husband of Mrs.E.Squires of 274, Holdenhurst Road, Bournemouth.

6176. SQUIRES, Wilfred Augustus; B: Burgess Hill, Sussex; E: Hastings; Pte. SD 3012; K: 30.6.16; Loos Mem. Pas-de-Calais; Age 20; Son of Mr.W.A.Squires of Victoria House, London Road, Balcombe, Sussex.

6177. STANDINGFORD, Alfred John; B: Enfield, Middlesex; E: Tottenham, London; Pte. G 20729; K: 27.9.17; Tyne Cot Mem. (Bel.); Age 19; Son of Mr. and Mrs.L.Sandingford of 93, Raynham Avenue, Edmonton, London.

6178. STAPLEHURST, Robert George; B: Eastbourne; E: Eastbourne; Pte. SD 1466; K: 26.4.18; Tyne Cot Mem. (Bel.).

6179. STAPLETON, Vincent James; B: Newport Pagnell, Buckinghamshire; E: Hastings; Pte. G 18232; K: 3.9.16; Hamel Mil. Cem. Somme; Age 31; Son of James and Eva Mercy Stapleton of 46, Belle Hill, Bexhill-on-Sea.

6180. STEBBINGS, William George; B: Babraham, Cambridgeshire; E: Cambridge; L/Cpl. G 14900; K: 23.3.18; Pozieres Mem. Somme; Age 21; Son of John Thomas Stebbings and Esther Winfield Stebbings (stepmother) of Trinity Cottages, Cheveley, Cambridgeshire.*

6181. STENNING, Lawrence; B: Sayers Common, Sussex; E: Haywards Heath, Sussex; Pte. SD 3023; K: 21.10.16; Grandcourt Road Cem. Somme; Age 32; Husband of Mrs.Reeves, formerly Stenning, of 8, Valebridge Terrace, Burgess Hill, Sussex.

6182. STENNING, William; B: Brighton; E: Brighton; Pte. L 10346; K: 26.9.17; Tyne Cot Mem. (Bel.); Age 24; Son of Harry and Elizabeth Stenning.

6183. STEPNEY, James; B: Pulborough, Sussex; E: Haywards Heath, Sussex; Pte. SD 3220; K: 24.9.17; Tyne Cot Mem. (Bel.); Age 37; Son of Marchant and Mary Arm Stepney of Royal George Road, Burgess Hill, Sussex; His brother, Jack, also fell.*

6184. STEVENS, Ernest Gordon; B: East Dean, Sussex; E: Hastings; Pte. SD 2781; K: 30.6.16; Cabaret-Rouge Brit. Cem. Pas-de-Calais; Age 23; Son of John and Ann Stevens of 45, East Dean, Chichester.

6185. STEVENS, Geoffrey William; B: Grenthorpe, Norfolk; E: Norwich; Pte. TF 202344; K: 26.4.18; Tyne Cot Mem. (Bel.); Age 20; Son of Charlotte Stevens of Grenthorpe.*

6186. STEVENSON, Charles Evan; B: Wymondham, Norfolk; E: Norwich; Pte. G 9362; K: 31.7.17; Ypres (Menin Gate) Mem. (Bel.).

6187. STEVENSON, James; B: Nutley, Sussex; E: Eastbourne; Pte. SD 3226; W: 17.4.16; Bethune Town Cem., Pas-de-Calais; Age 25; Son of Richard and Alice Stevenson of Sweet Briar Cottage, Dane Hill, Sussex; Brother, Jesse, also fell (see 6188).

6188. STEVENSON, Jesse; B: Uckfield, Sussex; E: Horsham, Sussex; Pte. SD 3691; K: 30.6.16; Cabaret-Rouge Brit. Cem. Pas-de-Calais; Age 21; Son of Alice Stevenson of Sweet Briar Cottage, Dane Hill, Sussex; Brother, James, also fell (see 6187).

6189. STEWART, Sidney Walter; B: South Heigham, Norfolk; E: Norwich; Pte. SD 5600; K: 27.10.16; Thiepval Mem. Somme; Age 27; Husband of Ada Florence Stewart of 88, William Street, Norwich.*

6190. STICKLAND, Alfred Augustus; B: Lewes; E: Eastbourne; Pte. G 15975; K: 24.10.17; Godewaersvelde Brit. Cem., Nord; Son of Henry and Martha Stickland of 9, Elmdoune Place, Hailsham, Sussex.

6191. STILL, William George; B: Croydon; E: Croydon; Pte. G 24445; K: 26.4.18; Tyne Cot Mem. (Bel.); Age 19; Son of Mrs.Alice Still of 3, Victoria Place, Duppas Hill Lane, Croydon.

6192. STILLWELL, Alfred James; B: Westbourne, Sussex; E: Chichester; L/Cpl. SD 3019; K: 26.9.17; Tyne Cot Mem. (Bel.).

6193. STOCKWELL, Stanley Frank; B: Penge, London; E: Maidstone; Pte. G 16949; K: 18.10.17; Tyne Cot Mem. (Bel.); Age 19; Son of Eli and Rose Stockwell of 28, Croydon Road, Penge.

6194. STOKES, John Thomas Nelson; B: –; E: Spalding, Lincolnshire; Pte. G 15314; K: 2.8.17; Buffs Road Cem., St.Jean-les-Ypres (Bel.); Age 25; Son of Tom and Susannah Stokes of 62, Little London, Spalding.

6195. STONE, Bernard Alfred; B: Amberley, Sussex; E: Bognor Regis, Sussex; R.S.M. TF 200023; D.C.M; K: 26.4.18; Tyne Cot Mem. (Bel.).

6196. STRATTON, Herbert; B: Coventry; E: Luton; L/Cpl. G 14868; K: 26.9.17; Tyne Cot Mem. (Bel.); Age 20; Son of Henry and Mary Stratton.*

6197. STREET, Albert James; B: Worthing; E: Worthing; L/Cpl. SD 4106; K: 30.6.16; Guards Cem. (Cuinchy) Pas-de-Calais.

6198. STREET, Claude Arthur; B: Poole, Dorset; E: Maidstone; L/Cpl. G 20224; K; 8.2.18; Gouzeaucourt New Brit. Cem., Nord.

6199. STREETER, John Vincent; B: St.Leonards-on-Sea, Sussex; E: Shepherd's Bush, London; Pte. G 6575; K: 26.4.18; Tyne Cot Mem. (Bel.); Age 28; Son of John Streeter of 2a, Commercial Road, Eastbourne.

6200. STRIDE, Henry James; B: Devonport; E: Plymouth; Pte. G 17127; W: 11.11.17; Lijssenthoek Mil. Cem. (Bel.).

6201. STRINGER, George Stephenson; B: Fishergate, Sussex; E: Worthing; L/Cpl. SD 3223; K: 26.4.18; Tyne Cot Mem. (Bel.).

6202. STRONG, Samuel Victor; B: Brighton; E: Hastings; Pte. G 17974; K: 3.9.16; Hamel Mil. Cem. Somme.

6203. STUBBERFIELD, Albert Henry; B: St.Leonards-on-Sea; E: Hastings; Pte. SD 4107; K: 30.6.16; St.Vaast Post Mil. Cem. Pas-de-Calais.

6204. SUMNER, Alfred William; B: Ashurst, Kent; E: Eastbourne; Pte. SD 3024; K: 21.10.16; Serre Road Cem. No.2, Somme; Age 39; Son of Albert and Katharine Sumner; Husband of Emma Jane Crittenden, formerly Sumner, Red House, Hartfield, Sussex.

6205. SUMNER, Harold; B: Stockport, Cheshire; E: Crawley, Sussex; Pte. SD 3224; K: 30.6.16; Loos Mem. Pas-de-Calais.

6206. SURRIDGE, Lester Thomas; B: Bow, London; E: Brighton; Pte. TF 260029; W: 1.8.17; Dozinghem Mil. Cem. (Bel.); Son of Mrs.E.L.Clary of 2, Wembley Road, Highgate, London.

6207. SUTTON, Albert Nathaniel; B: – ; E: Lincoln; Pte. G 15315; K: 21.10.16; Thiepval Mem. Somme; Age 30; Son of Emily Sutton of New Bolingbroke, Lincolnshire.*

6208. SWAIN, Thomas; B: Wisbech, Cambridgeshire; E: Cambridge; Pte. G 14901; K: 5.8.17; Ypres (Menin Gate) Mem. (Bel.).

6209. SWATTON, Stephen; B: Wickham, Berkshire; E: Hastings; Pte. G 17975; K: 23.9.16; Euston Road Cem. Somme; Killed with eight others in the front line trench on the Redan Ridge by an enemy trench mortar explosion.

T

6210. TAILBY, Walter Sidney; B: Kentish Town, London; E: Tottenham, London; Pte. SD 5585; K: 21.10.16; Grandcourt Road Cem. Somme; Age 25; Husband of Mrs. Ethel Tailby of Pagnatin Street, Queenstown, Port Adelaide, South Australia.

6211. TAPNER, William; B: Mundham, Sussex; E: Chichester; Cpl. SD 3473; W: 8.7.16; Boulogne Eastern Cem. Pas-de-Calais.

6212. TAPP, Henry William; B: Tunbridge Wells; E: Tunbridge Wells; Pte. SD 4111; K: 21.6.16; St.Vaast Post Mil. Cem. Pas-de-Calais; Age 19; Son of Walter Henry and Essie A.E.Tapp of 28, Rochdale Road, Tunbridge Wells.

6213. TASKER, Frederick Joseph; B: Withyham, Sussex; E: Hastings; Pte. SD 4138; K: 30.6.16; Loos Mem. Pas-de-Calais; Age 20; Son of Mr. and Mrs.Joseph Tasker of Hole Farm, Lye Green, Withyham.

6214. TASKER, William; B: Ringmer, Sussex; E: Lewes; Pte. G 2234; K: 29.3.18; Pozieres Mem. Somme; Age 25; Son of Philemon and Agnes Tasker of Broyle Lane, Ringmer.

6215. TATE, Percy; B: March, Cambridgeshire; E: March; L/Cpl. G 14883; K: 31.7.17; Ypres (Menin Gate) Mem. (Bel.).

6216. TATLOW, John Bertram; B: Aston, Warwickshire; E: Newhaven, Sussex; Pte. G 17762; W: 20.9.16; Bertrancourt Mil. Cem. Somme; Age 24; Son of John and Clara Tatlow of 224, Newcombe Road, Handsworth, Birmingham.*

6217. TAYLOR, Percy; B: Rotherfield, Sussex; E: Eastbourne; Pte. SD 2797; W: 3.6.17; Hop Store Cem. (Bel.); Age 24; Son of Arthur and Mary Ann Taylor of Rotherfield.

6218. TAYLOR, Walter; B: Guildford; E: West London; Pte. G 14888; K: 31.7.17; Buffs Road Cem., St.Jean-les-Ypres (Bel.); Age 24; Son of Frederick John and Ellen Taylor of Guildford.

6219. TAYLOR, William; B: Chichester; E: Hastings; Pte. SD 4110; K: 30.6.16; Loos Mem. Pas-de-Calais; Age 33; Son of Mrs.W.Taylor of 11, Market Road, Chichester; Husband of Mrs.L.C.Wilton, formerly Taylor, of 24, Little London, Chichester.

6220. TAYLOR, William Ernest Ewart; 2nd Lt.; K: 27.3.18; Delville Wood Cem. Somme; Age 19; Son of Alfred Ernest Edward and Eliza Jane Taylor of "Hillside", Queen's Corner, Iping, Sussex.

6221. TEAGUE, Ernest Alfred; B: Brighton; E: Brighton; Pte. G 18242; K: 23.3.18; Pozieres Mem. Somme; Age 33; Husband of Ada Eleanor Teague of 134, Hartington Road, Brighton.

6222. TEESDALE, Harry; B: – ; E: Lincoln; Pte. G 15316; K: 13.1.18; St.Julien Dressing Station Cem. (Bel.); Age 22; Son of Joseph and Sarah Teesdale of Cameringham, Lincoln.

6223. TERRY, Frank; B: Angmering, Sussex; E: Littlehampton, Sussex; Pte. G 15982; K: 26.9.16; Euston Road Cem. Somme;.

6224. THEOFF, William Harry; B: Canterbury; E: Charlton, Kent; Pte. G 6248; K: 16.7.17; Ypres (Menin Gate) Mem. (Bel.).*

6225. THICK, Douglas; B: Brentford, Middlesex; E: Croydon; L/Cpl. SD 3244; K: 30.6.16; Loos Mem. Pas-de-Calais; Age 34; Son of Frederick and Martha Thick. *

6226. THOMAS, Ernest Leslie; B: Hastings; E: Hastings; Pte. SD 3237; K: 30.6.16; Cabaret-Rouge Brit. Cem. Pas-de-Calais; Age 26; Son of Zachariah and Emily Thomas of 6, The Creek, All Saints Street, Hastings.*

6227. THOMAS, Robert William; B: Westfield, Sussex; E: Hastings; Pte. SD 2799; K: 30.6.16; Loos Mem. Pas-de-Calais.

6228. THOMAS, Sydney Edwin Bailey; Lt.; K: 3.9.16; Ancre Brit. Cem. Somme; Age 21; Son of E. and Alice Thomas of 123, Westbourne Terrace, Hyde Park, London.

6229. TICE, Thomas Harry; B: Hastings; E: Brighton; Pte. SD 3699; K: 30.6.16; St.Vaast Post Mil. Cem. Pas-de-Calais.

6230. TINLEY, Herbert Henry; B: Hampstead, London; E: Mill Hill, London; Pte. G 21510; K: 22.3.18; Pozieres Mem. Somme; Age 19; Son of Herbert and Annie Tinley of 58, Ravenston Road, Hendon, London.*

6231. TITE, Ernest; B: Brisworth, Northamptonshire; E: Northampton; Pte. G 17467; K: 26.4.18; Tyne Cot Mem. (Bel.); Age 20; Son of Thomas H. and Charlotte Tite of Spratton, Northampton; Enlisted with brother, Reginald George, who was also killed and also has no known grave (see 6232).

6232. TITE, Reginald George; B: All Saints, Northamptonshire; E: Northampton; Pte. G 17468; K: 27.9.17; Tyne Cot Mem. (Bel.); Son of Thomas H. and Charlotte Tite of Spratton, Northampton; Enlisted with brother, Ernest, who was also killed and also has no known grave (see 6231).*

6233. TITE, Reginald Thomas; B: – ; E: – ; Pte. – 4242; K: 25.11.16; Poperinghe New Mil. Cem. (Bel.); 'Shot at Dawn' after having been tried at Court Marshal for desertion and found guilty (see text).

6234. TODD, Reginald George; B: Enfield, Middlesex; E: Mill Hill, London; Pte. G 17423; K: 27.9.17; Tyne Cot Mem. (Bel.).

6235. TOLHURST, Frederick Herbert; B: Lewisham, London; E: Bournemouth; Pte. G 17116; K: 27.9.17; Bedford House Cem. Enclosure No.4, (Bel.); Age 28; Son of Frederick Tolhurst of "Ilford", Waterloo Road, Bournemouth.

6236. TOMPKINS, Frederick; B: Meopham, Kent; E: Gravesend, Kent; Pte. G 23233; K: 23.3.18; Pozieres Mem. Somme; Age 21; Son of Frederick and Jane Tompkins of 2, Neville Cottages, Meopham.*

6237. TOOGOOD, Sidney; B: Mitcham, Surrey; E: Mitcham; L/Cpl. SD 5649; M.M.; K: 27.9.17; Tyne Cot Mem. (Bel.).

6238. TOON, Reginald; B: Nunhead, Kent; E: St.Paul's Churchyard, London; Pte. SD 2802; K: 30.6.16; St.Vaast Post Mil. Cem. Pas-de-Calais.

6239. TOPLISS, Basil Rupert; B: – ; E: Lincoln; Pte. G 15318; K: 21.10.16; Grandcourt Road Cem. Somme; Son of Mrs.A.Topliss of 6, Queen Street, Market Rasen, Lincolnshire.*

6240. TOY, Percy William; B: Islington, London; E: Wood Green, London; Pte. G 13919; W: 27.9.17; Westoutre Churchyard Ext. (Bel.).

6241. TOYE, Claude Leonard; B: Haywards Heath, Sussex; E: Bexhill-on-Sea; L/Cpl. SD 3034; K: 30.6.16; Cabaret-Rouge Brit. Cem. Pas-de-Calais; Age 27; Husband of Mrs.C.M.Moody, formerly Toye, of 17, Henderson Avenue, Scunthorpe, Lincolnshire.

6242. TOYNE, George Henry; B: – ; E: Lincoln; Pte. G 15317; K: 19.10.16; Thiepval Mem. Somme.

6243. TREAGUS, Frank; B: Worthing; E: Worthing; Pte. G 17018; K: 27.3.18; Pozieres Mem. Somme; Age 19; Son of Mr. and Mrs.A.Treagus of 5, Stanhope Road, Worthing.

6244. TRILL, Clement; B: Brighton; E: Hove; Pte. SD 2803; W: 1.7.16; Merville Com Cem., Nord; Age 29; Son of Henry J. and Elizabeth Trill; Husband of Violet J.A.Trill of 40, Marlborough Place, Brighton.

6245. TROTT, Charles Edmund; B: Clerkenwell, London; E: Tottenham, London; L/Cpl . G 13910; K: 19.10.17; Ypres Reservoir Cem. (Bel.); Age 38; Son of Edmund Thomas and Annie Trott of London; Husband of Florence Katherine Trott of 65, Chesterfield Gardens, Harringay, London.*

6246. TROWER, Frank; B: Hove; E: Hove; Pte. G 15980; K: 19.6.17; Vlamertinghe New Mil. Cem. (Bel.); Brother of J.Trower of 2, Oxford Place, Brighton.

6247. TUGWELL, Frederick; B: Brighton; E: Hove; Pte. G 17912; K: 27.3.18; Pozieres Mem. Somme.

6248. TUNSTALL, Frederick Thomas; B: Holloway, London; E: Kingston-on-Thames; Pte. SD 5664; K: 27.9.17; Tyne Cot Mem. (Bel.); Age 23; Son of Mr.E.A. and Mary Ellen Tunstall of 135, Endlesham Road, Balham, London.

6249. TURNER, Albury Charles; B: Coventry; E: Brighton; Pte. SD 2804; K: 30.6.16; Cabaret-Rouge Brit. Cem. Pas-de-Calais; Age 32; Son of Charles Thomas Turner and Maria Georgina Turner.

6250. TURNER, Arthur Ernest; B: Forest Gate, London; E: Bexhill-on-Sea; L/Cpl. SD 2793; K: 26.9.17; Tyne Cot Mem. (Bel.); Age 34; Son of William Turner of 2, Avenue Road, Forest Gate; Husband of Violet Turner of 13, Credon Road, Upton Park, London.

6251. TURNER, Edward Richard; B: Isfield, Sussex; E: Hastings; L/Cpl. SD 3036; K: 30.6.16; Loos Mem. Pas-de-Calais; Age 39; Husband of Susan Clara Turner of Rose Cottage, Buckham Hill, Uckfield, Sussex.

6252. TURNER, George; B: Clare, Suffolk; E: Gravesend, Kent; L/Cpl. TF 201698; K: 31.7.17; Buffs Road Cem., St.Jean-les-Ypres; Age 26; Husband of May Turner of 15, Stonebridge Road, Northfleet, Kent.

6253. TWITCHETT, Harry Charles; B: Brentwood, Essex; E: Chadwell Heath, Essex; Pte. TF 201836; K: 24.3.18; Pozieres Mem. Somme; Age 20; Son of George and Abigail Twitchett of 182, Victoria Road, Romford, Essex.

6254. TYE, Sydney George; B: Swanton, Norfolk; E: Norwich; Pte. TF 290872; K: 16.4 18; Tyne Cot Mem. (Bel.); Age 37; Son of George and Sarah Tye of The Angel Inn, Swanton Morley; Husband of Mrs.J.E.Watkins, formerly Tye, of Woodside, Swanton Morley.

6255. TYLER, Jesse Benjamin; B: – ; E: Uckfield, Sussex; Pte. G 8265; K: 26.9.17; Tyne Cot Mem. (Bel.); Son of Mrs.Benjamin Tyler of Dodds Bottom, Nutley, Sussex; Husband of Mrs.D.M.Best, formerly Tyler, of Dodds Bank, Nutley.

U

6256. UPFOLD, Percival Courtney; B: Haslemere, Surrey, E: Guildford; Pte. G 16954; K: 24.9.17; Tyne Cot Mem. (Bel.); Age 19; Son of Mr.C.J.Upfold of 3, Fieldway, Haslemere.

V

6257. VANSITTART, William French; B: Sydenham, London; E: Aldershot; Pte. G 24511; K: 26.4.18; Tyne Cot Mem. (Bel.); Age 19; Son of Frank French Vansittart and Amy Vansittart of Lodge Farm, Morden, Surrey.*

6258. VEASEY, Thomas; B: Regent's Park, London; E: Tottenham, London; Pte. G 15662; W: 29.3.18; Namps-au-Val Brit. Cem. Somme; Age 22; Son of Helen S.Veasey of 78, Waverley Road, Walthamstow, London.

6259. VENESS, Robert Charles; B: Herstmonceux, Sussex; E: Hastings; L/Cpl. SD 4120; K: 30.6.16; Loos Mem. Pas-de-Calais; Age 21; Son of Thomas Herbert and Philadelphia Fanny Veness of Oak Cottage, Gardner Street, Herstmonceux.

6260. VENNI, Harry; B: Outwell, Norfolk ; E: Norwich; Pte. TF 4002; W: 31.7.16; Le Touret Mil. Cem., Pas-de-Calais; Age 22; Son of William and Eliza Venni of The Common, Upwell, Cambridgeshire.*

6261. VERNEY, George Edward; B: Brixton, London; E: Wandsworth, London; Pte. G 13935; K: 28.9.17; Tyne Cot Mem. (Bel.); Age 33; Son of George Verney of 53, Dalberg Road, Brixton.*

6262. VICK, Sydney Edward; B: St.Peter's, Sussex; E: Chichester; Pte. G 9600; K: 26.4.18; Tyne Cot Mem. (Bel.); Age 27; Son of Edward Thomas and Maud Wilmot Vick of 27, Quay Lane, Exeter, Devon.

6263. VIGAR, Robert; B: Copthorne, Sussex; E: East Grinstead; Pte. G 12995; K: 31.7.17; Buffs Road Cem., St.Jean-les-Ypres (Bel.); Age 39; Son of Edward and Mary Vigar of Copthorne; Husband of Rose Marion Vigar of "Viola", Church Lane, Copthorne.*

6264. VINE, Edward; B: Cross-in-Hand, Sussex; E: Chichester; Pte. G 13357; K: 1.8.17; Ypres (Menin Gate) Mem. (Bel.).

6265. VINE, Edward; B: Eastbourne; E: Eastbourne; Pte. SD 3708; K: 30.6.16; Loos Mem. Pas-de-Calais; Age 28; Husband of Rosina Vine of 6, Beltring Road, Eastbourne.

6266. VOICE, Albert; B: Emsworth, Hampshire; E: Chichester; Pte. SD 3247; K: 16.4.16; Post Office Rifles Cem. Pas-de-Calais; Husband of Charlotte May Voice of 24, King Street, Emsworth.

6267. VOITES, Ernest Augustus; B: Dublin, Ireland; E: Seaford; Pte. G 15984; K: 21.10.16; Grandcourt Road Cem. Somme; Son of Mr.M.C.Voites of 1, Mayfield Grove, Harrogate, Yorkshire.

W

6268. WABY, Edward; B: – ; E: Lincoln; Pte. G 15325; K: 1.3.17; Railway Dugouts Burial Ground (Bel.).

6269. WAIGHT, Sidney; B: Aveley, Essex; E: Warley, Essex; Pte. SD 5841; K: 21.10.16; Grandcourt Road Cem. Somme; Son of Mr.W.Waight of Mill Road, Aveley.

6270. WALDOCK, Frederick George; B: – ; E: Hertford; Pte. G 15694; K: 21.10.16; Grandcourt Road Cem. Somme; Age 21; Son of Edward George and Lucy Waldock of 71, Albert Street, Stevenage, Hertfordshire.

6271. WALDRON, William Herbert; B: Kidderminster, Worcestershire; E: Bexhill-on-Sea; L/Cpl. SD 3503; M.M; W: 1.8.17; Brandhoek New Mil. Cem. (Bel.).

6272. WALKER, Ernest George; B: Wandsworth, London; E: Eastbourne; Cpl; SD 1624; K: 23.3.18; Pozieres Mem. Somme.

6273. WALLER, Alfred; B: Swanley, Kent; E: Cambridge; Pte. G 14906; W: 26.10.16; Aveluy Wood Cem. Somme; Age 21; Son of Mrs.Emily Waller of 8, Barleycorn Lane, Old Chesterton, Cambridge.

6274. WALLER, Frederick James; B: Hove; E: Brighton; Pte. SD 4124; K: 3.9.16; Englebelmer Com. Cem. Ext. Somme; Son of Mrs.E.Waller of 53, Clyde Road, Brighton.

6275. WALLER, Harry James William; B: Ditchling, Sussex; E: Brighton; Pte G 12097; K: 23.7.17; Essex Farm Cem. (Bel.).

6276. WALLIS, Joseph; B: Crowborough, Sussex; E: Hastings; Pte.TF 202272; W: 17.6.17; Vlamertinghe New Mil. Cem. (Bel.); Age 19; Son of Reginald and Fanny Wallis of The Forge, Rotherfield, Sussex.

6277. WALSGROVE, Frederick; B: – ; E: Hastings; Pte. G 16084; K: 23.9.16; Euston Road Cem. Somme; Enlisted with brother, Henry, who was killed in the same action on the same day; Both buried side by side in the same cemetery (see 6278). *

6278. WALSGROVE, Henry; B: Hastings; E: Hastings; Pte G 16085; K: 23.9.16; Euston Road, Cem. Somme; Enlisted with brother, Frederick, who was killed in the same action on the same day; Both buried side by side in the same cemetery (see 6277).

6279. WALSH, Arthur; B: Wigston, Leicestershire; E: Leicester; Pte. G 22906; K: 23.3.18; Pozieres Mem. Somme.

6280. WALTERS, Herbert Edwin Thomas; B: Bognor Regis, Sussex; E: Bognor Regis; Pte. SD 3260; K: 30.6.16; Cabaret-Rouge Brit. Cem. Pas-de-Calais; Age 28; Son of Ephraim and Sarah Walters of North Bersted, Sussex; Husband of Emily Eliza Johnson, formerly, Walters, of 6, Wishfield Terrace, Chichester Road, Bognor Regis.

6281. WARD, Harry Edward Charles; B: Sheerness, Kent; E: Sittingbourne, Kent; Cpl. K: 10.3.18; Fins New Brit. Cem. Somme; Age 21; Son of William and Georgina S.Ward of 123, High Street, Mile Town, Sheerness.

6282. WARD, Thomas William; B: Hatfield,

Hertfordshire; E: Hertford; Pte. G 15563; W: 28.7.18; – .

6283. WARE, Roy Kenneth; B: Eastbourne; E: Eastbourne; Pte. SD 1492; W: 27.4.18; Harlebeke New Brit. Cem. (Bel.); Age 22; Son of William and Sarah Ware of 65, Sidley Road, Eastbourne.*

6284. WATTS, Thomas Ernest; B: Leyton, London; E: London; Pte. G 16956; W: 18.10.17; Godewaersvelde Brit. Cem., Nord; Age 19; Son of Ernest and Mary Ann Watts of 18, Yeatman Road, Highgate, London; Died at Casualty Clearing Station.

6285. WATTS, Walter; B: Frant, Sussex; E: Hastings; Cpl. SD 3253; K: 30.6.16; Cabaret-Rouge Brit. Cem. Pas-de-Calais.

6286. WATTS, William; B: Croydon; E: Battersea, London; Pte. G 10851; K: 27.9.17; Spoilbank Cem. (Bel.).*

6287. WATTS, William Herbert; B: King's Lynn, Norfolk; E: Norwich; Pte. G 9312; K: 31.7.17; Buffs Road Cem., St.Jean-les-Ypres (Bel.); Brother of Mr.C.A.Watts of 43, Whitehall Street, Wakfield, Yorkshire.

6288. WEAVER, Alfred Ernest; B: Plumpton, Sussex; E: Lewes; Pte. G 1669; K: 16.4.18; Tyne Cot Mem. (Bel.).

6289. WEBB, Richard Lloyd; B: Bosham, Sussex; E: Worthing; Pte. SD 3484; K: 30.6.16; Loos Mem. Pas-de-Calais; Age 33; Son of Allan and Frances Alice Webb.

6290. WELCH, Frederick; B: Chichester; E: Chichester; Pte. G 15986; K: 26.9.17; Tyne Cot Cem. (Bel.); Age 19; Son of Mr.G.J. and Mrs.M.E.Welch of 102, Victoria Road, Portfield, Sussex.

6291. WELLCOME, Walter; B: Chichester; E: Chichester; Pte. SD 5035; W: 16.7.16; Cabaret-Rouge Brit. Cem. Pas-de-Calais; Age 31; Son of Walter and Sarah Wellcome of Chichester; Husband of May Mary Bartlett, formerly Wellcome, of Tanyard Cottage, West Lavington, Sussex; Died while a Prisoner of War.*

6292. WELLER, Harry William; B: Hassocks, Sussex; E: Brighton; Pte. SD 3483; K: 26.10.16; Thiepval Mem. Somme.

6293. WELLS, Frank William; B: Coventry; E: Coventry; Pte. G 17145; D: 3.10.18; Glageon Com. Cem. Ext., Nord; Age 21; Son of Frank W. and Alice Wells of 64, Arden Street, Earlsdon, Coventry.

6294. WELLS, George Frederick; B: Boston, Lincolnshire; E: Boston; Pte. G 15322; W: 15.6.17; Vlamertinghe New Mil. Cem. (Bel.); Age 26; Brother of Mrs.F.Cox of 2, Chapel Street, Scunthorpe, Lincolnshire.

6295. WEST, Alfred Robert; B: Northampton; E: Long Buckby, Northamptonshire; Pte. TF 201803; D: 23.9.17; Outtersteene Com. Cem. Ext., Bailleul, Nord.

6296. WEST, Frederick Louis; B: Gravesend, Kent; E: Gravesend; L/Cpl. G 20226; K: 31.7.17; Ypres (Menin Gate) Mem. (Bel.); Age 28; Son of James and Ruth West; Husband of Florence May West of 9, Northcote Road, Gravesend.

6297. WEST, James Henry; B: Eastbourne; E: Eastbourne; Pte. SD 4166; K: 21.10.16; Thiepval Mem. Somme.

6298. WEST, Leonard; B: Eastbourne; E: Eastbourne; Pte. SD 2819; M.M.; K: 31.7.17; Ypres (Menin Gate) Mem. (Bel.); Son of George and Ellen West of 177, Langney Road, Eastbourne.

6299. WHIBLEY, Alfred Victor; B: Eastling, Kent; E: Hastings; L/Cpl. SD 2820; K: 30.6.16; Cabaret-Rouge Brit. Cem. Pas-de-Calais; Age 22; Son of Edwin Richard and Phillis Whibley of Fairbourne Manor Farm, Harrietsham, Kent.

6300. WHITE, Charles Robert; B: Walworth, London; E: Lewisham, London; L/Cpl. G 11420; K: 27.9.17; Tyne Cot Mem. (Bel.).

6301. WHITE, Frederick Edwin; B: St.Mary's, Bedfordshire; E: Bedford; Pte. G 14875; K: 2.8.17; Ypres (Menin Gate) Mem. (Bel.).

6302. WHITE, Herbert; B: Glossop, Derbyshire; E: Glossop; Pte. SD 4141; K: 13.5.16; Le Touret Mil. Cem. Pas-de-Calais.

6303. WHITE, Horace; B: Clophill, Bedfordshire; E: Bedford; Pte. G 14876; K: 21.10.16; Thiepval Mem. Somme.

6304. WHITE, Joseph; B: East Grinstead, Sussex; E: Haywards Heath, Sussex; Sgt. SD 3495; K: 12.7.16; Loos Mem. Pas-de-Calais; Age 27; Son of Mrs.Annie White of 4, Oak Cottage, Burgess Hill, Sussex; Husband of Rosetta White of 4, Windermere Lane, Haywards Heath; Buried by a heavy trench mortar at Cuinchy where desperate efforts to save him failed when all hope had to be abandoned.*

6305. WHITE, William; B: Southgate, London; E: Chichester; Sgt. G 17764; K; 2.8.17; Ypres (Menin Gate) Mem. (Bel.).

6306. WHITEWAY, Francis Robert; B: – ; E: Lincoln; Pte. G 15324; K: 27.9.17; Tyne Cot Cem. (Bel.); Age 22; Son of John Ridgway Whiteway and Mary Jane Whiteway of 26, South Street, Boston, Lincolnshire.

6307. WHITTAKER, Roger D'Arcy; Capt. and Adjutant; K: 30.6.16; Loos Mem. Pas-de-Calais.

6308. WHITWELL, Russell; B: Ramsey, Hampshire; E: Ponders Bridge, Huntingdonshire; Pte. G 14908; K: 13.9.16; Euston Road Cem. Somme.

6309. WILKINS, Charles Harrison; B: Penton, Hampshire; E: Eastbourne; Pte. G 15992; K: 15.10.16; Euston Road Cem. Somme.

6310. WILLIAMS, Frederick Thomas; B: Lamborn, Berkshire; E: Basingstoke, Hampshire; Pte. G 17118; K: 24.9.17; Bedford House Cem. Enclosure No.4 (Bel.); Age 19; Son of Ralph Williams of Bankers Cottage, The Woodland, Lamborn.

6311. WILLIAMS, John Thomas; B: Chatham, Kent; E: Maidstone; Pte. G 202772; K: 3.8.18; New Irish Farm Cem. (Bel.).*

6312. WILLIS, Francis; B: Woolwich, London; E: Tenterden, Kent; Pte. SD 5926; K: 31.7.17; Ypres (Menin Gate) Mem. (Bel.).

6313. WILLMER, Percy Leonard; B: Hove; E: Hove; Pte.

SD 3712; W: 22.6.16; Merville Com. Cem., Nord; Age 20; Son of Arthur and Eliza Willmer of 47, Shakespeare Street, Hove.

6314. WILSHER, George William; B: Northill, Bedfordshire; E: Bedford; Pte. G 14879; K: 26.9.17; Tyne Cot Mem. (Bel.).

6315. WILSON, Edward Thomas; B: Yapton, Sussex; E: Chichester; L/Sgt. G 17924; K: 25.3.18; Pozieres Mem. Somme.

6316. WILSON, John; B: Sleaford, Lincolnshire; E: Luton; L/Cpl. G 15321; K: 23.3.18; Ste.Emilie Valley Cem., Villers-Faucon, Somme; Son of Mrs.M.Wilson of 8, Williams Square, Sleaford.

6317. WILSON, Sydney; B: Hurstpierpoint, Sussex; E: Brighton; Pte. SD 3262; K: 30.6.16; Loos Mem. Pas-de-Calais.

6318. WINCHESTER, Hubert; B: Ashburnham, Sussex; E: Eastbourne; Pte. SD 3486; K: 30.6.16; Loos Mem. Pas-de-Calais.

6319. WINCHESTER, William Amos; B: Ticehurst, Sussex; E: Hastings; Pte. SD 3259; W: 16.4.16; Bethune Town Cem. Pas-de-Calais; Age 35; Son of William and Jane Winchester of Mereworth, Kent; Husband of Mrs.D.B.Winchester of Swan Cottage, West Peckham, Kent.

6320. WINCHESTER, William Frank; B: Catsfield, Sussex; E: Hastings; Pte. SD 5021; K: 30.6.16; Loos Mem. Pas-de-Calais; Age 23; Son of William and Grace Winchester of Oakland, Ninfield, Sussex.*

6321. WINGFIELD, Herbert; B: Bow, London; E: Hove; Sgt. SD 3499; K: 30.6.16; Loos Mem. Pas-de-Calais; Age 28; Son of Samuel Wingfield of 59a, Geer Road, Stratford, London; Husband of Mary Elizabeth Wingfield of 228, Hessle Road, Hull.

6322. WISEMAN, Leonard; B: Hemel Hempstead, Hertfordshire; E: Watford; Pte. G 17257; K: 26.3.18; Pozieres Mem. Somme; Age 19; Son of Samuel and Mary Ann Wiseman of 3, Victoria Terrace, Albion Hill, Hertfordshire.

6323. WOOD, Albert Vallance; B: Dane Hill, Sussex; E: Hastings; L/Sgt. S 2248; W: 4.4.18; Wimereux Com. Cem. Pas-de-Calais; Age 27; Son of Jeremiah and Caroline Smith of Chelwood Gate, Sussex.

6324. WOOD, George; B: Goring-by-Sea, Sussex; E: Worthing; Pte. SD 5018; K: 30.6.16; Cabaret-Rouge Brit. Cem. Pas-de-Calais.

6325. WOOD, Harry Joseph; B: Croydon; E: Hastings; Pte. SD 3710; K: 30.6.16; St.Vaast Post Mil. Cem. Pas-de-Calais; Age 27; Son of Joseph and Eliza Wood of Croydon; Husband of Alice Edith Wood of 58, Whitehorse Lane, South Norwood, London.

6326. WOOD, Walter; B: Brighton; E: Brighton; Pte. SD 5045; K: 30.5.16; Cambrin Churchyard Ext. Pas-de-Calais; Age 33; Son of Charles Alfred and Emily Wood of Brighton; Husband of Emily Wood of 95, Bonchurch Road, Brighton; Buried alive by an enemt mine explosion at Cuinchy.

6327. WOODFORD, Arthur; B: Gravesend, Kent; E: Hove; Pte. SD 3047; K: 30.6.16; St.Vaast Post Mil. Cem. Pas-de-Calais; Age 35; Son of

Robert Woodford of Gravesend; Husband of Mrs.A.Burchell, formerly Woodford, of Brighton.

6328. WRATHMALL, Edward; B: Sunderland; E: Sunderland; Pte. G 8068; K: 18.10.17; Tyne Cot Mem. (Bel.); Son of William Gibson Wrathmall; Husband of Ada Preston, formerly Wrathmall, of 65, Inkerman Street, Vauxhall, Birmingham.

6329. WRIGHT, Alfred; B: Norwood, London; E: Gillingham, Kent; Pte. TF 201693; K: 31.7.17; Buffs Road Cem., St.Jean-les-Ypres (Bel.); Husband of Mrs.L.A.Wright of 22, North Terrace, Sydenham, London.

6330. WRIGHT, Bernard George; B: Berkswell, Warwickshire; E: Horsham, Sussex; Pte. G 13994; K: 21.10.16; Villers-Bretonneux Mil. Cem. Somme; Age 37; Son of Walter Henry and Catherine Wright.

6331. WRIGHT, James; B: Woodford, Essex; E: Stratford, London; Pte G 22699; K: 5.11.17; Tyne Cot Mem. (Bel.).

Y

6332. YARDLEY, Frederick William George; B: Bermondsey, London; E: Camberwell, London; Pte. G 24314; K: 29.3.18; Pozieres Mem. Somme.

6333. YEATMAN, William George; B: Wimbourne, Dorset; E: Bognor Regis, Sussex; Sgt. SD 3402; W: 12.9.16; Couin Brit. Cem. Pas-de-Calais; Age 38; Husband of Alice Yeatman of 18, Bedford Street, Bognor Regis.

6334. YORKE, Arthur; B: Leicester; E: Leicester; L/Cpl. G 15029; K: 23.3.18; Pozieres Mem. Somme; Son of Mr. and Mrs.A.Yorke of 4, Mellor Street, Belgrave, Leicester.

6335. YOUNG, Ernest George; B: – ; E: Cambridge; Pte. G 14897; K: 24.12.16; Essex Farm Cem, (Bel.). Killed by shell fire at Hill Top Farm.

16th Battalion
A

6336. APPS, Herbert Edward Vincent Baldock; B: Salehurst, Sussex; E: Bexhill-on-Sea; Pte. TF 315357; W: 14.9.18; Etretat Churchyard Ext., Seine-Maritime.

6337. AXTELL, Thomas Alfred; B: Camberwell, London; E: Camberwell; Pte. G 22126; K: 3.9.18; Peronne Com. Cem. Ext., Ste.Radegonde, Somme.

B

6338. BAKER, Harry; B: Brighton; E: Brighton; Pte. G 5396; K: 2.9.18; Peronne Com. Cem. Ext., Ste. Radegonde, Somme; Age 33; Husband of Annie Baker of 141, Westbourne Street, Hove.

6339. BEACON, Edward John; B: Gravesend, Kent; E: Chatham, Kent; Pte. G 21788; K: 21.9.18; Le Cateau Mil. Cem., Nord; Age 32; Son of Thomas and Jessie Beacon of Gravesend; Husband of Georgina A.Beacon of 31, Bryant Street, Chatham.

6340. BEAL, Albert Edward; B: Brighton; E: Brighton;

Sgt. TF 320302; K: 21.9.18; Vis-en-Artois Mem., Haucourt, Pas-de-Calais; Age 25; Son of Charles Arthur Beal of 27, Caledonian Road, Brighton.

6341. BELL, William John; B: Bexleyheath, Kent; E: Woolwich, London; Pte. G 14402; K: 15.9.18; Roisel Com. Cem. Ext., Somme; Age 38; Son of John Losh Bell and Sarah Bell of Higham House, Brampton Road, Bexleyheath; Husband of Rebecca Bell of 38, Rowan Road, Bexleyheath.

6342. BLACKMAN, Walter; B: Halling, Kent; E: Gravesend, Kent; Pte. G 20187; K: 21.9.18; Vis-en-Artois mem., Haucourt, Pas-de-Calais.

6343. BLAKE, Charles Arthur; B: West Ham, London; E: Hurstpierpoint, Sussex; Pte. TF 315492; K: 2.9.18; Peronne Com. Cem. Ext., Ste.Radegonde, Somme; Age 24; Son of Thoma and Emma Blake.

6344. BOARDMAN, Arthur; 2nd Lt.; K: 21.9.18; Vis-en-Artois Mem., Haucourt, Pas-de-Calais; Age 29; Son of Thomas and Sarah Boardman.*

6345. BONIFACE, William Alfred; B: Portslade, Sussex; E: Brighton; Pte. TF 320391; K: 16.9.18; Peronne Com. Cem. Ext., Ste.Radegonde, Somme; Age 24; Son of Alfred Boniface of 1, St.Andrew's Road, Portslade.

6346. BOTTING, Frederick Charles; B: Brighton; E: Hove; L/Cpl. L 10883; W: 2.9.18; Fouquescourt Brit. Cem., Somme; Age 20; Son of Harry and Catherine Botting of 100, Tamworth Road, Hove.*

6347. BRACE, Victor John; B: Worthing; E: Worthing; L/Cpl. TF 320427; K: 2.9.18; Peronne Com. Cem. Ext., Ste.Radegonde, Somme; Age 21; Son of Albert and Elizabeth Brace of Worthing.

6348. BRIDGER, Percy; B: Abinger, Surrey; E: Guildford; Pte. G 18055; K: 21.9.18; Hargicourt Com. Cem. Ext., Aisne; Age 30; Son of Edwin and Sarah Bridger of King George's Hill, Wotton, Surrey.

6349. BRISTOW, Frank; B: Brighton; E: Brighton; Pte. TF 320320; D at Home: 20.9.18; Patcham (All Saints) Churchyard, Sussex (UK); Age 24; Son of Edwin and Jane Bristow.

6350. BROOKES, Frank Trevor; B: Ross-on-Wye, Herefordshire; E: Brighton; Sgt. TF 320169; D at Home: 23.10.18; Durrington Cem., Wiltshire (UK); Age 25; Son of David and Mabel Brookes of The Cottage, Amberley, Bury Road, Newmarket, Cambridgeshire.*

6351. BRUCE, Frank; B: Rotherham, Yorkshire; E: Peterborough, Northamptonshire; Pte. TF 315031; W: 12.7.18; St.Venant-Robecq Road Brit. Cem., Robecq, Pas-de-Calais; Age 23; Son of John William and Sarah bruce of Pilsgate Grange, Stamford, Northamptonshire.

6352. BURBRIDGE, Arthur Allen; B: Horley, Surrey; E: Brighton; Pte. TF 320195; K: 21.9.18; Vis-en-Artois Mem., Haucourt, Pas-de-Calais.*

6353 BUTLER, Thomas Patrick; B: Dublin, Ireland; E: Brighton; L/Cpl. TF 320396; K: 21.9.18; Ste.Emilie Valley Cem., Villers-Faucon, Somme; Age 42; Son of Dr.N.J. and Mrs.W.Butler of Dublin; Husband of Mrs.A.W.Butler of 183, Elm Grove, Brighton.

C

6354. CARRIER, Jesse; B: Horningham, Wiltshire; E: Findon, Sussex; Pte. TF 315272; D: 19.9.18; St.Sever Cem. Ext., Rouen, Seine Maritime.

6355. CHATFIELD, Herbert Dixon; B: Eastbourne; E: Eastbourne; Sgt. TF 320094; K: 2.9.18; Vis-en-Artois Mem., Haucourt, Pas-de-Calais.

6356. CHILES, Charles; B: Seaford, Sussex; E: Eastbourne; Pte. TF 315262; D at Home: 24.7.18; Nottingham General; Cem., Nottinghamshire (UK).*

6357. CLACK, Percy Dumbrill; B: Eastbourne; E: Eastbourne; Pte. SD 156; K: 18.9.18; Ste.Emilie Valley Cem., Villers-Faucon, Somme; Age 21; Son of Mr.C.S. and Mrs.C.I.B.Clack of 10, Clarence Road, Eastbourne; Killed during the attack at Templeux-le-Guerard.*

6358. CLARK, Alexander Edward; B: Wandsworth, London; E: Kingston-on-Thames; Pte. G 20170; K: 23.9.18; Templeux-Le-Guerard Brit. Cem., Somme; Age 31; Son of James W. and Charlotte E.Clark of 20, Coombe Lane, Wimbledon, London.*

6359. CLARK, George; B: Chelmsford, Essex; E: Chelmsford; L/Cpl. G 14667; W: 24.7.18; St.Venant-Robecq Road Brit. Cem., Robecq, Pas-de-Calais; Age 20; Son of Frederick and Susannah Clark of 1, Starr Terrace, Baddow Road, Chelmsford.

6360. CLARKE, Ernest Alber t Guy; B: Gloucester; E: Cricklewood, London; Pte. TF 203353; W: 22.9.18; Doingt Com. Cem., Somme; Age 40; Husband of Helen Livingstone Clarke of 77, Oakwood Road, Golders Green, London; Died at Casualty Clearing Station, Doingt.

6361. COZENS, Arthur George; B: Goring-b-Sea, Sussex; E: Worthing; Cpl. TF 320255; K: 2.9.18; Peronne Com. Cem. Ext., Ste.Radegonde, Somme; Age 23; Son of Mrs.S.A.Cozens of "Rosemount", Tarring Road, Worthing.

6362. CROSS, Charles William; B: Postland, Lincolnshire; E: Peterborough, Northamptonshire; Pte. TF 203368; K: 15.9.18; Roisel Com. Cem. Ext., Somme; Age 39; Son of John and Ellen cross of Postland; Husband of Florence Ada cross of 9, South Parade, Peretborough.

6363. CUMMINS, Hedley John; B: Betchworth, Surrey; E: Reigate, Surrey; Pte. TF 315169; K: 10.10.18; Aubers Ridge Brit. Cem., Nord; Age 41; Son of George and Sarah Cummins; Husband of Emily Cummins of 64, Allingham Road, Reigate.

D

6364. DANIELS, Gilbert Joseph; B: Hadlow Down, Sussex; E: Eridge, Kent; L/Cpl; TF 320083; K: 21.9.18; Hargicourt Com. Cem. Ext., Aisne.

6365. DENGATE, James; B: Hastings; E: Hastings; Pte. G 4236; K: 21.9.18; Vis-en-Artois Mem., Haucourt, Pas-de-Calais.

6366. DIVE, Stephen; B: Westfield, Sussex; E: Brighton;

L/Cpl. TF 320428; K: 16.9.18; Peronne Com. Cem. Ext., Ste.Radegonde, Somme.

6367. DUCK, William; B: Petworth, Sussex; E: Brighton; Cpl. TF 320155; K: 14.10.18; Aubers Ridge Brit. Cem., Nord.

E

6368. EDWARDS, Cyril Victor Gladwin; B: – ; E: Uckfield, Sussex; Pte. TF 315036; K: 18.9.18; Vis-en-Artois Mem., Haucourt, Pas-de-Calais; Killed in the attack on Templeux-le-Guerard.

6369. ELDRIDGE, Bertram; B: Westfield, Sussex; E: Hastings; Pte. SD 5037; K: 2.9.18; Peronne Com. Cem. Ext., Ste.Radegonde, Somme; Age 22; Son of Jesse David and Frances Agnes Eldridge of Dagg Lane, Ewhurst, Sussex.

6370. ELGAR, Reginald Jack; B: Cambridge; E: Bury St.Edmunds, Suffolk; Pte. G 17368; K: 25.9.18; Templeux-Le-Guerard Brit. Cem., Somme; Age 20; Son of Mrs.L.H.Elgar of 19, Doric Street, Cambridge.

6371. ELLIS, R.B.; B; – ; E: – ; Pte. G 36092; D at Home: 1.11.18; Seend (Holy Cross) Churchyard, Wiltshire (UK); Age 30; Son of Albert and Jane Ellis of Seend; Died of pneumonia.

F

6372. FIELDWICK, Percy Frank; B: Newick, Sussex; E: Worthing; Pte. G 17821; K: 21.9.18; Ste.Emilie Valley Cem., Villers-Faucon, Somme; Husband of Mrs.A.N.Fieldwick of Church Road, Newick.

6373. FLINT, William Robert; B: Putney, London; E: Whitehall, London; Pte. G 20656; K: 21.9.18; Vis-en-Artois Mem., Haucourt, Pas-de-Calais.

6374. FRENCH, George Henry; B: Billingshurst, Sussex; E: Brighton; Pte. TF 315222; K: 21.9.18; Vis-en-Artois Mem., Haucourt, Pas-de-Calais.

6375. FROUD, Archie John; B: Cowes, Isle of Wight; E: Brighton; Cpl. TF 320472; W: 26.9.18; St.Sever Cem. Ext., Rouen, Seine-Maritime.

G

6376. GARDNER, Herbert; B: – ; E: Brighton; L/Cpl. TF 320212; M.M.; W: 3.10.18; Le cateau Mil. Cem., Nord; Age 36; Husband of Ethel Gertrude Gardner of 3, The Broadway, Crouch End, London.

6377. GASTON, Frank; B: Lindfield, Sussex; E: Haywards Heath, Sussex; Pte. G 12151; W: 18.9.18; Doingt Com. Cem., Somme; Husband of Mrs.A.S.Gaston of 4, Frederick Cottages, Lewes Road, Lindfield; Mortally wounded in the attack at Templeux-le-Guerard.

H

6378. HALL, William; B: Balcombe, Sussex; E: Canterbury; Pte. TF 320151; K: 16.9.18; Peronne Com. Cem. Ext., Ste.Radegonde, Somme.

6379. HANNANT, William Kelter; B: – ; E: East Dereham, Norfolk; Pte. G 15283; K: 21.9.18; Vis-en-Artois Mem., Haucourt, Pas-de-Calais; Age 25; Son of

William and Blanche Emma Hannant of Honing, Norfolk.

6380. HANSON, William; B: Hull; E: Horsham, Sussex; Pte. G 8457; W: 19.9.18; Doingt Com. Cem., Somme; Died at Casualty Clearing Station, Doingt.

6381. HARBOROUGH, Ernest Victor; B: Hastings; E: Hastings; L/Cpl. G 20626; K: 15.9.18; Roisel Com. Cem. Ext., Somme; Age 21; Son of Mr. and Mrs. Russell H.Harborough of Rose Cottage, Guestling Thorn, Sussex.

6382. HARKER, John Gordon; 2nd Lt.; K: 28.9.18; Thilloy Road Cem., Pas-de-Calais.

6383. HARVEY, Arthur Vincent; B: Reading, Berkshire; E: Brighton; Sgt. TF 320388; W: 15.9.18; Peronne Com. Cem. Ext., Ste.Radegonde, Somme; Age 42.

6384. HARVEY, Reginald; B: Haywards Heath, Sussex; E: Lewes; Pte. TF 315508; K: 21.9.18; Vis-en-Artois Mem., Haucourt, Pas-de-Calais; Age 29; Son of John and Alice Harvey of The Fire Station, Lewes; Husband of Maria Esther Harvey of Little Gassons, Cranleigh, Surrey.

6385. HEATHER, Frank; B: Hove; E: Brighton; L/Cpl. TF 320050; K: 10.10.18; Aubers Ridge Brit. Cem., Nord; Age 26.*

6386. HEDGER, Edmund John; B: Eastbourne; E: Chichester; Pte. G 14143; K: 21.9.18; Vis-en-Artois Mem., Haucourt, Pas-de-Calais; Age 20; Son of William and Harriet Hedger of High Haly. Petworth, Sussex.

6387. HOAD, Fred; B: Bethersden, Kent; E: Maidstone; Pte. TF 315125; K: 4.9.18; Peronne Com. Cem. Ext., Ste.Radegonde, Somme.

6388. HOADLEY, James Victor; B: Burgess Hill, Sussex; E: Brighton; Pte. TF 320379; K: 2.9.18; Peronne Com. Cem. Ext., Ste.Radegonde, Somme; Age 21; Son of James Hoadley of 39, Church Road, Burgess Hill.

6389. HOGBIN, James; B: Sutton, Kent; E: Maidstone; Pte. G 13551; K: 21.9.18; Vis-en-Artois Mem., Haucourt, Pas-de-Calais.

6390. HOOK, Bertram; B: Ashburnham, Sussex; E: Hastings; Pte. SD 2926; W: 19.9.18; Doingt Com. Cem., Somme; Husband of Mrs.R.Fairman, formerly Hook, of 1467, Finlayson Avenue, Victoria, British Columbia, Canada; Died at Casualty Clearing Station, Doingt.

6391. HOPKINS, Herbert Edward; B: Lewes; E: Brighton; L/Cpl. TF 320429; W: 4.9.18; Heilly Station Cem., Mericourt-L'Abbé, Somme; Died at No.20 Casualty Clearing Station, Heilly Station.

6392. HOPKINS, Percy; B: Brighton; E: Brighton; Cpl. TF 320425; K: 2.9.18; Vis-en-Artois Mem., Haucourt, Pas-de-Calais.

6393. HUNT, Charles William; B: Richmond, London; E: Cricklewood, London; Pte. G 21494; K: 21.9.18; Ste.Emilie Valley Cem., Villers-Faucon, Somme.

J

6394. JENKINS, Alfred; B: Slinfold, Sussex; E: Guildford; Pte. SD 3792; W: 29.9.18; Doingt Com. Cem.,

Somme; Age 33; Husband of Mrs.M.Jenkins of Ellen's Green, Rudgwick, Sussex; Died at Casualty Clearing Station, Doingt.

6395. JOHNSON, Sidney Ernest; B: Crofton, Kent; E: Bromley, Kent; Pte. TF 203359; K: 8.9.18; Tincourt New Brit. cem., Somme; Age 24; Son of John and Hannah Johnson of The Bungalow, Fairfield Road, Crofton.

6396. JONES, Joseph George William; B: – ; E: Kettering, Northamptonshire; Pte. TF 201758; K: 21.9.18; Vis-en-Artois mem., Haucourt, Pas-de-Calais.

K

6397. KLAWIER, Albert Edwin; B: Grimsby; E: Grimsby; Pte. TF 315133; K: 2.9.18; Peronne Com. Cem. Ext., Ste.Radegonde, Somme; Age 23; Son of Charles and Hannah Klawier of 54, Buller Street, Grimsby.

6398. KNIGHT, Edward James; B: Southborne, Hampshire; E: Chichester; Pte. TF 315320; K: 21.9.18; Unicorn Cem., Aisne; Age 30; Son of Frederick and Emily Knight of 70, Osborne Villas, Hove.

L

6399. LAKE, Basil; B: Freethorpe, Norfolk; E: Norwich; Pte. G 11712; K: 2.9.18; Vis-en-Artois Mem., Haucourt, Pas-de-Calais; Age 19; Son of Robert and Elizabeth A.Lake of Halvargate Road, Freethorpe.

M

6400. MARE, Cyril Ronald Charles John; B: Littlehampton, Sussex; E: Hove; Pte. TF 315205; K: 6.10.18; Sucrerie Cem., Ablain-St.Nazaire, Pas-de-Calais; Age 24; Son of Charles John Salmon Peter Mare and Clara Egerton Mare of "Rothesay", 24, Hartington Villas, Hove.*

6401. McDONALD, William Paterson; B: Row, Dumbartonshire; E: Dumbarton; Pte. TF 315049; K: 13.10.18; Aubers Ridge Brit. Cem., Nord.

6402. MIDDLETON, Samuel; B: Stratford, London; E: Stratford; Pte. G 9732; K: 2.9.18; Peronne Com. Cem. Ext., Ste.Radegonde, Somme.

6403. MILLS, James Walter; B: – ; E: Littlehampton, Sussex; Pte. TF 315146; M.M.; D: 7.10.18; St.Sever Cem. Ext., Rouen, Seine-Maritime; Age 23; Son of Louisa Tuggs, formerly Mills, of 265, High Street, Wick, Sussex, and the late Charles Mills; Died from pneumonia.

6404. MORGAN, Thomas James; B: – ; E: Horsham, Sussex; Sgt. TF 315183; K: 18.9.18; Ste.Emilie Valley Cem., Villers-Faucon, Somme; Age 29; Son of George and Matilda Morgan of High Street, New Romney, Kent; Killed in the attack at Templeux-le-Guerard.

6405. MORTON, Herbert Charles; B: Anerley, Surrey; E: Brighton; Pte. TF 320309; W: 4.9.18; Heath Cem., Harbonnieres, Somme.

6406. MUNDAY, William Henry; B: Bognor Regis, Sussex; E: Chichester; Pte. TF 315324; K: 16.9.18; Peronne Com. Cem. Ext., Ste.Radegonde, Somme.

P

6407. PAGE, Ernest; B: Lyminster, Sussex; E: Arundel, Sussex; Pte. TF 320100; K: 16.9.18; Peronne Com. Cem. Ext., Ste.Radegonde, Somme; Age 22; Son of Arthur and Ellen Page of Fir Tree House, Boxgrove, Sussex.*

6408. PENFOLD, James; B: Burgess Hill, Sussex; E: Brighton; L/Cpl. TF 320465; W: 20.9.18; Doingt Com. Cem. Ext., Somme; Husband of Mrs.R.Penfold of Nightingale Hall, Henfield, Sussex.

6409. POTTER, Walter Edward; B: Epsom, Surrey; E: Brighton; Pte. TF 320485; K: 21.9.18; Vis-en-Artois Mem., Haucourt, Pas-de-Calais; Age 27; Son of William and Emily Potter.

6410. PRESTON, Joseph; B: Berkhamsted, Hertfordshire; E: Berkhamsted; Pte. TF 315419; K: 18.9.18; Ste. Emily Valley Cem., Villers-Faucon, Somme; Brother of Mr.J.Preston of 71, Ellesmere Road, Berkamsted; Killed in the attack at Templeux-le-Guerard.

R

6411. RALPH, Ernest Alfred; B: Surbiton, Surrey; E: Kingston-on-Thames; Pte. TF 315128; K: 2.9.18; Peronne Com. Cem. Ext., Ste.Radegonde, Somme.

6412. RATHBORN, Thomas Edmund; B: Horsham, Sussex; E: Horsham; Pte. TF 315190; D: 9.10.18; Harlebeke New Brit. Cem. (Bel.); Age 20; Son of Thomas William and Sarah Margaret Rathborn of 13, Clarence Road, Horsham.*

6413. REEVES, George; B: Brighton; E: Whitehall, London; Pte. G 14243; K: 21.9.18; Unicorn Cem., Aisne.

6414. RIDLEY, Edward John; B: Brighton; E: Brighton; L/Cpl. TF 320308; K: 18.9.18; Ste.Emilie Valley Cem., Villers-Faucon, Somme; Son of Mr.T.Ridley of 111, Portland Road, Hove; Killed in the attack at Templeux-le-Guerard.

6415. RILEY, George Henry; B: Brighton; E: Brighton; Pte. TF 320350; K: 17.9.18; Bronfay Farm Mil. Cem., Somme; Age 42; Husband of Julia Riley of 59, Totland Road, Brighton.

6416. ROBINSON, Arthur; B: Holbeach, Lincolnshire; E: Hammersmith, London; Pte. G 10446; K: 21.9.18; Ste.Emilie Valley Cem., Villers-Faucon, Somme.

6417. RODGERS, James Francis; B: Cardiff; E: Hastings; Pte. TF 315422; K: 21.9.18; Vis-en-Artois Mem., Haucourt, Pas-de-Calais.

S

6418. SAUNDERS, Arthur Charles; B: Croydon; E: Hove; Pte. TF 315282; K: 21.9.18; Vis-en-Artois Mem., Haucourt, Pas-de-Calais.

6419. SCHOLES, Thomas; B: – ; E: Manchester; Pte. TF 201933; W: 16.9.18; Bronfay Farm Mil. Cem., Somme; Age 29; Son of Thomas and Mary Scholes of 4, Brovis Road, Chorlton-cum-Hardy,

Manchester; Husband of Lydia Booth, formerly Scholes.

6420. SMITH, Thomas Albert Straughan; B: Hove; E: West London; Pte. G 20608; W: 18.7.18; Aire Com. Cem., Pas-de-Calais; Age 25; Son of William James Napier Smith and Harriett Annie Smith of Hove; Died at No.54 Casualty Clearing Station (known as 1/2nd London C.C.S.), Aire.*

6421. SPENCER-MAYNARD, Sydney; B: Eastbourne; E: Eastbourne; Pte. TF 315182; D: 27.10.18; Étaples Mil. Cem., Pas-de-Calais; Age 21; Son of Charles and Clara Spencer-Maynard of 18, Cornfield Road, Eastbourne.*

6422. SQUIRES, Walter Robert; B: Ashwellthorpe, Norfolk; E: Chichester; Pte.TF 315252; K: 16.9.18; Peronne Com. Cem. Ext., Ste.Radegonde, Somme; Age 34; Husband of Louise Marie Squires of Steel Cross House, Tunbridge Wells.

6423. SUDDS, William John; B: Burwash, Sussex; E: Battle, Sussex; Sgt. TF 320060; K: 18.9.18; Ste. Emilie Valley Cem., Villers-Faucon, Somme; Age 31; Son of Henry and Mary Sudds of The Lodge, Magdalen Road, St.Leonards-on-Sea; Killed in the attack at Templeux-le-Guerard.

T

6424. TAYLOR, Alexander John; 2nd Lt.; W: 8.8.18; Aire Com. Cem., Pas-de-Calais; Age 25; Son of Mr.W.J. and Mrs.M.Taylor of 5, Grange Road, Eastbourne; Died at No.54 Casualty Clearing Station (known as 1/2nd London C.C.S.), Aire; Mortally wounded during the previous night.

6425. TAYLOR, Thomas William Henry; B: Brighton; E: Hove; C.S.M. G 1177; W: 19.9.18; Doingt Com. Cem., Somme; Died at Casualty Clearing Station, Doingt.*

6426. THOMAS, Walter Edward; 2nd Lt.; K: 21.9.18; Unicorn Cem., Aisne.

6427. THURLOW, John James; B: Camden Town, London; E: Tooting, London; Pte. TF 203340; K: 18.9.18; Templeux-le-Guerard Com. Cem. Ext., Somme; Killed in the attack at Templeux-le-Guerard.

6428. TIMLICK, William George; B: Brighton; E: Brighton; Pte. TF 320177; D: 30.5.18; Abbeville Com. Cem. Ext., Somme; Age 23; Son of T.N.Timlick of "Hill View", Aldingbourne, Sussex.

6429. TOTTEM, Albert Edward Victor; B: Hornsey, London; E: Mill Hill, London; Pte. G 22255; K: 20.9.18; Unicorn Cem., Aisne; Age 21; Son of Charles William and Katherine Tottem of 111, Roslyn Road, South Tottenham, London.

6430. TURNER, Frank; B: Holloway, London; E: Mill Hill, London; Pte. G 22254; K: 2.9.18; Peronne Com. Cem. Ext., Ste.Radegonde, Somme.

6431. TYLER, Henry; B: – ; E: Worthing; Pte. TF 315430; W: 2.11.18; Don Com. Cem., Nord; Son of Mrs. Harriett Tyler of 63, Brunswick Place, Hove; Died at No.15 Casualty Clearing Station, Don.

V

6432. VERRION, Richard; B: Brighton; E: Brighton; Pte. TF 315196; K: 15.9.18; Roisel Com. Cem. Ext., Somme; Age 20; Son of Edwin and Elizabeth Verrion of Brighton.

W

6433. WAKEFORD, Horace; B: Wadhurst, Sussex; E: Hastings; Pte. TF 315431; K: 18.9.18; Ste.Emilie Valley Cem., Villers-Faucon, Somme; Age 21; Son of Charles and Emily Wakeford of Latters Farm Cottage, Tudeley, Hale, Kent; Killed in the attack at Templeux-le-Guerard.

6434. WALLIS, William John James; B: Dartford, Kent; E: Tonbridge, Kent; Pte. G 21520; W: 18.10.18; Cambrin Mil. Cem., Pas-de-Calais; Age 33; Son of William and Emma Wallis of Dartford; Husband of Clara Wallis of 105, High Street, Tonbridge; Died at No.54 Casualty Clearing Station (known as 1/2nd London C.C.S.), Cambrin.*

6435. WATSON, Charles Percy; B: Burwash, Sussex; E: Eastbourne; Pte. SD 3711; W: 24.9.18; Vis-en-Artois Mem., Haucourt, Pas-de-Calais.

6436. WATSON, Harry; B: Icklesham, Sussex; E: March, Cambridgeshire; L/Cpl. TF 320045; K: 16.9.18; Peronne Com. Cem. Ext., Ste.Radegonde, Somme; Age 24; Son of Robert and Martha Dennis Watson of Rye Harbour, Sussex; Husband of Gladys Watson of 2, Judge Place, Rye; Killed during enemy air raid.*

6437. WATTS, Charles Edwin; B; Wadhurst, Sussex; E: Chichester; Pte. TF 315156; K: 21.9.18; Le Cateau Mil. Cem., Nord; Age 27; Son of Mrs.Lois Watts of Stonebridge, Wadhurst.

6438. WHITEWOOD, Frank; B: Fairwarp, Sussex; E: Brighton; L/Cpl. TF 320459; W: 5.10.18; Le Cateau Mil. Cem., Nord; Age 24; Son of James William and Frances D.Whitewood of 87, Reginald Road, Bexhill-on-Sea.

6439. WIGHTMAN, Hector; B: Belgrave, Leicestershire; E: Cheetham, Lancashire; Pte. TF 201929; D: 31.10.18; Hautmont Com. Cem., Nord.

6440. WILES, Thomas Abel; B: Wood Green, London; E: West London; L/Cpl. G 10427; K: 21.9.18; Ste. Emilie Valley Cem., Villers-Faucon, Somme; Age 43; Son of Frederick and Amy Wiles of 13, Colsterworth Road, Tottenham, London.*

6441. WILEY, Donald Willam; Lt.; K: 12.10.18; Busigny Com. Cem. Ext., Nord.

6442. WINCHESTER, Charley; B: Ashburnham, Sussex; E: Horsham, Sussex; Pte. SD 752; W: 14.12.18; Cambrin Mil. Cem., Pas-de-Calais; Age 27; Son of Mark and Lucy Winchester of 14, Ringwood Road, Sidley, Bexhill-on-Sea.*

6443. WINTERMAN, William Robert; B: Widmore, Kent; E: Woolwich, London; Pte. TF 203354; K: 21.9.18; Templeux-le-Guerard Com. Cem. Ext., Somme; Age 28; Husband of Everelda White, formerly Winterman, of 2, Wakering Avenue, Shoeburyness, Essex.*

6444. WOOD, Frederick William; B: Tandridge, Surrey; E: Dover, Kent; Pte. TF 315081; K: 21.9.18; Vis-en-Artois Mem., Haucourt, Pas-de-Calais; Husband of Mabel E.Wood of 12, Park View, Tandridge.

6445. WOOD, Henry James; B: Marylebone, London; E: Marylebone; Pte. G 22260; K: 21.9.18; Vis-en-Artois Mem., Haucourt, Pas-de-Calais; Age 20; Son of Henry Wood of 8, Aybrook Street, Marylebone.

6446. WOODCOCK, Edward H.C.; B: Warrington, Lancashire; E: Warrington; Pte. TF 201930; W: 16.9.18; Bronfay Farm Mil. Cem., Somme; Age 21; Son of Edward E. and Martha Woodcock of 6, Dudley Street, Warrington.

6447. WOODIN, William; B: Yardley, Warwickshire; E: Northampton; Pte. TF 203372; K: 2.9.18; Peronne Com. Cem. Ext., Ste.Radegonde, Somme; Age 38.

17th Battalion
A

6448. ASHTON, Albert Edward; B: Bow, London; E: Bow; Sgt. G 30749; D: 8.11.18; Lille Southern Cem., Nord; Age 30.

6449. AUSTEN, John; B: – ; E: Brighton; Pte. TF 266412; K: 22.8.18; Beacon Cem., Somme.

B

6450. BARTLETT, James; B: Eastbourne; E: Eastbourne; C.S.M. G 3841; D.C.M.; D at Home: 26.10.18; Eastbourne (Ocklynge) Cem., Sussex (UK).

6451. BROTHERTON, Frederick Charles; B: – ; E: Worcester; Pte. TF 2631114; D: 5.7.18; Aire Com. Cem., Pas-de-Calais; Age 30; Son of Harry and Jane Brotherton of 29, Bendley Street, Evesham, Worcestershire.

6452. BUCHAN, J.; B: – ; E: Peterhead, Scotland; Pte. TF 263149; W: 23.8.18; Cabaret-Rouge Brit. Cem., Pas-de-Calais.*

C

6453. CLARKE, Herbert Lance; B: Nottingham; E: Edmonton, London; Pte. G 26111; D: 24.11.18; Terlincthun Brit. Cem., Pas-de-Calais.

6454. COOK, Sydney; B: Whitchurch, Hampshire; E: Winchester; Pte. L 11562; K: 29.7.18; Bellacourt Mil. Cem., Pas-de-Calais; Age 18; Son of Harvey and Fanny Cook of Round House, London Road, Whitchurch.

D

6455. DALTON, Walter; B:– ; E: Chennies Street, London; Pte. TF 263148; K: 29.7.18; Bellacourt Mil. Cem., Pas-de-Calais; Age 38; Husband of Mrs.Dalton of "Dudley", Fairfield Road, Grove Park, Kent.

F

6456. FRASER, James; B: Carlisle; E: Hamilton, Scotland;

Pte. G 30177; W: 31.7.18; Gezaincourt Com. Cem. Ext., Somme; Died at Casualty Clearing Station, Gezaincourt.

6457. FURNELL, Phillip John; B: Walthamstow, London; E: Bunhill Row, London; Pte. TF 263152; K: 29.7.18; Bellacourt Mil. Cem., Pas-de-calais.

G

6458. GEE, John; B: Salford, Lancashire; E: Bury, Lancashire; Pte. G 30031; K: 16.10.18; Houplines Com. Cem. Ext., Nord; Age 19; Son of William and Teresa Gee of Manchester.

6459. GRAHAM, Joseph Bernard; B: Dulwich, London; E: St.Swithin's Lane, London; Pte. G 31018; K: 6.10.18; Ploegsteert Mem. (Bel.); Age 39; Son of James and Agnes Graham of Ashbourne House, Upland Road, Dulwich.

H

6460. HARDWICK, William; B: – ; E: – ; Pte. – 2001172; D: 3.10.18; Ste.Marie Cem., Le Havre, Seine-Maritime; Age 42; Husband of Bessie Frances Hardwick of 28, Regent's Street, St.Helen's, Ipswich, Suffolk; Labour Corps.

L

6461. LATHAN, William; 2nd Lt.; K: 24.9.18; Y Farm Mil. Cem., Bois-Grenier, Nord; Age 23; Son of George and Sarah A.Lathan of Norwich; Joined the Battalion only on 14.9.18.

6462. LUMSDEN, George; B: Castle Eden, County Durham; E: Durham; Pte. G 30643; K: 16.9.18; Pont-du-Hem Mil. Cem., Nord; Husband of Jane Lumsden of 2, Institute Terrace, Ouston, County Durham.

M

6463. MARKS, Leonard George; B: Jesmond, Northumberland; E: Newcastle-on-Tyne; L/Cpl. G 26028; K: 12.10.18; Ration Farm Mil. Cem., Nord; Age 24; Son of Simon Marks of 38, Grainger Street, Newcastle-on-Tyne.*

P

6464. PARKER, Albert; B: Manchester; E: Manchester; Pte. G 30076; K: 6.10.18; Ploegsteert Mem. (Bel.); Age 19; Son of John and Mary Ellen Parker of 9, Langness Street, Clayton, Manchester.

6465. PARSLOW, Joseph; B: Throckley, Northumberland; E: Ashington, Northumberland; Pte. G 30268; K: 12.10.18; Ration Farm Mil. Cem., Nord.*

6466. PINK, Edward; B: East Ham, London; E: Ilford, Essex; C.S.M. L 11561; D.C.M.; W: 29.7.18; Bellacourt Mil. Cem., Pas-de-Calais.*

R

6467. RODD, George; B: Exeter; E: Cardiff; Pte. G 30470; D: 25.10.18; Étaples Mil. Cem., Pas-de-Calais; Died at Military Hospital, Étaples.

T

6468. TAPLIN, Charles; B: Botley, Hampshire; E: Gosport, Hampshire; Pte. G 30492; W: 3.8.18; Bagneux Brit. Cem., Somme.

W

6469. WILDMAN, Joseph Walter; B: Barby, Warwickshire; E: Rugby, Warwickshire; Pte. G 31015; W: 2.11.18; Terlincthun Brit. Cem., Pas-de-Calais; Age 34; Son of Joseph and Emma Noble Wildman of East Keal, Spilsby, Linclonshire; Husband of Catherine Wildman of East Keal.

6470. WILSON, John; B: – ; E: Preston, Lancashire; Pte. G 26065; K: 5.10.18; Ration Farm Mil. Cem., Nord.

6471. WILSON, Thomas; B: Stalybridge, Cheshire; E: Ashton-under-Lyne, Lancashire; Pte. G 30106; D: 26.6.18; Aire Com. Cem., Pas-de-Calais; Age 18; Son of Robert and Florence Wilson of Ashton-under-Lyne; Died at No.39 Stationary Military Hospital, Aire.

6472. WRIGHT, William Lake; 2nd Lt.; K: 21.10.18; Lille Southern Cem., Nord; Age 34; Son of Edward and Eliza Wright of Bexley, Kent; Husband of Emily Constance Wright of 8, Mornington Road, Chingford, Essex; Last man of the Battalion to be killed in action.*

OTHER MEN ATTACHED TO, OR FROM, ROYAL SUSSEX UNITS BUT WHOSE RECORDS DO NOT APPEAR AMONG THOSE OF WESTERN FRONT ROYAL SUSSEX BATTALIONS

— BADDELEY, Alfred James; Lt.; K: 23.10.18; Vis-en-Artois Mem., Haucourt, Pas-de-Calais; Age 19; Brother of the Rev.Walter H.Baddeley of The Vicarage, South Bank, Yorkshire; Attached to 2nd Trench Mortar Battery, Royal Sussex Regiment.

— BALL, A.H.; Lt.; K: 9.4.18 at Guinchy; Cambrin Mil. Cem., Pas-de-Calais; Age 29; Son of Mr.W.E. and Mrs.M.A.Ball of Brasted, Kent; Husband of Sylvia N.Row, formerly Ball, of Dudwell House, Burwash, Sussex.

— BARROW, L.A.H.; 2nd Lt.; K: 31.8.16; Englebelmer Com. Cem. Ext., Somme; Age 21; Son of the Rev.A.H. and Mrs.Emily Mary Barrow of Ashfield, Beckenham, Kent; Attached from 10th Battalion Royal Sussex Regiment.*

— BOURNE, Rowland Hurst; 2nd Lt.; K: 24.10.18; Valenciennes (St.Roch) Com. Cem., Nord; Age 19; Son of Rowland Manlove Bourne and Gertrude Bourne of 26, Bath Road, Bedford Park, Chiswick, London; Attached from Royal Army Service Corps.

— CATMER, Harry Albert Frederick Valentine; Lt.; K: 1.7.16; Thiepval Mem., Somme; Attached to Machine Gun Corps (Infantry) from 3rd Battalion Royal Sussex Regiment.

— CRAWLEY-BOEVEY, Edward Martin; Capt.; K: 24.12.14; Kemmel Chateau Mil. Cem. (Bel.); Age 41; Son of Sir Thomas Crawley-Boevey, Bart., of Flaxley Abbey, Gloucestershire; Husband of Mrs.W.Crawle-Boevey of 56, Barkston Gardens, London; Attached to Royal Fusiliers (City of London Regiment) from 1st Battalion Royal Sussex Regiment.

— DIXON, Albert Ernest Lucas; 2nd Lt.; K: 8.5.18; Bucquoy Road Cem., Pas-de-Calais; Age 20; Son of Albert and Emma Sophia Dixon of 46/47, Frederick Street, Brighton; Attached to 23rd Battalion Royal Fusiliers from 3rd Battalion Royal Sussex Regiment.

— DU MOULIN, Francis Louis; Lt.Col.; M.C.; K: 7.11.18; Berlaimont Com. Cem., Nord; Age 29; Son of Louis Eugene and Katherine Parrell Du Moulin of Fishbourne Lodge, Chichester; Attached to East Yorkshire Regiment from Royal Sussex Regiment.

— FERGUSON, James Arthur Ross; Lt.; K: 9.5.15; Ypres (Menin Gate) Mem. (Bel.); Age 18; Son of Robert James and Gertrude K.Ferguson of 10, St.George's Place, Canterbury; Attached to 1st Battalion Kings Own Yorkshire Light Infantry from 3rd Battalion Royal Sussex Regiment.

— FISHER, Percy Harold; 2nd Lt.; W: 4.7.16; Couin Brit. Cem., Pas-de-Calais; Age 23; Son of Tom P. and Kate Mary Fisher of 205, St.Margaret's Road, St.Margarets-on-Thames, Middlesex; Attached to Machine Gun Corps from 10th Battalion Royal Sussex Regiment.

— GRAY, Percy Tom William; Pte. – 20892; W: 18.9.16; Heilly Station Cem., Mericourt-L'Abbé, Somme; Age 18; Son of Mr. and Mrs.Gray of 108, Cromwell Road, New Southgate, London; Died at Casualty Clearing Station, Mericourt-L'Abbé; Attached to Middlesex Regiment from 20th Battalion Royal Sussex Regiment.

— HAWKRIDGE, Joseph Arnold; B: Sydenham, London; 2nd Lt.; W: 6.11.16; Barlin Com. Cem., Pas-de-Calais; Age 21; Son of Joseph and Mary Louisa Hawkridge; Attached to Royal Fusiliers (City of London) Regiment from Royal Sussex Regiment.

— HOLLINGSWORTH, John Frederick; 2nd Lt.; B: Wallington, Surrey; W: 2.10.16; Grove Town Cem., Somme; Age 31; Son of Frederick J. and Rebecca Hollingsworth of Strawberry Lodge, Carshalton, Surrey; Died at Casualty Clearing Station, Grove Town; Attached 7th Battalion East Surrey Regiment from 14th Battalion Royal Sussex Regiment.

— KENYON, Charles Wilton; 2nd. Lt.;K: 16.3.16; Cabaret-Rouge Brit. Cem., Pas-de-calais; Age 22; Son of George Herbert and Annie Caroline Kenyon of "Holme Lea", 26, Rusper Road, Horsham, Sussex; Attached to 47th Trench Mortar Battery Royal Sussex Regiment from 10th Battalion Royal Sussex Regiment.

— LOTT, William; 2nd Lt.; K: 7.10.16; Thiepval Mem, Somme; Attached from 14th Battalion Royal Sussex Regiment.

— ORME, Owen Felix; Capt.; K: 25.9.15; Dud Corner Cem., Pas-de-calais; Age 27; Son of Mrs.Louisa Orme of Lowfield, Clitheroe, Lancashire.

— OXLEY, Fergus Richard; Lt.; K: 20.9.16; Vlamertinghe Mil. Cem. (Bel.); Age 28; Son of George E. and Alice D.Oxley of Brighton; Attached to 1st Battalion Royal

Dublin Fusiliers and Trench Mortar Battery Royal Sussex Regiment from 10th Battalion Royal Sussex Regiment.

— PHELPS, Duncan; 2nd Lt.; K: 29.9.18; Tyne Cot Mem. (Bel.); Attached to Hampshire Regiment from Royal Sussex Regiment.

— PIERCE, Henry; Pte. – 3038; K: 31.8.16; Thiepval Mem., Somme; Age 29; Son of Mr. and Mrs.A.J.Pierce of 10, Hartington Road, Brighton; Sussex Yeomanry; Attached from 16th to 9th Battalion.

— POWELL, E.I.; Capt.; K: 22.3.18; Villers-Faucon Com. Cem. Ext., Somme; Attached from 6th Battalion Royal Sussex Regiment.

— RAMSBOTHAM, Geoffrey Bury; Lt.; K: 16.5.15; Le Touret Mem., Pas-de-Calais; Age 21; Son of Philip Bury and Florence Elizabeth Ramsbotham of The Manor House, Ottery St.Mary, Devonshire; Killed at Festubert; Attached to South Staffordshire Regiment from 3rd Battalion Royal Sussex Regiment.

— RAYNES, Albert Brainerd; 2nd Lt.; K: 10.3.15; Le Touret Mem., Pas-de-Calais; Age 20; Son of Albert Edward and Alice Mary Raynes of 201, Denman Street, Nottingham; Attached to 2nd Battalion Royal Berkshire Regiment from Royal Sussex Regiment.

— STEWARD, Thomas Henry; Pte. G 3950; W at Home: 23.4.18; Birmingham (Witton) Cem., Warwickshire (UK); Age 22; Son of Thomas Henry and Elizabeth Steward of 43, Brantley Road, Witton; Attached from 3rd Battalion Royal Sussex Regiment.

— THOMSON, Alfred Maurice; Capt.; K: 7.7.16; Thiepval Mem., Somme; Age 30; Son of Alfred and Florence C.Thomson of 9, Osborne Mansions, Northumberland Street, London; Attached to Royal Sussex Regiment from Royal Army Medical Corps.

— ULOTH, Arthur Curtis Wilmot; B: London; Lt.; M.C.; W: 19.9.18; Doingt Com. Cem., Somme; Age 20; Son of H.Wilmot Uloth and Susannah H.Uloth of Great Tylers, Reigate, Surrey; Died at Casualty Clearing Station, Doingt; Attached from 3rd Battalion Royal Sussex Regiment.

— WALLIS, Edward Percy; Capt.; K: 18.10.16; Bapaume Post Mil. Cem., Somme; Age 22; Son of Dr. and Mrs.P.E.Wallis of East Grinstead, Sussex; Attached to Kings Own (Royal Lancaster) Regiment from Royal Sussex Regiment.

— WIGSTON, Geoffrey Herbert; Capt.; K: 9.9.16; Caterpillar Valley Cem., Somme; Age 21; Son of William Jebb Wigston and Lucy Sophia Wigston of Rushmere, Ashtead, Surrey; Attached to East Surrey Regiment from 1st Battalion Royal Sussex Regiment.

— WILSON, George Andrew Glanville; Captain; K: 31.7.17; Ypres (Menin Gate) Mem. (Bel.); Attached from 6th Battalion Royal Sussex Regiment.

BV - #0036 - 110324 - C0 - 297/210/30 [32] - CB - 9781908336309 - Gloss Lamination